**MINITAB INC**
Making Data Analysis Easier

A student version of Minitab is also available. This CD-ROM contains the student version of Release 12 (for Windows® 95), Release 9 (for Windows® 3.1), and the necessary documentation and data files.

*Please use ISBN 0-13-083103-4 to order this special package.*

## Visit Our Web Site:

### http://www.prenhall.com/berenson

◆ **Study Hall:** A student resource guide including Ask the Tutor, Career Center, Writing Center, and Study Skills Center.

◆ **Faculty Lounge:** This Faculty page is password protected and provides a wealth of resources, which includes downloadable supplements, teaching tips, and current events articles. It also offers help with computers, teaching archives, Internet skills, and a conference and chat system.

◆ **Research Area:** Links to domestic and international news organizations, Web browsers, and Web tutorials.

Companion Website

## Every chapter features the following additional interactive materials:

◆ **Interactive Study Guide:** On a chapter-by-chapter basis, we give student tips and provide a variety of graded quizzes as a self-review of each chapter. These quizzes include multiple choice questions, true/false questions, and Internet essays.

◆ **Internet Exercises** Exercises for each chapter to encourage you to use the Internet for learning and research.

◆ **Internet Resources:** Specific Internet resources linked to the chapter and topic you are studying.

◆ **Current Events:** A summary and analysis of current statistics news events, discussion questions, group activities, a glossary, and a bibliography.

◆ **PowerPoint Slides:** A multitude of PowerPoint slides to help you review text material and organize your studies.

◆ **Contest Submissions:** Additional exercises, problems, case studies, and student projects from your colleagues are posted here.

# Would you like to customize this book?

Utilizing our **Just-in-Time Program**, you have the option of creating your own version of this text, or mixing and matching chapters of this text and those texts listed on the following page. You can choose chapters from any of these titles to create a custom textbook that will fulfill your course needs exactly. In addition, you have the option to include your own material or material from other publishers. Plus, your custom book can be packaged with any Prentice Hall Decision Science or Business Statistics software, or shrink-wrapped with any Prentice Hall textbook. The Harvard Business Cases are also available as part of the JIT Program.

## THE JIT PROGRAM OFFERS:

### FLEXIBILITY:
You can revise and update your book every semester.

### INSTRUCTIONAL SUPPORT:
You have access to all instructor's materials that accompany the traditional textbook and desk copies of your JIT book.

### COST SAVINGS:
Because you use only the material you select, JIT books are often less expensive than traditional textbooks.

### QUICK TURNAROUND:
You can have your custom book delivered in four weeks.

### ADDITIONAL RESOURCES:
You can package your JIT book with Prentice Hall Decision Science/Business Statistics software and shrink-wrap your book with other Prentice Hall books.

### ADDITIONAL ACCESS:
All Harvard Business Cases are available to include in your custom text.

## The Highest Quality Production Available Includes:

- Custom cover and title page: including your name, school, department, course title, and section number
- Paperback, perfect bound, black-and-white laser printed text
- Customized table of contents and index
- Sequential pagination throughout the text
- Chapters, text figures, and problems renumbered to correspond with custom organization
- Solutions to selected problems included at the end of each chapter

*Please see the next page for our current list of available titles!*

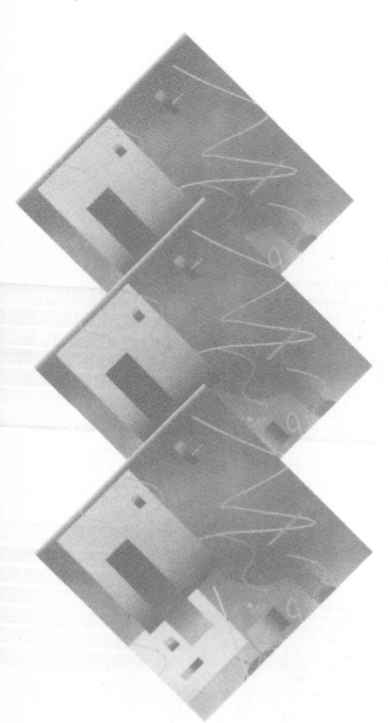

## OPERATIONS MANAGEMENT

Handfield/Nichols Jr., *Introduction to Supply Chain Management*
Heineke/Meile, *Games and Exercises in Operations Management*
Heizer/Render, *Operations Management,* Fifth Edition
Heizer/Render, *Principles of Operations Management,* Third Edition
Latona/Nathan, *Cases and Readings in POM*
Russell/Taylor, *Operations Management,* Second Edition
Schmenner, *Plant and Service Tours in Operations Management,* Fifth Edition

## MANAGEMENT SCIENCE/OPERATIONS RESEARCH

Eppen/Gould, *Introductory Management Science,* Fifth Edition
Render/Stair, *Quantitative Analysis for Management,* Sixth Edition
Render/Stair, *Introduction to Management Science*
Render et al., *Cases and Readings in Management Science*
Taylor, *Introduction to Management Science,* Sixth Edition
Wright et al., *Strategic Management: Texts and Cases*

## BUSINESS STATISTICS

Berenson/Levine, *Basic Business Statistics,* Seventh Edition
Klimberg et al., *Cases in Business Statistics*
Levin/Rubin, *Statistics for Management,* Seventh Edition
Levine et al., *Statistics for Managers Using Microsoft Excel,* Updated and
     Second Edition
McClave/Benson, *Statistics for Business and Economics,* Seventh Edition
Neter, *Applied Statistics,* Fourth Edition
Watson et al., *Statistics for Management and Economics,* Fifth Edition

## SOFTWARE

Weiss, *POM for Windows*
Weiss, *QM for Windows*
Weiss, *DS for Windows*

If you are interested in creating your own JIT book,
please give us a call at **1-800-777-6872** or email us at
**JIT_DecScience@prenhall.com.** For further information on this program,
you can visit our Web site at **www.sscp.com/just_in_time.html**.

# Basic Business Statistics

# Basic Business Statistics

## Concepts and Applications

Seventh Edition

Mark L. Berenson

David M. Levine

*Department of Statistics and Computer Information Systems*
*Baruch College, Zicklin School of Business, City University*
*of New York*

**Prentice-Hall**
Upper Saddle River, New Jersey 07458

Acquisitions Editor: Tom Tucker
Editorial Assistant: Melissa Back
Editor-in-Chief: Natalie E. Anderson
Marketing Manager: Debbie Clare
Senior Production Editor: Cynthia Regan
Managing Editor: Dee Josephson
Manufacturing Buyer: Arnold Vila
Manufacturing Manager: Vincent Scelta
Senior Designer: Cheryl Asherman
Design Manager: Patricia Smythe
Interior/Cover Design: Jill Little
Cover Illustration/Photo: Marjory Dressler
Composition/Illustrator (Interior): GTS Graphics, Inc.

MINITAB is a registered trademark of Minitab, Inc., at
3081 Enterprise Drive
State College, PA 16801 USA
ph. 814.238.3280     fax. 814.238.4383
e-mail: Info@minitab.com
URL: http://www.minitab.com

LIBRARY OF CONGRESS CATALOGING-IN-PUBLICATION DATA

Berenson, Mark L.
    Basic business statistics : concepts and applications / Mark L. Berenson, David M. Levine. — 7th ed.
        p.          cm.
    Includes bibliographical references and index.
    ISBN 0-13-795618-5
    1. Commercial statistics.   2. Statistics.   I. Levine, David M.,              II. Title.
HF1017.B38   1999
519.5—dc21          98-38873
                    CIP

Prentice-Hall International (UK) Limited, *London*
Prentice-Hall of Australia Pty. Limited, *Sydney*
Prentice-Hall Canada, Inc., *Toronto*
Prentice-Hall Hispanoamericana, S.A., *Mexico*
Prentice-Hall of India Private Limited, *New Delhi*
Prentice-Hall of Japan, Inc., *Tokyo*
Simon & Schuster Asia Pte. Ltd., *Singapore*
Editora Prentice-Hall do Brasil, Ltda., *Rio de Janeiro*

*To our wives,*
*Rhoda B. and Marilyn L.*
*and to our children,*
*Kathy B., Lori B., and Sharyn L.*

# Brief Contents

# Contents

## ◆10 Confidence Interval Estimation   365

## ◆11 Fundamentals of Hypothesis Testing: One-Sample Tests   411

# Preface

Over the various editions of the text we have attempted to keep up with changes that have occurred in the teaching of business statistics, and have been active participants in a series of conferences called *Making Statistics More Effective in Schools of Business*. In this seventh edition major changes have been made that reduce the focus on computations and increase the emphasis on concepts and the proper use of statistics to analyze data, assuming that computer software is an integral feature of any analysis that takes place.

Among the new features of this seventh edition of *Basic Business Statistics* are:

- Business Scenarios: Each chapter begins with a *Using Statistics* example that demonstrates how statistics can be used in one of the functional areas of business—accounting, finance, management, or marketing. The scenario is then applied to topics within the chapter.
- An increased focus on data analysis and interpretation of computer output. There is a reduced focus on hand calculations.
- Instructions on using Microsoft Excel 97 and Minitab, which are included in chapter appendices.
- A statistics add-in for Microsoft Excel, *PHStat*, which is included on the CD-ROM that accompanies this text.
- A running case study, the *Springville Herald*, which is carried through the entire text as an integrating theme.
- An additional chapter on multiple regression that emphasizes model building.
- A new chapter on decision making.
- New sections of importance in business applications, including principles of graphical excellence, sampling in auditing, and the application of the covariance in finance.

Among the features of our text that distinguish it from other competing texts are:

 ## MAIN FEATURE: COMPREHENSIVE COVERAGE OF STATISTICAL METHODS WITH AN APPLIED APPROACH

The seventh edition is a comprehensive 19-chapter text that provides sufficient breadth of coverage for a one- or two-semester course in business statistics. It takes an applied approach that focuses on the concepts and applications of statistics to the functional areas of business—accounting, economics and finance, management, and marketing.

 ## MAIN FEATURE: EMPHASIS ON DATA ANALYSIS AND INTERPRETATION OF COMPUTER OUTPUT

The personal computer revolution has dramatically changed how information is analyzed in the workplace, and how statistics should be taught in the classroom. In this edition, we take the position that the use of computer software in the form of a spreadsheet application such as Microsoft Excel or a statistical package such as Minitab is an integral part of learning statistics. Our focus emphasizes analyzing data, interpreting the output from Microsoft Excel and Minitab, and explaining how to use this software while reducing emphasis on doing computations. In order to carry out our approach, we have added a great deal of computer output and integrated this output into the fabric of the text. For example, in our coverage of tables and charts in chapter 3, our focus is on the interpretation of various charts, not on their construction by hand. In our coverage of hypothesis testing in chapters 11–14, we have made sure to include extensive computer output so that the $p$-value approach can be used. In our coverage of simple linear regression in chapter 16, we assume that software such as Microsoft Excel or Minitab will be used and thus our focus is on the interpretation of the output, not on hand calculations (which have been placed in a separate section of the chapter).

 ## MAIN FEATURE: PROBLEMS, CASE STUDIES, AND TEAM PROJECTS

"Learning" results from "doing." This text provides the student with the opportunity to select and solve from among the 1,100 problems (most with multiple parts) presented at the end of sections as well as the end of chapters. Most of these problems apply to realistic situations (using real data whenever possible) in various fields, including accounting, economics, finance, health care administration, information systems, management, marketing, and public administration.

- The end-of-section problems give the students the opportunity to reinforce what they have just learned. These are divided into two types—Learning the Basics and Applying the Concepts.
- The Checking Your Understanding problems provide short discussion questions that examine understanding of concepts.
- The Chapter Review Problems included at the end of each chapter are based on the concepts and methods learned throughout the chapter.
- Answers to selected problems appear at the end of the text.
- Detailed case studies are included at the end of nine chapters.
- The *Springville Herald* Case is included at the end of most chapters as an integrating theme.
- A Team Project relating to mutual funds is included at the end of most chapters as an integrating theme.

 ## MAIN FEATURE: APPENDICES ON USING MICROSOFT EXCEL AND MINITAB

The availability of powerful personal computers has created an environment of relatively easy access to statistical and spreadsheet software. Rather than rely on supplementary manuals, it is a much better pedagogical approach to provide an explanation of how the software is used in the text, employing the in-chapter examples. Detailed appendices that explain how to use Minitab, the most popular statistical software for introductory business statistics, and Microsoft Excel, the dominant spreadsheet package, are included at the end of most chapters. In addition, an appendix that explains the basics of the Windows operating environment is provided after chapter 1.

## MAIN FEATURE: STATISTICS ADD-IN FOR MICROSOFT EXCEL: PHSTAT

The CD-ROM that accompanies the text includes a statistics add-in for Microsoft Excel to facilitate its use in business statistics courses. Although Microsoft Excel is a spreadsheet package, it contains features that enable it to perform statistical analysis for most of the topics in this text. However, in some cases such analyses are cumbersome in the off-the-shelf version of Excel. The PHStat statistics add-in provides a custom menu of choices that lead to dialog boxes in which users make entries and selections to perform specific analyses. PHStat minimizes the work associated with setting up statistical solutions in Microsoft Excel by automating the creation of spreadsheets and charts. PHStat, along with Microsoft Excel's Data Analysis tool, now allows users to perform statistical analysis in most topics covered in a two-term introductory business statistics course. For a complete list of topics on the PHStat custom menu, please refer to the pages inside the front cover of this text.

 ## MAIN FEATURE: PEDAGOGICAL AIDS

Among the many features for creating a better learning environment throughout the text are:

- Conversational writing style
- A *Using Statistics* example that illustrates the application of at least one of the statistical methods covered in each chapter in accounting, finance, management, or marketing
- Real data for as many examples and problems as possible
- Exhibit boxes that highlight important concepts
- Set-off examples that provide reinforcement for learning concepts
- Comment boxes that focus on assumptions of statistical methods
- Problem sets with varied levels of difficulty and complexity
- Chapter summary charts
- Key terms
- Explanation and illustration of statistical tables
- Side notes in which additional material appears adjacent to where it is referenced

 ## MAIN FEATURE: FULL SUPPLEMENT PACKAGE

The supplement package that accompanies this text includes:

- **Instructor's Solution Manual**—written by Priscilla Chaffe-Stengel and Donald Stengel, this solutions manual is enriched with extra detail in the problem solutions.
- **Student Solutions Manual**—to order this supplement for your students use ISBN 0-13-083073-9.
- **Test Item File**—also prepared by Priscilla Chaffe-Stengel and Donald Stengel.
- **Prentice Hall's Custom Test Manager.**
- **Instructor's CD-ROM**—The instructor's CD contains PowerPoint slides, the Instructor's Solutions Manual and Test Item File, and Presentation Manager.

- **Presentation Manager**—a totally new supplement on a CD-ROM. Presentation Manager allows users to build their own multimedia lecture using resources provided on the CD-ROM. The CD contains color figures, photos, and PowerPoint slides, organized by chapter. Many of these resources come directly from the text. With Presentation Manager's easy navigation, users can view and select each resource, and integrate their own resources to build new customized multimedia lectures.
- **PHStat** (a statistical add-in for Microsoft Excel) and the data files for the examples and exercises are contained on the CD-ROM that accompanies the text.
- **World Wide Web** site that contains alternative course outlines, additional problems, teaching tips, tips for students, and links to other sites containing statistical data. This site can be found at **www.prenhall.com/berenson**.
- *The New York Times* **supplement** of articles related to text material.
- **Student version of Minitab**—a student version of Minitab's release 12 can be packaged with this text for a reasonable additional cost. To order this package, use ISBN 0-13-083103-4.

 ## CONTENT CHANGES IN THE SEVENTH EDITION

- Chapter 1 (Introduction) now includes appendices on using Windows, using Microsoft Excel, and using Minitab.
- Chapter 2 (Data Collection) now includes stratified, systematic, and cluster sampling.
- Chapter 3 (Presenting Data in Tables and Charts) now combines material on numerical and categorical tables and charts. There is an increased focus on interpretation of output and a decreased focus on construction of charts. New sections include the scatter diagram and time series plot, the side-by-side bar chart, Tufte's principles of graphical excellence, and appendices on Excel and Minitab.
- Chapter 4 (Summarizing and Describing Numerical Data) integrates computer output into the chapter with a focus on interpretation and a reduced emphasis on computations. There is a new section on obtaining the mean and standard deviation from a frequency distribution as well as appendices on Excel and Minitab.
- Chapter 5 (Basic Probability) changes the chapter example from playing cards to a business application and streamlines and combines sections.
- Chapter 6 (Some Important Discrete Probability Distributions) changes the chapter example from playing cards to a business application and adds sections on the hypergeometric distribution, the covariance applied to finance, and appendices on Excel and Minitab.
- Chapter 7 (Decision Making) consists of a complete chapter on decision making, including payoff and opportunity loss tables, the return to risk ratio, and decision making with sample information. Specific examples are applied to finance and marketing.
- Chapter 8 (The Normal Distribution and Other Continuous Distributions) uses the cumulative normal table and adds the exponential distribution and appendices on Excel and Minitab.
- Chapter 9 (Sampling Distributions) adds appendices on Excel and Minitab.
- Chapter 10 (Confidence Interval Estimation) adds a section on applications in auditing and appendices on Excel and Minitab.
- Chapter 11 (Fundamentals of Hypothesis Testing: One-Sample Tests) combines all one-sample tests and integrates computer output. Appendices on Excel and Minitab are also included.

- Chapter 12 (Two-Sample Tests with Numerical Data) integrates computer output throughout the chapter and places all nonparametric tests at the end of the chapter. In addition, appendices on Excel and Minitab are included.
- Chapter 13 (ANOVA and Other *c*-Sample Tests with Numerical Data) reduces computations, increases the focus on the interpretation of output, and places all nonparametric tests at the end of the chapter. In addition, appendices on Excel and Minitab are included.
- Chapter 14 (Two-Sample and *c*-Sample Tests with Categorical Data) adds appendices on Excel and Minitab.
- Chapter 15 (Statistical Applications in Quality and Productivity Management) integrates computer output, and streamlines coverage of control charts. A new multipart case is added along with an exhibit on the themes of quality management. In addition, appendices on Excel and Minitab are included.
- Chapter 16 (Simple Linear Regression and Correlation) provides integration of computer output and focuses on interpretation rather than hand calculations. Most computations are moved to a separate section. The *SSXY, SSX, SSY* notation is used for sum of squares. Correlation is separated from regression and moved to the end of the chapter. Influence analysis is moved to the first chapter on multiple regression. In addition, appendices on Excel and Minitab are included.
- Chapter 17 (Introduction to Multiple Regression) contains the first of two chapters on multiple regression. There is an additional focus on output interpretation and reduction in computations and an additional case study along with appendices on Excel and Minitab.
- Chapter 18 (Multiple Regression Model Building) contains expanded coverage of dummy variables and model building using best subsets regression and stepwise regression along with appendices on Excel and Minitab.
- Chapter 19 (Time-Series Analysis) provides a simplification of moving averages and autoregressive models and a reduction in computations and more focus on interpreting computer output. The dummy variable approach to seasonal data is now used and appendices on Excel and Minitab are included.

 ## ABOUT THE WORLD WIDE WEB ICON

The text has a home page on the World Wide Web with an address of
**http://www.prenhall.com/berenson**
This site incorporates the features of PHLIP (Prentice Hall's Learning on the Internet Partnership), a robust Web site containing many resources for both faculty and student. A partial list of the features includes:

- Teaching tips
- Alternative course outlines
- Links to other sites containing data appropriate for statistics courses
- Additional team projects
- Questions relating to *The New York Times* supplement

 ## ACKNOWLEDGMENTS

We are extremely grateful to the many organizations and companies that allowed us to use their data in developing problems and examples throughout the text. We would like to thank *The New York Times*, Consumers' Union (publishers of *Consumer Reports*), Moody's

Investor Service (publishers of *Moody's Handbook of Common Stocks*), CEEPress, and Gale Research.

In addition we would like to thank the Biometrika Trustees, American Cyanimid Company, the Rand Corporation, and the American Society for Testing and Materials for their kind permission to publish various tables in Appendix E, and the American Statistical Association for its permission to publish diagrams from the *American Statistician*. Finally, we are grateful to Professors George A. Johnson and Joanne Tokle of Idaho State University and Ed Conn, Mountain States Potato Company, for their kind permission to incorporate parts of their work as our Mountain States Potato Company case in chapter 18.

## A Note of Thanks

We would like to thank Ann Brandwein, Baruch College; Alan S. Chesen, Wright State University; John McKenzie, Babson College; Raymond Raab, University of Minnesota–Duluth; Don R. Robinson, Illinois State University; Lillian M. Russell, University of Delaware; Priscilla Chaffe-Stengel and Donald Stengel, California State University–Fresno; James A. Swanson, Central Missouri State University; Larry Tatum, Baruch College; Kent D. Smith, California Polytechnic State University–San Luis Obispo; William L. Seaver, University of Tennessee–Knoxville; David Mathiason, Rochester Institute of Technology; Kathryn Ernstberger, Indiana University Southeast; Alireza Tahai, Mississippi State University; and T. Henry Jablonski Jr., East Tennessee State University for their constructive comments during the writing of this text.

We would like to especially thank Tom Tucker, Debbie Clare, Cynthia Regan, Melissa Back, Dee Josephson, Kristen Imperatore, Steve Deitmer, Natalie Anderson, and Sandy Steiner of the editorial, marketing, and production teams at Prentice-Hall. We would also like to thank our developmental editor Zanae Rodrigo for her many ideas in the development of this edition, Susan L. Reiland, our statistical reader, for her diligence in checking the accuracy of our work, Gretlyn Cline for her proofreading, and Katy Spining of GTS Graphics for work in the compositing of the text. Finally, we would like to thank our wives and children for patience, understanding, love, and assistance in making this book a reality. It is to them that we dedicate this book.

## Concluding Remarks

We have gone to great lengths to make this text both pedagogically sound and error free. If you have any suggestions, or material requiring clarification, or should you find any errors, please contact us at DMLBB@CUNYVM.CUNY.EDU

*Mark L. Berenson*
*David M. Levine*

# Basic Business Statistics

# Introduction

## CHAPTER OBJECTIVES

✓ *To present a broad overview of the subject of statistics and its applications*
✓ *To distinguish between descriptive and inferential statistics*
✓ *To introduce the basic features of the Microsoft Excel spreadsheet software and the Minitab statistical software*

 ## 1.1 WHY A MANAGER NEEDS TO KNOW ABOUT STATISTICS

A century ago H. G. Wells commented that "statistical thinking will one day be as necessary as the ability to read and write." As we approach the next millennium, the issue facing managers is not a shortage of information but how to use the available information to make better decisions.

It is from this perspective of informed decision making that we consider why a manager needs to know about statistics. Managers need an understanding of statistics for the following four key reasons:

**1.** To know how to properly present and describe information
**2.** To know how to draw conclusions about large populations based only on information obtained from samples
**3.** To know how to improve processes
**4.** To know how to obtain reliable forecasts

On the next page is a road map of this text from the perspective of these four reasons for learning statistics. From this road map we observe that the first four chapters include coverage of methods involved in the collection, presentation, and description of information. Chapters 5–9 provide coverage of the basic concepts of probability; the binomial, normal, and other distributions; decision making; and sampling distributions so that in chapters 10–14 the reader will learn how to draw conclusions about large populations based only on information obtained from samples. Chapter 15 contains coverage of statistical applications in quality and productivity management that is essential for process improvement. Chapters 16–19 focus on regression, multiple regression, modeling, and time-series analysis that provide methods for obtaining forecasts.

We may apply statistical methods in the functional areas of business: accounting, finance, management, and marketing. Accounting uses statistical methods to select samples for auditing purposes and to understand the cost drivers in cost accounting. Finance uses statistical methods to choose between alternative portfolio investments and to track trends in financial measures over time. Management uses statistical methods to improve the quality of the products manufactured or the services delivered by an organization. Marketing uses statistical methods to estimate the proportion of customers who prefer one product to another and why they do and to draw conclusions about what advertising strategy might be most useful in increasing sales of a product.

 ## 1.2 THE GROWTH AND DEVELOPMENT OF MODERN STATISTICS

Historically, the growth and development of modern statistics can be traced to three separate phenomena: the needs of government to collect data on its citizenry (see references 5, 6, 11, 12, and 15), the development of the mathematics of probability theory, and the advent of the computer.

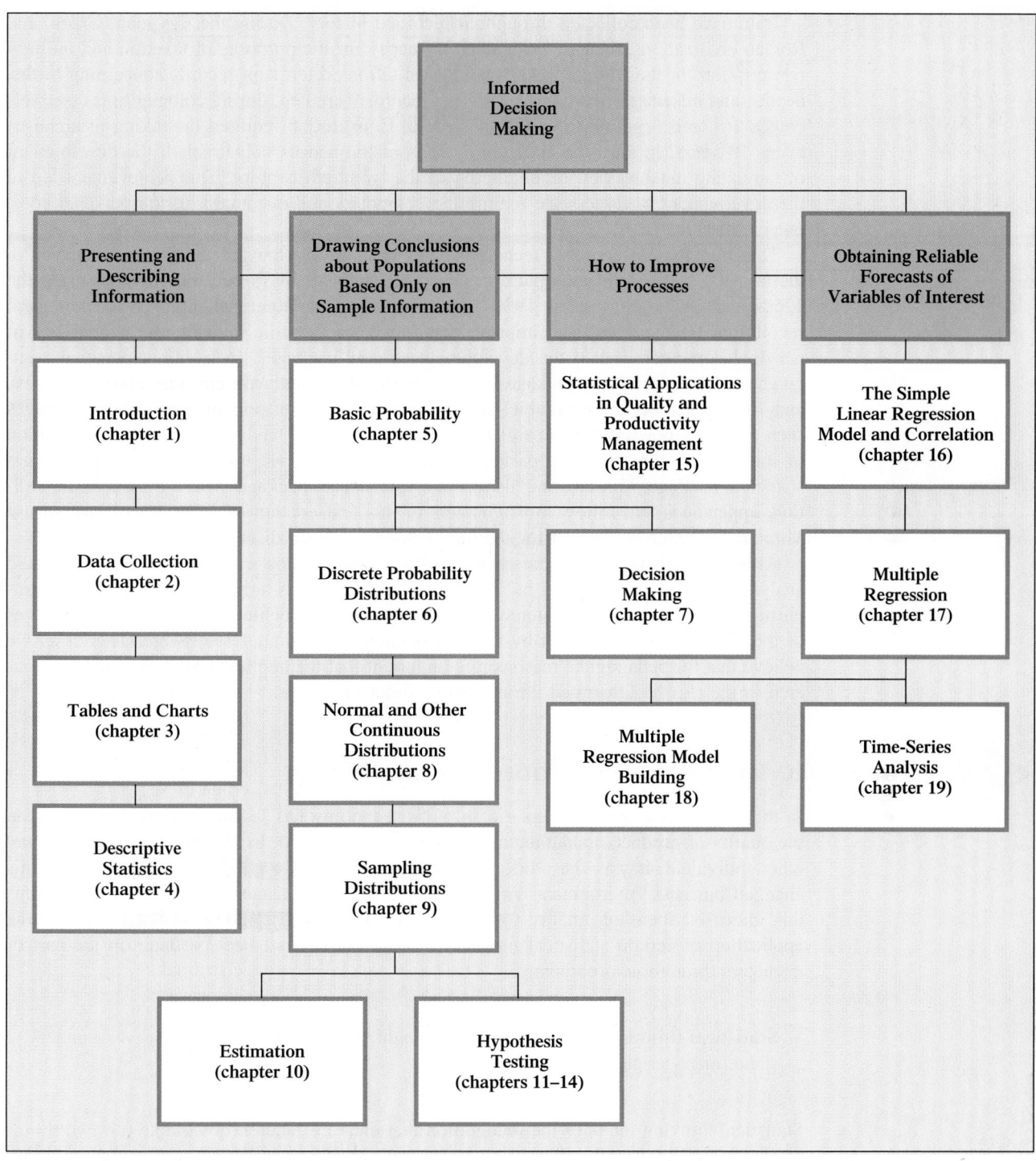

Road map for the text

Data have been collected throughout recorded history. During the Egyptian, Greek, and Roman civilizations, data were obtained primarily for the purposes of taxation and military conscription. In the Middle Ages, church institutions often kept records concerning births, deaths, and marriages. In America, various records were kept during colonial times (see reference 16), and beginning in 1790 the federal Constitution required the taking of a census every 10 years. In fact, the expanding needs of the census helped spark the development of tabulating machines at the beginning of the twentieth century. This achievement led to the development of large-scale mainframe computers and eventually to the personal computer.

This infusion of computer technology has profoundly changed the field of statistics in the last 30 years. Mainframe packages such as SAS and SPSS became popular during the 1960s and 1970s. During the 1980s, statistical software experienced a vast technological revolution. Besides the usual improvements made in periodic updates, the availability of personal computers led to the development of new packages. In addition, personal computer versions of existing packages such as SAS, SPSS, and Minitab (see references 9, 10, and 14) quickly became available, and the increasing use of popular spreadsheet packages such as Lotus 1-2-3 and Microsoft Excel (see references 7 and 8) led to the incorporation of statistical features in these packages. Thus, in this text we will illustrate output from a statistical package, Minitab, and also from a spreadsheet package, Microsoft Excel. In addition, appendices that follow most chapters of this text contain explanations of how to use Minitab and Microsoft Excel for the topics that have been discussed in the chapter.

Although statistical and spreadsheet software have made even the most sophisticated analyses feasible, we need to be aware that problems may arise when statistically unsophisticated users who do not understand the assumptions behind the statistical procedures or their limitations are misled by results obtained from computer software. Therefore, we believe that for pedagogical reasons it is important that the applications of the methods covered in the text be illustrated through worked-out examples.

## 1.3 STATISTICAL THINKING AND MODERN MANAGEMENT

In the past decade the emergence of a global economy has led to an increasing focus on the quality of products manufactured and services delivered. In fact, more than that of any other individual, it was the work of a statistician, W. Edwards Deming, that led to this changed business environment. An integral part of the managerial approach that contains this increased focus on quality (often referred to as **Total Quality Management**) is the application of certain statistical methods and the use of statistical thinking on the part of managers throughout a company.

> **Statistical thinking** can be defined as thought processes that focus on ways to understand, manage, and reduce variation.

Statistical thinking includes the recognition that data are inherently variable (no two things or people will be exactly alike in all ways) and that the identification, measurement, control, and reduction of variation provide opportunities for quality improvement. Statistical methods can provide the vehicle for taking advantage of these opportunities. The role of statistical methods in the context of quality improvement can be better understood if we refer to a model of quality improvement as presented in Figure 1.1. We may observe from

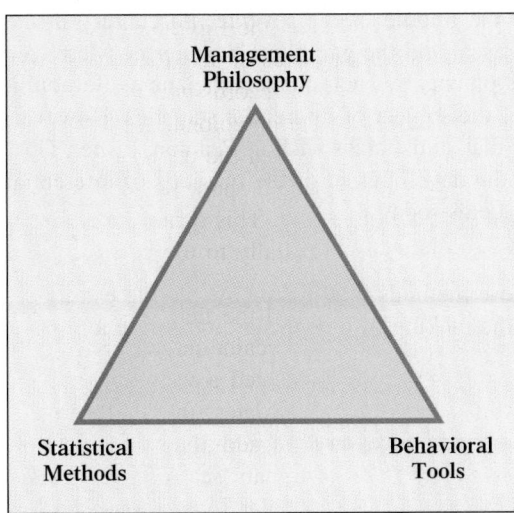

**FIGURE 1.1**
A model of the quality improvement process

Management
Philosophy

Statistical
Methods

Behavioral
Tools

Figure 1.1 that the triangle consists of three parts: at the top we have management philosophy, and at the two lower corners we have statistical methods and behavioral tools. Each of these three aspects is indispensable for long-term quality improvement of either the products manufactured or the services provided by an organization. A management philosophy provides a constant foundation for quality improvement efforts. Among the approaches available are those advocated by W. Edwards Deming (see references 1 and 2 and section 15.2) and Joseph Juran (see references 3 and 4).

In order to implement a quality improvement approach in an organization, one needs to use both behavioral tools and statistical methods. Each of these aids in understanding and improving processes. Among the useful behavioral tools are process flow and fishbone diagrams, brainstorming, nominal group decision making, and team building. (For further discussion, see references 1, 3, and 13.) Among the most useful statistical methods for quality improvement are the numerous tables and charts and descriptive statistics discussed in chapters 3 and 4 and the control charts developed in chapter 15.

 **DESCRIPTIVE VERSUS INFERENTIAL STATISTICS**

The need for data on a nationwide basis was closely intertwined with the development of descriptive statistics.

> **Descriptive statistics** can be defined as those methods involving the collection, presentation, and characterization of a set of data in order to describe the various features of that set of data properly.

Although descriptive statistical methods are important for presenting and characterizing data (see chapters 3 and 4), it has been the development of inferential statistical methods as an outgrowth of probability theory that has led to the wide application of statistics in all fields of research today.

The initial impetus for the formulation of the mathematics of probability theory came from the investigation of games of chance during the Renaissance. The foundations of the subject of probability can be traced back to the middle of the seventeenth century in the correspondence between the mathematician Pascal and the gambler Chevalier de Mere (see references 11 and 12). These and other developments by such mathematicians as Bernoulli, DeMoivre, and Gauss were the forerunners of the subject of inferential statistics. However, it has only been since the turn of this century that statisticians such as Pearson, Fisher, Gosset, Neyman, Wald, and Tukey pioneered in the development of the methods of inferential statistics that are widely applied in so many fields today.

**Inferential statistics** can be defined as those methods that make possible the estimation of a characteristic of a population or the making of a decision concerning a population based only on sample results.

To clarify this definition, a few more definitions are necessary.

A **population** (or **universe**) is the totality of items or things under consideration.
A **sample** is the portion of the population that is selected for analysis.
A **parameter** is a summary measure that is computed to describe a characteristic of an entire population.
A **statistic** is a summary measure that is computed to describe a characteristic from only a sample of the population.

Suppose that the president of your college wanted to conduct a survey to learn about student perceptions concerning the quality of life on campus. The population, or universe, in this instance would be all currently enrolled students, whereas the sample would consist only of those students who had been selected to participate in the survey. The goal of the survey would be to describe various attitudes or characteristics of the entire population (the parameters). This would be achieved by using the statistics obtained from the sample of students to estimate various attitudes or characteristics of interest in the population. Thus, one major aspect of inferential statistics is the process of using sample statistics to draw conclusions about the population parameters.

The need for inferential statistical methods derives from the need for sampling. As a population becomes large, it is usually too costly, too time consuming, and too cumbersome to obtain our information from the entire population. Decisions about the population's characteristics have to be based on the information contained in a sample of that population. Probability theory provides the link by determining the likelihood that the results from the sample reflect the results from the population.

As you can see in the chapter summary chart on the following page, this chapter provided an introduction to statistics, provided definitions of various terms that will be used throughout the text, and discussed the role of computer software. Chapter 2 will focus on data collection and the selection of samples. These two introductory chapters provide the background for descriptive statistics, which will be discussed in chapters 3 and 4.

## *Key Terms*

| | | |
|---|---|---|
| descriptive statistics 5 | population 6 | statistical thinking 4 |
| inferential statistics 6 | sample 6 | Total Quality Management 4 |
| parameter 6 | statistic 6 | universe 6 |

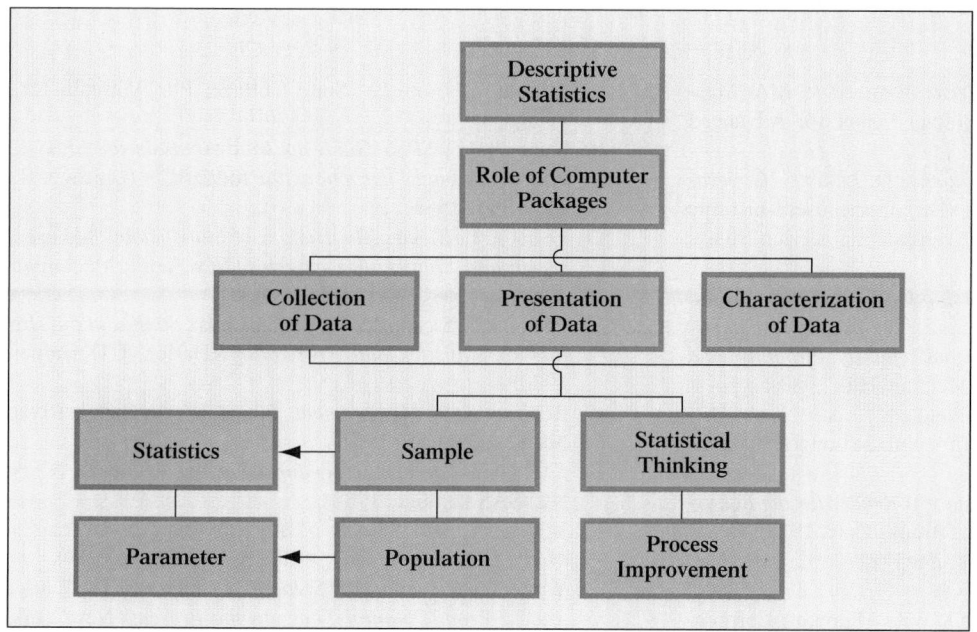

Chapter 1 summary chart

## Checking Your Understanding

**1.1** What is the difference between a sample and a population?

**1.2** What is the difference between a statistic and a parameter?

**1.3** What is the difference between descriptive and inferential statistics?

**1.4** How can statistical methods be useful to a manager?

**1.5** How has the field of statistics been changed by the development of computer technology?

**1.6** How was the development of the field of statistics intertwined with the needs of the census?

**1.7** How have statistical software packages changed in the past 30 years?

**1.8** What are the three aspects of quality improvement?

## Chapter Review Problems

**1.9** The Data and Story Library (DASL)(http://lib.stat.cmu.edu/DASL) is an on-line library of data files and stories that illustrate the use of basic statistical methods. Each data set has one or more associated stories. The stories are classified by method and by subject. Access this World Wide Web (WWW) site and, after reading a story, summarize how statistics have been used in one of the subject areas.

**1.10** Access one of the following two World Wide Web sites provided by Microsoft Corporation for Microsoft Excel (http://www.microsoft.com/msexcel and http://www.microsoft.com/msexcelsupport). Explain how you think Microsoft Excel could be useful in the field of statistics.

**1.11** Access the World Wide Web site for Minitab (http://www.minitab.com). Explain how the use of a statistical software package such as Minitab might be useful to a manager.

# References

1. Deming, W. E., *Out of the Crisis* (Cambridge, MA: Massachusetts Institute of Technology Center for Advanced Engineering Study, 1986).
2. Deming, W. E*., The New Economics for Industry, Government, Education* (Cambridge, MA: Massachusetts Institute of Technology Center for Advanced Engineering Study, 1993).
3. Juran, J. M., *Juran on Leadership for Quality* (New York: The Free Press, 1989).
4. Juran, J. M., and F. M. Gryna, *Quality Planning and Analysis*, 2d ed. (New York: McGraw-Hill, 1980).
5. Kendall, M. G., and R. L. Plackett, eds., *Studies in the History of Statistics and Probability,* vol. 2 (London: Charles W. Griffin, 1977).
6. Kirk, R. E., ed., *Statistical Issues: A Reader for the Behavioral Sciences* (Monterey, CA: Brooks/Cole, 1972).
7. *Lotus 1-2-3 Release 5* (Cambridge, MA: Lotus Development Corporation, 1994).
8. *Microsoft Excel 97* (Redmond, WA: Microsoft Corporation, 1997).
9. *Minitab Version 12* (State College, PA: Minitab, Inc., 1998).
10. Norusis, M., *SPSS Guide to Data Analysis for SPSS-X: With Additional Instructions for SPSS/PC+* (Chicago, IL: SPSS Inc., 1986).
11. Pearson, E. S., ed., *The History of Statistics in the Seventeenth and Eighteenth Centuries* (New York: Macmillan, 1978).
12. Pearson, E. S., and M. G. Kendall, eds., *Studies in the History of Statistics and Probability* (Darien, CT: Hafner, 1970).
13. Robbins, S. P., *Management,* 5th ed. (Upper Saddle River, NJ: Prentice Hall, 1997).
14. *SAS Language and Procedures Usage, Version 6* (Cary, NC: SAS Institute, 1988).
15. Walker, H. M., *Studies in the History of the Statistical Method* (Baltimore, MD: Williams & Wilkins, 1929).
16. Wattenberg, B. E., ed., *Statistical History of the United States: From Colonial Times to the Present* (New York: Basic Books, 1976).

## ❖ APPENDIX 1.1    BASICS OF THE WINDOWS USER INTERFACE

In this appendix we first provide an orientation to the basic concepts necessary to operate any program, such as Microsoft Excel or Minitab, that runs in a Windows user interface in which windows or frames are used as containers to subdivide the screen. In this user interface, although communication can be done with some combination of keystrokes, many pointing or choosing tasks are more easily done using a pointer device such as a mouse, trackball, or touchpad. Moving a pointer device moves the **mouse pointer**, an on-screen graphic that in its most common form takes the shape of an arrow. Moving the mouse pointer over another object and pressing one of the buttons on the pointer device defines a mouse operation. Four types of mouse operations used in Microsoft Excel or Minitab are defined in Exhibit A1.1.1.

In a window environment, mouse operations are applied to a variety of on-screen objects. First and foremost among these objects are **windows**, frames that serve as containers for other windows or for the objects described in this appendix. Many windows can be selected and dragged from one position on the screen to another and sometimes are capable of being **resized,** or having their length and width dimensions changed.

Other common objects in a window environment include free-floating icons, task or tool bars, menu bars, and dialog boxes.

### Free-Floating Icons

**Free-floating icons,** graphics that represent a specific application or document, can be selected and dragged from one position to another. Activating an icon representing Microsoft Excel would be a typical way of starting the Excel program.

## Exhibit A1.1.1  Types of Mouse Operations

✓ **1.** To **select** an on-screen object, move the mouse pointer (by moving the mouse) directly over an object and then press the left mouse button (or click the single button, if your mouse contains only one button). If the on-screen object being selected is a button, **click** is often used as an alternative to the verb *select*, as in the phrase "click the OK button."

✓ **2.** To **drag** or move an object, first move the mouse pointer over an object and then, while holding down the left (or single) mouse button, move the mouse. After the object has been dragged, release the mouse button.

✓ **3.** To **double-click** an object, move the mouse pointer directly over an object and press the left (or single) mouse button twice in rapid succession.

✓ **4.** To **right-click** an object, move the mouse pointer directly over an object and press the right mouse button. If your mouse contains only one mouse button, right-clicking is the same as simultaneously holding down the control key and pressing the mouse button.

## Menu Bars

**Menu bars** are the horizontal lists of words that represent a set of command choices. Selection of one of the choices results in the display of a **pull-down menu**, a list containing more word choices.

## Task or Tool Bars

**Task** or **tool bars** are groups of fixed-position icons or *buttons*, clickable graphics that simulate the operation of a mechanical push button. Tool bars can either be free floating or fixed—"snapped" into an on-screen position. In applications such as Microsoft Excel, there are tool bars that represent different categories of user actions such as formatting, editing, or drawing.

## Dialog Boxes

Making a certain selection on a menu or tool bar often results in a special type of window called a **dialog box**. Dialog boxes are used to display status messages or to prompt you to make choices or supply additional information. Common to many dialog boxes are the objects listed in Exhibit A1.1.2.

---

*COMMENT: Abbreviated Notation for Menu Selection*

In this text, the authors will abbreviate menu selections by using the vertical slash character | to separate menu choices. For example, **File | Open** will be used instead of the longer "select the File menu and then select the Open choice." In addition, as was done with **File | Open,** the actual commands will be in **bold-faced** type.

- **Drop-down list** boxes allow selection from a nonscrollable list that appears when the drop-down button, located on the right edge of the box, is clicked.
- **Scrollable list** boxes display a list of items, in this case, files or folders, for selection. When the list is too long to be seen in its entirety in the box, clicking the right scroll button or dragging the slider on the scroll bar at the bottom of the list box reveals the rest of the choices.
- **Edit** boxes provide an area into which a value can be edited or typed. Edit boxes are often combined with either a scroll-down list box or spinner buttons to provide an alternative to the typing of a value.
- **Option** buttons represent a set of mutually exclusive choices. Selecting an option button (also known as a radio button) always deselects, or clears, the other option buttons in the set, thereby allowing only one choice at any time.
- **Check** boxes allow the selection of optional actions. Unlike option buttons, more than one check box in a set can be selected at a given time.
- Clicking the **Open** or **OK** buttons causes an application to execute an operation with the current values and choices as shown in the dialog box.
- Clicking the **Cancel** button closes a dialog box and cancels the operation.

# ❖ APPENDIX 1.2 INTRODUCTION TO MICROSOFT EXCEL

## Microsoft Excel and This Text

Microsoft Excel is an example of a spreadsheet application, the personal productivity program best suited for the interactive manipulation of numerical data. Spreadsheet applications allow users to make entries into electronic versions of paper spreadsheets, or worksheets, ruled paper containing rows and columns long employed for the management and analysis of financial data by accountants. Not surprisingly, accountants were among the first professionals to understand the advantage of using an electronic worksheet in which calculations could be preprogrammed and the effects of changing data values immediately computed and displayed.

Today, the flexibility of spreadsheet applications makes them a common tool in many business professions and a good way of introducing statistical problem solving to students in an introductory business statistics course. This flexibility allows Microsoft Excel to be used in conjunction with the teaching of statistics in this text in two ways:

- As an application development tool that allows the implementation of original Excel-based solutions.

- As a "black box" that performs statistical analyses on command similar to the way a statistical package operates.

Either of these approaches can be used with this text. To support the first approach, many of the chapters contain a Microsoft Excel appendix that provides step-by-step instructions for walking through the implementation of an original design. To support the second approach, the CD-ROM that accompanies this text contains a special type of program, called an Add-In, that supports the black box approach to using Excel. If you are unsure which approach to use, the authors suggest that for at least some statistical topics, you develop and implement your own workbook. Using this approach will reinforce your understanding of the statistical topic involved, with the added benefit of also enhancing your Microsoft Excel skills.

## Getting Familiar with the Microsoft Excel Application Window

When Microsoft Excel is loaded and run, an Excel application window appears. Figure A1.2.1 shows such a window.

Users can configure the exact combination and placements of objects that appear in this window. In Figure A1.2.1, as in all illustrations of the Excel application window in this text, the standard and formatting tool bars and the formula bar have been configured to appear below the menu bar. The workbook displayed in the workspace area has been maximized, opened to cover the entire workspace area. Sets of resizing and closing buttons appear on the title bar and the menu bar. Scroll bars, both horizontal and vertical, allow for the display of parts of the worksheet currently offscreen. Sheet tabs, identifying the names of individual sheets, provide a means of "turning" to another sheet in the workbook. A status bar displays information about the current operation and the state of certain keyboard toggles.

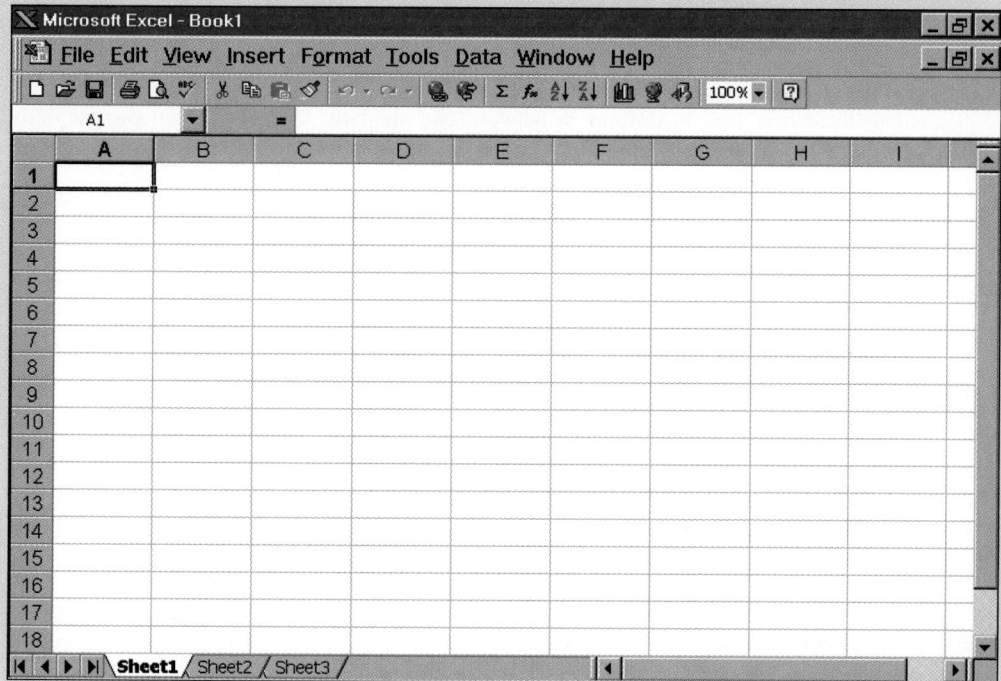

**FIGURE A1.2.1**

## Specifying Worksheet Locations

Part of the design process when using a spreadsheet application involves placing the data, calculations, and results required, along with title and labels such as column headings, into a grid formed by individual worksheets. Using a standard notation for worksheets, we can refer to the columns of a worksheet with letters and refer to rows with numbers to identify into which cells, the intersections of the rows and columns, entries should be placed. In this system, the cell reference A1 refers to the cell in the first column and the first row (the upper-left-corner cell); cell reference B4 refers to the cell in the second column and the fourth row.

Because a Microsoft Excel workbook can contain multiple worksheets, this column letter and row number format is, in certain contexts, insufficient to specify the particular cell of interest. When a workbook design calls for cell entries on one worksheet to refer to cells on another worksheet, the cell reference must be written in the form

*Sheetname!ColumnRow*

Using this notation, one can distinguish between two similarly located cells of two different sheets in the workbook. For example, Data!A1 and Calculations!A1 refer to the upper-left-corner cell of the Data and Calculations sheets, respectively. This extended notation is necessary only when the cell reference is to a worksheet other than the current one into which entries are being made.

Besides individual cells, references can be made to cell ranges which are rectangular groups of adjacent cells. Cell ranges are written using the cell references to the upper-leftmost and lower-rightmost cells in the block. The cell range form is

*UpperLeft:LowerRight*

For example, the cell range A1:B3 refers to the six-cell worksheet block containing the cells A1, B1, A2, B2, A3, and B3, and the range A1:A8 refers to the first eight cells in the first column of the worksheet. Ranges in the form

*Sheetname!UpperLeft:LowerRight*

are allowed and refer to ranges not on the current active sheet.

Sometimes there is a need to distinguish between two similarly located cells on two similarly named worksheets in two different workbooks located in the same folder or directory. In such cases, cell references are written in the form

*'[Workbookname]Sheetname'!ColumnRow*

as in '[MUTUAL]Data'!A1 referring to the upper-left-corner cell on the Data worksheet in the MUTUAL workbook.

## Configuring Microsoft Excel

Microsoft Excel allows for the custom configuration of the Excel application window. Readers of this text may want to make their Excel windows appear as similar as possible to Figure A1.2.1 and other illustrations of the application window that appear in this text. To configure Microsoft Excel so that the application window matches the illustrations in this text, load and run Excel and then follow the steps in Exhibit A1.2.1.

## Renaming Worksheets

Giving self-descriptive names to individual workbook objects can make using the workbook easier. By default, Microsoft Excel names worksheets serially in the form of Sheet1, Sheet2, and so on. Better names are ones that reflect the content of the sheets, such as Data for a sheet that contains the data to be analyzed, and Calculations for a sheet that holds the necessary calculations for an analysis. To give a sheet a descriptive name, we double-click the **sheet tab** of the sheet to be renamed, type a new sheet name, and press the **Enter** key.

---

### Exhibit A1.2.1 Commands for Configuring Microsoft Excel

✓ **1.** To display the formula and status bars and the standard and formatting toolbars:
- Select **View**. If the **Formula** bar is not checked, select it. If the **Status** bar is not checked, select it.
- Select **View | Toolbars**. If the **Standard** choice is not checked, select it. If the **Formatting** choice is not checked, select it.
- If any bar is not aligned to the top of the Excel application window, drag the bar toward the top of the screen until the dragged border of the bar changes to a slender band of small dots. The bar will then snap into place when the mouse button is released.

✓ **2.** To standardize the display of the worksheet area:
- Select **Tools | Options**. In the Options dialog box, select the **View** tab (if another tab's options are visible). Select the **Gridlines, Zero Values, Row & Column Headers, Horizontal Scroll Bar, Vertical Scroll Bar**, and **Sheet Tabs** check boxes. Deselect (uncheck) the **Formulas** check box if it has been selected. Click the **OK** button.

✓ **3.** To verify calculation, edit, and general display options that are used in the text:
- Select **Tools | Options**. In the Options dialog box, select the **Calculation** tab and verify that the **Automatic** option button of the Calculation group has been selected. Select the **Edit** tab and verify that all check boxes except the **Fixed Decimal** and **Provide Feedback with Animation** check boxes have been selected. Select the **General** tab. Verify that the **R1C1 Reference Style** box is deselected (unchecked). Change the value in the **Sheets in New Workbook** edit box to **3** if it is some other value. Select **Arial** (or a similar font) from the **Standard Font** list box. Select **10** from the **Size** drop-down list box.

✓ **4.** To verify the installation of the Data Analysis ToolPak Add-In:
- Select **Tools**. Select **Data Analysis** if it appears on the Tools menu and verify that the dialog box that appears contains an Analysis Tools scrollable list box. Click the **Cancel** button. This verifies the installation of the tools.
- If Data Analysis does not appear on the Tools menu, select **Add-Ins** from the menu. In the Add-Ins dialog box select the **Analysis ToolPak** and the **Analysis ToolPak-VBA** check boxes—if these check boxes appear—from the **Add-Ins Available:** list. Click the **OK** button. Exit Excel (select **File | Exit**); rerun Excel and follow the instructions in the previous paragraph to verify installation. *continued*

---

- If you cannot find the Analysis ToolPak or the Analysis ToolPak-VBA check box in the Add-Ins Available: list, most likely these special add-in files were not included when your copy of Excel was installed. You may need to rerun the Excel setup program. (See the "Install and use the Analysis ToolPak" on-line help topic for further information.)

## Entering Data in Excel Workbooks

Now that we have provided a basic orientation to Microsoft Excel and its user interface, we are ready to use Excel in an illustrative example. Suppose that data are available concerning the amount of money spent by five customers at a department store. The results are illustrated in Table A1.2.1.

**Table A1.2.1** *Amount spent by a sample of five customers at a department store*

| NAME | AMOUNT($) |
|------|-----------|
| Allen | 125 |
| Barry | 250 |
| Diane | 72 |
| Kim | 105 |
| Susan | 48 |

We are now ready to use Microsoft Excel to perform statistical analysis for these data. For our data of Table A1.2.1 we decide that the first column heading (Name) should appear in cell A1. Using the same reasoning, we determine that the amount heading should appear in cell B1 and the values indicating the amount of money spent by the five customers should appear in the next five rows (2 through 6). Having specified cell addresses for the various parts of the Data worksheet, we are now ready to enter values into the cells of a sheet that we will name Data. To do this, activate the Microsoft Excel application and select **File | New** to create a new, blank worksheet window. Rename Sheet1 as **Data**.

Select cell **A1** by clicking its interior. A special border, the **cell highlight**, appears around the cell. This highlight indicates that cell A1 is now the **active cell**, the cell into which the next value to be typed will be entered. (Also note that A1, the address of the active cell, appears in the cell reference box.) Type the column heading Name. As you type, notice that your keystrokes appear both in the edit box of the formula bar and in cell A1 itself. Press the **Enter** key (or click the check button to the left of the edit box) to complete the entry. (Users of keyboards that do not contain an Enter key should press the Return key when instructions in this text call for pressing the Enter key.) Continue by selecting cell B1 and entering the column heading Amount.

Now that the column headings have been entered, we can begin to enter the values that will appear underneath them. We will type in values by columns, using the feature of the Enter (return) key to automatically advance the cell highlight down one row after each entry. (If we wished to enter values by rows, we could end each entry by pressing the Tab key, which would advance the cell highlight one column to the right.)

Select cell A2 and type the name Allen and press the Enter key (or Return) key. Then type the remainder of the names in cells A3–A6, being sure to press the enter key after each name. Select cell B2 and enter the purchase amount of $125 from Table A1.2.1 into cell B2. Then continue and enter the corresponding amounts of 250, 72, 105, and 48 into cells B3 through B6. Having now entered all the data from our source table into the Data worksheet, we should **save** a copy of our work on disk, using **File | Save** or **File | Save As**, before continuing.

## COMMENT: *Correcting Errors*

As you make entries into a worksheet, you will probably at some point make a typing error. To correct typing errors, you can do one of the following:

- To cancel the current entry while typing it, press the Escape key or click the "X" button on the formula bar.
- To erase characters to the left of the cursor one character at a time, press the Backspace key.
- To erase characters to the right of the cursor one character at a time, press the Delete key.
- To replace an in-text error, first click at the start of the error, drag the mouse pointer over the rest of the error, and type the replacement text. If you change your mind, you can undo your last edit by selecting the command **Edit | Undo.** If you change your mind again and wish to keep the edit after all, select **Edit | Redo.**

## Developing Formulas to Perform Calculations

Now that we have saved our work, we are ready to compute a simple statistic, the total amount spent by the five customers. One way to generate the total amount value would be to just manually sum the values, adding 125, 250, 72, 105, and 48 to get 600 as the value for the total amount.

Although it might be argued that for this very small and very simple problem, manual calculation would be the best method to obtain the total amount, more generally it is wiser to have Microsoft Excel generate the values than to do it yourself. To have Excel generate these values, we will need to develop and enter formulas, or instructions to perform a calculation or some other task, in the appropriate cells of our Data worksheet (cell B7 in this example).

To distinguish them from other types of cell entries, all formulas always begin with the = (equal sign) symbol. Creating formulas requires knowledge of the **operators**, or special symbols, used to express arithmetic operations. Operators used in formulas in this text include addition (+), subtraction (−), multiplication (∗), division (/), and exponentiation [a number raised to a power (^)].

Because our definition of the total amount calls for the addition of five quantities, we will use the + (plus sign) in our total amount formula, combining it with the cell addresses containing the values we wish to add. In the case of calculating the total amount spent for the five customers, cells B2, B3, B4, B5, and B6 on the Data sheet are added together.

Assembling these pieces, we can form the formula

=Data!B2 + Data!B3 + Data!B4 + Data!B5 + Data!B6

and enter it into cell B7. However, since we are entering a formula in the same sheet as the sheet to which it refers, we also can write the formula using the shorthand notation

=B2 + B3 + B4 + B5 + B6

and Microsoft Excel will correctly interpret the addresses as referring to the current (Data) sheet.

## Using Functions in Formulas

In our discussion of formulas, we used the plus sign arithmetic operator to construct our formula. We could have just as easily used the sum function, one of many such preprogrammed instructions that can be selected when solving a variety of common arithmetic, business, engineering, and statistical problems.

To use the Sum function we would have typed the formula =SUM(B2:B6) into cell B7 instead of the formula =B2 + B3 + B4 + B5 + B6. In the formula =SUM(B2:B6) the word SUM identifies the sum function, the pair of parentheses () bracket the cells of interest, and B2:B6 is the address of the cell range of interest, the cells whose values will be used by the function.

---

*COMMENT:* **Copying Objects in Microsoft Excel**

Objects ranging from a single cell to an entire worksheet can be copied to simplify or speed implementation of a worksheet design. Generally, copying involves first selecting the object and then selecting the appropriate copy and paste commands.

- To copy a single cell entry or a range of entries, select the cell containing the entry to be copied or the cell range by dragging the mouse pointer through all cells of the range. Select **Edit | Copy**. Select the cell (or select the first cell of the range) to receive the copy. Select **Edit | Paste**. (Note: Copying entries that contain formulas may not result in duplicate entries. See appendix 3.1 for an explanation of absolute addresses.)
- To copy an entire worksheet, select the worksheet to be copied by clicking on its sheet tab. Select **Edit | Move or Copy Sheet**. In the Move or Copy dialog box, select the **Create a Copy** check box. Select **New Book** from the To book: drop-down list box if the copy of the worksheet is to be placed in a new workbook. Select the workbook position for the copy by selecting the appropriate choice from the Before sheet: list box. Click the **OK** button.

---

## Wizards

Wizards are sets of linked dialog boxes that step the user through some tasks. Users advance through the set of dialog boxes by making choices, supplying values, clicking the Next button to go forward, and ultimately a Finish button to complete a task. One example of a Microsoft Excel wizard is the Text Import Wizard, which assists in the importing or transferring of data from a text file—a file containing unlabeled and unformatted values that are separated by delimiters such as spaces, commas, or tab characters—into a worksheet. (This wizard would be particularly useful when seeking to avoid the reentry of the observations from a large data set that has previously been stored by a program other than Excel.)

To illustrate this wizard, consider the case of the mutual fund data that will be discussed in chapters 3 and 4. This data set has been stored in the text file MUTUAL.TXT. To import the data from this text file, select the command **File | Open**. In the Open dialog box, select **Text files** from the Files of type: drop-down list box (All Files can also be chosen). Select from the **Look In: drop-down list box** the folder that contains the file MUTUAL.TXT. Enter the name MUTUAL.TXT in the File Name edit box (or select it from the File Name list box). Click the **OK** button. This begins the three-step Text Import Wizard. In the Text Import Wizard Step 1 dialog box, select the **Fixed Width** option button (because the data values for the variables in this file have been placed in aligned, fixed-width columns). Click the **Next** button. In the Text Import Wizard Step 2 dialog box, click the **Next** button to accept the wizard's placement of the data from each line of the text file into the columns.

(Dragging the vertical column separator line would alter the placement had it been necessary.) In the Text Import Wizard Step 3 dialog box, select the **General** option button under the Column data format heading. Click the **Finish** button. The data of the text file have now been transferred to a Microsoft Excel worksheet.

## Add-Ins

Add-ins are optional components that can be combined with ("added into") Microsoft Excel in order to extend the functionality of Excel. Some add-ins, such as the Data Analysis ToolPak previously discussed, are supplied by Microsoft and can be installed, made permanently available to users, by running the Microsoft Excel setup program. Other, "third party" add-ins, such as the Prentice Hall/PHStat add-in that is supplied on the CD-ROM that accompanies this text, are loaded and installed separately.

For example, the Data Analysis ToolPak add-in inserts the choice Data Analysis to the preexisting Tools menu, while the Prentice Hall/PHStat add-in inserts the PHStat pull-down menu to the Menu bar. Selecting Tools | Data Analysis causes the ToolPak add-in to display the Data Analysis dialog box in which the statistical analysis of interest can be selected. Selecting PHStat from the Menu bar pulls down a menu of choices in which the operation of interest can be selected. These selections can lead to one or more dialog boxes or the generation of some workbook object.

### COMMENT:  *The PHStat Add-In That Accompanies This Text*

Third-party add-ins, such as the PHStat add-in supplied on the CD-ROM that accompanies this text, can either be permanently installed or loaded every time Excel is run. Because of possible performance issues, the authors suggest loading and not installing any third-party add-ins. To load an add-in, select **File | Open**, and then select the add-in file from the **File | Open** dialog box. (Add-ins have the extension .xla.)

Loading add-in files using the File | Open method may trigger the Microsoft macro virus dialog box that warns of the possibility of viruses. As provided on the CD-ROM that accompanies this text, the PHStat add-in is certified virus free, so if this dialog box appears, the **Enable Macros** button that allows the PHStat add-in to be loaded can be safely chosen.

To load the Prentice Hall PHStat add-in, use the setup program on the CD-ROM that accompanies this text to install the PHStat add-in, if this has not been done previously. (You must be able to write to your System's Windows directories in order to properly install the add-in. See the detailed instructions in Appendix F.)

If Microsoft Excel is not running, click the **Windows Desktop Start** button. Select Programs/Prentice Hall Add-In/PHStat Add-In. If Microsoft Excel is running, select **File | Open**. In the File | Open dialog box, select the folder containing the Prentice Hall PHStat add-in and open the Prentice Hall PHStat add-in file (PHSA.XLA). As the PHStat add-in loads, if the Macros Virus dialog box appears, click the Enable Macros button.

If the PHStat add-in loads successfully a new PHStat menu is added to the Excel application menu bar and a title dialog box appears. Click the **Continue** button to continue using Excel and this add-in.

To use the Prentice Hall PHStat add-in after it has been loaded, select PHStat from the Excel application menu bar. Select the menu choice, and submenu choice, if necessary, until the add-in dialog box for the procedure is displayed. Enter information and make selections, as is necessary into these dialog boxes. Click the **OK** button to perform the analysis.

## Summary

In this appendix we have provided an introduction to the basic features of the Microsoft Excel application. For additional details concerning various features of Microsoft Excel, see references 1–3. In the remainder of the Excel appendices in this text we will be learning about many additional aspects of Microsoft Excel in the context of specific statistical analyses.

## References

1. Grauer, R., and M. Barber, *Exploring Microsoft Excel 97* (Upper Saddle River, NJ: Prentice Hall, 1997).
2. Levine, D. M., M. L. Berenson, and D. Stephan, *Statistics for Managers using Microsoft Excel,* 2d ed. (Upper Saddle River, NJ: Prentice Hall, 1999).
3. *Microsoft Excel 97 for Windows* (Redmond, WA: Microsoft Corporation, 1997).

## ❖ APPENDIX 1.3    INTRODUCTION TO MINITAB

### What Are Statistical Software Application Programs?

In section 1.2 when we discussed how software could help the manager use data to make decisions, we stated that the statistical software package Minitab would be illustrated in this text.

Statistical software application programs contain a collection of statistical methods that help provide solutions to managerial problems. These programs allow users who are relatively unskilled in statistics to access a wide variety of statistical methods for their data sets of interest. In this text, we will be illustrating and explaining the use of the Minitab statistical software in appendices to many of the chapters. The latest version of Minitab operates in a windowing environment. Readers who are not familiar with such an operating environment should read appendix A1.1, which explains the basic features of this environment.

### Entering Data Using Minitab

There are two fundamental methods for obtaining data for use with Minitab, entering data at a keyboard, or importing data from a file. To begin, open Minitab to obtain a window that should look similar to Figure A1.3.1.

This window contains several features that need to be discussed. At the top of the window is a Menu bar from which you choose commands that allow you to obtain statistics, graphs, store and save data, and perform many other operations. Below the Menu bar is a Session window that displays text output such as tables of statistics. Below the Session window is the Data window, a rectangular array of rows and columns where you enter, edit, and view data. Note that the first row in the Data window lists the columns, which are generically labeled C1, C2, and so on. The following row contains an arrow in the first column and then a set of blank columns. This row serves as a place holder in which labels for variable names are entered.

Data may be entered via the keyboard in the cells in the Data window. If the arrow points down, pressing Enter moves the active cell (into which numbers are entered) down; if the arrow points right, pressing Enter moves the active cell to the right. Clicking the arrow will change the direction of the data entry.

As an illustrative example, suppose that data are available concerning the amount of money spent by five customers at a department store. The results are illustrated in Table A1.3.1.

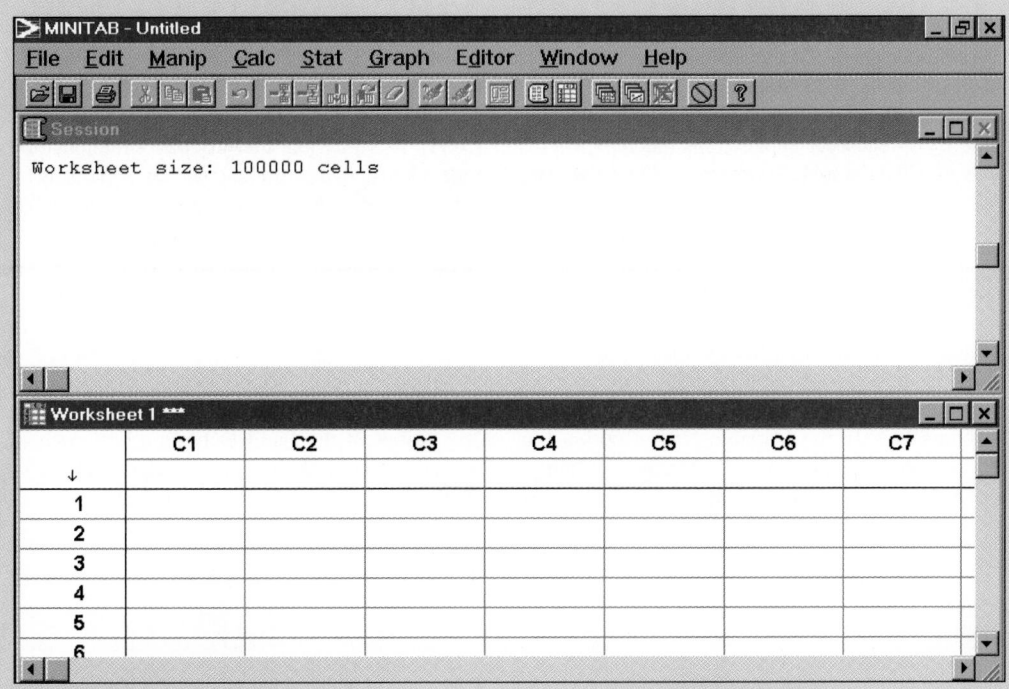

**FIGURE A1.3.1**

**Table A1.3.1** *Amount spent by a sample of five customers at a department store*

| NAME | AMOUNT($) |
|---|---|
| Allen | 125 |
| Barry | 250 |
| Diane | 72 |
| Kim | 105 |
| Susan | 48 |

Begin in the row above the horizontal line containing numbered rows. This row is used to provide the labels for each variable. In the first column (labeled C1) enter the label of the first variable (Name) and press the Enter key. This moves the cursor to the first row of this column. Enter Allen in row 1, Barry in row 2, Diane in row 3, Kim in row 4, and Susan in row 5. Move the cursor to the heading area at the top of column 2 (under C2) and enter Amount ($) as the label for this column. After pressing Enter to move to row 1 in column C2, we enter 125, the amount spent by Allen. Continuing, we enter the amounts spent by the other four customers in rows 2 to 5, respectively.

When performing statistical analyses throughout this text, we often encounter data sets with a large number of observations. When such sets have previously been entered and stored in a data file, it makes sense to try to import the contents of the file into our Data sheet to avoid having to reenter each observation one at a time. Each data set in this text has been stored in several different formats, including the Minitab format (.MTW or .MTP). To import the contents of a Minitab worksheet, open the Minitab file of interest located in the appropriate directory. This is done by selecting **File | Open Worksheet** on the Menu bar and then selecting the appropriate file from the directory in which we have stored the data sets for this text.

Although Minitab can import data that have been stored in any one of various special file types used by spreadsheet applications (such as Microsoft Excel), it is possible that in other situations you will find data stored as text files, files that contain unlabeled and unformatted values separated by *delimiters* such as spaces, commas, or tab characters. To open data from a text file, we need to use the command **File | Open Worksheet**. This will provide us with the Open Worksheet dialog box. Many different files, including Minitab files (.MTW or .MTP), Microsoft Excel (.XLS), data (.DAT), and text (.TXT), can be opened from this dialog box. Making sure that the proper file type appears in the List of Files of Type Box, select the file that you wish to open. To see how the file will look on the worksheet, click the Preview option.

If the first row of the file begins with data and does not contain the variable names (as is the case with the files ending in .TXT that are contained on the disk that accompanies this text), click the **Options** box. In the Variable Names option box, select **None**. In the Field Definition options box, select **Free Format**. Click the **OK** box. When you are ready to open the selected file, click **Open** so that the data will appear in the Data window. Enter labels for each variable as appropriate.

## References

1. *Minitab Version 12* (State College, PA: Minitab, Inc., 1998).

# 2

# Data Collection

# CHAPTER OBJECTIVES

✓ *To discuss sources of data*
✓ *To discuss types of data*
✓ *To introduce methods of sample selection*
✓ *To study how to evaluate survey worthiness*

## Introduction

Collecting, understanding, and analyzing data are central to the success of many businesses. In this chapter we discuss how data are collected and measured. We then discuss how and for whom surveys are designed as well as how the resulting data are prepared. Finally, we discuss the various errors inherent in data obtained from surveys and how to avoid them so that we can present good survey results and avoid any ethical problems that may arise.

## ◆ USING STATISTICS: *Exchange International Resort Evaluation*

Exchange International offers a vacation exchange network for time-share resort owners throughout the world. Members of Exchange International may use its services to arrange for vacation exchanges with other time-share resort owners. Exchange International recognizes the importance of offering its members high-quality resort destinations. To monitor the quality of its affiliated resorts, Exchange International provides a survey to all members prior to their vacation departures and offers the possibility of a free vacation exchange as an incentive to respond. By evaluating their perceptions and opinions, Exchange International seeks to improve member services and to affiliate with only the finest vacation resorts. This survey is partially reproduced here.

• How would you rate the following aspects of your vacation?

|  | EXCELLENT | GOOD | FAIR | DISAPPOINTING | UNACCEPTABLE |
|---|---|---|---|---|---|
| Quality of area | 5 | 4 | 3 | 2 | 1 |
| Quality of unit | 5 | 4 | 3 | 2 | 1 |
| Quality of resort | 5 | 4 | 3 | 2 | 1 |
| Quality of services | 5 | 4 | 3 | 2 | 1 |

• Would you be likely to return to this resort again?   Yes ☐    No ☐
• About how much money (in U.S. dollars) did you pay for your time-share? _____

## ◆ 2.1  WHY DO WE NEED DATA?

Obtaining appropriate information is essential to conducting business. We may think of **data** as the information needed to help us make a more informed decision in a particular situation. There are many instances in which data are needed.

- A market researcher needs to assess product characteristics to distinguish one product from another.
- A pharmaceutical manufacturer needs to determine whether a new drug is more effective than those currently in use.
- A manager wants to monitor a process on a regular basis to find out whether the quality of service being provided or products being manufactured are conforming to company standards.
- An auditor wants to review the financial transactions of a company in order to ascertain whether or not it is in compliance with generally accepted accounting principles.
- A potential investor wants to determine which firms within which industries are likely to have accelerated growth in a period of economic recovery.
- A student wants to get data on his classmates' favorite rock group to satisfy his curiosity.

There are six main reasons for data collection, as illustrated in Exhibit 2.1.

**Exhibit 2.1  Reasons for Obtaining Data**

✓ **1.** Data are needed to provide the necessary input to a survey.

✓ **2.** Data are needed to provide the necessary input to a study.

✓ **3.** Data are needed to measure performance of an ongoing service or production process.

✓ **4.** Data are needed to evaluate conformance to standards.

✓ **5.** Data are needed to assist in formulating alternative courses of action in a decision-making process.

✓ **6.** Data are needed to satisfy our curiosity.

The Exchange International survey in our opening Using Statistics example illustrates reasons 1, 3, 4, and 5. For example, Exchange International compiles data as the result of a survey. It then analyzes the data to measure performance, to evaluate standards, and to help formulate alternative courses of action should this be required.

It is extremely important that we begin our statistical analysis by identifying the most appropriate data collection sources. If the data are flawed by biases, ambiguities, or other types of errors, even the fanciest and most sophisticated statistical methodologies would not likely be enough to compensate for such deficiencies.

 **SOURCES OF DATA**

There are four key data collection sources as illustrated in Exhibit 2.2.

Data collectors are labeled **primary sources,** while data compilers are called **secondary sources.** As illustrated in Exhibit 2.2, the first method of obtaining data is via governmental, industrial, or individual sources. Of these three, the federal government is the major collector and compiler of data for both public and private purposes.

Many governmental agencies facilitate this work. The Bureau of Labor Statistics is responsible for collecting data on employment as well as for establishing the well-known monthly *Consumer Price Index*. In addition to its constitutional requirement for conducting a decennial census, the Bureau of the Census oversees a variety of ongoing surveys regarding population, housing, and manufacturing. Additionally, it undertakes special studies on topics such as crime, travel, and health care.

---

**Exhibit 2.2  Key Data Collection Sources**

✓ **1.** We may obtain data already published by governmental, industrial, or individual sources.

✓ **2.** We may design an experiment to obtain the necessary data.

✓ **3.** We may conduct a survey.

✓ **4.** We may make observations through an observational study.

---

In addition to the federal government, various trade publications present data pertaining to specific industrial groups. Investment services such as Moody's display financial data on a company basis. Syndicated services such as A. C. Nielsen provide clients with information enabling the comparison of client products with their competitors. Daily newspapers are filled with numerical information regarding stock prices, weather conditions, and sports statistics.

The second data collection source is through experimentation. In an experiment, strict control is exercised over the treatments given to participants. For example, in a study testing the effectiveness of toothpaste, the researcher would determine which participants in the study would use the new brand and which would not, instead of leaving the choice to the subjects. Proper experimental designs are usually the subject matter of more advanced texts, since they often involve sophisticated statistical procedures. However, in order to develop a feeling for testing and experimentation, the fundamental experimental design concepts will be considered in chapters 11–14.

The third data collection source is by conducting a survey. Here no control is exercised over the behavior of the people being surveyed. They are merely asked questions about their beliefs, attitudes, behaviors, and other characteristics. Responses are then edited, coded, and tabulated for analysis.

The fourth method for obtaining data is through an observational study. A researcher observes the behavior directly, usually in its natural setting. Most knowledge of animal behavior is developed in this way, as is our scientific knowledge in many fields, such as astronomy and geology, in which experimentation and surveys are impractical if not impossible.

Observational study has many formats in business, all of which are intended to collect information in a group setting to assist in the decision-making process. As one example, the **focus group** is a popular marketing research tool that is used for eliciting unstructured responses to open-ended questions. A moderator leads the discussion and all the participants respond to the questions asked. Other, more structured formats involving group dynamics for obtaining information (and consensus building) include various organizational behavior/industrial psychology tools such as brainstorming, the Delphi technique, and the nominal-group method (see reference 13). These tools have become more popular in recent years owing to the impact of the total quality management (TQM) philosophy on business, because TQM emphasizes the importance of teamwork and employee empowerment in an attempt to improve every product and service.

In order to design an experiment, conduct a survey, or perform an observational study, one must understand the different types of data and measurement levels. To demonstrate some of the issues involved in obtaining data, we will present them in the context of a survey, although most of the same issues will arise in other types of research.

## 2.3 TYPES OF DATA

Statisticians develop surveys to deal with a variety of phenomena or characteristics. These phenomena or characteristics are called **random variables**. The data, which are the observed outcomes of these random variables, will undoubtedly differ from response to response.

As illustrated in Figure 2.1, there are two types of random variables that yield the observed outcomes or data: categorical and numerical.

**Categorical random variables** yield categorical responses, such as yes or no answers. An example is the response to the question "Do you currently own U.S. Government Savings Bonds?" because it is limited to a simple yes or no answer. Another example is the response to the question on the Exchange International survey "Would you be likely to return to this resort again?"

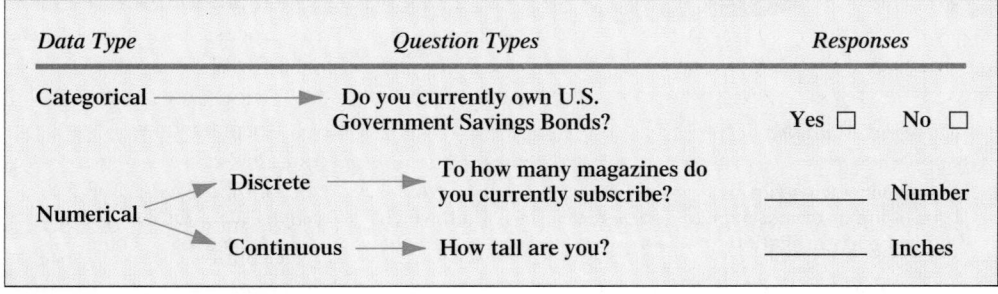

*FIGURE 2.1* Types of data

**Numerical random variables** yield numerical responses such as your height in inches. Other examples are how much money you paid for your time-share from the Exchange International survey or the response to the question "To how many magazines do you currently subscribe?"

There are two types of numerical variables: discrete and continuous.

**Discrete random variables** produce numerical responses that arise from a counting process. "The number of magazines subscribed to" is an example of a discrete numerical variable, because the response is one of a finite number of integers. You subscribe to zero, one, two, and so on, magazines.

**Continuous random variables** produce numerical responses that arise from a measuring process. Your height is an example of a continuous numerical variable, because the response takes on any value within a continuum or interval, depending on the precision of the measuring instrument. For example, your height may be 67 inches, $67\frac{1}{4}$ inches, $67\frac{7}{32}$ inches, or $67\frac{58}{250}$ inches depending on the precision of the available instruments.

Theoretically, no two persons could have exactly the same height, since the finer the measuring device used, the greater the likelihood of detecting differences among them. However, most measuring devices are not sophisticated enough to detect small differences. Hence, *tied observations* are often found in experimental or survey data even though the random variable is truly continuous.

## Levels of Measurement and Types of Measurement Scales

We could also describe our resulting data in accordance with the level of measurement attained. There are four widely recognized levels of measurement: nominal, ordinal, interval, and ratio scales.

◆ *Nominal and Ordinal Scales*   Data obtained from a categorical variable are said to have been measured on a **nominal scale** or on an **ordinal scale**. A nominal scale (Figure 2.2) classifies data into various distinct categories in which no ordering is implied. In the Exchange International survey, the answer to the question "Would you be likely to return to this resort again?" is an example of a nominally scaled variable, as is your favorite soft drink, your political party affiliation, and your gender. Nominal scaling is the weakest form of measurement because no attempt can be made to account for differences within a particular category or to specify any ordering or direction across the various categories.

An ordinal scale classifies data into distinct categories in which ordering is implied. In the Exchange International survey, the answers to the question "How would you rate the following aspects of your vacation: overall quality of the area, overall quality of the unit, overall quality of the resort, and overall quality of services?" are all ordinal scaled variables because the responses excellent, good, fair, disappointing, and unacceptable are ranked

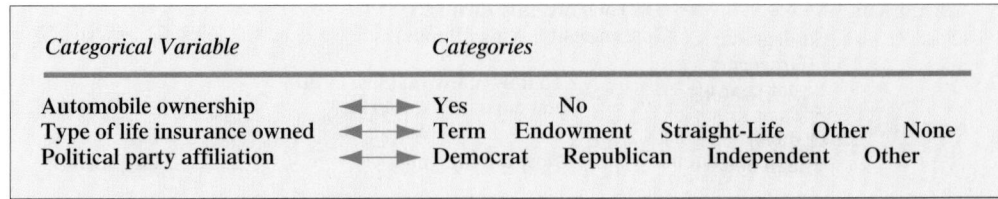

***FIGURE 2.2***   Examples of nominal scaling

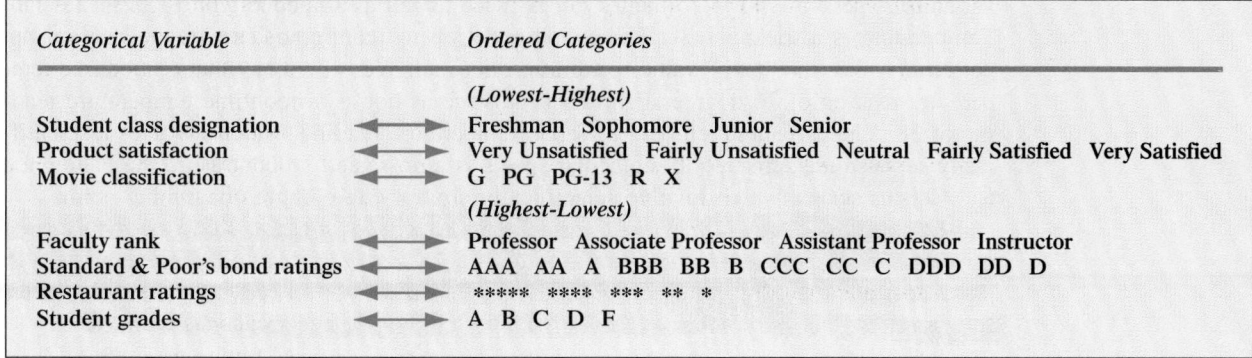

| Categorical Variable | | Ordered Categories |
|---|---|---|
| | | *(Lowest-Highest)* |
| Student class designation | ← → | Freshman  Sophomore  Junior  Senior |
| Product satisfaction | ← → | Very Unsatisfied  Fairly Unsatisfied  Neutral  Fairly Satisfied  Very Satisfied |
| Movie classification | ← → | G  PG  PG-13  R  X |
| | | *(Highest-Lowest)* |
| Faculty rank | ← → | Professor  Associate Professor  Assistant Professor  Instructor |
| Standard & Poor's bond ratings | ← → | AAA  AA  A  BBB  BB  B  CCC  CC  C  DDD  DD  D |
| Restaurant ratings | ← → | *****  ****  ***  **  * |
| Student grades | ← → | A  B  C  D  F |

***FIGURE 2.3***  Examples of ordinal scaling

in order of satisfaction level. Other examples of ordinal scaled variables such as bond ratings and grades are depicted in Figure 2.3.

Ordinal scaling is a somewhat stronger form of measurement, because an observed value classified into one category is said to possess more of a property being scaled than does an observed value classified into another category. Nevertheless, ordinal scaling is still a relatively weak form of measurement because no attempt is made to account for differences *between* the classified values. This is because no meaningful numerical statements can be made about differences between the categories. The ordering implies only *which* category is "greater," "better," or "more preferred"—not by *how much*. For example, ratings of college basketball and football teams rank who is in first, second, or third place. However, the differences between the teams ranked first and second might not be the same as the differences between the teams ranked second and third, and so on.

◆ *Interval and Ratio Scales*   An **interval scale** (Figure 2.4) is an ordered scale in which the difference between measurements is a meaningful quantity that does not involve a true zero point. For example, a noontime temperature reading of 67 degrees Fahrenheit is 2 degrees Fahrenheit warmer than a noontime reading of 65 degrees Fahrenheit. In addition, the 2 degrees Fahrenheit difference in the noontime temperature readings is the same quantity that would be obtained if the two noontime temperature readings were 74 and 76 degrees Fahrenheit, so the difference has the same meaning anywhere on the scale.

A **ratio scale** is an ordered scale in which the difference between the measurements involves a true zero point as in height, weight, age, or salary measurements. In the Exchange International survey the amount paid for a time-share unit is an example of a ratio scaled

| Numerical Variable | | Level of Measurement |
|---|---|---|
| Temperature (in degrees Celsius or Fahrenheit) | ———→ | Interval |
| Calendar time (Gregorian, Hebrew, or Islamic) | ———→ | Interval |
| Height (in inches or centimeters) | ———→ | Ratio |
| Weight (in pounds or kilograms) | ———→ | Ratio |
| Age (in years or days) | ———→ | Ratio |
| Salary (in American dollars or Japanese yen) | ———→ | Ratio |

***FIGURE 2.4***  Examples of interval and ratio scaling

variable. A person who is 76 inches tall is twice as tall as someone who is 38 inches tall. Temperature is a trickier case: Fahrenheit and Celsius (centigrade) scales are interval but not ratio scales; the "zero" value is arbitrary, not real. We cannot say that a noontime temperature reading of 76 degrees Fahrenheit is twice as hot as a noontime temperature reading of 38 degrees Fahrenheit. But a Kelvin temperature reading, which involves a scientifically set absolute zero tied to molecular speed, is ratio-scaled, in contrast to the Fahrenheit and Celsius scales, which involve scientifically arbitrary zero-degree beginning points.

Data obtained from a numerical variable are usually assumed to have been measured either on an interval scale or on a ratio scale. These scales constitute the highest levels of measurement. They are stronger forms of measurement than an ordinal scale because we can determine not only which observed value is the largest but also by how much.

## Problems for Section 2.3

### Learning the Basics

• **2.1** Suppose that three different beverages are sold at a fast-food restaurant—soft drinks, tea, and coffee.
(a) Explain why the type of beverage sold is an example of a categorical variable.
(b) Explain why the type of beverage sold is an example of a nominal scaled variable.

**2.2** Suppose that soft drinks are sold in three sizes in a fast-food restaurant—small, medium, and large. Explain why the size of the soft drink is an ordinal scaled variable.

**2.3** Suppose that we measure the time of airplane flight from New York to Los Angeles from takeoff to landing.
(a) Explain why the time of airplane flight is a numerical variable.
(b) Explain why the time of airplane flight is a ratio scaled variable.

### Applying the Concepts

• **2.4** For each of the following random variables determine
1. Whether the variable is categorical or numerical. If the variable is numerical, determine whether the phenomenon of interest is discrete or continuous.
2. The level of measurement.
   (a) Number of telephones per household
   (b) Type of telephone primarily used
   (c) Number of long-distance calls made per month
   (d) Length (in minutes) of longest long-distance call made per month
   (e) Color of telephone primarily used
   (f) Monthly charge (in dollars and cents) for long-distance calls made
   (g) Ownership of a cellular phone
   (h) Number of local calls made per month
   (i) Length (in minutes) of longest local call per month
   (j) Whether there is a telephone line connected to a computer modem in the household
   (k) Whether there is a FAX machine in the household

**2.5** Suppose that the following information is obtained from students upon exiting from the campus bookstore during the first week of classes:
(a) Amount of money spent on books
(b) Number of textbooks purchased
(c) Amount of time spent shopping in the bookstore
(d) Academic major
(e) Gender
(f) Ownership of a personal computer
(g) Ownership of a videocassette recorder
(h) Number of credits registered for in the current semester
(i) Whether or not any clothing items were currently purchased at the bookstore
(j) Method of payment

1. Classify each of these variables as categorical or numerical. If the variable is numerical, determine whether the variable is discrete or continuous.
2. Provide the level of measurement.

**2.6** For each of the following random variables determine
1. Whether the variable is categorical or numerical. If the variable is numerical, determine whether the phenomenon of interest is discrete or continuous.
2. The level of measurement.
   (a) Brand of personal computer primarily used
   (b) Cost of personal computer system
   (c) Amount of time the personal computer is used per week
   (d) Primary use for the personal computer
   (e) Number of persons in the household who use the personal computer
   (f) Number of computer magazine subscriptions
   (g) Word processing package primarily used
   (h) Whether the personal computer is connected to the Internet

**2.7** For each of the following random variables determine
1. Whether the variable is categorical or numerical. If the variable is numerical, determine whether the phenomenon of interest is discrete or continuous.
2. The level of measurement.
   (a) Amount of money spent on clothing in the last month
   (b) Number of winter coats owned
   (c) Favorite department store
   (d) Amount of time spent shopping for clothing in the last month
   (e) Most likely time period during which shopping for clothing takes place (weekday, weeknight, or weekend)
   (f) Number of pairs of gloves owned
   (g) Primary type of transportation used when shopping for clothing

**2.8** Suppose the following information is obtained from Robert Keeler on his application for a home mortgage loan at the Metro County Savings and Loan Association:

(a) Place of Residence: Stony Brook, New York
(b) Type of Residence: Single-family home
(c) Date of Birth: April 9, 1962
(d) Monthly Payments: $1,427
(e) Occupation: Newspaper reporter/author
(f) Employer: Daily newspaper
(g) Number of Years at Job: 14
(h) Number of Jobs in Past 10 Years: 1
(i) Annual Family Salary Income: $66,000
(j) Other Income: $16,000
(k) Marital Status: Married
(l) Number of Children: 2
(m) Mortgage Requested: $120,000
(n) Term of Mortgage: 30 years
(o) Other Loans: Car
(p) Amount of Other Loans: $8,000

Classify each of the responses by type of data and level of measurement.

**2.9** One of the variables most often included in surveys is income. Sometimes the question is phrased "What is your income (in thousands of dollars)?" In other surveys, the respondent is asked to "Place an X in the circle corresponding to your income level."

    ○ Under $20,000?    ○ $20,000–$39,999    ○ $40,000 or more

(a) For each of these formats, state whether the measurement level for the variable is nominal, ordinal, interval, or ratio.
(b) In the first format, explain why income might be considered either discrete or continuous.
(c) Which of these two formats would you prefer to use if you were conducting a survey? Why?
(d) Which of these two formats would likely bring you a greater rate of response? Why?

**2.10** If two students both score a 90 on the same examination, what arguments could be used to show that the underlying random variable—test score—is continuous?

**2.11** Suppose that the director of market research at a large department store chain wanted to conduct a survey throughout a metropolitan area to determine the amount of time working women spend shopping for clothing in a typical month.

(a) Describe both the population and the sample of interest and indicate the type of data the director might wish to collect.

(b) Develop a first draft of the questionnaire needed in (a) by writing a series of three categorical questions and three numerical questions that you feel would be appropriate for this survey.

 **2.4** **DESIGN OF SURVEY RESEARCH**

As noted in our Using Statistics example at the beginning of the chapter, the market researchers at Exchange International use surveys to distinguish product or service characteristics from those of their competitors and to improve on them. If customers are "loyal," company management does not want them to switch to the competition. How do businesses maintain this loyalty? One way is to design and conduct surveys that are geared to identifying the characteristics of a product or service that customers find essential. Survey design is an art that improves with experience. The general procedure for designing a survey involves five basic steps as outlined in Exhibit 2.3.

 **Exhibit 2.3 Survey Design**

✓ **1.** Choose an appropriate mode of response.

✓ **2.** Identify broad categories that reflect the theme of the survey.

✓ **3.** Carefully formulate accurate questions.

✓ **4.** Test the survey for clarity and length. Revise as necessary.

✓ **5.** Write a cover letter. The letter should include question instructions and offer an incentive gift to respondents, if needed.

A discussion of these steps follows.

### Choosing a Mode of Response

The particular questionnaire format to be selected and the specific question wording are affected by the intended mode of response. There are three primary modes of response: personal interview, telephone interview, and mail. The personal interview and the telephone interview usually produce a higher response rate than does the mail survey—but at a higher cost.

Other modes of response to surveys are based on self-selection. These include television surveys, which provide 900 numbers, Internet surveys developed by specific search engines or companies and by groups with home pages; newspapers or magazines with printed surveys that can be clipped and mailed by readers who wish to comply; and product or service questionnaires often found in hotel rooms or restaurants, on trains or planes, or attached to products purchased in stores.

Self-selection response methods are usually not reliable because the respondents who choose to participate in such surveys often do not represent the views of the general population. Thus it is not appropriate to use such data to make inferences about the general population.

## Identifying Broad Categories

As an organizing tool, first list the broad categories that reflect the theme of the survey. These categories should not overlap and should be complete.

## Formulating Accurate Questions

Working through the broad categories usually generates a long list of questions, called a questionnaire. Because of the inverse relationship between the length of a questionnaire and the rate of response to the survey, it is imperative that we carefully evaluate the merits of each question to determine whether the question is really necessary. Then, if the question is deemed necessary, we must determine how best to word it, remembering that questions should be as short and clear as possible. This is so important that researchers have coined a term for it—**GIGO**, which stands for "garbage in, garbage out." Essentially, if the questions are ambiguous, the resulting data will be flawed.

To be accurate, data cannot be flawed by ambiguities that arise from misinterpretations of the questions asked in a survey. For example, consider the question "What is your age?" To avoid problems of ambiguity, we must clarify whether age should be reported to the nearest birthday or as of the last birthday. Young respondents are likely to choose their nearest birthdays. Older respondents are much more likely to report their current age. Therefore, the question avoids ambiguity if it simply asks, "What was your age on your last birthday?"

Clear, unambiguous questions that ask for specific information use commonly accepted operational definitions.

An **operational definition** is a universally accepted definition that provides meaning to a concept or variable and can be communicated to other individuals.

## Testing the Survey

Once the pros and cons of each question have been discussed, the survey is organized and readied for pilot testing. Such testing on a small group of participants is essential to assess the survey for clarity and length. Not only will this group provide an estimate of the time needed for responding to the survey, but they also may shed light on any perceived question ambiguities or on whether additional questions are needed.

## Writing a Cover Letter

If the survey is being conducted by mail, a cover letter must be included, and it should be as brief as possible. The cover letter should state the goal and purpose of the survey and why it is important that the selected individuals respond. It should also give any necessary assurance of respondent anonymity and, in some cases involving regular mail rather than in-house surveys, offer an incentive gift for respondent participation.

## Problems for Section 2.4

### Learning the Basics

• **2.12** Give an operational definition of what you would consider to be fast service in a fast-food restaurant.

**2.13** Provide three different ways that the question "What was your income last year?" could be asked in a survey conducted by mail.

### Applying the Concepts

**2.14** Provide an operational definition for each of the following:
(a) An outstanding teacher
(b) A hard worker
(c) A nice day
(d) Fast service at a bank
(e) A leader
(f) Commuting time to school or work
(g) A fine quarterback

**2.15** Provide an operational definition for each of the following:
(a) A dynamic individual
(b) A boring class
(c) An interesting book
(d) An outstanding performance
(e) A manager
(f) An on-time plane arrival
(g) Study time

**2.16** A question often asked in surveys relates to how much education a person has.
(a) Write three versions of the question that give different levels of detail.
(b) Which question would you be more likely to ask in a personal interview?
(c) Which question would you be more likely to ask in a telephone interview?
(d) Which question would you be more likely to ask in a mail survey?

## 2.5 TYPES OF SAMPLING METHODS

As mentioned in chapter 1, a sample is the portion of the population that has been selected for analysis. Rather than taking a complete census of the whole population, statistical sampling procedures focus on a small representative group of the larger population. The resulting sample provides information that can be used to estimate characteristics of the entire population.

The sampling process begins by locating appropriate data sources, such as population lists, directories, maps, and other sources, which are called **frames**. Samples are drawn from these frames. If the frame is inadequate because certain groups of individuals or items in the targeted population were not properly included, then the samples will be inaccurate and biased. Using different frames to generate data can lead to opposite conclusions, as illustrated in Example 2.1.

### Example 2.1  *A Case of Opposing Conclusions*

Consider the following headline that appeared in a suburban New York newspaper a decade ago: "Off, With a Head Count: Is Suffolk More Populous than Nassau? LILCO and the Census Bureau Disagree" (*Newsday*, April 25, 1988). Given Suffolk's survey data, the Suffolk county executive felt it was more populous, whereas the Nassau county executive disagreed, citing Nassau's own survey data. Who was right?

*SOLUTION*

The differences in the two estimates come from the fact that the Census Bureau and the Long Island Lighting Company (LILCO) used different frames and formulas to estimate population in the two counties. The Census Bureau used birth and death rates, migration patterns as shown on income tax returns, and a demographic formula that estimated that the average number of people per household had been shrinking in the past several years. For its definition, LILCO used the number of year-round electric and gas meters, building permits, and a factor for the number of people in each house.

---

There are three main reasons for drawing a sample, as depicted in Exhibit 2.4.

### Exhibit 2.4  *Reasons for Drawing a Sample*

✓ **1.** A sample is less time consuming than a census.

✓ **2.** A sample is less costly to administer than a census.

✓ **3.** A sample is less cumbersome and more practical to administer than a census of the targeted population.

As depicted in Figure 2.5, there are basically two kinds of samples: the **nonprobability sample** and the **probability sample**.

A **nonprobability sample** is one in which the items or individuals included are chosen without regard to their probability of occurrence.

Since nonprobability samples have chosen participants without knowing their probabilities of selection (and in some cases participants have self-selected), the theory that has been

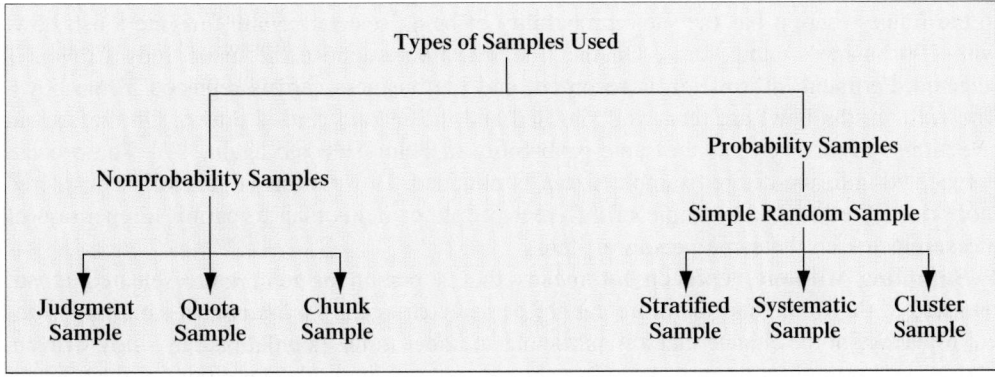

*FIGURE 2.5*  Types of samples

developed for probability sampling cannot be applied. For many studies, only a nonprobability sample such as a judgment sample is available. In these instances, the opinion of an expert in the subject matter of a study is crucial to being able to use the results obtained to make changes in a process. Some other common procedures of nonprobability sampling are quota sampling and chunk sampling; these are discussed in detail in specialized books on sampling methods (see references 1, 3, and 8).

Nonprobability samples can have certain advantages such as convenience, speed, and lower cost. On the other hand, two major disadvantages—a lack of accuracy due to selection bias and a lack of generalizability of the results—more than offset the advantages. Therefore, we should restrict our use of nonprobability sampling methods to situations in which we want to obtain rough approximations at low cost in order to satisfy our curiosity about a particular subject or to small-scale initial or pilot studies that will later be followed up by more rigorous investigations.

Probability sampling should be used whenever possible because it is the only method by which correct statistical inferences can be made from a sample.

A **probability sample** is one in which the subjects of the sample are chosen on the basis of known probabilities.

The four types of probability samples most commonly used are the simple random, systematic, stratified, and cluster. These sampling methods vary from one another in their cost, accuracy, and complexity. A discussion of these types of samples follows.

## Simple Random Sample

A **simple random sample** is one in which every individual or item from a population has the same chance of selection as every other individual or item. In addition, every sample of a fixed size has the same chance of selection as every other sample of that size. Simple random sampling is the most elementary random sampling technique and as such forms the basis for the other random sampling techniques.

With simple random sampling, we use $n$ to represent the sample size and $N$ to represent the population size. Every item or person in the frame is numbered from 1 to $N$. The chance that any particular member of the population is selected on the first draw is $1/N$.

There are two basic methods by which samples are selected: with replacement or without replacement.

**Sampling with replacement** means that once a person or item is selected, it is returned to the frame where it has the same probability of being selected again. Imagine a fish bowl with 100 business name cards. On the first selection, suppose the name Judy Craven is selected. Pertinent information is recorded, and the business card is replaced in the bowl. The cards in the bowl are then well shuffled and the second card is drawn. On the second selection, Judy Craven has the same probability of being selected again, $1/N$. The process is repeated until the desired sample size $n$ is obtained. However, it is generally considered more desirable to have a sample of different people or items than to permit a repetition of measurements on the same person or item.

**Sampling without replacement** means that a person or item once selected is not returned to the frame and therefore cannot be selected again. As before, in sampling without replacement the chance that any particular member in the population, say, Judy Craven, is selected on the first draw is $1/N$. The chance that any individual not previously selected will be selected on the second draw is now 1 out of $N - 1$. This process continues until the desired sample of size $n$ is obtained.

Regardless of whether we sample with or without replacement, such "fish bowl" methods for sample selection have a major drawback—our ability to thoroughly mix the cards and randomly pull the sample. As a result, fish bowl methods are not very useful. Less cumbersome and more scientific methods of selection are desirable.

One such method uses a **table of random numbers** (see Table E.1 of appendix E) for obtaining the sample. A table of random numbers consists of a series of digits randomly generated and listed in the sequence in which the digits were generated (see references 8 and 12). Since our numeric system uses 10 digits (0, 1, 2, . . . , 9), the chance of randomly generating any particular digit is equal to the probability of generating any other digit. This probability is 1 out of 10. Hence, if a sequence of 800 digits were generated, we would expect about 80 of them to be the digit 0, 80 to be the digit 1, and so on. In fact, researchers who use tables of random numbers usually test out such generated digits for randomness before employing them. Table E.1 has met all such criteria for randomness. Since every digit or sequence of digits in the table is random, we may use the table by reading either horizontally or vertically. The margins of the table designate row numbers and column numbers. The digits themselves are grouped into sequences of five to make reading the table easier.

To use such a table instead of a fish bowl for selecting the sample, it is first necessary to assign code numbers to the individual members of the population. We then obtain our random sample by reading the table of random numbers and selecting those individuals from the population frame whose assigned code numbers match the digits found in the table. To better understand the process of sample selection from its inception, consider Example 2.2.

## Example 2.2 *Selecting a Simple Random Sample Using a Table of Random Numbers*

Suppose that a company wants to select a sample size of 32 full-time workers out of a population of 800 full-time employees in order to obtain information on expenditures from a company-sponsored dental plan. We assume that not everyone will be willing to respond to the survey, so we reason that we must have a larger mailing than 32 to get our desired 32 responses. If we assume that 8 out of 10 full-time workers are expected to respond to such a survey (that is, a rate of return of 80%), we calculate that a total of 40 such employees must be contacted to obtain the desired 32 responses. Therefore, our survey will be distributed to 40 full-time employees drawn from the personnel files of the company. How will the simple random sample actually be drawn?

### SOLUTION

To select the random sample, we use a table of random numbers. The population frame consists of a listing of the names and company mailbox numbers of all $N = 800$ full-time employees obtained from the company personnel files. Since the population size (800) is a three-digit number, each assigned code number must also be three digits so that every full-time worker has an equal chance for selection. Thus, a code of 001 is given to the first full-time employee in the population listing, a code of 002 is given to the second full-time employee in the population listing, and so on, until a code of 800 is given to the $N$th full-time worker in the listing. Since $N = 800$ is the largest possible coded value, all three-digit code sequences greater than $N$ (i.e., 801 through 999 and 000) are discarded.

To select the simple random sample, a random starting point for the table of random numbers is chosen. One such method is to close one's eyes and strike the table of random numbers with a pencil. Suppose we use such a procedure and thereby select row 06, column 05, of Table 2.1 (which is a replica of Table E.1) as the starting point. Although we can go in any direction in the table, suppose we read from left to right in sequences of three digits without skipping.

The individual with code number 003 is the first full-time employee in the sample (row 06 and columns 05–07), the second individual has code number 364 (row 06 and columns 08–10), and the third individual has code number 884. Since the highest code for any employee is 800, this number is discarded. Individuals with code numbers 720, 433, 463, 363, 109, 592, 470, and 705 are selected third through tenth, respectively.

The selection process continues in a similar manner until the needed sample size of 40 full-time employees is obtained. During the selection process, if any three-digit coded

**Table 2.1**  *Using a table of random numbers*

| | Row | COLUMN | | | | | | | |
|---|---|---|---|---|---|---|---|---|---|
| | | *00000* *12345* | *00001* *67890* | *11111* *12345* | *11112* *67890* | *22222* *12345* | *22223* *67890* | *33333* *12345* | *33334* *67890* |
| | 01 | 49280 | 88924 | 35779 | 00283 | 81163 | 07275 | 89863 | 02348 |
| | 02 | 61870 | 41657 | 07468 | 08612 | 98083 | 97349 | 20775 | 45091 |
| | 03 | 43898 | 65923 | 25078 | 86129 | 78496 | 97653 | 91550 | 08078 |
| | 04 | 62993 | 93912 | 30454 | 84598 | 56095 | 20664 | 12872 | 64647 |
| | 05 | 33850 | 58555 | 51438 | 85507 | 71865 | 79488 | 76783 | 31708 |
| Begin | 06 | 97340 | 03364 | 88472 | 04334 | 63919 | 36394 | 11095 | 92470 |
| Selection | 07 | 70543 | 29776 | 10087 | 10072 | 55980 | 64688 | 68239 | 20461 |
| (Row 06, Column 05) | 08 | 89382 | 93809 | 00796 | 95945 | 34101 | 81277 | 66090 | 88872 |
| | 09 | 37818 | 72142 | 67140 | 50785 | 22380 | 16703 | 53362 | 44940 |
| | 10 | 60430 | 22834 | 14130 | 96593 | 23298 | 56203 | 92671 | 15925 |
| | 11 | 82975 | 66158 | 84731 | 19436 | 55790 | 69229 | 28661 | 13675 |
| | 12 | 39087 | 71938 | 40355 | 54324 | 08401 | 26299 | 49420 | 59208 |
| | 13 | 55700 | 24586 | 93247 | 32596 | 11865 | 63397 | 44251 | 43189 |
| | 14 | 14756 | 23997 | 78643 | 75912 | 83832 | 32768 | 18928 | 57070 |
| | 15 | 32166 | 53251 | 70654 | 92827 | 63491 | 04233 | 33825 | 69662 |
| | 16 | 23236 | 73751 | 31888 | 81718 | 06546 | 83246 | 47651 | 04877 |
| | 17 | 45794 | 26926 | 15130 | 82455 | 78305 | 55058 | 52551 | 47182 |
| | 18 | 09893 | 20505 | 14225 | 68514 | 46427 | 56788 | 96297 | 78822 |
| | 19 | 54382 | 74598 | 91499 | 14523 | 68479 | 27686 | 46162 | 83554 |
| | 20 | 94750 | 89923 | 37089 | 20048 | 80336 | 94598 | 26940 | 36858 |
| | 21 | 70297 | 34135 | 53140 | 33340 | 42050 | 82341 | 44104 | 82949 |
| | 22 | 85157 | 47954 | 32979 | 26575 | 57600 | 40881 | 12250 | 73742 |
| | 23 | 11100 | 02340 | 12860 | 74697 | 96644 | 89439 | 28707 | 25815 |
| | 24 | 36871 | 50775 | 30592 | 57143 | 17381 | 68856 | 25853 | 35041 |
| | 25 | 23913 | 48357 | 63308 | 16090 | 51690 | 54607 | 72407 | 55538 |
| | ⋮ | ⋮ | ⋮ | ⋮ | ⋮ | ⋮ | ⋮ | ⋮ | ⋮ |

*Source: Partially extracted from The Rand Corporation,* A Million Random Digits with 100,000 Normal Deviates *(Glencoe, IL: The Free Press, 1955) and displayed in Table E.1 in appendix E at the back of this text.*

sequence repeats, the employee corresponding to that coded sequence is included again as part of the sample if we are sampling with replacement; however, the repeating coded sequence is discarded if we are sampling without replacement.

◆ **Systematic Sample** In a **systematic sample**, the $N$ individuals or items in the population frame are partitioned into $k$ groups by dividing the size of the population frame $N$ by the desired sample size $n$. That is,

$$k = \frac{N}{n}$$

where $k$ is rounded to the nearest integer. To obtain a systematic sample, the first individual or item to be selected is chosen at random from the $k$ individuals or items in the first partitioned group in the population frame, and the rest of the sample is obtained by selecting every $k$th individual or item thereafter from the entire population frame listing.

If the population frame consists of a listing of prenumbered checks, sales receipts, or invoices or if the population frame pertains to club membership listings, student registration listings, or perhaps a preset number of consecutive items coming off an assembly line, a systematic sample is faster and easier to obtain than a simple random sample. In such situations, the systematic sample would be a convenient mechanism for obtaining the desired data.

## Example 2.3 *Selecting a Systematic Sample*

As in Example 2.2, suppose that a company wants to select a sample size of 32 full-time workers out of a population of 800 full-time employees in order to obtain information on expenditures from a company-sponsored dental plan. If we again assume an overall 80% response rate, our survey will be distributed to 40 full-time employees taken from the personnel files of the company to obtain the desired 32 responses. How will the systematic sample actually be selected?

### SOLUTION

The population frame consists of a listing of the names and company mailbox numbers of all $N = 800$ full-time employees obtained from the company personnel files. Since the population size (800) is a three-digit number, each assigned code number must also be three digits, so that every full-time worker has an equal chance for selection. Thus, a code of 001 is given to the first full-time employee in the population listing and a code of 800 is given to the $N$th full-time worker in the listing.

To obtain a systematic sample, the $N = 800$ full-time employees who make up the population frame are partitioned into $k = 20$ groups by dividing the size of the population frame (800) by the desired number of employees to be sampled (40) in order to obtain the anticipated number of responses to the questionnaire. That is,

$$k = \frac{N}{n} = \frac{800}{40} = 20$$

In this situation, $k = 20$ is itself an integer and no rounding is needed.

To conduct a systematic sample, the first full-time employee to be selected is chosen at random from among the $k = 20$ individuals in the first partitioned group, and the rest of the sample is obtained by selecting every twentieth (that is, $k$th) full-time employee thereafter from the population frame listing.

We use a table of random numbers to select the first full-time employee in our systematic sample from among the 20 in the first partitioned group. To expedite the sampling process, the first 20 individuals are assigned temporary code numbers of 01 through 20, respectively. If from Table E.1, we select row 12, column 01, as the starting point, we read from left to right in sequences of two digits without skipping until we obtain a random number that corresponds to one of the 20 full-time employees in the first partitioned group from the population frame listing. From the table we note that the first two-digit sequence is 39 (too large) but the second two-digit sequence is 08 (row 12 and columns 03–04). Therefore, the eighth individual in the first partitioned group is the first full-time employee selected for the survey. Note that this employee's three-digit code number is actually 008 since he or she is the eighth full-time employee listed in the entire population frame.

The remainder of the systematic sample may be selected by locating every $k = 20$th individual thereafter from the population frame listing. Thus this systematic sample would consist of the 40 full-time employees with code numbers 008, 028, 048, 068, 088, 108, 128, 148, 168, 188, 208, 228, 248, 268, 288, 308, 328, 348, 368, 388, 408, 428, 448, 468, 488, 508, 528, 548, 568, 588, 608, 628, 648, 668, 688, 708, 728, 748, 768, and 788. Each of these employees will be given a questionnaire, and it is anticipated that approximately 80%, or 32 individuals, will actually respond.

---

Although they are simpler to use, simple random sampling methods and systematic sampling methods are generally less efficient than other, more sophisticated probability sampling methods. That is, for any one sample obtained by either simple random sampling or systematic sampling, the data obtained may or may not be a good representation of the population's underlying characteristics (parameters). Although most simple random samples are representative of their underlying population, it is not possible to know if the particular sample taken is in fact representative.

Even greater possibilities for selection bias and lack of representation of the population characteristics occur from systematic samples. If a pattern were to exist in the population frame listing, severe selection biases could result. To overcome the potential problem of disproportionate representation of specific groups in a sample, we can use either stratified sampling methods or cluster sampling methods.

◆ *Stratified Sample*   In a **stratified sample**, the $N$ individuals or items in the population are first subdivided into separate subpopulations, or *strata,* according to some common characteristic. A simple random sample is conducted within each of the strata and the results from the separate simple random samples are then combined. Such sampling methods are more efficient than either simple random sampling or systematic sampling because they ensure representation of individuals or items across the entire population, which ensures a greater precision in the estimates of underlying population parameters. It is the homogeneity of individuals or items within each stratum that when combined across strata provides the precision.

## Example 2.4 *Selecting a Stratified Sample*

As in Example 2.2, suppose that a company wants to select a sample size of 32 full-time workers out of a population of 800 full-time employees in order to obtain information on expenditures from a company-sponsored dental plan. If we again assume an (overall) 80% response rate, our survey will be distributed to 40 full-time employees taken from the personnel files of the company to obtain the desired 32 responses. How will the stratified sample actually be selected?

### SOLUTION

The population frame consists of a listing of the names and company mailbox numbers of all $N = 800$ full-time employees obtained from the company personnel files. Since 25% of the full-time employees are considered to be managerial, the first step is to separate the population frame into two strata: a subpopulation listing of all 200 managerial-level personnel and a separate subpopulation listing of all 600 full-time nonmanagerial workers. Since the first stratum consists of a listing of 200 managers, three-digit code numbers from 001 to 200 are assigned. Since the second stratum contains a listing of 600 nonmanagerial-level workers, three-digit code numbers from 001 to 600 are assigned.

To obtain a stratified sample proportional to the sizes of the strata, 25% of the overall sample are drawn from the first stratum and 75% of the overall sample are taken from the second stratum. To accomplish this, two separate simple random samples are drawn, each of which is based on a distinct random starting point from a table of random numbers (Table E.1). This results in the selection of 10 managers from the listing of 200 in the first stratum and 30 nonmanagerial workers from the listing of 600 in the second stratum. The results are then combined to reflect the composition of the entire company.

◆ *The Cluster Sample* In a **cluster sample**, the $N$ individuals or items in the population are divided into several *clusters* so that each cluster is representative of the entire population. A random sampling of clusters is then taken and all individuals or items in each selected cluster are then studied. Clusters can be naturally occurring designations, such as counties, election districts, city blocks, apartment buildings, or families.

Cluster sampling methods can be more cost effective than simple random sampling methods, particularly if the underlying population is spread over a wide geographic region. However, cluster sampling methods tend to be less efficient than either simple random sampling methods or stratified sampling methods and would require a larger overall sample size to obtain results as precise as those that would be obtained from the more efficient procedures.

## Example 2.5 *Selecting a Cluster Sample*

As in Example 2.2, suppose that a company wants to select a sample size of 32 full-time workers out of a population of 800 full-time employees in order to obtain information on expenditures from a company-sponsored dental plan. If we again assume an (overall) 80% response rate, the survey will be distributed to 40 full-time employees taken from the personnel files of the company to obtain the desired 32 responses. How will the cluster sample actually be selected?

### SOLUTION

Suppose the company is organized into 10 project centers each of which contains 80 full-time employees, 25% of whom are considered to be management level. Since each project center contains both managerial and nonmanagerial-level personnel, these 10 project centers represent clusters that can be used to facilitate the cluster sampling process.

To obtain a cluster sample, the first step is to identify and number the 10 clusters using two-digit code numbers from 01 to 10. Using a random starting point in a table of random numbers (Table E.1), a cluster is then selected.

Progressing to the next step involves our making some logical decisions. For example, each cluster contains 80 individuals and the desired sample size is 40 individuals. Thus, a complete sample of one cluster is expected to yield 64 responses (that is, 80% of 80 people), which is twice as many as initially desired. We also reason that it is more logical to sample two clusters to better ensure overall population representation. However, a complete sample of two clusters is expected to yield 128 responses, which is four times as many as desired. To satisfy the constraints of our problem, we decide to conduct a *two-stage* cluster sample in which we choose 20 individuals from each of the two randomly selected clusters. With this method, the 20 individuals can be selected using random sampling, systematic sampling, or any other efficient, timesaving scheme.

A detailed discussion of systematic sampling, stratified sampling, and cluster sampling procedures can be found in references 1, 3, and 8.

## Problems for Section 2.5

### Learning the Basics

**2.17** For a population list containing $N = 902$ individuals, what code number would you assign for
(a) the first person on the list?
(b) the fortieth person on the list?
(c) the last person on the list?

**2.18** For a population of $N = 902$, verify that by starting in row 05 of the table of random numbers (Table E.1), only six rows are needed to draw a sample of size $n = 60$ *without* replacement.

• **2.19** Given a population of $N = 93$, starting in row 29 of the table of random numbers (Table E.1) and reading across the row, draw a sample of size $n = 15$
(a) *without* replacement.
(b) *with* replacement.

### Applying the Concepts

**2.20** For a study that would involve doing personal interviews with participants (rather than mail or phone surveys), tell why a simple random sample might be less practical than some other methods.

**2.21** Suppose that I want to select a random sample of size 1 from a population of three items (which we can call A, B, and C). My rule for drawing the sample is: Flip a coin; if it is heads, pick item A; if it is tails, flip the coin again; this time, if it is heads, choose B; if tails, choose C. Explain why this is a random sample but not a simple random sample.

**2.22** Suppose that a population has four members (call them A, B, C, and D). I would like to draw a random sample of size 2, which I decide to do in the following way: Flip a coin; if it is heads, my sample will be items A and B; if it is tails, the sample will be items C and D. Although this is a random sample, it is not a simple random sample. Explain why. (If you did Problem 2.21, compare the procedure described there with the procedure described in this problem.)

● **2.23** Suppose that the registrar of a college with a population of $N = 4,000$ full-time students is asked by the president to conduct a survey to measure satisfaction with the quality of life on campus. The following table contains a breakdown of the 4,000 registered full-time students by gender and class designation:

| GENDER | CLASS DESIGNATION | | | | TOTALS |
|---|---|---|---|---|---|
| | FR. | SO. | JR. | SR. | |
| Female | 700 | 520 | 500 | 480 | 2,200 |
| Male | 560 | 460 | 400 | 380 | 1,800 |
| Totals | 1,260 | 980 | 900 | 860 | 4,000 |

The registrar intends to take a probability sample of $n = 200$ students and project the results from the sample to the entire population of full-time students.

(a) If the population frame available from the registrar's files is an alphabetical listing of the names of all $N = 4,000$ registered full-time students, what type of samples could be taken? Discuss.

(b) What would be the advantage of selecting a simple random sample in (a)?

(c) What would be the advantage of selecting a systematic sample in (a)?

(d) If the population frame available from the registrar's files is a listing of the names of all $N = 4,000$ registered full-time students compiled from eight separate alphabetical lists based on the gender and class designation breakdowns shown in the above table, what type of sample should be taken? Discuss.

(e) Suppose that all $N = 4,000$ registered full-time students lived in one of the 20 campus dormitories. Each dormitory contains four floors with 50 beds per floor, thereby accommodating 200 students. It is college policy to fully integrate students by gender and class designation in each floor of each dormitory. If the registrar was able to compile a population frame through a listing of all student occupants on each floor within each dormitory, what type of sample should be taken? Discuss.

**2.24** Prenumbered sales invoices are kept in a sales journal. The invoices are numbered from 0001 to 5000.

(a) Beginning in row 16, column 1, and proceeding horizontally in Table E.1, select a simple random sample of 50 invoice numbers.

(b) Select a systematic sample of 50 invoice numbers. Use the random numbers in row 20, columns 5–7 as the starting point for your selection.

(c) Are the invoices selected in (a) the same as those selected in (b)? Why or why not?

**2.25** Suppose that 5,000 sales invoices are separated into four strata. Stratum 1 contains 50 invoices, stratum 2 contains 500 invoices, stratum 3 contains 1,000 invoices, and stratum 4 contains 3,450 invoices. All 50 invoices in stratum 1 are to be selected, and 50 invoices from each of the other strata are to be selected.

(a) What type of sampling should be done? Why?

(b) Explain how you would carry out the sampling according to the method stated in (a).

(c) Why is the type of sampling in (a) not a simple random sample?

Nearly every day, we read or hear about survey or opinion poll results in our newspapers or on radio or television. Clearly, advances in information technology have led to a proliferation of survey research. Not all this research is good, meaningful, or important (reference 2), however.

To avoid those surveys lacking in objectivity or credibility, we must critically evaluate what we read and hear by examining the worthiness of the survey. First, we must evaluate the purpose of the survey, why it was conducted, and for whom. An opinion poll or survey conducted to satisfy curiosity is mainly for entertainment. Its result is an end in itself rather than a means to an end. We should be more skeptical of such a survey because the result should not be put to further use.

The second step in evaluating the worthiness of a survey is to determine whether it was based on a probability or a nonprobability sample (as discussed in section 2.5). You may recall that the only way for us to make correct statistical inferences from a sample to a population is through the use of a probability sample. Surveys employing nonprobability sampling methods are subject to serious, perhaps unintentional, interview biases that may render the results meaningless, as illustrated in the following.

*COMMENT:* ***A Nonprobability Sampling Disaster***

In 1948, major pollsters predicted the outcome of the American presidential election between Harry S. Truman, the incumbent president, and Thomas E. Dewey, then governor of New York, as going to Dewey. *The Chicago Tribune* was so confident of the polls' predictions that it printed its early edition based on the predictions rather than waiting for the ballots to be counted.

An embarrassed newspaper and the pollsters they had relied on had a lot of explaining to do. How had the pollsters been so wrong? Intent on discovering the source of the error, the pollsters found that their use of a nonprobability sampling method was the culprit (see reference 11). As a result, polling organizations adopted probability sampling methods for future elections.

## Survey Errors

Even when surveys employ random probability sampling methods, they are subject to potential errors. As illustrated in Exhibit 2.5, there are four types of survey errors (reference 7). Good survey research design attempts to reduce or minimize these various survey errors, often at considerable cost.

### Exhibit 2.5  *Survey Errors*

✓ **1.** Coverage error or selection bias
✓ **2.** Nonresponse error or nonresponse bias
✓ **3.** Sampling error
✓ **4.** Measurement error

◆ *Coverage Error*   The key to proper sample selection is an adequate population frame or up-to-date list of all the subjects from which the sample will be drawn. **Coverage error** occurs if we exclude certain groups of subjects from this population listing so that they have no chance of being selected in the sample. Coverage error results in a **selection bias**. If the listing is inadequate because certain groups of subjects in the population were not properly included, any random probability sample selected will provide an estimate of the characteristics of the *target* population, not the *actual* population. For a presentation of a famous case of selection bias we turn to the comment box on page 44.

◆ *Nonresponse Error*   Not everyone will be willing to respond to a survey. In fact, research has indicated that individuals in the upper and lower economic classes tend to respond less frequently to surveys than do people in the middle class. **Nonresponse error** arises from the failure to collect data on all subjects in the sample and results in a **nonresponse bias**. Since it cannot be generally assumed that persons who do not respond to surveys are similar to those who do, it is extremely important to follow up on the nonresponses after a specified period of time. Several attempts should be made, either by mail or by telephone, to convince such individuals to change their minds. Based on these results, the estimates obtained from the initial respondents are subsequently tied to those obtained from the follow-ups so that the inferences made from the survey are valid (reference 1).

   As stated in section 2.4, the mode of response affects the rate of response. The personal interview and the telephone interview usually produce a higher response rate than does the mail survey—but at a higher cost. The comment on the 1936 *Literary Digest* poll (page 44) also addresses nonresponse bias.

◆ *Sampling Error*   There are three main reasons for drawing a sample rather than taking a complete census: It is more expedient, less costly, and more efficient. However, chance dictates who in the population frame will or will not be included. **Sampling error** reflects the heterogeneity, or "chance differences," from sample to sample based on the probability of particular individuals or items being selected in the particular samples.

   When we read about the results of surveys or polls in newspapers or magazines, there is often a statement regarding margin of error or precision; for example, "the results of this poll are expected to be within $\pm 4$ percentage points of the actual value." This margin of error is our sampling error. Sampling error can be reduced by taking larger sample sizes, although this will increase the cost of conducting the survey.

---

**COMMENT:** *A Case of Selection Bias and Nonresponse Bias*

In 1936, the magazine Literary Digest predicted that Governor Alf Landon of Kansas would receive 57% of the votes and overwhelmingly defeat President Franklin D. Roosevelt's ambition for a second term. However, Landon was soundly defeated when he received only 38% of the vote. Such an unprecedented error by a magazine with respect to a major poll had never occurred before. As a result, the prediction devastated the magazine's credibility with the public, eventually bankrupting it.

The Literary Digest poll thought it had done everything right. It had based its prediction on a huge sample size, 2.4 million respondents, out of a survey sent to 10 million registered voters. What went wrong? There are two answers, selection bias and nonresponse bias.

To understand the role of selection bias, some historical background must be provided. In 1936, the United States was still suffering from the Great Depression. Not accounting for this, the Literary Digest compiled its population frame from such sources as telephone books, club membership lists, magazine subscriptions, and automobile registrations (reference 5). Inadvertently they chose a population frame composed of the rich and excluded the majority of the voting population who, during the Great Depression, could not afford telephones, club memberships, magazine subscriptions, and automobiles. Thus, the 57% estimate for the Landon vote may have been very close to the target population but certainly not the actual population.

Nonresponse bias resulted when the huge sample of 10 million registered voters only produced 2.4 million responses. A response rate of only 24% is far too low to yield accurate estimates of the population parameters without some mechanism to assure that the 7.6 million individual nonrespondents have similar opinions. However, the problem of nonresponse bias was secondary to the problem of selection bias. Even if all 10 million registered voters in the sample had responded, this would not have compensated for the fact that the target population differed substantially in composition from the actual voting population.

---

◆ *Measurement Error* In the practice of good survey research, a questionnaire is designed with the intent that it will allow meaningful information to be gathered. The obtained data must be *valid*; that is, the "right" responses must be assessed, and in a manner that will elicit meaningful measurements.

But there is a dilemma here—obtaining meaningful measurements is often easier said than done. Consider the following proverb:

*A man with one watch always knows what time it is;*
*A man with two watches always searches to identify the correct one;*
*A man with ten watches is always reminded of the difficulty in measuring time.*

Unfortunately, the process of obtaining a measurement is often governed by what is convenient, not what is needed. And the measurements obtained are often only a proxy for the ones really desired.

> **Measurement error** refers to inaccuracies in the recorded responses that occur because of a weakness in question wording, an interviewer's effect on the respondent, or the effort made by the respondent.

Much attention has been given to measurement error that occurs because of a weakness in question wording (reference 6). A question should be clear, not ambiguous. It should be objectively presented in a neutral manner; "leading questions" must be avoided.

There are three sources of measurement error: ambiguous wording of questions, the halo effect, and respondent error. As an example of ambiguous wording, in November 1993 the Labor Department reported that the unemployment rate in the United States had been underestimated for more than a decade because of poor questionnaire wording in the Current Population Survey. In particular, the wording led to a significant undercount of women in the labor force. Since unemployment rates are tied to benefit programs such as state unemployment compensation systems, it was imperative that government survey researchers rectify the situation by adjusting the questionnaire wording.

The "halo effect" occurs when the respondent feels obligated to please the interviewer. This type of error can be minimized by proper interviewer training.

Respondent error occurs as a result of overzealous or underzealous effort by the respondent. We can minimize this type of error in two ways: (1) by carefully scrutinizing the data and calling back those individuals whose responses seem unusual and (2) by establishing a program of random callbacks in order to ascertain the reliability of the responses.

## Ethical Issues

With respect to the proliferation of survey research (reference 2), Eric Miller, editor of the newsletter *Research Alert*, stated that "There's been a slow sliding in ethics. The scary part is that people make decisions based on this stuff. It may be an invisible crime, but it's not a victimless one." Not all survey research is good, meaningful, or important and not all survey research is ethical. We must try to distinguish between poor survey design and unethical survey design.

Ethical considerations arise with respect to the four types of potential errors that may occur when designing surveys that use random probability samples: coverage error or selection bias, nonresponse error or nonresponse bias, sampling error, and measurement error. Coverage error or selection bias becomes an ethical issue only if particular groups or individuals are *purposely* excluded from the population frame so that the survey results are skewed, indicating a position more favorable to that of the survey's sponsor.

In a similar vein, nonresponse error or nonresponse bias becomes an ethical issue only if particular groups or individuals are less likely to respond to a particular survey format and the sponsor knowingly designs the survey in a manner aimed at excluding such groups or individuals. Sampling error becomes an ethical issue only if the findings are purposely presented without reference to sample size and margin of error so that the sponsor can promote a viewpoint that might otherwise be truly insignificant. Measurement error becomes an ethical issue in one of three ways. (1) A survey sponsor may purposely choose loaded, leading questions that would guide the responses in a particular direction. (2) An interviewer, through mannerisms and tone, may purposely create a halo effect or otherwise guide the responses in a particular direction. (3) A respondent having a disdain for the survey process may willfully provide false information.

## Problems for Section 2.6

### Applying the Concepts

**2.26** "A survey indicates that Americans overwhelmingly preferred a Chrysler to a Toyota after test-driving both." What information would you want to know before you accept the results of this survey?

**2.27** "A survey indicates that the vast majority of college students picked Gap jeans as the most 'in' clothing." What information would you want to know before you accept the results of this survey?

**2.28** A simple random sample of $n = 300$ full-time employees is drawn from a company list containing the names of all $N = 5,000$ full-time employees in order to evaluate job satisfaction.
(a) Give an example of possible coverage error.
(b) Give an example of possible nonresponse error.
(c) Give an example of possible sampling error.
(d) Give an example of possible measurement error.

 **SUMMARY**

As you can see in the summary chart on the following page, this chapter discussed data collection. We have studied different modes of response to a survey, various types of data, and different ways of selecting random samples. In addition, we examined several aspects of survey worthiness.

Once they have been collected, the data must be organized and prepared in order to assist us in making various analyses. In the next two chapters, methods of tabular and chart presentation will be demonstrated, various "exploratory data analysis" techniques will be described, and a variety of descriptive summary measures useful for data analysis and interpretation will be developed.

## *Key Terms*

categorical random variable   25

cluster sample   39

continuous random variables   26

coverage error   43

data   22

discrete random variables   26

focus group   24

frame   32

GIGO   31

interval scale   27

measurement error   45

nominal scale   26

nonprobability sample   33

nonresponse bias   43

nonresponse error   43

numerical random variable   26

operational definition   31

ordinal scale   26

primary and secondary sources   23

probability sample   34

random variable   25

ratio scale   27

sample with replacement   34

sample without replacement   34

sampling error   43

selection bias   43

simple random sample   34

stratified sample   38

systematic sample   37

table of random numbers   35

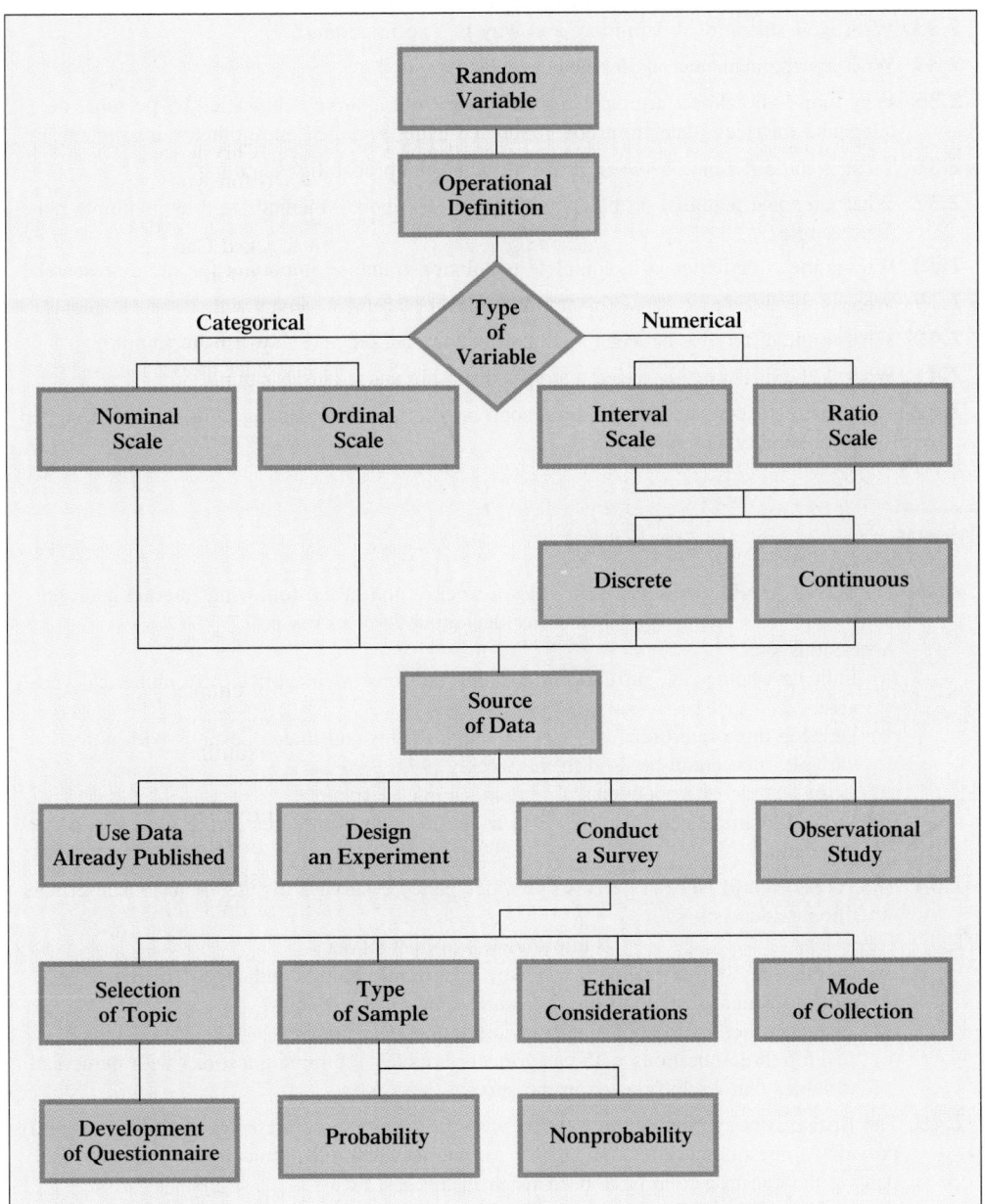

Chapter 2 summary chart

## Checking Your Understanding

**2.29** What is the difference between a categorical and a numerical random variable?

**2.30** What is the difference between discrete and continuous data?

**2.31** What is the difference between a nominal scale and an ordinal scale?

**2.32** What is the difference between an interval scale and a ratio scale?

**2.33** What is an operational definition, and why is it so important?

**2.34** What are the main reasons for obtaining data?

**2.35** Why might you expect a greater response rate from a survey conducted by personal or telephone interview than from one conducted using a mailed questionnaire instrument?

**2.36** What is the difference between probability and nonprobability sampling?

**2.37** What are some potential problems with using "fish bowl" methods to draw a simple random sample?

**2.38** Why is the compilation of a complete population frame so important for survey research?

**2.39** What is the difference between sampling with replacement versus without replacement?

**2.40** What is the difference between a simple random sample and a systematic sample?

**2.41** What is the difference between a stratified sample and a cluster sample?

**2.42** What distinguishes the four potential sources of error when dealing with surveys designed using probability sampling?

## Chapter Review Problems

**2.43** The AT&T World Net Service provides a weekly poll at the following Internet address:
http://www.worldnet.att.net/poll/survey.poll
Access this site.
(a) Indicate whether the current poll question concerns a categorical or a numerical variable.
(b) Develop three questions with categorical variables and three questions with numerical variables that could be used in the weekly poll.
(c) Is the sample of respondents a random sample? Explain.
(d) What difficulties can you foresee in trying to apply the results of the survey to a population?

**2.44** The AT&T World Net Service also provides periodic surveys of interest to its subscribers at its home address:
http://www.worldnet.att.net/
Access this site, and determine if a survey is currently being conducted. If it is,
(a) indicate which of the poll questions are categorical variables.
(b) indicate which of the poll questions are numerical variables.
(c) develop three questions with categorical variables and three questions with numerical variables that could be used in the survey.

**2.45** The British Airways Internet site (http://www.britishairways.com/feedback/feedback.shtml) provides a questionnaire instrument that can be answered electronically.
Among the questions that have been listed in the past are:
1. How did you first hear about the British Airways Internet site?
2. What was your age at your last birthday?
3. What is the speed of your Internet connection?
(a) Does the survey on the British Airways Internet site represent a random sample? Explain.
(b) How can a random sample be obtained?
(c) Define the target population for British Airways.
(d) On the basis of the wording of the age question in this survey, what is the level of measurement?
(e) If the survey has not already done so, write a question that presents age as a numerical variable.
(f) Is "How did you first hear about the British Airways Internet site?" a categorical or a numerical variable? Explain.

(g) Is the question "How did you first hear about the British Airways Internet site?" a nominal scaled or interval scaled variable? Explain.

(h) List three questions not currently part of the British Airways survey that you believe should be included.

**2.46** Suppose that the manager of the customer service division of a consumer electronics company was interested in determining whether customers who had purchased a videocassette recorder over the past 12 months were satisfied with their products. Using the warranty cards submitted after the purchase, the manager was planning to survey these customers.

(a) Describe the target population.

(b) Describe the frame.

(c) What differences are there between the target population and the frame? How might these differences affect the results?

(d) Develop three categorical questions that you feel would be appropriate for this survey.

(e) Develop three numerical questions that you feel would be appropriate for this survey.

(f) How could a simple random sample of warranty cards be selected?

(g) If the manager wanted to select a sample of warranty cards for each brand of videocassette recorder sold, how should the sample be selected? Explain.

**2.47** Political polls are taken to try to predict the outcome of an election. The results of such polls are routinely reported in newspapers and on television in the weeks and months prior to an election. For a specific election such as for president of the United States,

(a) what is the population to which we usually want to generalize?

(b) how might we get a random sample from that population?

(c) from what you know about how such polls are actually conducted, what might be some problems with the sampling in these polls?

**2.48** The following questionnaire is placed in each room of a well-known and widely respected hotel. The intent of management is to evaluate guest satisfaction.

| How well did we serve you? | 😊 | 🙂 | 😐 | 🙁 |
|---|---|---|---|---|
| Reservations | | | | |
| Doorman | | | | |
| Front desk | | | | |
| Room | | | | |
| Cleanliness | | | | |
| Restaurant | | | | |

(a) Do you feel that this four-category ordinal scaling device with "faces" provides management with enough information on each service or facility being rated? Discuss.

(b) Would the addition of another "frown face" to balance the two "smile faces" improve this questionnaire instrument? Discuss.

(c) Of what value are such self-selecting surveys? Can they be used to project the opinions of all guests during a particular interval of time (say, a week or a month)? Discuss.

(d) How could a random sample of guests be selected?

(e) What categorical question would you add to the survey?

(f) What numerical question would you add to the survey?

**2.49** Suppose that a manufacturer of cat food was planning to survey households in the United States to determine purchase habits of cat owners. Among the questions to be included are those that relate to

1. where cat food is primarily purchased.
2. whether dry or moist cat food is purchased.
3. the number of cats living in the household.
4. whether or not the cat is pedigreed.

(a) Describe the target population.
(b) Define the frame.
(c) Indicate the type of sampling that you would use and why you would select it.
(d) For each of the four questions listed, indicate whether the variable is categorical or numerical.
(e) Develop five categorical questions for the survey, and provide an operational definition for each variable.
(f) Develop five numerical questions for the survey.

## TEAM PROJECTS

**TP2.1**  Suppose the following information is obtained for F. Jay Mori upon his admittance to the Brandwein College infirmary:

(a) Gender: Male
(b) Residence or Dorm: Mogelever Hall
(c) Class: Sophomore
(d) Temperature: 102.2°F (oral)
(e) Pulse: 70 beats per minute

(f) Blood Pressure: 130/80 mg/mm(g)
(g) Blood Type: B Positive
(h) Known Allergies to Medicines: No
(i) Preliminary Diagnosis: Influenza
(j) Estimated Length of Stay: 3 days

Classify each of the 10 responses by type of data and level of measurement. Provide an operational definition for each variable. (*Hint*: Be careful with blood pressure; it's tricky.)

**TP2.2**  Provide an operational definition for each of the following:

(a) A good student
(b) The number of children per household
(c) An excellent movie
(d) A light-tasting beer

(e) A cute dress or outfit
(f) A quality product
(g) A smooth-riding automobile

## *Case Study* — ALUMNI ASSOCIATION SURVEY

Suppose that the president of the alumni association of a state university wishes to take a survey of its membership from the classes of 1988 and 1989 to determine their past achievements, current activities, and future aspirations. Toward this end, information pertaining to the following areas is desired: gender of the alumnus; major area of study; undergraduate grade-point index; further educational pursuits (i.e., master's degree or doctorate); current employment status; current annual salary; number of full-time positions held since graduation; annual salary anticipated in five years; political party affiliation; and marital status.

As director of institutional research you are asked to write a proposal demonstrating how you plan to conduct the survey. Included in this proposal must be

1. A statement of objectives (i.e., what you want to find out and why)
2. A discussion of *how* and *when* the survey will be conducted (i.e., how you plan to sample 300 alumni from the list of 3,000 alumni association members in the two classes)
3. A first draft of the questionnaire instrument (containing an organized sequence of both nu-

merical and categorical questions—including operational definitions for each variable, all category labels).

4. A first draft of the cover letter to be used with the questionnaire
5. A first draft of any special instructions to respondents to aid them in filling out the questionnaire
6. A discussion of *how* you plan to test the questionnaire for validity and/or ambiguity
7. A discussion of the type of sampling to be used in the survey

8. A statement that you have taken into consideration such things as the costs involved in conducting the survey, personnel needs, and the amount of time required for implementation and completion
9. A statement regarding the target population of alumni association members versus the actual population of graduates from the two classes, 1988 and 1989, and whether the survey results can be projected to all graduates from these two classes

## References

1. Cochran, W. G., *Sampling Techniques*, 3d ed. (New York: Wiley, 1977).
2. Crossen, C., "Margin of Error: Studies and Surveys Proliferate, but Poor Methodology Makes Many Unreliable," *The Wall Street Journal*, November 14, 1991, A1 and A9.
3. Deming, W. E., *Sample Design in Business Research* (New York: Wiley, 1960).
4. Deming, W. E., *Out of the Crisis* (Cambridge, MA: Massachusetts Institute of Technology Center for Advanced Engineering Study, 1986).
5. Gallup, G. H., *The Sophisticated Poll-Watcher's Guide* (Princeton, NJ: Princeton Opinion Press, 1972).
6. Goleman, D., "Pollsters Enlist Psychologists in Quest for Unbiased Results," *The New York Times*, September 7, 1993, C1 and C11.
7. Groves, R. M., *Survey Errors and Survey Costs* (New York: Wiley, 1989).
8. Hansen, M. H., W. N. Hurwitz, and W. G. Madow, *Sample Survey Methods and Theory*, vols. 1 and 2 (New York: Wiley, 1953).
9. *Microsoft Excel 97* (Redmond, WA: Microsoft Corporation, 1997).
10. *Minitab for Windows Version 12* (State College, PA: Minitab, Inc., 1997).
11. Mosteller, F., et al., *The Pre-Election Polls of 1948* (New York: Social Science Research Council, 1949).
12. Rand Corporation, *A Million Random Digits with 100,000 Normal Deviates* (New York: The Free Press, 1955).
13. Robbins, S. P., *Management*, 5th ed. (Upper Saddle River, NJ: Prentice Hall, 1997).

## ❖ APPENDIX 2.1   USING MICROSOFT EXCEL TO SELECT A RANDOM SAMPLE

In section 2.5 we learned how to use a table of random numbers to select a simple random sample. Now we will use Microsoft Excel to obtain a sample of random numbers of any desired size.

There are two Excel functions, RANDBETWEEN and RAND, that provide random numbers based on simple random sampling. The RANDBETWEEN function produces integer values; the RAND function provides values that are between 0 and 1.

The RANDBETWEEN function takes the form

RANDBETWEEN(lower limit, upper limit)

The RAND function takes the form

RAND()

and provides a random number between 0 and 1. If we wish to change the range of the numbers, we may do so by multiplying the RAND function by the value of the desired upper limit. For example, to generate a random number between 0 and 1000, we would enter =RAND()*1000 into the appropriate cell.

To use the RANDBETWEEN function to select a set of 40 employees from a population of 800 employees as we did in section 2.5, open a new workbook and rename the active sheet Sample. After first entering the heading SAMPLE in cell A1, enter the formula =RANDBETWEEN(1,800) in cell A2 and copy this formula down an additional 39 cells, from cells A3 through A41. You will observe that the cell range A2:A41 now contains random numbers between 001 and 800. However, depending on your results, you may also observe that some random numbers have been repeated. This is due to the fact that the RANDBETWEEN function generates random numbers by sampling with replacement. If you wish to sample without replacement, you need to remove any random numbers that have been repeated and for those cells perform the random selection again until none of the random numbers obtained represent repeating numbers.

If a population of values is already stored on a worksheet, the Sampling option of the Data Analysis tool can be used to obtain a sample of size $n$ from the population of $N$ items with replacement. This may be illustrated by referring to the population of 194 domestic general stock funds introduced in appendix 1.2. Suppose we wanted to select a random sample of 10 stock funds from this population. To do so, **open** the **MUTUAL.XLS** workbook and select **Tools | Data Analysis | Sampling**.

Because sampling is conducted over the entire cell range specified, we first need to define the variable to be sampled. To select a sample of the Net Asset Values in column C, in the Sampling dialog box, enter **Data!C2:C195** in the Input Range edit box. Select the **Random** option button and enter **10** in the Number of Samples edit box. Select the **New Worksheet Ply** option button and enter the name *Sample* in this edit box. Click the **OK** button. You will observe that a sample of 10 stock funds has been selected and the Net Asset Values for the selected funds is provided on the Sample worksheet.

## ❖ APPENDIX 2.2   USING MINITAB TO SELECT A RANDOM SAMPLE

In section 2.5, we learned how to use a table of random numbers to select a simple random sample. Now we will use Minitab to obtain a sample of random numbers of any desired size. In order to select a random sample, we first must open the Minitab file that contains the population from which the sample is to be selected. One such file that will be used extensively in chapters 3 and 4 is a file that contains 194 domestic general stock funds (see appendix D). This file (MUTUAL.MTP) will be used here for illustrative purposes.

To open this file, select **File | Open Worksheet** and then open this MUTUAL.MTP file. You will note that the file contains eight columns, of which the first represents the name of the stock fund, and 194 rows, one for each of the stock funds. Select **Calc | Random Data | Sample from Column**.

In the Sample from Column dialog box, to select a sample of 10 without replacement from the 194 stock funds, enter **10** in the Sample Rows from Column(s): edit box. Enter **C1−C8** into the edit box below the Sample Rows from Column(s): edit box. In the **Store Samples In:** edit box enter **C9−C16**. Leave the Sample with Replacement check box unchecked for sampling without replacement. Click the **OK** button. You will observe that a sample of 10 stock funds has been selected with replacement and the results have been stored in columns C9−C16.

# 3

# Presenting Data in Tables and Charts

# CHAPTER OBJECTIVES

✓ *To demonstrate how to organize numerical data*
✓ *To develop tables and charts for numerical data*
✓ *To develop graphs for bivariate numerical data*
✓ *To develop tables and charts for categorical data*
✓ *To develop tables and charts for bivariate categorical data*
✓ *To demonstrate the principles of proper graphical presentation*

# Introduction

In chapter 2 we learned about data collection. As a general rule, whenever a set of data contains about 20 or more observations, it is best to examine it in summary form by constructing appropriate tables and charts. We can then extract the important features of the data from these tables and charts. In this chapter we demonstrate how large sets of data can be organized and most effectively presented in the form of tables and charts in order to enhance data analysis and interpretation—two key aspects of the decision-making process. We begin with an example concerning equity mutual funds.

# ◆ USING STATISTICS: *Comparing the Performance of Equity Mutual Funds*

In recent years millions of individuals have invested billions of dollars in a variety of mutual funds. These investments have been made for a variety of reasons involving short-term objectives and long-term objectives. Suppose that you were employed by a financial investment service that was evaluating currently traded domestic general stock funds so that it could make purchase recommendations to potential investors. If you were to study the financial performance measures of these domestic general stock funds based on various features such as fund objective (growth versus blend), fee structure (no load versus fee payment), and capitalization size (large, mid, small) of companies making up a fund's portfolio, how might this help in pinpointing funds for possible investment as part of a long-term financial plan?

## 3.1 ORGANIZING NUMERICAL DATA

How can we go about answering the question raised in our Using Statistics example? One way is by obtaining recent data on the performance of a sample of 194 domestic general stock funds with high Morningstar Inc. dual ratings of 4 or 5. These data are described in detail in appendix D. The data relating to these 194 mutual funds are stored under the name MUTUAL in a variety of formats on the CD-ROM that accompanies this text.

One way we may wish to compare performance, as measured by the 1-year return percentage, is based on fund objective (growth versus blend). There are 59 growth funds and 135 blend funds in our sample. The data contained in the file are in **raw form**; they are listed alphabetically by name of the mutual fund. In addition to the name of the mutual fund, information is provided on a variety of variables (see appendix D).

As the number of observations gets large, it becomes more and more difficult to focus on the major features in a set of data. We need ways to organize the observations so that we can better understand what information the data are conveying. Two commonly used methods for accomplishing this are the *ordered array* and the *stem-and-leaf display*.

## The Ordered Array

If we place the raw data in rank order, from the smallest to the largest observation, the ordered sequence obtained is called an **ordered array**. As we begin our analysis with the growth funds, Table 3.1 indicates the 1-year total returns achieved by the 59 sampled growth funds. When data are sorted into an ordered array, it becomes easier to pick out extremes, typical values, and concentrations of values.

Although it is useful to place the raw data into an ordered array prior to developing summary tables and charts or computing descriptive summary measures (see chapter 4), the greater the number of observations present in a data set, the more useful it is to organize the data set into a stem-and-leaf display in order to study its characteristics (references 1, 14, and 15).

**Table 3.1** *Ordered array of 1-year total percentage returns achieved by 59 growth funds*

| | | | | | | | | | |
|---|---|---|---|---|---|---|---|---|---|
| 20.4 | 23.8 | 25.6 | 26.2 | 27.6 | 27.7 | 28.3 | 28.6 | 28.8 | 28.9 |
| 28.9 | 29.3 | 29.3 | 29.5 | 29.9 | 30.1 | 31.5 | 31.6 | 31.6 | 31.8 |
| 31.9 | 32.1 | 32.3 | 32.3 | 32.4 | 32.8 | 32.9 | 32.9 | 33.0 | 33.3 |
| 33.4 | 33.7 | 33.8 | 34.0 | 34.0 | 34.3 | 34.7 | 34.7 | 34.8 | 35.0 |
| 38.2 | 39.0 | 39.4 | 40.7 | 41.1 | 42.8 | 42.9 | 43.3 | 43.4 | 43.5 |
| 43.6 | 43.7 | 44.6 | 44.7 | 45.4 | 45.7 | 46.6 | 48.0 | 48.6 | |

**DATA FILE**
MUTUAL

## The Stem-and-Leaf Display

The **stem-and-leaf display** is a valuable and versatile tool for organizing a set of data and understanding how the values distribute and cluster over the range of the observations in the set of data. A stem-and-leaf display separates data entries into leading digits, or stems, and trailing digits, or leaves. For example, since the 1-year total returns in the growth fund data set all have two-digit integer numbers, the 10s and units columns are the leading digits, and the remaining column (the 10ths column) is the trailing digit. Thus, an entry of 32.3 (corresponding to a 1-year total percentage return of 32.3) has a stem of 32 and a trailing digit, or leaf, of 3.

Figure 3.1 depicts the stem-and-leaf display of the 1-year total returns achieved by the 59 growth funds obtained from Minitab. The second column of numbers is the stem, or leading digits, of the data while the leaves, or trailing digits, branch out to the right of these numbers. The first column of numbers represents the cumulative number of values below or equal to the stem that contains the middle ranked value, or for stems above the middle ranked value, the cumulative number of values equal to or above a particular stem. Thus,

FIGURE 3.1

Stem-and-leaf display of the 1-year total returns (in percentages) achieved by 59 growth funds obtained from Minitab

*Source: Data are taken from Table 3.1.*

```
Character Stem-and-Leaf Display

Stem-and-leaf of 1Yr%Grow   N  = 59
Leaf Unit =0.10


     1      20  4
     1      21
     1      22
     2      23  8
     2      24
     3      25  6
     4      26  2
     6      27  67
    11      28  36899
    15      29  3359
    16      30  1
    21      31  56689
    28      32  1334899
    (5)     33  03478
    26      34  003778
    20      35  0
    19      36
    19      37
    19      38  2
    18      39  04
    16      40  7
    15      41  1
    14      42  89
    12      43  34567
     7      44  67
     5      45  47
     3      46  6
     2      47
     2      48  06
```

a value of 4 next to a stem of 26 means that there are 4 values at or below a stem of 26, while a value of 14 next to a stem of 42 means that there are 14 values of 42 or above.

An examination of Figure 3.1 allows us to begin drawing conclusions about the 1-year percentage returns of the growth funds. Among the conclusions we can reach from the stem-and-leaf display are:

**1.** The lowest 1-year percentage return is 20.4.

**2.** The highest 1-year percentage return is 48.6.

**3.** The returns of the 59 growth funds are spread out between the lowest and highest returns with some concentration of percentage returns between 28 and 34.

**4.** There seem to be more growth funds that have a high percentage return above 40 than a low percentage return below 25.

**5.** Some mutual funds have the same percentage return; for example, there are two mutual funds for each percentage return of 28.9, 31.6, 32.3, 32.9, 34.0, and 34.7.

To understand how the stem-and-leaf display is constructed, refer to Example 3.1.

## Example 3.1 *Constructing a Stem-and-Leaf Display*

The following raw data represent the weekly salary checks earned by a sample of eight secretaries in a large law firm:

$555  $490  $648  $832  $710  $590  $576  $627

Construct the stem-and-leaf display.

### SOLUTION

Since all the values are three-digit integers, to form the stem-and-leaf display, two approaches are demonstrated.

First, we may use the 100s column as the stems and the 10s column as the leaves and ignore the units column:

$555  $490  $648  $832  $710  $590  $576  $627

```
4 | 9
5 | 597
6 | 42
7 | 1
8 | 3
```

or, second, we may use the 100s column as the stems and the 10s column as the leaves after rounding the units column:

$555  $490  $648  $832  $710  $590  $576  $627

```
4 | 9
5 | 698
6 | 53
7 | 1
8 | 3
```

In the first approach, the values listed in the second row indicate that these weekly salaries are in the 550s, 590s, and 570s. In the second approach, the values listed in the second row show that these weekly salaries are rounded to $560, $590, and $580.

## Problems for Section 3.1

### Learning the Basics

● **3.1** Form the ordered array given the following raw data from a sample of $n = 7$ midterm exam scores in accounting:

68  94  63  75  71  88  64

● **3.2** Form the stem-and-leaf display given the following raw data from a sample of $n = 7$ midterm exam scores in finance:

80  54  69  98  93  53  74

**3.3** Form the ordered array given the following raw data from a sample of $n = 7$ midterm exam scores in marketing:

88 78 78 73 91 78 85

**3.4** Form the stem-and-leaf display given the following raw data from a sample of $n = 7$ midterm exam scores in organizational behavior:

76 68 76 87 95 63 87

**3.5** Form the stem-and-leaf display given the following ordered array from a sample of $n = 7$ midterm exam scores in economics:

46 58 69 76 82 82 96

**3.6** Form the ordered array given the following stem-and-leaf display from a sample of $n = 7$ midterm exam scores in information systems:

```
5 | 0
6 |
7 | 464
8 | 91
9 | 2
```

## Applying the Concepts

**3.7** Given the following stem-and-leaf display representing the amount of gasoline purchased in gallons (with leaves in 10ths of gallons) for a sample of 25 cars that use a particular service station on the New Jersey Turnpike:

```
 9 | 714
10 | 82230
11 | 561776735
12 | 394282
13 | 20
```

(a) Place the data into an ordered array.
(b) Which of these two displays seems to provide more information? Discuss.
(c) What amount of gasoline (in gallons) is most likely to be purchased?
(d) Is there a concentration of the purchase amounts in the center of the distribution?
(e) Do you think these 25 purchase amounts are representative of larger population amounts? Explain.

**3.8** Upon examining the monthly billing records of a mail-order CD and cassette company, the auditor takes a sample of 20 of its unpaid accounts. The amounts owed the company are

**DATA FILE**
MAILORD

$4, $18, $11, $7, $7, $10, $5, $33, $9, $12
$3, $11, $10, $6, $26, $37, $15, $18, $10, $21

(a) Develop the ordered array.
(b) Form the stem-and-leaf display.
(c) What conclusions can you reach about the amounts owed in the unpaid accounts?

**3.9** The following data represent the retail price (in dollars) of a sample of 29 different types of attaché cases that were being sold in department stores:

**DATA FILE**
ATTACHE

395 395 215 40 75 140 250 240 450 245 410 130 120 200 65 130
258 485 75 55 220 30 60 80 70 135 150 100 70

*Source: "Attaché Cases," Copyright 1996 by Consumers Union of U.S., Inc. Adapted from* CONSUMER REPORTS, *December 1996, 30–32, by permission of Consumers Union of U.S., Inc., Yonkers, NY 10703-1057. Although these data sets originally appeared in* CONSUMER REPORTS, *the selective adaptation and resulting conclusions presented are those of the authors and are not sanctioned or endorsed in any way by Consumers Union, the publisher of* CONSUMER REPORTS.

(a) Develop the ordered array.

(b) Form the stem-and-leaf display.

(c) Are you more likely to encounter an expensive attaché case or an inexpensive attaché case? Explain.

(d) Do you think that if you are interested in purchasing an attaché case for under $100, you will be able to do so in a department store? Explain.

• **3.10** The following data are the book values (in dollars, i.e., net worth divided by number of outstanding shares) for a random sample of 50 stocks from the New York Stock Exchange:

| 7 | 9 | 8 | 6 | 12 | 6 | 9 | 15 | 9 | 16 |
|---|---|---|---|----|---|---|----|---|----|
| 8 | 5 | 14 | 8 | 7 | 6 | 10 | 8 | 11 | 4 |
| 10 | 6 | 16 | 5 | 10 | 12 | 7 | 10 | 15 | 7 |
| 10 | 8 | 8 | 10 | 18 | 8 | 10 | 11 | 7 | 10 |
| 7 | 8 | 15 | 23 | 13 | 9 | 8 | 9 | 9 | 13 |

**DATA FILE**
STOCK

(a) Develop the ordered array.

(b) Form the stem-and-leaf display.

(c) On the basis of these data, are the book values on the New York Stock Exchange likely to be high or low? Explain.

(d) Are you more likely to find a stock with a book value below $10 or above $20? Explain.

**3.11** The following data represent the annual family premium rates (in thousands of dollars) charged by 36 randomly selected HMOs throughout the United States:

| 3.8 | 4.1 | 4.7 | 5.2 | 2.8 | 5.6 | 4.9 | 6.7 | 9.2 |
|-----|-----|-----|-----|-----|-----|-----|-----|-----|
| 4.9 | 4.9 | 4.9 | 5.2 | 5.9 | 5.2 | 4.8 | 4.8 | 9.1 |
| 4.6 | 8.0 | 4.9 | 4.2 | 4.1 | 5.3 | 5.5 | 8.0 | 7.2 |
| 7.2 | 4.1 | 4.5 | 8.0 | 4.4 | 4.2 | 4.6 | 4.2 | 4.8 |

**DATA FILE**
HMOFRATE

*Source: "HMO Annual Family Premium Rates," Copyright 1996 by Consumers Union of U.S., Inc. Adapted from* CONSUMER REPORTS, *October 1996, 35, by permission of Consumers Union of U.S., Inc., Yonkers, NY 10703-1057. Although these data sets originally appeared in* CONSUMER REPORTS, *the selective adaptation and resulting conclusions presented are those of the authors and are not sanctioned or endorsed in any way by Consumers Union, the publisher of* CONSUMER REPORTS.

(a) Develop the ordered array.

(b) Form the stem-and-leaf display.

(c) Does there appear to be a concentration of premium rates in the center of the distribution?

(d) Your friend Kathy Rae said that her family has been considering whether or not to join an HMO. On the basis of your findings in parts (a) and (b), what would you tell her?

**3.12** The following data are the retail prices for a random sample of 22 VCR models:

| 350 | 300 | 340 | 220 | 320 | 450 | 270 | 265 |
|-----|-----|-----|-----|-----|-----|-----|-----|
| 210 | 250 | 180 | 300 | 190 | 170 | 190 | |
| 170 | 170 | 200 | 180 | 220 | 200 | 250 | |

**DATA FILE**
VCR

*Source: "VCRs," Copyright 1996 by Consumers Union of U.S., Inc. Adapted from* CONSUMER REPORTS, *November 1996, 36–38, by permission of Consumers Union of U.S., Inc., Yonkers, NY 10703-1057. Although these data sets originally appeared in* CONSUMER REPORTS, *the selective adaptation and resulting conclusions presented are those of the authors and are not sanctioned or endorsed in any way by Consumers Union, the publisher of* CONSUMER REPORTS.

(a) Develop the ordered array.

(b) Form the stem-and-leaf display.

(c) Are you more likely to find a VCR for under $200 or over $300?

(d) From the stem-and-leaf display, does there seem to be a concentration of prices around or near any specific dollar amount? Explain.

## The Frequency Distribution

Regardless of whether an ordered array (see Table 3.1) or a stem-and-leaf display (see Figure 3.1) is selected for organizing the data, as the number of observations obtained gets large, it becomes necessary to further condense the data into appropriate summary tables in order to properly present, analyze, and interpret the findings. Thus, we may wish to arrange the data into **class groupings** (i.e., categories) according to conveniently established divisions of the range of the observations. Such an arrangement of data in tabular form is called a frequency distribution.

> A **frequency distribution** is a summary table in which the data are arranged into conveniently established, numerically ordered class groupings or categories.

When the observations are grouped or condensed into frequency distribution tables, the process of data analysis and interpretation is made much more manageable and meaningful. The major data characteristics can be approximated, which compensates for the fact that when the data are so grouped, the initial information pertaining to individual observations that was previously available is lost through the grouping process.

In constructing the frequency distribution table, attention must be given to selecting the appropriate *number* of class groupings for the table, obtaining a suitable *class interval*, or *width* of each class grouping, and establishing the *boundaries* of each class grouping to avoid overlapping.

◆ *Selecting the Number of Classes*   The number of class groupings to be used is primarily dependent on the number of observations in the data. Larger numbers of observations require a larger number of class groups. In general, however, the frequency distribution should have at least 5 class groupings but no more than 15. If there are not enough class groupings or if there are too many, little new information would be learned.

◆ *Obtaining the Class Intervals*   When developing the frequency distribution table, it is desirable that each class grouping has the same width. To determine the **width of each class interval**, the *range* of the data is divided by the number of class groupings desired:

### Determining the Width of a Class Interval

$$\text{Width of interval} \cong \frac{\text{range}}{\text{number of desired class groupings}} \qquad (3.1)$$

Since there were only 59 growth funds sampled, six class groupings are sufficient. From the ordered array in Table 3.1 on page 55 the range is computed as $48.6 - 20.4 = 28.2$. Using equation (3.1), the width of the class interval is approximated by

$$\text{Width of interval} \cong \frac{28.2}{6} = 4.7$$

For convenience and ease of reading, the selected interval or width of each class grouping is rounded to 5.0.

♦ **Establishing the Boundaries of the Classes**   To construct the frequency distribution table, it is necessary to establish clearly defined **class boundaries** for each class grouping so that the observations can be properly tallied into the classes. Overlapping of classes must be avoided.

Since the width of each class interval for the 1-year total return data has been set at 5.0%, the boundaries of the various class groupings must be established so as to include the entire range of observations. Whenever possible, these boundaries should be chosen to facilitate the reading and interpreting of data. Thus, the first class interval ranges from 20.0 to under 25.0%, the second from 25.0 to under 30.0%, and so on, until they have been tallied into six classes, each having an interval width of 5.0%, without overlapping. By establishing these boundaries, all 59 observations can be tallied into each class as shown in Table 3.2.

The main advantage of using this summary table is that the major data characteristics should become immediately clear to the reader. For example, we see from Table 3.2 that the *approximate range* in the 1-year total percentage returns achieved by these 59 sampled growth funds is from 20.0 to 50.0 and, typically, the 1-year total percentage returns tend to cluster between 30.0 and 35.0%.

On the other hand, the major disadvantage of this summary table is that we cannot know how the individual values are distributed within a particular class interval without access to the original data. Thus, for the four funds whose 1-year total returns are between 35.0 and 40.0%, it is not clear from Table 3.2 whether the values are distributed throughout the interval, cluster near 35.0%, or cluster near 40.0%. The *class midpoint* (37.5%), however, is the value used to represent the 1-year total percentage returns for all four funds contained in the particular interval.

The **class midpoint** is the point halfway between the boundaries of each class and is representative of the data within that class.

The class midpoint for the interval "20.0 but less than 25.0" is 22.5%. (The other class midpoints are, respectively, 27.5, 32.5, 37.5, 42.5, and 47.5%.)

**Table 3.2**   *Frequency distribution of 1-year total percentage returns achieved by 59 growth funds*

| 1-Year Total Percentage Return | Number of Funds |
|---|---|
| 20.0 but less than 25.0 | 2 |
| 25.0 but less than 30.0 | 13 |
| 30.0 but less than 35.0 | 24 |
| 35.0 but less than 40.0 | 4 |
| 40.0 but less than 45.0 | 11 |
| 45.0 but less than 50.0 | 5 |
| Total | 59 |

*Source: Data are taken from Table 3.1.*

◆ *Subjectivity in Selecting Class Boundaries*   The selection of class boundaries for frequency distribution tables is highly subjective. For data sets that do not contain many observations the choice of a particular set of class boundaries over another might yield a different picture to the reader. For example, for the 1-year total percentage return data, using a class-interval width of 6.0 instead of 5.0 (as was used in Table 3.2) may cause shifts in the way in which the observations distribute among the classes. This is particularly true if the number of observations in the data set is not very large.

Such shifts in data concentration do not occur only because the width of the class interval is altered. We may keep the interval width at 5.0% but choose different lower and upper class boundaries. Such manipulation may also cause shifts in the way in which the data distribute—especially if the size of the data set is not very large. Fortunately, as the number of observations in a data set increases, alterations in the selection of class boundaries affect the concentration of data less and less.

## The Relative Frequency Distribution and the Percentage Distribution

The frequency distribution is a summary table into which the original data are grouped to facilitate data analysis. To enhance the analysis, however, it is almost always desirable to form either the relative frequency distribution or the percentage distribution, depending on whether we prefer proportions or percentages. These two equivalent distributions are shown in Table 3.3.

The **relative frequency distribution** is formed by dividing the frequencies in each class of the frequency distribution (Table 3.2 on page 61) by the total number of observations. A **percentage distribution** may then be formed by multiplying each relative frequency or proportion by 100.0. Thus, the proportion of growth funds that achieved 1-year total percentage returns of 35.0 to under 40.0 is .068, while it can be seen that 6.8% of the funds have achieved such performance results.

Working with a base of 1 for proportions or 100.0 for percentages is usually more meaningful than using the frequencies themselves. Indeed, the use of the relative frequency distribution or percentage distribution becomes essential whenever one set of data is being compared with other sets of data, especially if the number of observations in each set differs. As a case in point, let us refer to Example 3.2.

**Table 3.3**   *Relative frequency distribution and percentage distribution of 1-year total percentage returns achieved by 59 growth funds*

| 1-YEAR TOTAL PERCENTAGE RETURN | PROPORTION OF FUNDS | PERCENTAGE OF FUNDS |
|---|---|---|
| 20.0 but less than 25.0 | .034 | 3.4 |
| 25.0 but less than 30.0 | .220 | 22.0 |
| 30.0 but less than 35.0 | .407 | 40.7 |
| 35.0 but less than 40.0 | .068 | 6.8 |
| 40.0 but less than 45.0 | .186 | 18.6 |
| 45.0 but less than 50.0 | .085 | 8.5 |
| Total | 1.000 | 100.0 |

*Source: Data are taken from Table 3.2.*

## Example 3.2 *Comparing Two Sets of Data*

Suppose that a personnel manager wanted to compare daily absenteeism among the clerical workers in two branches of a department store. If, on a given day, 6 clerical workers out of 60 in store A were absent and 3 clerical workers out of 10 in store B were absent, what conclusions could be drawn? Demonstrate why it is important to compare two or more sets of data on a relative basis.

### SOLUTION

It is inappropriate to say that *more* absenteeism occurred in store A. Although there were twice as many absences in store A as there were in store B, there were also six times as many clerical workers employed in store A. Hence, in these types of comparisons, we must formulate our conclusions from the *relative rates* of absenteeism, not from the actual counts. Thus, we can state that the absenteeism rate is three times higher in store B (30.0%) than it is in store A (10.0%).

---

Now suppose that in order to make purchase recommendations to potential investors we want to compare the 1-year total percentage returns achieved by the 59 sampled growth funds with those from the 135 sampled blend funds. To compare the 1-year total percentage returns achieved by the 59 growth funds with those from the 135 blend funds, we develop a percentage distribution for the latter group. This new table will then be compared with Table 3.3.

Table 3.4 depicts both the frequency distribution and the percentage distribution of the 1-year total returns achieved by the 135 blend funds. Note that the class groupings selected in Table 3.4 match, where possible, those selected in Table 3.3 for the growth funds. The boundaries of the classes should match or be multiples of each other in order to facilitate comparisons.

With the use of the percentage distributions of Tables 3.3 and 3.4, it is now meaningful to compare the differences in the 1-year total returns achieved by growth funds versus blend funds. Even though the 1-year total returns achieved by growth funds and by blend funds are typically clustering between 30 and 35% and, secondarily, are clustering between 25 and 30%, there is a vast difference in the manner in which the two sets of data distribute. The 1-year total percentage returns achieved by growth funds are generally at a substan-

---

## Table 3.4 *Frequency distribution and percentage distribution of 1-year total percentage returns achieved by 135 blend funds*

| 1-YEAR TOTAL PERCENTAGE RETURN | NUMBER OF FUNDS | PERCENTAGE OF FUNDS |
|---|---|---|
| 10.0 but less than 15.0 | 1 | 0.7 |
| 15.0 but less than 20.0 | 3 | 2.2 |
| 20.0 but less than 25.0 | 9 | 6.7 |
| 25.0 but less than 30.0 | 41 | 30.4 |
| 30.0 but less than 35.0 | 67 | 49.6 |
| 35.0 but less than 40.0 | 14 | 10.4 |
| Total | 135 | 100.0 |

tially higher level than those attained by blend funds. We can observe this if we evaluate the ranges in 1-year total returns for both types of funds. In growth funds, the range in 1-year total percentage returns is approximated to be 30.0 (i.e., the difference between 50.0, the upper boundary of the last class, and 20.0, the lower boundary of the first class). In blend funds, however, even though the range in 1-year total percentage returns also is approximated as 30.0, the difference in the extreme boundaries here is 40.0 − 10.0. Other descriptive summary measures that would enhance a comparative analysis of the 1-year total returns achieved by growth funds versus blend funds will be discussed in chapter 4.

## The Cumulative Distribution

Another useful method of data presentation that facilitates analysis and interpretation is the **cumulative distribution** table. This may be formed from the frequency distribution, the relative frequency distribution, or the percentage distribution. In this text, we will focus on the percentage distribution.

Since we already have the percentage distributions of 1-year total returns achieved by 59 growth funds and 135 blend funds (see Tables 3.3 and 3.4), we can use these tables to construct the respective cumulative percentage distributions as depicted in Tables 3.5 and 3.6.

A comparison of these two tables demonstrates that the growth funds have achieved a higher level of 1-year total returns. For example, we see from Table 3.5 that only 25.4% of the growth funds have achieved a 1-year total percentage return of less than 30.0, whereas from Table 3.6 we observe that 40.0% of the blend funds have attained a 1-year total percentage return of less than 30.0. In addition, only 72.9% of the growth funds have achieved a 1-year total percentage return of less than 40.0, whereas all the blend funds have performance records less than that level.

A **cumulative percentage distribution table** is constructed by first recording the lower boundaries of each class from the percentage distribution and then inserting an extra boundary at the end. We compute the cumulative percentages in the "less than" column by determining the percentage of observations less than each of the stated boundary values.

In Example 3.3 we demonstrate how the cumulative percentage distribution shown in Table 3.5 is constructed by using the percentage distribution of 1-year total returns achieved by 59 growth funds displayed in Table 3.3 on page 62.

**Table 3.5** *Cumulative percentage distribution of 1-year total percentage returns achieved by 59 growth funds*

| 1-YEAR TOTAL PERCENTAGE RETURN | PERCENTAGE OF FUNDS "LESS THAN" INDICATED VALUE |
|---|---|
| 20.0 | 0.0 |
| 25.0 | 3.4 |
| 30.0 | 25.4 |
| 35.0 | 66.1 |
| 40.0 | 72.9 |
| 45.0 | 91.5 |
| 50.0 | 100.0 |

*Source: Data are taken from Table 3.3 on page 62.*

**Table 3.6** *Cumulative percentage distribution of 1-year total percentage returns achieved by 135 blend funds*

| 1-Year Total Percentage Return | Percentage of Funds "Less Than" Indicated Value |
|---|---|
| 10.0 | 0.0 |
| 15.0 | 0.7 |
| 20.0 | 2.9 |
| 25.0 | 9.6 |
| 30.0 | 40.0 |
| 35.0 | 89.6 |
| 40.0 | 100.0 |

*Source: Data are taken from Table 3.4 on page 63.*

## Example 3.3 *Forming the Cumulative Percentage Distribution*

Using the percentage distribution of Table 3.3 on page 62, form the cumulative percentage distribution.

### SOLUTION

From Table 3.5, we see that 0.0% of the 1-year total returns in growth funds are less than 20.0%; 3.4% of the 1-year total returns in growth funds are less than 25.0%; 25.4% of the 1-year total returns in growth funds are less than 30.0%; and so on, until all (100.0%) of the 1-year total returns in growth funds are less than 50.0%. This cumulating process is observed in the accompanying table.

| 1-Year Total Return (in %) | Percentage of Funds in Class Interval | Percentage of Funds "Less Than" Lower Boundary of Class Interval |
|---|---|---|
| 20.0 but less than 25.0 | 3.4 | 0.0 |
| 25.0 but less than 30.0 | 22.0 | 3.4 |
| 30.0 but less than 35.0 | 40.7 | 25.4 = 3.4 + 22.0 |
| 35.0 but less than 40.0 | 6.8 | 66.1 = 3.4 + 22.0 + 40.7 |
| 40.0 but less than 45.0 | 18.6 | 72.9 = 3.4 + 22.0 + 40.7 + 6.8 |
| 45.0 but less than 50.0 | 8.5 | 91.5 = 3.4 + 22.0 + 40.7 + 6.8 + 18.6 |
| 50.0 but less than 55.0 | 0.0 | 100.0 = 3.4 + 22.0 + 40.7 + 6.8 + 18.6 + 8.5 |

## The Histogram

A saying sometimes mistakenly attributed to Confucius is that "one picture is worth a thousand words." Indeed, statisticians often employ graphic techniques to more vividly describe sets of data. In particular, a histogram is used to describe numerical data that have been grouped into frequency, relative frequency, or percentage distributions.

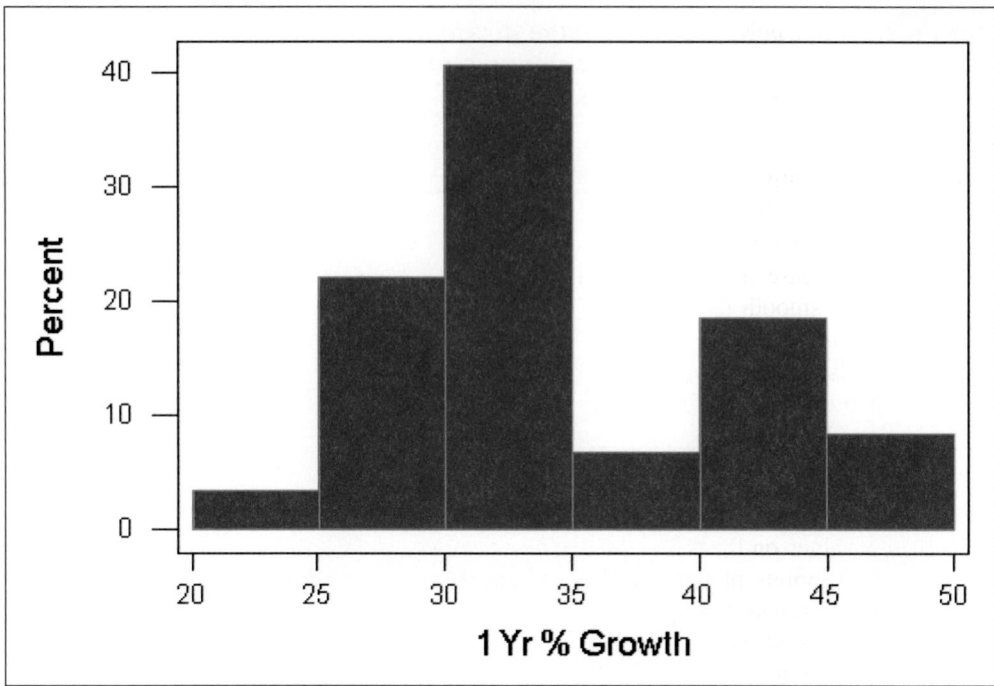

*FIGURE 3.2* Percentage histogram of 1-year total percentage returns achieved by 59 growth funds obtained from Minitab

A **histogram** is a vertical bar chart in which the rectangular bars are constructed at the boundaries of each class.

When plotting a histogram, we display the random variable of interest along the horizontal axis; the vertical axis represents the number, proportion, or percentage of observations per class interval.

A percentage histogram of the 1-year total percentage returns achieved by just the 59 growth funds is presented in Figure 3.2, which has been obtained from Minitab. We can observe a strong concentration of funds with a return between 30 and 35%, smaller concentrations of funds with returns between 25 and 30% and between 40 and 45%, and little concentration of funds in the other class groupings.

When comparing two or more sets of data, we can construct neither stem-and-leaf displays nor histograms on the same graph. For example, superimposing the vertical bars of one histogram on another would cause difficulty in interpretation. For such cases it is necessary to construct relative frequency or percentage polygons.

## The Polygon

As with histograms, when plotting polygons, we display the phenomenon of interest along the horizontal axis, and the vertical axis represents the number, proportion, or percentage of observations per class interval. In this text, we will concern ourselves with the latter.

The **percentage polygon** is formed by having the midpoint of each class represent the data in that class and then connecting the sequence of midpoints at their respective class percentages.

Because consecutive midpoints are connected by a series of straight lines, the **polygon** is sometimes jagged in appearance. However, when dealing with a very large set of data, were we to make the boundaries of the classes in its frequency distribution closer together (and thereby increase the number of classes in that distribution), the jagged lines of the polygon would "smooth out."

Figure 3.3 shows the percentage polygons for the 1-year total returns achieved by the 59 growth funds and the 135 blend funds obtained from Excel. The differences in the structure of the two distributions, previously discussed when comparing Tables 3.3 and 3.4, are clearly indicated here.

◆ *Polygon Construction*    Notice that the polygon in Figure 3.3 by Microsoft Excel has points whose values on the *X* axis represent the upper limit of the class interval. For example, observe the points plotted on the *X* axis at 34.99. The value for the blend funds (the higher value) represents the fact that 49.6% of these funds have 1-year percentage returns of between 30 and 34.99. The value for the growth funds (the lower value) represents the fact that 40.7% of these funds have 1-year percentage returns of between 30 and 34.99.

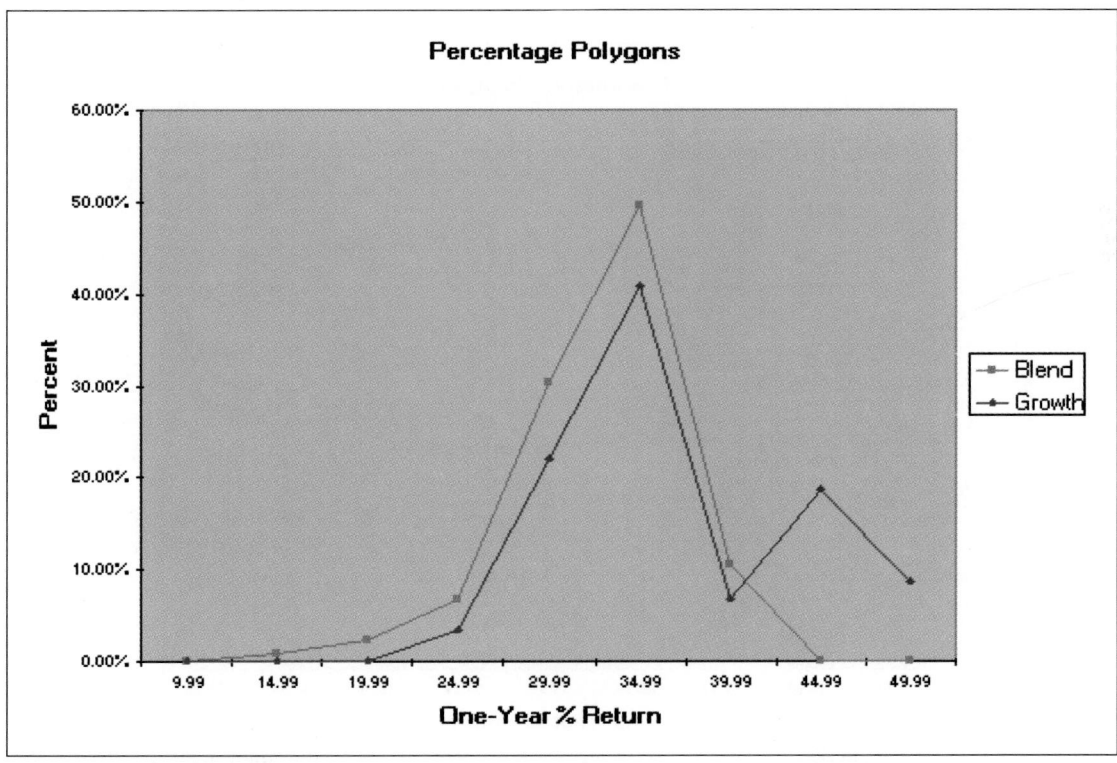

**FIGURE 3.3**    Percentage polygons of 1-year total percentage returns achieved by 59 growth funds and 135 blend funds obtained from Microsoft Excel

Notice, too, that when polygons or histograms are constructed, the vertical axis should show the true zero or "origin" so as not to distort or otherwise misrepresent the character of the data. The horizontal axis, however, does not need to specify the zero point for the phenomenon of interest. For aesthetic reasons, the range of the random variable should constitute the major portion of the chart.

## The Cumulative Polygon (Ogive)

The **cumulative percentage polygon**, or **ogive**, is a graphic representation of a cumulative distribution table. As with histograms and polygons, when plotting cumulative polygons, we display the phenomenon of interest along the horizontal axis, and the vertical axis represents the number, proportion, or percentage of cumulated observations. Again, we will concern ourselves here with the latter.

To construct a cumulative percentage polygon (also known as a percentage ogive), we note that our random variable of interest—1-year total percentage returns—is again plotted on the horizontal axis, while the cumulative percentages (from the "less than" column) are plotted on the vertical axis.

Figure 3.4 illustrates the cumulative percentage polygons of the 1-year total percentage returns achieved by the 59 growth companies and the 135 blend funds obtained from Microsoft Excel. As was the case with the percentage polygons obtained from Excel, the

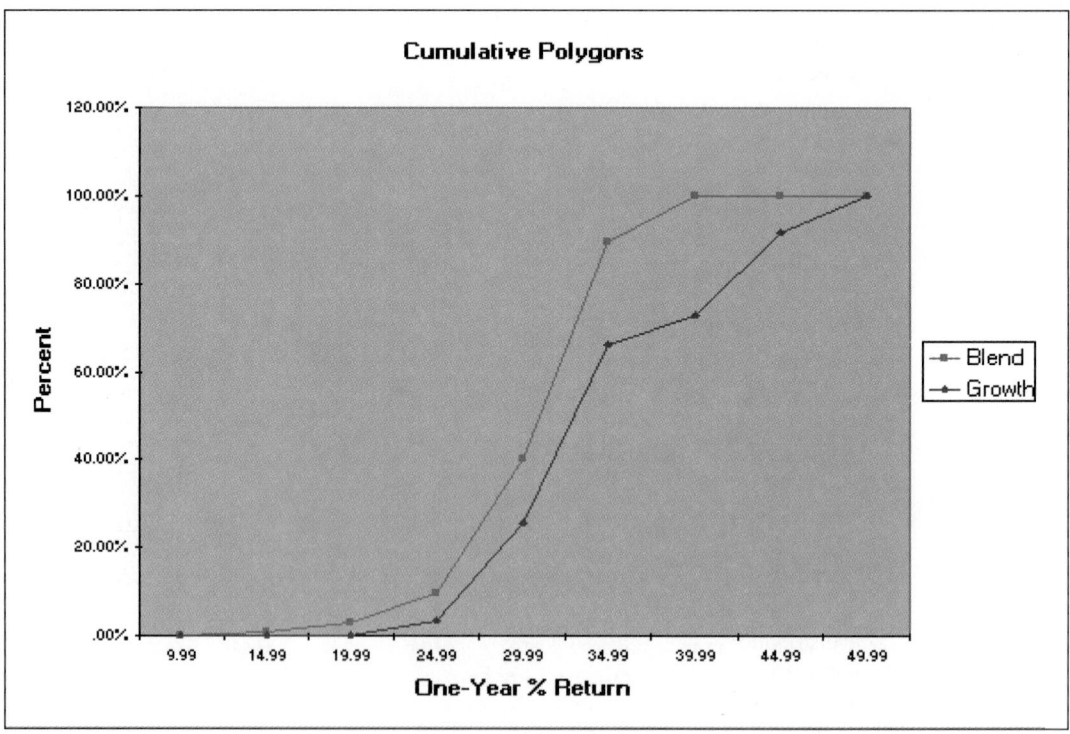

**FIGURE 3.4**    Cumulative percentage polygons of 1-year total percentage returns achieved by 59 growth funds and 135 blend funds obtained from Microsoft Excel

upper limits of the classes are noted on the $X$ axis. Thus, for example, for the blend funds 9.6% had a 1-year percentage return of less than or equal to 24.99, while for the growth funds the percentage was 3.4. From Figure 3.4 we note that in general the blend funds ogive is drawn to the left of the growth funds ogive. For example, 25% of all growth funds have attained 1-year total returns below 30.0%, while 25% of all blend funds have attained 1-year total returns below 27.5%. In addition, 50% of all growth funds have attained 1-year total returns below 33.0%, while 50% of all blend funds have attained 1-year total returns below 31.5%. Furthermore, 75% of all growth funds have attained 1-year total returns below 41.0%, while 75% of all blend funds have attained 1-year total returns below 34.0%. These comparisons enable us to confirm our earlier impression that the 1-year total percentage return achieved by growth funds is at a higher level than that attained by blend funds.

## Problems for Section 3.2

### Learning the Basics

**3.13** The price-to-earnings ratios from a sample of 50 companies whose stocks are traded on the New York Stock Exchange range from 5.2 to 63.4.
  (a) What should be the width of each of your class intervals if you wanted to construct a frequency distribution having six class groupings?
  (b) For convenience, and ease of reading the table, how would you round off the width of the interval obtained in part (a), and what value would you assign to the lowest class boundary in the table you would be constructing?
  (c) On the basis of part (b), what would the class midpoints for each of the class groupings be?

**3.14** A random sample of 50 executive vice presidents is selected from various public universities in the United States, and the annual salaries of these officials are obtained. The salaries range from $62,000 to $247,000. Set up the class boundaries for a frequency distribution
  (a) if five class intervals are desired.
  (c) if seven class intervals are desired.
  (b) if six class intervals are desired.
  (d) if eight class intervals are desired.

• **3.15** The asking price of one-bedroom cooperative and condominium apartments in Queens, a borough of New York City, varies from $103,000 to $295,000.
  (a) Indicate the class boundaries of 10 classes into which these values can be grouped.
  (b) What class-interval width did you choose?
  (c) What are the 10 class midpoints?

**3.16** A frequency distribution is constructed on the basis of a sample of 40 observations. The most typical, or *modal*, class grouping contains 12 observations.
  (a) When the corresponding relative frequency distribution is constructed, what value will appear in the table for this class grouping?
  (b) When the corresponding percentage distribution is constructed, what value will appear in the table for this class grouping?

**3.17** A percentage distribution is constructed on the basis of a sample of 60 observations. The value that appears in the table for the first class grouping is 20%.
  (a) When the corresponding relative frequency distribution is constructed, what value will appear in the table for this class grouping?
  (b) When the corresponding frequency distribution is constructed, what value will appear in the table for this class grouping?

**3.18** In differentiating the histogram from the polygon:
   (a) Which of the two diagrams is plotted at the class midpoints from a frequency distribution?
   (b) Which of the two diagrams is plotted at the class boundaries from a frequency distribution?
   (c) Which of the two diagrams contains a series of vertical rectangular bars?
   (d) Which of the two diagrams results from connecting a set of consecutive plotted points?
   (e) Which of the two diagrams can be used for comparing two or more sets of data that have been tallied into corresponding frequency distributions?

• **3.19** In constructing either a histogram or polygon, on which axis (vertical or horizontal) must the true zero, or "origin," be shown so as not to visually distort or otherwise misrepresent the characteristics of the data?

• **3.20** In constructing an ogive, on which axis (vertical or horizontal) must the true zero, or "origin," be shown so as not to visually distort or otherwise misrepresent the characteristics of the data?

**3.21** In constructing a percentage ogive (i.e., a cumulative percentage polygon):
   (a) What must be the largest value denoted on the scale along the vertical axis?
   (b) What value does the first plotted point on the horizontal axis represent?

**3.22** In constructing a percentage ogive (i.e., a cumulative percentage polygon) pertaining to the GMAT scores from a sample of 50 applicants to an MBA program, it was noted from a previously obtained frequency distribution that none of the applicants scored below 450 and that the frequency distribution was formed by choosing class intervals $450 < 500$, $500 < 550$, and so on, with the last class grouping $700 < 750$. If two applicants scored in the interval $450 < 500$ and 16 applicants scored in the interval $500 < 550$:
   (a) What percentage of applicants scored below 500?
   (b) What percentage of applicants scored below 550?
   (c) What percentage of applicants scored between 500 and 550?
   (d) How many applicants scored between 500 and 550?
   (e) What percentage of applicants scored below 750?

## Applying the Concepts

**DATA FILE**
UTILITY

• **3.23** The data displayed here represent the electricity cost during the month of July 1997 for a random sample of 50 two-bedroom apartments in a large city.

Raw Data on Utility Charges ($)

| | | | | | | | | | |
|---|---|---|---|---|---|---|---|---|---|
| 96 | 171 | 202 | 178 | 147 | 102 | 153 | 197 | 127 | 82 |
| 157 | 185 | 90 | 116 | 172 | 111 | 148 | 213 | 130 | 165 |
| 141 | 149 | 206 | 175 | 123 | 128 | 144 | 168 | 109 | 167 |
| 95 | 163 | 150 | 154 | 130 | 143 | 187 | 166 | 139 | 149 |
| 108 | 119 | 183 | 151 | 114 | 135 | 191 | 137 | 129 | 158 |

   (a) Form a frequency distribution
      (1) having five class intervals.
      (2) having six class intervals.
      (3) having seven class intervals.
   [*Hint:* To help you decide how best to set up the class boundaries, you should first place the raw data either in a stem-and-leaf display (by letting the leaves be the trailing digits) or in an ordered array.]
   (b) Form a frequency distribution having seven class intervals with the following class boundaries: $80 but less than $100, $100 but less than $120, and so on.
   (c) Form the percentage distribution from the frequency distribution developed in part (b).
   (d) Plot the percentage histogram.

(e) Plot the percentage polygon.
(f) Form the cumulative frequency distribution.
(g) Form the cumulative percentage distribution.
(h) Plot the ogive (cumulative percentage polygon).
(i) Around what amount does the monthly electricity cost seem to be concentrated?
(j) Which of the graphs do you think is best in presenting the distribution of electricity cost? Explain.

**3.24** Given the ordered arrays in the accompanying table dealing with the lengths of life (in hours) of a sample of forty 100-watt light bulbs produced by manufacturer A and a sample of forty 100-watt light bulbs produced by manufacturer B:

| Manufacturer A | | | | | Manufacturer B | | | | |
|---|---|---|---|---|---|---|---|---|---|
| 684 | 697 | 720 | 773 | 821 | 819 | 836 | 888 | 897 | 903 |
| 831 | 835 | 848 | 852 | 852 | 907 | 912 | 918 | 942 | 943 |
| 859 | 860 | 868 | 870 | 876 | 952 | 959 | 962 | 986 | 992 |
| 893 | 899 | 905 | 909 | 911 | 994 | 1,004 | 1,005 | 1,007 | 1,015 |
| 922 | 924 | 926 | 926 | 938 | 1,016 | 1,018 | 1,020 | 1,022 | 1,034 |
| 939 | 943 | 946 | 954 | 971 | 1,038 | 1,072 | 1,077 | 1,077 | 1,082 |
| 972 | 977 | 984 | 1,005 | 1,014 | 1,096 | 1,100 | 1,113 | 1,113 | 1,116 |
| 1,016 | 1,041 | 1,052 | 1,080 | 1,093 | 1,153 | 1,154 | 1,174 | 1,188 | 1,230 |

DATA FILE
BULBS

(a) Form the frequency distribution for each brand. (*Hint*: For purposes of comparison, choose class-interval widths of 100 hours for each distribution.)
(b) For purposes of answering part (d), form the frequency distribution for each brand according to the following schema [if you have not already done so in part (a) of this problem]:
   (1) Manufacturer A: 650 but less than 750, 750 but less than 850, and so on.
   (2) Manufacturer B: 750 but less than 850, 850 but less than 950, and so on.
(c) Change the class-interval width in (b) to 50 so that you have intervals from 650 to under 700, 700 to under 750, 750 to under 800, and so on. Comment on the results of these changes.
(d) Form the percentage distributions from the frequency distributions developed in (b).
(e) Plot the percentage histograms on separate graphs.
(f) Plot the percentage polygons on one graph.
(g) Form the cumulative frequency distributions.
(h) Form the cumulative percentage distributions.
(i) Plot the ogives (cumulative percentage polygons) on one graph.
(j) Which manufacturer has bulbs with a longer life, manufacturer A or manufacturer B? Explain.

• **3.25** Given the following stem-and-leaf display representing the amount of gasoline purchased in gallons (with leaves in 10ths of gallons) for a sample of 25 cars that use a particular service station on the New Jersey Turnpike:

```
 9 | 714
10 | 82230
11 | 561776735
12 | 394282
13 | 20
```

(a) Construct a frequency distribution and a percentage distribution.
(b) Form the cumulative frequency distribution and the cumulative percentage distribution.
(c) Plot the percentage histogram.
(d) Plot the percentage polygon.
(e) Plot the ogive (cumulative percentage polygon).
(f) Around what amount of gasoline do most of the purchases seem to be concentrated?

**3.26** The following data are the book values (in dollars, i.e., net worth divided by number of outstanding shares) for a random sample of 50 stocks from the New York Stock Exchange:

| | | | | | | | | | |
|---|---|---|---|---|---|---|---|---|---|
| 7 | 9 | 8 | 6 | 12 | 6 | 9 | 15 | 9 | 16 |
| 8 | 5 | 14 | 8 | 7 | 6 | 10 | 8 | 11 | 4 |
| 10 | 6 | 16 | 5 | 10 | 12 | 7 | 10 | 15 | 7 |
| 10 | 8 | 8 | 10 | 18 | 8 | 10 | 11 | 7 | 10 |
| 7 | 8 | 15 | 23 | 13 | 9 | 8 | 9 | 9 | 13 |

(a) Construct a frequency distribution and a percentage distribution.
(b) Form the cumulative frequency distribution and the cumulative percentage distribution.
(c) Plot the percentage histogram.
(d) Plot the percentage polygon.
(e) Plot the ogive (cumulative percentage polygon).
(f) Are there any book values that seem to be more likely to occur than others? Explain.

**3.27** The following data represent the number of cases of salad dressing purchased per week by a local supermarket chain over a period of 30 weeks:

| Week | Cases Purchased | Week | Cases Purchased | Week | Cases Purchased |
|---|---|---|---|---|---|
| 1 | 81 | 11 | 86 | 21 | 91 |
| 2 | 61 | 12 | 133 | 22 | 99 |
| 3 | 77 | 13 | 91 | 23 | 89 |
| 4 | 71 | 14 | 111 | 24 | 96 |
| 5 | 69 | 15 | 86 | 25 | 108 |
| 6 | 81 | 16 | 84 | 26 | 86 |
| 7 | 66 | 17 | 131 | 27 | 84 |
| 8 | 111 | 18 | 71 | 28 | 76 |
| 9 | 56 | 19 | 118 | 29 | 83 |
| 10 | 81 | 20 | 88 | 30 | 76 |

(a) Construct a stem-and-leaf display.
(b) Construct the frequency distribution and the percentage distribution.
(c) Plot the percentage histogram.
(d) Plot the percentage polygon.
(e) Form the cumulative percentage distribution.
(f) Plot the cumulative percentage polygon.
(g) On the basis of the results of (a)–(f), does there appear to be any concentration of the number of cases of salad dressing ordered by the supermarket chain around specific values?
(h) If you had to make a prediction of the number of cases of salad dressing that would be ordered next week, how many cases would you predict? Why?

**3.28** The following data represent the amount of soft drink filled in a sample of 50 consecutive 2-liter bottles. The results, listed horizontally in the order of being filled, were:

| | | | | | | | | | |
|---|---|---|---|---|---|---|---|---|---|
| 2.109 | 2.086 | 2.066 | 2.075 | 2.065 | 2.057 | 2.052 | 2.044 | 2.036 | 2.038 |
| 2.031 | 2.029 | 2.025 | 2.029 | 2.023 | 2.020 | 2.015 | 2.014 | 2.013 | 2.014 |
| 2.012 | 2.012 | 2.012 | 2.010 | 2.005 | 2.003 | 1.999 | 1.996 | 1.997 | 1.992 |
| 1.994 | 1.986 | 1.984 | 1.981 | 1.973 | 1.975 | 1.971 | 1.969 | 1.966 | 1.967 |
| 1.963 | 1.957 | 1.951 | 1.951 | 1.947 | 1.941 | 1.941 | 1.938 | 1.908 | 1.894 |

(a) Construct a stem-and-leaf display.

(b) Construct the frequency distribution and the percentage distribution.

(c) Plot the frequency histogram.

(d) Plot the percentage polygon.

(e) Form the cumulative percentage distribution.

(f) Plot the cumulative percentage polygon.

(g) On the basis of the results of (a)–(f), does there appear to be any concentration of the amount of soft drink filled in the bottles around specific values?

(h) If you had to make a prediction of the amount of soft drink filled in the next bottle, what would you predict? Why?

 **3.3**   ## GRAPHING BIVARIATE NUMERICAL DATA

When studying and describing data from a numerical random variable such as 1-year total percentage returns, the histogram, the polygon, and the ogive developed in the preceding section are the appropriate graphical tools to use. In this section we will illustrate some appropriate graphical tools that may be used when dealing with **bivariate numerical data**—the outcomes from two numerical random variables studied simultaneously. The oldest and most widely used of these bivariate graphical displays is the **time-series plot**, popularized by William Playfair, which illustrates how a series of numerical data changes over time (see chapter 19). Typically, the data evaluated pertain to some business or economic indicator or financial characteristic.

Related to the time-series plot is the **scatter diagram** (also called **scatterplot**) that was popularized by Sir Francis Galton's work in regression and correlation analysis (see chapter 16). The scatter diagram is a two-dimensional graph depicting how two numerical variables relate to each other.

## The Scatter Diagram

To demonstrate the scatter diagram, let us refer to the special data set in appendix D that presents various characteristics from a sample of 194 domestic general stock funds with high Morningstar Inc. dual ratings of 4 or 5. Aside from the 1-year total returns that we have been studying in this chapter, a second measure of performance is also displayed, the net asset value or price paid for purchasing a share in a fund at a specific time. If for each of our domestic general stock funds we plot this pair of points on a two-dimensional graph so that the 1-year total percentage return represents the $X$ coordinate and the corresponding net asset value represents the $Y$ coordinate, the scatter diagram shown in Figure 3.5 obtained from Minitab is developed. As we might expect, although there is a great deal of variation, there is some evidence that a *direct* or *positive* relationship between these two measures of financial performance exists.

## The Time-Series Plot

The time-series plot is a two-dimensional graph, widely used in business, that illustrates how a series of numerical data changes over time. The horizontal ($X$) axis indicates the time period dimension—usually years, quarters, months, weeks, days, or hours—listed consecutively from left to right. Often the corresponding data values plotted on the vertical ($Y$)

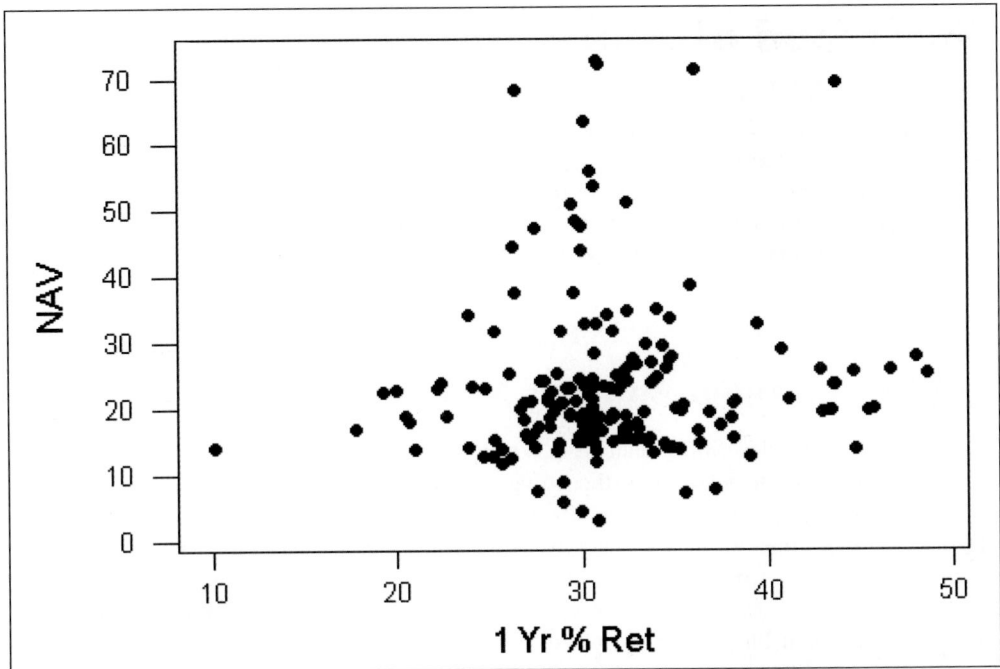

**FIGURE 3.5** Scatter diagram depicting net asset value and 1-year total percentage returns of 194 domestic general stock funds obtained from Minitab

axis pertain to some financial characteristic or economic indicator collected in sequence over time (that is, the "time series"). These consecutively plotted points are then connected in order to help us visually interpret how the series changes over time.

Figure 3.6 displays a time-series plot of the annual average of monthly cash flows into equity mutual funds, expressed as a percentage of assets, from 1955 through 1996. This is an example of a well-designed time-series plot. The extra embellishments assist in the analysis of the series. The bottom portion is darkened to reflect negative cash flows, and the summary discussion draws the eye to key data points.

## Problems for Section 3.3

### Learning the Basics

● **3.29** Given the following set of data from a sample of $n = 11$ items,

| X | 7 | 5 | 8 | 3 | 6 | 10 | 12 | 4 | 9 | 15 | 18 |
|---|---|---|---|---|---|----|----|---|---|----|----|
| Y | 21 | 15 | 24 | 9 | 18 | 30 | 36 | 12 | 27 | 45 | 54 |

(a) Plot the scatter diagram.
(b) Is there a relationship between $X$ and $Y$? Explain.

**3.30** Given the following series of real annual sales (in millions of constant 1995 dollars) over an 11-year period (1987–1997),

| Year | 1987 | 1988 | 1989 | 1990 | 1991 | 1992 | 1993 | 1994 | 1995 | 1996 | 1997 |
|------|------|------|------|------|------|------|------|------|------|------|------|
| Sales | 13.0 | 17.0 | 19.0 | 20.0 | 20.5 | 20.5 | 20.5 | 20.0 | 19.0 | 17.0 | 13.0 |

(a) Construct a time-series plot.
(b) Does there appear to be any change in real annual sales over time? Explain.

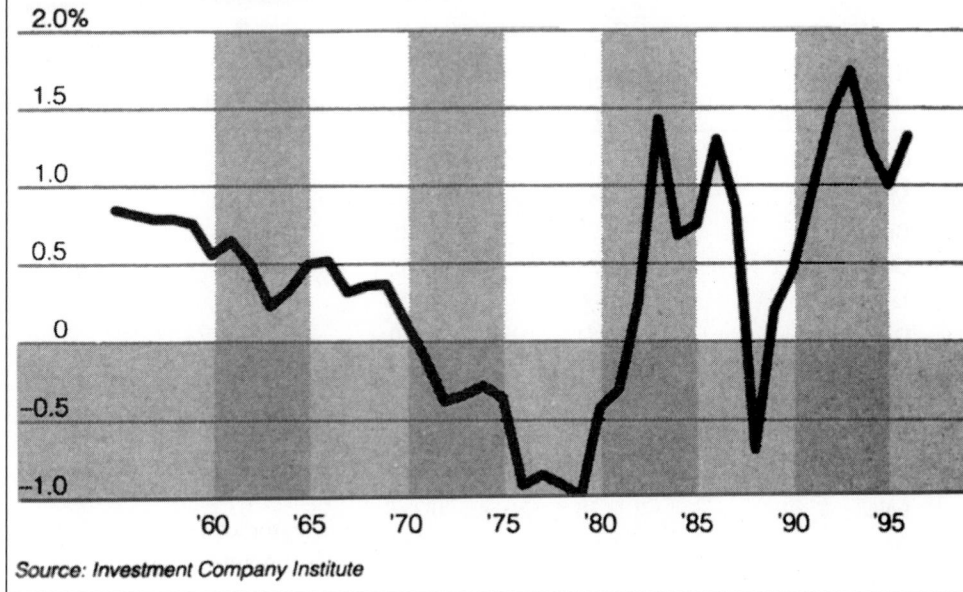

# The Flood of Fund Flows

More than $200 billion flowed into equity mutual funds in 1996, 60 percent more than a year ago and an all-time record for stock funds. But when measured as a percentage of assets, last year's average monthly cash flows were only the fourth largest in history, falling short of the levels seen in 1983, 1992 and 1993. Below is the annual average of monthly cash flows, expressed as a percentage of assets, since 1955.

Source: Investment Company Institute

**FIGURE 3.6**
Time-series plot of annual average of monthly cash flows into equity mutual funds, expressed as percentage of assets, from 1955 through 1996

*Source: Reprinted by permission of* The New York Times. The New York Times, *January 2, 1997, C35.*

## Applying the Concepts

**3.31** The following data represent the approximate retail price (in $) and the energy cost per year (in $) of nine large side-by-side refrigerators.

| BRAND | PRICE ($) | ENERGY COST PER YEAR ($) |
|---|---|---|
| KitchenAidSuperbaKSRS25QF | 1,600 | 73 |
| Kenmore(Sears)5757 | 1,200 | 73 |
| WhirlpoolED25DQXD | 1,550 | 78 |
| AmanaSRD25S3 | 1,350 | 85 |
| Kenmore(Sears)5647 | 1,700 | 93 |
| GEProfileTPX24PRY | 1,700 | 93 |
| FrigidaireGalleryFRS26ZGE | 1,500 | 95 |
| MaytagRSW2400EA | 1,400 | 96 |
| GETFX25ZRY | 1,200 | 94 |

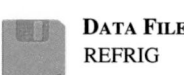

**DATA FILE**
REFRIG

*Source: "The Kings of Cool," Copyright 1997 by Consumers Union of U.S., Inc. Adapted from CON-SUMER REPORTS, January 1998, 52, by permission of Consumers Union U.S., Inc., Yonkers, NY 10703-1057. Although these data sets originally appeared in CONSUMER REPORTS, the selective adaptation and resulting conclusions presented are those of the authors and are not sanctioned or endorsed in any way by Consumers Union, the publisher of CONSUMER REPORTS.*

(a) With energy cost on the horizontal $X$ axis and price on the vertical $Y$ axis, set up a scatter diagram.

(b) Does there appear to be a relationship between price and energy cost? If so, is the relationship positive or negative?

(c) Would you expect the higher-priced refrigerators to have greater energy efficiency? Is this borne out by the data?

**3.32** The following data represent the average charge (in dollars and cents per minute) and the amount of minutes expended (in billions) for all telephone calls placed from the United States to 20 different countries during 1996.

| COUNTRY | CHARGE PER MINUTE (IN DOLLARS) | MINUTES (IN BILLIONS) |
|---|---|---|
| Canada | 0.34 | 3.049 |
| Mexico | 0.85 | 2.012 |
| Britain | 0.73 | 1.025 |
| Germany | 0.88 | 0.662 |
| Japan | 1.00 | 0.576 |
| Dominican Republic | 0.84 | 0.410 |
| France | 0.81 | 0.364 |
| South Korea | 1.09 | 0.319 |
| Hong Kong | 0.90 | 0.317 |
| Philippines | 1.29 | 0.297 |
| India | 1.38 | 0.287 |
| Brazil | 0.96 | 0.284 |
| Italy | 1.00 | 0.279 |
| Taiwan | 0.97 | 0.273 |
| Colombia | 1.00 | 0.257 |
| China | 1.47 | 0.232 |
| Israel | 1.16 | 0.214 |
| Australia | 1.01 | 0.201 |
| Jamaica | 1.03 | 0.188 |
| Netherlands | 0.78 | 0.167 |

*Source: Reprinted by permission of* The New York Times. The New York Times, *February 17, 1997, 46. Copyright by The New York Times Company.*

(a) With charge per minute on the horizontal $X$ axis and minutes on the vertical $Y$ axis, set up a scatter diagram.

(b) Does there appear to be a relationship between charge per minute and minutes? If so, is the relationship positive or negative?

(c) One might expect that the higher the charge per minute, the lower the number of minutes that would be used. Does the scatter diagram reflect this expected relationship? Explain.

**3.33** The following data represent the retail price (in dollars) and the printing speed (in number of pages per minute of double-spaced black text with standard margins) for a sample of 19 computer printers:

| BRAND | PRICE (IN DOLLARS) | TEXT SPEED (PAGES PER MINUTE) |
|---|---|---|
| Hewlett-PackardDeskJet855Cse | 500 | 3.0 |
| Hewlett-PackardDeskJet682C | 300 | 2.5 |
| Hewlett-PackardDeskJet600C | 250 | 2.6 |
| EpsonStylusColorII | 230 | 2.5 |
| Hewlett-PackardDeskWriter600 | 250 | 3.0 |
| CanonBJC-610 | 430 | 1.3 |
| CanonBJC-210 | 150 | 2.9 |
| AppleColorStyleWriter1500 | 280 | 3.1 |
| CanonBJC-4100 | 230 | 1.7 |
| AppleColorStyleWriter2500 | 380 | 3.4 |
| EpsonStylusColorIIs | 190 | 0.7 |
| Lexmark2070Jetprinter | 350 | 2.1 |
| Lexmark1020Jetprinter | 150 | 1.3 |
| NECSuperScript860 | 500 | 7.9 |
| PanasonicKX-P6500 | 450 | 5.5 |
| Hewlett-PackardLaserJet5L | 480 | 4.2 |
| TexasInstrumentsMicroLaserWin/4 | 380 | 4.2 |
| CanonLBP-460 | 350 | 4.1 |
| OkidataOL600e | 400 | 3.9 |

DATA FILE
PRINTER

*Source: "Computer Printers," Copyright 1996 by Consumers Union of U.S., Inc. Adapted from* CONSUMER REPORTS, *October 1996, 60–61, by permission of Consumers Union U.S., Inc., Yonkers, NY 10703-1057. Although these data sets originally appeared in* CONSUMER REPORTS, *the selective adaptation and resulting conclusions presented are those of the authors and are not sanctioned or endorsed in any way by Consumers Union, the publisher of* CONSUMER REPORTS.

(a) With price on the horizontal $X$ axis and text speed on the vertical $Y$ axis, set up a scatter diagram.

(b) Does there appear to be a relationship between price and text speed? If so, is the relationship positive or negative?

(c) One might expect that the higher the price, the higher the text speed. Does the scatter diagram reflect this expected relationship? Explain.

**3.34** The following data represent the number of cases of salad dressing purchased per week by a local supermarket chain over a period of 30 weeks:

| WEEK | CASES PURCHASED | WEEK | CASES PURCHASED | WEEK | CASES PURCHASED |
|---|---|---|---|---|---|
| 1 | 81 | 11 | 86 | 21 | 91 |
| 2 | 61 | 12 | 133 | 22 | 99 |
| 3 | 77 | 13 | 91 | 23 | 89 |
| 4 | 71 | 14 | 111 | 24 | 96 |
| 5 | 69 | 15 | 86 | 25 | 108 |
| 6 | 81 | 16 | 84 | 26 | 86 |
| 7 | 66 | 17 | 131 | 27 | 84 |
| 8 | 111 | 18 | 71 | 28 | 76 |
| 9 | 56 | 19 | 118 | 29 | 83 |
| 10 | 81 | 20 | 88 | 30 | 76 |

DATA FILE
SALAD

(a) Plot the number of cases purchased per week in a time-series plot.

(b) Does there appear to be any pattern in the number of cases purchased over time? Explain.

(c) If you had to make a prediction of the number of cases of salad dressing that would be ordered next week, how many cases would you predict? Why?

(d) Compare your prediction in (c) with the one made in Problem 3.27 (h) on page 72. What might account for the difference in the two predictions?

• **3.35** The following data represent the amount of soft drink filled in a sample of 50 consecutive 2-liter bottles. The results, listed horizontally in the order of being filled, were:

| | | | | | | | | | |
|---|---|---|---|---|---|---|---|---|---|
| 2.109 | 2.086 | 2.066 | 2.075 | 2.065 | 2.057 | 2.052 | 2.044 | 2.036 | 2.038 |
| 2.031 | 2.029 | 2.025 | 2.029 | 2.023 | 2.020 | 2.015 | 2.014 | 2.013 | 2.014 |
| 2.012 | 2.012 | 2.012 | 2.010 | 2.005 | 2.003 | 1.999 | 1.996 | 1.997 | 1.992 |
| 1.994 | 1.986 | 1.984 | 1.981 | 1.973 | 1.975 | 1.971 | 1.969 | 1.966 | 1.967 |
| 1.963 | 1.957 | 1.951 | 1.951 | 1.947 | 1.941 | 1.941 | 1.938 | 1.908 | 1.894 |

**DATA FILE**
**DRINK**

(a) Plot the amount of soft drink filled in a time-series plot.

(b) Does there appear to be any pattern in the amount of soft drink filled over time? Explain.

(c) If you had to make a prediction of the amount of soft drink that would be filled in the next bottle, what amount would you predict? Why?

(d) Compare your prediction in (c) with the one made in Problem 3.28 (h) on page 72. What might account for the difference in the two predictions?

**3.36** A large chain of toy stores has a policy of distributing "store dollars" for any merchandise returned without a sales receipt. The following data represent the amount of "store dollars" distributed during a 1-month period in April of a recent year at a branch of this chain in a large metropolitan area.

| DATE | AMOUNT OF "STORE DOLLARS" DISTRIBUTED ($) | DATE | AMOUNT OF "STORE DOLLARS" DISTRIBUTED ($) | DATE | AMOUNT OF "STORE DOLLARS" DISTRIBUTED ($) |
|---|---|---|---|---|---|
| 4–1 | 2,008 | 4–11 | 3,499 | 4–22 | 2,675 |
| 4–2 | 1,982 | 4–12 | 1,524 | 4–23 | 1,954 |
| 4–3 | 1,766 | 4–13 | 2,686 | 4–24 | 1,764 |
| 4–4 | 2,072 | 4–14 | 2,464 | 4–25 | 2,919 |
| 4–5 | 1,732 | 4–15 | 2,162 | 4–26 | 2,133 |
| 4–6 | 2,177 | 4–16 | 2,009 | 4–27 | 2,371 |
| 4–7 | 2,130 | 4–17 | 2,572 | 4–28 | 1,659 |
| 4–8 | 1,809 | 4–18 | 3,420 | 4–29 | 2,432 |
| 4–9 | 1,827 | 4–20 | 3,409 | 4–30 | 1,943 |
| 4–10 | 2,115 | 4–21 | 2,700 | | |

**DATA FILE**
**STOREDOL**

*Note: The store was closed on April 19, which was Easter Sunday.*

(a) Plot the amount of "store dollars" distributed in a time-series plot.

(b) Does there appear to be any pattern in the amount of "store dollars" distributed over time? Explain.

(c) If you had to make a prediction of the amount of "store dollars" distributed on the next day, what amount would you predict? Why?

**3.37** Referring to the financial section of your local newspaper, obtain a time-series plot. What is the chart intending to convey to its readers? Discuss.

## ◆ 3.4 TABLES AND CHARTS FOR CATEGORICAL DATA

Thus far in this chapter we have learned that when collecting a large set of numerical data, the best way to examine it is first to organize and present it in appropriate tabular and chart format. Often, however, the data we collect are categorical, not numerical. Thus, in this and the following section we will demonstrate how categorical data can be organized and presented in the form of tables and charts.

In order to do this, let us suppose once again that we want to evaluate various features pertaining to domestic general stock funds. In addition to net asset value and the two performance measures (1-year total percentage return and 3-year annualized total return) and fund objective (growth versus blend), the data set in appendix D displays information on fee schedule and fund size. We note that net asset value (in dollars) and the two performance measure variables (in percentages) are *numerical*, whereas the fund objective variable along with fee schedule and fund size are *categorical*. Earlier in this chapter we were concerned only with the tabular and chart presentation of numerical data. A detailed study of the responses to the categorical variables will be undertaken here.

When dealing with categorical phenomena, we may tally the observations into summary tables and then graphically display them as bar charts, pie charts, or Pareto diagrams.

### The Summary Table

A **summary table** for categorical data is similar in format to the frequency distribution table for numerical data that we studied in section 3.2. To illustrate the development of a summary table, let us consider the data obtained on fee schedule. By tallying the observations from Special Data Set 1 in appendix D, we see that of the 194 sampled domestic general stock funds, 17 have fees covering marketing costs paid from fund assets, 5 have deferred sales charges or redemption fees, 19 have "front-load" sales charges, 46 are classified as charging multiple fees, and 107 are categorized as "no-load" funds (that is, there are no fee charges). This information is presented in Table 3.7.

**Table 3.7** *Frequency and percentage summary table pertaining to fee schedule for 194 domestic general stock funds*

| FEE SCHEDULE | NUMBER OF FUNDS | PERCENTAGE OF FUNDS |
|---|---|---|
| Fees from fund assets | 17 | 8.8 |
| Deferred fees | 5 | 2.6 |
| Front-load fees | 19 | 9.8 |
| Multiple fees | 46 | 23.7 |
| No-load funds | 107 | 55.2 |
| Total | 194 | 100.1[a] |

[a] *Error due to rounding.*
*Source: Data are taken from Special Data Set 1 in appendix D.*

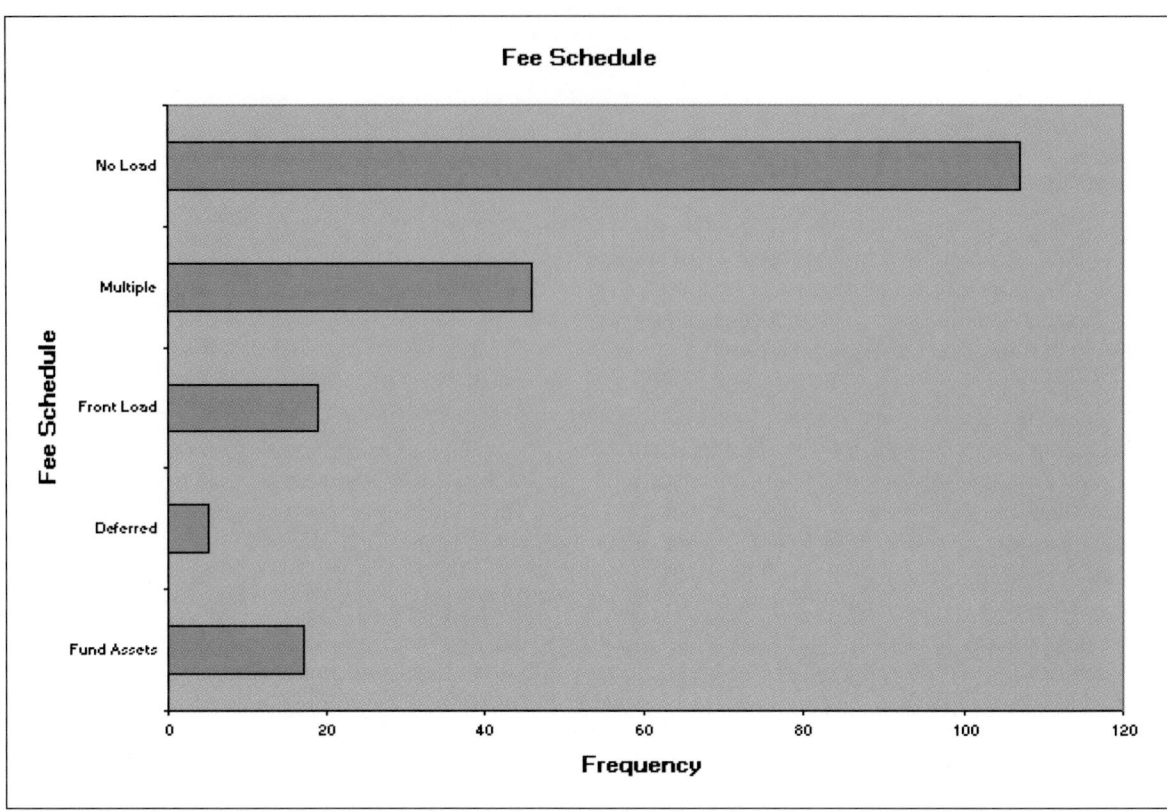

**FIGURE 3.7**  Frequency bar chart pertaining to fee schedule for 194 sampled domestic general stock funds obtained from Microsoft Excel

*Source: Data are taken from Table 3.7 on page 79.*

## The Bar Chart

To express the information provided in Table 3.7 graphically, a percentage bar chart can be displayed. Figure 3.7 depicts a percentage bar chart obtained from Microsoft Excel for the fee schedule data presented in Table 3.7. In **bar charts**, each category is depicted by a bar, the length of which represents the frequency or percentage of observations falling into a category. From Figure 3.7 we observe that the bar chart allows us to directly compare the percentage of funds in terms of the type of fee schedule. More than half the funds are no-load funds, while almost 25% of the funds are multiple-fee funds. Very few funds receive fees from fund assets, deferred fees, or front-load fees.

## The Pie Chart

Another widely used graphical display to visually express categorical data from a summary table is the **pie chart.** Figure 3.8 depicts a percentage pie chart for the fee schedule data presented in Table 3.7.

The pie chart is based on the fact that the circle has 360°. The pie is divided into slices according to the percentage in each category. As an example, in Table 3.7, 23.7% of the domestic general stock funds sampled are classified as charging multiple fees. Thus, in constructing the pie chart, 360° is multiplied by .237, resulting in a sector that takes up 85° of

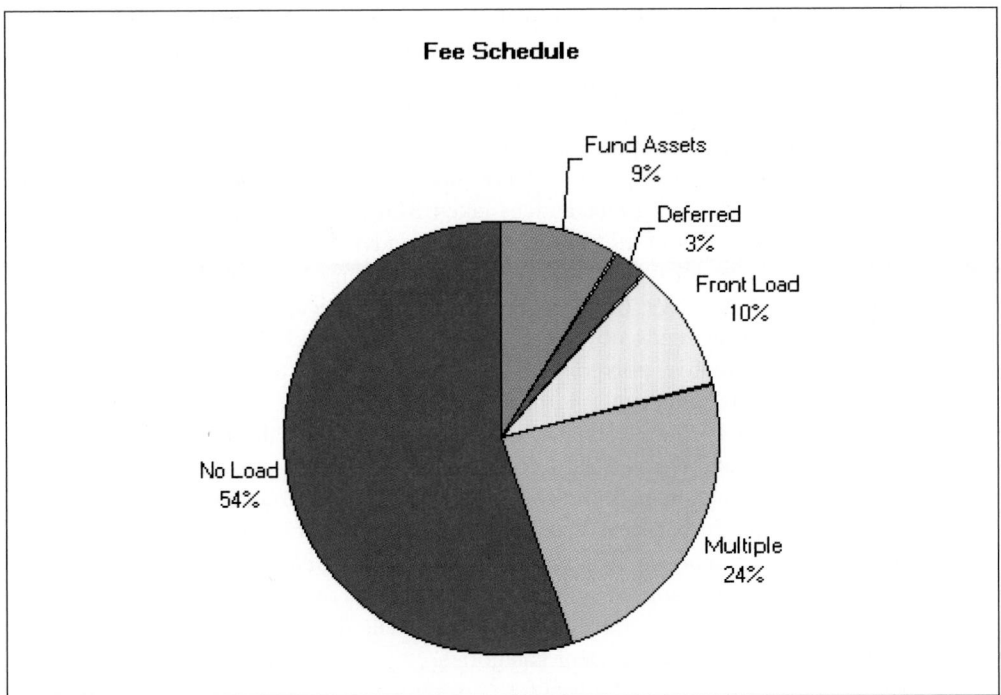

**FIGURE 3.8**   Percentage pie chart pertaining to fee schedule for 194 sampled domestic general stock funds obtained from Microsoft Excel

*Source: Data are taken from Table 3.7 on page 79.*

the 360° of the circle. From Figure 3.8 we observe that the pie chart lets us visualize the portion of the entire pie that is in each category. We can see that no-load funds take up more than half the pie and multiple-fee funds almost one-quarter.

The purpose of graphical presentation is to display data accurately and clearly. Figures 3.7 and 3.8 attempt to convey the same information with respect to fee schedule. Whether these charts succeed, however, has been a matter of much concern (see references 2–4, 11, 12). In particular, some research in the human perception of graphs (reference 4) concludes that the pie chart presents the weaker display. The bar chart is preferred to the pie chart because it has been observed that the human eye can more accurately judge length comparisons against a fixed scale (as in a bar chart) than angular measures (as in a pie chart). Nevertheless, the pie chart has two distinct advantages: (1) it is aesthetically pleasing, and (2) it clearly shows that the total for all categories or slices of the pie comes to 100%. Thus, the selection of a particular chart is still highly subjective and often dependent on the aesthetic preferences of the user.

## The Pareto Diagram

A graphical device for portraying categorical data that often provides more visual information than either the bar chart or the pie chart is the Pareto diagram. This is particularly true as the number of classifications or groupings for our categorical variable of interest increases. The **Pareto diagram** is a special type of vertical bar chart in which the categorized responses are plotted in the descending rank order of their frequencies and combined with a cumulative polygon on the same scale. The main principle behind this graphical device is its ability to separate the "vital few" from the "trivial many," enabling us to focus on the important responses. Hence, the chart achieves its greatest utility when the categorical variable of interest contains many categories. The Pareto diagram is widely used in the statistical control of process and product quality (see chapter 15).

To illustrate the Pareto diagram, we observe that in Figure 3.7 the bar chart pertaining to fee schedule presents the categories as fees taken from fund assets, deferred fees, front-load fees, multiple fees, and no fees (that is, no-load funds). Since no-load funds dominate, a Pareto diagram may be formed by changing the ordering. Such a plot obtained from Minitab is depicted in Figure 3.9. From the lengths of the vertical bars we observe that five out of every nine of these funds do not charge fees and are classified as no-load funds (code 5). From the cumulative polygon we note that 78.9% of these funds are classified either as no-load or as charging multiple fees (code 4).

In the construction of the Pareto diagram, the vertical axis on the left contains the frequencies or percentages and the vertical axis on the right contains the cumulative percentages (from 100 on top to 0 on bottom) and the horizontal axis contains the categories of interest. The equally spaced bars are of equal width. The point on the cumulative percentage polygon for each category is centered at the midpoint of each respective bar. Hence, when studying a Pareto diagram, we should be focusing on two things: the magnitudes of the differences in bar lengths corresponding to adjacent descending categories and the cumulative percentages of these adjacent categories.

The Pareto diagram is a very useful tool for presenting categorical data, particularly when the number of classifications or groupings increases. To further demonstrate its value in these situations, we turn to Example 3.4, which is an application in operations management.

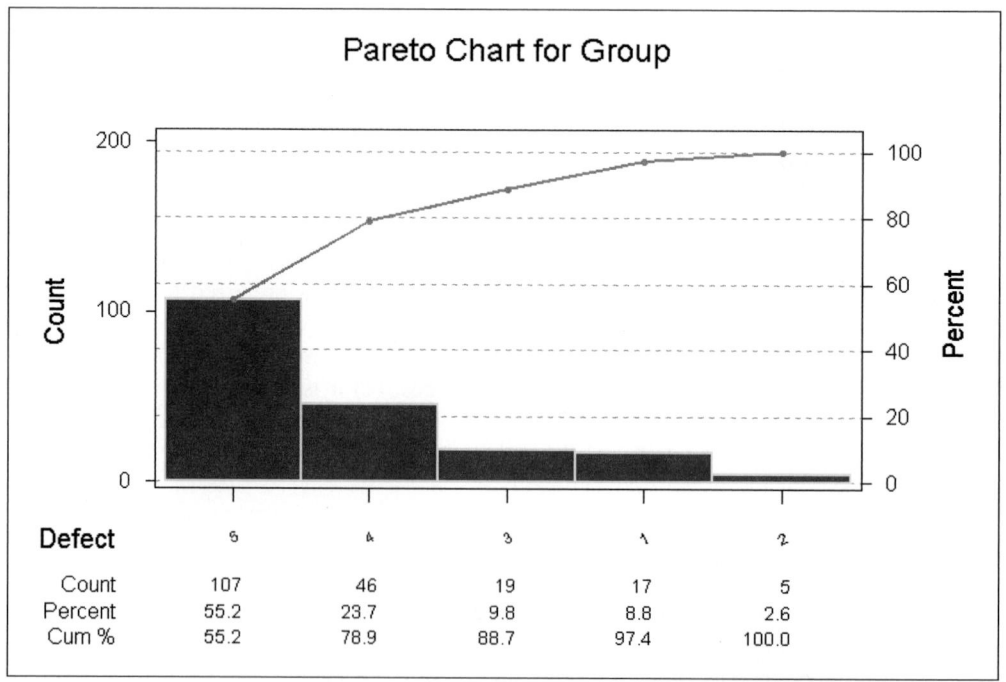

**FIGURE 3.9** Pareto diagram depicting fee schedule for 194 sampled domestic general stock funds obtained from Minitab

## Example 3.4 *The Pareto Diagram*

The operations manager at a cereal packaging plant said that in her experience, typically there are nine reasons that result in the production of unacceptable cereal cartons at the end of the packaging process: broken carton (R), bulging carton (G), cracked carton (C), dirty carton (D), hole in carton (H), improper package weight (I), printing error (P), unreadable label (U), and unsealed box top (S).

The raw data below represent a sample of 50 unacceptable cereal cartons taken from the past week's production, and the reasons for nonconformance are indicated:

U G U S H D D R I  U S U S U G C S U D R S U D U S
S D P R S I S U D G S S U S D G S C U D D S S S U

Using these data, construct the Pareto diagram.

### SOLUTION

First, a summary and percentage table is developed. Then, after rank-ordering the categories in the table from its alphabetical listing to one representing the reasons for nonconformance in descending order of importance, a Pareto diagram is constructed.

*Summary and percentage table of reasons for nonconformance*

| REASON FOR NONCONFORMANCE | No. | % |
|---|---|---|
| Broken carton (R) | 3 | 6.0 |
| Bulging carton (G) | 4 | 8.0 |
| Cracked carton (C) | 2 | 4.0 |
| Dirty carton (D) | 9 | 18.0 |
| Hole in carton (H) | 1 | 2.0 |
| Improper package weight (I) | 2 | 4.0 |
| Printing error (P) | 1 | 2.0 |
| Unreadable label (U) | 12 | 24.0 |
| Unsealed box top (S) | 16 | 32.0 |
| Total | 50 | 100.0 |

*Summary and percentage table of ranked reasons for nonconformance*

| REASON FOR NONCONFORMANCE | No. | % |
|---|---|---|
| Unsealed box top (S) | 16 | 32.0 |
| Unreadable label (U) | 12 | 24.0 |
| Dirty carton (D) | 9 | 18.0 |
| Bulging carton (G) | 4 | 8.0 |
| Broken carton (R) | 3 | 6.0 |
| Cracked carton (C) | 2 | 4.0 |
| Improper package weight (I) | 2 | 4.0 |
| Hole in carton (H) | 1 | 2.0 |
| Printing error (P) | 1 | 2.0 |
| Total | 50 | 100.0 |

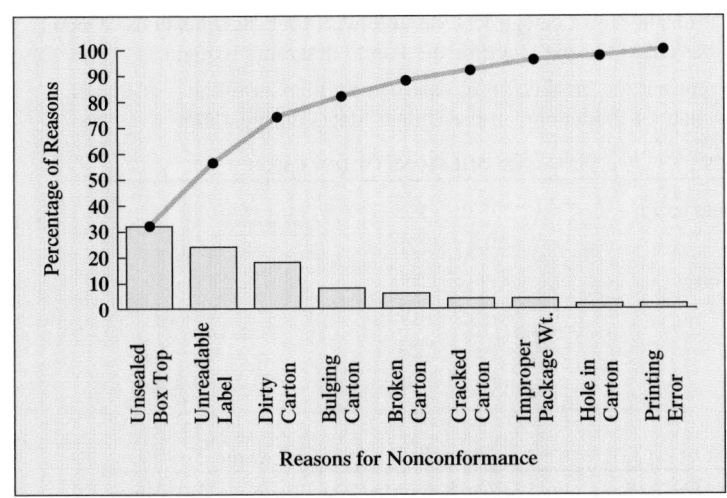

Separating the "vital few" from the "trivial many," we may determine that unsealed box tops (32.0%), unreadable labels (24.0%), and dirty cartons (18.0%) together account for 74.0% of the reasons for nonconformance. The remaining six reasons account for 26.0%.

## Problems for Section 3.4

### Learning the Basics

• **3.38** Suppose that a categorical variable had three categories with the following frequency of occurrence:

| CATEGORY | FREQUENCY |
|----------|-----------|
| A | 13 |
| B | 28 |
| C | 9 |

(a) Compute the percentage of values in each category.
(b) Construct a bar chart.
(c) Construct a pie chart.
(d) Form a Pareto diagram.

**3.39** Suppose that a categorical variable had four categories with the following percentage of occurrence:

| CATEGORY | PERCENTAGE |
|----------|------------|
| A | 12 |
| B | 29 |
| C | 35 |
| D | 24 |

(a) Construct a bar chart.
(b) Construct a pie chart.
(c) Form a Pareto diagram.

### Applying the Concepts

**3.40** If you were going to make a presentation in front of an audience of 100 people and needed to use a visual display for a categorical variable with four classifications, which would you use—the bar chart, the pie chart, or the Pareto diagram? Explain.

**3.41** The following data represent the breakdown of sales (in millions of dollars) of organic foods purchased from natural food stores in the United States during 1995:

| FOOD PRODUCT | SALES (IN MILLIONS OF DOLLARS) |
|--------------|--------------------------------|
| Grocery, soy foods, and dairy | 512 |
| Herbs | 228 |
| Food service and bakery | 208 |
| Produce | 402 |
| Bulk | 231 |
| Frozen foods | 98 |
| Miscellaneous | 192 |
| Total | 1,871 |

*Sources:* Natural Foods Merchandiser; New Product News Magazine; The New York Times.

(a) Construct a bar chart.
(b) Construct a pie chart.
(c) Form a Pareto diagram.
(d) Which of these charts do you prefer to use here? Why?
(e) On the basis of the results of (a)–(c), in what categories does the major portion of the sales of organic foods purchased from natural food stores occur? Explain.

**3.42** The following data represent the percentage of sales by various companies in the music industry during 1995:

| COMPANY | % OF SALES |
| --- | --- |
| Sony | 13.6 |
| Warner, Elektra, Atlantic | 22.1 |
| Polygram | 13.8 |
| Bertelsmann Music | 12.0 |
| MCA | 10.1 |
| Capital/EMI | 9.2 |
| Independents | 19.1 |
| Total | 99.9[a] |

[a] Due to rounding.
Sources: Soundscan; Nielsen Media Research; Exhibitor Relations Company; The New York Times, December 6, 1995.

(a) Construct a bar chart.
(b) Construct a pie chart.
(c) Form a Pareto diagram.
(d) Which of these charts do you prefer to use here? Why?
(e) Would you conclude that any one company dominates sales in the music industry? Explain.

**3.43** During the year 1995, oil consumption in the United States was 17.7 million barrels per day. The following data represent the percentage breakdown of the sources of that consumption:

| SOURCE OF CONSUMPTION | % USAGE |
| --- | --- |
| Electric utilities | 1.4 |
| Highway transportation | 53.4 |
| Jet fuel | 8.5 |
| Plastics and fertilizers | 10.2 |
| Railroad, boat, and some construction equipment | 4.8 |
| Other uses for homes, industry, and businesses | 21.7 |
| Total | 100.0 |

Source: U.S. Department of Energy.

(a) Construct a bar chart.
(b) Construct a pie chart.
(c) Form a Pareto diagram.
(d) Which of these charts do you prefer to use here? Why?
(e) What sources account for the bulk of oil consumption in the United States? Explain.

**3.44** The following data represent the number of accidental deaths in the United States due to various causes during a recent year:

| CAUSE OF DEATH | NUMBER |
|---|---|
| Agricultural machines | 553 |
| Airplanes | 39 |
| Buses | 23 |
| Caught in or between objects | 119 |
| Dog bites | 13 |
| Domestic wiring and appliances | 66 |
| Drowning (other than bathtub) | 4,186 |
| Drowning in bathtub | 345 |
| Falling objects | 712 |
| Falls | 12,646 |
| Falls into holes and openings | 99 |
| Fire and burns | 3,958 |
| Inhalation and ingestion of food | 1,196 |
| Lightning | 53 |
| Passenger cars and taxis | 21,257 |
| Side effects of therapeutic drug use | 156 |
| Suffocation by falling earth | 58 |
| Venomous plants and animals | 68 |
| Total | 45,547 |

*Source: National Safety Council.*

(a) Form a Pareto diagram.
(b) What causes accounted for most of the accidental deaths? Explain.

**3.45** The following data represent daily water consumption per household in a suburban water district during a recent summer.

| REASON FOR WATER USAGE | GALLONS PER DAY |
|---|---|
| Bathing and showering | 99 |
| Dish washing | 13 |
| Drinking and cooking | 11 |
| Laundering | 33 |
| Lawn watering | 150 |
| Toilet | 88 |
| Miscellaneous | 20 |
| Total | 414 |

(a) Form a Pareto diagram.
(b) If the water district wanted to develop a water reduction plan, which reasons for water usage should be focused on?

• **3.46** A patient-satisfaction survey conducted for a sample of 210 individuals discharged from a large urban hospital during the month of June led to the following list of 384 complaints:

| REASON FOR COMPLAINT | NUMBER |
|---|---|
| Anger with other patients/visitors | 13 |
| Failure to respond to buzzer | 71 |
| Inadequate answers to questions | 38 |
| Lateness for tests | 34 |
| Noise | 28 |
| Poor food service | 117 |
| Rudeness of staff | 62 |
| All others | 21 |
| Total | 384 |

(a) Form a Pareto diagram.
(b) Which reasons for complaint do you think the hospital should focus on if it wishes to reduce the number of complaints? Explain.

**3.47** From a study of commercial properties conducted in March 1996 the following data represent the mix of retail establishments in the 32-block Times Square area of New York City:

| TYPE OF RETAIL ESTABLISHMENT | NUMBER |
|---|---|
| Accessories | 13 |
| Adult use | 25 |
| Bar, lounge, or nightclub | 15 |
| Beauty/barber | 15 |
| Books/news | 6 |
| Clothing | 18 |
| Electronics | 27 |
| Entertainment | 8 |
| Fabric | 5 |
| Gifts | 49 |
| Grocery/convenience | 34 |
| Hardware | 7 |
| Health and fitness | 4 |
| Health, beauty, and housewares | 10 |
| Music | 18 |
| Quick-service (food) | 83 |
| Restaurant | 149 |
| Services | 45 |
| Theater-movies | 6 |
| Wines and liquor | 5 |
| Other | 14 |
| Vacant store | 69 |
| Total | 625 |

*Source: Reprinted by permission of* The New York Times. The New York Times, *March 10, 1996, R11.*

(a) Form a Pareto diagram.

(b) What type of retail establishments make up the major portion of commercial properties in the Times Square area of New York City? Explain.

(c) If you were employed by a public relations firm whose goal was to promote business opportunities in New York City for tourists, what would you say about this renovated Times Square district?

 ## 3.5 TABULATING AND GRAPHING BIVARIATE CATEGORICAL DATA

Often we need to examine simultaneously the responses to two categorical variables. For example, we might be interested in examining whether or not there is any pattern or relationship between fund objective (i.e., growth or blend) and the fee schedule. In this section we will examine some tabular and graphical methods of cross-classifying and presenting such data. In particular, we will develop the contingency table and the side-by-side bar chart.

### The Contingency Table

In order to simultaneously study the responses to two categorical variables, we first form a two-way table of cross-classification known as a **contingency** or **cross-classification table**. For example, using the data set in appendix D, we can cross-classify the responses to the two categorical variables fund objective and fee schedule in order to determine if there is a pattern or relationship between them. Table 3.8 depicts this information for all 194 sampled domestic general stock funds.

To construct this contingency table, the joint responses for each of the 194 domestic general stock funds with respect to fund objective and fee schedule are tallied into one of the 10 possible "cells" of the table. Thus, from the data set in appendix D, the first fund listed (AARP Investment GrowInc) is classified as a blend fund for which there is no fee (that is, it is a no-load fund). These joint responses are tallied into the cell composed of the second row and fifth column. The second institution (AIM BlueCh A) is a growth fund charging multiple fees. These joint responses are tallied into the cell composed of the first row and fourth column. The remaining 192 joint responses are recorded in a similar manner.

**Table 3.8** *Contingency table displaying fund objective and fee schedule*

| FUND OBJECTIVE | FEE SCHEDULE | | | | | |
| --- | --- | --- | --- | --- | --- | --- |
| | FUND ASSETS | DEFERRED FEES | FRONT LOAD | MULTIPLE FEES | NO LOAD | TOTAL |
| Growth | 4 | 0 | 7 | 16 | 32 | 59 |
| Blend | 13 | 5 | 12 | 30 | 75 | 135 |
| Total | 17 | 5 | 19 | 46 | 107 | 194 |

*Source: Data are taken from Special Data Set 1 in appendix D.*

In order to explore any possible pattern or relationship between fund objective and fee schedule, it is useful to first convert these results into percentages based on the following three totals:

1. The overall total (i.e., the 194 sampled domestic general stock funds)
2. The row totals (i.e., growth or blend funds)
3. The column totals (i.e., the five fee schedule classifications)

This is accomplished in Tables 3.9, 3.10, and 3.11, respectively.

Let us examine some of the many findings present in these tables. From Table 3.9 we note that 30.4% of the domestic general stock funds sampled are growth funds, 55.2% are no-load funds, and 16.5% are growth funds that are no-load. From Table 3.10 we note that 0.0% of the growth funds have a deferred-fee schedule, and 22.2% of the blend funds have a multiple-fee schedule. From Table 3.11 we note that 36.8% of the funds with a front-load fee schedule are growth funds and 76.5% of the funds whose fees are paid from fund assets are blend funds. The tables, therefore, do not reveal any major patterns: blend funds predominate over growth funds, regardless of the fee schedule. In addition, no-load funds and those with multiple-fee schedules predominate over other fee schedules, regardless of the objective of the fund (i.e., growth versus blend).

**Table 3.9** *Contingency table displaying fund objective and fee schedule (percentages based on overall total)*

| FUND OBJECTIVE | FEE SCHEDULE | | | | | |
| | FUND ASSETS | DEFERRED FEES | FRONT LOAD | MULTIPLE FEES | NO LOAD | TOTAL |
|---|---|---|---|---|---|---|
| Growth | 2.1 | 0.0 | 3.6 | 8.2 | 16.5 | 30.4 |
| Blend | 6.7 | 2.6 | 6.2 | 15.5 | 38.7 | 69.6 |
| Total | 8.8 | 2.6 | 9.8 | 23.7 | 55.2 | 100.0 |

*Source: Data are taken from Table 3.8.*

**Table 3.10** *Contingency table displaying fund objective and fee schedule (percentages based on row totals)*

| FUND OBJECTIVE | FEE SCHEDULE | | | | | |
| | FUND ASSETS | DEFERRED FEES | FRONT LOAD | MULTIPLE FEES | NO LOAD | TOTAL |
|---|---|---|---|---|---|---|
| Growth | 6.8 | 0.0 | 11.9 | 27.1 | 54.2 | 100.0 |
| Blend | 9.6 | 3.7 | 8.9 | 22.2 | 55.6 | 100.0 |
| Total | 8.8 | 2.6 | 9.8 | 23.7 | 55.2 | 100.0 |

*Source: Data are taken from Table 3.8.*

**Table 3.11** *Contingency table displaying fund objective and fee schedule (percentages based on column totals)*

| | FEE SCHEDULE | | | | | |
| FUND OBJECTIVE | FUND ASSETS | DEFERRED FEES | FRONT LOAD | MULTIPLE FEES | NO LOAD | TOTAL |
|---|---|---|---|---|---|---|
| Growth | 23.5 | 0.0 | 36.8 | 34.8 | 29.9 | 30.4 |
| Blend | 76.5 | 100.0 | 63.2 | 65.2 | 70.1 | 69.6 |
| Total | 100.0 | 100.0 | 100.0 | 100.0 | 100.0 | 100.0 |

We may now wish to condense these $2 \times 5$ contingency tables (i.e., 2 rows by 5 columns) into a set of $2 \times 2$ tables of cross-classification by simplifying the fee schedule variable into only two categories—funds that charge fees versus those that do not (i.e., the no-load funds).

## The Side-by-Side Bar Chart

A useful way to visually display bivariate categorical data when looking for patterns or relationships is by constructing a **side-by-side bar chart**. This graphic form is best suited when primary interest is in demonstrating differences in magnitude rather than differences in percentages. Thus, for example, using the data from Table 3.8, Figure 3.10 is a side-by-side bar chart obtained from Excel that enables a comparison of the two fund objectives based on the various fee schedules. From Figure 3.10 and Table 3.11 we observe that although about 70% of all the mutual funds have a blend fund objective, a slightly larger proportion of mutual funds whose fees are paid from fund assets have a blend objective, whereas a slightly smaller proportion of funds whose fees are front-loaded or are from multiple sources have a blend objective. In addition, all five funds with a deferred fee schedule have a blend fund objective.

## Problems for Section 3.5

### Learning the Basics

● **3.48** The following data represent the bivariate responses to two questions asked in a survey of 40 college students majoring in business—Gender (Male = M; Female = F) and Major (Accountancy = A; Computer Information Systems = C; Retailing = R):

Gender: M M M F M F F M F M F M F M M M M F F M F F
Major:  A  C  C  R A C A A C A A A R C R A A A C

Gender: M M M M F M F F M M F M M M M F M F M M
Major:  C  C  A A R R C A A A C C A A A A C C A C

(a) Tally the data into a $2 \times 3$ contingency table where the two rows represent the gender categories and the three columns represent the student-major categories.
(b) Form a contingency table based on percentages of all 40 student responses.
(c) Form a contingency table based on row percentages.
(d) Form a contingency table based on column percentages.
(e) Using the results from (a), construct a side-by-side bar chart of gender based on student major.

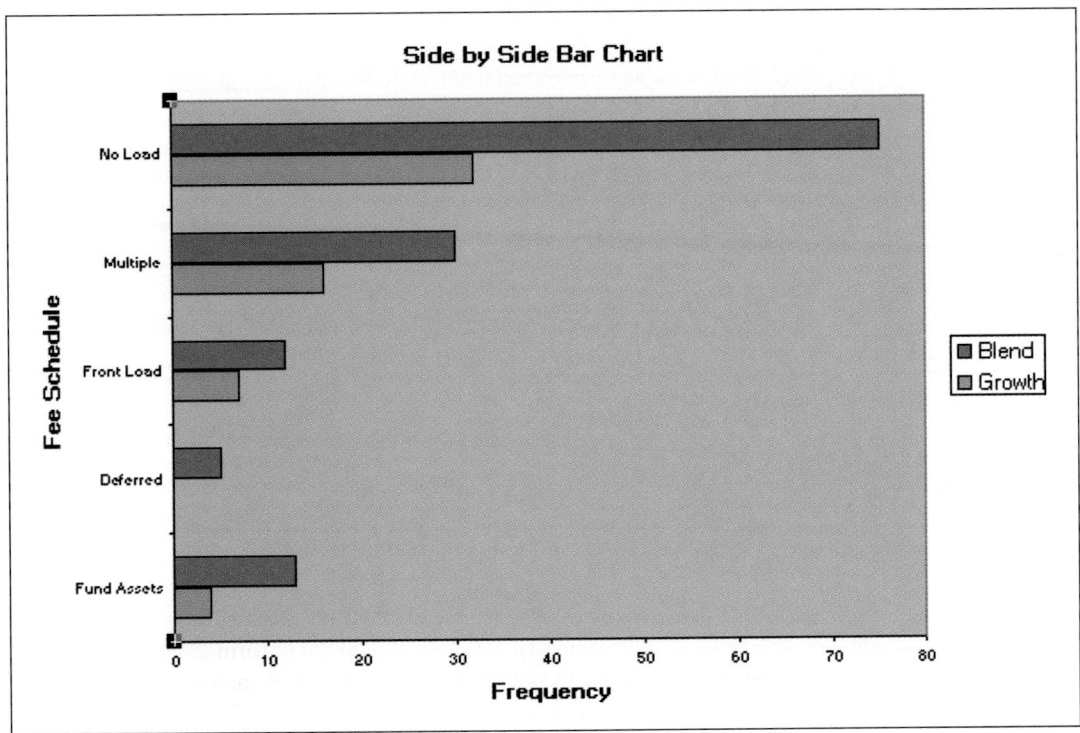

FIGURE 3.10   A side-by-side bar chart of fund objective based on fee schedule obtained from Microsoft Excel

**3.49** Given the following two-way cross-classification table, construct a side-by-side bar chart comparing A and B for each of the three column categories.

|   | 1 | 2 | 3 | TOTAL |
|---|---|---|---|-------|
| A | 20 | 40 | 40 | 100 |
| B | 80 | 80 | 40 | 200 |

## Applying the Concepts

● **3.50** An employee survey was conducted by the Human Resources Department at Leonel Industries. Responses to a questionnaire from 400 full-time employees yielded the following breakdown with respect to gender and occupational title:

| GENDER | MGT. | PROF. | SALES | ADM. | SUPPORT SERVICE | PRODUCTION | LABORER | TOTAL |
|--------|------|-------|-------|------|-----------------|------------|---------|-------|
| Male | 36 | 33 | 34 | 14 | 18 | 51 | 47 | 233 |
| Female | 29 | 33 | 23 | 51 | 11 | 3 | 17 | 167 |
| Total | 65 | 66 | 57 | 65 | 29 | 54 | 64 | 400 |

(OCCUPATIONAL TITLE spans MGT. through LABORER)

(a) Construct a table of row percentages.

(b) Construct a side-by-side bar chart for the results in (a).

(c) Does there seem to be an overrepresentation of males in some categories and an underrepresentation in others? Explain.

• **3.51** The victory of the incumbent, Bill Clinton, in the 1996 presidential election was attributed to improved economic conditions and low unemployment. Suppose that a survey of 800 adults taken soon after the election resulted in the following cross-classification of financial condition with education level:

| | EDUCATION LEVEL | | | |
| FINANCIAL CONDITIONS | H.S. DEGREE OR LOWER | SOME COLLEGE | COLLEGE DEGREE OR HIGHER | TOTAL |
| --- | --- | --- | --- | --- |
| Worse off now than before | 91 | 39 | 18 | 148 |
| No difference | 104 | 73 | 31 | 208 |
| Better off now than before | 235 | 48 | 161 | 444 |
| Total | 430 | 160 | 210 | 800 |

(a) Construct a table of column percentages.

(b) Construct a side-by-side bar chart to visually highlight the results in (a).

(c) On the basis of the results of (a) and (b), do you think there is a clear difference in the current financial condition as compared with before based on level of education?

**3.52** Using Special Data Set 1 from appendix D:

(a) Set up a 2 × 3 table of cross-classifications of fund objective (growth versus blend) and size of fund capitalization (large, medium, or small).

(b) Construct a table based on total percentages.

(c) Construct a table based on row percentages.

(d) Construct a table based on column percentages.

(e) Construct a side-by-side bar chart of fund objective based on size of fund capitalization.

(f) On the basis of your results in (e), does there appear to be a pattern or relationship between fund objective and size of fund capitalization? Discuss.

**3.53** Each day at a large hospital several hundred laboratory tests are performed. The rate at which these tests are improperly done for a variety of reasons (and therefore need to be redone) seems steady at about 4%. In an effort to get to the root cause of these nonconformances (tests that need to be redone), the director of the lab decides to keep records for a period of one week of the nonconformances subdivided by the shift of workers who performed the lab tests. The results were as follows:

| | SHIFT | | |
| LAB TESTS PERFORMED | DAY | EVENING | TOTAL |
| --- | --- | --- | --- |
| Nonconforming | 16 | 24 | 40 |
| Conforming | 654 | 306 | 960 |
| Total | 670 | 330 | 1,000 |

(a) Construct a table of row percentages.

(b) Construct a table of column percentages.

(c) Construct a table of total percentages.

(d) Which type of percentage—row, column, or total—do you think is most informative for these data? Explain.

(e)  What conclusions concerning the pattern of nonconforming laboratory tests can the laboratory director reach?

● **3.54**  A savings bank conducted a customer satisfaction survey on a monthly basis to measure satisfaction with several areas of services offered by a branch office. The results from a sample of 200 customers were as follows:

| AREA OF SERVICE | NUMBER SATISFIED | NUMBER DISSATISFIED |
|---|---|---|
| Waiting time for tellers | 123 | 65 |
| Automatic teller machine (ATM) | 73 | 7 |
| Investment advisement | 43 | 6 |
| Traveler's-check service | 25 | 11 |
| Safe deposits | 24 | 5 |
| Account maintenance services | 46 | 4 |

*Note: Because all customers did not use each service, the number of responses for each area of service is different.*

(a)  Construct a table of row percentages.
(b)  Construct a table of column percentages.
(c)  Construct a table of total percentages.
(d)  Which type of percentage—row, column, or total—do you think is most helpful in understanding these data. Why?
(e)  Construct a side-by-side bar chart of customer satisfaction by area of service.
(f)  Do customers seem equally satisfied with all areas of service? Which areas seem to need improvement more than others? Discuss.

## 3.6 ◆ GRAPHICAL EXCELLENCE

To this point we have studied how a collected set of data is presented in tabular and chart form. Among the methods for describing and communicating statistical information, well-designed graphical displays are usually the simplest and the most powerful. Good graphical displays reveal what the data are conveying. If our analysis is to be enhanced by visual displays of data, it is essential that the tables and charts be presented clearly and carefully. Tabular frills and other "**chart junk**" must be eliminated so as not to cloud the message given by the data with unnecessary adornments (references 7, 11, 12, and 13).

The widespread use of spreadsheet applications and graphics software has led to a proliferation of graphics in recent years. While much of the graphics presented have served as useful representations of the data, unfortunately the inappropriate and improper nature of many presentations has often hindered understanding and analysis.

### Principles of Graphical Excellence

Perhaps the most well-known proponent of the proper presentation of data in graphs is Professor Edward R. Tufte, who has written a series of books devoted to proper methods of graphical design (see references 11, 12, and 13). It is the work of Tufte that we will focus on in this section.

Exhibit 3.1 lists the essential features of graphing data.

### Exhibit 3.1 Features of Graphing Data

The basic features of a proper graph include the following:

✓ **1.** Showing the data

✓ **2.** Getting the viewer to focus on the substance of the graph, not on how the graph was developed

✓ **3.** Avoiding distortion

✓ **4.** Encouraging comparisons of data

✓ **5.** Serving a clear purpose

✓ **6.** Being integrated with the statistical and verbal descriptions of the graph

In *The Visual Display of Quantitative Information* (reference 11), Tufte has suggested five principles of graphical excellence. These are listed in Exhibit 3.2.

### Exhibit 3.2 Principles of Graphical Excellence

✓ **1.** Graphical excellence is a well-designed presentation of data that provides substance, statistics, and design.

✓ **2.** Graphical excellence communicates complex ideas with clarity, precision, and efficiency.

✓ **3.** Graphical excellence gives the viewer the largest number of ideas in the shortest time with the least ink.

✓ **4.** Graphical excellence almost always involves several dimensions.

✓ **5.** Graphical excellence requires telling the truth about the data.

There are several ways in which the excellence of a graph can be evaluated. One important measure is the **data-ink ratio**.

### Data-Ink Ratio

The data-ink ratio is the proportion of the graphic's ink that is devoted to nonredundant display of data information.

$$\text{Data-ink ratio} = \frac{\text{data-ink}}{\text{total ink used to print the graphic}}$$

The objective is to maximize the proportion of the ink used in the graph that is devoted to the data. Within reasonable limits, non-data-ink and redundant data-ink should be eliminated. Non-data-ink includes aspects of the graph that do not relate to the substantive features of the data as well as grid lines that may be imposed on the graph. We refer to such adornments as chartjunk, which can be defined as follows.

**Chartjunk** is decoration that is non-data-ink or redundant data-ink.

In its extreme form, chartjunk represents self-promoting graphics that focuses the viewer on the style of the graph, not the data presented in the graph. Tufte has referred to this type of graph as "The Duck."

A central feature of graphical excellence is the importance of not using a graph to distort the data that it represents. A graph does not distort if its visual representation is consistent with its numerical representation. The amount of distortion can be measured by the **lie factor**.

## Lie Factor

The lie factor is the ratio of the size of the effect shown in the graph to the size of the effects shown in the data.

One principle involved here is that any variation in the design of a graph must be consistent with the variation that exists in the data. Often changes in the graph are not consistent with variations in the data, producing a distortion between what the data represent and what the graph is showing.

In order to better understand these principles, it is useful to study several examples of graphs that are deficient in graphical excellence.

Figure 3.11 is a graph printed in *The New York Times* of the annual oyster catch in Chesapeake Bay in millions of bushels for a time period that stretches more than a century, from the 1890s until 1992. The icon representing the estimated 20 million bushels of oysters caught in the 1890s does not appear to be five times the size of the icon representing the estimated 4 million bushels caught in 1962. Such an illustration may catch the eye, but it usually doesn't show anything that could not be presented better in a summary table or a plot of the data over time (see section 3.3).

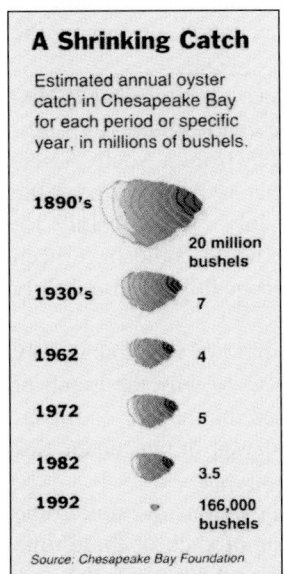

**FIGURE 3.11**

"Improper" display of estimated oyster catch (in millions of bushels) in Chesapeake Bay over various time periods

*Source: Reprinted by permission of* The New York Times. The New York Times, *October 17, 1993, 26.*

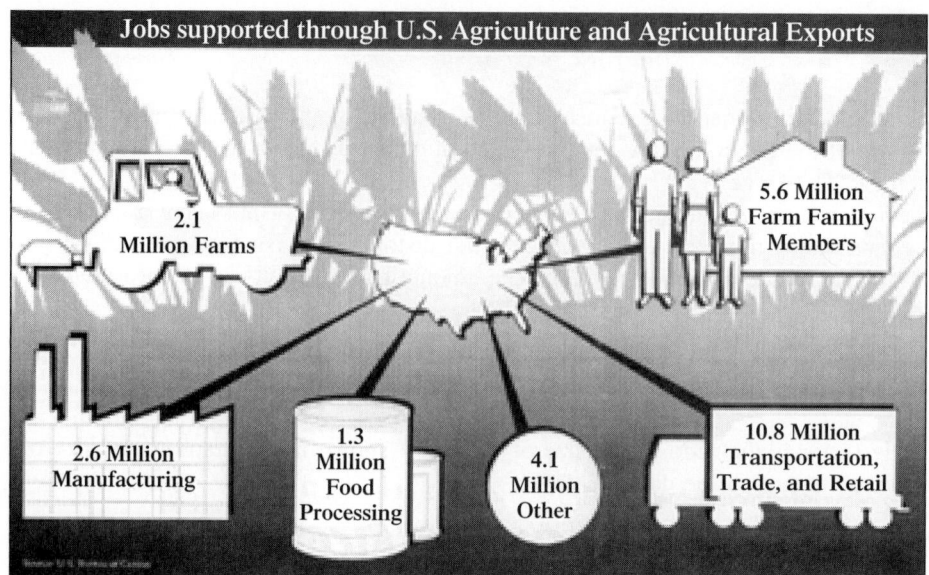

**FIGURE 3.12** "Improper" display of jobs supported through United States agriculture and agricultural exports

*Source: Reprinted by permission of* The New York Times. The New York Times, *October 19, 1993, Advertising Supplement, D18.*

Exaggerated icons and symbols are chartjunk. They result in a distortion of the visual impact. Let's examine Figure 3.12, a display of jobs supported through U.S. agriculture and agricultural exports. Note that in this chart the magnitude of the 10.8 million transportation, trade, and retail jobs is underrepresented by a truck icon that is smaller than the icon representing the 5.6 million jobs for farm family members. Also, the can icon representing the 1.3 million food processing jobs is far too large compared with the icons representing the 2.1 million farm worker jobs, the 2.6 million manufacturing jobs, and the 4.1 million jobs in other areas of agriculture and exporting. A simple summary table or a bar chart, a pie chart, or a Pareto diagram would have been more effective in accurately portraying the data.

If we do not display the zero point on the vertical axis it becomes easy to visually distort a set of data. In what at first glance appears to be an attractive chart, Figure 3.13 provides a clear demonstration of such distortion. The five graphs, taken from a South American newspaper, are intended to depict the negative impact of what is referred to as the "caipirinha effect" on various Latin American stock markets from July 7 through July 15, 1997. The chart is so poorly drawn, however, that the same information could have been better presented in a small table highlighting the downward trends from July 7 through July 15.

There are numerous problems with this graphical display. First, the eye is automatically drawn to the São Paulo, Brazil, graph, and there is no explanation as to why the graph of the Indice Bovespa is drawn to dwarf the other four graphed indexes that appear comparable in size. Moreover, we have no explanation as to why an icon was drawn under this graph but not under any of the others.

As we examine the five graphs more closely and try to make comparisons, we note some inconsistencies in the description of data points. Although the levels of each of these time series are provided for the first and last recorded days (i.e., July 7 and July 15), the per-

**FIGURE 3.13** "Improper" displays of time-series data

centage declines indicated in the five red boxes represent the percentage change in the respective indexes only over the most recently recorded day, July 14 to July 15. The reader is not told that. In fact, the only percentage calculation that the reader can actually make and verify from what is shown in the boxes is the 8.5% drop in the Indice Bovespa from its level of 12.698 on July 14 to 11.617 on July 15. Inexplicably, the Indice Merval from Buenos Aires, Argentina, and the Indice de Valores from Mexico also show the high points reached in this time period, but the Indice IGPA from Santiago, Chile, and the Indice IGB from Lima, Peru, do not give these values.

Even if none of the above-mentioned deficiencies had been observed, the chart still suffers from a very major flaw—improper compression of the vertical axes that present major distortions in the visual statements provided. If the designer felt it important enough to highlight in red boxes the most recent day percentage declines, the graphics depicting these declines need to correspond to the size of the declines. To the eye, the final downward slope segments in each of the five graphs do not correspond to the magnitudes of the percentage changes displayed in the red boxes. Because of the vertical compression of the axes, to the eye the steepest negative slope appears to have occurred in Lima (a 5.6% drop), then in Buenos Aires (a 3.3% drop), then in São Paulo (an 8.5% drop), then in Santiago (a 1.4% drop), and, finally, in Mexico (a 1.7% drop).

Other types of eye-catching displays that we typically see in magazines and newspapers often include information that is not necessary and just adds excessive data-ink. Figure 3.14 is an example of one such display. The partial male-female icons do not adequately portray

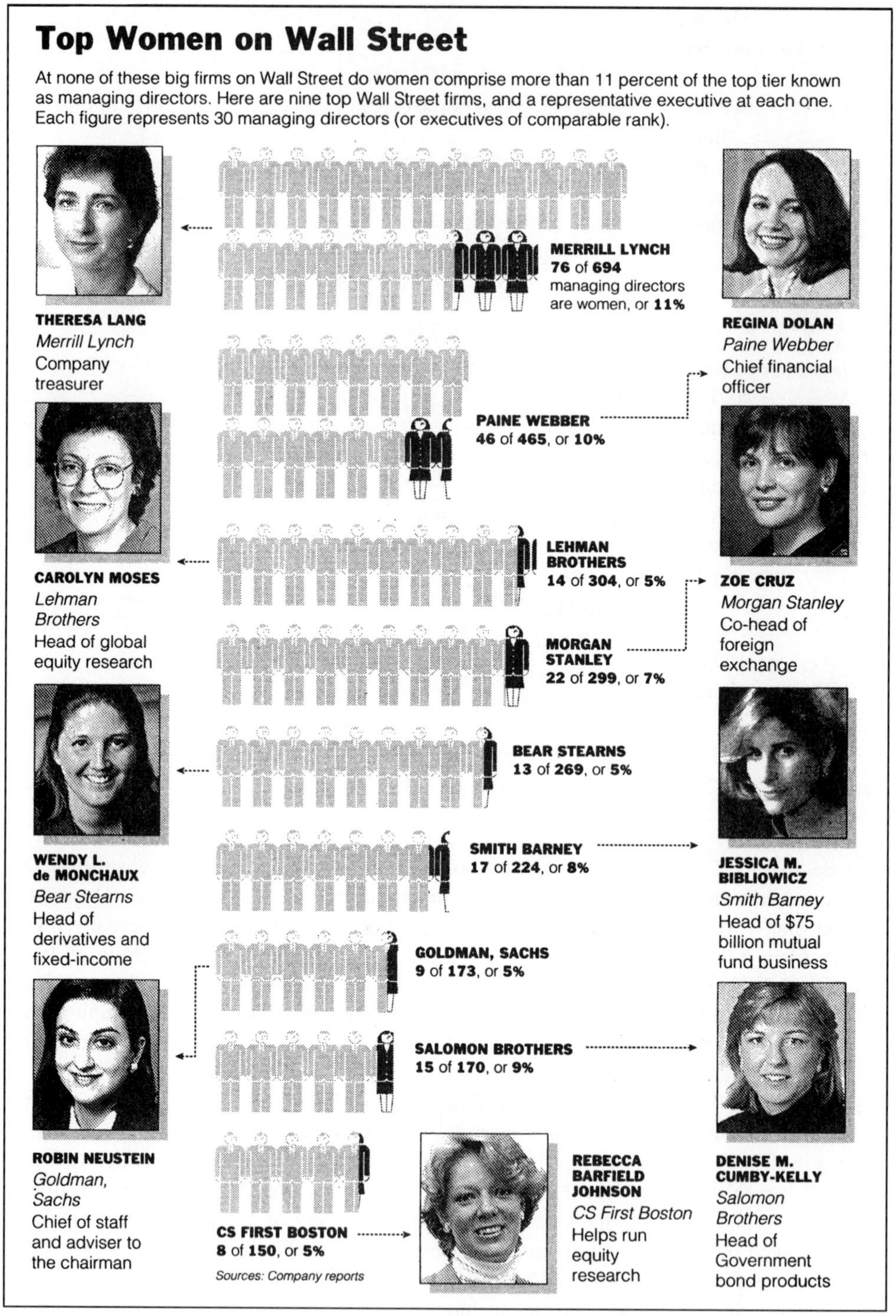

# Top Women on Wall Street

At none of these big firms on Wall Street do women comprise more than 11 percent of the top tier known as managing directors. Here are nine top Wall Street firms, and a representative executive at each one. Each figure represents 30 managing directors (or executives of comparable rank).

**THERESA LANG**
*Merrill Lynch*
Company treasurer

**CAROLYN MOSES**
*Lehman Brothers*
Head of global equity research

**WENDY L. de MONCHAUX**
*Bear Stearns*
Head of derivatives and fixed-income

**ROBIN NEUSTEIN**
*Goldman, Sachs*
Chief of staff and adviser to the chairman

**MERRILL LYNCH**
**76** of **694** managing directors are women, or **11%**

**PAINE WEBBER**
**46** of **465**, or **10%**

**LEHMAN BROTHERS**
**14** of **304**, or **5%**

**MORGAN STANLEY**
**22** of **299**, or **7%**

**BEAR STEARNS**
**13** of **269**, or **5%**

**SMITH BARNEY**
**17** of **224**, or **8%**

**GOLDMAN, SACHS**
**9** of **173**, or **5%**

**SALOMON BROTHERS**
**15** of **170**, or **9%**

**CS FIRST BOSTON**
**8** of **150**, or **5%**

*Sources: Company reports*

**REGINA DOLAN**
*Paine Webber*
Chief financial officer

**ZOE CRUZ**
*Morgan Stanley*
Co-head of foreign exchange

**JESSICA M. BIBLIOWICZ**
*Smith Barney*
Head of $75 billion mutual fund business

**DENISE M. CUMBY-KELLY**
*Salomon Brothers*
Head of Government bond products

**REBECCA BARFIELD JOHNSON**
*CS First Boston*
Helps run equity research

**FIGURE 3.14** "Improper" display of workforce size for each of 30 managing directors at nine large Wall Street firms

*Source: Reprinted by permission of* The New York Times. The New York Times, *July 2, 1996, D1 and D4.*

the gender composition of top management at the nine Wall Street firms. The same information could be conveyed more clearly through the use of the contingency table or the side-by-side bar chart.

In summation, we are active consumers of information that we hear or see daily through the various media. Since much of what we hear or read is junk, we must learn to evaluate critically and discard that which has no real value. We must also keep in mind that sometimes the junk we are provided is based on ignorance; other times, it is planned and malicious. The bottom line: Be critical and be skeptical of information provided.

## Ethical Issues

According to Tufte (reference 11), for many people the first word that comes to mind when they think about statistical charts is "lie." Too many graphics distort the underlying data, making it hard for the reader to learn the truth. Ethical considerations arise when we are deciding what data to present in tabular and chart format and what not to present. It is vitally important when presenting data to document both good and bad results. When making oral presentations and presenting written reports, it is essential that the results be given in a fair, objective, and neutral manner. Thus, we must try to distinguish between poor data presentation and unethical presentation. Again, as in our discussion of ethical considerations in data collection (section 2.6), the key is *intent*. Often, when fancy tables and chart junk are presented or pertinent information is omitted, it is simply done out of ignorance. However, unethical behavior occurs when an individual willfully hides the facts by distorting a table or chart or by failing to report pertinent findings.

## Problems for Section 3.6

### Applying the Concepts

**3.55** (Student Project) Bring a chart to class from a newspaper or magazine that you believe to be a poorly drawn representation of some numerical variable. Be prepared to submit the chart to the instructor with comments as to why you feel it is inappropriate. Also, be prepared to present and comment on this in class.

**3.56** (Student Project) Bring a chart to class from a newspaper or magazine that you believe to be a poorly drawn representation of some categorical variable. Be prepared to submit the chart to the instructor with comments as to why you feel it is inappropriate. Also, be prepared to present and comment on this in class.

**3.57** (Student Project) Bring a chart to class from a newspaper or magazine that you believe to contain too much "chart junk" that may cloud the message given by the data. Be prepared to submit the chart to the instructor with comments as to why you feel it is inappropriate. Also, be prepared to present and comment on this in class.

**3.58** Cassie and Lori were reading the following advertisement that appeared in a New York newspaper and was intended to interest prospective clients in purchasing advertising time on a New York radio station.

Cassie looks at the graph and says, "Lori, this graph does not accurately present the intended information to its readers." Lori replies, "Aside from being inaccurate, the graph has failed to demonstrate the projected growth in buying power that would make the radio station even more attractive to potential purchasers of advertising time." Cassie says, "I agree with you."

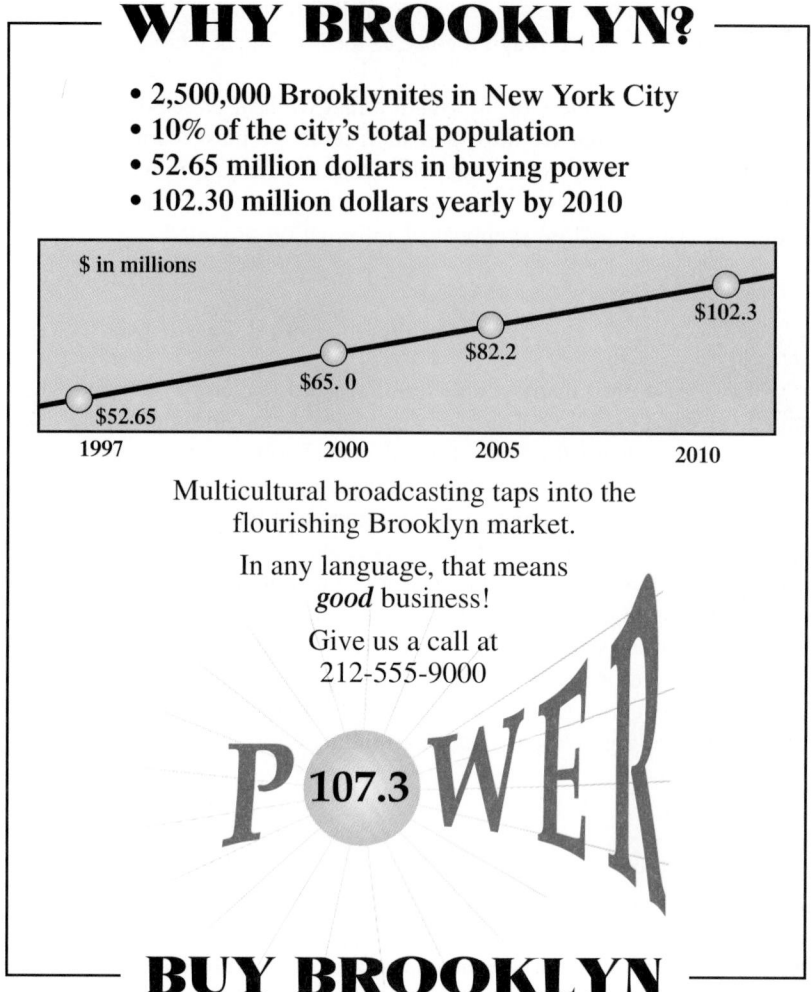

## WHY BROOKLYN?

- **2,500,000 Brooklynites in New York City**
- **10% of the city's total population**
- **52.65 million dollars in buying power**
- **102.30 million dollars yearly by 2010**

$ in millions

$52.65   $65. 0   $82.2   $102.3

1997    2000    2005    2010

Multicultural broadcasting taps into the
flourishing Brooklyn market.

In any language, that means
*good* business!

Give us a call at
212-555-9000

P**O**WER
107.3

## BUY BROOKLYN

A newspaper advertisement

(a) Redraw this graph by properly plotting the time series.

(b) Do you agree with the conclusions reached by Cassie and Lori? Discuss.

**3.59** The visual display on page 101 (top) contains an overembellished time series that appeared as part of an article in *The New York Times* dealing with the decline of market share for Crest toothpaste.

(a) Describe at least one good feature of this visual display.

(b) Describe at least one bad feature of this visual display.

(c) Locate the errors in the time-series portion of this visual display. Discuss.

(d) Redraw the graph using the principles of graphical excellence.

**3.60** The visual display on page 101 (bottom) appeared in *The New York Times* and permits a comparison of the relative size of police departments in major U.S. cities.

(a) Indicate a feature of this chart that violates Tufte's principles of graphical excellence.

(b) Set up an alternative graph for the data provided in this figure.

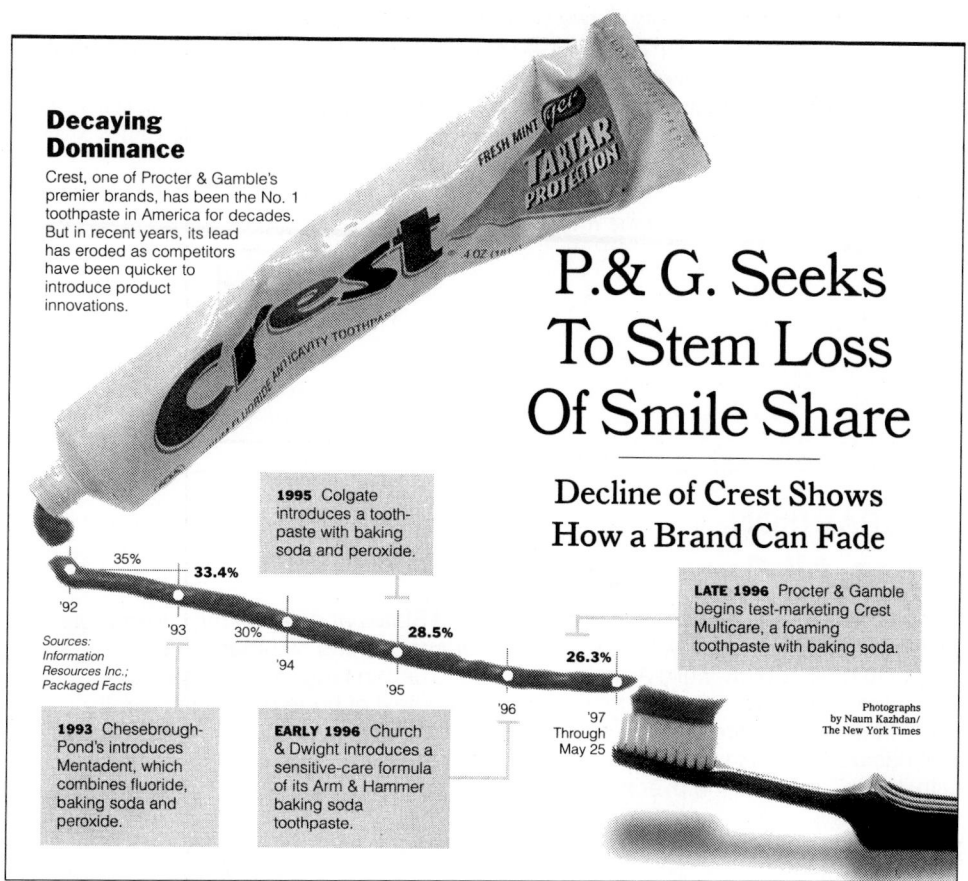

**Decaying Dominance**

Crest, one of Procter & Gamble's premier brands, has been the No. 1 toothpaste in America for decades. But in recent years, its lead has eroded as competitors have been quicker to introduce product innovations.

# P.& G. Seeks To Stem Loss Of Smile Share

## Decline of Crest Shows How a Brand Can Fade

**1995** Colgate introduces a toothpaste with baking soda and peroxide.

**LATE 1996** Procter & Gamble begins test-marketing Crest Multicare, a foaming toothpaste with baking soda.

35%

33.4%

'92

30%

28.5%

26.3%

'93

'94

'95

'96

'97 Through May 25

*Sources: Information Resources Inc.; Packaged Facts*

**1993** Chesebrough-Pond's introduces Mentadent, which combines fluoride, baking soda and peroxide.

**EARLY 1996** Church & Dwight introduces a sensitive-care formula of its Arm & Hammer baking soda toothpaste.

Photographs by Naum Kazhdan/ The New York Times

P&G seeks to stem loss of market share

*Source: Reprinted by permission of* The New York Times. The New York Times, *June 20, 1997, D1.*

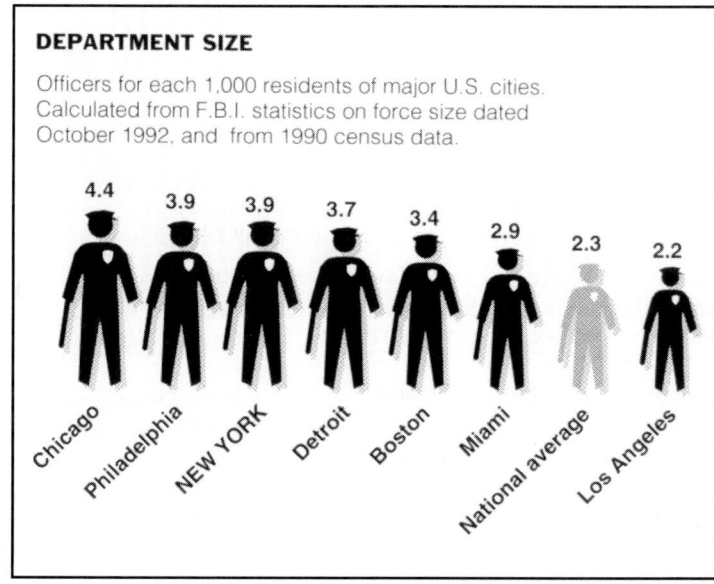

**DEPARTMENT SIZE**

Officers for each 1,000 residents of major U.S. cities. Calculated from F.B.I. statistics on force size dated October 1992, and from 1990 census data.

| Chicago | Philadelphia | NEW YORK | Detroit | Boston | Miami | National average | Los Angeles |
|---|---|---|---|---|---|---|---|
| 4.4 | 3.9 | 3.9 | 3.7 | 3.4 | 2.9 | 2.3 | 2.2 |

"Improper" display of police department size for each 1,000 residents of major cities in the United States

*Source: Reprinted by permission of* The New York Times. *Extracted from R. Powell, "A Statistical Portrait of the N.Y.P.D.,"* The New York Times, *October 10, 1993, 35.*

**3.61** The following visual display of two side-by-side time series appeared in *The New York Times* and permits a comparison of U.S. trade with both Japan and China on an annual basis for more than a quarter of a century.

  (a) Defend or refute the following statement: "This is an attractive, well-designed visual display that permits direct comparisons of trade over time between the United States and China and between the United States and Japan."

  (b) Defend or refute the following statement: "The graphic 'keys' for both China and Japan adequately assist the reader in interpreting the data."

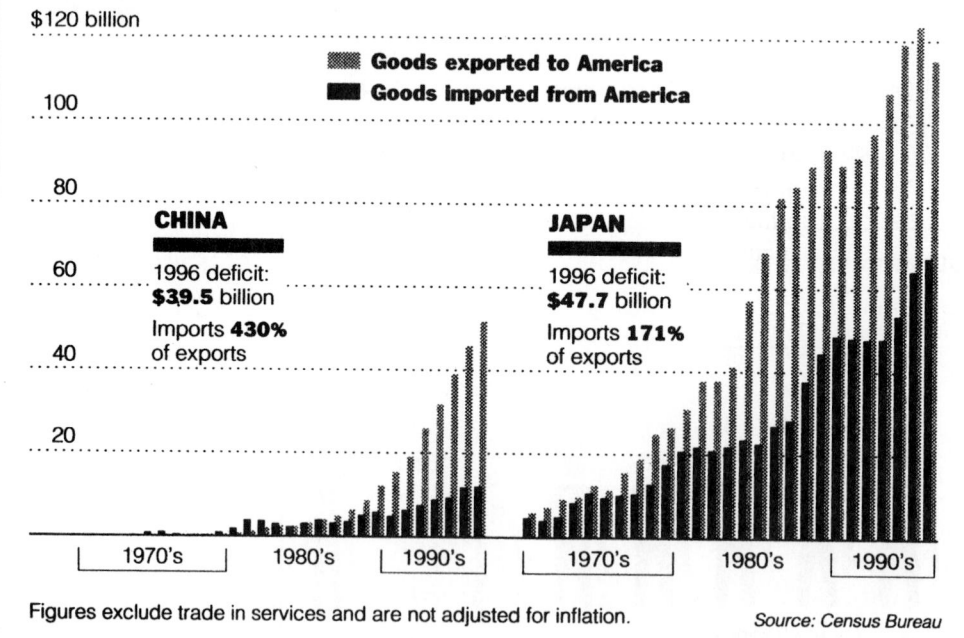

Comparing U.S. trade with Japan and China

*Source: Reprinted by permission of* The New York Times. *The New York Times,* March 2, 1997, 14.

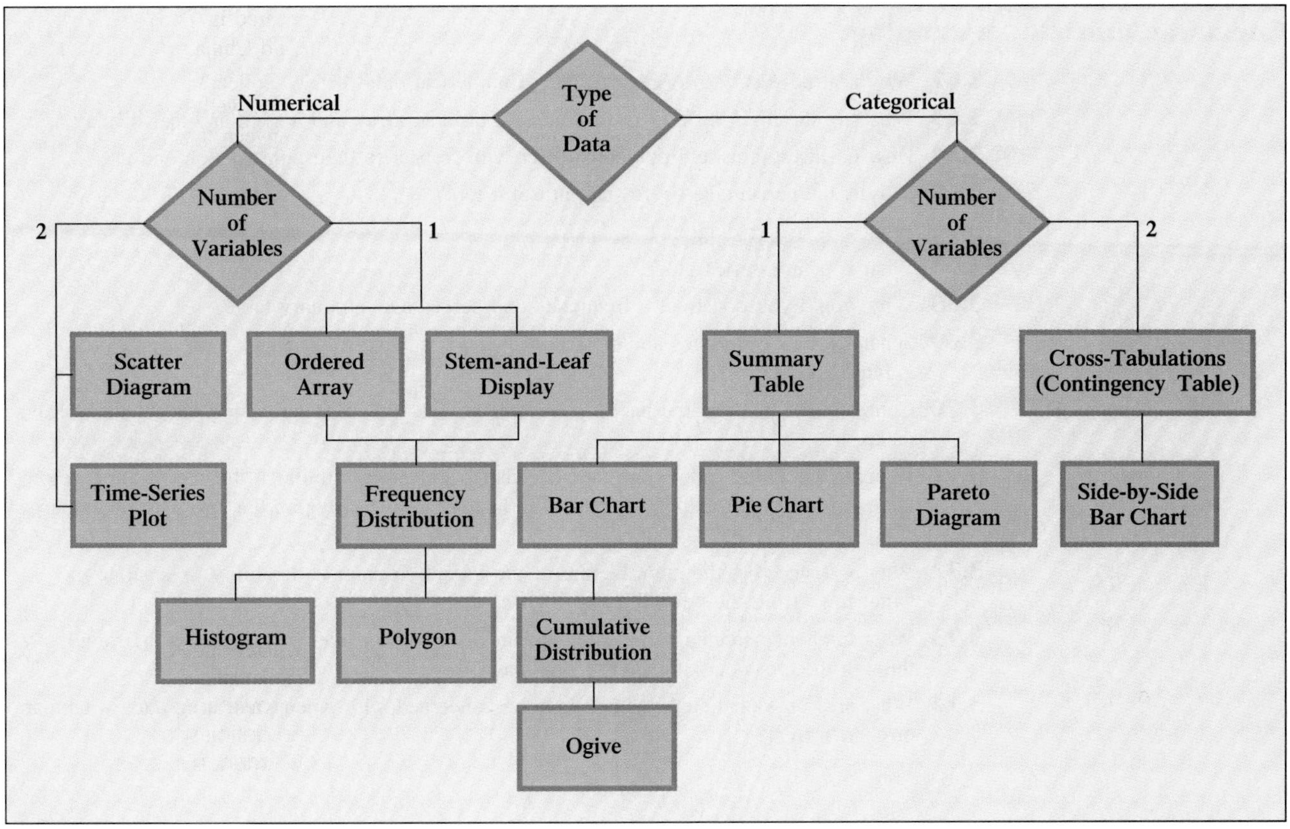

```
                          ┌──────────┐
                          │  Type    │
      Numerical           │   of     │           Categorical
                          │  Data    │
                          └──────────┘

   ┌──────────┐                          ┌──────────┐
   │ Number   │                          │ Number   │
 2 │   of     │ 1                      1 │   of     │ 2
   │ Variables│                          │ Variables│
   └──────────┘                          └──────────┘

┌─────────┐ ┌─────────┐ ┌──────────────┐   ┌─────────┐   ┌──────────────────┐
│ Scatter │ │ Ordered │ │Stem-and-Leaf │   │ Summary │   │ Cross-Tabulations│
│ Diagram │ │  Array  │ │   Display    │   │  Table  │   │(Contingency Table)│
└─────────┘ └─────────┘ └──────────────┘   └─────────┘   └──────────────────┘

┌─────────┐ ┌──────────────┐ ┌──────────┐ ┌──────────┐ ┌──────────┐ ┌──────────────┐
│Time-    │ │ Frequency    │ │Bar Chart │ │Pie Chart │ │ Pareto   │ │ Side-by-Side │
│Series   │ │ Distribution │ │          │ │          │ │ Diagram  │ │  Bar Chart   │
│Plot     │ │              │ │          │ │          │ │          │ │              │
└─────────┘ └──────────────┘ └──────────┘ └──────────┘ └──────────┘ └──────────────┘

  ┌──────────┐ ┌─────────┐ ┌────────────┐
  │Histogram │ │ Polygon │ │ Cumulative │
  │          │ │         │ │Distribution│
  └──────────┘ └─────────┘ └────────────┘

                          ┌─────────┐
                          │  Ogive  │
                          └─────────┘
```

Chapter 3 summary chart

## ◆ SUMMARY

As you can see in the summary chart above, this chapter was about data presentation. Once the collected data have been presented in tabular and chart format, we are ready to make various analyses. In the following chapter, a variety of descriptive summary measures useful for data analysis and interpretation will be developed.

## *Key Terms*

bar chart   80
bivariate categorical data   88
bivariate numerical data   73
chart junk   93
class boundaries   61
class groupings   60
class midpoint   61
contingency table or cross-classification table   88
cumulative distribution   64
cumulative percentage distribution table   64

cumulative polygon   68
data-ink ratio   94
frequency distribution   60
graphical excellence   93
histogram   66
lie factor   95
ogive (cumulative percentage polygon)   68
ordered array   55
Pareto diagram   81
percentage distribution   62

percentage polygon   67
pie chart   80
polygon   67
raw form   54
relative frequency distribution   62
scatter diagram or scatterplot   73
side-by-side bar chart   90
stem-and-leaf display   55
summary table   79
time-series plot   73
width of the class interval   60

## Checking Your Understanding

**3.62** Why is it necessary to organize a set of numerical data that we collect?

**3.63** What are the main differences between an ordered array and a stem-and-leaf display?

**3.64** How do histograms and polygons differ with respect to their construction and use?

**3.65** Why is the percentage ogive such a useful tool?

**3.66** What is a scatter diagram?

**3.67** What is a time-series plot?

**3.68** Why would you construct a frequency and percentage summary table?

**3.69** What are the advantages and/or disadvantages for using a bar chart, a pie chart, or a Pareto diagram?

**3.70** Compare and contrast the bar chart for categorical data with the histogram for numerical data.

**3.71** Which ones of the following graphical displays are most similar in format to the Pareto diagram—the stem-and-leaf display, the histogram, the polygon, the ogive, the bar chart, and/or the pie chart? Discuss.

**3.72** Why is it said that the main feature of the Pareto diagram is its ability to separate the "vital few" from the "trivial many"? Discuss.

**3.73** What kinds of percentage breakdowns can assist you in interpreting the results found through the cross-classification of data based on two categorical variables?

**3.74** What are some of the ethical issues to be concerned with when presenting data in tabular or chart format?

## Chapter Review Problems

**DATA FILE**
FURNCOMP

• **3.75** One of the major measures of the quality of service provided by any organization is the speed with which it responds to customer complaints. A large family-held department store selling furniture and flooring including carpeting had undergone a major expansion in the past several years. In particular, the flooring department had expanded from 2 installation crews to an installation supervisor, a measurer, and 15 installation crews. During a recent year there were 50 complaints concerning carpeting installation. The following data represent the number of days between the receipt of the complaint and the resolution of the complaint.

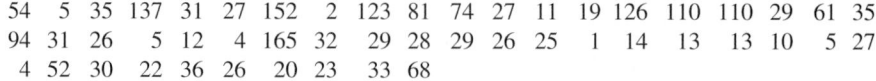

```
54   5  35 137  31  27 152   2 123  81  74  27  11  19 126 110 110  29  61  35
94  31  26   5  12   4 165  32  29  28  29  26  25   1  14  13  13  10   5  27
 4  52  30  22  36  26  20  23  33  68
```

(a) Form the frequency distribution and percentage distribution.
(b) Plot the histogram.
(c) Plot the percentage polygon.
(d) Form the cumulative percentage distribution.
(e) Plot the ogive (cumulative percentage polygon).
(f) On the basis of the results of (a)–(e), does there appear to be a great deal of variation in the time it takes to resolve complaints? Explain.
(g) On the basis of the results of (a)–(e), if you had to tell the president of the company how long a customer should expect to wait to have a complaint resolved, what would you say? Explain.

| AMERICAN EXCHANGE (25 ISSUES) | | NEW YORK EXCHANGE (50 ISSUES) | | | |
|---|---|---|---|---|---|
| $ 6.88 | $ 4.88 | $36.50 | $26.00 | $ 8.75 | $29.38 |
| .75 | 6.38 | 23.50 | 19.00 | 8.62 | 3.75 |
| 3.88 | 33.62 | 8.25 | 46.00 | 5.75 | 64.75 |
| 4.12 | 4.88 | 57.50 | 23.50 | 21.88 | 14.25 |
| 11.88 | 9.00 | 27.12 | 22.62 | 6.12 | 46.38 |
| 15.88 | 2.00 | 3.75 | 12.88 | 25.00 | 4.75 |
| 16.50 | 20.00 | 25.00 | 5.50 | 15.88 | 25.00 |
| 8.75 | 14.25 | 15.50 | 37.50 | 24.00 | 35.00 |
| 9.25 | 4.00 | 36.12 | 9.88 | 10.88 | 9.00 |
| 7.50 | 15.25 | 6.00 | 59.12 | 18.75 | 12.38 |
| 5.38 | 2.38 | 9.12 | 35.25 | 53.88 | 31.00 |
| 14.38 | 49.50 | 33.38 | 20.62 | 20.38 | |
| 2.50 | | 22.50 | 24.00 | 80.50 | |

**DATA FILE**
NYSEAX

**3.76** The above sets of data are based on closing stock price for random samples of 25 issues traded on the American Exchange and 50 issues traded on the New York Exchange:
(a) Using interval widths of $10, form the frequency distribution and percentage distribution for each exchange.
(b) Plot the frequency histogram for each exchange.
(c) On one graph, plot the percentage polygon for each exchange.
(d) Form the cumulative percentage distribution for each exchange.
(e) On one graph, plot the ogive (cumulative percentage polygon) for each exchange.
(f) On the basis of parts (a)–(e), can you conclude that there is a difference in the closing prices of stocks traded on both exchanges? Explain.

**3.77** For a sample of 40 pizza products, the data on the next page represent pie weight in ounces (PWt), cost of a slice in dollars (SCost), amount of calories per slice (SCal), and amount of fat in grams (SFat) per slice for three types of products—pizza-chain cheese (type-1), supermarket cheese (type-2), and supermarket pepperoni (type-3):
(a) For each of the four numerical variables in the data set (weight, cost, calories, and fat)
   (1) develop the ordered array.
   (2) form the stem-and-leaf display.
(b) On the basis of whether the pizza product is classified as either chain or supermarket cheese versus supermarket pepperoni, for each of the four numerical variables in the data set (weight, cost, calories, and fat)
   (1) develop the ordered array.
   (2) form the stem-and-leaf display.
(c) Construct separate frequency distributions and percentage distributions for weight, cost, and calories.
(d) Form the respective cumulative frequency distributions and cumulative percentage distributions for weight, cost, and calories.
(e) Plot the respective percentage polygons.
(f) Plot the respective ogives (cumulative percentage polygons).
(g) Construct scatter diagrams of weight and cost, weight and calories, weight and fat, cost and calories, cost and fat, and calories and fat.

| PRODUCT | PWT | SCOST | SCAL | SFAT | TYPE |
|---|---|---|---|---|---|
| Pizza Hut Hand Tossed | 31 | 1.51 | 305 | 9 | 1 |
| Domino's Deep Dish | 29 | 1.53 | 382 | 16 | 1 |
| Pizza Hut Pan Pizza | 31 | 1.51 | 338 | 14 | 1 |
| Domino's Hand Tossed | 21 | 1.90 | 327 | 9 | 1 |
| Little Caesars Pan! Pan! | 26 | 1.23 | 309 | 10 | 1 |
| Little Caesars Pizza! Pizza! | 25 | 1.28 | 313 | 11 | 1 |
| Pizza Hut Stuffed Crust | 47 | 1.23 | 349 | 13 | 1 |
| DiGiorno Rising Crust Four Cheese | 29 | 0.90 | 332 | 10 | 2 |
| Tombstone Special Order Four Cheese | 26 | 0.85 | 364 | 17 | 2 |
| Red Baron Premium 4-Cheese | 22 | 0.80 | 393 | 19 | 2 |
| Boboli crust with Boboli sauce | 29 | 1.00 | 347 | 12 | 2 |
| Jack's Super Cheese | 17 | 0.69 | 350 | 17 | 2 |
| Pappalo's Three Cheese | 19 | 0.75 | 353 | 12 | 2 |
| Tombstone Original Extra Cheese | 21 | 0.81 | 357 | 16 | 2 |
| Master Choice Gourmet Four Cheese | 17 | 0.90 | 296 | 13 | 2 |
| Celeste Pizza For One | 7 | 0.92 | 358 | 16 | 2 |
| Totino's Party | 10 | 0.64 | 322 | 14 | 2 |
| The New Weight Watchers Extra Cheese | 6 | 1.54 | 337 | 10 | 2 |
| Jeno's Crisp 'N Tasty | 7 | 0.72 | 323 | 14 | 2 |
| Stouffer's French Bread2—Cheese | 10 | 1.15 | 333 | 13 | 2 |
| Ellio's 9-slice | 24 | 0.52 | 299 | 9 | 2 |
| Kroger | 7 | 0.72 | 316 | 7 | 2 |
| Healthy Choice French Bread | 6 | 1.50 | 275 | 4 | 2 |
| Lean Cuisine French Bread | 6 | 1.49 | 288 | 7 | 2 |
| DiGiorno Rising Crust | 30 | 0.87 | 360 | 15 | 3 |
| Tombstone Special Order | 27 | 0.81 | 394 | 21 | 3 |
| Pappalo's | 20 | 0.73 | 390 | 17 | 3 |
| Jack's New More Cheese! | 18 | 0.64 | 372 | 21 | 3 |
| Tombstone Original | 22 | 0.77 | 387 | 20 | 3 |
| Red Baron Premium | 22 | 0.80 | 409 | 22 | 3 |
| Tony's Italian Style Pastry Crust | 15 | 0.83 | 436 | 25 | 3 |
| Red Baron Deep Dish Singles | 12 | 1.13 | 442 | 26 | 3 |
| Totino's Party | 10 | 0.62 | 367 | 20 | 3 |
| The New Weight Watchers | 6 | 1.52 | 348 | 11 | 3 |
| Jeno's Crisp 'N Tasty | 7 | 0.71 | 365 | 19 | 3 |
| Stouffer's French Bread | 11 | 1.14 | 370 | 18 | 3 |
| Celeste Pizza For One | 7 | 1.11 | 381 | 20 | 3 |
| Tombstone For One French Bread | 12 | 1.11 | 361 | 15 | 3 |
| Healthy Choice French Bread | 6 | 1.46 | 264 | 3 | 3 |
| Lean Cuisine French Bread | 5 | 1.71 | 312 | 7 | 3 |

**DATA FILE**
PIZZA

*Source: "Pizza," Copyright 1997 by Consumers Union of U.S., Inc. Adapted from* CONSUMER REPORTS, *January 1997, 26–28, by permission of Consumers Union of U.S., Inc., Yonkers, NY 10703-1057.*
*Although these data sets originally appeared in* CONSUMER REPORTS, *the selective adaptation and resulting conclusions presented are those of the authors and are not sanctioned or endorsed in any way by Consumers Union, the publisher of* CONSUMER REPORTS.

(h) What is the typical pie weight for these pizzas? Explain.

(i) What is the typical cost per slice for these pizzas? Explain.

(j) What is the typical amount of calories per slice for these pizzas? Explain.

(k) On the basis of the results of (g), do any of the variables of weight, cost, calories, and fat seem to be related? Explain.

**3.78** The following data are intended to show the gap between families with the highest income and families with the lowest income in each of the 50 states and the District of Columbia as measured by the average of the top fifth and the bottom fifth of families with children during 1994–1996. The results classified by states were as follows:

| STATE | BOTTOM FIFTH ($000) | TOP FIFTH ($000) | STATE | BOTTOM FIFTH ($000) | TOP FIFTH ($000) |
|---|---|---|---|---|---|
| New York | 6.787 | 132.390 | Kansas | 10.790 | 110.341 |
| Louisiana | 6.430 | 102.339 | Oregon | 9.627 | 97.589 |
| New Mexico | 6.408 | 91.741 | New Jersey | 14.211 | 143.010 |
| Arizona | 7.273 | 103.392 | Indiana | 11.115 | 110.876 |
| Connecticut | 10.415 | 147.594 | Montana | 9.051 | 89.902 |
| California | 9.033 | 127.719 | South Dakota | 9.474 | 93.822 |
| Florida | 7.705 | 107.811 | Idaho | 10.721 | 104.725 |
| Kentucky | 7.364 | 99.210 | Delaware | 12.041 | 116.965 |
| Alabama | 7.531 | 99.062 | Arkansas | 8.995 | 83.434 |
| West Virginia | 6.439 | 84.479 | Colorado | 14.326 | 131.368 |
| Tennessee | 8.156 | 106.966 | Hawaii | 12.735 | 116.060 |
| Texas | 8.642 | 113.149 | Missouri | 11.090 | 100.837 |
| Mississippi | 6.257 | 80.980 | Alaska | 14.868 | 129.065 |
| Michigan | 9.257 | 117.107 | Wyoming | 11.174 | 94.845 |
| Oklahoma | 7.483 | 94.380 | Minnesota | 14.655 | 120.344 |
| Massachusetts | 10.694 | 132.962 | Nebraska | 12.546 | 102.992 |
| Georgia | 9.978 | 123.837 | Maine | 11.275 | 92.457 |
| Illinois | 10.002 | 123.233 | New Hampshire | 14.299 | 116.018 |
| Ohio | 9.346 | 111.894 | Nevada | 12.276 | 98.693 |
| South Carolina | 8.146 | 96.712 | Iowa | 13.148 | 104.253 |
| Pennsylvania | 10.512 | 124.537 | Wisconsin | 13.398 | 103.551 |
| North Carolina | 9.363 | 107.490 | Vermont | 13.107 | 97.898 |
| Rhode Island | 9.914 | 111.015 | North Dakota | 12.424 | 91.041 |
| Washington | 10.116 | 112.501 | Utah | 15.709 | 110.938 |
| Maryland | 13.346 | 147.971 | District of Columbia | 5.293 | 149.508 |
| Virginia | 10.816 | 116.202 | | | |

*Source: United States Census Bureau.*

DATA FILE
STATEINC

(a) For each of the numerical variables

  (1) develop the ordered array

  (2) form the stem-and-leaf display

(b) Construct separate frequency distributions and percentage distributions for income of the bottom fifth and top fifth of families.

(c) Form the respective cumulative frequency distributions and cumulative percentage distributions for income of the bottom fifth and top fifth of families.

(d) Plot the respective percentage polygons.

(e) Plot the respective ogives (cumulative percentage polygons).

(f) What conclusions can you reach concerning the average income in the bottom fifth of families?

(g) What conclusions can you reach concerning the average income in the top fifth of families?

(h) Construct a scatter diagram of the income of the bottom fifth and top fifth of families.

(i) What seems to be the relationship between the average income in the top fifth of families and the average income in the bottom fifth of families?

(j) For each state, obtain the ratio of the income of the top fifth divided by the income of the bottom fifth. Set up a stem-and-leaf display of this ratio.

(k) What conclusions can you reach concerning the ratio of the average income in the top fifth of families divided by the average income in the bottom fifth of families?

**3.79** The following data represent the number of daily calls received at a toll-free telephone number of a large European airline over a period of 30 consecutive nonholiday workdays (Monday to Friday):

| DAY | NUMBER OF CALLS | DAY | NUMBER OF CALLS | DAY | NUMBER OF CALLS | DAY | NUMBER OF CALLS |
|---|---|---|---|---|---|---|---|
| 1 | 3,060 | 9 | 3,235 | 17 | 2,685 | 25 | 3,252 |
| 2 | 3,370 | 10 | 3,174 | 18 | 3,618 | 26 | 3,161 |
| 3 | 3,087 | 11 | 3,603 | 19 | 3,369 | 27 | 3,186 |
| 4 | 3,135 | 12 | 3,256 | 20 | 3,353 | 28 | 3,347 |
| 5 | 3,805 | 13 | 3,075 | 21 | 3,277 | 29 | 3,275 |
| 6 | 3,234 | 14 | 3,187 | 22 | 3,066 | 30 | 3,129 |
| 7 | 3,105 | 15 | 3,060 | 23 | 3,341 | | |
| 8 | 3,168 | 16 | 3,004 | 24 | 3,181 | | |

DATA FILE
CALLSDLY

(a) Set up a time-series plot of the number of daily calls. Are the number of daily calls stable over the 30 days?

(b) Form the frequency distribution and percentage distribution.

(c) Plot the percentage histogram.

(d) Plot the percentage polygon.

(e) Form the cumulative percentage distribution.

(f) Plot the ogive (cumulative percentage polygon).

(g) On the basis of the results of (a)–(f), does there appear to be a great deal of variation in the daily number of calls?

**3.80** The following data indicate fat and cholesterol information concerning popular protein foods (fresh red meats, poultry, and fish):

| FOOD | CALORIES (G) | PROTEIN | % CALORIES FROM FAT | % CALORIES FROM SATURATED FAT | CHOLESTEROL (MG) |
|---|---|---|---|---|---|
| Beef, ground, extra lean | 250 | 25 | 58 | 23 | 82 |
| Beef, ground, regular | 287 | 23 | 66 | 26 | 87 |
| Beef, round | 184 | 28 | 24 | 12 | 82 |

*continued*

| FOOD | CALORIES (G) | PROTEIN | % CALORIES FROM FAT | SATURATED FAT | CHOLESTEROL (MG) |
|---|---|---|---|---|---|
| Brisket | 263 | 28 | 54 | 21 | 91 |
| Flank steak | 244 | 28 | 51 | 22 | 71 |
| Lamb leg roast | 191 | 28 | 38 | 16 | 89 |
| Lamb loin chop, broiled | 215 | 30 | 42 | 17 | 94 |
| Liver, fried | 217 | 27 | 36 | 12 | 482 |
| Pork loin roast | 240 | 27 | 52 | 18 | 90 |
| Sirloin | 208 | 30 | 37 | 15 | 89 |
| Spareribs | 397 | 29 | 67 | 27 | 121 |
| Veal cutlet, fried | 183 | 33 | 42 | 20 | 127 |
| Veal rib roast | 175 | 26 | 37 | 15 | 131 |
| Chicken, no skin, roasted | 239 | 27 | 51 | 14 | 88 |
| Chicken, no skin, roast | 190 | 29 | 37 | 10 | 89 |
| Turkey, light meat, no skin | 157 | 30 | 18 | 6 | 69 |
| Clams | 98 | 16 | 6 | 0 | 39 |
| Cod | 98 | 22 | 8 | 1 | 74 |
| Flounder | 99 | 21 | 12 | 2 | 54 |
| Mackerel | 199 | 27 | 77 | 20 | 100 |
| Ocean perch | 110 | 23 | 13 | 3 | 53 |
| Salmon | 182 | 27 | 24 | 5 | 93 |
| Scallops | 112 | 23 | 8 | 1 | 56 |
| Shrimp | 116 | 24 | 15 | 2 | 156 |
| Tuna | 181 | 32 | 41 | 10 | 48 |

DATA FILE
PROTEIN

*Source: United States Department of Agriculture.*

For the data relating to the amount of calories, protein, the percentage of calories from fat and from saturated fat, and the cholesterol for the popular protein foods:

(a) Construct the stem-and-leaf display.

(b) Construct the frequency distribution and the percentage distribution.

(c) Plot the percentage histogram.

(d) Plot the percentage polygon.

(e) Form the cumulative percentage distribution.

(f) Plot the cumulative percentage polygon.

(g) Construct scatter diagrams for each pair of variables.

(h) What conclusions can you reach concerning the amount of calories in these foods?

(i) What conclusions can you reach concerning the amount of protein in these foods?

(j) What conclusions can you reach concerning the percentage of calories from fat and saturated fat in these foods?

(k) Are there any foods that seem very different from the others in terms of these variables? Explain.

(l) On the basis of (g), what conclusions can you reach about the relationship among these five variables?

**3.81** A wholesale appliance-distributing firm wished to study its accounts receivable for two successive months. Two independent samples of 50 accounts were selected for each of the two months. The results are summarized in the table at the top of page 110.

### Frequency distributions for accounts receivable

| AMOUNT | MARCH FREQUENCY | APRIL FREQUENCY |
|---|---|---|
| $0 to under $2,000 | 6 | 10 |
| $2,000 to under $4,000 | 13 | 14 |
| $4,000 to under $6,000 | 17 | 13 |
| $6,000 to under $8,000 | 10 | 10 |
| $8,000 to under $10,000 | 4 | 0 |
| $10,000 to under $12,000 | 0 | 3 |
| Total | 50 | 50 |

(a) Plot the frequency histogram for each month.
(b) On one graph, plot the percentage polygon for each month.
(c) Form the cumulative percentage distribution for each month.
(d) On one graph, plot the ogive (cumulative percentage polygon) for each month.
(e) On the basis of parts (a)–(d), do you think the distribution of the accounts receivable has changed from March to April? Explain.

**3.82** The following table contains the cumulative distributions and cumulative percentage distributions of braking distance (in feet) at 80 miles per hour for a sample of 25 U.S.-manufactured automobile models and for a sample of 72 foreign-made automobile models obtained in a recent year:

### Cumulative frequency and percentage distributions for the braking distance (in feet) at 80 mph for U.S.-manufactured and foreign-made automobile models

| BRAKING DISTANCE (IN FT) | U.S.-MADE AUTOMOBILE MODELS "LESS THAN" INDICATED VALUES | | FOREIGN-MADE AUTOMOBILE MODELS "LESS THAN" INDICATED VALUES | |
|---|---|---|---|---|
| | NUMBER | PERCENTAGE | NUMBER | PERCENTAGE |
| 210 | 0 | 0.0 | 0 | 0.0 |
| 220 | 1 | 4.0 | 1 | 1.4 |
| 230 | 2 | 8.0 | 4 | 5.6 |
| 240 | 3 | 12.0 | 19 | 26.4 |
| 250 | 4 | 16.0 | 32 | 44.4 |
| 260 | 8 | 32.0 | 54 | 75.0 |
| 270 | 11 | 44.0 | 61 | 84.7 |
| 280 | 17 | 68.0 | 68 | 94.4 |
| 290 | 21 | 84.0 | 68 | 94.4 |
| 300 | 23 | 92.0 | 70 | 97.2 |
| 310 | 25 | 100.0 | 71 | 98.6 |
| 320 | 25 | 100.0 | 72 | 100.0 |

On the basis of these data, answer the following questions:
(a) How many models of U.S.-made automobiles have braking distances of 240 feet or more?
(b) What is the percentage of U.S.-made automobiles with braking distances less than 260 feet?

(c) Which group of car models—U.S.-made or foreign-made—have the wider range in braking distance?

(d) How many foreign-made automobile models have braking distances between 260 feet and 269.9 feet (inclusive)?

(e) Use the cumulative distributions to construct the frequency distributions and percentage distributions for each group of car models.

(f) On one graph, plot the two percentage ogives.

(g) Do you think there is a difference in the braking distance between the two groups of car models? Explain.

**3.83** The article and graph (see below) appeared in *The New York Times* a few weeks after the 1996 presidential election.

(a) Using the 24 available pairs of coordinates corresponding to presidential election years, construct a scatter diagram with percentage change in the Dow Jones Industrial Average for the 12 trading days following the election on the *X* axis and percentage change in the Dow Jones Industrial average for the following year on the *Y* axis.

(b) Describe your findings in this scatter diagram.

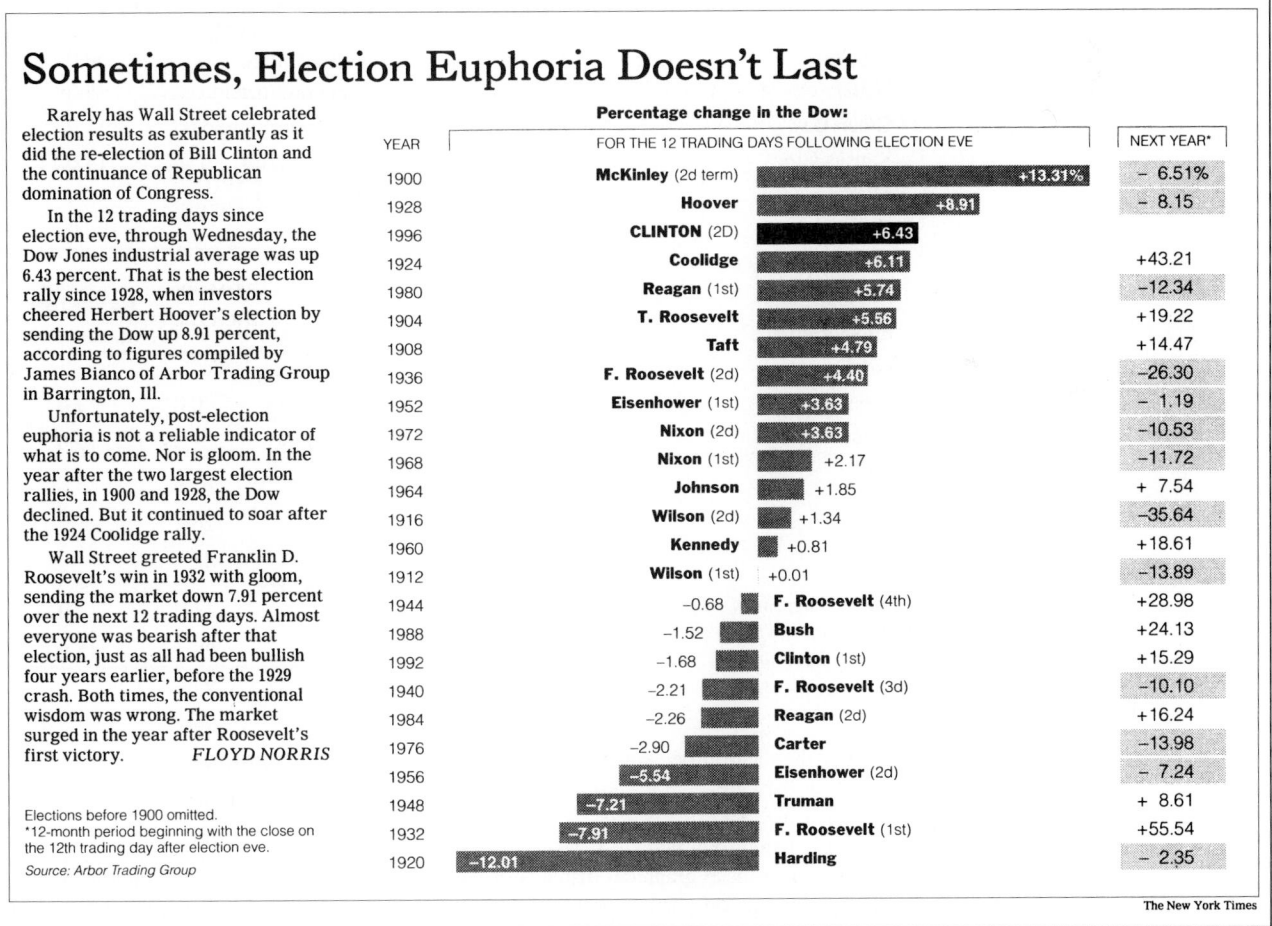

# Sometimes, Election Euphoria Doesn't Last

Rarely has Wall Street celebrated election results as exuberantly as it did the re-election of Bill Clinton and the continuance of Republican domination of Congress.

In the 12 trading days since election eve, through Wednesday, the Dow Jones industrial average was up 6.43 percent. That is the best election rally since 1928, when investors cheered Herbert Hoover's election by sending the Dow up 8.91 percent, according to figures compiled by James Bianco of Arbor Trading Group in Barrington, Ill.

Unfortunately, post-election euphoria is not a reliable indicator of what is to come. Nor is gloom. In the year after the two largest election rallies, in 1900 and 1928, the Dow declined. But it continued to soar after the 1924 Coolidge rally.

Wall Street greeted Franklin D. Roosevelt's win in 1932 with gloom, sending the market down 7.91 percent over the next 12 trading days. Almost everyone was bearish after that election, just as all had been bullish four years earlier, before the 1929 crash. Both times, the conventional wisdom was wrong. The market surged in the year after Roosevelt's first victory.   *FLOYD NORRIS*

Elections before 1900 omitted.
*12-month period beginning with the close on the 12th trading day after election eve.
*Source: Arbor Trading Group*

**Percentage change in the Dow:**

| YEAR | FOR THE 12 TRADING DAYS FOLLOWING ELECTION EVE | | NEXT YEAR* |
|---|---|---|---|
| 1900 | McKinley (2d term) | +13.31% | − 6.51% |
| 1928 | Hoover | +8.91 | − 8.15 |
| 1996 | CLINTON (2D) | +6.43 | |
| 1924 | Coolidge | +6.11 | +43.21 |
| 1980 | Reagan (1st) | +5.74 | −12.34 |
| 1904 | T. Roosevelt | +5.56 | +19.22 |
| 1908 | Taft | +4.79 | +14.47 |
| 1936 | F. Roosevelt (2d) | +4.40 | −26.30 |
| 1952 | Eisenhower (1st) | +3.63 | − 1.19 |
| 1972 | Nixon (2d) | +3.63 | −10.53 |
| 1968 | Nixon (1st) | +2.17 | −11.72 |
| 1964 | Johnson | +1.85 | + 7.54 |
| 1916 | Wilson (2d) | +1.34 | −35.64 |
| 1960 | Kennedy | +0.81 | +18.61 |
| 1912 | Wilson (1st) | +0.01 | −13.89 |
| 1944 | F. Roosevelt (4th) | −0.68 | +28.98 |
| 1988 | Bush | −1.52 | +24.13 |
| 1992 | Clinton (1st) | −1.68 | +15.29 |
| 1940 | F. Roosevelt (3d) | −2.21 | −10.10 |
| 1984 | Reagan (2d) | −2.26 | +16.24 |
| 1976 | Carter | −2.90 | −13.98 |
| 1956 | Eisenhower (2d) | −5.54 | − 7.24 |
| 1948 | Truman | −7.21 | + 8.61 |
| 1932 | F. Roosevelt (1st) | −7.91 | +55.54 |
| 1920 | Harding | −12.01 | − 2.35 |

The New York Times

Election Euphoria

*Sources: Reprinted by permission of* The New York Times. *Arbor Trading Group and* The New York Times, *Sunday, November 24, 1996.*

(c) Using the various presidential election years in proper sequence as the time variable on the $X$ axis, on one graph construct separate time-series plots of percentage change in the Dow Jones Industrial averages for the 12 trading days following the election as well as for the following year.

(d) Describe your findings by comparing and contrasting the two time series.

(e) Which of the graphical presentations—the original chart from *The New York Times*, the scatter diagram, or the two time-series plots—seems to give the most information about the data? Discuss.

**3.84** At the start of the 1995 National Football League season, Jerry Jones, owner of the Dallas Cowboys, argued that since his team was more popular than other teams and generated the most revenues from sales of team products, it deserved a proportionally higher share in earnings that, under league policy, are distributed equally to all 30 teams by NFL properties. The following summary tables respectively display the percentage market share of sales of licensed products by the various teams, the percentage of sales attributed to the specific kinds of products sold, and, lastly, the amount of revenues generated (in millions of dollars) from various sources:

| TEAM | % SALES OF LICENSED PRODUCTS |
|---|---|
| Carolina | 5.0 |
| Dallas | 20.8 |
| Green Bay | 5.1 |
| Kansas City | 4.8 |
| Miami | 6.6 |
| New England | 3.6 |
| New York Giants | 3.2 |
| Oakland | 4.7 |
| Pittsburgh | 4.7 |
| San Francisco | 11.3 |
| Other 20 teams | 30.2 |
| Total | 100.0 |

| TYPE OF PRODUCT | % SALES |
|---|---|
| Clothing/hats | 50.0 |
| Home products | 7.0 |
| Toys/sporting goods | 11.0 |
| Trading cards | 14.0 |
| Other | 18.0 |
| Total | 100.0 |

| SOURCE | REVENUES (IN MILLIONS OF $) |
|---|---|
| International marketing | 14.9 |
| Publishing | 10.6 |
| Retail licensing | 94.3 |
| Special events | 3.8 |
| Sponsorships | 58.8 |
| Trading cards | 15.3 |
| Other operations | 17.9 |
| Total | 215.6 |

*Sources: Reprinted by permission of* The New York Times. *NFL Properties;* The New York Times, *September 24, 1995, D1.*

(a) For the data on percentage of sales of licensed products, construct
   (1) a bar chart.
   (2) a pie chart.
   (3) a Pareto diagram.

(b) Which of these graphical displays do you prefer for purposes of presentation? Why?

(c) For the data on percentage of sales by type of product, develop the appropriate graph to pinpoint the "vital few" from the "trivial many."

(d) For the data on the amount of revenues generated (in millions of dollars) from various sources, develop the appropriate graph to pinpoint the "vital few" from the "trivial many."

(e) Analyze the data and summarize your findings.

• **3.85** The following data represent the trade relationships (in billions of dollars) between the United States and China in the year 1996:

### Chinese and U.S. trade in 1996

| CHINESE GOODS EXPORTED TO U.S. | BILLIONS OF $ |
|---|---|
| Apparel, fabrics, and fibers | 7.38 |
| Electrical components, equipment, and parts | 9.22 |
| Food, agriculture, and forest products | 1.77 |
| Footwear | 6.70 |
| Furniture, bedding, and lighting | 2.62 |
| Leather goods (other than footwear) | 2.76 |
| Machinery, equipment, and parts (incl. computers) | 4.64 |
| Mineral, chemical, plastic, and rubber goods | 3.99 |
| Toys, games, and sporting goods | 7.99 |
| All other goods | 7.33 |
| Total | 54.40 |

| U.S. GOODS EXPORTED TO CHINA | BILLIONS OF $ |
|---|---|
| Aircraft, spacecraft, and parts | 1.71 |
| Electronic components, equipment, and parts | 1.43 |
| Food and other farm produce | 1.34 |
| Leather, fur, tobacco, wood, cork, and paper | 0.60 |
| Machinery, equipment, and parts (incl. computers) | 2.31 |
| Mineral, chemical, plastic, and rubber goods | 1.96 |
| Textiles, apparel, and fibers | 0.95 |
| All other goods | 1.69 |
| Total | 11.99 |

*Sources: Reprinted by permission of* The New York Times. *National Trade Data Bank,* The New York Times, *March 2, 1997, 14.*

(a) For the data on U.S. goods exported to China, construct
    (1) a bar chart.
    (2) a pie chart.
    (3) a Pareto diagram.
(b) For the data on Chinese goods exported to the U.S., construct
    (1) a bar chart.
    (2) a pie chart.
    (3) a Pareto diagram.
(c) Which pair of graphs do you prefer for purposes of presentation? Why?
(d) What differences are there between Chinese goods exported to the United States and U.S. goods exported to China? Explain.

**3.86** It has been noted by consumer researchers that where people buy computers depends on whether they are buying one for the first time. First-time buyers tend to buy at big retail stores, whereas repeat buyers favor catalogues, small stores that assemble computers, and manufacturers that market directly.

    The table at the top of page 114 provides a percentage breakdown of where first-time buyers and repeat buyers purchased personal computers in 1996:

| WHERE PURCHASED | FIRST-TIME BUYERS | REPEAT BUYERS |
|---|---|---|
| Assembly stores | 15% | 23% |
| Catalogues/resellers | 5 | 10 |
| Computer superstores | 23 | 21 |
| Consumer electronics stores | 28 | 11 |
| Manufacturers | 8 | 20 |
| Mass merchants | 11 | 4 |
| Office superstores | 4 | 5 |
| Other | 6 | 6 |
| Total | 100 | 100 |

*Sources: Reprinted by permission of* The New York Times. *Computer Intelligence and* The New York Times, *January 8, 1997, D1–D2.*

In addition, the following table displays the percentage of sales of personal computers that were purchased in various types of stores in 1996:

| STORE CATEGORY | % 1996 SALES |
|---|---|
| Assembly stores | 20 |
| Catalogues/resellers | 8 |
| Computer superstores | 22 |
| Consumer electronics stores | 18 |
| Manufacturers | 15 |
| Mass merchants | 7 |
| Office superstores | 5 |
| Other | 5 |
| Total | 100 |

*Sources: Reprinted by permission of* The New York Times. *Computer Intelligence and* The New York Times, *January 8, 1997, D1–D2.*

(a) For each table, construct an appropriate graph and analyze the data.
(b) Discuss the implications of these shifting trends in repeat purchases and how this may affect product promotion and advertising. What marketing strategy might be useful for selling to people buying computers for the first time? Explain.

**3.87** The owner of a restaurant serving Continental-style entrées was interested in studying patterns of demand by patrons for the Friday to Sunday weekend time period. Records were maintained that indicated the number of entrées ordered for each type. The following data were obtained:

| TYPE OF ENTRÉE | NUMBER SERVED |
|---|---|
| Beef | 187 |
| Chicken | 103 |
| Duck | 25 |
| Fish | 122 |
| Pasta | 63 |
| Shellfish | 74 |
| Veal | 26 |

(a) Construct a bar chart for the types of entrées ordered.

(b) Construct a Pareto diagram for the types of entrées ordered.

(c) Construct a pie chart for the types of entrées ordered.

(d) Do you prefer a Pareto diagram or a pie chart for these data? Why?

(e) What conclusions can the owner draw concerning demand for different types of entrées?

Suppose that the owner was also interested in studying the demand for dessert during the same time period. She decided that two other variables were to be studied along with whether a dessert was ordered, the gender of the individual, and whether a beef entrée was ordered. The results were as follows:

| DESSERT ORDERED | GENDER | | TOTAL |
| | MALE | FEMALE | |
| --- | --- | --- | --- |
| Yes | 96 | 40 | 136 |
| No | 224 | 240 | 464 |
| Total | 320 | 280 | 600 |

| DESSERT ORDERED | BEEF ENTRÉE | | TOTAL |
| | YES | NO | |
| --- | --- | --- | --- |
| Yes | 71 | 65 | 136 |
| No | 116 | 348 | 464 |
| Total | 187 | 413 | 600 |

Concerning each of the two cross-classification tables:

(f) Construct a table of row percentages.

(g) Construct a table of column percentages.

(h) Construct a table of total percentages.

(i) Which type of percentage (row, column, or total) do you think is most informative for each table? Explain.

(j) What conclusions concerning the pattern of dessert ordering can the owner of the restaurant reach?

**3.88** (Class Project) Let each student in the class respond to the question "Which type of carbonated soft drink do you most prefer?" so that the teacher may tally the results into a summary table on the blackboard.

(a) Convert the data to percentages and construct a Pareto diagram.

(b) Analyze the findings.

**3.89** (Class Project) Let each student in the class be cross-classified on the basis of gender (male, female) and current employment status (yes, no) so that the results are tallied on the blackboard.

(a) Construct a table with either row or column percentages, depending on which you think is more informative.

(b) What would you conclude from this study?

(c) What other variables would you want to know regarding employment in order to enhance your findings?

 # TEAM PROJECT

**TP3.1** A financial investment service is evaluating the list of domestic general stock funds so that it can make purchase recommendations to potential investors. The vice president for research has hired your group, the _____ Corporation, to study the financial characteristics of currently traded domestic general stock funds. The vice president is interested in a comparison of some features of

**DATA FILE**
MUTUAL

these funds based on fee structure (no load versus fee payment), objective (growth fund versus blend fund), and capitalization size of companies making up a fund's portfolio (large, mid, or small). Having access to Special Data Set 1 in appendix D pertaining to various characteristics from a sample of 194 domestic general stock funds with high Morningstar Inc. dual ratings of 4 or 5, the ———————— Corporation is ready to

(a) outline how the group members will proceed with their tasks.

(b) form the respective frequency and percentage distributions of net asset value (in dollars) and 3-year annualized total returns (in percentage rates) for the 107 no-load funds versus the 87 fee-payment funds.

(c) form the respective frequency and percentage distributions of net asset value (in dollars) and 3-year annualized total returns (in percentage rates) for the 59 growth funds versus the 135 blend funds.

(d) form the respective frequency and percentage distributions of net asset value (in dollars) and 3-year annualized total returns (in percentage rates) for the 119 large-size funds, the 44-mid size funds, and the 31 small-size funds.

(e) On the basis of parts (b), (c), and (d), plot the various percentage polygons.

(f) Form the needed cumulative percentage distributions.

(g) Plot the various percentage ogives.

(h) Additionally, form a contingency table cross-classifying type of fee schedule (fees from fund assets, deferred fee, front-load fee, multiple fees, or no load) with type of fund (large-growth, mid-growth, small-growth, large-blend, mid-blend, or small-blend). Discuss the results.

(i) Form a Pareto diagram for the type of fund (large-growth, mid-growth, small-growth, large-blend, mid-blend, or small-blend). Discuss.

(j) Write and submit a summary of your descriptive analysis, attaching all tables and charts.

(k) Prepare and deliver a 15-minute oral presentation to the vice president for research at this financial investment service.

*Note:* Additional team projects can be found on the World Wide Web site for this text

**http://www.prenhall.com/berenson**

These team projects deal with characteristics of 80 universities and colleges (see the UNIV&COL file) and the features of 89 automobiles (see the AUTO96 file).

# THE SPRINGVILLE HERALD CASE

## Background

Springville represents a suburban area that is about 50 miles outside a large city in the western United States. The area was heavily agricultural before World War II and experienced a great expansion in population and industry between 1950 and 1980, with little growth in the years since 1980. The *Herald* was originally a family-owned newspaper that has only published a daily and Sunday edition since 1957. Current circulation is 250,000 on weekdays (Monday–Saturday) and 300,000 on Sunday, growing only moderately since 1980. The financial status of the company is healthy, but senior management has become more conscious of costs and the need to improve the efficiency of operations.

## Phase 1

A task force consisting of corporate-level officers and department heads was formed to consider how to go about the quality improvement effort. There was agreement that the first step was the development of a mission statement for the newspaper that could succinctly communicate its mission to both customers and employees.

Once the mission statement was developed with the aid of both customers and employees at all levels of the organization, the task force turned to a discussion of which areas of operations should be examined for improvement opportunities. After much brainstorming and discussion, the task force decided by consensus that one critical area for improvement was represented by errors that were made in the process of filling advertising orders (which represented a critical revenue source for the newspaper) from the time the advertisement was ordered to when it actually appeared in the newspaper. Unfortunately, under certain circumstances, errors had been made and incorrect ads were displayed in the newspaper or may have been printed on the wrong day. Such occurrences called for an immediate effort to satisfy the customer by a variety of sometimes costly devices including refunds and rerunning the ads on other days. Members of the task force realized that data relating to the occurrence of these errors were already available from periodic reports that were routinely generated by the advertising production department. One such report containing the number of occurrences for each type of error in the most recent calendar year is presented in Table SH3.1.

**Table SH3.1**  *Summary table of errors for advertising production, composing room, policy, and sales for last calendar year*

| TYPE OF ERROR | TALLY | TOTAL |
|---|---|---|
| Copy error | 卌 卌 卌 卌 卌 卌 卌 卌 卌 卌 IIII | 54 |
| Layout | 卌 II | 7 |
| Omits | 卌 卌 III | 13 |
| Paste-up | 卌 卌 I | 11 |
| Poor reproduction | 卌 III | 8 |
| Ran in error | 卌 卌 卌 卌 卌 卌 | 30 |
| Rate quote | 卌 卌 III | 13 |
| Space not ordered | 卌 II | 7 |
| Typesetting | 卌 卌 卌 卌 卌 卌 卌 卌 卌 卌 III | 53 |
| Velox | 卌 卌 卌 卌 卌 III | 28 |
| Wrong ad | 卌 卌 卌 卌 卌 | 25 |
| Wrong date | 卌 卌 IIII | 14 |
| Wrong position | 卌 卌 卌 卌 卌 卌 卌 卌 卌 | 45 |
| Wrong manual paste-up | 卌 | 5 |
| Wrong size | 卌 I | 6 |
| Total | | 319 |

## Exercises

**3.1** Develop the appropriate table for the data presented in Table SH3.1.

**3.2 (a)** Construct the graphical presentation you feel is most appropriate and useful in gaining insights from the data of Table SH3.1.

(b) Explain in detail why you chose the graph in (a) instead of other alternative graphical presentations.

(c) On the basis of results of the frequency and percentage distribution and the graph that was constructed in (a), write a report to management concerning the frequency of different types of advertising errors.

**3.3** At this stage of the analysis, what other information concerning the different types of errors would be useful to obtain?

 **Do not continue until the Phase 1 exercises have been completed.**

## Phase 2

At the first meeting of the task force after the data of Table SH3.1 were made available, Bob Tatum, the head of advertising production, suggested that this was not the most appropriate way of examining the problem. He stated that the frequency of the errors was not the only issue. He argued that certain types of errors, although perhaps less frequent, might involve much greater costs than other errors. Fortunately, data concerning the cost of each type of error were also available. The data for the most recent year are summarized in Table SH3.2.

**Table SH3.2** *Cost of advertising errors for last calendar year*

| TYPE OF ERROR | AMOUNT ($000) | TYPE OF ERROR | AMOUNT ($000) |
|---|---|---|---|
| Copy error | 32.6 | Typesetting | 53.1 |
| Layout | 3.0 | Velox | 23.3 |
| Omits | 36.5 | Wrong ad | 53.6 |
| Paste-up | 59.4 | Wrong date | 35.9 |
| Poor reproduction | 13.0 | Wrong position | 74.9 |
| Ran in error | 108.2 | Wrong manual paste-up | 16.5 |
| Rate quote | 5.3 | Wrong size | 5.3 |
| Space not ordered | 12.9 | Total | 533.5 |

### Exercises

**3.4** Prepare the appropriate table for the data presented in Table SH3.2.

**3.5 (a)** Construct the graphical presentation you feel is most appropriate for the data presented in Table SH3.2.

   **(b)** Explain in detail why you chose the graph in (a) instead of other alternative graphical presentations.

   **(c)** On the basis of results of the percentage distribution and the graph that was constructed in (a), write a report to management concerning the dollar amount of the different types of advertising errors.

**3.6** On the basis of your analysis in Exercise 3.5 (c), what action would you recommend be taken next to study the reasons for advertising errors?

 **Do not continue until the Phase 2 exercises have been completed.**

## Phase 3

Once the data of Table SH3.2 had been analyzed, it became evident that the most costly error involved the ran-in-error category, which accounted for over $100,000, or more than 20% of the total cost of the errors for the year. Further investigation of the errors in this category subdivided errors into different types. This is presented in Table SH3.3 on page 119.

### Exercises

**3.7** Prepare a percentage summary table for the data of Table SH3.3.

**3.8 (a)** Construct the graphical presentation you feel is most appropriate for the data of Table SH3.3.

**Table SH3.3** *Frequency and dollar amount of different types of ran-in-error problems in most recent calendar year*

| TYPE | FREQUENCY | AMOUNT ($000) |
|------|-----------|---------------|
| Composing room | 10 | 12.8 |
| Policy | 16 | 88.7 |
| Sales | 4 | 6.6 |
| Total | 30 | 108.1 |

**(b)** Explain in detail why you chose the graph in (a) instead of other alternative graphical presentations.

**(c)** If the graph chosen in (a) was not the same one selected in Exercises 3.2(a) and 3.5(a), explain why you chose it.

**(d)** On the basis of results of the percentage distribution and the graph that was constructed in (a), write a report to management concerning the dollar amount of the different types of ran-in-error problems.

**(e)** What course of action would you recommend be taken next to reduce these types of errors in the future?

 **Do not continue until the Phase 3 exercises have been completed.**

## Phase 4

One of the functions of the computer systems department of the newspaper relates to the reporting of the activities of the mainframe computer system. Typically, in any given day more than 100 different jobs need to be processed on the system. These jobs vary in requirements, from very small jobs that require a minimum of access to data cartridge storage devices, to large complex jobs that need to access in excess of 200 different data cartridges. The data presented in Table SH3.4 consist of an ordered array of the number of data cartridges that needed to be accessed by 111 jobs on a recent day.

**Table SH3.4** *Ordered array of number of data cartridges accessed per job on a recent day*

| | | | | | | | | | | | | | | | | | | |
|--|--|--|--|--|--|--|--|--|--|--|--|--|--|--|--|--|--|--|
| 1 | 1 | 1 | 1 | 1 | 1 | 2 | 2 | 2 | 2 | 2 | 3 | 3 | 3 | 3 | 4 | 4 | 4 | 4 |
| 4 | 4 | 5 | 5 | 5 | 5 | 5 | 5 | 5 | 6 | 6 | 6 | 7 | 7 | 7 | 7 | 8 | 8 | 8 |
| 8 | 9 | 10 | 10 | 10 | 10 | 10 | 11 | 12 | 12 | 13 | 14 | 14 | 15 | 17 | 18 | 18 | 18 | 18 |
| 19 | 20 | 20 | 20 | 20 | 21 | 22 | 23 | 24 | 28 | 28 | 29 | 30 | 30 | 30 | 30 | 31 | 32 | 33 |
| 35 | 37 | 40 | 40 | 42 | 43 | 50 | 52 | 55 | 56 | 59 | 60 | 60 | 67 | 74 | 80 | 86 | 91 | 94 |
| 96 | 100 | 111 | 126 | 127 | 131 | 137 | 140 | 144 | 147 | 164 | 166 | 170 | 182 | 212 | 237 | | | |

**DATA FILE SH3&4**

## Exercises

**3.9 (a)** Set up all appropriate tables and charts for the number of data cartridges accessed by jobs on a recent day.

**(b)** Write a report to management that summarizes the results obtained from the tables and charts developed in (a).

# References

1. Chambers, J. M., W. S. Cleveland, B. Kleiner, and P. A. Tukey, *Graphical Methods for Data Analysis* (Boston, MA: Duxbury Press, 1983).
2. Cleveland, W. S., "Graphs in Scientific Publications," *The American Statistician* 38 (November 1984), 261–269.
3. Cleveland, W. S., "Graphical Methods for Data Presentation: Full Scale Breaks, Dot Charts, and Multibased Logging," *The American Statistician* 38 (November 1984), 270–280.
4. Cleveland, W. S., and R. McGill, "Graphical Perception: Theory, Experimentation, and Application to the Development of Graphical Methods," *Journal of the American Statistical Association* 79 (September 1984), 531–554.
5. Croxton, F., D. Cowden, and S. Klein, *Applied General Statistics*, 3d ed. (Englewood Cliffs, NJ: Prentice Hall, 1967).
6. Ehrenberg, A. S. C., "Rudiments of Numeracy," *Journal of the Royal Statistical Society*, series A, vol. 140 (1977), 277–297.
7. Huff, D., *How to Lie with Statistics* (New York: W. W. Norton, 1954).
8. Kimble, G. A., *How to Use (and Misuse) Statistics* (Englewood Cliffs, NJ: Prentice Hall, 1978).
9. *Microsoft Excel 97* (Redmond, WA: Microsoft Corporation, 1997).
10. *Minitab for Windows Version 12* (State College, PA: Minitab, Inc., 1998).
11. Tufte, E. R., *The Visual Display of Quantitative Information* (Cheshire, CT: Graphics Press, 1983).
12. Tufte, E. R., *Envisioning Information* (Cheshire, CT: Graphics Press, 1990).
13. Tufte, E. R., *Visual Explanations* (Cheshire, CT: Graphics Press, 1997).
14. Tukey, J., *Exploratory Data Analysis* (Reading, MA: Addison-Wesley, 1977).
15. Velleman, P. F., and D. C. Hoaglin, *Applications, Basics, and Computing of Exploratory Data Analysis* (Boston, MA: Duxbury Press, 1981).
16. Wainer, H., "How to Display Data Badly," *The American Statistician* 38 (May 1984), 137–147.
17. Wainer, H., *Visual Revelations: Graphical Tales of Fate and Deception from Napoleon Bonaparte to Ross Perot* (Newark: Copernicus/Springer-Verlag, 1997).

## ❖ APPENDIX 3.1   USING MICROSOFT EXCEL FOR TABLES AND CHARTS

In this chapter we have developed a variety of tables and charts for the 1-year total returns of domestic general stock funds. Each of these tables and charts can be obtained by accessing Microsoft Excel.

> **COMMENT:   *Instructions for PHStat Add-in Users (see appendix 1.2 and appendix F for further details)***
>
> If Microsoft Excel is not running, click the **PHStat** add-in icon. If Microsoft Excel is running, select **File | Open**. Select the PHStat add-in file **PHSA.XLA**. Click the **Open** button.
>
> To obtain a stem-and-leaf display, select **PHStat | Stem-and-Leaf Display**. In the **Variable Cell Range** edit box, enter the cell range for the data. In the Stem Unit edit box, either let the add-in calculate the stem unit or enter the stem unit. Select **Summary Statistics** and provide a title in the Output Title edit box. Click the **OK** button.
>
> To obtain one-way tables and charts for categorical data, select **PHStat | One-Way Tables & Charts**. Enter the range of the data in the Cell Range edit box. Select the **Bar Chart**, **Pie Chart**, and **Pareto Diagram** check boxes as desired and enter an output title. Click the **OK** button.
>
> To obtain two-way tables and charts for categorical variables, select **PHStat | Two-Way Tables & Charts**. Enter the Row Variable Cell range and the Column Variable Cell range in the appropriate edit boxes. Select the Side-by-Side Bar Chart if desired and enter an output title. Click the **OK** button.

## Obtaining an Ordered Array

Open the MUTUAL.XLS workbook. Select **Data | Sort**. In the Sort By list box select the name **1Yr$Ret**. Select the **Ascending** button for data ordered from lowest to highest. Select the **Header Row** option button, and click the **OK** button. You will observe that the 1-year percentage returns are sorted in ascending order.

## Using the Data Analysis Tool to Obtain Frequency and Cumulative Frequency Distributions and Histograms

The Data Analysis tool is an add-in supplied by Microsoft Excel that can be used to perform many of the statistical procedures we will discuss in the text. The Histogram option of the Data Analysis tool can be used to obtain both a frequency distribution and charts such as a histogram and cumulative percentage polygon. To use the Histogram option of the Data Analysis tool, the upper class boundaries of the class intervals must be entered on the Data sheet that contains the data to be analyzed. Open the **MUTUAL.XLS** workbook, and select the Data sheet by clicking on the Data Sheet tab. If you have not already done so, sort the data so that the 59 growth funds are in rows 2–60. Enter the desired upper class limits of 9.99, 14.99, 19.99, 24.99, 29.99, 34.99, 39.99, 44.99, and 49.99 in cells J2–J10.

To create the histogram and cumulative percentage polygon for the 1-year percentage return of the 59 growth funds, select **Tools | Data Analysis**. Select **Histogram** from the Analysis Tools list box that appears. Click the **OK** button to display the Histogram dialog box. If Data Analysis is not a choice on your Tools menu, the Data Analysis component of Excel is probably not properly installed (review appendix 1.2 before continuing). Enter **Data!D2:D60** in the Input Range edit box. Enter **Data!J2:J10** in the Bin Range edit box. In the Output edit box select the **New Worksheet Ply** button and enter Histogram as the name of the new sheet. Select the **Cumulative Percentages** and **Chart Output** check boxes and leave the Pareto check box unselected. Click the **OK** button.

Excel will generate both a frequency distribution and cumulative percentage distribution and superimpose the cumulative percentage polygon onto the histogram. Observe that the frequencies and cumulative percentages provided refer to the upper boundaries of the class. This means that 3.39% of the mutual funds have 1-year percentage returns less than 25, 25.42% have 1-year percentage returns less than 30, and so on. Observe also that a different vertical axis is included for each chart since the two graphs are superimposed. The vertical axis on the left side of the chart provides frequencies for the histogram, while the vertical axis on the right provides percentages for the cumulative percentage polygon. Observe that this chart may contain four mistakes: the $X$ axis labels cannot be clearly seen; there are gaps between the bars that correspond to the class intervals; there is an additional class labeled More by Excel that has been incorrectly plotted; and the secondary $Y$ axis scale exceeds 100%.

To expand the chart to clearly display the $X$ axis labels, select a cell in the Histogram sheet that is outside the chart box. Then click in the white area inside the chart box. Move the mouse pointer directly over the lower left corner of the chart box until the mouse pointer changes to a small double-sided arrow. With the pointer still a double-sided arrow, drag the mouse pointer toward cell D15. As you drag the mouse pointer, it changes to a simple plus sign and the area of the chart expands. When the mouse pointer is over cell D15, release the mouse button. The chart is now enlarged and $X$ axis labels appear.

To eliminate the gaps between bars, click inside one of the bars to select the plotted frequencies. Right-click over the bar to display a shortcut menu. Select **Format Data Series** from this menu. In the Format Data Series dialog box, click the **Options** tab. Change the value in the Gap Width edit box to **0**. Click the **OK** button. The bars are now plotted without gaps.

To delete the additional class, click inside one of the bars to select the plotted frequencies. Right-click over the bar to display a shortcut menu. Select **Source Data** from the menu. In the Source Data dialog box, click the **Series** tab. In the Series: list box of this tab, select **Frequency**. Enter

**Histogram!B2:B10** in the Values: edit box, and **=Histogram!A2:A10** in both the Category (*X*) axis labels and Second category (*X*) axis labels: edit boxes. Be sure to include the equals sign as part of these entries. Select **Cumulative %** from the Series: list box. In the Values: edit box, enter **Histogram!C2:C10**. Click the **OK** button.

To correct the secondary *Y* axis scale, right-click the secondary axis on the right side of the chart. Select **Format Axis** from the shortcut menu that appears. In the Format Axis dialog box, select the **Scale** tab. Change the value in the Maximum edit box to **1**. Click the **OK** button.

Further refinement of the chart is possible by selecting and then editing the title and axis labels.

## Using the Chart Wizard to Obtain Polygons and Histograms

The Microsoft Excel 97 Chart Wizard is a series of four dialog boxes, displayed one at a time, that allow you to create a variety of charts for both numerical and categorical variables. The first dialog box asks you to select the type of chart desired. The second dialog box asks you to specify the orientation of your data and the cell ranges containing the data and data labels for the chart. The third dialog box gives you control over most of the formatting options including the content and placement of titles and a legend. The fourth dialog box allows you to choose between placing a chart on its own (new) chart sheet or in a preexisting worksheet. (Charts created in this text are always placed on new sheets.) Charts created by the Chart Wizard can be refined by further editing.

To use the Chart Wizard to generate a frequency polygon for the 1-year total percentage return for the 59 growth funds, open the **MUTUAL.XLS** workbook that was used to generate the histogram using the Data Analysis Tool. Click the Histogram sheet tab since we need to use the bins, and either the frequency or cumulative percentage in each of the bins. To obtain the percentage polygon from the Chart Wizard, start the Chart Wizard by selecting **Insert | Chart**. In the first dialog box, select the **Standard Types** tab and then select **Line** from the Chart type: list box. Note that the choices under the Chart subtype: heading change as a selection from the Chart type: list is made and that a description of the currently selected subtype appears below the choices. Select the first choice in the second row of subtypes, the choice described as "Line with markers displayed at each data value." Click the **Next** button to continue to the second dialog box.

In the second dialog box, select the Data Range tab, enter **Histogram!B2:B10** in the Data range: edit box. Select the **Columns** option button in the Series in: group. Select the **Series** tab. In the Category (*X*) axis labels: edit box enter **=Histogram!A2:A10**. Note that this entry must include the equals sign (=). Click the **Next** button.

In the third dialog box, select the **Titles** tab. Enter Growth Funds 1-Year Percentage Return in the Chart Title: edit box, enter 1-Year Percentage Return in the Category (*X*) axis: edit box, and enter Frequency in the Value (*Y*) axis: edit box. Select the **Axes** tab. Select both the (*X*) axis and (*Y*) axis check boxes. Select the Automatic option under the (*X*) axis check box. Select the **Gridlines** tab. Deselect all gridlines. Select the **Legend** tab. Deselect the Show legend check box since there is only one group plotted. Select the **Data labels** tab. Select the **None** option button under the Data labels heading. Select the **Data Table** tab. Deselect the **Show data table** check box. Click the **Next** button.

In the fourth dialog box, select the **As new sheet:** option button and enter Frequency Polygon in the edit box to the right of the option button. Click the **Finish** button to create the chart. If we examine this frequency polygon, we note that the category markings on the *X* axis refer to the upper limits of the classes, not the class midpoints.

In addition, if we wanted to obtain a percentage polygon or a cumulative percentage polygon, we would use the column of percentages or cumulative percentages instead of the column of frequencies when we define the range for the data. To obtain a histogram from the Chart Wizard, we would follow steps similar to those described for the polygon.

If we want to obtain a percentage polygon or histogram, we need to calculate relative frequencies and then percentages. On the Histogram sheet, with the cursor in column C, select **Insert | Columns** to insert a new column. In cell B12, enter the formula **=SUM(B2:B10)** to obtain the total frequency. To calculate the relative frequencies, first enter **=B2/$B$12** in cell C2. In this formula, note that the address in the denominator has been entered as an *absolute address*. This is an address that will not be adjusted by Excel during the copying operation. We use this here because we want to divide each frequency by the same total frequency. Copy cell C2 down the column through cell C10. Change the values in column C to percentages by clicking the % button. Click the **Increase decimal** button twice to obtain two-decimal-place accuracy.

The Chart Wizard can also be used to superimpose two polygons on the same graph as was done in Figure 3.3 on page 67 for the percentage polygons and in Figure 3.4 on page 68 for the cumulative percentage polygons for the growth and blend funds. To do so, we must first use the Data Analysis Tool for the 135 blend funds in a manner similar to how the histogram, frequency distribution, and cumulative frequencies were obtained on the Histogram sheet for the growth funds. On the Data sheet, the 1-year total percentage returns should already be sorted in cells D61:D195. Enter the bin values of 9.99, 14.99, 19.99, 24.99, 29.99, 34.99, 39.99, 44.99, and 49.99 in cells J2:J10. Follow the same instructions for these blend funds as was used for the growth funds, naming the New Worksheet Ply BlendReturn.

On the BlendReturn sheet, insert two new columns after column C. Copy the frequencies and percentages for the growth funds from the Histogram sheet to cells D2:E10 of the BlendReturn sheet. Enter a label for Blend in cell C1 and Growth in cell E1.

To obtain the two percentage polygons, start the Chart Wizard by selecting the command **Insert | Chart.** In the first dialog box, select the **Custom Types** tab and then select **Line on Two Axes** from the Chart type: list box. Click the **Next** button to continue to the second dialog box.

In the second dialog box, select the **Data Range** tab, and enter **BlendReturn!C1:C10, BlendReturn!E1:E10** in the Data range: edit box. Note that since the ranges were not located in adjacent columns, their cell ranges are separated by a comma. Select the Columns option button in the Series in: group. Continue by selecting the Series tab. In the Category (*X*) axis labels: edit box enter =BlendReturn!A2:A10. Note that this entry must include the equals sign (=). Click the **Next** button.

In the third dialog box, select the Titles tab. Enter Percentage Polygons in the Chart Title: edit box, enter 1-Year Percentage Return in the Category (*X*) axis: edit box, and enter Percent in the Value (*Y*) axis: edit box. Select the Axes tab. Select the (*X*) axis and (*Y*) axis check boxes for Primary axis, but deselect the secondary *X* and *Y* axes. Select the Gridlines tab. Deselect all the choices. Select the Legend tab. Select the Show legend check box. Select the Data labels tab. Select the None option button under the Data labels heading. Select the Data Table tab. Deselect the Show data table check box. Click the **Next** button.

In the fourth dialog box, select the **As new sheet:** option button and enter Percentage Polygons in the edit box to the right of the option button. Click the **Finish** button to create the chart. A chart similar to Figure 3.4 can be obtained by using the two sets of cumulative percentages.

## Using the Chart Wizard to Obtain a Scatter Diagram

To use the Chart Wizard to generate a scatter diagram of the net asset value and the 1-year total percentage return for the 194 mutual funds, open the MUTUAL.XLS workbook. Click the **Data sheet** tab.

To obtain the scatter diagram from the Chart Wizard, start the Chart Wizard by selecting the command Insert | Chart. In the first dialog box, select the Standard Types tab and then select *XY* (Scatter) from the Chart type: list box. Select the first choice of subtypes, the one described as "Scatter: Compares pairs of values." Click the **Next** button to continue to the second dialog box.

In the second dialog box, select the Data Range tab, enter Data!C2:D195 in the Data range: edit box, and select the Columns option button in the Series in: group. Unless instructed otherwise, Excel will consider the first variable in the cell range as *X* and the second variable as *Y*. To switch this designation so that 1-Year Percentage Return is on the *X* axis and Net Asset Value is on the *Y* axis, click the **Series** tab and enter =Data!D2:D195 in the *X* values edit box and =Data!C2:C195 in the *Y* values edit box. Click the **Next** button.

In the third dialog box, select the Titles tab. Enter Scatter Diagram in the Chart Title: edit box, enter 1-Year Percentage Return in the Category (*X*) axis: edit box, and enter Net Asset Value in the Value (*Y*) axis: edit box. Select the Axis tab. Select both the (*X*) axis and (*Y*) axis check boxes. Select the Gridlines tab. Deselect check boxes. Select the Legend tab. Deselect the Show legend check box. Select the Data labels tab. Select the None option button under the Data labels heading. Click the Next button.

In the fourth dialog box, select the As new sheet: option button and enter Scatter in the edit box to the right of the Option button. Click the Finish button to create the chart.

## Using the PivotTable Wizard to Obtain a One-Way Summary Table

Using the PivotTable Wizard can automate the process of tabulating categorical variables. The Wizard, a series of four dialog boxes displayed one at a time, allows you to specify the organization, contents, and workbook location of summary tables called PivotTables. In Table 3.7 on page 79, we developed a summary table for the fee schedule for the 194 mutual funds. To generate a PivotTable similar to Table 3.7, open the **MUTUAL.XLS** file and click on the Data sheet tab. Note that each mutual fund has been placed in its own row and that the first row contains column headings.

Select **Data | PivotTable Report** to start the PivotTable Wizard. In the first dialog box, select the Microsoft Excel List or database option button, seeing that the data to be summarized already exists in the workbook. Click the **Next** button to continue to the second dialog box. In the second dialog box, enter **Data!B1:H195** in the Range: edit box. Click the **Next** button.

In the third dialog box, first note the labels on the right side of the dialog box that correspond to the headings for the variables under study (type, net asset value, 1-year total percentage return, groups of fee schedules, fee group coded into load and no-load, objective, and size). Drag the Group label into the Row box. A copy of the Group label snaps into the Row box. Now drag another copy of the Group label (at the right) and drop it into the Data box. The wording on the label changes to Count of Group, indicating that the frequency of the variable will be calculated in the PivotTable. (If the label reads something other than Count of Group, double-click on the label to display the PivotTable Field dialog box. In this dialog box, select Count from the Summarize by: list box and then click the Options button. In the Show data as: drop-down list box that appears, select **Normal**. Click the **OK** button to return to the third dialog box of the Wizard.) Click the **Next** button.

In the fourth dialog box, select the **New Worksheet** option button and then select the **Options** button. In the PivotTable options dialog box, enter OneWayTable in the Name: edit box. Select **Grand Total for columns, Autoformat** table, and **Preserve formatting** check boxes in the Format options group. Select the For empty cells, show: check box and enter **0** in its edit box. Select the **Save data with table layout** and **Enable drilldown** option buttons under the Data sources options: heading. Click the **OK** button to return to the fourth dialog box. Click the **Finish** button. Rename the sheet containing the PivotTable OneWayTable.

## Using the Chart Wizard to Obtain Bar Charts, Pie Charts, and Pareto Diagrams

The Chart Wizard can be used in conjunction with the output of the PivotTable Wizard or an available summary table to generate a bar chart, pie chart, or Pareto diagram. To obtain these charts for the mutual fund data, open the **MUTUAL.XLS** workbook and click on the OneWayTable sheet tab. Change the numbered category labels to Fund Assets, Deferred, Front-Load, Multiple, and No-Load.

To obtain the bar chart generated in Figure 3.7 on page 80, start the Chart Wizard by selecting Insert | Chart. In the first dialog box, select the Standard Types tab and then select Bar from the Chart type: list box. Select the first choice in the top row of subtypes, the choice described as "Clustered Bar." Click the **Next** button to continue to the second dialog box.

In the second dialog box, select the Data Range tab. Enter **OneWayTable!B3:B7** in the Data range: edit box, and select the **Columns** option button in the Series in: group. Select the **Series** tab. In the Category (*X*) axis labels: edit box enter **=OneWayTable!A3:A7.** Note that this entry must include the equals sign (=). Click the **Next** button.

In the third dialog box, select the **Titles** tab. Enter Fee Schedule in the Chart Title: edit box, enter **Fee Schedule** in the Category (*X*) axis: edit box, and enter **Frequency** in the Value (*Y*) axis: edit box. Select the **Axes** tab. Select both the (*X*) axis and (*Y*) axis check boxes. Select the **Gridlines** tab. Deselect all gridlines. Select the **Legend** tab. Deselect the Show legend check box. Select the **Data labels** tab. Select the **None** option button under the Data labels heading. Select the **Data Table** tab. Deselect the Show data table check box. Click the **Next** button.

In the fourth dialog box, select the **As new sheet:** option button and enter **Bar** in the edit box to the right of the option button. Click the **Finish** button to create the chart.

To obtain the pie chart generated in Figure 3.8 on page 81, start the Chart Wizard by selecting **Insert | Chart.** In the first dialog box, select the Standard Types tab and then select **Pie** from the Chart type: list box. Select the first choice in the top row of subtypes, the choice described as "Pie." Click the **Next** button to continue to the second dialog box.

In the second dialog box, select the **Data Range** tab. Enter **OneWayTable!B3:B7** in the Data range: edit box, and select the **Columns** option button in the Series in: group. Select the **Series** tab. In the Category labels: edit box enter **=OneWayTable!A3:A7**. Note that this entry must include the equals sign (=). Click the **Next** button.

In the third dialog box, select the **Titles** tab. Enter Fee Schedule in the Chart Title: edit box. Select the **Legend** tab. Select the **Show legend** check box. Select the **Data labels** tab. Select the Show label and Percent option button. Click the **Next** button.

In the fourth dialog box, select the **As new sheet:** option button and enter **Pie** in the edit box to the right of the option button. Click the **Finish** button to create the chart.

To obtain a Pareto diagram, we need to implement Excel formulas to obtain cumulative frequencies and then obtain a combination chart from the Chart Wizard. To do this, we first need to copy the PivotTable into columns C and D. To do this, click on the OneWayTable sheet to make it active. Select cell **A1** of this sheet. Select **Edit | Copy.** Select cell **C1.** Select **Edit | Paste.** A copy of the PivotTable now occupies the range C1:D8.

To sort the copy of the PivotTable, select cell **C1.** Change the value of the cell to Count of Group Sorted. Right-click cell **C1.** Select **Refresh Data** from the shortcut menu that appears. Select cell **C2,** then right-click this cell. Select **Field** from the shortcut menu that appears. In the PivotTable Field dialog box that appears, click the **Advanced** button. This causes the PivotTable Field Advanced Options dialog box to appear. Select the **Descending** option button of the AutoSort group. In the Using field: list box of the AutoSort group, select **Count of Group Sorted**. Click the **OK** button, then click the **OK** button of the PivotTable Field dialog box. The frequencies in column D are now sorted in descending order.

To obtain cumulative percentages, enter the formula **=D3/$D$8** in cell E3 and copy this formula to the cell range E4:E7. To change to percentage style, select the cell range **E3:E7** and click the **Percent Style** button on the formatting toolbar. Click the **Increase Decimal** button twice to get two decimal places. Enter the title Percentage in cell E2. Enter the formula **=E3** in cell F3. Enter the formula **=F3+E4** into cell F4. Copy this formula from cell F4 to the cell range F5:F7. Enter the heading Cumulative Percentage in cell F2.

To obtain the Pareto diagram from the Chart Wizard, with the OneWayTable sheet active, start the Chart Wizard by selecting the command **Insert | Chart.** In the first dialog box, select the **Custom Types** tab and then select **Line-Column on Two Axes** from the Chart type: list box. Click the **Next** button to continue to the second dialog box.

In the second dialog box, select the Data range tab. Enter **OneWayTable!E3:F7** in the Data range: edit box. Select the Columns option button in the Series in: group. Continue by selecting the **Series** tab. In the Category (*X*) axis labels: edit box enter **=OneWayTable!C3:C7.** Click the **Next** button.

In the third dialog box, select the Titles tab. Enter Pareto Diagram in the Chart Title: edit box, enter Group in the Category (*X*) axis: edit box: Select the **Axes** tab. Select the Primary axis, Category

(*X*) axis, and both of the Value (*Y*) axis check boxes. Select the **Gridlines** tab. Deselect all the choices. Select the **Legend** tab. Deselect the Show legend check box. Select the Data labels tab. Select the None option button under the Data labels heading. Select the Data Table tab. Deselect the Show data table check box. Click the **Next** button.

In the fourth dialog box, select the **As new sheet:** option button and enter Pareto in the edit box to the right of the option button. Click the **Finish** button to create the chart. To correct the secondary *Y* axis scale, double-click the Secondary Axis on the right side of the chart. In the Format Axis dialog box, click the **Scale** tab. Change the value in the Maximum edit box to **1.**

## Using the PivotTable Wizard to Obtain a Two-Way Summary Table

To generate a PivotTable similar to Table 3.8 on page 88, open the **MUTUAL.XLS** file. Click on the Data sheet tab. Select **Data | PivotTable Report** to start the PivotTable Wizard. In the first dialog box, select the Microsoft Excel List or database option button, seeing that the data to be summarized already exists in the workbook. Click the **Next** button to continue to the second dialog box. In the second dialog box, enter **Data!B1:H195** in the Range: edit box. Click the **Next** button.

In the third dialog box, first note the labels on the right side of the dialog box that correspond to the headings for the variables under study (type, net asset value, 1-year total percentage return, groups of fee schedules, fee group coded into load and no-load, objective, and size). Drag the Object label into the Row box. A copy of the Object label snaps into the Row box. Drag the Group label into the Column box. Now again drag the Group label (at the right) and drop it into the Data box. The wording on the label changes to Count of Group, indicating that the frequency of the variable will be calculated in the PivotTable. (If the label reads something other than Count of Group, double-click on the label to display the PivotTable Field dialog box. In this dialog box, select Count from the Summarize by: list box and then click the Options button. In the Show data as: drop-down list box that appears, select Normal. Click the **OK** button to return to the third dialog box of the Wizard.) Click the **Next** button.

In the fourth dialog box, select the **New Worksheet** option button and then click the **Options** button. In the PivotTable options dialog box, enter TwoWayTable in the Name: edit box. Select **Grand total for columns, Grand totals for rows, Autoformat** table, and Preserve formatting check boxes in the Format options group. Select the For empty cells, show: check box and enter **0** in its edit box. Select the **Save data with table layout** and **Enable drilldown** option buttons under the Data Sources options: heading. Click the **OK** button to return to the fourth dialog box. Click the **Finish** button. Rename the sheet containing the PivotTable TwoWayTable.

If the results were desired in terms of total percentages, row percentages, or column percentages as in Tables 3.9–3.11, we would repeat the above procedure but in the third dialog box we would double-click on the Count of Group Label dropped into the data box in order to display the Pivot-Table field dialog box. In that dialog box we would click the Options button and select either % of total, % of row, or % of column from the Show data as: list box before clicking the OK button to return to the third dialog box of the Wizard.

## Using the Chart Wizard to Obtain a Side-by-Side Bar Chart

The Chart Wizard can be used in conjunction with the output of the PivotTable Wizard or an available contingency table to generate a side-by-side bar chart. To obtain this chart for the mutual fund data, open the MUTUAL.XLS workbook. Click on the TwoWayTables sheet tab. Change the numbered column category labels to fund assets, Deferred, Front-Load, Multiple, and No-Load. Change the numbered row catagory labels to Growth and Blend.

To obtain the side-by-side bar chart generated in Figure 3.10 on page 91, start the Chart Wizard by selecting **Insert | Chart.** In the first dialog box, select the **Standard Types** tab and then select

**Bar** from the Chart type: list box. Select the first choice in the top row of subtypes, the choice described as "Clustered Bar." Click the Next button to continue to the second dialog box.

In the second dialog box, select the **Data Range** tab. Enter **TwoWayTable!A3:F4** in the Data range: edit box. Select the **Rows** option button in the Series in: group. Select the **Series** tab. In the Category (*X*) axis labels: edit box enter **=TwoWayTable!B2:F2.** Click the Next button.

In the third dialog box, select the **Titles** tab. Enter Side-by-Side Bar Chart in the Chart Title: edit box, enter Fee Schedule in the Category (*X*) axis: edit box, and enter Frequency in the Value (*Y*) axis: edit box. Select the **Axes** tab. Select both the (*X*) axis and (*Y*) axis check boxes. Select the **Gridlines** tab. Deselect all gridlines. Select the **Legend** tab. Select the Show legend check box. Select the **Data labels** tab. Select the None option button under the Data labels heading. Select the **Data Table** tab. Deselect the Show data table check box. Click the **Next** button.

In the fourth dialog box, select the **As new sheet:** option button and enter **Side** in the edit box to the right of the option button. Click the **Finish** button to create the chart.

## ❖ APPENDIX 3.2  USING MINITAB FOR TABLES AND CHARTS

In this chapter we have developed a variety of tables and charts for the 1-year total returns of domestic general stock funds. Many of these tables and charts can be obtained by accessing Minitab.

### Obtaining a Stem-and-Leaf Display

To obtain the stem-and-leaf display of Figure 3.1 on page 56, we need to unstack the data to separate the 1-year percentage return of the 59 growth funds from those of the 135 blend funds. To unstack the mutual funds data, open the MUTUAL.MTP file and select **MANIP | Stack/Unstack | Unstack One Column**. In the Unstack dialog box, enter **C4** or 1Yr%Ret in the Unstack the data in edit box. Enter **C9 C10** in the Store Unstacked data in edit box. Enter **C7** or Obj in the Using Subscripts in: edit box. Click the **OK** button.

The 1-year percentage returns are now stored in columns C9 and C10. After providing labels for these variables (1Yr%RetGrow and 1Yr%RetBlen), select **Stat | EDA | Stem-and-Leaf**. In the Stem-and-Leaf dialog box, enter **C9** or 1Yr%RetGrow in the Variables edit box and **1** in the Increment edit box (to have the stems equal to 1). Click the **OK** button.

### Obtaining a Histogram

With the data unstacked as was the case with the stem-and-leaf display, to obtain the histogram depicted in Figure 3.2 on page 66, select **Graph | Histogram.** In the Histogram dialog box, in the Graph variables edit box enter **C9** or 1Yr%RetGrow. Click the **Options** button. Under Type of Histogram, select **Percent**. Under Type of Interval, select **Cutpoint**. Under Definition of Interval, select **Midpoint/cutpoint** position and enter the values 20 25 30 35 40 45 50. Click the **OK** button to return to the Histogram dialog box. To obtain colors for the histogram, click **Edit Attributes** and select a Fill Type, Fore Color, Back Color, and Edge Type. Click **OK** to return to the Histogram dialog box. Click the **OK** button to obtain the histogram.

### Obtaining a Scatter Diagram

To obtain the scatter diagram illustrated in Figure 3.5 on page 74, open the file MUTUAL.MTP. Select **Graph | Plot**. In the Plot dialog box, in the Graph variables edit box, in row 1, enter **C3** or NAV in the *Y* column, and C4 or 1Yr%Ret in the *X* column. Click the **OK** button.

### Obtaining a Bar Chart

To obtain a bar chart for a categorical variable, open the file MUTUAL.MTP. Select **Graph | Bar Chart**. In the Graph Variables edit box, select **C5** or Group and enter this variable in row 1 in the *X* column. Click the **OK** button.

### Obtaining a Pie Chart

To obtain a pie chart for a categorical variable, open the file MUTUAL.MTP. Select **Graph | Pie Chart**. In the Chart data in edit box, select **C5** or Group. Enter a title in the Title edit box. Click the **OK** button.

### Obtaining a Pareto Diagram

To obtain a Pareto diagram for a categorical variable, open the file MUTUAL.MTP. Select **Stat | Quality Tools | Pareto Chart**. In the Chart Defects data in edit box, select **C5** or Group. Click the **OK** button.

### Obtaining a Contingency Table

To obtain a two-way contingency table, open the MUTUAL.MTP file. Select **Stat | Tables | Cross Tabulation**. In the Classification Variables edit box, select **C7** or Obj and **C5** or Group. In the Display check box, select **Counts, Row percents, Column percents**, and **Total percents**. Click the **OK** button.

### Obtaining a Side-by Side Bar Chart

To obtain a side-by-side bar chart, open the MUTUAL.MTP file. Select **Graph | Chart**. Enter **C5** or Group in the Graph Variables edit box in row 1 in the *X* column. In the Data display edit box, be sure that in row 1 the Display column indicates **Bar** and the For each column indicates **Graph**. In the Group variables column select **C7** or Obj. Click the **Options** button. In the Options dialog box, in the Groups within *X* edit box, select **Cluster** and enter **C7** or Obj. Under Order Groups Based on, select the **Total Y to 100%** within each *X* category box to obtain percentages for each group. Click the **OK** button to return to the Chart dialog box. To obtain colors for each bar, click **Edit Attributes** and select a Fill Type, Fore Color, Back Color, and Edge Type. Click the **OK** button to return to the Chart dialog box. Click the **OK** button again to obtain the side-by-side bar chart.

# 4

# Summarizing and Describing Numerical Data

## CHAPTER OBJECTIVES

✓ *To describe central tendency in numerical data*
✓ *To describe variation in numerical data*
✓ *To describe the shape of a distribution*
✓ *To introduce the box-and-whisker plot as a graphical tool for describing the characteristics of numerical data*
✓ *To calculate descriptive summary measures from a population*
✓ *To calculate descriptive summary measures from a frequency distribution*

## Introduction

In the preceding chapter we learned how to present numerical and categorical data in both tabular and chart format. Now, how do we make sense out of such information? Although presenting data is an essential component of descriptive statistics, it does not tell the whole story. When dealing with numerical information, good **data analysis** involves not only *presenting* the data and *observing* what the data are trying to convey, but also *computing* and *summarizing* the key features and *analyzing* the findings.

In this chapter we explore numerical data and their properties. Next we discuss measures of central tendency, variation, and shape. Then we explore data analysis and how to calculate descriptive summary measures from a population and from a frequency distribution. Finally we address how to recognize and practice proper descriptive summarization and deal with pertinent ethical issues.

---

## ◆ USING STATISTICS: *Evaluating the Performance of Equity Mutual Funds*

To introduce the relevant ideas of this chapter, let us return to our study of the performance of currently traded domestic general stock funds. In determining an investment strategy, it would be useful to compare the 1-year total percentage return of the stock funds based on their fee structures. To illustrate such an evaluation, we will first study the 17 funds whose fee structure consists of marketing fees paid from fund assets and subsequently compare the returns for all five fee structures.

## ◆ 4.1 EXPLORING NUMERICAL DATA AND THEIR PROPERTIES

The 1-year total percentage returns are given in Table 4.1. We note that the 17 funds (recorded in alphabetical order) are presented along with their attained 1-year total returns (in percents). What can be learned from such data that will assist us in an evaluation for future investment purposes? On the basis of this sample, we can make the following three observations:

**Table 4.1** *1-year total percentage returns for stocks funds whose fee structure consists of marketing fees paid from funds assets*

| FUND | 1-YEAR TOTAL PERCENTAGE RETURNS |
|---|---|
| Amcore Vintage Equity | 32.2 |
| Baron Funds Asset | 29.5 |
| Berger SmCoGrow | 29.9 |
| Chicago Trust GrowInc | 32.4 |
| Dodge & Cox DominiSo | 30.5 |
| Federated Institut MaxCapSvc | 30.1 |
| First Funds GroInc III | 32.1 |
| Harris Insight Inst Haven | 35.2 |
| Mentor Merger | 10.0 |
| Rainler Reich Tang | 20.6 |
| Robertson Stephens ValGrow | 28.6 |
| SSgA S&P500Idx | 30.5 |
| SSgA SmallCap | 38.0 |
| 1784 GrowInc | 33.0 |
| Stagecoach CorpStk | 29.4 |
| Westwood Eq R | 37.1 |
| Wright Yacktman | 28.6 |

DATA FILE
MUTUAL

1. Two of the funds achieved 1-year total percentage returns of 28.6 and two other funds attained 1-year total percentage returns of 30.5. These are the *most typical*, or *modal*, values, and this data set is considered to be *bimodal*. The 1-year total returns achieved by each of the other funds differ from one another.

2. The *spread* in the one year total returns ranges from 10.0% to 38.0%.

3. There appears to be at least one unusual or extraordinarily low 1-year total return in this data set—that attained by Mentor Merger. Arranged in an ordered array, the 1-year total percentage returns attained by these domestic general stock funds (in percents) are

   10.0, 20.6, 28.6, 28.6, 29.4, 29.5, 29.9, 30.1, 30.5, 30.5, 32.1, 32.2, 32.4, 33.0, 35.2, 37.1, 38.0

   Here the 10.0 and, perhaps, the 20.6 would be considered **outliers**, or **extreme values**.

We might want to explore the reasons why the 1-year total percentage return attained by Mentor Merger was so much lower than that achieved by any of the other funds whose marketing fees were paid from fund assets. A comparison of the prospectus for this fund against those with higher-achieving performance records might provide some useful insight for future investment purposes.

Nevertheless, had we been asked to examine the data and present a short summary of our findings, statements similar to the three preceding are basically all that we could be expected to make without more knowledge of statistics.

We can add to our understanding of what the data are telling us by more formally examining the three major properties that describe a set of numerical data: *central tendency*, *variation*, and *shape*.

## 4.2 MEASURES OF CENTRAL TENDENCY, VARIATION, AND SHAPE

In any analysis and/or interpretation, a variety of descriptive measures representing the properties of central tendency, variation, and shape may be used to summarize the major features of the data set. If these descriptive summary measures are computed from a sample of data, they are called *statistics*; if they are computed from an entire population of data, they are called *parameters*. Since statisticians usually take samples rather than use entire populations, our primary emphasis in this text when describing the properties of central tendency, variation, and shape is on statistics, rather than on parameters.

### Measures of Central Tendency

Most sets of data show a distinct tendency to group or cluster about a certain central point. Thus, for any particular set of data, it usually becomes possible to select some typical value, or **average**, to describe the entire set. Such a descriptive typical value is a measure of **central tendency**, or **location**.

Five types of averages often used as measures of central tendency are the *arithmetic mean*, the *median*, the *mode*, the *midrange*, and the *midhinge*.

◆ *The Arithmetic Mean* The **arithmetic mean** (also called the **mean**) is the most commonly used *average*[1] or measure of central tendency. It is calculated by summing all the observations in a set of data and then dividing the total by the number of items involved. Thus, for a sample containing a set of $n$ observations $X_1, X_2, X_3, \ldots, X_n$, the arithmetic mean (given by the symbol $\overline{X}$—called "$X$ bar") can be written as

$$\overline{X} = \frac{X_1 + X_2 + X_3 + \cdots + X_n}{n}$$

To simplify the notation, the term

$$\sum_{i=1}^{n} X_i$$

(meaning the *summation of all the $X_i$ values*) is used whenever we wish to add together a series of observations. That is,

$$\sum_{i=1}^{n} X_i = X_1 + X_2 + X_3 + \cdots + X_n$$

Rules pertaining to summation notation are presented in appendix B. Using this summation notation, the arithmetic mean of the sample can be expressed as follows.

[1]*Although the word* average *refers to any summary measure of central tendency, it is most often used as a synonym for the mean.*

## Arithmetic Mean

The arithmetic mean is the sum of the values divided by the number of values.

$$\overline{X} = \frac{\displaystyle\sum_{i=1}^{n} X_i}{n} \qquad\qquad (4.1)$$

where

$\overline{X}$ = sample arithmetic mean

$n$ = sample size

$X_i$ = $i$th observation of the random variable $X$

$\displaystyle\sum_{i=1}^{n} X_i$ = summation of all $X_i$ values in the sample (see appendix B)

## Example 4.1 *Computing the Arithmetic Mean*

Compute the arithmetic mean of the 1-year total percentage returns of the 17 domestic general stock funds presented in Table 4.1.

### SOLUTION

We begin by assigning $X_i$ values to the 17 funds.

$X_1$ = 32.2 at Amcore Vintage Equity

$X_2$ = 29.5 at Baron Funds Asset

$X_3$ = 29.9 at Berger SmCoGrow

$X_4$ = 32.4 at Chicago Trust GrowInc

$X_5$ = 30.5 at Dodge & Cox DominiSo

$X_6$ = 30.1 at Federated Institut MaxCapSvc

$X_7$ = 32.1 at First Funds GroInc III

$X_8$ = 35.2 at Harris Insight Inst Haven

$X_9$ = 10.0 at Mentor Merger

$X_{10}$ = 20.6 at Rainler Reich Tang

$X_{11}$ = 28.6 at Robertson Stephens ValGrow

$X_{12}$ = 30.5 at SSgA S&P500Idx

$X_{13}$ = 38.0 at SSgA SmallCap

$X_{14}$ = 33.0 at 1784 GrowInc

$X_{15}$ = 29.4 at Stagecoach CorpStk

$X_{16}$ = 37.1 at Westwood Eq R

$X_{17}$ = 28.6 at Wright Yacktman

The arithmetic mean for this sample is then calculated as follows.

$$\overline{X} = \frac{\sum\limits_{i=1}^{n} X_i}{n} = \frac{32.2 + 29.5 + 29.9 + \cdots + 28.6}{17} = 29.86$$

We observe here that the mean 1-year total percentage return is computed as 29.86 even though not one particular fund in the sample actually had that value. In addition, we see from the **dot scale** of Figure 4.1 that for this set of data, 6 observations are smaller than the mean and 11 are larger. The mean acts as a *balancing point* so that smaller observations balance out larger ones. Note that the calculation of the mean is based on all of the observations $(X_1, X_2, X_3, \ldots, X_n)$ in the set of data. No other commonly used measure of central tendency possesses this characteristic.

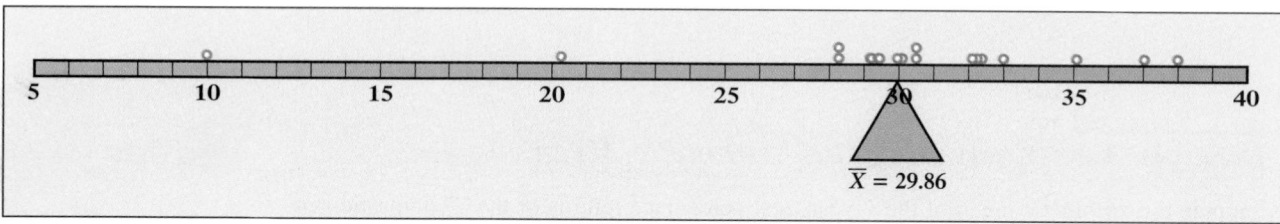

**FIGURE 4.1** Dot scale representing the 1-year total percentage returns achieved by 17 domestic general stock funds with marketing fees paid from fund assets

**COMMENT: When to Use the Arithmetic Mean**

Since its computation is based on every observation, the arithmetic mean is greatly affected by any extreme value or values. In such instances, the arithmetic mean presents a distorted representation of what the data are conveying; hence, the mean is not the best average to use for describing or summarizing a set of data that has extreme values. This is what has happened in Example 4.1.

To demonstrate the effect that extreme values can have when summarizing and describing the property of central tendency, suppose that the outlier Mentor Merger is removed. How the arithmetic mean of the 1-year total percentage returns changes is explored in Example 4.2.

## Example 4.2 *Computing the Arithmetic Mean*

Compute the arithmetic mean of the 1-year total percentage returns after removing the outlier Mentor Merger.

### SOLUTION

The arithmetic mean for this sample of 16 funds is calculated as follows.

$$\overline{X} = \frac{\sum\limits_{i=1}^{n} X_i}{n} = \frac{32.2 + 29.5 + 29.9 + \cdots + 28.6}{16} = 31.11$$

By the removal of Mentor Merger, the arithmetic mean increased from 29.86 to 31.11.

The dot scale is displayed in Figure 4.2.

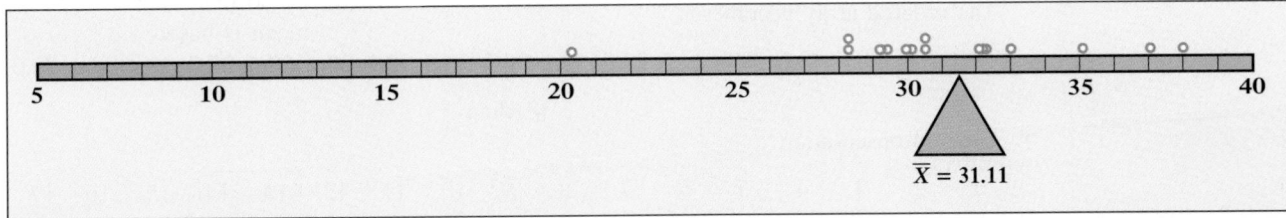

**FIGURE 4.2**   Dot scale representing the 1-year total percentage returns achieved by 16 domestic general stock funds with marketing fees paid from fund assets

◆ *The Median*   The **median** is the middle value in an ordered array of data. If there are no ties, half of the observations will be smaller and half will be larger. The median is unaffected by any extreme observations in a set of data. Thus, whenever an extreme observation is present, it is appropriate to use the median rather than the mean to describe a set of data.

To calculate the median from a set of data, we must first organize the data into an ordered array. Then the median can be obtained as:

## Median

The median is the value such that 50% of the observations are smaller and 50% of the observations are larger.

$$\text{Median} = \frac{n + 1}{2} \text{ ranked observation} \qquad (4.2)$$

Equation (4.2) is used to find the place in the ordered array that corresponds to the median value by following one of two rules:

**RULE 1:** If the size of the sample is an *odd* number, then the median is represented by the numerical value corresponding to the positioning point—the $(n + 1)/2$ ordered observation.
**RULE 2:** If the size of the sample is an *even* number, then the positioning point lies between the two middle observations in the ordered array. The median is the average of the numerical values corresponding to these two middle observations.

## Example 4.3  *Computing the Median from an Odd-Sized Sample*

From our sample of 1-year total percentage returns achieved by domestic general stock funds whose marketing fees are paid from fund assets, the raw data are presented as follows.

32.2 29.5 29.9 32.4 30.5 30.1 32.1 35.2 10.0 20.6 28.6 30.5 38.0 33.0 29.4 37.1 28.6

Compute the median.

### SOLUTION

The ordered array becomes

10.0 20.6 28.6 28.6 29.4 29.5 29.9 30.1 30.5 30.5 32.1 32.2 32.4 33.0 35.2 37.1 38.0
↑
Median

Ordered observation                                    ↑

  1   2   3   4   5   6   7   8   9   10   11   12   13   14   15   16   17

Median = 30.5

For these data, the positioning point is the ninth ordered observation [that is, $(n + 1)/2 = (17 + 1)/2 = 9$]. Therefore, the median is 30.5.

---

As can be seen from the ordered array in Example 4.3, the median is unaffected by extreme observations. Regardless of whether the smallest 1-year total percentage return is 1.0, 10.0, or 20.0, the median is still 30.5.

In addition, when computing the median, we ignore the fact that tied values may be present in the data. In Example 4.3, two of the funds (Robertson Stephens ValGrow and Wright Yacktman) achieved the same 1-year total percentage returns of 28.6. However, this amount had no impact on the actual median value. On the other hand, two other funds (Dodge & Cox DominiSo and SSgA S&P500Idx) attained the same 1-year total percentage returns of 30.5, which happens to be equal to the median performance value. Thus, for this odd-sized sample, the median positioning point is the $(n + 1)/2 = 9$th ordered observation and the median is 30.5, the middle value in the ordered sequence, even though the 10th ordered observation is also 30.5.

## Example 4.4  *Computing the Median from an Even-Sized Sample*

Suppose that our sample consists of the net asset values of 14 domestic general stock funds that are classified as small capitalization blend funds. The raw data, displaying the net asset values (in dollars) for these funds, are as follows.

$$X_1 = 7.35 \text{ at Baron Funds BanRosSC}$$
$$X_2 = 17.30 \text{ at Citizens Trust CloverEqV}$$
$$X_3 = 11.62 \text{ at DFA US9-10Sm}$$

$$X_4 = 26.10 \text{ at FPA Fasciano}$$
$$X_5 = 21.69 \text{ at GT Global Equity AmerGroA}$$
$$X_6 = 21.17 \text{ at GP Global Equity AmerGroB}$$
$$X_7 = 14.07 \text{ at Galaxy Retail SmCapVal}$$
$$X_8 = 14.09 \text{ at Galaxy Trust SmCapVal}$$
$$X_9 = 24.01 \text{ at Heritage SmCapStkA}$$
$$X_{10} = 20.34 \text{ at HighMark Fid HomePAGr}$$
$$X_{11} = 18.26 \text{ at T Rowe Price OTCSec}$$
$$X_{12} = 37.61 \text{ at Princor EmgGro A}$$
$$X_{13} = 18.60 \text{ at SSgA SmallCap}$$
$$X_{14} = 16.95 \text{ at Wasatch Growth}$$

Compute the median.

## SOLUTION

The ordered array becomes

7.35  11.62  14.07  14.09  16.95  17.30  18.26  18.60  20.34  21.17  21.69  24.01  26.10  37.61

Ordered observation

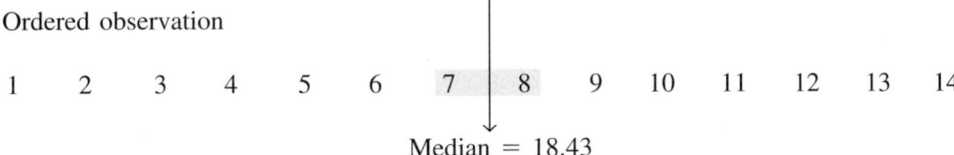

For these data, the positioning point is $(n + 1)/2 = (14 + 1)/2 = 7.5$. Therefore, the median is obtained by averaging the seventh and eighth ordered observations:

$$\frac{18.26 + 18.60}{2} = \$18.43$$

To summarize, the calculation of the median value is affected by the number of observations, not by the magnitude of any extreme(s). Ignoring the possibility of tied data values, which are usually attributable to imprecise measurements, any observation selected at random is just as likely to exceed the median as it is to be exceeded by it.

◆ *The Mode*  The **mode** is the value in a set of data that appears most frequently. Unlike the arithmetic mean, the mode is not affected by the occurrence of any extreme values. However, the mode is used only for descriptive purposes because it is more variable from sample to sample than other measures of central tendency.

## Example 4.5  *Obtaining the Mode*

Using the ordered array for the 1-year total percentage returns achieved by the domestic general stock funds whose marketing fees are paid from fund assets (see Example 4.3), obtain the mode.

**SOLUTION**

The ordered array for these data is

10.0  20.6  28.6  28.6  29.4  29.5  29.9  30.1  30.5  30.5  32.1  32.2  32.4  33.0  35.2  37.1  38.0

We see that there are two "most typical" values, or two modes—28.6 and 30.5. Such data are described as *bimodal*.

A set of data may have no mode if none of the values is "most typical." This is illustrated in our next example.

## Example 4.6   *Data with No Mode*

Using the ordered array of net asset values (in dollars) of 14 domestic general stock funds that are classified as small capitalization blend funds (see Example 4.4 on page 136), obtain the mode.

**SOLUTION**

The ordered array for these data is

7.35  11.62  14.07  14.09  16.95  17.30  18.26  18.60  20.34  21.17  21.69  24.01  26.10  37.61

Here there is no mode. None of the net asset values is "most typical."

◆ ***The Midrange***   The **midrange** is the average of the *smallest* and *largest* observations in a set of data. This can be written as follows.

### Midrange

The midrange is obtained by adding the smallest and largest values and dividing by 2.

$$\text{Midrange} = \frac{X_{smallest} + X_{largest}}{2} \tag{4.3}$$

## Example 4.7   *Computing the Midrange*

Using the ordered array for the 1-year total percentage returns achieved by the domestic general stock funds whose marketing fees are paid from fund assets (see Example 4.3 on page 136), compute the midrange.

**SOLUTION**

The ordered array for these data is

10.0  20.6  28.6  28.6  29.4  29.5  29.9  30.1  30.5  30.5  32.1  32.2  32.4  33.0  35.2  37.1  38.0

The midrange is computed from equation (4.3) as

$$\text{Midrange} = \frac{X_{smallest} + X_{largest}}{2}$$

$$= \frac{10.0 + 38.0}{2} = 24.0$$

The midrange is often used as a summary measure both by financial analysts and by weather reporters, since it can provide an adequate, quick, and simple measure to characterize the *entire* data set. Nevertheless, despite these advantages, the midrange must be used cautiously.

**COMMENT: *When to Use the Midrange***

In our dealing with data such as daily closing stock prices or hourly temperature readings, an extreme value is not likely to occur. Nevertheless, in most applications, despite its simplicity, the midrange must be used cautiously. Since it involves only the smallest and largest observations in a data set, the midrange becomes distorted as a summary measure of central tendency if an outlier is present (as in Example 4.7). In such situations, the midrange is inappropriate.

Aside from the measures of central tendency, **quartiles** are the most widely used measures of "noncentral" location (also called **quantiles**) and are employed particularly when summarizing or describing the properties of large sets of numerical data. Whereas the median is a value that splits the ordered array in half (50.0% of the observations are smaller and 50.0% of the observations are larger), the quartiles are descriptive measures that split the ordered data into four quarters. Other often used quantiles are deciles, which split the ordered data into 10ths, and percentiles, which split the data into 100ths.

The quartiles can be defined as in equations (4.4) and (4.5).

**First Quartile, $Q_1$**

The first quartile, $Q_1$, is a value such that 25.0% of the observations are smaller and 75.0% of the observations are larger.

$$Q_1 = \frac{(n + 1)}{4} \text{ ordered observation} \tag{4.4}$$

**Third Quartile, $Q_3$**

The third quartile, $Q_3$, is a value such that 75.0% of the observations are smaller and 25.0% of the observations are larger.

$$Q_3 = \frac{3(n + 1)}{4} \text{ ordered observation} \tag{4.5}$$

Three rules are used for obtaining the quartile values.

**Rule 1:** If the resulting positioning point is an integer, the particular numerical observation corresponding to that positioning point is chosen for the quartile.

**Rule 2:** If the resulting positioning point is halfway between two integers, the average of their corresponding values is selected.

**Rule 3:** If the resulting positioning point is neither an integer nor a value halfway between two integers, a simple rule used to approximate the particular quartile is to *round up or down* to the nearest integer positioning point and select the numerical value of the corresponding observation.

The computation of the quartiles is illustrated in Example 4.8.

## Example 4.8 *Obtaining the Quartiles*

Using the ordered array for the 1-year total percentage returns achieved by the domestic general stock funds whose marketing fees are paid from fund assets (see Example 4.3 on page 136), compute the quartiles.

### SOLUTION

The ordered array is

10.0  20.6  28.6  28.6  29.4  29.5  29.9  30.1  30.5  30.5  32.1  32.2  32.4  33.0  35.2  37.1  38.0

For these data we have

$$Q_1 = \frac{n+1}{4} \text{ ordered observation}$$

$$= \frac{17+1}{4} = 4.5\text{th ordered observation}$$

Therefore, using rule 2, $Q_1$ can be approximated as the average of the fourth and fifth ordered observations.

$$Q_1 = \frac{28.6 + 29.4}{2} = 29.0$$

In addition,

$$Q_3 = \frac{3(n+1)}{4} \text{ ordered observation}$$

$$= \frac{3(17+1)}{4} = 13.5\text{th ordered observation}$$

Therefore, using rule 2, $Q_3$ can be approximated as the average of the 13th and 14th ordered observations.

$$Q_3 = \frac{32.4 + 33.0}{2} = 32.7$$

♦ *The Midhinge* The **midhinge** is a summary measure used to overcome potential problems introduced by extreme values in the data. The midhinge is computed as the average of the *first* and *third quartiles* in a set of data.

## Midhinge

The midhinge is obtained by adding the first and third quartiles and dividing by 2.

$$\text{Midhinge} = \frac{Q_1 + Q_3}{2} \tag{4.6}$$

where

$$Q_1 = \text{first quartile}$$
$$Q_3 = \text{third quartile}$$

To compute the midhinge, we first need to compute $Q_1$ and $Q_3$. This is demonstrated in Example 4.9.

## Example 4.9 *Computing the Midhinge*

Using the ordered array for the 1-year total percentage returns achieved by the domestic general stock funds whose marketing fees are paid from fund assets (see Example 4.3 on page 136), compute the midhinge.

### SOLUTION

From Example 4.8 we determined that $Q_1 = 29.0$ and $Q_3 = 32.7$. Returning to equation (4.6), we may now compute the midhinge as

$$\text{Midhinge} = \frac{Q_1 + Q_3}{2}$$

$$= \frac{29.0 + 32.7}{2} = 30.85$$

It is important to note that the midhinge, the average of $Q_1$ and $Q_3$, two measures of noncentral location, cannot be affected by potential outliers since no observation smaller than $Q_1$ or larger than $Q_3$ is considered. Summary measures such as the midhinge and the median, which cannot be affected by outliers, are called **resistant measures**.

## Measures of Variation

A second important property that describes a set of numerical data is variation. **Variation** is the amount of *dispersion,* or "spread," in the data. Two sets of data may differ in both central tendency and variation; or, as shown in the polygons of Figure 4.3, two sets of data

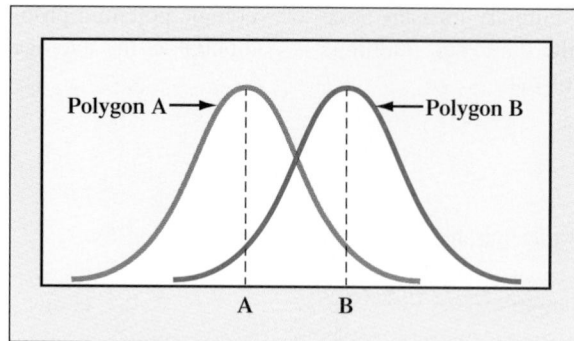

**FIGURE 4.3**
Two symmetrical bell-shaped distributions differing only in central tendency

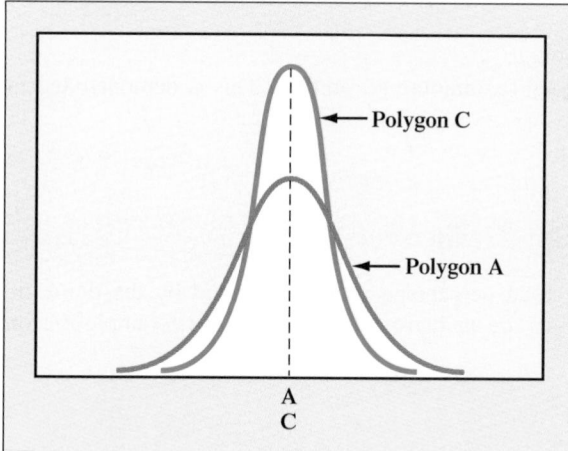

**FIGURE 4.4**
Two symmetrical bell-shaped distributions differing only in variation

may have the same measures of variation but differ in central tendency; or, as depicted in the polygons of Figure 4.4, two sets of data may have the same measures of central tendency but differ greatly in terms of variation. The data set depicted in polygon C of Figure 4.4 is much less variable than that depicted in polygon A.

Five measures of variation include the *range*, the *interquartile range*, the *variance*, the *standard deviation*, and the *coefficient of variation*.

◆ **The Range**   The **range** is the difference between the *largest* and *smallest* observations in a set of data.

### Range

The range is equal to the largest value minus the smallest value.

$$\text{Range} = X_{largest} - X_{smallest} \tag{4.7}$$

We apply equation (4.7) in Example 4.10.

## Example 4.10   *Computing the Range*

Using the ordered array for the 1-year total percentage returns achieved by the domestic general stock funds whose marketing fees are paid from fund assets (see Example 4.3 on page 136), compute the range.

### SOLUTION

The ordered array is

10.0  20.6  28.6  28.6  29.4  29.5  29.9  30.1  30.5  30.5  32.1  32.2  32.4  33.0  35.2  37.1  38.0

For these data, the range is $38.0 - 10.0 = 28.0$.

The range measures the *total spread* in the set of data. Although the range is a simple measure of total variation in the data, its distinct weakness is that it does not take into account *how* the data are actually distributed between the smallest and largest values. This can be observed from Figure 4.5. As evidenced in scale C, it would be improper to use the range as a measure of variation when at least one of its components is an extreme observation.

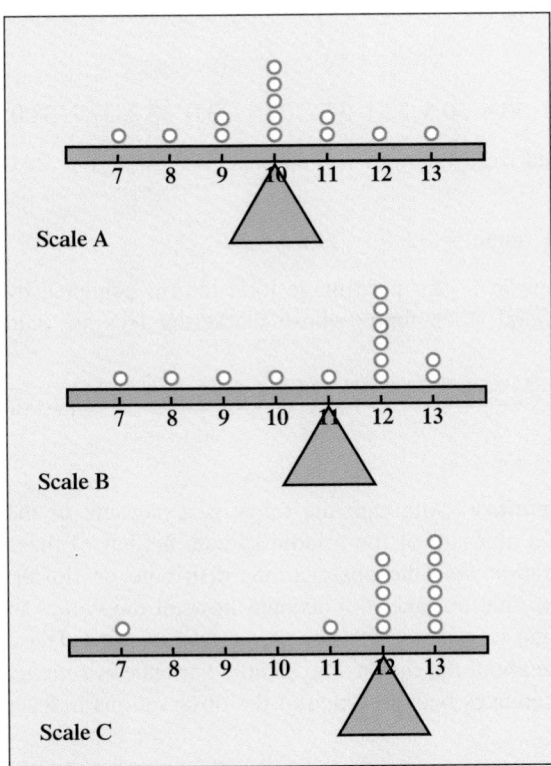

**FIGURE 4.5**   Comparing three data sets with the same range

♦ **The Interquartile Range** The **interquartile range** (also called **midspread**) is the difference between the *third* and *first quartiles* in a set of data.

> **Interquartile Range**
>
> The interquartile range is obtained by subtracting the first quartile from the third quartile.
>
> $$\text{Interquartile range} = Q_3 - Q_1 \qquad\qquad (4.8)$$

This measure considers the spread in the middle 50% of the data; therefore, it is not influenced by extreme values.

## Example 4.11 *Computing the Interquartile Range*

Using the ordered array for the 1-year total percentage returns achieved by the domestic general stock funds whose marketing fees are paid from fund assets (see Example 4.3 on page 136), compute the interquartile range.

**SOLUTION**

The ordered array is

10.0 20.6 28.6 28.6 29.4 29.5 29.9 30.1 30.5 30.5 32.1 32.2 32.4 33.0 35.2 37.1 38.0

For these data, we have already determined from Example 4.8 on page 140 that $Q_1 = 29.0$ and $Q_3 = 32.7$. Returning to equation (4.8),

$$\text{Interquartile range} = 32.7 - 29.0 = 3.7$$

This is the midspread or interquartile range in 1-year percentage total returns achieved by the *middle group* of the 17 domestic general stock funds whose marketing fees are paid from fund assets.

♦ **The Variance and the Standard Deviation** Although the range is a measure of the total spread and the interquartile range is a measure of the middle spread, neither of these measures of variation takes into consideration *how* the observations distribute or cluster. Two commonly used measures of variation that do take into account how all the values in the data are distributed are the *variance* and its square root, the *standard deviation*. These measures evaluate how the values fluctuate about the mean. The sample variance is *roughly* (or *almost*) the average of the squared differences between each of the observations in a set of data and the mean.

Thus, for a sample containing $n$ observations, $X_1, X_2, X_3, \ldots, X_n$, the sample variance (given by the symbol $S^2$) can be written as

$$S^2 = \frac{(X_1 - \overline{X})^2 + (X_2 - \overline{X})^2 + (X_3 - \overline{X})^2 + \cdots + (X_n - \overline{X})^2}{n - 1}$$

Using summation notation, this formula can be expressed as follows:

## Sample Variance

The sample variance is the sum of the squared differences around the arithmetic mean divided by the sample size minus 1.

$$S^2 = \frac{\displaystyle\sum_{i=1}^{n} (X_i - \overline{X})^2}{n - 1} \tag{4.9}$$

where

$\overline{X}$ = sample arithmetic mean

$n$ = sample size

$X_i$ = $i$th observation of the random variable $X$

$\displaystyle\sum_{i=1}^{n} (X_i - \overline{X})^2$ = summation of all the squared differences between the $X_i$ values and $\overline{X}$

Had the denominator been $n$ instead of $n - 1$, the average of the squared differences around the mean would have been obtained. However, $n - 1$ is used here because of certain desirable mathematical properties possessed by the statistic $S^2$ that make it appropriate for statistical inference (which will be discussed in chapter 9). As the sample size increases, the difference between dividing by $n$ or $n - 1$ becomes smaller and smaller.

Now let us turn our attention to the more practical of the two measures, the sample standard deviation. This measure, given by the symbol $S$, is the square root of the sample variance. It is expressed as follows.

## Sample Standard Deviation

The standard deviation is the square root of the sum of the squared differences around the arithmetic mean divided by the sample size minus 1.

$$S = \sqrt{\frac{\displaystyle\sum_{i=1}^{n} (X_i - \overline{X})^2}{n - 1}} \tag{4.10}$$

The steps for computing both the sample variance and the sample standard deviation are presented in Exhibit 4.1.

## Exhibit 4.1  Computing $S^2$ and $S$

To compute $S^2$, the sample variance, complete the following:

✓ **1.** Obtain the difference between each observation and the mean.

✓ **2.** Square each difference.

✓ **3.** Add the squared differences.

✓ **4.** Divide this total by $n - 1$.

To compute $S$, the sample standard deviation, we take the square root of the variance.

Let us now apply these steps to our domestic general stock funds data in Example 4.12.

## Example 4.12  *Computing the Sample Variance and Sample Standard Deviation*

For our sample containing the 17 domestic general stock funds with marketing fees paid from fund assets, the raw data pertaining to achieved 1-year total percentage returns are as follows.

32.2 29.5 29.9 32.4 30.5 30.1 32.1 35.2 10.0 20.6 28.6 30.5 38.0 33.0 29.4 37.1 28.6

The arithmetic mean for this sample is calculated as $\overline{X} = 29.86$. Compute the sample variance $S^2$ and sample standard deviation $S$.

### SOLUTION

Using the four-step procedure, the sample variance $S^2$ is computed on the basis of the following tabular layout:

### 1-year total percentage returns

| DOMESTIC GENERAL STOCK FUND | $X_i$ | $\overline{X}$ | $(X_i - \overline{X})$ | $(X_i - \overline{X})^2$ |
|---|---|---|---|---|
| Amcore Vintage Equity | $X_1 = 32.2$ | 29.86 | +2.34 | 5.4756 |
| Baron Funds Asset | $X_2 = 29.5$ | 29.86 | −0.36 | 0.1296 |
| Berger SmCoGrow | $X_3 = 29.9$ | 29.86 | +0.04 | 0.0016 |
| Chicago Trust GrowInc | $X_4 = 32.4$ | 29.86 | +2.54 | 6.4516 |
| Dodge & Cox DominiSo | $X_5 = 30.5$ | 29.86 | +0.64 | 0.4096 |
| Federated Institut MaxCapSvc | $X_6 = 30.1$ | 29.86 | +0.24 | 0.0576 |
| First Funds GroInc III | $X_7 = 32.1$ | 29.86 | +2.24 | 5.0176 |
| Harris Insight Inst Haven | $X_8 = 35.2$ | 29.86 | +5.34 | 28.5156 |
| Mentor Merger | $X_9 = 10.0$ | 29.86 | −19.86 | 394.4196 |
| Rainler Reich Tang | $X_{10} = 20.6$ | 29.86 | −9.26 | 85.7476 |
| Robertson Stephens ValGrow | $X_{11} = 28.6$ | 29.86 | −1.26 | 1.5876 |

*continued*

## 1-year total percentage returns *(Continued)*

| DOMESTIC GENERAL STOCK FUND | $X_i$ | $\overline{X}$ | $(X_i - \overline{X})$ | $(X_i - \overline{X})^2$ |
|---|---|---|---|---|
| SSgA S&P500Idx | $X_{12} = 30.5$ | 29.86 | +0.64 | 0.4096 |
| SSgA SmallCap | $X_{13} = 38.0$ | 29.86 | +8.14 | 66.2596 |
| 1784 GrowInc | $X_{14} = 33.0$ | 29.86 | +3.14 | 9.8596 |
| Stagecoach CorpStk | $X_{15} = 29.4$ | 29.86 | −0.46 | 0.2116 |
| Westwood Eq R | $X_{16} = 37.1$ | 29.86 | +7.24 | 52.4176 |
| Wright Yacktman | $X_{17} = 28.6$ | 29.86 | −1.26 | 1.5876 |
| Total | | | $0^a$ | 658.5592 |
| | | | $\displaystyle\sum_{i=1}^{n}(X_i - \overline{X})$ | $\displaystyle\sum_{i=1}^{n}(X_i - \overline{X})^2$ |

[a] *Result differs from 0 due to rounding.*

From equation (4.9), the sample variance is

$$
\begin{aligned}
S^2 &= \frac{\displaystyle\sum_{i=1}^{n}(X_i - \overline{X})^2}{n - 1} \\[2mm]
&= \frac{(32.2 - 29.86)^2 + (29.5 - 29.86)^2 + (29.9 - 29.86)^2 + \cdots + (28.6 - 29.86)^2}{17 - 1} \\[2mm]
&= \frac{658.5592}{16} \\[2mm]
&= 41.15995
\end{aligned}
$$

From equation (4.10), the sample standard deviation $S$ is computed as

$$
S = \sqrt{S^2} = \sqrt{\frac{\displaystyle\sum_{i=1}^{n}(X_i - \overline{X})^2}{n - 1}} = \sqrt{41.15995} = 6.42
$$

In making our computations in Example 4.12 we are squaring the differences between each of the observations and the mean; therefore, *neither the variance nor the standard deviation can ever be negative.* The only time $S^2$ and $S$ can be zero is when there is no variation at all in the data—when each observation in the sample is exactly the same. In such an unusual case, the range and interquartile range would also be zero.

But numerical data are inherently variable—not constant. Any random phenomenon of interest that we can think of usually takes on a variety of values. For example, different domestic general stock funds achieve different 1-year rates of return, attain different 3-year annualized rates of return, have different net asset values, and have different expense ratios. It is because numerical data inherently vary that it becomes so important to study not only measures of central tendency that summarize the data but also measures of variation that reflect how the numerical data are dispersed.

The standard deviation helps tell us how a set of data clusters or distributes around its mean. For almost all sets of data, the majority of the observed values lie within an interval of plus and minus one standard deviation above and below the arithmetic mean. This means that the interval between $\overline{X} \pm 1S$ usually captures at least a majority of the data values. Therefore, a knowledge of the arithmetic mean and the standard deviation usually helps define where at least the majority of the data values are clustering.

We should note that the formulas for variance and standard deviation [equations (4.9) and (4.10)] could not use

$$\sum_{i=1}^{n}(X_i - \overline{X})$$

as a numerator because, as you may recall, the mean acts as a *balancing point* for observations larger and smaller than it. Therefore, the sum of the deviations about the mean is always zero;[2] that is,

$$\sum_{i=1}^{n}(X_i - \overline{X}) = 0$$

[2]*See appendix B for the proof.*

To demonstrate this, let us again refer to Example 4.12 on page 146. We see from the tabular layout in the fourth column that the summation of the differences between each value and the mean [that is, $\sum_{i=1}^{n}(X_i - \overline{X})$] is, except for rounding error, equal to zero. The sum of the squared deviations allows us to study the variation in the data. Hence we use

$$\sum_{i=1}^{n}(X_i - \overline{X})^2$$

when computing the variance and standard deviation. In the squaring process, observations that are farther from the mean get more weight than observations closer to the mean.

The respective squared deviations for the 17 domestic general stock funds are displayed in the last column of the tabular layout in Example 4.12 on page 146. We note that the 9th observation, $X_9 = 10.0$ attained by Mentor Merger, is 19.86 lower than the mean performance measure of 29.86 and the 10th observation, $X_{10} = 20.6$ attained by Rainler Reich Tang, is 9.26 lower. In the squaring process, both these values, along with the 13th and 16th observations (SSgA SmallCap and Westwood Eq R), contribute substantially more to the calculation of $S^2$ and $S$ than do the other observations in the sample, which are much closer to the mean. Therefore, we may generalize as in Exhibit 4.2.

---

### Exhibit 4.2  *Understanding Variation in Data*

✓ **1.** The more spread out, or dispersed, the data are, the larger will be the range, the interquartile range, the variance, and the standard deviation.

✓ **2.** The more concentrated, or *homogeneous*, the data are, the smaller will be the range, the interquartile range, the variance, and the standard deviation.

✓ **3.** If the observations are all the same (so that there is no variation in the data), the range, interquartile range, variance, and standard deviation will all be zero.

✓ **4.** *None* of the measures of variation (the range, interquartile range, standard deviation, variance) can *ever* be negative.

---

◆ *The Coefficient of Variation*  Unlike the previous measures we have studied, the **coefficient of variation** is a *relative measure* of variation. It is always expressed as a percentage rather than in terms of the units of the particular data.

The coefficient of variation, denoted by the symbol $CV$, measures the scatter in the data relative to the mean. It may be computed as follows:

### Coefficient of Variation

The coefficient of variation is equal to the standard deviation divided by the arithmetic mean, multiplied by 100%.

$$CV = \left( \frac{S}{\overline{X}} \right) 100\% \tag{4.11}$$

where

$S$ = standard deviation in a set of numerical data

$\overline{X}$ = arithmetic mean in a set of numerical data

---

## Example 4.13  *Computing the Coefficient of Variation*

For our sample containing the 17 domestic general stock funds with marketing fees paid from fund assets, the raw data pertaining to achieved 1-year total returns (in percents) are

32.2 29.5 29.9 32.4 30.5 30.1 32.1 35.2 10.0 20.6 28.6 30.5 38.0 33.0 29.4 37.1 28.6

Compute the coefficient of variation.

## SOLUTION

From these data, the mean 1-year total percentage return $\bar{X}$ is 29.86 and the standard deviation $S$ is 6.42. Using equation (4.11), the coefficient of variation is

$$CV = \left(\frac{S}{\bar{X}}\right)100\% = \left(\frac{6.42}{29.86}\right)100\% = 21.5\%$$

For this sample, the relative size of the "average spread around the mean" to the mean is 21.5%.

As a relative measure, the coefficient of variation is particularly useful when comparing the variability of two or more data sets that are expressed in different units of measurement. This is demonstrated in Example 4.14.

## Example 4.14  *Comparing Two Coefficients of Variation*

Suppose that the operations manager of a package delivery service is contemplating the purchase of a new fleet of trucks. When packages are efficiently stored in the trucks in preparation for delivery, there are two major constraints that have to be considered—the weight (in pounds) and the volume (in cubic feet) for each item.

Now suppose that in a sample of 200 packages the average weight is 26.0 pounds with a standard deviation of 3.9 pounds. In addition, suppose that the average volume for each of these packages is 8.8 cubic feet with a standard deviation of 2.2 cubic feet. How can we compare the variation of the weight and the volume?

## SOLUTION

Because the units of measurement differ for the weight and volume constraints, to compare the fluctuations in these measurements it would be appropriate for the operations manager to consider the relative variability in the two types of measurements. For weight, the coefficient of variation is $CV_W = (3.9/26.0)100\% = 15.0\%$; for volume, the coefficient of variation is $CV_V = (2.2/8.8)100\% = 25.0\%$. Thus, relative to the mean, the volume of a package is much more variable than the weight of the package.

The coefficient of variation is also very useful when comparing two or more sets of data that are measured in the same units but differ to such an extent that a direct comparison of the respective standard deviations is not very helpful. This is illustrated in Example 4.15.

## Example 4.15  *Comparing Two Coefficients of Variation*

Suppose that a potential investor is considering purchasing shares of stock in one of two companies, A or B, that are listed on the American Stock Exchange. If neither company offers dividends to its stockholders and if both companies are rated equally high (by various investment services) in terms of potential growth, the potential investor might want to consider the volatility (*variability*) of the two stocks to aid in the investment decision.

Now suppose that each share of stock in company A has averaged $50 over the past few months with a standard deviation of $10. In addition, suppose that in this same time period, the price per share for company B stock averaged $12 with a standard deviation of $4. How can the investor determine which stock is more variable?

### SOLUTION

In terms of the actual standard deviations, the price of company A shares seems to be more volatile than that of company B shares. However, since the average prices per share for the two stocks are so different, it would be more appropriate for the potential investor to consider the variability in price relative to the average price in order to examine the volatility/stability of the two stocks.

For company A, the coefficient of variation is $CV_A =$ ($10/$50)100% = 20.0%; for company B, the coefficient of variation is $CV_B =$ ($4/$12)100% = 33.3%. Thus, relative to the mean, the price of stock B is much more variable than the price of stock A.

## Shape

A third important property of a set of data is its **shape**—the manner in which the data are distributed. Either the distribution of the data is **symmetrical** or it is not. If the distribution of data is not symmetrical, it is called asymmetrical, or **skewed**.

To describe the shape, we need only compare the mean and the median. If these two measures are equal, we may generally consider the data to be symmetrical (or zero-skewed). On the other hand, if the mean exceeds the median, the data may generally be described as *positive,* or **right-skewed**. If the mean is exceeded by the median, those data can generally be called *negative,* or **left-skewed**. That is,

> mean > median: positive, or right-skewness
>
> mean = median: symmetry, or zero-skewness
>
> mean < median: negative, or left-skewness

Positive skewness arises when the mean is increased by some unusually high values; negative skewness occurs when the mean is reduced by some extremely low values. Data are symmetrical when there are no really extreme values in a particular direction so that low and high values balance each other out.

Figure 4.6 on page 152 depicts the shapes of three data sets. The data in panel A are negative or left-skewed. In this panel we observe a long tail and distortion to the left that is caused by extremely small values. These extremely small values pull the mean downward so that the mean is less than the median.

The data in panel B are symmetrical since each half of the curve is a mirror image of the other half of the curve. The low and high values on the scale balance, and the mean equals the median. The data in panel C are positive or right-skewed. In this panel we observe a long tail on the right of the distribution and a distortion to the right that is caused by extremely large values. These extremely large values pull the mean upward so that the mean is greater than the median. How a data set's shape is determined is discussed in our next example.

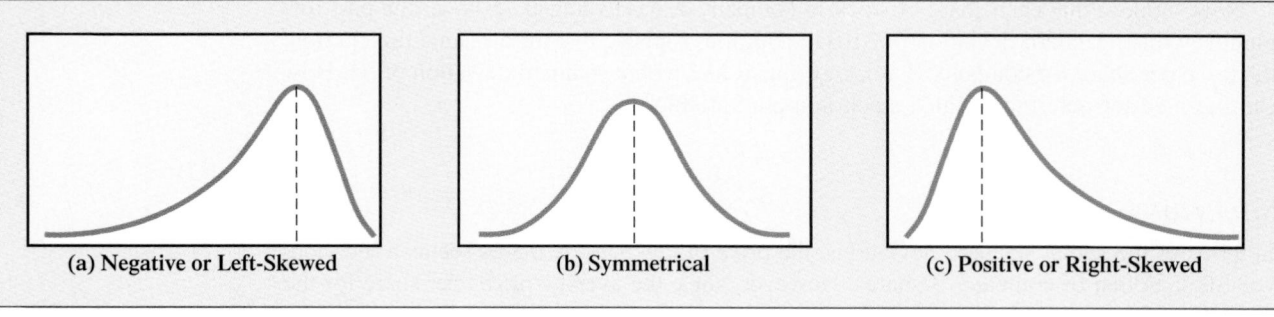

| (a) Negative or Left-Skewed | (b) Symmetrical | (c) Positive or Right-Skewed |

**FIGURE 4.6**    A comparison of three data sets differing in shape

**Example 4.16**  *Determining the Shape of the Data Set*

For our sample containing the 17 domestic general stock funds with marketing fees paid from fund assets, the raw data pertaining to achieved 1-year total percentage returns are

32.2  29.5  29.9  32.4  30.5  30.1  32.1  35.2  10.0  20.6  28.6  30.5  38.0  33.0  29.4  37.1  28.6

and the data are displayed along the dot scale in Figure 4.1 on page 134. What can be said about the shape of this data set?

*SOLUTION*

Note that there is one outlier in this data set and that the 17 observations do not cluster symmetrically around their arithmetic mean. The 1-year total percentage return of 10.0 attained by Mentor Merger is greatly exceeded by that achieved by all other domestic general stock funds in this sample. In Example 4.1 on page 133 the mean was computed to be 29.86. In Example 4.3 on page 136 the median was computed to be 30.5. Therefore, since the mean is exceeded by the median, this data set may be described as negative, or left-skewed.

## Interpreting Microsoft Excel and Minitab Descriptive Statistics Output

Now that we have discussed the characteristics of central tendency, variation, and shape, we can examine descriptive statistics output of achieved 1-year total percentage returns that has been obtained for the sample of 17 domestic general stock funds using Microsoft Excel and also using Minitab.

◆ *Microsoft Excel Output*  Figure 4.7 represents output obtained from the Descriptive Statistics option of the Data Analysis tool of Microsoft Excel. We note that Excel has provided the (arithmetic) mean, median, mode, standard deviation, variance, range, minimum, maximum, and count (sample size), all of which have been discussed in this section. In addition, Excel has computed the Standard Error, along with statistics for Kurtosis and Skewness and what it calls Confidence Level (95.0%). The *standard error* is the standard deviation divided by the square root of the sample size and will be discussed in chapter 9.

| | A | B |
|---|---|---|
| 1 | | *1Yr$Ret* |
| 2 | | |
| 3 | **Mean** | 29.86470588 |
| 4 | Standard Error | 1.556011615 |
| 5 | **Median** | 30.5 |
| 6 | **Mode** | 30.5 |
| 7 | **Standard Deviation** | 6.415600242 |
| 8 | **Sample Variance** | 41.15992647 |
| 9 | Kurtosis | 5.546604844 |
| 10 | Skewness | -2.011159015 |
| 11 | **Range** | 28 |
| 12 | **Minimum** | 10 |
| 13 | **Maximum** | 38 |
| 14 | Sum | 507.7 |
| 15 | **Count** | 17 |
| 16 | Largest(1) | 38 |
| 17 | Smallest(1) | 10 |
| 18 | Confidence Level(95.0%) | 3.298596523 |

**FIGURE 4.7** Descriptive statistics of achieved 1-year total percentage returns from sample of 17 domestic general stock funds using Microsoft Excel

*Skewness* is a measure of lack of symmetry in the data and is based on a statistic that is a function of the *cubed* differences around the arithmetic mean. *Kurtosis* is a measure of the relative concentration of values in the center of the distribution as compared with the tails and is based on the differences around the arithmetic mean raised to the fourth power. This measure is not discussed in this text (see reference 4). *Confidence intervals* will be discussed in chapter 10. What is actually provided in this output next to the label Confidence Level (95.0%) is a multiple of the standard error.

◆ *Minitab Output* Figure 4.8 on page 154 represents descriptive statistics output obtained from Minitab of the 1-year total percentage returns for the domestic general stock funds classified according to fee schedule. The five fee schedule classifications are, respectively, fees paid from fund assets, deferred fees, front-load fees, multiple fees, and no-load funds. We may observe that for each of these five fee schedule classifications, Minitab has computed the sample size *n*, (arithmetic) mean, median, standard deviation (labeled StDev), minimum, maximum, and first and third quartiles, all of which have been discussed in this section. In addition, Minitab has computed the *trimmed mean* (labeled as TrMean), which trims possible outliers by removing the smallest and largest 5% of the observations and averaging the remaining values. In addition, Minitab computes the *standard error of the mean* (labeled SE Mean), which is equal to the standard deviation divided by the square root of the sample size. This will be discussed in chapter 9.

From Figure 4.8 there appears to be very little difference in the mean, median, first quartile, and third quartile 1-year total percentage return for the various types of fee structures, with the exception of the mean for the fees paid by fund assets. The standard deviation of the funds whose fees are deferred is substantially less than those of the other groups.

## Descriptive Statistics

| Variable | Group | N | Mean | Median | TrMean | StDev |
|---|---|---|---|---|---|---|
| 1Yr%Ret | 1 | 17 | 29.86 | 30.50 | 30.65 | 6.42 |
| | 2 | 5 | 31.22 | 30.40 | 31.22 | 2.42 |
| | 3 | 19 | 32.48 | 30.50 | 32.08 | 5.97 |
| | 4 | 46 | 32.035 | 31.400 | 31.929 | 6.445 |
| | 5 | 107 | 31.111 | 30.500 | 30.934 | 5.065 |

| Variable | Group | SE Mean | Minimum | Maximum | Q1 | Q3 |
|---|---|---|---|---|---|---|
| 1Yr%Ret | 1 | 1.56 | 10.00 | 38.00 | 29.00 | 32.70 |
| | 2 | 1.08 | 29.60 | 35.50 | 29.85 | 33.00 |
| | 3 | 1.37 | 23.80 | 48.00 | 28.70 | 34.70 |
| | 4 | 0.950 | 19.200 | 46.600 | 27.875 | 34.625 |
| | 5 | 0.490 | 17.700 | 48.600 | 28.800 | 32.900 |

FIGURE 4.8 Descriptive statistics of achieved 1-year total returns (in percents) for domestic general stock funds classified according to fee schedule using Minitab

## Problems for Section 4.2

### Learning the Basics

**4.1** Given the following set of data from a sample of size $n = 5$:

7   4   9   8   2

(a) Compute the mean, median, mode, midrange, and midhinge.
(b) Compute the range, interquartile range, variance, standard deviation, and coefficient of variation.
(c) Describe the shape.

• **4.2** Given the following set of data from a sample of size $n = 6$:

7   4   9   7   3   12

(a) Compute the mean, median, mode, midrange, and midhinge.
(b) Compute the range, interquartile range, variance, standard deviation, and coefficient of variation.
(c) Describe the shape.

• **4.3** Given the following set of data from a sample of size $n = 7$:

12   7   4   9   0   7   3

(a) Compute the mean, median, mode, midrange, and midhinge.
(b) Compute the range, interquartile range, variance, standard deviation, and coefficient of variation.
(c) Describe the shape.

**4.4** Given the following set of data from a sample of size $n = 5$:

7   −5   −8   7   9

(a) Compute the mean, median, mode, midrange, and midhinge.
(b) Compute the range, interquartile range, variance, standard deviation, and coefficient of variation.
(c) Describe the shape.

**4.5** Given the following set of data from a sample of size $n = 7$:

   3   3   3   3   3   3   3

(a) Compute the mean, median, mode, midrange, and midhinge.
(b) Compute the range, interquartile range, variance, standard deviation, and coefficient of variation.
(c) What is unusual about this set of data?

● **4.6** Given the following two sets of data—each with samples of size $n = 7$:

   Set 1:   10   2   3   2   4   2   5
   Set 2:   20   12   13   12   14   12   15

(a) For each set, compute the mean, median, mode, midrange, and midhinge.
(b) Compare your results and summarize your findings.
(c) Compare the first sampled item in each set, compare the second sampled item in each set, and so on. Briefly describe your findings here in light of your summary in part (b).
(d) For each set, compute the range, interquartile range, variance, standard deviation, and coefficient of variation.
(e) Describe the shape.
(f) Compare your results in (d) and (e) and discuss your findings.
(g) On the basis of your answers to (a)–(f) above, what can you generalize about the properties of central tendency, variation, and shape?

## Applying the Concepts

**4.7** The operations manager of a plant that manufactures tires wishes to compare the actual inner diameter of two grades of tires, each of which is expected to be 575 millimeters. A sample of five tires of each grade was selected, and the results representing the inner diameters of the tires, ordered from smallest to largest, were as follows:

   Grade X                 Grade Y
568 570 575 578 584    573 574 575 577 578

(a) For each of the two grades of tires, compute the
    (1) arithmetic mean    (2) median    (3) standard deviation
(b) Which grade of tire is providing better quality? Explain.
(c) What would be the effect on your answers in (a) and (b) if the last value for grade Y was 588 instead of 578? Explain.

**4.8** Suppose that owing to an error, a data set containing the price-to-earnings (PE) ratios from nine companies traded on the American Stock Exchange was recorded as 13, 15, 14, 17, 13, 16, 15, 16, and 61, where the last value should have been 16 instead of 61.

(a) Show how much the mean, median, and midrange are affected by the error (i.e., compute these statistics for the "bad" and "good" data sets, and compare the results of using different estimators of central tendency).
(b) Compute the range, interquartile range, variance, standard deviation, and coefficient of variation for the data set with the error (61) and then recompute these statistics after the PE ratio is corrected to 16.
(c) Discuss the differences in your findings in (b) for each measure of variation.
(d) Which measure in (b) seems to be affected most by the error?
(e) How would you describe the shape of the data set with and without the error?

● **4.9** A manufacturer of flashlight batteries took a sample of 13 batteries from a day's production and used them continuously until they were drained. The numbers of hours they were used until failure were

   342, 426, 317, 545, 264, 451, 1049, 631, 512, 266, 492, 562, 298

**DATA FILE**
FLASHBAT

(a) Compute the mean, median, mode, midrange, and midhinge. Looking at the distribution of times to failure, which measures of location do you think are best and which worst? (And why?)

(b) In what ways would this information be useful to the manufacturer? Discuss.

(c) Calculate the range, variance, and standard deviation.

(d) For many sets of data the range is about six times the standard deviation. Is this true here? (If not, why do you think it is not?)

(e) Using the information above, what would you advise if the manufacturer wanted to be able to say in advertisements that these batteries "should last 400 hours"? (*Note*: There is no right answer to this question; the point is to consider how to make such a statement precise.)

(f) Suppose that the first value was 1,342 instead of 342. Repeat (a), using this value. Comment on the difference in the results.

(g) Do (c)–(e) with the first value equal to 1,342 instead of 342. Comment on the difference in the results.

(h) How would you describe the shape of the data set if the first value were 342?

(i) How would you describe the shape of the data set if the first value were 1,342?

**4.10** The following data are the monthly rental prices for a sample of 10 unfurnished studio apartments in the center of a large city and a sample of 10 unfurnished studio apartments in an outlying part of the city:

**DATA FILE**
STUDIO

Center City
$955 $1,000 $985 $980 $940 $975 $965 $999 $1,247 $1,119
Outlying Area
$750    $775 $725 $705 $694 $725 $690 $745    $575    $800

(a) For each set of data, compute the mean, median, midhinge, range, interquartile range, standard deviation, and coefficient of variation.

(b) What can be said about unfurnished studio apartments renting in the center city versus those renting in an outlying area? Compare and contrast the rents in these two areas.

• **4.11** A bank branch located in a commercial district of a city has developed an improved process for serving customers during the 12:00 P.M. to 1 P.M. peak lunch period. The waiting time in minutes (operationally defined as the time the customer enters the line until he or she is served) of all customers during this hour is recorded over a period of 1 week. A random sample of 15 customers is selected and the results are as follows:

**DATA FILE**
BANK1

4.21 5.55 3.02 5.13 4.77 2.34 3.54 3.20 4.50 6.10 0.38 5.12 6.46 6.19 3.79

(a) Compute the
    (1) arithmetic mean
    (2) median
    (3) midrange
    (4) first quartile
    (5) third quartile
    (6) midhinge

    (7) range
    (8) interquartile range
    (9) variance
    (10) standard deviation
    (11) coefficient of variation

(b) Are the data skewed? If so, how?

(c) As a customer walks into the branch office during the lunch hour, she asks the branch manager how long she can expect to wait. The branch manager replies, "Almost certainly not longer than five minutes." On the basis of the results of (a), evaluate this statement.

(d) Suppose that the branch manager would like to guarantee a certain level of service during the peak lunch hour period. Failure to obtain service within a specified time would result in a small monetary payment or gift to the customer. What waiting time do you think should be used as a cutoff above which this small payment or gift would be provided? Explain your answer.

**4.12** Suppose that another branch located in a residential area is most concerned with the Friday evening hours from 5 P.M. to 7 P.M. The waiting time in minutes (operationally defined as the time the customer enters the line until he or she is served) of all customers during these hours is recorded over a period of 1 week. A random sample of 15 customers is selected and the results are as follows:

DATA FILE
BANK2

9.66  5.90  8.02  5.79  8.73  3.82  8.01  8.35  10.49  6.68  5.64  4.08  6.17  9.91  5.47

(a) Compute the
  (1) arithmetic mean
  (2) median
  (3) midrange
  (4) first quartile
  (5) third quartile
  (6) midhinge
  (7) range
  (8) interquartile range
  (9) variance
  (10) standard deviation
  (11) coefficient of variation

(b) Are the data skewed? If so, how?

(c) As a customer walks into the branch office during the Friday evening hours, he asks the branch manager how long he can expect to wait. The branch manager replies, "Almost certainly not longer than five minutes." On the basis of the results of (a), evaluate this statement.

(d) Suppose that the branch manager would like to guarantee a certain level of service during the Friday evening hours. Failure to obtain service within a specified time would result in a small monetary payment or gift to the customer. What waiting time do you think should be used as a cutoff above which this small payment or gift would be provided? Explain your answer.

(e) What arguments can be raised that would make it inappropriate to compare the waiting times in Problem 4.11 with those in this problem?

**4.13** For the last 10 days in June, the "Shore Special" train arrived late at its destination by the times (in minutes) listed here. (A negative number means that the train was early by that number of minutes.)

DATA FILE
TRAIN1

−3, 6, 4, 10, −4, 124, 2, −1, 4, 1

(a) If you were hired by the railroad to show that the railroad is providing good service, what are some of the summary measures pertaining to central tendency that you would use to accomplish this?

(b) If you were hired by a TV station that was producing a documentary to show that the railroad is providing bad service, what summary measures pertaining to central tendency would you use?

(c) If you were trying to be objective and unbiased in assessing the railroad's performance, which summary measures pertaining to central tendency would you use? (This is the hardest part, because you cannot answer without making additional assumptions about the relative costs of being late by various amounts of time.)

(d) Compute the range, interquartile range, variance, standard deviation, and coefficient of variation for "lateness" (in minutes).

(e) Discuss the property of variation for these data.

(f) What would be the effect on your conclusions in (a)–(e) if the value of 124 had been incorrectly recorded and should have been 12?

(g) Describe the shape of the data shown above.

(h) Describe the shape of the data if the value 124 is replaced by 12.

**4.14** In order to estimate how much water will be needed to supply the community of Falling Rock in the next decade, the town council asked the city manager to find out how much water a sample of families currently uses. The sample of 15 families used the following number of gallons (in thousands) in the past year as shown at the top of page 158:

11.2, 21.5, 16.4, 19.7, 14.6, 16.9, 32.2, 18.2, 13.1, 23.8, 18.3, 15.5, 18.8, 22.7, 14.0

(a) What is the mean amount of water used per family? The median? The midrange? The midhinge?

(b) Suppose the town council expects that 10 years from now, there will be 4,500 families living in Falling Rock. How many gallons of water will be needed annually if the rate of consumption per family stays the same?

(c) In what ways would the information provided in (a) and (b) be useful to the town council? Discuss.

(d) Why might the town council have used the data from a survey rather than just measuring the total consumption in the town? (Think about what types of users are not yet included in the estimation process.)

(e) Compute the range, interquartile range, variance, standard deviation, and coefficient of variation in water consumption.

(f) Discuss the property of variation for these data.

(g) Describe the shape.

## 4.3  EXPLORATORY DATA ANALYSIS

Now that we have studied the three major properties of numerical data (central tendency, variation, and shape), it is important that we identify and describe the major features of the data in a summarized format. One approach to such an "exploratory data analysis" is to develop a *five-number summary* and to construct a *box-and-whisker plot* (references 6 and 7).

### The Five-Number Summary

A **five-number summary** consists of

$$X_{smallest} \quad Q_1 \quad Median \quad Q_3 \quad X_{largest}$$

From the five-number summary we can obtain three measures of central tendency (the median, midhinge, and midrange) and two measures of variation (the interquartile range and range) to provide us with a better idea as to the shape of the distribution.

If the data are perfectly symmetrical, the relationship among the various measures of location can be expressed as in Exhibit 4.3.

**Exhibit 4.3   Using the Five-Number Summary to Recognize Symmetry in Data**

✓ **1.** The distance from $Q_1$ to the median equals the distance from the median to $Q_3$.

✓ **2.** The distance from $X_{smallest}$ to $Q_1$ equals the distance from $Q_3$ to $X_{largest}$.

✓ **3.** The median, the midhinge, and the midrange are all equal. (These measures also equal the mean in the data.)

On the other hand, for nonsymmetrical distributions the relationship among the various measures of location can be expressed as in Exhibit 4.4.

We determine the five-number summary in Example 4.17.

## Example 4.17    *Determining the Five-Number Summary*

For our sample representing the 1-year total percentage returns achieved by the 17 domestic general stock funds whose marketing fees are paid from fund assets, the ordered array is

10.0 20.6 28.6 28.6 29.4 29.5 29.9 30.1 30.5 30.5 32.1 32.2 32.4 33.0 35.2 37.1 38.0

State the five-number summary for these data.

### SOLUTION

In Example 4.3 on page 136 the median was computed to be 30.5. In Example 4.8 on page 140 the first quartile was computed to be 29.0 and the third quartile 32.7. Therefore, the five-number summary is

    10.0    29.0    30.5    32.7    38.0

We may now use the five-number summary to study the shape of this distribution. From the guidelines presented in Exhibits 4.3 and 4.4 it is clear that the 1-year total returns data for our sample are left-skewed because the distance from $X_{smallest}$ to $Q_1$ (that is, 19.0) greatly exceeds the distance from $Q_3$ to $X_{largest}$ (that is, 5.3). Also, if we compare the median (30.5), the midhinge (30.85), and the midrange (24.0), we observe that the midrange is distorted by the outlier 10.0 and is by far the smallest of these summary measures. The midhinge and the median, which are resistant to outliers, are very close in value.

## Box-and-Whisker Plot

In its simplest form, a **box-and-whisker plot** provides a graphical representation of the data through its five-number summary. The box-and-whisker plot is depicted in Figure 4.9 for the 1-year total returns achieved by the sample of 17 domestic general stock funds whose marketing fees are paid from fund assets.

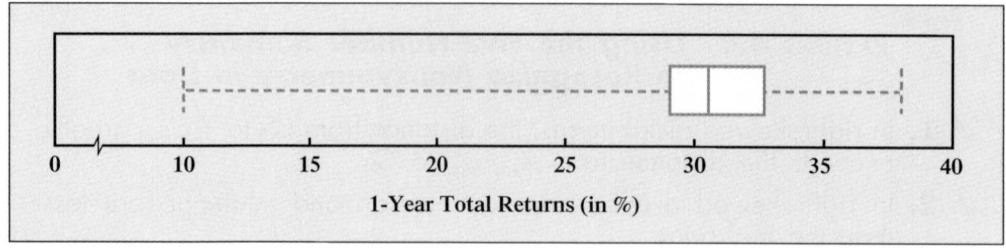

**FIGURE 4.9**  Box-and-whisker plot representing the 1-year total percentage returns achieved by 17 domestic general stock funds whose marketing fees are paid from fund assets

The vertical line drawn within the box represents the location of the median value in the data. Note further that the vertical line at the left side of the box represents the location of $Q_1$ and the vertical line at the right side of the box represents the location of $Q_3$. Therefore, we see that the box contains the middle 50% of the observations in the distribution. The lower 25% of the data are represented by a dashed line (i.e., a *whisker*) connecting the left side of the box to the location of the smallest value, $X_{smallest}$. Similarly, the upper 25% of the data are represented by a dashed line connecting the right side of the box to $X_{largest}$.

> **COMMENT:  *Interpreting the Box-and-Whisker Plot***
>
> The visual representation of the 1-year total returns depicted in Figure 4.9 indicates that the shape of this data set is left-skewed. Although we observe that the vertical median line is unexpectedly closer to the left side of the box, we also see that the left-side whisker length is clearly much larger than the right-side whisker length. This has occurred here because the 1-year total percentage return of 10.0 attained by Mentor Merger is an outlier.

To summarize what we have learned about graphical representation of our data, Figure 4.10 demonstrates the relationship between exploratory data analysis methods such as the box-and-whisker plot and graphical displays such as polygons. Four different types of distributions are depicted with their box-and-whisker plots and corresponding polygons.

When a data set is perfectly symmetrical, as is the case in Figure 4.10(a) and (d), the mean, median, midrange, and midhinge will be the same. In addition, the length of the left whisker will equal the length of the right whisker, and the median line will divide the box in half. In practice, it is unlikely that we will observe a data set that is perfectly symmetrical. However, we should be able to state that our data set is approximately symmetrical if the lengths of the two whiskers are almost equal and the median line almost divides the box in half.

On the other hand, when our data set is left-skewed as in Figure 4.10(b), the few small observations distort the midrange and mean toward the left tail. In such cases, it would be expected that we have the following sequence among the five measures of central tendency:

$$midrange < mean < midhinge < median < mode$$

For this hypothetical left-skewed distribution, we observe from Figure 4.10(b) that the skewed (i.e., distorted) nature of the data set indicates that there is a heavy clustering of observations at the high end of the scale (i.e., the right side); 75% of all data values are found between the left edge of the box ($Q_1$) and the end of the right whisker ($X_{largest}$).

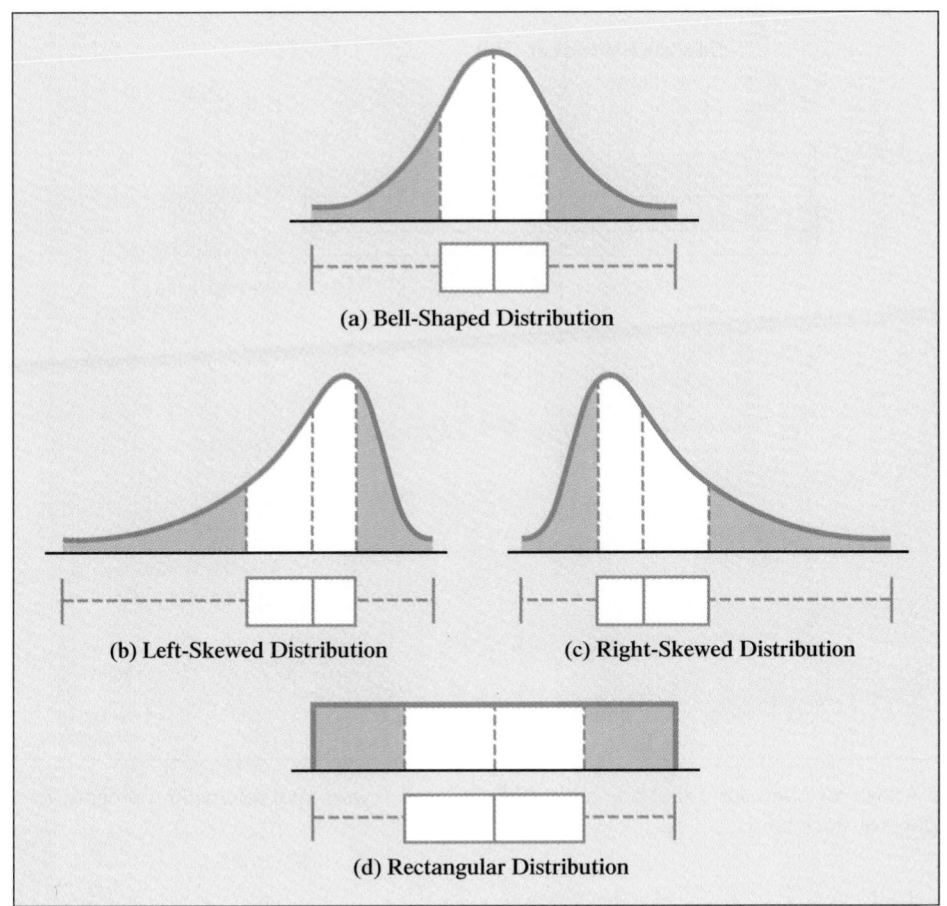

FIGURE **4.10**

Four hypothetical distributions examined through their box-and-whisker plots and their corresponding polygons.

*Note: Area under each polygon is split into quartiles corresponding to the five-number summary for the respective box-and-whisker plot*

(a) Bell-Shaped Distribution

(b) Left-Skewed Distribution

(c) Right-Skewed Distribution

(d) Rectangular Distribution

Therefore, the long left whisker contains the distribution of only the smallest 25% of the observations, demonstrating the distortion from symmetry in this data set.

If the data set is right-skewed as in Figure 4.10(c), the few large observations distort the midrange and mean toward the right tail. In such cases, it would be expected that we have the following sequence among the five measures of central tendency:

$$\text{mode} < \text{median} < \text{midhinge} < \text{mean} < \text{midrange}$$

For the right-skewed data set in Figure 4.10(c), the concentration of data points will be on the low end of the scale (i.e., the left side of the box-and-whisker plot). Here, 75% of all data values are found between the beginning of the left whisker ($X_{smallest}$) and the right edge of the box ($Q_3$), and the remaining 25% of the observations are dispersed along the long right whisker at the upper end of the scale.

Instead of depicting the box-and-whisker plot horizontally from left (low) to right (high), as in Figures 4.9 and 4.10, output from several spreadsheet and statistical packages, including Microsoft Excel and Minitab, display the box-and-whisker plot vertically from bottom (low) to top (high). Figure 4.11 demonstrates the box-and-whisker plot for the 1-year total percentage returns achieved by our 17 domestic general stock funds using the PHStat Add-In for Microsoft Excel. We observe that Microsoft Excel has plotted a vertical box-and-whisker plot, rather than the horizontal plot of Figure 4.9. Figure 4.11 provides a line that connects the minimum and maximum values which are shown with a short dash.

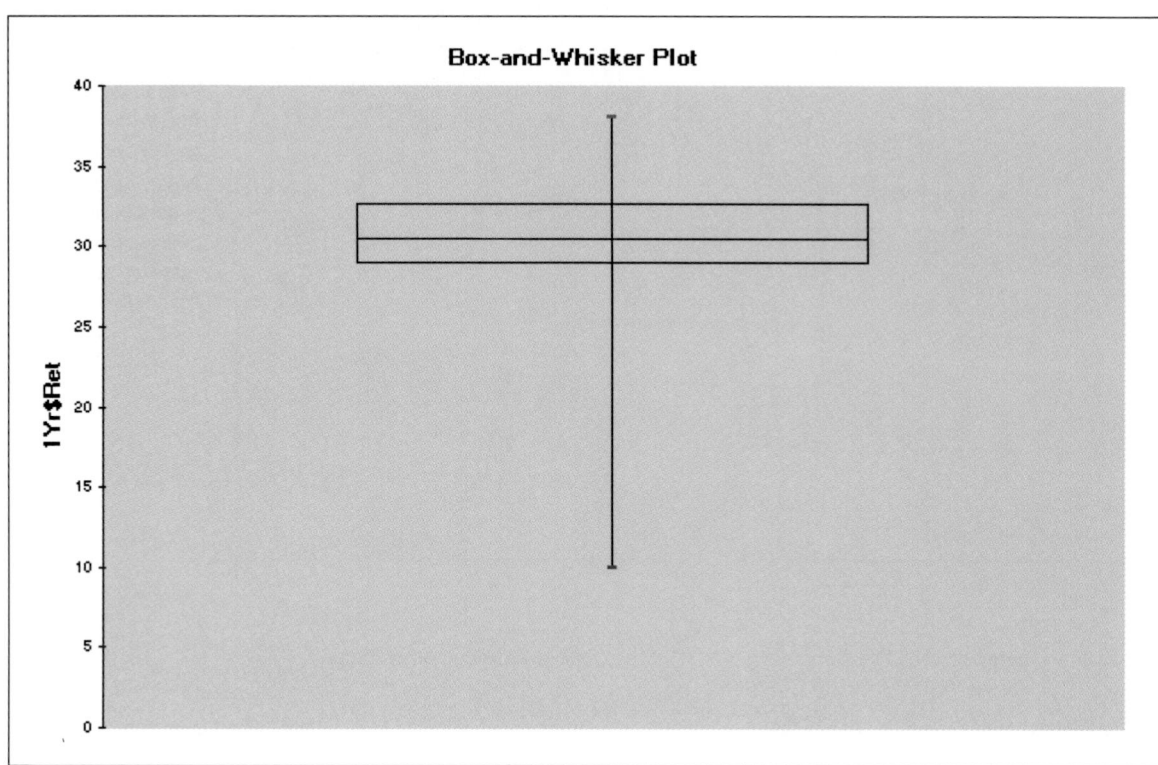

**FIGURE 4.11** PHStat Add-In for Microsoft Excel box-and-whisker plot of 1-year total returns (in percents) for 17 sampled domestic general stock funds

Figure 4.12 on page 163 represents the side-by-side box-and-whisker plot of the 1-year percentage returns classified by fee payment schedule using Minitab. This side-by-side plot is especially valuable in providing us with a comparison of several groups. We note that although the medians of the five fee payment groups appear to be similar, there are some differences in the first and third quartiles and substantial differences in the extreme values. In addition, it seems clear that the groups differ in both their variability as measured by the range and interquartile range and in their shape. Note that the asterisk (*) in the fee schedule groups 1 (fees from fund assets), 3 (front-load fees), 4 (multiple fees), and 5 (no-load funds) indicate the presence of outlier values.

## Problems for Section 4.3

### Learning the Basics

**4.15** Given the following set of data from a sample of size $n = 5$:

　　7　　4　　9　　8　　2

(a) List the five-number summary.
(b) Form the box-and-whisker plot and describe the shape.
(c) Compare your answer in (b) with that from Problem 4.1(c) on page 154. Discuss.

● **4.16** Given the following set of data from a sample of size $n = 6$:

　　7　　4　　9　　7　　3　　12

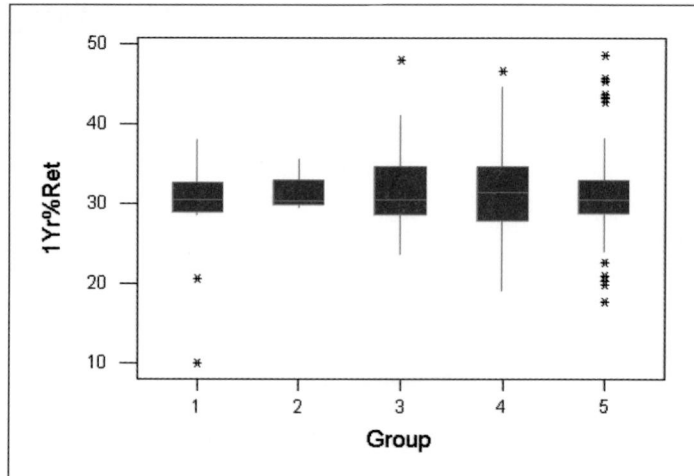

**FIGURE 4.12**
Side-by-side box-and-whisker plots of achieved 1-year total returns (in percents) for the domestic general stock funds classified according to fee schedule using Minitab

(a) List the five-number summary.
(b) Form the box-and-whisker plot and describe the shape.
(c) Compare your answer in (b) with that from Problem 4.2(c) on page 154. Discuss.

**4.17** Given the following set of data from a sample of size $n = 7$:

   12    7    4    9    0    7    3

(a) List the five-number summary.
(b) Form the box-and-whisker plot and describe the shape.
(c) Compare your answer in (b) with that from Problem 4.3(c) on page 154. Discuss.

**4.18** Given the following set of data from a sample of size $n = 5$:

   7    −5    −8    7    9

(a) List the five-number summary.
(b) Form the box-and-whisker plot and describe the shape.
(c) Compare your answer in (b) with that from Problem 4.4(c) on page 154. Discuss.

**4.19** Given the following set of data from a sample of size $n = 7$:

   3    3    3    3    3    3    3

(a) List the five-number summary.
(b) Why can't you form the box-and-whisker plot here?

## Applying the Concepts

**4.20** A manufacturer of flashlight batteries took a sample of 13 batteries from a day's production and used them continuously until they were drained. The numbers of hours they were used until failure were

   342, 426, 317, 545, 264, 451, 1049, 631, 512, 266, 492, 562, 298

**DATA FILE**
FLASHBAT

(a) List the five-number summary.
(b) Form the box-and-whisker plot and describe the shape.
(c) Compare your answer in (b) with that from Problem 4.9(h) on page 156. Discuss.

**4.21** The data at the top of page 164 are the annual percentage yields on money market accounts from a sample of 15 commercial banks in the New York metropolitan area as of February 12, 1997, the day before the Dow Jones Industrial Average passed 7,000 for the first time:

| Bank Name | MM Acct. Yield | Bank Name | MM Acct. Yield |
|---|---|---|---|
| Banco Popular | 3.10 | Fleet Bank | 2.28 |
| Bank of N.Y. | 2.63 | Key Bank of N.Y. | 3.01 |
| Bank of Tokyo-Mitsubishi | 3.05 | Marine Midland | 2.73 |
| Chase Manhattan | 2.79 | North Fork Bank | 2.53 |
| Citibank | 3.25 | PNC Bank (N.J.) | 2.00 |
| CoreStates NJ National Bank | 1.90 | Republic National | 3.05 |
| EAB | 2.79 | Summit Bank | 2.02 |
| First Union | 2.90 | | |

**DATA FILE
MONEYMKT**

(a) List the five-number summary.
(b) Form the box-and-whisker plot and describe the shape.
(c) If someone said to you, "Money market rates don't vary much from bank to bank," on the basis of these data, what would you say?

**4.22** The following data are the monthly rental prices for a sample of 10 unfurnished studio apartments in the center of a large city and a sample of 10 unfurnished studio apartments in an outlying part of the city:

**DATA FILE
STUDIO**

Center City
$955  $1,000  $985  $980  $940  $975  $965  $999  $1,247  $1,119
Outlying Area
$750    $775  $725  $705  $694  $725  $690  $745    $575    $800

For each of the two areas,
(a) List the five-number summary.
(b) Form the box-and-whisker plot and describe the shape.
(c) Does the distribution of the rents in the two areas appear to be similar? Explain.

**4.23** For the last 10 days in June, the "Shore Special" train arrived late at its destination by the times (in minutes) listed here. (A negative number means that the train was early by that number of minutes.)

**DATA FILE
TRAIN1**

$-3, 6, 4, 10, -4, 124, 2, -1, 4, 1$

(a) List the five-number summary.
(b) Form the box-and-whisker plot and describe the shape.
(c) Compare your answer in (b) with that from Problem 4.13(g) on page 157. Discuss.

**4.24** In order to estimate how much water will be needed to supply the community of Falling Rock in the next decade, the town council asked the city manager to find out how much water a sample of families currently uses. The sample of 15 families used the following number of gallons (in thousands) in the past year:

**DATA FILE
WATER**

11.2, 21.5, 16.4, 19.7, 14.6, 16.9, 32.2, 18.2, 13.1, 23.8, 18.3, 15.5, 18.8, 22.7, 14.0

(a) List the five-number summary.
(b) Form the box-and-whisker plot and describe the shape.
(c) Compare your answer in (b) with that from Problem 4.14(g) on page 158. Discuss.

## 4.4  OBTAINING DESCRIPTIVE SUMMARY MEASURES FROM A POPULATION

In section 4.2 we examined various *statistics* that summarize or describe numerical information from a *sample*. In particular, we used these statistics to describe the properties of central tendency, variation, and shape.

## Table 4.2  Amounts for a population of 50 sales vouchers

| | | | | | | | | | |
|---|---|---|---|---|---|---|---|---|---|
| 127.43 | 372.68 | 349.03 | 213.45 | 326.55 | 148.93 | 213.54 | 409.61 | 211.01 | 290.87 |
| 219.76 | 429.05 | 328.44 | 215.62 | 462.45 | 389.04 | 234.65 | 543.67 | 176.43 | 435.32 |
| 430.32 | 278.93 | 436.72 | 327.80 | 354.11 | 265.76 | 216.87 | 654.32 | 345.45 | 213.65 |
| 399.05 | 324.55 | 451.23 | 287.60 | 219.06 | 214.54 | 278.96 | 378.90 | 368.02 | 319.06 |
| 267.90 | 265.78 | 345.11 | 379.01 | 417.89 | 267.91 | 210.32 | 277.62 | 321.81 | 334.22 |

**DATA FILE**
VOUCHER

Suppose, however, that the data set we have access to is not a sample but rather a collection of numerical measurements from an entire *population*. For example, suppose that a wholesale plumbing supply company had a population of 50 sales vouchers from a particular day. The amount (in $) of these vouchers was as illustrated in Table 4.2.

When dealing with a set of data making up an entire population, we again consider the arithmetic mean, the variance, and the standard deviation.

## The Population Mean

The **population mean** is given by the symbol $\mu$, the Greek lowercase letter *mu*. It is obtained as follows.

### Population Mean

The population mean is equal to the sum of all the values in the population divided by the population size.

$$\mu = \frac{\sum_{i=1}^{N} X_i}{N} \qquad (4.12)$$

where

$N$ = population size

$X_i$ = $i$th value of the random variable $X$

$\sum_{i=1}^{N} X_i$ = summation of all $X_i$ values in the population

Example 4.18 illustrates how we compute the population mean.

## Example 4.18  *Computing the Population Mean*

Compute the population mean of the amount of sales of plumbing supplies for the data of Table 4.2.

### SOLUTION

The population mean is computed from equation (4.12) as shown at the top of page 166.

$$\mu = \frac{\sum\limits_{i=1}^{N} X_i}{N} = \frac{127.43 + 372.68 + 349.03 + \cdots + 334.22}{50} = \frac{15,950}{50} = \$319.00$$

Thus, the average sales voucher amount in this population is $319.

## The Population Variance and Standard Deviation

The **population variance** is given by the symbol $\sigma^2$, the Greek lowercase letter *sigma* squared, and the **population standard deviation** is given by the symbol $\sigma$. These measures are obtained as follows.

### Population Variance

The population variance is equal to the sum of the squared differences around the population mean, divided by the population size.

$$\sigma^2 = \frac{\sum\limits_{i=1}^{N} (X_i - \mu)^2}{N} \tag{4.13}$$

where

$$N = \text{population size}$$
$$X_i = i\text{th value of the random variable } X$$

$$\sum_{i=1}^{N} (X_i - \mu)^2 = \text{summation of all the squared differences between the } X_i \text{ values and } \mu$$

and the population standard deviation is the square root of the population variance

### Population Standard Deviation

$$\sigma = \sqrt{\frac{\sum\limits_{i=1}^{N} (X_i - \mu)^2}{N}} \tag{4.14}$$

We note that the formulas for the population variance and standard deviation differ from those for the sample variance and standard deviation in that $(n - 1)$ in the denominator of $S^2$ and $S$ [see equations (4.9) and (4.10)] is replaced by $N$ in the denominator of $\sigma^2$ and $\sigma$. Example 4.19 demonstrates how to compute the population variance and standard deviation.

## Example 4.19 *Computing the Population Variance and Standard Deviation*

Compute the population variance and standard deviation of the amount of sales of plumbing supplies for the data of Table 4.2.

### SOLUTION

Using equation (4.13), the population variance is computed as follows.

**Variance**

$$\sigma^2 = \frac{\sum_{i=1}^{N}(X_i - \mu)^2}{N}$$

$$= \frac{(127.43 - 319)^2 + (372.68 - 319)^2 + (349.03 - 319)^2 + \cdots + (334.22 - 319)^2}{50}$$

$$= \frac{518,008.2}{50} = 10,360.16 \text{ (in squared dollars)}$$

The population standard deviation is just the square root of the population variance. Using equation (4.14), we have

$$\sigma = \sqrt{\frac{\sum_{i=1}^{N}(X_i - \mu)^2}{N}} = \sqrt{10,360.16} = \$101.78$$

## Using the Standard Deviation: The Empirical Rule

In most data sets, a large portion of the observations tend to cluster somewhat near the median. In right-skewed data sets, this clustering occurs to the left of (i.e., *below*) the median, and in left-skewed data sets, the observations tend to cluster to the right of (i.e., *above*) the median. In symmetrical data sets, where the median and mean are the same, the observations tend to distribute equally around these measures of central tendency. When extreme skewness is not present and such clustering is observed in a data set, we can use the so-called *empirical rule* to examine the property of data variability and get a better sense of what the standard deviation is measuring.

### Empirical Rule

The empirical rule states that for most data sets, we will find that roughly two out of every three observations (i.e., 67%) are contained within a distance of 1 standard deviation around the mean and roughly 90%–95% of the observations are contained within a distance of 2 standard deviations around the mean.

Hence, the standard deviation, as a measure of average variation around the mean, helps us to understand how the observations distribute above and below the mean and helps us to focus on and flag unusual observations (i.e., *outliers*) when analyzing a set of numerical data.

From the data of Table 4.2, for the population of 50 sales vouchers, the mean amount $\mu$ is \$319.00 and the standard deviation $\sigma$ is \$101.78. From Table 4.2 we observe that 31 sales vouchers (62%) are between $\mu - 1\sigma$ and $\mu + 1\sigma$ (i.e., between \$217.22 and \$420.78). We also see that 48 sales vouchers (96%) are between $\mu - 2\sigma$ and $\mu + 2\sigma$ (i.e., between \$115.44 and \$522.56). In addition, we note that all but one of the sales vouchers (98%) were between $\mu - 3\sigma$ and $\mu + 3\sigma$ (i.e., between \$13.66 and \$624.34).

## Using the Standard Deviation: The Bienaymé-Chebyshev Rule

[3] *The Bienaymé-Chebyshev rule can apply only to distances beyond $\pm 1$ standard deviation about the mean.*

More than a century ago, the mathematicians Bienaymé and Chebyshev (reference 2) independently examined the property of data variability around the mean.[3] They found that regardless of how skewed a set of data is distributed, the percentage of observations that are contained within distances of $k$ standard deviations around the mean must be at least

$$\left(1 - \frac{1}{k^2}\right)100\%$$

Therefore, regardless of the shape of the distribution of data

- At least $[1 - (1/2^2)]100\% = 75.0\%$ of the observations must be contained within distances of $\pm 2$ standard deviations around the mean.
- At least $[1 - (1/3^2)]100\% = 88.89\%$ of the observations must be contained within distances of $\pm 3$ standard deviations around the mean.
- At least $[1 - (1/4^2)]100\% = 93.75\%$ of all the observations must be included within distances of $\pm 4$ standard deviations about the mean.

Although the Bienaymé-Chebyshev rule is general in nature and applies to any kind of distribution of data, we will see in chapter 8 that if the data form the *bell-shaped* normal or Gaussian distribution, 68.26% of all the observations will be contained within distances of $\pm 1$ standard deviation around the mean, while 95.44%, 99.73%, and 99.99% of the observations will be included, respectively, within distances of $\pm 2$, $\pm 3$, and $\pm 4$ standard deviations around the mean.

Specifically, if we knew that a particular random phenomenon followed the pattern of the bell-shaped distribution—as many do, at least approximately—we would then know (as will be shown in chapter 8) *exactly* how likely it is that any particular observation was close to or far from its mean. Generally, however, for any kind of distribution, the Bienaymé-Chebyshev rule tells us *at least* how likely it must be that any particular observation falls within a given distance about the mean.

It is interesting to note that even though the amount of the sales vouchers may not be normally distributed, the percentages falling within 1 or more standard deviations about the mean are not very different from what would be expected had the data been distributed as a perfectly symmetrical, bell-shaped distribution. These results (among others) are summarized in Table 4.3.

## Table 4.3 *How data vary around the mean*

| NUMBER OF STANDARD DEVIATION UNITS $k$ | PERCENTAGE OF OBSERVATIONS CONTAINED BETWEEN THE MEAN AND $k$ STANDARD DEVIATIONS BASED ON | | |
| --- | --- | --- | --- |
| | BIENAYMÉ-CHEBYSHEV RULE FOR ANY DISTRIBUTION | NORMAL DISTRIBUTION | SALES VOUCHERS |
| 1 | Not calculable | Exactly 68.26% | Exactly 62% |
| 2 | At least 75.00% | Exactly 95.44% | Exactly 96% |
| 3 | At least 88.89% | Exactly 99.73% | Exactly 98% |
| 4 | At least 93.75% | Exactly 99.99% | Exactly 100.0% |

## Problems for Section 4.4

### Learning the Basics

**4.25** Given the following set of data for a population of size $N = 10$:

  7  5  11  8  3  6  2  1  9  8

(a) Compute the mean, median, mode, midrange, and midhinge.
(b) Compute the range, interquartile range, variance, standard deviation, and coefficient of variation.
(c) Are these data skewed? If so, how?

**4.26** Given the following set of data for a population of size $N = 10$:

  7  5  6  6  6  4  8  6  9  3

(a) Compute the mean, median, mode, midrange, and midhinge.
(b) Compute the range, interquartile range, variance, standard deviation, and coefficient of variation.
(c) Are these data skewed? If so, how?
(d) Compare the measures of central tendency to those of Problem 4.25(a). Discuss.
(e) Compare the measures of variation to those of Problem 4.25(b). Discuss.

### Applying the Concepts

**• 4.27** The following data represent the quarterly sales tax receipts (in $000) submitted to the comptroller of Gmoserville Township for the period ending March 1998 by all 50 business establishments in that locale:

| | | | | |
| --- | --- | --- | --- | --- |
| 10.3 | 11.1 | 9.6 | 9.0 | 14.5 |
| 13.0 | 6.7 | 11.0 | 8.4 | 10.3 |
| 13.0 | 11.2 | 7.3 | 5.3 | 12.5 |
| 8.0 | 11.8 | 8.7 | 10.6 | 9.5 |
| 11.1 | 10.2 | 11.1 | 9.9 | 9.8 |
| 11.6 | 15.1 | 12.5 | 6.5 | 7.5 |
| 10.0 | 12.9 | 9.2 | 10.0 | 12.8 |
| 12.5 | 9.3 | 10.4 | 12.7 | 10.5 |
| 9.3 | 11.5 | 10.7 | 11.6 | 7.8 |
| 10.5 | 7.6 | 10.1 | 8.9 | 8.6 |

DATA FILE
TAX

(a) Organize the data into an ordered array or stem-and-leaf display.
(b) Compute the arithmetic mean for this population.
(c) Compute the variance and standard deviation for this population.

(d) What proportion of these businesses have quarterly sales tax receipts
  (1) within $\pm 1$ standard deviation of the mean?
  (2) within $\pm 2$ standard deviations of the mean?
  (3) within $\pm 3$ standard deviations of the mean?

(e) Are you surprised at the results in (d)? (*Hint*: Compare and contrast your findings versus what would be expected on the basis of the empirical rule.)

**4.28** Suppose that a population of 1,024 domestic general stock funds was obtained, and it was determined that $\mu$, the mean 1-year total percentage return achieved by all the funds, is 28.20 and that $\sigma$, the standard deviation, is 6.75. In addition, suppose it was determined that the range in 1-year total returns is from 0.3 to 60.3 and that the quartiles are, respectively, 23.9 ($Q_1$) and 32.3 ($Q_3$).

(a) According to the empirical rule, what proportion of these funds are expected to be
  (1) within $\pm 1$ standard deviation of the mean?
  (2) within $\pm 2$ standard deviations of the mean?
  (3) within $\pm 3$ standard deviations of the mean?

(b) According to the Bienaymé-Chebyshev rule, what proportion of these funds are expected to be
  (1) within $\pm 1$ standard deviation of the mean?
  (2) within $\pm 2$ standard deviations of the mean?
  (3) within $\pm 3$ standard deviations of the mean?

(c) According to the Bienaymé-Chebyshev rule, at least 93.75% of these funds are expected to have 1-year total percentage returns between what two amounts?

**4.29** The following data are intended to show the gap between families with the highest income and families with the lowest income in each of the 50 states and the District of Columbia as measured by the average of the top fifth and the bottom fifth of families with children during 1994–96. The results classified by states were as follows:

| STATE | BOTTOM FIFTH ($000) | TOP FIFTH ($000) | STATE | BOTTOM FIFTH ($000) | TOP FIFTH ($000) |
|---|---|---|---|---|---|
| New York | 6.787 | 132.390 | Pennsylvania | 10.512 | 124.537 |
| Louisiana | 6.430 | 102.339 | North Carolina | 9.363 | 107.490 |
| New Mexico | 6.408 | 91.741 | Rhode Island | 9.914 | 111.015 |
| Arizona | 7.273 | 103.392 | Washington | 10.116 | 112.501 |
| Connecticut | 10.415 | 147.594 | Maryland | 13.346 | 147.971 |
| California | 9.033 | 127.719 | Virginia | 10.816 | 116.202 |
| Florida | 7.705 | 107.811 | Kansas | 10.790 | 110.341 |
| Kentucky | 7.364 | 99.210 | Oregon | 9.627 | 97.589 |
| Alabama | 7.531 | 99.062 | New Jersey | 14.211 | 143.010 |
| West Virginia | 6.439 | 84.479 | Indiana | 11.115 | 110.876 |
| Tennessee | 8.156 | 106.966 | Montana | 9.051 | 89.902 |
| Texas | 8.642 | 113.149 | South Dakota | 9.474 | 93.822 |
| Mississippi | 6.257 | 80.980 | Idaho | 10.721 | 104.725 |
| Michigan | 9.257 | 117.107 | Delaware | 12.041 | 116.965 |
| Oklahoma | 7.483 | 94.380 | Arkansas | 8.995 | 83.434 |
| Massachusetts | 10.694 | 132.962 | Colorado | 14.326 | 131.368 |
| Georgia | 9.978 | 123.837 | Hawaii | 12.735 | 116.060 |
| Illinois | 10.002 | 123.233 | Missouri | 11.090 | 100.837 |
| Ohio | 9.346 | 111.894 | Alaska | 14.868 | 129.065 |
| South Carolina | 8.146 | 96.712 | Wyoming | 11.174 | 94.845 |

*continued*

| STATE | BOTTOM FIFTH ($000) | TOP FIFTH ($000) | STATE | BOTTOM FIFTH ($000) | TOP FIFTH ($000) |
|---|---|---|---|---|---|
| Minnesota | 14.655 | 120.344 | Wisconsin | 13.398 | 103.551 |
| Nebraska | 12.546 | 102.992 | Vermont | 13.107 | 97.898 |
| Maine | 11.275 | 92.457 | North Dakota | 12.424 | 91.041 |
| New Hampshire | 14.299 | 116.018 | Utah | 15.709 | 110.938 |
| Nevada | 12.276 | 98.693 | District of Columbia | 5.293 | 149.508 |
| Iowa | 13.148 | 104.253 | | | |

**DATA FILE**
STATEINC

*Source: United States Census Bureau.*

For each of these numerical variables
(a) organize the data into an ordered array or stem-and-leaf display.
(b) compute the arithmetic mean for the population.
(c) compute the variance and standard deviation for the population.
(d) What proportion of these states have average incomes
  (1) within ±1 standard deviation of the mean?
  (2) within ±2 standard deviations of the mean?
  (3) within ±3 standard deviations of the mean?
(e) Are you surprised at the results in (d)? (*Hint*: Compare and contrast your findings versus what would be expected based on the empirical rule.)
(f) Remove the District of Columbia from consideration. Do parts (a)–(e) with the District of Columbia removed. How have the results changed?

 **4.5** ## OBTAINING DESCRIPTIVE SUMMARY MEASURES FROM A FREQUENCY DISTRIBUTION (*OPTIONAL TOPIC*)

It is sometimes the case that raw data are not available and the only source of data is a frequency distribution. In such a situation, approximations to descriptive summary measures such as the arithmetic mean and standard deviation can be obtained.

### Approximating the Arithmetic Mean

When data have been summarized into a frequency distribution, we can obtain an approximation of the arithmetic mean by assuming that all values within each class interval are located at the midpoint of the class. Thus, for a sample of $n$ observations, we would have

**Approximating the Arithmetic Mean from a Frequency Distribution**

$$\overline{X} \cong \frac{\sum_{j=1}^{c} m_j f_j}{n}$$ (4.15)

where

$\overline{X}$ = arithmetic mean of the sample

$n$ = number of observations in the sample

$c$ = number of classes in the frequency distribution

$m_j$ = midpoint of the *j*th class

$f_j$ = frequencies tallied into the *j*th class

To calculate the standard deviation from a frequency distribution we also assume that all values within each class interval are located at the midpoint of the class. Thus, for a sample of $n$ observations, we would have

**Approximating the Standard Deviation from a Frequency Distribution**

$$S \cong \sqrt{\frac{\sum_{j=1}^{c} (m_j - \overline{X})^2 f_j}{n - 1}} \qquad (4.16)$$

We may illustrate the computation of the arithmetic mean and the standard deviation from a frequency distribution by looking at Example 4.20.

**Example 4.20** *Approximating the Arithmetic Mean and Standard Deviation from a Frequency Distribution*

In Table 3.2 on page 61, the following frequency distribution of the 1-year total percentage return of the 59 growth funds was presented.

*Frequency distribution of the 1-year total percentage returns achieved by 59 growth funds*

| 1-YEAR TOTAL PERCENTAGE RETURN | NUMBER OF FUNDS |
|---|---|
| 20.0 but less than 25.0 | 2 |
| 25.0 but less than 30.0 | 13 |
| 30.0 but less than 35.0 | 24 |
| 35.0 but less than 40.0 | 4 |
| 40.0 but less than 45.0 | 11 |
| 45.0 but less than 50.0 | 5 |
| Total | 59 |

Approximate the arithmetic mean and standard deviation of the 1-year total percentage return of these 59 growth funds.

**SOLUTION**

For these data, we compute

| PERCENTAGE RETURN | $f_j$ NUMBER OF FUNDS | $m_j$ MIDPOINT | $m_j f_j$ | $(m_j - \overline{X})$ | $(m_j - \overline{X})^2$ | $(m_j - \overline{X})^2 f_j$ |
|---|---|---|---|---|---|---|
| 20.0 but less than 25.0 | 2 | 22.5 | 45.0 | −12.03 | 144.7209 | 289.4418 |
| 25.0 but less than 30.0 | 13 | 27.5 | 357.5 | −7.03 | 49.4209 | 642.4717 |
| 30.0 but less than 35.0 | 24 | 32.5 | 780.0 | −2.03 | 4.1209 | 98.9016 |
| 35.0 but less than 40.0 | 4 | 37.5 | 150.0 | +2.97 | 8.8209 | 35.2836 |
| 40.0 but less than 45.0 | 11 | 42.5 | 467.5 | +7.97 | 63.5209 | 698.7299 |
| 45.0 but less than 50.0 | 5 | 47.5 | 237.5 | +12.97 | 168.2209 | 841.1045 |
| Total | 59 | | 2,037.5 | | | 2,605.9331 |

Using equation (4.15), we have

$$\overline{X} \cong \frac{\sum_{j=1}^{c} m_j f_j}{n}$$

$$\overline{X} \cong \frac{2,037.5}{59} = 34.53$$

and

$$S \cong \sqrt{\frac{\sum_{j=1}^{c} (m_j - \overline{X})^2 f_j}{n - 1}}$$

$$S \cong \sqrt{\frac{2,605.9331}{59 - 1}} = 6.70$$

## Problems for Section 4.5

### Learning the Basics

• **4.30** Suppose you were given the following frequency distribution

| CLASS INTERVALS | FREQUENCY |
|---|---|
| 0–Under 10 | 10 |
| 10–Under 20 | 20 |
| 20–Under 30 | 40 |
| 30–Under 40 | 20 |
| 40–Under 50 | 10 |
| | 100 |

Approximate
(a) the arithmetic mean.
(b) the standard deviation.

**4.31** Suppose you were given the following frequency distribution

| CLASS INTERVALS | FREQUENCY |
| --- | --- |
| 0–Under 10 | 40 |
| 10–Under 20 | 25 |
| 20–Under 30 | 15 |
| 30–Under 40 | 15 |
| 40–Under 50 | 5 |
| | 100 |

Approximate
(a) the arithmetic mean.
(b) the standard deviation.

## Applying the Concepts

**4.32** A wholesale appliance distributing firm wished to study its accounts receivable for 2 successive months. Two independent samples of 50 accounts were selected for each of the 2 months. The results are summarized in the following table:

*Frequency distributions for accounts receivable*

| AMOUNT | MARCH FREQUENCY | APRIL FREQUENCY |
| --- | --- | --- |
| $0 to under $2,000 | 6 | 10 |
| $2,000 to under $4,000 | 13 | 14 |
| $4,000 to under $6,000 | 17 | 13 |
| $6,000 to under $8,000 | 10 | 10 |
| $8,000 to under $10,000 | 4 | 0 |
| $10,000 to under $12,000 | 0 | 3 |
| Total | 50 | 50 |

For each month, approximate the
(a) arithmetic mean.
(b) standard deviation.
(c) On the basis of parts (a)–(b), do you think the arithmetic mean and standard deviation of the accounts receivable have changed substantially from March to April? Explain.

**4.33** The following table contains the cumulative distributions and cumulative percentage distributions of braking distance (in feet) at 80 miles per hour for a sample of 25 U.S.-manufactured automobile models and for a sample of 72 foreign-made automobile models obtained in a recent year:

*Cumulative frequency and percentage distributions for braking distance (in feet) at 80 mph for U.S.-manufactured and foreign-made automobile models*

| BRAKING DISTANCE (IN FT) | U.S.-MADE AUTOMOBILE MODELS "LESS THAN" INDICATED VALUES | | FOREIGN-MADE AUTOMOBILE MODELS "LESS THAN" INDICATED VALUES | |
|---|---|---|---|---|
| | NUMBER | PERCENTAGE | NUMBER | PERCENTAGE |
| 210 | 0 | 0.0 | 0 | 0.0 |
| 220 | 1 | 4.0 | 1 | 1.4 |
| 230 | 2 | 8.0 | 4 | 5.6 |
| 240 | 3 | 12.0 | 19 | 26.4 |
| 250 | 4 | 16.0 | 32 | 44.4 |
| 260 | 8 | 32.0 | 54 | 75.0 |
| 270 | 11 | 44.0 | 61 | 84.7 |
| 280 | 17 | 68.0 | 68 | 94.4 |
| 290 | 21 | 84.0 | 68 | 94.4 |
| 300 | 23 | 92.0 | 70 | 97.2 |
| 310 | 25 | 100.0 | 71 | 98.6 |
| 320 | 25 | 100.0 | 72 | 100.0 |

For U.S.- and for foreign-made automobiles
(a) construct a frequency distribution for each group.
(b) On the basis of the results of (a), approximate the arithmetic mean of the braking distance.
(c) On the basis of the results of (a), approximate the standard deviation of the braking distance.
(d) On the basis of the results of (b) and (c), do U.S.- and foreign-made automobiles seem to differ in their braking distance? Explain.

• **4.34** The following data represent the distribution of the ages of employees within two different divisions of a publishing company.

| AGE OF EMPLOYEES (YEARS) | A FREQUENCY | B FREQUENCY |
|---|---|---|
| 20–Under 30 | 8 | 15 |
| 30–Under 40 | 17 | 32 |
| 40–Under 50 | 11 | 20 |
| 50–Under 60 | 8 | 4 |
| 60–Under 70 | 2 | 0 |

For each of the two divisions, approximate the
(a) arithmetic mean.
(b) standard deviation.
(c) On the basis of the results of (a) and (b), do you think there are differences in the age distribution between the two divisions? Explain.

# RECOGNIZING AND PRACTICING PROPER DESCRIPTIVE SUMMARIZATION AND EXPLORING ETHICAL ISSUES

In this chapter we have studied how a set of numerical data can be characterized by various statistics that measure the properties of central tendency, variation, and shape. The next step is data analysis and interpretation; the former is *objective*, the latter is *subjective*. We must avoid errors that may arise either in the objectivity of what is being analyzed or in the subjectivity of what is being interpreted (references 1 and 3).

## Avoiding Errors in Analysis and Interpretation

You may recall that in section 4.1 we examined and described a set of numerical data pertaining to 1-year total percentage returns achieved by 17 domestic general stock funds whose marketing fees are paid from fund assets. Without a knowledge of the contents of this chapter, we attempted to analyze and interpret what the data were trying to convey.

Our analysis was *objective*; we should all have agreed with our limited visual findings: The *modal* values or most typical 1-year total percentage returns were 28.6 and 30.5; the *spread* in the 1-year total return performance indicator ranged from 10.0% to 38.0%; and there was one *outlier* present in the data, the 10.0% return attained by Mentor Merger, and one *potential outlier*, the 20.6% return achieved by Rainler Reich Tang.

Having now read the chapter and thus gained a knowledge about various descriptive summary measures and their strengths and weaknesses, how could we improve on our previous objective analysis? Since the data distribute in a slightly nonsymmetrical manner, shouldn't we report the median or midhinge rather than the mean? Doesn't the standard deviation provide more information about the property of variation than the range? Shouldn't we describe the data set as negative, or left-skewed, in shape? Objectivity in data analysis means reporting the most appropriate summary measures for a given data set—those that best meet the assumptions about the given data set.

On the other hand, our data interpretation was *subjective*; we could have formed different conclusions when interpreting our analytical findings. We all see the world from different perspectives. Some of us will look at the ordered array of 1-year total returns in percents (10.0, 20.6, 28.6, 28.6, 29.4, 29.5, 29.9, 30.1, 30.5, 30.5, 32.1, 32.2, 32.4, 33.0, 35.2, 37.1, and 38.0) and be satisfied with the performances achieved by the domestic general stock funds whose marketing fees are paid from fund assets; others, particularly those who have invested in either Mentor Merger (with its 10.0% return) or Rainler Reich Tang (with its 20.6% return), or those individuals who simply expect greater performance to compensate for investment risks taken, will look at the same data set and conclude that the performance has been too low. Thus, since data interpretation is subjective, it must be done in a fair, neutral, and clear manner.

## Ethical Issues

Ethical issues are vitally important to all data analysis. As daily consumers of information, we owe it to ourselves to question what we read in newspapers and magazines and what we hear on the radio or television. Over time, much skepticism has been expressed about the purpose, the focus, and the objectivity of published studies. Perhaps no comment on this topic was ever more telling than a quip often attributed to the famous nineteenth-century British statesman Benjamin Disraeli: "There are three kinds of lies: lies, damned lies, and statistics."

Again, as was mentioned in sections 2.4 and 3.6, ethical considerations arise when we are deciding what results to present in a report and what not to present. It is vitally important to document both good and bad results. In addition, when making oral presentations and presenting written reports, it is essential that the results be given in a fair, objective, and neutral manner. Thus, we must try to distinguish between poor presentation of results and unethical presentation. Once more, as in our prior discussions on ethical considerations, the key is intent. When pertinent information is omitted, often it is simply done out of ignorance. However, unethical behavior occurs when one willfully chooses an inappropriate summary measure (e.g., the mean or midrange for a very skewed set of data) to distort the facts in order to support a particular position. In addition, unethical behavior occurs when one selectively fails to report pertinent findings because it would be detrimental to the support of a particular position.

## Problems for Section 4.6

### Applying the Concepts

**4.35** You receive a telephone call from a friend who is also studying statistics this semester. Your friend has just used Microsoft Excel to obtain descriptive summary measures for several numerical variables pertaining to a survey concerning student life on campus. He says, "I've been asked to write a report and prepare a 5-minute classroom presentation on student life on campus. I'm looking at my computer printout—I've got all these descriptive summary measures for each of my seven numerical variables. There's so much information here, I just can't get started. Do you have any suggestions?" You think for a moment, and then reply . . .

**4.36** An arbitrator is asked to examine a dispute over salaries paid to professional baseball players. The owner of a particular team claims that the average salary per annum is too high. The agent for the players argues that the average salary for the players on this team is too low. How should the arbitrator evaluate these two conflicting statements? (*Hint*: To which *average* do you think the agent would be referring and to which *average* do you think the owner would be referring?)

## ◆ SUMMARY

As you can see from the summary chart on page 178, this chapter was about data summarization and description. In this and the previous two chapters, we have studied the subject matter of descriptive statistics: how data are collected, presented in tabular or chart format, and then summarized, described, analyzed, and interpreted. In the next chapter, we will study the basic principles of probability in order to bridge the gap between the subject of descriptive statistics and the subject of inferential statistics.

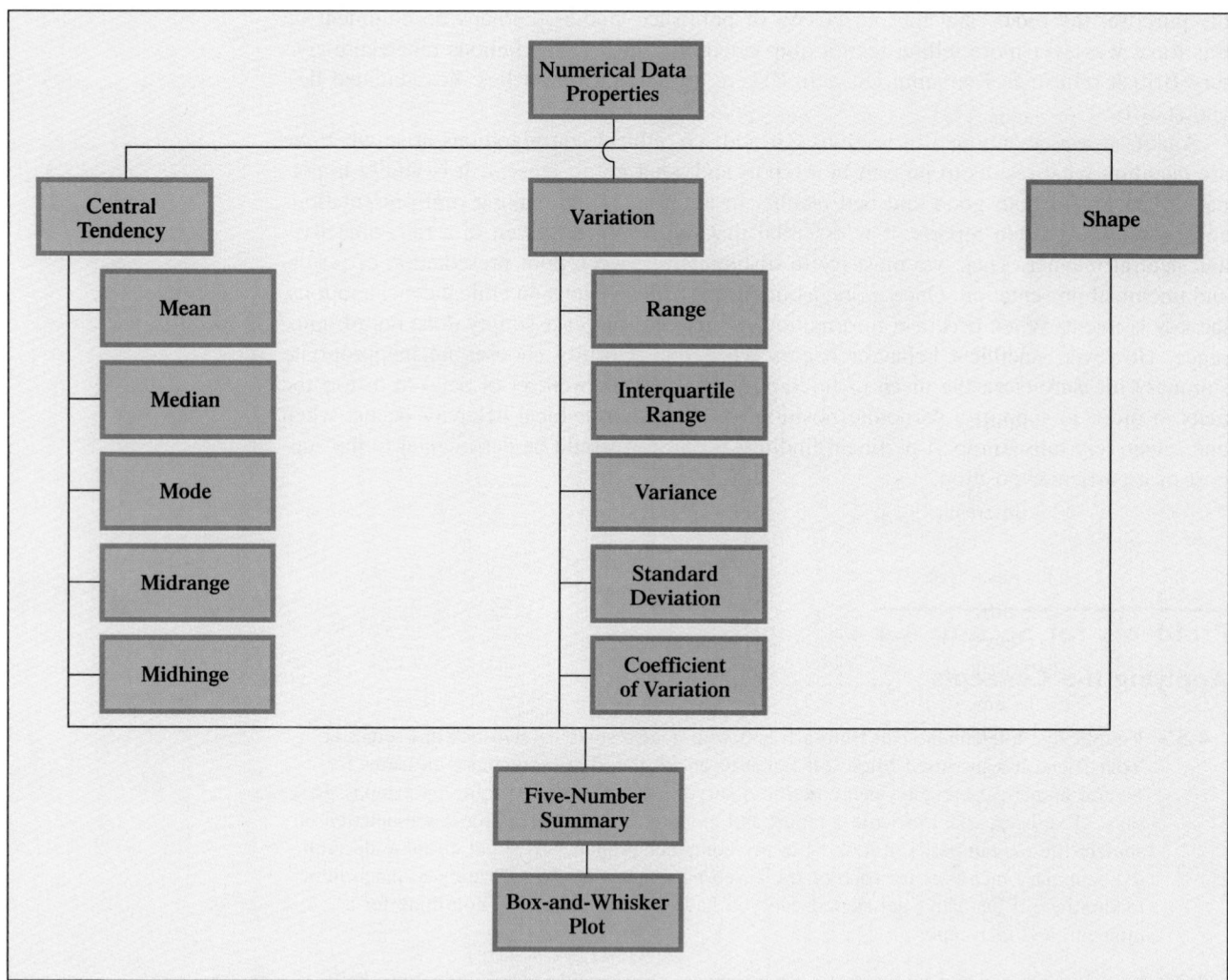

Chapter 4 summary chart

## *Key Terms*

## Checking Your Understanding

**4.37** What should we be looking for when we attempt to characterize and describe the properties of a set of numerical data?

**4.38** What do we mean by the property of location or central tendency?

**4.39** What are the differences among the various measures of central tendency such as the mean, median, mode, midrange, and midhinge, and what are the advantages and disadvantages to each?

**4.40** What is the difference between measures of central tendency and measures of noncentral tendency?

**4.41** What do we mean by the property of variation?

**4.42** What are the differences among the various measures of variation such as the range, interquartile range, variance, standard deviation, and coefficient of variation, and what are the advantages and disadvantages of each?

**4.43** How does the empirical rule help explain the ways in which the observations in a set of numerical data cluster and distribute?

**4.44** What do we mean by the property of shape?

**4.45** Why are such exploratory data analysis techniques as the five-number summary and the box-and-whisker plot so useful?

**4.46** What are some of the ethical issues to be concerned with when distinguishing between the use of appropriate and inappropriate descriptive summary measures reported in newspapers and magazines?

## Chapter Review Problems

**4.47** A college was conducting a phonathon to raise money for the building of a center for the study of international business. The provost hoped to obtain half a million dollars for this purpose. The following data represent the amounts pledged (in thousands of dollars) by all alumni who were called during the first nine nights of the campaign.

**DATA FILE**
FUNRAISE

16, 18, 11, 17, 13, 10, 22, 15, 16

(a) Compute the mean, median, and standard deviation.
(b) Describe the shape of this set of data.
(c) Estimate the total amount that will be pledged (in thousands of dollars) by all alumni if the campaign is to last 30 nights. (*Hint*: Total $= N\overline{X}$.)
(d) Do you think that the phonathon will raise the half a million dollars that the provost hoped to obtain? Explain.

• **4.48** The data at the top of page 180 represent the monthly long-distance phone rates charged to residential customers across the United States from a sample of 34 different plans (based on 36 calls per month for a total of 318 minutes spread out over the day):

| PLAN | RATE | PLAN | RATE |
|------|------|------|------|
| AT&T Dial-1 Standard | 74.68 | Matrix SBN Flat Rate | 54.03 |
| Frontier Dial-1 | 76.41 | Matrix Smartworld Flat | 49.46 |
| LCI Basic | 71.50 | Sprint Sense | 55.50 |
| Matrix Dial-1 | 59.58 | Worldcom Home Advantage | 49.10 |
| MCI Dial-1 Standard | 74.29 | AT&T True Reach Savings | 56.01 |
| Sprint Dial-1 Standard | 74.68 | AT&T True Savings | 55.21 |
| Worldcom MTS | 63.92 | Matrix Smartworld Basic | 55.76 |
| AT&T One Rate | 58.35 | MCI Friends and Family | 60.98 |
| AT&T One Rate Plus | 47.90 | MCI Friends and Family Free | 58.09 |
| LCI Single Rate | 53.97 | Sprint Sense With Most Option | 53.70 |
| Matrix Flat Rate 1 | 51.85 | Sprint the Most II | 60.31 |
| MCI One | 47.57 | Matrix Smartworld Basic With Discount | 52.78 |
| Sprint Sense Day | 56.05 | Sprint Sense With Cash Back | 49.95 |
| AT&T Simple Rate | 56.55 | Sprint Sense With Most and Cash Back | 48.33 |
| Frontier Homesaver | 49.36 | AT&T One Rate With True Rewards | 57.18 |
| LCI All-American | 52.71 | AT&T True Reach With True Rewards | 54.89 |
| LCI Two-Rate | 53.10 | AT&T True Savings With True Rewards | 54.11 |

**DATA FILE**
PHONRATE

Sources: *Reprinted by permission of* The New York Times. *Telecommunications Research and Action Center;* The New York Times, *March 2, 1997, E5.*

(a) Compute all appropriate measures of location.
(b) Compute all appropriate measures of variation.
(c) Construct a box-and-whisker plot.
(d) On the basis of the results of (a) and (c), how would you describe the shape of the distribution? Explain.
(e) On the basis of the results of (a) and (c), if you were summarizing the results in a written report, which measures of location would you provide? Explain.

● **4.49** The data at the top of page 181 display the price (in dollars), the actual number of cups that can be made, the price to replace a carafe (in dollars), and the type (basic function versus programmable) for a random sample of 19 brands of coffeemakers.

(a) Using the entire sample of 19 coffeemakers, develop stem-and-leaf displays for each of the three numerical variables.
(b) Compute the mean, median, mode, midrange, and midhinge for each of the three numerical variables.
(c) Repeat part (a) for each type of coffeemaker—the 12 basic function machines versus the 7 programmable models.
(d) Repeat part (b) for each type of coffeemaker—the 12 basic function machines versus the 7 programmable models.
(e) Compute the range, interquartile range, variance, standard deviation, and coefficient of variation for each of the three numerical variables.
(f) Repeat part (e) for each type of coffeemaker—the 12 basic function machines versus the 7 programmable models.
(g) Describe the shape for each of the three numerical variables.
(h) Repeat part (g) for each type of coffeemaker—the 12 basic function machines versus the 7 programmable models.
(i) Form the box-and-whisker plot and describe the shape for each of the numerical variables.
(j) Repeat part (i) for each type of coffeemaker—the 12 basic function machines versus the 7 programmable models.

(k) What differences are there in location, variation, and shape between basic and programmable coffeemakers for each of the three variables?

| BRAND | PRICE | ACTUAL CUPS | CARAFE | TYPE |
|---|---|---|---|---|
| Mr. Coffee Accel PR15 | 22 | 11.0 | 9 | Basic |
| Braun KF157 | 52 | 10.5 | 16 | Basic |
| Mr. Coffee AD10 | 20 | 9.0 | 9 | Basic |
| Proctor-Silex 42301 | 20 | 11.0 | 14 | Basic |
| Melitta IBS-10C | 50 | 8.5 | 11 | Basic |
| Krups CompacTherm 206 | 85 | 8.5 | 45 | Basic |
| Bunn GR | 60 | 8.5 | 9 | Basic |
| Oster 3272 | 50 | 10.5 | 17 | Basic |
| Black & Decker DCM902 | 20 | 9.5 | 10 | Basic |
| West Bend 56660 | 30 | 9.0 | 7 | Basic |
| Regal K7617 | 20 | 9.0 | 8 | Basic |
| Betty Crocker BC-1733 | 25 | 11.5 | 12 | Basic |
| Braun FlavorSelect KF185 | 90 | 10.5 | 16 | Progm |
| Mr. Coffee Accel PRX20 | 37 | 11.0 | 9 | Progm |
| Krups Crystal Aroma Time 458 | 90 | 9.0 | 20 | Progm |
| Black & Decker ODC300 | 65 | 9.5 | 11 | Progm |
| Proctor-Silex 42461 | 30 | 11.0 | 14 | Progm |
| Black & Decker DCM903 | 40 | 9.5 | 10 | Progm |
| Hamilton Beach 47261 | 40 | 11.0 | 12 | Progm |

*Source: "Coffee Makers," Copyright 1996 by Consumers Union of U.S., Inc. Adapted from* CONSUMER REPORTS, *November 1996, 40–41 by permission of Consumers Union of U.S., Inc., Yonkers, NY 10703-1057. Although these data sets originally appeared in* CONSUMER REPORTS, *the selective adaptation and resulting conclusions presented are those of the authors and are not sanctioned or endorsed in any way by Consumers Union, the publisher of* CONSUMER REPORTS.

**DATA FILE**
COFMKR

• **4.50** The following data represent the price, an overall performance score, the battery life, and the battery cost per hour of usage (in cents) for a sample of 22 brands of portable CDs:

| BRAND | PRICE | SCORE | BATTLIFE | BCOST/HR |
|---|---|---|---|---|
| RCA RP-7913 | 86 | 92 | 8.50 | 18 |
| Panasonic SL-S290 | 134 | 91 | 9.50 | 16 |
| Panasonic SL-S160 | 92 | 91 | 8.50 | 18 |
| RCA RP-7926A w/car kit | 125 | 87 | 7.00 | 21 |
| Panasonic SL-S490 | 195 | 85 | 7.50 | 20 |
| Sony D-141 | 89 | 79 | 8.00 | 19 |
| Sony D-335 | 283 | 79 | 8.50 | 18 |
| Sony D-143 | 110 | 72 | 8.00 | 19 |
| Craig JC6111 | 68 | 72 | 4.50 | 33 |

*continued*

| BRAND | PRICE | SCORE | BATTLIFE | BCOST/HR |
|---|---|---|---|---|
| JVC XL-P41 | 136 | 72 | 5.75 | 52 |
| Fisher PCD-60 w/car kit | 183 | 72 | 3.25 | 46 |
| Sony D-421SP | 258 | 71 | 6.50 | 23 |
| Aiwa XP-559 w/car kit | 152 | 71 | 13.50 | 22 |
| JVC XL-P61CR w/car kit | 143 | 70 | 6.50 | 46 |
| Aiwa XP-33 | 94 | 69 | 11.50 | 26 |
| Onkyo DX-F71 w/car kit | 179 | 68 | 3.50 | 43 |
| Kenwood DPC-151 | 94 | 63 | 6.50 | 46 |
| Optimus CD-3450 | 130 | 61 | 8.00 | 38 |
| Kenwood DPC-951 w/car kit | 263 | 61 | 4.75 | 32 |
| Magnavox AZ 6827C w/car kit | 149 | 61 | 6.50 | 46 |
| Kenwood DPC-751 w/car kit | 213 | 60 | 4.75 | 32 |
| Emerson HD6825 w/car kit | 85 | 57 | 7.50 | 40 |

**DATA FILE**
PORTCD

*Source: "Portable CDs," Copyright 1995 by Consumers Union of U.S., Inc. Adapted from* CONSUMER REPORTS, *December 1995, 782–783 by permission of Consumers Union of U.S., Inc., Yonkers, NY 10703-1057. Although these data sets originally appeared in* CONSUMER REPORTS, *the selective adaptation and resulting conclusions presented are those of the authors and are not sanctioned or endorsed in any way by Consumers Union, the publisher of* CONSUMER REPORTS.

(a) Develop all the appropriate displays, tables, and charts and thoroughly analyze each of the numerical variables in the data set.

(b) On the basis of your findings in part (a), what conclusions can you reach about the central tendency, variation, and shape of the price, performance score, battery life, and battery cost per hour of these portable CDs?

• **4.51** A problem with a telephone line that prevents a customer from receiving or making calls is disconcerting both to the customer and the telephone company. These problems can be of two types: those that are located inside a central office and those located on lines between the central office and the customer's equipment. The following data represent samples of 20 problems reported to two different offices of a telephone company and the time to clear these problems (in minutes) from the customers' lines:

*Central Office I Time to Clear Problems (minutes)*

| | | | | | | | | | |
|---|---|---|---|---|---|---|---|---|---|
| 1.48 | 1.75 | 0.78 | 2.85 | 0.52 | 1.60 | 4.15 | 3.97 | 1.48 | 3.10 |
| 1.02 | 0.53 | 0.93 | 1.60 | 0.80 | 1.05 | 6.32 | 3.93 | 5.45 | 0.97 |

*Central Office II Time to Clear Problems (minutes)*

**DATA FILE**
PHONE

| | | | | | | | | | |
|---|---|---|---|---|---|---|---|---|---|
| 7.55 | 3.75 | 0.10 | 1.10 | 0.60 | 0.52 | 3.30 | 2.10 | 0.58 | 4.02 |
| 3.75 | 0.65 | 1.92 | 0.60 | 1.53 | 4.23 | 0.08 | 1.48 | 1.65 | 0.72 |

For each of the two central office locations,

(a) Compute the
  (1) arithmetic mean
  (2) median
  (3) midrange
  (4) first quartile
  (5) third quartile
  (6) midhinge
  (7) range
  (8) interquartile range
  (9) variance
  (10) standard deviation
  (11) coefficient of variation

(b) Construct a box-and-whisker plot.
(c) Are the data skewed? If so, how?
(d) Based on the results of (a)–(c), are there any differences between the two central offices? Explain.

(e) What would be the effect on your results and your conclusions if the first value for central office II was incorrectly recorded as 27.55 instead of 7.55?

**4.52** In many manufacturing processes there is a term called work in process (often abbreviated as WIP). In a book manufacturing plant this represents the time it takes for sheets from a press to be folded, gathered, sewn, tipped on endsheets, and bound. The following data represent samples of 20 books at each of two production plants and the processing time (operationally defined as the time in days from when the books came off the press to when they were packed in cartons) for these jobs.

*Plant A*

| 5.62 | 5.29 | 16.25 | 10.92 | 11.46 | 21.62 | 8.45 | 8.58 | 5.41 | 11.42 |
| 11.62 | 7.29 | 7.50 | 7.96 | 4.42 | 10.50 | 7.58 | 9.29 | 7.54 | 8.92 |

*Plant B*

| 9.54 | 11.46 | 16.62 | 12.62 | 25.75 | 15.41 | 14.29 | 13.13 | 13.71 | 10.04 |
| 5.75 | 12.46 | 9.17 | 13.21 | 6.00 | 2.33 | 14.25 | 5.37 | 6.25 | 9.71 |

DATA FILE
WIP

For each of the two plants,
(a) Compute the
    (1) arithmetic mean
    (2) median
    (3) midrange
    (4) first quartile
    (5) third quartile
    (6) midhinge
    (7) range
    (8) interquartile range
    (9) variance
    (10) standard deviation
    (11) coefficient of variation
(b) Construct a box-and-whisker plot.
(c) Are the data skewed? If so, how?
(d) On the basis of the results of (a)–(c), are there any differences between the two plants? Explain.

**4.53** In New York State, savings banks are permitted to sell a form of life insurance called Savings Bank Life Insurance (SBLI). The approval process consists of underwriting, which includes a review of the application, a medical information bureau check, possible requests for additional medical information and medical exams, and a policy compilation stage where the policy pages are generated and sent to the bank for delivery. The ability to deliver approved policies to customers in a timely manner is critical to the profitability of this service to the bank. During a period of 1 month, a random sample of 27 approved policies was selected and the total processing time in days was recorded with the following results:

73 19 16 64 28 28 31 90 60 56 31 56 22 18
45 48 17 17 17 91 92 63 50 51 69 16 17

DATA FILE
BANKTIME

(a) Compute the
    (1) arithmetic mean
    (2) median
    (3) midrange
    (4) first quartile
    (5) third quartile
    (6) midhinge
    (7) range
    (8) interquartile range
    (9) variance
    (10) standard deviation
    (11) coefficient of variation
(b) Construct a box-and-whisker plot.
(c) Are the data skewed? If so, how?
(d) If a customer enters the bank to purchase this type of insurance policy, and asks how long the approval process takes, what would you tell him?

**4.54** One of the major measures of the quality of service provided by any organization is the speed with which it responds to customer complaints. A large family-held department store selling furniture and flooring, including carpeting, had undergone a major expansion in the past several years. In particular, the flooring department had expanded from 2 installation crews to an installation supervisor, a measurer, and 15 installation crews. A sample of 50 complaints concerning carpeting installation was selected during a recent year. The following data represent the number of days between the receipt of the complaint and the resolution of the complaint.

54    5 35 137 31  27 152   2 123 81 74 27  11  19 126 110 110 29 61 35 94 31 26   5 12
  4 165 32  29 28 29  26 25   1  14 13 13 10   5  27   4  52 30 22 36 26 20 23 33 68

(a) Compute the
    (1) arithmetic mean
    (2) median
    (3) midrange
    (4) first quartile
    (5) third quartile
    (6) midhinge
    (7) range
    (8) interquartile range
    (9) variance
    (10) standard deviation
    (11) coefficient of variation

(b) Construct a box-and-whisker plot.

(c) Are the data skewed? If so, how?

(d) On the basis of the results of (a)–(c), if you had to tell the president of the company how long a customer should expect to wait to have a complaint resolved, what would you say? Explain.

**4.55** As an illustration of the misuse of statistics, an article by Glenn Kramon ("Coaxing the Stanford Elephant to Dance," *The New York Times* Sunday Business Section, November 11, 1990) implied that costs at Stanford Medical Center had been driven up higher than at competing institutions because the former was more likely to treat indigent, Medicare, Medicaid, sicker, and more complex patients. To illustrate this, a chart was provided that depicted a comparison of average 1989–90 hospital charges for three medical procedures (coronary bypass, simple birth, and hip replacement) at three competing institutions (El Camino, Sequoia, and Stanford).

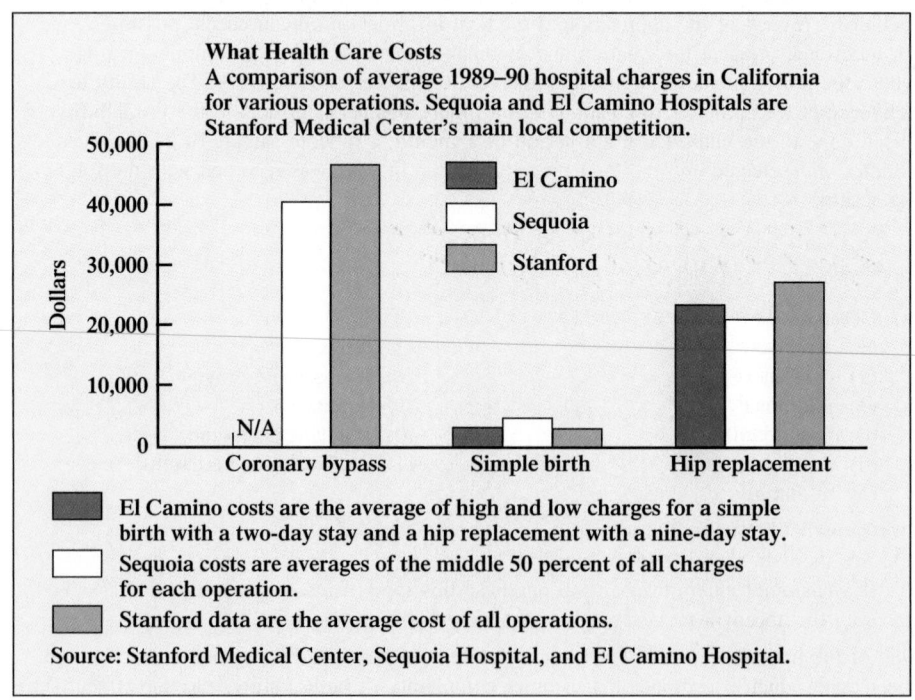

Reprinted by permission of The New York Times.

Suppose you were working in a medical center. Your CEO knows you are currently taking a course in statistics and calls you in to discuss this. She tells you that the article was presented in a discussion group setting as part of a meeting of regional area medical center CEOs last night and that one of them mentioned that this chart was totally meaningless and asked her opinion. She now requests that you prepare her response. You smile, take a deep breath, and reply . . .

**4.56** You are planning to study for your statistics examination with a group of classmates, one of whom you particularly want to impress. This individual has volunteered to use a software package to get the needed summary information, tables, and charts for a data set containing several numerical and categorical variables assigned by the instructor for study purposes. This person comes over to you with the printout and exclaims, "I've got it all—the means, the medians, the standard deviations, the stem-and-leafs, the box-and-whisker plots, the pie charts—for all our variables. The problem is, some of the output looks weird—like the stem-and-leafs and the box-and-whisker plots for gender and for major and the pie charts for grade point index and for height. Also, I can't understand why Professor McKenzie said we can't get the descriptive stats for some of our variables—I got it for everything! See, the mean for height is 68.23, the mean for grade point index is 2.76, the mean for gender is 1.50, the mean for major is 4.33." You look at your would-be friend, take a deep breath, and reply . . .

# TEAM PROJECT

**TP4.1**  Refer to TP3.1 on page 115. Your group, the _____ Corporation, has been hired by the vice president for research at a financial investment service to study the financial characteristics of currently traded domestic general stock funds. The investment service is interested in evaluating the list of domestic general stock funds so that it can make purchase recommendations to potential investors. In particular, the vice president is interested in a comparison of some features of these funds based on fee structure (no-load versus fee payment), objective (growth fund versus blend fund), and capitalization size of companies making up a fund's portfolio (large, mid, or small). Having prepared the appropriate tables and charts (see TP3.1), the _____ Corporation is ready to enhance its preliminary analysis. Armed with Special Data Set 1 of appendix D pertaining to various characteristics from a sample of 194 domestic general stock funds with high Morningstar Inc. dual ratings of 4 or 5:

**DATA FILE**
MUTUAL

(a) Outline how the group members will proceed with their tasks.
(b) Obtain various descriptive summary measures of the net asset value (in dollars), the total year-to-date return (in percents), the 3-year annualized total return (in percents), and the expense ratios (in percents) for the 107 no-load funds versus the 87 fee payment funds.
(c) Obtain various descriptive summary measures of the net asset value (in dollars), the total year-to-date return (in percents), the 3-year annualized total return (in percents), and the expense ratios (in percents) for the 59 growth funds versus the 135 blend funds.
(d) Obtain various descriptive summary measures of the net asset value (in dollars), the total year-to-date return (in percents), the 3-year annualized total return (in percents), and the expense ratios (in percents) for the 119 large-size funds, the 44 mid-size funds, and the 31 small-size funds.
(e) Write and submit an executive summary describing the results.
(f) Prepare and deliver a 10-minute oral presentation to the vice president for research at this financial investment service.

*Note*: Additional Team Projects can be found at the following World Wide Web address:
**http://www.prenhall.com/berenson**
These Team Projects deal with the characteristics of 80 universities and colleges (see the UNIV&COL file) and the features in 89 automobile models (see the AUTO96 file).

## Case Study — STATE ALCOHOLIC BEVERAGES OVERSIGHT BOARD STUDY ON BEERS

Dan Oates, director of research for the State Alcoholic Beverages Oversight Board, held a meeting with Manus Rabb, the newly appointed manager of the Ale and Beer Division, and Dr. Arnold Matlin, professor of nutrition at State University and a leading research consultant on beverage products, whom Mr. Rabb has just hired. "We now have access to the data from the June 1996 *Consumer Reports* beer taste testing study," commented Mr. Oates as he distributed copies of the article and the data. "As I recently said to Mr. Rabb, it is important that the Oversight Board evaluate the data and publish information that would be of interest and use to consumers. The Board has not done such a study during my tenure — the last such evaluation was made in 1990. According to this *Consumer Reports* article (June 1996, page 10), one billion dollars worth of beer is sold every week, and in the past decade there has been a nine-fold increase in the number of breweries in operation in the United States. As popularity with variants of this beverage has increased, it is important for the consumer to be made aware of the products' features." "I agree with you," Mr. Rabb stated. "I myself was appointed by the Board only 3 weeks ago and since then I have been reading the logs of the various studies directed by my predecessor, David Valinski, who managed this division for almost 40 years. Mr. Oates then asked Dr. Matlin to conduct the study and to report his findings to Mr. Rabb in 2 weeks. Dr. Matlin requested that a student assistant be provided.

Dr. Matlin has hired you to assist him in this study and has provided you with the *Consumer Reports* data on 69 different beers, broken down by type of product and origin of product. The data represent the price of a six-pack of 12-ounce bottles, the calories per 12 fluid ounces, the percent alcoholic content per 12 fluid ounces, the type of beer (craft lagers, craft ales, imported lagers, regular and ice beers, and light and nonalcoholic beers), and the country of origin (U.S.A. versus imported) for each of the 69 beers that were sampled (the first four are shown below).

Your task is to write a report based on a complete descriptive evaluation of each of the numerical variables—price, calories, and alcoholic content—regardless of type of product or origin. Then perform a similar evaluation comparing and contrasting each of these numerical variables based on type of product—craft lagers, craft ales, imported lagers, regular and ice beers, and light or nonalcoholic beers. In addition, perform a similar evaluation comparing and contrasting each of these numerical variables based on the origin of the beers—those brewed in the United States versus those that were imported. Appended to your report should be all appropriate tables, charts, and descriptive statistical information obtained from the survey results.

**DATA FILE**
BEER

| PRODUCT | PRICE | CALORIES | PCTALC | TYPE | ORIG |
|---------|-------|----------|--------|------|------|
| Brooklyn Brand | 6.24 | 159 | 5.2 | Craft Lgrs | USA |
| Leinenkugel's Red | 4.79 | 160 | 5.0 | Craft Lgrs | USA |
| Samuel Adams Boston | 5.96 | 160 | 4.9 | Craft Lgrs | USA |
| George Killian's Irish Red | 4.70 | 162 | 4.9 | Craft Lgrs | USA |

*Source: "Beers," Copyright 1996 by Consumers Union of U.S.. Adapted from* CONSUMER REPORTS, *June 1996, 10–17, by permission of Consumers Union of U.S., Inc., Yonkers, NY 10703-1057. Although these data sets originally appeared in* CONSUMER REPORTS, *the selective adaptation and resulting conclusions presented are those of the authors and are not sanctioned or endorsed in any way by Consumers Union, the publisher of* CONSUMER REPORTS.

# THE SPRINGVILLE HERALD CASE

Walter Fairfax, the head of the computer systems department, realized that in addition to the numerous tables and charts that had been prepared on the basis of Table SH3.4 (see page 119) concerning the number of data cartridges accessed for jobs, there was a need for various descriptive summary measures relating to location, variation, and skewness to make any report provided for management more useful.

## Exercise

**4.1 (a)** Compute all descriptive summary measures, stem-and-leaf displays, and box-and-whisker plots relating to the number of data cartridges accessed for jobs that you believe would be useful in preparing a report to management.

**DATA FILE**
SH3&4

**(b)** Write a report to management that summarizes the results obtained from the descriptive summary measures, stem-and-leaf displays, and box-and-whisker plots developed in (a).

## References

1. Huff, D., *How to Lie with Statistics* (New York: W.W. Norton, 1954).
2. Kendall, M. G., and A. Stuart, *The Advanced Theory of Statistics,* vol. 1 (London: Charles W. Griffin, 1958).
3. Kimble, G. A., *How to Use (and Misuse) Statistics* (Englewood Cliffs, NJ: Prentice Hall, 1978).
4. *Microsoft Excel 97* (Redmond, WA: Microsoft Corporation, 1997).
5. *Minitab for Windows Version 12* (State College, PA: Minitab, Inc., 1998).
6. Tukey, J., *Exploratory Data Analysis* (Reading, MA: Addison-Wesley, 1977).
7. Velleman, P. F., and D. C. Hoaglin, *Applications, Basics, and Computing of Exploratory Data Analysis* (Boston, MA: Duxbury Press, 1981).

## ❖ APPENDIX 4.1    USING MICROSOFT EXCEL FOR DESCRIPTIVE STATISTICS

### Using the Data Analysis Tool

Although various Microsoft Excel functions such as AVERAGE, MEDIAN, and STDEV can be used to obtain individual statistics, the Data Analysis tool can be used to simultaneously obtain a set of descriptive statistics as displayed in Figure 4.7 on page 153.

To obtain the descriptive statistics for the 17 domestic general stock funds whose fee structure consists of marketing fees paid from fund assets, open the MUTUAL.XLS workbook. Since we only wish to obtain statistics for the 17 domestic general funds whose fee structure consists of marketing fees paid from fund assets (those whose Group code = 1), we need to sort the data by group so that all the stock funds with a Group = 1 code will be in adjacent rows. To do this, select **Data | Sort**. In the Sort dialog box in the Sort By drop-down list box select **Group** and select the **Ascending** button. Click the **OK** button. The data have been sorted in ascending order by fee structure group.

Now we are ready to compute descriptive statistics for the 17 domestic general stock funds whose fee structure consists of marketing fees paid from fund assets (i.e., those whose Group code = 1). Select **Tools | Data Analysis**. Select **Descriptive Statistics** from the Analysis Tools list box and click the **OK** button. Enter **D1:D18** in the Input Range edit box because the 1-year percentage returns for the domestic general stock funds are in rows 2–18 and the variable label is in row 1. Select the

**Grouped By Columns** option button. Select the **Labels in First Row** check box. Leave the Confidence Levels for Mean check box unchecked because it will be discussed in chapter 10. To obtain the minimum and maximum values, select the **Kth Largest** and the **Kth Smallest** check boxes and enter **1** in their edit boxes. Select the **New Worksheet Ply** option button and enter the name **Descriptive** in its edit box. Select the **Summary Statistics** check box. Click the **OK** button.

### Using the PHStat Add-In to Obtain a Box-and-Whisker Plot

If Microsoft Excel is not running, click the **PHStat** add-in icon. If Microsoft Excel is running, select **File | Open**. Select the **PHStat** add-in file **PHSA.XLA**. Click the **Open** button. To obtain the box-and-whisker plot select **PHStat | Box-and-Whisker Plot**. If a single group is involved, in the Input Range edit box, enter the cell range for the data. If multiple groups are involved enter the cell range for the data variable and the cell range for the grouping variable. Select the **Five-Number Summary** button. Click the **OK** button.

## ❖ APPENDIX 4.2   USING MINITAB FOR DESCRIPTIVE STATISTICS

### Obtaining Descriptive Statistics

To obtain the descriptive statistics for the 17 domestic general stock funds whose fee structure consists of marketing fees paid from fund assets, open the MUTUAL.MTP file by selecting **File | Open Worksheet**.

Now we are ready to compute descriptive statistics for the 17 domestic general stock funds whose fee structure consists of marketing fees paid from fund assets (i.e., those whose Group code = 1), along with descriptive statistics for the other group codes (see Figure 4.8 on page 154). To obtain these statistics, select **Stat | Basic Statistics | Display Descriptive Statistics**. In the Display Descriptive Statistics dialog box, in the Variables List box, enter the **1Yr%Ret** or **C4**. Select the **By Variable** check box and enter **Group** or **C5**. Click the **OK** button.

### Obtaining a Box-and-Whisker Plot

To obtain the box-and-whisker plot illustrated in Figure 4.12 on page 163, with the MUTUAL.MTP file open, select **Graph | Boxplot**. In the Boxplot dialog box, in the Graph list box, in row 1 of the $Y$ column, enter **1Yr%Ret** or **C4**. In row 1 of the $X$ column, enter **Group** or **C5**. To obtain colors for each box-and-whisker plot, select **Edit Attributes** and select a **Fill Type**, **Fore Color**, **Back Color**, and **Edge Type**. Click the **OK** button to return to the Boxplot dialog box. Click the **OK** button.

# 5

# Basic Probability

# CHAPTER OBJECTIVES

✓ *To develop an understanding of the basic probability concepts*
✓ *To introduce conditional probability*
✓ *To use Bayes' theorem to revise probabilities in the light of new information*

## Introduction

In chapters 2 to 4 we studied data collection, tables and charts, and descriptive summary measures. In this chapter we turn our attention to the subject of probability, which serves as the link between describing and presenting information obtained from samples and being able to make inferences to larger populations. We discuss three different approaches to determining the probability of occurrence of different phenomena: *a priori* classical probability, empirical classical probability, and subjective probability. We then learn how to compute a variety of types of probabilities and to revise probabilities in the light of new information. Let us begin with a look at how a company uses probability to help plan its activities and processes.

## ◆ USING STATISTICS *The Consumer Electronics Company*

Numerous intensive studies have been conducted of consumer planning for the purchase of durable goods such as television sets, refrigerators, washing machines, stoves, and automobiles. Suppose that a marketing director for a consumer electronics company was interested in studying the intention of consumers to purchase a new large television (defined as 27 inches or larger) in the next 12 months and, as a follow up, whether they in fact actually purchase the television. On the basis of a survey of consumers, some of the questions the marketing director would like to answer include the following:

- What is the probability that the consumer is planning to purchase a large television in the next year?
- What is the probability that the consumer will actually purchase the large television?
- What is the probability that the consumer is planning to purchase the television and actually purchases the television?
- What is the probability that the consumer is planning to purchase the television or actually purchased the television?
- Given that the consumer is planning to purchase the television, what is the probability that the purchase is made?
- Does knowledge of whether the consumer plans to purchase the large television change the likelihood of predicting whether the consumer will purchase the large television?

Answers to these questions and others can help management develop future sales and marketing strategies.

## ◆ 5.1 ◆ BASIC PROBABILITY CONCEPTS

What do we mean by the word probability? **Probability** is the likelihood or chance that a particular event will occur. It could refer to the chance of picking a black card from a deck of cards, the chance that an individual prefers one product over another, or the chance that a new consumer product on the market will be successful. In each of these examples, the probability is a proportion or fraction whose values range between 0 and 1, inclusively. We note that an event that has no chance of occurring (i.e., the **null event**) has a probability of 0, while an event that is sure to occur (i.e., the **certain event**) has a probability of 1.

Each of the above examples refers to one of three approaches to the subject of probability. The first is often called the *a priori* **classical probability** approach. Here the probability of success is based on prior knowledge of the process involved. In the simplest case, where each outcome is equally likely, this chance of occurrence of the event is defined as follows:

## Probability of Occurrence

$$\text{Probability of occurrence} = \frac{X}{T} \tag{5.1}$$

where

$X$ = number of outcomes in which the event we are looking for occurs

$T$ = total number of possible outcomes

What does this probability tell us? In a standard deck of cards that has 26 red cards and 26 black cards, if we replace each card after it is drawn, does it mean that one out of the next two cards selected will be black? No, because we cannot say for sure what will happen on the next several selections. However, we can say that in the long run, if this selection process is continually repeated, the proportion of black cards selected will approach .50.

In this example, the number of successes and the number of outcomes are known from the composition of the deck of cards. However, in the second approach to probability, called the **empirical classical probability** approach, although the probability is still defined as the ratio of the number of favorable outcomes to the total number of outcomes, these outcomes are based on observed data, not upon prior knowledge of a process. This type of probability could refer to the proportion of individuals in a survey who actually purchase a television, who prefer a certain political candidate, or who have a part-time job while attending school.

The third approach to probability is called the **subjective probability** approach. Whereas the probability of a favorable event in the previous two approaches was computed objectively, either from prior knowledge or from actual data, subjective probability refers to the chance of occurrence assigned to an event by a particular individual. This chance may be quite different from the subjective probability assigned by another individual. For example, the inventor of a new toy may assign quite a different probability to the chance of success for the toy than the president of the company that is considering marketing the toy. The assignment of subjective probabilities to various events is usually based on a combination of an individual's past experience, personal opinion, and analysis of a particular situation. Subjective probability is especially useful in making decisions in situations in which the probability of various events cannot be determined empirically.

## Sample Spaces and Events

The basic elements of probability theory are the outcomes of the process or phenomenon under study. Each possible type of occurrence is referred to as an event.

A **simple event** can be described by a single characteristic. The collection of all the possible events is called the **sample space**.

We can achieve a better understanding of these terms by referring to the Consumer Electronics Company discussed in the Using Statistics example on page 190. Suppose that a sample of 1,000 households was initially selected and the respondents were asked whether they planned to purchase a large television. Twelve months later the same respondents were asked whether they actually purchased the television. The results are summarized in Table 5.1.

**Table 5.1**   *Purchase behavior for large televisions*

| | ACTUALLY PURCHASED | | |
|---|---|---|---|
| PLANNED TO PURCHASE | YES | NO | TOTAL |
| Yes | 200 | 50 | 250 |
| No | 100 | 650 | 750 |
| Total | 300 | 700 | 1,000 |

The sample space consists of the entire set of 1,000 respondents. The events within the sample space depend on how we wish to classify the different outcomes. For example, if we are interested in purchase plans, the events are "plan to purchase" and "do not plan to purchase." If we are interested in actual purchases, the events are "purchase" and "did not purchase." Thus, the manner in which the sample space is subdivided depends on the types of probabilities that are to be determined. With this in mind, it is of interest to define both the complement of an event and a joint event as follows:

The **complement** of event $A$ includes all events that are not part of event $A$. It is given by the symbol $A'$.

The complement of the event "plans to purchase" is "does not plan to purchase."

A **joint event** is an event that has two or more characteristics.

The event "planned to purchase" and "actually purchases" is a joint event, since the respondent must plan to purchase the television *and* actually purchase it.

## Contingency Tables and Venn Diagrams

There are several ways in which a particular sample space can be viewed. The first method involves assigning the appropriate events to a **table of cross-classifications** such as that displayed in Table 5.1. Such a table is also called a **contingency table** (see section 3.5). The values in the cells of the table were obtained by subdividing the sample space of 1,000 respondents according to whether someone planned to purchase and actually purchased the large television. Thus, for example, 200 of the respondents planned to purchase a large television and subsequently did purchase the large television.

A second way to present the sample space is by using a **Venn diagram**. This diagram graphically represents the various events as "unions" and "intersections" of circles. Figure 5.1 presents a typical Venn diagram for a two-variable situation, with each variable having only two events ($A$ and $A'$, $B$ and $B'$). The circle on the left (the red one) represents all events that are part of $A$. The circle on the right (the lighter one) represents all events that are part of $B$. The area contained within circle $A$ and circle $B$ (center area) is the **intersection** of $A$ and $B$ (written as $A \cap B$), since it is part of $A$ and also part of $B$. The total area of the two circles is the **union** of $A$ and $B$ (written as $A \cup B$) and contains all outcomes that are just part of event $A$, just part of event $B$, or part of both $A$ and $B$. The area in the diagram outside of $A \cup B$ contains those outcomes that are neither part of $A$ nor part of $B$.

In order to develop a Venn diagram, $A$ and $B$ must be defined. It does not matter which event is defined as $A$ or $B$, as long as we are consistent in evaluating the various events. For the consumer electronics example, the events can be defined as follows:

$A$ = planned to purchase             $B$ = actually purchased
$A'$ = did not plan to purchase          $B'$ = did not actually purchase

In drawing the Venn diagram (see Figure 5.2), the value of the intersection of $A$ and $B$ must be determined so that the sample space can be divided into its parts. $A \cap B$ consists of all 200 respondents who planned to purchase and actually purchased a large television. The remainder of event $A$ (planned to purchase) consists of the 50 respondents who planned to purchase and did not actually purchase a large television. The remainder of event $B$ (actually purchased) consists of the 100 respondents who did not plan to purchase and actually purchased the large television. The remaining 650 respondents represent those who neither planned to purchase nor actually purchased a large television. Let us apply a Venn diagram to analyzing a domestic general stock fund as in Example 5.1.

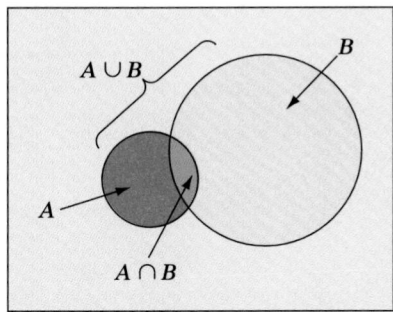

**FIGURE 5.1**
Venn diagram for events $A$ and $B$

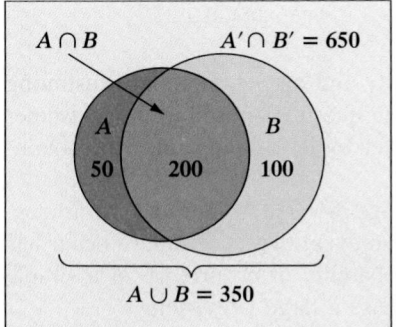

**FIGURE 5.2**
Venn diagram for the consumer electronics example

## Example 5.1 *Forming a Venn Diagram from a Domestic General Stock Fund Contingency Table*

In Table 3.8 on page 88 we cross-classified the objective (growth versus blend) and fee schedule for 194 domestic general stock funds. Suppose that we combine the five classes of fees so that there are only two categories, no load and other. We then form the following contingency table:

| | **FEE SCHEDULE** | | |
|---|---|---|---|
| **FUND OBJECTIVE** | **NO LOAD** | **OTHER** | **TOTAL** |
| Growth | 32 | 27 | 59 |
| Blend | 75 | 60 | 135 |
| Total | 107 | 87 | 194 |

Form the Venn diagram.

### SOLUTION

Using the following definitions:

$$A = \text{growth fund} \qquad B = \text{no-load fee structure}$$
$$A' = \text{blend fund} \qquad B' = \text{other than no-load fee structure}$$

we have the following Venn diagram:

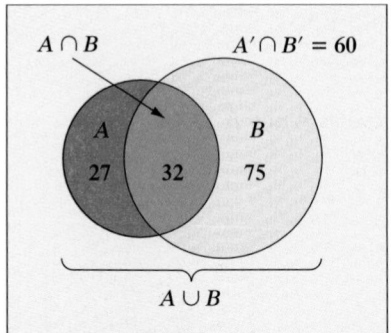

Venn diagram for the domestic general stock fund example

## Simple (Marginal) Probability

Thus far, we have focused on the meaning of probability and on defining and illustrating sample spaces. We will now begin to answer some of the questions posed in the consumer electronics example given at the beginning of the chapter by developing rules for obtaining different types of probability.

The most obvious rule for probabilities is that they range in value from 0 to 1. An impossible event has a probability of occurrence of zero, and an event that is certain to occur has a probability of 1. **Simple probability** refers to the probability of occurrence of a simple event $P(A)$, such as the probability of planning to purchase a large television.

How would we find the probability of selecting a respondent who planned to purchase a large television? Using equation (5.1) we have the following:

$$P(\text{planned to purchase}) = \frac{\text{number who planned to purchase}}{\text{total number of respondents}}$$

$$= \frac{250}{1,000} = .25$$

Thus, there is a .25 (or 25%) chance that a respondent planned to purchase a large television. Let us compute the probability of purchasing a large television set as in Example 5.2.

## Example 5.2 Computing the Probability of Purchasing a Large Television

Suppose instead that we were interested in those respondents who actually purchased a large television. Find the probability of selecting a respondent who actually purchased a large television.

### SOLUTION

$$P(\text{actually purchased}) = \frac{\text{number who actually purchased}}{\text{total number of respondents}}$$

$$= \frac{300}{1,000} = .30$$

There is a .30 (30%) chance of selecting a respondent who actually purchased the television.

Simple probability is also called **marginal probability**, since the total number of successes (those who plan to purchase) can be obtained from the appropriate margin of the contingency table (see Table 5.1 on page 192). Example 5.3 illustrates.

## Example 5.3 Computing the Probability That a Domestic General Stock Fund Will Be a No-Load Fund

In Example 5.1, we cross-classified the type of fund and whether the fund had a no-load fee structure. Find the probability that if a fund is randomly selected, it will have a no-load fee structure.

### SOLUTION

$$P(\text{no-load fee structure}) = \frac{\text{number of no-load funds}}{\text{total number of funds}}$$

$$= \frac{107}{194} = .552$$

There is a 55.2% chance that a randomly selected fund will have a no-load fee structure.

## Joint Probability

Whereas marginal probability refers to the occurrence of simple events, **joint probability** refers to phenomena containing two or more events, such as the probability of planning to purchase *and* actually purchasing a large television.

Recall that a joint event *A and B* means that both event *A and* event *B* must occur simultaneously. With reference to Table 5.1 on page 192, those individuals who planned to purchase and actually purchased a large television consist only of the outcomes in the single cell "yes—planned to purchase *and* yes—actually purchased." Since this consists of 200 respondents, the probability of picking a respondent who planned to purchase *and* actually purchased a large television is

$P$(planned to purchase *and* actually purchased

$$= \frac{\text{number who planned to purchase } and \text{ actually purchased}}{\text{total number of respondents}}$$

$$= \frac{200}{1,000} = .20$$

Example 5.4 demonstrates how to determine joint probability.

### Example 5.4 *Determining the Joint Probability for the Domestic General Stock Fund Example*

In Example 5.1 on page 194, we cross-classified the type of fund and whether the fund had a no-load fee structure. Find the probability that a randomly selected domestic general stock fund will have a growth objective *and* a no-load fee structure.

#### SOLUTION

$P$(growth objective *and* no-load fee structure)

$$= \frac{\text{number that have growth objective } and \text{ no-load fee structure}}{\text{total number of funds}}$$

$$= \frac{32}{194} = .165$$

There is a 16.5% chance that a randomly selected domestic general stock fund will have a growth objective and a no-load fee structure.

Now that we have discussed the concept of joint probability, the marginal probability of a particular event can be viewed in an alternative manner. In fact, the marginal probability of an event consists of a set of joint probabilities. For example, if $B$ consists of two events, $B_1$ and $B_2$, then we can observe that $P(A)$, the probability of event $A$, consists of the joint probability of event $A$ occurring with event $B_1$ and the joint probability of event $A$ occurring with event $B_2$. Thus, in general,

## Computing Marginal Probability

$$P(A) = P(A \text{ and } B_1) + P(A \text{ and } B_2) + \cdots + P(A \text{ and } B_k) \qquad (5.2)$$

where $B_1, B_2, \ldots, B_k$ are the $k$ mutually exclusive and collectively exhaustive events.

Events are **mutually exclusive** if the events cannot both occur.
Events are **collectively exhaustive** if one of the events must occur.

For example, being male and being female are mutually exclusive and collectively exhaustive events. No one is both (they are mutually exclusive), and everyone is one or the other (they are collectively exhaustive).

Suppose now that we want to use equation (5.2) to compute the marginal probability of planning to purchase a large television. We would have

$$P(\text{planned to purchase}) = P(\text{planned to purchase } and \text{ purchased})$$
$$+ P(\text{planned to purchase } and \text{ did not purchase})$$
$$= \frac{200}{1,000} + \frac{50}{1,000}$$
$$= \frac{250}{1,000} = .25$$

This is the same result that we obtain if we add up the number of outcomes that make up the simple event "planned to purchase."

## General Addition Rule

Having developed a means of finding the probability of event $A$ and the probability of event "$A$ and $B$," we should like to examine a rule that is used for finding the probability of event "$A$ or $B$," the union of $A$ and $B$ ($A \cup B$). This rule considers the occurrence of either event $A$ or event $B$ or both $A$ and $B$.

How would we find the probability that a respondent planned to purchase or actually purchased a large television? The event "planned to purchase or actually purchased" would include all respondents who had planned to purchase and all respondents who had actually purchased the large television. Each cell of the contingency table (Table 5.1 on page 192) can be examined to determine whether it is part of the event in question. If we want to study the event "planned to purchase or actually purchased" from Table 5.1, the cell "planned to purchase and did not actually purchase" is part of the event, since it includes respondents who planned to purchase. The cell "did not plan to purchase and actually purchased" is included because it contains respondents who actually purchased. Finally, the cell "planned to purchase *and* actually purchased" has both characteristics of interest. Therefore, the probability of planned to purchase or actually purchased can be obtained as follows:

$$P(\text{planned to purchase } or \text{ actually purchased}) = P(\text{planned to purchase } and \text{ did not actually purchase})$$
$$+ P(\text{did not plan to purchase } and \text{ actually purchased})$$
$$+ P(\text{planned to purchase } and \text{ actually purchased})$$
$$= \frac{50}{1,000} + \frac{100}{1,000} + \frac{200}{1,000} = \frac{350}{1,000}$$

The computation of $P(A \ or \ B)$, the probability of the event $A \ or \ B$, can be expressed in the following general addition rule:

## General Addition Rule

The probability of $A \ or \ B$ is equal to the probability of $A$ plus the probability of $B$ minus the probability of $A \ and \ B$.

$$P(A \ or \ B) = P(A) + P(B) - P(A \ and \ B) \tag{5.3}$$

Applying this addition rule to our previous example, we obtain the following result:

$$P(\text{planned to purchase } or \text{ actually purchased}) = P(\text{planned to purchase})$$
$$+ P(\text{actually purchased})$$
$$- P(\text{planned to purchase } and \text{ actually purchased})$$
$$= \frac{250}{1,000} + \frac{300}{1,000} - \frac{200}{1,000}$$
$$= \frac{350}{1,000} = .35$$

The **addition rule** consists of taking the probability of $A$ and adding it to the probability of $B$; the intersection of $A$ and $B$ must then be subtracted from this total because it has already been included twice in computing the probability of $A$ and the probability of $B$. This can be demonstrated by referring to Table 5.1 on page 192. If the outcomes of the event "planned to purchase" are added to those of the event "actually purchased," then the joint event planned to purchase *and* actually purchased has been included in each of these simple events. Therefore, since this has been "double-counted," it must be subtracted to provide the correct result. Example 5.5 illustrates.

## Example 5.5 *Using the Addition Rule for the Domestic General Stock Fund Example*

In Example 5.1 on page 194, we cross-classified the type of fund and whether the fund had a no-load fee structure. Find the probability that a randomly selected domestic general stock fund will have a growth objective or a no-load fee structure.

### SOLUTION

$$P\left(\begin{array}{l}\text{growth objective } or \\ \text{no-load fee structure}\end{array}\right) = P(\text{growth objective})$$
$$+ P(\text{no-load fee structure})$$
$$- P(\text{growth objective } and \text{ no-load fee structure})$$

$$= \frac{59}{194} + \frac{107}{194} - \frac{32}{194}$$

$$= \frac{134}{194} = .691$$

There is a 69.1% chance that a randomly selected domestic general stock fund will have a growth objective *or* a no-load fee structure.

## Addition Rule for Mutually Exclusive Events

In certain circumstances, the joint probability need not be subtracted because it is equal to zero as is discussed in Example 5.6.

**Example 5.6** *Using the Addition Rule for Mutually Exclusive Events*

Suppose that we wanted to know the probability of picking either a heart *or* a spade if we were selecting only one card from a standard deck of 52 playing cards. Find this probability using the addition rule.

*SOLUTION*

$$P(\text{heart } or \text{ spade}) = P(\text{heart}) + P(\text{spade}) - P(\text{heart } and \text{ spade})$$

$$= \frac{13}{52} + \frac{13}{52} - \frac{0}{52} = \frac{26}{52} = .50$$

There is a 50% chance that a randomly selected card is a heart or a spade.

We realize that the probability that a card will be both a heart *and* a spade simultaneously is zero, because in a standard deck each card belongs to only one particular suit. The joint occurrence in this case is nonexistent (called the **null set**) because it contains no outcomes—a card cannot be a heart and a spade simultaneously. As mentioned previously, whenever the joint event cannot occur, the events involved are considered to be *mutually exclusive*. This refers to the fact that the occurrence of one event (a heart) means that the other event (a spade) cannot occur. Thus, the addition rule for mutually exclusive events reduces to

### Addition Rule for Mutually Exclusive Events

The probability of *A or B* is equal to the probability of *A* plus the probability of *B*.

$$P(A \text{ } or \text{ } B) = P(A) + P(B) \qquad (5.4)$$

## Addition Rule for Collectively Exhaustive Events

Now consider what the probability would be of selecting a card that was red *or* black. Since red *and* black are mutually exclusive events, using equation (5.4) we would have

$$P(\text{red } or \text{ black}) = P(\text{red}) + P(\text{black})$$

$$= \frac{26}{52} + \frac{26}{52} = \frac{52}{52} = 1.0$$

The probability of red or black adds up to 1.0. This means that the card selected must be red or black, because these are the only colors in a standard deck. Since one of these events must occur, they are considered to be collectively exhaustive events. Finding such a probability is depicted in Example 5.7.

**Example 5.7** *Using the Addition Rule for Collectively Exhaustive Events in the Domestic General Stock Fund Example*

In Example 5.1 on page 194, we cross-classified the type of fund and whether the fund had a no-load fee structure. Find the probability that a randomly selected domestic general stock fund will have a no-load or other fee structure.

**SOLUTION**

$$P(\text{no-load } or \text{ other}) = P(\text{no-load}) + P(\text{other})$$

$$= \frac{107}{194} + \frac{87}{194}$$

$$= \frac{194}{194} = 1.0$$

The probability that a randomly selected domestic general stock fund will have a no-load *or* other fee structure is 100% because these are the only two categories listed for fund objective.

## Problems for Section 5.1

### Learning the Basics

• **5.1** Suppose that two coins are tossed.
(a) Give an example of a simple event.
(b) Give an example of a joint event.
(c) What is the complement of a head on the first toss?

**5.2** Suppose that an urn contains 12 red balls and 8 white balls.
(a) Give an example of a simple event.
(b) What is the complement of a red ball?

**5.3** Suppose that the following contingency table was set up:

|      | B  | B' |
|------|----|----|
| A    | 10 | 20 |
| A'   | 20 | 40 |

What is the probability of

(a) event $A$?

(b) event $B$?

(c) event $A'$?

(d) event $A$ and $B$?

(e) event $A$ and $B'$?

(f) event $A'$ and $B'$?

(g) event $A$ or $B$?

(h) event $A$ or $B'$?

(i) event $A'$ or $B'$?

● **5.4** Suppose that the following contingency table was set up:

|       | $B$ | $B'$ |
|-------|-----|------|
| $A$   | 10  | 30   |
| $A'$  | 25  | 35   |

What is the probability of

(a) event $A$?

(b) event $B$?

(c) event $A'$?

(d) event $A$ and $B$?

(e) event $A$ and $B'$?

(f) event $A'$ and $B'$?

(g) event $A$ or $B$?

(h) event $A$ or $B'$?

(i) event $A'$ or $B'$?

## Applying the Concepts

**5.5** For each of the following, indicate whether the type of probability involved is an example of *a priori* classical probability, empirical classical probability, or subjective probability.

(a) That the next toss of a fair coin will land on heads

(b) That Italy will win soccer's World Cup the next time the competition is held

(c) That the sum of the faces of two dice will be 7

(d) That the train taking a commuter to work will be more than 10 minutes late

(e) That a Republican will win the next presidential election in the United States

**5.6** For each of the following, state whether the events created are mutually exclusive and/or collectively exhaustive. If they are not, either reword the categories to make them mutually exclusive and/or collectively exhaustive or explain why this would not be useful.

(a) Registered voters were asked whether they registered as Republican or Democrat.

(b) Respondents were classified on car ownership into the categories American, European, Japanese, or none.

(c) People were asked, "Do you currently live in (i) an apartment, (ii) a house?"

(d) A product was classified as defective or not defective.

(e) People were asked, "Do you intend to purchase a new car in the next 6 months?" (i) yes, (ii) no.

**5.7** The probability of each of the following events is zero. For each, state why. Tell what common characteristic of these events makes their probability zero.

(a) A person who is registered as a Republican and a Democrat

(b) A product that is defective and not defective

(c) A house that is a ranch style and split-level style

● **5.8** In the past several years, credit card companies have made an aggressive effort to solicit new accounts from college students. Suppose that a sample of 200 students at your college indicated the following information as to whether the student possessed a bank credit card and/or a travel and entertainment credit card:

| BANK CREDIT CARD | TRAVEL AND ENTERTAINMENT CREDIT CARD | |
|------------------|------|------|
|                  | YES  | NO   |
| Yes              | 60   | 60   |
| No               | 15   | 65   |

(a) Give an example of a simple event.
(b) Give an example of a joint event.
(c) What is the complement of having a bank credit card?
(d) Why is "having a bank credit card *and* having a travel and entertainment credit card" a joint event?

If a student is selected at random, what is the probability that
(e) the student has a bank credit card?
(f) the student has a travel and entertainment credit card?
(g) the student has a bank credit card *and* a travel and entertainment card?
(h) the student has neither a bank credit card *nor* a travel and entertainment card?
(i) the student has a bank credit card *or* has a travel and entertainment card?
(j) the student does not have a bank credit card *or* has a travel and entertainment card?

**5.9** The director of a large employment agency wishes to study various characteristics of its job applicants. A sample of 150 applicants has been selected, and the following information is provided as to whether the applicants have had their current jobs for at least 5 years and whether or not the applicants are college graduates:

| HELD CURRENT JOB AT LEAST 5 YEARS | COLLEGE GRADUATE | | |
|---|---|---|---|
| | YES | NO | TOTAL |
| Yes | 25 | 45 | 70 |
| No | 55 | 25 | 80 |
| Total | 80 | 70 | 150 |

(a) Set up a Venn diagram to evaluate the probabilities.
(b) Give an example of a simple event.
(c) Give an example of a joint event.
(d) What is the complement of "had current job for at least 5 years"?

If an applicant is selected at random, what is the probability that he or she
(e) is a college graduate?
(f) has held the current job less than 5 years?
(g) is a college graduate *and* has held the current job less than five years?
(h) is not a college graduate *and* has held the current job less than five years?
(i) is a college graduate *or* has held the current job less than 5 years?
(j) is not a college graduate *or* has held the current job less than 5 years?

• **5.10** A sample of 500 respondents was selected in a large metropolitan area to determine various information concerning consumer behavior. Among the questions asked was "Do you enjoy shopping for clothing?" Of 240 males, 136 answered yes. Of 260 females, 224 answered yes.
(a) Set up a 2 $\times$ 2 table or a Venn diagram to evaluate the probabilities.
(b) Give an example of a simple event.
(c) Give an example of a joint event.
(d) What is the complement of "enjoy shopping for clothing"?

What is the probability that a respondent chosen at random
(e) is a male?
(f) enjoys shopping for clothing?
(g) is a female *and* enjoys shopping for clothing?
(h) is a male *and* does not enjoy shopping for clothing?
(i) is a female *or* enjoys shopping for clothing?
(j) is a male *or* does not enjoy shopping for clothing?
(k) is a male *or* a female?

**5.11** A company has made available to its employees (without charge) extensive health club facilities that may be used before work, during the lunch hour, after work, and on weekends. Records for the last year indicate that of 250 employees, 110 used the facilities at some time. Of 170 males employed by the company, 65 used the facilities.
   (a) Set up a 2 × 2 table or a Venn diagram to evaluate the probabilities of using the facilities.
   (b) Give an example of a simple event.
   (c) Give an example of a joint event.
   (d) What is the complement of "used the health club facilities"?
   What is the probability that an employee chosen at random
   (e) is a male?
   (f) has used the health club facilities?
   (g) is a female *and* has used the health club facilities?
   (h) is a female *and* has not used the health club facilities?
   (i) is a female *or* has used the health club facilities?
   (j) is a male *or* has not used the health club facilities?
   (k) has used the health club facilities *or* has not used the health club facilities?

**5.12** Each year, ratings are compiled concerning the performance of new cars during the first 90 days of use. Suppose that the cars have been categorized according to two attributes, whether or not the car needs warranty-related repair (yes or no) and the country in which the company manufacturing the car is based (United States, not United States). Based on the data collected, the probability that the new car needs a warranty repair is .04, the probability that the car is manufactured by an American-based company is .60, and the probability that the new car needs a warranty repair *and* was manufactured by an American-based company is .025.
   (a) Set up a 2 × 2 table or a Venn diagram to evaluate the probabilities of a warranty-related repair.
   (b) Give an example of a simple event.
   (c) Give an example of a joint event.
   (d) What is the complement of "manufactured by an American-based company"?
   What is the probability that a new car selected at random
   (e) needs a warranty-related repair?
   (f) is not manufactured by an American-based company?
   (g) needs a warranty repair *and* is manufactured by a company based in the United States?
   (h) does not need a warranty repair *and* is not manufactured by a company based in the United States?
   (i) needs a warranty repair *or* was manufactured by an American-based company?
   (j) needs a warranty repair *or* was not manufactured by an American-based company?
   (k) needs a warranty repair *or* does not need a warranty repair?

 **5.2  CONDITIONAL PROBABILITY**

## Computing Conditional Probabilities

Each situation we have examined thus far in this chapter has involved the probability of a particular event when sampling from the entire sample space. However, how would we find various probabilities if certain information about the events involved is already known?

When we are computing the probability of a particular event $A$, given information about the occurrence of another event $B$, this probability is referred to as **conditional probability**, $P(A \mid B)$. The conditional probability $P(A \mid B)$ can be defined as follows:

## Conditional Probability

The probability of A given B is equal to the probability of A *and* B divided by the probability of B

$$P(A \mid B) = \frac{P(A \text{ and } B)}{P(B)} \qquad (5.5a)$$

or

$$P(B \mid A) = \frac{P(A \text{ and } B)}{P(A)} \qquad (5.5b)$$

where

$$P(A \text{ and } B) = \text{joint probability of } A \text{ and } B$$
$$P(A) = \text{marginal probability of } A$$
$$P(B) = \text{marginal probability of } B$$

Before using equation (5.5a) or (5.5b) to find a conditional probability, we could use either the contingency table or a Venn diagram. In the consumer electronics example we have been discussing, suppose we were told that a respondent planned to purchase the large television. What would be the probability that the respondent actually purchased the television? In this example, we wish to find $P$(actual purchase | planned to purchase). Here the information is given that the respondent planned to purchase the large television. Therefore, the sample space does not consist of all 1,000 respondents in the survey; it consists only of those respondents who planned to purchase the large television. Of 250 such respondents, 200 actually purchased the large television. Therefore, the probability that a respondent actually purchased the large television given that he or she planned to purchase is

$$P(\text{actually purchased} \mid \text{planned to purchase}) = \frac{\text{planned to purchase } and \text{ actually purchased}}{\text{planned to purchase}}$$

$$= \frac{200}{250}$$

This result (200/250) can also be obtained by using equation (5.5b):

If

$$P(B \mid A) = \frac{P(A \text{ and } B)}{P(A)}$$

where

$$\text{event } A = \text{planned to purchase}$$
$$\text{event } B = \text{actually purchased}$$

then

$$P(\text{actually purchased} \mid \text{planned to purchase}) = \frac{200/1,000}{250/1,000}$$

$$= \frac{200}{250} = 0.80$$

Example 5.8 further illustrates this process.

## Example 5.8 *Finding a Conditional Probability in the Domestic General Stock Fund Example*

In Example 5.1 on page 194, we cross-classified the type of fund and whether the fund had a no-load fee structure. Suppose that we know that a particular fund is a no-load fund. What then is the probability that it has a growth fund objective?

### SOLUTION

Since we know that the domestic general stock fund is a no-load fund, the sample space has been reduced to 107 funds. Of these 107 funds, we observe that 32 have growth objectives. Therefore, the probability that a fund has a growth objective given that it is a no-load fund is obtained as follows:

$P$(growth objective | no-load fee structure)

$$= \frac{\text{number of funds with growth objective } and \text{ no-load fee structure}}{\text{number of funds with no-load fee structure}}$$

$$= \frac{32}{107} = .299$$

If we were to use equation (5.5a) and define

$$A = \text{growth fund} \qquad B = \text{no-load fee structure}$$
$$A' = \text{blend fund} \qquad B' = \text{other than no-load fee structure}$$

then, using equation (5.5a)

$$P(\text{growth objective | no-load fee structure}) = \frac{P(\text{growth objective } and \text{ no-load fee structure})}{P(\text{no-load fee structure})}$$

$$= \frac{32/194}{107/194} = \frac{32}{107} = .299$$

Therefore, given that a fund has a no-load fee structure, there is a 29.9% chance that it will have a growth objective.

## Decision Trees

In Table 5.1 respondents were classified according to whether they planned to purchase and whether they actually purchased a large television. An alternative way to view the breakdown of the possibilities into four cells is through the use of a **decision tree**. Figure 5.3 represents the decision tree for this example.

In Figure 5.3, beginning at the left with the entire set of respondents, there are two "branches" according to whether or not the respondent planned to purchase a large television. Each of these branches has two subbranches, corresponding to whether the respondent actually purchased or did not actually purchase the large television. The probabilities at the end of the initial branches represent the marginal probabilities of $A$ and $A'$. The probabilities at the end of each of the four subbranches represent the joint probability for each

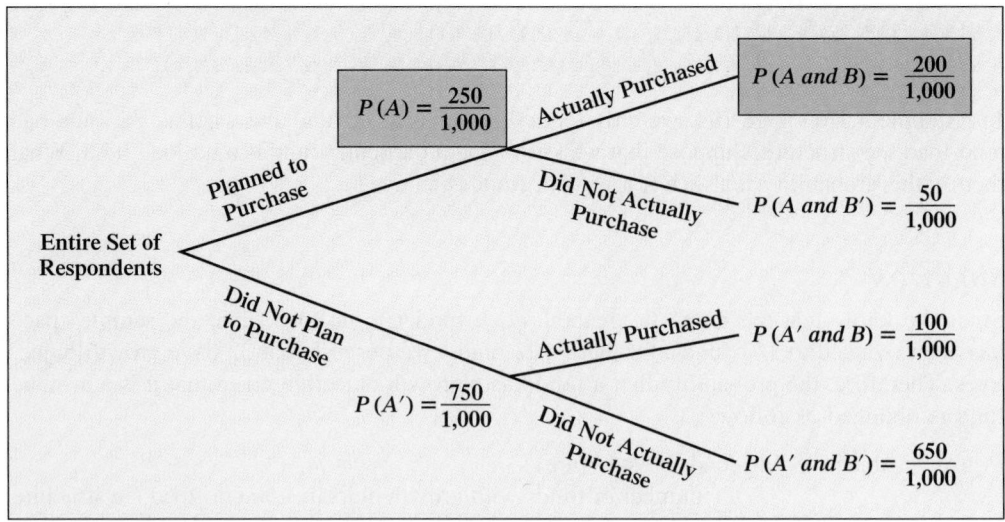

**FIGURE 5.3** Decision tree for the consumer electronics example

combination of events $A$ and $B$. The conditional probability can be obtained by dividing the joint probability by the appropriate marginal probability.

For example, to obtain the probability the respondent actually purchased given that the respondent planned to purchase the large television, we would take $P$(planned to purchase *and* actually purchased) and divide it by $P$(planned to purchase). From Figure 5.3 we would have

$$P(\text{actually purchased} \mid \text{planned to purchase}) = \frac{200/1{,}000}{250/1{,}000}$$

$$= \frac{200}{250}$$

Example 5.9 illustrates how to form a decision tree.

## Example 5.9 *Forming the Decision Tree for the Domestic General Stock Fund Example*

In Example 5.1 on page 194, we cross-classified the type of fund and whether the fund had a no-load fee structure. Form the decision tree and use the decision tree to find the probability that a fund has a growth fund objective given that the fund is a no-load fund.

### SOLUTION

Using the following definitions:

$$A = \text{growth fund} \qquad B = \text{no-load fee structure}$$
$$A' = \text{blend fund} \qquad B' = \text{other than no-load fee structure}$$

the decision tree is at the top of page 207

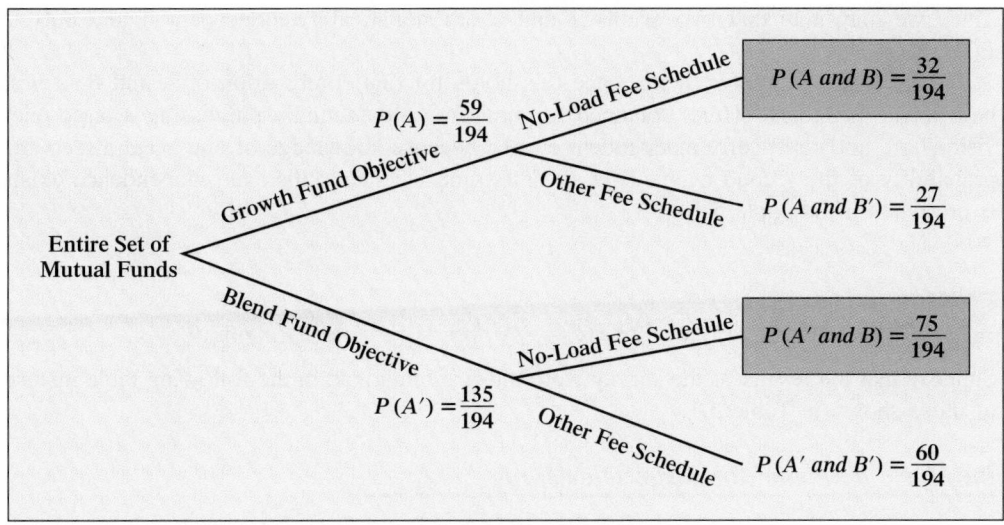

Decision tree for the domestic general stock fund example

Using equation (5.5a)

$$P(\text{growth objective} \mid \text{no-load fee structure}) = \frac{P(\text{growth objective } and \text{ no-load fee structure})}{P(\text{no-load fee structure})}$$

$$= \frac{32/194}{107/194} = \frac{32}{107} = .299$$

## Statistical Independence

In our example concerning the purchase of large televisions, we observed that the probability that the respondent selected actually purchased the large television, given that the respondent planned to purchase, is 200/250 = .80. We may remember that the probability of selecting a respondent who actually purchases is 300/1,000, which reduces to .30. This result reveals some important information. The prior knowledge that the respondent planned to purchase affected the probability that the respondent actually purchased the television. The outcome is conditional on prior information. Unlike this example, when the outcome of one event does not affect the probability of occurrence of another event, the events are said to be statistically independent. **Statistical independence** can be defined as follows:

**Statistical Independence**

$$P(A \mid B) = P(A) \qquad (5.6)$$

where

$P(A \mid B)$ = conditional probability of $A$ given $B$

$P(A)$ = marginal probability of $A$

Thus, we may note that two events $A$ and $B$ are statistically independent if and only if $P(A \mid B) = P(A)$.

In a $2 \times 2$ contingency table, once this holds for one combination of $A$ and $B$, it will be true for all others.[1] Here, "planned to purchase" and "actually purchasing a large television" are not statistically independent events, because knowledge of one event affects the probability of the second event. How to determine whether statistical independence exists is presented in Example 5.10:

[1] *In a contingency table with R rows and C columns, the rule would have to be examined for $(R - 1)(C - 1)$ separate combinations of A and B.*

## Example 5.10 *Determining Statistical Independence*

Suppose that the results of the survey were those summarized in the following table instead of those shown in Table 5.1.

*Purchase behavior for large televisions*

| | ACTUALLY PURCHASED | | |
| PLANNED TO PURCHASE | YES | NO | TOTAL |
| --- | --- | --- | --- |
| Yes | 75 | 175 | 250 |
| No | 225 | 525 | 750 |
| Total | 300 | 700 | 1,000 |

Determine whether planning to purchase and actually purchasing a new television are statistically independent.

### SOLUTION
For these data,

$$P(\text{actually purchased} \mid \text{planned to purchase}) = \frac{75/1,000}{250/1,000}$$

$$= \frac{75}{250} = .30$$

which is equal to $P(\text{actually purchased}) = 300/1,000 = .30$. Thus, in this case, planning to purchase and actually purchasing a large television are statistically independent. Knowledge of one event in no way affects the probability of the second event.

## Multiplication Rule

The formula for conditional probability can be manipulated algebraically so that the joint probability $P(A \text{ and } B)$ can be determined from the conditional probability of an event. Using equation (5.5a),

$$P(A \mid B) = \frac{P(A \text{ and } B)}{P(B)}$$

and solving for the joint probability $P(A \text{ and } B)$, we have the **general multiplication rule**.

## General Multiplication Rule

The probability of A *and* B is equal to the probability of A given B times the probability of B.

$$P(A \text{ and } B) = P(A \mid B)P(B) \qquad (5.7)$$

To demonstrate the use of this multiplication rule, we turn to Examples 5.11 and 5.12.

## Example 5.11 *Using the Multiplication Rule*

Suppose that 20 marking pens are displayed in a stationery store. Six are red and 14 are blue. We are to select 2 markers randomly from the set of 20. Find the probability that both markers selected are red.

### SOLUTION

Here the multiplication rule can be used in the following way:

$$P(A \text{ and } B) = P(A \mid B)P(B)$$

Therefore if

$$A_R = \text{second marker selected is red}$$
$$B_R = \text{first marker selected is red}$$

we have

$$P(A_R \text{ and } B_R) = P(A_R \mid B_R)P(B_R)$$

The probability that the first marker is red is 6/20, because 6 of the 20 markers are red. However, the probability that the second marker is also red depends on the result of the first selection. If the first marker is not returned to the display after its color is determined (sampling *without* replacement), then the number of markers remaining will be 19. If the first marker is red, the probability that the second is also red is 5/19, because 5 red markers remain in the display. Therefore, using equation (5.7), we have the following:

$$P(A_R \text{ and } B_R) = \left(\frac{5}{19}\right)\left(\frac{6}{20}\right)$$
$$= \frac{30}{380} = .079$$

There is a 7.9% chance that both markers will be red.

## Example 5.12 *Using the Multiplication Rule When Sampling with Replacement*

What if the first marker selected is returned to the display after its color is determined? Find the probability of selecting red markers on both selections.

*SOLUTION*

In this example, the probability of picking a red marker on the second selection is the same as on the first selection (sampling *with* replacement), because there are 6 red markers out of 20 in the display. Therefore, we have the following:

$$P(A_R \text{ and } B_R) = P(A_R \mid B_R)P(B_R)$$
$$= \left(\frac{6}{20}\right)\left(\frac{6}{20}\right)$$
$$= \frac{36}{400} = .09$$

There is a 9% chance that both markers will be red.

---

This example of sampling *with* replacement illustrates that the second selection is independent of the first, because the second probability was not influenced by the first selection. Therefore, the **multiplication rule for independent events** can be expressed as follows [by substituting $P(A)$ for $P(A \mid B)$].

If $A$ and $B$ are statistically independent, the probability of $A$ *and* $B$ is equal to the probability of $A$ times the probability of $B$.

$$P(A \text{ and } B) = P(A)P(B) \tag{5.8}$$

If this rule holds for two events, $A$ and $B$, then $A$ and $B$ are statistically independent. Therefore, there are two ways to determine statistical independence.

**1.** Events $A$ and $B$ are statistically independent if and only if $P(A \mid B) = P(A)$.

**2.** Events $A$ and $B$ are statistically independent if and only if $P(A \text{ and } B) = P(A)P(B)$.

It should be noted that for a $2 \times 2$ contingency table, if this is true for one joint event, it will be true for all joint events.[2]

Now that we have discussed the multiplication rule, we can write the formula for marginal probability [equation (5.2)] as follows.

If

$$P(A) = P(A \text{ and } B_1) + P(A \text{ and } B_2) + \cdots + P(A \text{ and } B_k)$$

then, using the multiplication rule, we have

**Marginal Probability**

$$P(A) = P(A \mid B_1)P(B_1) + P(A \mid B_2)P(B_2) + \cdots + P(A \mid B_k)P(B_k) \tag{5.9}$$

where $B_1, B_2, \ldots, B_k$ are the $k$ mutually exclusive and collectively exhaustive events.

This formula may be illustrated by referring to Table 5.1 on page 192. Using equation (5.9), we compute the probability of planning to purchase as follows:

$$P(A) = P(A \mid B_1)P(B_1) + P(A \mid B_2)P(B_2)$$

[2] *See footnote 1.*

where

$P(A)$ = probability of planned to purchase

$P(B_1)$ = probability of actually purchased

$P(B_2)$ = probability of did not actually purchase

$$P(A) = \left(\frac{200}{300}\right)\left(\frac{300}{1,000}\right) + \left(\frac{50}{700}\right)\left(\frac{700}{1,000}\right)$$

$$= \frac{200}{1,000} + \frac{50}{1,000} = \frac{250}{1,000}$$

## Problems for Section 5.2

### Learning the Basics

**5.13** Suppose that the following contingency table was set up:

|  | Purch B | Didn't Pur B' |  |
|---|---|---|---|
| Plan to Pur A | 10 | 20 | 30 |
| Didn't Plan A' | 20 | 40 | 60 |
|  | 30 | 60 | 90 |

What is the probability of
(a) $A \mid B$?
(b) $A \mid B'$?
(c) $A' \mid B'$?
(d) Are events $A$ and $B$ statistically independent?

• **5.14** Suppose that the following contingency table was set up:

|  | B | B' |
|---|---|---|
| A | 10 | 30 |
| A' | 25 | 35 |

What is the probability of
(a) $A \mid B$?
(b) $A \mid B'$?
(c) $A' \mid B'$?
(d) Are $A$ and $B$ statistically independent?

• **5.15** If $P(A \text{ and } B) = .4$ and $P(B) = .8$, find $P(A \mid B)$.

**5.16** If $P(A) = .7$ and $P(B) = .6$, and $A$ and $B$ are statistically independent, find $P(A \text{ and } B)$?

**5.17** If $P(A) = .3$ and $P(B) = .4$, and $P(A \text{ and } B) = .20$, are $A$ and $B$ statistically independent?

### Applying the Concepts

• **5.18** In the past several years, credit card companies have made an aggressive effort to solicit new accounts from college students. Suppose that a sample of 200 students at your college indicated the following information as to whether the student possessed a bank credit card and/or a travel and entertainment credit card:

| | TRAVEL AND ENTERTAINMENT CREDIT CARD | |
|---|---|---|
| BANK CREDIT CARD | YES | NO |
| Yes | 60 | 60 |
| No | 15 | 65 |

(a) Assume that we know that the student has a bank credit card. What is the probability, then, that he or she has a travel and entertainment card?

(b) Assume that we know that the student does not have a travel and entertainment card. What then is the probability that he or she has a bank credit card?

(c) Are the two events, having a bank credit card and having a travel and entertainment card, statistically independent? Explain.

**5.19** The director of a large employment agency wishes to study various characteristics of its job applicants. A sample of 150 applicants has been selected and the following information is provided as to whether the applicants have had their current jobs for at least 5 years and whether or not the applicants are college graduates:

| HELD CURRENT JOB AT LEAST 5 YEARS | COLLEGE GRADUATE | | |
|---|---|---|---|
| | YES | NO | TOTAL |
| Yes | 25 | 45 | 70 |
| No | 55 | 25 | 80 |
| Total | 80 | 70 | 150 |

(a) Given that the applicant is a college graduate, what is the probability that he or she has held a current job less than 5 years?

(b) If the applicant has held a current job less than 5 years, what is the probability that he or she is a college graduate?

(c) Explain the difference in the results in (a) and (b).

(d) Are being a college graduate and holding the current job at least 5 years statistically independent? Explain.

**5.20** A sample of 500 respondents was selected in a large metropolitan area to determine various information concerning consumer behavior. The following contingency table was obtained:

| ENJOYS SHOPPING FOR CLOTHING | GENDER | | |
|---|---|---|---|
| | MALE | FEMALE | TOTAL |
| Yes | 136 | 224 | 360 |
| No | 104 | 36 | 140 |
| Total | 240 | 260 | 500 |

(a) Suppose the respondent chosen is a female. What then is the probability that she does not enjoy shopping for clothing?

(b) Suppose the respondent chosen enjoys shopping for clothing. What then is the probability that the individual is a male?

(c) Are enjoying shopping for clothing and the gender of the individual statistically independent? Explain.

**5.21** A company has made available to its employees (without charge) extensive health club facilities that may be used before work, during the lunch hour, after work, and on weekends. Records for the last year indicate that of 250 employees, 110 used the facilities at some time. Of 170 males employed by the company, 65 used the facilities.

(a) Suppose that we select a female employee of the company. What then is the probability that she has used the health club facilities?

(b) Suppose that we select a male employee of the company. What then is the probability that he has not used the health club facilities?

(c) Are the gender of the individual and the use of the health club facilities statistically independent? Explain.

**5.22** Each year, ratings are compiled concerning the performance of new cars during the first 90 days of use. Suppose that the cars have been categorized according to two attributes, whether or not the car needs warranty-related repair (yes or no) and the country in which the company manufacturing the car is based (United States, not United States). Based on the data collected, the probability that the new car needs a warranty repair is .04, the probability that the car is manufactured by an American-based company is .60, and the probability that the new car needs a warranty repair *and* was manufactured by an American-based company is .025.

(a) Suppose we know that the car was manufactured by a company that is based in the United States. What then is the probability that the car needs a warranty repair?

(b) Suppose we know that the car was not manufactured by a company that is based in the United States. What then is the probability that the car needs a warranty repair?

(c) Are need for a warranty repair and location of the company manufacturing the car statistically independent?

**5.23** Suppose you believe that the probability that you will get an A in Statistics is .6 and the probability that you will get an A in Organizational Behavior is .8. If these events are independent, what is the probability that you will get an A in both Statistics *and* Organizational Behavior? Give some plausible reasons why these events may not be independent, even though the teachers of these two subjects may not communicate about your work.

**5.24** A standard deck of cards is being used to play a game. There are four suits (hearts, diamonds, clubs, and spades), each having 13 faces (ace, 2, 3, 4, 5, 6, 7, 8, 9, 10, jack, queen, and king), making a total of 52 cards. This complete deck is thoroughly mixed, and you will receive the first two cards from the deck without replacement.

(a) What is the probability that both cards are queens?

(b) What is the probability that the first card is a 10 *and* the second card is a 5 or 6?

(c) If we were sampling *with* replacement, what would be the answer in (a)?

(d) In the game of blackjack, the picture cards (jack, queen, king) count as 10 points and the ace counts as either 1 or 11 points. All other cards are counted at their face value. Blackjack is achieved if your two cards total 21 points. What is the probability of getting blackjack in this problem?

**5.25** A box of nine golf gloves contains two left-handed gloves and seven right-handed gloves.

(a) If two gloves are randomly selected from the box without replacement, what is the probability that

(1) both gloves selected will be right-handed?

(2) there will be one right-handed glove *and* one left-handed glove selected?

(b) If three gloves are selected, what is the probability that all three will be left-handed?

(c) If we were sampling with replacement, what would be the answers to (a)(1) and (b)?

## 5.3 BAYES' THEOREM

Conditional probability takes into account information about the occurrence of one event to find the probability of another event. This concept can be extended to revise probabilities based on new information and to determine the probability that a particular effect was due to a specific cause. The procedure for revising these probabilities is known as **Bayes'**

**theorem**, having been originally developed by the Rev. Thomas Bayes in the eighteenth century (see references 1 and 2).

Bayes' theorem can be applied in the following situation that relates to toy marketing. The marketing manager of a toy manufacturing company is considering the marketing of a new toy. In the past, 40% of the toys introduced by the company have been successful and 60% have been unsuccessful. Before the toy is marketed, market research is conducted and a report, either favorable or unfavorable, is compiled. In the past, 80% of the successful toys had received a favorable market research report and 30% of the unsuccessful toys received a favorable market research report. The marketing manager wants to know the probability the toy will be successful if it receives a favorable report.

Bayes' theorem can be developed from the definition of conditional probability [see equations (5.5a and b) on page 204 and (5.9) on page 210]. To find $P(B \mid A)$, we use equation (5.5b) to obtain

$$P(B \mid A) = \frac{P(A \mid B)P(B)}{P(A)}$$

We substitute equation (5.9) for $P(A)$ and obtain Bayes' theorem in equation (5.10).

---

**Bayes' Theorem**

$$P(B_i \mid A) = \frac{P(A \mid B_i)P(B_i)}{P(A \mid B_1)P(B_1) + P(A \mid B_2)P(B_2) + \cdots + P(A \mid B_k)P(B_k)} \quad (5.10)$$

where $B_i$ is the $i$th event out of $k$ mutually exclusive events.

---

To use equation (5.10), let

$$\text{event } S = \text{successful toy} \qquad \text{event } F = \text{favorable report}$$
$$\text{event } S' = \text{unsuccessful toy} \qquad \text{event } F' = \text{unfavorable report}$$

and

$$P(S) = .40 \qquad P(F \mid S) = .80$$
$$P(S') = .60 \qquad P(F \mid S') = .30$$

Then, using equation (5.10),

$$P(S \mid F) = \frac{P(F \mid S)P(S)}{P(F \mid S)P(S) + P(F \mid S')P(S')}$$
$$= \frac{(.80)(.40)}{(.80)(.40) + (.30)(.60)}$$
$$= \frac{.32}{.32 + .18} = \frac{.32}{.50}$$
$$= .64$$

The probability of a successful toy, given that a favorable report was received, is .64. Thus, the probability of an unsuccessful toy, given that a favorable report was received, is $1 - .64 = .36$. The computation of the probabilities is summarized in tabular form in Table 5.2 and displayed in the form of a decision tree in Figure 5.4.

**Table 5.2**  *Bayes' theorem calculations for the toy marketing problem*

| EVENT $S_i$ | PRIOR PROBABILITY $P(S_i)$ | CONDITIONAL PROBABILITY $P(F \mid S_i)$ | JOINT PROBABILITY $P(F \mid S_i)P(S_i)$ | REVISED PROBABILITY $P(S_i \mid F)$ |
|---|---|---|---|---|
| $S$ = successful toy | .40 | .80 | .32 | $.32/.50 = .64 = P(S \mid F)$ |
| $S'$ = unsuccessful toy | .60 | .30 | $\underline{.18}$ | $.18/.50 = .36 = P(S' \mid F)$ |
|  |  |  | .50 |  |

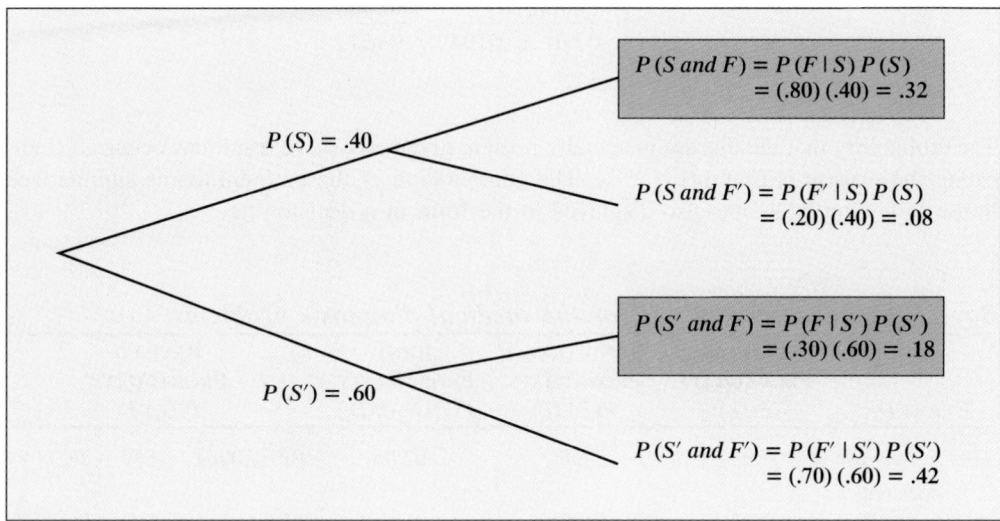

**FIGURE 5.4**  Decision tree for the toy marketing problem

Bayes' theorem is applied to a medical diagnosis problem in Example 5.13.

## Example 5.13  *Using Bayes' Theorem in a Medical Diagnosis Problem*

Suppose that the probability a person has a certain disease is .03. Medical diagnostic tests are available to determine whether the person actually has the disease. If the disease is actually present, the probability that the medical diagnostic test will give a positive result (indicating the disease is present) is .90. If the disease is not actually present, the probability of a positive test result (indicating that the disease is present) is .02. Suppose the medical diagnostic test has given a positive result (indicating the disease is present). What is the probability that the disease is actually present?

### SOLUTION

Let        event $D$ = has disease                 event $T$ = test is positive

event $D'$ = does not have disease        event $T'$ = test is negative

and

$$P(D) = .03 \qquad P(T \mid D) = .90$$
$$P(D') = .97 \qquad P(T \mid D') = .02$$

Using equation (5.10), we have

$$P(D \mid T) = \frac{P(T \mid D)P(D)}{P(T \mid D)P(D) + P(T \mid D')P(D')}$$
$$= \frac{(.90)(.03)}{(.90)(.03) + (.02)(.97)}$$
$$= \frac{.0270}{.0270 + .0194} = \frac{.0270}{.0464}$$
$$= .582$$

The probability that the disease is actually present given a positive result has occurred (indicating the disease is present) is .582. The computation of the probabilities is summarized in the following table and also displayed in the form of a decision tree.

*Bayes' theorem calculations for the medical diagnosis problem*

| EVENT $D_i$ | PRIOR PROBABILITY $P(D_i)$ | CONDITIONAL PROBABILITY $P(T \mid D_i)$ | JOINT PROBABILITY $P(T \mid D_i)P(D_i)$ | REVISED PROBABILITY $P(D_i \mid T)$ |
|---|---|---|---|---|
| $D$ = has disease | .03 | .90 | .0270 | .0270/.0464 = .582 = $P(D \mid T)$ |
| $D'$ = does not have disease | .97 | .02 | .0194 | .0194/.0464 = .418 = $P(D' \mid T)$ |
| | | | .0464 | |

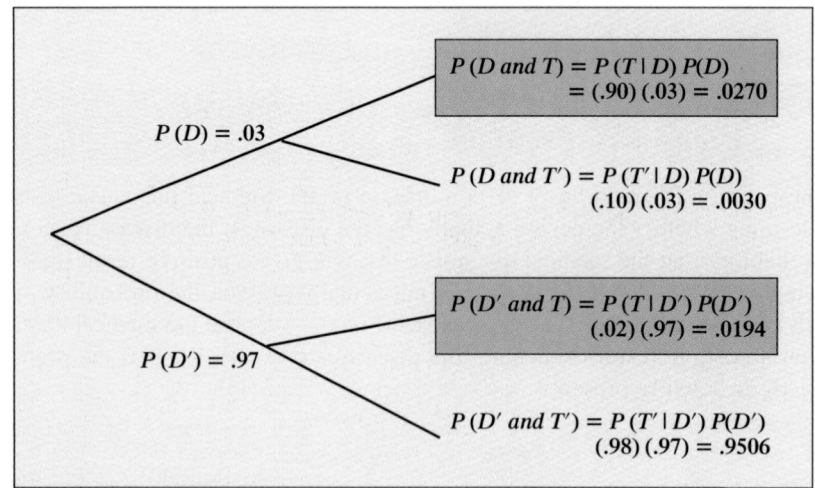

Decision tree for the medical diagnosis test problem

## Example 5.14 *Finding the Proportion of Medical Diagnostic Tests That Are Positive*

Using the data from Example 5.13, determine the proportion of medical diagnostic tests that are positive.

### SOLUTION

The denominator in Bayes' theorem represents $P(T)$, the probability of a positive test result, which in this case is .0464. Therefore, the probability of a positive test result is 4.64%.

## Problems for Section 5.3

### Learning the Basics

**5.26** If $P(B) = .05$, $P(A \mid B) = .80$, $P(B') = .95$, and $P(A \mid B') = .40$, find $P(B \mid A)$.

**5.27** If $P(B) = .30$, $P(A \mid B) = .60$, $P(B') = .70$, and $P(A \mid B') = .50$, find $P(B \mid A)$.

### Applying the Concepts

**5.28** In Example 5.13 on page 215, suppose that the probability that a medical diagnostic test will give a positive result if the disease is not present is reduced from .02 to .01. Given this information, we would like to know the following:
   (a) If the medical diagnostic test has given a positive result (indicating the disease is present), what is the probability that the disease is actually present?
   (b) If the medical diagnostic test has given a negative result (indicating the disease is not present), what is the probability that the disease is not present?

**5.29** An advertising executive is studying television viewing habits of married men and women during prime-time hours. On the basis of past viewing records, the executive has determined that during prime time, husbands are watching television 60% of the time. It has also been determined that when the husband is watching television, 40% of the time the wife is also watching. When the husband is not watching television, 30% of the time the wife is watching television. Find the probability that
   (a) if the wife is watching television, the husband is also watching television.
   (b) the wife is watching television in prime time.

**5.30** The Olive Construction Company is determining whether it should submit a bid for a new shopping center. In the past, Olive's main competitor, Base Construction Company, has submitted bids 70% of the time. If Base Construction Company does not bid on a job, the probability that the Olive Construction Company will get the job is .50. If Base Construction Company does bid on a job, the probability that the Olive Construction Company will get the job is .25.
   (a) If the Olive Construction Company gets the job, what is the probability that the Base Construction Company did not bid?
   (b) What is the probability that the Olive Construction Company will get the job?

**5.31** The editor of a major textbook publishing company is trying to decide whether to publish a proposed business statistics textbook. Previous textbooks published indicate that 10% are huge successes, 20% are modest successes, 40% break even, and 30% are losers. However, before a publishing decision is made, the book will be reviewed. In the past, 99% of the huge successes received favorable reviews, 70% of the moderate successes received favorable reviews, 40% of the break-even books received favorable reviews, and 20% of the losers received favorable reviews.

(a) If the proposed text receives a favorable review, how should the editor revise the probabilities of the various outcomes to take this information into account?

(b) What proportion of textbooks receive favorable reviews?

**5.32** A municipal bond service has three rating categories (A, B, and C). Suppose that in the past year, of the municipal bonds issued throughout the United States, 70% were rated A, 20% were rated B, and 10% were rated C. Of the municipal bonds rated A, 50% were issued by cities, 40% by suburbs, and 10% by rural areas. Of the municipal bonds rated B, 60% were issued by cities, 20% by suburbs, and 20% by rural areas. Of the municipal bonds rated C, 90% were issued by cities, 5% by suburbs, and 5% by rural areas.

(a) If a new municipal bond is to be issued by a city, what is the probability it will receive an A rating?

(b) What proportion of municipal bonds are issued by cities?

(c) What proportion of municipal bonds are issued by suburbs?

 **5.4** **ETHICAL ISSUES AND PROBABILITY**

 Ethical issues may arise when any statements relating to probability are being presented for public consumption, particularly when these statements are part of an advertising campaign for a product or service. Unfortunately, a substantial portion of the population is not very comfortable with any type of numerical concept (see reference 3) and misinterprets the meaning of the probability. In some instances, the misinterpretation is not intended, but in other cases, advertisements may unethically try to mislead potential customers.

One example of a potentially unethical application of probability relates to the sales of tickets to a state lottery in which the customer typically selects a set of numbers (such as 6) from a larger list of numbers (such as 54). Although virtually all participants know that they are unlikely to win the lottery, they also have very little idea of how unlikely it is for them to select all 6 winning numbers out of the list of 54 numbers. In addition, they have even less of an idea of how likely it is that they can win a consolation prize by selecting either 4 winning numbers or 5 winning numbers.

Given this background, it seems to us that a recent advertising campaign in which a commercial for a state lottery said, "We won't stop until we have made everyone a millionaire" is at the very least deceptive and at the very worst unethical. Actually, given the fact that the lottery brings millions of dollars in revenue into the state treasury, the state is never going to stop running it, although in anyone's lifetime no one can be sure of becoming a millionaire by winning the lottery.

Another example of a potentially unethical application of probability relates to an investment newsletter promising a 20% annual return on investment with a 90% probability. In such a situation, it seems imperative that the investment service needs to (a) explain the basis on which this probability estimate rests, (b) provide the probability statement in another format such as 9 chances in 10, and (c) explain what happens to the investment in the 10% of the cases in which a 20% return is not achieved. Is the entire investment lost?

## Problems for Section 5.4

### Applying the Concepts

**5.33** Write an advertisement for the state lottery that describes in an ethical fashion the probability for winning.

**5.34** Write an advertisement for the investment newsletter that states in an ethical fashion the probability for a 20% annual return.

As shown in the chapter summary chart, this chapter was about basic probability, conditional probability, and Bayes' theorem. Probability theory is the foundation for statistical inference. The concepts learned in this chapter will be extended to a variety of situations in subsequent chapters to develop probability distributions, use probabilities for decision making, and make inferences concerning populations.

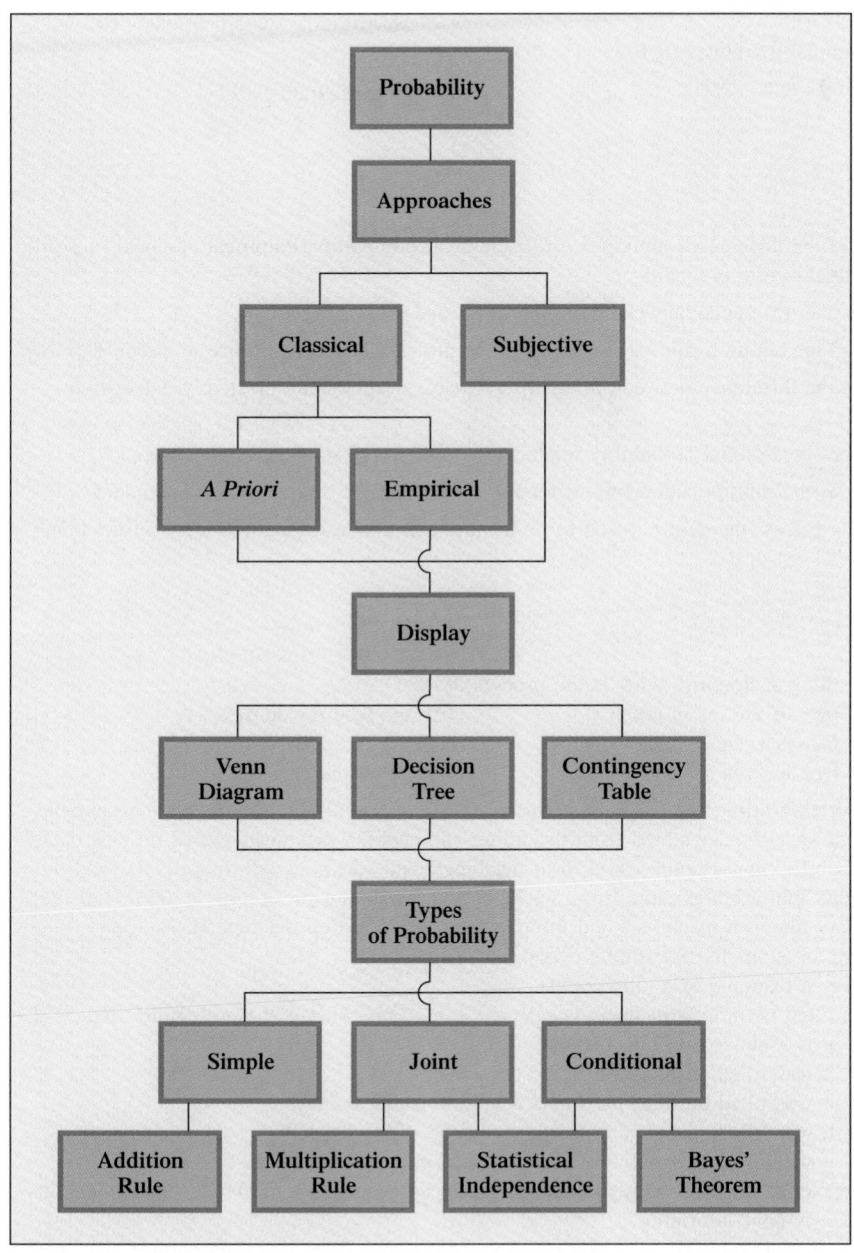

Chapter 5 summary chart

## Key Terms

addition rule   198
*a priori* classical probability   191
Bayes' theorem   214
certain event   191
collectively exhaustive   197
complement   192
conditional probability   203
contingency table   192
decision tree   205
empirical classical probability   191

general addition rule   198
general multiplication rule   209
intersection   193
joint event   192
joint probability   196
marginal probability   195
multiplication rule for independent events
    210
mutually exclusive   197
null event   191

null set   199
probability   190
sample space   192
simple event   192
simple probability   194
statistical independence   207
subjective probability   191
table of cross-classifications   192
union   193
Venn diagram   193

## Checking Your Understanding

**5.35** What are the differences among *a priori* classical probability, empirical classical probability, and subjective probability?

**5.36** What is the difference between a simple event and a joint event?

**5.37** How can the addition rule be used to find the probability of occurrence of event *A or B*?

**5.38** What is the difference between mutually exclusive events and collectively exhaustive events?

**5.39** How does conditional probability relate to the concept of statistical independence?

**5.40** How does the multiplication rule differ for events that are and are not independent?

**5.41** How can Bayes' theorem be used to revise probabilities in the light of new information?

## Chapter Review Problems

**5.42** When rolling a die once, what is the probability that
(a) the face of the die is odd?
(b) the face is even *or* odd?
(c) the face is even *or* a 1?
(d) the face is odd *or* a 1?
(e) the face is both even *and* a 1?
(f) given the face is odd, it is a 1?

• **5.43** A soft-drink bottling company maintains records concerning the number of unacceptable bottles of soft drink obtained from the filling and capping machines. Based on past data, the probability that a bottle came from machine I and was nonconforming is .01 and the probability that a bottle came from machine II and was nonconforming is .025. Half the bottles are filled on machine I and the other half are filled on machine II.
(a) Give an example of a simple event.
(b) Give an example of a joint event.
(c) If a filled bottle of soft drink is selected at random, what is the probability that
(1) it is a nonconforming bottle?
(2) it was filled on machine II?
(3) it was filled on machine I *and* is a conforming bottle?
(4) it was filled on machine II *and* is a conforming bottle?
(5) it was filled on machine I *or* is a conforming bottle?
(d) Suppose we know that the bottle was produced on machine I. What is the probability that it is nonconforming?
(e) Suppose we know that the bottle is nonconforming. What is the probability that it was produced on machine II?

(f) Explain the difference in the answers to (d) and (e).

(*Hint*: Set up a 2 × 2 table or a Venn diagram to evaluate the probabilities.)

**5.44** Suppose that a survey has been undertaken to determine if there is a relationship between place of residence and ownership of a foreign-made automobile. A random sample of 200 car owners from large cities, 150 from suburbs, and 150 from rural areas was selected with the following results.

| CAR OWNERSHIP | TYPE OF AREA | | | TOTAL |
|---|---|---|---|---|
| | LARGE CITY | SUBURB | RURAL | |
| Own foreign car | 90 | 60 | 25 | 175 |
| Do not own foreign car | 110 | 90 | 125 | 325 |
| Total | 200 | 150 | 150 | 500 |

(a) If a car owner is selected at random, what is the probability that he or she
  (1) owns a foreign car?
  (2) lives in a suburb?
  (3) owns a foreign car *or* lives in a large city?
  (4) lives in a large city *or* a suburb?
  (5) lives in a large city *and* owns a foreign car?
  (6) lives in a rural area *or* does not own a foreign car?
(b) Assume that we know that the person selected lives in a suburb. What is the probability that he or she owns a foreign car?
(c) Is area of residence statistically independent of whether the person owns a foreign car? Explain.

**5.45** The finance society at a college of business at a large state university would like to determine whether there is a relationship between a student's interest in finance and his or her ability in mathematics. A random sample of 200 students is selected and they are asked whether their interest in finance and ability in mathematics are low, average, or high. The results are as follows:

| INTEREST IN FINANCE | ABILITY IN MATHEMATICS | | | TOTAL |
|---|---|---|---|---|
| | LOW | AVERAGE | HIGH | |
| Low | 60 | 15 | 15 | 90 |
| Average | 15 | 45 | 10 | 70 |
| High | 5 | 10 | 25 | 40 |
| Total | 80 | 70 | 50 | 200 |

(a) Give an example of a simple event.
(b) Give an example of a joint event.
(c) Why is high interest in finance *and* high ability in mathematics a joint event?
(d) If a student is selected at random, what is the probability that he or she
  (1) has a high ability in mathematics?
  (2) has an average interest in finance?
  (3) has a low ability in mathematics?
  (4) has a high interest in finance?
  (5) has a low interest in finance *and* a low ability in mathematics?
  (6) has a high interest in finance *and* a high ability in mathematics?
  (7) has a low interest in finance *or* a low ability in mathematics?
  (8) has a high interest in finance *or* a high ability in mathematics?
  (9) has a low ability in mathematics *or* an average ability in mathematics *or* a high

ability in mathematics? Are these events mutually exclusive? Are they collectively exhaustive? Explain.

(e) Assume we know that the person selected has a high ability in mathematics. What is the probability that the person has a high interest in finance?

(f) Assume we know that the person selected has a high interest in finance. What is the probability that the person has a high ability in mathematics?

(g) Explain the difference in your answers in (e) and (f).

(h) Are interest in finance and ability in mathematics statistically independent? Explain.

• **5.46** The owner of a restaurant serving Continental-style entrées was interested in studying ordering patterns of patrons for the Friday to Sunday weekend time period. Records were maintained that indicated the demand for dessert during the same time period. The owner decided that two other variables were to be studied along with whether a dessert was ordered: the gender of the individual and whether a beef entrée was ordered. The results were as follows:

| | GENDER | | |
| DESSERT ORDERED | MALE | FEMALE | TOTAL |
|---|---|---|---|
| Yes | 96 | 40 | 136 |
| No | 224 | 240 | 464 |
| Total | 320 | 280 | 600 |

| | BEEF ENTRÉE | | |
| DESSERT ORDERED | YES | NO | TOTAL |
|---|---|---|---|
| Yes | 71 | 65 | 136 |
| No | 116 | 348 | 464 |
| Total | 187 | 413 | 600 |

(a) A waiter approaches a table to take an order. What is the probability that the first customer to order at the table
   (1) orders a dessert?
   (2) does not order a beef entrée?
   (3) orders a dessert *or* a beef entrée?
   (4) is a female *and* does not order a dessert?
   (5) orders a dessert *and* a beef entrée?
   (6) is a female *or* does not order a dessert?

(b) Suppose the first person that the waiter takes the dessert order from is a female. What is the probability that she does not order dessert?

(c) Suppose the first person that the waiter takes the dessert order from ordered a beef entrée. What is the probability that this person orders dessert?

(d) Is gender statistically independent of whether the person orders dessert?

(e) Is ordering a beef entrée statistically independent of whether the person orders dessert?

# References

1. Bernstein, P. L. *Against the Gods: The Remarkable Story of Risk* (New York: John Wiley, 1996).
2. Kirk, R. L., ed., *Statistical Issues: A Reader for the Behavioral Sciences* (Belmont, CA: Wadsworth, 1972).
3. Paulos, J. A. *Innumeracy* (New York: Hill and Wang, 1988).
4. Render, B., and R. M. Stair, *Quantitative Analysis for Management*, 6th ed. (Upper Saddle River, NJ: Prentice Hall, 1997).

# 6

# Some Important Discrete Probability Distributions

## CHAPTER OBJECTIVES

✓ *To provide an understanding of the basic concepts of discrete probability distributions and their characteristics*
✓ *To develop the concept of mathematical expectation for a discrete random variable*
✓ *To present applications of the binomial distribution in business*
✓ *To present applications of the Poisson distribution in business*
✓ *To present applications of the hypergeometric distribution in business*
✓ *To introduce the covariance and illustrate its application in finance*

## Introduction

In chapter 5 we established various rules of probability. In this chapter we will use this information to develop the discrete probability distribution and the concept of mathematical expectation. We will then develop the binomial, the Poisson, and the hypergeometric distributions and illustrate applications in business.

---

 **USING STATISTICS** *The Customer Services Department of a Natural Gas Utility Company*

Customer surveys for natural gas companies have indicated that customer satisfaction is strongly related to a repair response time of no more than 2 hours from the initial call requesting service. The arrival of the repair person within 2 hours is considered an *acceptable* waiting period. Recent data collected by the company indicate that the likelihood is .60 that a repair person will reach the customer's home within a 2-hour period. The company is interested in determining the likelihood of obtaining a certain number of service calls in the acceptable waiting period for a given sample of service calls. How can such probabilities be determined?

## 6.1 THE PROBABILITY DISTRIBUTION FOR A DISCRETE RANDOM VARIABLE

As discussed in section 2.3, a *numerical random variable* is some phenomenon of interest whose responses or outcomes may be expressed numerically. Such a random variable may also be classified as *discrete* or *continuous*—the former arising from a counting process and the latter from a measuring process. This chapter deals with some probability distributions that represent discrete random variables.

We define the probability distribution for a discrete random variable as follows:

> A **probability distribution for a discrete random variable** is a mutually exclusive listing of all possible numerical outcomes for that random variable such that a particular probability of occurrence is associated with each outcome.

| NUMBER OF CARS SOLD PER DAY | FREQUENCY OF OCCURRENCE |
|:---:|:---:|
| 0 | 40 |
| 1 | 100 |
| 2 | 142 |
| 3 | 66 |
| 4 | 36 |
| 5 | 30 |
| 6 | 26 |
| 7 | 20 |
| 8 | 16 |
| 9 | 14 |
| 10 | 8 |
| 11 | 2 |
| Total | 500 |

(a) Form the empirical probability distribution (that is, relative frequency distribution) for the discrete random variable $X$, the number of cars sold per day.
(b) Compute the mean or expected number of cars sold per day.
(c) Compute the standard deviation.
(d) What is the probability that on any given day
    (1) fewer than four cars will be sold?
    (2) at most four cars will be sold?
    (3) at least four cars will be sold?
    (4) exactly four cars will be sold?
    (5) more than four cars will be sold?

• **6.4** The following table contains the probability distribution of the number of traffic accidents daily in a small city.

| NUMBER OF ACCIDENTS DAILY ($X$) | $P(X)$ |
|:---:|:---:|
| 0 | .10 |
| 1 | .20 |
| 2 | .45 |
| 3 | .15 |
| 4 | .05 |
| 5 | .05 |

(a) Compute the mean or expected number of accidents per day.
(b) Compute the standard deviation.

**6.5** The manager of a large computer network has developed a probability distribution of the number of interruptions per day. This is displayed at the top of page 230.

| Interruptions ($X$) | $P(X)$ |
|---|---|
| 0 | .32 |
| 1 | .35 |
| 2 | .18 |
| 3 | .08 |
| 4 | .04 |
| 5 | .02 |
| 6 | .01 |

(a) Compute the mean or expected number of interruptions per day.

(b) Compute the standard deviation.

**6.6** In the carnival game Under-or-over-seven, a pair of fair dice are rolled once, and the resulting sum determines whether or not the player wins or loses his or her bet. For example, the player can bet $1.00 that the sum is under 7—that is, 2, 3, 4, 5, or 6. For such a bet the player will lose $1.00 if the outcome equals or exceeds 7 or will win $1.00 if the result is under 7. Similarly, the player can bet $1.00 that the sum is over 7—that is, 8, 9, 10, 11, or 12. Here the player wins $1.00 if the result is over 7 but loses $1.00 if the result is 7 or under. A third method of play is to bet $1.00 on the outcome 7. For this bet the player will win $4.00 if the result of the roll is 7 and lose $1.00 otherwise.

(a) Form the probability distribution function representing the different outcomes that are possible for a $1.00 bet on being under 7.

(b) Form the probability distribution function representing the different outcomes that are possible for a $1.00 bet on being over 7.

(c) Form the probability distribution function representing the different outcomes that are possible for a $1.00 bet on 7.

(d) Show that the expected long-run profit (or loss) to the player is the same—no matter which method of play is used.

 ## BINOMIAL DISTRIBUTION

The **binomial distribution** is a discrete probability distribution function with many everyday applications. The binomial distribution possesses four essential properties:

### Exhibit 6.1 *Properties of the Binomial Distribution*

✓ **1.** The possible observations may be obtained by two different sampling methods. Each observation may be considered as having been selected either from an *infinite population without replacement* or from a *finite population with replacement*.

✓ **2.** Each observation may be classified into one of two mutually exclusive and collectively exhaustive categories, usually called *success* and *failure*.

✓ **3.** The probability of an observation's being classified as success, *p*, is constant from observation to observation. Thus, the probability of an observation's being classified as failure, 1 − *p*, is constant over all observations.

✓ **4.** The outcome (i.e., success or failure) of any observation is independent of the outcome of any other observation.

The discrete random variable or phenomenon of interest that follows the binomial distribution is the number of successes obtained in a sample of $n$ observations. Returning to our Using Statistics example concerning the natural gas utility company (see page 224), *success* is the arrival of the repair person within the acceptable 2-hour period and *failure* is any other outcome. In the example, we stated that we were interested in the likelihood that the repair person would arrive within the acceptable period in a certain number of service calls that have been monitored.

What results can occur? If, for example, we consider a sample of four service calls, the service could be provided in an acceptable time period at none of the houses, at one house, at two houses, at three houses, or at all four houses. Can the binomial random variable, the number of arrivals within an acceptable time period, take on any other value? That would be impossible because the number of successful arrivals cannot exceed the sample size $n$, nor can it be lower than zero. Hence, the range of a binomial random variable is from 0 to $n$.

Suppose that the following result is observed in a sample of four monitored service calls:

| FIRST SERVICE CALL | SECOND SERVICE CALL | THIRD SERVICE CALL | FOURTH SERVICE CALL |
|---|---|---|---|
| Acceptable | Acceptable | Not Acceptable | Acceptable |

What is the probability of obtaining three successes (service calls within an acceptable time) in a sample of four monitored service calls in this particular sequence? Because it may be assumed that making a service call is a stable process with a historical probability of .60 occurring within the acceptable time period, the probability that each service call occurs as noted is

| FIRST SERVICE CALL | SECOND SERVICE CALL | THIRD SERVICE CALL | FOURTH SERVICE CALL |
|---|---|---|---|
| $p = .60$ | $p = .60$ | $1 - p = .40$ | $p = .60$ |

Because each outcome is independent of the others, the probability of obtaining this particular sequence is

$$pp(1 - p)p = p^3(1 - p) = p^3(1 - p)^1 = (.60)^3(.40)^1 = .0864$$

However, this only tells us the probability of obtaining three acceptable service calls within 2 hours (successes) out of a sample of four monitored service calls *in a specific order*. If we now want to find the number of ways of selecting $X$ objects out of $n$ objects *irrespective of order* we must use the **rule of combinations**.

## Combinations

The *number of combinations* of selecting $X$ objects out of $n$ objects is given by

$$\frac{n!}{X!(n - X)!} \tag{6.4}$$

where $n! = n(n - 1) \ldots (1)$ is called $n$ factorial and $0! = 1$.

This expression may be denoted by the symbol $\binom{n}{X}$. Therefore, with $n = 4$ and $X = 3$, we have

$$\binom{n}{X} = \frac{n!}{X!(n-X)!} = \frac{4!}{3!(4-3)!} = \frac{4 \times 3 \times 2 \times 1}{(3 \times 2 \times 1)(1)} = 4$$

such sequences. These four possible sequences are

**Sequence 1** = *acceptable, acceptable, acceptable, not acceptable* with probability $ppp(1-p) = p^3(1-p)^1 = .0864$

**Sequence 2** = *acceptable, acceptable, not acceptable, acceptable* with probability $pp(1-p)p = p^3(1-p)^1 = .0864$

**Sequence 3** = *acceptable, not acceptable, acceptable, acceptable* with probability $p(1-p)pp = p^3(1-p)^1 = .0864$

**Sequence 4** = *not acceptable, acceptable, acceptable, acceptable* with probability $(1-p)ppp = p^3(1-p)^1 = .0864$

Note that ours is the second of these four possible sequences.

Therefore, the probability of obtaining exactly three service calls within the acceptable time period is equal to

(number of possible sequences) $\times$ (probability of a particular sequence)

(4) $\times$ (.0864) = .3456

A similar, intuitive derivation can be obtained for the other four possible outcomes of the random variable—zero, one, two, and four service calls within the acceptable time period. However, as $n$, the number of observations, gets large, this type of intuitive approach becomes quite laborious and a mathematical model is more appropriate. In general, the following mathematical model represents the binomial probability distribution for obtaining a number of successes ($X$), given a knowledge of this distribution's parameters $n$ and $p$.

## Binomial Distribution

$$P(X) = \frac{n!}{X!(n-X)!} p^X (1-p)^{n-X} \tag{6.5}$$

where

$P(X)$ = the probability of $X$ successes given a knowledge of $n$ and $p$

$n$ = sample size

$p$ = probability of success

$1-p$ = probability of failure

$X$ = number of successes in the sample ($X = 0, 1, 2, \ldots, n$)

We note, however, that the generalized form shown in equation (6.5) is merely a restatement of what we had intuitively derived. The binomial random variable $X$ can have any integer value $X$ from 0 through $n$. In equation (6.5) the product

$$p^X(1-p)^{n-X}$$

tells us the probability of obtaining exactly $X$ successes out of $n$ observations in *a particular sequence*, whereas the term

$$\frac{n!}{X!(n-X)!}$$

tells us *how many combinations* of the $X$ successes out of $n$ observations are possible. Hence, given the number of observations $n$ and the probability of success $p$, we determine the probability of $X$ successes:

$$P(X) = \text{(number of possible sequences)} \times \text{(probability of a particular sequence)}$$

$$= \frac{n!}{X!(n-X)!} p^X (1-p)^{n-X}$$

by substituting the desired values for $n$, $p$, and $X$ and computing the result. In Example 6.2 we illustrate the use of equation (6.5).

## Example 6.2 *Determining $P(X = 3)$, given $n = 4$ and $p = .6$*

If the likelihood of an acceptable service call is .6, what is the probability that three acceptable service calls are made out of the sample of four that are monitored?

**SOLUTION**

As previously shown, using equation (6.5), the probability of obtaining exactly three service calls within the acceptable time period from a sample of four monitored service calls is

$$P(X = 3) = \frac{4!}{3!(4-3)!} (.6)^3 (1 - .6)^1$$

$$= \frac{4!}{3!1!} (.6)^3 (.4)^1$$

$$= 4(.6)(.6)(.6)(.4) = .3456$$

Other computations concerning different values of $X$ can also be obtained as in Examples 6.3 and 6.4.

## Example 6.3 *Determining $P(X \geq 3)$, given $n = 4$ and $p = .6$*

If the likelihood of an acceptable service call is .6, what is the probability that three or more (i.e., at least three) acceptable service calls are made out of the sample of four that are monitored?

**SOLUTION**

As previously shown, using equation (6.5), the probability of obtaining exactly three service calls within the acceptable time period from a sample of four monitored service calls is .3456. To obtain the probability of at least three acceptable service calls, we need to add the probability of three acceptable service calls to the probability of four acceptable service calls. The probability of four acceptable service calls is

$$P(X = 4) = \frac{4!}{4!(4-4)!} (.6)^4 (1 - .6)^0$$

$$= \frac{4!}{4!0!} (.6)^4 (.4)^0$$

$$= 1(.6)(.6)(.6)(.6) = .1296$$

Thus the probability of at least three acceptable service calls is

$$P(X \geq 3) = P(X = 3) + P(X = 4)$$
$$= .3456 + .1296$$
$$= .4752$$

There is a .4752 chance that there will be at least three acceptable service calls in a sample of four calls.

## Example 6.4   *Determining $P(X < 3)$, given $n = 4$ and $p = .6$*

If the likelihood of an acceptable service call is .6, what is the probability that fewer than three acceptable service calls are made out of the sample of four that are monitored?

### SOLUTION

The probability that fewer than three acceptable service calls are made is

$$P(X < 3) = P(X = 0) + P(X = 1) + P(X = 2)$$

Using equation (6.5) to obtain each of these probabilities, we have

$$P(X = 0) = \frac{4!}{0!(4 - 0)!}(.6)^0(1 - .6)^4 = .0256$$

$$P(X = 1) = \frac{4!}{1!(4 - 1)!}(.6)^1(1 - .6)^3 = .1536$$

$$P(X = 2) = \frac{4!}{2!(4 - 2)!}(.6)^2(1 - .6)^2 = .3456$$

Therefore, we have

$$P(X < 3) = .0256 + .1536 + .3456 = .5248$$

Rather than using equation (6.5) to compute $P(X < 3)$, because we have already computed $P(X \geq 3)$, we could obtain $P(X < 3)$ as its complement as follows:

$$P(X < 3) = P(X = 0) + P(X = 1) + P(X = 2)$$
$$= 1 - P(X \geq 3)$$
$$= 1 - .4752 = .5248$$

Such computations can become quite tedious, especially as $n$ gets large. However, we can obtain the probabilities by using Microsoft Excel or Minitab (see appendices 6.1 and 6.2) and thereby avoid any computational drudgery. Figure 6.2 represents output from Microsoft Excel, and Figure 6.3 represents output from Minitab for the binomial distribution example with parameters $n = 4$ and $p = .6$.

## Characteristics of the Binomial Distribution

Each time a set of parameters—$n$ and $p$—is specified, a particular binomial probability distribution can be generated.

| | A | B | C | D | E | F |
|---|---|---|---|---|---|---|
| 1 | **Calculating Binomial Probabilities** | | | | | |
| 2 | | | | | | |
| 3 | **n** | **p** | **Mean** | **Variance** | **Std. Deviation** | |
| 4 | 4 | 0.6 | 2.4 | 0.96 | 0.979795897 | |
| 5 | | | | | | |
| 6 | **X** | **P(x)** | **P(<=X)** | **P(<X)** | **P(>X)** | **P(>=X)** |
| 7 | 0 | 0.0256 | 0.0256 | 0 | 0.9744 | 1 |
| 8 | 1 | 0.1536 | 0.1792 | 0.0256 | 0.8208 | 0.9744 |
| 9 | 2 | 0.3456 | 0.5248 | 0.1792 | 0.4752 | 0.8208 |
| 10 | 3 | 0.3456 | 0.8704 | 0.5248 | 0.1296 | 0.4752 |
| 11 | 4 | 0.1296 | 1 | 0.8704 | 0 | 0.1296 |

**FIGURE 6.2**
Binomial distribution calculations
for $n = 4$ and $p = .6$
obtained from the PHStat Add-In for
Microsoft Excel

### Probability Density Function

Binomial with n = 4 and p = 0.600000

| x | P( X = x) |
|---|---|
| 0.00 | 0.0256 |
| 1.00 | 0.1536 |
| 2.00 | 0.3456 |
| 3.00 | 0.3456 |
| 4.00 | 0.1296 |

**FIGURE 6.3**
Binomial distribution calculations
for $n = 4$ and $p = .6$
obtained from Minitab

◆ **Shape** We note that a binomial distribution may be symmetric or skewed. Whenever $p = .5$, the binomial distribution will be symmetric regardless of how large or small the value of $n$. However, when $p \neq .5$, the distribution will be skewed. The closer $p$ is to .5 and the larger the number of observations $n$, the less skewed the distribution will be. Thus, the distribution of the number of service calls within the acceptable time period is skewed to the left because $p = .60$. This can be observed in Figure 6.4, which is a plot of the distribution for $n = 4$ and $p = .60$.

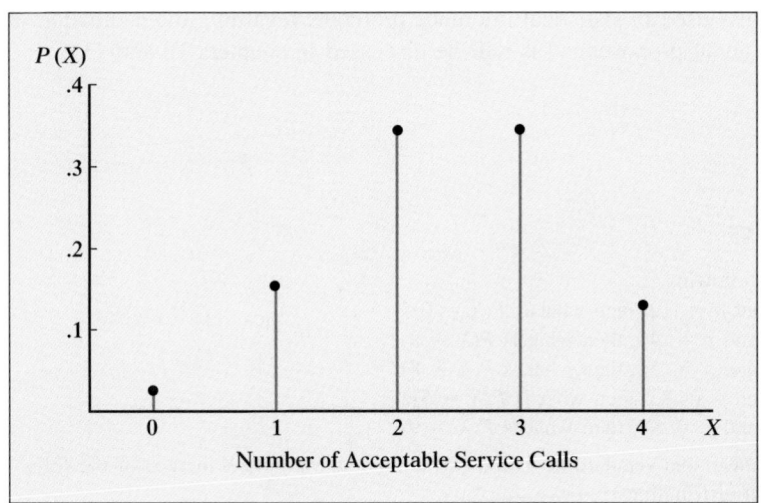

**FIGURE 6.4**
Binomial distribution for $n = 4$
and $p = .6$

◆ **The Mean**   The mean of the binomial distribution can be obtained as the product of its two parameters $n$ and $p$. Instead of using equation (6.1), which holds for all discrete probability distributions, we use the following to compute the mean for data that are binomially distributed:

## The Mean of the Binomial Distribution

The mean $\mu$ of the binomial distribution is equal to the sample size $n$ multiplied by the probability of success $p$.

$$\mu = E(X) = np \tag{6.6}$$

Intuitively, this makes sense. On the average, over the long run, we would theoretically expect $\mu = E(X) = np = (4)(.6) = 2.4$ service calls within the acceptable time period out of a sample of four monitored service calls.

◆ **The Standard Deviation**   The standard deviation of the binomial distribution is calculated using the following

## The Standard Deviation of the Binomial Distribution

$$\sigma = \sqrt{\sigma^2} = \sqrt{Var(X)} = \sqrt{np(1 - p)} \tag{6.7}$$

Referring to our service calls example, we compute

$$\sigma = \sqrt{(4)(.6)(.4)} = \sqrt{.96} = .98$$

This is the same result that would be obtained from the more general expression shown in equation (6.3).

In this section we have developed the binomial model as a useful discrete probability distribution and demonstrated its characteristics through an application involving service calls by a gas utility company. However, the binomial distribution plays an even more important role when it is used in statistical inference problems regarding the estimation or testing of hypotheses about proportions (as will be discussed in chapters 10 and 11).

## Problems for Section 6.2

### Learning the Basics

● **6.7**   Determine the following:
  (a) If $n = 4$ and $p = .12$, then what is $P(X = 0)$?
  (b) If $n = 10$ and $p = .40$, then what is $P(X = 9)$?
  (c) If $n = 10$ and $p = .50$, then what is $P(X = 8)$?
  (d) If $n = 6$ and $p = .83$, then what is $P(X = 5)$?
  (e) If $n = 10$ and $p = .90$, then what is $P(X = 9)$?

**6.8**   Determine the mean and standard deviation of the random variable $X$ in each of the following binomial distributions:

(a) If $n = 4$ and $p = .10$
(b) If $n = 4$ and $p = .40$
(c) If $n = 5$ and $p = .80$
(d) If $n = 3$ and $p = .50$

## Applying the Concepts

**6.9**   Suppose that the increase or decrease in the price of a stock between the beginning and the end of a trading day is considered to be an equally likely random event. What is the probability that a stock will show an increase in its closing price on five consecutive days?

**6.10**  Suppose that warranty records show the probability that a new car needs a warranty repair in the first 90 days is .05. If a sample of three new cars is selected,
(a) what is the probability that
  (1) none needs a warranty repair?
  (2) at least one needs a warranty repair?
  (3) more than one needs a warranty repair?
(b) What assumptions are necessary in (a)?
(c) What are the mean and the standard deviation of the probability distribution in (a)?
(d) What would be your answers to (a)–(c) if the probability of needing a warranty repair was .10?

**6.11**  Suppose that the likelihood that someone who logs onto a particular site in a "shopping mall" on the World Wide Web will purchase an item is .20. If the site has 10 people accessing it in the next minute, what is the probability that
(a) none of the individuals will purchase an item?
(b) exactly two individuals will purchase an item?
(c) at least two individuals will purchase an item?
(d) at most two individuals will purchase an item?
(e) If 20 people accessed the site in the next minute, what would be your answers to (a)–(d)?
(f) If the probability of purchasing an item was only .10, what would be your answers to (a)–(d)?

**6.12**  An important part of the customer service responsibilities of a telephone company relate to the speed with which troubles in residential service can be repaired. Suppose that past data indicate that the likelihood is .70 that troubles in residential service can be repaired on the same day.
(a) For the first five troubles reported on a given day, what is the probability that
  (1) all five will be repaired on the same day?
  (2) at least three will be repaired on the same day?
  (3) fewer than two will be repaired on the same day?
(b) What assumptions are necessary in (a)?
(c) What are the mean and standard deviation of the probability distribution in (a)?
(d) What would be your answers in (a) and (c) if the probability is .80 that troubles in residential service can be repaired on the same day?
(e) Compare the results of (a) and (d).

**6.13**  Suppose that a student is taking a multiple-choice exam in which each question has four choices. Assuming that she has no knowledge of the correct answers to any of the questions, she has decided on a strategy in which she will place four balls (marked A, B, C, and D) into a box. She randomly selects one ball for each question and replaces the ball in the box. The marking on the ball will determine her answer to the question.
(a) If there are five multiple-choice questions on the exam, what is the probability that she will get
  (1) five questions correct?
  (2) at least four questions correct?
  (3) no questions correct?
  (4) no more than two questions correct?

(b) What assumptions are necessary in (a)?

(c) What are the average and the standard deviation of the number of questions that she will get correct in (a)?

(d) Suppose that the exam has 50 multiple-choice questions and 30 or more correct answers is a passing score. What is the probability that she will pass the exam by following her strategy? (Use Microsoft Excel or Minitab to compute this probability.)

 **6.3** POISSON DISTRIBUTION

The Poisson distribution is another discrete probability distribution with many important practical applications. Numerous discrete phenomena are represented by a Poisson process as described in Exhibit 6.2.

---

 **Exhibit 6.2   A Poisson Process**

A **Poisson process** is said to exist if we can observe discrete events in an *area of opportunity*—a continuous interval (of time, length, surface area, etc.)—in such a manner that if we shorten the area of opportunity or interval sufficiently,

✓ **1.** the probability of observing exactly one success in the interval is stable.

✓ **2.** the probability of observing more than one success in the interval is 0.

✓ **3.** the occurrence of a success in any one interval is statistically independent of that in any other interval.

---

To better understand the Poisson process, suppose we examine the number of customers arriving during the 12 noon to 1 P.M. lunch hour at a bank located in the central business district in a large city. Any arrival of a customer is a *discrete* event at a particular point in time over the *continuous* 1-hour interval. Over such an interval of time, there might be an average of 180 arrivals. Now if we were to break up the 1-hour interval into 3,600 consecutive 1-second intervals,

- the expected (or average) number of customers arriving in any 1-second interval would be .05.
- the probability of having more than one customer arriving in any 1-second interval approaches 0.
- the arrival of one customer in any 1-second interval has no effect on (i.e., is statistically independent of) the arrival of any other customer in any other 1-second interval.

The Poisson distribution has one parameter, called $\lambda$ (the Greek lowercase letter lambda), which is the average or expected number of successes per unit. Interestingly, the variance of a Poisson distribution is also equal to $\lambda$ and the standard deviation is equal to $\sqrt{\lambda}$. Moreover, the number of successes $X$ of the Poisson random variable ranges from 0 to $\infty$.

The mathematical expression for the Poisson distribution for obtaining $X$ successes, given that $\lambda$ successes are expected, is

## Poisson Distribution

$$P(X) = \frac{e^{-\lambda}\lambda^X}{X!}$$ (6.8)

where

$P(X)$ = the probability of $X$ successes given a knowledge of $\lambda$

$\lambda$ = expected number of successes

$e$ = mathematical constant approximated by 2.71828

$X$ = number of successes per unit

To demonstrate Poisson model applications, let us return to the example of the bank lunch-hour customer arrivals:

## Example 6.5 *Determining Poisson Process Probabilities*

If, on average, three customers arrive per minute at the bank during the lunch hour, what is the probability that in a given minute exactly two customers will arrive? Also, what is the chance that more than two customers will arrive in a given minute?

### SOLUTION

Using equation (6.8), we have, for the first question

$$P(X = 2) = \frac{e^{-3.0}(3.0)^2}{2!} = \frac{9}{(2.71828)^3(2)} = .2240$$

To answer the second question—the probability that in any given minute more than two customers will arrive—we have

$$P(X > 2) = P(X = 3) + P(X = 4) + \cdots + P(X = \infty)$$

Because all the probabilities in a probability distribution must sum to 1, the terms on the right side of the equation $P(X > 2)$ also represent the complement of the probability that $X$ is less than or equal to 2 [that is, $1 - P(X \le 2)$]. Thus,

$$P(X > 2) = 1 - P(X \le 2) = 1 - [P(X = 0) + P(X = 1) + P(X = 2)]$$

Now, using equation (6.8), we have

$$P(X > 2) = 1 - \left[\frac{e^{-3.0}(3.0)^0}{0!} + \frac{e^{-3.0}(3.0)^1}{1!} + \frac{e^{-3.0}(3.0)^2}{2!}\right]$$
$$= 1 - [.0498 + .1494 + .2240]$$
$$= 1 - .4232 = .5768$$

Thus, we see that there is roughly a 42.3% chance that two or fewer customers will arrive at the bank per minute. Therefore, a 57.7% chance exists that more than two customers will arrive.

Such computations can become quite tedious, especially as $\lambda$ gets large. However, we can obtain the probabilities by using Microsoft Excel or Minitab (see appendices 6.1 and 6.2) and thereby avoid any computational drudgery. Figure 6.5 represents output from Microsoft Excel, and Figure 6.6 represents output from Minitab for the Poisson distribution example with $\lambda = 3$.

|   | A | B | C | D | E | F |
|---|---|---|---|---|---|---|
| 5 |   |   | Mean: | 3 |   |   |
| 6 | X | P(X) | P(<=X) | P(<X) | P(>X) | P(>=X) |
| 7 | 0 | 0.049787068 | 0.049787068 | 0 | 0.950212932 | 1 |
| 8 | 1 | 0.149361205 | 0.199148273 | 0.049787068 | 0.800851727 | 0.950212932 |
| 9 | 2 | 0.224041808 | 0.423190081 | 0.199148273 | 0.576809919 | 0.800851727 |
| 10 | 3 | 0.224041808 | 0.647231889 | 0.423190081 | 0.352768111 | 0.576809919 |
| 11 | 4 | 0.168031356 | 0.815263245 | 0.647231889 | 0.184736755 | 0.352768111 |
| 12 | 5 | 0.100818813 | 0.916082058 | 0.815263245 | 0.083917942 | 0.184736755 |
| 13 | 6 | 0.050409407 | 0.966491465 | 0.916082058 | 0.033508535 | 0.083917942 |
| 14 | 7 | 0.021604031 | 0.988095496 | 0.966491465 | 0.011904504 | 0.033508535 |
| 15 | 8 | 0.008101512 | 0.996197008 | 0.988095496 | 0.003802992 | 0.011904504 |
| 16 | 9 | 0.002700504 | 0.998897512 | 0.996197008 | 0.001102488 | 0.003802992 |
| 17 | 10 | 0.000810151 | 0.999707663 | 0.998897512 | 0.000292337 | 0.001102488 |
| 18 | 11 | 0.00022095 | 0.999928613 | 0.999707663 | 7.13866E-05 | 0.000292337 |
| 19 | 12 | 5.52376E-05 | 0.999983851 | 0.999928613 | 1.6149E-05 | 7.13866E-05 |
| 20 | 13 | 1.27471E-05 | 0.999996598 | 0.999983851 | 3.40191E-06 | 1.6149E-05 |
| 21 | 14 | 2.73153E-06 | 0.99999933 | 0.999996598 | 6.70386E-07 | 3.40191E-06 |
| 22 | 15 | 5.46306E-07 | 0.999999876 | 0.99999933 | 1.2408E-07 | 6.70386E-07 |

**FIGURE 6.5**  Poisson distribution calculations for $\lambda = 3$ obtained from the PHStat Add-In for Microsoft Excel

```
Poisson with mu = 3.00000

     x         P( X = x)
  0.00          0.0498
  1.00          0.1494
  2.00          0.2240
  3.00          0.2240
  4.00          0.1680
  5.00          0.1008
  6.00          0.0504
  7.00          0.0216
  8.00          0.0081
  9.00          0.0027
 10.00          0.0008
 11.00          0.0002
 12.00          0.0001
 13.00          0.0000
 14.00          0.0000
 15.00          0.0000
 16.00          0.0000
 17.00          0.0000
 18.00          0.0000
 19.00          0.0000
 20.00          0.0000
 21.00          0.0000
```

**FIGURE 6.6**

Poisson distribution calculations for $\lambda = 3$ obtained from Minitab (Note: Minitab uses $\mu$ to represent $\lambda$.)

# Problems for Section 6.3

## Learning the Basics

• **6.14** Determine the following:

    (a) If $\lambda = 2.5$, then what is $P(X = 2)$?     (d) If $\lambda = 3.7$, then what is $P(X = 0)$?
    (b) If $\lambda = 8.0$, then what is $P(X = 8)$?     (e) If $\lambda = 4.4$, then what is $P(X = 7)$?
    (c) If $\lambda = 0.5$, then what is $P(X = 1)$?

**6.15** Determine the following:

    (a) If $\lambda = 2.0$, then what is $P(X \geq 2)$?     (d) If $\lambda = 4.0$, then what is $P(X \geq 1)$?
    (b) If $\lambda = 8.0$, then what is $P(X \geq 3)$?     (e) If $\lambda = 5.0$, then what is $P(X \leq 3)$?
    (c) If $\lambda = 0.5$, then what is $P(X \leq 1)$?

## Applying the Concepts

• **6.16** The average number of claims per hour made to the C - G - N Insurance Company for damages or losses incurred in moving is 3.1. What is the probability that in any given hour

    (a) fewer than three claims will be made?     (c) three or more claims will be made?
    (b) exactly three claims will be made?     (d) more than three claims will be made?

**6.17** Based on past records, the average number of two-car accidents in a New York City police precinct is 3.4 per day. What is the probability that there will be

    (a) at least six such accidents in this precinct on any given day?
    (b) not more than two such accidents in this precinct on any given day?
    (c) fewer than two such accidents in this precinct on any given day?
    (d) at least two but no more than six such accidents in this precinct on any given day?
    (e) what would be your answers to (a)–(d) if the average is five such accidents per day?

• **6.18** The quality control manager of Marilyn's Cookies is inspecting a batch of chocolate-chip cookies that have just been baked. If the production process is in control, the average number of chip parts per cookie is 6.0. What is the probability that in any particular cookie being inspected

    (a) fewer than five chip parts will be found?     (d) four or five chip parts will be found?
    (b) exactly five chip parts will be found?     (e) What would be your answers to (a)–(d) if the average number of chip parts per cookie is 5.0?
    (c) five or more chip parts will be found?

**6.19** Refer to Problem 6.18. How many cookies in a batch of 100 being sampled should the manager expect to discard if company policy requires that all chocolate-chip cookies sold must have at least four chocolate-chip parts?

**6.20** Suppose that the number of claims for missing baggage for a well-known airline in a small city averages nine per day. What is the probability that on a given day, there will be

    (a) seven claims?     (c) fewer than five claims?
    (b) seven or eight or nine claims?

**6.21** Based on past experience, it is assumed that the number of flaws per foot in rolls of grade 2 paper follows a Poisson distribution with an average of one flaw per 5 feet of paper (.2 flaw per foot). What is the probability that in a

    (a) 1-foot roll there will be at least 2 flaws?
    (b) 12-foot roll there will be at least 1 flaw?
    (c) 50-foot roll there will be between 5 and 15 (inclusive) flaws?

Both the binomial distribution and the **hypergeometric distribution** are concerned with the same thing—the number of successes in a sample containing $n$ observations. What differentiates these two discrete probability distributions is the manner in which the data are obtained. For the binomial model, the sample data are drawn *with* replacement from a *finite* population or *without* replacement from an *infinite* population. On the other hand, for the hypergeometric model, the sample data are drawn *without* replacement from a *finite* population. Hence, while the probability of success $p$ is constant over all observations of a binomial experiment, and the outcome of any particular observation is independent of any other, the same cannot be said for a hypergeometric experiment; here the outcome of one observation is affected by the outcomes of the previous observations.

In general, a mathematical expression of the hypergeometric distribution for obtaining $X$ successes, given a knowledge of the parameters $n$, $N$, and $A$, is

### Hypergeometric Distribution

$$P(X) = \frac{\binom{A}{X}\binom{N-A}{n-X}}{\binom{N}{n}}$$

(6.9)

where

$$P(X) = \text{the probability of } X \text{ successes given a knowledge of } n, N, \text{ and } A$$
$$n = \text{sample size}$$
$$N = \text{population size}$$
$$A = \text{number of successes in the population}$$
$$N - A = \text{number of failures in the population}$$
$$X = \text{number of successes in the sample}$$

The number of successes in the sample $X$ cannot exceed the number of successes in the population $A$ or the sample size $n$. Thus, the range of the hypergeometric random variable is limited to the sample size (as was the range for the binomial random variable) or to the number of successes in the population—whichever is smaller.

◆ *The Mean*   Like the binomial distribution, the mean of the hypergeometric distribution can be computed from

### The Mean of the Hypergeometric Distribution

$$\mu = E(X) = \frac{nA}{N}$$

(6.10)

◆ *The Standard Deviation*   The standard deviation of the hypergeometric distribution is obtained from equation (6.11).

## The Standard Deviation of the Hypergeometric Distribution

$$\sigma = \sqrt{\frac{nA(N-A)}{N^2}} \times \sqrt{\frac{N-n}{N-1}} \qquad (6.11)$$

The expression $\sqrt{\frac{N-n}{N-1}}$ is a **finite population correction factor**, which arises because of the process of sampling without replacement from finite populations. (This correction factor will be discussed in greater detail in section 9.3.) To illustrate the hypergeometric distribution, let us consider Example 6.6.

## Example 6.6 *Determining Probabilities from the Hypergeometric Distribution*

Suppose an investment company employs 52 researchers with Ph.D. degrees—13 of whom have their doctorates in finance. A delegation of five researchers is to be randomly chosen by a lottery drawing to attend an international investments conference, all expenses paid. What is the probability that the delegation will contain exactly two researchers with doctorates in finance?

### SOLUTION

Here the population of $N = 52$ researchers is finite. In addition, $A = 13$ of these researchers hold doctorates in finance. The delegation to the international conference is to contain $n = 5$ members. Using equation (6.9), we have

$$P(X = 2) = \frac{\binom{13}{2}\binom{39}{3}}{\binom{52}{5}}$$

$$= \frac{\dfrac{13!}{2!11!} \times \dfrac{39!}{3!36!}}{\dfrac{52!}{5!47!}}$$

$$= .2743$$

Thus, the probability that the delegation contains exactly two doctorates in finance is .2743.

Such computations can become quite tedious, especially as $N$ gets large. However, we can obtain the probabilities by using Microsoft Excel (see appendix 6.1) and thereby avoid any computational drudgery. Figure 6.7 represents output from Microsoft Excel for the hypergeometric distribution of Example 6.6.

| | A | B | C | D |
|---|---|---|---|---|
| 1 | **Calculating Hypergeometric Probabilities** | | | |
| 2 | | | | |
| 3 | n | A | N | |
| 4 | 5 | 13 | 52 | |
| 5 | | | | |
| 6 | X | P(x) | | |
| 7 | 0 | 0.221534 | | |
| 8 | 1 | 0.411420 | | |
| 9 | 2 | 0.274280 | | |
| 10 | 3 | 0.081543 | | |
| 11 | 4 | 0.010729 | | |
| 12 | 5 | 0.000495 | | |

**FIGURE 6.7**

Hypergeometric distribution calculations for Example 6.6 obtained from the PHStat Add-In for Microsoft Excel

---

# Problems for Section 6.4

## Learning the Basics

• **6.22** Determine the following:
    (a) If $n = 4$, $N = 10$, and $A = 5$, then find $P(X = 3)$.
    (b) If $n = 4$, $N = 6$, and $A = 3$, then find $P(X = 1)$.
    (c) If $n = 5$, $N = 12$, and $A = 3$, then find $P(X = 0)$.
    (d) If $n = 3$, $A = 3$, and $N = 10$, then find $P(X = 3)$.

**6.23** Refer to Problem 6.22:
    (a) Compute the mean and standard deviation for the hypergeometric distribution described in (a).
    (b) Compute the mean and standard deviation for the hypergeometric distribution described in (b).
    (c) Compute the mean and standard deviation for the hypergeometric distribution described in (c).
    (d) Compute the mean and standard deviation for the hypergeometric distribution described in (d).

## Applying the Concepts

• **6.24** An auditor for the Internal Revenue Service is selecting a sample of six tax returns from persons in a particular profession for possible audit. If two or more of these indicate "improper" deductions, the entire group (population) of 100 tax returns will be audited.
    (a) What is the probability that the entire group will be audited if the true number of improper returns in the population is
        (1) 25?    (2) 30?    (3) 5?    (4) 10?
    (b) Discuss the differences in your results depending on the true number of improper returns in the population.

**6.25** The dean of a business school wishes to form an executive committee of five from among the 40 tenured faculty members at the school. The selection is to be random, and at the school there are eight tenured faculty members in accounting.
    (a) What is the probability that the committee will contain
        (1) none of them?
        (2) at least one of them?
        (3) not more than one of them?
    (b) What would be your answers to (a) if the committee consisted of seven members?

**6.26** From an inventory of 48 cars being shipped to local automobile dealers, suppose 12 have had defective radios installed.
   (a) What is the probability that one particular dealership receiving eight cars
      (1) obtains all with defective radios?
      (2) obtains none with defective radios?
      (3) obtains at least one with a defective radio?
   (b) What would be your answer to (a) if six cars have had defective radios installed?

**• 6.27** A state lottery is conducted in which six winning numbers are selected from a total of 54 numbers. What is the probability that if six numbers are randomly selected,
   (a) all six numbers will be winning numbers?
   (b) five numbers will be winning numbers?
   (c) four numbers will be winning numbers?
   (d) three numbers will be winning numbers?
   (e) none of the numbers will be winning numbers?
   (f) What would be your answers to (a)–(e) if the six winning numbers were selected from a total of 40 numbers?

**6.28** In a shipment of 15 hard disks, five are defective. If four of the disks are inspected,
   (a) what is the probability that
      (1) exactly one is defective?
      (2) at least one is defective?
      (3) no more than two are defective?
   (b) What is the average number of defective hard disks that you would expect to find in the sample of four hard disk drives?

## 6.5    COVARIANCE AND ITS APPLICATION IN FINANCE (OPTIONAL TOPIC)

In section 6.1 we studied the expected value, variance, and standard deviation of a discrete random variable in a probability distribution. In this section we introduce the concept of the covariance between two variables and illustrate how it is applied in portfolio management in finance.

### The Covariance

The **covariance** $\sigma_{XY}$ between two discrete random variables $X$ and $Y$ may be defined as:

**Covariance**

$$\sigma_{XY} = \sum_{i=1}^{N} [X_i - E(X)][Y_i - E(Y)]P(X_iY_i) \qquad (6.12)$$

where

$$X = \text{discrete random variable } X$$
$$X_i = i\text{th outcome of } X$$
$$P(X_iY_i) = \text{probability of occurrence of the } i\text{th outcome of } X \text{ and the } i\text{th outcome of } Y$$
$$Y = \text{discrete random variable } Y$$
$$Y_i = i\text{th outcome of } Y$$
$$i = 1, 2, \ldots, N$$

We illustrate the covariance in Example 6.7.

---

### Example 6.7 *Computing the Covariance*

Suppose that you are deciding between two alternative investments for the coming year. The first investment is a mutual fund whose portfolio consists of a combination of stocks that make up the Dow Jones Industrial Average. The second investment consists of shares of a growth stock. Suppose you estimate the following returns (per \$1,000 investment) under three economic conditions, each with a given probability of occurrence.

| $P(X_iY_i)$ | ECONOMIC CONDITION | INVESTMENT | |
|---|---|---|---|
| | | DOW JONES FUND | GROWTH STOCK |
| .2 | Recession | −\$100 | −\$200 |
| .5 | Stable economy | + 100 | + 50 |
| .3 | Expanding economy | + 250 | + 350 |

Compute the expected value and standard deviation for each investment and the covariance of the two investments.

#### SOLUTION

If $X$ = Dow Jones fund and $Y$ = growth stock

$E(X) = \mu_X = (-100)(.2) + (100)(.5) + (250)(.3) = \$105$

$E(Y) = \mu_Y = (-200)(.2) + (50)(.5) + (350)(.3) = \$90$

$Var(X) = \sigma_X^2 = (.2)(-100 - 105)^2 + (.5)(100 - 105)^2 + (.3)(250 - 105)^2$

$\sigma_X^2 = 14{,}725$

$\sigma_X = 121.35$

$Var\ (Y) = \sigma_Y^2 = (.2)(-200 - 90)^2 + (.5)(50 - 90)^2 + (.3)(350 - 90)^2$

$\sigma_Y^2 = 37{,}900$

$\sigma_Y = 194.68$

$\sigma_{XY} = (.2)(-100 - 105)(-200 - 90) + (.5)(100 - 105)(50 - 90)$
$$+ (.3)(250 - 105)(350 - 90)$$

$= 11{,}890 + 100 + 11{,}310$

$= 23{,}300$

Thus, the Dow Jones fund has a higher expected value or return than the growth fund and also has a lower standard deviation. The covariance of 23,300 between the two investments indicates a large positive relationship in which the two investments are covarying together in the same direction. When one investment is increasing, the other is also increasing.

---

## The Expected Value, Variance, and Standard Deviation of the Sum of Two Random Variables

Having computed the covariance between two variables $X$ and $Y$, we can now find the expected value and standard deviation of the sum of two random variables.

## Expected Value of the Sum of Two Random Variables

The expected value of the sum of two random variables is equal to the sum of the expected values.

$$E(X + Y) = E(X) + E(Y) \qquad (6.13)$$

## Variance of the Sum of Two Random Variables

The variance of the sum of two random variables is equal to the sum of the variances plus twice the covariance.

$$Var(X + Y) = \sigma^2_{X+Y} = \sigma^2_X + \sigma^2_Y + 2\sigma_{XY} \qquad (6.14)$$

The standard deviation is just the square root of the variance.

## Standard Deviation of the Sum of Two Random Variables

$$\sigma_{X+Y} = \sqrt{\sigma^2_{X+Y}} \qquad (6.15)$$

The expected value, variance, and standard deviation of the sum of two random variables are illustrated in Example 6.8.

### Example 6.8 *The Expected Value, Variance, and Standard Deviation of the Sum of Two Random Variables*

In Example 6.7 on page 246, we studied the expected value, standard deviation, and covariance of two different investments. Suppose that we want to determine the expected value, variance, and standard deviation of the sum of these two investments.

#### SOLUTION

If $X$ = Dow Jones fund and $Y$ = growth stock, using equations (6.13), (6.14), and (6.15),

$$E(X + Y) = E(X) + E(Y) = 105 + 90 = \$195$$
$$\sigma^2_{X+Y} = \sigma^2_X + \sigma^2_Y + 2\sigma_{XY} = 14{,}725 + 37{,}900 + (2)(23{,}300)$$
$$= 99{,}225$$
$$\sigma_{X+Y} = \$315$$

The expected return of the sum of the Dow Jones fund and the growth stock is $195 with a standard deviation of $315.

## Portfolio Expected Return and Portfolio Risk

Now that we have defined the covariance and the expected return and standard deviation of the sum of two random variables, we are ready to apply these concepts to the study of a group of assets referred to as a **portfolio**. By diversifying their investments, investors combine securities into portfolios to reduce the risk (see references 1 and 2). Often the objective is to maximize the return while minimizing the risk. For such portfolios, rather than studying the sum of two random variables, we weight each investment by the proportion of assets assigned to that investment. This enables us to compute the **portfolio expected return** and the **portfolio risk** as defined in equations (6.16) and (6.17).

## Portfolio Expected Return

The portfolio expected return for a two-asset investment is equal to the weight assigned to asset $X$ multiplied by the expected return of asset $X$ plus the weight assigned to asset $Y$ multiplied by the expected return of asset $Y$.

$$E(P) = wE(X) + (1 - w)E(Y) \tag{6.16}$$

where

$$
\begin{aligned}
E(P) &= \text{portfolio expected return}\\
w &= \text{the proportion of portfolio value assigned to asset } X\\
(1 - w) &= \text{the proportion of portfolio value assigned to asset } Y\\
E(X) &= \text{expected return of asset } X\\
E(Y) &= \text{expected return of asset } Y
\end{aligned}
$$

## Portfolio Risk

$$\sigma_p = \sqrt{[w^2\sigma_X^2 + (1 - w)^2\sigma_Y^2 + 2w(1 - w)\sigma_{XY}]} \tag{6.17}$$

The application of equations (6.16) and (6.17) to the evaluation of a portfolio is presented in Example 6.9.

## Example 6.9 *Determining Portfolio Expected Return and Portfolio Risk*

In Example 6.7 we evaluated the expected return of two different investments, a Dow Jones indexed fund and a growth stock, and also computed the standard deviation of the return of each investment and the covariance of the two investments. Now suppose that we wish to form a portfolio of these two investments that consisted of an equal investment in each of these two assets. Compute the portfolio expected return and the portfolio risk.

### SOLUTION

Using equations (6.16) and (6.17) with $w = .50$, $E(X) = \$105$, $E(Y) = \$90$, $\sigma_X^2 = 14{,}725$, $\sigma_Y^2 = 37{,}900$, and $\sigma_{XY} = 23{,}300$

$$E(P) = (.5)(105) + (1 - .5)(90) = \$97.50$$

$$\sigma_p = \sqrt{[(.5)^2(14{,}725) + (1 - .5)^2(37{,}900) + 2(.5)(1 - .5)(23{,}300)]}$$

$$\sigma_p = \sqrt{24{,}806.25} = \$157.50$$

Thus, the portfolio has an expected return of $97.50 for each $1,000 invested (a return of 9.75%) but has a portfolio risk of $157.50. Note here that the portfolio risk is higher than the expected return.

## Problems for Section 6.5

### Learning the Basics

**• 6.29** Given the following probability distribution for variables $X$ and $Y$

| $P(X_i Y_i)$ | $X$ | $Y$ |
|---|---|---|
| .4 | 100 | 200 |
| .6 | 200 | 100 |

Compute
(a) $E(X)$
(b) $E(Y)$
(c) $\sigma_X$
(d) $\sigma_Y$
(e) $\sigma_{XY}$
(f) $E(X + Y)$
(g) $\sigma_{X + Y}$

**6.30** Given the following probability distribution for variables $X$ and $Y$

| $P(X_i Y_i)$ | $X$ | $Y$ |
|---|---|---|
| .2 | −100 | 50 |
| .4 | 50 | 30 |
| .3 | 200 | 20 |
| .1 | 300 | 20 |

Compute
(a) $E(X)$
(b) $E(Y)$
(c) $\sigma_X$
(d) $\sigma_Y$
(e) $\sigma_{XY}$
(f) $E(X + Y)$
(g) $\sigma_{X + Y}$

**6.31** Suppose that two investments $X$ and $Y$ have the following characteristics: $E(X) = \$50$, $E(Y) = \$100$, $\sigma_X^2 = 9,000$, $\sigma_Y^2 = 15,000$, and $\sigma_{XY} = 7,500$. If the weight assigned to investment $X$ of portfolio assets is .4, compute the
(a) portfolio expected return
(b) portfolio risk

### Applying the Concepts

**6.32** A vendor at a local baseball stadium must determine whether to sell ice cream or soft drinks at today's game. The vendor estimates the following profits that will be made under cool weather and warm weather.

| $P$(EVENT) | EVENT | SELL SOFT DRINKS | SELL ICE CREAM |
|---|---|---|---|
| .4 | Cool weather | $50 | $30 |
| .6 | Warm weather | 60 | 90 |

Compute the
(a) expected return for selling soft drinks.
(b) expected return for selling ice cream.
(c) standard deviation of selling soft drinks.
(d) standard deviation of selling ice cream.
(e) covariance of selling soft drinks and selling ice cream.
(f) Do you think the vendor should sell soft drinks or ice cream? Explain.
(g) How would you describe the relationship between selling soft drinks and selling ice cream?

**6.33** In Example 6.9 on page 248, we assumed that half the portfolio assets were invested in the Dow Jones index fund and half in a growth stock. Recalculate the portfolio expected return and the portfolio risk if
(a) 30% are invested in the Dow Jones index fund and 70% in the growth stock.
(b) 70% are invested in the Dow Jones index fund and 30% in the growth stock.
(c) Which of the three investment strategies (30%, 50%, or 70% in the Dow Jones index stock) would you recommend? Why?

• **6.34** You are trying to develop a strategy for investing in two different stocks. The anticipated annual return for a $1,000 investment in each stock has the following probability distribution:

| | RETURNS | |
|---|---|---|
| PROBABILITY | STOCK $X$ | STOCK $Y$ |
| 0.1 | $-$100 | $50 |
| 0.3 | 0 | 100 |
| 0.3 | 80 | $-$20 |
| 0.3 | 150 | 100 |

Compute the
(a) expected return for stock $X$.
(b) expected return for stock $Y$.
(c) standard deviation for stock $X$.
(d) standard deviation for stock $Y$.
(e) covariance of stock $X$ and stock $Y$.
(f) Do you think you will invest in stock $X$ or stock $Y$? Explain.
(g) Suppose you wanted to create a portfolio that consists of stock $X$ and stock $Y$. Compute the portfolio expected return and portfolio risk for each of the following proportions invested in stock $X$.
    (1) .10        (4) .70
    (2) .30        (5) .90
    (3) .50
(h) On the basis of the results of (g), which portfolio would you recommend? Explain.

**6.35** You are trying to develop a strategy for investing in two different stocks. The anticipated annual return for a $1,000 investment in each stock has the following probability distribution:

| | RETURNS | |
|---|---|---|
| PROBABILITY | STOCK $X$ | STOCK $Y$ |
| 0.1 | $-$50 | $-$100 |
| 0.3 | 20 | 50 |
| 0.4 | 100 | 130 |
| 0.2 | 150 | 200 |

Compute the
(a) expected return for stock $X$.
(b) expected return for stock $Y$.
(c) standard deviation for stock $X$.
(d) standard deviation for stock $Y$.
(e) covariance of stock $X$ and stock $Y$.
(f) Do you think you should invest in stock $X$ or stock $Y$? Explain.
(g) Suppose you wanted to create a portfolio that consists of stock $X$ and stock $Y$. Compute the portfolio expected return and portfolio risk for each of the following proportions invested in stock $X$.
   (1) .10          (4) .70
   (2) .30          (5) .90
   (3) .50
(h) On the basis of the results of (g), which portfolio would you recommend? Explain.

**6.36** You are trying to set up a portfolio that consists of a corporate bond fund and a common stock fund. The following information about the annual return (per $1,000) of each of these investments under different economic conditions is available along with the probability that each of these economic conditions will occur.

| PROBABILITY | STATE OF THE ECONOMY | CORPORATE BONDS | COMMON STOCKS |
|---|---|---|---|
| .10 | Recession | −$30 | −$150 |
| .15 | Stagnation | 50 | −20 |
| .35 | Slow growth | 90 | 120 |
| .30 | Moderate growth | 100 | 160 |
| .10 | High growth | 110 | 250 |

Compute the
(a) expected return for corporate bonds.
(b) expected return for common stocks.
(c) standard deviation for corporate bonds.
(d) standard deviation for common stocks.
(e) covariance of corporate bonds and common stocks.
(f) Do you think you should invest in corporate bonds or common stocks? Explain.
(g) Suppose you wanted to create a portfolio that consists of corporate bonds and common stocks. Compute the portfolio expected return and portfolio risk for each of the following proportions invested in corporate bonds.
   (1) .10          (4) .70
   (2) .30          (5) .90
   (3) .50
(h) On the basis of the results of (g), which portfolio would you recommend? Explain.

# SUMMARY

As shown in the chapter summary chart on page 252, this chapter was about mathematical expectation and covariance and the development and application of some important discrete probability distributions—the binomial, Poisson, and hypergeometric distributions. In the following chapter we will concern ourselves with using probability distributions to make decisions among alternative courses of action.

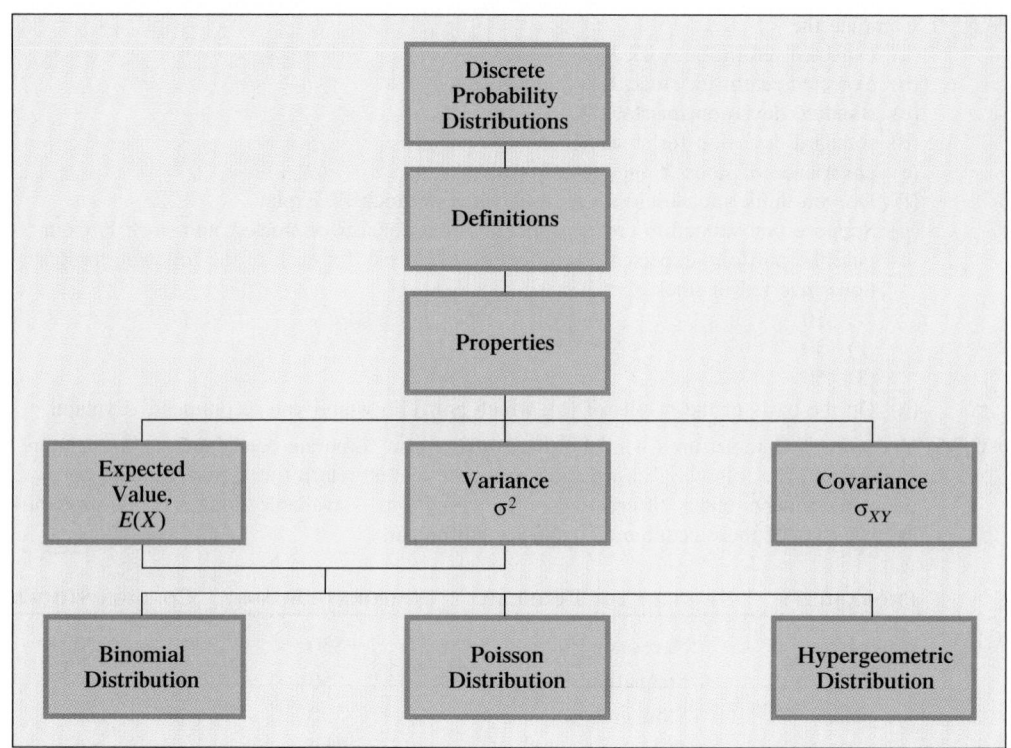

Chapter 6 summary chart

## Key Terms

binomial distribution   230, 232

covariance   245

expected value of a discrete random variable   225, 226

expected value of the sum of two random variables   247

finite population correction factor   243

hypergeometric distribution   242

mathematical model   227

model   227

Poisson distribution   239

Poisson process   238

portfolio   247

portfolio expected return   248

portfolio risk   248

probability distribution for a discrete random variable   224

probability distribution function   227

rule of combinations   231

standard deviation $\sigma$ of a discrete random variable   227

standard deviation of the sum of two random variables   247

uniform probability distribution   227

variance of the sum of two random variables   247

variance ($\sigma^2$) of a discrete random variable   226

## Checking Your Understanding

**6.37**  What is the meaning of the expected value of a probability distribution?

**6.38**  What are the assumptions of the binomial distribution?

**6.39**  What are the assumptions of the Poisson distribution, and how do they differ from those of the binomial distribution?

**6.40**  Under what circumstances should the hypergeometric distribution be used instead of the binomial distribution?

**6.41**  Why is it important to know the covariance when determining the portfolio risk?

## Chapter Review Problems

**6.42** Using the summation rules (see appendix B) show that the expression for $\sigma^2$ given in equation (6.2) can also be written as

$$\sigma^2 = \sum_{i=1}^{N} X_i^2 P(X_i) - \mu^2$$

Verify your results using the data presented in Table 6.1 on page 225.

**6.43** A natural gas exploration company averages four strikes (that is, natural gas is found) per 100 holes drilled. If 20 holes are to be drilled, what is the probability that
(a) exactly one strike will be made?       (b) at least two strikes will be made?

**6.44** On the basis of past experience, 2% of the telephone bills mailed to suburban households are incorrect. If a sample of 20 bills is selected, find the probability that
(a) at least one bill will be incorrect.       (b) at most one bill will be incorrect.

**6.45** Records provided by the vice president for human resources at a large urban hospital indicate that on any given workday 10% of the nonclinical workforce (i.e., kitchen, house-keeping and janitorial, electrical and plumbing, security, mailroom, laundry, clerical, and administrative) are absent from work. What is the probability that in a random sample of 15 nonclinical workers,
(a) exactly one will be absent today?       (b) at least two will be absent?

**6.46** On the basis of past experience, 15% of the bills of a large mail-order book company are incorrect. A random sample of three current bills is selected.
(a) What is the probability that
  (1) exactly two bills are incorrect?
  (2) no more than two bills are incorrect?
  (3) at least two bills are incorrect?
(b) What assumptions about the probability distribution are necessary to solve this problem?
(c) What would be your answers to (a) if the percentage of incorrect bills was 10%?

**6.47** On the basis of past experience, printers in a university computer lab are available 90% of the time. If a random sample of 10 time periods is selected
(a) what is the probability that printers are available
  (1) exactly nine times?       (4) more than nine times?
  (2) at least nine times?       (5) fewer than nine times?
  (3) at most nine times?
(b) How many times can the printers be expected to be available?
(c) What would be your answers to (a) and (b) if the printers were available 95% of the time?

**6.48** Suppose that on a very long mathematics test, Lauren would get 70% of the items right.
(a) For a 10-item quiz, calculate the probability that Lauren will get
  (1) at least 7 items right.
  (2) fewer than 6 items right (and therefore fail the quiz).
  (3) 9 or 10 items right (and get an A on the quiz).
(b) What is the expected number of items that Lauren will get right? What proportion of the time will she get that number right?
(c) What is the standard deviation of the number of items that Lauren will get right?
(d) What would be your answers to (a)–(c) if she typically got 80% correct?

**6.49** The manufacturer of the disk drives used in one of the well-known brands of microcomputers expects 2% of the disk drives to malfunction during the microcomputer's warranty period. In a sample of 10 disk drives, what is the probability that
(a) none will malfunction during the warranty period?

(b) exactly one will malfunction during the warranty period?

(c) at least two will malfunction during the warranty period?

(d) What would be your answers to (a)–(c) if 1% of the disk drives were expected to malfunction?

# THE SPRINGVILLE HERALD CASE

The marketing department of the newspaper has attempted to apply a strategic initiative to increase home-delivery sales through an aggressive direct-marketing campaign that has included mailings, discount coupons, and telephone solicitations. One issue that has emerged on the basis of telephone solicitation of new customers relates to the time at which the newspaper is delivered in the morning. Prospective as well as existing customers are very concerned with obtaining an early delivery of the newspaper, especially during weekdays, primarily for two reasons. First, many customers would like to bring the newspaper with them while commuting to work. Second, and more critically, many customers do not want a newspaper left on their driveway when they are not at home during the day since they believe that an unattended newspaper is a signal to a potential burglar that no one is home.

After several brainstorming sessions, a team consisting of managers and sales associates in the marketing department decided that a policy had to be developed to guarantee delivery by a specific time. After collecting data from a focus group of customers, the team decided that delivery had to be guaranteed by 7 A.M. and that the customer would not be charged for the newspaper on any day that it was not delivered by that time.

Before instituting such a policy, the team needed to determine what percentage of home-delivery customers would be entitled to a free newspaper if this policy was applied to the current delivery process. Al Leslie, the research director, suggested that data maintained on a regular basis could be used to estimate the current delivery times to customers. At a subsequent meeting, he reported to the group that on the basis of data collected from all home-delivery customers in the past week, 7% of the customers did not receive delivery by 7 A.M.

## Exercises

**6.1** Suppose that the group would like to further study the process before instituting any changes. If a sample of 50 customers is selected on a given day, what is the probability that

(a) fewer than three customers would receive a free newspaper?

(b) between two and four customers (inclusive) would receive a free newspaper?

(c) more than five customers would receive a free newspaper?

**6.2** If the process of delivering newspapers could be improved so that only 5% of the customers did not receive delivery by 7 A.M., what would be the probability that in a sample of 50 customers

(a) fewer than three customers would receive a free newspaper?

(b) between two and four customers (inclusive) would receive a free newspaper?

(c) more than five customers would receive a free newspaper?

## References

1. Bernstein, P. L., *Against the Gods: The Remarkable Story of Risk* (New York: Wiley, 1996).
2. Emery, D. R., and J. D. Finnerty, *Corporate Financial Management* (Upper Saddle River, NJ: Prentice Hall, 1997).
3. Mendenhall, W., and T. Sincich, *Statistics for Engineering and the Sciences*, 4th ed. (Upper Saddle River, NJ: Prentice Hall, 1995).
4. *Microsoft Excel 97* (Redmond, WA: Microsoft Corp., 1997).
5. *Minitab for Windows Version 12* (State College, PA: Minitab, Inc., 1998).

❖❖ **APPENDIX 6.1** **USING MICROSOFT EXCEL WITH DISCRETE PROBABILITY DISTRIBUTIONS**

In this chapter we studied the binomial, Poisson, and hypergeometric distributions and used equations (6.5), (6.8), and (6.9) to compute various probabilities. Rather than using these equations, which involve tedious calculations, we can use Microsoft Excel functions.

### COMMENT: PHStat Add-In Users

If Microsoft Excel is not running, click the **PHStat** add-in icon. If Microsoft Excel is running, select **File | Open**. Select the **PHStat** add-in file PHSA.XLA. Click the **Open** button.

To obtain a binomial probability select **PHStat | Probability Distributions | Binomial**. In the Sample Size edit box enter the value for $n$. In the Probability of success edit box, enter the value for $p$. Select the Cumulative Probabilities check box and Histogram check box if these are desired. Click the **OK** button.

To obtain a Poisson probability, select **PHStat | Probability Distributions | Poisson**. In the Avg. | Expected no. of successes edit box, enter a value for $\lambda$. Select the Cumulative Probabilities check box and Histogram check box if these are desired. Click the **OK** button.

To obtain a hypergeometric probability, select **PHStat | Probability Distributions | Hypergeometric**. In the Sample Size edit box, enter a value for $n$. In the No. of successes in population edit box, enter a value for $A$. In the Population Size edit box, enter a value for $N$. Select the Histogram edit box if a histogram is desired. Click the **OK** button.

### The Binomial Distribution

We can use the BINOMDIST function of Microsoft Excel. The format of this function is as follows:

$$\text{BINOMDIST } (X, n, p, \text{cumulative})$$

where
    $X$ = the number of successes

    $n$ = the sample size

    $p$ = the probability of success

    cumulative = False if you wish to compute the probability of exactly $X$ successes or True if you wish to compute the probability of $X$ or fewer successes

To illustrate the use of this formula, suppose we return to Example 6.2. We computed the probability of obtaining three acceptable service calls in a sample of four calls as .3456. To obtain this result using Excel, we would enter the formula **=BINOMDIST(3,4,6,False)** in a cell. If we wanted the probability of three or fewer acceptable service calls, the cumulative selection would have been set equal to True.

## The Poisson Distribution

Using Microsoft Excel, the POISSON function can be used to obtain Poisson probabilities. The format of this function is POISSON ($X$, $\lambda$, cumulative)

where          $X$ = the number of successes

            $\lambda$ = the expected or average number of successes in an area of opportunity

cumulative = False if you wish to compute the probability of exactly $X$ successes or
                    True if you wish to compute the probability of $X$ or fewer successes

To illustrate the POISSON function, suppose we return to Example 6.5 concerning the bank lunch-hour customer arrivals in section 6.3. We computed the probability that two customers would arrive at the bank in the next minute if the average arrivals were three per minute as .2240. To obtain this result using Excel, we would enter the formula **=POISSON(2,3,False)** in a cell. If we wanted the probability of two or fewer arrivals, the cumulative selection would have been set equal to True **[=POISSON(2,3,True)]**.

## The Hypergeometric Distribution

The HYPGEOMDIST function can be used to obtain the probability of $X$ successes in the hypergeometric distribution. The format of this function is

$$\text{HYPGEOMDIST } (X, n, A, N)$$

where     $X$ = the number of successes in the sample

        $n$ = the sample size

        $A$ = the number of successes in the population

        $N$ = the population size

As an example of computing a hypergeometric probability using this function, suppose we return to Example 6.6. We computed the desired probability to be .2743. To obtain this result using Excel, we would enter the formula **=HYPGEOMDIST(2,5,13,52)** in a cell and would obtain the value .27428.

## ❖ APPENDIX 6.2    USING MINITAB WITH DISCRETE PROBABILITY DISTRIBUTIONS

In this chapter we studied the binomial, Poisson, and hypergeometric distributions and used equations (6.5), (6.8), and (6.9) to compute various probabilities. Rather than using these equations, which involve tedious calculations, we can use Minitab.

## The Binomial Distribution

To illustrate the use of Minitab, suppose we return to Example 6.2. We computed the probability of obtaining three acceptable service calls in a sample of four calls as .3456. To obtain this result using Minitab, enter the values 0, 1, 2, 3, and 4 in rows 1–5 of column C1. Select **Calc | Probability Distributions | Binomial** to compute binomial probabilities. In the Binomial dialog box, select the **Probability** option button to obtain the exact probabilities of $X$ successes for all values of $X$. In the Number of trials edit box enter the sample size of **4**. In the Probability of success edit box enter **.6**. Select the **Input column** edit box and enter **C1**. Click the **OK** button.

## The Poisson Distribution

To illustrate how to obtain Poisson probabilities using Minitab, suppose we return to Example 6.5 concerning the bank lunch-hour customer arrivals in section 6.3. We computed the probability that two customers would arrive at the bank in the next minute if the average arrivals were three per minute as .2240. To obtain this result using Minitab, enter the values 0 through 22 in rows 1–23 of column C1. Select **Calc | Probability Distributions | Poisson** to compute Poisson probabilities. In the Poisson dialog box, select the **Probability** option button to obtain the exact probabilities of $X$ successes for all values of $X$. In the Mean edit box enter the $\lambda$ value of **3**. Select the **Input column** dialog box and enter **C1**. Click the **OK** button.

# Decision Making

## CHAPTER OBJECTIVES

✓ *To develop the payoff table to evaluate alternative courses of action using expected monetary value, expected opportunity loss, and risk to return criteria*
✓ *To revise prior probabilities in the light of new information*
✓ *To introduce the concept of utility*

## Introduction

In chapter 5 we studied various rules of probability and used Bayes' theorem to revise probabilities. In chapter 6 we defined and developed discrete probability distributions. In this chapter we will apply these rules and distributions to develop a decision-making process for evaluating whether a specific course of action should or should not be taken. In this context we may consider the four basic features of any decision-making situation:

1. **Alternative courses of action**. The decision maker must have two or more possible choices to evaluate prior to selecting one course of action. For example, a company must decide whether or not to market a new product or an investor must decide which portfolio to select for investment.

2. **Events or states of the world.** The decision maker must list the events that can occur and consider each event's probability of occurrence.

3. **Payoffs.** In order to evaluate each course of action, the decision maker must associate a value or payoff with the result of each event. In business applications, this payoff is usually expressed in terms of profits or costs, although other payoffs such as units of satisfaction or utility may be considered.

4. **Decision criteria.** The decision maker must determine how the best course of action is to be selected. Several criteria will be discussed in this chapter.

## ◆ USING STATISTICS: *The BerLev Mutual Fund Portfolio Strategy*

Suppose that the manager of a mutual fund was trying to decide between various alternative collections of stocks to purchase for short-term investment of up to 1 year. In putting together such a portfolio or collection of stocks there are dual objectives of wanting to maximize the return to investors while minimizing the risk. Different portfolios will have different returns under different economic conditions. Some portfolios will do better in a recession, while others may do best under conditions of moderate growth or in boom times. Suppose that the manager of the mutual fund evaluated each portfolio under four economic conditions—recession, stability, moderate growth, and boom. How can we determine which portfolio to choose so that we maximize our return and keep our risk to a minimum?

In order to consider the various alternative courses of action for the complete set of events, we can either develop a payoff table or construct a decision tree. A **payoff table** contains each possible event that can occur for each alternative course of action. For each combination of an event with a course of action, a payoff must be available. Example 7.1 provides an application of the payoff table in marketing a toy.

## Example 7.1 *A Payoff Table for Deciding Whether or Not to Market a Toy*

Suppose that the marketing manager of a toy company is considering whether or not a particular toy should be introduced into the market. The manager is aware that there are risks in deciding whether or not to market this toy. For example, it is possible that the toy will be marketed and it will be unsuccessful. Alternatively, a decision could be made not to market a toy that would have been successful. Suppose that there is a fixed cost of $3,000 incurred prior to making a final decision to market the toy. On the basis of past experience, if the toy is successful, a profit of $45,000 ($48,000 − $3,000 in fixed costs) would be obtained. If the toy is not considered successful, a loss of $36,000 ($33,000 in marketing the toy and $3,000 in fixed costs) would be incurred. Set up a payoff table for these two alternative courses of action.

### SOLUTION

A payoff table assuming only two possible events (a successful toy or an unsuccessful toy) with two possible courses of action (market the toy or do not market the toy) is shown below.

*Payoff table for the toy marketing example*

| EVENT $E_i$ | ALTERNATIVE COURSES OF ACTION | |
|---|---|---|
| | MARKET $A_1$ | DO NOT MARKET $A_2$ |
| Successful Toy $E_1$ | +$45,000 | −$3,000 |
| Unsuccessful Toy $E_2$ | −$36,000 | −$3,000 |

A **decision tree** is another way of representing the events for each alternative course of action. The decision tree pictorially represents the events and courses of action through a set of branches and nodes. The decision tree is illustrated in Example 7.2.

**Example 7.2** *The Decision Tree for the Toy*
*Marketing Decision*

Given the payoff table for the toy marketing example, set up a decision tree.

**SOLUTION**

The accompanying figure is the decision tree for the payoff table of Example 7.1.

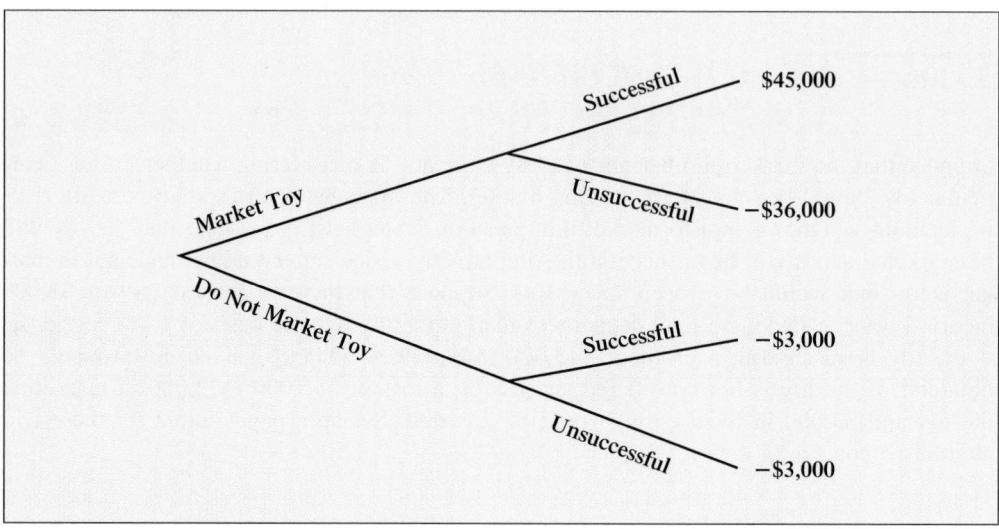

Decision tree for the toy marketing example

We observe that the first set of branches relate to the two alternative courses of action, market the toy or do not market the toy. The second set of branches represent the possible events of successful toy and unsuccessful toy. These events occur for each of the alternative courses of action on the decision tree.

Our decision structure for this toy marketing example contained only two possible alternative courses of action and two possible events. In general, there can be any number of alternative courses of action and events.

In the Using Statistics example presented at the beginning of the chapter, a manager of a mutual fund wants to decide between various alternative collections of stocks to purchase for short-term investment of up to 1 year. Suppose that the manager evaluates two portfolios under the four economic conditions of recession, stability, moderate growth, and boom. The predicted 1-year return of a $1,000 investment in each portfolio under each economic condition is presented in Table 7.1. The decision tree for this payoff table is depicted in Figure 7.1.

We use payoff tables as decision-making tools; that is, they help to determine a course of action. For example, when deciding whether to market a toy, we would of course market it if we knew that the toy was going to be successful. Conversely, we would not market it if we knew that it was not going to be successful. For each event, we can determine

**Table 7.1** *Predicted 1-year return of investment of $1,000 in each of two portfolios under four economic conditions*

| | PORTFOLIOS | |
|---|---|---|
| ECONOMIC CONDITIONS | A | B |
| Recession | $30 | −$50 |
| Stable economy | 70 | 30 |
| Moderate growth | 100 | 250 |
| Boom | 150 | 400 |

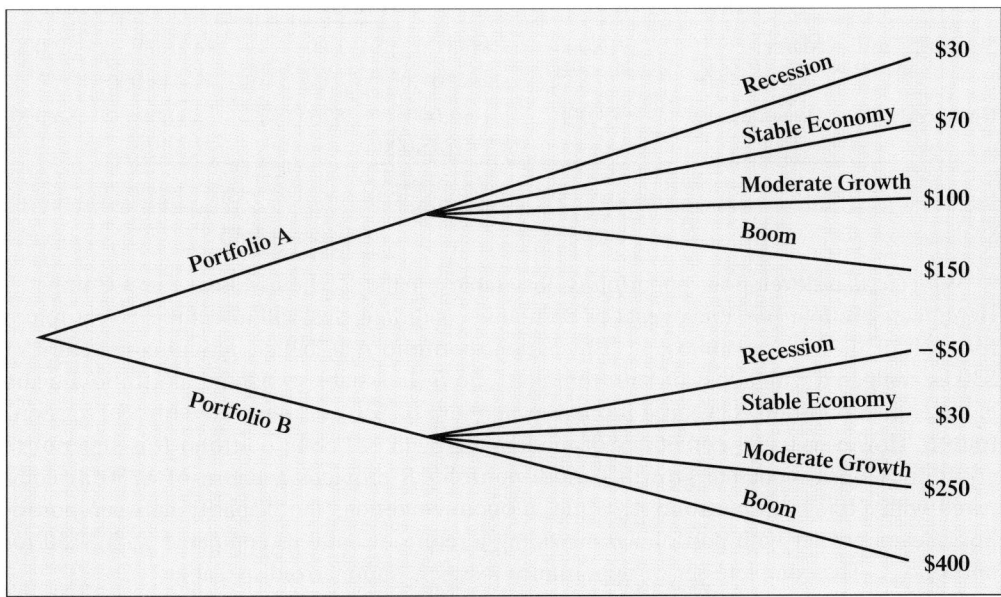

**FIGURE 7.1** Decision tree for the portfolio selection payoff table

the amount of profit that will be lost if the best alternative course of action is not taken. This is called opportunity loss and is defined as follows:

> The **opportunity loss** is the difference between the highest possible profit for an event and the actual profit obtained for an action taken.

Opportunity loss is illustrated in Example 7.3.

## Example 7.3 *Finding Opportunity Loss in Toy Marketing*

Using the payoff table of Example 7.1 on page 261, set up the opportunity loss table.

### SOLUTION

For the event "successful toy," the maximum profit is achieved when the product is marketed (+$45,000). The opportunity that is lost by not marketing the toy is the difference between $45,000 and $-$3,000, which is $48,000. If the toy is unsuccessful, the best action is not to market the toy ($-$3,000 profit). The opportunity that is lost by making the incorrect decision of marketing the toy is $-$3,000 $-$ ($-$36,000) $=$ $33,000. Note here that the opportunity loss will *always be a nonnegative number* because it represents the difference between the profit under the best action and any other course of action that is taken for the particular event. The complete opportunity loss table for the toy marketing example is summarized below.

*Opportunity loss table for the toy marketing example*

| EVENT $E_i$ | OPTIMUM ACTION | PROFIT OF OPTIMUM ACTION | ALTERNATIVE COURSES OF ACTION | |
|---|---|---|---|---|
| | | | MARKET | DO NOT MARKET |
| Successful toy | Market | $45,000 | $45,000 $-$ $45,000 = $0 | $45,000 $-$ ($-$3,000) = $48,000 |
| Unsuccessful toy | Do not market | $-$3,000 | $-$3,000 $-$ ($-$36,000) = $33,000 | $-$3,000 $-$ ($-$3,000) = $0 |

We can also develop an opportunity loss table for the BerLev Mutual Fund Company. Here, there are four possible events or economic conditions that will affect the 1-year return for each of the two portfolios. In a recession, portfolio $A$ is better, providing a return of $30 as compared with a loss of $50 from portfolio $B$. In a stable economy, portfolio $A$ again is better than portfolio $B$ because it provides a return of $70 as compared with $30 for portfolio $B$. However, under conditions of moderate growth or boom, portfolio $B$ is superior to portfolio $A$. In a moderate growth period, portfolio $B$ provides a return of $250 as compared with $100 from portfolio $A$, while in boom conditions the disparity between portfolios is even greater with portfolio $B$ providing a return of $400 as compared with $150 for portfolio $A$. The complete set of opportunity losses is summarized in Table 7.2.

**Table 7.2**  *Opportunity loss table for two portfolios under four economic conditions*

| EVENT $E_i$ | OPTIMUM ACTION | PROFIT OF OPTIMUM ACTION | ALTERNATIVE COURSES OF ACTION | |
|---|---|---|---|---|
| | | | A | B |
| Recession | A | $ 30 | 30 $-$ 30 = 0 | 30 $-$ ($-$50) = 80 |
| Stable economy | A | 70 | 70 $-$ 70 = 0 | 70 $-$ 30 = 40 |
| Moderate growth | B | 250 | 250 $-$ 100 = 150 | 250 $-$ 250 = 0 |
| Boom | B | 400 | 400 $-$ 150 = 250 | 400 $-$ 400 = 0 |

## Problems for Section 7.1

### Learning the Basics

• **7.1**  For the following payoff table

| EVENT | ACTION A | ACTION B |
|:-----:|:--------:|:--------:|
| 1 | 50 | 100 |
| 2 | 200 | 125 |

(a) Set up the opportunity loss table.     (b) Construct a decision tree.

**7.2** For the following payoff table

| EVENT | ACTION A | ACTION B |
|:-----:|:--------:|:--------:|
| 1 | 50 | 10 |
| 2 | 300 | 100 |
| 3 | 500 | 200 |

(a) Set up the opportunity loss table.     (b) Construct a decision tree.

## Applying the Concepts

**7.3** The manufacturer of designer jeans must decide whether to build a large factory or a small factory in a particular location. The profit per pair of jeans manufactured is estimated as $10. A small factory will have an amortized annual cost of $200,000 with a production capacity of 50,000 jeans per year. A large factory will have an amortized annual cost of $400,000 with a production capacity of 100,000 jeans per year. Four levels of manufacturing demand are considered likely, 10,000, 20,000, 50,000, and 100,000 pairs of jeans per year.
  (a) Indicate the possible levels of production for a small factory and the payoffs for each possible level of production.
  (b) Indicate the possible levels of production for a large factory and the payoffs for each possible level of production.
  (c) Based on the results of (a) and (b), set up the payoff table indicating the events and alternative courses of action.
  (d) Set up the decision tree.
  (e) Set up the opportunity loss table.

• **7.4** An author is trying to choose between two publishing companies that are competing for the marketing rights to her new novel. Company A has offered the author $10,000 plus $2 per book sold. Company B has offered the author $2,000 plus $4 per book sold. The author believes that five levels of demand for the book are possible, 1,000, 2,000, 5,000, 10,000, and 50,000 books sold.
  (a) Compute the payoffs for each level of demand for company A and for company B.
  (b) Set up the payoff table indicating the events and alternative courses of action.
  (c) Set up the decision tree.
  (d) Set up the opportunity loss table.

**7.5** The LeFleur Garden Center chain purchases Christmas trees for sale during the holiday season. The trees are purchased for $10 each and are sold for $20 each. Any trees not sold by Christmas Day can be disposed of for $2 each. The garden center estimates that four levels of demand are possible, 100, 200, 500, 1,000 trees.
  (a) Compute the payoffs for purchasing 100, 200, 500, or 1,000 trees for each of the four levels of demand.
  (b) Set up the payoff table indicating the events and alternative courses of action.
  (c) Set up the decision tree.
  (d) Set up the opportunity loss table.

Now that the profit and opportunity loss for each event under each alternative course of action has been provided in the payoff and opportunity loss tables, we need to determine the criteria for selecting the most desirable course of action. To determine which alternative to choose, the decision maker first assigns a probability to each event. Such probabilities are based on information available from past data, on the opinions of the decision maker, or on knowledge about the probability distribution that the event may follow. Using these probabilities, along with the payoffs or opportunity losses of each event-action combination, we can select the best course of action according to particular criteria.

In section 6.1 on page 226, we used equation (6.1) to compute the expected value of a probability distribution. Now we extend this formula to compute the expected monetary value for each alternative course of action.

The **expected monetary value (*EMV*)** for a course of action $j$ is the profit for each combination ($x_{ij}$) of event $i$ and action $j$ times the probability of occurrence of the event ($P_i$) summed over all events. This expression is given by

**Expected Monetary Value**

$$EMV_j = \sum_{i=1}^{N} x_{ij}P_i \qquad (7.1)$$

where

$EMV_j$ = expected monetary value of action $j$

$x_{ij}$ = the payoff that occurs when course of action $j$ is selected and event $i$ occurs

$P_i$ = probability of occurrence of event $i$

We illustrate the application of expected monetary value in Example 7.4, which refers to toy marketing.

---

### Example 7.4 *Computing the Expected Monetary Value for Toy Marketing*

Returning to the payoff table for deciding whether to market a toy (Example 7.1 on page 261), suppose that a probability of .40 is assigned to the event that the toy will be successful (so that a probability of .60 is assigned to the complementary event that the toy will not be successful). Compute the expected monetary value for each alternative course of action, and determine whether the toy should be marketed.

#### SOLUTION

The expected monetary value for each alternative course of action can be determined using equation (7.1). These computations are summarized at the top of page 267.

## Expected monetary value for each alternative in the toy marketing example

| EVENT $E_i$ | $P_i$ | MARKET $A_1$ | $x_{ij}P_i$ | DO NOT MARKET $A_2$ | $x_{ij}P_i$ |
|---|---|---|---|---|---|
| | | **ALTERNATIVE COURSES OF ACTION** | | | |
| Successful toy $E_1$ | .40 | +$45,000 | $45,000(.4) $\\$ = -$18,000 | -$3,000 | -$3,000(.4) $\\$ = -$1,200 |
| Unsuccessful toy $E_2$ | .60 | -$36,000 | -$36,000(.6) $\\$ = -$21,600 | -$3,000 | -$3,000(.6) $\\$ = -$1,800 |
| | | $EMV(A_1)$ = | -$3,600 | $EMV(A_2)$ = | -$3,000 |

The expected monetary value for marketing the toy is −$3,600, whereas the expected monetary value for not marketing the toy is −$3,000. Thus, if our objective is to choose the action that maximizes the expected monetary value, we would choose the action of not marketing the toy because its profit is higher (or in this case its loss is lower).

As a second application of expected monetary value, we can return to the BerLev Mutual Fund Company whose payoff table was presented in Table 7.1 on page 263. Suppose the mutual fund manager assigns the following probabilities to the different economic conditions:

$$P(\text{recession}) = .10$$

$$P(\text{stable economy}) = .40$$

$$P(\text{moderate growth}) = .30$$

$$P(\text{boom}) = .20$$

With the information provided in Table 7.1 on page 263, the expected monetary value for each of the two portfolios can be developed as in Table 7.3. Thus, the expected monetary value or profit for portfolio A is $91, whereas the expected monetary value or profit for portfolio B is $162. Using this criterion, the manager of the mutual fund would choose portfolio B because the expected rate of return on portfolio B is 162/1,000, or 16.2%, almost twice that of portfolio A, which has an expected rate of return of 91/1,000, or 9.1%, on the $1,000 investment.

## Table 7.3  Expected monetary value for each alternative for each of two portfolios under four economic conditions

| EVENT $E_i$ | $P_i$ | A | $x_{ij}P_i$ | B | $x_{ij}P_i$ |
|---|---|---|---|---|---|
| | | **ALTERNATIVE COURSES OF ACTION** | | | |
| Recession | .10 | 30 | 30(.1) = 3 | -50 | -50(.1) = -5 |
| Stable economy | .40 | 70 | 70(.4) = 28 | 30 | 30(.4) = 12 |
| Moderate growth | .30 | 100 | 100(.3) = 30 | 250 | 250(.3) = 75 |
| Boom | .20 | 150 | 150(.2) = 30 | 400 | 400(.2) = 80 |
| | | | $EMV(A)$ = 91 | | $EMV(B)$ = 162 |

Another way of evaluating the alternative courses of action involves using the opportunity loss table that was developed in section 7.1. The **expected opportunity loss (EOL)** of action $j$ is equal to

---

## Expected Opportunity Loss

$$EOL_j = \sum_{i=1}^{N} l_{ij}P_i \qquad (7.2)$$

where

$l_{ij}$ = opportunity loss that occurs when course of action $j$ is selected and event $i$ occurs

$P_i$ = probability of occurrence of event $i$

---

We illustrate the application of expected monetary value in Example 7.5, which refers to toy marketing.

---

## Example 7.5 *Computing the Expected Opportunity Loss for Toy Marketing*

Referring to the opportunity loss table developed in Example 7.3 on page 263, and assuming that a probability of .40 is assigned to the event that the toy will be successful, compute the expected opportunity loss for each alternative course of action and determine whether the toy should be marketed.

*Expected opportunity loss for each alternative in the toy marketing example*

| EVENT $E_i$ | $P_i$ | ALTERNATIVE COURSES OF ACTION | | | |
| | | MARKET $A_1$ | $l_{ij}P_i$ | DO NOT MARKET $A_2$ | $l_{ij}P_i$ |
| --- | --- | --- | --- | --- | --- |
| Successful toy $E_1$ | .40 | 0 | 0(.4) = 0 | $48,000 | $48,000(.4) = $19,200 |
| Unsuccessful toy $E_2$ | .60 | $33,000 | $33,000(.6) = $19,800 | 0 | 0(.6) = 0 |
| | | | $EOL(A_1) = $19,800$ | | $EOL(A_2) = $19,200$ |

The expected opportunity loss is lower for not marketing the toy ($19,200) than for marketing the toy ($19,800).

---

This *expected opportunity loss from the best decision* has a special meaning in the decision-making context. It is defined as the **expected value of perfect information (EVPI)**. This expected value of perfect information is determined as follows:

## Expected Value of Perfect Information

$EVPI$ = expected profit under certainty − expected monetary value of the best
   alternative                                                              (7.3)

The **expected profit under certainty** represents the expected profit that we could make if we have perfect information about which event will occur. To illustrate the expected value of perfect information, we turn to Example 7.6.

## Example 7.6  *Computing the Expected Value of Perfect Information*

Referring to Example 7.5, compute the expected profit under certainty and the expected value of perfect information.

### SOLUTION

If the marketing manager in the toy example could always predict the future, a profit of $45,000 would be made for the 40% of the toys that are successful, whereas a loss of $3,000 would be incurred for the 60% of the toys that would not be successful. Thus, we have

$$\text{Expected profit under certainty} = .40(\$45,000) + .60(-\$3,000)$$
$$= \$18,000 - \$1,800$$
$$= \$16,200$$

This value, $16,200, represents the profit that we could make if the marketing manager knew with *certainty* whether the toy was going to be successful. The expected value of perfect information can now be obtained using equation (7.3) as follows:

$EVPI$ = expected profit under certainty − expected monetary value of the best
   alternative

$EVPI = \$16,200 - (-\$3,000) = \$19,200$

which is the expected opportunity loss of not marketing the toy. This *EVPI* value of $19,200 represents the maximum amount that the marketing manager should be willing to pay to obtain perfect information.

As a second application of expected opportunity loss, we can return to the BerLev Mutual Fund Company, whose opportunity loss table was presented in Table 7.2 on page 264. These computations are presented in Table 7.4 on page 270.

The expected opportunity loss is lower for portfolio *B*, so consistent with our decision when we used expected monetary value, we would choose portfolio *B*. The expected value of perfect information is $24 (per $1,000 invested), meaning that the mutual fund manager should be willing to pay up to this amount to obtain perfect information.

Unfortunately neither the expected monetary value nor the expected opportunity loss criterion take into account the variability of the payoffs of alternative courses of action under different events. From Table 7.1 on page 263, we determine that the return for portfolio *A*

**Table 7.4**  *Expected opportunity loss for each alternative for the portfolio selection example*

| EVENT $E_i$ | $P_i$ | A | $l_{ij} P_i$ | B | $l_{ij} P_i$ |
|---|---|---|---|---|---|
| | | ALTERNATIVE COURSES OF ACTION | | | |
| Recession | .10 | 0 | 0(.1) = 0 | 80 | 80(.1) = 8 |
| Stable economy | .40 | 0 | 0(.4) = 0 | 40 | 40(.4) = 16 |
| Moderate growth | .30 | 150 | 150(.3) = 45 | 0 | 0(.3) = 0 |
| Boom | .20 | 250 | 250(.2) = 50 | 0 | 0(.2) = 0 |
| | | | $EOL(A) = 95$ | | $EOL(B) = EVPI = 24$ |

varies from $30 in a recession to $150 in boom economic times, whereas portfolio $B$ (the one chosen according to the expected monetary value and expected opportunity loss criteria) varies from a loss of $50 in a recession to a profit of $400 under boom economic conditions.

If we wish to take into account the variability of the events (in this case the economic conditions), we can compute the variance and standard deviation of each portfolio or alternative course of action using equations (6.2) and (6.3) on pages 226 and 227. Using the portfolio selection data of Table 7.3, for portfolio $A$ we have

$$\sigma_A^2 = \sum_{i=1}^{N} [X_i - E(X)]^2 P(X_i)$$

$$= (30 - 91)^2(.1) + (70 - 91)^2(.4) + (100 - 91)^2(.3) + (150 - 91)^2(.2)$$

$$= 1,269$$

and

$$\sigma_A = 35.623$$

so that the standard deviation of portfolio $A$ is $35.62. For portfolio $B$ we have

$$\sigma_B^2 = \sum_{i=1}^{N} [X_i - E(X)]^2 P(X_i)$$

$$= (-50 - 162)^2(.1) + (30 - 162)^2(.4) + (250 - 162)^2(.3) + (400 - 162)^2(.2)$$

$$= 25,116$$

and

$$\sigma_B = 158.48$$

so that the standard deviation of portfolio $B$ is $158.48.

Now that we have obtained the standard deviation of the return from each portfolio, because we are comparing two sets of data with vastly different means, the coefficient of variation discussed in section 4.2 on page 149 can be computed. From equation (4.11) the coefficient of variation for portfolio $A$ is equal to

$$CV_A = \frac{\sigma_A}{EMV_A} 100\%$$

$$= \frac{35.62}{91} \cdot 100\% = 39.1\%$$

while the coefficient of variation for portfolio $B$ is equal to

$$CV_B = \frac{\sigma_B}{EMV_B} \cdot 100\%$$

$$= \frac{158.48}{162} \cdot 100\% = 97.8\%$$

Thus we see that there is much more variation in the returns from portfolio $B$ than from portfolio $A$.

Since the coefficient of variation shows the relative size of the variation as compared with the arithmetic mean (or expected monetary value), a different criterion is needed to express the relationship between the return (or payoff) and the *risk* (as expressed by the standard deviation). One such criterion is the **return to risk ratio**, which represents the expected monetary value divided by the standard deviation and is presented in equation (7.4).

## Return to Risk Ratio

$$\text{Return to risk ratio} = \frac{EMV_j}{\sigma_j} \tag{7.4}$$

where

$EMV_j$ = the expected monetary value for alternative course of action $j$

$\sigma_j$ = the standard deviation for alternative course of action $j$

For each of the two portfolios discussed previously, the return to risk ratios are computed as follows: For portfolio $A$, the return to risk ratio is equal to

$$\text{Return to risk ratio} = \frac{91}{35.62} = 2.55$$

whereas for portfolio $B$, the return to risk ratio is equal to

$$\text{Return to risk ratio} = \frac{162}{158.48} = 1.02$$

Thus, relative to the risk as expressed by the standard deviation, the return seems much higher for portfolio $A$ than for portfolio $B$. Although portfolio $A$ had a smaller expected monetary value than portfolio $B$ it also had a much smaller risk. The return to risk ratio shows $A$ to be preferable to $B$.

## Problems for Section 7.2

### Learning the Basics

• **7.6** For the following payoff table

| | ACTION | |
|---|---|---|
| EVENT | *A* | *B* |
| 1 | 50 | 100 |
| 2 | 200 | 125 |

suppose the probability of event 1 is .5 and the probability of event 2 is also .5.
(a) Compute the expected monetary value (*EMV*) for actions *A* and *B*.
(b) Compute the expected opportunity loss (*EOL*) for actions *A* and *B*.
(c) Explain the meaning of the expected value of perfect information (*EVPI*) in this problem.
(d) Based on the results of (a) or (b), which action would you choose? Why?
(e) Compute the coefficient of variation for each action.
(f) Compute the return to risk ratio for each action.
(g) Based on (e) and (f), which action would you choose? Why?
(h) Compare the results of (d) and (g), and explain any differences.

**7.7** For the following payoff table

| | ACTION | |
|---|---|---|
| EVENT | *A* | *B* |
| 1 | 50 | 10 |
| 2 | 300 | 100 |
| 3 | 500 | 200 |

suppose the probability of event 1 is .8, the probability of event 2 is .1, and the probability of event 3 is .1.
(a) Compute the expected monetary value (*EMV*) for actions *A* and *B*.
(b) Compute the expected opportunity loss (*EOL*) for actions *A* and *B*.
(c) Explain the meaning of the expected value of perfect information (*EVPI*) in this problem.
(d) Based on the results of (a) or (b), which action would you choose? Why?
(e) Compute the coefficient of variation for each action.
(f) Compute the return to risk ratio for each action.
(g) Based on (e) and (f), which action would you choose? Why?
(h) Compare the results of (d) and (g), and explain any differences.
(i) Would your answers to (d) and (g) be different if the probabilities for the three events were .1, .1, and .8, respectively? Discuss.

**7.8** For a potential investment of $1,000, if a portfolio has an *EMV* of $100 and a standard deviation of $25, what is the
(a) rate of return?          (c) return to risk ratio?
(b) coefficient of variation?

• **7.9** If a portfolio has the following returns under the following economic conditions,

| ECONOMIC CONDITION | PROBABILITY | RETURN |
|---|---|---|
| Recession | .30 | $50 |
| Stable economy | .30 | 100 |
| Moderate growth | .30 | 120 |
| Boom | .10 | 200 |

compute the
(a) expected monetary value.        (c) coefficient of variation.
(b) standard deviation.             (d) return to risk ratio.

**7.10** Given the following results for two portfolios

|                          | A    | B    |
| ------------------------ | ---- | ---- |
| Expected monetary value  | $90  | $60  |
| Standard deviation       | 10   | 10   |

which portfolio would you choose and why?

**7.11** Given the following results for two portfolios

|                          | A    | B    |
| ------------------------ | ---- | ---- |
| Expected monetary value  | $60  | $60  |
| Standard deviation       | 20   | 10   |

which portfolio would you choose and why?

## Applying the Concepts

• **7.12** A vendor at a local baseball stadium must determine whether to sell ice cream or soft drinks at today's game. The vendor believes that the profit made will depend on the weather. The payoff table is as follows:

|              | ACTION           |                |
| ------------ | ---------------- | -------------- |
| EVENT        | SELL SOFT DRINKS | SELL ICE CREAM |
| Cool weather | $50              | $30            |
| Warm weather | 60               | 90             |

On the basis of her past experience at this time of year, the vendor estimates the probability of warm weather as .60.

(a) Compute the expected monetary value (*EMV*) for selling soft drinks and selling ice cream.

(b) Compute the expected opportunity loss (*EOL*) for selling soft drinks and selling ice cream.

(c) Explain the meaning of the expected value of perfect information (*EVPI*) in this problem.

(d) On the basis of the results of (a) or (b), which should the vendor choose to sell, soft drinks or ice cream? Why?

(e) Compute the coefficient of variation for selling soft drinks and selling ice cream.

(f) Compute the return to risk ratio for selling soft drinks and selling ice cream.

(g) On the basis of (e) and (f), which should the vendor choose to sell, soft drinks or ice cream? Why?

(h) Compare the results of (d) and (g), and explain any differences.

• **7.13** The Islander Fishing Company purchases clams for $1.50 per pound from Peconic Bay fishermen for sale to various New York restaurants for $2.50 per pound. Any clams not sold to the restaurants by the end of the week can be sold to a local soup company for $0.50 per pound. The probabilities of various levels of demand are as follows:

| DEMAND (POUNDS) | PROBABILITY |
| --------------- | ----------- |
| 500             | .2          |
| 1,000           | .4          |
| 2,000           | .4          |

(*Hint*: The company can purchase 500, 1,000, or 2,000 pounds.)

(a) For each possible purchase level (500, 1,000, or 2,000 pounds) compute the profit (or loss) for each level of demand.

(b) Using the expected monetary value criterion, determine the optimal number of pounds of clams that the company should purchase from the fishermen. Discuss.

(c) Compute the standard deviation for each possible purchase level.

(d) Compute the expected opportunity loss (*EOL*) for purchasing 500, 1,000, and 2,000 pounds of clams.

(e) Explain the meaning of the expected value of perfect information (*EVPI*) in this problem.

(f) Compute the coefficient of variation for purchasing 500, 1,000, and 2,000 pounds of clams.

(g) Compute the return to risk ratio for purchasing 500, 1,000, and 2,000 pounds of clams.

(h) On the basis of (b) and (d), what would you choose to purchase, 500, 1,000, or 2,000 pounds of clams? Why?

(i) Compare the results of (b), (d), (f), and (g), and explain any differences.

(j) Suppose that clams can be sold for $3 per pound. Do (a)–(i) with this selling price for clams and compare the results with those obtained in (i).

(k) What would be the effect on the results in (a)–(i) if the probability of the demand for 500, 1,000, and 2,000 pounds were .4, .4, and .2 respectively?

**7.14** An investor has a certain amount of money available to invest now. Three alternative portfolio selections are available. The estimated profits of each portfolio under each economic condition are indicated in the following payoff table:

| EVENT | PORTFOLIO SELECTION | | |
| --- | --- | --- | --- |
| | *A* | *B* | *C* |
| Economy declines | $ 500 | $−2,000 | $−7,000 |
| No change | 1,000 | 2,000 | −1,000 |
| Economy expands | 2,000 | 5,000 | 20,000 |

On the basis of his own past experience, the investor assigns the following probabilities to each economic condition:

$$P(\text{economy declines}) = .30$$
$$P(\text{no change}) = .50$$
$$P(\text{economy expands}) = .20$$

(a) Determine the best portfolio selection for the investor according to the expected monetary value criterion. Discuss.

(b) Compute the standard deviation for each possible portfolio selection.

(c) Compute the expected opportunity loss (*EOL*) for portfolios *A*, *B*, and *C*.

(d) Explain the meaning of the expected value of perfect information (*EVPI*) in this problem.

(e) Compute the coefficient of variation for portfolios *A*, *B*, and *C*.

(f) Compute the return to risk ratio for portfolios *A*, *B*, and *C*.

(g) On the basis of (e) and (f), which would you choose, portfolio *A*, *B*, or *C*? Why?

(h) Compare the results of (a) and (g), and explain any differences.

(i) Suppose the probabilities of the different economic conditions were as follows:

(1) .1, .6, and .3     (3) .4, .4, and .2
(2) .1, .3, and .6     (4) .6, .3, and .1

Do (a)–(g) with each of these sets of probabilities and compare the results with those obtained in (h). Discuss.

**7.15** In Problem 7.3 on page 265, a payoff table was developed for building a small factory or a large factory for manufacturing designer jeans. Given the results obtained in that problem, suppose that the probability of the levels of manufacturing demand are

| DEMAND | PROBABILITY |
|--------|-------------|
| 10,000 | .1 |
| 20,000 | .4 |
| 50,000 | .2 |
| 100,000 | .3 |

(a) Compute the expected monetary value (*EMV*) for building a small factory or building a large factory.

(b) Compute the expected opportunity loss (*EOL*) for building a small factory or building a large factory.

(c) Explain the meaning of the expected value of perfect information (*EVPI*) in this problem.

(d) On the basis of the results of (a) and (b), which would you choose to build, a small factory or a large factory? Why?

(e) Compute the coefficient of variation for building a small factory or building a large factory.

(f) Compute the return to risk ratio for building a small factory or building a large factory.

(g) On the basis of (e) and (f), which would you choose to build, a small factory or a large factory? Why?

(h) Compare the results of (d) and (g), and explain any differences.

(i) Suppose that the probabilities of demand were .4, .2, .2, and .2, respectively. Do (a)–(h) with these probabilities and compare your results.

**● 7.16** In Problem 7.4 on page 265, a payoff table was developed to assist an author in choosing between signing with company A or with company B. Given the results obtained in that problem, suppose that the probability of the levels of demand for the novel are

| DEMAND | PROBABILITY |
|--------|-------------|
| 1,000 | .45 |
| 2,000 | .20 |
| 5,000 | .15 |
| 10,000 | .10 |
| 50,000 | .10 |

(a) Compute the expected monetary value (*EMV*) for signing with company A and with company B.

(b) Compute the expected opportunity loss (*EOL*) for signing with company A and with company B.

(c) Explain the meaning of the expected value of perfect information (*EVPI*) in this problem.

(d) On the basis of the results of (a) and (b), if you were the author, which company would you choose to sign with, company A or company B? Why?

(e) Compute the coefficient of variation for signing with company A and with company B.

(f) Compute the return to risk ratio for signing with company A and with company B.

(g) Based on (e) and (f), which company would you choose to sign with, company A or company B? Why?

(h) Compare the results of (d) and (g), and explain any differences.

(i) Suppose that the probabilities of demand were .3, .2, .2, .1, and .2, respectively. Do (a)–(h) with these probabilities and compare your results.

**7.17** In Problem 7.5 on page 265, a payoff table was developed for purchasing 100, 200, 500, and 1,000 Christmas trees. Given the results obtained in that problem, suppose that the probability of the demand for the different number of trees was as follows

| DEMAND (NUMBER OF TREES) | PROBABILITY |
|---|---|
| 100 | .20 |
| 200 | .50 |
| 500 | .20 |
| 1,000 | .10 |

(a) Compute the expected monetary value (*EMV*) for purchasing 100, 200, 500, and 1,000 trees.

(b) Compute the expected opportunity loss (*EOL*) for purchasing 100, 200, 500, and 1,000 trees.

(c) Explain the meaning of the expected value of perfect information (*EVPI*) in this problem.

(d) On the basis of the results of (a) and (b), which would you choose to purchase, 100, 200, 500, or 1,000 trees? Why?

(e) Compute the coefficient of variation for purchasing 100, 200, 500, and 1,000 trees.

(f) Compute the return to risk ratio for purchasing 100, 200, 500, and 1,000 trees.

(g) On the basis of (e) and (f), what would you choose to purchase, 100, 200, 500, or 1,000 trees? Why?

(h) Compare the results of (d) and (g), and explain any differences.

(i) Suppose that the probabilities of demand were .4, .2, .2, and .2, respectively. Do (a)–(h) with these probabilities, and compare your results.

## 7.3 DECISION MAKING WITH SAMPLE INFORMATION

In sections 7.1 and 7.2 we developed the framework for making decisions when there are several courses of action. We used different criteria for choosing between alternatives and discussed the expected value of perfect information. For each criterion discussed, the probabilities of the various events were obtained using the past experience and/or the subjective judgment of the decision maker. Recall that in section 5.3 Bayes' theorem was used to revise the prior probabilities on the basis of sample information. We will illustrate decision making with sample information in Example 7.7.

### Example 7.7 *Decision Making Using Sample Information for Toy Marketing*

In section 5.3 on page 214, we found that the probability of a successful toy, given that a favorable report was received, is .64. Thus, the probability of an unsuccessful toy, given that a favorable report was received, is $1 - .64 = .36$. Using these revised probabilities, compute the expected monetary value for each alternative course of action and determine whether the toy should be marketed.

## SOLUTION

Because the original subjective probabilities were used in Example 7.4 on page 266 to determine the best decision based on the expected monetary value criterion, the expected profit of each alternative must be reevaluated by using the revised probabilities. The revised expected monetary value computations are illustrated below.

*Expected monetary value using revised probabilities for each alternative in the toy marketing example*

| EVENT $E_i$ | $P_i$ | MARKET $A_1$ | $x_{ij}P_i$ | DO NOT MARKET $A_2$ | $x_{ij}P_i$ |
|---|---|---|---|---|---|
| Successful toy $E_1$ | .64 | +$45,000 | $45,000(.64) = $28,800 | −$3,000 | −$3,000(.64) = −$1,920 |
| Unsuccessful toy $E_2$ | .36 | −$36,000 | −$36,000(.36) = −$12,960 | −$3,000 | −$3,000(.36) = −$1,080 |
| | | $EMV(A_1) = $ | $15,840 | $EMV(A_2) = $ | −$3,000 |

In this case, the optimal decision is to market the product, because an average profit of $15,840 can be expected as compared with a loss of $3,000 if the toy is not marketed. This decision is different from the one considered optimal prior to the collection of the sample information in the form of the market research report. The favorable recommendation contained in the report has a substantial effect on the prior assessment of the marketing manager, so that the optimal decision is one in which the product is marketed.

Just as the marketing manager of the toy company is able to use sample information prior to making a decision, the mutual fund manager wants to obtain a forecast of the economic conditions in the upcoming year because the relative desirability of the two portfolios is directly affected by economic conditions. Suppose that a forecast can be obtained that predicts either an expanding economy ($F_1$) or a declining or stagnant economy ($F_2$). Past experience indicates that, when there is a recession, prior forecasts predicted an expanding economy 20% of the time. When there has been a stable economy, prior forecasts predicted an expanding economy 40% of the time. When there is moderate growth, prior forecasts predicted an expanding economy 70% of the time. Finally, when there is a boom economy, prior forecasts predicted an expanding economy 90% of the time. The mutual fund manager wants to know how the prior probabilities of economic conditions should be revised if the forecast is for an expanding economy. To use equation (5.10), let

event $E_1$ = recession    event $F_1$ = expanding economy

event $E_2$ = stable economy    event $F_2$ = declining or stagnant economy

event $E_3$ = moderate growth

event $E_4$ = boom economy

and

$$P(E_1) = .10 \quad P(F_1|E_1) = .20$$
$$P(E_2) = .40 \quad P(F_1|E_2) = .40$$
$$P(E_3) = .30 \quad P(F_1|E_3) = .70$$
$$P(E_4) = .20 \quad P(F_1|E_4) = .90$$

Then, using equation (5.10)

$$P(E_1|F_1) = \frac{P(F_1|E_1)P(E_1)}{P(F_1|E_1)P(E_1) + P(F_1|E_2)P(E_2) + P(F_1|E_3)P(E_3) + P(F_1|E_4)P(E_4)}$$

$$= \frac{(.20)(.10)}{(.20)(.10) + (.40)(.40) + (.70)(.30) + (.90)(.20)}$$

$$= \frac{.02}{.57} = .035$$

$$P(E_2|F_1) = \frac{P(F_1|E_2)P(E_2)}{P(F_1|E_1)P(E_1) + P(F_1|E_2)P(E_2) + P(F_1|E_3)P(E_3) + P(F_1|E_4)P(E_4)}$$

$$= \frac{(.40)(.40)}{(.20)(.10) + (.40)(.40) + (.70)(.30) + (.90)(.20)}$$

$$= \frac{.16}{.57} = .281$$

$$P(E_3|F_1) = \frac{P(F_1|E_3)P(E_3)}{P(F_1|E_1)P(E_1) + P(F_1|E_2)P(E_2) + P(F_1|E_3)P(E_3) + P(F_1|E_4)P(E_4)}$$

$$= \frac{(.70)(.30)}{(.20)(.10) + (.40)(.40) + (.70)(.30) + (.90)(.20)}$$

$$= \frac{.21}{.57} = .368$$

$$P(E_4|F_1) = \frac{P(F_1|E_4)P(E_4)}{P(F_1|E_1)P(E_1) + P(F_1|E_2)P(E_2) + P(F_1|E_3)P(E_3) + P(F_1|E_4)P(E_4)}$$

$$= \frac{(.90)(.20)}{(.20)(.10) + (.40)(.40) + (.70)(.30) + (.90)(.20)}$$

$$= \frac{.18}{.57} = .316$$

The computation of these probabilities is summarized in Table 7.5 and displayed in the form of a decision tree in Figure 7.2.

**Table 7.5** *Bayes' theorem calculations for the BerLev mutual funds*

| EVENT $E_i$ | PRIOR PROBABILITY $P(E_i)$ | CONDITIONAL PROBABILITY $P(F_1|E_i)$ | JOINT PROBABILITY $P(F_1|E_i)P(E_i)$ | REVISED PROBABILITY $P(E_i|F_1)$ |
|---|---|---|---|---|
| $E_1$ = Recession | .10 | .20 | .02 | .02/.57 = .035 = $P(E_1|F_1)$ |
| $E_2$ = Stable economy | .40 | .40 | .16 | .16/.57 = .281 = $P(E_2|F_1)$ |
| $E_3$ = Moderate growth | .30 | .70 | .21 | .21/.57 = .368 = $P(E_3|F_1)$ |
| $E_4$ = Boom | .20 | .90 | .18 | .18/.57 = .316 = $P(E_4|F_1)$ |
| | | | .57 | |

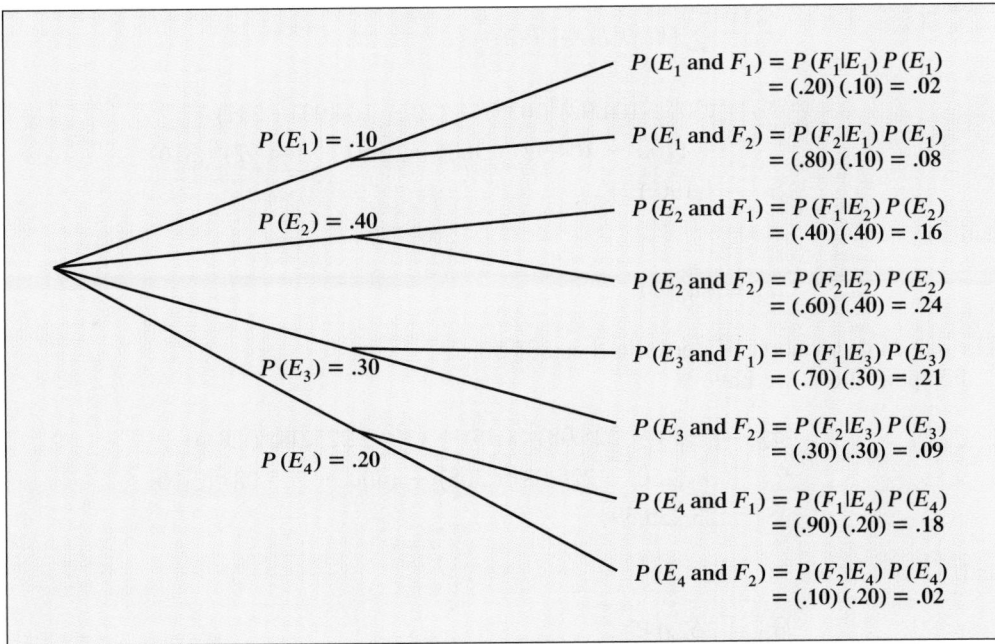

$$P(E_1 \text{ and } F_1) = P(F_1|E_1) P(E_1)$$
$$= (.20)(.10) = .02$$

$$P(E_1 \text{ and } F_2) = P(F_2|E_1) P(E_1)$$
$$= (.80)(.10) = .08$$

$$P(E_2 \text{ and } F_1) = P(F_1|E_2) P(E_2)$$
$$= (.40)(.40) = .16$$

$$P(E_2 \text{ and } F_2) = P(F_2|E_2) P(E_2)$$
$$= (.60)(.40) = .24$$

$$P(E_3 \text{ and } F_1) = P(F_1|E_3) P(E_3)$$
$$= (.70)(.30) = .21$$

$$P(E_3 \text{ and } F_2) = P(F_2|E_3) P(E_3)$$
$$= (.30)(.30) = .09$$

$$P(E_4 \text{ and } F_1) = P(F_1|E_4) P(E_4)$$
$$= (.90)(.20) = .18$$

$$P(E_4 \text{ and } F_2) = P(F_2|E_4) P(E_4)$$
$$= (.10)(.20) = .02$$

$P(E_1) = .10$    $P(E_2) = .40$    $P(E_3) = .30$    $P(E_4) = .20$

**FIGURE 7.2**  Decision tree with revised probabilities for BerLev mutual funds

Because the original subjective probabilities were used to determine the best decision based on the expected monetary value criterion, the expected profit of each alternative is reevaluated by using these revised probabilities. The revised expected monetary value computations are illustrated in Table 7.6.

**Table 7.6**  *Expected monetary value using revised probabilities for each alternative for each of two portfolios under four economic conditions*

| EVENT $E_i$ | $P_i$ | ALTERNATIVE COURSES OF ACTION | | | | |
|---|---|---|---|---|---|---|
| | | A | $x_{ij}P_i$ | B | $x_{ij}P_i$ | |
| Recession | .035 | $ 30 | 30(.035) = 1.05 | −$50 | −50(.035) = −1.75 | |
| Stable economy | .281 | 70 | 70(.281) = 19.67 | 30 | 30(.281) = 8.43 | |
| Moderate growth | .368 | 100 | 100(.368) = 36.80 | 250 | 250(.368) = 92.00 | |
| Boom | .316 | 150 | 150(.316) = 47.40 | 400 | 400(.316) = 126.40 | |
| | | | EMV(A) = $104.92 | | EMV(B) = $225.08 | |

Thus, the expected monetary value or profit for portfolio A is $104.92, whereas the expected monetary value or profit for portfolio B is $225.08. Using this criterion, the manager of the mutual fund once again chooses portfolio B because the expected monetary value is much higher for this portfolio. However, we should also examine the return to risk criterion in light of these revised probabilities. Using equations (6.2) and (6.3) on pages 226 and 227, we have the following for portfolio A:

$$\sigma_A^2 = \sum_{i=1}^{N} [X_i - E(X)]^2 P(X_i)$$

$$= (30 - 104.92)^2(.035) + (70 - 104.92)^2(.281)$$
$$+ (100 - 104.92)^2(.368) + (150 - 104.92)^2(.316)$$
$$= 1{,}190.194$$

and

$$\sigma_A = 34.499$$

The standard deviation of portfolio $A$ is \$34.50.

For portfolio $B$ we have

$$\sigma_B^2 = (-50 - 225.08)^2(.035) + (30 - 225.08)^2(.281)$$
$$+ (250 - 225.08)^2(.368) + (400 - 225.08)^2(.316)$$
$$= 23{,}239.39$$

and

$$\sigma_B = 152.445$$

The standard deviation of portfolio $B$ is \$152.45.

Now that the standard deviation of the return from each portfolio has been obtained, the coefficient of variation can be computed. From equation (4.11), the coefficient of variation for portfolio $A$ is equal to

$$CV_A = \frac{\sigma_A}{EMV_A}\, 100\%$$

$$= \frac{34.499}{104.92} \cdot 100\% = 32.88\%$$

while the coefficient of variation for portfolio $B$ is equal to

$$CV_B = \frac{\sigma_B}{EMV_B}\, 100\%$$

$$= \frac{152.445}{225.08} \cdot 100\% = 67.73\%$$

Thus, we can see that there is still much more variation in the returns from portfolio $B$ than from portfolio $A$.

For each of these two portfolios the return to risk ratios are calculated as follows. For portfolio $A$ the return to risk ratio is equal to

$$\text{Return to risk ratio} = \frac{104.92}{34.499} = 3.041$$

while for portfolio $B$ the return to risk ratio is equal to

$$\text{Return to risk ratio} = \frac{225.08}{152.445} = 1.476$$

Thus, relative to the risk as expressed by the standard deviation, the return still seems much higher for portfolio *A* than for portfolio *B*. Portfolio *A* has a smaller expected monetary value than portfolio *B* but also has a much smaller risk than portfolio *B*. The return to risk ratio still shows *A* to be preferable to *B*.

## Problems for Section 7.3

### Learning the Basics

**7.18** In the following payoff table

|        | ACTION | |
|--------|------|------|
| EVENT  | *A*  | *B*  |
| 1      | 50   | 100  |
| 2      | 200  | 125  |

suppose $P(E_1)$, the probability of event 1, were equal to .5 and $P(E_2)$, the probability of event 2, were also equal to .5. Suppose that $P(F|E_1) = .6$ and $P(F|E_2) = .4$ and event $F$ occurs.
(a) Revise the probabilities $P(E_1)$ and $P(E_2)$ in light of this information.
(b) Compute the expected monetary value (*EMV*) for actions *A* and *B*.
(c) Compute the expected opportunity loss (*EOL*) for actions *A* and *B*.
(d) Explain the meaning of the expected value of perfect information (*EVPI*) in this problem.
(e) Based on the results of (b) or (c), which action would you choose? Why?
(f) Compute the coefficient of variation for each action.
(g) Compute the return to risk ratio for each action.
(h) Based on (f) and (g), what action would you choose? Why?
(i) Compare the results of (e) and (h), and explain any differences.
(j) Compare the results obtained in (b) with those of Problem 7.6 on page 271.

**7.19** In the following payoff table

|        | ACTION | |
|--------|------|------|
| EVENT  | *A*  | *B*  |
| 1      | 50   | 10   |
| 2      | 300  | 100  |
| 3      | 500  | 200  |

suppose $P(E_1)$, the probability of event 1 were equal to .8, $P(E_2)$, the probability of event 2 were equal to .1, and $P(E_3)$, the probability of event 3 were equal to .1. Suppose that $P(F|E_1) = .2$, $P(F|E_2) = .4$, and $P(F|E_3) = .4$, and event $F$ occurs.
(a) Revise the probabilities $P(E_1)$, $P(E_2)$, and $P(E_3)$ in light of this information.
(b) Compute the expected monetary value (*EMV*) for actions *A* and *B*.
(c) Compute the expected opportunity loss (*EOL*) for actions *A* and *B*.
(d) Explain the meaning of the expected value of perfect information (*EVPI*) in this problem.
(e) Based on the results of (b) or (c), which action would you choose? Why?
(f) Compute the coefficient of variation for each action.

(g) Compute the return to risk ratio for each action.
(h) Based on (f) and (g), what action would you choose? Why?
(i) Compare the results of (e) and (h), and explain any differences.
(j) Compare the results obtained in (b) with those of Problem 7.7 on page 272.

## Applying the Concepts

• **7.20** A vendor at a baseball stadium must decide whether to sell ice cream or soft drinks at today's game. The vendor believes that the profit made will depend on the weather. The payoff table is as follows:

| | ACTION | |
| EVENT | SELL SOFT DRINKS | SELL ICE CREAM |
| --- | --- | --- |
| Cool weather | $50 | $30 |
| Warm weather | 60 | 90 |

On the basis of her past experience at this time of year, the vendor estimates the probability of warm weather as .60. Suppose that prior to making her decision, she decides to listen to the forecast of the local weather reporter. In the past, when it has been cool, the weather reporter has forecast cool weather 80% of the time. When it has been warm, the weather reporter has forecast warm weather 70% of the time. If today's forecast is for cool weather,
(a) revise the prior probabilities of the vendor in light of this information.
Based on these revised probabilities:
(b) Compute the expected monetary value (*EMV*) for selling soft drinks and selling ice cream.
(c) Compute the expected opportunity loss (*EOL*) for selling soft drinks and selling ice cream.
(d) Explain the meaning of the expected value of perfect information (*EVPI*) in this problem.
(e) On the basis of the results of (b) or (c), which should the vendor choose to sell, soft drinks or ice cream? Why?
(f) Compute the coefficient of variation for selling soft drinks and selling ice cream.
(g) Compute the return to risk ratio for selling soft drinks and selling ice cream.
(h) On the basis of (f) and (g), which should the vendor choose to sell, soft drinks or ice cream? Why?
(i) Compare the results of (e) and (h), and explain any differences.
(j) Compare the results obtained in (i) with those of Problem 7.12 on page 273.

**7.21** An investor was trying to determine the optimal investment decision among three portfolios. The estimated profits of each portfolio under each economic condition are indicated in the following payoff table:

| | PORTFOLIO SELECTION | | |
| EVENT | *A* | *B* | *C* |
| --- | --- | --- | --- |
| Economy declines | $ 500 | −$2,000 | −$ 7,000 |
| No change | 1,000 | 2,000 | −1,000 |
| Economy expands | 2,000 | 5,000 | 20,000 |

On the basis of his own past experience, the investor assigns the following probabilities to each economic condition:

$$P(\text{economy declines}) = .30$$
$$P(\text{no change}) = .50$$
$$P(\text{economy expands}) = .20$$

Suppose that prior to making his investment decision, the investor decided to consult with his stockbroker. In the past when the economy has declined, the stockbroker has given a rosy forecast 20% of the time (with a gloomy forecast 80% of the time). When there has been no change in the economy, the stockbroker has given a rosy forecast 40% of the time. When there has been an expanding economy, the stockbroker has given a rosy forecast 70% of the time. The stockbroker in this case gives a gloomy forecast for the economy.

(a) Revise the probabilities of the investor in light of this economic forecast by the stockbroker.

(b) Determine the best portfolio selection for the investor according to the expected monetary value criterion. Discuss.

(c) Compute the standard deviation for each possible portfolio selection.

(d) Compute the expected opportunity loss (*EOL*) for portfolios *A, B,* and *C.*

(e) Explain the meaning of the expected value of perfect information (*EVPI*) in this problem.

(f) Compute the coefficient of variation for portfolios *A, B,* and *C.*

(g) Compute the return to risk ratio for portfolios *A, B,* and *C.*

(h) On the basis of (f) and (g), which would you choose, portfolio *A, B,* or *C?* Why?

(i) Compare the results of (b) and (h), and explain any differences.

(j) Suppose the probabilities of the different economic conditions were as follows:

(1) .1, .6, and .3        (3) .4, .4, and .2
(2) .1, .3, and .6        (4) .6, .3, and .1

Do (b)–(i) with each of these sets of probabilities and compare the results with those obtained in (i). Discuss.

(k) Compare the results obtained in (b) to those of Problem 7.14 on page 274.

**7.22** In Problem 7.16 on page 275, an author was deciding which of two competing publishing companies should be selected to publish her new novel. Suppose that prior to making a final decision, the author has decided to have an experienced reviewer examine her novel. This reviewer has an outstanding reputation for predicting success for a novel. In the past, for novels that sold 1,000 copies, only 1% received favorable reviews. Of novels that sold 2,000 copies, only 1% received favorable reviews. Of novels that sold 5,000 copies, 25% received favorable reviews. Of novels that sold 10,000 copies, 60% received favorable reviews. Of novels that sold 50,000 copies, 99% received favorable reviews. After examining the author's novel, the reviewer gives it an unfavorable review.

(a) Revise the probabilities of the number of books sold in light of this unfavorable review.

(b) Use these revised probabilities to do Problem 7.16.

(c) Compare the results obtained in (b) with those of Problem 7.16.

 **7.4 UTILITY**

Thus far we have assumed that each incremental amount of profit or loss has the same value as the previous amounts of profits attained or losses incurred. In fact, under many circumstances this is not the case in the business world. Most individuals make special efforts to avoid large losses. At the same time, many individuals place less value on extremely large profits as compared with initial profits. Such differential evaluation of incremental profits or losses is referred to as **utility**, a concept first discussed by Daniel Bernoulli in the eighteenth century (see reference 1). To illustrate this concept, suppose that you are faced with the following two choices:

**CHOICE 1** A fair coin is to be tossed: If it lands on heads, you will receive $.60; if it lands on tails, you will pay $.40.

**CHOICE 2** Do not play the game.

What decision should you choose? The expected value of playing this game would be $(.60)(.50) + (-.40)(.50) = +\$.10$, whereas the expected value of not playing the game is 0.

If forced to make a choice based solely on monetary value, most people will decide to play the game because the expected value is positive and only small amounts of money are involved. Suppose, however, that the game is formulated with a payoff of $600,000 when the coin lands on heads and a loss of $400,000 when the coin lands on tails. The expected value of playing this game is +$100,000. With these payoffs, even though the expected value is positive, most individuals will not play the game because of the severe negative consequences of losing $400,000. Each additional dollar amount of either profit or loss does not have the same utility as the previous amount. Large negative amounts for most individuals have severely negative utility, whereas conversely the extra value of each incremental dollar of profit decreases, once high enough profit levels are reached.

An important part of the decision problem, which is beyond the scope of this text (see references 2 and 3), is to develop a utility curve for the decision maker that represents the utility of each specified dollar amount.

There are three basic types of utility curves: those of the risk averter, the risk seeker, and the risk-neutral person (Figure 7.3).

The **risk averter's curve** shows a rapid increase in utility for initial amounts of money followed by a gradual leveling off for increasing dollar amounts. This curve is appropriate for most individuals or businesses because the value of each additional dollar is not as great once large amounts of money have been earned.

The **risk seeker's curve** represents the utility of one who enjoys taking risks. The utility is greater for large dollar amounts. This curve represents an individual who is interested only in "striking it rich" and is willing to take large risks to obtain the opportunity of making large profits.

The **risk-neutral's curve** represents the expected monetary value approach. Each additional dollar of profit has the same value as the previous dollar.

Once a utility curve has been developed for a particular decision maker in a specific situation, the dollar amounts are converted to utilities and the decision maker uses the utility of each alternative course of action along with the decision criteria of expected utility, expected opportunity loss, and return to risk to make a decision.

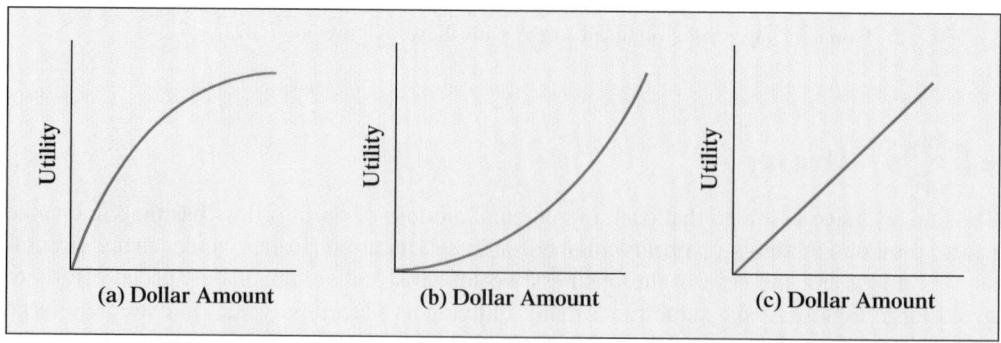

**FIGURE 7.3** Three types of utility curves: (a) risk averter, (b) risk seeker, (c) risk-neutral

## Problems for Section 7.4

### Applying the Concepts

**7.23** Do you consider yourself a risk taker, risk-neutral, or a risk averter? Explain.

**7.24** Refer to Problems 7.3–7.5, and 7.12–7.17 on pages 265 and 273–276. In which problems do you think the expected monetary value (risk-neutral) criteria may be inappropriate? Why?

 **SUMMARY**

As shown in the summary chart, this chapter was about decision making. We developed payoff tables and decision trees, used various criteria to choose between alternative courses of action, and revised probabilities in the light of sample information.

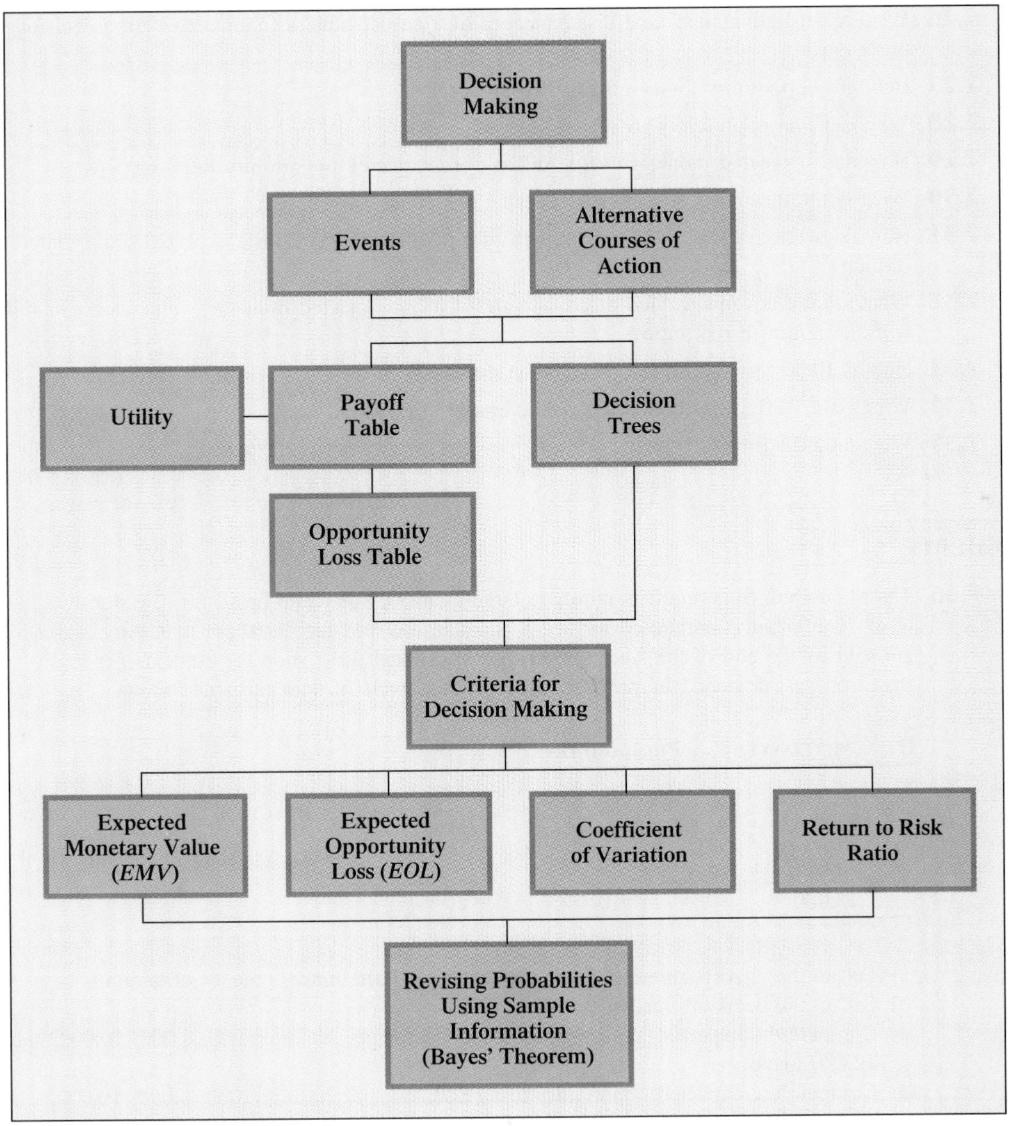

Chapter 7 summary chart

## Key Terms

alternative courses of action 260

decision criteria 260

decision tree 261

events or states of the world 260

expected monetary value (*EMV*) 266

expected opportunity loss (*EOL*) 268

expected profit under certainty 269

expected value of perfect information (*EVPI*) 268

opportunity loss 263

payoff table 261

payoffs 260

return to risk ratio 271

risk averter's curve 284

risk neutral's curve 284

risk seeker's curve 284

utility 283

## Checking Your Understanding

**7.25** What is the difference between an event and an alternative course of action?

**7.26** What are the advantages and disadvantages of a payoff table as compared with a decision tree?

**7.27** How are opportunity losses obtained from payoffs?

**7.28** Why can't an opportunity loss be negative?

**7.29** How does expected monetary value differ from expected opportunity loss?

**7.30** What is the meaning of the expected value of perfect information?

**7.31** How does the expected value of perfect information differ from the expected profit under certainty?

**7.32** What are the advantages and disadvantages of using expected monetary value as compared with the return to risk ratio?

**7.33** How is Bayes' theorem used to revise probabilities in the light of sample information?

**7.34** What is the difference between a risk averter and a risk seeker?

**7.35** Why should utilities be used instead of payoffs in certain circumstances?

## Chapter Review Problems

**7.36** The Shop-Quik Supermarkets purchase large quantities of white bread for sale during a week. The bread is purchased for $0.75 per loaf and sold for $1.10 per loaf. Any loaves not sold by the end of the week can be sold to a local thrift shop for 40 cents per loaf. Based on past demand, the probability of various levels of demand is as follows:

| DEMAND (LOAVES) | PROBABILITY |
|---|---|
| 6,000 | .10 |
| 8,000 | .50 |
| 10,000 | .30 |
| 12,000 | .10 |

(a) Set up the payoff table indicating the events and alternative courses of action.

(b) Set up the decision tree.

(c) Compute the expected monetary value (*EMV*) for purchasing 6,000, 8,000, 10,000, and 12,000 loaves.

(d) Compute the expected opportunity loss (*EOL*) for purchasing 6,000, 8,000, 10,000, and 12,000 loaves.

(e) Explain the meaning of the expected value of perfect information (*EVPI*) in this problem.

(f) On the basis of the results of (c) or (d), how many loaves would you purchase? Why?

(g) Compute the coefficient of variation for each purchase level.

(h) Compute the return to risk ratio for each purchase level.

(i) On the basis of (g) and (h), what action would you choose? Why?

(j) Compare the results of (f) and (i), and explain any differences.

(k) Suppose that the demand level for loaves was as follows:

| DEMAND (LOAVES) | PROBABILITY |
|---|---|
| 6,000 | .30 |
| 8,000 | .40 |
| 10,000 | .20 |
| 12,000 | .10 |

Do (c)–(j) of this problem with these new probabilities. Compare the results obtained with these new probabilities with those of (c)–(j).

**7.37** The owner of a home heating oil delivery company would like to determine whether to offer a solar heating installation service to its customers. The owner of the company has determined that a startup cost of $150,000 would be necessary, but a profit of $2,000 could be made on each solar heating system installed. The owner estimates the probability of various demand levels as follows:

| NUMBER OF UNITS INSTALLED | PROBABILITY |
|---|---|
| 50 | .40 |
| 100 | .30 |
| 200 | .30 |

(a) Set up the payoff table indicating the events and alternative courses of action.

(b) Set up the decision tree.

(c) Set up the opportunity loss table.

(d) Compute the expected monetary value (*EMV*) for offering this solar heating system installation service.

(e) Compute the expected opportunity loss (*EOL*) for offering this solar heating system installation service.

(f) Explain the meaning of the expected value of perfect information (*EVPI*) in this problem.

(g) Compute the return to risk ratio for offering this solar heating system installation service.

(h) On the basis of the results of (d) or (e) and (g), should the company offer this solar heating system installation service? Why?

(i) How would your answers to (a)–(h) be affected if the startup cost were $200,000?

**• 7.38** The manufacturer of a nationally distributed brand of potato chips would like to determine the feasibility of changing the product package from a cellophane bag to an unbreakable container. The product manager believes that there would be three possible national market responses to a change in product package: weak, moderate, and strong. The projected payoffs, in increased or decreased profit as compared with the current package, are shown at the top of page 288.

| EVENT | STRATEGY | |
| --- | --- | --- |
| | USE NEW PACKAGE | KEEP OLD PACKAGE |
| Weak national response | −$4,000,000 | 0 |
| Moderate national response | 3,000,000 | 0 |
| Strong national response | 5,000,000 | 0 |

On the basis of past experience, the product manager assigns the following probabilities to the different levels of national response:

$$P(\text{weak national response}) = .30$$

$$P(\text{moderate national response}) = .60$$

$$P(\text{strong national response}) = .10$$

(a) Set up the decision tree.
(b) Set up the opportunity loss table.
(c) Compute the expected monetary value (*EMV*) for offering this new product package.
(d) Compute the expected opportunity loss (*EOL*) for offering this new product package.
(e) Explain the meaning of the expected value of perfect information (*EVPI*) in this problem.
(f) Compute the return to risk ratio for offering this new product package.
(g) On the basis of the results of (c) or (d) and (f), should the company offer this new product package? Why?
(h) What would your answers to parts (c)–(g) be if the probabilities were .6, .3, and .1, respectively?
(i) What would your answers to parts (c)–(g) be if the probabilities were .1, .3, and .6, respectively?

   Prior to making a final decision, the product manager would like to test-market the new package in a selected city. In this selected city, the new package is substituted for the old package and a determination is made as to whether sales have increased, decreased, or stayed the same in a specified period of time. In previous test marketing of other products, when there has been a subsequent weak national response, sales in the test city have decreased 60% of the time, stayed the same 30% of the time, and increased 10% of the time. When there has been a moderate national response, sales in the test city have decreased 20% of the time, stayed the same 40% of the time, and increased 40% of the time. When there has been a strong national response, sales in the test city have decreased 5% of the time, stayed the same 35% of the time, and increased 60% of the time.
(j) If sales in the test city stayed the same, revise the original probabilities in light of this new information.
(k) Use the revised probabilities obtained in (j) to do (c)–(g).
(l) If sales in the test city decreased, revise the original probabilities in light of this new information.
(m) Use the revised probabilities obtained in (l) to do (c)–(g).

**7.39** An entrepreneur would like to determine whether it would be profitable to establish a gardening service in a local suburb. The entrepreneur believes that there are four possible levels of demand for this gardening service:
1. Very low demand—1% of the households would use the service
2. Low demand—5% of the households would use the service
3. Moderate demand—10% of the households would use the service
4. High demand—25% of the households would use the service
On the basis of past experiences in other suburbs, the entrepreneur assigns the following probabilities to the various demand levels:

$$P(\text{very low demand}) = .20$$

$$P(\text{low demand}) = .50$$

$$P(\text{moderate demand}) = .20$$

$$P(\text{high demand}) = .10$$

The entrepreneur has calculated the following profits or losses of this garden service for each demand level (over a period of 1 year):

|  | ACTION | |
| --- | --- | --- |
| DEMAND | PROVIDE GARDEN SERVICE | NO GARDEN SERVICE |
| Very low ($p = .01$) | $-\$\ 5,000$ | 0 |
| Low ($p = .05$) | 6,000 | 0 |
| Moderate ($p = .10$) | 13,000 | 0 |
| High ($p = .25$) | 30,000 | 0 |

(a) Set up the decision tree.
(b) Set up the opportunity loss table.
(c) Compute the expected monetary value (*EMV*) for offering this garden service.
(d) Compute the expected opportunity loss (*EOL*) for offering this garden service.
(e) Explain the meaning of the expected value of perfect information (*EVPI*) in this problem.
(f) Compute the return to risk ratio for offering this garden service.
(g) On the basis of the results of (c) or (d) and (f), should the company offer this garden service? Why?
   The entrepreneur decides that prior to a final decision, a survey of households in this suburb should be taken to determine demand for the gardening service. If a random sample of 20 households is selected and 3 would use this gardening service:
(h) Revise the prior probabilities in light of this sample information.
(*Hint:* Use the binomial distribution to determine the probability of the outcome that occurred given a particular level of demand.)
(i) Use the revised probabilities obtained in (h) to do (c)–(g).

● **7.40** The manufacturer of a brand of inexpensive felt tip pens maintains a production process that produces 10,000 pens per day. In order to maintain the highest quality of this product, the manufacturer guarantees free replacement of any defective pen sold. It has been calculated that each defective pen produced costs 20 cents for the manufacturer to replace. On the basis of past experience, four rates of producing defective pens are possible:
1. Very low—1% of the pens manufactured will be defective.
2. Low—5% of the pens manufactured will be defective.
3. Moderate—10% of the pens manufactured will be defective.
4. High—20% of the pens manufactured will be defective.
The manufacturer can reduce the rate of defective pens produced by having a mechanic fix the machines at the end of the day. This mechanic can reduce the rate to 1%, but his services will cost $80.
   A payoff table based on the daily production of 10,000 pens, indicating the replacement costs for each of the two alternatives (calling in the mechanic and not calling in the mechanic), is presented at the top of page 290.

| DEFECTIVE RATE | ACTION | |
|---|---|---|
| | DO NOT CALL MECHANIC | CALL MECHANIC |
| Very low (1%) | $ 20 | $100 |
| Low (5%) | 100 | 100 |
| Moderate (10%) | 200 | 100 |
| High (20%) | 400 | 100 |

On the basis of past experience, each defective rate is assumed to be equally likely to occur.

(a) Set up the decision tree.

(b) Set up the opportunity loss table.

(c) Compute the expected monetary value (*EMV*) for calling and not calling the mechanic.

(d) Compute the expected opportunity loss (*EOL*) for calling and not calling the mechanic.

(e) Explain the meaning of the expected value of perfect information (*EVPI*) in this problem.

(f) Compute the return to risk ratio for not calling the mechanic.

(g) On the basis of the results of (c) or (d) and (f), should the company call the mechanic? Why?

At the end of a day's production, suppose that a sample of 15 pens is selected, of which 2 are defective.

(h) Revise the prior probabilities in light of this sample information.

(*Hint:* Use the binomial distribution to determine the probability of the outcome that occurred given a particular defective rate.)

(i) Use the revised probabilities obtained in (h) to do (c)–(g).

# References

1. Bernstein, P. L., *Against the Gods: The Remarkable Story of Risk* (New York: Wiley, 1996).
2. Render, B., and R. M. Stair, *Quantitative Analysis for Management*, 6th ed. (Upper Saddle River, NJ: Prentice Hall, 1997).
3. Tversky, A., and D. Kahneman, " Rational Choice and the Framing of Decisions," *Journal of Business* 59 (1986): 251–278.

# 8

# The Normal Distribution and Other Continuous Distributions

# CHAPTER OBJECTIVES

✓ *To show how the normal probability distribution can be used to represent certain types of continuous phenomena*
✓ *To show how the normal probability plot can be used to assess whether a distribution is normally distributed*
✓ *To introduce the exponential distribution*

## Introduction

In chapter 6 we developed the concept of a probability distribution for a discrete random variable. In this chapter we turn our attention to the most important probability distribution in statistics, the *Gaussian*, or **normal distribution,** which involves a continuous random variable. The normal distribution is one of many such distributions called **continuous probability density functions**—those that arise due to some measuring process on various phenomena of interest.

When a mathematical expression is available to represent some underlying continuous phenomenon, the probability that various values of the random variable occur within certain ranges or intervals may be calculated. However, the *exact* probability of a *particular value* from a continuous distribution is zero. This is what distinguishes continuous phenomena, which are measured, from discrete phenomena, which are counted. As an example, time (in seconds) is measured, not counted. Thus, we can compute the probability that a task can be completed in between 70 and 80 seconds. Narrowing this interval, we can compute the probability that a task can be accomplished in between 74 and 76 seconds. With more refined or precise measuring instruments, we can even compute the probability that a task can be completed in between 74.99 and 75.01 seconds. However, the probability that a task can be completed in *exactly* 75 seconds is zero.

Continuous models have important applications in engineering and the physical sciences as well as in business and the social sciences. Some examples of continuous random phenomena are height; weight; daily changes in closing prices of stocks; time between arrivals of planes landing on a runway, of telephone calls into a switchboard, of customers at a bank, etc.; and customer servicing times.

However, obtaining probabilities or computing expected values and standard deviations for continuous phenomena involves mathematical expressions that require a knowledge of integral calculus and are beyond the scope of this book. Nevertheless, the normal distribution has been deemed so important for applications that special probability tables [such as Tables E.2(a) and E.2(b) of appendix E] were devised to eliminate the need for what otherwise would require laborious mathematical computations. Many continuous random phenomena are either normally distributed or can be approximated by a normal distribution. Thus, we begin this chapter by discussing the properties of the normal distribution. We also study a simple graphical tool, the normal probability plot, that can be used to evaluate whether a set of data appears to be normally distributed. In addition, we introduce another continuous distribution, the exponential distribution.

## ◆ USING STATISTICS: *Applying the Normal Distribution to Study a Production Process*

Suppose that the operations manager in an automobile assembly plant is interested in studying the process of assembling a particular part of the automobile, with a goal of reducing the amount of time that it takes for assembly. A team of individuals involved in the process is formed. One of the first steps needed for process improvement involves the determination of how long it takes to assemble the part in the current process in which workers are trained with an individual learning approach. After studying the process and collecting data, the team determines that the assembly time approximately follows a normal distribution with an arithmetic mean ($\mu$) of 75 seconds and a standard deviation ($\sigma$) of 6 seconds. How can the team use this information to answer questions about the current process such as what proportion of the parts will be assembled in less than 62 seconds and how many seconds it will take to assemble 10% of the parts?

## 8.1 THE NORMAL DISTRIBUTION

The normal distribution is vitally important in statistics for three main reasons:

1. Numerous continuous phenomena seem to follow it or can be approximated by it.

2. We can use it to approximate various discrete probability distributions.

3. It provides the basis for *classical statistical inference* because of its relationship to the *central limit theorem* (which we discuss in section 9.1).

The normal distribution has several important theoretical properties as illustrated in Exhibit 8.1.

---

### Exhibit 8.1   *Properties of the Normal Distribution*

There are four key properties associated with the normal distribution.

✓ **1.** It is bell-shaped (and thus symmetrical) in its appearance.

✓ **2.** Its measures of central tendency (mean, median, mode, midrange, and midhinge) are all identical.

✓ **3.** Its "middle spread" is equal to 1.33 standard deviations. This means that the interquartile range is contained within an interval of two-thirds of a standard deviation below the mean to two-thirds of a standard deviation above the mean.

✓ **4.** Its associated random variable has an infinite range ($-\infty < X < +\infty$).

---

In practice, some of the variables we observe may only approximate these theoretical properties. This occurs for two reasons: (1) the underlying population distribution may be only approximately normal, and (2) any actual sample may deviate from the theoretically expected characteristics. When variables are approximately normally distributed, they are

**Table 8.1** *Thickness of 10,000 brass washers manufactured by Eastern Metal Company*

| THICKNESS (INCHES) | RELATIVE FREQUENCY |
|---|---|
| Under .0180 | 48/10,000 = .0048 |
| .0180 < .0182 | 122/10,000 = .0122 |
| .0182 < .0184 | 325/10,000 = .0325 |
| .0184 < .0186 | 695/10,000 = .0695 |
| .0186 < .0188 | 1,198/10,000 = .1198 |
| .0188 < .0190 | 1,664/10,000 = .1664 |
| .0190 < .0192 | 1,896/10,000 = .1896 |
| .0192 < .0194 | 1,664/10,000 = .1664 |
| .0194 < .0196 | 1,198/10,000 = .1198 |
| .0196 < .0198 | 695/10,000 = .0695 |
| .0198 < .0200 | 325/10,000 = .0325 |
| .0200 < .0202 | 122/10,000 = .0122 |
| .0202 or above | 48/10,000 = .0048 |
| Total | 1.0000 |

only approximately bell-shaped and symmetrical in appearance; their measures of central tendency may differ slightly from each other; their interquartile range may differ slightly from 1.33 standard deviations; and their *practical range* will not be infinite but will generally lie within 3 standard deviations above and below the mean (i.e., range ≅ 6 standard deviations).

As a case in point, let us refer to Table 8.1. The data in Table 8.1 represent the thickness (in inches) of 10,000 brass washers manufactured by a large company. The continuous random phenomenon of interest, thickness, is said to follow the Gaussian or **normal probability density function**. The measurements of the thickness of the 10,000 brass washers cluster in the interval (.0190 < .0192) inch and distribute symmetrically around that grouping, forming a "bell-shaped" pattern. As demonstrated in this table, if the nonoverlapping (*mutually exclusive*) listing contains all possible class intervals (is *collectively exhaustive*), the probabilities will again sum to 1. Such a probability distribution may be considered as a relative frequency distribution as described in section 3.2, where, except for the two open-ended classes, the midpoint of every other class interval represents the data in that interval.

Figure 8.1 depicts the relative frequency histogram and polygon for the distribution of the thickness of 10,000 brass washers. For these data, the first three theoretical properties of the normal distribution seem to be satisfied; however, the fourth does not hold. The random variable of interest, thickness, cannot possibly take on values of zero or below, nor can a washer be so thick that it becomes unusable. From Table 8.1 we note that only 48 out of every 10,000 brass washers manufactured are expected to have a thickness of 0.0202 inch or more, whereas an equal number are expected to have a thickness under 0.0180 inch. Thus, the chance of randomly obtaining a washer so thin or so thick is .0048 + .0048 = .0096—or almost 1 in 100.

The mathematical model or expression representing a probability density function is denoted by the symbol $f(X)$. For the normal distribution, the model used to obtain the desired probabilities is

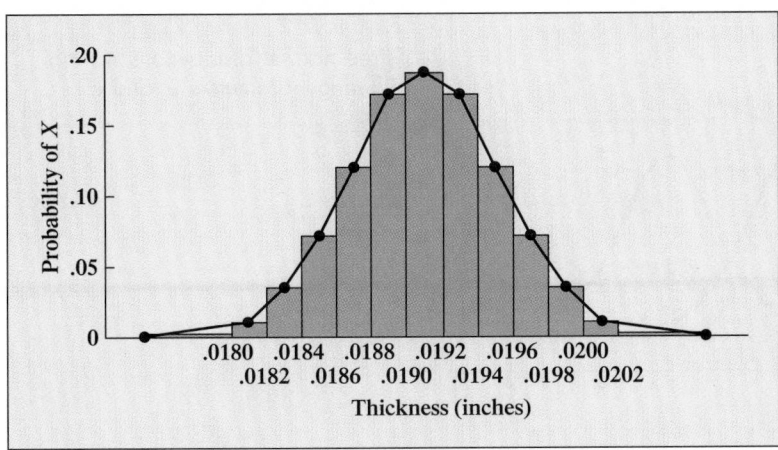

**FIGURE 8.1** Relative frequency histogram and polygon of the thickness of 10,000 brass washers

*Source: Data are taken from Table 8.1.*

## The Normal Distribution

$$f(X) = \frac{1}{\sqrt{2\pi}\sigma} e^{-(1/2)[(X-\mu)/\sigma]^2} \tag{8.1}$$

where

  $e$ = the mathematical constant approximated by 2.71828

  $\pi$ = the mathematical constant approximated by 3.14159

  $\mu$ = population mean

  $\sigma$ = population standard deviation

  $X$ = any value of the continuous random variable, where $-\infty < X < +\infty$

Note that because $e$ and $\pi$ are mathematical constants, the probabilities of the random variable $X$ are dependent only upon the two parameters of the normal distribution—the population mean $\mu$ and the population standard deviation $\sigma$. Every time we specify a *particular combination* of $\mu$ and $\sigma$, a *different* normal probability distribution is generated. We illustrate this in Figure 8.2 on page 296, which depicts three different normal distributions. Distributions A and B have the same mean ($\mu$) but have different standard deviations. On the other hand, distributions A and C have the same standard deviation ($\sigma$) but have different means. Furthermore, distributions B and C depict two normal probability density functions that differ with respect to both $\mu$ and $\sigma$.

Unfortunately, the mathematical expression in equation (8.1) is computationally tedious. To avoid such computations, it is useful to have a set of tables that provide the desired probabilities. However, because an infinite number of combinations of the parameters $\mu$ and $\sigma$ exists, an infinite number of such tables would be required.

By *standardizing* the data, we need only one table [see Table E.2(a) or E.2(b)]. By the use of the **transformation formula,** any normal random variable $X$ is converted to a standardized normal random variable $Z$.

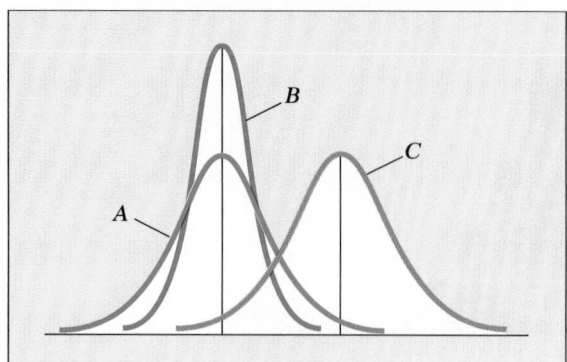

### The Transformation Formula

The $Z$ value is equal to the difference between $X$ and the population mean $\mu$, divided by the standard deviation $\sigma$.

$$Z = \frac{X - \mu}{\sigma} \qquad (8.2)$$

While the original data for the random variable $X$ had mean $\mu$ and standard deviation $\sigma$, the standardized random variable $Z$ will always have mean $\mu = 0$ and standard deviation $\sigma = 1$.

A **standardized normal distribution** is one whose random variable $Z$ always has a mean $\mu = 0$ and a standard deviation $\sigma = 1$.

Substituting in equation (8.1), we see that the probability density function of a standard normal variable $Z$ is

### The Standardized Normal Distribution

$$f(Z) = \frac{1}{\sqrt{2\pi}} e^{-(1/2)Z^2} \qquad (8.3)$$

Thus, we can always convert any set of normally distributed data to its standardized form and then determine any desired probabilities either from a table of the standardized normal distribution, Table E.2(a), or the cumulative standardized normal distribution, Table E.2(b).

To see how the transformation formula is applied and the results used to find probabilities from a table of the standardized normal distribution, Table E.2(a) or E.2(b), let us return to the Using Statistics example on page 293 in which the operations manager of an automobile assembly plant has determined that the assembly time for the current process in which workers receive individual training is normally distributed with a mean $\mu$ of 75 seconds and a standard deviation $\sigma$ of 6 seconds.

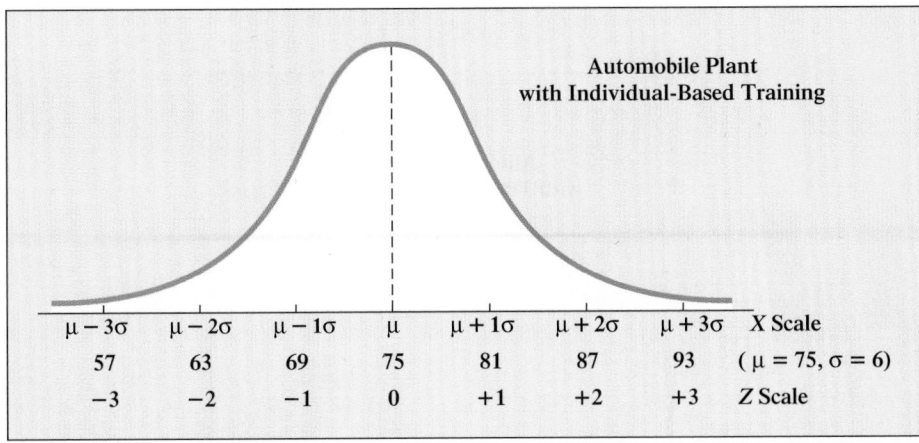

**FIGURE 8.3** Transformation of scales

We see from Figure 8.3 that every measurement $X$ has a corresponding standardized measurement $Z$ obtained from the transformation formula [equation (8.2)]. Hence, from Figure 8.3 it is clear that the 81 seconds required for a factory worker to complete the task is equivalent to 1 standardized unit (i.e., 1 *standard deviation*) above the mean, because

$$Z = \frac{81 - 75}{6} = +1$$

and that the 57 seconds required for a worker to assemble the part is equivalent to 3 standardized units (i.e., 3 *standard deviations*) below the mean because

$$Z = \frac{57 - 75}{6} = -3$$

Thus, the standard deviation has become the unit of measurement. In other words, a time of 81 seconds is 6 seconds (i.e., 1 standard deviation) higher, or *slower,* than the average time of 75 seconds and a time of 57 seconds is 18 seconds (i.e., 3 standard deviations) lower, or *faster,* than the average time.

Suppose now that the team decides that it would like to experiment with a small group of workers who will be provided with additional team-based learning. Suppose that after they receive this training, the time to assemble the part for this group of workers is normally distributed with mean $\mu$ of 60 seconds and standard deviation $\sigma$ of 3 seconds. The data are depicted in Figure 8.4 on page 298. Comparing these results with those of the workers who have individual-based training, we note, for example, that for the workers whose training is team-based, an assembly time of 57 seconds is only 1 standard deviation below the mean for the group because

$$Z = \frac{57 - 60}{3} = -1$$

We may also note that a time of 63 seconds is 1 standard deviation above the mean assembly time because

$$Z = \frac{63 - 60}{3} = +1$$

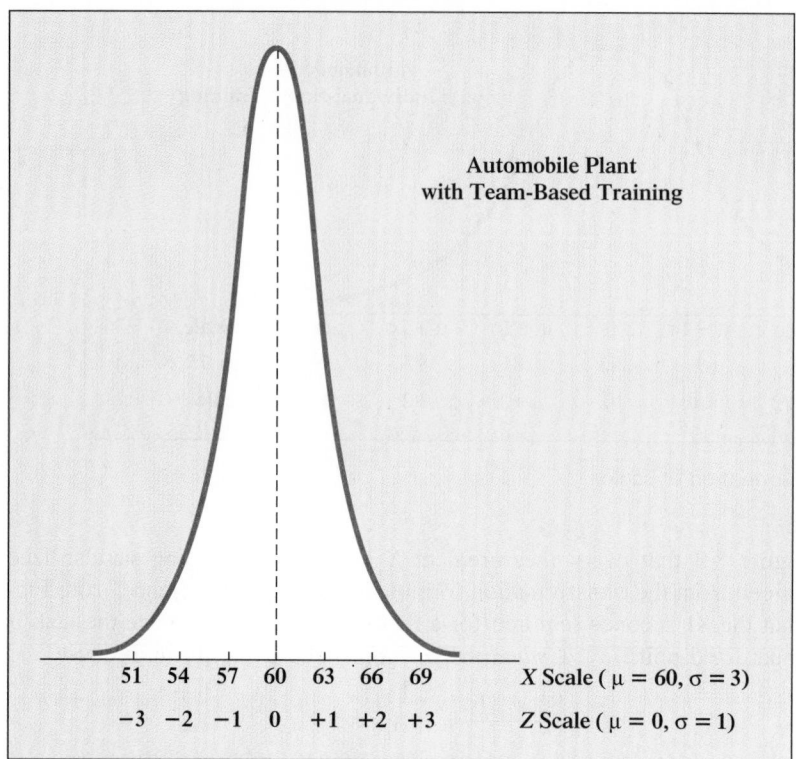

**FIGURE 8.4**  A different transformation of scales

and a time of 51 seconds is 3 standard deviations below the group mean because

$$Z = \frac{51 - 60}{3} = -3$$

The two bell-shaped curves in Figures 8.3 and 8.4 depict the relative frequency polygons of the normal distributions representing the assembly time (in seconds) for the two groups of workers, one in which workers received individual-based training and the other in which workers received team-based training. Because the times to assemble the part are known for every factory worker in each group, the data represent the entire population and, therefore, the *probabilities* or proportion of area under the entire curve must add up to 1. Thus, the area under the curve between any two reported time values represents only a portion of the total area possible.

Now suppose the operations manager wishes to determine the probability that a factory worker selected at random from those who underwent individual-based training should require between 75 and 81 seconds to assemble the part. That is, what is the likelihood that the worker's time is between the mean and 1 standard deviation above the mean? This answer is found by using Table E.2(a).

Table E.2(a) represents the probabilities, or areas, under the normal curve calculated from the mean $\mu$ to the particular values of interest $X$. Using equation (8.2), this corresponds to the probabilities or areas under the standardized normal curve from 0 to the transformed values of interest $Z$. Only positive entries for $Z$ are listed in the table because for such a symmetrical distribution having a mean of 0, the area from the mean to $+Z$ (i.e., $Z$

## Table 8.2  *Obtaining an area under the normal curve*

| Z | .00 | .01 | .02 | .03 | .04 | .05 | .06 | .07 | .08 | .09 |
|---|-----|-----|-----|-----|-----|-----|-----|-----|-----|-----|
| 0.0 | .0000 | .0040 | .0080 | .0120 | .0160 | .0199 | .0239 | .0279 | .0319 | .0359 |
| 0.1 | .0398 | .0438 | .0478 | .0517 | .0557 | .0596 | .0636 | .0675 | .0714 | .0753 |
| 0.2 | .0793 | .0832 | .0871 | .0910 | .0948 | .0987 | .1026 | .1064 | .1103 | .1141 |
| 0.3 | .1179 | .1217 | .1255 | .1293 | .1331 | .1368 | .1406 | .1443 | .1480 | .1517 |
| 0.4 | .1554 | .1591 | .1628 | .1664 | .1700 | .1736 | .1772 | .1808 | .1844 | .1879 |
| 0.5 | .1915 | .1950 | .1985 | .2019 | .2054 | .2088 | .2123 | .2157 | .2190 | .2224 |
| 0.6 | .2257 | .2291 | .2324 | .2357 | .2389 | .2422 | .2454 | .2486 | .2518 | .2549 |
| 0.7 | .2580 | .2612 | .2642 | .2673 | .2704 | .2734 | .2764 | .2794 | .2823 | .2852 |
| 0.8 | .2881 | .2910 | .2939 | .2967 | .2995 | .3023 | .3051 | .3078 | .3106 | .3133 |
| 0.9 | .3159 | .3186 | .3212 | .3238 | .3264 | .3289 | .3315 | .3340 | .3365 | .3389 |
| 1.0 → | .3413 | .3438 | .3461 | .3485 | .3508 | .3531 | .3554 | .3577 | .3599 | .3621 |

*Source: Extracted from Table E.2(a).*

standard deviations above the mean) must be identical to the area from the mean to $-Z$ (i.e., $Z$ standard deviations below the mean).

To use Table E.2(a), we note that all $Z$ values must first be recorded to two decimal places. Thus, our particular $Z$ value of interest is recorded as $+1.00$. To read the probability or area under the curve from the mean to $Z = +1.00$, we scan down the $Z$ column from Table E.2(a) until we locate the $Z$ value of interest (in 10ths). Hence, we stop in the row $Z = 1.0$. Next we read across this row until we intersect the column that contains the 100ths place of the $Z$ value. Therefore, in the body of the table the tabulated probability for $Z = 1.00$ corresponds to the intersection of the row $Z = 1.0$ with the column $Z = .00$ as shown in Table 8.2 which is a replica of Table E.2(a). This probability is .3413. As depicted in Figure 8.5, there is a 34.13% chance that a factory worker selected at random who has had individual-based training will require between 75 and 81 seconds to assemble the part.

On the other hand, we know from Figure 8.4 that for the workers who received team-based training, a time of 63 seconds is 1 standardized unit above the mean time of 60 seconds. Thus, the likelihood that a randomly selected factory worker who receives team-based training will complete the assemblage in between 60 and 63 seconds is also .3413. These

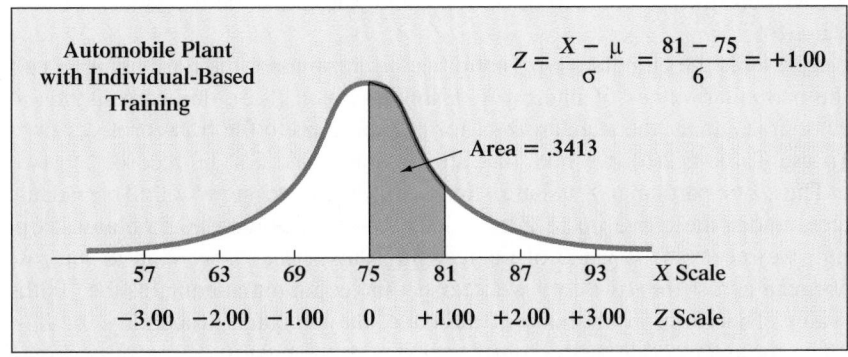

**FIGURE 8.5**  Determining the area between the mean and $Z$ from a standardized normal distribution

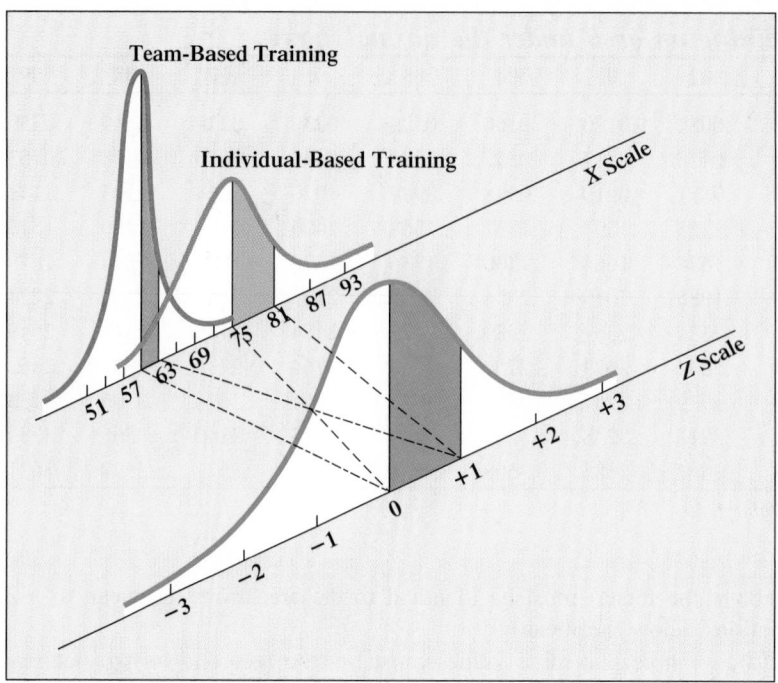

**FIGURE 8.6** Demonstrating a transformation of scales for corresponding portions under two normal curves

results are illustrated in Figure 8.6, which demonstrates that regardless of the value of the mean $\mu$ and standard deviation $\sigma$ of a particular set of normally distributed data, a transformation to a standardized scale can always be made from equation (8.2) and, by using Table E.2(a), any probability or portion of area under the curve can be obtained. From Figure 8.6 we see that the probability or area under the curve from 60 to 63 seconds for the workers who had team-based training is identical to the probability or area under the curve from 75 to 81 seconds for the workers who had individual-based training.

Now suppose the operations manager wishes to determine the probability that a factory worker selected at random from those who underwent individual-based training should require at most 81 seconds to complete the task. That is, what is the likelihood that the worker's time is no more than 1 standard deviation above the mean? This answer is found by using Table E.2(b).

Table E.2(b) represents the cumulative probabilities or areas under the normal curve calculated up to the particular values of interest $X$. Using equation (8.2), this corresponds to the probabilities or areas under the standardized normal curve up to the transformed values of interest $Z$. To use Table E.2(b), we note that all $Z$ values must first be recorded to two decimal places. Thus, our particular $Z$ value of interest is recorded as $+1.00$. To read the probability or area under the curve up to $Z = +1.00$, we scan down the $Z$ column from Table E.2(b) until we locate the $Z$ value of interest (in 10ths). Hence, we stop in the row $Z = 1.0$. Next we read across this row until we intersect the column that contains the 100ths place of the $Z$ value. Therefore, in the body of the table, the tabulated probability for $Z = 1.00$ corresponds to the intersection of the row $Z = 1.0$ with the column $Z = .00$ as shown in Table 8.3, which duplicates Table E.2(b). This probability is .8413. As depicted in Figure 8.7, there is an 84.13% chance that a factory worker selected at random who has had individual-based training will require at most 81 seconds to assemble the part.

**Table 8.3**  *Obtaining a cumulative area under the normal curve*

| Z | .00 | .01 | .02 | .03 | .04 | .05 | .06 | .07 | .08 | .09 |
|---|-----|-----|-----|-----|-----|-----|-----|-----|-----|-----|
| 0.0 | .5000 | .5040 | .5080 | .5120 | .5160 | .5199 | .5239 | .5279 | .5319 | .5359 |
| 0.1 | .5398 | .5438 | .5478 | .5517 | .5557 | .5596 | .5636 | .5675 | .5714 | .5753 |
| 0.2 | .5793 | .5832 | .5871 | .5910 | .5948 | .5987 | .6026 | .6064 | .6103 | .6141 |
| 0.3 | .6179 | .6217 | .6255 | .6293 | .6331 | .6368 | .6406 | .6443 | .6480 | .6517 |
| 0.4 | .6554 | .6591 | .6628 | .6664 | .6700 | .6736 | .6772 | .6808 | .6844 | .6879 |
| 0.5 | .6915 | .6950 | .6985 | .7019 | .7054 | .7088 | .7123 | .7157 | .7190 | .7224 |
| 0.6 | .7257 | .7291 | .7324 | .7357 | .7389 | .7422 | .7454 | .7486 | .7518 | .7549 |
| 0.7 | .7580 | .7612 | .7642 | .7673 | .7704 | .7734 | .7764 | .7794 | .7823 | .7852 |
| 0.8 | .7881 | .7910 | .7939 | .7967 | .7995 | .8023 | .8051 | .8078 | .8106 | .8133 |
| 0.9 | .8159 | .8186 | .8212 | .8238 | .8264 | .8289 | .8315 | .8340 | .8365 | .8389 |
| 1.0 | .8413 | .8438 | .8461 | .8485 | .8508 | .8531 | .8554 | .8577 | .8599 | .8621 |

*Source: Extracted from Table E.2(b).*

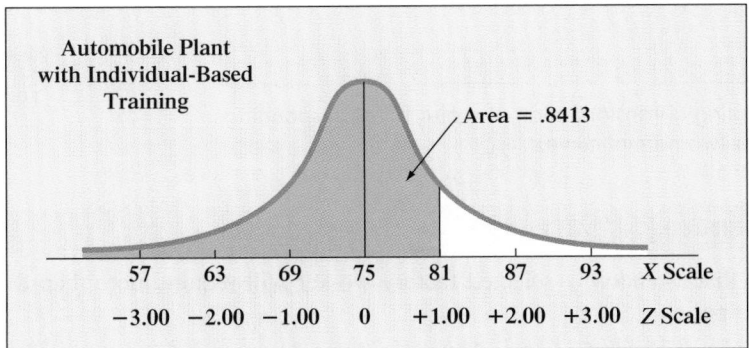

**FIGURE 8.7**  Determining the area up to $Z$ from a cumulative standardized normal distribution

On the other hand, we know from Figure 8.4 on page 298 that for the workers who received team-based training, a time of 63 seconds is 1 standardized unit above the mean time of 60 seconds. Thus, the likelihood that a randomly selected factory worker who received team-based training will assemble the part in at most 63 seconds is also .8413. These results are illustrated in Figure 8.8 on page 302, which demonstrates that regardless of the value of the mean $\mu$ and standard deviation $\sigma$ of a particular set of normally distributed data, a transformation to a standardized scale can always be made from equation (8.2) and, by using Table E.2(b), any probability or portion of area under the curve can be obtained. From Figure 8.8 we see that the probability or area under the curve up to 63 seconds for the workers who had team-based training is identical to the probability or area under the curve up to 81 seconds for the workers who had individual-based training.

Now that we have learned to use Tables E.2(a) and E.2(b) in conjunction with equation (8.2), many different types of probability questions pertaining to the normal distribution can be resolved. To illustrate this for workers who have the individual-based training, we turn to Examples 8.1–8.8. Although either Table E.2(a) or E.2(b) could be used in these examples, we will use Table E.2(b) because we will be referring to this **cumulative normal distribution** table in the remainder of the text.

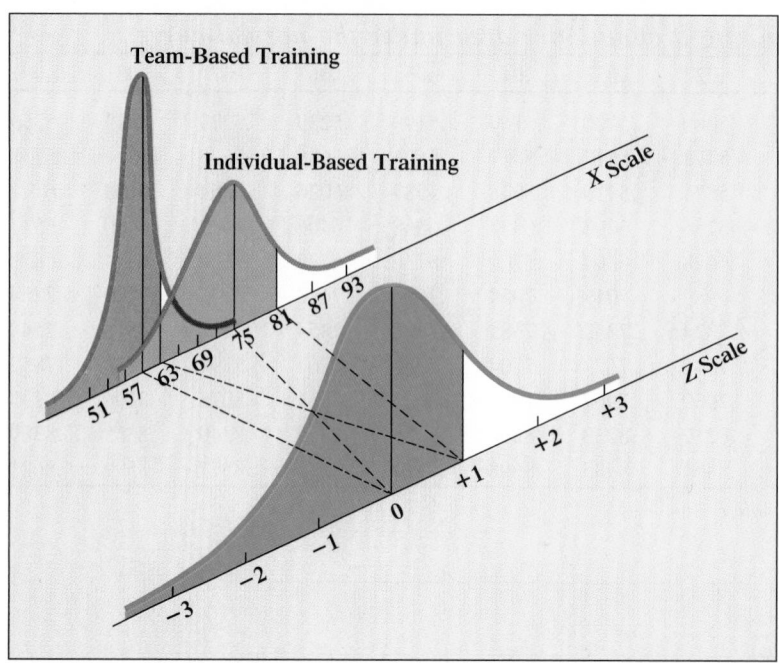

**FIGURE 8.8** Demonstrating a transformation of scales for corresponding cumulative portions under two normal curves

## Example 8.1 *Finding P(X > 81)*

What is the probability that a randomly selected factory worker will require more than 81 seconds to assemble the part?

### SOLUTION

Because we already determined the probability that a randomly selected factory worker will need up to 81 seconds to assemble the part, from Figure 8.7 on page 301 we observe that our desired probability must be its *complement*, that is, $1 - .8413 = .1587$. This is depicted in the following diagram.

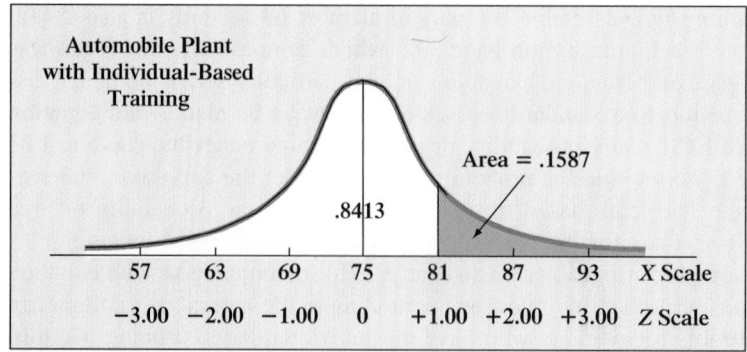

Finding $P(X > 81)$

## Example 8.2 *Finding P(75 < X < 81)*

What is the probability that a randomly selected factory worker will perform the task in 75 to 81 seconds?

**SOLUTION**

From Figure 8.7 on page 301 we already determined the probability that a randomly selected factory worker will need up to 81 seconds to assemble the part is .8413. To obtain our desired results we now must determine the probability of assembling the part in under 75 seconds and subtract this from the probability of assembling the part in under 81 seconds. This is depicted in the following diagram.

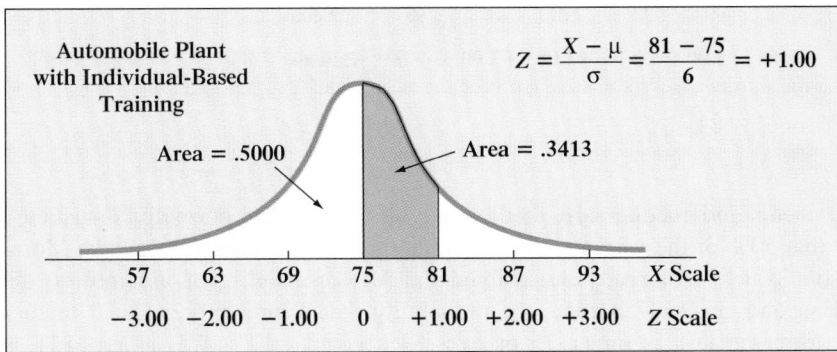

Finding $P(75 < X < 81)$

Because the mean and median are theoretically the same for normally distributed data, it follows that 50% of the workers can assemble the part in under 75 seconds. To show this, from equation (8.2) we have

$$Z = \frac{X - \mu}{\sigma} = \frac{75 - 75}{6} = 0.00$$

Using Table E.2(b), we see that the area under the normal curve up to the mean of $Z = 0.00$ is .5000. Hence, the area under the curve between $Z = 0.00$ and $Z = 1.00$ must be $.8413 - .5000 = .3413$. This is the same result we obtained when using the standardized normal distribution table, Table E.2(a), depicted in Figure 8.5 on page 299.

## Example 8.3 *Finding P(X < 75 or X > 81)*

What is the probability that a randomly selected factory worker will perform the task in under 75 seconds or over 81 seconds?

**SOLUTION**

Because we already determined that the probability is .3413 that a randomly selected factory worker will need between 75 and 81 seconds to assemble the part, from Figure 8.5 we observe that our desired probability must be its *complement*, that is, $1 - .3413 = .6587$.

Another way to view this problem, however, is to separately obtain both the probability of assembling the part in under 75 seconds and the probability of assembling the part in over 81 seconds and to then add these two probabilities together to obtain the desired result. This is depicted in the following diagram.

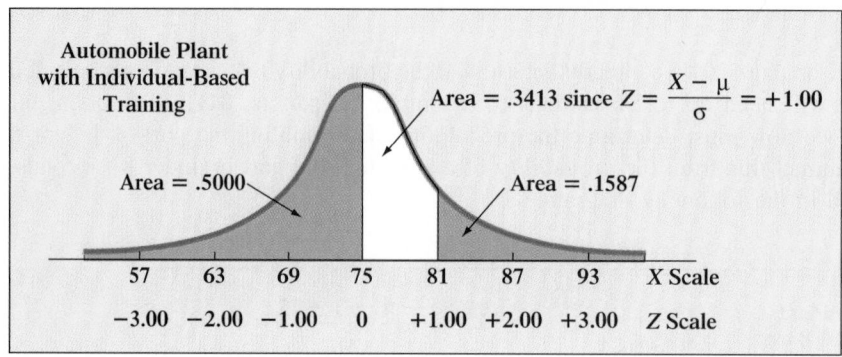

Finding $P(X < 75$ or $X > 81)$

Because the mean and median are theoretically the same for normally distributed data, it follows that 50% of the workers can assemble the part in under 75 seconds. Moreover, from Example 8.1 we already determined that the probability of assembling the part in over 81 seconds is .1587. Hence, the probability that a randomly selected factory worker will perform the task is under 75 or over 81 seconds, $P(X < 75$ or $X > 81)$, is .5000 + .1587 = .6587.

### Example 8.4  Finding $P(69 < X < 81)$

What is the probability that a randomly selected factory worker can complete the part in 69–81 seconds, that is, $P(69 < X < 81)$?

#### SOLUTION

We note from our diagram that one of the values of interest is above the mean assembly time of 75 seconds and the other value is below it. Since our transformation formula equation (8.2) permits us only to find probabilities up to a particular value of interest, we can obtain our desired probability in three steps:

**1.** Determine the probability up to 81 seconds.

**2.** Determine the probability up to 69 seconds.

**3.** Subtract the smaller result from the larger.

For this example, we already completed step 1; the area under the normal curve up to 81 seconds is .8413. To find the area under the normal curve up to 69 seconds (step 2), we have

$$Z = \frac{X - \mu}{\sigma} = \frac{69 - 75}{6} = -1.00$$

Using Table E.2(b), we look up the value $Z = -1.00$ and find the probability to be .1587. Hence, from step 3, the probability that the part can be assembled in between 69 and 81 seconds is $.8413 - .1587 = .6826$. This is displayed in the following diagram.

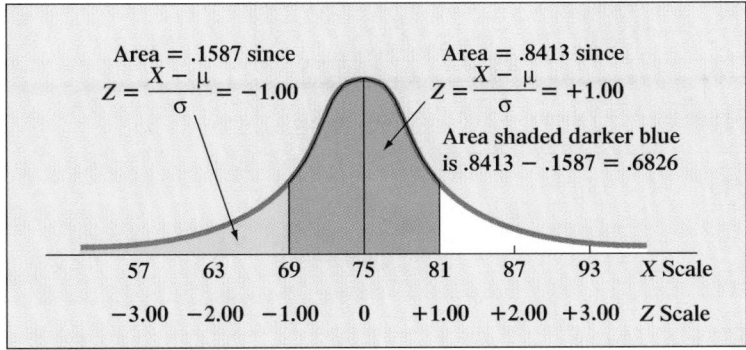

Finding $P(69 < X < 81)$

The result of Example 8.4 is rather important and allows us to generalize our findings. We can see that for any normal distribution there is a .6826 chance that a randomly selected item will fall within $\pm 1$ standard deviation above or below the mean. We know that slightly more than two out of every three (68.26%) of the factory workers who receive individual-based training can be expected to complete the task within $\pm 1$ standard deviation from the mean. Moreover, from Figure 8.9 slightly more than 19 out of every 20 factory workers (95.44%) can be expected to complete the assembly within $\pm 2$ standard deviations from the mean (i.e., between 63 and 87 seconds), and, from Figure 8.10 on page 306, practically all factory workers (99.73%) can be expected to assemble the part within $\pm 3$ standard deviations from the mean (i.e., between 57 and 93 seconds).

From Figure 8.10 it is indeed quite unlikely (.0027, or only 27 factory workers in 10,000) that a randomly selected factory worker will be so fast or so slow that he or she could be expected to complete the assembly of the part in under 57 seconds or over 93 seconds. Thus, it is clear why $6\sigma$ (i.e., 3 standard deviations above the mean to 3 standard deviations below the mean) is often used as a *practical approximation of the range* for normally distributed data.

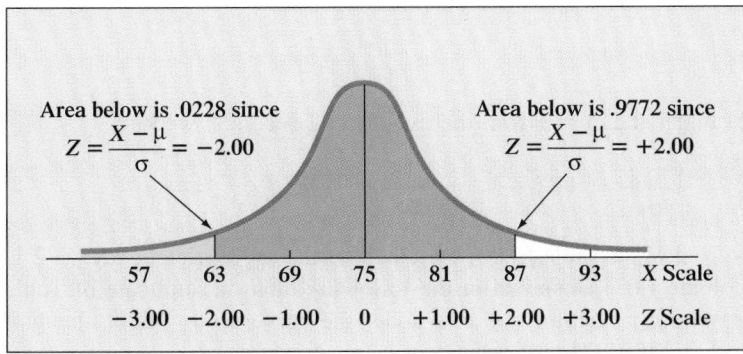

**FIGURE 8.9**   Finding $P(63 < X < 87)$

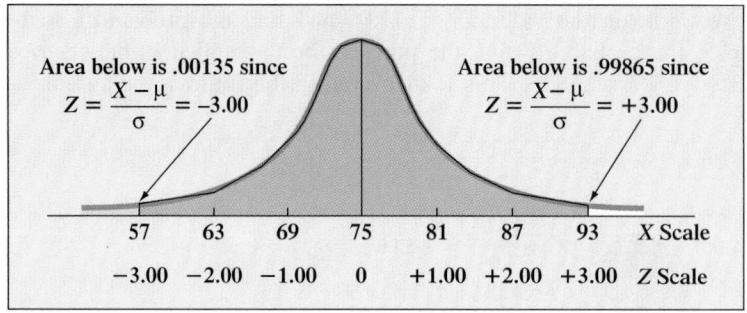

**FIGURE 8.10**   Finding $P(57 < X < 93)$

## Example 8.5   *Finding* $P(X < 62)$

What is the probability that a randomly selected factory worker can assemble the part in under 62 seconds?

### SOLUTION

We should examine the shaded lower left-tailed region of the accompanying diagram. The transformation formula equation (8.2) permits us to find areas under the standardized normal distribution up to $Z$.

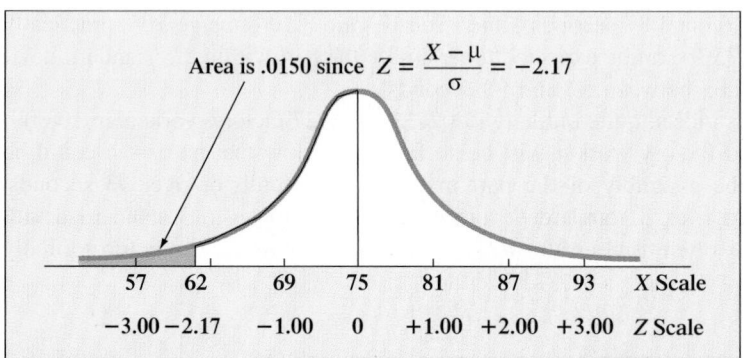

Finding $P(X < 62)$

To determine the area under the curve from the mean to 62 seconds, we have

$$Z = \frac{X - \mu}{\sigma} = \frac{62 - 75}{6} = \frac{-13}{6} = -2.17$$

We look up the $Z$ value of $-2.17$ in Table E.2(b) by matching the appropriate $Z$ row $(-2.1)$ with the appropriate $Z$ column $(.07)$ as shown in the following table [a duplicate of Table E.2(b)]. Therefore, the resulting probability or area under the curve up to $-2.17$ standard deviations below the mean is .0150. This is indicated in our diagram.

*Obtaining a cumulative area under the normal curve*

| Z | .00 | .01 | .02 | .03 | .04 | .05 | .06 | .07 | .08 | .09 |
|---|---|---|---|---|---|---|---|---|---|---|
| . | . | . | . | . | . | . | . | . | . | . |
| . | . | . | . | . | . | . | . | . | . | . |
| . | . | . | . | . | . | . | . | . | . | . |
| −2.4 | .0082 | .0080 | .0078 | .0075 | .0073 | .0071 | .0069 | .0068 | .0066 | .0064 |
| −2.3 | .0107 | .0104 | .0102 | .0099 | .0096 | .0094 | .0091 | .0089 | .0087 | .0084 |
| −2.2 | .0139 | .0136 | .0132 | .0129 | .0125 | .0122 | .0119 | .0116 | .0113 | .0110 |
| −2.1 | .0179 | .0174 | .0170 | .0166 | .0162 | .0158 | .0154 → | .0150 | .0146 | .0143 |

*Source: Extracted from Table E.2(b).*

In Examples 8.1–8.5, we sought to determine the probabilities associated with various measured values. Now we wish to determine particular numerical values of the variable of interest that correspond to known probabilities. To illustrate this, we turn to Examples 8.6–8.8.

## Example 8.6 *Finding the Median*

How much time (in seconds) will elapse before 50% of the factory workers assemble the part?

### SOLUTION

Because this time value corresponds to the median, and the mean and median are equal in all symmetrical distributions, the median must be 75 seconds.

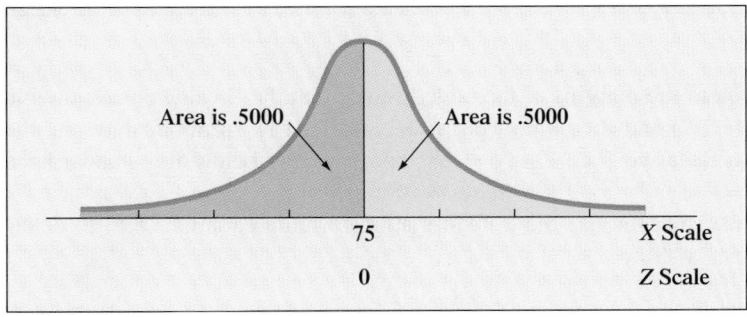

Finding X

## Example 8.7 *Finding the X Value for a Cumulative Probability of .10*

How much time (in seconds) will elapse before 10% of the factory workers assemble the part?

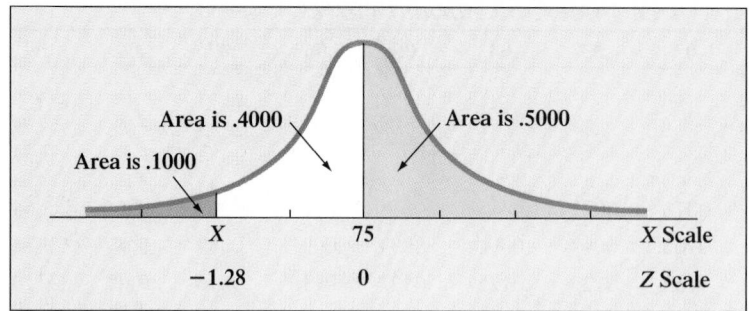

Finding *Z* to determine *X*

## SOLUTION

Since 10% of the factory workers are expected to complete the task in under *X* seconds, the area under the normal curve up to this *Z* value must be .1000. Using the body of Table E.2(b), we search for the area or probability .1000. The closest result is .1003, as shown in the following table [a replica of Table E.2(b)].

*Obtaining a Z value corresponding to a particular cumulative area (.10) under the normal curve*

| Z | .00 | .01 | .02 | .03 | .04 | .05 | .06 | .07 | .08 | .09 |
|------|-------|-------|-------|-------|-------|-------|-------|-------|-------|-------|
| . | . | . | . | . | . | . | . | . | . | . |
| . | . | . | . | . | . | . | . | . | . | . |
| . | . | . | . | . | . | . | . | . | . | . |
| −1.5 | .0668 | .0655 | .0643 | .0630 | .0618 | .0606 | .0594 | .0582 | .0571 | .0559 |
| −1.4 | .0808 | .0793 | .0778 | .0764 | .0749 | .0735 | .0721 | .0708 | .0694 | .0681 |
| −1.3 | .0968 | .0951 | .0934 | .0918 | .0901 | .0885 | .0869 | .0853 | .0838 | .0823 |
| −1.2 | .1151 | .1131 | .1112 | .1093 | .1075 | .1056 | .1038 | .1020 → | .1003 | .0985 |

*Source: Extracted from Table E.2(b).*

Working from this area to the margins of the table, we see that the *Z* value corresponding to the particular *Z* row (−1.2) and *Z* column (.08) is −1.28. That is, from our diagram, the *Z* value is recorded as a negative (i.e., *Z* = −1.28) because it is below the standardized mean of 0.

Once *Z* is obtained, we can now use the transformation formula equation (8.2) to determine the value of interest, *X*. Since

$$Z = \frac{X - \mu}{\sigma}$$

then

$$Z\sigma = X - \mu$$

and

$$\mu + Z\sigma = X$$

or

$$X = \mu + Z\sigma$$

Substituting, we compute

$$X = 75 + (-1.28)(6) = 67.32 \text{ seconds}$$

Thus, we can expect that 10% of the workers will be able to complete the task in less than 67.32 seconds.

From Example 8.7 we note the following:

The $X$ value is equal to the population mean $\mu$ plus the product of the $Z$ value and the standard deviation $\sigma$.

$$X = \mu + Z\sigma \qquad (8.4)$$

To find a *particular* value associated with a known probability, take the steps as displayed in Exhibit 8.2.

**Exhibit 8.2  *Finding a Particular Value Associated with a Known Probability***

To find a particular value associated with a known probability, follow these steps:

✓ **1.** Sketch the normal curve and then place the values for the means on the respective $X$ and $Z$ scales.

✓ **2.** Find the cumulative area less than the desired $X$.

✓ **3.** Shade the area of interest.

✓ **4.** Using Table E.2(b), determine the appropriate $Z$ value corresponding to the area under the normal curve up to the desired $X$.

✓ **5.** Using equation (8.4), solve for $X$; that is,

$$X = \mu + Z\sigma$$

**Example 8.8  *Obtaining the Interquartile Range***

What is the interquartile range?

**SOLUTION**

To obtain the interquartile range, we first find the value for $Q_1$ and the value for $Q_3$. Then subtract the former from the latter.

To find the first quartile value, we determine the time (in seconds) for which only 25% of the factory workers can be expected to assemble the part in less time. This is depicted in the diagram at the top of page 310.

Although we do not know $Q_1$, we can obtain the corresponding standardized value $Z$, because the area under the normal curve up to this $Z$ must be .2500. Using the body of Table E.2(b), we search for the area or probability .2500. The closest result is .2514, as shown in the table on page 310 which is a replica of Table E.2(b).

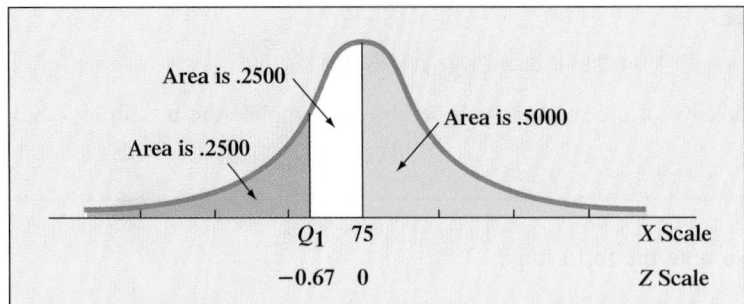

Finding $Q_1$

*Obtaining a Z value corresponding to a cumulative area of .25 under the normal curve*

| Z | .00 | .01 | .02 | .03 | .04 | .05 | .06 | .07 | .08 | .09 |
|---|---|---|---|---|---|---|---|---|---|---|
| . | . | . | . | . | . | . | . | | . | . |
| . | . | . | . | . | . | . | . | | . | . |
| . | | | . | | | | | | . | . |
| −0.9 | .1841 | .1814 | .1788 | .1762 | .1736 | .1711 | .1685 | .1660 | .1635 | .1611 |
| −0.8 | .2119 | .2090 | .2061 | .2033 | .2005 | .1977 | .1949 | .1922 | .1894 | .1867 |
| −0.7 | .2420 | .2388 | .2358 | .2327 | .2296 | .2266 | .2236 | .2006 | .2177 | .2148 |
| −0.6 | .2743 | .2709 | .2676 | .2643 | .2611 | .2578 | .2546 | .2514 | .2482 | .2451 |

*Source: Extracted from Table E.2(b).*

Working from this area to the margins of the table, we see that the Z value corresponding to the particular Z row (−0.6) and Z column (.07) is −0.67. From our diagram the Z value is recorded as a negative (i.e., $Z = −0.67$) because it lies to the left of the standardized mean of 0.

Once Z is obtained, the final step is to use equation (8.4). Hence,

$$Q_1 = X = \mu + Z\sigma$$
$$= 75 + (−0.67)(6)$$
$$= 75 − 4$$
$$= 71 \text{ seconds}$$

To find the third quartile, we determine the time (in seconds) for which 75% of the factory workers can be expected to assemble the part in less time (and 25% could complete the task in more time). This is displayed in the following diagram.

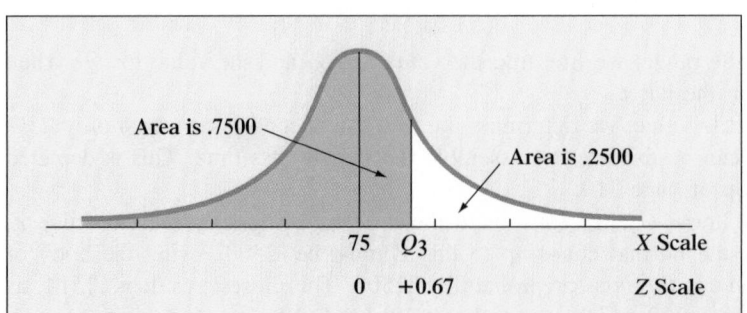

Finding $Q_3$

From the symmetry of the normal distribution, our desired $Z$ value must be $+0.67$ (since $Z$ lies to the right of the standardized mean of 0). However, this also can be seen in the following replica of Table E.2(b), where we note that .7486 of the area under the normal curve (that is, the closest value to .75) is less than the standardized $Z$ value of $+0.67$.

*Obtaining a Z value corresponding to a cumulative area of .75 under the normal curve*

| Z | .00 | .01 | .02 | .03 | .04 | .05 | .06 | .07 | .08 | .09 |
|---|---|---|---|---|---|---|---|---|---|---|
| . | . | . | . | . | . | . | . | | . | . |
| . | . | . | . | . | . | . | . | | . | . |
| . | . | . | . | . | . | . | . | | . | . |
| 0.3 | .6179 | .6217 | .6255 | .6293 | .6331 | .6368 | .6406 | .6443 | .6480 | .6517 |
| 0.4 | .6554 | .6591 | .6628 | .6664 | .6700 | .6736 | .6772 | .6808 | .6844 | .6879 |
| 0.5 | .6915 | .6950 | .6985 | .7019 | .7054 | .7088 | .7123 | .7157 | .7190 | .7224 |
| 0.6 | .7257 | .7291 | .7324 | .7357 | .7389 | .7422 | .7454 → | .7486 | .7518 | .7549 |

*Source: Extracted from Table E.2(b).*

Therefore, using equation (8.4), we compute

$$Q_3 = X = \mu + Z\sigma$$
$$= 75 + (+0.67)(6)$$
$$= 75 + 4$$
$$= 79 \text{ seconds}$$

The interquartile range or middle spread of the distribution is

$$\text{Interquartile range} = Q_3 - Q_1$$
$$= 79 - 71$$
$$= 8 \text{ seconds}$$

Now that we have used Table E.2(a) and E.2(b), we will illustrate how Microsoft Excel and Minitab can be used to obtain normal probabilities. Figure 8.11 on page 312 illustrates output obtained from Microsoft Excel for Examples 8.4 and 8.7, while Figure 8.12 on page 312 illustrates Minitab output.

## Problems for Section 8.1

### Learning the Basics

**8.1** Given a standardized normal distribution [with a mean of 0 and a standard deviation of 1 as in Table E.2(b)], answer the following:
(a) What is the probability that
(1) $Z$ is less than 1.57?
(2) $Z$ exceeds 1.84?
(3) $Z$ is between 1.57 and 1.84?
(4) $Z$ is less than 1.57 or greater than 1.84?
(5) $Z$ is between $-1.57$ and 1.84?
(6) $Z$ is less than $-1.57$ or greater than 1.84?

| | A | B |
|---|---|---|
| 1 | **Calculating Normal Probabilities** | |
| 2 | | |
| 3 | **Arithmetic Mean** | 75 |
| 4 | **Standard Deviation** | 6 |
| 5 | **Left Tail Probability** | |
| 6 | **First X Value** | 69 |
| 7 | **Z Value** | -1 |
| 8 | P(X<=69) | 0.15865526 |
| 9 | **Right Tail Probability** | |
| 10 | P(X>=69) | 0.84134474 |
| 11 | **Interval Probability** | |
| 12 | **Second X value** | 81 |
| 13 | P(X<=81) | 0.84134474 |
| 14 | P(69<X<81) | 0.68268948 |
| 15 | **Finding a X Value** | |
| 16 | **Cumulative Percent** | 0.1 |
| 17 | **Z Value** | -1.281550794 |
| 18 | **X Value** | 67.31069523 |

**FIGURE 8.11**

Obtaining normal probabilities from Microsoft Excel

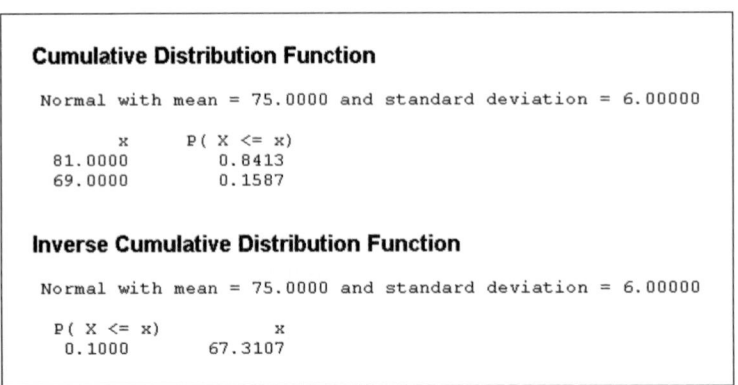

**Cumulative Distribution Function**

Normal with mean = 75.0000 and standard deviation = 6.00000

```
       x       P( X <= x)
 81.0000        0.8413
 69.0000        0.1587
```

**Inverse Cumulative Distribution Function**

Normal with mean = 75.0000 and standard deviation = 6.00000

```
 P( X <= x)          x
   0.1000       67.3107
```

**FIGURE 8.12**   Obtaining normal probabilities from Minitab

(b) What is the value of $Z$ if 50.0% of all possible $Z$ values are larger?

(c) What is the value of $Z$ if only 2.5% of all possible $Z$ values are larger?

(d) Between what two values of $Z$ (symmetrically distributed around the mean) will 68.26% of all possible $Z$ values be contained?

**8.2** Given a standardized normal distribution [with a mean of 0 and a standard deviation of 1 as in Table E.2(b)], determine the following probabilities.

(a) $P(Z > +1.34)$

(b) $P(Z < +1.17)$

(c) $P(0 < Z < +1.17)$

(d) $P(Z < -1.17)$

(e) $P(-1.17 < Z < +1.34)$

(f) $P(-1.17 < Z < -0.50)$

• **8.3** Given a standardized normal distribution [with a mean of 0 and a standard deviation of 1 as in Table E.2(b)],

(a) what is the probability that
- (1) $Z$ is between the mean and $+1.08$?
- (2) $Z$ is less than the mean or greater than $+1.08$?
- (3) $Z$ is between $-0.21$ and the mean?
- (4) $Z$ is less than $-0.21$ or greater than the mean?
- (5) $Z$ is at most $+1.08$?
- (6) $Z$ is at least $-0.21$?
- (7) $Z$ is between $-0.21$ and $+1.08$?
- (8) $Z$ is less than $-0.21$ or greater than $+1.08$?

(b) determine the following probabilities:
- (1) $P(Z > +1.08)$
- (2) $P(Z < -0.21)$
- (3) $P(-1.96 < Z < -0.21)$
- (4) $P(-1.96 < Z < +1.08)$
- (5) $P(+1.08 < Z < +1.96)$

(c) what is the value of $Z$ if 50.0% of all possible $Z$ values are smaller?

(d) what is the value of $Z$ if only 15.87% of all possible $Z$ values are smaller?

(e) what is the value of $Z$ if only 15.87% of all possible $Z$ values are larger?

**8.4** Verify the following:
- (a) The area under the normal curve between the mean and 2 standard deviations above and below it is .9544.
- (b) The area under the normal curve between the mean and 3 standard deviations above and below it is .9973.

**8.5** Given a normal distribution with $\mu = 100$ and $\sigma = 10$,
- (a) what is the probability that
  - (1) $X > 75$?
  - (2) $X < 70$?
  - (3) $75 < X < 85$?
  - (4) $X > 112$?
  - (5) $X < 80$ or $X > 110$?
- (b) 10% of the values are less than what $X$ value?
- (c) 80% of the values are between what two $X$ values (symmetrically distributed around the mean)?
- (d) 70% of the values will be above what $X$ value?

**8.6** Given a normal distribution with $\mu = 50$ and $\sigma = 4$,
- (a) what is the probability that
  - (1) $X > 43$?
  - (2) $X < 42$?
  - (3) $42 < X < 48$?
  - (4) $X > 57.5$?
  - (5) $X < 40$ or $X > 55$?
- (b) 5% of the values are less than what $X$ value?
- (c) 60% of the values are between what two $X$ values (symmetrically distributed around the mean)?
- (d) 85% of the values will be above what $X$ value?

## Applying the Concepts

**8.7** Monthly food expenditures for families of four in a large city average $420 with a standard deviation of $80. Assuming the monthly food expenditures are normally distributed,
- (a) what percentage of these expenditures are less than $350?
- (b) what percentage of these expenditures are between $250 and $350?
- (c) what percentage of these expenditures are between $250 and $450?
- (d) what percentage of these expenditures are less than $250 or greater than $450?
- (e) determine $Q_1$ and $Q_3$ from the normal curve.
- (f) What will your answers be to (a)–(e) if the standard deviation is $100?

**8.8** Toby's Trucking Company determined that on an annual basis, the distance traveled per truck is normally distributed with a mean of 50.0 thousand miles and a standard deviation of 12.0 thousand miles.

(a) What proportion of trucks can be expected to travel between 34.0 and 50.0 thousand miles in the year?

(b) What is the probability that a randomly selected truck travels between 34.0 and 38.0 thousand miles in the year?

(c) What percentage of trucks can be expected to travel either below 30.0 or above 60.0 thousand miles in the year?

(d) How many of the 1,000 trucks in the fleet are expected to travel between 30.0 and 60.0 thousand miles in the year?

(e) How many miles will be traveled by at least 80% of the trucks?

(f) What will your answers be to (a)–(e) if the standard deviation is 10.0 thousand miles?

**8.9** Plastic bags used for packaging produce are manufactured so that the breaking strength of the bag is normally distributed with a mean of 5 pounds per square inch and a standard deviation of 1.5 pounds per square inch.

(a) What proportion of the bags produced have a breaking strength of
    (1) between 5 and 5.5 pounds per square inch?
    (2) between 3.2 and 4.2 pounds per square inch?
    (3) at least 3.6 pounds per square inch?
    (4) less than 3.17 pounds per square inch?

(b) Between what two values symmetrically distributed around the mean will 95% of the breaking strengths fall?

(c) What will your answers be to (a) and (b) if the standard deviation is 1.0 pound per square inch?

**8.10** A set of final examination grades in an introductory statistics course was found to be normally distributed with a mean of 73 and a standard deviation of 8.

(a) What is the probability of getting a grade no higher than 91 on this exam?

(b) What percentage of students scored between 65 and 89?

(c) What percentage of students scored between 81 and 89?

(d) Only 5% of the students taking the test scored higher than what grade?

(e) If the professor "curves" (gives A's to the top 10% of the class regardless of the score), are you better off with a grade of 81 on this exam or a grade of 68 on a different exam where the mean is 62 and the standard deviation is 3? Show statistically and explain.

**8.11** A statistical analysis of 1,000 long-distance telephone calls made from the headquarters of Johnson & Shurgot Corporation indicates that the length of these calls is normally distributed with $\mu = 240$ seconds and $\sigma = 40$ seconds.

(a) What percentage of these calls lasted less than 180 seconds?

(b) What is the probability that a particular call lasted between 180 and 300 seconds?

(c) How many calls lasted less than 180 seconds or more than 300 seconds?

(d) What percentage of the calls lasted between 110 and 180 seconds?

(e) What is the length of a particular call if only 1% of all calls are shorter?

• **8.12** A building contractor claims he can renovate a 200-square-foot kitchen and dining room in 40 work hours, plus or minus 5 hours (i.e., the mean and standard deviation, respectively). The work includes plumbing, electrical installation, cabinets, flooring, painting, and the installation of new appliances. Assuming, from past experience, that times to complete similar projects are normally distributed with mean and standard deviation as estimated above,

(a) what is the likelihood the project will be completed in less than 35 hours?

(b) what is the likelihood the project will be completed in between 28 hours and 32 hours?

(c) what is the likelihood the project will be completed in between 35 hours and 48 hours?

(d) 10% of such projects require more than how many hours?

(e) Determine the midhinge for completion time.

(f) Determine the interquartile range for completion time.

(g) What will your answers be to (a)–(f) if the standard deviation is 10 hours?

**8.13** Wages for workers in a particular industry average $11.90 per hour and the standard deviation is $0.40. If the wages are assumed to be normally distributed,

    (a) what percentage of workers receive wages between $10.90 and $11.90?

    (b) what percentage of workers receive wages between $10.80 and $12.40?

    (c) what percentage of workers receive wages between $12.20 and $13.10?

    (d) what percentage of workers receive wages less than $11.00?

    (e) what percentage of workers receive wages more than $12.95?

    (f) what percentage of workers receive wages less than $11.00 or more than $12.95?

    (g) What must the wage be if only 10% of all workers in this industry earn more?

    (h) What must the wage be if 25% of all workers in this industry earn less?

    (i) Determine the midhinge and interquartile range of the wages in this industry.

## 8.2   ASSESSING THE NORMALITY ASSUMPTION

Now that we have discussed the importance of the normal distribution and described its properties as well as demonstrated how it may be applied, a very practical question must be considered. That is, we must be able to assess the likelihood that a particular data set can be assumed as coming from an underlying normal distribution or, at least, can be adequately approximated by it.

The reader must be cautioned—*not all continuous random variables are normally distributed!* Often the continuous random phenomenon that we are interested in studying will neither follow the normal distribution nor be adequately approximated by it. Although some methods for studying such continuous phenomena are outside the scope of this text (see reference 4), *nonparametric* techniques (see reference 3) that do not depend on the particular form of the underlying random variable will be discussed in chapters 12 and 13.

Hence, for a descriptive analysis of any particular set of data, the practical question remains: How can we decide whether our data set seems to follow or at least approximate the normal distribution sufficiently to permit it to be examined using the methodology of this chapter? Two descriptive *exploratory* approaches will be taken here to evaluate the *goodness-of-fit*:

**1.** A comparison of the data set's characteristics with the properties of an underlying normal distribution

**2.** The construction of a normal probability plot

More formal *confirmatory* approaches to the *goodness-of-fit* of a normal distribution can be found in references 3 and 7.

### Evaluating the Properties

In section 8.1 we noted that the normal distribution has several theoretical properties. We recall that it is bell-shaped and symmetrical in appearance; its measures of central tendency are all identical; its interquartile range is equal to 1.33 standard deviations; and its random variable is continuous and has an infinite range.

We also noted that in actual practice, some of the continuous random phenomena we observe may only approximate these theoretical properties, either because the underlying population distribution may be only approximately normal or because any obtained sample data set may deviate from the theoretically expected characteristics. In such circumstances, the data may not be perfectly bell-shaped and symmetrical in appearance. The measures of central tendency will differ slightly, and the interquartile range will not be exactly equal to

1.33 standard deviations. In addition, in practice, the range of the data will not be infinite—it will be approximately equal to 6 standard deviations.

However, many continuous phenomena are neither normally distributed nor approximately normally distributed. For such phenomena, the descriptive characteristics of the respective data sets do not match well with these four properties of a normal distribution.

What then should we do to investigate the assumption of normality in our data? One approach is to check for normality by comparing and contrasting the actual data characteristics against the corresponding properties from an underlying normal distribution as illustrated in Exhibit 8.3.

### Exhibit 8.3   *Checking for Normality*

✓ **1.** Make some tallies and plots and observe their appearance.

  A. For small- or moderate-sized data sets, construct a stem-and-leaf display and box-and-whisker plot.

  B. For large data sets, construct the frequency distribution and plot the histogram or polygon.

✓ **2.** Compute descriptive summary measures and compare the characteristics of the data with the theoretical and practical properties of the normal distribution.

  A. Obtain the mean, median, mode, midrange, and midhinge and note the similarities or differences in these five measures of central tendency.

  B. Obtain the interquartile range and standard deviation. Note how well the interquartile range can be approximated by 1.33 times the standard deviation.

  C. Obtain the range and note how well it can be approximated by 6 times the standard deviation.

✓ **3.** Make some tallies to evaluate how the observations in the data set distribute themselves.

  A. Determine whether approximately two-thirds of the observations lie between the mean ±1 standard deviation.

  B. Determine whether approximately four-fifths of the observations lie between the mean ±1.28 standard deviations.

  C. Determine whether approximately 19 out of every 20 observations lie between the mean ±2 standard deviations.

A second approach to evaluating the assumption of normality in our data is through the construction of a *normal probability plot*.

## Constructing the Normal Probability Plot

You may recall that *quantiles* are defined as measures of "noncentral" location that are usually computed for summarizing large sets of numerical data. In section 4.2 we stressed the median (which splits the ordered observations in half) and the quartiles (which split the ordered observations in fourths) and mentioned other quantiles such as the deciles (which split the ordered observations in 10ths) and the percentiles (which split the ordered observations in 100ths). With this in mind, we define a normal probability plot:

> A **normal probability plot** is a two-dimensional plot of the observed data values on the *vertical* axis with their corresponding quantile values from a standardized normal distribution on the *horizontal* axis (see references 2 and 8).

If the plotted points lie either on or close to an imaginary straight line rising from the lower left corner of the graph to the upper right corner, then the data set is (at least approximately) normally distributed. On the other hand, if the plotted points deviate from this imaginary straight line in some patterned fashion, then the data set is not normally distributed and the methodology presented in this chapter may not be appropriate.

To construct and use a normal probability plot, follow the steps presented in Exhibit 8.4:

### Exhibit 8.4    Steps Used in Constructing a Normal Probability Plot

To construct a normal probability plot follow these steps.

✓ **1.** Place the values in the data set into an ordered array.

✓ **2.** Find the corresponding standard normal quantile values.

✓ **3.** Plot the corresponding pairs of points using the observed data values on the vertical axis and the associated standard normal quantile values on the horizontal axis.

✓ **4.** Assess the likelihood that the random variable of interest is (at least approximately) normally distributed by inspecting the plot for evidence of linearity (i.e., a straight line).

These steps will be described in detail.

◆ *Obtaining the Ordered Array*    Since the original data set is likely to be obtained in raw form, the observations must be rearranged from smallest to largest so that the corresponding standard normal quantile values can be obtained. Thus, the original data are placed into an ordered array.

◆ *Finding the Standard Normal Quantile Values*    We know that a standard normal distribution is characterized by a mean of 0 and standard deviation of 1. Owing to its symmetry, the median from a standard normal distribution must also be 0. Therefore, in dealing with a standard normal distribution, the quantile values below the median will be negative and the quantile values above the median will be positive. However, the question we must still answer is: How can we obtain the quantile values from this distribution? The process by which we can accomplish this is known as an **inverse normal scores transformation** (see reference 3).

The following is noted: Given a data set containing $n$ observations from a standardized normal distribution, let the symbol $O_1$ represent the first (and smallest) ordered or quantile value, let the symbol $O_2$ represent its second smallest ordered value, let the symbol $O_i$ represent the $i$th smallest ordered value, and let the symbol $O_n$ represent the largest ordered value. Because of symmetry, the standard normal quantiles $O_1$ and $O_n$ will have the same numerical value—except for sign: $O_1$ will be negative and $O_n$ will be positive.

- The **first standard normal quantile,** $O_1$, is the $Z$ value on a standard normal distribution below which the proportion $1/(n + 1)$ of the area under the curve is contained.
- The **second standard normal quantile,** $O_2$, is the $Z$ value on a standard normal distribution below which the proportion $2/(n + 1)$ of the area under the curve is contained.
- The **$i$th standard normal quantile,** $O_i$, is the $Z$ value on a standard normal distribution below which the proportion $i/(n + 1)$ of the area under the curve is contained.
- The **$n$th (and largest) standard normal quantile,** $O_n$, is the $Z$ value on a standard normal distribution below which the proportion $n/(n + 1)$ of the area under the curve is contained.

◆ *Making the Inverse Normal Scores Transformation* As in section 8.1, once we know the probability or area under the curve, we may use the body of Table E.2(b) to locate the appropriate area and then its corresponding standard normal ordered value in the margins of this table. Thus, in general, to find the $i$th standard normal ordered value from a data set containing $n$ observations, we sketch the standard normal distribution and locate the value $O_i$ such that the proportion $i/(n + 1)$ of the area under the curve is contained below that value. We then find this area in the body of Table E.2(b), a table of cumulative normal probabilities, and working to the margins of that table, we locate the corresponding standard normal ordered value.

Example 8.9 illustrates how to obtain standard normal ordered values.

## Example 8.9 *Obtaining Standard Normal Ordered Values*

Suppose we wish to obtain the 1st, 2nd, and 10th standard normal ordered values corresponding to a sample of 19 observations.

### SOLUTION

The first standard normal ordered value, $O_1$, is that value below which the proportion $\dfrac{1}{n + 1} = \dfrac{1}{19 + 1} = \dfrac{1}{20} = .05$ of the area under the normal curve is contained. From our diagram at the top of the next page, we see that the area up to $O_1$ is .05 so that from the body of our table that follows, $O_1$ would fall halfway between $-1.65$ and $-1.64$. Because the standard normal ordered values are usually reported with two decimal places, the value $-1.65$ is chosen here.

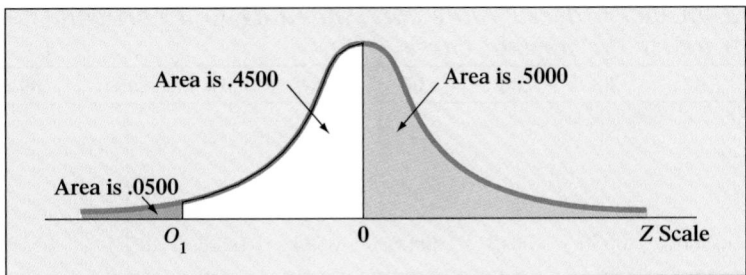

Finding the first standard normal ordered value from a data set with 19 observations

*Obtaining a standard normal ordered value corresponding to a particular cumulative area (.05) under the normal curve*

| Z | .00 | .01 | .02 | .03 | .04 | .05 | .06 | .07 | .08 | .09 |
|------|-------|-------|-------|-------|-------|-------|-------|-------|-------|-------|
| . | . | . | . | . | . | . | . | . | . | . |
| . | . | . | . | . | . | . | . | . | . | . |
| . | . | . | . | . | . | . | . | . | . | . |
| −1.9 | .0287 | .0281 | .0274 | .0268 | .0262 | .0256 | .0250 | .0244 | .0239 | .0233 |
| −1.8 | .0359 | .0351 | .0344 | .0336 | .0329 | .0322 | .0314 | .0307 | .0301 | .0294 |
| −1.7 | .0446 | .0436 | .0427 | .0418 | .0409 | .0401 | .0392 | .0384 | .0375 | .0367 |
| −1.6 | .0548 | .0537 | .0526 | .0516 → | .0505 | .0495 | .0485 | .0475 | .0465 | .0455 |

*Source: Extracted from Table E.2(b).*

The second standard normal ordered value, $O_2$, is that value below which the proportion $\frac{2}{n+1} = \frac{2}{19+1} = \frac{2}{20} = .10$ of the area under the normal curve is obtained. From the following diagram and table at the top of page 320, $O_2$ would fall between $-1.29$ and $-1.28$ but closer to the latter. Hence, $-1.28$ is selected here.

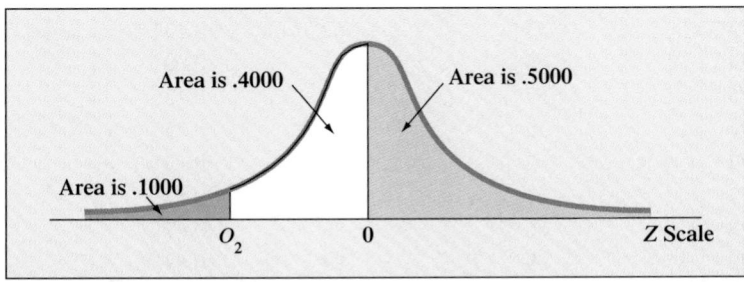

Finding the second standard normal ordered value from a data set with 19 observations

*Obtaining a standard normal ordered value corresponding to a particular cumulative area (.10) under the normal curve*

| Z | .00 | .01 | .02 | .03 | .04 | .05 | .06 | .07 | .08 | .09 |
|---|-----|-----|-----|-----|-----|-----|-----|-----|-----|-----|
| . | . | . | . | . | . | . | . | . | . | . |
| . | . | . | . | . | . | . | . | . | . | . |
| . | . | . | . | . | . | . | . | . | . | . |
| −1.5 | .0668 | .0655 | .0643 | .0630 | .0618 | .0606 | .0594 | .0582 | .0571 | .0559 |
| −1.4 | .0808 | .0793 | .0778 | .0764 | .0749 | .0735 | .0721 | .0708 | .0694 | .0681 |
| −1.3 | .0968 | .0951 | .0934 | .0918 | .0901 | .0885 | .0869 | .0853 | .0838 | .0823 |
| −1.2 | .1151 | .1131 | .1112 | .1093 | .1075 | .1056 | .1038 | .1020 → | .1003 | .0985 |

*Source: Extracted from Table E.2(b).*

Continuing in a similar manner, for example, the 10th standard normal ordered value, $O_{10}$, is that value below which the proportion $\dfrac{10}{n+1} = \dfrac{10}{19+1} = \dfrac{10}{20} = .50$ of the area under the normal curve is contained. Since we have located the median, this standard normal ordered value must be 0.00.

**Table 8.4** *Ordered arrays of midterm test scores obtained from 19 students in each of four sections (I–IV) of a course in introductory finance and corresponding standard normal ordered values*

| (I) BELL-SHAPED NORMAL DISTRIBUTION | (II) LEFT-SKEWED DISTRIBUTION | (III) RIGHT-SKEWED DISTRIBUTION | (IV) RECTANGULAR-SHAPED DISTRIBUTION | $O_i$ |
|---|---|---|---|---|
| 48 | 47 | 47 | 38 | −1.65 |
| 52 | 54 | 48 | 41 | −1.28 |
| 55 | 58 | 50 | 44 | −1.04 |
| 57 | 61 | 51 | 47 | −0.84 |
| 58 | 64 | 52 | 50 | −0.67 |
| 60 | 66 | 53 | 53 | −0.52 |
| 61 | 68 | 53 | 56 | −0.39 |
| 62 | 71 | 54 | 59 | −0.25 |
| 64 | 73 | 55 | 62 | −0.13 |
| 65 | 74 | 56 | 65 | 0.00 |
| 66 | 75 | 57 | 68 | 0.13 |
| 68 | 76 | 59 | 71 | 0.25 |
| 69 | 77 | 62 | 74 | 0.39 |
| 70 | 77 | 64 | 77 | 0.52 |
| 72 | 78 | 66 | 80 | 0.67 |
| 73 | 79 | 69 | 83 | 0.84 |
| 75 | 80 | 72 | 86 | 1.04 |
| 78 | 82 | 76 | 89 | 1.28 |
| 82 | 83 | 83 | 92 | 1.65 |

Table 8.4 presents ordered arrays of midterm test scores from 19 students in each of four sections (sections I–IV) of a course in introductory finance. Also shown in Table 8.4 are the corresponding standard normal ordered values obtained from the previously described inverse normal scores transformation. If we construct normal probability plots for these four distinct data sets, what would they show us and how would we interpret the plots?

The normal probability plots for the four class sections are depicted in parts (a)–(d) of Figure 8.13. From (a) we observe that the points appear to deviate from a straight line in a random manner, so we conclude that the data set from class section I is approximately normally distributed. [Note the corresponding polygon and box-and-whisker plot from Figure 4.10(a) on page 161.]

On the other hand, in Figure 8.13(b) we observe a nonlinear pattern to the plot. The points seem to rise somewhat more steeply at first and then increase at a decreasing rate. This pattern is an example of a left-skewed data set. The steepness of the left side of the plot is indicative of the elongated left tail of the distribution of test scores from class section II. [Note the corresponding polygon and box-and-whisker plot from Figure 4.10(b).]

In Figure 8.13(c) we observe the opposite nonlinear pattern. The points here seem to rise more slowly at first and then seem to increase at an increasing rate. This pattern is an example of a right-skewed data set. The steepness of the right side of the plot is indicative of the elongated right tail of the distribution of test scores from class section III. [Note the corresponding polygon and box-and-whisker plot from Figure 4.10(c).]

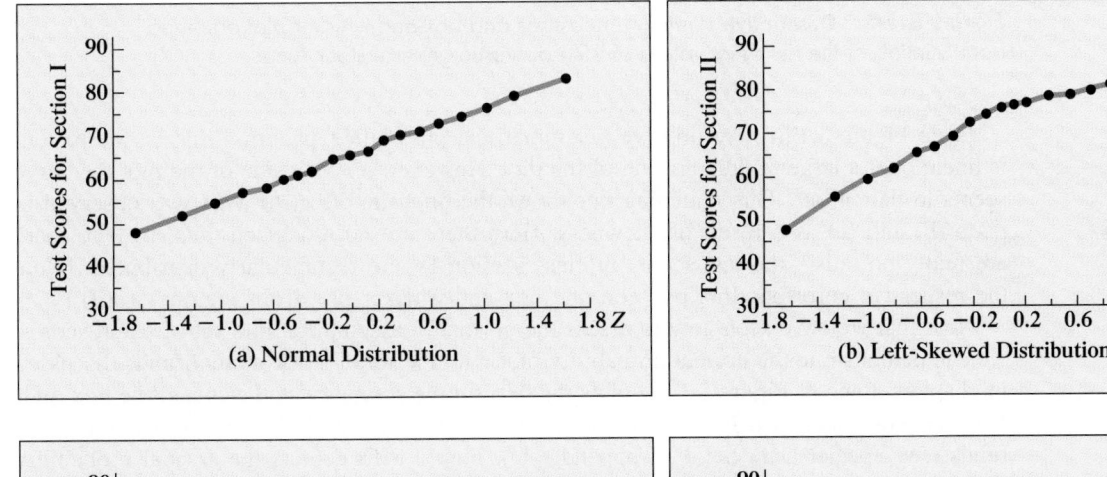

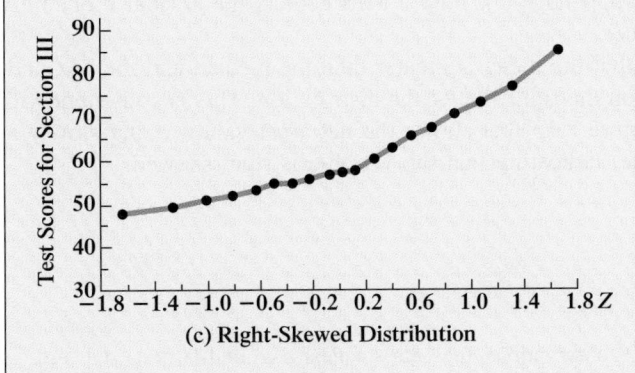

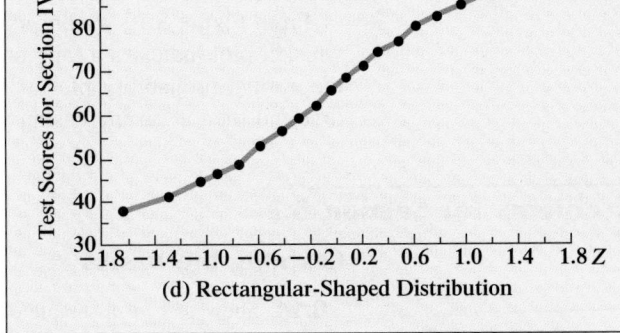

**FIGURE 8.13**  Normal probability plots for four data sets

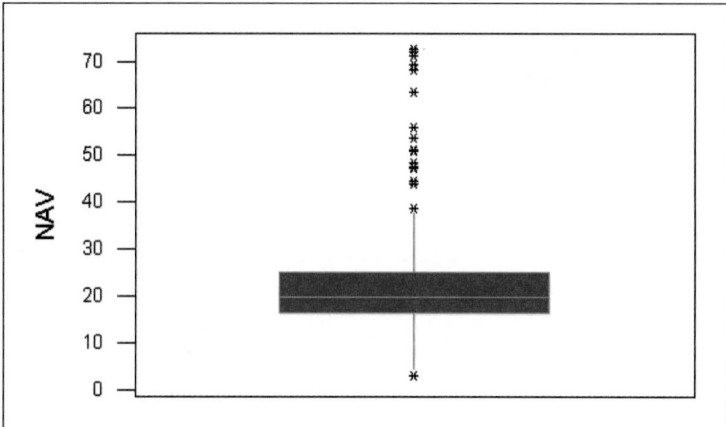

```
Descriptive Statistics

Variable       N       Mean     Median    TrMean      StDev   SE Mean
NAV          194     23.029     19.735    21.598     12.029     0.864

Variable   Minimum   Maximum         Q1         Q3
NAV          2.990    72.520     16.315     25.003
```

FIGURE 8.14   Descriptive summary measures and box-and-whisker plot obtained
from Minitab of the net asset values of 194 domestic general stock funds

From Figure 8.13(d) we observe a symmetrical plot with a pattern—that is, the pattern
is linear over a large middle portion of the plot. However, on each side of the plot the curve
seems to flatten out. This flattening out shows the opposite effect to what was observed in
parts (b) and (c) as a result of skewness. Here there are no elongated tails. In fact, there
are really no tails—the test scores in class section IV are rectangularly distributed. [Note
the respective corresponding polygon and box-and-whisker plot from Figure 4.10(d).]

Now that we have seen how to assess the normality assumption in a set of exam scores,
we can demonstrate the normal probability plot with the set of stock mutual funds discussed
in chapters 3 and 4. Figure 8.14 depicts the descriptive summary statistics and the box-and-
whisker plot obtained from Minitab of the net asset values of 194 domestic general stock
funds (see Special Data Set 1 of appendix D). Figure 8.15 depicts the normal probability
plot obtained from Microsoft Excel.

From Figure 8.14 we observe that the mean is greater than the median and the box-and-
whisker plot indicates a long tail on the right side of the distribution. This is consistent with
the normal probability plot of Figure 8.15 that shows the net asset values rising slowly at
first and then at an increasing rate, indicating that the variable is right-skewed.

## Problems for Section 8.2

### Learning the Basics

**8.14** Show that for a sample of 19 observations, the 18th-smallest (i.e., 2nd-largest) standard
normal ordered value obtained from the inverse normal scores transformation is $+1.28$ and
the 19th (i.e., largest) standard normal ordered value is $+1.65$.

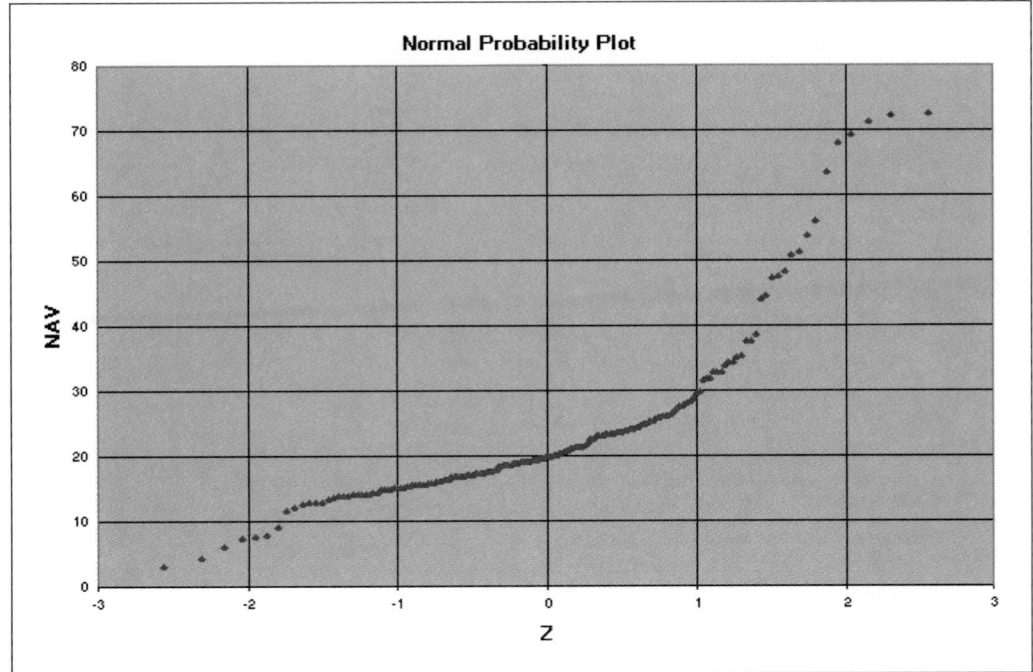

**FIGURE 8.15**  Normal probability plot obtained from Microsoft Excel of the net asset values of 194 domestic general stock funds

**8.15**  Show that for a sample of 39 observations, the smallest and largest standard normal ordered values obtained from the inverse normal scores transformation are, respectively, −1.96 and +1.96 and the middle (i.e., 20th) standard normal ordered value is 0.00.

**8.16**  Using the inverse normal scores transformation on a sample of 6 observations, list the 6 expected proportions or areas under the standardized normal curve along with their corresponding standard normal ordered values.

## Applying the Concepts

**8.17**  The following ordered array (from left to right) depicts the amount of money (in dollars) withdrawn from a cash machine by 25 customers at a local bank:

| 40 | 50 | 50 | 70 | 70 | 80 | 80 | 90 | 100 | 100 |
|----|----|----|----|----|----|----|----|-----|-----|
| 100 | 100 | 100 | 100 | 110 | 110 | 120 | 120 | 130 | 140 |
| 140 | 150 | 160 | 160 | 200 | | | | | |

**DATA FILE**
ATM1

Decide whether or not the data appear to be approximately normally distributed by
(a)  evaluating the actual versus theoretical properties.
(b)  constructing a normal probability plot.

**8.18**  The following data indicate the amount spent (in dollars) by a random sample of 28 customers in a local supermarket:

| 44.24 | 35.56 | 45.93 | 49.92 | 38.94 | 41.16 | 44.84 |
|-------|-------|-------|-------|-------|-------|-------|
| 27.28 | 50.66 | 50.97 | 45.93 | 46.58 | 28.73 | 25.93 |
| 24.21 | 23.84 | 54.58 | 52.62 | 47.36 | 30.84 | 48.62 |
| 31.15 | 38.58 | 34.96 | 45.32 | 53.81 | 40.22 | 37.19 |

**DATA FILE**
GROCERY

Decide whether or not the data appear to be approximately normally distributed by
(a) evaluating the actual versus theoretical properties.
(b) constructing a normal probability plot.

• **8.19** The following data indicate the amount of gasoline (in gallons) purchased at a highway gasoline station for a random sample of 24 automobile owners:

**DATA FILE**
GAS1

| 12.78 | 8.89 | 10.09 | 10.64 | 15.98 | 13.95 | 9.48 | 10.84 |
| 10.88 | 9.93 | 7.74 | 5.80 | 11.84 | 10.29 | 10.89 | 6.68 |
| 12.09 | 8.28 | 8.83 | 7.95 | 7.33 | 12.56 | 8.86 | 9.15 |

Decide whether or not the data appear to be approximately normally distributed by
(a) evaluating the actual versus theoretical properties.
(b) constructing a normal probability plot.

• **8.20** A problem with a telephone line that prevents a customer from receiving or making calls is disconcerting to both the customer and the telephone company. These problems can be of two types: those located inside a central office and those located on lines between the central office and the customer's equipment. The following data represent samples of 20 problems reported to two different offices of a telephone company and the time to clear these problems (in minutes) from the customers' lines:

*Central Office I Time to Clear Problems (minutes)*

1.48  1.75  0.78  2.85  0.52  1.60  4.15  3.97  1.48  3.10

1.02  0.53  0.93  1.60  0.80  1.05  6.32  3.93  5.45  0.97

**DATA FILE**
PHONE

*Central Office II Time to Clear Problems (minutes)*

7.55  3.75  0.10  1.10  0.60  0.52  3.30  2.10  0.58  4.02

3.75  0.65  1.92  0.60  1.53  4.23  0.08  1.48  1.65  0.72

For each of the two central office locations, decide whether or not the data appear to be approximately normally distributed by
(a) evaluating the actual versus theoretical properties.
(b) constructing a normal probability plot.

**8.21** In many manufacturing processes there is a term called *work in process* (often abbreviated as WIP). In a book manufacturing plant, this represents time it takes for sheets from a press to be folded, gathered, sewn, tipped on endsheets, and bound. The following data represent samples of 20 books at each of two production plants and the processing time (operationally defined as the time in days from when the books came off the press to when they were packed in cartons) for these jobs.

*Plant A*

5.62  5.29  16.25  10.92  11.46  21.62  8.45  8.58  5.41  11.42

11.62  7.29  7.50  7.96  4.42  10.50  7.58  9.29  7.54  8.92

*Plant B*

**DATA FILE**
WIP

9.54  11.46  16.62  12.62  25.75  15.41  14.29  13.13  13.71  10.04

5.75  12.46  9.17  13.21  6.00  2.33  14.25  5.37  6.25  9.71

For each of the two plants, decide whether or not the data appear to be approximately normally distributed by
(a) evaluating the actual versus theoretical properties.
(b) constructing a normal probability plot.

## ◆8.3 THE EXPONENTIAL DISTRIBUTION (*OPTIONAL TOPIC*)

In this section we introduce another continuous probability distribution, the exponential distribution, that is useful in a variety of circumstances in business, particularly in evaluating manufacturing and service processes. As examples, the exponential distribution has been widely used in waiting line or queuing theory to model the length of time between arrivals in a process such as automobiles at a toll bridge crossing, customers at a bank's automatic teller machine (ATM), clients at a restaurant, or patients at a hospital emergency room.

The **exponential distribution** is defined by a single parameter, its mean, $\lambda$, the average number of arrivals per unit of time. The probability that the length of time before the next arrival is less than $X$ is given by the following:

### The Exponential Distribution

The probability of an arrival in *less than or equal to* $X$ amount of time is equal to 1 minus the mathematical constant $e$ raised to a power equal to minus 1 times the product of the average number of arrivals $\lambda$ and the value of $X$.

$$P(\text{arrival time} \leq X) = 1 - e^{-\lambda X} \tag{8.5}$$

where

$\quad e$ = the mathematical constant approximated by 2.71828

$\quad \lambda$ = the population mean number of arrivals

$\quad X$ = any value of the continuous random variable, where $0 < X < +\infty$

We illustrate the exponential distribution with the following example. Suppose customers arrive at a bank's ATM at the rate of 20 per hour. If a customer has just arrived, what is the probability that the next customer arrives within 6 minutes (that is, 0.1 hour)?

For this example we have $\lambda = 20$ and $X = 0.1$. Using equation (8.5), we have

$$P(\text{arrival time} \leq 0.1) = 1 - e^{-20(.1)}$$
$$P(\text{arrival time} \leq 0.1) = 1 - e^{-2}$$
$$P(\text{arrival time} \leq 0.1) = 1 - .1353 = .8647$$

Thus, the probability that a customer will arrive within 6 minutes is .8647, or 86.47%.

Now that we have used equation (8.5) to obtain exponential probabilities, we will illustrate how Microsoft Excel and Minitab can be used. Figure 8.16 illustrates output obtained from Microsoft Excel, while Figure 8.17 on page 326 illustrates Minitab output.

| | A | B |
|---|---|---|
| 1 | Exponential Calculations | |
| 2 | | |
| 3 | X Value | 0.1 |
| 4 | Mean | 20 |
| 5 | Probability | 0.864664717 |
| 6 | | |

**FIGURE 8.16**

Obtaining exponential probabilities from Microsoft Excel

**FIGURE 8.17**  Obtaining exponential probabilities from Minitab
*Note: The mean assigned using Minitab is $1/\lambda$.*

---

## Problems for Section 8.3

### Learning the Basics

• **8.22** Given an exponential distribution with mean of $\lambda = 10$, what is the probability that the
   (a) arrival time is less than $X = .1$?
   (b) arrival time is greater than $X = .1$?
   (c) arrival time is between .1 and .2?
   (d) arrival time is less than $X = .1$ or greater than $X = .2$?

**8.23** Given an exponential distribution with mean of $\lambda = 30$, what is the probability that the
   (a) arrival time is less than $X = .1$?
   (b) arrival time is greater than $X = .1$?
   (c) arrival time is between .1 and .2?
   (d) arrival time is less than $X = .1$ or greater than $X = .2$?

**8.24** Given an exponential distribution with mean of $\lambda = 20$, what is the probability that the
   (a) arrival time is less than $X = .4$?
   (b) arrival time is greater than $X = .4$?
   (c) arrival time is between .4 and .5?
   (d) arrival time is less than $X = .4$ or greater than $X = .5$?

### Applying the Concepts

**8.25** Suppose autos arrive at a toll booth located at the entrance to a bridge at the rate of 50 per minute during the 5–6 P.M. hour. If an auto has just arrived,
   (a) what is the probability that the next auto arrives within 3 seconds (0.05 minute)?
   (b) what is the probability that the next auto arrives within 1 second (0.0167 minute)?
   (c) What would be your answers to (a) and (b) if the rate of arrival of autos was 60 per minute?
   (d) What would be your answers to (a) and (b) if the rate of arrival of autos was 30 per minute?

• **8.26** Customers arrive at the drive-up window of a fast-food restaurant at the rate of 2 per minute during the lunch hour.
   (a) What is the probability that the next customer arrives within 1 minute?
   (b) What is the probability that the next customer arrives within 5 minutes?
   (c) During the dinner time period, the arrival rate is 1 per minute. What would be your answers to (a) and (b) for this period?

• **8.27** Telephone calls arrive at the information desk of a large computer software company at the rate of 15 per hour.
   (a) What is the probability that the next call arrives within 3 minutes (0.05 hour)?
   (b) What is the probability that the next call arrives within 15 minutes (0.25 hour)?
   (c) Suppose the company has just introduced an updated version of one of its software

programs and telephone calls are now arriving at the rate of 25 per hour. Given this information, what would be your answers to (a) and (b)?

**8.28** An on-the-job injury occurs once every 10 days on average at an automobile plant. What is the probability that the next on-the-job injury occurs within

    (a)  10 days?

    (b)  5 days?

    (c)  1 day?

**8.29** Suppose golfers arrive at the starter's booth of a public golf course at the rate of 8 per hour during the Monday-to-Friday midweek period. If a golfer has just arrived,

    (a)  what is the probability that the next golfer arrives within 15 minutes (0.25 hour)?

    (b)  what is the probability that the next golfer arrives within 3 minutes (0.05 hour)?

    (c)  Suppose the actual arrival rate on Fridays is 15 per hour. What would be your answers for (a) and (b) on Fridays?

 ## SUMMARY

As seen in the summary chart, in this chapter we have introduced the subject of continuous probability distributions and, in particular, focused on the normal distribution and the exponential distribution. The normal distribution was shown to be useful in enabling probability estimates to be made for the numerous phenomena whose random variables yield outcomes that are bell-shaped. In the next chapter, we shall investigate how the normal distribution provides the basis for classical statistical inference.

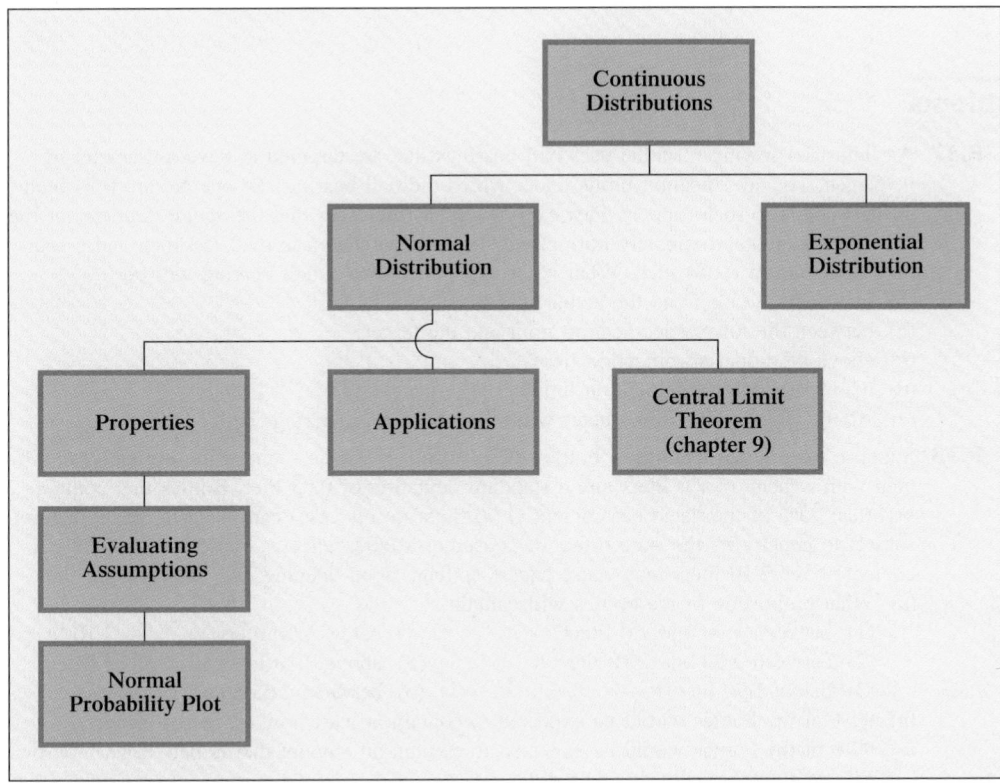

Chapter 8 summary chart

## Key Terms

continuous probability density function 292

cumulative normal distribution 301

exponential distribution 325

inverse normal scores transformation 318

normal distribution 292

normal probability density function 294

normal probability plot 317

standard normal quantile 318

standardized normal distribution 296

transformation formula 295

## Checking Your Understanding

**8.30** Why is it that only one table of the normal distribution such as Table E.2(a) or E.2(b) is needed to find any probability under the normal curve?

**8.31** How would you find the area between two values under the normal curve when both values are on the same side of the mean?

**8.32** How would you find the $X$ value that corresponds to a given percentile of the normal distribution?

**8.33** Why do the individual observations have to be converted to standard normal ordered values in order to develop a normal probability plot?

**8.34** What are some of the distinguishing properties of a normal distribution?

**8.35** How does the normal probability plot allow one to evaluate whether a set of data is normally distributed?

**8.36** Under what circumstances can the exponential distribution be used?

## Chapter Review Problems

**8.37** An industrial sewing machine uses ball bearings that are targeted to have a diameter of 0.75 inch. The specification limits under which the ball bearing can operate are 0.74 inch (lower) and 0.76 inch (upper). Past experience has indicated that the actual diameter of the ball bearings is approximately normally distributed with a mean of 0.753 inch and a standard deviation of 0.004 inch. What is the probability that a ball bearing will be
(a) between the target and the actual mean?
(b) between the lower specification limit and the target?
(c) above the upper specification limit?
(d) below the lower specification limit?
(e) Above which value in diameter will 93% of the ball bearings be?

**8.38** Suppose that the fill amount of bottles of soft drink has been found to be normally distributed with a mean of 2.0 liters and a standard deviation of 0.05 liter. Bottles that contain less than 95% of the listed net content (1.90 liters in this case) can make the manufacturer subject to penalty by the state office of consumer affairs, whereas bottles that have a net content above 2.10 liters may cause excess spillage upon opening.
(a) What proportion of the bottles will contain
    (1) between 1.90 and 2.0 liters?      (4) below 1.90 liters or above 2.10 liters?
    (2) between 1.90 and 2.10 liters?      (5) above 2.10 liters?
    (3) below 1.90 liters?      (6) between 2.05 and 2.10 liters?
(b) 99% of the bottles would be expected to contain at least how much soft drink?
(c) 99% of the bottles would be expected to contain an amount that is between which two values (symmetrically distributed)?
(d) Explain the difference in the results in (b) and (c).

(e) Suppose that in an effort to reduce the number of bottles that contain less than 1.90 liters, the bottler sets the filling machine so that the mean is 2.02 liters. Under these circumstances, what would be your answers in (a), (b), and (c)?

**8.39** A city agency that processes building renovation permits has a policy that states that the permit is free if it is not ready at the end of 5 business days from when the application is made. Processing time is measured from when the permit is received (the time is stamped) to when the application has been fully processed.
(a) If the process has a mean of 3 days and a standard deviation of 1 day, what proportion of the permits will be free?
(b) If the process has a mean of 2 days and a standard deviation of 1.5 days, what proportion of the permits will be free?
(c) Which process, (a) or (b), will result in more free permits? Explain.
(d) For the process described in (a), would it be better to focus on reducing the average to 2 days or the standard deviation to 0.75 day? Explain.

• **8.40** Sally D. is 67 inches tall and weighs 135 pounds. If the heights of women are normally distributed with $\mu = 65$ inches and $\sigma = 2.5$ inches and if the weights of women are normally distributed with $\mu = 125$ pounds and $\sigma = 10$ pounds, determine whether Sally's more unusual characteristic is her height or her weight. Discuss.

**8.41** The life of a type of transistor battery is normally distributed with $\mu = 100$ hours and $\sigma = 20$ hours.
(a) What proportion of the batteries will last between 100 and 115 hours?
(b) What proportion of the batteries will last more than 90 hours?
(c) 90% of the batteries will last more than how many hours?
(d) What is the interquartile range in battery life?

**8.42** An orange juice producer buys all his oranges from a large orange orchard. The amount of juice squeezed from each of these oranges is approximately normally distributed with a mean of 4.70 ounces and a standard deviation of 0.40 ounce.
(a) What is the probability that a randomly selected orange will contain between 4.70 and 5.00 ounces?
(b) What is the probability that a randomly selected orange will contain between 5.00 and 5.50 ounces?
(c) 77% of the oranges will contain at least how many ounces of juice?
(d) Between what two values (in ounces) symmetrically distributed around the population mean will 80% of the oranges fall?

• **8.43** Suppose the governor projects that on a weekly basis a state football lottery program she has proposed is expected to average 10.0 million dollars in profits (to be turned over to the state for educational programs) with a standard deviation of 2.5 million dollars. Suppose further that the weekly profits data are assumed to be (approximately) normally distributed. The following questions may be raised (or anticipated at the governor's next press conference):
(a) What is the probability that in any given week profits will be
   (1) between 10.0 and 12.5 million dollars?   (4) at least 7.5 million dollars?
   (2) between 7.5 and 10.0 million dollars?   (5) under 7.5 million dollars?
   (3) between 7.5 and 12.5 million dollars?   (6) between 12.5 and 14.3 million dollars?
(b) 50% of the time weekly profits (in millions of dollars) are expected to be above what value?
(c) 90% of the time weekly profits (in millions of dollars) are expected to be above what value?
(d) What is the interquartile range in weekly profits expected from the state football lottery program?

**8.44** **(Class Project)** According to Burton G. Malkiel, the daily changes in the closing price of stock follow a *random walk*—that is, these daily events are independent of each other and move upward or downward in a random manner—and can be approximated by a normal distribution.

To test this theory, each student should use either a newspaper or the Internet to select one company traded on the New York Stock Exchange, one company traded on the American Stock Exchange, and one company traded "over the counter" (NASDAQ national market) and then do the following:

1. Record the daily closing stock price of each of these companies for 6 consecutive weeks (so that you have 30 observations per company).
2. Record the daily changes in the closing stock price of each of these companies for 6 consecutive weeks (so that you have 30 observations per company).

For each of your six data sets, decide whether or not the data appear to be approximately normally distributed by

(a) examining the stem-and-leaf, histogram or polygon, and box-and-whisker plot.
(b) evaluating the actual versus theoretical properties.
(c) constructing a normal probability plot.
(d) Discuss the results of (a), (b), and (c).

*Note:* The random-walk theory pertains to the daily changes in the closing stock price, not the daily closing stock price.

(e) Based on your conclusions in (d), what can you now say about your three distributions of each type—daily closing prices and daily changes in closing prices? Which, if any, of the data sets appear to be approximately normally distributed?

## TEAM PROJECT

**TP8.1** Refer to TP3.1 on page 115. A financial investment service is evaluating the list of domestic general stock funds so that it can make purchase recommendations to potential investors. The vice president for research has hired your group, the _____ Corporation, to study the financial characteristics of currently traded domestic general stock funds and gives you access to Special Data Set 1 of appendix D containing various characteristics from a sample of 194 such funds. In particular, the vice president is interested in a comparison of some features of these funds based on fee structure (no-load versus fee payment). As part of your analysis of the 107 no-load funds versus the 87 fee payment funds, you want to decide whether or not both the net asset value (in dollars) and the total year-to-date return (in percentage rates) appear to be approximately normally distributed. You accomplish this by

**DATA FILE**
MUTUAL

(a) evaluating the actual versus theoretical properties.
(b) constructing a normal probability plot.
(c) stating your conclusions based on (a) and (b).

*Note*: Additional team projects can be found at the following World Wide Web address:
**http://www.prenhall.com/berenson**

## THE SPRINGVILLE HERALD CASE

The production department of the newspaper has embarked on a quality improvement effort and has chosen as its first project an issue that relates to the blackness of the newspaper print. Each day a determination needs to be made concerning how "black" the newspaper is printed. This is measured on a standard scale in which the target value is 1.0. Data collected over the past year indicates that the blackness is normally distributed with an average of 1.005 and a standard deviation of 0.10.

## Exercises

**8.1** Each day, one spot on the first newspaper printed is chosen and the blackness of the spot is measured. Suppose the blackness of the newspaper is considered acceptable if the blackness of the spot is between 0.95 and 1.05. Assuming that the distribution has not changed from what it has been in the past year, what is the probability that the blackness of the spot is

(a) less than 1.0?

(c) between 1.0 and 1.05?

(b) between .95 and 1.0?

(d) less than .95 or greater than 1.05?

**8.2** If the objective of the production team is to reduce the probability that the blackness is below 0.95 or above 1.05, would it be better off focusing on process improvement that lowers the blackness to the target value of 1.0 or on process improvement that reduces the standard deviation to 0.075? Explain.

## References

1. Cochran, W. G., *Sampling Techniques*, 3d ed. (New York: Wiley, 1977).
2. Gunter, B., "Q-Q Plots," *Quality Progress* (February 1994), 81–86.
3. Marascuilo, L. A., and M. McSweeney, *Nonparametric and Distribution-Free Methods for the Social Sciences* (Monterey, CA: Brooks/Cole, 1977).
4. Mendenhall, W., and T. Sincich, *Statistics for Engineering and the Sciences*, 4th ed. (Englewood Cliffs, NJ: Prentice Hall, 1995).
5. *Microsoft Excel 97* (Redmond, WA: Microsoft Corp., 1997).
6. *Minitab for Windows Version 12* (State College, PA: Minitab, Inc., 1998).
7. Ramsey, P. P., and P. H. Ramsey, "Simple Tests of Normality in Small Samples," *Journal of Quality Technology* 22 (1990): 299–309.
8. Sievers, G. L., "Probability Plotting." In *Encyclopedia of Statistical Sciences*, vol. 7, edited by S. Kotz and N. L. Johnson, (New York: Wiley, 1986), 232–237.

## ❖ APPENDIX 8.1 USING MICROSOFT EXCEL WITH CONTINUOUS PROBABILITY DISTRIBUTIONS

### COMMENT: PHStat Add-In Users

If Microsoft Excel is not running, click the **PHStat** add-in icon. If Microsoft Excel is running select **File | Open**. Select the **PHStat** add-in file PHSA.XLA. Click the **Open** button.

To obtain probabilities from the normal distribution, select **PHStat | Probability Distributions | Normal**. In the Arithmetic Mean edit box enter a value for $\mu$. In the Standard Deviation edit box, enter a value for $\sigma$. To obtain an area below an $X$ value, select the Probability for: $X <$ check box and enter an $X$ value in the edit box. To obtain an area between two $X$ values, select the Probability for range: edit boxes, and enter values in their edit boxes. To obtain the $X$ value corresponding to a cumulative percentage below $X$, select the $X$ for **Cumulative Percentage** check box and enter a value (in percent) in the edit box. Click the **OK** button.

To obtain a normal probability plot, select **PHStat | Probability Distributions | Normal Probability Plot**. Enter the cell range in the Variable Cell Range edit box. Click the **OK** button.

To obtain a probability from the exponential probability distribution, select **PHStat | Probability Distributions | Exponential**. In the Mean edit box enter a value for $\lambda$. In the $X$ value edit box enter a value for $X$. Click the **OK** button.

## Using Microsoft Excel to Obtain Normal Probabilities

In section 8.1, we studied the bell-shaped normal distribution and examined numerous applications in which we computed the probability or area under the normal curve. Rather than using equations (8.2) and (8.3) and Table E.2(a) or E.2(b) to compute these probabilities, we can use several Microsoft Excel functions. There are five functions that are useful for obtaining probabilities under the normal curve.

The first function related to the normal distribution is the STANDARDIZE function, which computes the $Z$ value for given values of $X$, $\mu$, and $\sigma$. The format of this function is

$$=\text{STANDARDIZE}(X, \mu, \sigma)$$

Referring to the example in section 8.1 in which $\mu = 75$ and $\sigma = 6$, to find the $Z$ value corresponding to $X = 81$, enter =STANDARDIZE (81,75,6) in a cell, and the value computed is 1.0.

The second function related to the normal distribution is the NORMSDIST function, which computes the area or probability less than a given $Z$ value. The format of this function is

$$=\text{NORMSDIST}(Z)$$

Referring to the example in section 8.1 in which $\mu = 75$ and $\sigma = 6$, to find the area below a $Z$ value of 1.0, enter =NORMSDIST(1.0) in a cell and the value computed is .8413.

The third function related to the normal distribution is the NORMSINV function, which computes the $Z$ value corresponding to a given cumulative area under the normal curve. The format of this function is

$$=\text{NORMSINV}(\text{Probability} < X)$$

where Probability $< X =$ the area under the curve less than $X$.

To find the $Z$ value corresponding to a cumulative area of .025, enter =NORMSINV(.025) in a cell and the value computed is $-1.96$.

The fourth function related to the normal distribution is the NORMDIST function, which computes the area or probability less than a given $X$ value. The format of this function is

$$=\text{NORMDIST}(X, \mu, \sigma, \text{True})$$

Referring to the example in section 8.1 in which $\mu = 75$ and $\sigma = 6$, to find the area below an $X$ value of 81, enter =NORMDIST(81,75,6,True) in a cell and the value computed is .8413.

The fifth function related to the normal distribution is the NORMINV function, which computes the $X$ value corresponding to a given cumulative area under the normal curve. The format of this function is

$$=\text{NORMINV}(\text{Probability} < X, \mu, \sigma)$$

where Probability $< X =$ the area under the curve less than $X$.

Referring to the example in section 8.1 in which $\mu = 75$ and $\sigma = 6$, to find the $X$ value corresponding to a cumulative area of .025, enter =NORMINV(.025,75,6) in a cell, and the value computed is 63.24.

## Using Microsoft Excel to Obtain a Normal Probability Plot

In section 8.2, we developed the normal probability plot to evaluate whether a given set of data was normally distributed. Although current versions of Microsoft Excel do not have the normal probability plot included as part of the Data Analysis tool, we can use Excel functions and the Chart Wizard to develop a normal probability plot.

Figure 8.15 on page 323 illustrates a normal probability plot of the net asset values of 194 domestic general stock funds. To obtain this normal probability plot, open the MUTUAL.XLS workbook and make Data the active sheet. First, be sure that the net asset value data have been sorted in ascending order. Insert a new worksheet and rename it Calculations. Enter the column headings in row 1 with Rank in column A, Ordered Value in column B, Z value in column C. and Net Asset Value in column 4.

To enter the ranks in column A, enter **1** in cell A2 and with A2 as the active cell, select **Edit | Fill | Series**. In the Series dialog box that appears, select the **Columns** and **Linear** option buttons. Enter **194** in the **Stop Value** edit box. Click the **OK** button. The ranks from 1 to 194 are now displayed in cells A2:A195 respectively.

The proportions $1/(n + 1)$, $2/(n + 1)$, . . . , $n/(n + 1)$ corresponding to each ordered value are obtained in column B by entering **=A2/195** in cell B2 and copying the formula through cell B195. Obtain the inverse normal values by using the NORMSINV function. Enter **=NORMSINV(B2)** in cell C2 and copy this formula through cell C195. Finally, copy the sorted net asset value data from the data sheet by entering **=DATA!:C2** in cell D2 and copying this formula through cell D195.

Now that the inverse normal values have been calculated for each net asset value, we can use Microsoft Excel's Chart Wizard (see appendix 3.1) to obtain the normal probability plot depicted in Figure 8.15. After selecting **Insert | Chart**, in the four dialog boxes for the Chart Wizard enter the following:

**DIALOG BOX 1** Select the **Standard Types** tab and then select *XY* **(Scatter)** from the Chart type: list box. Select the first choice Chart subtypes choice, the one described as "Scatter, Compares pairs of values." Click the **Next** button.

**DIALOG BOX 2** Select the **Data Range** tab and enter **Calculations!C2:D195** in the Data Range edit box. Select the **Columns** option button in the **Series in:** group. Select the **Series** tab. Enter **=Calculations!C2:C195** in the *X* **Values:** edit box. Click the **Next** button.

**DIALOG BOX 3** Select the **Titles** tab. Enter **Normal Probability Plot** in the Chart title: edit box. Enter **Z** in the Value (*X*) axis: edit box, and enter **Net Asset Value** in the Value (*Y*) axis: edit box. Select the **Axes** tab. Select both the (*X*) **axis** and (*Y*) **axis** check boxes. Select the **Gridlines** tab. Deselect all check boxes. Select the **Legend** tab. Deselect the **Show legend** check box. Select the **Data labels** tab. Select the **None** option button under the Data labels heading. Click the **Next** button.

**DIALOG BOX 4** In the fourth dialog box, select the **As new sheet:** option button and enter **Normal Plot** in the edit box to the right of the option button. Click the **Finish** button.

You will notice that the tick marks for the *Y* axis (the Net Asset Value variable) are placed midway across the chart along the vertical line that corresponds to the *X* axis value 0. To move the *Y* axis tick marks to the left edge of the chart, double-click those tick marks. In the Format Axis dialog box that appears, select the **Patterns** tab and then select the **Low** option button for the Tick mark labels group. Click the **OK** button. Double-click on the *X* axis. Select the **Scale** tab. Select the Value (*Y*) axis crosses at maximum value. Click the **OK** button. The chart will now be similar to the one shown in Figure 8.15.

## Using Microsoft Excel to Obtain Exponential Probabilities

Rather than using equation (8.5) to model the length of time between arrivals and compute probabilities from the exponential distribution, we can use the appropriate Microsoft Excel function.

The EXPONDIST function can be used to compute the probability of obtaining a value that is less than $X$ in the exponential distribution. The format of this function is

$$\text{EXPONDIST}(X, \lambda, \text{True})$$

where $\lambda$ = the mean of the exponential distribution.

To illustrate this function, suppose we return to the ATM customer-arrival application. In that example, with an arrival rate of 20 per hour, given that a customer has just arrived, we wanted to determine the probability that the next customer would arrive within 6 minutes (or, 0.1 hour). For this example we have $\lambda = 20$ and $X = 0.1$ and, on page 325, we computed this probability to be .8647. To obtain this result using Excel, we would enter the formula =EXPONDIST(.1,20,True) in a cell. The results are also displayed in Figure 8.16 on page 325.

## ❖ APPENDIX 8.2  USING MINITAB WITH CONTINUOUS PROBABILITY DISTRIBUTIONS

### Obtaining Normal Probabilities

In section 8.1, we studied the bell-shaped normal distribution and examined numerous applications in which we computed the probability or area under the normal curve. Rather than using equations (8.2) and (8.3) and Table E.2(a) or E.2(b) to compute these probabilities, we can use Minitab. Referring to the example in section 8.1 in which $\mu = 75$ and $\sigma = 6$, to find the area between 69 and 81, we separately find the area below an $X$ value of 81, and also below an $X$ value of 69. To do so, first enter 81 and 69 in the first two rows in column C1. Select **Calc | Probability Distributions | Normal**. Select **Cumulative probability**. Enter **75** in the **Mean** edit box and **6** in the **Standard Deviation** edit box. Enter **C1** in the Input column edit box. Click the **OK** button. You will obtain the output displayed in Panel A of Figure 8.12 on page 312.

To obtain the $Z$ value corresponding to a cumulative area of .10, enter **.10** in row 1 of column C2. Select **Calc | Probability Distributions | Normal**. Select **Inverse Cumulative probability**. Enter **75** in the **Mean** edit box and **6** in the **Standard Deviation** edit box. Enter **C2** in the Input column edit box. Click the **OK** button. You will obtain the output displayed in Panel B of Figure 8.12.

### Using Minitab to Obtain a Normal Probability Plot

In section 8.2, we developed the normal probability plot to evaluate whether a given set of data was normally distributed. To obtain a normal probability plot in Minitab for the mutual fund data, open the file titled, **MUTUAL.MTP**. Select **Graph | Probability Plot**. In the Distribution drop-down list box, select **Normal**. In the **Variables:** edit box, enter **NAV** (the net asset value variable name). Click the **OK** button. Note that the normal probability plot is different from the one described in section 8.2. Minitab provides a plot in which the variable is plotted on the $X$ axis and the cumulative percentage is plotted on the $Y$ axis on a special scale so that if the variable is normally distributed the data will plot along a straight line.

### Using Minitab to Obtain Exponential Probabilities

Rather than using equation (8.5) on page 325 to model the length of time between arrivals and compute probabilities from the exponential distribution, we can use Minitab. Suppose we return to the ATM customer-arrival application. In that example, we have $\lambda = 20$ and $X = 0.1$. To obtain this result using Minitab, enter **.1** in column C1. Select **Calc | Probability Distributions | Exponential**. Select **Cumulative probability**. In the **Mean** edit box we enter $1/\lambda = 1/20 = $ **.05**. Enter **C1** in the Input column edit box. Click the **OK** button. You will obtain the output displayed in Figure 8.17 on page 326.

# 9

# Sampling Distributions

# CHAPTER OBJECTIVES

✓ *To develop the concept of a sampling distribution for both numerical and categorical variables*
✓ *To examine the central limit theorem for cases in which a population is either normally or not normally distributed*
✓ *To provide the foundation for statistical inference*

## Introduction

A major goal of data analysis is to use statistics such as the sample mean and the sample proportion to estimate the corresponding parameters in the respective populations. We should realize that when making a statistical inference, we are concerned with drawing conclusions about a population, not about a sample. For example, a political pollster is interested in the sample results only as a way of estimating the actual proportion of the votes that each candidate will receive from the population of voters. Likewise, an auditor, in selecting a sample of vouchers, is interested only in using the sample mean for estimating the population average amount.

In practice, a single sample of a predetermined size is selected at random from the population. The items that are to be included in the sample are determined through the use of a random number generator, such as a table of random numbers (see section 2.5 and Table E.1), or by using random number functions in Microsoft Excel or Minitab (see appendices 2.1 and 2.2).

Hypothetically, to use the sample statistic to estimate the population parameter, we should examine *every* possible sample that could occur. If this selection of all possible samples were actually done, the distribution of the results would be referred to as a **sampling distribution**.

## ◆ USING STATISTICS: *Cereal-Fill Packaging Process*

In a food processing plant, each day thousands of boxes of cereal are filled. If the machinery is not working properly, there will be either boxes that are underfilled or boxes that are overfilled. Because it would be too time-consuming, costly, and inefficient to monitor and weigh every single box, the operations manager must plan on taking a sample of boxes and making a decision regarding the likelihood that the cereal-filling process is in control and working properly. Each time a sample of boxes is selected and the individual boxes are weighed, a decision needs to be made as to the likelihood that such a sample with mean $\overline{X}$ could have been randomly drawn from a population whose true mean $\mu$ is 368 grams. Based on this assessment, a decision will be made as to whether to keep the production process going or shut down the equipment and call in a mechanic.

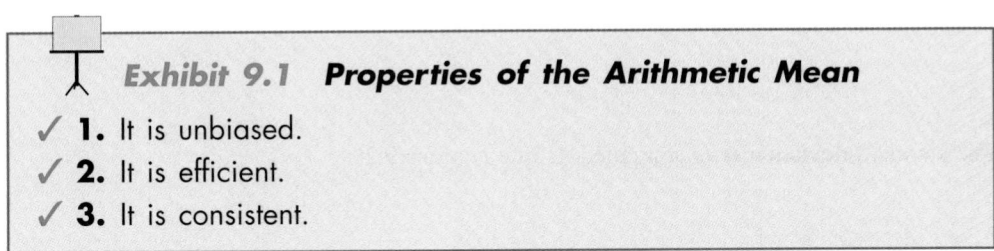

# 9.1 ◆ SAMPLING DISTRIBUTION OF THE MEAN

In chapter 4 we discussed several measures of central tendency. Undoubtedly, the most widely used measure of central tendency is the arithmetic mean. It is also the best measure if the population can be assumed to be normally distributed.

## Properties of the Arithmetic Mean

When computed from a set of normally distributed data, the arithmetic mean contains several important mathematical properties.

> ⊤ **Exhibit 9.1  Properties of the Arithmetic Mean**
>
> ✓ **1.** It is unbiased.
> ✓ **2.** It is efficient.
> ✓ **3.** It is consistent.

The first property, **unbiasedness**, involves the fact that the average of all the possible sample means (of a given sample size $n$) will be equal to the population mean $\mu$. This property can be demonstrated empirically by the following example: Suppose that each of the four typists making up a population of secretarial support service in a company is asked to type the same page of a manuscript. The number of errors made by each typist is presented in Table 9.1 and the population distribution is shown in Figure 9.1.

**Table 9.1**  *Listing of number of errors made by each of four typists*

| TYPIST | NUMBER OF ERRORS |
|---|---|
| Ann | $X_1 = 3$ |
| Bob | $X_2 = 2$ |
| Carla | $X_3 = 1$ |
| Dave | $X_4 = 4$ |

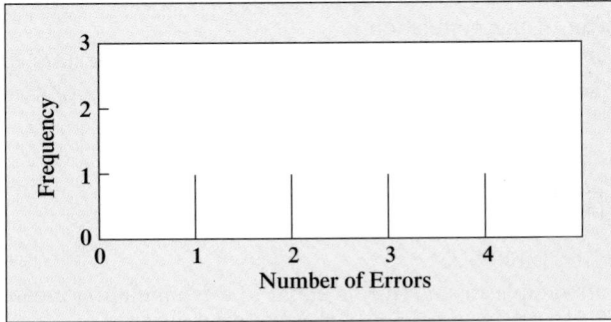

**FIGURE 9.1**    Number of errors made by population of four typists

You may recall from section 4.4 that when the data from a population are available, the mean is computed as illustrated in equation (9.1):

## Population Mean

The population mean $\mu$ is equal to the sum of the $X$ values in the population divided by the population size $N$.

$$\mu = \frac{\sum_{i=1}^{N} X_i}{N} \qquad (9.1)$$

The standard deviation $\sigma$ is computed as in equation (9.2):

## Population Standard Deviation

$$\sigma = \sqrt{\frac{\sum_{i=1}^{N} (X_i - \mu)^2}{N}} \qquad (9.2)$$

Thus, for the data of Table 9.1,

$$\mu = \frac{3 + 2 + 1 + 4}{4} = 2.5 \text{ errors}$$

and

$$\sigma = \sqrt{\frac{(3 - 2.5)^2 + (2 - 2.5)^2 + (1 - 2.5)^2 + (4 - 2.5)^2}{4}} = 1.12 \text{ errors}$$

If samples of two typists are selected *with* replacement from this population, there are 16 possible samples that are selected ($N^n = 4^2 = 16$). These possible sample outcomes are shown in Table 9.2. If all these 16 sample means are averaged, the mean of these values ($\mu_{\bar{x}}$) is equal to 2.5, which is the mean of the population $\mu$.

On the other hand, if sampling was being done *without* replacement, using the *rule of combinations* from section 6.2, we note that there would be six possible samples of two typists:

$$\frac{N!}{n!(N - n)!} = \frac{4!}{2!2!} = 6$$

These six possible samples are listed in Table 9.3.

In this case, also, the average of all sample means ($\mu_{\bar{x}}$) is equal to the population mean, 2.5. Therefore, the sample arithmetic mean is an unbiased estimator of the population mean. This tells us that although we do not know how close the average of any particular sample

**Table 9.2** *All sixteen samples of n = 2 typists from population of N = 4 typists when sampling with replacement*

| SAMPLE | TYPISTS | SAMPLE OUTCOMES | SAMPLE MEAN $\overline{X}_i$ |
|--------|---------|-----------------|------------------------------|
| 1 | Ann, Ann | 3, 3 | $\overline{X}_1 = 3$ |
| 2 | Ann, Bob | 3, 2 | $\overline{X}_2 = 2.5$ |
| 3 | Ann, Carla | 3, 1 | $\overline{X}_3 = 2$ |
| 4 | Ann, Dave | 3, 4 | $\overline{X}_4 = 3.5$ |
| 5 | Bob, Ann | 2, 3 | $\overline{X}_5 = 2.5$ |
| 6 | Bob, Bob | 2, 2 | $\overline{X}_6 = 2$ |
| 7 | Bob, Carla | 2, 1 | $\overline{X}_7 = 1.5$ |
| 8 | Bob, Dave | 2, 4 | $\overline{X}_8 = 3$ |
| 9 | Carla, Ann | 1, 3 | $\overline{X}_9 = 2$ |
| 10 | Carla, Bob | 1, 2 | $\overline{X}_{10} = 1.5$ |
| 11 | Carla, Carla | 1, 1 | $\overline{X}_{11} = 1$ |
| 12 | Carla, Dave | 1, 4 | $\overline{X}_{12} = 2.5$ |
| 13 | Dave, Ann | 4, 3 | $\overline{X}_{13} = 3.5$ |
| 14 | Dave, Bob | 4, 2 | $\overline{X}_{14} = 3$ |
| 15 | Dave, Carla | 4, 1 | $\overline{X}_{15} = 2.5$ |
| 16 | Dave, Dave | 4, 4 | $\overline{X}_{16} = 4$ |
| | | | $\mu_{\overline{x}} = 2.5$ |

**Table 9.3** *All six possible samples of n = 2 typists from population of N = 4 typists when sampling without replacement*

| SAMPLE | TYPISTS | SAMPLE OUTCOMES | SAMPLE MEAN $\overline{X}_i$ |
|--------|---------|-----------------|------------------------------|
| 1 | Ann, Bob | 3, 2 | $\overline{X}_1 = 2.5$ |
| 2 | Ann, Carla | 3, 1 | $\overline{X}_2 = 2$ |
| 3 | Ann, Dave | 3, 4 | $\overline{X}_3 = 3.5$ |
| 4 | Bob, Carla | 2, 1 | $\overline{X}_4 = 1.5$ |
| 5 | Bob, Dave | 2, 4 | $\overline{X}_5 = 3$ |
| 6 | Carla, Dave | 1, 4 | $\overline{X}_6 = 2.5$ |
| | | | $\mu_{\overline{x}} = 2.5$ |

selected comes to the population mean, we are at least assured that the average of all the possible sample means that could have been selected will be equal to the population mean.

The second property possessed by the mean, **efficiency**, refers to the precision of the sample statistic as an estimator of the population parameter. For distributions such as the normal, the arithmetic mean is considered more stable from sample to sample than are other measures of central tendency. For a sample of size *n*, the sample mean will, on average, come closer to the population mean than any other unbiased estimator, so that the sample mean is a better estimator of the population mean.

The third property, **consistency**, refers to the effect of the sample size on the usefulness of an estimator. As the sample size increases, the variation of the sample mean from the population mean becomes smaller so that the sample arithmetic mean becomes a better estimator of the population mean.

## Standard Error of the Mean

The fluctuation in the average number of typing errors that was obtained from all 16 possible samples when sampling *with* replacement is illustrated in Figure 9.2. In this small example, although we can observe a good deal of fluctuation in the sample mean—depending on which typists were selected—there is not nearly as much fluctuation as in the actual population itself. The fact that the sample means are less variable than the population data follows directly from the **law of large numbers**. A particular sample mean averages together all the values in the sample. A population may consist of individual outcomes that can take on a wide range of values from extremely small to extremely large. However, if an extreme value falls into the sample, although it will have an effect on the mean, the effect will be reduced because it is being averaged in with all the other values in the sample. As the sample size increases, the effect of a single extreme value gets even smaller because it is being averaged with more observations.

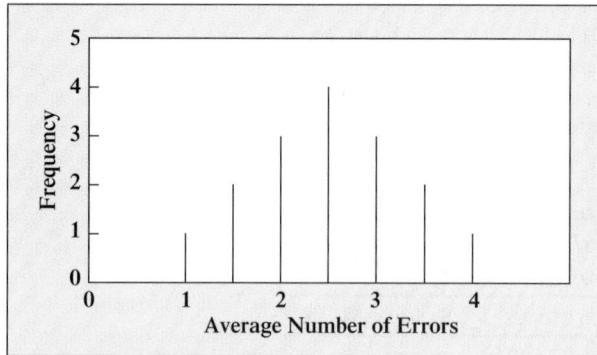

**FIGURE 9.2**
Sampling distribution of average number of errors based on all possible samples containing two typists
*Source: Data are from Table 9.2.*

How the arithmetic mean fluctuates from sample to sample is expressed statistically by the value of the standard deviation of all possible sample means. This measure of variability in the mean from sample to sample is referred to as the **standard error of the mean**, $\sigma_{\bar{x}}$. When sampling *with* replacement, we define the standard error of the mean as in equation (9.3):

### Standard Error of the Mean

The standard error of the mean $\sigma_{\bar{x}}$ is equal to the standard deviation in the population $\sigma$ divided by the square root of the sample size *n*.

$$\sigma_{\bar{x}} = \frac{\sigma}{\sqrt{n}} \tag{9.3}$$

Therefore, as the sample size increases, the standard error of the mean decreases by a factor equal to the square root of the sample size. This relationship between the standard error of the mean and the sample size is further examined in chapter 10 when we address the issue of sample size determination.

## Example 9.1    *Computing the Standard Error of the Mean*

Suppose we consider the various withdrawal transactions made from the ATM (automatic teller machine) of a particular bank over a 1-year period to represent a population and, over the year, 36,500 such transactions are made. If this population's standard deviation of the amount of money withdrawn per transaction is $50, what is the standard error of the mean if samples of size 400 are selected *with* replacement?

### SOLUTION

From equation (9.3) we have $\sigma_{\bar{x}} = \dfrac{\sigma}{\sqrt{n}}$. Here, $\sigma = \$50$ and $n = 400$ so that

$$\sigma_{\bar{x}} = \frac{\sigma}{\sqrt{n}} = \frac{\$50}{\sqrt{400}} = \frac{\$50}{20} = \$2.50$$

Note how much smaller the spread in the means based on samples of size 400 is compared with the spread in the original 36,500 ATM withdrawal transactions.

Finally, we should note that when we sample *with* replacement from a finite population, the size of the population is not important. In this example, the population size is $N = 36,500$ transactions. However, this value is not part of equation (9.3).

## Sampling from Normally Distributed Populations

Now that we have introduced the idea of a sampling distribution and defined the standard error of the mean, we need to explore the question of what distribution the sample mean $\bar{X}$ will follow if we compute the average from all possible samples, each of size $n$. It can be shown that if we sample *with* replacement from a population that is normally distributed with mean $\mu$ and standard deviation $\sigma$, the **sampling distribution of the mean** will also be normally distributed for *any size n* with mean $\mu_{\bar{x}} = \mu$ and have a standard error of the mean $\sigma_{\bar{x}}$.

In the most elementary case, if we draw samples of size $n = 1$, each possible sample mean is a single observation from the population because

$$\bar{X} = \frac{\displaystyle\sum_{i=1}^{n} X_i}{n} = \frac{X_i}{1} = X_i$$

If we know that the population is normally distributed with mean $\mu$ and standard deviation $\sigma$, then the sampling distribution of $\bar{X}$ for samples of $n = 1$ must also follow the normal distribution with mean $\mu_{\bar{x}} = \mu$ and standard error of the mean $\sigma_{\bar{x}} = \sigma/\sqrt{1} = \sigma$. In addition, we note that as the sample size increases, the sampling distribution of the mean still follows a normal distribution with mean $\mu_{\bar{x}} = \mu$. However, as the sample size increases, the standard error of the mean decreases, so that a larger proportion of sample means are closer to the population mean. This can be observed by referring to Figure 9.3 where 500

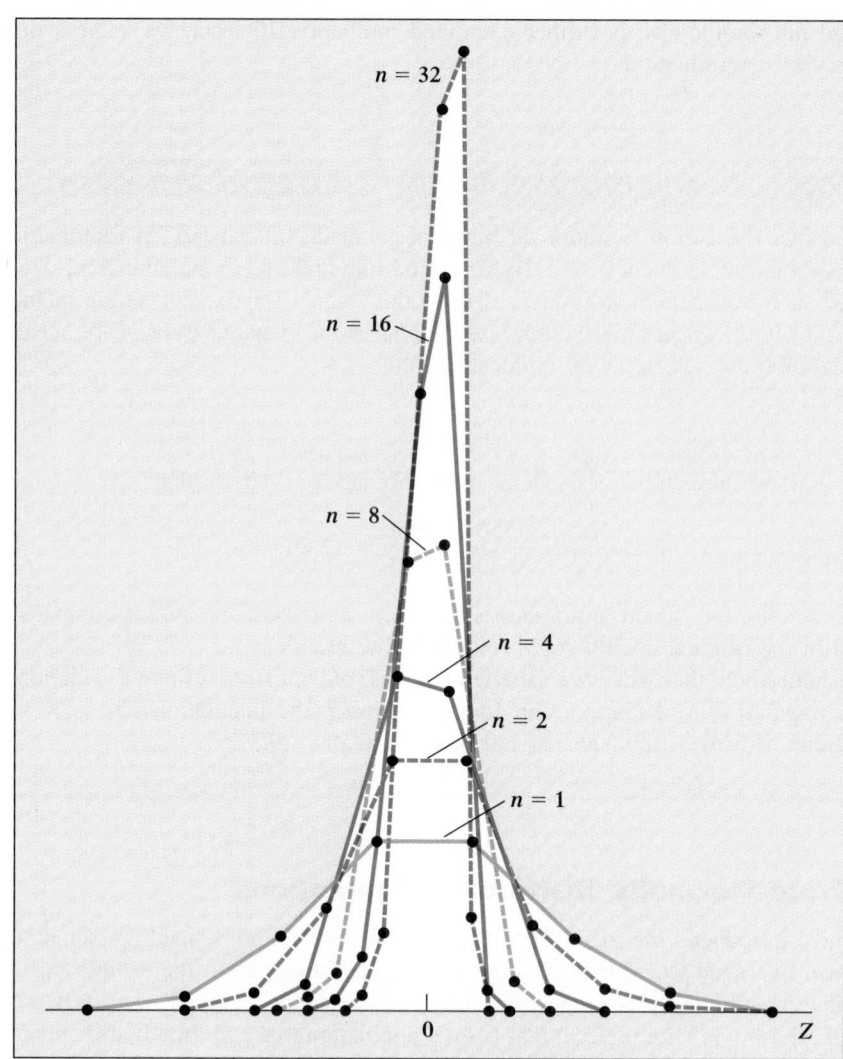

*FIGURE 9.3* Sampling distributions of the mean from 500 samples of sizes
$n$ = 1, 2, 4, 8, 16, and 32 selected from a normal population

[1]We must remember that
"only" 500 samples out of
an infinite number of samples have been selected, so
that the sampling distributions shown are only
approximations of the true
distributions.

samples of sizes 1, 2, 4, 8, 16, and 32 were randomly selected from a normally distributed
population. We can see clearly from the polygons in Figure 9.3 that although the sampling
distribution of the mean is approximately[1] normal for each sample size, the sample means
are distributed more tightly around the population mean as the sample size is increased.

For a deeper insight into the concept of the sampling distribution of the mean let us reexamine the Using Statistics scenario described on page 336. Suppose the packaging equipment in a manufacturing process that is filling 368-gram (that is, 13-ounce) boxes of cereal
is set so that the amount of cereal in a box is normally distributed with a mean of 368
grams. From past experience the population standard deviation for this filling process is
known to be 15 grams.

If a sample of 25 boxes is randomly selected from the many thousands that are filled in
a day and the average weight is computed for this sample, what type of result could be

expected? For example, do you think that the sample mean would be 368 grams? 200 grams? 365 grams?

The sample acts as a miniature representation of the population so that if the values in the population are normally distributed, the values in the sample should be approximately normally distributed. Thus, if the population mean is 368 grams, the sample mean has a good chance of being close to 368 grams.

To explore this even further, how can we determine the probability that the sample of 25 boxes will have a mean below 365 grams? We know from our study of the normal distribution (section 8.1) that the area below any value $X$ can be found by converting to standardized $Z$ units and finding the appropriate value in the table of the normal distribution, Table E.2(b).

## Computing the Standardized Z Value

$$Z = \frac{X - \mu}{\sigma} \qquad (9.4)$$

In the examples in section 8.1 we studied how any single value $X$ deviates from the mean. Now, in the cereal-fill example, the value involved is a sample mean, $\overline{X}$, and we wish to determine the likelihood of obtaining a sample mean below 365. Thus, by substituting $\overline{X}$ for $X$, $\mu_{\overline{x}}$ for $\mu$, and $\sigma_{\overline{x}}$ for $\sigma$, we have the following:

## Finding Z for the Sampling Distribution of the Mean

The $Z$ value is equal to the difference between the sample mean $\overline{X}$ and the population mean $\mu$, divided by the standard error of the mean $\sigma_{\overline{x}}$.

$$Z = \frac{\overline{X} - \mu_{\overline{x}}}{\sigma_{\overline{x}}} = \frac{\overline{X} - \mu}{\frac{\sigma}{\sqrt{n}}} \qquad (9.5)$$

Note that on the basis of the property of *unbiasedness*, it is always true that $\mu_{\overline{x}} = \mu$. To find the area below 365 grams (Figure 9.4), we have from equation 9.5

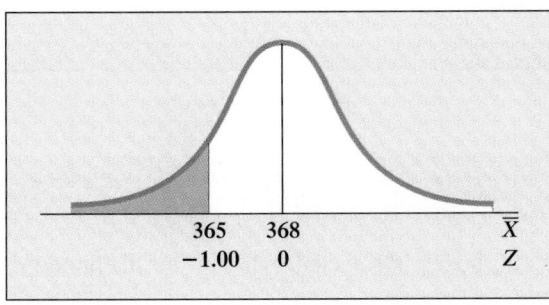

**FIGURE 9.4**
Diagram of sampling distribution of the mean needed to find area below 365 grams

$$Z = \frac{\overline{X} - \mu}{\frac{\sigma}{\sqrt{n}}} = \frac{365 - 368}{\frac{15}{\sqrt{25}}} = \frac{-3}{3} = -1.00$$

Looking up $-1.00$ in Table E.2(b), we find an area of .1587. Therefore, 15.87% of all the possible samples of size 25 would have a sample mean below 365 grams.

We must realize that this is not the same as saying that a certain percentage of *individual* boxes will have less than 365 grams of cereal. In fact, that percentage can be computed from equation (9.4) as follows:

$$Z = \frac{X - \mu}{\sigma} = \frac{365 - 368}{15} = \frac{-3}{15} = -0.20$$

The area corresponding to $Z = -0.20$ in Table E.2(b) is .4207. Therefore, 42.07% of the *individual* boxes are expected to contain less than 365 grams. Comparing these results, we may observe that many more *individual boxes* than *sample means* will be below 365 grams. This result can be explained by the fact that each sample consists of 25 different values, some small and some large. The averaging process dilutes the importance of any individual value, particularly when the sample size is large. Thus, the chance that the mean of a sample of 25 will be far away from the population mean is less than the chance that a *single individual* value will be.

Our results are affected by using a different sample size as observed in Examples 9.2 and 9.3.

<hr>

## Example 9.2 *The Effect of Sample Size n on the Computation of $\sigma_{\overline{x}}$*

How is the standard error of the mean affected by increasing the sample size from 25 to 100 boxes?

### SOLUTION

If *n* is 100 boxes, we have the following:

$$\sigma_{\overline{x}} = \frac{\sigma}{\sqrt{n}} = \frac{15}{\sqrt{100}} = \frac{15}{10} = 1.5$$

We observe that a fourfold increase in the sample size from 25 to 100 results in reducing the standard error of the mean by half—from 3 grams to 1.5 grams. This demonstrates that taking a larger sample results in less variability in the possible sample means from sample to sample.

<hr>

## Example 9.3 *The Effect of Sample Size n on the Clustering of Means in the Sampling Distribution*

In the cereal-fill example, if a sample of 100 boxes is selected, what is the likelihood of obtaining a sample mean below 365 grams?

## SOLUTION

Using equation (9.5), we have the following:

$$Z = \frac{\overline{X} - \mu}{\dfrac{\sigma}{\sqrt{n}}} = \frac{365 - 368}{\dfrac{15}{\sqrt{100}}} = \frac{-3}{1.5} = -2.00$$

From Table E.2(b), the area less than $Z = -2.00$ is .0228. Therefore, 2.28% of the samples of size 100 would be expected to have means below 365 grams, as compared with 15.87% for samples of size 25.

This important relationship between sample size $n$ and the variability in the sample means from sample to sample in the sampling distribution of the mean is further highlighted in Example 9.4.

## Example 9.4 *Computing the Standard Error of the Mean*

In Example 9.1 we considered the various withdrawal transactions made from the ATM (automatic teller machine) of a particular bank over a 1-year period to represent a population, and, over the year, 36,500 such transactions were made. This population's standard deviation of the amount of money withdrawn per transaction was $50. Using equation (9.3), based on samples of size 400 transactions selected *with* replacement, the standard error of the mean was computed to be

$$\sigma_{\overline{x}} = \frac{\sigma}{\sqrt{n}} = \frac{\$50}{\sqrt{400}} = \frac{\$50}{20} = \$2.50$$

Now suppose the sample size had been smaller. For example, suppose that samples of size $n = 100$ transactions were selected *with* replacement. Here

$$\sigma_{\overline{x}} = \frac{\sigma}{\sqrt{n}} = \frac{\$50}{\sqrt{100}} = \frac{\$50}{10} = \$5.00$$

so that when the sample size is smaller, the standard error is larger.

Sometimes we are more interested in finding out the interval within which a fixed proportion of the samples (means) fall. Analogously to section 8.1, we are determining a distance below and above the population mean containing a specific area of the normal curve. From equation (9.5), we have

$$Z_L = \frac{\overline{X}_L - \mu}{\dfrac{\sigma}{\sqrt{n}}}$$

where

$$Z_L = -Z$$

and

$$Z_U = \frac{\overline{X}_U - \mu}{\frac{\sigma}{\sqrt{n}}}$$

where

$$Z_U = +Z$$

Therefore, the lower value of $\overline{X}$ is

**Finding the Lower Value of $\overline{X}$**

$$\overline{X}_L = \mu - Z\frac{\sigma}{\sqrt{n}} \qquad\qquad (9.6)$$

and the upper value of $\overline{X}$ is

**Finding the Upper Value of $\overline{X}$**

$$\overline{X}_U = \mu + Z\frac{\sigma}{\sqrt{n}} \qquad\qquad (9.7)$$

This is observed in Example 9.5.

## Example 9.5  *Determining the Interval that Includes a Fixed Proportion of the Means*

For our cereal-fill example suppose we want to find an interval around the population mean that will include 95% of the sample means based on samples of 25 boxes.

### SOLUTION

The 95% is divided into two equal parts, half below the mean and half above the mean, as shown in the diagram on the next page. Because $\sigma = 15$ and $n = 25$, the value of $Z$ corresponding to an area of .0250 in the lower tail of the normal curve in Table E.2(b) is $-1.96$ and the value of $Z$ corresponding to a cumulative area of .975 (that is, .025 in the upper tail of the normal curve) in Table E.2(b) is $+1.96$. The lower and upper values of $\overline{X}$ are found using equations (9.6) and (9.7) as follows:

$$\overline{X}_L = 368 - (1.96)\frac{15}{\sqrt{25}} = 368 - 5.88 = 362.12$$

$$\overline{X}_U = 368 + (1.96)\frac{15}{\sqrt{25}} = 368 + 5.88 = 373.88$$

We conclude that 95% of all sample means based on samples of 25 boxes will fall between 362.12 and 373.88 grams.

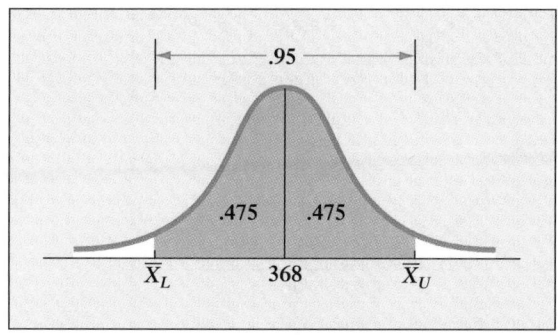

Diagram of sampling distribution of the mean needed to find upper and lower limits to include 95% of sample means

## Sampling from Nonnormally Distributed Populations

In this section, we have explored the sampling distribution of the mean for the case in which the population itself was normally distributed. However, in many instances, either we will know that the population is not normally distributed or it is unrealistic to assume a normal distribution. Thus, we need to examine the sampling distribution of the mean for populations that are not normally distributed. This issue brings us to an important theorem in statistics, the *central limit theorem.*

> **Central limit theorem:** As the sample size (number of observations in each sample) gets *large enough*, the sampling distribution of the mean can be approximated by the normal distribution. This is true regardless of the shape of the distribution of the individual values in the population.

What sample size is large enough? A great deal of statistical research has gone into this issue. As a general rule, statisticians have found that for many population distributions, once the sample size is at least 30, the sampling distribution of the mean will be approximately normal. However, we may be able to apply the central limit theorem for even smaller sample sizes if some knowledge of the population is available (e.g., if the distribution is symmetrical).[2]

The application of the central limit theorem to different populations can be illustrated by referring to Figures 9.5 to 9.7. Each of the depicted sampling distributions has been obtained by selecting 500 different samples from their respective population distributions. These samples were selected for varying sizes ($n$ = 2, 4, 8, 16, 32) from three different continuous distributions (normal, uniform, and exponential).

Figure 9.5 on page 348 illustrates the sampling distribution of the mean selected from a normal population. In the preceding section we stated that if the population is normally distributed, the sampling distribution of the mean is normally distributed, regardless of the sample size. An examination of the sampling distributions shown in Figure 9.5 gives empirical evidence for this statement. For each sample size studied the sampling distribution of the mean is *close* to the normal distribution that has been superimposed.

[2]*In some cases, sample sizes of 300 may not be enough to ensure normality.*

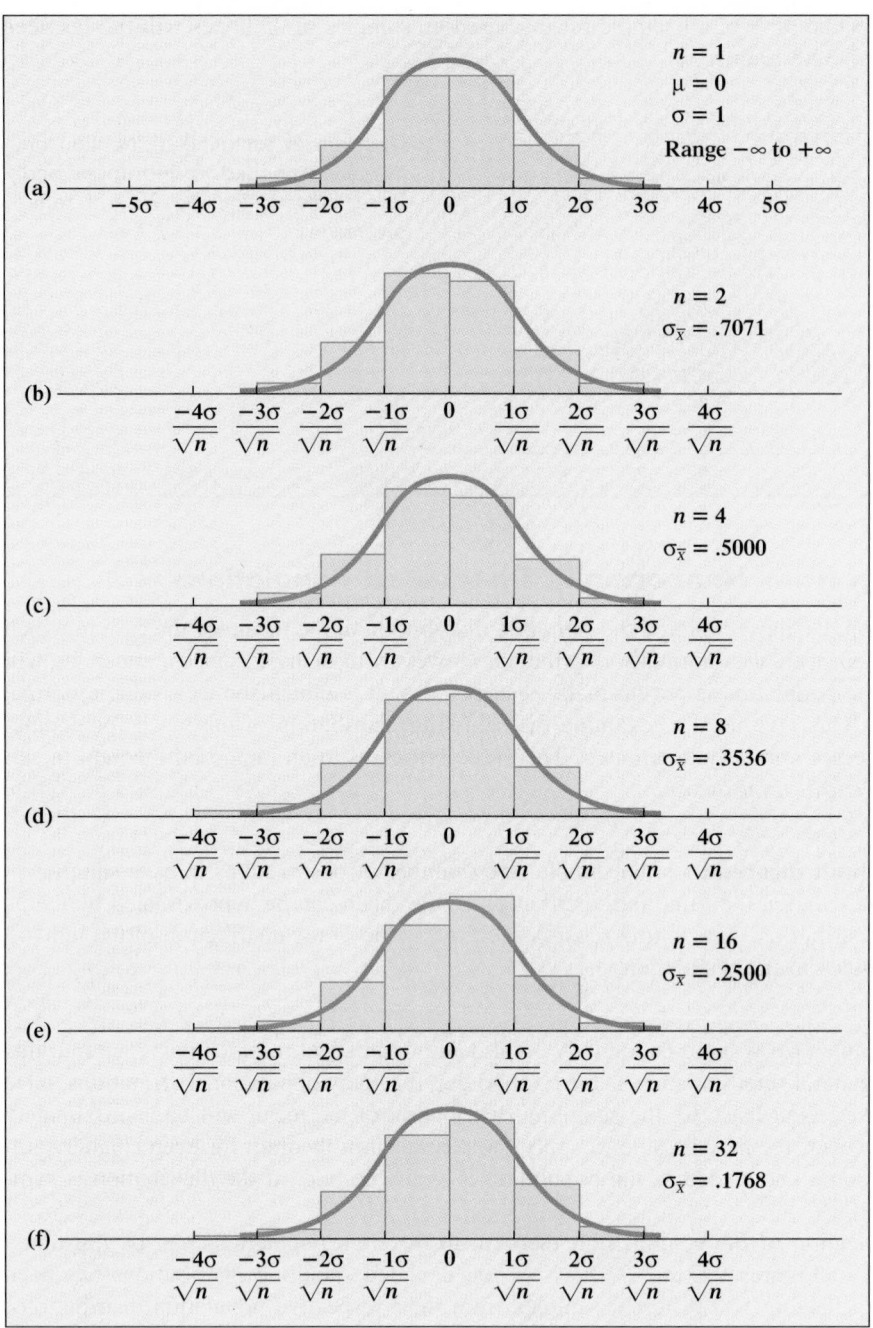

**FIGURE 9.5** Normal distribution and sampling distribution of the mean from 500 samples of sizes $n = 2, 4, 8, 16, 32$

Figure 9.6 presents the sampling distribution of the mean based on a population that follows a continuous uniform (or rectangular) distribution. As depicted in part (a), for samples of size $n = 1$, each value in the population is equally likely. However, when samples of only two are selected, there is a peaking or *central limiting* effect already working. In this case, we observe more values close to the mean of the population than far out at the

$$Z \cong \frac{p_s - p}{\sqrt{\dfrac{p(1-p)}{n}}}$$

$$= \frac{.30 - .40}{\sqrt{\dfrac{(.40)(.60)}{200}}} = \frac{-.10}{\sqrt{\dfrac{.24}{200}}} = \frac{-.10}{.0346}$$

$$= -2.89$$

Using Table E.2(b), the area under the normal curve up to $Z = -2.89$ is .0019. Therefore, the probability of obtaining a sample proportion of at most .30 is .0019—a highly unlikely event! That is, if the true proportion of successes in the population were .40, then less than one-fifth of 1% of the samples of size 200 are expected to have sample proportions of at most .30. This is depicted in the accompanying diagram.

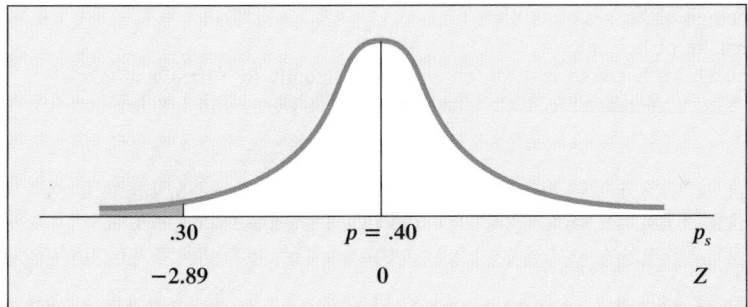

Diagram of the sampling distribution of the proportion to find area up to sample proportion of .30

## Problems for Section 9.2

### Learning the Basics

• **9.10** In a random sample of 64 people, 48 were classified as "successful."
   (a) Determine the sample proportion $p_s$ of "successful" people.
   (b) Determine the standard error of the sample proportion $\sigma_{p_s}$.

**9.11** A random sample of 50 households was selected for a telephone survey. The key question asked was, "Do you or any member of your household own a cellular telephone?" Of the 50 respondents, 15 said "yes" and 35 said "no."
   (a) Determine the sample proportion $p_s$ of households with cellular telephones.
   (b) Determine the standard error of the sample proportion $\sigma_{p_s}$.

**9.12** The following raw data represent the responses ("Y" for "yes" and "N" for "no") from a sample of 40 college students to the question "Do you currently own shares in any stocks?"

   N N Y N N Y N Y N Y N N Y N Y Y Y N N N Y

   N Y N N N N Y N N Y Y N N N Y N N Y N N

   (a) Determine the sample proportion $p_s$ of college students who own shares of stock.
   (b) Determine the standard error of the sample proportion $\sigma_{p_s}$.

## Applying the Concepts

*marginal handwritten notes:*

50.1 = $\alpha$ = Pop proportion = true % = P

(n=100)

$P_s = .55$

tricky myself

**9.13** Historically, 10% of a large shipment of machine parts are defective. If random samples of 400 parts are selected, what proportion of the samples will have
(a) between 9% and 10% defective parts?
(b) less than 8% defective parts?
(c) If a sample size of only 100 were selected, what would your answers have been in (a) and (b)?
(d) Which is more likely to occur—a percent defective above 13% in a sample of 100 or a percent defective above 10.5% in a sample of 400? Explain.

**9.14** A political pollster is conducting an analysis of sample results in order to make predictions on election night. Assuming a two-candidate election, if a specific candidate receives at least 55% of the vote in the sample, then that candidate will be forecast as the winner of the election. If a random sample of 100 voters is selected, what is the probability that a candidate will be forecast as the winner when
(a) the true percentage of her vote is 50.1%?
(b) the true percentage of her vote is 60%?
(c) the true percentage of her vote is 49% (and she will actually lose the election)?
(d) If the sample size is increased to 400, what will your answers be to (a), (b), and (c)? Discuss.

**9.15** Based on past data, 30% of the credit card purchases at a large department store are for amounts above $100. If random samples of 100 credit card purchases are selected,
(a) what proportion of samples are likely to have between 20% and 30% of the purchases over $100?
(b) within what symmetrical limits of the population percentage will 95% of the sample percentages fall?

**9.16** Suppose a marketing experiment is to be conducted in which students are to taste two different brands of soft drink. Their task is to correctly identify the brand tasted. Random samples of 200 students are selected and it is assumed that the students have no ability to distinguish between the two brands.
(*Hint*: If an individual has no ability to distinguish between the two soft drinks, then each one is equally likely to be selected.)
(a) What proportion of the samples will have between 50% and 60% of the identifications correct?
(b) Within what symmetrical limits of the population percentage will 90% of the sample percentages fall?
(c) What is the probability of obtaining a sample percentage of correct identifications in excess of 65%?
(d) Which is more likely to occur—more than 60% correct identifications in the sample of 200 or more than 55% correct identifications in a sample of 1,000? Explain.

**9.17** Historically, 93% of the deliveries of an overnight mail service arrive before 10:30 the following morning. If random samples of 500 deliveries are selected, what proportion of the samples will have
(a) between 93% and 97% of the deliveries arriving before 10:30 the following morning?
(b) more than 95% of the deliveries arriving before 10:30 the following morning?
(c) If samples of size 1,000 are selected, what will your answers be in (a) and (b)?
(d) Which is more likely to occur—more than 95% of the deliveries in a sample of 500 or less than 90% in a sample of 1,000 arriving before 10:30 the following morning? Explain.

## ◆ 9.3 SAMPLING FROM FINITE POPULATIONS

The central limit theorem and the standard errors of the mean and of the proportion are based on the premise that the samples selected are chosen *with* replacement. However, in virtually all survey research, sampling is conducted *without* replacement from populations that are of a finite size $N$. In these cases, particularly when the sample size $n$ is not *small* in comparison with the population size $N$ (i.e., more than 5% of the population is sampled) so that $n/N > .05$, a **finite population correction factor** (*fpc*) is used to define both the standard error of the mean and the standard error of the proportion. The finite population correction factor is expressed as

**Finite Population Correction Factor (*fpc*)**

$$fpc = \sqrt{\frac{N - n}{N - 1}} \qquad (9.11)$$

where

$$n = \text{sample size}$$
$$N = \text{population size}$$

Therefore, when dealing with means, we have

**Standard Error of the Mean for Finite Populations**

$$\sigma_{\bar{x}} = \frac{\sigma}{\sqrt{n}} \sqrt{\frac{N - n}{N - 1}} \qquad (9.12)$$

When we are referring to proportions, we have

**Standard Error of the Proportion for Finite Populations**

$$\sigma_{p_s} = \sqrt{\frac{p(1 - p)}{n}} \sqrt{\frac{N - n}{N - 1}} \qquad (9.13)$$

Examining the formula for the finite population correction factor [equation (9.11)], we see that the numerator is always smaller than the denominator, so the correction factor is less than 1. Because this finite population correction factor is multiplied by the standard error, the standard error becomes smaller when corrected. This means that we get more precise estimates because we are sampling a large segment of the population.

We illustrate the application of the finite population correction factor using two examples previously discussed in this chapter.

## Example 9.7  *Using the Finite Population Correction Factor with the Mean*

In the cereal-filling example on page 344, a sample of 25 cereal boxes was selected from a filling process. Suppose that 2,000 boxes (that is, the population) are filled on this particular day. Using the finite population correction factor, determine the probability of obtaining a sample whose mean is below 365 grams.

### SOLUTION

Using the finite population correction factor, we have

$$\sigma = 15, \ n = 25, \ N = 2,000$$

so that

$$\sigma_{\bar{x}} = \frac{\sigma}{\sqrt{n}}\sqrt{\frac{N-n}{N-1}}$$

$$= \frac{15}{\sqrt{25}}\sqrt{\frac{2,000-25}{2,000-1}}$$

$$= 3\sqrt{.988} = 2.982$$

The probability of obtaining a sample whose mean is between 365 and 368 grams is computed as follows.

$$Z = \frac{\bar{X} - \mu_{\bar{x}}}{\sigma_{\bar{x}}} = \frac{-3}{2.982} = -1.01$$

From Table E.2(b), the area below 365 grams is .1562.

It is evident in this example that the use of the finite population correction factor has a very small effect on the standard error of the mean and the subsequent area under the normal curve because the sample size (that is, $n = 25$ boxes) is only 1.25% of the population size (that is, $N = 2,000$ boxes).

## Example 9.8  *Using the Finite Population Correction Factor with the Proportion*

In Example 9.6 on page 354, concerning multiple banking accounts, suppose there are a total of 1,000 different depositors at the bank. Using the finite population correction factor, determine the probability of obtaining a sample whose proportion is less than .30.

### SOLUTION

With the use of the finite population correction factor, the previous sample of size 200 out of this finite population results in the following.

$$\sigma_{p_s} = \sqrt{\frac{p(1-p)}{n}}\sqrt{\frac{N-n}{N-1}}$$

$$= \sqrt{\frac{(.40)(.60)}{200}}\sqrt{\frac{1,000-200}{1,000-1}}$$

$$= \sqrt{\frac{.24}{200}}\sqrt{\frac{800}{999}} = \sqrt{.0012}\sqrt{.801}$$

$$= (.0346)(.895) = .031$$

With $\sigma_{p_s} = .031$ as the standard error of the sample proportion, from equation (9.10) we have, $Z = -.10/.031 = -3.23$. From Table E.2(b), the appropriate area below .30 is .00062. In this example, the use of the finite population correction factor has a moderate effect on the standard error of the proportion and on the area under the normal curve because the sample size is 20% (i.e., $n/N = .20$) of the population.

## Problems for Section 9.3

### Learning the Basics

• **9.18** Given that $N = 80$ and $n = 10$ and the sample is obtained *without* replacement, determine the finite population correction factor.

**9.19** Which of the following finite population factors will have a greater effect in reducing the standard error—one based on a sample of size 100 selected *without* replacement from a population of size 400 or one based on a sample of size 200 selected *without* replacement from a population of size 900? Explain.

**9.20** Given that $N = 60$ and $n = 20$ and the sample is obtained *with* replacement, should the finite population correction factor be used? Explain.

### Applying the Concepts

• **9.21** The diameter of Ping-Pong balls manufactured at a large factory is expected to be approximately normally distributed with a mean of 1.30 inches and a standard deviation of 0.04 inch. If many random samples of 16 Ping-Pong balls are selected from a population of 200 Ping-Pong balls *without* replacement, what proportion of the sample means would be between 1.31 and 1.33 inches?

**9.22** The amount of time a bank teller spends with each customer has a population mean $\mu = 3.10$ minutes and standard deviation $\sigma = 0.40$ minute. If a random sample of 16 customers is selected *without* replacement from a population of 500 customers,
  (a) what is the probability that the average time spent per customer will be at least 3 minutes?
  (b) there is an 85% chance that the sample mean will be below how many minutes?

• **9.23** Historically, 10% of a large shipment of machine parts are defective. If random samples of 400 parts are selected *without* replacement from a shipment that included 5,000 machine parts, what proportion of the samples will have
  (a) between 9% and 10% defective parts?
  (b) less than 8% defective parts?

**9.24** Historically, 93% of the deliveries of an overnight mail service arrive before 10:30 the following morning. If random samples of 500 deliveries are selected *without* replacement from a population that consisted of 10,000 deliveries, what proportion of the samples will have
  (a) between 93% and 97% of the deliveries arriving before 10:30 the following morning?
  (b) more than 95% of the deliveries arriving before 10:30 the following morning?

# ◆ SUMMARY

As seen in the summary chart, in this chapter we studied the sampling distribution of the sample mean and the sampling distribution of the sample proportion. The importance of the normal distribution in statistics is further emphasized by examining the central limit theorem. Knowledge of a population distribution is not always necessary in drawing conclusions from a sampling distribution of the mean or proportion.

The concepts concerning sampling distributions are central to the development of statistical inference. The main objective of statistical inference is to take information based only on a sample and use this information to draw conclusions and make decisions about various population values. The statistical techniques developed to achieve these objectives are discussed fully in the next five chapters (confidence intervals and tests of hypotheses).

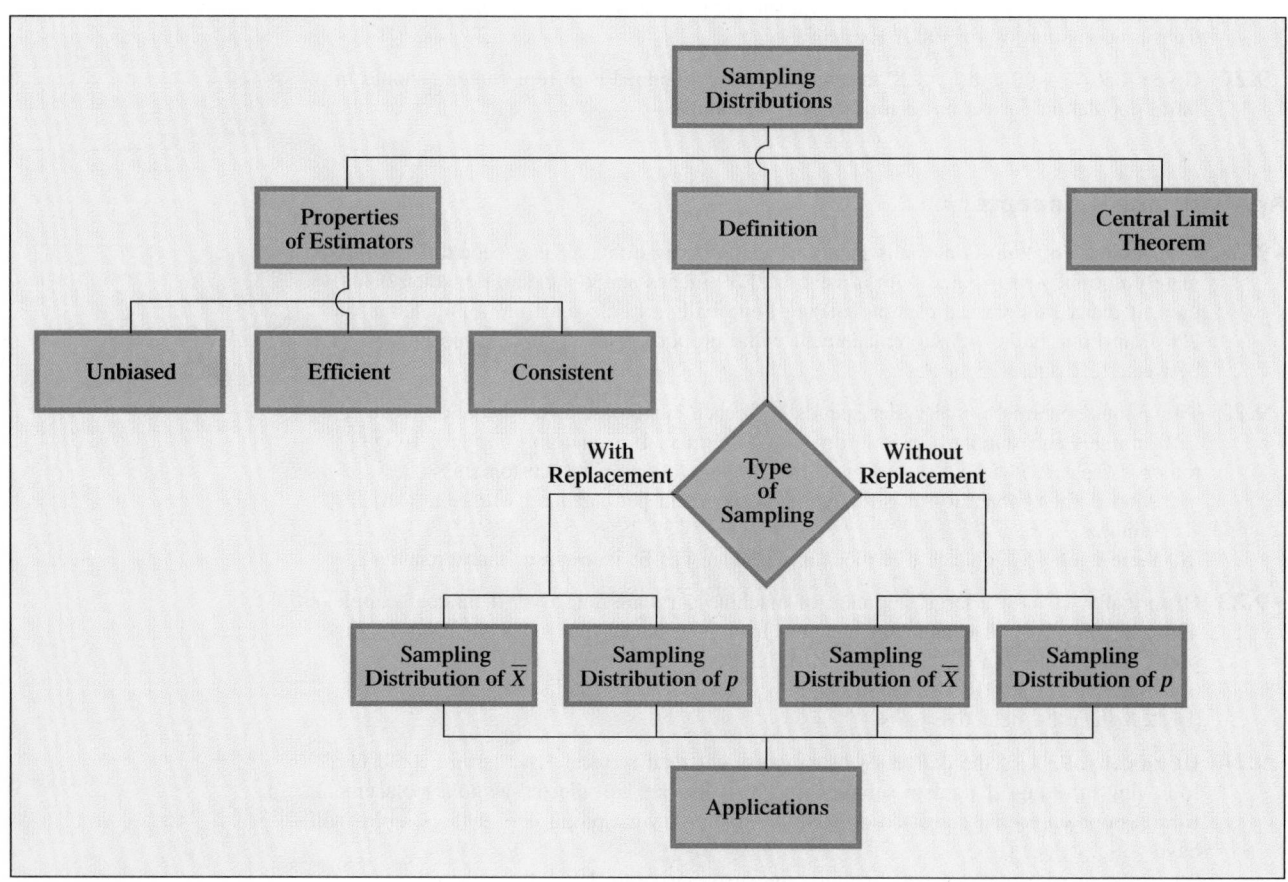

Chapter 9 summary chart

## Key Terms

central limit theorem   347
consistency   340
efficiency   339
finite population correction factor   357
law of large numbers   340

sampling distribution   336
sampling distribution of the mean   341
sampling distribution of the proportion   354
standard error of the mean   340

standard error of the proportion   353
unbiasedness   337

---

## Checking Your Understanding

**9.25** Why is the sample arithmetic mean an unbiased estimator of the population arithmetic mean?

**9.26** Why does the standard error of the mean decrease as the sample size $n$ increases?

**9.27** Why does the sampling distribution of the mean follow a normal distribution for a *large enough* sample size even though the population may not be normally distributed?

**9.28** Explain why a statistician would be interested in drawing conclusions about a population rather than merely describing the results of a sample.

**9.29** What is the difference between a probability distribution and a sampling distribution?

**9.30** Under what circumstances does the sampling distribution of the proportion approximately follow the normal distribution?

**9.31** What is the effect on the standard error of using the finite population correction factor?

---

## Chapter Review Problems

**9.32** A soft-drink machine is regulated so that the amount dispensed is normally distributed with $\mu = 7$ ounces and $\sigma = .5$ ounce. If samples of nine cups are taken, what value will be exceeded by 95% of the sample means?

**9.33** The life of a type of transistor battery is normally distributed with $\mu = 100$ hours and $\sigma = 20$ hours.
(a) What proportion of the batteries will last between 100 and 115 hours?
(b) If random samples of 16 batteries are selected,
   (1) what proportion of the sample means will be between 100 and 115 hours?
   (2) what proportion of the sample means will be more than 90 hours?
   (3) within what limits around the population mean will 90% of sample means fall?
(c) Is the central limit theorem necessary to answer (b)(1), (2), and (3)? Explain.

**9.34** An orange juice producer buys all his oranges from a large orange orchard. The amount of juice squeezed from each of these oranges is approximately normally distributed with a mean of 4.70 ounces and a standard deviation of .40 ounce.
(a) What is the probability that a randomly selected orange will contain
   (1) between 4.70 and 5.00 ounces?   (2) between 5.00 and 5.50 ounces?
(b) 77% of the oranges will contain at least how many ounces of juice?
Suppose that a sample of 25 oranges is selected:
(c) What is the probability that the sample mean will be at least 4.60 ounces?
(d) Between what two values symmetrically distributed around the population mean will 70% of the sample means fall?
(e) 77% of the sample means will be above what value?
(f) Are the results of (b) and (e) different? Explain why.

**9.35** **(Class Project)** The table of random numbers is an example of a uniform distribution because each digit is equally likely to occur. Starting in the row corresponding to the day of the month in which you were born, use the table of random numbers (Table E.1) to take *one digit* at a time.

Select samples of sizes $n = 2$, $n = 5$, $n = 10$. Compute the sample mean $\overline{X}$ of each sample. For each sample size, each student selects five different samples so that a frequency distribution of the sample means is developed for the results of the entire class based on samples of sizes $n = 2$, $n = 5$, and $n = 10$.

What can be said about the shape of the sampling distribution for each of these sample sizes?

**9.36** **(Class Project)** A coin having one side heads and the other side tails is to be tossed 10 times and the number of heads obtained is to be recorded. If each student performs this experiment five times, a frequency distribution of the number of heads can be developed from the results of the entire class. Does this distribution seem to approximate the normal distribution?

**9.37** **(Class Project)** The number of cars waiting in line at a car wash is distributed as follows:

### Length of waiting line

| NUMBER OF CARS | PROBABILITY |
|---|---|
| 0 | .25 |
| 1 | .40 |
| 2 | .20 |
| 3 | .10 |
| 4 | .04 |
| 5 | .01 |

The table of random numbers (Table E.1) can be used to select samples from this distribution by assigning numbers as follows:
1. Start in the row corresponding to the day of the month in which you were born.
2. *Two-digit* random numbers are to be selected.
3. If a random number between 00 and 24 is selected, record a length of 0; if between 25 and 64, record a length of 1; if between 65 and 84, record a length of 2; if between 85 and 94, record a length of 3; if between 95 and 98, record a length of 4; if it is 99, record a length of 5.

Select samples of sizes $n = 2$, $n = 10$, $n = 25$. Compute the sample mean for each sample. For example, if a sample of size 2 results in random numbers 18 and 46, these would correspond to lengths of 0 and 1, respectively, producing a sample mean of 0.5. If each student selects five different samples for each sample size, a frequency distribution of the sample means (for each sample size) can be developed from the results of the entire class.

What conclusions can you draw about the sampling distribution of the mean as the sample size is increased?

**9.38** **(Class Project)** The table of random numbers can simulate the selection of different colored balls from a bowl as follows:
1. Start in the row corresponding to the day of the month in which you were born.
2. Select *one-digit* numbers.
3. If a random digit between 0 and 6 is selected, consider the ball white; if a random digit is a 7, 8, or 9, consider the ball red.

Select samples of sizes $n = 10$, $n = 25$, and $n = 50$ digits. In each sample, count the number of white balls and compute the proportion of white balls in the sample. If each student in the class selects five different samples for each sample size, a frequency distribution of the proportion of white balls (for each sample size) can be developed from the results of the entire class.

What conclusions can be drawn about the sampling distribution of the proportion as the sample size is increased?

**9.39** **(Class Project)** Suppose that step 3 of Problem 9.38 uses the following rule: If a random digit between 0 and 8 is selected, consider the ball to be white; if a random digit of 9 is selected, consider the ball to be red. Compare and contrast the results obtained in this problem and in Problem 9.38.

# THE SPRINGVILLE HERALD CASE

Recall from chapter 8 (page 330) that the production department of the newspaper has embarked on a quality improvement effort and has chosen as its first project an issue that relates to the blackness of the newspaper print. Suppose that instead of selecting only one spot on the newspaper on which to measure blackness, a sample of 25 spots is selected.

## Exercises

**9.1** Assuming that the distribution has not changed from what it has been in the past year, what is the probability that the average blackness of the spots is:

**(a)** less than 1.0?

**(c)** between 1.0 and 1.05?

**(b)** between .95 and 1.0?

**(d)** less than .95 or greater than 1.05?

**9.2** Suppose that the average blackness of today's sample of 25 spots is 0.952. What conclusion would you draw about the blackness of the newspaper based on this result? Explain.

# References

1. Cochran, W. G., *Sampling Techniques*, 3d ed. (New York: Wiley, 1977).
2. Larsen, R. L., and M. L. Marx, *An Introduction to Mathematical Statistics and Its Applications,* 2d ed. (Englewood Cliffs, NJ: Prentice Hall, 1986).
3. *Microsoft Excel 97* (Redmond, WA: Microsoft Corp., 1996).
4. *Minitab for Windows Version 12* (State College, PA: Minitab, Inc., 1998).

# ❖ APPENDIX 9.1    USING MICROSOFT EXCEL FOR SAMPLING DISTRIBUTIONS

In appendix 2.1 we explained how to use Microsoft Excel to select random numbers. To illustrate the use of the Random Number Generator tool for simulating sampling distributions, we will develop sampling distributions of the mean based on a uniform population and a normal population.

To develop a simulation of the sampling distribution of the mean with a uniformly distributed population of 100 samples of $n = 30$, select **Tools | Data Analysis**. Then select **Random Number Generation**. Click the **OK** button. Enter **100** in the Number of Variables edit box. Enter **30** in the Number of Random Numbers edit box. Choose **Uniform** from the Distribution drop-down list box. In the Parameters edit box enter **0** and **1**. Select the **New Worksheet Ply** option button, and enter **Uniform** in the edit box to its right. Click the **OK** button.

The data you obtain on the Uniform worksheet will display the 30 values selected from a uniform distribution for each of 100 samples. To obtain the sampling distribution of the mean, you need to first enter the label **Sample Means:** in cell A31. Then, compute the sample means by entering **=AVERAGE(A1:A30)** in cell A32 and copy this across all 100 columns (for the 100 samples) through cell CV32. Then enter the label **Overall Average** in cell A33 and compute the average of all 100 sample averages by entering **=AVERAGE(A32:CV32)** in cell A34. Note the closeness of the overall average obtained to the population average of 0.5 (the average of 0 and 1).

With the Uniform worksheet active, select **Tools | Data Analysis**. Select **Histogram** from the Analysis Tools list box. Click the **OK** button. Enter **A32:CV32** for the Input Range. Select the **New Worksheet Ply** option button. Enter **Uniform Histogram** in the edit box. Select the **Chart Output** check box. Click the **OK** button. (By not providing an entry for Bin Range, Excel will create class intervals of equal width.) Gaps in the resulting bar chart can be eliminated by using the procedure discussed in appendix 3.1.

Now that we have obtained the sampling distribution of the mean for a uniformly distributed population, we can turn to a normally distributed population. To develop a simulation of the sampling distribution of the mean with a normally distributed population, insert a new worksheet into your workbook and rename it Normal and select **Tools | Data Analysis**. Then follow the instructions given for the uniform distribution except for the following: (1) select Normal in the Distribution drop-down edit box; (2) enter **0** in the Mean= edit box and **1** in the Standard Deviation = edit box; (3) on the Normal worksheet, enter the label **Standard Error of the Mean:** in cell A35 and compute the standard deviation of all 100 sample means by entering **=STDEV(A32:CV32)** in cell A36. Note the closeness of this standard error of the mean to the population standard error of the mean equal to $1/\sqrt{30} = .18257$.

## ❖ APPENDIX 9.2    USING MINITAB FOR SAMPLING DISTRIBUTIONS

In appendix 2.2, we explained how to use Minitab to select random numbers. To illustrate the use of the Random Number Generator tool for simulating sampling distributions, we will develop sampling distributions of the mean based on a uniform population, a normal population, and an exponential population.

To develop a simulation of the sampling distribution of the mean from a uniformly distributed population with 100 samples of $n = 30$, select **Calc | Random Data | Uniform**. Enter **100** in the Generate edit box. Enter **C1–C30** in the Store in column(s): edit box. Enter **0.0** in the Lower endpoint edit box and **1.0** in the Upper endpoint edit box. Click the **OK** button. You will observe that 100 rows of values are entered in columns C1–C30.

To calculate row statistics for each of the 100 samples, select **Calc | Row Statistics**. Select the **Mean** option button. Enter **C1–C30** in the Input variables edit box. Enter **C31** in the Store result in: edit box. Click the **OK** button. The mean for each of the 100 samples is stored in column C31. To compute statistics for the set of 100 sample means, select **PHStat | Basic Statistics | Display Descriptive Statistics**. Enter **C31** in the Variables edit box. Click the **OK** button.

To obtain a histogram of the 100 sample means, select **Graph | Histogram**. Enter **C31** in row 1 of the Graph Variables edit box. Click the **Options** button. Click **Density** for type of histogram. Click the **OK** button to return to the Histogram dialog box. Click the **OK** button again.

To obtain a simulation of the sampling distribution of the mean for a normal population, select **Calc | Random Data | Normal**. Enter a value for $\mu$ in the Mean edit box and for $\sigma$ in the Standard Deviation edit box. Follow the remainder of the instructions given for the Uniform population.

To obtain a simulation of the sampling distribution of the mean for an exponential population, select **Calc | Random Data | Exponential**. Enter a value for $1/\lambda$ in the Mean edit box. Follow the remainder of the instructions given for the Uniform population.

# Confidence Interval Estimation

10

## Introduction 366

## CHAPTER OBJECTIVES

✓ *To develop confidence interval estimates for the mean and the proportion*
✓ *To determine the sample size necessary to obtain a desired confidence interval*
✓ *To examine the effect of a finite population on the confidence interval and the sample size*
✓ *To demonstrate the application of confidence intervals in auditing*

## Introduction

Statistical inference is the process of using sample results to draw conclusions about the characteristics of a population. In this chapter we examine statistical procedures that will enable us to *estimate* either a population mean or a population proportion.

There are two major types of estimates: point estimates and interval estimates. A **point estimate** consists of a single sample statistic that is used to estimate the true value of a population parameter. For example, the sample mean $\overline{X}$ is a point estimate of the population mean $\mu$ and the sample variance $S^2$ is a point estimate of the population variance $\sigma^2$. Recall from section 9.1 that the sample mean $\overline{X}$ possesses the highly desirable properties of *unbiasedness* and *efficiency*. Although in practice only one sample is selected, we know that the average value of all possible sample means is $\mu$, the true population parameter.[1] A sample statistic such as $\overline{X}$ varies from sample to sample because it depends on the items selected in the sample, so we must take this into consideration when providing an estimate of the population characteristic. To accomplish this, we develop an **interval estimate** of the true population mean by taking into account the sampling distribution of the mean. The interval that we construct will have a specified confidence or probability of correctly estimating the true value of the population parameter $\mu$. Similar interval estimates are also developed for the population proportion $p$ and the population total.

In this chapter, we also discuss how to determine the size of the sample that should be selected in a survey. In addition, we discuss how a finite population affects the width of the confidence interval developed and the sample size selected.

We begin with a look at how a business uses confidence interval estimation to draw conclusions.

[1] *It is for this reason that the denominator of the sample variance is n − 1 instead of n, so that $S^2$ is an unbiased estimator of $\sigma^2$, that is, the average of all possible sample variances is $\sigma^2$.*

---

◆ **USING STATISTICS:** *Auditing Sales Invoices at Saxon Plumbing Company*

Saxon Plumbing Company is a large distributor of wholesale plumbing supplies in a suburban area outside a city in the northeastern United States. In an effort to maintain internal controls on sales, the company has prenumbered sales invoices that include a warehouse removal slip that must be used for each sale. Goods are not to be removed from the warehouse without an authorized warehouse removal slip. At the end of each month a sample of the sales invoices is selected to determine the following:

- The average amount listed on the sales invoices for the warehouse in that month.
- The total amount listed on the sales invoices for the warehouse in that month.
- Any differences between the actual amounts on the sales invoice and the amounts entered into the accounting system for the warehouse.
- The frequency of occurrence of various types of errors that violate the internal control policy of the warehouse. These errors may include failure to use the warehouse removal slip, failure to attach a duplicate sales invoice to the item being shipped, failure to include the correct account number of the customer, and shipment of the incorrect plumbing supply item.

 ## 10.1 ▶ CONFIDENCE INTERVAL ESTIMATION OF THE MEAN (σ KNOWN)

In section 9.1 we observed that we can use the central limit theorem and/or knowledge of the population distribution to determine the percentage of sample means that fall within certain distances of the population mean. For instance, in the cereal-filling-process example (see page 346) we observed that 95% of all sample means fall between 362.12 and 373.88 grams. This statement is based on *deductive reasoning*. However, it is exactly opposite to the type of reasoning that is needed here: *inductive reasoning*.

Inductive reasoning is needed because, in statistical inference, we must take the results of a single sample and draw conclusions about the population, not vice versa. In practice, the population mean is the unknown quantity that is to be estimated. Suppose that in the cereal-filling-process example, the true population mean $\mu$ is unknown but the true population standard deviation $\sigma$ is known to be 15 grams. Thus, rather than taking $\mu \pm (1.96)(\sigma/\sqrt{n})$ to find the upper and lower limits around $\mu$ as in section 9.1, we determine the consequences of substituting the sample mean $\overline{X}$ for the unknown $\mu$ and using $\overline{X} \pm (1.96)(\sigma/\sqrt{n})$ as an interval within which we estimate the unknown $\mu$. Although in practice a single sample of size $n$ is selected and the mean $\overline{X}$ is computed, we need to obtain a hypothetical set of all possible samples, each of size $n$, in order to understand the full meaning of the interval estimate to be obtained.

Suppose, for example, that our sample of size $n = 25$ boxes has a mean of 362.3 grams. The interval developed to estimate $\mu$ is $362.3 \pm (1.96)(15)/(\sqrt{25})$ or $362.3 \pm 5.88$. That is, the estimate of $\mu$ is

$$356.42 \le \mu \le 368.18$$

Because the population mean $\mu$ (equal to 368) is included within the interval, this sample has led to a correct statement about $\mu$ (see Figure 10.1 on page 368).

To continue our hypothetical example, suppose that for a different sample of $n = 25$ boxes, the mean is 369.5. The interval developed from this sample is $369.5 \pm (1.96)(15)/(\sqrt{25})$ or $369.5 \pm 5.88$. That is, the estimate is

$$363.62 \le \mu \le 375.38$$

Because the true population mean $\mu$ (equal to 368) is also included within this interval, we conclude that this statement about $\mu$ is correct.

Now, before we begin to think that we will *always* make correct statements about $\mu$ by developing a confidence interval estimate from the sample $\overline{X}$, suppose we draw a third hypothetical sample of size $n = 25$ boxes in which the sample mean is equal to 360 grams. The

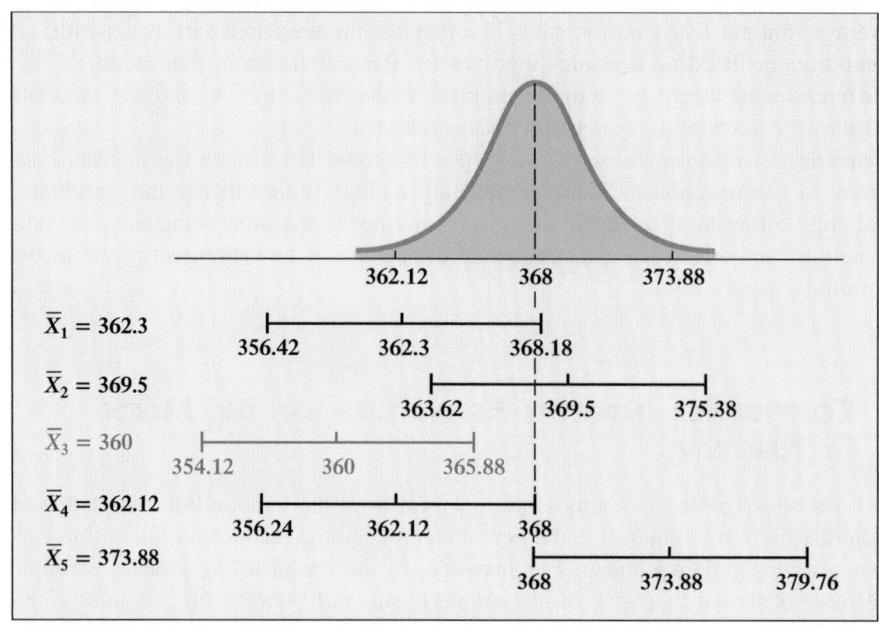

**FIGURE 10.1** Confidence interval estimates from five different samples of size $n = 25$ taken from population where $\mu = 368$ and $\sigma = 15$

interval developed here is $360 \pm (1.96)(15)/(\sqrt{25})$ or $360 \pm 5.88$. In this case, the estimate of $\mu$ is

$$354.12 \le \mu \le 365.88$$

Observe that this estimate is *not* a correct statement because the population mean $\mu$ is not included in the interval developed from this sample (see Figure 10.1). Thus, we are faced with a dilemma. For some samples the interval estimate of $\mu$ will be correct, and for others it will be incorrect. In addition, we must realize that in practice we select only one sample, and because we do not know the true population mean, we cannot determine whether our particular statement is correct.

What can we do to resolve this dilemma? We can determine the proportion of samples producing intervals that result in correct statements about the population mean $\mu$. To do this, we need to examine two other hypothetical samples: the case in which $\overline{X} = 362.12$ grams and the case in which $\overline{X} = 373.88$ grams. If $\overline{X} = 362.12$, the interval is $362.12 \pm (1.96)(15)/(\sqrt{25})$ or $362.12 \pm 5.88$. That is,

$$356.24 \le \mu \le 368.00$$

Since the population mean of 368 is at the upper limit of the interval, the statement is a correct one (see Figure 10.1). Finally, if $\overline{X} = 373.88$, the interval is $373.88 \pm (1.96)(15)/(\sqrt{25})$ or $373.88 \pm 5.88$. That is,

$$368.00 \le \mu \le 379.76$$

In this case, because the population mean of 368 is included at the lower limit of the interval, the statement is a correct one.

Thus, from these examples (see Figure 10.1), we can determine that if the sample mean based on a sample of $n = 25$ boxes falls anywhere between 362.12 and 373.88 grams, the population mean is included *somewhere* within the interval. However, we know from our discussion of the sampling distribution in section 9.1 that 95% of the sample means fall between 362.12 and 373.88 grams. Therefore, 95% of all samples of $n = 25$ boxes have sample means that include the population mean within the interval developed. The interval from 362.12 to 373.88 is referred to as a 95% confidence interval.

> In general, a 95% **confidence interval estimate** is interpreted as follows: If all possible samples of the same size $n$ are taken and their sample means are computed, 95% of them include the true population mean somewhere within the interval around their sample means, and only 5% of them do not.

Because only one sample is selected in practice and $\mu$ is unknown, we never know for sure whether our specific interval obtained includes the population mean. However, we can state that we have 95% confidence that we have selected a sample whose interval does include the population mean.

In some situations, we might desire a higher degree of assurance (such as 99%) of including the population mean within the interval. In other cases, we might be willing to accept less assurance (such as 90%) of correctly estimating the population mean.

In general, the level of confidence is symbolized by $(1 - \alpha) \times 100\%$, where $\alpha$ is the proportion in the tails of the distribution that is outside the confidence interval. Therefore, to obtain the $(1 - \alpha) \times 100\%$ confidence interval estimate of the mean with $\sigma$ known, we have

## Confidence Interval for a Mean (σ Known)

$$\overline{X} \pm Z \frac{\sigma}{\sqrt{n}}$$

*or*

$$\overline{X} - Z\frac{\sigma}{\sqrt{n}} \le \mu \le \overline{X} + Z\frac{\sigma}{\sqrt{n}} \qquad (10.1)$$

where

$Z$ = the value corresponding to an area of $(1 - \alpha)/2$ from the center of a standardized normal distribution

To construct a 95% confidence interval estimate of the mean, the $Z$ value corresponding to an area of $.95/2 = .4750$ from the center of the standard normal distribution is 1.96 because there is .025 in the upper tail of the distribution and the cumulative area less than $+Z$ is .975. The value of $Z$ selected for constructing such a confidence interval is called the **critical value** for the distribution.

There is a different critical value for each **level of confidence** $1 - \alpha$. A level of confidence of 95% leads to a $Z$ value of $\pm 1.96$ (see Figure 10.2 on page 370). If a level of confidence of 99% is desired, the area of .99 is divided in half, leaving .495 between each limit and $\mu$ (see Figure 10.3 on page 370). The $Z$ value corresponding to an area of .495 from the center of the normal curve is approximately 2.58 because the upper tail area is .005 and the cumulative area below $+Z$ is .995.

Now that we have considered various levels of confidence, why would we not want to make the confidence level as close to 100% as possible? We would not because any increase

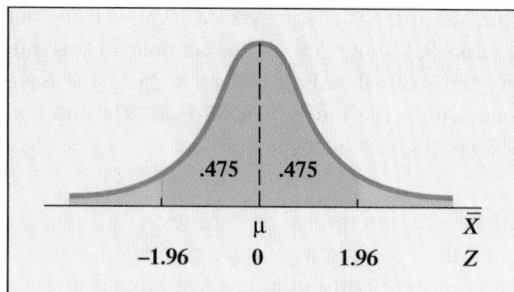

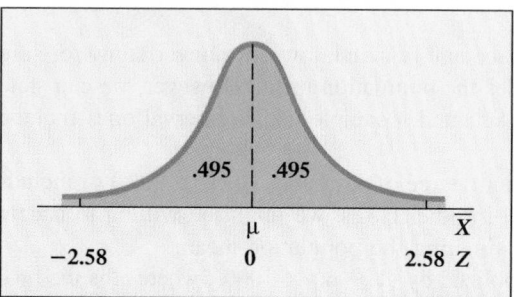

in the level of confidence is achieved only by simultaneously widening (and making less precise) the confidence interval obtained. Thus, we would have more confidence that the population mean is within a broader range of values but this is less useful for decision-making purposes. This trade-off between the width of the confidence interval and the level of confidence will be discussed in greater depth when we investigate how the sample size $n$ is determined (see section 10.4).

To illustrate the application of the confidence interval estimate, we turn to Example 10.1.

## Example 10.1  *Estimating the Mean Paper Length with 95% Confidence*

A manufacturer of computer paper has a production process that operates continuously throughout an entire production shift. The paper is expected to have an average length of 11 inches, and the standard deviation is known to be 0.02 inch. At periodic intervals, samples are selected to determine whether the average paper length is still equal to 11 inches or whether something has gone wrong in the production process to change the length of the paper produced. If such a situation has occurred, corrective action is needed. Suppose a random sample of 100 sheets is selected, and the average paper length is found to be 10.998 inches. Set up a 95% confidence interval estimate of the population average paper length.

### SOLUTION

Using Equation (10.1), with $Z = 1.96$ for 95% confidence, we have

$$\overline{X} \pm Z\frac{\sigma}{\sqrt{n}} = 10.998 \pm (1.96)\frac{0.02}{\sqrt{100}}$$

$$= 10.998 \pm .00392$$

$$10.99408 \leq \mu \leq 11.00192$$

Thus, we estimate, with 95% confidence, that the population mean is between 10.99408 and 11.00192 inches. Since 11, the value that indicates the production process is working properly, is included within the interval, there is no reason to believe that anything is wrong with the production process. There is 95% confidence that the sample selected is one in which the true population mean is included somewhere within the interval developed.

To observe the effect of using a 99% confidence interval, let us look at Example 10.2.

## Example 10.2 *Estimating the Mean Paper Length with 99% Confidence*

Suppose that 99% confidence is desired. Set up a 99% confidence interval estimate of the population average paper length.

### SOLUTION

Using equation (10.1), with $Z = 2.58$, we have

$$\overline{X} \pm Z \frac{\sigma}{\sqrt{n}} = 10.998 \pm (2.58) \frac{0.02}{\sqrt{100}}$$

$$= 10.998 \pm .00516$$

$$10.99284 \le \mu \le 11.00316$$

Once again, because 11 is included within this wider interval, there is no reason to believe that anything is wrong with the production process.

## Problems for Section 10.1

### Learning the Basics

- **10.1** If $\overline{X} = 85$, $\sigma = 8$, and $n = 64$, set up a 95% confidence interval estimate of the population mean $\mu$.

  **10.2** If $\overline{X} = 125$, $\sigma = 24$, and $n = 36$, set up a 99% confidence interval estimate of the population mean $\mu$.

  **10.3** A market researcher states that she has 95% confidence that the true average monthly sales of a product are between $170,000 and $200,000. Explain the meaning of this statement.

  **10.4** Why is it not possible for the production manager in Example 10.1 on page 370 to have 100% confidence? Explain.

  **10.5** From the results of Example 10.1 on page 370 regarding paper production, is it true that 95% of the sample means will fall between 10.99408 and 11.00192 inches? Explain.

  **10.6** Is it true in Example 10.1 on page 370 that we do not know for sure whether the true population mean is between 10.99408 and 11.00192 inches? Explain.

### Applying the Concepts

- **10.7** Suppose that the manager of a paint supply store wants to estimate the actual amount of paint contained in 1-gallon cans purchased from a nationally known manufacturer. It is known from the manufacturer's specifications that the standard deviation of the amount of paint is equal to 0.02 gallon. A random sample of 50 cans is selected, and the average amount of paint per 1-gallon can is 0.995 gallon.

(a) Set up a 99% confidence interval estimate of the true population average amount of paint included in a 1-gallon can.

(b) On the basis of your results, do you think that the store owner has a right to complain to the manufacturer? Why?

(c) Does the population amount of paint per can have to be normally distributed here? Explain.

(d) Explain why an observed value of 0.98 gallon for an individual can is not unusual, even though it is outside the confidence interval you calculated.

(e) Suppose that you used a 95% confidence interval estimate. What would be your answers to (a) and (b)?

**10.8** The quality control manager at a light bulb factory needs to estimate the average life of a large shipment of light bulbs. The process standard deviation is known to be 100 hours. A random sample of 64 light bulbs indicated a sample average life of 350 hours.

(a) Set up a 95% confidence interval estimate of the true average life of light bulbs in this shipment.

(b) Do you think that the manufacturer has the right to state that the light bulbs last an average of 400 hours? Explain.

(c) Does the population of light bulb life have to be normally distributed here? Explain.

(d) Explain why an observed value of 320 hours is not unusual, even though it is outside the confidence interval you calculated.

(e) Suppose that the process standard deviation changed to 80 hours. What would be your answers in (a) and (b)?

**10.9** The inspection division of the Lee County Weights and Measures Department is interested in estimating the actual amount of soft drink that is placed in 2-liter bottles at the local bottling plant of a large nationally known soft-drink company. The bottling plant has informed the inspection division that the standard deviation for 2-liter bottles is 0.05 liter. A random sample of one hundred 2-liter bottles obtained from this bottling plant indicates a sample average of 1.99 liters.

(a) Set up a 95% confidence interval estimate of the true average amount of soft drink in each bottle.

(b) Does the population of soft-drink fill have to be normally distributed here? Explain.

(c) Explain why an observed value of 2.02 liters is not unusual, even though it is outside the confidence interval you calculated.

(d) Suppose that the sample average had been 1.97 liters. What would be your answer to (a)?

## 10.2 CONFIDENCE INTERVAL ESTIMATION OF THE MEAN ($\sigma$ UNKNOWN)

Just as the mean of the population $\mu$ is usually not known, the actual standard deviation of the population $\sigma$ is also usually unknown. Therefore, we need to obtain a confidence interval estimate of $\mu$ by using only the sample statistics of $\bar{X}$ and $S$. To achieve this, we turn to the work of William S. Gosset.

### Student's $t$ Distribution

At the turn of the century, a statistician named William S. Gosset, an employee of Guinness Breweries in Ireland (see reference 3), was interested in making inferences about the mean when $\sigma$ was unknown. Since Guinness employees were not permitted to publish research work under their own names, Gosset adopted the pseudonym "Student." The distribution that he developed has come to be known as **Student's $t$ distribution.**

If the random variable $X$ is normally distributed, then the statistic

$$\frac{\overline{X} - \mu}{\dfrac{S}{\sqrt{n}}}$$

has a $t$ distribution with $n - 1$ **degrees of freedom.** Notice that this expression has the same form as equation (9.5), on page 343, except that $S$ is used to estimate $\sigma$, which is presumed to be unknown in this case.

## Properties of the $t$ Distribution

In appearance, the $t$ distribution is very similar to the normal distribution. Both distributions are bell-shaped and symmetrical. However, the $t$ distribution has more area in the tails and less in the center than does the normal distribution (see Figure 10.4). This is because $\sigma$ is unknown, and we are using $S$ to estimate it. Because we are uncertain of the value $\sigma$, the values of $t$ that we observe will be more variable than for $Z$.

However, as the number of degrees of freedom increases, the $t$ distribution gradually approaches the normal distribution until the two are virtually identical. This happens because $S$ becomes a better estimate of $\sigma$ as the sample size gets larger. With a sample size of about 120 or more, $S$ estimates $\sigma$ precisely enough that there is little difference between the $t$ and $Z$ distributions. For this reason, most statisticians use $Z$ instead of $t$ when the sample size is over 120.

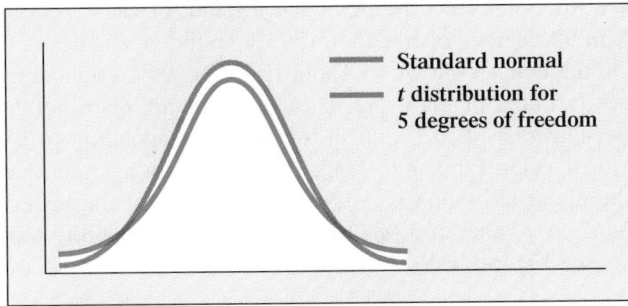

Standard normal
$t$ distribution for
5 degrees of freedom

**FIGURE 10.4**
Standard normal distribution and $t$ distribution for 5 degrees of freedom

### COMMENT: *Checking the Assumptions*

Recall that the $t$ distribution assumes that the random variable $X$ being studied is normally distributed. In practice, however, as long as the sample size is large enough and the population is not very skewed, the $t$ distribution can be used to estimate the population mean when $\sigma$ is unknown. We should be concerned about the validity of the confidence interval primarily when we are dealing with a small sample size and a skewed population distribution. However, we can assess the assumption of normality in the population by evaluating the shape of the sample data using a histogram, stem-and-leaf display, box-and-whisker plot, or normal probability plot (see section 8.2).

**Table 10.1**  *Determining the critical value from the t table for an area of .025 in each tail with 99 degrees of freedom*

| DEGREES OF FREEDOM | UPPER-TAIL AREAS | | | | | |
| | .25 | .10 | .05 | .025 | .01 | .005 |
|---|---|---|---|---|---|---|
| 1 | 1.0000 | 3.0777 | 6.3138 | 12.7062 | 31.8207 | 63.6574 |
| 2 | 0.8165 | 1.8856 | 2.9200 | 4.3027 | 6.9646 | 9.9248 |
| 3 | 0.7649 | 1.6377 | 2.3534 | 3.1824 | 4.5407 | 5.8409 |
| 4 | 0.7407 | 1.5332 | 2.1318 | 2.7764 | 3.7469 | 4.6041 |
| 5 | 0.7267 | 1.4759 | 2.0150 | 2.5706 | 3.3649 | 4.0322 |
| . | . | . | . | . | . | . |
| . | . | . | . | . | . | . |
| . | . | . | . | . | . | . |
| 96 | 0.6771 | 1.2904 | 1.6609 | 1.9850 | 2.3658 | 2.6280 |
| 97 | 0.6770 | 1.2903 | 1.6607 | 1.9847 | 2.3654 | 2.6275 |
| 98 | 0.6770 | 1.2902 | 1.6606 | 1.9845 | 2.3650 | 2.6269 |
| 99 | 0.6770 | 1.2902 | 1.6604 | → 1.9842 | 2.3646 | 2.6264 |
| 100 | 0.6770 | 1.2901 | 1.6602 | 1.9840 | 2.3642 | 2.6259 |

*Source: Extracted from Table E.3.*

The critical values of $t$ for the appropriate degrees of freedom can be obtained from the table of the $t$ distribution (see Table E.3). The top of each column of the table indicates the area in the right tail of the $t$ distribution (because positive entries for $t$ are supplied, the values for $t$ are for the upper tail); each row represents the particular $t$ value for each specific degree of freedom. For example, with 99 degrees of freedom, if 95% confidence is desired, the appropriate value of $t$ is found in the manner shown in Table 10.1. The 95% confidence level means that 2.5% of the values (an area of .025) are in each tail of the distribution. Looking in the column for an upper-tail area of .025 and in the row corresponding to 99 degrees of freedom results in a critical value for $t$ of 1.9842. Because $t$ is a symmetrical distribution with a mean of 0, if the upper-tail value is +1.9842, the value for the lower-tail area (lower .025) will be −1.9842. A $t$ value of 1.9842 means that the probability that $t$ exceeds +1.9842 is .025 or 2.5% (see Figure 10.5).

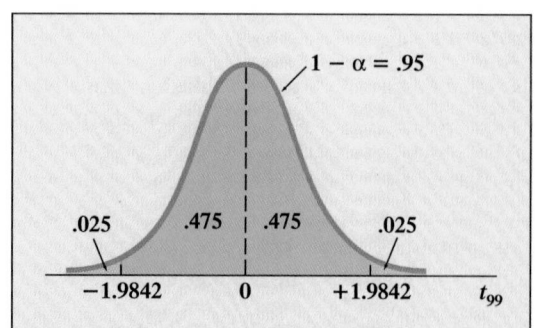

**FIGURE 10.5**
$t$ distribution with 99 degrees of freedom

## The Concept of Degrees of Freedom

You may recall from chapter 4 that the sample variance $S^2$ requires the computation of

$$\sum_{i=1}^{n}(X_i - \overline{X})^2$$

Thus, in order to compute $S^2$, we first need to know $\overline{X}$. Therefore, we can say that only $n - 1$ of the sample values are free to vary. That is, there are $n - 1$ degrees of freedom.

This concept is illustrated as follows. Suppose we have a sample of five values that have a mean of 20. How many distinct values do we need to know before we can obtain the remainder? The fact that $n = 5$ and $\overline{X} = 20$ also tells us that

$$\sum_{i=1}^{n} X_i = 100$$

because

$$\sum_{i=1}^{n} X_i / n = \overline{X}$$

Thus, once we know four of the values, the fifth one will *not* be free to vary because the sum must add to 100. For example, if four of the values are 18, 24, 19, and 16, the fifth value can only be 23 so that the sum equals 100.

## The Confidence Interval Statement

The $(1 - \alpha) \times 100\%$ confidence interval estimate for the mean with $\sigma$ unknown is expressed as follows:

### Confidence Interval for a Mean ($\sigma$ Unknown)

$$\overline{X} \pm t_{n-1}\frac{S}{\sqrt{n}}$$

*or*

$$\overline{X} - t_{n-1}\frac{S}{\sqrt{n}} \leq \mu \leq \overline{X} + t_{n-1}\frac{S}{\sqrt{n}} \qquad (10.2)$$

where

$t_{n-1}$ is the critical value of the $t$ distribution with $n - 1$ degrees of freedom for an area of $\alpha/2$ in the upper tail.

To illustrate the application of the confidence interval estimate for the mean when the standard deviation $\sigma$ is unknown, let us return to the Saxon Plumbing Company example presented earlier. Suppose that we select a sample of 100 sales invoices from the population of sales invoices during the month and the average amount of each sales invoice is \$110.27 with a sample standard deviation of \$28.95. The auditor in this case wants 95% confidence of estimating the population mean.

Using $\overline{X} = \$110.27$ and $S = \$28.95$, we obtain the critical value from the $t$ distribution as shown in Table 10.1. The critical value of $t$ is 1.9842. Using equation (10.2), we have

$$\overline{X} \pm t_{n-1}\frac{S}{\sqrt{n}}$$

$$= 110.27 \pm (1.9842)\frac{28.95}{\sqrt{100}}$$

$$= 110.27 \pm 5.74$$

$$\$104.53 \le \mu \le \$116.01$$

Thus, we conclude with 95% confidence that the average amount of the sales invoice is between $104.53 and $116.01. The 95% confidence interval states that we are 95% sure that the sample we have selected is one in which the population mean $\mu$ is located within the interval. This 95% confidence means that if all possible samples of size 100 were selected (something that would never be done in practice), 95% of the intervals developed would include the true population mean somewhere within the interval. The validity of this confidence interval estimate depends on the assumption of normality for the distribution of the amount of the sales invoices. With a sample of 100, as we have noted on page 373, the use of the $t$ distribution is likely to be appropriate. In practice, the results of this interval based on the actual invoices would be compared with the average invoice as entered into the computer system of the company. If there appeared to be large differences, further investigation would be undertaken.

To further illustrate how confidence intervals for a mean are constructed when the population standard deviation is unknown, let us turn to Example 10.3.

## Example 10.3 Estimating the Mean Annual Usage of Home Heating Oil

A marketing manager for a company that supplies home heating oil wants to estimate the average annual usage (in gallons) by single-family homes in a particular geographical area. A random sample of 35 single-family homes is selected, and the annual usage for these homes is summarized in the following table.

**ANNUAL AMOUNT OF HEATING OIL CONSUMED (IN GALLONS) IN A SAMPLE OF 35 SINGLE-FAMILY HOUSES**

| | | | | | | |
|---|---|---|---|---|---|---|
| 1150.25 | 1352.67 | 983.45 | 1365.11 | 942.71 | 1577.77 | 330.00 |
| 872.37 | 1126.57 | 1184.17 | 1046.35 | 1110.50 | 1050.86 | 851.60 |
| 1459.56 | 1252.01 | 373.91 | 1047.40 | 1064.46 | 1018.23 | 996.92 |
| 941.96 | 767.37 | 1598.57 | 1598.66 | 1343.29 | 1617.73 | 1300.76 |
| 1013.27 | 1402.59 | 1069.32 | 1108.94 | 1326.19 | 1074.86 | 975.86 |

**DATA FILE**
OILUSE

Set up a 95% confidence interval estimate of the population average amount of heating oil consumed per year.

### SOLUTION

For these data, the accompanying figure, obtained from Minitab, shows that the sample average is $\overline{X} = 1{,}122.7$ gallons and the sample standard deviation is $S = 295.7$ gallons. To obtain the confidence interval of 1,021.2 to 1,224.3 provided by Minitab, we first determine the critical value from the $t$ table for an area of .025 in each tail with 34 degrees of freedom. From Table E.3 we have $t_{34} = 2.0322$.

## T Confidence Intervals

| Variable | N | Mean | StDev | SE Mean | 95.0 % CI |
|---|---|---|---|---|---|
| Gallons | 35 | 1122.7 | 295.7 | 50.0 | ( 1021.2, 1224.3) |

| | UPPER-TAILED AREAS | | | | | |
|---|---|---|---|---|---|---|
| **DEGREES OF FREEDOM** | **.25** | **.10** | **.05** | **.025** | **.01** | **.005** |
| 1 | 1.0000 | 3.0777 | 6.3138 | 12.7062 | 31.8207 | 63.6574 |
| 2 | 0.8165 | 1.8856 | 2.9200 | 4.3027 | 6.9646 | 9.9248 |
| 3 | 0.7649 | 1.6377 | 2.3534 | 3.1824 | 4.5407 | 5.8409 |
| 4 | 0.7407 | 1.5332 | 2.1318 | 2.7764 | 3.7469 | 4.6041 |
| 5 | 0.7267 | 1.4759 | 2.0150 | 2.5706 | 3.3649 | 4.0322 |
| . | . | . | . | . | . | . |
| . | . | . | . | . | . | . |
| . | . | . | . | . | . | . |
| 31 | 0.6825 | 1.3095 | 1.6955 | 2.0395 | 2.4528 | 2.7440 |
| 32 | 0.6822 | 1.3086 | 1.6939 | 2.0369 | 2.4487 | 2.7385 |
| 33 | 0.6820 | 1.3077 | 1.6924 | 2.0345 | 2.4448 | 2.7333 |
| 34 | 0.6818 | 1.3070 | 1.6909 | → 2.0322 | 2.4411 | 2.7284 |
| 35 | 0.6816 | 1.3062 | 1.6896 | 2.0301 | 2.4377 | 2.7238 |

*Source: Extracted from Table E.3.*

Thus, using $\bar{X} = 1,122.7$, $S = 295.7$, $n = 35$, and $t_{34} = 2.0322$, we have

$$\bar{X} \pm t_{n-1}\frac{S}{\sqrt{n}}$$

$$= 1,122.7 \pm (2.0322)\frac{295.7}{\sqrt{35}}$$

$$= 1,122.7 \pm 101.57$$

$$1,021.13 \le \mu \le 1,224.27$$

We thus conclude with 95% confidence that the average amount of heating oil consumed per year is between 1,021.13 and 1,224.27 gallons. The 95% confidence interval states that we are 95% sure that the sample we have selected is one in which the population mean $\mu$ is located within the interval. This 95% confidence means that if all possible samples of size 35 were selected (something that would never be done in practice), 95% of the intervals developed would include the true population mean. The validity of this confidence interval estimate depends on the assumption of normality of the heating oil usage data. With a sample of 35, as we have noted on page 373, the use of the $t$ distribution is likely to be appropriate.

## Problems for Section 10.2

### Learning the Basics

**10.10** Determine the critical value of $t$ in each of the following circumstances:
(a) $1 - \alpha = .95$, $n = 10$.
(b) $1 - \alpha = .99$, $n = 10$.
(c) $1 - \alpha = .95$, $n = 32$.
(d) $1 - \alpha = .95$, $n = 65$.
(e) $1 - \alpha = .90$, $n = 16$.

• **10.11** If $\overline{X} = 75$, $S = 24$, and $n = 36$, assuming the population is normally distributed, set up a 95% confidence interval estimate of the population mean $\mu$.

**10.12** If $\overline{X} = 50$, $S = 15$, and $n = 16$, assuming the population is normally distributed, set up a 99% confidence interval estimate of the population mean $\mu$.

**10.13** Set up a 95% confidence interval estimate for the population mean, based on each of the following sets of data, assuming the population is normally distributed:

Set 1: 1, 1, 1, 1, 8, 8, 8, 8

Set 2: 1, 2, 3, 4, 5, 6, 7, 8

Explain why they have different confidence intervals even though they have the same mean and range.

**10.14** Compute a 95% confidence interval for the population mean, based on the numbers 1, 2, 3, 4, 5, 6, 20. Change the number 20 to 7, and recalculate the confidence interval. Using these results, describe the effect of an outlier (or extreme value) on the confidence interval.

### Applying the Concepts

• **10.15** The United States Department of Transportation requires tire manufacturers to provide tire performance information on the sidewall of the tire so that a prospective customer can be better informed when making a purchasing decision. One very important measure of tire performance is the tread wear index, which indicates the tire's resistance to tread wear compared with a tire graded with a base of 100. This means that a tire with a grade of 200 should last twice as long, on average, as a tire graded with a base of 100. Suppose that a consumer organization wishes to estimate the actual tread wear index of a brand name of tires graded 200 that are produced by a certain manufacturer. A random sample of 18 of these tires indicates a sample average tread wear index of 195.3 and a sample standard deviation of 21.4.
(a) Assuming the population of tread wear indices is normally distributed, set up a 95% confidence interval estimate of the population average tread wear index for tires produced by this manufacturer under this brand name.
(b) Do you think that the consumer organization should accuse the manufacturer of producing tires that do not meet the performance information provided on the sidewall of the tire? Explain.
(c) Tell why an observed tread wear index of 210 for a particular tire is not unusual, even though it is outside the confidence interval developed in (a).

**10.16** The manager of a branch of a local savings bank wants to estimate the average amount held in passbook savings accounts by depositors at the bank. A random sample of 30 depositors is selected, and the results indicate a sample average of $4,750 and a sample standard deviation of $1,200.
(a) Assuming a normal distribution, set up a 95% confidence interval estimate of the average amount held in all passbook savings accounts.

(b) If an individual had \$4,000 in a passbook savings account, is this considered unusual? Explain your answer.

**10.17** A stationery store wants to estimate the average retail value of greeting cards that it has in its inventory. A random sample of 20 greeting cards indicates an average value of \$1.67 and a standard deviation of \$0.32.

(a) Assuming a normal distribution, set up a 95% confidence interval estimate of the average value of all greeting cards in the store's inventory.

(b) How might the results obtained in (a) be useful in assisting the store owner to estimate the total value of her inventory?

**10.18** The personnel department of a large corporation wants to estimate the family dental expenses of its employees to determine the feasibility of providing a dental insurance plan. A random sample of 10 employees reveals the following family dental expenses (in dollars) for the preceding year:

DATA FILE
DENTAL

110, 362, 246, 85, 510, 208, 173, 425, 316, 179

(a) Set up a 90% confidence interval estimate of the average family dental expenses for all employees of this corporation.

(b) What assumption about the population distribution must be made in (a)?

(c) Give an example of a family dental expense that is outside the confidence interval but is not unusual for an individual family, and explain why this is not a contradiction.

(d) Suppose you used a 95% confidence interval in (a). What would be your answer to (a)?

(e) Suppose the fourth value was \$585 instead of \$85. What would be your answer to (a)? What effect does this change have on the confidence interval?

**10.19** The customer service department of a local gas utility wants to estimate the average length of time between the entry of the service request and the connection of service. A random sample of 15 houses is selected from the records available during the past year. The results recorded in number of days are as follows:

| 114 | 78 | 96 | 137 | 78 | 103 | 117 |    |
|-----|----|----|-----|----|-----|-----|----|
| 126 | 86 | 99 | 114 | 72 | 104 | 73  | 86 |

DATA FILE
GASERVE

(a) Set up a 95% confidence interval estimate of the population average waiting time in the past year.

(b) If the service department has been advising customers that the average waiting time is 90 days, can you say that the results obtained in (a) are consistent with such advice? Explain.

(c) What assumption about the population distribution must be made in (a)?

(d) Suppose the last value was 286 days instead of 86 days. What would be your answers to (a) and (b)? What effect does this change have on the confidence interval?

**10.20** The director of patient services of a large health maintenance organization wants to evaluate patient waiting time at a local facility. A random sample of 25 patients is selected from the appointment book. The waiting time is defined as the time from when the patient signs in to when he or she is seen by the doctor. The following data represent the waiting times (in minutes):

| 19.5 | 30.5 | 45.6 | 39.8 | 29.6 |
|------|------|------|------|------|
| 25.4 | 21.8 | 28.6 | 52.0 | 25.4 |
| 26.1 | 31.1 | 43.1 | 4.9  | 12.7 |
| 10.7 | 12.1 | 1.9  | 45.9 | 42.5 |
| 41.3 | 13.8 | 17.4 | 39.0 | 36.6 |

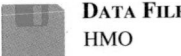

DATA FILE
HMO

(a) Set up a 95% confidence interval estimate of the population average waiting time.

(b) The director of patient services at the health maintenance organization wants to tell prospective patients that average waiting time is 15 minutes. On the basis of the results of (a) can this statement be made? Explain.

(c) What assumption about the population distribution must be made in (a)?

(d) Suppose that the recorded value of 1.9 minutes was actually 101.9 minutes. What would be your answers to (a) and (b)? What effect does this change have on the confidence interval?

## 10.3 CONFIDENCE INTERVAL ESTIMATION FOR THE PROPORTION

In this section we extend the concept of the confidence interval to categorical data to estimate the population proportion $p$ from the sample proportion $p_s = X/n$. Recall from section 9.2 that when both $np$ and $n(1 - p)$ are at least 5, the binomial distribution can be approximated by the normal distribution. Hence, we can set up the following $(1 - \alpha) \times 100\%$ confidence interval estimate for the population proportion $p$:

---

### Confidence Interval Estimate for the Proportion

$$p_s \pm Z \sqrt{\frac{p_s(1 - p_s)}{n}}$$

*or*

$$p_s - Z \sqrt{\frac{p_s(1 - p_s)}{n}} \leq p \leq p_s + Z \sqrt{\frac{p_s(1 - p_s)}{n}} \qquad (10.3)$$

where

$p_s$ = sample proportion

$p$ = population proportion

$Z$ = critical value from the normal distribution

$n$ = sample size

---

To see how this confidence interval estimate of the proportion is utilized, we return to our Saxon Plumbing Company example. Recall that the auditor wants to determine the frequency of occurrence of various types of errors that violate the internal control policy of the warehouse. Suppose that in the sample of 100 sales invoices, 10 contain an error. The auditor wants to develop a 95% confidence interval estimate of the population proportion of sales invoices that contain errors that are in violation of company policy. For these data we have $p_s = 10/100 = .10$. With 95% confidence $Z = 1.96$, so that using equation (10.3),

$$p_s \pm Z \sqrt{\frac{p_s(1 - p_s)}{n}} = .10 \pm (1.96)\sqrt{\frac{(.10)(.90)}{100}}$$

$$= .10 \pm (1.96)(.03)$$

$$= .10 \pm .0588$$

$$.0412 \leq p \leq .1588$$

Therefore, the auditor estimates with 95% confidence that between 4.12% and 15.88% of the sales invoices have errors that violate company policy.

To study another application of a confidence interval estimate for the proportion, consider Example 10.4.

## Example 10.4 *Estimating the Proportion of Nonconforming Newspapers Printed*

The operations manager for a large city newspaper wants to determine the proportion of newspapers printed that have a nonconforming attribute, such as excessive ruboff, improper page setup, missing pages, duplicate pages, and so on. The operations manager determines that a random sample of 200 newspapers should be selected for analysis. Suppose that of this sample of 200, thirty-five contain some type of nonconformance. If the operations manager wants to have 90% confidence in estimating the true population proportion, set up the confidence interval estimate.

### SOLUTION

The confidence interval is computed as follows:

$$p_s = 35/200 = .175 \text{ and with a 90\% level of confidence } Z = 1.645$$

Using equation (10.3), we have

$$p_s \pm Z \sqrt{\frac{p_s(1 - p_s)}{n}}$$

$$= .175 \pm (1.645) \sqrt{\frac{(.175)(.825)}{200}}$$

$$= .175 \pm (1.645)(.0269)$$

$$= .175 \pm .0442$$

$$.1308 \le p \le .2192$$

Therefore, the operations manager estimates with 90% confidence that between 13.08% and 21.92% of the newspapers printed on that day have some type of nonconformance.

### COMMENT: *Checking the Assumptions*

In Example 10.4 the number of successes and failures is sufficiently large that the normal distribution provides an excellent approximation for the binomial distribution. However, if the sample size is not large or the percentage of successes is either very low or very high, then the binomial distribution is used rather than the normal distribution (references 1 and 7). The exact confidence intervals for various sample sizes and proportions of successes have been tabulated by Fisher and Yates (reference 2).

For a given sample size, confidence intervals for proportions often seem to be wider than those for continuous variables. With continuous variables, the measurement on each respondent contributes more information than for a categorical variable. In other words, a categorical variable with only two possible values is a very crude measure compared with a continuous variable, so each observation contributes less information about the parameter we are estimating.

## Problems for Section 10.3

### Learning the Basics

● **10.21** If $n = 200$ and $X = 50$, set up a 95% confidence interval estimate of the population proportion.

**10.22** If $n = 400$ and $X = 25$, set up a 99% confidence interval estimate of the population proportion.

### Applying the Concepts

● **10.23** The manager of a bank in a small city wants to determine the proportion of its depositors who have more than one account at the bank. A random sample of 100 depositors is selected, and 30 state that they have more than one account at the bank.
   (a) Set up a 90% confidence interval estimate of the population proportion of the bank's depositors who have more than one account at the bank.
   (b) How can the results in (a) be used in a marketing strategy for a new type of investment that targets current depositors at the bank?

**10.24** An auditor for the state insurance department wants to determine the proportion of claims that are paid by a health insurance company within 2 months of receipt of the claim. A random sample of 200 claims is selected, and it is determined that 80 were paid out within 2 months of the receipt of the claim.
   (a) Set up a 99% confidence interval estimate of the population proportion of the claims paid within 2 months.
   (b) If 90% or more claims are supposed to be paid within 2 months of their receipt, what should the auditor report to the state insurance department about the payment performance of the health insurance company?

● **10.25** An automobile dealer wants to estimate the proportion of customers who still own the cars they purchased 5 years earlier. A random sample of 200 customers selected from the automobile dealer's records indicated that 82 still own cars that had been purchased 5 years earlier.
   (a) Set up a 95% confidence interval estimate of the population proportion of all customers who still own the cars 5 years after they were purchased.
   (b) How can the results in (a) be used by the automobile dealer to study satisfaction with cars purchased at the dealership?

– **10.26** A stationery supply store receives a shipment of a certain brand of inexpensive ball-point pens from a manufacturer. The owner of the store wishes to estimate the proportion of pens that are defective. A random sample of 300 pens is tested, and 30 are found to be defective.
   (a) Set up a 90% confidence interval estimate of the proportion of defective pens in the shipment.
   (b) The shipment can be returned if it is more than 5% defective; on the basis of the sample results, can the owner return this shipment?
   (c) Suppose that a 99% confidence interval estimate was desired in (a). What would be the effect of this change on your answers to (a) and (b)?

**10.27** The marketing manager for a fast-food chain wants to estimate the proportion of high school students who have eaten at one of the chain's restaurants in the last month. A random sample of 400 high school students indicates that 90 have eaten at one of the chain's restaurants in the last month.
   (a) Set up a 95% confidence interval estimate of the population proportion of high school students who have eaten at one of the chain's restaurants in the last month.
   (b) How can the marketing manager use the results in (a) to increase the proportion of high school students who will eat at one of the chain's restaurants?

**10.28** The telephone company wants to estimate the proportion of households that would purchase an additional telephone line if it were made available at a substantially reduced installation cost. A random sample of 500 households is selected. The results indicate that 135 of the households would purchase the additional telephone line at a reduced installation cost.

(a) Set up a 99% confidence interval estimate of the population proportion of households who would purchase the additional telephone line.

(b) How would the manager in charge of promotional programs concerning residential customers use the results in (a)?

**10.29** The dean of a graduate school of business wishes to estimate the proportion of MBA students enrolled who have access to a personal computer outside the school (either at home or at work). A sample of 150 students reveals that 135 have access to a personal computer outside the school (either at home or at work).

(a) Set up a 90% confidence interval estimate of the population proportion of students who have access to a personal computer outside the school.

(b) How can the dean use the results in (a) to determine whether additional personal computers should be purchased for the computer lab?

##  DETERMINING SAMPLE SIZE

In each of our examples concerning confidence interval estimation, the sample size was arbitrarily determined without regard to the size of the confidence interval. In the business world, the determination of the proper sample size is a complicated procedure subject to the constraints of budget, time, and ease of selection. As a case in point, if, in the Saxon Plumbing Company example, the auditor wants to estimate the average sales invoice or the proportion of sales invoices that contain errors, he would try to determine in advance how good an estimate would be required. This means that he must decide how much error he is willing to allow in estimating each of these variables. The auditor must also determine in advance how sure (confident) he wants to be of correctly estimating the true population parameter.

### Sample Size Determination for the Mean

To determine the sample size needed for estimating the mean, we must keep in mind the amount of sampling error we are willing to accept and the level of confidence desired. In addition, we need some information about the standard deviation.

To develop a formula for determining sample size, recall equation (9.5):

$$Z = \frac{\bar{X} - \mu}{\dfrac{\sigma}{\sqrt{n}}}$$

where $Z$ is the critical value corresponding to an area of $(1 - \alpha)/2$ from the center of a standardized normal distribution. Multiplying both sides of equation (9.5) by $\sigma/\sqrt{n}$, we have

$$Z \frac{\sigma}{\sqrt{n}} = \bar{X} - \mu$$

Thus, the value of $Z$ is positive or negative depending on whether $\bar{X}$ is larger or smaller than $\mu$. The difference between the sample mean $\bar{X}$ and the population mean $\mu$, denoted by $e$, is called the **sampling error**. The sampling error $e$ is defined as

$$e = Z \frac{\sigma}{\sqrt{n}}$$

Solving for $n$ gives us the sample size needed to develop the confidence interval estimate for the mean.

## Sample Size Determination for the Mean

The sample size $n$ is equal to the product of the $Z$ value squared and the variance $\sigma^2$, divided by the sampling error ($e$) squared.

$$n = \frac{Z^2 \sigma^2}{e^2} \qquad \text{(10.4)}$$

To determine the sample size, we must know the following three factors:

**1.** The desired confidence level, which determines the value of $Z$, the critical value from the normal distribution[2]

**2.** The acceptable sampling error $e$

**3.** The standard deviation $\sigma$

[2]We use Z instead of t because to determine the critical value of t, we would need to know the sample size, which we don't know yet, and for most studies, the sample size needed will be large enough that the normal distribution is a good approximation of the t distribution.

In practice, it is usually not easy to determine these three quantities. How can we know what level of confidence to use and what sampling error is desired? Typically, these questions are answered only by the subject matter expert, that is, the individual most familiar with the variables to be analyzed. Although 95% is the most common confidence level used (in which case $Z = 1.96$), if a greater confidence is desired, then 99% might be more appropriate; if less confidence is deemed acceptable, then 90% might be used. For the sampling error, we should be thinking not of how much sampling error we would like to have (we really do not want any error) but of how much we can tolerate and still be able to provide adequate conclusions from the data.

Even when the confidence level and the sampling error are specified, an estimate of the standard deviation must be available. Unfortunately, the population standard deviation $\sigma$ is rarely known. In some instances, we can estimate the standard deviation from past data. In other situations, we can develop an educated guess by taking into account the range and distribution of the variable. For example, if we assume a normal distribution, the range is approximately equal to 6 $\sigma$ (i.e., $\pm 3\sigma$ around the mean), so that $\sigma$ is estimated as range/6. If we cannot estimate $\sigma$ in this manner, a *pilot* study can be conducted and the standard deviation estimated from the resulting data.

To explore how to determine the sample size needed for estimating the population mean, let us again consider the audit to be performed this month at Saxon Plumbing Company. In section 10.2, we saw that a sample of 100 sales invoices was selected and a 95% confidence interval estimate of the population average sales invoice amount was developed. How was this sample size determined? Should we have selected a different sample size?

Suppose that after consultation with company officials, it is determined that a sampling error of no more than $\pm\$5$ is desired along with 95% confidence. The auditor notes that the standard deviation of the sales amount has been approximately $25 for a substantial period of time. Thus, $e = \$5$, $\sigma = \$25$, and $Z = 1.96$ (for 95% confidence). Using equation (10.4), we have

$$n = \frac{Z^2 \sigma^2}{e^2} = \frac{(1.96)^2 (25)^2}{(5)^2}$$

$$n = 96.04$$

Therefore, $n = 97$ because the general rule is to round the sample size up to the next integer to slightly oversatisfy the criteria. Thus, the sample size of 100 that was taken is close to the one necessary to satisfy the needs of the company based on the estimated standard deviation, desired confidence level, and sampling error. However, we note from the confidence interval obtained on page 376 that because the sample standard deviation is $28.95, the width of the confidence interval was slightly more than was desired.

We provide another application on how to determine the sample size needed to develop a confidence interval estimate for the mean in Example 10.5.

## Example 10.5  *Determining the Sample Size for the Mean*

To return to Example 10.3 on page 376, suppose the marketing manager wishes to estimate the population mean annual usage of home heating oil to within $\pm 50$ gallons of the true value and he desires to be 95% confident of correctly estimating the true mean. On the basis of a study taken the previous year, he feels that the standard deviation can be estimated as 325 gallons. Find the sample size needed.

### SOLUTION

With this information, the sample size is determined in the following manner for $e = 50$, $\sigma = 325$, and 95% confidence ($Z = 1.96$):

$$n = \frac{Z^2 \sigma^2}{e^2} = \frac{(1.96)^2 (325)^2}{(50)^2}$$

$$n = 162.31$$

Therefore, $n = 163$. We choose a sample size of 163 homes because the general rule for determining sample size is to always round up to the *next integer value* in order to slightly oversatisfy the criteria desired.

We may note that if the marketing manager uses these criteria, a sample of 163 homes will be taken—not a sample of 35 as was used in Example 10.3. However, the standard deviation that was used was estimated at 325 based on a previous survey. If the standard deviation obtained in the actual survey is very different from this value, the computed sampling error will be directly affected.

## Sample Size Determination for a Proportion

Thus far in this section we have discussed how to determine the sample size needed for estimating the population mean. Now suppose that the auditor of Saxon Plumbing Company also wishes to determine the sample size necessary for estimating the population proportion of sales invoices that have errors violating company policy. The methods of sample size determination that are used in estimating a population proportion are similar to those employed in estimating a mean.

To develop a formula for determining sample size, recall from equation (9.10) that

$$Z \cong \frac{p_s - p}{\sqrt{\dfrac{p(1 - p)}{n}}}$$

where $Z$ is the critical value corresponding to an area of $(1 - \alpha)/2$ from the center of a standardized normal distribution. Multiplying both sides of equation (9.10) by $\sqrt{p(1 - p)/n}$, we have

$$Z\sqrt{\frac{p(1 - p)}{n}} = p_s - p$$

The sampling error $e$ is equal to $(p_s - p)$, the difference between the sample proportion $(p_s)$ and the parameter to be estimated $(p)$. This sampling error can be defined as

$$e = Z\sqrt{\frac{p(1 - p)}{n}}$$

Solving for $n$, we obtain the sample size necessary to develop a confidence interval estimate for a proportion.

## Sample Size Determination for a Proportion

The sample size $n$ is equal to the $Z$ value squared times the true proportion $p$, times 1 minus the true proportion $p$, divided by the sampling error $(e)$ squared.

$$n = \frac{Z^2 p(1 - p)}{e^2} \tag{10.5}$$

To determine the sample size for estimating a proportion, three unknowns must be defined:

1. The desired level of confidence
2. The acceptable sampling error, $e$
3. The true proportion of "success," $p$

In practice, the selection of these quantities requires some planning. Once we determine the desired level of confidence, we can obtain the appropriate $Z$ value from the normal distribution. The sampling error $e$ indicates the amount of error that we are willing to accept or tolerate in estimating the population proportion. The third quantity—the true proportion of success, $p$—is actually the population parameter that we want to find! Thus, how do we state a value for the very thing that we are taking a sample in order to determine?

Here there are two alternatives. First, in many situations, past information or relevant experiences may be available that enable us to provide an educated estimate of $p$. Second, if past information or relevant experiences are not available, we can try to provide a value for $p$ that would never *underestimate* the sample size needed. Referring to equation (10.5), we observe that the quantity $p(1 - p)$ appears in the numerator. Thus, we must determine the value of $p$ that will make the quantity $p(1 - p)$ as large as possible. It can be shown that when $p = .5$, then the product $p(1 - p)$ achieves its maximum result. Several values of $p$ along with the accompanying products of $p(1 - p)$ are

When $p = .9$, then $p(1 - p) = (.9)(.1) = .09$

When $p = .7$, then $p(1 - p) = (.7)(.3) = .21$

When $p = .5$, then $p(1 - p) = (.5)(.5) = .25$

When $p = .3$, then $p(1 - p) = (.3)(.7) = .21$

When $p = .1$, then $p(1 - p) = (.1)(.9) = .09$

Therefore, when we have no prior knowledge or estimate of the true proportion $p$, we should use $p = .5$ as the most conservative way of determining the sample size. This produces the largest possible sample size but unfortunately results in the highest possible cost of sampling. That is, the use of $p = .5$ may result in an overestimate of the sample size because the actual sample proportion is used in developing the confidence interval. If the actual sample proportion is very different from .5, the width of the confidence interval may be substantially narrower than originally intended. The increased precision comes at the cost of spending more time and money for an increased sample size.

Returning to the auditor for Saxon Plumbing Company, suppose that he wants to have 95% confidence of estimating the population proportion of sales invoices with errors to within ±.07 of the true population proportion. The results from past months indicate that the largest proportion has been no more than .15. Thus, $e = .07$, $p = .15$, and $Z = 1.96$ (for 95% confidence). Using equation (10.5), we have

$$n = \frac{Z^2 p(1 - p)}{e^2}$$

$$= \frac{(1.96)^2(.15)(.85)}{(.07)^2}$$

$$= 99.96$$

Therefore, $n = 100$ because the general rule is to round the sample size up to the next whole integer to slightly oversatisfy the criteria. Thus, the sample size of 100 that was taken was exactly what was needed to satisfy the requirements of the company based on the estimated proportion, desired confidence level, and sampling error. However, we note from the confidence interval obtained on page 380 that because the sample proportion was .10, the width of the confidence level is actually narrower than desired.

A second application of determining the sample size for estimating the population proportion is provided in Example 10.6.

## Example 10.6 *Determining the Sample Size for the Proportion*

In Example 10.4 on page 381, suppose the operations manager wants to have 90% confidence of estimating the proportion of nonconforming newspapers to within ±.05 of its true value. In addition, because the publisher of the newspaper has not previously undertaken such a survey, no information is available from past data. Determine the sample size needed.

### SOLUTION

Because there is no information available from past data, we will set $p = .50$. With this and other criteria in mind, the sample size needed can be determined in the following manner when $e = .05$, $p = .5$, and for 90% confidence, $Z = 1.645$.

$$n = \frac{(1.645)^2(.5)(.5)}{(.05)^2}$$

$$= 270.6$$

Thus, $n = 271$. Therefore, in order to be 90% confident of estimating the proportion to within $\pm.05$ of its true value, a sample size of 271 newspapers is needed.

## Problems for Section 10.4

### Learning the Basics

● **10.30** If you want to be 95% confident of estimating the population mean to within a sampling error of $\pm 5$ and the standard deviation was assumed to be equal to 15, what sample size is required?

**10.31** If you want to be 99% confident of estimating the population mean to within a sampling error of $\pm 20$ and the standard deviation was assumed to be equal to 100, what sample size is required?

**10.32** If you want to be 99% confident of estimating the population proportion to within an error of $\pm.04$, what sample size is needed?

**10.33** If you want to be 95% confident of estimating the population proportion to within an error of $\pm.02$ and there is historical evidence that the population proportion is approximately .40, what sample size is needed?

### Applying the Concepts

**10.34** A survey is planned to determine the average annual family medical expenses of employees of a large company. The management of the company wishes to be 95% confident that the sample average is correct to within $\pm\$50$ of the true average annual family medical expenses. A pilot study indicates that the standard deviation can be estimated as \$400.
(a) How large a sample size is necessary?
(b) If management wants to be correct to within $\pm\$25$, what sample size is necessary?

**10.35** If the manager of a paint supply store wants to estimate the average amount in a 1-gallon can to within $\pm 0.004$ gallon with 95% confidence and also assumes that the standard deviation is 0.02 gallon, what sample size is needed?

● **10.36** If a quality control manager wants to estimate the average life of light bulbs to within $\pm 20$ hours with 95% confidence and also assumes that the process standard deviation is 100 hours, what sample size is needed?

**10.37** If the inspection division of a county weights and measures department wants to estimate the average amount of soft-drink fill in 2-liter bottles to within $\pm 0.01$ liter with 95% confidence and also assumes that the standard deviation is 0.05 liter, what sample size is needed?

● **10.38** A consumer group wishes to estimate the average electric bills for the month of July for single-family homes in a large city. Based on studies conducted in other cities, the standard deviation is assumed to be \$25. The group wants to estimate the average bill for July to within $\pm\$5$ of the true average with 99% confidence.
(a) What sample size is needed?
(b) If 95% confidence is desired, what sample size is necessary?

**10.39** A pharmaceutical company is considering a request to pay for the continuing education of its research scientists. It would like to estimate the average amount spent by these scientists for professional memberships. Based on a pilot study, the standard deviation is estimated to be $35.
  (a) What sample size is required to be 90% confident of being correct to within ±$10?
  (b) If 95% confidence of being correct to within ±$20 is desired, what sample size is necessary?

**10.40** An advertising agency that serves a major radio station wants to estimate the average amount of time that the station's audience spends listening to radio on a daily basis. From past studies, the standard deviation is estimated as 45 minutes.
  (a) What sample size is needed if the agency wants to be 90% confident of being correct to within ±5 minutes?
  (b) If 99% confidence is desired, what sample size is necessary?

**10.41** Suppose that a gas utility wishes to estimate its average waiting time for installation of service to within ±5 days with 95% confidence. Because it does not have access to previous data, it makes its own independent estimate of the standard deviation, which it believes to be 20 days. What sample size is needed?

**10.42** A political pollster wants to estimate the proportion of voters who will vote for the Democratic candidate in a presidential campaign. The pollster wishes to have 90% confidence that her prediction is correct to within ±.04 of the population proportion.
  (a) What sample size is needed?
  (b) If the pollster wants to have 95% confidence, what sample size is needed?
  (c) If she wants to have 95% confidence and a sampling error of ±.03, what sample size is needed?
  (d) On the basis of your answers to (a)–(c), what general conclusions can be reached about the effects of the confidence level desired and the acceptable sampling error on the sample size needed? Discuss.

**•10.43** A cable television company wants to estimate the proportion of its customers who would purchase a cable television program guide. The company would like to have 95% confidence that its estimate is correct to within ±.05 of the true proportion. Past experience in other areas indicates that 30% of the customers will purchase the program guide. What sample size is needed?

**•10.44** A bank manager wants to be 90% confident of being correct to within ±.05 of the true population proportion of depositors who have both savings and checking accounts at the bank. How many depositors need to be sampled?

**10.45** An audit test to establish the percentage of occurrence of failures to follow a specific internal control procedure is to be undertaken. The auditor decides that the maximum tolerable error rate that is permissible is 5%.
  (a) What size sample is required to achieve a sample precision of ±2% with 99% confidence?
  (b) What would be your answer in (a) if the maximum tolerable error rate is
    (1) 10%?
    (2) 15%?
    (3) 20%?

**10.46** A large shipment of air filters is received by Joe's Auto Supply Company. The air filters are to be sampled to estimate the proportion that are unusable. From past experience the proportion of unusable air filters is estimated to be .10.
  (a) How large a random sample should be taken to estimate the true proportion of unusable air filters to within ±.07 with 99% confidence?
  (b) If 95% confidence is desired with a sampling error of ±.06, what sample size should be taken?

**10.47** Suppose that Matt's Motors wants to conduct a survey to determine the proportion of its customers who still own their cars 5 years after purchasing them. Suppose it wants to be 95% confident of being correct to within ±.025 of the true proportion. What sample size is needed?

## 10.5 ESTIMATION AND SAMPLE SIZE DETERMINATION FOR FINITE POPULATIONS

### Estimating the Mean

In section 9.3 we saw that in sampling without replacement from finite populations, the **finite population correction (fpc) factor** serves to reduce the standard error by a value equal to $\sqrt{(N - n)/(N - 1)}$. When developing confidence interval estimates for population parameters and samples are selected without replacement, the fpc factor is used. Thus, the $(1 - \alpha) \times 100\%$ confidence interval estimate for the mean is calculated as in equation (10.6).

> **Confidence Interval Estimate for the Mean ($\sigma$ Unknown) for a Finite Population**
>
> $$\overline{X} \pm t_{n-1}\frac{S}{\sqrt{n}}\sqrt{\frac{N-n}{N-1}} \qquad (10.6)$$

To illustrate the finite population correction factor, we refer to the confidence interval estimate for the mean developed for Saxon Plumbing Company on page 375. Suppose that in this month there are 5,000 sales invoices. Using $\overline{X} = \$110.27$, $S = \$28.95$, $N = 5,000$, $n = 100$, and with 95% confidence, $t_{99} = 1.9842$. From equation (10.6) we have

$$\overline{X} \pm t_{n-1}\frac{S}{\sqrt{n}}\sqrt{\frac{N-n}{N-1}}$$

$$= 110.27 \pm (1.9842)\frac{28.95}{\sqrt{100}}\sqrt{\frac{5,000 - 100}{5,000 - 1}}$$

$$= 110.27 \pm 5.74(.99)$$

$$= 110.27 \pm 5.68$$

$$\$104.59 \leq \mu \leq \$115.95$$

In this case, because the sample is a very small fraction of the population, the correction factor has a minimal effect on the width of the confidence interval. To examine the effect of the correction factor when the sample size is more than 5% of the population size, we present Example 10.7.

---

### Example 10.7 *Estimating the Mean Annual Usage for Home Heating Oil*

In Example 10.3, on page 376, a sample of 35 single-family homes was selected. Suppose there is a population of 500 single-family homes served by the company. Set up a 95% confidence interval estimate of the population mean.

## SOLUTION

Using the finite population correction factor, we have, with $\bar{X} = 1,122.7$ gallons, $S = 295.72$, $n = 35$, $N = 500$, and $t_{34} = 2.0322$ (for 95% confidence):

$$\bar{X} \pm t_{n-1}\frac{S}{\sqrt{n}}\sqrt{\frac{N-n}{N-1}}$$

$$= 1,122.7 \pm (2.0322)\frac{295.72}{\sqrt{35}}\sqrt{\frac{500-35}{500-1}}$$

$$= 1,122.7 \pm 101.58(.9653)$$

$$= 1,122.7 \pm 98.05$$

$$1,024.65 \leq \mu \leq 1,220.75$$

Here, because more than 5% of the population is to be sampled, the fpc factor has a moderate effect on the confidence interval estimate.

## Estimating the Proportion

In sampling without replacement, the $(1 - \alpha) \times 100\%$ confidence interval estimate of the proportion is found as in equation (10.7).

### Confidence Interval Estimate for the Proportion Using the Finite Population Correction Factor

$$p_s \pm Z\sqrt{\frac{p_s(1-p_s)}{n}}\sqrt{\frac{N-n}{N-1}} \tag{10.7}$$

To illustrate the use of the finite population correction factor when developing a confidence interval estimate of the population proportion, consider again the estimate developed for Saxon Plumbing Company on page 380. For these data, we have $N = 5,000$, $n = 100$, $p_s = 10/100 = .10$, and with 95% confidence, $Z = 1.96$. Using equation (10.7),

$$p_s \pm Z\sqrt{\frac{p_s(1-p_s)}{n}}\sqrt{\frac{N-n}{N-1}} = .10 \pm (1.96)\sqrt{\frac{(.10)(.90)}{100}}\sqrt{\frac{5,000-100}{5,000-1}}$$

$$= .10 \pm (1.96)(.03)(.99)$$

$$= .10 \pm .0582$$

$$.0418 \leq p \leq .1582$$

In this case, because the sample is a very small fraction of the population, the fpc factor has virtually no effect on the confidence interval estimate.

## Determining the Sample Size

Just as the fpc factor is used to develop confidence interval estimates, it also is used to determine sample size when sampling without replacement. For example, in estimating the mean, the sampling error is

$$e = \frac{Z\sigma}{\sqrt{n}}\sqrt{\frac{N-n}{N-1}}$$

and in estimating the proportion, the sampling error is

$$e = Z\sqrt{\frac{p(1-p)}{n}}\sqrt{\frac{N-n}{N-1}}$$

To determine the sample size in estimating the mean or the proportion, we have, from equations (10.4) and (10.5),

$$n_0 = \frac{Z^2\sigma^2}{e^2} \text{ and } n_0 = \frac{Z^2p(1-p)}{e^2}$$

where $n_0$ is the sample size without considering the finite population correction factor. Applying the fpc factor to this results in the actual sample size $n$, computed as in equation (10.8).

### Sample Size Determination Using the Finite Population Correction Factor

$$n = \frac{n_0 N}{n_0 + (N-1)} \tag{10.8}$$

In the auditor's determination of sample size for Saxon Plumbing Company, a sample size of 97 was needed for the mean and a sample of 100 was needed for the proportion (see pages 385 and 387). Using the fpc factor in equation (10.8) for the mean, with $N = 5,000$, $e = \$5$, $\sigma = \$25$, and $Z = 1.96$ (for 95% confidence), leads to

$$n = \frac{(96.04)(5,000)}{96.04 + (5,000 - 1)} = 94.25$$

Thus, $n = 95$.

Using the fpc factor in equation (10.8) for the proportion, with $N = 5,000$, $e = .07$, $p = .15$, and $Z = 1.96$ (for 95% confidence),

$$n = \frac{(99.96)(5,000)}{99.96 + (5,000 - 1)} = 98.02$$

Thus, $n = 99$.

To satisfy *both requirements simultaneously with one sample*, we need to take the larger sample size of 99.

## Problems for Section 10.5

### Learning the Basics

● **10.48** If $\bar{X} = 75$, $S = 24$, $n = 36$, and $N = 200$, set up a 95% confidence interval estimate of the population mean $\mu$ if sampling is done without replacement.

**10.49** For a population of 1,000, we want 95% confidence with a sampling error of 5, and the standard deviation is assumed equal to 20. What sample size would be required if sampling is done without replacement?

## Applying the Concepts

- **10.50** The quality control manager at a light bulb factory needs to estimate the average life of a large shipment of light bulbs. The process standard deviation is known to be 100 hours. Assuming the shipment contains a total of 2,000 light bulbs, if sampling is done without replacement,
  - (a) set up a 95% confidence interval estimate of the true average life of light bulbs in this shipment if a random sample of 50 light bulbs selected from the shipment indicates a sample average life of 350 hours
  - (b) determine the sample size needed to estimate the average life to within $\pm 20$ hours with 95% confidence
  - (c) What are your answers in (a) and (b) if the shipment contains 1,000 light bulbs?

**10.51** A survey is planned to determine the average annual family medical expenses of employees of a large company. The management of the company wishes to be 95% confident that the sample average is correct to within $\pm \$50$ of the true average annual family medical expenses. A pilot study indicates that the standard deviation is estimated as $400. How large a sample size is necessary if the company has 3,000 employees and if sampling is done without replacement?

- **10.52** The manager of a bank that has 1,000 depositors in a small city wants to determine the proportion of its depositors with more than one account at the bank.
  - (a) Set up a 90% confidence interval estimate of the population proportion of the bank's depositors who have more than one account at the bank if a random sample of 100 depositors is selected without replacement and 30 state that they have more than one account at the bank.
  - (b) A bank manager wants to be 90% confident of being correct to within $\pm .05$ of the true population proportion of depositors who have more than one account at the bank. What sample size is needed if sampling is done without replacement?
  - (c) What are your answers to (a) and (b) if the bank has 2,000 depositors?

- **10.53** An automobile dealer wants to estimate the proportion of customers who still own the cars they purchased 5 years earlier. Sales records indicate that the population of owners is 4,000.
  - (a) Set up a 95% confidence interval estimate of the population proportion of all customers who still own cars 5 years after they were purchased if a random sample of 200 customers selected without replacement from the automobile dealer's records indicate that 82 still own cars that were purchased 5 years earlier.
  - (b) What sample size is necessary to estimate the true proportion to within $\pm .025$ with 95% confidence?
  - (c) What are your answers to (a) and (b) if the population consists of 6,000 owners?

**10.54** The inspection division of the Lee County Weights and Measures Department is interested in estimating the actual amount of soft drink that is placed in 2-liter bottles at the local bottling plant of a large nationally known soft-drink company. The population consists of 2,000 bottles. The bottling plant has informed the inspection division that the standard deviation for 2-liter bottles is 0.05 liter.
  - (a) Set up a 95% confidence interval estimate of the population average amount of soft drink in each bottle if a random sample of one hundred 2-liter bottles obtained without replacement from this bottling plant indicates a sample average of 1.99 liters.
  - (b) Determine the sample size necessary to estimate the population average amount to within $\pm 0.01$ liter with 95% confidence.
  - (c) What are your answers to (a) and (b) if the population consists of 1,000 bottles?

**10.55** A stationery store wishes to estimate the average retail value of greeting cards that it has in its inventory which consists of 300 greeting cards.

(a) Set up a 95% confidence interval estimate of the population average value of all greeting cards that are in its inventory if a random sample of 20 greeting cards selected without replacement indicates an average value of $1.67 and a standard deviation of $0.32.

(b) What is your answer to (a) if the store has 500 greeting cards in its inventory?

## 10.6  APPLICATIONS OF CONFIDENCE INTERVAL ESTIMATION IN AUDITING

In our discussion of estimation procedures, we have focused on estimating either the population mean or the population proportion when sampling with replacement or without replacement from finite populations. One of the areas in business that makes widespread use of statistical sampling for the purposes of estimation is auditing.

**Auditing** may be defined as the collection and evaluation of evidence about information relating to an economic entity such as a sole business proprietor, a partnership, a corporation, or a government agency in order to determine and report on how well the information obtained corresponds to established criteria.

Exhibit 10.1 lists six advantages of statistical sampling in auditing.

### Exhibit 10.1  Advantages of Statistical Sampling in Auditing

✓ **1.** The sample result is objective and defensible. Because the sample size is based on demonstrable statistical principles, the audit is defensible before one's superiors and in a court of law.

✓ **2.** The method provides a way of estimating the sample size in advance on an objective basis.

✓ **3.** The method provides an estimate of the sampling error.

✓ **4.** This approach may turn out to be more accurate in drawing conclusions about the population due to the fact that the examination of large populations may be time-consuming and subject to more nonsampling error than a statistical sample.

✓ **5.** Statistical samples may be combined and evaluated even though accomplished by different auditors. This is because there is a scientific basis for the sample so that the samples may be treated as if they have been done by a single auditor.

✓ **6.** Objective evaluation of the results of an audit is possible. The results can be projected with a known sampling error.

### Estimating the Population Total Amount

In auditing applications, we are more interested in obtaining estimates of the population **total amount** than the population mean. Equation (10.9) shows how to estimate a population total amount.

## Estimating the Population Total Amount

The population total is equal to the population size $N$ times the sample mean $\overline{X}$

$$\text{Total} = N\overline{X} \qquad (10.9)$$

Because the estimated total is $N\overline{X}$, a confidence interval estimate for the population total can be obtained as in equation (10.10).

## Confidence Interval Estimate for the Total

$$N\overline{X} \pm N(t_{n-1}) \frac{S}{\sqrt{n}} \sqrt{\frac{N-n}{N-1}} \qquad (10.10)$$

To demonstrate the application of the confidence interval estimate for the total, let us return to the Saxon Plumbing Company example. The auditor needs an estimate of the total amount listed on all sales invoices for the warehouse in that month (i.e., the population). Using equations (10.9) and (10.10), with $N = 5{,}000$, $\overline{X} = \$110.27$, and $S = \$28.95$, for 95% confidence, $t_{99} = 1.9842$, and we have

$$\text{Total} = (5{,}000)(\$110.27) = \$551{,}350$$

so that

$$N\overline{X} \pm N(t_{n-1}) \frac{S}{\sqrt{n}} \sqrt{\frac{N-n}{N-1}} = 551{,}350 \pm (5{,}000)(1.9842) \frac{28.95}{\sqrt{100}} \sqrt{\frac{5{,}000-100}{5{,}000-1}}$$

$$= 551{,}350 \pm 28{,}721.3(.99)$$

$$= 551{,}350 \pm 28{,}434.09$$

$$\$522{,}915.91 \le \text{population total} \le \$579{,}784.09$$

Thus, we estimate with 95% confidence that the total amount of sales invoices is between $522,915.91 and $579,784.09.

To further illustrate the population total, let us turn to Example 10.8.

## Example 10.8 *Developing a Confidence Interval Estimate for the Population Total*

Suppose that an auditor is faced with a population of 1,000 vouchers and wishes to estimate the total value of the population of vouchers. A sample of 50 vouchers is selected with the following results:

$$\text{Average voucher amount } (\overline{X}) = \$1{,}076.39$$
$$\text{Standard deviation } (S) = \$273.62$$

Set up a 95% confidence interval estimate of the total amount for the population of vouchers.

### SOLUTION
Using equation (10.9), the total is computed as

$$\text{Total} = (1{,}000)(1{,}076.39) = \$1{,}076{,}390$$

From equation (10.10), a 95% confidence interval estimate of the population total amount is obtained as follows:

$$(1,000)(1,076.39) \pm (1,000)(2.0096) \frac{(273.62)}{\sqrt{50}} \sqrt{\frac{1,000 - 50}{1,000 - 1}}$$

$$= 1,076,390 \pm 77,762.9(.975)$$

$$= 1,076,390 \pm 75,818.83$$

$$\$1,000,571.17 \leq \text{population total} \leq \$1,152,208.83$$

Thus, we estimate with 95% confidence that the total amount of the vouchers is between $1,000,571.17 and $1,152,208.83.

## Difference Estimation

**Difference estimation** is used when an auditor believes that errors exist in a set of items being audited and the auditor wishes to estimate the magnitude of the errors based only on a sample. The following steps are used in difference estimation.

**1.** Determine the sample size required.

**2.** Compute the average difference in the sample ($\overline{D}$) by dividing the total difference by the sample size as shown in equation (10.11).

**Average Difference**

$$\overline{D} = \frac{\sum\limits_{i=1}^{n} D_i}{n} \tag{10.11}$$

**3.** Compute the standard deviation of the differences ($S_D$) as shown in equation (10.12).

**Standard Deviation of the Difference**

$$S_D = \sqrt{\frac{\sum\limits_{i=1}^{n} (D_i - \overline{D})^2}{n - 1}} \tag{10.12}$$

Be sure to remember that any item that is not in error has a difference value of 0.

**4.** Set up a confidence interval estimate of the total difference in the population, as shown in equation (10.13).

**Confidence Interval Estimate for the Total Difference**

$$N\overline{D} \pm N(t_{n-1}) \frac{S_D}{\sqrt{n}} \sqrt{\frac{N - n}{N - 1}} \tag{10.13}$$

Recall from the Saxon Plumbing Company example that the auditor wants to obtain a 95% confidence interval estimate of the difference between the actual amounts on the sales invoice and the amounts entered into the accounting system for the warehouse. Suppose that in the sample of 100 sales invoices, there are 12 invoices in which the actual amount on the sales invoice and the amount entered into the accounting system for the warehouse are different. These 12 differences are:

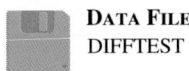

**DATA FILE**
PLUMBINV

$9.03 $7.47 $17.32 $8.30 $5.21 $10.80 $6.22 $5.63 $4.97 $7.43 $2.99 $4.63

The other 88 invoices are not in error. The *differences* are each 0. Thus,

$$\overline{D} = \frac{\sum\limits_{i=1}^{n} D_i}{n} = \frac{90}{100} = .90$$

and

$$S_D = \sqrt{\frac{\sum\limits_{i=1}^{n}(D_i - \overline{D})^2}{n-1}}$$

$$S_D = \sqrt{\frac{(9.03 - .9)^2 + (7.47 - .9)^2 + \cdots + (0 - .9)^2}{100 - 1}}$$

$$S_D = 2.752$$

To obtain the confidence interval estimate for the total difference in the population, we use equation (10.13), so that we have

$$(5,000)(.90) \pm 5,000(1.9842)\frac{2.752}{\sqrt{100}}\sqrt{\frac{5,000 - 100}{5,000 - 1}}$$

$$= 4,500 \pm 2,703.09$$

$$\$1,796.91 \le \text{total difference} \le \$7,203.09$$

Thus, the auditor estimates with 95% confidence that the total difference between the sales invoices and the actual amount entered into the accounting system is between $1,796.91 and $7,203.09.

In the Saxon Plumbing Company example, all 12 differences are positive because the actual amount on the sales invoice is more than the amount entered into the accounting system. It is possible that the error could have been negative. To illustrate such an occurrence, we present Example 10.9.

## Example 10.9 *Difference Estimation*

Returning to Example 10.8 on page 395, suppose that in the sample of 50 vouchers there are 14 vouchers that contain errors. Suppose that the values of the 14 errors are as follows, in which two differences are negative.

$75.41,  $38.97,  $108.54,  −$37.18,  $62.75,  $118.32,  −$88.84,

$127.74,  $55.42,  $39.03,  $29.41,  $47.99,  $28.73,  $84.05

**DATA FILE**
DIFFTEST

Set up a 95% confidence interval estimate of the total difference in the population of vouchers.

## SOLUTION

For these data,

$$\overline{D} = \frac{\sum\limits_{i=1}^{n} D_i}{n} = \frac{690.34}{50} = 13.8068$$

and

$$S_D = \sqrt{\frac{\sum\limits_{i=1}^{n} (D_i - \overline{D})^2}{n - 1}}$$

$$S_D = \sqrt{\frac{(75.41 - 13.8068)^2 + (38.97 - 13.8068)^2 + \cdots + (0 - 13.8068)^2}{50 - 1}}$$

$$S_D = 37.427$$

To obtain the confidence interval estimate for the total difference in the population, we use equation (10.13), so that we have

$$(1{,}000)(13.8068) \pm 1{,}000(2.0096) \frac{37.427}{\sqrt{50}} \sqrt{\frac{1{,}000 - 50}{1{,}000 - 1}}$$

$$= 13{,}806.8 \pm 10{,}372.63$$

$$\$3{,}434.17 \leq \text{total difference} \leq \$24{,}179.43$$

Thus, we estimate with 95% confidence that the total difference in the population of vouchers is between $3,170.03 and $24,179.43.

---

## Problems for Section 10.6

### Learning the Basics

• **10.56** Suppose that a sample of 25 is selected from a population of 500 items. The sample mean is 25.7 and the sample standard deviation is 7.8. Set up a 99% confidence interval estimate of the population total.

**DATA FILE**
ITEMERR

**10.57** Suppose that a sample of 200 items is selected from a population of 10,000 items. Ten items are found to have errors of the following amounts:

| 13.76 | 42.87 | 34.65 | 11.09 | 14.54 | 22.87 | 25.52 | 9.81 | 10.03 | 15.49 |

Set up a 95% confidence interval estimate of the total difference in the population.

### Applying the Concepts

**10.58** The manager of a branch of a local savings bank that has 2,000 depositors wants to estimate the total amount held in passbook savings accounts by depositors at the bank. A random sample of 30 depositors is selected, and the results indicate a sample average of $4,750 and a sample standard deviation of $1,200. Set up a 95% confidence interval estimate of the total amount held in passbook savings accounts in the branch.

• **10.59** A stationery store wants to estimate the total retail value of greeting cards that it has in its inventory, which consists of 300 greeting cards. Set up a 95% confidence interval estimate of the population total value of all greeting cards that are in its inventory if a random sample of 20 greeting cards indicates an average value of $1.67 and a standard deviation of $0.32.

**10.60** The personnel department of a large corporation employing 3,000 workers wishes to estimate the family dental expenses of its employees to determine the feasibility of providing a dental insurance plan. A random sample of 10 employees reveals the following family dental expenses (in dollars) for the preceding year:

DATA FILE
DENTAL

110, 362, 246, 85, 510, 208, 173, 425, 316, 179

Set up a 90% confidence interval estimate of the total family dental expenses for all employees in the preceding year.

**10.61** A branch of a chain of large electronics stores is conducting an end-of-month inventory of the merchandise in stock. It has been determined that there are 1,546 items in inventory at that time. A sample size of 50 items was randomly selected and an audit was conducted with the following results:

Value of Merchandise

$\overline{X} = \$252.28 \quad S = \$93.67$

Set up a 95% confidence interval estimate of the total estimated value of the merchandise in inventory at the end of the month.

● **10.62** A customer in the wholesale garment trade is often entitled to a discount for a cash payment for goods. The amount of discount varies by vendor. A sample of 150 items selected from a population of 4,000 invoices at the end of a period of time revealed that in 13 cases the customer failed to take the discount to which he or she was entitled. The amounts of the 13 discounts that were not taken were as follows:

DATA FILE
DISCOUNT

$6.45, 15.32, 97.36, 230.63, 104.18, 84.92, 132.76, 66.12, 26.55, 129.43, 88.32, 47.81, 89.01

Set up a 99% confidence interval estimate of the population total amount of discount not taken.

**10.63** Econe Dresses is a small company manufacturing woman's dresses for sale to specialty stores. There are 1,200 inventory items in which the historical cost is recorded on a first in, first out (FIFO) basis. In the past, approximately 15% of the inventory items were incorrectly priced. However, any misstatements were usually not significant. A sample of 120 items was selected and the historical cost of each item was compared with the audited value. The results indicated that 15 items differed in their historical costs and audited values. These differences were as follows:

| SAMPLE NUMBER | HISTORICAL COST ($) | AUDITED VALUE ($) | SAMPLE NUMBER | HISTORICAL COST ($) | AUDITED VALUE ($) |
|---|---|---|---|---|---|
| 5 | 261 | 240 | 60 | 21 | 210 |
| 9 | 87 | 105 | 73 | 140 | 152 |
| 17 | 201 | 276 | 86 | 129 | 112 |
| 18 | 121 | 110 | 95 | 340 | 216 |
| 28 | 315 | 298 | 96 | 341 | 402 |
| 35 | 411 | 356 | 107 | 135 | 97 |
| 43 | 249 | 211 | 119 | 228 | 220 |
| 51 | 216 | 305 | | | |

DATA FILE
FIFO

Set up a 95% confidence interval estimate of the total population difference in the historical cost and audited value.

## 10.7 ◆ CONFIDENCE INTERVAL ESTIMATION AND ETHICAL ISSUES

Ethical issues relating to the selection of samples and the inferences that accompany them from sample surveys can arise in several ways. The major ethical issue relates to whether or not confidence interval estimates are provided along with the point estimates of the sample statistics obtained from a survey. To indicate a point estimate of a sample statistic without also including the confidence interval limits (typically set at 95%), the sample size used, and an interpretation of the meaning of the confidence interval in terms that a layperson can understand raises ethical issues because of their omission. Failure to include a confidence interval estimate might mislead the user of the survey results into thinking that the point estimate obtained from the sample is all that is needed to predict the population characteristics with certainty. Thus, it is important that the interval estimate be indicated in a prominent place in any written communication along with a simple explanation of the meaning of the confidence interval. In addition, the size of the sample should be highlighted so that the reader clearly understands the magnitude of the survey that has been undertaken.

One of the most common areas where ethical issues concerning estimation from sample surveys occurs is in the publication of the results of political polls. All too often, the results of the polls are highlighted on page 1 of the newspaper and the sampling error involved along with the methodology used is printed on the page where the article is typically continued (often in the middle of the newspaper). To ensure an ethical interpretation of statistical results, the confidence levels, sample size, and confidence limits should be made available for all surveys.

## ◆ SUMMARY

As observed in the summary chart on the next page, in this chapter we have developed a confidence interval approach for estimating the characteristics of a population. In addition, we have investigated how we can determine the necessary sample size for a survey.

Now that we have made estimates of population characteristics such as the mean, proportion, total, and difference using confidence intervals, in the next four chapters we turn to a hypothesis-testing approach in which we make decisions about population parameters.

## *Key Terms*

auditing   394
confidence interval estimate   369
critical value   369
degrees of freedom   373
difference estimation   396

finite population correction
    factor (fpc)   390
interval estimate   366
level of confidence   369

point estimate   366
sampling error   383
Student's *t* distribution   373
total amount   394

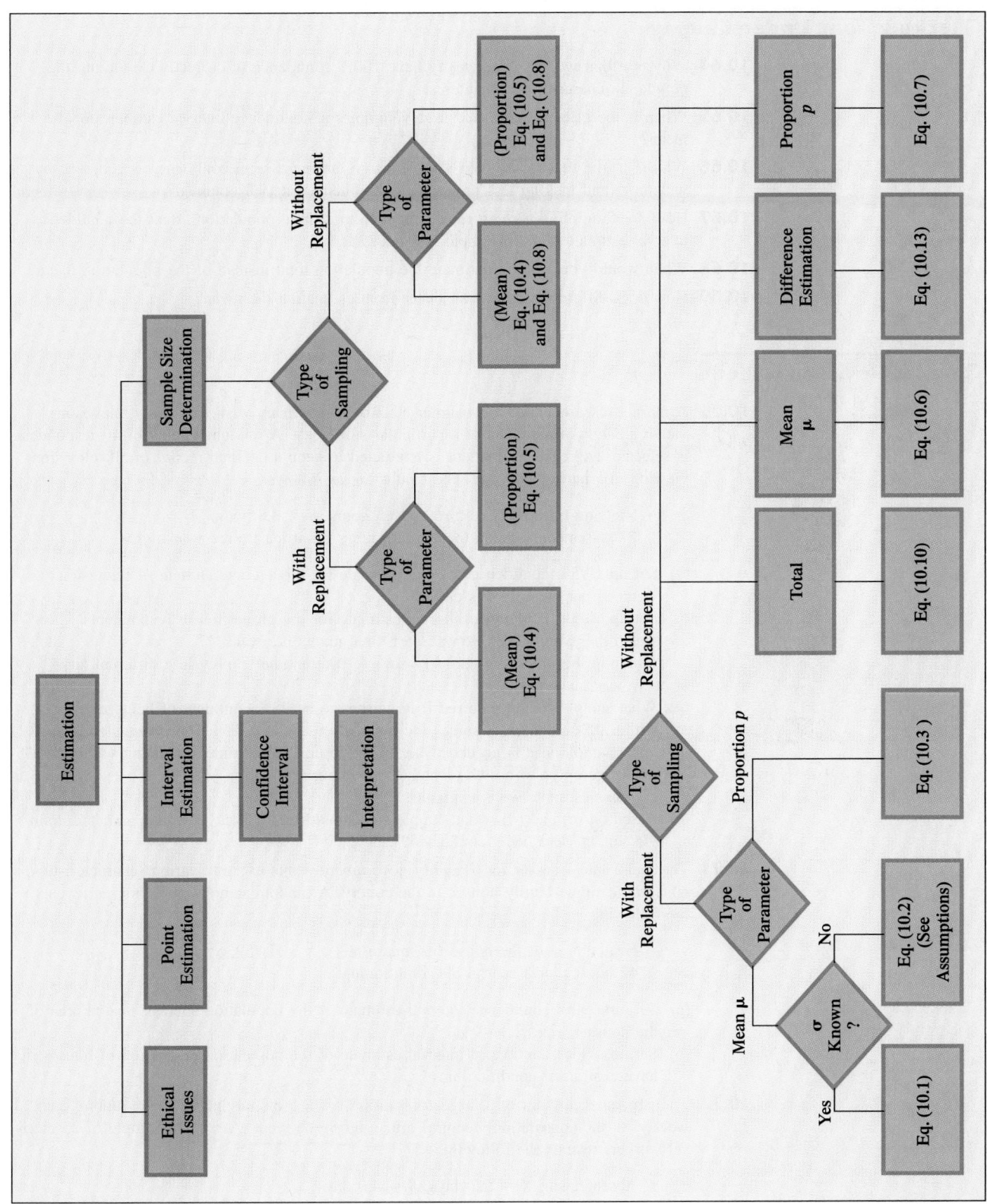

Chapter 10 summary chart

## Checking Your Understanding

**10.64** Why is it that we can never really have 100% confidence of correctly estimating the population characteristic of interest?

**10.65** When is the *t* distribution used in developing the confidence interval estimate for the mean?

**10.66** Why is it true that for a given sample size *n*, an increase in confidence is achieved by widening (and making less precise) the confidence interval obtained?

**10.67** How does sampling *without* replacement from a finite population affect the confidence interval estimate and the sample size necessary?

**10.68** When would you want to estimate the population total instead of the population mean?

**10.69** How does difference estimation differ from estimating the mean?

## Chapter Review Problems

**10.70** A market researcher for a consumer electronics company wishes to study television viewing habits of residents of a particular small city. A random sample of 40 respondents is selected, and each respondent is instructed to keep a detailed record of all television viewing in a particular week. The results are as follows:

- Viewing time per week: $\overline{X} = 15.3$ hours, $S = 3.8$ hours.
- 27 respondents watch the evening news on at least three weeknights.

(a) Set up a 95% confidence interval estimate for the average amount of television watched per week in this city.
(b) Set up a 95% confidence interval estimate for the proportion of respondents who watch the evening news on at least three nights per week.
  Assuming the market researcher wants to take another survey in a different city, answer these questions:
(c) What sample size is required if he wishes to be 95% confident of being correct to within ±2 hours and assumes the population standard deviation is equal to 5 hours?
(d) What sample size is needed if he wishes to be 95% confident of being within ±.035 of the true proportion who watch the evening news on at least three weeknights if no previous estimate were available?
(e) Based on (c) and (d), what sample size should the market researcher select if a single survey were being conducted?

**10.71** The real estate assessor for a county government wants to study various characteristics concerning single-family houses in the county. A random sample of 70 houses reveals the following:

- Heated area of the house (in square feet): $\overline{X} = 1,759$, $S = 380$.
- 42 houses have central air conditioning.

(a) Set up a 99% confidence interval estimate of the population average heated area of the house.
(b) Set up a 95% confidence interval estimate of the population proportion of houses that have central air conditioning.

**10.72** The personnel director of a large corporation wishes to study absenteeism among clerical workers at the corporation's central office during the year. A random sample of 25 clerical workers reveals the following:

- Absenteeism: $\overline{X} = 9.7$ days, $S = 4.0$ days.
- 12 clerical workers were absent more than 10 days.

(a) Set up a 95% confidence interval estimate of the average number of absences for clerical workers last year.

(b) Set up a 95% confidence interval estimate of the population proportion of clerical workers absent more than 10 days last year.

Assuming that the personnel director also wishes to take a survey in a branch office, answer these questions:

(c) What sample size is needed if the director wishes to be 95% confident of being correct to within $\pm 1.5$ days and the population standard deviation is assumed to be 4.5 days?

(d) What sample size is needed if the director wishes to be 90% confident of being correct to within $\pm .075$ of the true proportion of workers who are absent more than 10 days if no previous estimate is available?

(e) Based on (c) and (d), what sample size should the personnel director select if a single survey is being conducted?

**10.73** The market research director for Dotty's department store wants to study women's spending per year on cosmetics. A survey is to be sent to a sample of the store's credit card holders to determine:

- The average yearly amount that women spend on cosmetics.
- The population proportion of women who purchase their cosmetics primarily from Dotty's department store.

(a) If the market researcher wants to have 99% confidence of estimating the true population average to within $\pm \$5$ and the standard deviation is assumed to be \$18 (based on previous surveys), what sample size is needed?

(b) If the market researcher wishes to have 90% confidence of estimating the true proportion to within $\pm .045$, what sample size is needed?

(c) Based on the results in (a) and (b), how many of the store's credit card holders should be sampled? Explain.

• **10.74** The branch manager of an outlet of a large, nationwide bookstore chain wants to study characteristics of customers of her store, which is located near the campus of a large state university. In particular, she decides to focus on two variables: the amount of money spent by customers and whether the customers would consider purchasing educational videotapes relating to specific courses such as statistics, accounting, or calculus or graduate preparation exams such as GMAT, GRE, or LSAT. The results from a sample of 70 customers are as follows:

- Amount spent: $\overline{X} = \$28.52$, $S = \$11.39$.
- 28 customers stated that they would consider purchasing educational videotapes.

(a) Set up a 95% confidence interval estimate of the population average amount spent in the bookstore.

(b) Set up a 90% confidence interval estimate of the population proportion of customers who would consider purchasing educational videotapes.

Assuming the branch manager of another store from a different bookstore chain wishes to conduct a similar survey in his store (which is located near another university), answer these questions:

(c) If he wants to have 95% confidence of estimating the true population average amount spent in his store to within $\pm \$2$ and the standard deviation is assumed to be \$10, what sample size is needed?

(d) If he wants to have 90% confidence of estimating the true proportion of shoppers who would consider the purchase of videotapes to within $\pm .04$, what sample size is needed?

(e) Based on your answers to (c) and (d), what size sample should be taken?

**10.75** The branch manager of an outlet (store #1) of a large, nationwide chain of pet supply stores wants to study characteristics of customers of her store. In particular, she decides to focus on two variables: the amount of money spent by customers and whether the customers own only one dog, only one cat, or more than one dog and/or one cat. The results from a sample of 70 customers are as follows.

- Amount of money spent: $\overline{X} = \$21.34$, $S = \$9.22$.
- 37 customers own only a dog.
- 26 customers own only a cat.
- 7 customers own more than one dog and /or one cat.

(a) Set up a 95% confidence interval estimate of the population average amount spent in the pet supply store.
(b) Set up a 90% confidence interval estimate of the proportion of customers who own only a cat.
   Assuming the branch manager of another outlet (store #2) wishes to conduct a similar survey in his store (and does not have any access to the information generated by the manager of store #1), answer these questions:
(c) If he wants to have 95% confidence of estimating the true population average amount spent in his store to within ±$1.50 and the standard deviation is assumed to be $10, what sample size is needed?
(d) If he wants to have 90% confidence of estimating the true proportion of customers who own only a cat to within ±.045, what sample size is needed?
(e) Based on your answers to (c) and (d), what size sample should be taken?

**10.76** The owner of a restaurant serving continental food wants to study characteristics of customers of his restaurant. In particular, he decides to focus on two variables: the amount of money spent by customers and whether or not customers order dessert. The results from a sample of 60 customers are as follows:

- Amount spent: $\overline{X} = \$38.54$, $S = \$7.26$.
- 18 customers purchased dessert.

(a) Set up a 95% confidence interval estimate of the population average amount spent per customer in the restaurant.
(b) Set up a 90% confidence interval estimate of the population proportion of customers who purchase dessert.
   Assuming the owner of a competing restaurant wishes to conduct a similar survey in her restaurant (and does not have access to the information obtained by the owner of the first restaurant), answer these questions:
(c) If she wants to have 95% confidence of estimating the true population average amount spent in her restaurant to within ±$1.50 and the standard deviation is assumed to be $8, what sample size is needed?
(d) If she wants to have 90% confidence of estimating the true proportion of customers who purchase dessert to within ±.04, what sample size is needed?
(e) Based on your answers to (c) and (d), what size sample should be taken?

**10.77** A representative for a large chain of hardware stores is interested in testing the product claims of a manufacturer of a product called "Ice Melt," which is reported to melt snow and ice at temperatures as low as 0° Fahrenheit. A shipment of 400 five-pound bags is purchased by the chain for distribution. The representative wants to know with 95% confidence, within ±.05, what proportion of bags of Ice Melt perform the job as claimed by the manufacturer.

(a) How many bags does the representative need to test? What assumption should be made concerning the true proportion in the population? (This is called *destructive testing*; that is, the product being tested is destroyed by the test and is then unavailable to be sold.)

The representative tests 50 bags, and 42 do the job as claimed.

(b) Construct a 95% confidence interval estimate for the population proportion that will do the job as claimed.

(c) How can the representative use the results of (b) to determine whether to sell the Ice Melt product?

**10.78** An audit test to establish the percentage of occurrence of failure to follow a specific internal control procedure is to be undertaken. Suppose a sample of 50 from a population of 1,000 items is selected and it is determined that in seven instances the internal control procedure was not followed.

(a) Set up a 90% confidence interval estimate of the population proportion of items in which the internal control procedure was not followed.

(b) Suppose that in an effort to objectively determine the sample size, the auditor decides that she would like to have 95% confidence of correctly estimating the population proportion to within ±.04 (4%) of the true population value. She also assumes from past experience that the maximum error rate is 10%. What sample size needs to be selected?

**10.79** In a test of an attribute from a population of 15,000 items, if the maximum rate of occurrence is not expected to exceed 5% and a sample precision of ±2% is deemed satisfactory:

(a) What sample size is required for 95% confidence if sampling without replacement?

(b) What sample size is required for 99% confidence if sampling without replacement?

(c) Compare the difference in your answers to (a) and (b).

(d) If you desire a precision of ±3%, what sample size is required for 95% confidence?

(e) What sample size is required in (a) if the population size is 5,000?

**10.80** An auditor for a government agency is assigned the task of evaluating reimbursement for office visits to doctors paid by Medicare. The audit is to be conducted for all Medicare payments in a particular geographical zip code during a certain month. A population of 25,056 visits exists in this area for this month. The auditor primarily wants to estimate the total amount paid by Medicare in this area for the month. He desires to have 95% confidence of estimating the true population average to within ±$5. On the basis of past experience, he estimates the standard deviation to be $30.

(a) What sample size should be selected?

Using the sample size selected in (a), an audit is conducted. It is discovered that in 12 of the office visits, an incorrect amount of reimbursement was provided.

Amount of Reimbursement

$\overline{X} = \$93.70 \qquad S = \$34.55$

For the 12 office visits in which incorrect reimbursement was provided, the differences between the amount reimbursed and the amount that the auditor determined should have been reimbursed were:

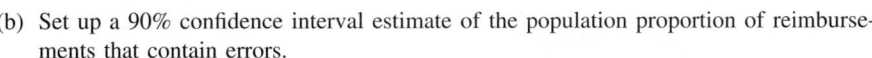

$17  $25  $14  -$10  $20  $40  $35  $30  $28  $22  $15  $5

(b) Set up a 90% confidence interval estimate of the population proportion of reimbursements that contain errors.

(c) Set up 95% confidence interval estimates of the
(1) average reimbursement per office visit.
(2) the total amount of reimbursements for this geographical area in this month.

(d) Set up a 95% confidence interval estimate of the total difference between the amount reimbursed and the amount that the auditor determined should have been reimbursed.

**10.81** A large computer store is conducting an end-of-month inventory of the computers in stock. It is determined that there were 258 computers in inventory at that time. An auditor for the store wants to estimate the average value of the computers in inventory at that time. She wants to have 99% confidence that her estimate of the average value is correct to within $\pm\$200$. On the basis of past experience, she estimates that the standard deviation of the value of a computer is $400.

(a) What sample size should be selected?

Using the sample size selected in (a), an audit was conducted with the following results:

Value of Computers

$$\overline{X} = \$3,054.13 \qquad S = \$384.62$$

(b) Set up a 99% confidence interval estimate of the total estimated value of the computers in inventory at the end of the month.

## TEAM PROJECT

**DATA FILE**
MUTUAL

**TP10.1** Refer to TP3.1 on page 115. Set up all appropriate estimates of population characteristics of currently traded domestic general stock funds. Include these estimates in any written and oral presentation to be made to the vice president for research at the financial investment service.

*Note:* Additional team projects can be found on the World Wide Web site for this text at

**http://www.prenhall.com/berenson**

These team projects deal with characteristics of 80 universities and colleges (see the UNIV&COL file) and the features of 89 automobiles (see the AUTO96 file).

## THE SPRINGVILLE HERALD CASE

The marketing department team met collectively to study the results of the new subscriptions forecasting model. Paul Kravitz, the market research director, asked the group to consider how new subscriptions could be increased and how those customers who agreed to trial subscription plans could be kept as subscribers after the trial period ended. Lauren Alfonso, a district sales manager, suggested that a survey be undertaken to determine various characteristics of readers of the newspaper who were not home-delivery subscribers. After a great deal of discussion by the group, a questionnaire was developed as follows.

1. Do you or a member of your household ever purchase the *Springville Herald*?
   (1) Yes  (2) No
   [If the respondent answers no, the interview is terminated.]
2. Do you receive the *Springville Herald* via home delivery?
   (1) Yes  (2) No
   [If no, skip to Question 4.]

3. Do you receive the *Springville Herald*:
   (1) Monday–Saturday  (2) Sunday only
   (3) Every day
   [Skip to Question 9.]
4. How often during the Monday–Saturday period do you purchase the *Springville Herald*?
   (1) Every day  (2) Most days
   (3) Occasionally
5. How often do you purchase the *Springville Herald* on Sundays?
   (1) Every Sunday  (2) 2–3 Sundays a month
   (3) Once a month
6. Where are you most likely to purchase the *Springville Herald*?
   (1) Convenience store/delicatessen
   (2) Stationery/candy store
   (3) Vending machine  (4) Supermarket
   (5) Other _____
7. Would you consider subscribing to the *Springville Herald* for a trial period if a discount was offered?
   (1) Yes  (2) No
   [If no, skip to Question 9.]

8. The *Springville Herald* currently costs 50 cents on Monday to Saturday and $1.50 on Sunday for a total of $4.50 per week. How much would you be willing to pay per week to obtain home delivery for a 90-day trial period? _____

9. Do you read a daily newspaper other than the *Springville Herald*?
   (1) Yes          (2) No

10. As an incentive to long-term subscribers, the newspaper is considering the possibility of offering all subscribers who pay for 6 months of home delivery in advance (about $100) a card that would provide discounts at a list of restaurants in Springville. Would you be likely to want to obtain such a card under the terms of this offer?
    (1) Yes          (2) No

A random sample of 500 households located in Springville was selected for a telephone survey that was to be conducted using the *random-digit dialing* method. In this approach, used to reach households that have unlisted telephone numbers, the last four digits of a telephone number are randomly selected to go with the telephone exchange that consists of the first three numbers. Only those exchanges that are contained in Springville are used. (For example, if the exchanges 676, 759, and 923 are available in Springville, the exchange would first be randomly selected among these three, and then the last four digits would be randomly selected to produce the telephone number to be dialed.)

Of the 500 households selected, 94 either refused to participate, could not be contacted after repeated attempts, or represented telephone numbers that were not in service or belonged to non-residences (remember that random digit dialing was used). The summary results were as follows:

| HOUSEHOLDS THAT PURCHASE THE *Springville Herald* | FREQUENCY |
|---|---|
| Yes | 352 |
| No | 54 |

| HOUSEHOLDS THAT RECEIVE THE *Springville Herald* VIA HOME DELIVERY | FREQUENCY |
|---|---|
| Yes | 136 |
| No | 216 |

| TYPE OF SUBSCRIPTION FOR HOME DELIVERY | FREQUENCY |
|---|---|
| Monday–Saturday | 18 |
| Sunday only | 25 |
| Every day | 93 |

| PURCHASE BEHAVIOR OF NONSUBSCRIBERS– MONDAY–SATURDAY EDITIONS | FREQUENCY |
|---|---|
| Every day | 78 |
| Most days | 95 |
| Occasionally | 43 |

| PURCHASE BEHAVIOR OF NONSUBSCRIBERS– SUNDAY EDITION | FREQUENCY |
|---|---|
| Every Sunday | 138 |
| 2–3 Sundays a month | 54 |
| Once a month | 24 |

| LOCATION OF PURCHASE | FREQUENCY |
|---|---|
| Convenience store/delicatessen | 74 |
| Stationery/candy store | 95 |
| Vending machine | 21 |
| Supermarket | 13 |
| Other | 13 |

| CONSIDER TRIAL PERIOD SUBSCRIPTION WITH DISCOUNT | FREQUENCY |
|---|---|
| Yes | 46 |
| No | 170 |

How much would you be willing to pay per week to obtain home delivery for a 90-day trial period?

$4.15 3.60 4.10 3.60 3.60 3.60 4.40
3.15 4.00 3.75 4.00 3.25 3.75 3.30
3.75 3.65 4.00 4.10 3.90 3.50 3.75
3.00 3.40 4.00 3.80 3.50 4.10 4.25
3.50 3.90 3.95 4.30 4.20 3.50 3.75
3.30 3.85 3.20 4.40 3.80 3.40 3.50
2.85 3.75 3.80 3.90

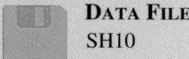
**DATA FILE**
SH10

| READ A DAILY NEWSPAPER OTHER THAN THE *Springville Herald* | FREQUENCY |
|---|---|
| Yes | 138 |
| No | 214 |

| WOULD PREPAY 6 MONTHS TO RECEIVE RESTAURANT DISCOUNT CARD | FREQUENCY |
|---|---|
| Yes | 66 |
| No | 286 |

## Exercises

**10.1** Some members of the marketing department team raised questions about the use of the random-digit dialing method used in the survey. Prepare a short report for the team that
  **(a)** indicates the advantages and disadvantages of conducting the survey using a random-digit dialing telephone survey.
  **(b)** suggests an alternative approach for conducting the survey. What would be the advantages and disadvantages of conducting the survey based on this alternative approach?

**10.2** Analyze the results of the survey of households in Springville. Write a report for the marketing department team that discusses the marketing implication of the survey results for the *Springville Herald*. In addition to the written report, prepare a summary that can be presented orally in less than 10 minutes.

## References

1. Cochran, W. G., *Sampling Techniques*, 3d ed. (New York: Wiley, 1977).
2. Fisher, R. A., and F. Yates, *Statistical Tables for Biological, Agricultural and Medical Research*, 5th ed. (Edinburgh: Oliver & Boyd, 1957).
3. Kirk, R. E., ed., *Statistical Issues: A Reader for the Behavioral Sciences* (Belmont, CA: Wadsworth, 1972).
4. Larsen, R. L., and M. L. Marx, *An Introduction to Mathematical Statistics and Its Applications*, 2d ed. (Englewood Cliffs, NJ: Prentice Hall, 1986).
5. *Microsoft Excel 97* (Redmond, WA: Microsoft Corporation, 1997).
6. *Minitab for Windows Version 12* (State College, PA: Minitab, Inc., 1998).
7. Snedecor, G. W., and W. G. Cochran, *Statistical Methods*, 7th ed. (Ames, IA: Iowa State University Press, 1980).

## Using the Data Analysis Tool

*COMMENT:   PHStat Add-in Users*

If Microsoft Excel is not running, click the **PHStat** add-in icon. If Microsoft Excel is running, select **File | Open**. Select the **PHStat** add-in file **PHSA.XLA**. Click the **Open** button.

To obtain a confidence interval estimate for the mean with σ known, select **PHStat | Confidence Intervals | Estimate for the Mean, Sigma known**. If the sample statistics are unknown, select the **Sample Statistics unknown** option button and enter the cell range for the data in the edit box. If the sample statistics are known, enter the sample size, the arithmetic mean, and the population standard deviation in their respective edit boxes. Enter the confidence level in percent in its edit box. If you have a finite population, select the **Finite Population Correction** check box and enter the population size in its edit box. Click the **OK** button.

To obtain a confidence interval estimate for the mean with σ unknown, select **PHStat | Confidence Intervals | Estimate for the Mean, Sigma unknown**. If the sample statistics are unknown, select the Sample Statistics unknown option button and enter the cell range for the data in the edit box. If the sample statistics are known, enter the sample size, the arithmetic mean, and the sample standard deviation in their respective edit boxes. Enter the confidence level in percent in its edit box. If you have a finite population, select the **Finite Population Correction** check box and enter the population size in its edit box. Click the **OK** button.

To obtain a confidence interval estimate for the proportion, select **PHStat | Confidence Intervals | Estimate for the Proportion**. Enter the sample size, number of successes, and confidence level in their respective edit boxes. If you have a finite population, select the **Finite Population Correction** check box and enter the population size in its edit box. Click the **OK** button.

To determine the sample size for the mean, select **PHStat | Sample Size | Determination for the Mean**. Enter values for the standard deviation, sampling error, and confidence level in their respective edit boxes. If you have a finite population, select the **Finite Population Correction** check box and enter the population size in its edit box. Click the **OK** button.

To determine the sample size for the proportion, select **PHStat | Sample Size | Determination for the Proportion**. Enter values for the estimated proportion, sampling error, and confidence level in their respective edit boxes. If you have a finite population, select the **Finite Population Correction** check box and enter the population size in its edit box. Click the **OK** button.

To determine a confidence interval estimate for the total, select **PHStat | Confidence Intervals | Estimate for the Population Total**. If the sample statistics are unknown, select the **Sample Statistics unknown** option button and enter the cell range for the data in the edit box. If the sample statistics are known, enter the sample size, the arithmetic mean, and the sample standard deviation in their respective edit boxes. Enter the population size in its edit box. Enter the confidence level in percent in its edit box. Click the **OK** button.

To determine a confidence interval estimate for the total difference, select **PHStat | Confidence Intervals | Estimate for the Total Difference**. Enter the cell range for the differences in its edit box. Enter the sample size and the confidence level in percent in their respective edit boxes. Enter the population size in its edit box. Click the **OK** button.

In appendix 4.1 we used the Data Analysis tool of Microsoft Excel to obtain a set of descriptive statistics. At that time, we stated that the confidence interval check box in the Descriptive Statistics list box should be left unchecked because confidence interval would not be discussed until chapter 10. If the confidence interval list box was checked, the output would include a line titled Confidence Level (95.0%). If we refer to the 17 mutual funds discussed in chapter 4, we can observe from Figure 4.7 on page 153 that the value listed for Confidence Level (95.0%) is 3.298597. This value represents the $t$ statistic for the 95% confidence level (with $n - 1$ degrees of freedom) multiplied by the standard error of the mean (1.556012). To obtain the 95% confidence interval estimate for the mean, we need to take the arithmetic mean given in cell B3 (29.86471) and add and subtract the value for Confidence Level (95.0%). Doing this manually or using an Excel formula results in a confidence interval from 26.566 to 33.163.

## ❖ APPENDIX 10.2    USING MINITAB FOR CONFIDENCE INTERVAL ESTIMATION

### Confidence Interval Estimation for the Mean ($\sigma$ Unknown)

Minitab can be used to obtain a confidence interval estimate for the mean when $\sigma$ is unknown by selecting **Stat | Basic Statistics | 1-Sample t** from the Menu bar.

We illustrate the confidence interval estimate for the mean when $\sigma$ is unknown by returning to the 17 mutual funds discussed in appendix 4.2. Because there are a total of 194 domestic general stock funds, if we want to obtain statistics only for those 17 mutual funds in group 1, we first need to unstack the variable 1Yr%Ret in column C4 so that the 1-year percentage returns for each of the five groups are in a separate column. To unstack the data, open the **MUTUAL.MTP** file and select **MANIP | Stack/Unstack | Unstack One Column**. In the Unstack One Column dialog box, select **C4** or **1Yr%Ret** and enter this variable in the Unstack the data in: edit box. Select **C5 or Group** and enter this variable in the first Using Subscripts in: edit box. In the Store Unstacked Data in: edit box enter **C9–C13** because there are five groups whose 1-year percentage returns need to be stored, noting that the last variable was previously stored in column C8. Click the **OK** button.

The 1-year percentage returns are now stored in columns C9–C13. After giving each of these new variables a label such as 1Yr%Ret-1 through 1Yr%Ret-5, select **Stat | Basic Statistics | 1-Sample t** and enter **C9** or **1Yr%Ret-1** in the Variables edit box. Select the **Confidence Interval** button and enter **95.0** in the Level edit box. Click the **OK** button.

# 11

# Fundamentals of Hypothesis Testing: One-Sample Tests

# CHAPTER OBJECTIVES

✓ *To develop hypothesis-testing methodology as a technique for making decisions about population parameters based on sample statistics*

✓ *To determine the risks involved in making these decisions based only on sample information*

✓ *To describe various practical tests of hypothesis in dealing with one sample*

✓ *To understand the conceptual differences between the traditional critical value approach versus the p-value approach to hypothesis testing*

## Introduction

In chapter 9 we began our discussion of statistical inference by developing the concept of a sampling distribution. In chapter 10 we considered studies in which a statistic (such as the sample mean or sample proportion) obtained from a random sample is used to *estimate* its corresponding population parameter.

In this chapter we focus on another phase of statistical inference that is also based on sample information—hypothesis testing. We develop a step-by-step methodology that enables us to make inferences about a population parameter by *analyzing differences* between the results we observe (our sample statistic) and the results we expect to obtain if some underlying hypothesis is actually true. Emphasis here is placed on the fundamental and conceptual underpinnings of **hypothesis-testing methodology**. In the three chapters that follow we present various hypothesis-testing procedures that are frequently employed in the analysis of data obtained from studies and experiments designed under a variety of conditions.

---

◆ **USING STATISTICS:** *Testing a Manufacturer's Claim Regarding Product Specifications*

To develop hypothesis-testing methodology, we continue our focus in this chapter on some issues based on the cereal box-filling process discussed in chapters 9 and 10. For example, the operations manager is concerned with evaluating whether or not the process is working in a way that ensures that, on average, the proper amount of cereal (i.e., 368 grams) is being filled in each box. He decides to select a random sample of 25 boxes from the filling process and examines their weights to determine how close each of these boxes comes to the company's specification of an average of 368 grams per box. The operations manager hopes to find that the process is working properly. However, he might find that the sampled boxes weigh too little or perhaps too much. As a result, he may then decide to halt the production process until the reason for the failure to adhere to the specified weight of 368 grams is determined.

By analyzing the differences between the weights obtained from the sample and the 368-gram expectation obtained from the company's specifications, he can reach a decision based on this sample information, and one of the following two conclusions can be drawn:

1. The average fill in the entire process is 368 grams. No corrective action is needed.

2. The average fill is not 368 grams; either it is less than 368 grams or it is more than 368 grams. Corrective action is needed.

 ## 11.1 ◆ HYPOTHESIS-TESTING METHODOLOGY

## The Null and Alternative Hypotheses

**Hypothesis testing** typically begins with some theory, claim, or assertion about a particular parameter of a population. For example, for purposes of statistical analysis, the operations manager at our cereal company chooses as his initial hypothesis that the process is in control; that is, the average fill is 368 grams and no corrective action is needed.

The hypothesis that the population parameter is equal to the company specification is referred to as the **null hypothesis**. A null hypothesis is always one of *status quo* or no difference. We commonly identify the null hypothesis by the symbol $H_0$. Our operations manager establishes as his null hypothesis that the filling process is in control and working properly, that the mean fill per box is the 368-gram specification. This can be stated as

$$H_0: \mu = 368$$

Note that even though the operations manager has information only from the sample, the null hypothesis is written in terms of the population parameter. This is because he is interested in the entire filling process, that is, (the population of) all cereal boxes being filled. The sample statistic will be used to make inferences about the entire filling process. One such inference may be that the results observed from the sample data indicate that the null hypothesis is false. If the null hypothesis is considered false, something else must be true. To anticipate this possibility, whenever we specify a null hypothesis, we must also specify an **alternative hypothesis**, or one that must be true if the null hypothesis is found to be false. The alternative hypothesis ($H_1$) is the opposite of the null hypothesis ($H_0$). For the operations manager, this is stated as

$$H_1: \mu \neq 368$$

The alternative hypothesis represents the conclusion reached by rejecting the null hypothesis if there is sufficient evidence from the sample information to decide that the null hypothesis is unlikely to be true. In our example, if the weights of the sampled boxes are sufficiently above or below the expected 368-gram average specified by the company, the operations manager rejects the null hypothesis in favor of the alternative hypothesis that the average amount of fill is different from 368 grams. He then stops production and takes whatever action is necessary to correct the problem.

Hypothesis-testing methodology is designed so that our rejection of the null hypothesis is based on evidence from the sample that our alternative hypothesis is far more likely to be true. However, failure to reject the null hypothesis is not proof that it is true. We can never prove that the null hypothesis is correct because our decision is based only on the sample information, not on the entire population. Therefore, if we fail to reject the null hypothesis, we can only conclude that there is insufficient evidence to warrant its rejection. A summary of the null and alternative hypotheses is presented in Exhibit 11.1.

## Exhibit 11.1 The Null and Alternative Hypotheses

The following two key points summarize the null and alternative hypotheses:

✓ **1.** The null hypothesis ($H_0$) is the hypothesis that is always tested.

✓ **2.** The alternative hypothesis ($H_1$) is set up as the opposite of the null hypothesis and represents the conclusion supported if the null hypothesis is rejected.

In what is known as *classical* hypothesis-testing methodology, we have the following three key points:

✓ **1.** The null hypothesis ($H_0$) always refers to a specified value of the *population parameter* (such as $\mu$), not a *sample statistic* (such as $\bar{X}$).

✓ **2.** The statement of the null hypothesis *always* contains an equal sign regarding the specified value of the population parameter (that is, $H_0: \mu = 368$ grams).

✓ **3.** The statement of the alternative hypothesis *never* contains an equal sign regarding the specified value of the population parameter (that is, $H_1: \mu \neq 368$ grams).

To illustrate the null and alternative hypotheses, consider Examples 11.1 and 11.2:

## Example 11.1 *Stating the Null and Alternative Hypotheses*

Suppose that Toyota claims that a new model car will average 30 miles per gallon in highway driving. If you are planning an experiment to test this claim, what are the null and alternative hypotheses?

### SOLUTION

$$H_0: \mu = 30 \text{ miles per gallon}$$
$$H_1: \mu \neq 30 \text{ miles per gallon}$$

## Example 11.2 *Stating the Null and Alternative Hypotheses*

In the past the average age of policyholders of term life insurance at Empire Insurance Company has been 48 years. As the company has expanded and provided more term policies across the nation, the chief financial officer believes the average age may have shifted. If you were planning a survey to test this claim, what would be the null and alternative hypotheses?

*SOLUTION*

$$H_0: \mu = 48 \text{ years}$$
$$H_1: \mu \neq 48 \text{ years}$$

## The Critical Value of the Test Statistic

We can develop the logic behind the hypothesis-testing methodology by contemplating how we can use only sample information to determine the plausibility of the null hypothesis.

Our operations manager states as his null hypothesis that the average amount of cereal per box over the entire filling process is 368 grams (i.e., the population parameter specified by the company). He then obtains a sample of boxes from the filling process, weighs each box, and computes the sample mean. We recall that a statistic from a sample is an estimate of the corresponding parameter from the population from which the sample is drawn. Even if the null hypothesis is in fact true, this statistic will likely differ from the actual parameter value because of chance or sampling error. Nevertheless, under such circumstances we expect the sample statistic to be close to the population parameter. In such a situation there would be insufficient evidence to reject the null hypothesis. If, for example, the sample mean is 367.9, our instinct is to conclude that the population mean has not changed (that is, $\mu = 368$), because a sample mean of 367.9 is very close to the hypothesized value of 368. Intuitively, we might think that it is likely that we could obtain a sample mean of 367.9 from a population whose mean is 368.

On the other hand, if there is a large discrepancy between the value of the statistic and its corresponding hypothesized parameter, our instinct is to conclude that the null hypothesis is unlikely to be true. For example, if the sample average is 320, our instinct is to conclude that the true population average is not 368 (that is, $\mu \neq 368$), because the sample mean is very far from the hypothesized value of 368. In such a case we reason that it is very unlikely that the sample mean of 320 can be obtained if the population mean is really 368 and, therefore, more logical to conclude that the population mean is not equal to 368. Here we reject the null hypothesis.

In either case our decision is reached because of our belief that randomly selected samples are truly representative of the underlying populations from which they are drawn.

Unfortunately, the decision-making process is not always so clear-cut and cannot be left to an individual's subjective judgment as to the meaning of "very close" or "very different." Determining what is very close and what is very different is very arbitrary without using definitions. Hypothesis-testing methodology provides clear definitions for evaluating such differences and enables us to quantify the decision-making process so that the probability of obtaining a given sample result can be found if the null hypothesis is true. This is achieved by first determining the sampling distribution for the sample statistic of interest (i.e., the sample mean) and then computing the particular **test statistic** based on the given sample result. Because the sampling distribution for the test statistic often follows a well-known statistical distribution, such as the normal or *t* distribution, we can use these distributions to determine the likelihood of a null hypothesis being true.

## Regions of Rejection and Nonrejection

The sampling distribution of the test statistic is divided into two regions, a **region of rejection** (sometimes called the **critical region**) and a **region of nonrejection** (see Figure 11.1 on page 416). If the test statistic falls into the region of nonrejection, the null hypothesis

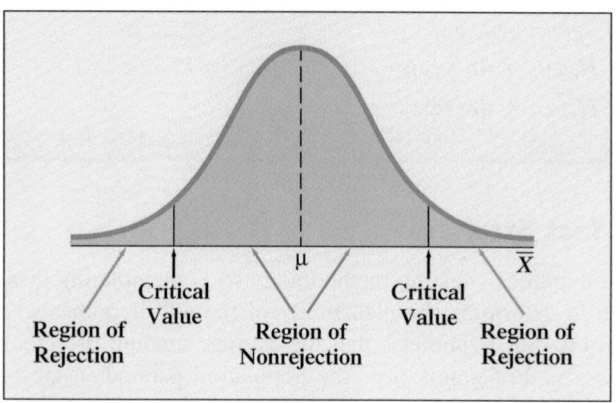

**FIGURE 11.1** Regions of rejection and nonrejection in hypothesis testing

cannot be rejected. In our example, the operations manager concludes that the average fill amount is not changed. If the test statistic falls into the rejection region, the null hypothesis is rejected. Here the operations manager concludes that the population mean is not 368.

The region of rejection may be thought of as consisting of the values of the test statistic that are unlikely to occur if the null hypothesis is true. On the other hand, these values are not so unlikely to occur if the null hypothesis is false. Therefore, if we observe a value of the test statistic that falls into this *rejection region*, we reject the null hypothesis because that value is unlikely if the null hypothesis is true.

To make a decision concerning the null hypothesis, we first determine the **critical value** of the test statistic. The critical value divides the nonrejection region from the rejection region. However, the determination of this critical value depends on the size of the rejection region. As we will see in the following section, the size of the rejection region is directly related to the risks involved in using only sample evidence to make decisions about a population parameter.

## Risks in Decision Making Using Hypothesis-Testing Methodology

When using a sample statistic to make decisions about a population parameter, there is a risk that an incorrect conclusion will be reached. Indeed, two different types of errors can occur when applying hypothesis-testing methodology, Type I and Type II.

A **Type I error** occurs if the null hypothesis $H_0$ is rejected when in fact it is true and should not be rejected. The probability of a Type I error occurring is $\alpha$.

A **Type II error** occurs if the null hypothesis $H_0$ is not rejected when in fact it is false and should be rejected. The **probability of a Type II error** occurring is $\beta$.

In our cereal-filling-process example, the Type I error occurs if the operations manager concludes (based on sample information) that the average population amount filled is *not* 368 when in fact it is 368. On the other hand, the Type II error occurs if he concludes (based on sample information) that the average population fill amount is 368 when in fact it is not 368.

◆ *The Level of Significance*  The probability of committing a Type I error, denoted by $\alpha$ (the lowercase Greek letter alpha), is referred to as the **level of significance** of the statistical test. Traditionally, one controls the Type I error rate by deciding the risk level $\alpha$ he or she is willing to tolerate in rejecting the null hypothesis when it is in fact true. Because the level of significance is specified before the hypothesis test is performed, the risk of committing a Type I error, $\alpha$, is directly under the control of the individual performing the test. Researchers traditionally select $\alpha$ levels of .05 or smaller. The choice of selecting a particular risk level for making a Type I error is dependent on the cost of making a Type I error. Once the value for $\alpha$ is specified, the size of the rejection region is known because $\alpha$ is the probability of rejection under the null hypothesis. From this fact, the critical value or values that divide the rejection and nonrejection regions are determined.

◆ *The Confidence Coefficient*  The complement $(1 - \alpha)$ of the probability of a Type I error is called the **confidence coefficient**, which, when multiplied by 100%, yields the confidence level that we studied in section 10.1.

The **confidence coefficient**, denoted by $1 - \alpha$, is the probability that the null hypothesis $H_0$ is not rejected when in fact it is true and should not be rejected.

In terms of hypothesis-testing methodology, this coefficient represents the probability of concluding that the specified value of the parameter being tested under the null hypothesis may be plausible when, in fact, it is true. In our cereal-filling-process example, the confidence coefficient measures the probability of concluding that the average fill per box is 368 grams when in fact it is 368 grams.

◆ *The $\beta$ Risk*  The probability of committing a Type II error, denoted by $\beta$ (the lowercase Greek letter beta), is often referred to as the *consumer's risk* level. Unlike the Type I error, which we control by our selection of $\alpha$, the probability of making a Type II error is dependent on the difference between the hypothesized and actual value of the population parameter. Because large differences are easier to find, if the difference between the sample statistic and the corresponding population parameter is large, $\beta$, the probability of committing a Type II error, will likely be small. For example, if the true population average (which is unknown to us) is 320 grams, there is a small chance ($\beta$) of concluding that the average has not changed from 368. On the other hand, if the difference between the statistic and the corresponding parameter value is small, the probability of committing a Type II error is large. Thus, if the true population average is really 367 grams, there is a high probability of concluding that the population average fill amount has not changed from the specified 368 grams (and we would be making a Type II error).

♦ **The Power of a Test**   The complement $(1 - \beta)$ of the probability of a Type II error is called the power of a statistical test.

> The **power of a statistical test**, denoted by $1 - \beta$, is the probability of rejecting the null hypothesis when in fact it is false and should be rejected.

In our cereal-filling-process example, the power of the test is the probability of concluding that the average fill amount is not 368 grams when in fact it actually is not 368 grams.

♦ **Risks in Decision Making: A Delicate Balance**   Table 11.1 illustrates the results of the two possible decisions (do not reject $H_0$ or reject $H_0$) that can occur in any hypothesis test. Depending on the specific decision, one of two types of errors may occur[1] or one of two types of correct conclusions may be reached.

One way in which we can control and reduce the probability of making a Type II error in a study is to increase the size of the sample. Larger sample sizes generally permit us to detect even very small differences between the sample statistics and the population parameters. For a given level of $\alpha$, increasing the sample size will decrease $\beta$ and therefore increase the power of the test to detect that the null hypothesis $H_0$ is false. Of course, however, there is always a limit to our resources and this will affect the decision as to how large a sample we can take. Thus, for a given sample size we must consider the trade-offs between the two possible types of errors. Because we can directly control our risk of Type I error, we can reduce our risk by selecting a lower level for $\alpha$ (for example, .01 instead of .05). However, when $\alpha$ is decreased, $\beta$ will be increased, so a reduction in risk of Type I error will result in an increased risk of Type II error. If, on the other hand, we wish to reduce $\beta$, our risk of Type II error, we could select a larger value for $\alpha$ (for example, .05 instead of .01).

In our cereal-filling-process example, the risk of a Type I error involves concluding that the average fill per box has changed from the hypothesized 368 grams when in fact it has not changed. The risk of a Type II error involves concluding that the average fill per box has not changed from the hypothesized 368 grams when in truth it has changed. The choice of reasonable values for $\alpha$ and $\beta$ depends on the costs inherent in each type of error. For example, if it were very costly to change the status quo, then we would want to be very sure that a change would be beneficial, so the risk of a Type I error might be most important and would be kept very low. On the other hand, if we wanted to be very certain of detecting changes from a hypothesized mean, the risk of a Type II error would be most important and we might choose a higher level of $\alpha$.

[1]*An easy way to remember which probability goes with which type of error is to note that $\alpha$ is the first letter of the Greek alphabet and is used to represent the probability of a Type I error. The letter $\beta$ is the second letter of the Greek alphabet and is used to represent the probability of a Type II error. (If you have trouble remembering the Greek alphabet, note that the word* alphabet *tells you its first two letters.)*

**Table 11.1**   *Hypothesis testing and decision making*

| | ACTUAL SITUATION | |
| STATISTICAL DECISION | $H_0$ TRUE | $H_0$ FALSE |
| --- | --- | --- |
| Do not reject $H_0$ | Correct decision<br>$P$ (confidence) $= 1 - \alpha$ | Type II error<br>$P$ (Type II error) $= \beta$ |
| Reject $H_0$ | Type I error<br>$P$ (Type I error) $= \alpha$ | Correct decision<br>$P$ (power) $= 1 - \beta$ |

## Problems for Section 11.1

### Learning the Basics

• **11.1**  The symbol $H_0$ is used to denote which hypothesis?

• **11.2**  The symbol $H_1$ is used to denote which hypothesis?

• **11.3**  The level of significance or chance of committing a Type I error is denoted by what symbol?

• **11.4**  The consumer's risk or chance of committing a Type II error is denoted by what symbol?

**11.5**  What does $1 - \beta$ represent?

**11.6**  What is the relationship of $\alpha$ to the Type I error?

**11.7**  What is the relationship of $\beta$ to the Type II error?

**11.8**  How is power related to the probability of making a Type II error?

### Applying the Concepts

**11.9**  Why is it possible for the null hypothesis to be rejected when in fact it is true?

**11.10**  Why is it possible that the null hypothesis will not always be rejected when it is false?

• **11.11**  For a given sample size, if $\alpha$ is reduced from .05 to .01, what will happen to $\beta$?

**11.12**  For $H_0$: $\mu = 100$, $H_1$: $\mu \neq 100$, and for a sample of size $n$, $\beta$ will be larger if the actual value of $\mu$ is 90 than if the actual value of $\mu$ is 75. Why?

**11.13**  In the American legal system, a defendant is presumed innocent until proved guilty. Consider a null hypothesis $H_0$ that the defendant is innocent and an alternative hypothesis $H_1$ that the defendant is guilty. A jury has two possible decisions: convict the defendant (i.e., reject the null hypothesis) or do not convict the defendant (i.e., do not reject the null hypothesis). Explain the meaning of the risks of committing either a Type I or Type II error in this example.

**11.14**  Suppose the defendant in Problem 11.13 is presumed guilty until proved innocent as in the French judicial system. How do the null and alternative hypotheses differ from those in Problem 11.13? What are the meanings of the risks of committing either a Type I or Type II error here?

• **11.15**  The CEO of a national clothing manufacturer claims that average profits per store are anticipated to be $1 million in the first quarter of the year. As market research director, you must evaluate the CEO's claim. State the null hypothesis $H_0$ and the alternative hypothesis $H_1$.

• **11.16**  Owing to complaints from both students and faculty about lateness, the registrar at a large university wants to adjust the scheduled class times to allow for adequate travel time between classes and is ready to undertake a study. Up until now, the registrar believed 20 minutes between the start of scheduled classes should be sufficient. State the null hypothesis $H_0$ and the alternative hypothesis $H_1$.

**11.17**  The manager of a local branch of a commercial bank believes that over the past few years the bank has been catering to a different clientele and that the average amount withdrawn from its ATMs is no longer $140. State the null hypothesis and the alternative hypothesis $H_1$.

Now that we have described the hypothesis-testing methodology, let us return to the question of interest to the operations manager at the cereal-packaging plant. You may recall that he wants to determine whether or not the cereal-filling process is under control—that the average fill per box throughout the entire packaging process remains at the specified 368 grams and no corrective action is needed. To study this, he plans to take a random sample of 25 boxes, weigh each one, and then evaluate the difference between the sample statistic and the hypothesized population parameter by comparing the mean weight (in grams) from the sample to the expected mean of 368 grams specified by the company. For this filling process, the null and alternative hypotheses are

$$H_0: \mu = 368$$
$$H_1: \mu \neq 368$$

If we assume that the standard deviation σ is known, then based on the central limit theorem, the sampling distribution of the mean follows the normal distribution resulting in the following **test statistic**:

---

### Z Test of Hypothesis for the Mean (σ Known)

$$Z = \frac{\overline{X} - \mu}{\dfrac{\sigma}{\sqrt{n}}} \tag{11.1}$$

---

In this equation the numerator measures how far (in an absolute sense) the observed sample mean $\overline{X}$ is from the hypothesized mean $\mu$. The denominator is the standard error of the mean, so $Z$ represents how many standard errors $\overline{X}$ is from $\mu$.

## The Critical Value Approach to Hypothesis Testing

If the operations manager decides to choose a level of significance of .05, the size of the rejection region would be .05 and the critical values of the normal distribution could be determined. These critical values can be expressed as standardized $Z$ values (i.e., in standard-deviation units). Because the rejection region is divided into the two tails of the distribution (this is called a **two-tailed test**), the .05 is divided into two equal parts of .025 each. A rejection region of .025 in each tail of the normal distribution results in a cumulative area of .025 below the lower critical value and a cumulative area of .975 below the upper critical value. Looking up these areas in the normal distribution [Table E.2(b)], we find that the critical values that divide the rejection and nonrejection regions are (in standard-deviation units) $-1.96$ and $+1.96$. Figure 11.2 illustrates this case; it shows that if the mean is actually 368 grams, as $H_0$ claims, then the values of the test statistic $Z$ have a standard normal distribution centered at $\mu = 368$ (which corresponds to a standardized $Z$ value of 0). Observed values of $Z$ greater than $+1.96$ or less than $-1.96$ indicate that $\overline{X}$ is so far from the hypothesized $\mu = 368$ that it is unlikely that such a value would occur if $H_0$ were true. Therefore, the decision rule is

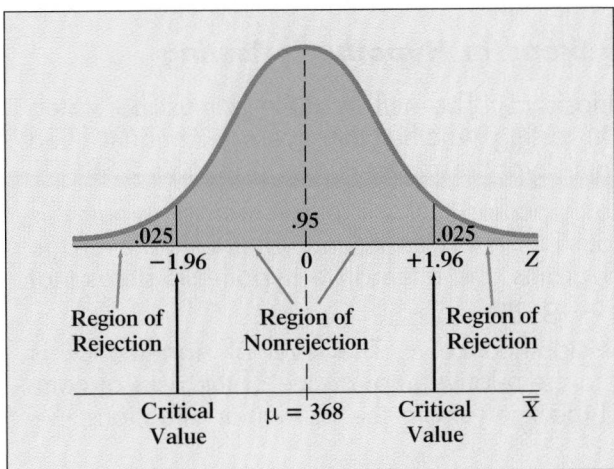

**FIGURE 11.2**
Testing a hypothesis about the mean (σ known) at the .05 level of significance

Reject $H_0$ if $Z > +1.96$

or if $Z < -1.96$;

otherwise do not reject $H_0$.

Suppose that the sample of 25 cereal boxes indicates a sample mean $\overline{X}$ of 372.5 grams and the population standard deviation σ is assumed to remain at 15 grams as specified by the company (see section 9.1). Using equation (11.1), we have

$$Z = \frac{\overline{X} - \mu}{\dfrac{\sigma}{\sqrt{n}}} = \frac{372.5 - 368}{\dfrac{15}{\sqrt{25}}} = +1.50$$

Since $Z = +1.50$, we see that $-1.96 < +1.50 < +1.96$. Thus, as seen in Figure 11.3, our decision is to not reject $H_0$. We would conclude that the average fill amount is 368 grams. Alternatively, to take into account the possibility of a Type II error, we may phrase the conclusion as "there is no evidence that the average fill is different from 368 grams."

Now that we have used hypothesis-testing methodology to draw a conclusion about the population mean in situations where the population standard deviation is known, we summarize the steps involved in Exhibit 11.2.

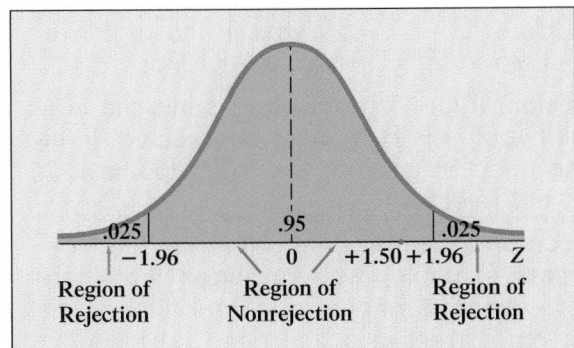

**FIGURE 11.3**
Testing a hypothesis about the mean (σ known) at the .05 level of significance

## Exhibit 11.2 The Steps in Hypothesis Testing

✓ **1.** State the null hypothesis $H_0$. The null hypothesis must be stated in statistical terms. In testing whether the average amount filled is 368 grams, the null hypothesis states that $\mu$ equals 368.

✓ **2.** State the alternative hypothesis $H_1$. The alternative hypothesis must be stated in statistical terms. In testing whether the average amount filled is 368 grams, the alternative hypothesis states that $\mu$ is not equal to 368 grams.

✓ **3.** Choose the level of significance $\alpha$. The level of significance is specified according to the relative importance of the risks of committing Type I and Type II errors in the particular situation. We chose $\alpha = .05$.

✓ **4.** Choose the sample size $n$. The sample size is determined after taking into account the specified risks of committing Type I and Type II errors (i.e., selected levels of $\alpha$ and $\beta$) and considering budget constraints in carrying out the study. Here 25 cereal boxes were randomly selected.

✓ **5.** Determine the appropriate statistical technique and corresponding test statistic to use. Since $\sigma$ is known (i.e., specified by the company to be 15 grams), a $Z$ test was selected.

✓ **6.** Set up the critical values that divide the rejection and nonrejection regions. Once we specify the null and alternative hypotheses and we determine the level of significance and the sample size, the critical values for the appropriate statistical distribution can be found so that the rejection and nonrejection regions can be indicated. Here the values $+1.96$ and $-1.96$ were used to define these regions because the $Z$ test statistic refers to the standard normal distribution.

✓ **7.** Collect the data and compute the sample value of the appropriate test statistic. Here, $\overline{X} = 372.5$ grams, so $Z = +1.50$.

✓ **8.** Determine whether the test statistic has fallen into the rejection or the nonrejection region. The computed value of the test statistic is compared with the critical values for the appropriate sampling distribution to determine whether it falls into the rejection or nonrejection region. Here, $Z = +1.50$ was in the region of nonrejection because $-1.96 < Z = +1.50 < +1.96$.

✓ **9.** Make the statistical decision. If the test statistic falls into the nonrejection region, the null hypothesis $H_0$ cannot be rejected. If the test statistic falls into the rejection region, the null hypothesis is rejected. Here, $H_0$ was not rejected.

✓ **10.** Express the statistical decision in terms of the particular situation. In our cereal-filling-process example, we concluded that there was no evidence that the average amount of cereal fill was different from 368 grams. No corrective action need be taken.

## Problems for Section 11.2

### Learning the Basics

**11.18** If a .05 level of significance is used in a (two-tailed) hypothesis test, what will you decide if the computed value of the test statistic $Z$ is $+2.21$?

**11.19** If a .10 level of significance is used in a (two-tailed) hypothesis test, what will be your decision rule for rejecting a null hypothesis that the population mean is 500 if you use the $Z$ test?

• **11.20** If a .01 level of significance were used in a (two-tailed) hypothesis test, what would be your decision rule for rejecting $H_0$: $\mu = 12.5$ if you were to use the $Z$ test?

• **11.21** What would be your decision in Problem 11.20 if the computed value of the test statistic $Z$ were $-2.61$?

### Applying the Concepts

**11.22** Suppose the director of manufacturing at a clothing factory needs to determine whether a new machine is producing a particular type of cloth according to the manufacturer's specifications, which indicate that the cloth should have a mean breaking strength of 70 pounds and a standard deviation of 3.5 pounds. A sample of 49 pieces reveals a sample mean of 69.1 pounds.
(a) State the null and alternative hypotheses.
(b) Is there evidence that the machine is not meeting the manufacturer's specifications for average breaking strength? (Use a .05 level of significance.)
(c) What will your answer be in (b) if the standard deviation is specified to be 1.75 pounds?
(d) What will your answer be in (b) if the sample mean is 69 pounds?

• **11.23** The purchase of a coin-operated laundry is being considered by a potential entrepreneur. The present owner claims that over the past 5 years the average daily revenue has been $675 with a standard deviation of $75. A sample of 30 selected days reveals a daily average revenue of $625.
(a) State the null and alternative hypotheses.
(b) Is there evidence that the claim of the present owner is not valid? (Use a .01 level of significance.)
(c) What will your answer be in (b) if the standard deviation is now $100?
(d) What will your answer be in (b) if the sample mean is $650?

• **11.24** A manufacturer of salad dressings uses machines to dispense liquid ingredients into bottles that move along a filling line. The machine that dispenses dressings is working properly when 8 ounces are dispensed. The standard deviation of the process is 0.15 ounce. A sample of 50 bottles is selected periodically, and the filling line is stopped if there is evidence that the average amount dispensed is different from 8 ounces. Suppose that the average amount dispensed in a particular sample of 50 bottles is 7.983 ounces.
(a) State the null and alternative hypotheses.
(b) Is there evidence that the population average amount is different from 8 ounces? (Use a .05 level of significance.)
(c) What will your answer be in (b) if the standard deviation is specified as 0.05 ounce?
(d) What will your answer be in (b) if the sample mean is 7.952 ounces?

• **11.25** ATMs must be stocked with enough cash to satisfy customers making withdrawals over an entire weekend. On the other hand, if too much cash is unnecessarily kept in the ATMs, the bank is forgoing the opportunity of investing the money and earning interest. Suppose that at a particular branch the expected (i.e., population) average amount of money withdrawn from ATM machines per customer transaction over the weekend is $160 with an expected (i.e., population) standard deviation of $30.
(a) State the null and alternative hypotheses.

(b) If a random sample of 36 customer transactions is examined and it is observed that the sample mean withdrawal is $172, is there evidence to believe that the true average withdrawal is no longer $160? (Use a .05 level of significance.)

(c) What will your answer be in (b) if the standard deviation is really $24?

(d) What will your answer be in (b) if you use a .01 level of significance?

 ## THE *p*-VALUE APPROACH TO HYPOTHESIS TESTING

In recent years, with the advent of widely available statistical and spreadsheet software, the concept of the *p*-value is an approach to hypothesis testing that has increasingly gained acceptance.

> The ***p*-value** is the probability of obtaining a test statistic equal to or more extreme than the result obtained from the sample data, given that the null hypothesis $H_0$ is really true.

The *p*-value is often referred to as the *observed level of significance*, which is the smallest level at which $H_0$ can be rejected for a given set of data. The decision rule for rejecting $H_0$ in the *p*-value approach is:

* If the *p*-value is greater than or equal to $\alpha$, the null hypothesis is not rejected.
* If the *p*-value is smaller than $\alpha$, the null hypothesis is rejected.

To understand the *p*-value approach, let us refer to the cereal-filling-process example of section 11.2. In that section, we tested whether or not the average fill amount was equal to 368 grams (page 421). We obtained a $Z$ value of $+1.50$ and did not reject the null hypothesis because $+1.50$ was greater than the lower critical value of $-1.96$ but less than the upper critical value of $+1.96$.

Now we use the *p*-value approach. For our *two-tailed test*, we wish to find the probability of obtaining a test statistic $Z$ that is equal to or more extreme than 1.50 standard deviation units from the center of a standardized normal distribution. This means that we need to compute the probability of obtaining a $Z$ value greater than $+1.50$ along with the probability of obtaining a $Z$ value less than $-1.50$. From Table E.2(b), the probability of obtaining a $Z$ value below $-1.50$ is .0668. The probability of obtaining a value below $+1.50$ is .9332. Therefore, the probability of obtaining a value equal to or above $+1.50$ is $1 - .9332 = .0668$. Thus, the *p*-value for this two-tailed test is $.0668 + .0668 = .1336$ (see Figure 11.4). This result may be interpreted to mean that the probability of obtaining

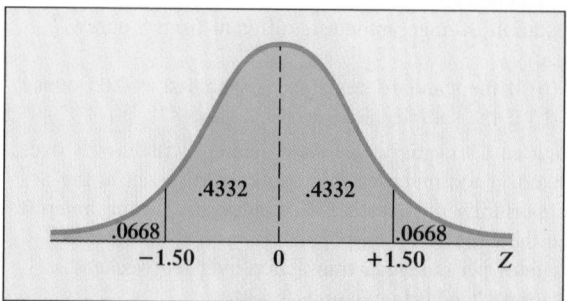

**FIGURE 11.4**
Finding the *p*-value for a two-tailed test

a result equal to or more extreme than the one observed is .1336. Because this is greater than $\alpha = .05$, the null hypothesis is not rejected.

Unless we are dealing with a test statistic that follows the normal distribution, the computation of the $p$-value can be very difficult. Thus, it is fortunate that software such as Microsoft Excel and Minitab (see references 4 and 5) routinely present the $p$-value as part of the output for hypothesis-testing procedures.

A summary of the $p$-value approach for hypothesis testing is displayed in Exhibit 11.3.

---

### Exhibit 11.3  *Steps in Determining the p-Value*

✓ **1.** State the null hypothesis $H_0$.

✓ **2.** State the alternative hypothesis $H_1$.

✓ **3.** Choose the level of significance $\alpha$.

✓ **4.** Choose the sample size $n$.

✓ **5.** Determine the appropriate statistical technique and corresponding test statistic to use.

✓ **6.** Collect the data and compute the sample value of the appropriate test statistic.

✓ **7.** Calculate the $p$-value based on the test statistic. This involves

    (a) sketching the distribution under the null hypothesis $H_0$.

    (b) placing the test statistic on the horizontal axis.

    (c) shading in the appropriate area under the curve, on the basis of the alternative hypothesis $H_1$.

✓ **8.** Compare the $p$-value to $\alpha$.

✓ **9.** Make the statistical decision. If the $p$-value is greater than or equal to $\alpha$, the null hypothesis is not rejected. If the $p$-value is smaller than $\alpha$, the null hypothesis is rejected.

✓ **10.** Express the statistical decision in terms of the particular situation.

---

## Problems for Section 11.3

### Learning the Basics

● **11.26** Suppose that in a two-tailed hypothesis test you compute the value of the test statistic $Z$ as $+2.00$. What is the $p$-value?

● **11.27** In Problem 11.26, what is your statistical decision if you test the null hypothesis at the .10 level of significance?

**11.28** Suppose that in a two-tailed hypothesis test you compute the value of the test statistic $Z$ as $-1.38$. What is the $p$-value?

**11.29** In Problem 11.28, what is your statistical decision if you test the null hypothesis at the .01 level of significance?

### Applying the Concepts

**11.30** The director of manufacturing at a clothing factory needs to determine whether a new machine is producing a particular type of cloth according to the manufacturer's specifications, which indicate that the cloth should have a mean breaking strength of 70 pounds and a standard deviation of 3.5 pounds. A sample of 49 pieces reveals a sample mean of 69.1 pounds.
  (a) Compute the *p*-value and interpret its meaning.
  (b) What is your statistical decision if you test the null hypothesis at the .05 level of significance?
  (c) Is there evidence that the machine is not meeting the manufacturer's specifications for average breaking strength?
  (d) Compare your conclusions here with those of part (b) of Problem 11.22 on page 423.

● **11.31** An entrepreneur is considering the purchase of a coin-operated laundry. The present owner claims that over the past 5 years, the average daily revenue has been $675 with a standard deviation of $75. A sample of 30 selected days reveals a daily average revenue of $625.
  (a) Compute the *p*-value and interpret its meaning.
  (b) What is your statistical decision if you test the null hypothesis at the .01 level of significance?
  (c) Is there evidence that the claim of the present owner is not valid?
  (d) Compare your conclusions here with those of part (b) of Problem 11.23 on page 423.

● **11.32** A manufacturer of salad dressings uses machines to dispense liquid ingredients into bottles that move along a filling line. The machine that dispenses dressings is working properly when 8 ounces are dispensed. The standard deviation of the process is 0.15 ounce. A sample of 50 bottles is selected periodically, and the filling line is stopped if there is evidence that the average amount dispensed is different from 8 ounces. Suppose that the average amount dispensed in a particular sample of 50 bottles is 7.983 ounces.
  (a) Compute the *p*-value and interpret its meaning.
  (b) What is your statistical decision if you test the null hypothesis at the .05 level of significance?
  (c) Is there evidence that the population average amount is different from 8 ounces?
  (d) Compare your conclusions here with those of part (b) of Problem 11.24 on page 423.

● **11.33** ATMs must be stocked with enough cash to satisfy customers making withdrawals over an entire weekend. On the other hand, if too much cash is unnecessarily kept in the ATMs, the bank is forgoing the opportunity of investing the money and earning interest. Suppose that at a particular branch the expected (i.e., population) average amount of money withdrawn from ATM machines per customer transaction over the weekend is $160 with an expected (i.e., population) standard deviation of $30. Suppose that a random sample of 36 customer transactions is examined and it is observed that the sample mean withdrawal is $172.
  (a) Compute the *p*-value and interpret its meaning.
  (b) What is your statistical decision if you test the null hypothesis at the .05 level of significance?
  (c) Is there evidence to believe that the true average withdrawal is no longer $160?
  (d) Compare your conclusions here with those of part (b) of Problem 11.25 on page 424.

## 11.4 A CONNECTION BETWEEN CONFIDENCE INTERVAL ESTIMATION AND HYPOTHESIS TESTING

Both in this chapter and in chapter 10 we examined the two major components of statistical inference—confidence interval estimation and hypothesis testing. Although they are based on the same set of concepts, we used them for different purposes. In chapter 10 we used confidence intervals to estimate parameters, and in this chapter we used hypothesis testing for making decisions about specified values of population parameters.

For example, in section 11.2 we first attempted to determine whether the population average fill amount was different from 368 grams by using equation (11.1)

$$Z = \frac{\overline{X} - \mu}{\dfrac{\sigma}{\sqrt{n}}}$$

Instead of testing the null hypothesis that $\mu = 368$ grams, we can also reach the conclusion by obtaining a confidence-interval estimate of $\mu$. If the hypothesized value of $\mu = 368$ falls into the interval, the null hypothesis is not rejected. That is, the value 368 would not be considered unusual for the data observed. On the other hand, if the hypothesized value does not fall into the interval, the null hypothesis is rejected, because 368 grams are then considered an unusual value. Using equation (10.1), the confidence interval estimate is set up from the following data:

$$n = 25, \overline{X} = 372.5 \text{ grams}, \sigma = 15 \text{ grams (specified by the company)}$$

For a confidence level of 95% (corresponding to a .05 level of significance—that is, $\alpha = .05$), we have

$$\overline{X} \pm Z\frac{\sigma}{\sqrt{n}}$$

$$372.5 \pm (1.96)\frac{15}{\sqrt{25}}$$

$$372.5 \pm 5.88$$

so that

$$366.62 \leq \mu \leq 378.38$$

Because the interval includes the hypothesized value of 368 grams, we do not reject the null hypothesis, and we would conclude that there is no evidence the mean fill amount over the entire filling process is not 368 grams. This is the same decision we reached by using hypothesis-testing methodology.

## Problems for Section 11.4

### Applying the Concepts

• **11.34** The manager of a paint supply store wants to estimate the correct amount of paint contained in 1-gallon cans purchased from a nationally known manufacturer. It is known from the manufacturer's specifications that the standard deviation of the amount of paint is equal to .02 gallon. A random sample of 50 cans is selected, and the average amount of paint per 1-gallon can is 0.995 gallon.
(a) State the null and alternative hypotheses.
(b) Is there evidence that the average amount is different from 1.0 gallon (use $\alpha = .01$)?
(c) Compare the conclusions reached in (b) with those from Problem 10.7 on page 371. Are the conclusions the same? Why?

**11.35** The quality control manager at a light bulb factory needs to estimate the average life of a large shipment of light bulbs. The process standard deviation is known to be 100 hours. A random sample of 64 light bulbs indicates a sample average life of 350 hours.

(a) State the null and alternative hypotheses.
(b) At the .05 level of significance is there evidence that the average life is different from 375 hours?
(c) Compare the conclusions reached in (b) with those from Problem 10.8 on page 372. Are the conclusions the same? Why?

**11.36** The inspection division of the Lee County Weights and Measures Department is interested in estimating the actual amount of soft drink that is placed in 2-liter bottles at the local bottling plant of a large nationally known soft-drink company. The bottling plant has informed the inspection division that the standard deviation for 2-liter bottles is .05 liter. A random sample of one hundred 2-liter bottles obtained from this bottling plant indicates a sample average of 1.99 liters.
(a) State the null and alternative hypotheses.
(b) At the .05 level of significance is there evidence that the average amount in the bottles is different from 2.0 liters?
(c) Compare the conclusions reached in (b) with those from Problem 10.9 on page 372. Are the conclusions the same? Why?

 **ONE-TAILED TESTS**

In section 11.2 we used hypothesis-testing methodology to examine the question of whether or not the average fill amount over the entire filling process (i.e., the population) is 368 grams. The alternative hypothesis ($H_1$: $\mu \neq 368$) contains two possibilities: Either the average is less than 368 grams or the average is more than 368 grams. For this reason, the rejection region is divided into the two tails of the sampling distribution of the mean. Furthermore, as we have just observed in the previous section, because a confidence interval estimate of the mean contains a lower and upper limit, respectively, corresponding to the left- and right-tail critical values from the sampling distribution of the mean, we are able to use the confidence interval to do a test of the null hypothesis that the average amount of fill over the entire filling process is 368 grams.

In some situations, however, the alternative hypothesis focuses in a *particular direction*. For example, the chief financial officer (CFO) of the food packaging company is mainly concerned with *excess* because if more than 368 grams of cereal are actually being filled per box but the price charged to the customer is based on the 368 grams labeled on the box, the company is losing money unnecessarily. Therefore, she is interested in whether the average fill for the entire filling process is *above* 368 grams. To her, strictly from a financial point of view with respect to her responsibility as CFO for the company, unless the sample mean is significantly above 368 grams, the process is working properly.

### The Critical Value Approach

For the CFO the null and alternative hypotheses are stated as follows:

$$H_0: \mu \leq 368 \text{ (process is working properly)}$$

$$H_1: \mu > 368 \text{ (process is not working properly)}$$

The rejection region here is entirely contained in the upper tail of the sampling distribution of the mean because we want to reject $H_0$ only when the sample mean is significantly above 368 grams. When such a situation occurs where the entire rejection region is contained in one tail of the sampling distribution of the test statistic, it is called a **one-tailed** or **direc-**

**tional test**. If we again choose a level of significance $\alpha$ of .05, the critical value on the Z distribution can be determined. As seen from Table 11.2 and Figure 11.5, because the entire rejection region is in the upper tail of the standard normal distribution and contains an area of .05, the area below the critical value must be .95; thus, the critical value of the Z test statistic is +1.645, the average of +1.64 and +1.65. (We should note here that some statisticians *round off* to two decimal places and select +1.64 as the critical value, whereas others *round up* to +1.65. We prefer to interpolate between the areas .9495 and .9505 so as to select the critical value with upper-tail area as close to .05 as possible. Thus, we take the average of +1.64 and +1.65.) The decision rule is

Reject $H_0$ if $Z > +1.645$;

otherwise do not reject $H_0$.

Using the Z test given by equation (11.1) on the information obtained from the sample drawn by the operations manager,

$$n = 25, \overline{X} = 372.5 \text{ grams}, \sigma = 15 \text{ grams (specified by the company)}$$

we have

$$Z = \frac{\overline{X} - \mu}{\dfrac{\sigma}{\sqrt{n}}} = \frac{372.5 - 368}{\dfrac{15}{\sqrt{25}}} = +1.50$$

**Table 11.2** *Obtaining the critical value of the Z test statistic from the standard normal distribution for a one-tailed test with* $\alpha = .05$

| Z | .00 | .01 | .02 | .03 | .04 | .05 | .06 | .07 | .08 | .09 |
|---|-----|-----|-----|-----|-----|-----|-----|-----|-----|-----|
| ⋮ | ⋮ | ⋮ | ⋮ | ⋮ | | | ⋮ | ⋮ | ⋮ | ⋮ |
| 1.3 | .9032 | .9049 | .9066 | .9082 | .9099 | .9115 | .9131 | .9147 | .9162 | .9177 |
| 1.4 | .9192 | .9207 | .9222 | .9236 | .9251 | .9265 | .9279 | .9292 | .9306 | .9319 |
| 1.5 | .9332 | .9345 | .9357 | .9370 | .9382 | .9394 | .9406 | .9418 | .9429 | .9441 |
| 1.6 | .9452 | .9463 | .9474 | .9484 | .9495 | .9505 | .9515 | .9525 | .9535 | .9545 |

*Source: Extracted from Table E.2(b)*

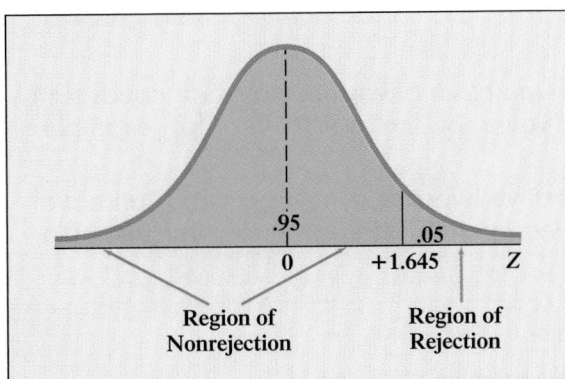

**FIGURE 11.5**

One-tailed test of hypothesis for a mean ($\sigma$ known) at the .05 level of significance

Because $Z = +1.50 < +1.645$, our decision is not to reject $H_0$, and we conclude that there is no evidence that the average fill per box over the entire filling process is above 368 grams. That is, even though the sample mean $\bar{X}$ exceeded 368 grams, the result from the sample is deemed due to *chance* or *sampling error*; it is not statistically significant.

## The *p*-Value Approach

To understand the *p*-value approach for the one-tailed test, we compute the probability of obtaining a value *either* greater than the computed test statistic *or* less than the computed test statistic, depending on the direction of the alternative hypothesis. To illustrate the computation of the *p*-value for the one-tailed test, we again refer to the cereal-filling-process example. For the chief financial officer (CFO), the null and alternative hypotheses are

$$H_0: \mu \le 368 \text{ (process is working properly)}$$

$$H_1: \mu > 368 \text{ (process is not working properly)}$$

Because the alternative hypothesis indicates a rejection region entirely in the *upper* tail of the sampling distribution of the $Z$ test statistic, we need only find the probability of obtaining a $Z$ value *above* $+1.50$. From Table E.2(b), the probability of obtaining a $Z$ value above $+1.50$ is $1 - .9332 = .0668$ (see Figure 11.6). Because this *p*-value is greater than the selected level of significance ($\alpha = .05$), the null hypothesis is not rejected.

To perform one-tailed tests of hypotheses, we must properly formulate $H_0$ and $H_1$. A summary of the null and alternative hypotheses for one-tailed tests is presented in Exhibit 11.4.

### Exhibit 11.4   *The Null and Alternative Hypotheses in One-Tailed Tests*

To summarize some key points about the null and alternative hypotheses in one-tailed tests:

✓ **1.** The null hypothesis ($H_0$) is the hypothesis that is always tested.

✓ **2.** The alternative hypothesis ($H_1$) is set up as the opposite of the null hypothesis and represents the conclusion supported if the null hypothesis is rejected.

✓ **3.** The null hypothesis ($H_0$) always refers to a specified value of the *population parameter* (such as $\mu$), not a *sample statistic* (such as $\bar{X}$).

✓ **4.** The statement of the null hypothesis *always* contains an equal sign regarding the specified value of the parameter (for example, $H_0: \mu \le 368$ grams).

✓ **5.** The statement of the alternative hypothesis *never* contains an equal sign regarding the specified value of the parameter (for example, $H_1: \mu > 368$ grams).

To further illustrate these points, consider Examples 11.3 and 11.4:

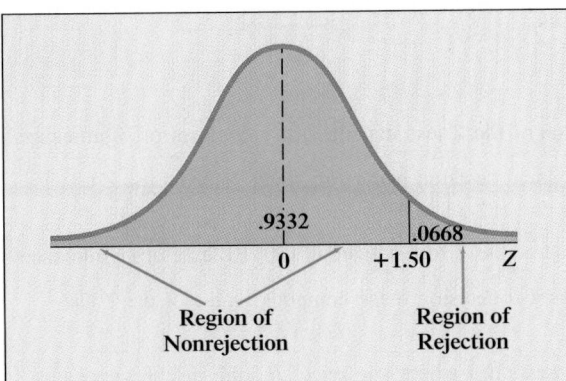

**FIGURE 11.6**
Determining the *p*-value for a one-tailed test

.9332   .0668
0   +1.50   *Z*

Region of
Nonrejection

Region of
Rejection

## Example 11.3  *Stating the Null and Alternative Hypotheses in One-Tailed Tests*

Toyota claims that a new model car will average *at least* 30 miles per gallon in highway driving. If you were planning an experiment to test this claim, what would be the null and alternative hypotheses?

### SOLUTION

The words *at least* contain an equal sign so this must be part of the null hypothesis. Therefore,

$$H_0: \mu \geq 30 \text{ miles per gallon}$$
$$H_1: \mu < 30 \text{ miles per gallon}$$

## Example 11.4  *Stating the Null and Alternative Hypotheses in One-Tailed Tests*

The average age of policyholders of term life insurance at Empire Insurance Company has been 48 for several years. As the company has expanded and provided more term policies across the nation, the chief financial officer would like to find evidence that the average age has *decreased*. If you were planning a survey to test this claim, what would be the null and alternative hypotheses?

### SOLUTION

The word *decreased* in what we would like to find evidence of does not have an equal sign so it must be part of the alternative hypothesis. Therefore,

$$H_0: \mu \geq 48 \text{ years}$$
$$H_1: \mu < 48 \text{ years}$$

# Problems for Section 11.5

## Learning the Basics

**11.37** What is the *upper-tail* critical value of the $Z$ test statistic at the .01 level of significance?

**11.38** In Problem 11.37 what is the statistical decision if the computed value of the $Z$ test statistic is 2.39?

● **11.39** What is the *lower-tail* critical value of the $Z$ test statistic at the .10 level of significance?

● **11.40** In Problem 11.39 what is the statistical decision if the computed value of the $Z$ test statistic is −1.15?

● **11.41** Suppose that in a one-tailed hypothesis test where you reject $H_0$ only in the *upper* tail, you compute the value of the test statistic $Z$ to be +2.00. What is the *p*-value?

● **11.42** In Problem 11.41 what would be your statistical decision if you tested the null hypothesis at the .10 level of significance?

**11.43** Suppose that in a one-tailed hypothesis test where you reject $H_0$ only in the *lower* tail, you compute the value of the test statistic $Z$ as −1.38. What would the *p*-value be?

**11.44** In Problem 11.43, what is your statistical decision if you tested the null hypothesis at the .01 level of significance?

## Applying the Concepts

**11.45** The CFO of a company selling computer software through megastores claims that average monthly profits throughout the country will *exceed* $1 billion. You are asked to test this claim by examining the monthly profits from a sample of megastores. State the null hypothesis $H_0$ and the alternative hypothesis $H_1$.

● **11.46** The Glen Valley Steel Company manufactures steel bars. If the production process is working properly, it turns out steel bars with an average length of *at least* 2.8 feet with a standard deviation of 0.20 foot (as determined from engineering specifications on the production equipment involved). Longer steel bars can be used or altered, but shorter bars must be scrapped. A sample of 25 bars is selected from the production line. The sample indicates an average length of 2.73 feet. The company wishes to determine whether the production equipment needs an immediate adjustment.
(a) State the null and alternative hypotheses.
(b) If the company wishes to test the hypothesis at the .05 level of significance, what decision would it make using the critical value approach to hypothesis testing?
(c) If the company wishes to test the hypothesis at the .05 level of significance, what decision would it make using the *p*-value approach to hypothesis testing?
(d) Interpret the meaning of the *p*-value in this problem.
(e) Compare your conclusions in parts (b) and (c).

**11.47** The director of manufacturing at a clothing factory needs to determine whether a new machine is producing a particular type of cloth according to the manufacturer's specifications, which indicate that the cloth should have a mean breaking strength of 70 pounds and a standard deviation of 3.5 pounds. The director is concerned that if the mean breaking strength is actually *less* than 70 pounds, the company will face too many lawsuits. A sample of 49 pieces reveals a sample mean of 69.1 pounds.
(a) State the null and alternative hypotheses.
(b) At the .05 level of significance, using the critical value approach to hypothesis testing, is there evidence that the mean breaking strength is less than 70 pounds?

(c) At the .05 level of significance, using the *p*-value approach to hypothesis testing, is there evidence that the mean breaking strength is less than 70 pounds?

(d) Interpret the meaning of the *p*-value in this problem.

(e) Compare your conclusions in parts (b) and (c).

● **11.48** A manufacturer of salad dressings uses machines to dispense liquid ingredients into bottles that move along a filling line. The machine that dispenses dressings is working properly when 8 ounces are dispensed. The standard deviation of the process is 0.15 ounce. A sample of 50 bottles is selected periodically, and the filling line is stopped if there is evidence that the average amount dispensed is actually *less* than 8 ounces. Suppose that the average amount dispensed in a particular sample of 50 bottles is 7.983 ounces.

(a) State the null and alternative hypotheses.

(b) At the .05 level of significance, using the critical value approach to hypothesis testing, is there evidence that the average amount dispensed is less than 8 ounces?

(c) At the .05 level of significance, using the *p*-value approach to hypothesis testing, is there evidence that the average amount dispensed is less than 8 ounces?

(d) Interpret the meaning of the *p*-value in this problem.

(e) Compare your conclusions in parts (b) and (c).

● **11.49** The policy of a particular bank branch is that its ATMs must be stocked with enough cash to satisfy customers making withdrawals over an entire weekend. Customer goodwill depends on such services meeting customer needs. At this branch the expected (i.e., population) average amount of money withdrawn from ATM machines per customer transaction over the weekend is $160 with an expected (i.e., population) standard deviation of $30. Suppose that a random sample of 36 customer transactions is examined and it is observed that the sample mean withdrawal is $172.

(a) State the null and alternative hypotheses.

(b) At the .05 level of significance, using the critical value approach to hypothesis testing, is there evidence to believe that the true average withdrawal is greater than $160?

(c) At the .05 level of significance, using the *p*-value approach to hypothesis testing, is there evidence to believe that the true average withdrawal is greater than $160?

(d) Interpret the meaning of the *p*-value in this problem.

(e) Compare your conclusions in parts (b) and (c).

**11.50** A pharmaceutical company claims to have produced a pill that if taken daily for 1 month will *reduce* systolic blood pressure of hypertensive patients by an average of 25 mg/mm. If you were asked to evaluate an experimental trial conducted by this company on a random sample of patients who consent to participate, what would the null hypothesis $H_0$ and alternative hypothesis $H_1$ be?

 **11.6** *t* **TEST OF HYPOTHESIS FOR THE MEAN (σ UNKNOWN)**

In most hypothesis-testing situations dealing with numerical data, the standard deviation σ of the population is unknown. However, the actual standard deviation of the population is estimated by computing $S$, the standard deviation of the sample. If the population is assumed to be normally distributed, you may recall from section 10.2 that the sampling distribution of the mean will follow a $t$ distribution with $n - 1$ degrees of freedom. The test statistic $t$ for determining the difference between the sample mean $\overline{X}$ and the population mean μ when the sample standard deviation $S$ is used is given by

## *t* Test of Hypothesis for the Mean (σ Unknown)

$$t = \frac{\overline{X} - \mu}{\dfrac{S}{\sqrt{n}}}$$

(11.2)

where the test statistic *t* follows a *t* distribution having *n* − 1 degrees of freedom.

To illustrate the use of this *t* test, we return to the Saxon Plumbing Company example presented on page 366. In one of the efforts to maintain internal controls on sales, the auditor takes a sample of sales invoices at the end of the month to evaluate the average amount listed on the sales invoices for the warehouse in that month. Over the past five years, the average amount of each sales invoice for customers outside the suburban area in which Saxon Plumbing Company is located is $120. Because shipping costs are affected by delivery distance, it is important that the auditor carefully monitors the average sales amount. The following data display the amounts listed (in dollars) in a random sample of 12 sales invoices that were selected from the population of sales invoices for customers outside the suburban area during the past month.

| 108.98 | 152.22 | 111.45 | 110.59 | 127.46 | 107.26 |
|--------|--------|--------|--------|--------|--------|
| 93.32  | 91.97  | 111.56 | 75.71  | 128.58 | 135.11 |

Because the auditor is interested in whether or not there is evidence of a change in the average amount of these sales invoices from the $120 amount that has been the monthly average over the past few years, the test is two-tailed and the following null and alternative hypotheses are established:

$$H_0: \mu = \$120$$
$$H_1: \mu \neq \$120$$

◆ **Critical Value Approach** For a given sample size *n*, the test statistic *t* follows a *t* distribution with *n* − 1 degrees of freedom. If a level of significance of α = .05 is selected, the critical values of the *t* distribution with 12 − 1 = 11 degrees of freedom can be obtained from Table E.3, as illustrated in Figure 11.7 and Table 11.3. Because the alternative

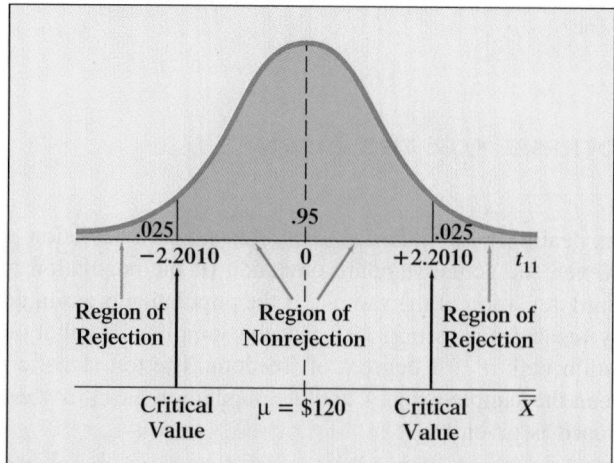

**FIGURE 11.7**
Testing a hypothesis about the mean (σ unknown) at the .05 level of significance with 11 degrees of freedom

## Table 11.3  Determining the critical value from the t table for an area of .025 in each tail with 11 degrees of freedom

| DEGREES OF FREEDOM | UPPER-TAIL AREAS | | | | | |
|---|---|---|---|---|---|---|
| | .25 | .10 | .05 | .025 | .01 | .005 |
| 1 | 1.0000 | 3.0777 | 6.3138 | 12.7062 | 31.8207 | 63.6574 |
| 2 | 0.8165 | 1.8856 | 2.9200 | 4.3027 | 6.9646 | 9.9248 |
| 3 | 0.7649 | 1.6377 | 2.3534 | 3.1824 | 4.5407 | 5.8409 |
| 4 | 0.7407 | 1.5332 | 2.1318 | 2.7764 | 3.7469 | 4.6041 |
| 5 | 0.7267 | 1.4759 | 2.0150 | 2.5706 | 3.3649 | 4.0322 |
| 6 | 0.7176 | 1.4398 | 1.9432 | 2.4469 | 3.1427 | 3.7074 |
| 7 | 0.7111 | 1.4149 | 1.8946 | 2.3646 | 2.9980 | 3.4995 |
| 8 | 0.7064 | 1.3968 | 1.8595 | 2.3060 | 2.8965 | 3.3554 |
| 9 | 0.7027 | 1.3830 | 1.8331 | 2.2622 | 2.8214 | 3.2498 |
| 10 | 0.6998 | 1.3722 | 1.8125 | 2.2281 | 2.7638 | 3.1693 |
| 11 | 0.6974 | 1.3634 | 1.7959 | → 2.2010 | 2.7181 | 3.1058 |

*Source: Extracted from Table E.3*

hypothesis $H_1$ that $\mu \neq \$120$ is *nondirectional*, the area in the rejection region of the $t$ distribution's left (lower) tail is .025 and the area in the rejection region of the $t$ distribution's right (upper) tail is also .025.

From the $t$ table as given in Table E.3, a replica of which is shown in Table 11.3, the critical values are $\pm2.2010$. The decision rule is

$$\text{Reject } H_0 \text{ if } t < -t_{11} = -2.2010$$
$$\text{or if } t > t_{11} = +2.2010;$$
$$\text{otherwise do not reject } H_0.$$

For the data set pertaining to the random sample of $n = 12$ sales invoices, using equations (4.1) and (4.10) on pages 133 and 145, respectively, we compute

$$\overline{X} = \frac{\sum\limits_{i=1}^{n} X_i}{n} = \$112.85 \quad \text{and} \quad S = \sqrt{\frac{\sum\limits_{i=1}^{n}(X_i - \overline{X})^2}{n-1}} = \$20.80$$

From equation (11.2) we then obtain

$$t = \frac{\overline{X} - \mu}{\dfrac{S}{\sqrt{n}}} = \frac{112.85 - 120}{\dfrac{20.80}{\sqrt{12}}} = -1.19$$

Because $t = -1.19$ falls within the nonrejection region between the critical values of $-2.2010$ and $2.2010$, we cannot reject $H_0$. There is no evidence to believe that the average monthly sales invoice has changed from the long-term average of $120—our observed difference is insignificant and due to chance.

◆ *p-Value Approach*   Software such as Microsoft Excel and Minitab (references 4 and 5) provides $p$-values as part of the output for various hypothesis-testing procedures. As an example, using Minitab for the sales invoice data, the two-tailed $p$-value is equal to .26 (see

```
Test of mu = 120.00 vs mu not = 120.00

Variable     N      Mean     StDev    SE Mean        T           P
Sales       12    112.85     20.80       6.00     -1.19        0.26
```

**FIGURE 11.8**   Minitab output with *p*-value for the one-sample *t* test of sales invoices

Figure 11.8). Because our *p*-value or *observed level of significance* is greater than α, our *specified level of significance*, we cannot reject $H_0$. (That is, .26 > .05, so we don't reject $H_0$.) If the null hypothesis were true, the probability that a sample of 12 invoices could have a monthly average that differs by $7.15 or more from the stated $120 is .26. This leads us to conclude that there is no evidence to believe that the average monthly sales invoice has changed from the long-term average of $120. The auditor need not make any recommendation to management about altering shipping policies for items purchased outside the suburban community.

Example 11.5 applies the 10 steps of hypothesis testing displayed in Exhibits 11.2 and 11.3 to the sales invoices example.

## Example 11.5   *t Test of Hypothesis for the Mean (σ Unknown)*

Using the sales invoice data on page 434, test the claim that the average monthly amount for items sold outside the suburban region is $120.

### SOLUTION

Steps 1 and 2:

$$H_0: \mu = \$120$$

$$H_1: \mu \neq \$120$$

Step 3:
$$\alpha = .05$$

Step 4:
$$n = 12$$

Step 5: Because σ is unknown, we choose the one-sample *t*-test with test statistic *t* given by equation (11.2):

$$t = \frac{\overline{X} - \mu}{\dfrac{S}{\sqrt{n}}}$$

Step 6: We use Table E.3 to develop the following decision rule as illustrated in Figure 11.7 on page 434:

Reject $H_0$ if $t < -t_{11} = -2.2010$ or if $t > t_{11} = +2.2010$;

otherwise do not reject $H_0$.

Step 7: We collect the data and evaluate the assumptions of the *t* test (to be described in the following section). We then compute the *t* test statistic:

$$t = \frac{\overline{X} - \mu}{\dfrac{S}{\sqrt{n}}} = \frac{112.85 - 120}{\dfrac{20.80}{\sqrt{12}}} = -1.19$$

Steps 8, 9, and 10:  The critical values for the *t* test statistic are $\pm 2.2010$. Because $-2.2010 < t = -1.19 < +2.2010$, we cannot reject $H_0$. (Alternatively, the *p*-value, .26, is greater than $\alpha$ of .05 so we cannot reject $H_0$). There is no evidence to believe that the average monthly sales invoice has changed from the long-term average of $120—our observed difference is insignificant and due to chance. The auditor need not make any recommendation to management about altering shipping policies for items purchased outside the suburban community.

The **one-sample *t* test** can be either a two-tailed test or a one-tailed test, depending on whether the alternative hypothesis is *nondirectional* or *directional*, respectively. If the alternative hypothesis is nondirectional, as in our sales invoice example, we are looking to reject the null hypothesis that the value of the parameter is a specified amount such as $\mu = \$120$. In this two-tailed test we reject $H_0$ if there is evidence from the sample that the value of the parameter being tested is likely to be either significantly more or significantly less than this hypothesized amount. In a one-tailed test, the alternative hypothesis is directional. We reject $H_0$ only if there is evidence from the sample that the value of the parameter being tested is too small or too large, depending on the direction specified in the alternative hypothesis. The regions of rejection and nonrejection for these one-sample *t* tests are depicted in Figure 11.9.

The one-sample *t* test is considered a **classical parametric** procedure—one that makes a variety of stringent assumptions that must hold if we are to be assured that the results we obtain from employing the test are valid. Assumptions of the one-sample *t* test are presented in the accompanying Comment box.

**COMMENT:  *Assumptions of the One-Sample t Test***

To use the one-sample *t* test, it is assumed that the obtained numerical data are independently drawn and represent a random sample from a population that is normally distributed. In practice, it has been found that as long as the sample size is not very small and the population is not very skewed, the *t* distribution gives a good approximation to the sampling distribution of the mean when $\sigma$ is unknown.

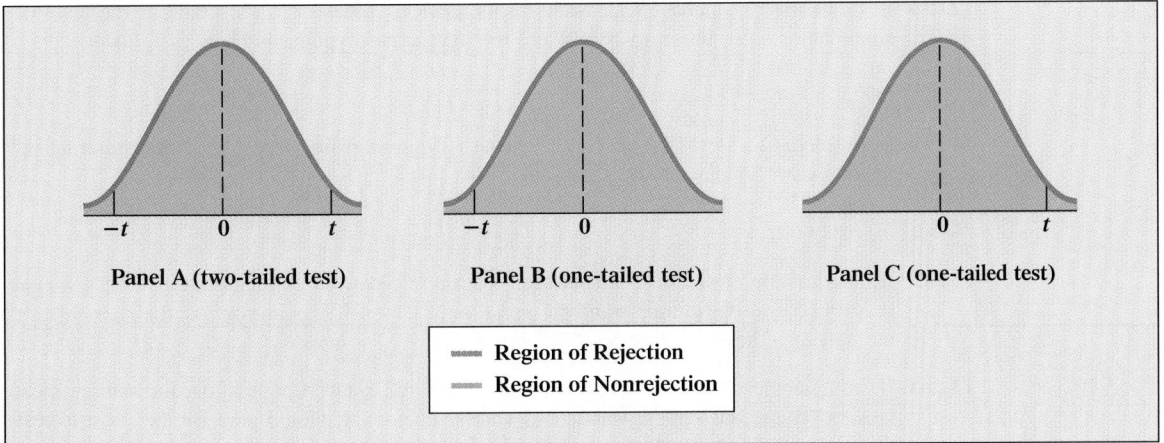

Panel A (two-tailed test)        Panel B (one-tailed test)        Panel C (one-tailed test)

---- Region of Rejection
---- Region of Nonrejection

**FIGURE 11.9**   Regions of rejection and nonrejection for one-sample *t* test

Software such as Microsoft Excel and Minitab enables us to evaluate the assumptions necessary for using the *t* test on the sales invoice data. As we learned in section 8.2, the normality assumption can be checked in several ways. A determination of how closely the actual data match the normal distribution's theoretical properties can be made by a descriptive analysis of the obtained statistics along with a graphical analysis to provide a visual interpretation. Thus, by exploring the sample data through a study of its descriptive summary measures along with a graphical analysis (a histogram, a stem-and-leaf display, a box-and-whisker plot, and a normal probability plot), we may draw our own conclusions as to the likelihood that the underlying population is at least approximately normally distributed.

Using the sales invoice data, Figure 11.10 presents Microsoft Excel output depicting the descriptive summary measures and a normal probability plot. From these, because the mean is very close to the median and the points on the normal probability plot appear to be increasing in an approximate straight line, there is no reason to believe that the assumption of underlying population normality of the sales invoice data is violated to any great degree, and we may conclude that the results obtained by the auditor are valid.

The *t* test is a **robust** test. That is, it does not lose power if the shape of the population from which the sample is drawn departs somewhat from a normal distribution, particularly when the sample size is large enough to enable the test statistic *t* to be influenced by the central limit theorem (see section 9.1). However, erroneous conclusions may be drawn and statistical power can be lost if the *t* test is incorrectly used. If the sample size $n$ is small (i.e., less than 30) and we cannot easily make the assumption that the underlying population from which the sample was drawn is at least approximately normally distributed, other, *nonparametric* testing procedures are likely to be more powerful (see references 1 and 2).

## Problems for Section 11.6

### Learning the Basics

• **11.51** If, in a sample of size $n = 16$ selected from an underlying normal population, the sample mean is $\overline{X} = 56$ and the sample standard deviation is $S = 12$, what is the value of the *t* test statistic if we are testing the null hypothesis $H_0$ that $\mu = 50$?

• **11.52** In Problem 11.51, how many degrees of freedom would there be in the one-sample *t* test?

**11.53** In Problems 11.51 and 11.52, what are the critical values from the *t* table if the level of significance $\alpha$ is chosen to be .05 and the alternative hypothesis $H_1$ is as follows:
(a) $\mu \neq 50$?
(b) $\mu > 50$?

**11.54** In Problems 11.51, 11.52, and 11.53, what is your statistical decision if your alternative hypothesis $H_1$ is as follows:
(a) $\mu \neq 50$?
(b) $\mu > 50$?

• **11.55** If, in a sample of size $n = 16$ selected from a left-skewed population, the sample mean is $\overline{X} = 65$ and the sample standard deviation is $S = 21$, would you use the *t* test to test the null hypothesis $H_0$ that $\mu = 60$? Discuss.

**11.56** If, in a sample of size $n = 160$ selected from a left-skewed population, the sample mean is $\overline{X} = 65$ and the sample standard deviation is $S = 21$, would you use the *t* test to test the null hypothesis $H_0$ that $\mu = 60$? Discuss.

| | A | B |
|---|---|---|
| 1 | Sales | |
| 2 | | |
| 3 | **Mean** | **112.8508333** |
| 4 | Standard Error | 6.003863082 |
| 5 | **Median** | **111.02** |
| 6 | Mode | #N/A |
| 7 | **Standard Deviation** | **20.7979918** |
| 8 | Sample Variance | 432.5564629 |
| 9 | Kurtosis | 0.172707598 |
| 10 | Skewness | 0.13363802 |
| 11 | **Range** | **76.51** |
| 12 | **Minimum** | **75.71** |
| 13 | Maximum | 152.22 |
| 14 | Sum | 1354.21 |
| 15 | Count | 12 |
| 16 | Confidence Level(95.0%) | 13.21442023 |

(a)

**FIGURE 11.10**

Excel output for studying assumptions necessary to employ the *t* test for the sales invoice data [panel (a): descriptive statistics; panel (b): normal probability plot]

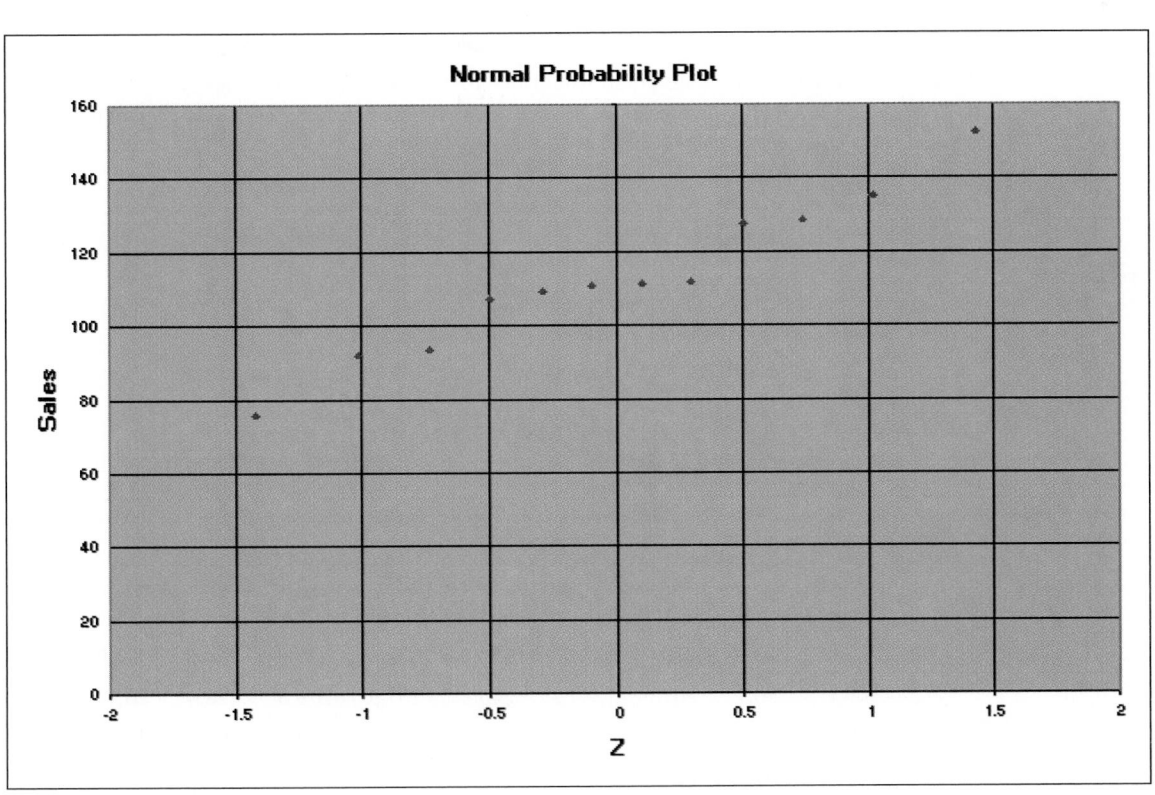

(b)

## Applying the Concepts

- **11.57** The manager of the credit department for an oil company would like to determine whether the average monthly balance of credit card holders is equal to $75. An auditor selects a random sample of 100 accounts and finds that the average owed is $83.40 with a sample standard deviation of $23.65.

(a) Using the .05 level of significance, should the auditor conclude that there is evidence that the average balance is different from $75?

(b) What is your answer in (a) if the standard deviation is $37.26?

(c) What is your answer in (a) if the sample mean is $78.81?

**11.58** A manufacturer of detergent claims that the mean weight of a particular box of detergent is 3.25 pounds. A random sample of 64 boxes reveals a sample average of 3.238 pounds and a sample standard deviation of 0.117 pound.

(a) Using the .01 level of significance, is there evidence that the average weight of the boxes is different from 3.25 pounds?

(b) What is your answer in (a) if the standard deviation is 0.05 pound?

(c) What is your answer in (a) if the sample mean is 3.211 pounds?

**11.59** The director of admissions at a large university advises parents of incoming students about the cost of textbooks during a typical semester. A sample of 100 students enrolled in the university indicates a sample average cost of $315.40 with a sample standard deviation of $43.20.

(a) Using the .10 level of significance, is there evidence that the population average is above $300?

(b) What is your answer in (a) if the standard deviation is $75 and the .05 level of significance is used?

(c) What is your answer in (a) if the sample average is $305.11?

• **11.60** A consumers' advocate group would like to evaluate the average energy efficiency rating (EER) of window-mounted, large-capacity (i.e., in excess of 7,000 Btu) air-conditioning units. A random sample of 36 such air-conditioning units is selected and tested for a fixed period of time. Their EER records are as follows:

| 8.9 | 9.1 | 9.2 | 9.1 | 8.4 | 9.5 | 9.0 | 9.6 | 9.3 |
|-----|-----|-----|-----|-----|-----|-----|-----|-----|
| 9.3 | 8.9 | 9.7 | 8.7 | 9.4 | 8.5 | 8.9 | 8.4 | 9.5 |
| 9.3 | 9.3 | 8.8 | 9.4 | 8.9 | 9.3 | 9.0 | 9.2 | 9.1 |
| 9.8 | 9.6 | 9.3 | 9.2 | 9.1 | 9.6 | 9.8 | 9.5 | 10.0 |

**DATA FILE**
EER

(a) Using the .05 level of significance, is there evidence that the average EER is different from 9.0?

(b) What assumptions are made to perform this test?

(c) If you are using Microsoft Excel or Minitab, find the *p*-value and interpret its meaning.

(d) What will be your answer in (a) if the last data value is 8.0 instead of 10.0?

**11.61** A manufacturer of plastics wants to evaluate the durability of rectangularly molded plastic blocks that are to be used in furniture. A random sample of 50 such plastic blocks is examined, and the hardness measurements (in Brinell units) are recorded as follows:

| 283.6 | 273.3 | 278.8 | 238.7 | 334.9 | 302.6 | 239.9 | 254.6 | 281.9 | 270.4 |
|-------|-------|-------|-------|-------|-------|-------|-------|-------|-------|
| 269.1 | 250.1 | 301.6 | 289.2 | 240.8 | 267.5 | 279.3 | 228.4 | 265.2 | 285.9 |
| 279.3 | 252.3 | 271.7 | 235.0 | 313.2 | 277.8 | 243.8 | 295.5 | 249.3 | 228.7 |
| 255.3 | 267.2 | 255.3 | 281.0 | 302.1 | 256.3 | 233.0 | 194.4 | 291.9 | 263.7 |
| 273.6 | 267.7 | 283.1 | 260.9 | 274.8 | 277.4 | 276.9 | 259.5 | 262.0 | 263.5 |

**DATA FILE**
PLASTIC

(a) Using the .05 level of significance, is there evidence that the average hardness of the plastic blocks exceeds 260 (in Brinell units)?

(b) What assumptions are made to perform this test?

(c) If you are using Microsoft Excel or Minitab, find the *p*-value and interpret its meaning.

(d) What will be your answer in (a) if the first data value is 233.6 instead of 283.6?

**11.62** A machine being used for packaging seedless golden raisins has been set so that on average 15 ounces of raisins will be packaged per box. The operations manager wishes to test the machine setting and selects a sample of 30 consecutive raisin packages filled during the production process. Their weights are recorded as follows:

| | | | | | | | | | |
|---|---|---|---|---|---|---|---|---|---|
| 15.2 | 15.3 | 15.1 | 15.7 | 15.3 | 15.0 | 15.1 | 14.3 | 14.6 | 14.5 |
| 15.0 | 15.2 | 15.4 | 15.6 | 15.7 | 15.4 | 15.3 | 14.9 | 14.8 | 14.6 |
| 14.3 | 14.4 | 15.5 | 15.4 | 15.2 | 15.5 | 15.6 | 15.1 | 15.3 | 15.1 |

DATA FILE
RAISINS

(a) Is there evidence that the mean weight per box is different from 15 ounces? (Use $\alpha = .05$.)

(b) To perform the test in part (a), we assume that the observed sequence in which the data were collected is random. What other assumptions must be made to perform the test? Discuss.

(c) What is your answer in (a) if the weights for the last two packages are 16.3 and 16.1 instead of 15.3 and 15.1?

**● 11.63** A manufacturer claims that the average capacity of a certain type of battery the company produces is at least 140 ampere-hours. An independent consumer protection agency wishes to test the credibility of the manufacturer's claim and measures the capacity of a random sample of 20 batteries from a recently produced batch. The results, in ampere-hours, are as follows:

| | | | | | | | | | |
|---|---|---|---|---|---|---|---|---|---|
| 137.4 | 140.0 | 138.8 | 139.1 | 144.4 | 139.2 | 141.8 | 137.3 | 133.5 | 138.2 |
| 141.1 | 139.7 | 136.7 | 136.3 | 135.6 | 138.0 | 140.9 | 140.6 | 136.7 | 134.1 |

DATA FILE
AMPHRS

(a) Using the .05 level of significance, is there evidence that the manufacturer's claim is being overstated?

(b) What assumption must hold in order to perform the test in part (a)?

(c) Evaluate this assumption through a graphical approach. Discuss.

(d) What is your answer in (a) if the last two values are 146.7 and 144.1 instead of 136.7 and 134.1?

**11.64** Suppose that the manager of a 500-car taxi fleet in a large city wishes to reevaluate the maintenance contract on its vehicles. A major part of the analysis considers the "wear and tear" on the vehicles—i.e., the daily usage as represented by miles logged per taxi per day. Upon examination of his contract, the manager feels that if the taxis are averaging more than 70 miles per day, he wants to renegotiate or change the contract. Because an odometer recording is made by management as each taxi departs and then returns to the terminal, the difference represents the total mileage driven per taxi per day. A sample of 16 taxis is selected at random from the fleet. The following table records their mileage for a particular day:

*mean 81.2125    standard deviation 19.93927*

| | | | | | | | |
|---|---|---|---|---|---|---|---|
| 107.1 | 121.0 | 71.2 | 76.1 | 95.7 | 92.8 | 74.8 | 92.1 |
| 94.4 | 42.5 | 82.3 | 56.5 | 74.6 | 91.7 | 63.7 | 62.9 |

DATA FILE
TAXI

(a) The manager knows you are studying statistics and asks you to completely analyze these data. Using an $\alpha = .05$ level of significance, what would you conclude about average daily mileage? What would you recommend to the manager?

(b) Present your findings in a memo to the manager. Be sure to attach an appendix describing the assumption that must hold in order for you to perform the test in part (a). Be sure to provide an evaluation of this assumption through a graphical approach.

In some situations, we want to test a hypothesis pertaining to the population proportion $p$ of values that are in a particular category. A random sample can be selected from the population, and the **sample proportion**, $p_s = X/n$, computed. The value of this statistic is then compared to the hypothesized value of the parameter $p$ so that a decision pertaining to the hypothesis can be made.

If certain assumptions are met, the sampling distribution of a proportion follows a standardized normal distribution (see section 9.2). To perform the hypothesis test in order to evaluate the magnitude of the difference between the sample proportion $p_s$ and the hypothesized population proportion $p$, the test statistic $Z$ given in equation (11.3) can be used.

---

**One-Sample Z Test for the Proportion**

$$Z \cong \frac{p_s - p}{\sqrt{\dfrac{p(1 - p)}{n}}} \tag{11.3}$$

where

$$p_s = \frac{X}{n} = \frac{\text{number of successes in sample}}{\text{sample size}}$$

$$= \text{observed proportion of successes}$$

$$p = \text{hypothesized proportion of successes}$$

---

This test statistic $Z$ is approximately normally distributed.

Alternatively, instead of examining the *proportion* of successes in a sample, as in equation (11.3), we can study the *number* of successes in a sample. The test statistic $Z$ for determining the magnitude of the difference between the number of successes in a sample and the hypothesized or expected number of successes in the population is presented in equation (11.4).

---

**One-Sample Z Test for the Proportion**

$$Z \cong \frac{X - np}{\sqrt{np(1 - p)}} \tag{11.4}$$

---

Aside from possible rounding errors, the test statistic $Z$ given by equations (11.3) and (11.4) provides exactly the same results. The two alternative forms of the test statistic are equivalent because the numerator of equation (11.4) is $n$ times the numerator of equation (11.3), and the denominator of equation (11.4) is also $n$ times the denominator of equation (11.3). The choice of which of these two formulas to employ is up to the user.

To illustrate the (one-sample) $Z$ test for a hypothesized proportion, let us return to the cereal-filling-process example discussed earlier in this chapter. Suppose that the operations manager is also concerned with the sealing process for filled boxes. Once the package inside the box is filled, it is supposed to be sealed so that it is airtight. On the basis of past experience, however, it is known that 1 out of 10 packages (i.e., 10% or .10) initially do not meet standards for sealing and must be "reworked" in order to pass inspection. To alter this situation, suppose the operations manager implements a newly developed sealing system on a trial basis. After a 1-day "break-in" period, he takes a random sample of 200 boxes that represent daily output at the plant and, through inspection, finds that 11 need rework. The operations manager wants to determine whether there is evidence that, under the new sealing system, the proportion of defective packages has improved (i.e., has decreased below .10).

In terms of proportions (rather than percentages), the null and alternative hypotheses can be stated as follows:

$$H_0: p \geq .10$$

$$H_1: p < .10$$

◆ **Critical Value Approach**   Because the operations manager is interested in whether or not there has been a significant reduction in the proportion of defective packages owing to the new sealing system, the test is one-tailed. If a level of significance $\alpha$ of .05 is selected, the rejection and nonrejection regions are set up as in Figure 11.11, and the decision rule is

Reject $H_0$ if $Z < -1.645$;

otherwise do not reject $H_0$.

From our data,

$$p_s = \frac{11}{200} = .055$$

Using equation (11.3), we have

$$Z \cong \frac{p_s - p}{\sqrt{\dfrac{p(1 - p)}{n}}} = \frac{.055 - .10}{\sqrt{\dfrac{(.10)(.90)}{200}}} = \frac{-.045}{\sqrt{.00045}} = \frac{-.045}{.0212} = -2.12$$

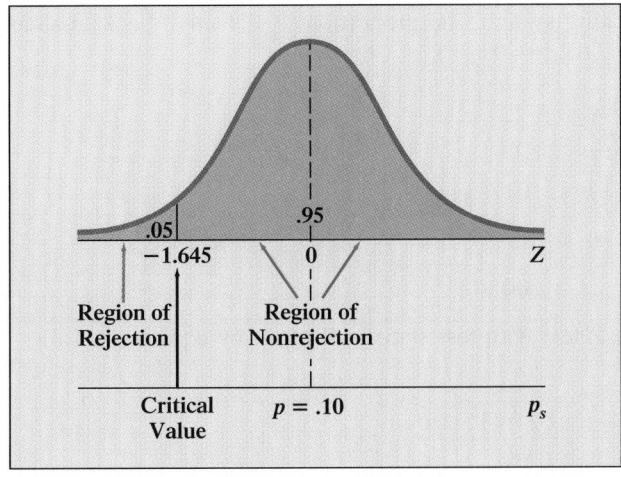

**FIGURE 11.11**
One-tailed test of hypothesis for a proportion at the .05 level of significance

or, using equation (11.4), we have

$$Z \cong \frac{X - np}{\sqrt{np(1 - p)}} = \frac{11 - (200)(.10)}{\sqrt{(200)(.10)(.90)}} = \frac{11 - 20}{\sqrt{18}} = \frac{-9}{4.243} = -2.12$$

Because $-2.12 < -1.645$, we reject $H_0$. Thus, the manager may conclude that there is evidence that the proportion of defectives with the new system is less than .10.

◆ *p-Value Approach*  As an alternative approach toward making a hypothesis-testing decision, we may also compute the *p*-value for this situation (see sections 11.3 and 11.5). Because a one-tailed test is involved in which the rejection region is located only in the lower tail (see Figure 11.12), we need to find the area below a $Z$ value of $-2.12$. From Table E.2(b) this probability will be .0170—our *observed* level of significance. Because this value is less than the *selected* level of significance ($\alpha = .05$), the null hypothesis can be rejected.

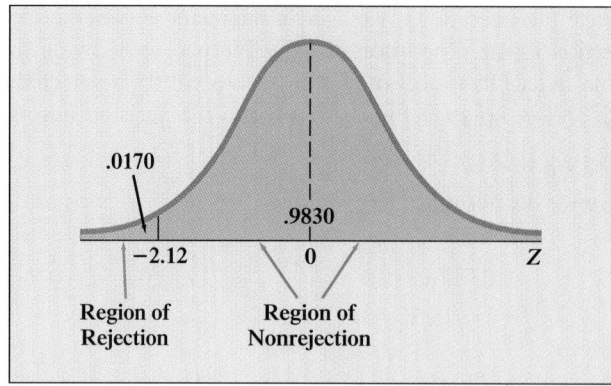

**FIGURE 11.12**
Determining the *p*-value for a one-tailed test

Example 11.6 applies the 10 steps in hypothesis testing developed in Exhibits 11.2 and 11.3.

## Example 11.6  *One-Sample Z Test for the Proportion*

Using the data available to the operations manager on page 443, determine whether there is evidence that, under the new sealing system, the proportion of defective packages has improved (i.e., has decreased below .10).

### SOLUTION

Steps 1 and 2: $\qquad\qquad\qquad H_0: p \geq .10$

$\qquad\qquad\qquad\qquad\qquad\quad H_1: p < .10$

Step 3: $\qquad\qquad\qquad\qquad \alpha = .05$

Step 4: $\qquad\qquad\qquad\qquad n = 200$

Step 5:  We choose the one-sample $Z$ test with test statistic $Z$ given by equation (11.3):

$$Z \cong \frac{p_s - p}{\sqrt{\dfrac{p(1 - p)}{n}}}$$

Step 6: We use Table E.2(b) to develop the following decision rule as illustrated in Figure 11.11:

$$\text{Reject } H_0 \text{ if } Z < -1.645;$$

$$\text{otherwise do not reject } H_0.$$

Step 7: We collect the data and compute the $Z$ test statistic:

$$Z \cong \frac{p_s - p}{\sqrt{\dfrac{p(1-p)}{n}}} = \frac{.055 - .10}{\sqrt{\dfrac{(.10)(.90)}{200}}} = \frac{-.045}{\sqrt{.00045}} = \frac{-.045}{.0212} = -2.12$$

Steps 8, 9, and 10: Because $-2.12 < -1.645$, we reject $H_0$. (Alternatively, the $p$-value, .0170, is less than $\alpha$ of .05, so we reject $H_0$.) Thus, the manager may conclude that there is evidence that the proportion of defectives with the new system is less than .10.

The one-sample $Z$ test for the proportion can be either a two-tailed test or a one-tailed test, depending on whether the alternative hypothesis is *nondirectional* or *directional*, respectively. If the alternative hypothesis is directional, as in our box-sealing example, we reject $H_0$ only if there is evidence from the sample that the value of the parameter being tested is too small or too large, depending on the direction specified in the alternative hypothesis. In a two-tailed test, the alternative hypothesis is nondirectional. We reject $H_0$ if there is evidence from the sample that the value of the parameter being tested is likely to be either significantly more or significantly less than this hypothesized amount. The regions of rejection and nonrejection for these one-sample $Z$ tests are depicted in Figure 11.13.

The one-sample $Z$ test for a proportion, sometimes called the **binomial test** is considered a **nonparametric** or distribution-free procedure—one whose test statistic does not depend on the form of the underlying population distribution from which the sample data were drawn and one whose data are categorical and measured on a nominal scale. Assumptions for the $Z$ test for a proportion are presented in the Comment box on page 446.

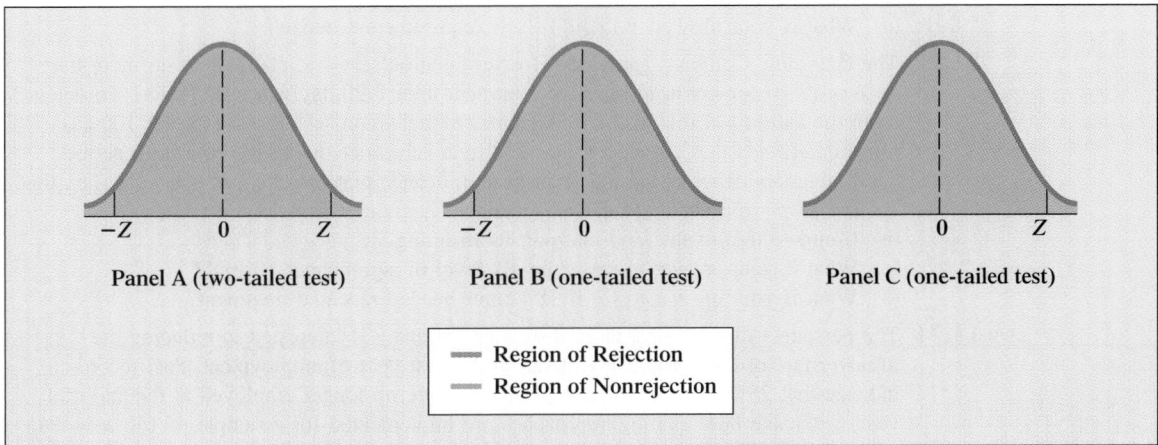

**FIGURE 11.13** Regions of rejection and nonrejection for the one-sample $Z$ test for a proportion

> **Comment:** **Checking the Assumptions of the Z Test for a Proportion**
>
> The test statistic $Z$ given in equations (11.3) and (11.4) is approximately normally distributed. You may recall from section 9.2 that although the random variable $X$ (the number of successes in the sample) follows a binomial distribution, if the sample size is large enough so that both $np \geq 5$ and $n(1 - p) \geq 5$, the normal distribution provides a good approximation of the binomial distribution.

## Problems for Section 11.7

### Learning the Basics

- **11.65** If in a random sample of 400 items, 88 are found to be defective, what is the sample proportion of defective items?

- **11.66** In Problem 11.65, if it is hypothesized that 20 percent of the items in the population are defective, what is the value of the $Z$ test statistic
  (a) computed from equation (11.3)?
  (b) computed from equation (11.4)?

- **11.67** In Problems 11.65 and 11.66, suppose you are testing the null hypothesis $H_0$: $p = .20$ against the two-tailed alternative hypothesis $H_1$: $p \neq .20$ and you choose the level of significance $\alpha$ to be .05. What is your statistical decision?

- **11.68** Prove that the formula on the right-hand side of equation (11.3) on page 442 is equivalent to the formula on the right-hand side of equation (11.4).

### Applying the Concepts

- **11.69** A television manufacturer claims in its warranty that in the past not more than 10% of its television sets needed any repair during their first 2 years of operation. To test the validity of this claim, a government testing agency selects a sample of 100 sets and finds that 14 sets required some repair within their first 2 years of operation. Using the .01 level of significance,
  (a) is the manufacturer's claim valid or is there evidence that the claim is not valid?
  (b) compute the *p*-value and interpret its meaning.
  (c) What is your answer in (a) if 18 sets required some repair?

- **11.70** The Giansante Company, provider of extermination services, claims that no more than 15% of its customers need repeated treatment after a 90-day warranty period. To determine the validity of this claim, a consumer organization selects a sample of 100 customers and finds that 22 needed repeated treatment after the 90-day warranty period.
  (a) Is there evidence at the .05 level of significance that the claim is not valid (i.e., that the proportion needing repeated treatment is greater than .15)?
  (b) Compute the *p*-value and interpret its meaning.
  (c) What is your answer to (a) if the .01 level of significance is used?
  (d) What is your answer to (a) if 18 homes needed repeated treatment?

- **11.71** The personnel director of a large insurance company is interested in reducing the turnover rate of data processing clerks in the first year of employment. Past records indicate that 25% of all new hires in this area are no longer employed at the end of 1 year. Extensive new training approaches are implemented for a sample of 150 new data processing clerks. At the end of a 1-year period, 29 of these 150 individuals are no longer employed.

(a) At the .01 level of significance, is there evidence that the proportion of data processing clerks who have gone through the new training and are no longer employed is less than .25?

(b) Compute the *p*-value and interpret its meaning.

(c) What is your answer to (a) if 22 of the individuals are no longer employed?

● **11.72** The marketing manager for an automobile manufacturer is interested in determining the proportion of new compact-car owners who would have purchased a passenger-side inflatable air bag if it had been available for an additional cost of $300. The manager believes from previous information that the proportion is .30. Suppose that a survey of 200 new compact-car owners is selected and 79 indicate that they would have purchased the inflatable air bags.

(a) At the .10 level of significance, is there evidence that the population proportion is different from .30?

(b) Compute the *p*-value and interpret its meaning.

(c) What is your answer to (a) if 70 new owners indicated that they would have purchased inflatable air bags?

**11.73** The marketing branch of the Mexican Tourist Bureau would like to increase the proportion of tourists who purchase silver jewelry while vacationing in Mexico from its present estimated value of .40. Toward this end, promotional literature describing both the beauty and value of the jewelry is prepared and distributed to all passengers on airplanes arriving at a certain seaside resort during a 1-week period. A sample of 500 passengers returning at the end of the 1-week period is randomly selected, and 227 of these passengers indicate that they purchased silver jewelry.

(a) At the .05 level of significance, is there evidence that the proportion has increased above the previous value of .40?

(b) Compute the *p*-value and interpret its meaning.

(c) What is your answer to (a) if 213 passengers indicated that they purchased silver jewelry?

**11.74** On the basis of industry sales of $1.5 billion recorded for the 1-year period ending May 25, 1997, *The New York Times* reported (June 20, 1997, D4) that Crest toothpaste was the market leader with a share of 26.3%.

(a) Suppose that a recently taken random sample of 250 individuals indicates that 68 are using Crest toothpaste. At the .05 level of significance, is there evidence that the proportion has changed from the previous 1996–1997 market share?

(b) What is the *p*-value? Interpret its meaning.

(c) Consider your class to be a sample of all students at your school. Determine the proportion of students in your class who use Crest toothpaste. At the .05 level of significance, is there evidence that this proportion is different from the 1996–1997 market share?

**11.75** There is an expression "the more things change, the more they stay the same." Over the 1-year period ending October 1992 *The New York Times* reported (November 17, 1992, D4) that Kellogg had been the market leader for ready-to-eat breakfast cereals with a share of 37.8%.

(a) Suppose that a recently taken random sample of 200 individuals indicates that 78 preferred Kellogg products to those from all other companies producing ready-to-eat cereals. At the .05 level of significance, is there evidence that the proportion has changed from the 1992 market share? On the basis of your findings, comment on the above expression.

(b) What is the *p*-value? Interpret its meaning.

(c) Consider your class to be a sample of all students at your school. Determine the proportion of students in your class who prefer Kellogg's products to those from all other companies producing ready-to-eat cereals. At the .05 level of significance, is there evidence that this proportion is different from the 1992 market share?

# $\chi^2$ Test of Hypothesis for the Variance or Standard Deviation (*Optional Topic*)

In analyzing numerical data, it is sometimes important to draw conclusions about the variability as well as the average of a characteristic of interest. For example, recall that in our cereal box-filling process (described in section 11.2), the operations manager assumes the company's 15-gram specification for the underlying process standard deviation $\sigma$ is correct and uses this parameter value to perform a $Z$ test that the population mean $\mu$ is 368 grams. Suppose, however, in monitoring whether the equipment used in the ongoing cereal fill process is working properly, the operations manager is now interested in determining whether there is evidence that the standard deviation has changed from the previously specified level of 15 grams. In such a situation, the operations manager would be interested in drawing conclusions about the population standard deviation $\sigma$.

In attempting to draw conclusions about the variability in the population, we first must determine what test statistic can be used to represent the distribution of the variability in the sample data. If the variable (amount of cereal filled in grams) is assumed to be normally distributed, then the $\chi^2$ **test statistic** for testing whether or not the population variance or standard deviation is equal to a specified value is

## $\chi^2$ Test for the Variance or Standard Deviation

$$\chi^2 = \frac{(n-1)S^2}{\sigma^2} \tag{11.5}$$

where

$n$ = sample size
$S^2$ = sample variance
$\sigma^2$ = hypothesized population variance

For a given sample size $n$, the test statistic $\chi^2$ follows a chi-square distribution with $n-1$ degrees of freedom. A **chi-square distribution** is a skewed distribution whose shape depends solely on its number of degrees of freedom. As the number of degrees of freedom increases, a chi-square distribution becomes more symmetrical. Table E.4 contains various upper-tail areas for chi-square distributions pertaining to different degrees of freedom. A portion of this table is displayed as Table 11.4.

The value at the top of each column indicates the area in the upper portion (or right side) of a particular chi-square distribution. As examples, with 24 degrees of freedom, the critical value of the $\chi^2$ test statistic corresponding to an upper-tail area of .025 is 39.364, whereas the critical value corresponding to an upper-tail area of .975 (i.e., a lower-tail area of .025) is 12.401. These are seen in Figure 11.14. This means that for 24 degrees of freedom, the probability of equaling or exceeding the critical value of 12.401 is .975, whereas the probability of equaling or exceeding the critical value of 39.364 is .025. By subtraction, the probability that a $\chi^2$ test statistic falls between the critical values of 12.401 and 39.364 is .95. Therefore, once we determine the level of significance and the degrees of freedom, any critical value of the $\chi^2$ test statistic can be found for a particular chi-square distribution.

**Table 11.4** *Obtaining critical values from chi-square distribution with 24 degrees of freedom*

| DEGREES OF FREEDOM | UPPER-TAIL AREA | | | | | | | | | |
|---|---|---|---|---|---|---|---|---|---|---|
| | .995 | .99 | .975 | .95 | .90 | .75 | .25 | .10 | .05 | .025 |
| 1 | ... | ... | 0.001 | 0.004 | 0.016 | 0.102 | 1.323 | 2.706 | 3.841 | 5.024 |
| 2 | 0.010 | 0.020 | 0.051 | 0.103 | 0.211 | 0.575 | 2.773 | 4.605 | 5.991 | 7.378 |
| 3 | 0.072 | 0.115 | 0.216 | 0.352 | 0.584 | 1.213 | 4.108 | 6.251 | 7.815 | 9.348 |
| · | · | · | · | · | · | · | · | · | · | · |
| · | · | · | · | · | · | · | · | · | · | · |
| · | · | · | · | · | · | · | · | · | · | · |
| 23 | 9.260 | 10.196 | 11.689 | 13.091 | 14.848 | 18.137 | 27.141 | 32.007 | 35.172 | 38.076 |
| 24 | 9.886 | 10.856 | 12.401 | 13.848 | 15.659 | 19.037 | 28.241 | 33.196 | 36.415 | 39.364 |
| 25 | 10.520 | 11.524 | 13.120 | 14.611 | 16.473 | 19.939 | 29.339 | 34.382 | 37.652 | 40.646 |

*Source: Extracted from Table E.4*

To apply the test of hypothesis, let us again return to the cereal-box-packaging example. The operations manager is interested in determining whether there is evidence that the standard deviation has changed from the previously specified level of 15 grams. Thus, we have a two-tailed test in which the null and alternative hypotheses can be stated as follows:

$$H_0\text{: } \sigma = 15 \text{ grams (or } \sigma^2 = 225 \text{ "grams squared")}$$
$$H_1\text{: } \sigma \neq 15 \text{ grams (or } \sigma^2 \neq 225 \text{ "grams squared")}$$

◆ *Critical Value Approach*   Because this is a two-tailed test based on a sample of 25 boxes, the null hypothesis is rejected if the $\chi^2$ test statistic falls into either the lower or upper tail of a chi-square distribution with 24 degrees of freedom as shown in Figure 11.14. From equation (11.5) the $\chi^2$ test statistic falls into the lower tail of the chi-square distribution if the sample standard deviation ($S$) is sufficiently smaller than the hypothesized $\sigma$ of 15 grams, and it falls into the upper tail if $S$ is sufficiently larger than 15 grams. From Table 11.4 (a replica of Table E.4, the table of the chi-square distribution) and Figure 11.14 we observe that if a level of significance of .05 is selected, the lower ($\chi^2_L$) and upper ($\chi^2_U$) critical values are 12.401 and 39.364, respectively. Therefore, the decision rule is

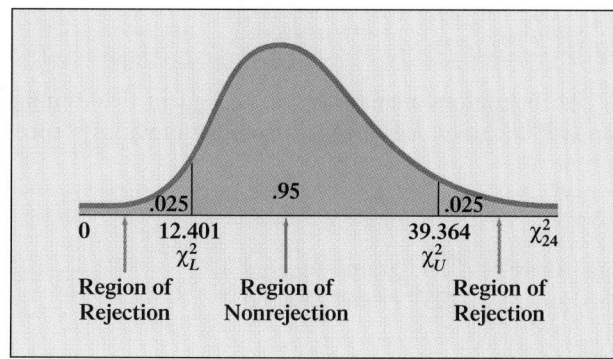

**FIGURE 11.14**
Determining the lower and upper critical values of a chi-square distribution with 24 degrees of freedom corresponding to a .95 level of confidence or a .05 level of significance for a two-tailed test of hypothesis about a population variance or standard deviation

$$\text{Reject } H_0 \text{ if } \chi^2 > \chi_U^2 = 39.364$$
$$\text{or if } \chi^2 < \chi_L^2 = 12.401;$$
$$\text{otherwise do not reject } H_0.$$

Suppose that from the operations manager's sample of 25 boxes, the standard deviation ($S$) is computed to be 17.7 grams. To test the null hypothesis at the .05 level of significance using equation (11.5), we have

$$\chi^2 = \frac{(n-1)S^2}{\sigma^2} = \frac{(25-1)(17.7^2)}{15^2} = 33.42$$

Note that 33.42, the computed value of the $\chi^2$ test statistic, falls between the lower- and upper-tailed critical values of 12.401 and 39.364. Since $\chi_L^2 = 12.401 < \chi^2 = 33.42 < \chi_U^2 = 39.364$, we do not reject $H_0$. The operations manager concludes that there is no evidence that the actual process (i.e., population) standard deviation is different from 15 grams.

◆ *p-Value Approach*   As an alternative approach toward making a hypothesis-testing decision, we may also compute the *p*-value for this situation. For a chi-square distribution with 24 degrees of freedom, we observe from Table E.4 that the probability of equaling or exceeding 33.196 is .10. With the *p*-value approach, the probability of obtaining a $\chi^2$ test statistic of 33.42 or larger is slightly less than .10 (see Figure 11.15). Because this value is greater than the upper-tail area of .025 (for the two-tailed test), the null hypothesis cannot be rejected.

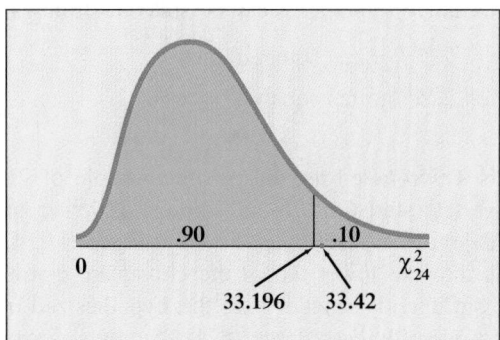

**FIGURE 11.15**
Determining the *p*-value

Example 11.7 applies the 10 steps in hypothesis testing displayed in Exhibits 11.2 and 11.3.

---

## Example 11.7   $\chi^2$ *Test for the Variance or Standard Deviation*

In the cereal-filling-process example the operations manager is interested in determining whether there is evidence that the standard deviation has changed from the previously specified level of 15 grams.

### SOLUTION

Steps 1 and 2:     $H_0$: $\sigma = 15$ grams (or $\sigma^2 = 225$ "grams squared")
                   $H_1$: $\sigma \neq 15$ grams (or $\sigma^2 \neq 225$ "grams squared")

Step 3:            $\alpha = .05$

Step 4:                                             $n = 25$ boxes

Step 5:  We choose the one-sample test for the variance or standard deviation with test statistic $\chi^2$ given by equation (11.5):

$$\chi^2 = \frac{(n-1)S^2}{\sigma^2}$$

Step 6:  We use Table E.4 to develop the following decision rule as illustrated in Figure 11.14 on page 449:

Reject $H_0$ if $\chi^2 > \chi_U^2 = 39.364$

or if $\chi^2 < \chi_L^2 = 12.401$;

otherwise do not reject $H_0$.

Step 7:  We collect the data and compute the $\chi^2$ test statistic:

$$\chi^2 = \frac{(n-1)S^2}{\sigma^2} = \frac{(25-1)(17.7)^2}{15^2} = 33.42$$

Steps 8, 9, and 10:  Because $\chi_L^2 = 12.401 < \chi^2 = 33.42 < \chi_U^2 = 39.364$, we do not reject $H_0$. Alternatively, the $p$-value, slightly less than .10 in the upper tail, is greater than the upper-tail area of .025 (for the two-tailed test), so the null hypothesis cannot be rejected. The operations manager would conclude that there is no evidence that the actual process (i.e., population) standard deviation is different from 15 grams.

The $\chi^2$ test for the variance or standard deviation can be either a two-tailed test or a one-tailed test, depending on whether the alternative hypothesis is *nondirectional* or *directional*, respectively. If the alternative hypothesis is nondirectional, as in our cereal-filling-process example, we are looking to reject the null hypothesis that the value of the parameter is a specified amount such as $\sigma = 15$ grams. In this two-tailed test, we reject $H_0$ if there is evidence from the sample that the value of the parameter being tested is likely to be either significantly more or significantly less than this hypothesized amount. In a one-tailed test, the alternative hypothesis is directional. We reject $H_0$ only if there is evidence from the sample that the value of the parameter being tested is too small or too large, depending on the direction specified in the alternative hypothesis. The regions of rejection and nonrejection for testing a hypothesis about the population variance or standard deviation are depicted in Figure 11.16 on page 452.

If, as shown in panel A of Figure 11.16, the test of hypothesis is two-tailed, the rejection region is split into both the lower and the upper tails of the chi-square distribution. However, if the test is one-tailed, the rejection region is either in the lower tail (panel B) or in the upper tail (panel C) of the chi-square distribution, depending on the direction of the alternative hypothesis. When testing a hypothesis about a population variance or standard deviation, it is frequently the case that we are interested in detecting whether the variation in a process has increased. In such circumstances, a one-tailed hypothesis test would be used (see reference 6) and the null hypothesis would be rejected at a chosen level of significance if the computed $\chi^2$ test statistic exceeds the upper-tail critical value ($\chi_U^2$) from a chi-square distribution with $n-1$ degrees of freedom as in panel C of Figure 11.16.

The $\chi^2$ test for the variance or standard deviation is considered a *classical parametric* procedure—one that makes a variety of stringent assumptions that must hold if we are to

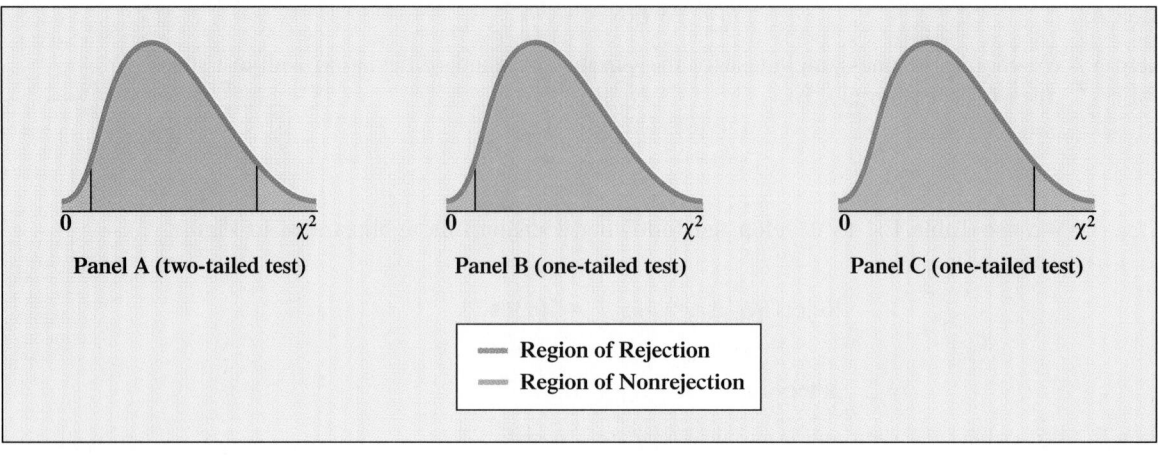

*FIGURE 11.16* Regions of rejection and nonrejection for testing a hypothesis about the population variance or standard deviation

be assured that the results we obtain from employing the test are valid. Assumptions for the $\chi^2$ test for the variance or standard deviation are presented in the following Comment box.

> ### Comment: Checking the Assumptions of the $\chi^2$ Test for the Variance or Standard Deviation
>
> In testing a hypothesis about a population variance or standard deviation, we assume the data in the population are normally distributed. Unfortunately, this $\chi^2$ test statistic is quite sensitive to departures from this assumption (i.e., it is not a *robust* test), so that if the population is not normally distributed, particularly for small sample sizes, the accuracy of the test can be seriously affected (see reference 6).

## Problems for Section 11.8

### Learning the Basics

**11.76** Determine the critical value of $\chi^2$ in each of the following circumstances:
   (a) Upper-tail area $= .01$, $n = 16$
   (b) Upper-tail area $= .025$, $n = 11$
   (c) Upper-tail area $= .05$, $n = 8$
   (d) Upper-tail area $= .95$, $n = 28$
   (e) Upper-tail area $= .975$, $n = 21$
   (f) Upper-tail area $= .99$, $n = 5$

**11.77** Determine the critical value of $\chi^2$ in each of the following circumstances:
   (a) Lower-tail area $= .01$, $n = 16$
   (b) Lower-tail area $= .025$, $n = 11$
   (c) Lower-tail area $= .05$, $n = 8$
   (d) Lower-tail area $= .95$, $n = 28$
   (e) Lower-tail area $= .975$, $n = 21$
   (f) Lower-tail area $= .99$, $n = 5$

**11.78** Determine the lower- and upper-tail critical values of $\chi^2$ for each of the following two-tailed tests:
  (a) $\alpha = .01$, $n = 26$
  (b) $\alpha = .05$, $n = 17$
  (c) $\alpha = .10$, $n = 14$

**11.79** If, in a sample of size $n = 16$ selected from an underlying normal population, the sample standard deviation is $S = 10$, what is the value of the $\chi^2$ test statistic if we are testing the null hypothesis $H_0$ that $\sigma = 12$?

**11.80** In Problem 11.79, how many degrees of freedom are there in the one-sample $\chi^2$ test?

**11.81** In Problems 11.79 and 11.80, what are the critical values from Table E.4 if the level of significance $\alpha$ is chosen to be .05 and the alternative hypothesis $H_1$ is as follows:
  (a) $\sigma \neq 12$?
  (b) $\sigma > 12$?

**11.82** In Problems 11.79, 11.80, and 11.81, what is your statistical decision if your alternative hypothesis $H_1$ is
  (a) $\sigma \neq 12$?
  (b) $\sigma > 12$?

**11.83** If, in a sample of size $n = 16$ selected from a very left-skewed population, the sample standard deviation is $S = 24$, would you use the one-sample $\chi^2$ test in order to test the null hypothesis $H_0$ that $\sigma = 20$? Discuss.

## Applying the Concepts

**11.84** A manufacturer of candy must monitor the temperature at which the candies are baked. Too much variation will cause inconsistency in the taste of the candy. Past records show that the standard deviation of the temperature has been 1.2°F. A random sample of 30 batches of candy is selected and the sample standard deviation of the temperature is 2.1°F.
  (a) At the .05 level of significance, is there evidence that the population standard deviation has increased above 1.2°F?
  (b) What assumptions are being made in order to perform this test?
  (c) Compute the $p$-value in part (a) and interpret its meaning.

**11.85** A market researcher for an automobile dealer intends to conduct a nationwide survey concerning car repairs. Among the questions to be included in the survey is the following: "What was the cost of all repairs performed on your car last year?" In order to determine the sample size necessary, he needs to obtain an estimate of the standard deviation. Using his past experience and judgment, he estimates that the standard deviation of the amount of repairs is $200. Suppose that a pilot study of 25 auto owners selected at random indicates a sample standard deviation of $237.52.
  (a) At the .05 level of significance, is there evidence that the population standard deviation is different from $200?
  (b) What assumptions are made in order to perform this test?
  (c) Compute the $p$-value in part (a) and interpret its meaning.

**11.86** The marketing manager of a branch office of a local telephone operating company wants to study characteristics of residential customers served by her office. In particular, she wants to estimate the average monthly cost of calls within the local calling region. In order to determine the sample size necessary, an estimate of the standard deviation must be made. On the basis of her past experience and judgment, she estimates that the standard deviation is equal to $12. Suppose that a pilot study of 15 residential customers indicates a sample standard deviation of $9.25.
  (a) At the .10 level of significance, is there evidence that the population standard deviation is different from $12?

(b) What assumptions are made in order to perform this test?

(c) Compute the *p*-value in part (a) and interpret its meaning.

**11.87** A manufacturer of doorknobs has a production process that is designed to provide a doorknob with a target diameter of 2.5 inches. In the past, the standard deviation of the diameter has been .035 inch. In an effort to reduce the variation in the process, various studies have resulted in a redesigned process. A sample of 25 doorknobs produced under the new process indicates a sample standard deviation of .025 inch.

(a) At the .05 level of significance, is there evidence that the population standard deviation is less than .035 inch in the new process?

(b) What assumptions are made in order to perform this test?

(c) Compute the *p*-value in part (a) and interpret its meaning.

**11.88** A machine used for packaging seedless golden raisins is set so that the standard deviation in the weight of raisins packaged per box is 0.25 ounce. The operations manager wishes to test the machine setting and selects a sample of 30 consecutive raisin packages filled during the production process. Their weights are recorded as follows:

**DATA FILE**
RAISINS

| 15.2 | 15.3 | 15.1 | 15.7 | 15.3 | 15.0 | 15.1 | 14.3 | 14.6 | 14.5 |
| 15.0 | 15.2 | 15.4 | 15.6 | 15.7 | 15.4 | 15.3 | 14.9 | 14.8 | 14.6 |
| 14.3 | 14.4 | 15.5 | 15.4 | 15.2 | 15.5 | 15.6 | 15.1 | 15.3 | 15.1 |

(a) At the .05 level of significance is there evidence that the population standard deviation differs from 0.25 ounce?

(b) What assumptions are made in order to perform this test?

(c) Obtain the *p*-value in part (a) and interpret its meaning.

**11.89** A manufacturer claims that the standard deviation in capacity of a certain type of battery the company produces is 2.5 ampere-hours. An independent consumer protection agency wishes to test the credibility of the manufacturer's claim and measures the capacity of a random sample of 20 batteries from a recently produced batch. The results, in ampere-hours, are as follows:

**DATA FILE**
AMPHRS

| 137.4 | 140.0 | 138.8 | 139.1 | 144.4 | 139.2 | 141.8 | 137.3 | 133.5 | 138.2 |
| 141.1 | 139.7 | 136.7 | 136.3 | 135.6 | 138.0 | 140.9 | 140.6 | 136.7 | 134.1 |

(a) At the .05 level of significance is there evidence that the population standard deviation in battery capacity exceeds 2.5 ampere-hours?

(b) What assumptions are made in order to perform this test?

(c) Obtain the *p*-value in part (a) and interpret its meaning.

## 11.9 ▸ THE POWER OF A TEST (*OPTIONAL TOPIC*)

In our initial discussions of statistical hypothesis testing we defined the two types of risks that are taken when decisions are made about population parameters based only on sample evidence. Recall from section 11.1 that $\alpha$ represents the probability that the null hypothesis is rejected when in fact it is true and should not be rejected and $\beta$ represents the probability that the null hypothesis is not rejected when in fact it is false and should be rejected. The power of the test, which is $1 - \beta$ (that is, the complement of $\beta$), indicates the sensitivity of the statistical test in detecting changes that have occurred by measuring the probability of rejecting the null hypothesis when in fact it is false and should be rejected. The power of the statistical test depends on how different the actual population mean really is from the value being hypothesized (under $H_0$). If there is a large difference between the actual population mean and the hypothesized mean, the power of the test will be much greater than if the difference between the actual population mean and the hypothesized mean is small.

In this section, we return to our cereal box-filling process to further develop the concept of the power of a statistical test. Suppose that the filling process is subject to periodic inspection from a representative of the local office of consumer affairs. It is this representative's job to detect the possible "short weighting" of boxes, a situation in which cereal boxes are sold at less than the specified 368 grams. Thus, the representative is interested in determining whether there is evidence that the cereal boxes have an average amount that is less than 368 grams. The null and alternative hypotheses are set up as follows:

$$H_0: \mu \geq 368 \text{ (filling process is working properly)}$$

$$H_1: \mu < 368 \text{ (filling process is not working properly)}$$

The representative of the office of consumer affairs is willing to accept the company's claim that the standard deviation $\sigma$ over the entire packaging process is equal to 15 grams; therefore, the $Z$ test is appropriate. If the level of significance $\alpha$ of .05 is selected and a random sample of 25 boxes is obtained, the value of $\overline{X}$ that enables us to reject the null hypothesis is found from equation (9.6) as follows:

$$\overline{X}_L = \mu - Z\frac{\sigma}{\sqrt{n}}$$

Because we have a one-tailed test with a level of significance of .05, the value of $Z$ equal to 1.645 standard deviations below the hypothesized mean is obtained from Table E.2(b) (see Figure 11.17). Therefore,

$$\overline{X}_L = 368 - (1.645)\frac{15}{\sqrt{25}} = 368 - 4.935 = 363.065$$

The decision rule for this one-tailed test is

$$\text{Reject } H_0 \text{ if } \overline{X} < 363.065;$$

$$\text{otherwise do not reject } H_0.$$

The decision rule states that if a random sample of 25 boxes reveals a sample mean of less than 363.065 grams, the null hypothesis is rejected, and the representative concludes that the process is not working properly. If in fact this is the case, the power of the test measures the probability of concluding that the process is not working properly for differing values of the true population mean.

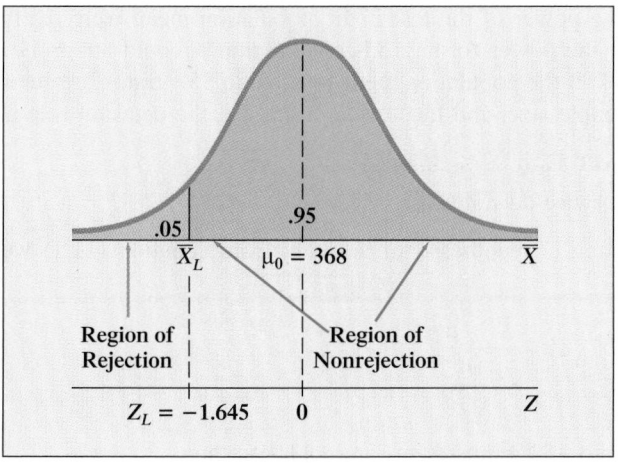

**FIGURE 11.17**

Determining the lower critical value for a one-tailed $Z$ test for a population mean at the .05 level of significance

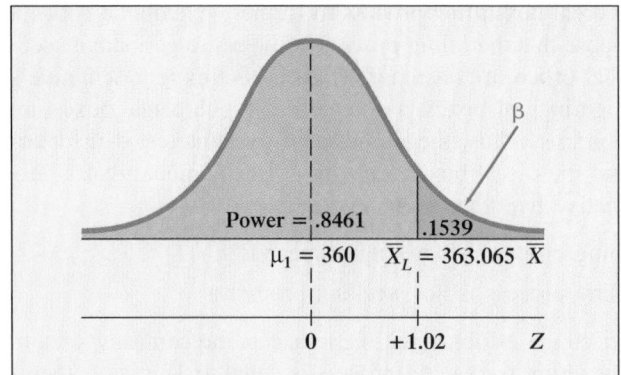

Suppose, for example, that we want to determine the chance of rejecting the null hypothesis when the population mean is actually 360 grams. On the basis of our decision rule, we need to determine the probability or area under the normal curve below 363.065 grams. From the central limit theorem and the assumption of normality in the population, we may assume that the sampling distribution of the mean follows a normal distribution. Therefore, the area under the normal curve below 363.065 grams can be expressed in standard deviation units, because we are finding the probability of rejecting the null hypothesis when the true mean has shifted to 360 grams. Using equation (11.1), we have

$$Z = \frac{\overline{X} - \mu_1}{\dfrac{\sigma}{\sqrt{n}}}$$

where $\mu_1$ is the actual population mean. Thus,

$$Z = \frac{363.065 - 360}{\dfrac{15}{\sqrt{25}}} = 1.02$$

From Table E.2(b), there is an 84.61% chance of observing a $Z$ value up to $+1.02$ standard deviations. This is the power of the test or area below 363.065 (see Figure 11.18). The probability ($\beta$) that the null hypothesis ($\mu = 368$) will not be rejected is $1 - .8461 = .1539$ (or 15.39%). This is the probability of committing a Type II error.

Now that we have determined the power of the test if the population mean were really equal to 360, we can also calculate the power for any other value that $\mu$ could attain. For example, what is the power of the test if the population mean is equal to 352 grams? Assuming the same standard deviation, sample size, and level of significance, the decision rule is

Reject $H_0$ if $\overline{X} < 363.065$;

otherwise do not reject $H_0$.

Once again, because we are testing a hypothesis for a mean, from equation (11.1) we have

$$Z = \frac{\overline{X} - \mu_1}{\dfrac{\sigma}{\sqrt{n}}}$$

If the population mean shifts down to 352 grams (see Figure 11.19), then

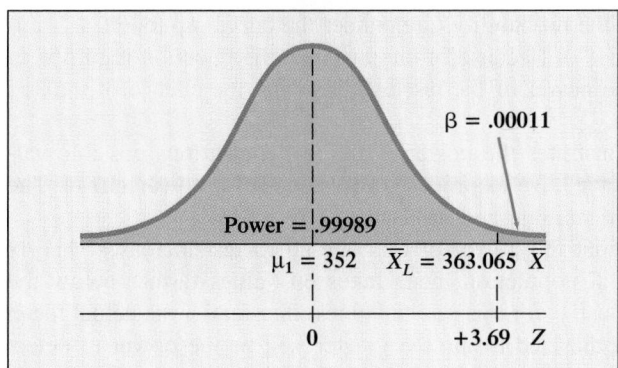

**FIGURE 11.19**
Determining power of the test
and the probability of a Type II
error when $\mu_1 = 352$ grams

$$Z = \frac{363.065 - 352}{\dfrac{15}{\sqrt{25}}} = 3.69$$

From Table E.2(b), there is a 99.989% chance of observing a $Z$ value up to $+3.69$ standard deviations. This is the power of the test or area below 363.065. The probability ($\beta$) that the null hypothesis ($\mu = 368$) will not be rejected is $1 - .99989 = .00011$ (or .011%). This is the probability of committing a Type II error.

In the preceding two cases we found that the power of the test was quite high, whereas, conversely, the chance of committing a Type II error was quite low. In our next example, we compute the power of the test if the population mean is really equal to 367 grams—a value that is very close to the hypothesized mean of 368 grams.

Once again, from equation (11.1), because we are testing a hypothesis about a mean (with $\sigma$ known), we have

$$Z = \frac{\overline{X} - \mu_1}{\dfrac{\sigma}{\sqrt{n}}}$$

If the population mean is really equal to 367 grams (see Figure 11.20), then

$$Z = \frac{363.065 - 367}{\dfrac{15}{\sqrt{25}}} = -1.31$$

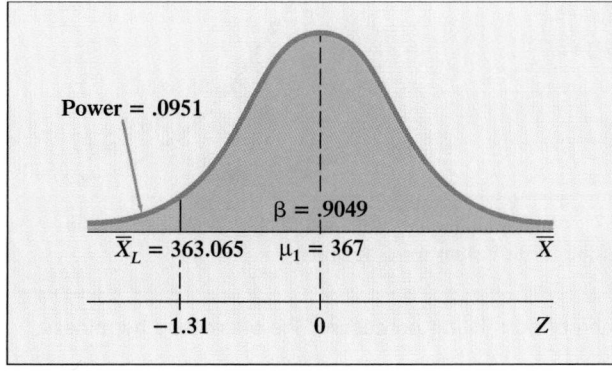

**FIGURE 11.20**
Determining power of the test
and the probability of a Type II
error when $\mu_1 = 367$ grams

From Table E.2(b), we observe that the probability (area under the curve) up to $-1.31$ standard deviation units is .0951 (or 9.51%). Because in this instance the rejection region is in the lower tail of the distribution, the power of the test is 9.51% and the chance of making a Type II error is 90.49%.

From Table E.2, Figure 11.21 illustrates the power of the test for various possible values of $\mu_1$ (including the three cases we have examined). This is called a **power curve**. The computations for our three cases are summarized in Figure 11.22.

From Figure 11.21 we observe that the power of this one-tailed test increases sharply (and approaches 100%) as the actual population mean takes on values farther below the hypothesized mean of 368 grams. Clearly, for this one-tailed test the smaller the actual mean $\mu_1$ is when compared with the hypothesized mean, the greater will be the power to detect this disparity.[2] On the other hand, for values of $\mu_1$ close to 368 grams the power is rather small because the test cannot effectively detect small differences between the actual population mean and the hypothesized value of 368 grams. Interestingly, if the population mean is actually 368 grams, the power of the test is equal to $\alpha$, the level of significance (which is .05 in this example), because the null hypothesis is actually true.

We can observe the drastic changes in the power of the test for differing values of the actual population means by reviewing the different panels of Figure 11.22. From panels A and B we can see that when the population mean does not greatly differ from 368 grams, the chance of rejecting the null hypothesis, based on the decision rule involved, is not large. However, once the actual population mean shifts substantially below the hypothesized 368 grams, the power of the test greatly increases, approaching its maximum value of 1 (or 100%).

In our discussion of the power of a statistical test, we have used a one-tailed test, a level of significance of .05, and a sample size of 25 boxes. With this in mind, we can determine

[2]*For situations involving one-tailed tests in which the actual mean $\mu_1$ really exceeds the hypothesized mean, the converse would be true. The larger the actual mean $\mu_1$ compared with the hypothesized mean, the greater is the power. On the other hand, for two-tailed tests, the greater the distance between the actual mean $\mu_1$ and the hypothesized mean, the greater the power of the test.*

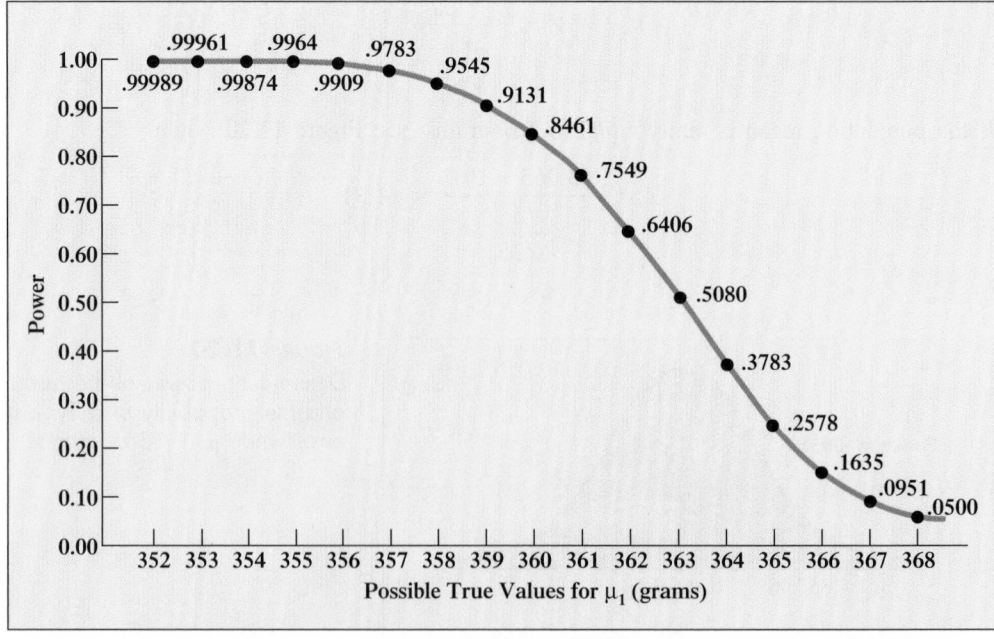

**FIGURE 11.21**  Power curve of the cereal box–filling process for the alternative hypothesis $H_1$: $\mu < 368$ grams

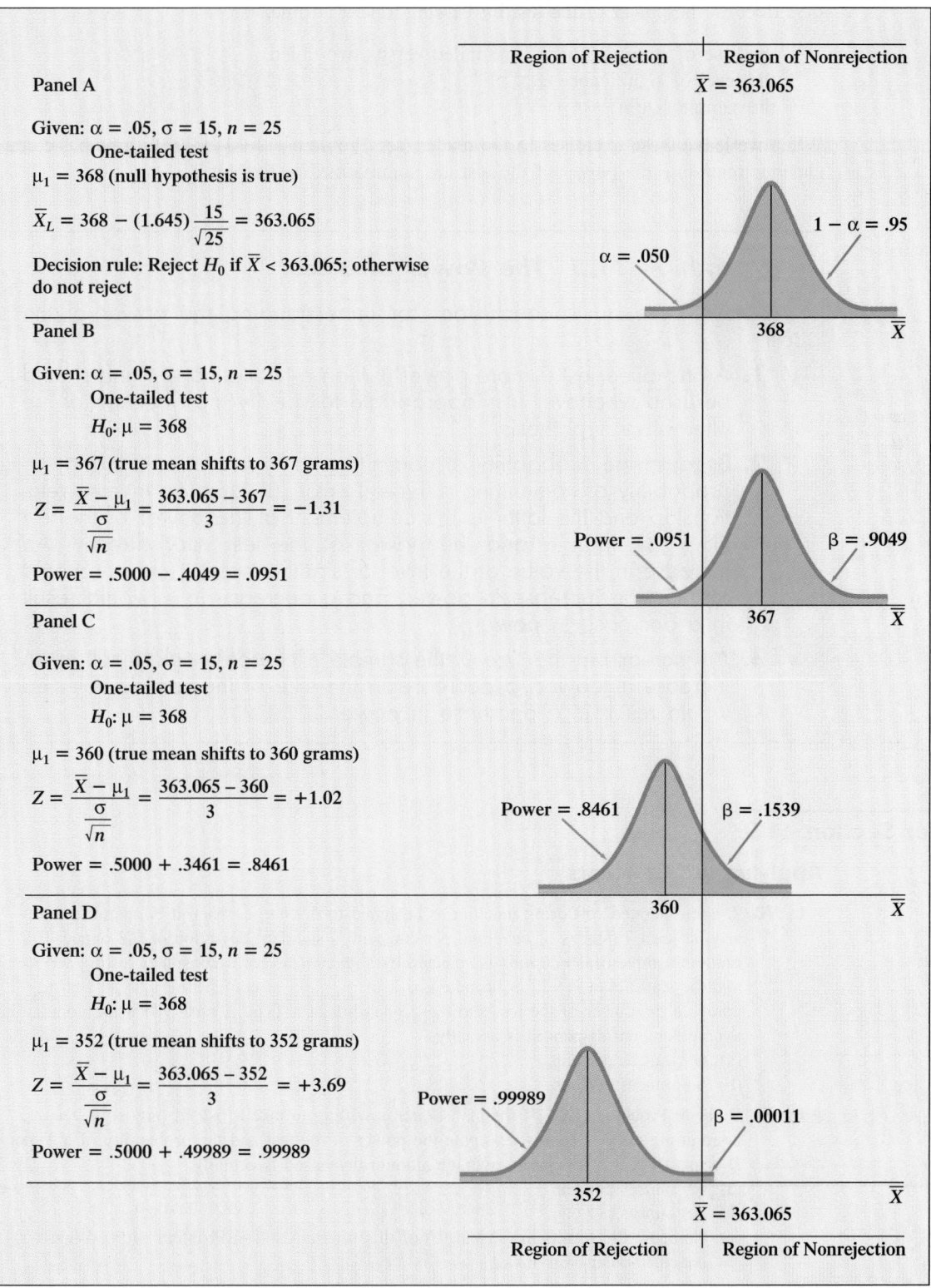

Region of Rejection | Region of Nonrejection

**Panel A**

Given: $\alpha = .05$, $\sigma = 15$, $n = 25$
    One-tailed test
$\mu_1 = 368$ (null hypothesis is true)

$\overline{X}_L = 368 - (1.645)\dfrac{15}{\sqrt{25}} = 363.065$

Decision rule: Reject $H_0$ if $\overline{X} < 363.065$; otherwise do not reject

$\overline{X} = 363.065$
$1 - \alpha = .95$
$\alpha = .050$
$368$   $\overline{X}$

**Panel B**

Given: $\alpha = .05$, $\sigma = 15$, $n = 25$
    One-tailed test
    $H_0: \mu = 368$

$\mu_1 = 367$ (true mean shifts to 367 grams)

$Z = \dfrac{\overline{X} - \mu_1}{\dfrac{\sigma}{\sqrt{n}}} = \dfrac{363.065 - 367}{3} = -1.31$

Power $= .5000 - .4049 = .0951$

Power $= .0951$
$\beta = .9049$
$367$   $\overline{X}$

**Panel C**

Given: $\alpha = .05$, $\sigma = 15$, $n = 25$
    One-tailed test
    $H_0: \mu = 368$

$\mu_1 = 360$ (true mean shifts to 360 grams)

$Z = \dfrac{\overline{X} - \mu_1}{\dfrac{\sigma}{\sqrt{n}}} = \dfrac{363.065 - 360}{3} = +1.02$

Power $= .5000 + .3461 = .8461$

Power $= .8461$
$\beta = .1539$
$360$   $\overline{X}$

**Panel D**

Given: $\alpha = .05$, $\sigma = 15$, $n = 25$
    One-tailed test
    $H_0: \mu = 368$

$\mu_1 = 352$ (true mean shifts to 352 grams)

$Z = \dfrac{\overline{X} - \mu_1}{\dfrac{\sigma}{\sqrt{n}}} = \dfrac{363.065 - 352}{3} = +3.69$

Power $= .5000 + .49989 = .99989$

Power $= .99989$
$\beta = .00011$
$352$   $\overline{X}$
$\overline{X} = 363.065$

Region of Rejection | Region of Nonrejection

**FIGURE 11.22** Determining statistical power for varying values of the actual population mean

the effect on the power of the test by varying, one at a time,

- the type of statistical test—one-tailed versus two-tailed.
- the level of significance $\alpha$.
- the sample size $n$.

While we leave these exercises to the reader (see Problems 11.90–11.96), three basic conclusions regarding the power of the test are summarized in Exhibit 11.5.

### Exhibit 11.5  *The Power of a Test*

We have three basic conclusions for understanding the power of the test.

✓ **1.** A one-tailed test is more powerful than a two-tailed test and should be used whenever it is appropriate to specify the direction of the alternative hypothesis.

✓ **2.** Because the probability of committing a Type I error ($\alpha$) and the probability of committing a Type II error ($\beta$) have an inverse relationship and the latter is the complement of the power of the test ($1 - \beta$), then $\alpha$ and the power of the test vary directly. An increase in the value of the level of significance ($\alpha$) chosen would result in an increase in power, and a decrease in $\alpha$ would result in a decrease in power.

✓ **3.** An increase in the size of the sample $n$ chosen would result in an increase in power; a decrease in the size of the sample selected would result in a decrease in power.

## Problems for Section 11.9

### Applying the Concepts

● **11.90** A coin-operated soft-drink machine is designed to discharge, when it is operating properly, at least 7 ounces of beverage per cup with a standard deviation of 0.2 ounce. If a random sample of 16 cupfuls is selected by a statistician for a consumer testing service and the statistician is willing to take a risk of $\alpha = .05$ of committing a Type I error, compute the power of the test and the probability of a Type II error ($\beta$) if the population average amount dispensed is actually
(a) 6.9 ounces per cup.
(b) 6.8 ounces per cup.

● **11.91** Refer to Problem 11.90. If the statistician is willing to take a risk of only $\alpha = .01$ of committing a Type I error, compute the power of the test and the probability of a Type II error ($\beta$) if the population average amount dispensed is actually
(a) 6.9 ounces per cup.
(b) 6.8 ounces per cup.
(c) Compare the results in (a) and (b) of this problem and in Problem 11.90. What conclusion can you draw?

● **11.92** Refer to Problem 11.90. If the statistician selects a random sample of 25 cupfuls and is willing to take a risk of $\alpha = .05$ of committing a Type I error, compute the power of the test and the probability of a Type II error (β) if the population average amount dispensed is actually

(a) 6.9 ounces per cup.

(b) 6.8 ounces per cup.

(c) Compare the results in (a) and (b) of this problem and in Problem 11.90. What conclusion can you draw?

**11.93** A tire manufacturer produces tires that last, on average, at least 25,000 miles when the production process is working properly. Based on past experience, the standard deviation of the tires is assumed to be 3,500 miles. The operations manager will stop the production process if there is evidence that the average tire life is below 25,000 miles. If a random sample of 100 tires is selected (to be subjected to *destructive testing*) and the operations manager is willing to take a risk of $\alpha = .05$ of committing a Type I error, compute the power of the test and the probability of a Type II error (β) if the population average life is actually

(a) 24,000 miles.

(b) 24,900 miles.

**11.94** Refer to Problem 11.93. If the operations manager is willing to take a risk of only $\alpha = .01$ of committing a Type I error, compute the power of the test and the probability of a Type II error (β) if the population average life is actually

(a) 24,000 miles.

(b) 24,900 miles.

(c) Compare the results in (a) and (b) of this problem and (a) and (b) in Problem 11.93. What conclusion can you draw?

**11.95** Refer to Problem 11.93. If the operations manager selects a random sample of 25 tires and is willing to take a risk of $\alpha = .05$ of committing a Type I error, compute the power of the test and the probability of a Type II error (β) if the population average life is actually

(a) 24,000 miles.

(b) 24,900 miles.

(c) Compare the results in (a) and (b) of this problem and (a) and (b) in Problem 11.93. What conclusion can you draw?

**11.96** Refer to Problem 11.93. If the operations manager will stop the process when there is evidence that the average life is different from 25,000 miles (either less than or greater than) and a random sample of 100 tires is selected along with a level of significance of $\alpha = .05$, compute the power of the test and the probability of a Type II error (β) if the population average life is actually

(a) 24,000 miles.

(b) 24,900 miles.

(c) Compare the results in (a) and (b) of this problem and (a) and (b) in Problem 11.93. What conclusion can you draw?

 ## POTENTIAL HYPOTHESIS-TESTING PITFALLS AND ETHICAL ISSUES

To this point, we have studied the fundamental concepts of hypothesis-testing methodology. We have learned how to use it for analyzing differences between sample estimates (i.e., statistics) of hypothesized population characteristics (i.e., parameters) in order to make decisions about the underlying characteristics. We have also learned how to evaluate the risks involved in making these decisions.

When planning to carry out a test of a hypothesis based on some designed experiment or research study under investigation, several questions must be asked to ensure that proper methodology is used. A listing of these questions appears in Exhibit 11.6 on page 462.

**Exhibit 11.6**    *Questions to Consider in the Planning Stage of Hypothesis Testing*

✓ **1.** What is the goal of the experiment or research? Can it be translated into a null and alternative hypothesis?

✓ **2.** Is the hypothesis test going to be two-tailed or one-tailed?

✓ **3.** Can a random sample be drawn from the underlying population of interest?

✓ **4.** What kinds of measurements will be obtained from the sample? Are the sampled outcomes of the random variable going to be numerical or categorical?

✓ **5.** At what significance level, or risk of committing a Type I error, should the hypothesis test be conducted?

✓ **6.** Is the intended sample size large enough to achieve the desired power of the test for the level of significance chosen?

✓ **7.** What statistical test procedure is to be used on the sampled data and why?

✓ **8.** What kinds of conclusions and interpretations can be drawn from the results of the hypothesis test?

Questions like these need to be raised and answered in the planning stage of a survey or designed experiment, so a person with substantial statistical training should be consulted and involved early in the process. All too often such an individual is consulted far too late in the process, after the data have been collected. Typically all that can be done at such a late stage is to choose the statistical test procedure that would be best for the obtained data. We are forced to assume that certain biases that have been built into the study (because of poor planning) are negligible. But this is a large assumption. Good research involves good planning. To avoid biases, adequate controls must be built in from the beginning.

We need to distinguish between what is poor research methodology and what is unethical behavior. Ethical considerations arise when a researcher is manipulative of the hypothesis-testing process. Some of the ethical issues that arise when dealing with hypothesis-testing methodology include the data collection method, informed consent from human subjects being "treated," the type of test—two-tailed or one-tailed, the choice of level of significance $\alpha$, data snooping, the cleansing and discarding of data, and reporting of findings.

◆ *Data Collection Method—Randomization*    To eliminate the possibility of potential biases in the results, we must use proper data collection methods. To draw meaningful conclusions, the data we obtain must be the outcomes of a random sample from some underlying population or the outcomes from some experiment in which a **randomization** process was employed. Potential subjects should not be permitted to self-select for a study. In a similar manner, a researcher should not be permitted to purposely select the subjects for the study. Aside from the potential ethical issues that may be raised, such a lack of randomization can result in serious coverage errors or selection biases and destroy the value of any study.

◆ **Informed Consent from Human Subjects Being "Treated"**   Ethical considerations require that any individual who is to be subjected to some "treatment" in an experiment be apprised of the research endeavor and any potential behavioral or physical side effects and provide informed consent with respect to participation. A researcher is not permitted to dupe or manipulate the subjects in a study.

◆ **Type of Test—Two-Tailed or One-Tailed**   If we have prior information that leads us to test the null hypothesis against a specifically directed alternative, then a one-tailed test will be more powerful than a two-tailed test. On the other hand, we should realize that if we are interested only in *differences* from the null hypothesis, not in the *direction* of the difference, the two-tailed test is the appropriate procedure to use. This is an important point. For example, if previous research and statistical testing have already established the difference in a particular direction or if an established scientific theory states that it is possible for results to occur in only one direction, then a one-tailed or directional test may be employed. However, these conditions are not often satisfied in practice, and it is recommended that one-tailed tests be used cautiously.

Using arguments based on ethical principles, Fleiss (see reference 3) and other statisticians have stated that in the overwhelming majority of research studies, a two-tailed test should be employed, particularly if the intention is to report the results to professional colleagues at meetings or in published journal articles. A major reason for this more conservative approach to testing is to enable us to draw more appropriate conclusions on data that may yield unexpected, counterintuitive results.

◆ **Choice of Level of Significance $\alpha$**   In a well-designed experiment or study, the level of significance $\alpha$ is selected in advance of data collection. One cannot be permitted to alter the level of significance, after the fact, to achieve a specific result. This would be **data snooping**. One answer to this issue of level of significance is to always report the $p$-value, not just the results of the test.

◆ **Data Snooping**   Data snooping is never permissible. It is unethical to perform a hypothesis test on a set of data, look at the results, and then select whether it should be two-tailed or one-tailed and/or choose the level of significance. These steps must be done first, as part of the planned experiment or study, before the data are collected, for the conclusions drawn to have meaning. In those situations in which a statistician is consulted by a researcher late in the process, with data already available, it is imperative that the null and alternative hypotheses be established and the level of significance chosen prior to carrying out the hypothesis test.

◆ **Cleansing and Discarding of Data**   Data cleansing is not data snooping. Data cleansing is an important part of an overall analysis—remember GIGO (garbage in, garbage out). In the data preparation stage of editing, coding, and transcribing, one has an opportunity to review the data for any observation whose measurement seems to be extreme or unusual. After this has been done, the outcomes of the numerical variables in the data set should be organized into stem-and-leaf displays and box-and-whisker plots in preparation for further data presentation and *confirmatory analysis*. This *exploratory data analysis* stage gives us another opportunity to cleanse the data set by flagging outlier observations that need to be checked against the original data. In addition, the exploratory data analysis enables us to examine the data graphically with respect to the assumptions underlying a particular hypothesis test procedure needed for confirmatory analysis.

The process of data cleansing raises a major ethical question. Should an observation be removed from a study? The answer is a qualified "yes." If it can be determined that a measurement is incomplete or grossly in error owing to some equipment problem or unusual behavioral occurrence unrelated to the study, a decision to discard the observation may be made. Sometimes there is no choice—an individual may decide to quit a particular study he has been participating in before a final measurement can be made. In a well-designed experiment or study, the researcher would decide, in advance, on all rules regarding the possible discarding of data.

◆ **Reporting of Findings**   In conducting research, it is vitally important to document both good and bad results so that individuals who follow up on such research do not have to "reinvent the wheel." It is inappropriate to report the results of hypothesis tests that show statistical significance but not those for which there was insufficient evidence in the findings.

Again, to summarize, we conclude that in discussing ethical issues concerning hypothesis-testing methodology, the key is *intent*. We must distinguish between poor confirmatory data analysis and unethical practice. Unethical behavior occurs when a researcher willfully causes a selection bias in data collection, manipulates the treatment of human subjects without informed consent, uses data snooping to select the type of test (two-tailed or one-tailed) and/or level of significance to his or her advantage, hides the facts by discarding observations that do not support a stated hypothesis, or fails to report pertinent findings.

◆ ## SUMMARY

As observed in the summary chart on page 465, this chapter presented the fundamental underpinnings of hypothesis-testing methodology. In the three chapters that follow we shall be building on the foundations of hypothesis testing that we have discussed here. We will present a set of procedures that may be employed to verify or confirm statistically the results of studies and experiments designed under a variety of conditions.

## *Key Terms*

$\alpha$ (level of significance)   417

alternative hypothesis ($H_1$)   413

$\beta$ risk   417

binomial test   445

chi-square distribution   448

$\chi^2$ test for a population variance or standard deviation   448

$\chi^2$ test statistic   448

confidence coefficient ($1 - \alpha$)   417

critical region   415

critical value   416

data snooping   463

hypothesis testing   413

hypothesis-testing methodology   412

level of significance ($\alpha$)   417

nonparametric test   445

null hypothesis ($H_0$)   413

one-sample $t$ test   437

one-tailed or directional test   428

$p$-value   424

parametric or classical test   437

power curve   458

power of a statistical test ($1 - \beta$)   418

probability of a Type II error ($\beta$)   416

randomization   462

region of nonrejection   415

region of rejection   415

robust   438

sample proportion   442

test statistic $t$   415

$t$ test for a population mean   433

$t$ test statistic   415

two-tailed or nondirectional test   420

Type I error   416

Type II error   416

$Z$ test for a population mean   420

$Z$ test for a population proportion   442

$Z$ test statistic   420

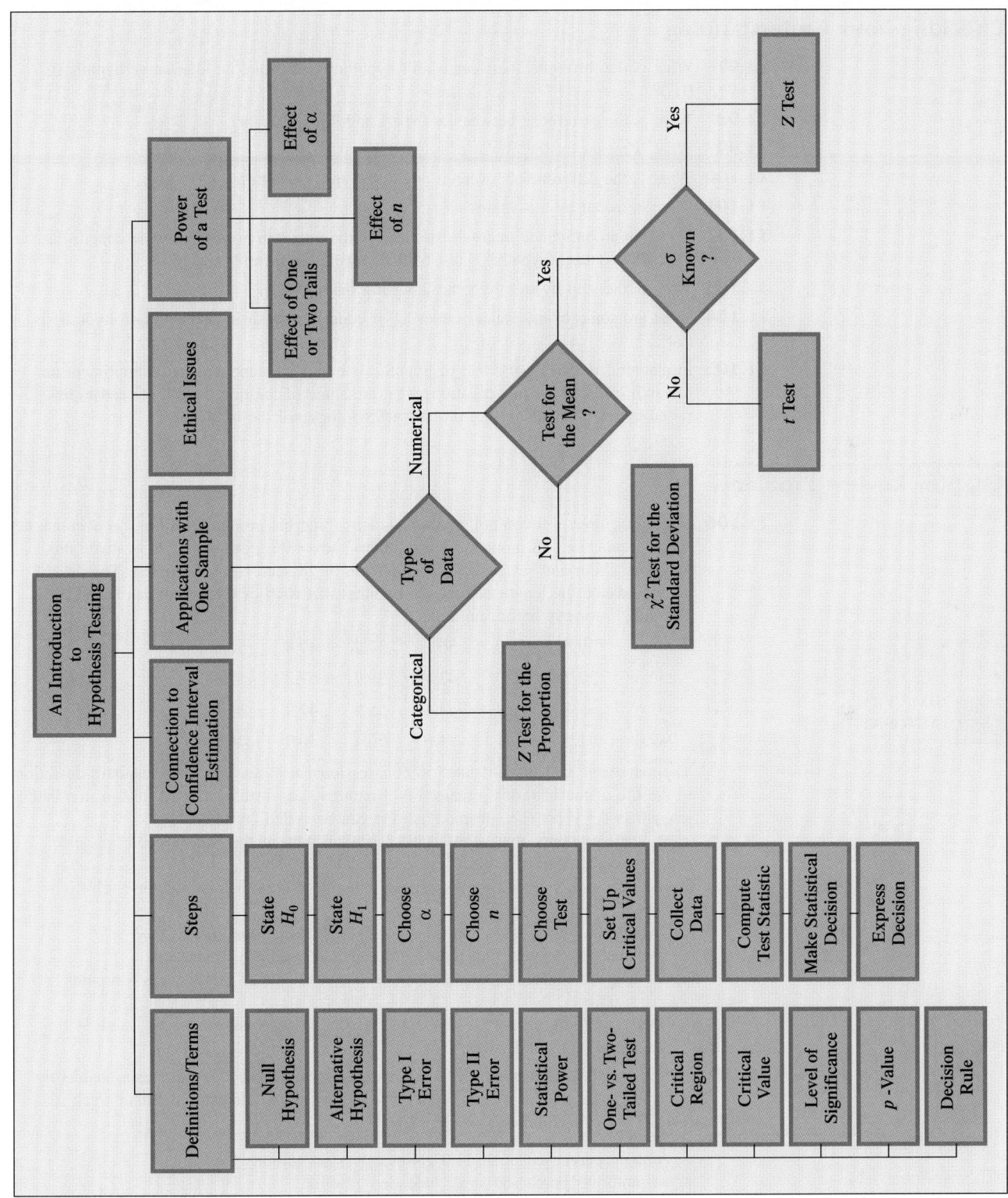

Chapter 11 summary chart

## Checking Your Understanding

**11.97** What is the difference between a null hypothesis ($H_0$) and an alternative hypothesis ($H_1$)?

**11.98** What is the difference between a Type I and Type II error?

**11.99** What is meant by the power of a test?

**11.100** What is the difference between a one-tailed and a two-tailed test?

**11.101** What is meant by a *p*-value?

**11.102** How can a confidence interval estimate for the population mean provide conclusions to the corresponding hypothesis test for the population mean?

**11.103** What is the step-by-step hypothesis-testing methodology?

**11.104** What are some of the ethical issues to be concerned with in performing a hypothesis test?

**11.105** In planning to carry out a test of hypothesis based on some designed experiment or research study under investigation, what are some of the questions that need to be raised in order to ensure that proper methodology will be used?

## Chapter Review Problems

**11.106** A manufacturer of automobile batteries claims that his product will last, on average, at least 4 years (i.e., 48 months). A consumers' advocate group wants to evaluate this longevity claim and selects a random sample of 28 such batteries to test. The data below indicate the length of time (in months) that each of these batteries lasted (i.e., performed properly before failure).

| | | | | | | |
|---|---|---|---|---|---|---|
| 42.3 | 39.6 | 25.0 | 56.2 | 37.2 | 47.4 | 57.5 |
| 39.3 | 39.2 | 47.0 | 47.4 | 39.7 | 57.3 | 51.8 |
| 31.6 | 45.1 | 40.8 | 42.4 | 38.9 | 42.9 | 34.1 |
| 49.0 | 41.5 | 60.1 | 34.6 | 50.4 | 30.7 | 44.1 |

**DATA FILE**
AUTOBAT

The manufacturer has also stated in congressional testimony that the standard deviation in the life of the batteries produced is 9 months and, further, at least 90% of the batteries will last 3 years (i.e., 36 months) and can be called "reliable."

(a) Is there evidence that significantly less than 90% of the batteries can be called "reliable"? (Use $\alpha = .05$.)

(b) Is there evidence that the average battery life is less than 48 months? (Use $\alpha = .05$.)

(c) What assumption must hold in order to perform the test in part (b)?

(d) Evaluate this assumption through a graphical approach. Discuss.

(e) Is there evidence that the standard deviation in battery life exceeds 9 months? (Use $\alpha = .05$.)

(f) What are your answers to (b) and (e) if the last two values are 50.7 and 54.1 instead of 30.7 and 44.1?

**11.107** The owner of a gasoline service station wants to study gasoline purchasing habits by motorists at his station. A random sample of 60 motorists during a certain week is selected with the following results:

- Amount purchased: $\overline{X} = 11.3$ gallons, $S = 3.1$ gallons.
- 11 motorists purchased super unleaded gasoline.

(a) At the .05 level of significance, is there evidence that the average purchase is different from 10 gallons?

(b) Find the *p*-value in part (a).

(c) At the .05 level of significance, is there evidence that the true standard deviation exceeds 2.9 gallons? (*Hint*: To obtain the critical value, follow the instructions for the footnote to Table E.4.

(d) Approximate the *p*-value in part (c).

(e) Discuss the underlying assumptions of the tests used in parts (a) and (c).

(f) At the .05 level of significance, is there evidence that less than 20% of the motorists purchase super unleaded gasoline?

(g) What is your answer to part (a) if the sample average is 10.3 gallons?

(h) What is your answer to part (f) if 7 motorists purchased super unleaded gasoline?

● **11.108** An auditor for a government agency is assigned the task of evaluating reimbursement for office visits to doctors paid by Medicare. The audit is to be conducted for all Medicare payments in a particular geographical area during a certain month. Suppose the audit is conducted on a sample of 75 of the reimbursements with the following results:

● In 12 of the office visits, an incorrect amount of reimbursement was provided; the amount of reimbursement: $\overline{X} = \$93.70$, $S = \$34.55$.

(a) At the .05 level of significance, is there evidence that the average reimbursement is less than $100?

(b) At the .05 level of significance, is there evidence that the proportion of incorrect reimbursements in the population is greater than .10?

(c) At the .05 level of significance, is there evidence that the standard deviation in reimbursements in the population differs from $30? (*Hint*: To obtain the critical value, follow the instructions for the footnote to Table E.4.)

(d) Discuss the underlying assumptions of the tests used in parts (a) and (c).

(e) What is your answer to part (a) if the sample average is $90?

(f) What is your answer to part (b) if 15 office visits had incorrect reimbursements?

● **11.109** A bank branch located in a commercial district of a city has developed an improved process for serving customers during the noon to 1 P.M. peak lunch period. The waiting time (operationally defined as the time the customer enters the line until he or she is served) of all customers during this hour is recorded over a period of 1 week. A random sample of 15 customers is selected, and the results are as follows:

**DATA FILE**
BANK1

4.21 5.55 3.02 5.13 4.77 2.34 3.54 3.20 4.50 6.10 0.38 5.12 6.46 6.19 3.79

(a) At the .05 level of significance, is there evidence that the average waiting time is less than 5 minutes?

(b) What assumption must hold in order to perform the test in (a)?

(c) Evaluate this assumption through a graphical approach. Discuss.

(d) At the .05 level of significance, is there evidence that the standard deviation of the waiting time is different from 1 minute?

(e) As a customer walks into the branch office during the lunch hour, she asks the branch manager how long she can expect to wait. The branch manager replies, "Almost certainly not longer than 5 minutes." On the basis of the results of (a), evaluate this statement.

**11.110** One of the major measures of the quality of service provided by any organization is the speed with which it responds to customer complaints. A large family-held department store selling furniture and flooring including carpeting had undergone a major expansion in the past several years. In particular, the flooring department had expanded from two installation crews to an installation supervisor, a measurer, and 15 installation crews. A sample of 50 complaints during a recent year concerning carpeting installation was selected. The data at the top of page 468 represent the number of days between the receipt of the complaint and the resolution of the complaint.

| 54 | 5 | 35 | 137 | 31 | 27 | 152 | 2 | 123 | 81 | 74 | 27 | 11 | 19 | 126 | 110 | 110 |
| 29 | 61 | 35 | 94 | 31 | 26 | 5 | 12 | 4 | 165 | 32 | 29 | 28 | 29 | 26 | 25 | 1 |
| 14 | 13 | 13 | 10 | 5 | 27 | 4 | 52 | 30 | 22 | 36 | 26 | 20 | 23 | 33 | 68 | |

(a) At the .05 level of significance, is there evidence that the average days between the receipt of the complaint and the resolution of the complaint is greater than 20 days?

(b) What assumption must hold in order to perform the test in (a)?

(c) Evaluate this assumption through a graphical approach. Discuss.

(d) At the .05 level of significance, is there evidence that the standard deviation of the time between the receipt of the complaint and the resolution of the complaint is greater than 10 days?

(e) What assumption is needed in (d)? On the basis of the results of (c), do you think this assumption is valid? Explain.

(f) Suppose a customer calls the department store with a complaint after the carpet has been installed. She asks the flooring department manager how long she can expect to wait to have her complaint resolved. The flooring department manager replies, "Almost certainly not longer than 20 days." On the basis of the results of (a), evaluate this statement.

● **11.111** A businessman is considering the establishment of a Sunday morning bagel and breakfast delivery service in a local suburb and wants to conduct a survey. On the basis of the cost of this service and the profits to be made, he has arrived at the following conclusion: If there is evidence that the average order will be more than $14 per household in this suburban area, then the delivery service will be instituted. If no evidence can be demonstrated, the delivery service will not be instituted. Based on past experience with several other suburbs, the standard deviation is estimated to be $3. The businessman is willing to take a .01 risk of committing a Type I error and institute the service when the actual average order is at most $14 per household. The businessman decides that a random sample of 36 households is to be surveyed.

(a) What is the probability of instituting the bagel and breakfast delivery service when the average order is actually
  (1) $15 per household?
  (2) $17 per household?

(b) If the businessman is willing to take a .05 risk (rather than a .01 risk) that the service will be instituted when the average order is at most $14 per household, compute the probability of instituting the bagel and breakfast delivery service when the average order is actually
  (1) $15 per household.
  (2) $17 per household.

(c) Compare the results in (a)(1) and (a)(2) with those in (b)(1) and (b)(2). What conclusions can you draw?

(d) If the businessman is willing to select a random sample of 64 households and is also willing to take a risk of $\alpha = .01$ of committing a Type I error, compute the probability of instituting the bagel and breakfast delivery service when the average order is actually
  (1) $15 per household.
  (2) $17 per household.

(e) Compare the results in (a)(1) and (a)(2) with those in (d)(1) and (d)(2). What conclusions can you draw here?

● **11.112** Referring to Problem 11.111, suppose a sample of 36 households is actually surveyed. From this sample the average order is $15.66. Assuming the population standard deviation ($\sigma$) in this suburb is $3:

(a) What decision should be made?

(b) What is the *p*-value?

**11.113** A large chain of discount toy stores wants to determine whether a certain toy should be sold and is considering a survey. On the basis of past experience with similar toys, the marketing director of the chain decides that the toy will be marketed only if there is evidence that monthly gross sales receipts for this toy will average more than $10,000 throughout the chain of stores. Based on past experience, the standard deviation is estimated to be $1,000. The marketing director is willing to take a .05 risk of committing a Type I error and market the toy when the average monthly gross sales receipts are actually no more than $10,000. Given a random sample of 25 stores selected for a test-marketing period of 1 month:

(a) Compute the probability that the toy will be marketed when the average monthly gross sales receipts are actually

   (1) $10,500.

   (2) $10,800.

(b) What might account for the slight discrepancies in your results in (a)(1) and (a)(2)?

(c) If the marketing director is willing to take a .10 risk (rather than a .05 risk) of selling the toy when the average monthly gross sales receipts are no more than $10,000, compute the probability that the toy will be marketed when the average monthly gross sales receipts are actually

   (1) $10,500.

   (2) $10,800.

(d) Compare the results in (a)(1) and (a)(2) with those in (c)(1) and (c)(2). What conclusions can you draw?

(e) If the marketing director could select a sample of only 16 stores in which to test-market the toy and was willing to take a risk of $\alpha = .05$ of committing a Type I error, compute the probability of marketing that toy when the average monthly gross sales receipts are actually

   (1) $10,500.

   (2) $10,800.

(f) Compare the results in (a)(1) and (a)(2) with those in (e)(1) and (e)(2). What conclusions can you draw here?

**11.114** Referring to Problem 11.113, suppose a sample of 25 stores is actually surveyed and the average gross sales receipts for the 1-month trial period is $10,420. Assuming the population standard deviation ($\sigma$) based on past experience with similar toys is $1,000:

(a) What decision should be made?

(b) What is the *p*-value?

## References

1. Bradley, J. V., *Distribution-Free Statistical Tests* (Englewood Cliffs, NJ: Prentice Hall, 1968).

2. Daniel, W., *Applied Nonparametric Statistics*, 2d ed. (Boston: Houghton Mifflin, 1990).

3. Fleiss, J. L., *Statistical Methods for Rates and Proportions*, 2d ed. (New York: Wiley, 1981).

4. *Microsoft Excel 97* (Redmond, WA: Microsoft Corporation, 1997).

5. *Minitab for Windows Version 12* (State College, PA: Minitab, Inc., 1998).

6. Solomon, H., and M. A. Stephens, "Sample Variance." In *Encyclopedia of Statistical Sciences*, vol. 9, edited by S. Kotz and N. L. Johnson (New York: Wiley, 1988), 477–480.

## APPENDIX 11.1   USING MICROSOFT EXCEL FOR ONE-SAMPLE TESTS OF HYPOTHESIS

### COMMENT:   PHStat Add-in Users

If Microsoft Excel is not running, click the **PHStat** add-in icon. If Microsoft Excel is running, select **File | Open**. Select the PHStat add-in file **PHSA.XLA**. Click the **Open** button.

To obtain a $Z$ test for the mean with $\sigma$ known, select **PHStat | One Sample Tests | Z test for the Mean, sigma known**. If the sample statistics are unknown, select the Sample Statistics unknown option button and enter the cell range for the data in the edit box. If the sample statistics are known, enter the sample size, the arithmetic mean, and the population standard deviation in their respective edit boxes.

Enter the hypothesized value for $\mu$ in its edit box. Enter the level of significance in its edit box (.05 is the default value). If a one-tailed test is desired, select the Upper-Tailed Test or Lower-Tail Test check box. If a two-tailed test is desired, select the Two-Tailed Test check box. Click the **OK** button.

To obtain a $t$ test for the mean with $\sigma$ unknown, select **PHStat | One Sample Tests | t Test for the Mean, Sigma unknown**. If the sample statistics are unknown, select the Sample Statistics unknown option button and enter the cell range for the data in the edit box. If the sample statistics are known, enter the sample size, the arithmetic mean, and the sample standard deviation in their respective edit boxes.

Enter the hypothesized value for $\mu$ in its edit box. Enter the level of significance in its edit box (.05 is the default value). If a one-tailed test is desired, select the Upper-Tail Test or Lower-Tail Test check box. If a two-tailed test is desired, select the Two-Tailed Test check box. Click the **OK** button.

To obtain a $Z$ test for the proportion, select **PHStat | One Sample Tests | Z Test for the Proportions**. Enter the sample size and number of successes in their respective edit boxes. Enter the hypothesized value in its edit box (0.00 is the default value). Enter the level of significance in its edit box (.05 is the default value). If a one-tailed test is desired, select the Upper-Tail Test or Lower-Tail Test check box. If a two-tailed test is desired, select the Two-Tailed Test check box. Click the **OK** button.

## APPENDIX 11.2   USING MINITAB FOR ONE-SAMPLE TESTS OF HYPOTHESIS

Minitab can be used for a test of the mean when $\sigma$ is unknown by selecting Stat | Basic Statistics | 1-Sample t from the Menu bar.

We illustrate the test of hypothesis for the mean when $\sigma$ is unknown by returning to the 12 sales invoices discussed in section 11.6. Open the **INVOICES.MTP** file and select **Stat | Basic Statistics | 1-Sample t**. Enter **C1** or **Amount** in the Variables edit box. Select the **Test Mean** option button and enter **120** in the Test Mean edit box. In the Alternative drop-down list box, select less than or more than for one-tailed tests or not equal for a two-tailed test. Click the **OK** button.

# Two-Sample Tests with Numerical Data

# CHAPTER OBJECTIVES

✓ *To extend the basic principles of hypothesis testing to two-sample tests involving numerical variables*
✓ *To describe some practical tests of hypothesis when dealing with two independent samples*
✓ *To describe some practical tests of hypothesis when dealing with two related samples*
✓ *To introduce nonparametric tests as alternative tests of hypothesis*

## Introduction

Hypothesis testing provides a *confirmatory* approach to data analysis. In the preceding chapter we focused on a variety of commonly used hypothesis-testing procedures that relate to a single sample of data drawn from a population. In this chapter we shall extend our discussion of hypothesis testing to procedures that enable us to compare statistics computed from two samples of numerical data. Such procedures are called two-sample tests and are used to make inferences about possible differences in the parameters of two populations.

To develop the relevant ideas for this and the next chapter, we begin with a specific application—an operations manager's concern for establishing appropriate equipment dial settings to meet product specifications in filling 1-liter soft-drink bottles at a bottling plant.

## ◆ USING STATISTICS: *Establishing Proper Equipment Dial Settings to Meet Product Specifications*

The operations manager for a soft-drink distributor is interested in obtaining more uniform fill heights in the bottles filled during the bottling process at a bottling plant. Available machinery fills each bottle; however, there is variation around the specified target. One variable that must be controlled in the filling process is the operating pressure. Two dial settings, 25 or 30 psi, are to be studied during an experiment in filling performance with 10 bottles filled at each of these two operating pressure levels.

One of the many questions that the operations manager will seek to answer is whether or not there is evidence of a significant difference in average deviation from the specified target based on bottles filled under equipment dial settings that permit either 25 or 30 psi of operating pressure. To answer this question, the appropriate *t* tests will be developed in the next section.

## 12.1 COMPARING TWO INDEPENDENT SAMPLES: *t* TESTS FOR DIFFERENCES IN TWO MEANS

### Pooled-Variance *t* Test for Differences in Two Means

Suppose that we have two **independent populations,** each with a mean and a standard deviation, symbolically represented as follows:

**POPULATION 1**    **POPULATION 2**

$\mu_1, \sigma_1$        $\mu_2, \sigma_2$

Let us also suppose that a random sample of size $n_1$ is taken from the first population, a random sample of size $n_2$ is drawn from the second population, and the data collected in each sample pertain to some numerical random variable of interest.

The test statistic used to determine the difference between the population means is based on the difference between the sample means $(\overline{X}_1 - \overline{X}_2)$. Because of the central limit theorem discussed in section 9.1, this test statistic follows the standard normal distribution for large enough sample sizes. The $Z$ test for the difference between two means is as follows:

## Z Test for Difference in Two Means

$$Z = \frac{(\overline{X}_1 - \overline{X}_2) - (\mu_1 - \mu_2)}{\sqrt{\dfrac{\sigma_1^2}{n_1} + \dfrac{\sigma_2^2}{n_2}}} \qquad (12.1)$$

where

$\overline{X}_1$ = mean of the sample taken from population 1

$\mu_1$ = mean of population 1

$\sigma_1^2$ = variance of population 1

$n_1$ = size of the sample taken from population 1

$\overline{X}_2$ = mean of the sample taken from population 2

$\mu_2$ = mean of population 2

$\sigma_2^2$ = variance of population 2

$n_2$ = size of the sample taken from population 2

In most cases we do not know the actual variance or standard deviation of either of the two populations. The only information usually obtainable is the sample means ($\overline{X}_1$ and $\overline{X}_2$), the sample variances ($S_1^2$ and $S_2^2$), and sample standard deviations ($S_1$ and $S_2$). If the assumptions are made that the samples are randomly and independently drawn from respective populations that are normally distributed and that the population variances are equal (that is, $\sigma_1^2 = \sigma_2^2$), a pooled-variance $t$ test can be used to determine whether there is a significant difference between the means of the two populations.

To test the null hypothesis of no difference in the means of two independent populations

$$H_0: \mu_1 = \mu_2 \text{ or } \mu_1 - \mu_2 = 0$$

against the alternative that the means are not the same

$$H_1: \mu_1 \neq \mu_2 \text{ or } \mu_1 - \mu_2 \neq 0$$

we use the pooled-variance $t$-test statistic for testing the difference in two means:

## Pooled-Variance *t* Test for the Difference in Two Means

$$t = \frac{(\overline{X}_1 - \overline{X}_2) - (\mu_1 - \mu_2)}{\sqrt{S_p^2 \left(\dfrac{1}{n_1} + \dfrac{1}{n_2}\right)}} \qquad (12.2)$$

where

$$S_p^2 = \frac{(n_1 - 1)S_1^2 + (n_2 - 1)S_2^2}{(n_1 - 1) + (n_2 - 1)}$$

and

$S_p^2$ = pooled variance

$\overline{X}_1$ = mean of the sample taken from population 1

$S_1^2$ = variance of the sample taken from population 1

$n_1$ = size of the sample taken from population 1

$\overline{X}_2$ = mean of the sample taken from population 2

$S_2^2$ = variance of the sample taken from population 2

$n_2$ = size of the sample taken from population 2

From equation (12.2) we observe that the pooled-variance *t* test gets its name because the test statistic requires that we pool or combine the two sample variances $S_1^2$ and $S_2^2$ to obtain $S_p^2$, the best estimate of the variance common to both populations under the assumption that the two population variances are equal.[1]

[1]*We should note that in our operations manager's study, the two groups had equal sample sizes. When the two sample sizes are equal (that is, $n_1 = n_2$), the formula for the pooled variance can be simplified to* $S_p^2 = \dfrac{S_1^2 + S_2^2}{2}$

The pooled-variance *t*-test statistic follows a *t* distribution with $n_1 + n_2 - 2$ degrees of freedom. For a given level of significance $\alpha$, we reject the null hypothesis if the computed *t*-test statistic exceeds the upper-tailed critical value $t_{n_1 + n_2 - 2}$ from the *t* distribution or if the computed test statistic falls below the lower-tailed critical value $-t_{n_1 + n_2 - 2}$ from the *t* distribution. That is, the decision rule is

Reject $H_0$ if $t > t_{n_1 + n_2 - 2}$

or if $t < -t_{n_1 + n_2 - 2}$;

otherwise do not reject $H_0$.

The decision rule and regions of rejection and nonrejection are displayed in Figure 12.1.

To demonstrate the use of the pooled-variance *t* test, let us return to our Using Statistics application. One of the many questions that the operations manager wants to answer is whether or not there is evidence of a significant difference in the average deviation from the specified target based on bottles filled under equipment dial settings that allow either 25 or 30 psi of operating pressure. The results in terms of deviation from a specified target (in millimeters) are shown in Table 12.1.

To answer this, the null and alternative hypotheses are

$H_0$: $\mu_1 = \mu_2$ or $\mu_1 - \mu_2 = 0$

$H_1$: $\mu_1 \neq \mu_2$ or $\mu_1 - \mu_2 \neq 0$

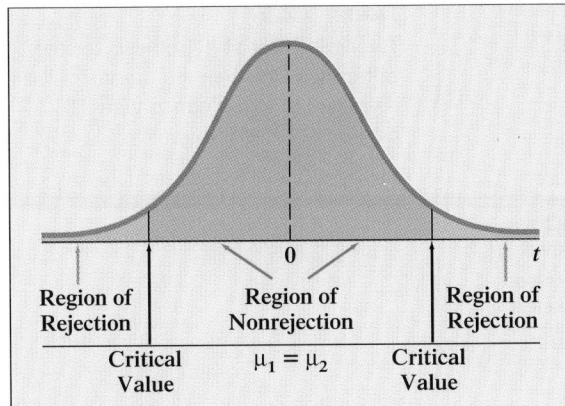

**FIGURE 12.1**
Rejection regions for a two-tailed test for the difference between two means

Region of Rejection | Region of Nonrejection | Region of Rejection

Critical Value     $\mu_1 = \mu_2$     Critical Value

**Table 12.1** *Comparing soft-drink bottle fills based on two different pressure settings*

| PRESSURE SETTINGS | | | |
| --- | --- | --- | --- |
| 25 PSI | | 30 PSI | |
| −2.8 | −1.0 | 0.2 | 3.3 |
| −1.6 | 1.4 | 2.1 | 1.6 |
| 0.2 | 3.4 | 2.6 | 4.0 |
| 1.2 | 0.6 | 0.4 | 2.7 |
| −2.0 | 0.9 | 1.7 | 3.4 |

*Note: A "negative deviation" from target indicates the amount a bottle is underfilled in millimeters, and a "positive deviation" shows the amount a bottle is overfilled in millimeters.*

DATA FILE
PRESSURE

Assuming that the manager takes samples from underlying normal populations having equal variances, the pooled-variance $t$ test can be used. If the test is conducted at the $\alpha = .05$ level of significance, the $t$-test statistic follows a $t$ distribution with $10 + 10 - 2 = 18$ degrees of freedom. From Table E.3 of appendix E the critical values for this two-tailed test are $+2.1009$ and $-2.1009$. As depicted in Figure 12.2 on page 476, the decision rule is

$$\text{Reject } H_0 \text{ if } t > t_{18} = +2.1009$$
$$\text{or if } t < -t_{18} = -2.1009;$$
$$\text{otherwise do not reject } H_0.$$

Using the data in Table 12.1, a set of summary statistics are computed and displayed in Table 12.2 on page 476.

For our data we have

$$t = \frac{(\bar{X}_1 - \bar{X}_2) - (\mu_1 - \mu_2)}{\sqrt{S_p^2 \left(\frac{1}{n_1} + \frac{1}{n_2}\right)}}$$

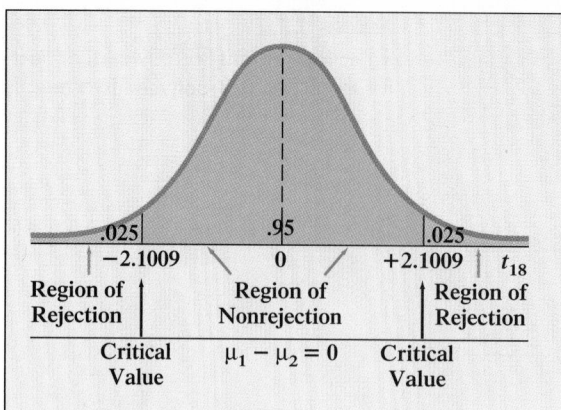

**FIGURE 12.2**

Two-tailed test of hypothesis for the difference between the means at the .05 level of significance with 18 degrees of freedom

**Table 12.2** *Some summary statistics on bottle fill (in mm)*

| PRESSURE SETTINGS | |
|---|---|
| **25 PSI** | **30 PSI** |
| $n_1 = 10$ | $n_2 = 10$ |
| $\overline{X}_1 = 0.03$ | $\overline{X}_2 = 2.20$ |
| $S_1^2 = 3.5068$ | $S_2^2 = 1.5733$ |
| $S_1 = 1.873$ | $S_2 = 1.254$ |

where

$$S_p^2 = \frac{(n_1 - 1)S_1^2 + (n_2 - 1)S_2^2}{(n_1 - 1) + (n_2 - 1)}$$

$$= \frac{9(3.5068) + 9(1.5733)}{9 + 9} = \frac{45.7209}{18} = 2.5401$$

or because $n_1 = n_2$,

$$S_p^2 = \frac{3.5068 + 1.5733}{2} = \frac{5.0801}{2} = 2.5401$$

Therefore

$$t = \frac{0.03 - 2.20}{\sqrt{2.5401\left(\frac{1}{10} + \frac{1}{10}\right)}} = \frac{-2.17}{\sqrt{0.5080}} = -3.04$$

Using a .05 level of significance, the null hypothesis ($H_0$) is rejected because $t = -3.04 < -t_{18} = -2.1009$.

If the null hypothesis were true, there would be an $\alpha = .05$ probability of obtaining a $t$-test statistic either larger than $+2.1009$ standard deviations from the center of the $t$ distribution or smaller than $-2.1009$ standard deviations from the center of the $t$ distribution. The $p$-value, or probability of obtaining a difference between the two sample means even larger than the 2.17 mm observed here, which translates to a test statistic $t$ with a distance even farther from the center of the $t$ distribution than $\pm 3.04$ standard deviations, is .007 (as obtained by Minitab) if the null hypothesis of no difference in the means were true. Because the $p$-value is less than $\alpha$, we have sufficient evidence that the null hypothesis is not true and we reject it.

The null hypothesis is rejected because the test statistic $t$ has fallen into the region of rejection. The operations manager can conclude that there is evidence of a difference in the average deviation from the target in the amount of soft drink filled under the two operating pressure levels. Using an operating pressure level of 25 psi results in significantly less deviation from the target than does a pressure level dial setting of 30 psi. Because the goal is to have the fill amount as close to the target as possible, a setting of 25 psi is preferred.

The pooled-variance $t$ test to be performed can be either two-tailed or one-tailed, depending on whether we are testing if the two population means are merely different or if one mean is greater than the other mean. This is seen below.

| TWO-TAILED TEST | ONE-TAILED TEST | ONE-TAILED TEST |
|---|---|---|
| $H_0$: $\mu_1 = \mu_2$ or $\mu_1 - \mu_2 = 0$ | $H_0$: $\mu_1 \geq \mu_2$ or $\mu_1 - \mu_2 \geq 0$ | $H_0$: $\mu_1 \leq \mu_2$ or $\mu_1 - \mu_2 \leq 0$ |
| $H_1$: $\mu_1 \neq \mu_2$ or $\mu_1 - \mu_2 \neq 0$ | $H_1$: $\mu_1 < \mu_2$ or $\mu_1 - \mu_2 < 0$ | $H_1$: $\mu_1 > \mu_2$ or $\mu_1 - \mu_2 > 0$ |

where

$\mu_1$ = mean of population 1

$\mu_2$ = mean of population 2

The appropriate regions of rejection are illustrated in Figure 12.3.

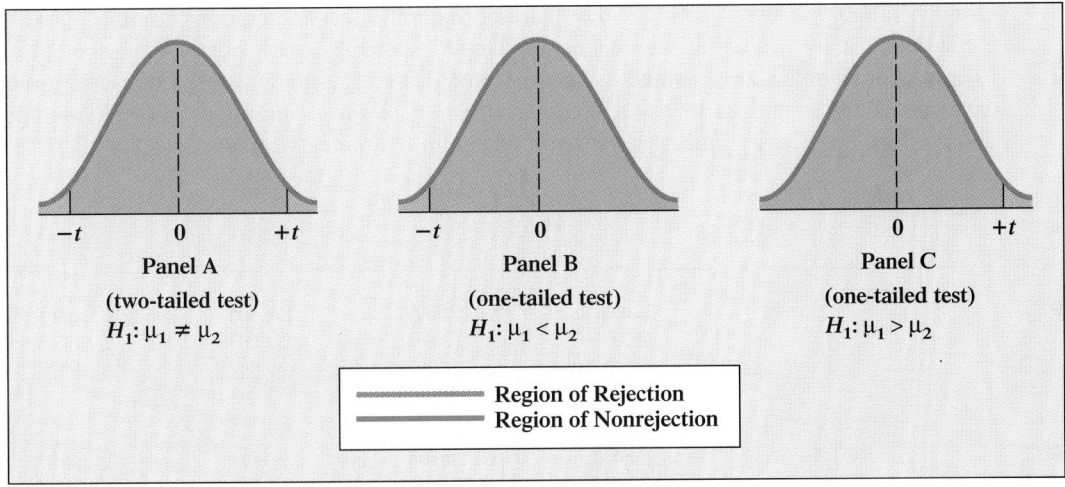

**FIGURE 12.3** Regions of rejection and nonrejection for the two sample $t$ tests for the difference in means

In Example 12.1 we undertake a thorough exploratory analysis of the soft-drink bottling data and illustrate the results of the pooled-variance *t* test obtained from Minitab.

## Example 12.1 *Pooled-Variance t Test*

Referring to the soft-drink bottling example, the operations manager wishes to answer the question as to whether there is evidence of a significant difference in average deviation from the specified target based on bottles filled under equipment dial settings of either 25 or 30 psi of operating pressure.

### SOLUTION

Using Minitab, we first "explore" the data and examine the assumptions for the pooled-variance *t* test by evaluating the set of descriptive statistics and a box-and-whisker plot. Even so, for sample sizes as small as 10 it is often difficult to get a clear picture. From our data, in neither sample is there an obvious violation of the assumption that the sampled observations are coming from a population whose measurements follow a normal distribution.

| Variable  | PSI | N  | Mean  | Median | TrMean | StDev |
|-----------|-----|----|-------|--------|--------|-------|
| Deviation | 25  | 10 | 0.030 | 0.400  | -0.037 | 1.873 |
|           | 30  | 10 | 2.200 | 2.350  | 2.225  | 1.254 |

| Variable  | PSI | SE Mean | Minimum | Maximum | Q1     | Q3    |
|-----------|-----|---------|---------|---------|--------|-------|
| Deviation | 25  | 0.592   | -2.800  | 3.400   | -1.700 | 1.250 |
|           | 30  | 0.397   | 0.200   | 4.000   | 1.300  | 3.325 |

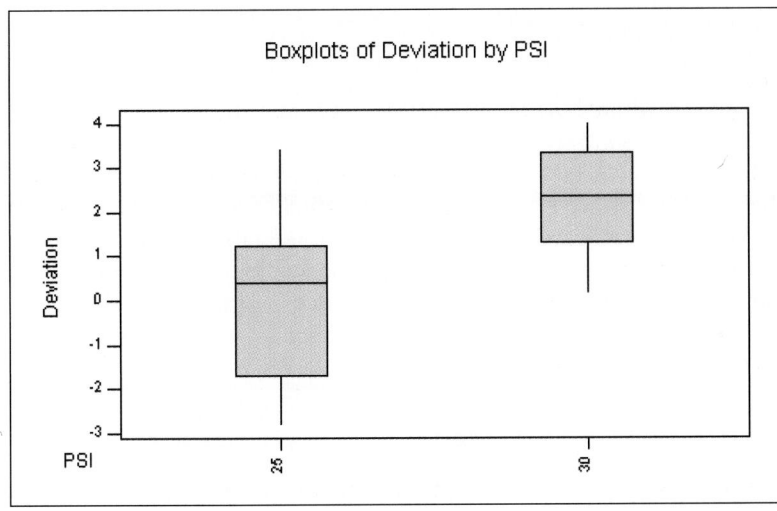

After we have performed an "exploratory data analysis" and examined the assumptions, the following Minitab printout displays the pooled-variance *t* test.

```
Two Sample T-Test and Confidence Interval

Two sample T for Deviation

PSI          N      Mean      StDev    SE Mean
25          10      0.03      1.87       0.59
30          10      2.20      1.25       0.40

95% CI for mu (25) - mu (30): ( -3.67,  -0.67)
T-Test mu (25) = mu (30) (vs not =): T = -3.04   P = 0.0070   DF = 18
Both use Pooled StDev = 1.59
```

Using the *steps in hypothesis testing* from Exhibits 11.2 and 11.3 on pages 422 and 425, we observe the following:

Steps 1 and 2:
$$H_0: \mu_1 = \mu_2 \text{ or } \mu_1 - \mu_2 = 0$$
$$H_1: \mu_1 \neq \mu_2 \text{ or } \mu_1 - \mu_2 \neq 0$$

Step 3:
$$\alpha = .05$$

Step 4:
$$n_1 = 10 \text{ and } n_2 = 10$$

Step 5: Assuming the samples are drawn from underlying normal populations with equal variances, we use the pooled-variance *t* test with test statistic *t* given by equation (12.2):

$$t = \frac{(\overline{X}_1 - \overline{X}_2) - (\mu_1 - \mu_2)}{\sqrt{S_p^2 \left(\frac{1}{n_1} + \frac{1}{n_2}\right)}}$$

Step 6: We use Table E.3 to develop the following decision rule as illustrated in Figure 12.2 on page 476:

$$\text{Reject } H_0 \text{ if } t > t_{18} = +2.1009 \text{ or if } t < -t_{18} = -2.1009;$$
otherwise do not reject $H_0$.

Step 7: We observe from the Minitab printout that the $t$-test statistic is $-3.04$ and the $p$-value is 0.007.

Steps 8, 9, and 10: Because $t = -3.04 < -2.1009$, we reject $H_0$. (Alternatively, the $p$-value .007 is less than $\alpha$ of .05 so we reject $H_0$.) The operations manager concludes that there is evidence of a difference in the average deviation from the target in the amount of soda filled under the two operating pressure levels. Using an operating pressure level of 25 psi results in significantly less deviation from the target than does a pressure level dial setting of 30 psi.

## Separate-Variance $t$ Test for Differences in Two Means

In our discussion of testing for the difference between the means of two independent populations in the previous section, we pooled the sample variances into a common estimate $S_p^2$ because we assumed that the population variances were equal (that is, $\sigma_1^2 = \sigma_2^2$). This situation is depicted in panel A of Figure 12.4 for the case in which normally distributed population 1 has a higher mean than does normally distributed population 2. However, if, as in panel B of Figure 12.4, we are either unwilling to assume that the two normally distributed populations have equal variances or we have evidence that the variances are not equal, then the pooled-variance $t$ test is inappropriate. As a result, the separate-variance $t$ test developed by Satterthwaite (see reference 6) is used. In the Satterthwaite approximation procedure, the two separate sample variances are included in the computation of the $t$-test statistic—hence the name separate-variance $t$ test.

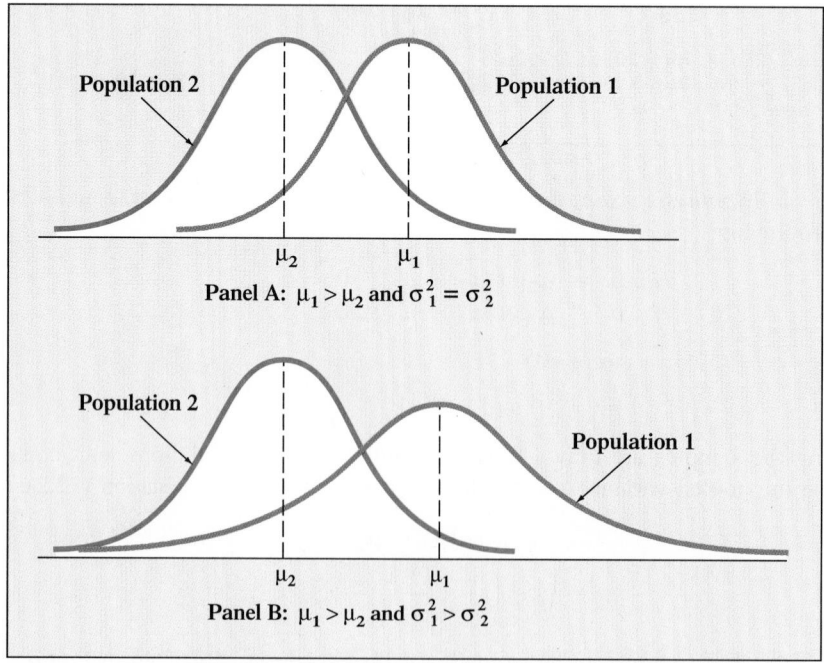

**FIGURE 12.4** Comparing the means from two normally distributed populations

To test the null hypothesis of no difference in the means of two independent populations

$$H_0: \mu_1 = \mu_2 \text{ or } \mu_1 - \mu_2 = 0$$

against the alternative that the means are not the same

$$H_1: \mu_1 \neq \mu_2 \text{ or } \mu_1 - \mu_2 \neq 0$$

we use the separate-variance $t$-test statistic for testing the difference in two means.

---

**Separate-Variance $t$ Test for the Difference in Two Means**

$$t = \frac{(\overline{X}_1 - \overline{X}_2) - (\mu_1 - \mu_2)}{\sqrt{\dfrac{S_1^2}{n_1} + \dfrac{S_2^2}{n_2}}} \qquad (12.3)$$

where

$\overline{X}_1 = $ mean of the sample taken from population 1

$S_1^2 = $ variance of the sample taken from population 1

$n_1 = $ size of the sample taken from population 1

$\overline{X}_2 = $ mean of the sample taken from population 2

$S_2^2 = $ variance of the sample taken from population 2

$n_2 = $ size of the sample taken from population 2

---

The separate-variance $t$-test statistic is approximated by a $t$ distribution with degrees of freedom $\nu$ taken to be the integer portion of the following computation.

---

**Obtaining Degrees of Freedom in Separate-Variance $t$ Test**

$$\nu = \frac{\left(\dfrac{S_1^2}{n_1} + \dfrac{S_2^2}{n_2}\right)^2}{\dfrac{\left(\dfrac{S_1^2}{n_1}\right)^2}{n_1 - 1} + \dfrac{\left(\dfrac{S_2^2}{n_2}\right)^2}{n_2 - 1}} \qquad (12.4)$$

---

For a given level of significance $\alpha$, we reject the null hypothesis if the computed $t$-test statistic exceeds the upper-tailed critical value $t_\nu$ from the $t$ distribution or if the computed test statistic falls below the lower-tailed critical value $-t_\nu$ from the $t$ distribution. That is, the decision rule is

$$\text{Reject } H_0 \text{ if } t > t_\nu$$
$$\text{or if } t < -t_\nu;$$
$$\text{otherwise do not reject } H_0.$$

The decision rule and regions of rejection and nonrejection are displayed in Figure 12.5 on page 482.

We can demonstrate the separate-variance $t$ test by referring to our soft-drink bottle fill example. Recall that the operations manager wants to determine whether or not there is evidence of a significant difference in average deviation from the specified target based on

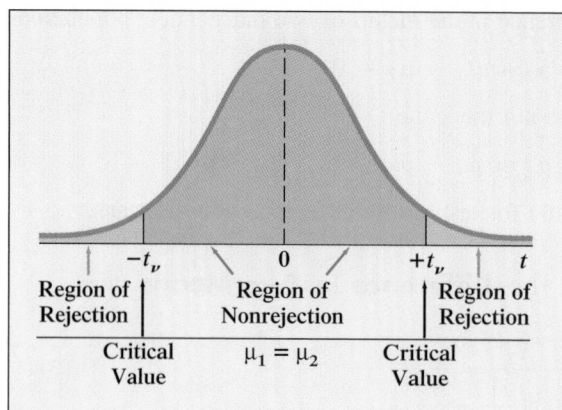

bottles filled under machinery and equipment dial settings that allow operating pressure levels of either 25 or 30 psi. Comparing the differences in average deviation from the specified target, the null and alternative hypotheses are

$$H_0: \mu_1 = \mu_2 \text{ or } \mu_1 - \mu_2 = 0$$
$$H_1: \mu_1 \neq \mu_2 \text{ or } \mu_1 - \mu_2 \neq 0$$

The data displaying the deviations from target based on random samples of 10 bottles filled using operating pressure levels of 25 or 30 psi are shown in Table 12.1 (page 475), and summary statistics are presented in Table 12.2 (page 476).

If we are willing to assume the possibility that the samples are taken from underlying normal populations but we are unwilling to assume that these populations have equal variances, the separate-variance $t$ test is employed. If the test is conducted at the $\alpha = .05$ level of significance, using equation (12.4), the separate-variance $t$-test statistic is approximated by a $t$ distribution with $\nu = 15$ degrees of freedom, the integer portion of the following computation.

$$\nu = \frac{\left( \dfrac{S_1^2}{n_1} + \dfrac{S_2^2}{n_2} \right)^2}{\dfrac{\left( \dfrac{S_1^2}{n_1} \right)^2}{n_1 - 1} + \dfrac{\left( \dfrac{S_2^2}{n_2} \right)^2}{n_2 - 1}}$$

$$= \frac{\left( \dfrac{3.5068}{10} + \dfrac{1.5733}{10} \right)^2}{\dfrac{\left( \dfrac{3.5068}{10} \right)^2}{9} + \dfrac{\left( \dfrac{1.5733}{10} \right)^2}{9}} = 15.72$$

From Table E.3 of appendix E the upper- and lower-critical values for this two-tailed test are, respectively, +2.1315 and −2.1315. As depicted in Figure 12.6, the decision rule is

$$\text{Reject } H_0 \text{ if } t > t_{15} = +2.1315$$
$$\text{or if } t < -t_{15} = -2.1315;$$
$$\text{otherwise do not reject } H_0.$$

Using the data of Table 12.2 on page 476, we have from equation (12.3)

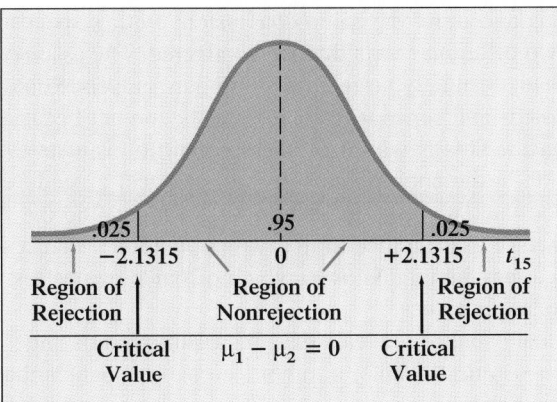

**FIGURE 12.6**
Two-tailed test of hypothesis for the difference between the means at the .05 level of significance with 15 degrees of freedom

$$t = \frac{(\overline{X}_1 - \overline{X}_2) - (\mu_1 - \mu_2)}{\sqrt{\dfrac{S_1^2}{n_1} + \dfrac{S_2^2}{n_2}}}$$

$$= \frac{0.03 - 2.20}{\sqrt{\left(\dfrac{3.5068}{10} + \dfrac{1.5733}{10}\right)}} = \frac{-2.17}{\sqrt{0.50801}} = -3.04$$

Rather than computing these results manually, as is illustrated in Figure 12.7, Minitab can be used.

Using a .05 level of significance, the null hypothesis ($H_0$) is rejected here because $t = -3.04 < -t_{15} = -2.1315$. The *p*-value, or probability of obtaining a difference between the two sample means even larger than the 2.17 mm observed here, which translates to a test statistic $t$ with a distance even farther from the center of the $t$ distribution than $\pm3.04$ standard deviations, is .0082 if the null hypothesis of no differences in the means were true. Because the *p*-value is less than $\alpha$ of .05, we have evidence to refute the null hypothesis.

The null hypothesis is rejected here because the test statistic $t$ has fallen into the region of rejection as depicted in Figure 12.6. The operations manager can conclude that there is evidence of a difference in the average deviation from the target in the amount of soda filled under the two operating pressure level dial settings. Using an operating pressure level of 25 psi results in significantly less average deviation than does a pressure level dial setting of 30 psi.

```
Two Sample T-Test and Confidence Interval

Two sample T for Deviation

PSI          N       Mean     StDev    SE Mean
25          10       0.03     1.87      0.59
30          10       2.20     1.25      0.40

95% CI for mu (25) - mu (30): ( -3.69,  -0.65)
T-Test mu (25) = mu (30) (vs not =): T = -3.04  P = 0.0082  DF = 15
```

**FIGURE 12.7**   Two-sample *t* test assuming unequal variances for the bottling fill example

Note that we made the same decisions and drew the same conclusions with respect to the two different dial settings from the two different $t$ tests that we conducted. The assumption of equality of population variances had absolutely no real effect on our analysis. Sometimes, however, the results from the pooled- and separate-variance $t$ tests conflict because the assumptions of one of them are violated. This is why it is so important to evaluate the assumptions and use those results to guide in the appropriate selection of a test procedure. Resolving such a dilemma is part of good data analysis. In section 12.2 we develop the $F$ test to determine whether there is evidence of a difference in the two population variances. On the basis of the results of that test, we may be guided as to which of our previous tests is more appropriate for the operations manager to use.

On the other hand, if our exploratory data analysis reveals that the assumption of underlying normality in the sampled populations is questionable, it might lead us to conclude that neither test is appropriate. In such a situation, either a *data transformation* (see reference 8) would be made (and then the assumptions rechecked to determine whether one of the $t$ tests is more appropriate) or a *nonparametric procedure*, which does not make these stringent assumptions, would be employed. One such nonparametric procedure, the *Wilcoxon rank sum test*, is presented in section 12.4.

## Problems for Section 12.1

### Learning the Basics

• **12.1** Given a sample of size $n_1 = 40$ from a population with known standard deviation $\sigma_1 = 20$, and an independent sample of size $n_2 = 50$ from another population with known standard deviation $\sigma_2 = 10$, what is the value of the $Z$-test statistic for testing differences in two population means if $\overline{X}_1 = 72$ and $\overline{X}_2 = 66$?

• **12.2** What is your decision in Problem 12.1 if you are testing $H_0$: $\mu_1 = \mu_2$ against the two-tailed alternative $H_1$: $\mu_1 \neq \mu_2$ using a level of significance $\alpha = .01$?

• **12.3** What is the $p$-value in Problem 12.1 if you are testing $H_0$: $\mu_1 = \mu_2$ against the two-tailed alternative $H_1$: $\mu_1 \neq \mu_2$?

**12.4** Given a sample of size $n_1 = 8$ with sample mean $\overline{X}_1 = 42$ and sample standard deviation $S_1 = 4$, and an independent sample of size $n_2 = 15$ from another population with sample mean $\overline{X}_2 = 34$ and sample standard deviation $S_2 = 5$, answer the following:
(a) What is the value of the pooled-variance $t$-test statistic for testing differences in two population means?
(b) In obtaining the critical value of the test statistic $t$, how many degrees of freedom are there?
(c) Using a level of significance $\alpha = .01$, what is the critical value for a one-tailed test of the hypothesis $H_0$: $\mu_1 \leq \mu_2$ against the alternative $H_1$: $\mu_1 > \mu_2$?
(d) What is your statistical decision?

**12.5** Given a sample of size $n_1 = 13$ with sample mean $\overline{X}_1 = 52$ and sample standard deviation $S_1 = 8$, and an independent sample of size $n_2 = 15$ from another population with sample mean $\overline{X}_2 = 48$ and sample standard deviation $S_2 = 16$, answer the following:
(a) What is the value of the separate-variance $t$-test statistic for testing differences in two population means?
(b) In obtaining the critical value of the separate-variance $t$-test statistic, how many degrees of freedom are there?
(c) Using a level of significance $\alpha = .01$, what is the critical value for a one-tailed test of the hypothesis $H_0$: $\mu_1 \leq \mu_2$ against the alternative $H_1$: $\mu_1 > \mu_2$?
(d) What is your statistical decision?

## Applying the Concepts

• **12.6** The operations manager at a light bulb factory wants to determine if there is any difference in the average life expectancy of bulbs manufactured on two different types of machines. The process standard deviation of machine I is 110 hours and of machine II is 125 hours. A random sample of 25 light bulbs obtained from machine I indicates a sample mean of 375 hours, and a similar sample of 25 from machine II indicates a sample mean of 362 hours.

    (a) Using the .05 level of significance, is there any evidence of a difference in the average life of bulbs produced by the two types of machines?

    (b) Compute the $p$-value in part (a) and interpret its meaning.

**12.7** The purchasing director for an industrial parts factory is investigating the possibility of purchasing a new type of milling machine. She determines that the new machine will be bought if there is evidence that the parts produced have a higher average breaking strength than those from the old machine. The process standard deviation of the breaking strength for the old machine is 10 kilograms and for the new machine is 9 kilograms. A sample of 100 parts taken from the old machine indicated a sample mean of 65 kilograms, whereas a similar sample of 100 from the new machine indicated a sample mean of 72 kilograms.

    (a) Using the .01 level of significance, is there evidence that the purchasing director should buy the new machine?

    (b) Compute the $p$-value in part (a) and interpret its meaning.

**12.8** In intaglio printing, a design or figure is carved beneath the surface of hard metal or stone. Suppose that an experiment is designed to compare differences in average surface hardness of steel plates used in intaglio printing (measured in indentation numbers) based on two different surface conditions—untreated versus treated by light polishing with emery paper. Based on past experience it is believed that the standard deviation in surface hardness (in indentation numbers) is 10.2 for untreated surfaces and 6.4 for lightly polished surfaces. If in the experiment 40 steel plates are randomly assigned, 20 that are untreated and 20 that are lightly polished, use a .05 level of significance to determine whether there is evidence of a significant treatment effect (i.e., a significant difference in average surface hardness between the untreated and the polished steel plates) if the sample mean for the untreated plates is 163.4 and the sample mean for the polished plates is 156.9.

• **12.9** Management of the Sycamore Steel Company wishes to determine if there is any difference in performance between the day shift of workers and the evening shift of workers. A sample of 100 day-shift workers reveals an average output of 74.3 parts per hour with a sample standard deviation of 16 parts per hour. A sample of 100 evening-shift workers reveals an average output of 69.7 parts per hour with a sample standard deviation of 18 parts per hour. Assume that the population variances are equal.

    (a) At the .10 level of significance, is there evidence of a difference in average output between the day shift and the evening shift?

    (b) Find the approximate $p$-value in part (a) and interpret its meaning.

**12.10** An independent testing agency has been contracted to determine whether there is any difference in gasoline mileage output from two different blends of gasoline used on the same model automobile. Gasoline A is tested on 200 cars and produces a sample average of 18.5 miles per gallon with a sample standard deviation of 4.6 miles per gallon. Gasoline B is tested on a sample of 100 cars and produces a sample average of 19.34 miles per gallon with a sample standard deviation of 5.2 miles per gallon. Assume that the population variances are equal.

    (a) At the .05 level of significance, is there evidence of a difference in average performance of the two blends of gasoline?

    (b) Find the approximate $p$-value in part (a) and interpret its meaning.

**12.11** A carpet manufacturer is studying differences between two of its major outlet stores. The company is particularly interested in the time it takes before customers receive carpeting that has been ordered from the plant. Data concerning a sample of delivery times for the most popular type of carpet are summarized as follows:

|  | STORE A | STORE B |
|---|---|---|
| $\overline{X}$ | 34.3 days | 43.7 days |
| $S$ | 2.4 days | 3.1 days |
| $n$ | 41 | 31 |

(a) Assuming that the population variances from both stores are equal, is there evidence of a difference in the average delivery time for the two outlet stores? (Use a .01 level of significance.)
(b) Find the $p$-value in part (a) and interpret its meaning.
(c) Assuming that the population variances from both stores are unequal, is there evidence of a difference in the average delivery time for the two outlet stores? (Use a .01 level of significance.)
(d) Find the $p$-value in part (c) and interpret its meaning.
(e) Compare the results obtained in part (a) with those in part (c).

**12.12** An industrial psychologist wishes to study the effects of motivation on sales in a particular firm. Of 24 new salespersons, 12 are paid an hourly rate and 12 are paid a commission. The 24 individuals are randomly assigned to the two groups. The following data represent the sales volume (in thousands of dollars) achieved during the first month on the job.

| HOURLY RATE | | COMMISSION | |
|---|---|---|---|
| 256 | 212 | 224 | 261 |
| 239 | 216 | 254 | 228 |
| 222 | 236 | 273 | 234 |
| 207 | 219 | 285 | 225 |
| 228 | 225 | 237 | 232 |
| 241 | 230 | 277 | 245 |

**DATA FILE**
**SALESVOL**

(a) Assuming that the population variances are equal, is there evidence that wage incentives (through commission) yield greater average sales volume? (Use $\alpha = .01$.)
(b) What other assumptions must be made in part (a) of this problem?
(c) Determine the $p$-value in part (a) and interpret its meaning.
(d) Assuming that the population variances are not equal, is there evidence that wage incentives (through commission) yield greater average sales volume? (Use $\alpha = .01$.)
(e) What other assumptions must be made in part (d) of this problem?
(f) Determine the $p$-value in part (d) and interpret its meaning.
(g) Compare the results obtained in part (a) with those in part (d).

**● 12.13** A manufacturer is developing a nickel-metal hydride battery that is to be used in cellular telephones in lieu of nickel-cadmium batteries. The director of quality control decides to evaluate the newly developed battery against the widely used nickel-cadmium battery with respect to performance. A random sample of 25 nickel-cadmium batteries and a random sample of 25 of the newly developed nickel-metal hydride batteries are placed in cellular telephones of the same brand and model. The performance measure of interest is the talking time (in minutes) prior to recharging. The results are shown at the top of page 487.

| NICKEL-CADMIUM BATTERY | | | NICKEL-METAL HYDRIDE BATTERY | | |
|---|---|---|---|---|---|
| 54.5 | 71.0 | 67.0 | 78.3 | 103.0 | 79.8 |
| 67.8 | 41.7 | 56.7 | 95.4 | 81.3 | 91.1 |
| 64.5 | 69.7 | 86.8 | 69.4 | 46.4 | 82.8 |
| 70.4 | 40.8 | 74.9 | 87.3 | 82.3 | 71.8 |
| 72.5 | 75.4 | 76.9 | 62.5 | 83.2 | 77.5 |
| 64.9 | 81.0 | 104.4 | 85.0 | 85.3 | 74.3 |
| 83.3 | 90.4 | 82.0 | 85.3 | 85.5 | 86.1 |
| 72.8 | 71.8 | 58.7 | 72.1 | 112.3 | 74.1 |
| 68.8 | | | 41.1 | | |

DATA FILE
NICKBAT

(a) Assuming that the population variances are equal, is there evidence of a difference in the two types of batteries with respect to average talking time (in minutes) prior to recharging? (Use $\alpha = .05$.)
(b) What other assumptions must be made in part (a) of this problem?
(c) Determine the $p$-value in part (a) and interpret its meaning.
(d) Assuming that the population variances are not equal, is there evidence of a difference in the two types of batteries with respect to average talking time (in minutes) prior to recharging? (Use $\alpha = .05$.)
(e) What other assumptions must be made in part (d) of this problem?
(f) Determine the $p$-value in part (d) and interpret its meaning.
(g) Compare the results obtained in part (a) with those in part (d).

● **12.14** A real estate agency wants to compare the appraised values of single-family homes in two Nassau County, New York, communities. A sample of 60 listings in Farmingdale and 99 listings in Levittown yield the following results (in thousands of dollars):

| | FARMINGDALE | LEVITTOWN |
|---|---|---|
| $\overline{X}$ | 191.33 | 172.34 |
| $S$ | 32.60 | 16.92 |
| $n$ | 60 | 99 |

Assuming that the population variances are not equal, at the .05 level of significance, is there evidence of a difference in the average appraised values for single-family homes in the two Nassau County communities?

**12.15** Shipments of meat, meat by-products, and other ingredients are mixed together in several filling lines at a pet food canning factory. Management suspects that although the average amount filled in the can of pet food is usually the same, the variability of the cans filled in line A is much greater than that of line B. The following sample data are obtained (from filling 8-ounce cans):

| | LINE A | LINE B |
|---|---|---|
| $\overline{X}$ | 8.005 | 7.997 |
| $S$ | 0.012 | 0.005 |
| $n$ | 11 | 16 |

Assuming that the population variances are not equal, at the .05 level of significance, is there evidence of a difference in the average weight of cans filled on the two lines?

**12.16** A public official working on health care reform policy wants to compare occupancy rates (i.e., average annual percentage of beds filled) in urban versus suburban hospitals within his state. A random sample of 16 urban hospitals and a random sample of 16 suburban hospitals are selected within the state and the occupancy rates are recorded, as follows:

| URBAN HOSPITALS | | SUBURBAN HOSPITALS | |
|---|---|---|---|
| 76.5 | 73.3 | 71.5 | 63.0 |
| 75.9 | 77.4 | 73.4 | 76.0 |
| 79.6 | 79.0 | 74.6 | 75.5 |
| 77.5 | 79.9 | 74.3 | 70.7 |
| 79.4 | 70.4 | 71.2 | 67.4 |
| 78.7 | 77.7 | 67.8 | 62.6 |
| 78.6 | 78.1 | 76.9 | 73.0 |
| 79.3 | 75.9 | 60.0 | 76.5 |

DATA FILE
HOSPITAL

(a) Assume that the variances in occupancy rates in the populations of hospital types (i.e., urban and suburban) are equal. Is there evidence of a difference in the average occupancy rates between urban and suburban hospitals in this state? (Use a .05 level of significance.)
(b) What assumptions must be made in part (a) of this problem?
(c) Assume that the variances in occupancy rates in the populations of hospital types (i.e., urban and suburban) are not equal. Is there evidence of a difference in the average occupancy rates between urban and suburban hospitals in this state? (Use a .05 level of significance.)
(d) What other assumptions must be made in order to do part (c) of this problem?
(e) Compare the results obtained in part (a) with those in part (c).

**12.17** The director of training for a company manufacturing electronic equipment is interested in determining whether different training methods have an effect on the productivity of assembly line employees. She randomly assigns 42 recently hired employees into two groups of 21, of which the first received a computer-assisted, individual-based training program and the other received a team-based training program. Upon completion of the training, the employees are evaluated on the time (in seconds) it takes to assemble a part. The results are as follows:

| COMPUTER-ASSISTED, INDIVIDUAL-BASED PROGRAM | | | TEAM-BASED PROGRAM | | |
|---|---|---|---|---|---|
| 19.4 | 16.7 | 16.5 | 22.4 | 13.8 | 23.7 |
| 20.7 | 19.3 | 17.7 | 18.7 | 18.0 | 17.4 |
| 21.8 | 16.8 | 16.2 | 19.3 | 20.8 | 23.2 |
| 14.1 | 17.7 | 17.4 | 15.6 | 17.1 | 20.1 |
| 16.1 | 19.8 | 16.4 | 18.0 | 28.2 | 12.3 |
| 16.8 | 19.3 | 16.8 | 21.7 | 20.8 | 15.2 |
| 14.7 | 16.0 | 18.5 | 30.7 | 24.7 | 16.0 |

DATA FILE
TRAINING

(a) Assuming that the variances in the populations of training methods are equal, is there evidence of a difference in the average assembly times (in seconds) between employees trained in a computer-assisted, individual-based program and those trained in a team-based program? (Use a .05 level of significance.)

(b) What other assumptions must be made in part (a) of this problem?

(c) Assuming that the variances in the populations of training methods are not equal, is there evidence of a difference in the average assembly times (in seconds) between employees trained in a computer-assisted, individual-based program and those trained in a team-based program? (Use a .05 level of significance.)

(d) What other assumptions must be made in part (c) of this problem?

(e) Compare the results obtained in part (a) with those in part (c).

 ## F TEST FOR DIFFERENCES IN TWO VARIANCES

Often we want to test whether two independent populations have the same variability. Either we may be interested in studying the variances of two populations to test the assumption of equal variances so we can determine whether to use the pooled-variance $t$ test or the separate-variance $t$ test or we may just be interested in studying the variances of two populations.

We use a statistical test based on the ratio of the two sample variances to test for the equality of the variances of two independent populations. If the data from each population are assumed to be normally distributed, then the ratio $S_1^2/S_2^2$ follows a distribution called the **F distribution** (see Table E.5), named after the famous statistician R. A. Fisher. From Table E.5 we see that the critical values of the $F$ distribution depend on two sets of degrees of freedom. The degrees of freedom in the numerator of the ratio pertain to the first sample, and the degrees of freedom in the denominator pertain to the second sample. The $F$-test statistic for testing the equality between two variances is found as follows.

### F Statistic for Testing the Equality of Two Variances

The $F$-test statistic is equal to the variance of sample 1 divided by the variance of sample 2.

$$F = \frac{S_1^2}{S_2^2} \qquad (12.5)$$

where

$n_1$ = size of sample taken from population 1

$n_2$ = size of sample taken from population 2

$n_1 - 1$ = degrees of freedom from sample 1 (i.e., the numerator degrees of freedom)

$n_2 - 1$ = degrees of freedom from sample 2 (i.e., the denominator degrees of freedom)

$S_1^2$ = variance of sample 1

$S_2^2$ = variance of sample 2

For a given level of significance $\alpha$, to test the null hypothesis of equality of variances

$$H_0: \sigma_1^2 = \sigma_2^2$$

against the alternative hypothesis that the two population variances are not equal

$$H_1: \sigma_1^2 \neq \sigma_2^2$$

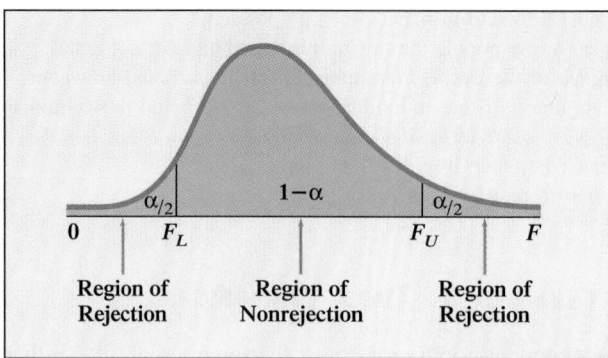

we reject the null hypothesis if the computed $F$-test statistic exceeds the upper-tailed critical value $F_U$ from the $F$ distribution with $n_1 - 1$ degrees of freedom from sample 1 in the numerator and $n_2 - 1$ degrees of freedom from sample 2 in the denominator, or if the computed $F$-test statistic falls below the lower-tailed critical value $F_L$ from the $F$ distribution with $n_1 - 1$ and $n_2 - 1$ degrees of freedom in the numerator and denominator. Thus, the decision rule is

$$\text{Reject } H_0 \text{ if } F > F_U \text{ or if } F < F_L;$$

$$\text{otherwise do not reject } H_0.$$

This decision rule and rejection region are displayed in Figure 12.8.

To demonstrate how we may use the $F$ test for the equality of two variances, we return to our Using Statistics application. The operations manager wants to determine whether or not there is evidence of a significant difference in average deviation from the specified target based on bottles filled under machinery and equipment dial settings that allow 25 or 30 psi operating pressure levels. The data are shown in Table 12.1 on page 475, and the summary measures for the two samples are presented in Table 12.2 on page 476.

To determine whether the pooled-variance $t$ test or the separate-variance $t$ test is more appropriate for analysis of the collected data, we first test for the equality of the two population variances. We have the following null and alternative hypotheses:

$$H_0: \sigma_1^2 = \sigma_2^2$$

$$H_1: \sigma_1^2 \neq \sigma_2^2$$

Because this is a two-tailed test, the rejection region is split into the lower and upper tails of the $F$ distribution. If a level of significance of $\alpha = .05$ is selected, each rejection region contains .025 of the distribution.

$F_U$, the upper-tail critical value of the $F$ distribution with 9 and 9 degrees of freedom, can be obtained directly from Table E.5, a replica of which is presented in Table 12.3. Because there are 9 degrees of freedom in the numerator and 9 degrees of freedom in the denominator, the upper-tail critical value $F_U$ is found by looking in the column labeled "9" and the row labeled "9," which pertain to an upper-tail area of .025. Thus, the upper-tail critical value of this $F$ distribution is 4.03.

## Obtaining Lower-Tail Critical Values

$F_L$, a lower-tail critical value on the $F$ distribution with the desired $n_1 - 1$ degrees of freedom from sample 1 in the numerator and $n_2 - 1$ degrees of freedom from sample 2 in the denominator, is computed by taking the reciprocal of $F_{U*}$, an upper-tail critical value on the

**Table 12.3** *Obtaining $F_U$, upper-tail critical value of F with 9 and 9 degrees of freedom for upper-tail area of .025*

| DENOMINATOR | NUMERATOR $df_1$ | | | | | | | |
|---|---|---|---|---|---|---|---|---|
| $df_2$ | 1 | 2 | 3 | ... | 7 | 8 | 9 |
| 1 | 647.8 | 799.5 | 864.2 | ... | 948.2 | 956.7 | 963.3 |
| 2 | 38.51 | 39.00 | 39.17 | ... | 39.36 | 39.37 | 39.39 |
| 3 | 17.44 | 16.04 | 15.44 | ... | 14.62 | 14.54 | 14.47 |
| ⋮ | ⋮ | ⋮ | ⋮ | ⋮ | ⋮ | ⋮ | ⋮ |
| 7 | 8.07 | 6.54 | 5.89 | ... | 4.99 | 4.90 | 4.82 |
| 8 | 7.57 | 6.06 | 5.42 | ... | 4.53 | 4.43 | 4.36 |
| 9 | 7.21 | 5.71 | 5.08 | ... | 4.20 | 4.10 | 4.03 |

*Source: Extracted from Table E.5.*

$F$ distribution with degrees of freedom "switched" (that is, $n_2 - 1$ degrees of freedom in the numerator and $n_1 - 1$ degrees of freedom in the denominator). This gives us equation (12.6).

### Obtaining Lower-Tail Critical Values from the *F* Distribution

$$F_L = \frac{1}{F_{U^*}} \qquad (12.6)$$

In our operations manager's example the degrees of freedom are 9 and 9 for the respective numerator sample and denominator sample so there is no "switching" of degrees of freedom: We just take the reciprocal. Therefore, to compute our desired lower-tail .025 critical value, we need to obtain the upper-tail .025 critical value of $F$ with 9 degrees of freedom in the numerator and 9 degrees of freedom in the denominator and take its reciprocal. As we have already observed in Table 12.3, this upper-tail value is 4.03 so that, from equation (12.6)

$$F_L = \frac{1}{F_{U^*}} = \frac{1}{4.03} = 0.248$$

As depicted in Figure 12.9 on page 492, the decision rule is

Reject $H_0$ if $F > F_U = 4.03$ or if $F < F_L = 0.248$;

otherwise do not reject $H_0$.

Using equation (12.5) for the operations manager's data (see Table 12.2 on page 476), we compute the following $F$-test statistic:

$$F = \frac{S_1^2}{S_2^2}$$

$$= \frac{3.5068}{1.5733} = 2.23$$

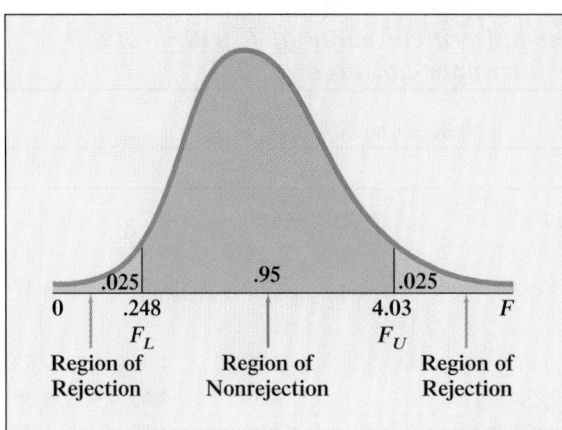

**FIGURE 12.9**
Regions of rejection and nonrejection for a two-tailed $F$ test for the equality of two variances at the .05 level of significance with 9 and 9 degrees of freedom

Therefore, because $F_L = 0.248 < F = 2.23 < F_U = 4.03$, we do not reject $H_0$. The operations manager concludes that there is no evidence of a difference in the variability in the deviation of soft-drink fill levels for the populations of bottles filled under the two operating pressure level dial settings.

Because there is no evidence that the population variances significantly differ, if we assume that the two populations are normally distributed, the pooled-variance $t$ test would be more appropriate than the separate-variance $t$ test for comparing differences in the average deviation from the specified fill target. In such situations the pooled-variance $t$ test has more statistical power in its ability to detect a significant difference between the means. On the other hand, if we do not feel that the normality assumption is viable, we can use the *Wilcoxon rank sum test* to determine if there are differences in the median deviation from the specified fill target. This test procedure is described in section 12.4.

In testing for the equality of variances, particularly as part of assessing the validity of that assumption for choosing the appropriate $t$-test procedure, the $F$ test is two-tailed. On the other hand, when interest focuses on process variability itself, the $F$ test is often one-tailed. Thus, in testing the equality of two variances, either two-tailed or one-tailed tests can be employed, depending on whether we are testing if the two population variances are *different* or if one variance is *greater than* the other variance. These situations are depicted in Figure 12.10.

It is often the case that the two sample sizes differ. To demonstrate how to obtain a lower-tail critical value from the $F$ distribution in a more general situation, we present a hypothesis test in Example 12.2.

## Example 12.2  *Obtaining the Lower-Tail Critical Value from the F Distribution in a Two-Tailed Test of Hypothesis*

Let us assume we have a sample of size $n_1 = 8$ from a normally distributed population. The sample variance is computed to be $S_1^2 = 56.0$. Now let us assume we have a sample of size $n_2 = 10$ from an independent, normally distributed population. The sample variance for this set of data is computed to be $S_2^2 = 24.0$. Using a level of significance of $\alpha = .05$,

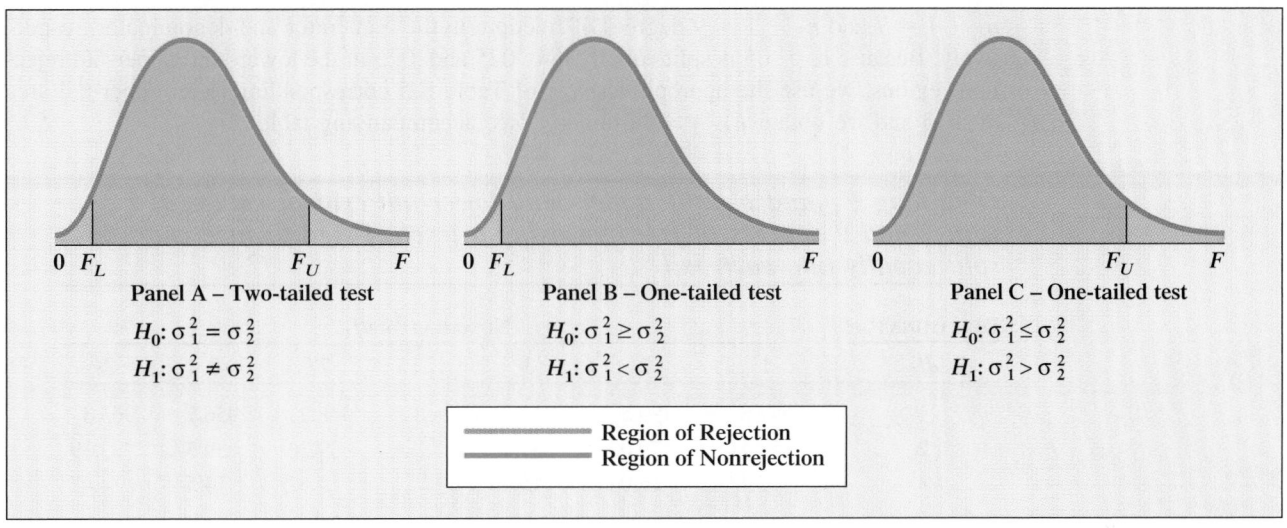

**FIGURE 12.10** Determining the rejection region for testing a hypothesis about the equality of two population variances

test the null hypothesis of no differences in the two population variances against the two-tailed alternative that there is evidence of a significant difference in the population variances.

## SOLUTION

Using the steps in hypothesis testing from Exhibits 11.2 and 11.3 on pages 422 and 425, we observe the following.

Steps 1 and 2:

$$H_0: \sigma_1^2 = \sigma_2^2$$
$$H_1: \sigma_1^2 \neq \sigma_2^2$$

Step 3: $\alpha = .05$

Step 4: $n_1 = 8$ and $n_2 = 10$

Step 5: Assuming the independent samples are drawn from underlying normal populations, the $F$-test statistic is given by equation (12.5):

$$F = \frac{S_1^2}{S_2^2}$$

Step 6: We use Table E.5 to develop the following decision rule: We reject the null hypothesis if the computed $F$-test statistic exceeds the upper-tailed critical value $F_U$ from the $F$ distribution with $n_1 - 1 = 7$ degrees of freedom from sample 1 in the numerator and $n_2 - 1 = 9$ degrees of freedom from sample 2 in the denominator or if the computed $F$-test statistic falls below the lower-tailed critical value $F_L$ from the $F$ distribution with

$n_1 - 1 = 7$ and $n_2 - 1 = 9$ degrees of freedom in the numerator and denominator, respectively. Because $\alpha = .05$ is split equally into .025 and .025 in the lower- and upper-tail rejection regions, we use the appropriate page of Table E.5 corresponding to an upper-tail area of .025 and we obtain $F_U = 4.20$ directly (see accompanying table).

***Obtaining $F_U$ and $F_L$, the upper- and lower-tail critical values of $F$ with 7 and 9 degrees of freedom using a level of significance $\alpha$ of .05 split equally into each tail***

| DENOMINATOR | NUMERATOR $df_1$ | | | | | | |
|---|---|---|---|---|---|---|---|
| $df_2$ | 1 | 2 | 3 | ... | 7 | 8 | 9 |
| 1 | 647.8 | 799.5 | 864.2 | ... | 948.2 | 956.7 | 963.3 |
| 2 | 38.51 | 39.00 | 39.17 | ... | 39.36 | 39.37 | 39.39 |
| 3 | 17.44 | 16.04 | 15.44 | ... | 14.62 | 14.54 | 14.47 |
| ⋮ | ⋮ | ⋮ | ⋮ | ⋮ | ⋮ | ⋮ | ⋮ |
| 7 | 8.07 | 6.54 | 5.89 | ... | 4.99 | 4.90 | 4.82 |
| 8 | 7.57 | 6.06 | 5.42 | ... | 4.53 | 4.43 | 4.36 |
| 9 | 7.21 | 5.71 | 5.08 | ... | 4.20 | 4.10 | 4.03 |

*Source: Extracted from Table E.5.*

For a computed value of the $F$-test statistic greater than 1, the decision rule is

$$\text{Reject } H_0 \text{ if } F > F_U = 4.20.$$

For a computed value of the $F$-test statistic below, the decision rule is

$$\text{Reject } H_0 \text{ if } F < F_L$$

where $F_L$ with the desired 7 and 9 degrees of freedom in the numerator and denominator, respectively, is obtained by taking the reciprocal of $F_{U*}$ with degrees of freedom "switched" to 9 in the numerator and 7 in the denominator. Thus, from equation (12.6) and the table above

$$F_L = \frac{1}{F_{U*}} = \frac{1}{4.82} = 0.207$$

If the computed value of the $F$-test statistic falls within the boundaries of $F_L = 0.207$ and $F_U = 4.20$, we do not reject $H_0$.

Step 7: From equation (12.5) we compute the $F$-test statistic to be

$$F = \frac{S_1^2}{S_2^2} = \frac{56.0}{24.0} = 2.33$$

Steps 8, 9, and 10: Because the $F$-test statistic of 2.33 falls within the boundaries of $F_L = 0.207$ and $F_U = 4.20$, we do not reject $H_0$. Using a .05 level of significance, we conclude that there is no evidence of a difference in the variation in these two independent populations. Although one of the samples has a variance 2.33 times the size of the other sample's variance, this observed difference is due to chance.

## COMMENT: *Checking the Assumptions*

In testing for the equality of two population variances, be aware that the test assumes that each of the two populations is normally distributed. That is, if the assumption of normality for each population is met, the $F$-test statistic follows an $F$ distribution with $n_1 - 1$ degrees of freedom from sample 1 in the numerator and $n_2 - 1$ degrees of freedom from sample 2 in the denominator. Unfortunately, this $F$-test statistic is not *robust* to departures from this assumption (reference 1), particularly when the sample sizes in the two groups are not equal. Therefore, if the populations are not at least approximately normally distributed, the accuracy of the procedure can be seriously affected. (References 1–3 present other procedures for testing the equality of two variances.)

---

## Problems for Section 12.2

### Learning the Basics

• **12.18** Determine $F_U$ and $F_L$, the upper- and lower-tail critical values of $F$ in each of the following two-tailed tests:
  (a) $\alpha = .10$, $n_1 = 16$, $n_2 = 21$
  (b) $\alpha = .05$, $n_1 = 16$, $n_2 = 21$
  (c) $\alpha = .02$, $n_1 = 16$, $n_2 = 21$
  (d) $\alpha = .01$, $n_1 = 16$, $n_2 = 21$
  (e) Given your results in parts (a)–(d), what do you conclude regarding the width of the region of nonrejection as the selected level of significance $\alpha$ gets smaller?

**12.19** Determine $F_U$, the upper-tail critical value of $F$ in each of the following one-tailed tests:
  (a) $\alpha = .05$, $n_1 = 16$, $n_2 = 21$
  (b) $\alpha = .025$, $n_1 = 16$, $n_2 = 21$
  (c) $\alpha = .01$, $n_1 = 16$, $n_2 = 21$
  (d) $\alpha = .005$, $n_1 = 16$, $n_2 = 21$
  (e) Given your results in parts (a)–(d), what do you conclude about the width of the region of nonrejection as the selected level of significance $\alpha$ gets smaller?

• **12.20** Determine $F_L$, the lower-tail critical value of $F$ in each of the following one-tailed tests:
  (a) $\alpha = .05$, $n_1 = 16$, $n_2 = 21$
  (b) $\alpha = .025$, $n_1 = 16$, $n_2 = 21$
  (c) $\alpha = .01$, $n_1 = 16$, $n_2 = 21$
  (d) $\alpha = .005$, $n_1 = 16$, $n_2 = 21$
  (e) Given your results in parts (a)–(d), what do you conclude regarding the width of the region of nonrejection as the selected level of significance $\alpha$ gets smaller?

**12.21** Suppose that the following information is available for two samples drawn from independent normally distributed populations:

$$n_1 = 25 \qquad S_1^2 = 133.7 \qquad n_2 = 25 \qquad S_2^2 = 161.9$$

What is the value of the $F$-test statistic if we are testing the null hypothesis $H_0$ of equality of population variances ($\sigma_1^2 = \sigma_2^2$)?

**12.22** In Problem 12.21 how many degrees of freedom are there in the numerator and denominator of the $F$ test?

**12.23** In Problems 12.21 and 12.22 what are the critical values for $F_U$ and $F_L$ from Table E.5 if the level of significance $\alpha$ is chosen to be .05 and the alternative hypothesis is $H_1$: $\sigma_1^2 \neq \sigma_2^2$?

**12.24** In Problems 12.21–12.23 what is your statistical decision?

- **12.25** Suppose that the following information is available for two samples drawn from independent but very right-skewed populations.

$$n_1 = 16 \qquad S_1^2 = 47.3 \qquad n_2 = 13 \qquad S_2^2 = 36.4$$

Would you use the $F$ test to test the null hypothesis of equality of variances ($H_0: \sigma_1^2 = \sigma_2^2$)? Discuss.

- **12.26** If the two samples are drawn from independent normally distributed populations in Problem 12.25:
  - (a) At the .05 level of significance, is there evidence of a difference between $\sigma_1^2$ and $\sigma_2^2$?
  - (b) Suppose that we wanted to perform a one-tailed test. At the .05 level of significance, what is the upper-tailed critical value of the $F$-test statistic to determine if there is evidence that $\sigma_1^2 > \sigma_2^2$? What is your statistical decision?
  - (c) Suppose that we wanted to perform a one-tailed test. At the .05 level of significance, what is the lower-tailed critical value of the $F$-test statistic to determine if there is evidence that $\sigma_1^2 < \sigma_2^2$? What is your statistical decision?

## Applying the Concepts

**12.27** A professor in the accounting department of a business school claims that there is much more variability in the final exam scores of students taking the introductory accounting course as a requirement than for students taking the course as part of their majors. Random samples of 13 nonaccounting majors and 10 accounting majors are taken from the professor's class roster in his large lecture, and the following results are computed based on the final exam scores:

$$n_1 = 13 \qquad S_1^2 = 210.2 \qquad n_2 = 10 \qquad S_2^2 = 36.5$$

  - (a) At the .05 level of significance, is there evidence to support the professor's claim?
  - (b) Using Table E.5, find upper and lower approximation limits on the $p$-value.
  - (c) What assumptions do you make here about the two populations in order to justify your use of the $F$ test?

**12.28** A carpet manufacturer is studying differences between two of its major outlet stores. The company is particularly interested in the time it takes customers to receive carpeting that was ordered from the plant. Data concerning a sample of delivery times for the most popular type of carpet are summarized as follows.

|                  | STORE A   | STORE B   |
|------------------|-----------|-----------|
| $\overline{X}$   | 34.3 days | 43.7 days |
| $S$              | 2.4 days  | 3.1 days  |
| $n$              | 41        | 31        |

  - (a) At the .01 level of significance, is there evidence of a difference in the variances of the shipping time between the two outlets?
  - (b) Using Table E.5, find upper and lower limits on the $p$-value.
  - (c) What assumptions do you make here about the two populations to justify your use of the $F$ test?
  - (d) On the basis of your findings in part (a), which of the two $t$ tests, the pooled-variance test or the separate-variance test, is more appropriate for comparing the means of the two outlets? Discuss.

**12.29** An industrial psychologist wishes to study the effects of motivation on sales in a particular firm. Of 24 new salespersons, 12 are paid an hourly rate and 12 are paid a commission. The 24 individuals are randomly assigned to the two groups. The following data represent the sales volume (in thousands of dollars) achieved during the first month on the job.

| HOURLY RATE | | | | COMMISSION | | | |
|---|---|---|---|---|---|---|---|
| 256 | 212 | 207 | 219 | 224 | 261 | 285 | 225 |
| 239 | 216 | 228 | 225 | 254 | 228 | 237 | 232 |
| 222 | 236 | 241 | 230 | 273 | 234 | 277 | 245 |

DATA FILE
SALESVOL

(a) Using a .01 level of significance, is there evidence of a difference in the variances in sales volume achieved by the two groups?
(b) On the basis of the results obtained in part (a), which test should be selected to compare the means of the two groups—the pooled-variance $t$ test or the separate-variance $t$ test? Discuss.

• **12.30** A manufacturer is developing a nickel-metal hydride battery that is to be used in cellular telephones in lieu of nickel-cadmium batteries. The director of quality control decides to evaluate the newly developed battery against the widely used nickel-cadmium battery with respect to performance. A random sample of 25 nickel-cadmium batteries and a random sample of 25 of the newly developed nickel-metal hydride batteries are placed in cellular telephones of the same brand and model. The performance measure of interest is the talking time (in minutes) prior to recharging. The results are as follows:

| NICKEL-CADMIUM BATTERY | | | NICKEL-METAL HYDRIDE BATTERY | | |
|---|---|---|---|---|---|
| 54.5 | 71.0 | 67.0 | 78.3 | 103.0 | 79.8 |
| 67.8 | 41.7 | 56.7 | 95.4 | 81.3 | 91.1 |
| 64.5 | 69.7 | 86.8 | 69.4 | 46.4 | 82.8 |
| 70.4 | 40.8 | 74.9 | 87.3 | 82.3 | 71.8 |
| 72.5 | 75.4 | 76.9 | 62.5 | 83.2 | 77.5 |
| 64.9 | 81.0 | 104.4 | 85.0 | 85.3 | 74.3 |
| 83.3 | 90.4 | 82.0 | 85.3 | 85.5 | 86.1 |
| 72.8 | 71.8 | 58.7 | 72.1 | 112.3 | 74.1 |
| 68.8 | | | 41.1 | | |

DATA FILE
NICKBAT

(a) Using a .05 level of significance, is there evidence of a difference in the variances in talking time (in minutes) prior to recharging between the two types of batteries?
(b) On the basis of the results obtained in part (a), which test should be selected to compare the means of the two groups—the pooled-variance $t$ test or the separate-variance $t$ test? Discuss.

**12.31** A public official working on health care reform policy wants to compare occupancy rates (i.e., average annual percentage of beds filled) in urban versus suburban hospitals within his state. A random sample of 16 urban hospitals and a random sample of 16 suburban hospitals are selected within the state and the occupancy rates are recorded as follows.

| URBAN HOSPITALS | | | | SUBURBAN HOSPITALS | | | |
|---|---|---|---|---|---|---|---|
| 76.5 | 73.3 | 79.4 | 70.4 | 71.5 | 63.0 | 71.2 | 67.4 |
| 75.9 | 77.4 | 78.7 | 77.7 | 73.4 | 76.0 | 67.8 | 62.6 |
| 79.6 | 79.0 | 78.6 | 78.1 | 74.6 | 75.5 | 76.9 | 73.0 |
| 77.5 | 79.9 | 79.3 | 75.9 | 74.3 | 70.7 | 60.0 | 76.5 |

DATA FILE
HOSPITAL

(a) Using a .05 level of significance, is there evidence of a difference in the variances in occupancy rates between urban and suburban hospitals in this state?

(b) On the basis of the results obtained in part (a), which test should be selected to compare the means of the two groups—the pooled-variance *t* test or the separate-variance *t* test? Discuss.

**12.32** The director of training for a company manufacturing electronic equipment is interested in determining whether different training methods have an effect on the productivity of assembly line employees. She randomly assigns 42 recently hired employees to two groups of 21, of which the first received a computer-assisted, individual-based training program and the other received a team-based training program. Upon completion of the training, the employees were evaluated on the time (in seconds) it took to assemble a part. The results are as follows:

| COMPUTER-ASSISTED, INDIVIDUAL-BASED PROGRAM | | | TEAM-BASED PROGRAM | | |
|---|---|---|---|---|---|
| 19.4 | 16.7 | 16.5 | 22.4 | 13.8 | 23.7 |
| 20.7 | 19.3 | 17.7 | 18.7 | 18.0 | 17.4 |
| 21.8 | 16.8 | 16.2 | 19.3 | 20.8 | 23.2 |
| 14.1 | 17.7 | 17.4 | 15.6 | 17.1 | 20.1 |
| 16.1 | 19.8 | 16.4 | 18.0 | 28.2 | 12.3 |
| 16.8 | 19.3 | 16.8 | 21.7 | 20.8 | 15.2 |
| 14.7 | 16.0 | 18.5 | 30.7 | 24.7 | 16.0 |

**DATA FILE**
**TRAINING**

(a) Using a .05 level of significance, is there evidence of a difference in the variances in assembly times (in seconds) between employees trained in a computer-assisted, individual-based program and those trained in a team-based program?

(b) On the basis of the results obtained in part (a), which test should be selected to compare the means of the two groups—the pooled-variance *t* test or the separate-variance *t* test? Discuss.

## 12.3 COMPARING TWO RELATED SAMPLES: *t* TEST FOR THE MEAN DIFFERENCE

The hypothesis-testing procedures examined thus far enable us to make comparisons and examine differences between two *independent* populations based on samples containing numerical data. In this section, we develop a procedure for analyzing the difference between the means of two groups when the sample data are obtained from populations that are **related,** that is, when results of the first group are *not* independent of the second group. This "dependency" characteristic of the two groups occurs either because the items or individuals are **paired** or **matched** according to some characteristic or because **repeated measurements** are obtained from the same set of items or individuals. In either case, the variable of interest becomes the *difference between the values* of the observations rather than the *values* of the observations themselves.

The first approach to the related-samples problem involves the matching or pairing of items or individuals according to some characteristic of interest. For example, in test-marketing a product under two different advertising and promotion strategies, a sample of test markets can be *matched* on the basis of the test-market population size and/or other socio-economic and demographic variables. By controlling these variables, we are better able to measure the effects of the two different advertising and promotion campaigns.

The second approach to the related-samples problem involves taking repeated measurements on the same items or individuals. Under the theory that the same items or individuals will behave alike if treated alike, the objective of the analysis is to show that any differences between two measurements of the same items or individuals are due to different treatment conditions. For example, when performing a taste-testing experiment, each subject in the sample can be used as his or her own control so that *repeated measurements* on the same individual are obtained.

Regardless of whether matched (paired) samples or repeated measurements are utilized, the objective is to study the difference between two measurements by reducing the effect of the variability that is due to the items or individuals themselves. In this section we develop an important test procedure to accomplish this: the *t* test for the mean difference in related samples.

To determine whether any difference exists between two related groups, the differences in the individual values in each group are obtained as shown in Table 12.4. To read this table, let $X_{11}, X_{12}, \ldots, X_{1n}$ represent the $n$ observations from a sample. Now let $X_{21}, X_{22}, \ldots, X_{2n}$ represent either the corresponding $n$ matched observations from a second sample or the corresponding $n$ repeated measurements from the initial sample. Then, $D_1, D_2, \ldots, D_n$ will represent the corresponding set of $n$ **difference scores** such that

$$D_1 = X_{11} - X_{21}, D_2 = X_{12} - X_{22}, \ldots, \text{and } D_n = X_{1n} - X_{2n}$$

From the central limit theorem, the average difference $\overline{D}$ follows a normal distribution when the population standard deviation of the difference $\sigma_D$ is known and the sample size is large enough. The Z-test statistic is computed as follows.

### Table 12.4    *Determining the difference between two related groups*

| OBSERVATION | GROUP 1 | GROUP 2 | DIFFERENCE |
|:---:|:---:|:---:|:---|
| 1 | $X_{11}$ | $X_{21}$ | $D_1 = X_{11} - X_{21}$ |
| 2 | $X_{12}$ | $X_{22}$ | $D_2 = X_{12} - X_{22}$ |
| . | . | . | . |
| . | . | . | . |
| . | . | . | . |
| $i$ | $X_{1i}$ | $X_{2i}$ | $D_i = X_{1i} - X_{2i}$ |
| . | . | . | . |
| . | . | . | . |
| . | . | . | . |
| $n$ | $X_{1n}$ | $X_{2n}$ | $D_n = X_{1n} - X_{2n}$ |

### Z Test for the Mean Difference

$$Z = \frac{\overline{D} - \mu_D}{\dfrac{\sigma_D}{\sqrt{n}}}$$

(12.7)

where

$$\overline{D} = \frac{\displaystyle\sum_{i=1}^{n} D_i}{n}$$

$\mu_D$ = hypothesized mean difference

$\sigma_D$ = population standard deviation of the difference scores

$n$ = sample size

As mentioned previously, in most cases we do not know the actual standard deviation in a population. The only information usually obtainable is the summary statistics such as the sample mean, the sample variance, and the sample standard deviation.

If we assume that the sample of difference scores is randomly and independently drawn from a population that is normally distributed, a $t$ test can be used to determine whether there is a significant population mean difference. Thus, analogous to the (one-sample) $t$ test developed in section 11.6 [see equation (11.2) on page 434], the $t$-test statistic developed here follows the $t$ distribution with $n - 1$ degrees of freedom.

---

**COMMENT:** *Assumptions of the t Test for the Mean Difference*

Although the population is assumed to be normally distributed, in practice it has been found that as long as the sample size is not very small and the population is not very skewed, the $t$ distribution gives a good approximation to the sampling distribution of the average difference $\overline{D}$.

---

To test the null hypothesis of no difference in the means of two related populations (i.e., the population mean difference $\mu_D$ is 0)

$$H_0: \mu_D = 0 \ (\text{where } \mu_D = \mu_1 - \mu_2)$$

against the alternative that the means are not the same (i.e., the population mean difference $\mu_D$ is not 0)

$$H_1: \mu_D \neq 0$$

the following $t$-test statistic is computed

## *t* Test for the Mean Difference

$$t = \frac{\overline{D} - \mu_D}{\frac{S_D}{\sqrt{n}}} \tag{12.8}$$

where

$$\overline{D} = \frac{\sum_{i=1}^{n} D_i}{n}$$

and

$$S_D = \sqrt{\frac{\sum_{i=1}^{n}(D_i - \overline{D})^2}{n-1}}$$

For a given level of significance $\alpha$ we reject the null hypothesis if the computed *t*-test statistic exceeds the upper-tailed critical value $t_{n-1}$ from the *t* distribution or if the computed test statistic falls below the lower-tailed critical value $-t_{n-1}$ from the *t* distribution. That is, the decision rule is

$$\text{Reject } H_0 \text{ if } t > t_{n-1}$$
$$\text{or if } t < -t_{n-1};$$
$$\text{otherwise do not reject } H_0.$$

To illustrate the use of the *t* test for the mean difference, suppose that a software applications company is developing a new financial applications package. Because computer processing time is an important decision criterion, the developer wants the new package to have the same features and capabilities as the current market leader while providing results faster than the current leading package. If the new financial package is effective, it will provide the same results as does the current market leader but use less computer processing time.

As a test of the worthiness of the new software package, an experiment is designed where particular financial applications projects will be used by the new software package as well as by the current market leader. By using a particular set of financial applications projects on both packages, each project is its own control. Therefore, we simply evaluate differences in the times required to achieve the desired results by comparing the average differences in the two time readings rather than comparing the difference in the average completion times from two independent samples of financial applications projects, one of which uses the new software package while the other uses the current market leading package.

This latter approach of comparing two independent samples is presented in sections 12.1, 12.2, and 12.4 . Here, however, we should note that obtaining the two time readings (one for the new software package and one for the current market leader) for each financial appli-

**Table 12.5**  *Repeated measurements of time in seconds to complete financial applications projects on two competing software packages*

| APPLICATIONS PROJECT USER | COMPLETION TIMES (IN SECONDS) | |
| --- | --- | --- |
| | BY CURRENT MARKET LEADER | BY NEW SOFTWARE PACKAGE |
| C.B. | 9.98 | 9.88 |
| T.F. | 9.88 | 9.86 |
| M.H. | 9.84 | 9.75 |
| R.K. | 9.99 | 9.80 |
| M.O. | 9.94 | 9.87 |
| D.S. | 9.84 | 9.84 |
| S.S. | 9.86 | 9.87 |
| C.T. | 10.12 | 9.86 |
| K.T. | 9.90 | 9.83 |
| S.Z. | 9.91 | 9.86 |

DATA FILE
COMPTIME

cations project serves to reduce the variability in the time readings compared with what would occur if two independent sets of financial applications projects were used. It also enables us to focus on the differences between the two time readings for each financial applications project in order to measure the effectiveness of the new software package.

The results displayed in Table 12.5 are for a sample of $n = 10$ financial applications projects used in the experiment.

The question that must be answered is whether or not this new software package is faster. That is, is there evidence that significantly more processing time is required on average when financial applications projects employ the current market leader rather than the new software package? Thus, we have the following null and alternative hypotheses:

$H_0$: $\mu_D \leq 0$ (average processing time for the old package is lower than or the same as that for the new package)

$H_1$: $\mu_D > 0$ (average processing time is higher for the old package than the new package)

Choosing a level of significance $\alpha$ of .05 and assuming the differences are normally distributed, we use the paired-sample $t$ test [equation (12.8)] to test the null hypothesis that the average processing time is not higher for the old package. For a sample of $n = 10$ projects using Table E.3, the decision rule is:

$$\text{Reject } H_0 \text{ if } t > t_9 = 1.8331$$

$$\text{otherwise do not reject } H_0.$$

For the data set pertaining to the random sample of $n = 10$ differences, we compute the sample mean difference

$$\overline{D} = \frac{\sum\limits_{i=1}^{n} D_i}{n} = \frac{0.84}{10} = 0.084$$

We then compute the sample standard deviation

$$S_D = \sqrt{\frac{\sum\limits_{i=1}^{n} (D_i - \overline{D})^2}{n-1}} = 0.0844$$

From equation (12.8) we then obtain

$$t = \frac{\overline{D} - \mu_D}{\dfrac{S_D}{\sqrt{n}}} = \frac{0.084 - 0}{\dfrac{0.0844}{\sqrt{10}}} = +3.15$$

Because $t = +3.15$ falls within the rejection region above 1.8331 we can reject the null hypothesis $H_0$ (see Figure 12.11). There is evidence to believe that the average processing time is higher for the current market leader than for the new package.

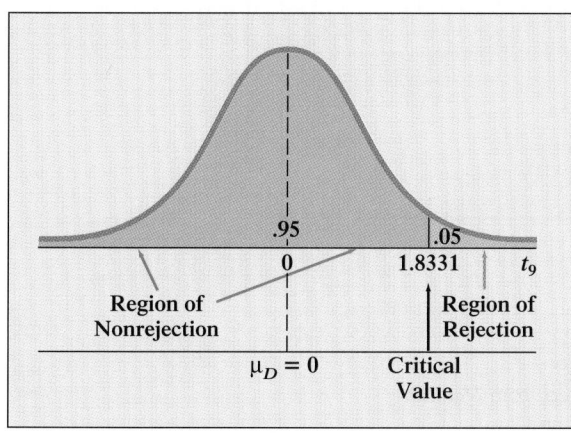

**FIGURE 12.11**
One-tailed $t$ test for the mean difference at the .05 level of significance with 9 degrees of freedom

Using Minitab (see Figure 12.12 on page 504), we can obtain this test statistic, along with the $p$-value and the box-and-whisker plot. Because the $p$-value $= .006 < \alpha = .05$, our conclusion is to reject $H_0$. We also observe that Minitab provides a confidence interval estimate of the average difference. The box-and-whisker plot of panel B shows symmetry between the first and third quartiles, with the presence of two extremely high values. In addition, the confidence interval for the average difference and the null hypothesis are displayed.

The $t$ test to be performed can be either two-tailed or one-tailed, depending on whether we are testing if the two population means are merely *different* (i.e., the population mean difference $\mu_D \neq 0$) or if one mean is *greater than* the other mean (i.e., the population mean difference $\mu_D < 0$ or the population mean difference $\mu_D > 0$). The three panels of Figure 12.13 on page 504 indicate the null and alternative hypotheses and rejection regions for the possible two-tailed and one-tailed tests. If, as shown in panel A, the test of hypothesis is two-tailed, the rejection region is split into the lower and upper tails of the $t$ distribution. However, if the test is one-tailed, the rejection region is either in the lower tail (panel B of Figure 12.13) or in the upper tail (panel C of Figure 12.13) of the $t$ distribution, depending on the direction of the alternative hypothesis.

```
               N      Mean      StDev    SE Mean
Current        10    9.9260    0.0863    0.0273
New            10    9.8420    0.0399    0.0126
Difference     10    0.0840    0.0844    0.0267

95% CI for mean difference: (0.0237, 0.1443)
T-Test of mean difference = 0 (vs > 0): T-Value = 3.15  P-Value = 0.006
```

**PANEL A**

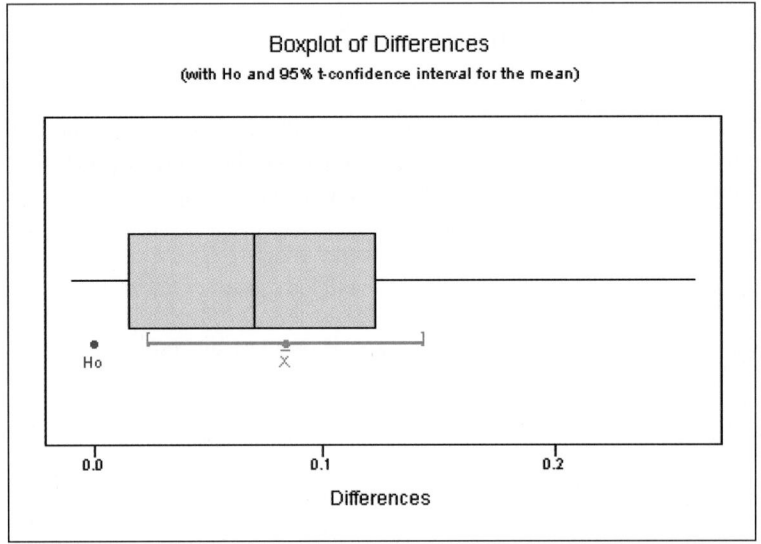

**PANEL B**

**FIGURE 12.12**   Paired *t* test for the financial packages data obtained from Minitab

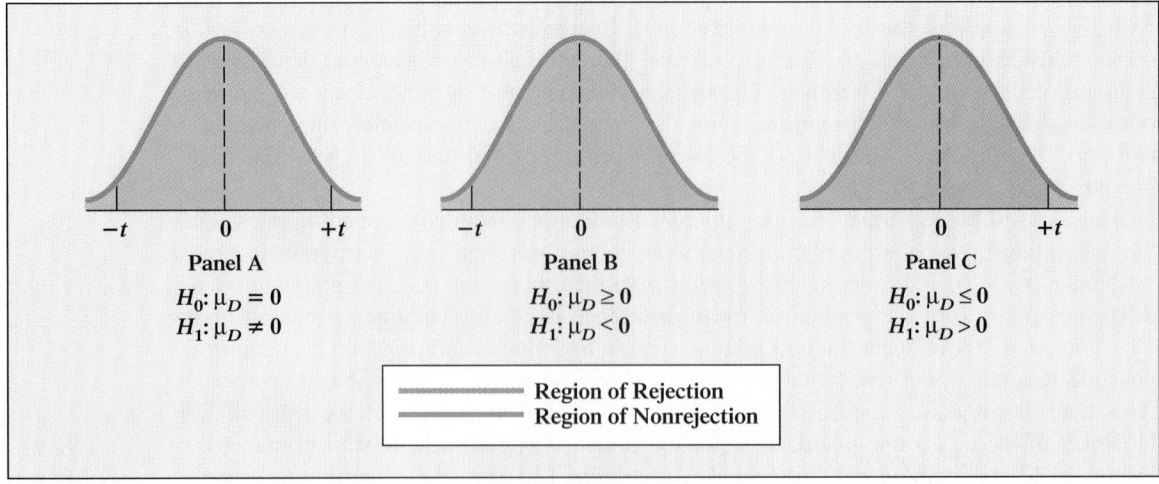

**FIGURE 12.13**   Regions of rejection and nonrejection when testing for the mean difference in related samples

## Problems for Section 12.3

### Learning the Basics

**12.33** An experimental design for a paired *t* test has, as a matched sample, 20 pairs of identical twins. How many degrees of freedom are there in this *t* test?

**12.34** An experimental design for a repeated-measures *t* test requires a measurement before and after the presentation of a stimulus on each of 15 subjects. How many degrees of freedom are there in this *t* test?

### Applying the Concepts

● **12.35** The manager of a nationally known real estate agency has just completed a training session on appraisals for two newly hired agents. To evaluate the effectiveness of his training, the manager wishes to determine whether there is any difference in the appraised values placed on houses by these two different individuals. A sample of 12 houses is selected by the manager, and each agent is assigned the task of placing an appraised value (in thousands of dollars) on the 12 houses. The results are as follows:

| HOUSE | AGENT 1 | AGENT 2 |
|-------|---------|---------|
| 1 | 181.0 | 182.0 |
| 2 | 179.9 | 180.0 |
| 3 | 163.0 | 161.5 |
| 4 | 218.0 | 215.0 |
| 5 | 213.0 | 216.5 |
| 6 | 175.0 | 175.0 |
| 7 | 217.9 | 219.5 |
| 8 | 151.0 | 150.0 |
| 9 | 164.9 | 165.5 |
| 10 | 192.5 | 195.0 |
| 11 | 225.0 | 222.7 |
| 12 | 177.5 | 178.0 |

DATA FILE
REAPPR

(a) At the .05 level of significance, is there evidence of a difference in the average appraised values given by the two agents?
(b) What assumption is necessary to perform this test?
(c) Find the *p*-value in (a) and interpret its meaning.

**12.36** Suppose that a shoe company wants to test material for the soles of shoes. For each pair of shoes the new material is placed on one shoe and the old material is placed on the other shoe. After a given period of time a random sample of 10 pairs of shoes is selected. The wear is measured on a 10-point scale (higher is better) with the following results:

DATA FILE
SHOESOLE

| | PAIR NUMBER | | | | | | | | | |
| MATERIAL | I | II | III | IV | V | VI | VII | VIII | IX | X |
|---|---|---|---|---|---|---|---|---|---|---|
| New | 2 | 4 | 5 | 7 | 7 | 5 | 9 | 8 | 8 | 7 |
| Old | 4 | 5 | 3 | 8 | 9 | 4 | 7 | 8 | 5 | 6 |
| Differences | −2 | −1 | +2 | −1 | −2 | +1 | +2 | 0 | +3 | +1 |

(a) At the .05 level of significance, is there evidence of a difference in the average wear for the new material and the old material?
(b) What assumption is necessary to perform this test?
(c) Find the *p*-value in (a) and interpret its meaning.

• **12.37** A few engineering students decide to see whether cars that supposedly do not need high-octane gasoline get more miles per gallon using regular or high-octane gas. They test several cars (under similar road surface, weather, and other driving conditions), using both types of gas in each car at different times. The mileage for each gas type for each car is as follows:

DATA FILE
GASMILE

| | CAR | | | | | | | | | |
| GAS TYPE | #1 | #2 | #3 | #4 | #5 | #6 | #7 | #8 | #9 | #10 |
|---|---|---|---|---|---|---|---|---|---|---|
| Regular | 15 | 23 | 21 | 35 | 42 | 28 | 19 | 32 | 31 | 24 |
| High-octane | 18 | 21 | 25 | 34 | 47 | 30 | 19 | 27 | 34 | 20 |

(a) Is there any evidence of a difference in the average gasoline mileage between regular and high-octane gas? (Use $\alpha = .05$.)
(b) What assumption is necessary to perform this test?
(c) Find the *p*-value in (a) and interpret its meaning.

**12.38** In order to measure the effect of a storewide sales campaign on nonsale items, the research director of a national supermarket chain took a random sample of 13 pairs of stores that were matched according to average weekly sales volume. One store of each pair (the experimental group) was exposed to the sales campaign, and the other member of the pair (the control group) was not. The following data indicate the results over a weekly period:

| STORE | WITH SALES CAMPAIGN | WITHOUT SALES CAMPAIGN |
|---|---|---|
| 1 | 67.2 | 65.3 |
| 2 | 59.4 | 54.7 |
| 3 | 80.1 | 81.3 |
| 4 | 47.6 | 39.8 |
| 5 | 97.8 | 92.5 |
| 6 | 38.4 | 37.9 |
| 7 | 57.3 | 52.4 |
| | | *(continued)* |

| STORE | WITH SALES CAMPAIGN | WITHOUT SALES CAMPAIGN |
|-------|---------------------|------------------------|
| 8 | 75.2 | 69.9 |
| 9 | 94.7 | 89.0 |
| 10 | 64.3 | 58.4 |
| 11 | 31.7 | 33.0 |
| 12 | 49.3 | 41.7 |
| 13 | 54.0 | 53.6 |

DATA FILE
SALESCMP

(a) At the .05 level of significance, can the research director conclude that there is evidence that the sales campaign has increased the average sales of nonsale items?
(b) What assumption is necessary to perform this test?
(c) Find the $p$-value in (a) and interpret its meaning.

**12.39** A professor in the school of business wants to investigate the prices of new textbooks in the campus bookstore and the competing off-campus store, which is a branch of a national chain. The professor randomly chooses the required texts for 12 business school courses and compares the prices in the two stores. The results are as follows:

| BOOK | CAMPUS STORE | OFF-CAMPUS STORE |
|------|--------------|------------------|
| #1 | $55.00 | $50.95 |
| #2 | 47.50 | 45.75 |
| #3 | 50.50 | 50.95 |
| #4 | 38.95 | 38.50 |
| #5 | 58.70 | 56.25 |
| #6 | 49.90 | 45.95 |
| #7 | 39.95 | 40.25 |
| #8 | 41.50 | 39.95 |
| #9 | 42.25 | 43.00 |
| #10 | 44.95 | 42.25 |
| #11 | 45.95 | 44.00 |
| #12 | 56.95 | 55.60 |

DATA FILE
BKPRICE

(a) At the .01 level of significance, is there any evidence of a difference in the average price of business textbooks between the two stores?
(b) What assumption is necessary to perform this test?
(c) Find the $p$-value in (a) and interpret its meaning.

**12.40** The National Association of Realtors reported that the median price of previously owned, single-family homes rose 5% on average in the third-quarter 1997, from the third-quarter 1996 (*USA Today*, November 14, 1997, 6B). The data at the top of page 508 are median prices (in thousands of dollars) of such homes in a random sample of 15 metropolitan areas selected across the United States over two time periods:
(a) At the .05 level of significance, is there any evidence of an increase in the average of median prices over the 1-year period?
(b) What assumption is necessary to perform this test?
(c) Find the $p$-value in (a) and interpret its meaning.

| METROPOLITAN AREA | THIRD-QTR 97 PRICE | THIRD-QTR 96 PRICE |
|---|---|---|
| Baltimore, MD | 120.8 | 115.4 |
| Buffalo, NY | 81.0 | 81.3 |
| Cincinnati, OH | 113.7 | 105.5 |
| Daytona Beach, FL | 73.6 | 74.3 |
| Fort Wayne, IN | 86.5 | 80.8 |
| Honolulu, HI | 315.0 | 335.1 |
| Kansas City, MO | 107.6 | 99.9 |
| Louisville, KY | 99.6 | 93.6 |
| Monmouth, NJ | 152.7 | 148.1 |
| Oklahoma City, OK | 80.0 | 76.7 |
| Portland, OR | 155.4 | 144.6 |
| Sacramento, CA | 119.3 | 116.7 |
| Shreveport, LA | 82.7 | 78.0 |
| Tallahassee, FL | 115.3 | 106.0 |
| West Palm Beach, FL | 137.8 | 129.0 |

**DATA FILE
NAR**

*Reprinted by permission of National Association of REALTORS®.*

(d) Using a .05 level of significance, test the National Association of Realtors' claim that the average rise in the median price over this 1-year period is 6.0 thousand dollars. (*Hint*: Under the null hypothesis $\mu_D = 6.0$ thousand dollars.)

(e) What are your conclusions? Discuss.

**12.41** Over the past year the vice president for human resources at a large medical center ran a series of 3-month programs and lectures aimed at increasing worker motivation and performance. As a check on the effectiveness of the programs, a random sample of 35 employees was selected from the personnel files and their most recent annual performance ratings were recorded along with the ratings attained prior to attending the programs. The following Minitab output provides both descriptive and inferential information so that you can examine the assumptions of the hypothesis test used and analyze the results.

**DATA FILE
PERFORM**

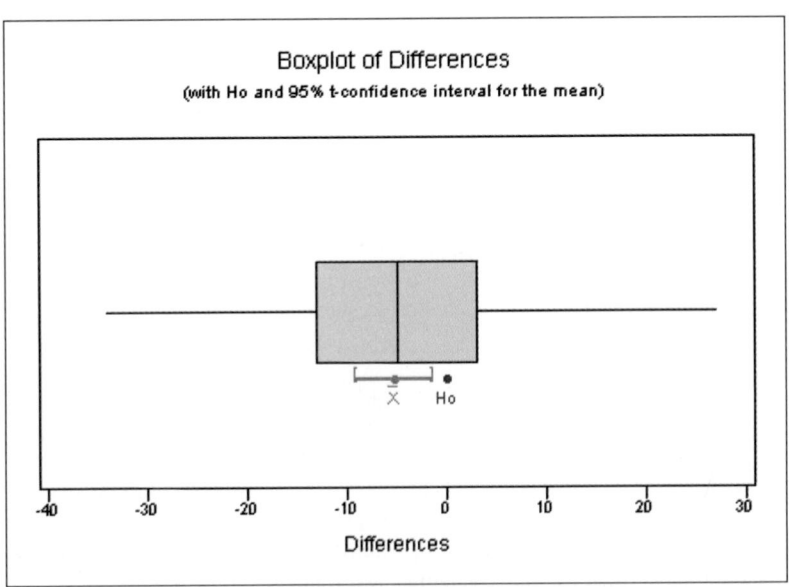

```
Paired T for Before - After

                N        Mean      StDev     SE Mean
Before          35       74.54     8.99       1.52
After           35       79.80     6.10       1.03
Difference      35       -5.26     11.52      1.95

95% CI for mean difference: (-9.22, -1.30)
T-Test of mean difference = 0 (vs < 0): T-Value = -2.70   P-Value = 0.005
```

State your findings and your conclusions in a report you are writing to the vice president for human resources.

 ## 12.4 WILCOXON RANK SUM TEST FOR DIFFERENCES IN TWO MEDIANS (*OPTIONAL TOPIC*)

In section 12.1 we evaluated the difference in the means of samples taken from two independent populations. If sample sizes are small and we cannot or do not wish to make the assumption that the data in each group are taken from normally distributed populations, two choices exist: (1) we can use either the pooled-variance $t$ test or separate-variance $t$ test following some *normalizing transformation* on the data (see reference 8); (2) we can employ some nonparametric procedure, which does not depend on the assumption of normality for the two populations.

In this section we introduce the **Wilcoxon rank sum test**, a widely used, simple, and powerful nonparametric procedure for testing for differences between the medians of two populations. The Wilcoxon rank sum test has proved to be almost as powerful as the pooled- and separate-variance $t$ tests under conditions appropriate to the latter and is likely to be more powerful when the stringent assumptions of those tests are not met. In addition, the Wilcoxon rank sum test is a procedure to choose when only ordinal-type data can be obtained, as is often the case when dealing with studies in consumer behavior and marketing research. The $t$ tests are not used in such situations because these procedures require that the obtained data be measured on at least an interval scale.

To perform the Wilcoxon rank sum test, we replace the observations in the two samples of size $n_1$ and $n_2$ with their combined ranks (unless the obtained data contained the ranks initially). Let $n = n_1 + n_2$ be the total number of observations in both samples. The ranks are assigned in such a manner that rank 1 is given to the smallest of the $n = n_1 + n_2$ combined observations, rank 2 is given to the second-smallest, and so on, until rank $n$ is given to the largest. If several values are tied, we assign each the average of the ranks that would otherwise have been assigned had there been no ties.

For convenience, whenever the two sample sizes are unequal, we let $n_1$ represent the smaller-sized sample and $n_2$ the larger-sized sample. The Wilcoxon rank sum test statistic $T_1$ is chosen as the sum of the ranks assigned to the $n_1$ observations in the smaller sample. (For equal-sized samples, either group may be selected for determining $T_1$.)

As a check on our assigned rankings, we should note that for any integer value $n$, the sum of the first $n$ consecutive integers is calculated as $n(n + 1)/2$. The test statistic $T_1$ plus the sum of the ranks assigned to the $n_2$ items in the second sample, $T_2$, must therefore be equal to this value, as illustrated in equation (12.9).

### Checking the Rankings

$$T_1 + T_2 = \frac{n(n + 1)}{2} \qquad (12.9)$$

The test of the null hypothesis can be either two-tailed or one-tailed, depending on whether we are testing if the two population medians are merely *different* or if one median is *greater than* the other median.

| TWO-TAILED TEST | ONE-TAILED TEST | ONE-TAILED TEST |
|---|---|---|
| $H_0: M_1 = M_2$ | $H_0: M_1 \geq M_2$ | $H_0: M_1 \leq M_2$ |
| $H_1: M_1 \neq M_2$ | $H_1: M_1 < M_2$ | $H_1: M_1 > M_2$ |

where    $M_1$ = median of population 1 having $n_1$ sample observations

$M_2$ = median of population 2 having $n_2$ sample observations

When the sizes of both samples $n_1$ and $n_2$ are not greater than 10, we can use Table E.7 to obtain the critical values of the test statistic $T_1$ for both one- and two-tailed tests at various levels of significance. For a two-tailed test and for a particular level of significance $\alpha$, if the computed value of $T_1$ equals or exceeds the upper critical value or is less than or equal to the lower critical value, the null hypothesis may be rejected. This is depicted in panel A of Figure 12.14.

For one-tailed tests having the alternative $H_1: M_1 < M_2$, the decision rule is to reject the null hypothesis if the observed value of $T_1$ is less than or equal to the lower critical value (see panel B of Figure 12.14).

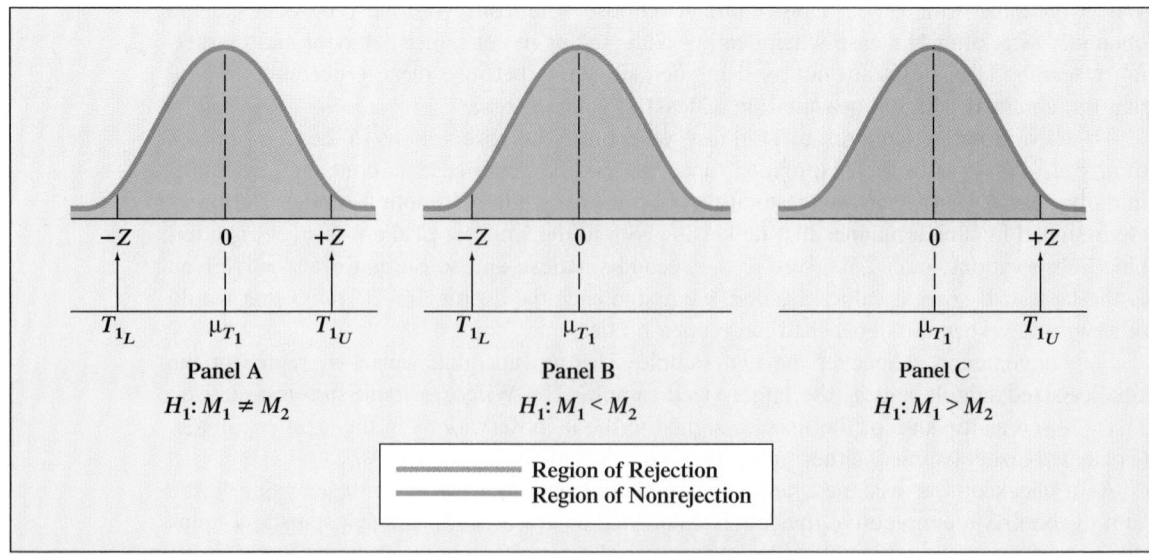

**FIGURE 12.14**   Regions of rejection and nonrejection using the Wilcoxon rank sum test

For one-tailed tests having the alternative $H_1$: $M_1 > M_2$, the decision rule is to reject the null hypothesis if the observed value of $T_1$ equals or exceeds the upper critical value (see panel C of Figure 12.14).

For large sample sizes, the test statistic $T_1$ is approximately normally distributed with mean $\mu_{T_1}$ and standard deviation $\sigma_{T_1}$. We note that $\mu_{T_1}$, the mean value of the test statistic $T_1$, is computed from

$$\mu_{T_1} = \frac{n_1(n + 1)}{2}$$

and $\sigma_{T_1}$, the standard deviation of $T_1$, is calculated from

$$\sigma_{T_1} = \sqrt{\frac{n_1 n_2(n + 1)}{12}}$$

Therefore, the standardized $Z$-test statistic can be defined in equation (12.10) as

## "Large-Sample" Wilcoxon Rank Sum Test

$$Z = \frac{T_1 - \mu_{T_1}}{\sigma_{T_1}} \qquad (12.10)$$

This large-sample approximation formula may be used for testing the null hypothesis when sample sizes are outside the range of Table E.7.

Based on $\alpha$, the level of significance selected, the null hypothesis may be rejected if the computed $Z$-value falls in the appropriate region of rejection, depending on whether a two-tailed or a one-tailed test is used (see Figure 12.14 on page 510).

To demonstrate how we may use the Wilcoxon rank sum test, we return to our Using Statistics application. If as a result of an exploratory data analysis (see the figure accompanying Example 12.1 on pages 478–479), the operations manager does not wish to make the stringent assumption that the samples were taken from populations that are normally distributed, the Wilcoxon rank sum test can be used for evaluating possible differences in the median deviations from the specified target amount of soda fill.[2] The operations manager wants to determine whether or not there is evidence of a significant difference in median deviation from the target based on bottles filled under machinery and equipment dial settings that permit operating pressure levels of either 25 or 30 psi. The data are shown in Table 12.1 on page 475.

Because the operations manager does not specify which of the dial settings is likely to possess a greater median deviation from the specified target, the test is two-tailed, and the following null and alternative hypotheses are established:

$H_0$: $M_1 = M_2$     (the median deviations from target are equal)

$H_1$: $M_1 \neq M_2$     (the median deviations from target are different)

To perform the Wilcoxon rank sum test, we form the combined ranking of the deviations from the specified target obtained from the $n_1 = 10$ bottles filled under an operating pressure level of 25 psi and the $n_2 = 10$ bottles filled under an operating pressure level of 30 psi. The combined ranking of the deviations is displayed in Table 12.6 on page 512.

We then obtain the test statistic $T_1$, the sum of the ranks assigned to the *smaller* sample. When the sample sizes are equal, as in our case, we select either sample as the group from which to obtain the test statistic $T_1$. The choice should not affect our ultimate

[2]*To test for differences in the median deviations from the specified target amount of soft-drink fill, it must be assumed that the distributions of soda fills in both populations from which the random samples were drawn are identical, except possibly for differences in location (i.e., the medians).*

**Table 12.6**    *Forming the combined ranks*

| PRESSURE SETTINGS | | | |
|---|---|---|---|
| **25 PSI** <br> ($n_1 = 10$) | **COMBINED** <br> **RANK** | **30 PSI** <br> ($n_2 = 10$) | **COMBINED** <br> **RANK** |
| $-2.8$ | 1.0 | 0.2 | 5.5 |
| $-1.6$ | 3.0 | 2.1 | 14.0 |
| 0.2 | 5.5 | 2.6 | 15.0 |
| 1.2 | 10.0 | 0.4 | 7.0 |
| $-2.0$ | 2.0 | 1.7 | 13.0 |
| $-1.0$ | 4.0 | 3.3 | 17.0 |
| 1.4 | 11.0 | 1.6 | 12.0 |
| 3.4 | 18.5 | 4.0 | 20.0 |
| 0.6 | 8.0 | 2.7 | 16.0 |
| 0.9 | 9.0 | 3.4 | 18.5 |

*Source: Data are taken from Table 12.1.*

decision. Here, we arbitrarily choose the dial setting with an operating pressure level of 25 psi as our first sample. Therefore,

$$T_1 = 1 + 3 + 5.5 + 10 + 2 + 4 + 11 + 18.5 + 8 + 9 = 72$$

As a check on the ranking procedure we also obtain $T_2$:

$$T_2 = 5.5 + 14 + 15 + 7 + 13 + 17 + 12 + 20 + 16 + 18.5 = 138$$

We then use equation (12.9) to show that the sum of the first $n = 20$ integers in the combined ranking is equal to $T_1 + T_2$:

$$T_1 + T_2 = \frac{n(n + 1)}{2}$$

$$72 + 138 = \frac{20(21)}{2} = 210$$

To test the null hypothesis of no difference in the median deviations from a specified target fill in the two populations, we use Table E.7 to determine the lower- and upper-tail critical values for the test statistic $T_1$ in our two-tailed test. From Table 12.7, a replica of Table E.7, we note that for a level of significance of .05, the critical values are 78 and 132. The decision rule is therefore

Reject $H_0$ if $T_1 \geq 132$ or if $T_1 \leq 78$;

otherwise do not reject $H_0$.

Because the test statistic $T_1 = 72$, we reject $H_0$. There is evidence of significant difference in the median deviations from the specified target fill level. The operating pressure level dial setting of 25 psi is superior to the setting of 30 psi because the sample median deviation (0.40 mm) obtained from the 25 psi dial setting is closer to the specified target than is

**Table 12.7** *Obtaining the lower- and upper-tail critical values for the Wilcoxon rank sum test statistic $T_1$ where $n_1 = 10$, $n_2 = 10$, and $\alpha = .05$*

| | $\alpha$ | | $n_1$ | | | | | | |
|---|---|---|---|---|---|---|---|---|---|
| $n_2$ | ONE-TAILED | TWO-TAILED | 4 | 5 | 6 | 7 | 8 | 9 | 10 |
| | | | | | | (LOWER, UPPER) | | | |
| | .05 | .10 | 16,40 | 24,51 | 33,63 | 43,76 | 54,90 | 66,105 | |
| 9 | .025 | .05 | 14,42 | 22,53 | 31,65 | 40,79 | 51,93 | 62,109 | |
| | .01 | .02 | 13,43 | 20,55 | 28,68 | 37,82 | 47,97 | 59,112 | |
| | .005 | .01 | 11,45 | 18,57 | 26,70 | 35,84 | 45,99 | 56,115 | |
| | .05 | .10 | 17,43 | 26,54 | 35,67 | 45,81 | 56,96 | 69,111 | 82,128 |
| 10 | .025 | .05 | 15,45 | 23,57 | 32,70 | 42,84 | 53,99 | 65,115 | 78,132 |
| | .01 | .02 | 13,47 | 21,59 | 29,73 | 39,87 | 49,103 | 61,119 | 74,136 |
| | .005 | .01 | 12,48 | 19,61 | 27,75 | 37,89 | 47,105 | 58,122 | 71,139 |

*Source: Extracted from Table E.7.*

the sample median deviation (2.35) obtained from the 30 psi dial setting. From the Minitab output in Figure 12.15 we observe that the *p*-value is .014, which is less than $\alpha = .05$.

We note that Minitab provides output for the *Mann-Whitney U test*, which is numerically equivalent to our Wilcoxon rank sum test (see references 2, 3, and 5). From Figure 12.15 we note that ETA1 and ETA2 refer to our hypothesized population medians $M_1$ and $M_2$. Also, the test statistic $W = 72$ is our test statistic $T_1$. The actual *p*-value for this two-tailed hypothesis test is .0139, adjusted for ties in the rankings. Although we should use these adjusted *p*-values in making our statistical decisions, a discussion of such adjustments is beyond the scope of this text (see references 1–3).

We note that Table E.7 (lower and upper critical values of the Wilcoxon rank sum test statistic $T_1$) provides critical values only for situations involving small samples, that is, where both $n_1$ and $n_2$ are less than or equal to 10. If either one or both of the sample sizes exceeds 10, the large-sample Z approximation formula [equation (12.10)] must be used to perform the test of hypothesis. Nevertheless, to demonstrate the effectiveness of the large-sample Z approximation formula, even for small sample sizes, we use it for our operations manager's data (Example 12.3).

```
Mann-Whitney Confidence Interval and Test

25PSI      N =  10      Median =      0.400
30PSI      N =  10      Median =      2.350
Point estimate for ETA1-ETA2 is      -2.150
95.5 Percent CI for ETA1-ETA2 is (-3.701,-0.600)
W = 72.0
Test of ETA1 = ETA2   vs   ETA1 not = ETA2 is significant at 0.0140
The test is significant at 0.0139 (adjusted for ties)
```

**FIGURE 12.15** Wilcoxon rank sum test for the soft-drink fill example obtained from Minitab

## Example 12.3 *Wilcoxon Rank Sum Test with Large-Sample Z Approximation Formula*

The operations manager wants to answer the question: Is there evidence of a significant difference in median deviation from the specified target based on bottles filled with equipment dial settings that allow either operating pressure levels of 25 or 30 psi? The data for this along with the corresponding ranks are shown in Table 12.6 on page 512.

### SOLUTION

Using the *steps in hypothesis testing* (Exhibits 11.2 and 11.3 on pages 422 and 425), we have the following:

Steps 1 and 2:

$H_0$: $M_1 = M_2$     (the median deviations from target are equal)

$H_1$: $M_1 \neq M_2$     (the median deviations from target are different)

Step 3:         $\alpha = .05$

Step 4:         $n_1 = 10$, $n_2 = 10$, and $n = 20$

Step 5:  We use the large-sample $Z$ approximation formula given by equation (12.10):

$$Z = \frac{T_1 - \mu_{T_1}}{\sigma_{T_1}}$$

Step 6:  We use Table E.2(b) to develop the following decision rule:

Reject $H_0$ if $Z > +1.96$ or if $Z < -1.96$;

otherwise do not reject $H_0$.

Step 7:  We collect the data and compute the $Z$-test statistic:

$$Z = \frac{T_1 - \mu_{T_1}}{\sigma_{T_1}}$$

where

$$\mu_{T_1} = \frac{n_1(n + 1)}{2} = \frac{10(21)}{2} = 105$$

$$\sigma_{T_1} = \sqrt{\frac{n_1 n_2(n + 1)}{12}} = \sqrt{\frac{10(10)(21)}{12}} = 13.23$$

and

$$Z = \frac{72 - 105}{13.23} = -2.49$$

Steps 8, 9 and 10: Because $Z = -2.49 < -1.96$, the decision is to reject $H_0$. The null hypothesis is rejected because the test statistic $Z$ has fallen into the region of rejection. The *p*-value, or probability of obtaining a test statistic $T_1$ even less than that observed here, which translates to a test statistic $Z$ with a distance even farther from the center of the standard normal distribution than $\pm 2.49$ standard deviations, is .0128 if the null hypothesis of no difference in the medians were true. Because the *p*-value is less than $\alpha = .05$, we reject the null hypothesis. Thus, without having to make the stringent assumption of normality in the original populations, the operations manager concludes that there is evidence of a difference in the median deviations from the specified targets for the two groups. Bottle fills under an operating pressure level of 25 psi are superior to those under an operating pressure level of 30 psi.

The conclusion we just reached using the Wilcoxon rank sum test agrees with our previous findings from the pooled-variance $t$ test. Because we also demonstrated that there is no evidence of a difference in the variability in the dial settings, we have sufficient reason to conclude that the results from this $t$ test and the Wilcoxon rank sum test are plausible. In this situation the viability of the assumption of underlying normality in the data did not affect the decision reached, regardless of the test procedure used.

As we concluded from our exploratory data analysis in Example 12.1, there is no reason to suspect that the underlying populations are not at least approximately normally distributed, so the pooled-variance $t$ test of section 12.1 is likely to be slightly more powerful than the Wilcoxon rank sum test in its ability to detect a false null hypothesis. This phenomenon is observed by comparing the $p$-values of both tests. The more powerful test procedure for a given set of data displays a smaller $p$-value. With the use of Minitab software (see Example 12.1), the $p$-value associated with the $t$ test is .007, whereas the $p$-value associated with the Wilcoxon rank sum test is .0139 (see Figure 12.15).

## COMMENT:  *Good Confirmatory Data Analysis*

Good confirmatory data analysis requires a careful examination of the assumptions made by various competing test procedures. A major criterion for the selection of an appropriate test is how well the obtained data seem to meet its assumptions.

In our analysis of differences in the average deviation from a specified target obtained from the two pressure-level dial settings, we first descriptively examine the measures of central tendency, dispersion, and shape for each of our samples.

In Example 12.1 Minitab is used to obtain box-and-whisker plots and descriptive statistics for each sample. These displays allow us to assess the reasonableness of the assumption of normality. If we feel the assumption of equal spread can be met and if it be plausible that the two populations are similar in shape (even if not bell-shaped), the Wilcoxon rank sum test for the difference in two population medians is the preferred procedure to use.

If on the other hand, through our visual and graphical exploration of the data sets, we have no reason to suspect major violations of the assumption of normality in the shapes of the populations, then the $F$ test is used to test that assumption of equality of population variances. The $F$ test is sensitive to departures from normality, particularly when the two sample sizes are unequal.

However, in the problem of interest to the operations manager, this was not the case—the sample sizes were each 10. In addition, both our descriptive analysis and the results from the $F$ test show no reason to suspect that the assumption of equal variances is violated. This result leads us to prefer the pooled-variance $t$ test to the separate-variance $t$ test if we wish to compare the mean deviation from the specified target because it is more powerful in detecting a significant difference in the population means.

## Problems for Section 12.4

### Learning the Basics

• **12.42** Using Table E.7, determine the lower- and upper-tail critical values for the Wilcoxon rank sum test statistic $T_1$ in each of the following two-tailed tests:

(a) $\alpha = .10$, $n_1 = 6$, $n_2 = 8$
(b) $\alpha = .05$, $n_1 = 6$, $n_2 = 8$
(c) $\alpha = .01$, $n_1 = 6$, $n_2 = 8$
(d) Given your results in parts (a)–(c), what do you conclude regarding the width of the region of nonrejection as the selected level of significance $\alpha$ gets smaller?

**12.43** Using Table E.7, determine the upper-tail critical value for the Wilcoxon rank sum test statistic $T_1$ in each of the following one-tailed tests:

(a) $\alpha = .05$, $n_1 = 6$, $n_2 = 8$
(b) $\alpha = .025$, $n_1 = 6$, $n_2 = 8$
(c) $\alpha = .01$, $n_1 = 6$, $n_2 = 8$
(d) $\alpha = .005$, $n_1 = 6$, $n_2 = 8$
(e) Given your results in parts (a)–(d), what do you conclude regarding the width of the region of nonrejection as the selected level of significance $\alpha$ gets smaller?

• **12.44** Using Table E.7, determine the lower-tail critical value for the Wilcoxon rank sum test statistic $T_1$ in each of the following one-tailed tests:

(a) $\alpha = .05$, $n_1 = 6$, $n_2 = 8$
(b) $\alpha = .025$, $n_1 = 6$, $n_2 = 8$
(c) $\alpha = .01$, $n_1 = 6$, $n_2 = 8$
(d) $\alpha = .005$, $n_1 = 6$, $n_2 = 8$
(e) Given your results in parts (a)–(d), what do you conclude regarding the width of the region of nonrejection as the selected level of significance $\alpha$ gets smaller?

**12.45** Suppose that the following information is available for two samples drawn from independent populations:

Sample 1:   $n_1 = 7$     Assigned ranks: 4 1 8 2 5 10 11

Sample 2:   $n_2 = 9$     Assigned ranks: 7 16 12 9 3 14 13 6 15

What is the value of the test statistic $T_1$ if we are testing the null hypothesis $H_0$ of equality of population medians ($M_1 = M_2$)?

**12.46** In Problem 12.45, what are the lower- and upper-tail critical values for the test statistic $T_1$ from Table E.7 if a .05 level of significance is chosen and the alternative hypothesis is $H_1$: $M_1 \neq M_2$?

**12.47** In Problems 12.45 and 12.46, what is your statistical decision?

• **12.48** Suppose that the following information is available for two samples drawn from independent and similarly shaped right-skewed populations:

Sample 1:   $n_1 = 5$     Data: 1.1 2.3 2.9 3.6 14.7

Sample 2:   $n_2 = 6$     Data: 2.8 4.4 4.4 5.2 6.0 18.5

(a) Replace the observed data by the corresponding ranks (where $1$ = smallest value, $n = n_1 + n_2 = 11$ = largest value) in the combined samples.
(b) What is the value of the test statistic $T_1$?
(c) Obtain the value of $T_2$, the sum of the ranks in the larger sample.
(d) As a check on the accuracy of your rankings, from equation (12.9) demonstrate that

$$T_1 + T_2 = \frac{n(n + 1)}{2}$$

● **12.49** From Problem 12.48, at a level of significance of .05, determine the lower-tail critical value for the Wilcoxon rank sum test statistic $T_1$ if we want to perform a test of the hypothesis $H_0: M_1 \geq M_2$ against the one-tail alternative $H_1: M_1 < M_2$.

● **12.50** From Problems 12.48 and 12.49 what is your statistical decision?

## Applying the Concepts

● **12.51** The vice president for marketing recently recruited 20 outstanding college graduates to be trained in sales and management. The 20 individuals are randomly assigned, 10 each, to one of two groups. A "traditional" method of training ($T$) is used in one group and an "experimental" method ($E$) in the other. After six months on the job, the vice president ranks the individuals on the basis of their performance from 1 (worst) to 20 (best).

| $T$: | 1 | 2 | 3 | 5 | 9 | 10 | 12 | 13 | 14 | 15 |
|------|---|---|---|---|---|----|----|----|----|----|
| $E$: | 4 | 6 | 7 | 8 | 11 | 16 | 17 | 18 | 19 | 20 |

 **DATA FILE TESTRANK**

Is there any evidence of a difference in performance based on the two methods? (Use $\alpha = .05$.)

**12.52** The director of human resources at a 1,200-bed New York City hospital is evaluating candidates for the position of administrator of the billings and payments department. Among the applicants 22 are invited for interviews. Following the interviews, the rankings (1 = most preferred) of the candidates (based on interview, academic record, and prior experience) are determined. They are presented below, broken down by "type" of master's degree obtained—MBA versus MPH.

| MBA CANDIDATES | | MPH CANDIDATES | |
|----------------|----|----------------|----|
| 1 | 2 | 3 | 6 |
| 4 | 5 | 7 | 10 |
| 8 | 9 | 13 | 14 |
| 11 | 12 | 16 | 18 |
| 15 | 17 | 19 | 20 |
| | | 21 | 22 |

 **DATA FILE INTRANK**

Is there evidence that the MBA candidates are more preferred than the MPH candidates? (Use $\alpha = .05$.)

**12.53** A New York television station decides to produce a story comparing two commuter railroads in the area—the Long Island Rail Road (LIRR) and New Jersey Transit (NJT). The researchers at the station sample the performance of several scheduled train runs of each railroad, 10 for the LIRR and 12 for NJT. The data on how many minutes each train is early (negative numbers) or late (positive numbers) are presented below:

| LIRR: | 5 | −1 | 39 | 9 | 12 | 21 | 15 | 52 | 18 | 23 | | |
|-------|---|----|----|---|----|----|----|----|----|----|----|---|
| NJT: | 8 | 4 | 10 | 4 | 12 | 5 | 4 | 9 | 15 | 33 | 14 | 7 |

 **DATA FILE TRAIN2**

(a) Is there evidence that the railroads differ in their median tendencies to be late? (Use $\alpha = .01$.)

(b) What assumptions must be made in order to do part (a) of this problem?

(c) What conclusions about the lateness of the two railroads can be made?

**12.54** An industrial psychologist wishes to study the effects of motivation on sales in a particular firm. Of 24 new salespersons being trained, 12 are to be paid at an hourly rate and 12 on a commission basis. The 24 individuals were randomly assigned to the two groups. The following data represent the sales volume (in thousands of dollars) achieved during the first month on the job.

| HOURLY RATE | | COMMISSION | |
|---|---|---|---|
| 256 | 212 | 224 | 261 |
| 239 | 216 | 254 | 228 |
| 222 | 236 | 273 | 234 |
| 207 | 219 | 285 | 225 |
| 228 | 225 | 237 | 232 |
| 241 | 230 | 277 | 245 |

(a) Using a .01 level of significance, is there evidence that wage incentives (through commission) yield greater median sales volume?
(b) What assumptions must be made to do part (a) of this problem?
(c) If you did Problem 12.12 on page 486, compare the results obtained in parts (a) and (d) of that problem with the results obtained in part (a) above. Discuss.

• **12.55** A manufacturer is developing a nickel-metal hydride battery that is to be used in cellular telephones in lieu of nickel-cadmium batteries. The director of quality control decides to evaluate the newly developed battery against the widely used nickel-cadmium battery with respect to performance. A random sample of 25 nickel-cadmium batteries and a random sample of 25 of the newly developed nickel-metal hydride batteries are placed in cellular telephones of the same brand and model. The performance measure of interest is the talking time (in minutes) prior to recharging. The results are presented in the following table.

| NICKEL-CADMIUM BATTERY | | | NICKEL-METAL HYDRIDE BATTERY | | |
|---|---|---|---|---|---|
| 54.5 | 71.0 | 67.0 | 78.3 | 103.0 | 79.8 |
| 67.8 | 41.7 | 56.7 | 95.4 | 81.3 | 91.1 |
| 64.5 | 69.7 | 86.8 | 69.4 | 46.4 | 82.8 |
| 70.4 | 40.8 | 74.9 | 87.3 | 82.3 | 71.8 |
| 72.5 | 75.4 | 76.9 | 62.5 | 83.2 | 77.5 |
| 64.9 | 81.0 | 104.4 | 85.0 | 85.3 | 74.3 |
| 83.3 | 90.4 | 82.0 | 85.3 | 85.5 | 86.1 |
| 72.8 | 71.8 | 58.7 | 72.1 | 112.3 | 74.1 |
| 68.8 | | | 41.1 | | |

(a) Using a .05 level of significance, is there evidence of a difference in the two types of batteries with respect to median talking time (in minutes) prior to recharging?
(b) What assumptions must be made in order to do part (a) of this problem?
(c) If you did Problem 12.13 on page 486, compare the results obtained in parts (a) and (d) of that problem with the results obtained in part (a) above. Discuss.

**12.56** A public official working on health care reform policy wants to compare occupancy rates (i.e., average annual percentage of beds filled) in urban versus suburban hospitals within his state. A random sample of 16 urban hospitals and a random sample of 16 suburban hospitals are selected within the state and the occupancy rates are recorded as follows:

| URBAN HOSPITALS | | SUBURBAN HOSPITALS | |
|---|---|---|---|
| 76.5 | 73.3 | 71.5 | 63.0 |
| 75.9 | 77.4 | 73.4 | 76.0 |
| 79.6 | 79.0 | 74.6 | 75.5 |
| 77.5 | 79.9 | 74.3 | 70.7 |
| 79.4 | 70.4 | 71.2 | 67.4 |
| 78.7 | 77.7 | 67.8 | 62.6 |
| 78.6 | 78.1 | 76.9 | 73.0 |
| 79.3 | 75.9 | 60.0 | 76.5 |

DATA FILE
HOSPITAL

(a) Using a .05 level of significance, is there evidence of a difference in the median occupancy rates between urban and suburban hospitals in this state?

(b) What assumptions must be made in order to do part (a) of this problem?

(c) If you did Problem 12.16 on page 488, compare the results obtained in parts (a) and (c) of that problem with the results obtained in part (a) above. Discuss.

**12.57** The director of training for a company manufacturing electronic equipment is interested in determining whether different training methods have an effect on the productivity of assembly line employees. She randomly assigned 42 recently hired employees into two groups of 21, of which the first received a computer-assisted, individual-based training program and the other received a team-based training program. Upon completion of the training, the employees were evaluated on the time (in seconds) it took to assemble a part. The results are as follows:

| COMPUTER-ASSISTED, INDIVIDUAL-BASED PROGRAM | | | TEAM-BASED PROGRAM | | |
|---|---|---|---|---|---|
| 19.4 | 16.7 | 16.5 | 22.4 | 13.8 | 23.7 |
| 20.7 | 19.3 | 17.7 | 18.7 | 18.0 | 17.4 |
| 21.8 | 16.8 | 16.2 | 19.3 | 20.8 | 23.2 |
| 14.1 | 17.7 | 17.4 | 15.6 | 17.1 | 20.1 |
| 16.1 | 19.8 | 16.4 | 18.0 | 28.2 | 12.3 |
| 16.8 | 19.3 | 16.8 | 21.7 | 20.8 | 15.2 |
| 14.7 | 16.0 | 18.5 | 30.7 | 24.7 | 16.0 |

DATA FILE
TRAINING

(a) Using a .05 level of significance, is there evidence of a difference in the median assembly times (in seconds) between employees trained in a computer-assisted, individual-based program and those trained in a team-based program?

(b) What assumptions must be made in order to do part (a) of this problem?

(c) If you did Problem 12.17 on page 488, compare the results obtained in parts (a) and (c) with the results obtained in part (a) above. Discuss.

## 12.5  WILCOXON SIGNED-RANKS TEST FOR THE MEDIAN DIFFERENCE (*OPTIONAL TOPIC*)

For situations involving either matched items or repeated measurements of the same item, the nonparametric **Wilcoxon signed-ranks test for the median difference** may be used when the *t* test for the mean difference described in section 12.3 is not appropriate. That is, the Wilcoxon signed-ranks test may be chosen over the *t* test when (1) we are able to obtain data measured at a higher level than an ordinal scale but (2) do not believe that the assumptions of the $t$ test are sufficiently met. When the assumptions of the $t$ test are violated, the Wilcoxon procedure, which makes fewer and less stringent assumptions, is likely to be the more powerful in detecting the existence of significant differences. Moreover, even under conditions appropriate to the $t$ test, the Wilcoxon signed-ranks test has proved to be almost as powerful.

To perform the Wilcoxon signed-ranks test for the median difference, we first obtain the test statistic $W$. As displayed in Exhibit 12.1, this is accomplished in six steps.

### Exhibit 12.1  Steps in Obtaining the Wilcoxon Signed-Ranks Test Statistic W

✓ **1.** For each item in a sample of $n$ items we obtain a *difference score* $D_i$ between two measurements.

✓ **2.** We then neglect the "+" and "−" signs and obtain a set of $n$ *absolute differences* $|D_i|$.

✓ **3.** We omit from further analysis any absolute difference score of zero, thereby yielding a set of $n'$ nonzero absolute difference scores, where $n' \le n$. Thus, $n'$ becomes the actual sample size—after we have removed observations with absolute difference scores of zero.

✓ **4.** We then assign ranks $R_i$ from 1 to $n'$ to each of the $|D_i|$ such that the smallest absolute difference score gets rank 1 and the largest gets rank $n'$. Owing to a lack of precision in the measuring process, if two or more $|D_i|$ are equal, they are each assigned the average rank of the ranks they would have been assigned individually had ties in the data not occurred.

✓ **5.** We now reassign the symbol "+" or "−" to each of the $n'$ ranks $R_i$, depending on whether $D_i$ was originally positive or negative.

✓ **6.** The Wilcoxon test statistic $W$ is obtained as the sum of the positive ranks [see equation (12.11)].

### Wilcoxon Signed-Ranks Test Statistic W

The Wilcoxon test statistic $W$ is obtained as the sum of the positive ranks.

$$W = \sum_{i=1}^{n'} R_i^{(+)}$$

(12.11)

Because the sum of the first $n'$ integers (1, 2, . . . , $n'$) is given by $n'(n' + 1)/2$, the Wilcoxon test statistic $W$ may range from a minimum of 0 (where all the observed difference scores are negative) to a maximum of $n'(n' + 1)/2$ (where all the observed difference scores are positive). If the null hypothesis is true, we expect the test statistic $W$ to take on a value close to its mean $\mu_W = n'(n' + 1)/4$. If the null hypothesis is false, we expect the observed value of the test statistic to be close to one of the extremes.

The test of the null hypothesis that the population median difference $M_D$ is zero may be two-tailed or one-tailed.

| Two-Tailed Test | One-Tailed Test | One-Tailed Test |
|---|---|---|
| $H_0: M_D = 0$ | $H_0: M_D \geq 0$ | $H_0: M_D \leq 0$ |
| $H_1: M_D \neq 0$ | $H_1: M_D < 0$ | $H_1: M_D > 0$ |

Table E.8 may be used for obtaining the critical values of the test statistic $W$ for both one- and two-tailed tests at various levels of significance for samples of $n' \leq 20$. For a two-tailed test and for a particular level of significance, if the observed value of $W$ equals or exceeds the upper critical value or is equal to or less than the lower critical value, the null hypothesis is rejected (panel A of Figure 12.16). For a one-tailed test in the negative direction, the decision rule is to reject the null hypothesis if the observed value of $W$ is less than or equal to the lower critical value (panel B of Figure 12.16). For a one-tailed test in the positive direction, the decision rule is to reject the null hypothesis if the observed value of $W$ equals or exceeds the upper critical value (panel C of Figure 12.16).

For samples of $n' > 20$, the test statistic $W$ is approximately normally distributed with mean $\mu_W$ and standard deviation $\sigma_W$. We note that $\mu_W$, the mean of the test statistic $W$, is computed from

$$\mu_W = \frac{n'(n' + 1)}{4}$$

and $\sigma_W$, the standard deviation of the test statistic $W$, is obtained from

$$\sigma_W = \sqrt{\frac{n'(n' + 1)(2n' + 1)}{24}}$$

Therefore, the standardized $Z$-test statistic is defined as in equation (12.12).

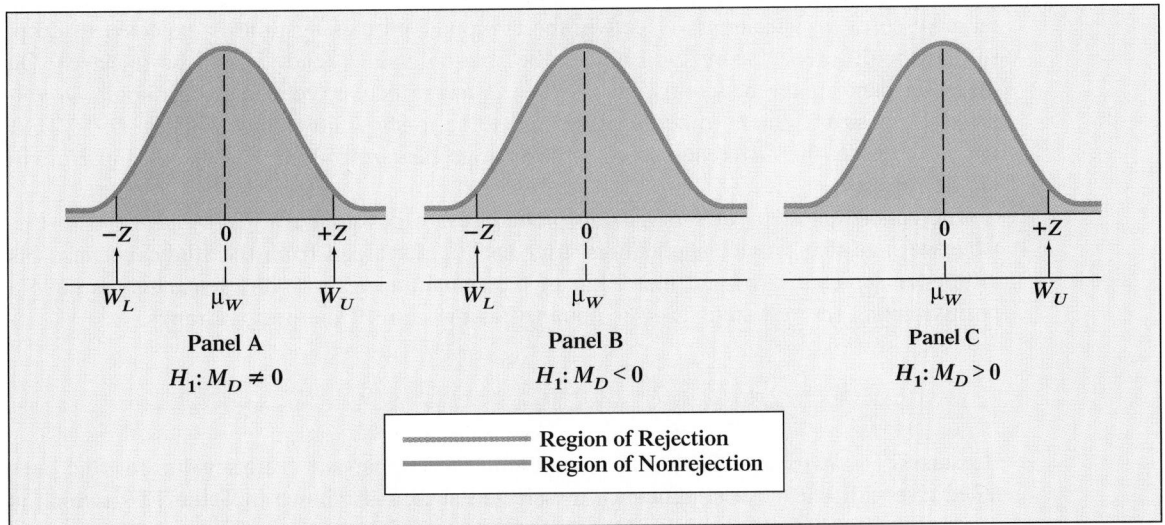

**FIGURE 12.16** Regions of rejection and nonrejection using the Wilcoxon signed-ranks test

## "Large-Sample" Wilcoxon Signed-Ranks Test

$$Z = \frac{W - \mu_W}{\sigma_W} \tag{12.12}$$

This large-sample approximation formula is used for testing the null hypothesis when sample sizes are outside the range of Table E.8.

Based on $\alpha$, the level of significance selected, the null hypothesis is rejected if the computed Z-value falls in the appropriate region of rejection, depending on whether a two-tailed or a one-tailed test is used—as shown in Figure 12.16.

To demonstrate how we may use the Wilcoxon signed-ranks test, we return to our example concerning the financial applications packages discussed in section 12.3. If as a result of an exploratory data analysis (see Figure 12.12 on page 504), we do not wish to make the stringent assumption that the differences were taken from populations that are normally distributed, the Wilcoxon signed-ranks test can be used for evaluating whether the current market leader uses more processing time than the new package.

The null and alternative hypotheses are:

$$H_0: M_D \leq 0$$
$$H_1: M_D > 0$$

and the test is one-tailed.

To compute the test statistic $W$ and perform the paired-sample test, the first step of the six-step procedure is to obtain a set of difference scores $D_i$ between each of the $n$ paired observations:

$$D_i = X_{1i} - X_{2i}$$

where

$$i = 1, 2, \ldots, n.$$

In our example, we obtain a set of $n$ difference scores from $D_i = X_{current_i} - X_{new_i}$. If the new software package is effective, the computer processing time is expected to drop, so that the difference scores will tend to be *positive* values (and $H_0$ will be rejected). On the other hand, if the new software package is not effective, we can expect some $D_i$ values to be positive, others to be negative, and some to show no change (that is, $D_i = 0$). If this is the case, the difference scores will average near zero (that is, $\overline{D} \cong 0$) and $H_0$ will not be rejected.

The remaining steps of the six-step procedure are developed in Table 12.8. From this table we note that project applications user D.S. is discarded from the study (because his difference score is zero) and that eight of the remaining $n' = 9$ difference scores have a positive sign. The test statistic $W$ is obtained as the sum of the positive ranks:

$$W = \sum_{i=1}^{n'} R_i^{(+)} = 7 + 2 + 6 + 8 + 4.5 + 9 + 4.5 + 3 = 44$$

Because $n' = 9$, we use Table E.8 to determine the upper-tail critical value for this one-tailed test with a level of significance $\alpha$, selected at .05. As shown in Table 12.9 (which is a replica of Table E.8), this upper-tail critical value is 37.

Because $W = 44 > 37$, the null hypothesis is rejected. There is evidence to support the

**Table 12.8** *Setting up the Wilcoxon signed-ranks test for the median difference*

| PROJECT APPLICATIONS USER | PROCESSING TIME (IN SECONDS) | | $D_i = X_{1i} - X_{2i}$ | $|D_i|$ | $R_i$ | SIGN OF $D_i$ |
| | CURRENT LEADER $X_{1i}$ | NEW PACKAGE $X_{2i}$ | | | | |
|---|---|---|---|---|---|---|
| C.B. | 9.98 | 9.88 | +0.10 | 0.10 | 7.0 | + |
| T.F. | 9.88 | 9.86 | +0.02 | 0.02 | 2.0 | + |
| M.H. | 9.84 | 9.75 | +0.09 | 0.09 | 6.0 | + |
| R.K. | 9.99 | 9.80 | +0.19 | 0.19 | 8.0 | + |
| M.O. | 9.94 | 9.87 | +0.07 | 0.07 | 4.5 | + |
| D.S. | 9.84 | 9.84 | 0.00 | 0.00 | — | Discard |
| S.S. | 9.86 | 9.87 | −0.01 | 0.01 | 1.0 | − |
| C.T. | 10.12 | 9.86 | +0.26 | 0.26 | 9.0 | + |
| K.T. | 9.90 | 9.83 | +0.07 | 0.07 | 4.5 | + |
| S.Z. | 9.91 | 9.86 | +0.05 | 0.05 | 3.0 | + |

**Table 12.9** *Obtaining upper-tail critical value for the Wilcoxon signed-ranks test statistic W where n' = 9 and α = .05*

| ONE-TAILED: | $\alpha = .05$ | $\alpha = .025$ | $\alpha = .01$ | $\alpha = .005$ |
| TWO-TAILED: | $\alpha = .10$ | $\alpha = .05$ | $\alpha = .02$ | $\alpha = .01$ |
|---|---|---|---|---|
| $n'$ | (LOWER, UPPER) | | | |
| 5 | 0,15 | — | — | — |
| 6 | 2,19 | 0,21 | — | — |
| 7 | 3,25 | 2,26 | 0,28 | — |
| 8 | 5,31 | 3,33 | 1,35 | 0,36 |
| 9 ⟶ | 8,37 | 5,40 | 3,42 | 1,44 |
| 10 | 10,45 | 8,47 | 5,50 | 3,52 |

*Source: Extracted from Table E.8.*

contention that the median processing time using the new finance software package is significantly faster than that using the current market leader. From the Minitab output in Figure 12.17 on page 524 we observe that the *p*-value is .006, which is less than .05.

We note that Table E.8 (lower and upper critical values of the Wilcoxon signed-ranks test statistic *W*) provides critical values for only situations involving small samples, that is, where $n'$ is less than or equal to 20. If our actual sample size $n'$ exceeds 20, the large-sample *Z* approximation formula [equation (12.12)] must be used to perform the test of hypothesis. Nevertheless, to demonstrate the effectiveness of the large-sample *Z* approximation formula, even for sample sizes as small as 9, we use it for our software applications manufacturer's data in Example 12.4.

```
Test of median = 0.000000 versus median  >  0.000000

                      N for    Wilcoxon                 Estimated
               N      Test     Statistic          P       Median
Difference     10       9          44.0        0.006      0.07000
```

**FIGURE 12.17**   Wilcoxon signed-ranks test for the financial applications software example obtained from Minitab

### Example 12.4   *Wilcoxon Signed-Ranks Test with Large-Sample Z Approximation Formula*

For the data of Table 12.8 concerning the financial applications packages, use the large sample approximation formula for the Wilcoxon signed-ranks test to determine if there is evidence at the .05 level of significance that the median processing time is higher for the current market leader than for the new package.

### SOLUTION

Using the *steps in hypothesis testing* (Exhibits 11.2 and 11.3 on pages 422 and 425), we have the following:

Steps 1 and 2:

$$H_0: M_D \leq 0$$
$$H_1: M_D > 0$$

Step 3: $\quad \alpha = .05$

Step 4: $\quad n = 10$

Step 5: We use the large-sample $Z$ approximation formula given by equation (12.12):

$$Z = \frac{W - \mu_W}{\sigma_W}$$

Step 6: We use Table E.2(b) to develop the following decision rule:

Reject $H_0$ if $Z > +1.645$;

otherwise do not reject $H_0$.

Step 7: We collect the data and compute the $Z$-test statistic for the sample of $n' = 9$ (nonzero differences):

$$Z = \frac{W - \mu_W}{\sigma_W}$$

where

$$\mu_W = \frac{n'(n' + 1)}{4} = \frac{9(10)}{4} = 22.5$$

$$\sigma_W = \sqrt{\frac{n'(n' + 1)(2n' + 1)}{24}} = \sqrt{\frac{9(10)(19)}{24}} = 8.44$$

and

$$Z = \frac{44 - 22.5}{8.44} = +2.55$$

Steps 8, 9, and 10: Because $Z = +2.55 > +1.645$, the decision is to reject $H_0$. The null hypothesis is rejected because the test statistic $Z$ has fallen into the region of rejection. The $p$-value, or probability of obtaining a test statistic $W$ even greater than what was observed here, which translates to a test statistic $Z$ with a distance even farther from the center of the standard normal distribution than 2.55 standard deviations, is .0054 if the null hypothesis of a median difference of zero were true. Because the $p$-value is less than $\alpha = .05$, we reject the null hypothesis. Thus, without having to make the stringent assumption of normality in the original population of difference scores, the software applications manufacturer may conclude that there is evidence of a significant median difference in the time to run the programs and that the new financial applications program is superior to the current market leader.

The Wilcoxon signed-ranks test for the median difference makes fewer and less stringent assumptions than does the $t$ test for the mean difference. The assumptions for the Wilcoxon signed-ranks test are listed in Exhibit 12.2.

## Exhibit 12.2 Wilcoxon Signed-Ranks Test for the Median Difference

The assumptions necessary for performing the test are that:

✓ **1.** The observed data either constitute a random sample of $n$ independent items or individuals, each with two measurements $(X_{11}, X_{21}), (X_{12}, X_{22}), \ldots, (X_{1n}, X_{2n})$, one taken *before* and the other taken *after* the presentation of some stimulus (i.e., treatment) or the observed data constitute a random sample of $n$ independent pairs of items or individuals so that $(X_{1i}, X_{2i})$ represents the observed values for each member of the matched pair ($i = 1, 2, \ldots, n$).

✓ **2.** The underlying variable of interest is continuous.

✓ **3.** The observed data are measured at a higher level than the ordinal scale—i.e., at the interval or ratio level.

✓ **4.** The distribution of the population of difference scores between repeated measurements or between matched items or individuals is approximately symmetric.

## Problems for Section 12.5

### Learning the Basics

• **12.58** Using Table E.8, determine the lower- and upper-tail critical values for the Wilcoxon signed-ranks test statistic $W$ in each of the following two-tailed tests:

(a) $\alpha = .10$, $n' = 11$

(b) $\alpha = .05$, $n' = 11$
(c) $\alpha = .02$, $n' = 11$
(d) $\alpha = .01$, $n' = 11$
(e) Given your results in parts (a)–(d), what do you conclude about the width of the region of nonrejection as the selected level of significance $\alpha$ gets smaller?

**12.59** Using Table E.8, determine the upper-tail critical value for the Wilcoxon signed-ranks test statistic $W$ in each of the following one-tailed tests:
(a) $\alpha = .05$, $n' = 11$
(b) $\alpha = .025$, $n' = 11$
(c) $\alpha = .01$, $n' = 11$
(d) $\alpha = .005$, $n' = 11$
(e) Given your results in parts (a)–(d), what do you conclude about the width of the region of nonrejection as the selected level of significance $\alpha$ gets smaller?

● **12.60** Using Table E.8, determine the lower-tail critical value for the Wilcoxon signed-ranks test statistic $W$ in each of the following one-tailed tests:
(a) $\alpha = .05$, $n' = 11$
(b) $\alpha = .025$, $n' = 11$
(c) $\alpha = .01$, $n' = 11$
(d) $\alpha = .005$, $n' = 11$
(e) Given your results in parts (a)–(d), what do you conclude about the width of the region of nonrejection as the selected level of significance $\alpha$ gets smaller?

**12.61** Suppose that the following information is available on the $n = 12$ difference scores from two related samples:

Difference scores ($D_i$): $+3.2$, $+1.7$, $+4.5$, $0.0$, $+11.1$, $-0.8$, $+2.3$, $-2.0$, $0.0$, $+14.8$, $+5.6$, $+1.7$

What is the value of the test statistic $W$ if we are testing the null hypothesis $H_0$: $M_D = 0$?

**12.62** In Problem 12.61 what are the lower- and upper-tail critical values for the test statistic $W$ from Table E.8 if the level of significance $\alpha$ is chosen to be .05 and the alternative hypothesis is $H_1$: $M_D \neq 0$?

**12.63** In Problems 12.61 and 12.62 what is your statistical decision?

● **12.64** Suppose that the following information is available on the $n' = 12$ signed ranks ($R_i$) obtained from the difference scores ($D_i$) from two related samples:

Signed ranks ($R_i$): $+5$, $+6.5$, $+4$, $+11$, $-8$, $+2.5$, $-2.5$, $+1$, $+12$, $+6.5$, $+10$, $+9$

What is the value of the test statistic $W$ if we are testing the null hypothesis $H_0$: $M_D \leq 0$?

● **12.65** From Problem 12.64, at a level of significance of .05, determine the upper-tail critical value for the Wilcoxon signed-ranks test statistic $W$ if we want to perform a test of the hypothesis $H_0$: $M_D \leq 0$ against the one-tail alternative $H_1$: $M_D > 0$.

● **12.66** From Problems 12.64 and 12.65 what is your statistical decision?

## Applying the Concepts

**12.67** A tax preparation company claims that taxpayers save money when the firm prepares their individual tax returns. To evaluate this claim, a consumer protection agency has people who had already prepared their tax forms go to this company's office to get their taxes done by the firm's preparers. The taxes, as calculated by both the firm and the individuals, are presented in the following table:

| | TAX-RETURN PREPARER | |
| --- | --- | --- |
| TAXPAYER | FIRM | SELF |
| Jose | 1,459 | 1,910 |
| Marcia | 3,250 | 2,900 |
| Alexis | 1,190 | 1,200 |
| Harry | 8,100 | 7,650 |
| Jean | 13,200 | 15,390 |
| Marc | 9,120 | 9,100 |
| JR | 255,970 | 33,120 |
| Billy | 210 | 140 |
| Richard | 1,290 | 1,320 |
| Ted | 130 | 0 |
| Bruce | 5,190 | 6,123 |

DATA FILE
TAXRET

(a) Is there evidence that the firm's claim is valid? (Use $\alpha = .05$.)

(b) Discuss the implications of your results.

**12.68** The following data represent the midterm and final examination scores from a sample of 11 students taking Introductory Finance. Both exams were 2 hours in length, and the final covered material learned since the midterm.

| | STUDENT | | | | | | | | | | |
| --- | --- | --- | --- | --- | --- | --- | --- | --- | --- | --- | --- |
| | N.A. | A.B. | L.B. | M.B. | W.B. | S.D. | T.J. | L.K. | J.M. | H.R. | D.R. |
| Midterm | 80 | 82 | 47 | 75 | 80 | 69 | 83 | 73 | 55 | 70 | 81 |
| Final Exam | 81 | 85 | 40 | 75 | 83 | 79 | 91 | 72 | 66 | 76 | 79 |

DATA FILE
FINTEST

(a) Is there evidence of an increase in median student performance in the second half of the semester? (Use $\alpha = .05$.)

(b) Discuss the implications of your results.

● **12.69** A group of engineering students decides to see whether cars that supposedly do not need high-octane gasoline get more miles per gallon using regular or high-octane gas. They test several cars (under similar road surface, weather, and other driving conditions), using both types of gas in each car at different times. The mileage for each gas type for each car is

| | CAR | | | | | | | | | |
| --- | --- | --- | --- | --- | --- | --- | --- | --- | --- | --- |
| GAS TYPE | #1 | #2 | #3 | #4 | #5 | #6 | #7 | #8 | #9 | #10 |
| Regular | 15 | 23 | 21 | 35 | 42 | 28 | 19 | 32 | 31 | 24 |
| High-octane | 18 | 21 | 25 | 34 | 47 | 30 | 19 | 27 | 34 | 20 |

DATA FILE
GASMILE

(a) At the .05 level of significance, is there evidence of a difference in the median gasoline mileage between regular and high-octane gas?

(b) What assumption is necessary to perform this test?

(c) If you did Problem 12.37 on page 506, is there any difference in your present findings from that obtained using the $t$ test? Discuss.

**12.70** In order to measure the effect of a storewide sales campaign on nonsale items, the research director of a national supermarket chain took a random sample of 13 pairs of stores that were matched according to average weekly sales volume. One store of each pair (the experimental group) was exposed to the sales campaign, and the other member of the pair (the control group) was not. The following data indicate the results over a weekly period:

### Sales ($000) of Nonsale Items

| STORE | WITH SALES CAMPAIGN | WITHOUT SALES CAMPAIGN |
|-------|---------------------|------------------------|
| 1     | 67.2                | 65.3                   |
| 2     | 59.4                | 54.7                   |
| 3     | 80.1                | 81.3                   |
| 4     | 47.6                | 39.8                   |
| 5     | 97.8                | 92.5                   |
| 6     | 38.4                | 37.9                   |
| 7     | 57.3                | 52.4                   |
| 8     | 75.2                | 69.9                   |
| 9     | 94.7                | 89.0                   |
| 10    | 64.3                | 58.4                   |
| 11    | 31.7                | 33.0                   |
| 12    | 49.3                | 41.7                   |
| 13    | 54.0                | 53.6                   |

**DATA FILE SALESCMP**

(a) At the .05 level of significance, can the research director conclude that there is evidence that the sales campaign has increased the median sales of nonsale items?

(b) What assumption is necessary to perform this test?

(c) If you did Problem 12.38 on page 506, is there any difference in your present findings from that obtained using the $t$ test? Discuss.

## SUMMARY

In this chapter we introduced four statistical test procedures that are commonly employed in analyzing possible differences between the parameters of two independent populations based on samples containing numerical data. In addition, we developed two test procedures that are frequently used when analyzing possible differences between the parameters of two related populations based on samples containing numerical data. Again, part of a good data analysis is to understand the assumptions underlying each of the hypothesis test procedures and, using these as well as other criteria, to select the one most appropriate for a given set of conditions.

As observed in the summary chart for this chapter, the major distinction for comparing two groups containing numerical data is based on whether the populations from which the samples were drawn are independent or related. We should not use test procedures designed for independent populations when dealing with paired data, and we should not use test procedures designed for related populations when dealing with two independent samples. After focusing on an appropriate grouping of similar test procedures, we need to look carefully at the assumptions and other criteria prior to selecting a particular procedure.

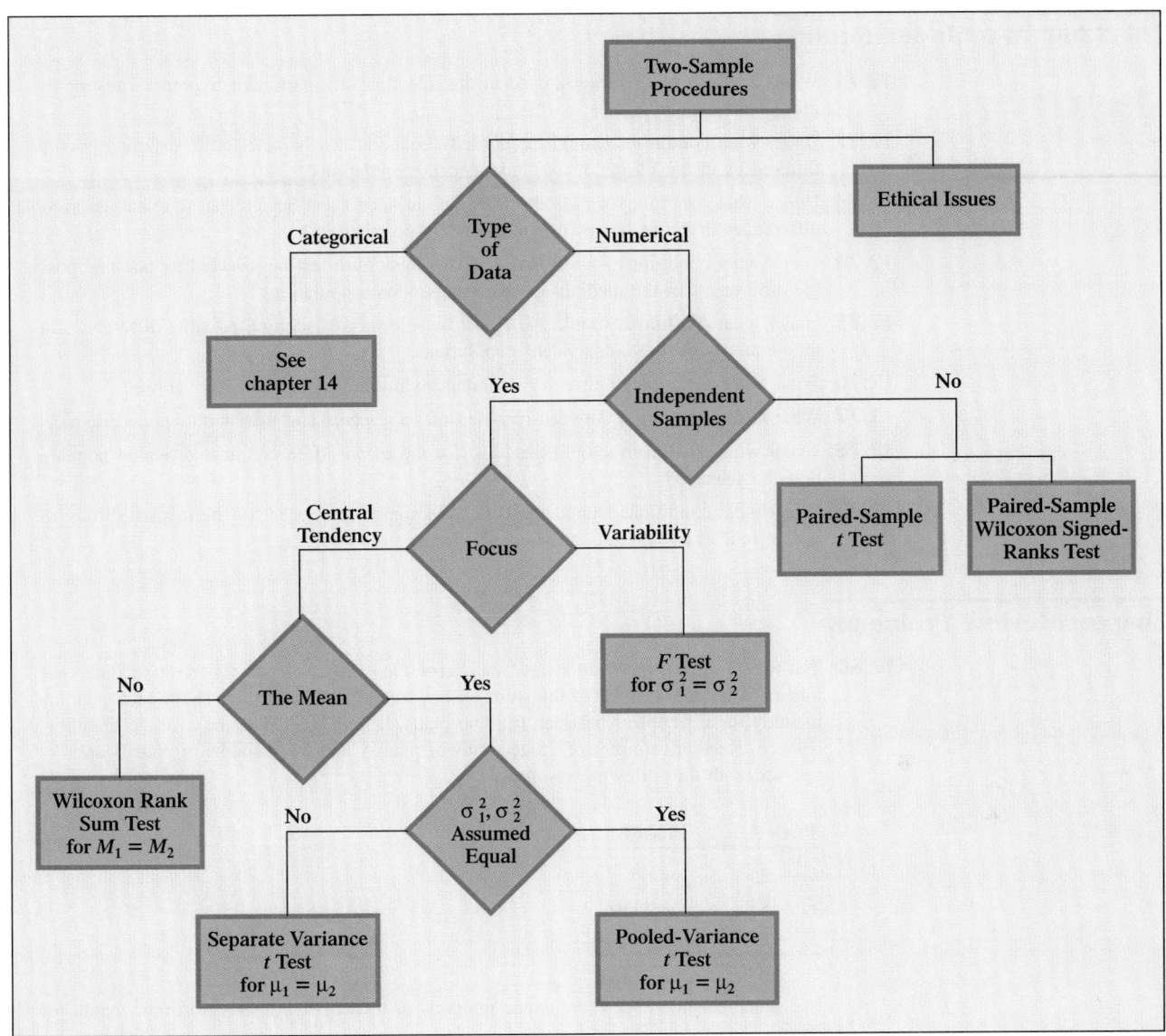

Chapter 12 summary chart

## *Key Terms*

difference score $D_i$   499

$F$ distribution   489

$F$ test for differences in two variances   489

independent populations   472

median difference   519

paired or matched items   498

pooled-variance $t$ test for the difference in two means   474

related populations   498

related samples   498

repeated measurements   498

robust   478

separate-variance $t$ test for the difference in two means   481

$t$ test for the mean difference   501

Wilcoxon rank sum test for differences in two medians   509

Wilcoxon signed-ranks test for the median difference   519

$Z$ test for differences in two means   473

$Z$ test for the mean difference   500

## Checking Your Understanding

**12.71** What are some of the criteria used in the selection of a particular hypothesis-testing procedure?

**12.72** Under what conditions should the pooled-variance $t$ test be selected to examine possible differences in the means of two independent populations?

**12.73** Under what conditions should the separate-variance $t$ test be selected to examine possible differences in the means of two independent populations?

**12.74** Under what conditions should the Wilcoxon rank sum test be selected to examine possible differences in the medians of two independent populations?

**12.75** Under what conditions should the $F$ test be selected to examine possible differences in the variances of two independent populations?

**12.76** What is the difference between two independent and two related populations?

**12.77** What is the distinction between repeated measurements and matched or paired items?

**12.78** Under what conditions should the $t$ test for the mean difference in two related populations be selected?

**12.79** Under what conditions should the Wilcoxon signed-ranks test for the median difference in two related populations be selected?

## Chapter Review Problems

**• 12.80** The R & M department store has two charge plans available for its credit-account customers. The management of the store wishes to collect information about each plan and to study the differences between the two plans. It is interested in the average monthly balance. Random samples of 25 accounts of plan A and 50 accounts of plan B are selected with the following results:

| PLAN A | PLAN B |
|---|---|
| $n_A = 25$ | $n_B = 50$ |
| $\overline{X}_A = \$75$ | $\overline{X}_B = \$110$ |
| $S_A = \$15$ | $S_B = \$14.14$ |

Use statistical inference (confidence intervals or tests of hypothesis) to draw conclusions about each of the following:

*Note*: Use a level of significance of .01 (or use 99% confidence) throughout.

(a) Average monthly balance of all plan B accounts.

(b) Is there evidence that the average monthly balance of plan A accounts is different from \$105?

(c) Is there evidence of a difference in the variances (in the monthly balances) between plan A and plan B?

(d) Is there evidence of a difference in the average monthly balances between plan A and plan B?

(e) Compute the $p$-values in parts (b)–(d) and interpret their meaning.

(f) On the basis of the results of parts (a)–(e), what will you tell the management about the two plans?

**12.81** A large public utility wishes to compare the consumption of electricity during the summer season for single-family homes in two counties that it services. For each household sampled, the monthly electric bill is recorded with the following results:

|  | COUNTY I | COUNTY II |
|---|---|---|
| $\overline{X}$ | $115 | $98 |
| $S$ | $30 | $18 |
| $n$ | 25 | 21 |

Choosing a level of significance of .05 (or 95% confidence), use statistical inference (confidence intervals or tests of hypothesis) to draw conclusions about each of the following:
(a) Population average monthly electric bill for county I.
(b) Is there evidence that the average bill in county II is above $80?
(c) Is there evidence of a difference in the variances between bills in county I and county II?
(d) Is there evidence that the average monthly bill is higher in county I than county II?
(e) Compute the $p$-values in parts (b)–(d) and interpret their meaning.
(f) On the basis of the results of parts (a)–(e), what would you tell the utility about the consumption of electricity in the two counties?

**12.82** The manager of computer operations of a large company wishes to study computer usage of two departments within the company, the accounting department and the research department. A random sample of five jobs from the accounting department in the last week and six jobs from the research department in the last week are selected, and the processing time (in seconds) for each job is recorded.

| DEPARTMENT | PROCESSING TIME (IN SECONDS) | | | | | |
|---|---|---|---|---|---|---|
| Accounting | 9 | 3 | 8 | 7 | 12 | |
| Research | 4 | 13 | 10 | 9 | 9 | 6 |

DATA FILE
ACCRES

Choosing a level of significance of .05 (or 95% confidence), use statistical inference (confidence intervals or tests of hypothesis) to draw conclusions about each of the following:
(a) Average processing time for all jobs in the accounting department.
(b) Is there evidence that the average processing time in the research department is greater than 6 seconds?
(c) Is there evidence of a difference in the variances in the processing time between the two departments?
(d) What must you assume to do in (c)?
(e) Is there evidence of a difference in the mean processing time between the accounting department and the research department?
(f) What must you assume to do in (e)?
(g) Compute the $p$-values in (b), (c), and (e) and interpret their meanings.
(h) On the basis of the results of (a)–(g), what should the manager write in his report to the director of information systems concerning the two departments?

**12.83** A computer professor is interested in studying the amount of time it would take students enrolled in the Introduction to Computers course to write and run a program in Visual Basic. The professor hires you to analyze the following results (in minutes) from a random sample of nine students:

DATA FILE
VB

    10  13  9  15  12  13  11  13  12

(a) At the .05 level of significance, is there evidence that the population average amount is greater than 10 minutes? What will you tell the professor?
(b) Suppose that when checking her results, the computer professor realizes that the fourth student needed 51 minutes rather than the recorded 15 minutes to write and

run the Visual Basic program. At the .05 level of significance, reanalyze the revised data in part (a). What will you tell the professor now?

(c) The professor is perplexed by these paradoxical results and requests an explanation from you regarding the justification for the difference in your findings in parts (a) and (b). Discuss.

(d) A few days later, the professor calls to tell you that the dilemma is completely resolved. The original number 15 [the fourth data value] was correct, and therefore your findings in part (a) are being used in the article she is writing for a computer magazine. Now she wants to hire you to compare the results from that group of Introduction to Computers students against those from a sample of 11 computer majors in order to determine whether there is evidence that computer majors can write a Visual Basic program (on average) in less time than introductory students. The sample mean for the computer majors is 8.5 minutes and the sample standard deviation is 2.0 minutes. At the .05 level of significance, completely analyze these data. What will you tell the professor?

(e) A few days later the professor calls again to tell you that a reviewer of her article wants her to include the $p$-value for the "correct" result in part (a). In addition, the professor inquires about an "unequal variances problem," which the reviewer wants her to discuss in her article. In your own words, discuss the concept of $p$-value and describe the unequal variances problem. Determine the $p$-value in part (a) and discuss whether or not the unequal variances problem had any meaning in the professor's study.

• **12.84** A bank with a branch located in a commercial district of a city has developed an improved process for serving customers during the noon to 1 P.M. peak lunch period. The waiting time (operationally defined as the time elapsed from when the customer enters the line until he or she is served) of all customers during this hour is recorded over a period of 1 week. A random sample of 15 customers is selected, and the results (in minutes) are as follows:

**DATA FILE**
**BANK1**

4.21   5.55   3.02   5.13   4.77   2.34   3.54   3.20   4.50   6.10   0.38   5.12   6.46
6.19   3.79

Suppose that another branch located in a residential area is most concerned with the Friday evening hours from 5 P.M. to 7 P.M. A random sample of 15 customers is selected, and the results are as follows:

**DATA FILE**
**BANK2**

9.66   5.90   8.02   5.79   8.73   3.82   8.01   8.35   10.49   6.68   5.64   4.08   6.17
9.91   5.47

Completely analyze the differences in the waiting times between the two branches, and write a summary of your findings to be presented to the vice president for operations of the bank. Be sure to include an explanation of why you think it is or is not appropriate to compare the two branches.

• **12.85** A problem with a telephone line that prevents a customer from receiving or making calls is disconcerting to both the customer and the telephone company. These problems can be of two types: those that are located inside a central office and those located on lines between the central office and the customer's equipment. The following data represent samples of 20 problems reported to two different offices of a telephone company and the time to clear these problems (in minutes) from the customers' lines:

| Central Office I Time to Clear Problems (minutes) | | | | | | | | | |
|------|------|------|------|------|------|------|------|------|------|
| 1.48 | 1.75 | 0.78 | 2.85 | 0.52 | 1.60 | 4.15 | 3.97 | 1.48 | 3.10 |
| 1.02 | 0.53 | 0.93 | 1.60 | 0.80 | 1.05 | 6.32 | 3.93 | 5.45 | 0.97 |

**DATA FILE**
**PHONE**

| Central Office II Time to Clear Problems (minutes) | | | | | | | | | |
|------|------|------|------|------|------|------|------|------|------|
| 7.55 | 3.75 | 0.10 | 1.10 | 0.60 | 0.52 | 3.30 | 2.10 | 0.58 | 4.02 |
| 3.75 | 0.65 | 1.92 | 0.60 | 1.53 | 4.23 | 0.08 | 1.48 | 1.65 | 0.72 |

Completely analyze the differences in the time to clear problems between the two central offices, and write a summary of your findings to be presented to the vice president for operations of the company.

**12.86** In many manufacturing processes there is a term called *work in process* (often abbreviated as WIP). In a book manufacturing plant this represents time it takes for sheets from a press to be folded, gathered, sewn, tipped on endsheets, and bound. The following data represent samples of 20 books at each of two production plants and the processing time (operationally defined as the time in days from when the books came off the press to when they were packed in cartons) for these jobs.

*Plant A*

| 5.62 | 5.29 | 16.25 | 10.92 | 11.46 | 21.62 | 8.45 | 8.58 | 5.41 | 11.42 |
| 11.62 | 7.29 | 7.50 | 7.96 | 4.42 | 10.50 | 7.58 | 9.29 | 7.54 | 8.92 |

*Plant B*

| 9.54 | 11.46 | 16.62 | 12.62 | 25.75 | 15.41 | 14.29 | 13.13 | 13.71 | 10.04 |
| 5.75 | 12.46 | 9.17 | 13.21 | 6.00 | 2.33 | 14.25 | 5.37 | 6.25 | 9.71 |

 **DATA FILE WIP**

Completely analyze the differences in the processing time between the two plants and write a summary of your findings to be presented to the vice president for operations of the book manufacturing company.

**12.87** Salaries in team sports have skyrocketed over the years and owners of major league baseball teams have had to increase ticket prices in order to meet payroll needs. Labor negotiations invariably get bogged down with discussions of average payroll. To the owners, the total payroll divided by 25 roster players represents the average (mean) payout per person. Because income is a right-skewed distribution, however, to the players the average payout per person has to be the median, a perceived fairer indicator of what typical player personnel receive.

The data below record the annual salaries and prorated signing bonuses (in millions of dollars) paid to each major league team's fourth-highest-salaried pitcher and third-highest-salaried outfielder. This table is intended for comparative analysis. Typically major league rosters contain 10 pitchers and 5 outfielders.

| TEAM | PITCHER | OUTFIELDER |
|---|---|---|
| American League | | |
| Anaheim Angels | 1.600 | 2.275 |
| Baltimore Orioles | 2.340 | 2.200 |
| Boston Red Sox | 1.126 | 1.100 |
| Cleveland Indians | 3.100 | 2.100 |
| Chicago White Sox | 0.817 | 0.225 |
| Detroit Tigers | 0.475 | 0.310 |
| Kansas City Royals | 1.700 | 1.750 |
| Milwaukee Brewers | 1.216 | 0.275 |
| Minnesota Twins | 0.450 | 0.260 |
| New York Yankees | 2.325 | 2.355 |
| Oakland A's | 0.240 | 0.165 |
| Seattle Mariners | 2.300 | 0.750 |
| Texas Rangers | 2.000 | 0.375 |
| Toronto Blue Jays | 3.300 | 1.050 |
| | | *(continued)* |

| TEAM | PITCHER | OUTFIELDER |
|---|---|---|
| National League | | |
| Atlanta Braves | 3.610 | 0.250 |
| Chicago Cubs | 1.050 | 0.450 |
| Cincinnati Reds | 2.100 | 0.190 |
| Colorado Rockies | 1.200 | 4.000 |
| Florida Marlins | 2.900 | 4.500 |
| Houston Astros | 0.413 | 0.750 |
| Los Angeles Dodgers | 1.600 | 1.733 |
| Montreal Expos | 0.525 | 0.500 |
| New York Mets | 1.100 | 0.212 |
| Philadelphia Phillies | 0.900 | 2.000 |
| Pittsburgh Pirates | 0.210 | 0.160 |
| St. Louis Cardinals | 1.750 | 3.300 |
| San Diego Padres | 0.835 | 2.987 |
| San Francisco Giants | 2.400 | 1.700 |

DATA FILE
BBSALARY

*Source: From* USA Today, *November 14, 1997, 14C.*

(a) At the .05 level of significance, is there evidence of a difference between American versus National League pitcher salaries?

(b) At the .05 level of significance, is there evidence of a difference between American versus National League outfielder salaries?

(c) At the .05 level of significance, is there evidence of a difference between pitcher and outfielder salaries in the American League?

(d) At the .05 level of significance, is there evidence of a difference between pitcher and outfielder salaries in the National League?

(e) On the basis of your results in parts (c) and (d), if appropriate, ignore league and, at the .05 level of significance, test to see if there is evidence of a difference between pitcher and outfielder salaries.

(f) What conclusions can be reached? What would you tell the commissioner of baseball regarding your findings? What would you tell the players' representatives?

# TEAM PROJECT

**TP12.1**   Refer to TP 3.1 on page 115. Your group, the _____ Corporation, has been hired by the vice president for research at a financial investment service to study the financial characteristics of currently traded domestic general stock funds. The investment service is interested in evaluating the list of domestic general stock funds so that it can make purchase recommendations to potential investors. Armed with Special Data Set 1 of appendix D, the _____ Corporation is ready to:

DATA FILE
MUTUAL

(a) Determine if there is evidence of a significant difference in average net asset value (in dollars) based on fee structure of the fund (no-load versus fee payment).

(b) Determine if there is evidence of a significant difference in average net asset value (in dollars) based on managerial objective (growth fund versus blend fund).

(c) Determine if there is evidence of a significant difference in average total year-to-date return based on fee structure of the fund (no-load versus fee payment).

(d) Determine if there is evidence of a significant difference in average total year-to-date return based on managerial objective (growth fund versus blend fund).

(e) Write and submit an executive summary describing the results in parts (a) through (d), clearly specifying all hypotheses, selected levels of significance, and the assumptions of the chosen test procedures.

(f) Prepare and deliver a 10-minute oral presentation to the vice president for research at this financial investment service.

*Note:* Additional Team Projects can be found at the following World Wide Web address:

**http://www.prenhall.com/Berenson**

These Team Projects deal with the characteristics of 80 universities and colleges (see the UNIV&COL file) and the features in 89 automobile models (see the AUTO96 file).

# THE SPRINGVILLE HERALD CASE

The marketing department team studying new home-delivery subscriptions wondered whether the telemarketing process itself could be improved to increase the number of home-delivery subscriptions sold. After several brainstorming sessions involving many individuals familiar with all aspects of the telemarketing process, including individuals who provide training for the callers and several of the callers themselves, it was decided that it was necessary to find ways to increase the length of the phone calls because it was clear that the longer a caller can speak to a respondent, the greater is the chance that a newspaper subscription will be sold.

Initially, the team decided it wanted to investigate the impact that time of call might have on subscription sales. Under current arrangements, calls were made in the evening hours between 5 P.M. and 9 P.M., Monday through Friday. The team wanted to compare length of calls made early in the evening (i.e., between 5 P.M. and 7 P.M.) with those made later in the evening (i.e., between 7 P.M. and 9 P.M.) to determine whether one of these time periods was more conducive to lengthier calls and, correspondingly, to increased subscription sales. The team selected a sample of 30 female callers who staff the telephone bank on Wednesday evenings and randomly assigned 15 of them to the "early" group and 15 to the "later" group. The callers knew that the team was observing their efforts that evening but didn't know which particular call was going to be monitored. The callers had been trained to make their telephone presentations in a structured manner. They were to read from a script and their greeting was personal but informal ("Hi, this is Mary Jones from the *Springville Herald*—may I speak to Bill Richards?").

Measurements were taken on the length of call (operationally defined as the difference, in seconds, between the time the person answers the phone and the time he or she hangs up). The results are presented in Table SH12.1 on page 536.

## Exercises

**12.1** Analyze these data and write a report for presentation to the team that indicates your findings. Be sure to include an attached appendix in which you discuss the reason you selected a particular statistical test to compare the two independent groups of callers. To solve this problem use either a software package or the following summary statistics:

| EVENING PERIOD: | EARLY | LATE |
|---|---|---|
| Sample means | 36.74 | 40.72 |
| Sample standard deviations | 2.98 | 3.57 |
| Rank sums | 166.50 | 298.50 |

**Table SH12.1** *Length of calls in seconds based on time of call—early versus later in the evening*

| TIME OF CALL | | TIME OF CALL | |
|---|---|---|---|
| EARLY | LATE | EARLY | LATE |
| 41.3 | 37.1 | 40.6 | 40.7 |
| 37.5 | 38.9 | 33.3 | 38.0 |
| 39.3 | 42.2 | 39.6 | 43.6 |
| 37.4 | 45.7 | 35.7 | 43.8 |
| 33.6 | 42.4 | 31.3 | 34.9 |
| 38.5 | 39.0 | 36.8 | 35.7 |
| 32.6 | 40.9 | 36.3 | 47.4 |
| 37.3 | 40.5 | | |

DATA FILE
SH12

**12.2** Suppose that instead of the research design described above, there were only 15 callers sampled and each caller was to be monitored twice in the evening, once in the early time period and once in the later time period. Suppose that in Table SH12.1 each row represents a particular caller's two measurements. Reanalyze these data and write a report for presentation to the team that indicates your findings. Be sure to include an attached appendix in which you discuss the reason you selected a particular statistical test to compare the average difference in the two related groups.

To solve this problem use either a software package or the following summary statistics:

| EVENING PERIOD: | EARLY | LATE | DIFFERENCE |
|---|---|---|---|
| Sample means | 36.74 | 40.72 | −3.98 |
| Sample standard deviations | 2.98 | 3.57 | 4.29 |
| Sum of positive signed ranks | | | 12 |

**12.3** What other variables should be investigated next? Discuss.

# References

1. Bradley, J. V., *Distribution-Free Statistical Tests* (Englewood Cliffs, NJ: Prentice Hall, 1968).
2. Conover, W. J., *Practical Nonparametric Statistics*, 2d ed. (New York: Wiley, 1980).
3. Daniel, W., *Applied Nonparametric Statistics*, 2d ed. (Boston: Houghton Mifflin, 1990).
4. *Microsoft Excel 97* (Redmond, WA: Microsoft Corporation, 1997).
5. *Minitab for Windows Version 12* (State College, PA: Minitab, Inc., 1998).
6. Satterthwaite, F. E., "An Approximate Distribution of Estimates of Variance Components," *Biometrics Bulletin 2*, (1946): 110–114.
7. Snedecor, G. W., and W. G. Cochran, *Statistical Methods*, 7th ed. (Ames, IA: Iowa State University Press, 1980).
8. Winer, B. J., *Statistical Principles in Experimental Design*, 2d ed. (New York: McGraw-Hill, 1971).

## Using Microsoft Excel for the *t* Test for the Difference between Two Means

If raw data are available, the *t* test: Two-Sample Assuming Equal Variances option or the *t* test: Two-Sample Assuming Unequal Variances option of the Data Analysis tool may be used to test for the difference in the means of two groups. To illustrate the use of the this tool for the *t* test, we refer to the soft drink example of Table 12.1 on page 475.

With the PRESSURE.XLS workbook open, select **Tools | Data Analysis**. Select **t test Two-Sample Assuming Equal Variances** from the Analysis tools list box. Click the **OK** button. In the Variable 1 Range edit box enter **A1:A11**. In the Variable 2 Range edit box enter **B1:B11**. In the Hypothesized Mean Difference edit box enter **0**. Select the **Labels** check box. In the Alpha edit box, enter the level of significance (.05 in this example). Select the **New Worksheet Ply** option button and enter the name *t***-Test for Two Means**. Click the **OK** button.

To test for the difference between two variances, use the same instructions as for the *t*-Test (except there is no entry involved for Mean Difference).

If only summary data are available, use the PHStat add-in for Two-Sample Tests by entering values for the sample size, arithmetic mean, and standard deviation for each group along with the type of test.

### Using Microsoft Excel for the Paired *t* Test

If raw data are available, the Paired *t*-test option of the Data Analysis tool may be used to test for the differences in related samples. The steps involved are similar to those of the *t* test for the difference between two means. To illustrate the use of the this tool for the *t* test, we refer to the financial applications example of Table 12.5 on page 502.

With the COMPTIME.XLS workbook open, select **Tools | Data Analysis**. Select **t Test: Paired Two Sample for Means** from the Analysis tools list box. Click the **OK** button. In the Variable 1 Range edit box enter **A1:A11**. In the Variable 2 Range edit box enter **B1:B11**. In the Hypothesized Mean Difference edit box enter **0**. Select the **Labels** check box. In the Alpha edit box, enter the level of significance (.05 in this example). Select the **New Worksheet Ply** option button and enter the name **t Test for Two Means**. Click the **OK** button.

## Using Minitab for the *t* Test for the Difference between Two Means

To illustrate the use of Minitab for the *t* test of the difference in two means, open the PRESSURE.MTP worksheet. Select **Stat | Basic Statistics | 2-Sample t**. If the data are stacked with the values in one column and the categories in a second column as they are in this worksheet, select **Samples in one column**. (If the samples are in different columns, select **Samples in different Columns** and enter the column numbers or names.) In the Sample edit box, enter **C1** or **Deviation**. In the Subscripts edit box, enter **C2** or **PSI**. If you wish to assume equal variances, select the **Assume equal variances** check box. In the Alternative drop-down list box, select less than or greater than for a one-tailed test or not equal for a two-tailed test. Click on **Graphs** and select **Boxplots of data**. Click the **OK** button to return to the 2-Sample t dialog box. Click the **OK** button.

## Using Minitab for the Paired *t* Test

To illustrate the use of Minitab for the paired *t* test, open the COMPTIME.MTW worksheet. Select **Stat | Basic Statistics | Paired t**. In the First Sample edit box, enter **C1** or **Current**. In the Second Sample edit box, enter **C2** or **New**. Click the **Options** button. In the Alternative drop-down list box, select less than or greater than for one-tailed test or not equal for a two-tailed test. Click the **OK** button to return to the Paired t dialog box. Click the **Graphs** button and select the **Boxplot of Differences** check box. Click the **OK** button to return to the Paired t dialog box. Click the **OK** button.

## Using Minitab for the Wilcoxon Rank Sum Test

To illustrate the use of Minitab for the Wilcoxon rank sum test of the difference in two medians, open the PRESSURE.MTP worksheet. If the data are stacked with the values in one column and the categories in a second column as they are in this worksheet, to unstack the data select **Manip | Stack/Unstack | Unstack One Column**. In the Unstack the data in edit box, enter **C1** or **Deviation**. In the Store the unstacked data in edit box, enter **C3–C4**. In the Using Subscripts in edit box, enter **C2** or **PSI**. Click the **OK** button. Enter 25 PSI as the label for C3 and 30PSI as the label for C4.

Select **Stat | Nonparametrics | Mann-Whitney**. In the First Sample edit box, enter **C3** or **25 PSI**. In the Second Sample edit box, enter **C4** or **30 PSI**. In the Alternative drop-down list box, select less than or greater than for one-tailed test or not equal for a two-tailed test. Click the **OK** button.

## Using Minitab for the Wilcoxon Signed-Ranks Test

To illustrate the use of Minitab for the Wilcoxon signed-ranks test, open the COMPTIME.MTW worksheet. To compute the differences, select **Calc | Calculator**. In the Store Result in Variable edit box, enter **C3**. In the Expression edit box, enter **C1–C2**. Click the **OK** button, Enter the label **Difference** for C3.

Select **Stat | Nonparametrics | One-Sample Wilcoxon** test. In the Variables edit box, enter **C3** or **Difference.** Select **Test Median**, and enter **0** in the edit box. In the Alternative drop-down list box, select less than or greater than for a one-tailed test or not equal for a two-tailed test. Click the **OK** button.

# 13

# ANOVA and Other c-Sample Tests with Numerical Data

# CHAPTER OBJECTIVES

✓ **To introduce the concepts of experimental design through the development of the completely randomized design model**

✓ **To describe the one-way ANOVA procedure used to test for differences among the means of c groups**

✓ **To describe the randomized block and factorial design models**

✓ **To develop the concept of interaction in a two-way factorial design**

✓ **To develop nonparametric alternatives for the one-way ANOVA procedure and the randomized block design**


## Introduction

In chapter 12 we used hypothesis-testing methodology to draw conclusions about possible differences between the parameters of two groups. Frequently, however, it is necessary to evaluate differences among the parameters of several ($c$) groups. We might want to compare alternative materials, methods, or treatments according to some predetermined criteria.

We begin this chapter by examining the *completely randomized design model* having only one *factor* with several groups (such as type of tire, marketing strategy, or brand of drug) and by developing procedures for evaluating differences in $c$ groups. We then extend this by describing the *randomized block design model* and the more sophisticated *factorial design model* (where more than one factor at a time is studied in one experiment) and by developing procedures for analyzing the numerical data. Throughout the chapter, emphasis is given to the assumptions behind the use of the various testing procedures.

To develop the relevant ideas for this chapter we again highlight the specific application described in chapter 12—an operations manager's concern for establishing appropriate machinery and equipment dial settings to meet product specifications in the process of filling 1-liter soft-drink bottles at a bottling plant.


◆ **USING STATISTICS:** *Establishing Proper Equipment Dial Settings to Meet Product Specifications*

The operations manager for a soft-drink distributor is interested in obtaining more uniform fill heights in the bottles filled during the bottling process at the bottling plant. Supposedly, available machinery fills each bottle to the correct level, but in practice there is variation around the specified target. In the preceding chapter we determined that an operating pressure of 25 psi is desirable for the equipment on hand. Two additional variables may still affect the filling process: line speed (210, 240, 270, or 300 bottles per minute) and/or the percent carbonation (10% or 12%). We will first examine the effect of line speed for a given percent carbonation. Later we will examine the effect of varying both line speed and percent carbonation.

## 13.1 ◆ THE COMPLETELY RANDOMIZED MODEL: ONE-FACTOR ANALYSIS OF VARIANCE

Many industrial applications involve experiments in which the groups or levels pertaining to only one **factor** of interest are considered. A factor such as baking temperature may have several *numerical levels* (for example, 300°, 350°, 400°, 450°) or a factor such as preferred placement for a product in a supermarket may have several *categorical levels* (front of aisle, middle of aisle, back of aisle). Such designed one-factor experiments in which subjects or *experimental units* are randomly assigned to groups or levels of a single factor are called **one-way** or **completely randomized design models**.

### F Test for Differences in c Means

When the numerical measurements across the $c$ groups are continuous and certain assumptions are met, a methodology known as **analysis of variance (ANOVA)** may be employed to compare the means of the groups. In a sense, the term "analysis of variance" appears to be a misnomer because the objective is to analyze differences among the group means. However, through an analysis of the variation in the data, both among and within the $c$ groups, we are able to draw conclusions about possible differences in group means. In ANOVA we subdivide the total variation in the measurements into that which is attributable to differences *among* the $c$ groups and that which is due to chance or attributable to inherent variation *within* the $c$ groups (see Figure 13.1). "Within group" variation is considered **experimental error**, while "among group" variation is attributable to **treatment effects**.

Under the assumptions that the $c$ groups or levels of the factor being studied represent populations whose measurements are randomly and independently drawn, follow a normal distribution, and have equal variances, the null hypothesis of no differences in the population means

$$H_0: \mu_1 = \mu_2 = \cdots = \mu_c$$

is tested against the alternative that not all the $c$ population means are equal.

$$H_1: \text{Not all } \mu_j \text{ are equal (where } j = 1, 2, \ldots, c)$$

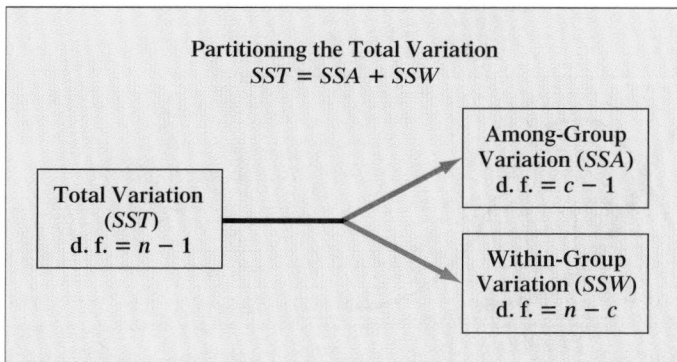

**FIGURE 13.1** Partitioning the total variation in a completely randomized model

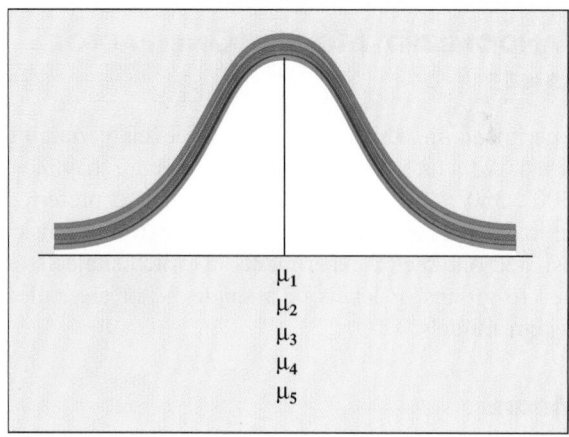

$\mu_1$
$\mu_2$
$\mu_3$
$\mu_4$
$\mu_5$

Figure 13.2 presents a picture of what a true null hypothesis looks like when five groups are compared and the assumptions of normality and equality of variances hold. The five populations representing the different levels of the factor are identical and therefore superimpose on one another. The properties of central tendency, variation, and shape are identical for each.

On the other hand, suppose that the null hypothesis is really false with level 4 having the largest mean, level 1 having the second-largest mean, and no differences in the other population means (see Figure 13.3). Note that except for differences in central tendency (that is, $\mu_4 > \mu_1 > \mu_2 = \mu_3 = \mu_5$), the five populations are the same in appearance.

To perform an ANOVA test of equality of population means we subdivide the total variation in the measurements into two parts, that which is attributable to differences among the groups and that which is due to inherent variation within the groups. The **total variation** is usually represented by the **sum of squares total** (or *SST*). Because under the null hypothesis the population means of the $c$ groups are presumed equal, a measure of the total variation among all the observations is obtained by summing the squared differences between each individual observation and the **overall** or **grand mean** $\overline{\overline{X}}$ that is based on all the observations in all the groups combined. The total variation is computed as in equation (13.1).

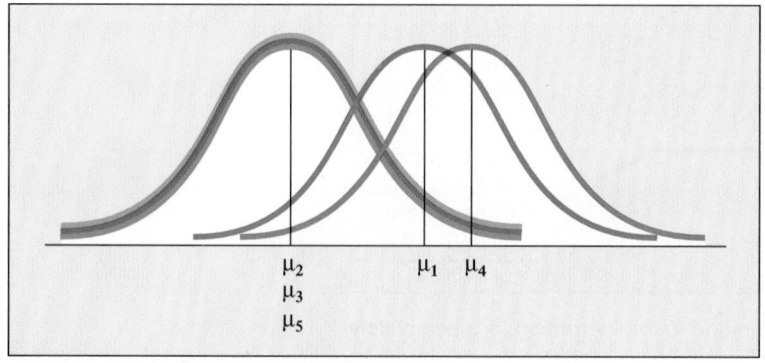

$\mu_2$
$\mu_3$
$\mu_5$

$\mu_1$   $\mu_4$

**FIGURE 13.3**   Treatment effect is present: $\mu_4 > \mu_1 > \mu_2 = \mu_3 = \mu_5$

## Total Variation

$$SST = \sum_{j=1}^{c} \sum_{i=1}^{n_j} (X_{ij} - \overline{\overline{X}})^2 \qquad (13.1)$$

where

$$\overline{\overline{X}} = \frac{\sum_{j=1}^{c} \sum_{i=1}^{n_j} X_{ij}}{n} \text{ is called the overall or grand mean}$$

$X_{ij}$ = the $i$th observation in group or level $j$

$n_j$ = the number of observations in group $j$

$n$ = the total number of observations in all groups combined
(that is, $n = n_1 + n_2 + \cdots + n_c$)

$c$ = the number of groups or levels of the factor of interest

The **among-group variation**, usually called the **sum of squares among groups** (or *SSA*), is measured by the sum of the squared differences between the sample mean of each group $\overline{X}_j$ and the overall or grand mean $\overline{\overline{X}}$, weighted by the sample size $n_j$ in each group. The among-group variation is computed as in equation (13.2).

## Among-Group Variation

$$SSA = \sum_{j=1}^{c} n_j (\overline{X}_j - \overline{\overline{X}})^2 \qquad (13.2)$$

where

$c$ = the number of groups or levels being compared

$n_j$ = the number of observations in group or level $j$

$\overline{X}_j$ = the sample mean of group $j$

$\overline{\overline{X}}$ = the overall or grand mean

The **within-group variation**, usually called the **sum of squares within groups** (or *SSW*), measures the difference between each observation and the mean of its own group and cumulates the squares of these differences over all groups. The within-group variation is computed as in equation (13.3).

## Within-Group Variation

$$SSW = \sum_{j=1}^{c} \sum_{i=1}^{n_j} (X_{ij} - \overline{X}_j)^2 \qquad (13.3)$$

where

$X_{ij}$ = the $i$th observation in group or level $j$

$\overline{X}_j$ = the sample mean of group $j$

Because $c$ levels of the factor are being compared, there are $c - 1$ degrees of freedom associated with the sum of squares among groups. Given that each of the $c$ levels contributes $n_j - 1$ degrees of freedom, there are $n - c$ degrees of freedom associated with the sum of squares within groups because

$$\sum_{j=1}^{c} (n_j - 1) = n - c$$

In addition, there are $n - 1$ degrees of freedom associated with the sum of squares total because each observation $X_{ij}$ is being compared with the overall or grand mean $\overline{\overline{X}}$ based on all $n$ observations.

If each of these sums of squares is divided by its associated degrees of freedom, we obtain three variances or **mean square** terms—*MSA*, *MSW*, and *MST*.

### Obtaining the Mean Squares

$$MSA = \frac{SSA}{c - 1} \tag{13.4a}$$

$$MSW = \frac{SSW}{n - c} \tag{13.4b}$$

$$MST = \frac{SST}{n - 1} \tag{13.4c}$$

Because a variance is computed by dividing the sum of squared differences by its appropriate degrees of freedom, the mean square terms are all variances.

Although our primary interest is in comparing the means of the $c$ groups or levels of a factor to determine whether a treatment effect exists among them, the ANOVA procedure derives its name from the fact that this is achieved by analyzing variances. If the null hypothesis is true and there are no real differences in the $c$ group means, all three mean square terms—*MSA*, *MSW*, and *MST*—which themselves are *variances*, provide estimates of the variance $\sigma^2$ inherent in the data. Thus, to test the null hypothesis

$$H_0\colon \mu_1 = \mu_2 = \cdots = \mu_c$$

against the alternative

$$H_1\colon \text{Not all } \mu_j \text{ are equal (where } j = 1, 2, \ldots, c)$$

we compute the test statistic $F$ as the ratio of two of the variances *MSA* to *MSW*, as in equation (13.5).

### The One-Way ANOVA *F*-Test Statistic

$$F = \frac{MSA}{MSW} \tag{13.5}$$

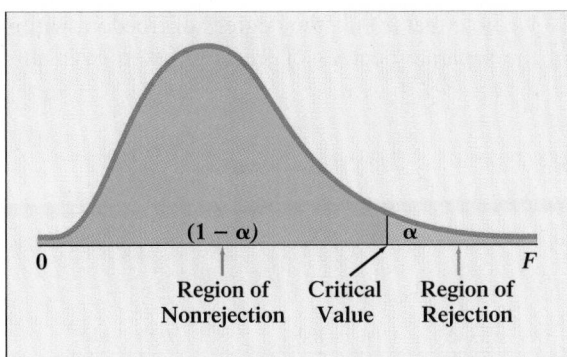

The $F$-test statistic follows an **$F$ distribution** with $c - 1$ degrees of freedom corresponding to $MSA$ in the numerator and $n - c$ degrees of freedom corresponding to $MSW$ in the denominator. For a given level of significance $\alpha$ we may reject the null hypothesis if the computed $F$-test statistic exceeds the upper-tailed critical value $F_U$ from the $F$ distribution having $c - 1$ degrees of freedom in the numerator and $n - c$ degrees of freedom in the denominator (see Table E.5). That is, as shown in Figure 13.4, our decision rule is

$$\text{Reject } H_0 \text{ if } F > F_U;$$
$$\text{otherwise don't reject } H_0.$$

If the null hypothesis is true, we expect the computed $F$ statistic to be approximately equal to 1 because both the numerator and denominator mean square terms are estimating the true variance $\sigma^2$ inherent in the data. On the other hand, if $H_0$ is false (and there are real differences in the means), we should expect the computed $F$ statistic to be substantially larger than 1 because the numerator, $MSA$, would be estimating the treatment effect or differences among groups in addition to the inherent variability in the data, whereas the denominator, $MSW$, would be measuring only the inherent variability. Hence, the ANOVA procedure yields an $F$ test in which the null hypothesis can be rejected at a selected $\alpha$ level of significance only if the computed $F$ statistic is large enough to exceed $F_U$, the upper-tail critical value of the $F$ distribution having $c - 1$ and $n - c$ degrees of freedom, as illustrated in Figure 13.4.

The one-factor ANOVA $F$ test is essentially an extension of the pooled-variance $t$ test. In section 12.1 we developed the pooled-variance $t$ test in order to compare differences in the means of two groups. When we introduced the $t$ test in equation (12.2), we defined $S_p^2$, the *pooled variance*, as

$$S_p^2 = \frac{(n_1 - 1)S_1^2 + (n_2 - 1)S_2^2}{(n_1 - 1) + (n_2 - 1)}$$

In the one-factor ANOVA $F$ test we are comparing differences in the means of $c$ groups. Therefore,

$$SSW = \sum_{j=1}^{c} \sum_{i=1}^{n_j} (X_{ij} - \overline{X}_j)^2$$

$$= \sum_{j=1}^{c} (n_j - 1)S_j^2 = (n_1 - 1)S_1^2 + (n_2 - 1)S_2^2 + \cdots + (n_c - 1)S_c^2$$

From the denominator of equation (13.4b) we note that $n - c$, the degrees of freedom within the groups, is equal to the summation of the separate degrees of freedom taken over all $c$ groups.

$$n - c = \sum_{j=1}^{c} (n_j - 1) = (n_1 - 1) + (n_2 - 1) + \cdots + (n_c - 1)$$

Equation (13.4b) can now be rewritten as follows:

$$MSW = \frac{SSW}{n - c} = \frac{\sum_{j=1}^{c} (n_j - 1)S_j^2}{\sum_{j=1}^{c} (n_j - 1)} = \frac{(n_1 - 1)S_1^2 + (n_2 - 1)S_2^2 + \cdots + (n_c - 1)S_c^2}{(n_1 - 1) + (n_2 - 1) + \cdots + (n_c - 1)}$$

Now that we have established a connection between the pooled-variance $t$ test and the one-factor ANOVA $F$ test, we address a frequently raised question: If the $F$ and $t$ tests *can* provide equivalent results, why discuss both procedures? The answer has two parts. If there are more than two groups whose means need to be compared, then only the $F$ test can be used, not the $t$ test. If there are only two groups to examine, the $t$ test can be employed if we are interested in testing the null hypothesis ($H_0$: $\mu_1 = \mu_2$) against either the general alternative that there are real differences ($H_1$: $\mu_1 \neq \mu_2$) or against a specific, ordered alternative ($H_1$: $\mu_1 > \mu_2$). The $F$ test is more limited. It can only be used to test the null hypothesis of no differences in the means ($H_0$: $\mu_1 = \mu_2$) against the general, two-sided alternative ($H_1$: $\mu_1 \neq \mu_2$).

The results of an analysis of variance are usually displayed in an **ANOVA summary table**, the format for which is presented in Table 13.1. The entries in this table include the sources of variation (i.e., among group, within group, and total), the degrees of freedom, the sums of squares, the mean squares (i.e., the variances), and the calculated $F$ statistic. In addition, the p-value (i.e., the probability of obtaining an $F$ statistic as large as or larger than the one obtained, given that the null hypothesis is true) is included in the ANOVA table of spreadsheet and statistical software packages. This allows us to make direct conclusions about the null hypothesis without referring to a table of critical values of the $F$ distribution. If the p-value is less than the chosen level of significance, the null hypothesis is rejected.

To illustrate the one-way ANOVA $F$ test, let us return to our Using Statistics application. In the previous chapter we determined that an operating pressure of 25 psi is desirable for the equipment on hand. If, in addition, a dial setting for 12% carbonation is also

**Table 13.1**    *Analysis-of-variance summary table*

| SOURCE | DEGREES OF FREEDOM | SUM OF SQUARES | MEAN SQUARE (VARIANCE) | F |
|---|---|---|---|---|
| Among groups | $c - 1$ | $SSA$ | $MSA = \dfrac{SSA}{c - 1}$ | $F = \dfrac{MSA}{MSW}$ |
| Within groups | $n - c$ | $SSW$ | $MSW = \dfrac{SSW}{n - c}$ | |
| Total | $n - 1$ | $SST$ | | |

**Table 13.2** *Deviations from specified target fill (in mm) under four line speeds*

| | LINE SPEED (IN BPM) | | | |
|---|---|---|---|---|
| | **210** | **240** | **270** | **300** |
| | $-3.5$ | $3.4$ | $-1.4$ | $4.3$ |
| | $2.0$ | $-2.1$ | $3.2$ | $3.3$ |
| | $-4.8$ | $0.6$ | $-1.2$ | $2.0$ |
| | $-2.1$ | $-4.5$ | $2.7$ | $-0.8$ |
| | $-4.0$ | $-1.6$ | $0.9$ | $2.5$ |
| *Mean* | $\overline{X}_1 = -2.48$ | $\overline{X}_2 = -0.84$ | $\overline{X}_3 = 0.84$ | $\overline{X}_4 = 2.26$ |
| *Variance* | $S_1^2 = 7.237$ | $S_2^2 = 8.903$ | $S_3^2 = 4.553$ | $S_4^2 = 3.683$ |
| *Std. Dev.* | $S_1 = 2.69$ | $S_2 = 2.98$ | $S_3 = 2.13$ | $S_4 = 1.92$ |

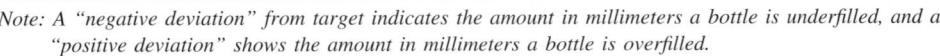

**DATA FILE LINESPD**

*Note: A "negative deviation" from target indicates the amount in millimeters a bottle is underfilled, and a "positive deviation" shows the amount in millimeters a bottle is overfilled.*

used, the operations manager will still want to determine the effect of different line speeds (in filled bottles per minute) on the average deviation from the specified target fill.

Suppose that the operations manager decides to perform an experiment with five bottles filled at each of the four levels of the line speed factor—210, 240, 270, and 300 bottles per minute (bpm). The results of this experiment (in terms of deviation from the target in millimeters) are displayed in Table 13.2 along with some summary computations of key descriptive statistics.

A *scatter plot* is depicted in Figure 13.5 on page 548 so that we can visually inspect the data and see how the measurements (in mm) distribute around their own group means as well as around the overall group mean $\overline{\overline{X}}$. We also get a sense for how each group mean compares with the overall mean. Thus, by examining Figure 13.5, we have the opportunity to observe possible trends or relationships across the groups as well as patterns within groups. In addition, we need to consider any potential violations of assumptions required by a particular testing procedure. Had the sample sizes in each group been larger, stem-and-leaf displays, box-and-whisker plots, and normal probability plots could be used for a visual evaluation. In addition, various tests of hypothesis are available for this purpose (see reference 2 and the Hartley test on pages 553–555).

We note from Table 13.2 and Figure 13.5 that there are differences in the sample means under the four line speeds. At a line speed of 210 bpm, the average deviation from specified target is $-2.48$ mm. At a line speed of 240 bpm, the average deviation is $-0.84$ mm. At a speed of 270 bpm, the average deviation is $+0.84$ mm and, at 300 bpm, the average deviation is $+2.26$ mm. The question that must be answered is whether these sample results are sufficiently different for the operations manager to decide that the *population* averages are not all equal.

The null hypothesis states that there is no difference among the four line speed levels in mean deviation from specified target fill.

$$H_0: \mu_1 = \mu_2 = \mu_3 = \mu_4$$

The alternative hypothesis states that there is a **treatment effect**; that is, at least one of the line speeds differs with respect to the average deviation from specified target fill.

$$H_1: \text{Not all the means are equal}$$

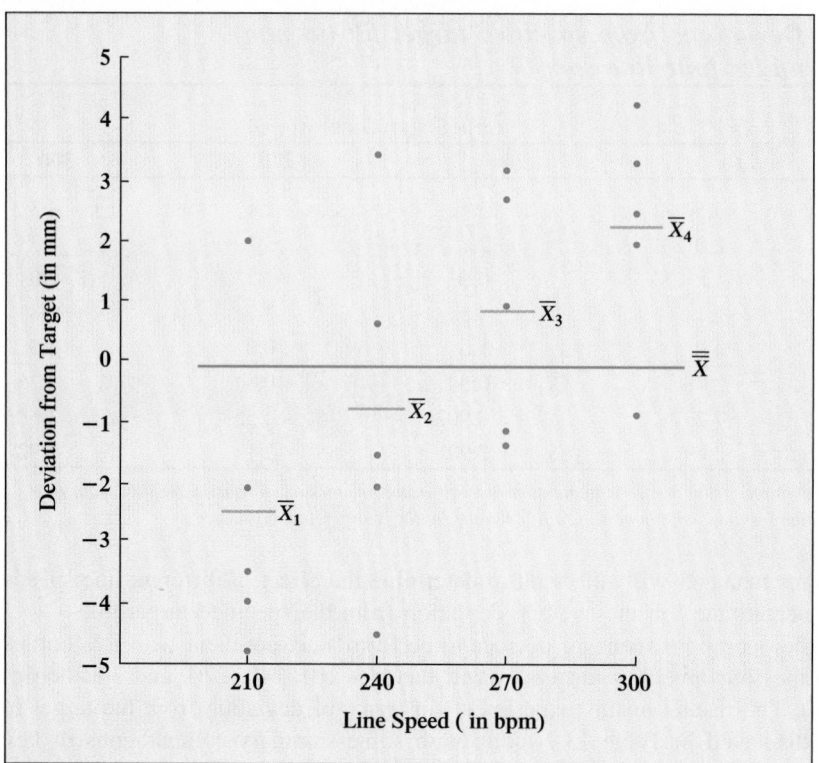

*FIGURE 13.5*

Scatter plot of deviations from specified target fill (in mm) under four different line speeds

*Source: Table 13.2*

To establish the ANOVA summary table, we first compute the sample means in each group (see Table 13.2 on page 547). Then, we compute the overall or grand mean by summing all 20 observations in Table 13.2 (being careful to include plus and minus signs).

$$\overline{\overline{X}} = \frac{\displaystyle\sum_{j=1}^{c}\sum_{i=1}^{n_j} X_{ij}}{n} = \frac{-1.10}{20} = -0.055$$

followed by the sums of squares:

$$SSA = \sum_{j=1}^{c} n_j(\overline{X}_j - \overline{\overline{X}})^2$$

$$= (5)[(-2.48) - (-0.055)]^2 + (5)[(-0.84) - (-0.055)]^2 + (5)[0.84 - (-0.055)]^2$$
$$+ (5)[2.26 - (-0.055)]^2$$

$$= 63.286$$

$$SSW = \sum_{j=1}^{c}\sum_{i=1}^{n_j} (X_{ij} - \overline{X}_j)^2$$

$$= (n_1 - 1)S_1^2 + (n_2 - 1)S_2^2 + (n_3 - 1)S_3^2 + (n_4 - 1)S_4^2$$

$$= (4)(7.237) + (4)(8.903) + (4)(4.553) + (4)(3.683)$$

$$= 97.504$$

the among-group variation will be larger. This fact forms the basis for the one-way ANOVA $F$ test of differences in group means.

Now let us review the soft-drink example. Again, from Table 13.2 on page 547 and Figure 13.5 on page 548 we note that there are differences among the four sample means. Using the one-way ANOVA $F$ test, the operations manager finds sufficient evidence to conclude that there is a significant treatment effect across the levels (or groups) of the factor of interest, line speeds. That is, there is evidence that the population means differ with respect to the average deviation from specified target fill based on the line speed used.

What we don't yet know, however, is which particular line speed or line speeds differ from the other(s). All we know is that there is sufficient evidence to state that the population means are not all the same; that is, at least one or some combination of them is significantly different. To determine exactly which line speed(s) differ, we will make all possible pairwise comparisons between the line speed dial settings and use a procedure developed by John Tukey (and later modified, independently, by Tukey and by C. Y. Kramer, for situations in which the sample sizes differ) to draw our conclusions (references 6, 7, 11, and 12).

## Multiple Comparisons: The Tukey-Kramer Procedure

In the soft-drink example discussed thus far in this chapter, the one-way ANOVA $F$ test was used to determine whether or not the selection of particular line speed levels affects fill heights. Once differences in the means of the groups or levels are found, it is important that we determine which particular groups or levels are different.

Although many procedures are available (see references 6 and 9), we now focus on the Tukey-Kramer procedure to determine which of the $c$ means are significantly different from each other. This method is an example of a *post hoc* (or **a posteriori**) comparison procedure, because the hypotheses of interest are formulated *after* the data have been inspected.

The Tukey-Kramer procedure enables us to simultaneously examine comparisons between all pairs of groups. The first step involved is to compute the differences $\overline{X}_j - \overline{X}_{j'}$ (where $j \neq j'$) among all $c(c - 1)/2$ pairs of means. The **critical range** for the Tukey-Kramer procedure is then obtained from the quantity given in equation (13.6).

### Obtaining the Critical Range

$$\text{Critical range} = Q_U \sqrt{\frac{MSW}{2}\left(\frac{1}{n_j} + \frac{1}{n_{j'}}\right)} \tag{13.6}$$

where $Q_U$ = the upper-tail critical value from a *Studentized range* distribution having $c$ degrees of freedom in the numerator and $n - c$ degrees of freedom in the denominator.

If the sample sizes differ, a critical range is then computed for each pairwise comparison of sample means. The final step is to compare each of the $c(c - 1)/2$ pairs of means against its corresponding critical range. A specific pair is then declared significantly different if the absolute difference in the sample means $\left|\overline{X}_j - \overline{X}_{j'}\right|$ exceeds the critical range.

To apply the Tukey-Kramer procedure, we return to the soft-drink example. Using the ANOVA procedure, we concluded that there was evidence of a significant treatment effect.

**Table 13.5**  *Obtaining Studentized range Q statistic for $\alpha = .05$ with 4 and 16 degrees of freedom*

| DENOMINATOR DEGREES OF FREEDOM | NUMERATOR DEGREES OF FREEDOM | | | | | | | |
|---|---|---|---|---|---|---|---|---|
| | 2 | 3 | 4 | 5 | 6 | 7 | 8 | 9 |
| . | . | . | . | . | . | . | . | . |
| . | . | . | . | . | . | . | . | . |
| . | . | . | . | . | . | . | . | . |
| 11 | 3.11 | 3.82 | 4.26 | 4.57 | 4.82 | 5.03 | 5.20 | 5.35 |
| 12 | 3.08 | 3.77 | 4.20 | 4.51 | 4.75 | 4.95 | 5.12 | 5.27 |
| 13 | 3.06 | 3.73 | 4.15 | 4.45 | 4.69 | 4.88 | 5.05 | 5.19 |
| 14 | 3.03 | 3.70 | 4.11 | 4.41 | 4.64 | 4.83 | 4.99 | 5.13 |
| 15 | 3.01 | 3.67 | 4.08 | 4.37 | 4.60 | 4.78 | 4.94 | 5.08 |
| 16 | 3.00 | 3.65 | 4.05 | 4.33 | 4.56 | 4.74 | 4.90 | 5.03 |

*Source: Extracted from Table E.10.*

Different line speed levels significantly affect bottle fill heights. Because there are four levels, there are $4(4 - 1)/2 = 6$ possible pairwise comparisons to be made. From Table 13.2 on page 547, the absolute mean differences are calculated as follows.

$$1.\ |\bar{X}_1 - \bar{X}_2| = |(-2.48) - (-0.84)| = 1.64$$
$$2.\ |\bar{X}_1 - \bar{X}_3| = |(-2.48) - 0.84| = 3.32$$
$$3.\ |\bar{X}_1 - \bar{X}_4| = |(-2.48) - 2.26| = 4.74$$
$$4.\ |\bar{X}_2 - \bar{X}_3| = |(-0.84) - 0.84| = 1.68$$
$$5.\ |\bar{X}_2 - \bar{X}_4| = |(-0.84) - 2.26| = 3.10$$
$$6.\ |\bar{X}_3 - \bar{X}_4| = |0.84 - 2.26| = 1.42$$

Only one critical range needs to be obtained here because the four groups had equal-sized samples. To determine the critical range, from our ANOVA summary table (Table 13.4 on page 550) we have $MSW = 6.094$ and also $n_j = 5$. From Table E.10, for $\alpha = .05$, $c = 4$ and $n - c = 20 - 4 = 16$, then $Q_U$, the upper-tailed critical value of the test statistic with 4 degrees of freedom in the numerator and 16 degrees of freedom in the denominator, is 4.05 (see Table 13.5). From equation (13.6), we have

$$\text{Critical range} = 4.05\sqrt{\left(\frac{6.094}{2}\right)\left(\frac{1}{5} + \frac{1}{5}\right)} = 4.471$$

Because $4.74 > 4.471$, we conclude that there is a significant difference between the means of groups 1 and 4. All other pairwise differences are due to chance. The operations manager therefore concludes that using a line speed of 210 bpm results in significantly less soda fill than does a line speed of 300 bpm.

## ANOVA Assumptions

In our soft-drink example we have not yet thoroughly evaluated the assumptions underlying the one-way $F$ test. How can the operations manager know whether the one-way $F$ test was an appropriate procedure for analyzing the experimental data?

In chapters 11 and 12 we mentioned the assumptions made in the application of each hypothesis-testing procedure and the consequences of departures from these assumptions. To employ the one-way ANOVA $F$ test, we must also make certain assumptions about the data being investigated. The three major assumptions are randomness and independence, normality, and homogeneity of variance.

The first assumption, **randomness and independence**, always must be met because the validity of any experiment depends on random sampling and/or the randomization process. To avoid biases in the outcomes, it is essential that either the obtained samples of data be considered as randomly and independently drawn from the $c$ populations or that the items or subjects in a study be randomly assigned to the $c$ levels of the factor of interest (i.e., the *treatment groups*). Departures from this assumption can seriously affect inferences from the analysis of variance. These problems are discussed more thoroughly in references 1 and 6.

The second assumption, **normality**, states that the values in each sampled group are drawn from normally distributed populations. Just as in the case of the $t$ test, the one-way ANOVA $F$ test is fairly robust against departures from the normal distribution. As long as the distributions are not extremely different from a normal distribution, the level of significance of the ANOVA $F$ test is usually not greatly affected by lack of normality, particularly for large samples. When only the normality assumption is seriously violated, *nonparametric* alternatives to the one-way ANOVA $F$ test are available (see section 13.4).

The third assumption, **homogeneity of variance**, states that the variance within each population should be equal for all populations (that is, $\sigma_1^2 = \sigma_2^2 = \cdots = \sigma_c^2$). This assumption is needed in order to combine or pool the variances within the groups into a single within-group source of variation *SSW*. If there are equal sample sizes in each group, inferences based on the $F$ distribution may not be seriously affected by unequal variances. If, however, there are unequal sample sizes in different groups, unequal variances from group to group can have serious effects on any inferences developed from the ANOVA procedures. Thus, when possible, there should be equal sample sizes in all groups.

When only the homogeneity-of-variance assumption is violated, procedures similar to those used in the separate-variance $t$ test of section 12.1 are available (see reference 1). However, if both the normality and homogeneity-of-variance assumptions have been violated, an appropriate *data transformation* may be used that will both normalize the data and reduce the differences in variances (see references 1 and 11) or, alternatively, a more general *nonparametric procedure* may be employed (see references 2 and 3).

## Hartley's $F_{max}$ Test for Homogeneity of Variance

Although the one-way ANOVA $F$ test is relatively robust with respect to the assumption of equal group variances, large departures from this assumption may seriously affect the level of significance and the power of the test. Therefore, various procedures have been developed to more formally test the assumption of homogeneity of variance. Perhaps the simplest and best known is Hartley's $F_{max}$ procedure (see reference 1). To test for the equality of the $c$ population variances

$$H_0: \sigma_1^2 = \sigma_2^2 = \cdots = \sigma_c^2$$

against the alternative

$$H_1: \text{Not all } \sigma_j^2 \text{ are equal } (j = 1, 2, \ldots, c)$$

we obtain the $F_{max}$ test statistic in equation (13.7).

## Hartley's $F_{max}$ Test

$$F_{max} = \frac{S^2_{max}}{S^2_{min}} \tag{13.7}$$

where

$$S^2_{max} = \text{largest sample variance}$$
$$S^2_{min} = \text{smallest sample variance}$$

The $F_{max}$ test statistic follows **Hartley's $F_{max}$ distribution** with $c$ degrees of freedom in the numerator and $(\bar{n} - 1)$ degrees of freedom in the denominator where $\bar{n}$ is the average sample size over the $c$ groups.[1]

[1] *The integer portion of the calculation for $\bar{n}$ is used for determining the degrees of freedom in the denominator of Hartley's $F_{max}$ distribution.*

$$\bar{n} = \frac{\sum_{j=1}^{c} n_j}{c} = \frac{n}{c}$$

Using a level of significance $\alpha$, the null hypothesis of the equality of group variances will be rejected only when the computed $F_{max}$ statistic exceeds $F_{max_U}$, the upper-tail critical value of Hartley's $F_{max}$ distribution based upon $c$ and $(\bar{n} - 1)$ degrees of freedom (see Table E.6, a replica of which is presented as Table 13.6). That is,

$$\text{Reject } H_0 \text{ if } F_{max} > F_{max_U};$$
$$\text{otherwise don't reject } H_0.$$

To illustrate Hartley's $F_{max}$ procedure, let us return to the data for the soft-drink example (see Table 13.2 on page 547). Using equation (4.9) on page 145, we compute the sample variances of the four groups as follows.

$$S^2_1 = 7.237 \qquad S^2_2 = 8.903 \qquad S^2_3 = 4.553 \qquad S^2_4 = 3.683$$

Because each group contains a sample of size 5, $\bar{n} = (5 + 5 + 5 + 5)/4 = 5$, and, testing the null hypothesis

$$H_0: \sigma^2_1 = \sigma^2_2 = \sigma^2_3 = \sigma^2_4$$

**Table 13.6** *Obtaining upper-tailed critical value of $F_{max}$ with 4 and 4 degrees of freedom at the .05 level of significance*

| | | | | Upper 5% Points ($\alpha = .05$) | | | | |
|---|---|---|---|---|---|---|---|---|
| $\bar{n} - 1 \backslash c$ | 2 | 3 | 4 | 5 | 6 | 7 | 8 | 9 |
| 2 | 39.0 | 87.5 | 142 | 202 | 266 | 333 | 403 | 475 |
| 3 | 15.4 | 27.8 | 39.2 | 50.7 | 62.0 | 72.9 | 83.5 | 93.9 |
| 4 | 9.60 | 15.5 | 20.6 | 25.2 | 29.5 | 33.6 | 37.5 | 41.1 |
| 5 | 7.15 | 10.8 | 13.7 | 16.3 | 18.7 | 20.8 | 22.9 | 24.7 |
| 6 | 5.82 | 8.38 | 10.4 | 12.1 | 13.7 | 15.0 | 16.3 | 17.5 |

*Source: Extracted from Table E.6.*

against the alternative

$$H_1: \text{Not all } \sigma_j^2 \text{ are equal (where } j = 1, 2, 3, 4)$$

the $F_{max}$ statistic is computed from equation (13.7) as follows.

$$F_{max} = \frac{8.903}{3.683} = 2.417$$

If the .05 level of significance is selected, the decision rule is to reject $H_0$ if $F_{max} > F_{max_U} = 20.6$, the upper-tail critical value of Hartley's $F_{max}$ distribution with $c = 4$ degrees of freedom in the numerator and $(\bar{n} - 1) = 4$ degrees of freedom in the denominator (see Table 13.6). In our soda fill study, because $F_{max} = 2.417 < F_{max_U} = 20.6$, we do not reject $H_0$. We therefore conclude that there is no evidence of a difference in the variances of the four groups.

---

**COMMENT:** *Assumptions of the Hartley $F_{max}$ test*

Although the $F_{max}$ test is simple to use, it is not robust because it is extremely sensitive to departures from normality in the data. Thus, in situations in which we are unable to assume normality for each group, other alternative procedures should be applied (see references 2 and 3).

---

## Problems for Section 13.1

### Learning the Basics

● **13.1** Given an experiment having a single factor of interest with five groups or levels and seven observations in each group, answer the following.
   (a) How many degrees of freedom are there in determining the among-group variation?
   (b) How many degrees of freedom are there in determining the within-group variation?
   (c) How many degrees of freedom are there in determining the total variation?

● **13.2** From Problem 13.1:
   (a) If $SSA = 60$ and $SST = 210$, what is $SSW$?
   (b) What is $MSA$?
   (c) What is $MSW$?
   (d) What is the value of the test statistic $F$?

● **13.3** From Problems 13.1 and 13.2:
   (a) Form the ANOVA summary table and fill in all values in the body of the table.
   (b) At the .05 level of significance, what is the upper-tailed critical value from the $F$ distribution?
   (c) State the decision rule for testing the null hypothesis that all five groups have equal population means.
   (d) What is your statistical decision?

**13.4** Given an experiment having one factor containing three treatment levels with seven observations in each, answer the following.
   (a) How many degrees of freedom are there in determining the among-group variation?

(b) How many degrees of freedom are there in determining the within-group variation?

(c) How many degrees of freedom are there in determining the total variation?

**13.5** From Problem 13.4, suppose we obtain the following summary information:

| Level 1 | Level 2 | Level 3 |
|---|---|---|
| $\bar{X}_1 = 33$ | $\bar{X}_2 = 38$ | $\bar{X}_3 = 37$ |
| $S_1^2 = 20$ | $S_2^2 = 18$ | $S_3^2 = 13$ |
| $S_1 = 4.47$ | $S_2 = 4.24$ | $S_3 = 3.61$ |

(a) What is the value of Hartley's $F_{max}$ statistic?

(b) How many degrees of freedom are there in the numerator of Hartley's $F_{max}$ distribution?

(c) How many degrees of freedom are there in the denominator of Hartley's $F_{max}$ distribution?

(d) At the .05 level of significance, what is $F_{max_U}$, the upper-tailed critical value of Hartley's $F_{max}$ distribution?

(e) What is your statistical decision when testing the assumption of equality of population variances?

**13.6** From Problem 13.4 and the data of Problem 13.5:

(a) When each group or level contains equal sample sizes, the overall or grand mean is obtained as the mean of the individual sample means. What is the value of $\bar{\bar{X}}$?

(b) What is the value of $MSW$?

(c) Form the ANOVA summary table and fill in all values in the body of the table.

(d) At the .05 level of significance, what is the upper-tailed critical value from the $F$ distribution?

(e) State the decision rule for testing the null hypothesis that all three groups have equal population means.

(f) What is your statistical decision?

**13.7** You are conducting an experiment with one factor of interest containing four groups or levels with eight observations in each group. From the ANOVA summary table below, fill in all the missing results.

| SOURCE | DEGREES OF FREEDOM | SUM OF SQUARES | MEAN SQUARE (VARIANCE) | F |
|---|---|---|---|---|
| Among groups | $c - 1 = ?$ | $SSA = ?$ | $MSA = 80$ | $F = ?$ |
| Within groups | $n - c = ?$ | $SSW = 560$ | $MSW = ?$ | |
| Total | $n - 1 = ?$ | $SST = ?$ | | |

**13.8** From Problem 13.7:

(a) At the .05 level of significance, what is the upper-tailed critical value from the $F$ distribution?

(b) State the decision rule for testing the null hypothesis that all four groups have equal population means.

(c) What is your statistical decision?

(d) To perform the Tukey-Kramer procedure, how many degrees of freedom are there in the numerator and how many degrees of freedom are there in the denominator of the Studentized range distribution?

(e) At the .05 level of significance, what is the upper-tailed critical value from the Studentized range distribution?

(f) To perform the Tukey-Kramer procedure, what is the critical range?

## Applying the Concepts

● **13.9** The personnel manager of a large insurance company wishes to evaluate the effectiveness of four different sales-training programs designed for new employees. A group of 32 recently hired college graduates are randomly assigned to the four programs so that there are 8 subjects in each program. At the end of the monthlong training period, a standard exam is administered to the 32 subjects; the scores are as follows:

| PROGRAMS | | | |
|---|---|---|---|
| **A** | **B** | **C** | **D** |
| 66 | 72 | 61 | 63 |
| 74 | 51 | 60 | 61 |
| 82 | 59 | 57 | 76 |
| 75 | 62 | 60 | 84 |
| 73 | 74 | 81 | 58 |
| 97 | 64 | 55 | 65 |
| 87 | 78 | 70 | 69 |
| 78 | 63 | 71 | 80 |

DATA FILE
INSPGM

Using either computer software or the following summary information:

| Programs: | **A** | **B** | **C** | **D** | |
|---|---|---|---|---|---|
| Sample means: | 79.000 | 65.375 | 64.375 | 69.500 | $\overline{\overline{X}} = 69.56$ |
| Sample standard deviations: | 9.592 | 8.815 | 8.815 | 9.487 | |

(a) Construct an appropriate graph, plot, or chart of the data.

(b) Describe any trends or relationships that might be apparent within or among the groups.

(c) Does the variation within the groups seem to be similar for all groups? Discuss.

(d) If conditions are appropriate, at an $\alpha = .05$ level of significance, use the one-way $F$ test to determine whether there is evidence of a significant difference in the four sales-training programs.

(e) On the basis of your results in (a), (b), and (d), if appropriate, which group or groups might you suspect to be significantly different from which other groups? Discuss.

**13.10** A statistics professor wants to study four different strategies of playing the game of Blackjack (Twenty-One). The four strategies are:

(1) Dealer's strategy

(2) 5-count strategy

(3) Basic 10-count strategy

(4) Advanced 10-count strategy

A calculator that could play Blackjack is used, and data from five sessions of each strategy are collected. The profits (or losses) from each session are shown at the top of page 558.

| | | STRATEGY | |
|---|---|---|---|
| **DEALER'S** | **5 COUNT** | **BASIC 10 COUNT** | **ADVANCED 10 COUNT** |
| −$56 | −$26 | +$16 | +$60 |
| −78 | −12 | +20 | +40 |
| −20 | +18 | −14 | −16 |
| −46 | −8 | +6 | +12 |
| −60 | −16 | −25 | +4 |

**DATA FILE**
**BLACKJ**

Using either computer software or the following summary information:

| Strategies: | 1 | 2 | 3 | 4 | |
|---|---|---|---|---|---|
| Sample means: | −52.00 | −8.80 | +0.60 | +20.00 | $\overline{\overline{X}} = -\$10.05$ |
| Sample standard deviations: | 21.31 | 16.41 | 19.44 | 30.07 | |

The professor wants to know whether there is evidence of a significant difference among the four strategies and, if so, which strategies seem to be superior with respect to potential profitability.
(a) Completely analyze the data. (Use $\alpha = .01$.)
(b) If you were to play Blackjack, what strategy would you choose? Explain.

**13.11** A snack foods company that supplies stores in a metropolitan area with "healthy" snack products was interested in improving the shelf life of its tortilla chip product. Six batches (each batch containing 1 pound) of the product were made under each of four different formulations. The batches were then kept under the same conditions of storage. Product condition was checked each day for freshness. The shelf life in days until the product was deemed to be lacking in freshness was as follows:

| | FORMULATION METHOD | | |
|---|---|---|---|
| **A** | **B** | **C** | **D** |
| 94 | 88 | 76 | 82 |
| 100 | 89 | 69 | 80 |
| 90 | 88 | 76 | 82 |
| 97 | 83 | 79 | 78 |
| 101 | 79 | 80 | 89 |
| 90 | 82 | 72 | 80 |

**DATA FILE**
**POTCHIP**

To solve, use either computer software or the following summary information:

| Formulation Method: | A | B | C | D | |
|---|---|---|---|---|---|
| Sample means: | 95.33 | 84.83 | 75.33 | 81.83 | $\overline{\overline{X}} = 84.33$ |
| Sample standard deviations: | 4.803 | 4.07 | 4.179 | 3.817 | |

(a) At the .05 level of significance, completely analyze the data to determine whether there is evidence of a difference in the average shelf life among the formulations.

(b)  If appropriate, determine which groups differ in average shelf life.

(c)  What conclusions about the shelf life of the formulations can the manager of the snack foods company reach? Explain.

● **13.12**  The retailing manager of a supermarket chain wishes to determine whether product location has any effect on the sale of pet toys. Three different aisle locations are considered: front, middle, and rear. A random sample of 18 stores is selected with 6 stores randomly assigned to each aisle location. The size of the display area and price of the product are constant for all stores. At the end of a 1-week trial period, the sales volume (in thousands of dollars) of the product in each store was as follows:

**AISLE LOCATION**

| FRONT | MIDDLE | REAR |
|-------|--------|------|
| 8.6 | 3.2 | 4.6 |
| 7.2 | 2.4 | 6.0 |
| 5.4 | 2.0 | 4.0 |
| 6.2 | 1.4 | 2.8 |
| 5.0 | 1.8 | 2.2 |
| 4.0 | 1.6 | 2.8 |

DATA FILE
LOCATE

| Aisle location: | FRONT | MIDDLE | REAR | |
|-----------------|-------|--------|------|---|
| Sample means: | 6.067 | 2.067 | 3.733 | $\overline{\overline{X}} = 3.956$ |
| Sample standard deviations: | 1.648 | .653 | 1.418 | |

(a)  At the .05 level of significance, is there evidence of a significant difference in average sales among the various aisle locations?

(b)  If appropriate, which aisle locations appear to differ significantly in average sales?

(c)  What should the retailing manager conclude? Describe fully the retailing manager's options with respect to aisle locations.

**13.13**  To examine effects of the work environment on attitude toward work, an industrial psychologist randomly assigns a group of 18 recently hired sales trainees to three "home rooms"—6 trainees per room. Each room is identical except for wall color. One is light green, another is light blue, and the third is deep red.

 During the weeklong training program, the trainees stay mainly in their respective home rooms. At the end of the program, an attitude scale is used to measure each trainee's attitude toward work (a low score indicates a poor attitude, a high score a good attitude). The following data are obtained:

**ROOM COLOR**

| LIGHT GREEN | LIGHT BLUE | DEEP RED |
|-------------|------------|----------|
| 46 | 59 | 34 |
| 51 | 54 | 29 |
| 48 | 47 | 43 |
| 42 | 55 | 40 |
| 58 | 49 | 45 |
| 50 | 44 | 34 |

DATA FILE
WORKATT

On the basis of these data, the industrial psychologist wants to determine whether there is significant evidence that work environment (i.e., color of room) has an effect on attitude toward work and, if so, which room color(s) appear(s) to significantly enhance attitude. To solve, use either computer software or the following summary information:

| Color: | GREEN | BLUE | RED | |
|---|---|---|---|---|
| Sample means: | 49.167 | 51.333 | 37.500 | $\overline{\overline{X}} = 46.000$ |
| Sample standard deviations: | 5.382 | 5.610 | 6.156 | |

(a) Completely analyze the data. (Use $\alpha = .05$.)
(b) On the basis of this thorough analysis, draft a report discussing the implications of the findings for office design in large firms, knowing that the industrial psychologist might use this when meeting with the vice president for human resources at the company.

**13.14** A senior partner in a brokerage firm wishes to determine whether there is really any difference between long-run performance of different categories of people hired as customers' representatives. The junior members of the firm are classified into four groups: professionals who have changed careers, recent business school graduates, former salespeople, and brokers hired from competing firms. A random sample of six individuals in each of these categories is selected, and a detailed performance score (a higher number indicates better performance) is obtained.

| CUSTOMER REPRESENTATIVE BACKGROUNDS | | | |
|---|---|---|---|
| **PROFESSIONALS** | **BUSINESS SCHOOL GRADS** | **SALESPEOPLE** | **BROKERS** |
| 88 | 65 | 61 | 83 |
| 85 | 73 | 67 | 87 |
| 95 | 54 | 74 | 90 |
| 96 | 72 | 65 | 84 |
| 91 | 81 | 68 | 92 |
| 88 | 69 | 77 | 94 |

DATA FILE
BROKER

To solve, use either computer software or the following summary information:

| Background: | 1 | 2 | 3 | 4 | |
|---|---|---|---|---|---|
| Sample means: | 90.50 | 69.00 | 68.67 | 88.33 | $\overline{\overline{X}} = 79.13$ |
| Sample standard deviations: | 4.32 | 9.06 | 5.89 | 4.41 | |

(a) Is there evidence of a significant difference in the average performance score for the various categories? (Use $\alpha = .05$.)
(b) If appropriate, which customer representative backgrounds seem to result in a significantly higher performance?

(c) What would you tell the senior partner concerning the long-run performance of people hired as customers' representatives?

**13.15** Suppose that the training director of a manufacturing company wanted to compare three different team-based approaches. Each member of a group of 26 new employees was randomly assigned to one of three team-based methods. After completing training, the employees in the study were evaluated on the time it took (in minutes) to assemble the product. The results are summarized as follows:

TIME TO ASSEMBLE PRODUCT

| METHODS | | |
|---|---|---|
| **A** | **B** | **C** |
| 8.82 | 8.21 | 8.57 |
| 9.26 | 6.65 | 8.50 |
| 8.70 | 7.44 | 9.11 |
| 8.97 | 7.95 | 8.20 |
| 8.64 | 8.20 | 8.32 |
| 8.29 | 7.75 | 7.88 |
| 9.45 | 8.84 | 9.90 |
| 9.42 | 8.40 | 9.43 |
| 9.25 | 7.98 | |

DATA FILE
TRAIN3G

To solve, use either computer software or the following summary information:

| Method: | **A** | **B** | **C** | |
|---|---|---|---|---|
| Sample sizes: | 9 | 9 | 8 | |
| Sample means: | 8.9778 | 7.9356 | 8.7387 | $\overline{\overline{X}} = 8.543$ |
| Sample standard deviations: | .3971 | .6239 | .6817 | |

(a) At the .05 level of significance, analyze the data to determine whether there is evidence of a difference in the average assembly time among the team-based methods.
(b) If the results you obtained in (a) indicate it is appropriate, determine which groups differ in average assembly time.
(c) What conclusions about the three team-based training methods should be reached by the training director?

**13.16** A manufacturer is developing a nickel-metal hydride battery that is to be used in cellular telephones in lieu of nickel-cadmium batteries. The director of quality control decides to evaluate the newly developed battery against the widely used nickel-cadmium battery with respect to performance. A random sample of 25 nickel-cadmium batteries and a random sample of 25 of the newly developed nickel-metal hydride batteries are placed in cellular telephones of the same brand and model. The performance measure of interest is the talking time (in minutes) prior to recharging. The results are as follows:

| NICKEL-CADMIUM BATTERY | | | NICKEL-METAL HYDRIDE BATTERY | | |
|---|---|---|---|---|---|
| 54.5 | 71.0 | 67.0 | 78.3 | 103.0 | 79.8 |
| 67.8 | 41.7 | 56.7 | 95.4 | 81.3 | 91.1 |
| 64.5 | 69.7 | 86.8 | 69.4 | 46.4 | 82.8 |
| 70.4 | 40.8 | 74.9 | 87.3 | 82.3 | 71.8 |
| 72.5 | 75.4 | 76.9 | 62.5 | 83.2 | 77.5 |
| 64.9 | 81.0 | 104.4 | 85.0 | 85.3 | 74.3 |
| 83.3 | 90.4 | 82.0 | 85.3 | 85.5 | 86.1 |
| 72.8 | 71.8 | 58.7 | 72.1 | 112.3 | 74.1 |
| 68.8 | | | 41.1 | | |

**DATA FILE
NICKBAT**

To solve, use either computer software or the following summary information:

| Battery: | NC | NMH | |
|---|---|---|---|
| Sample means: | 70.75 | 79.73 | $\overline{\overline{X}} = 75.24$ |
| Sample standard deviations: | 13.99 | 15.03 | |

(a) Use the one-way ANOVA $F$ test to determine if there is evidence of a difference in the two types of batteries with respect to average talking time (in minutes) prior to recharging. (Use $\alpha = .05$.)

(b) What assumptions are necessary to perform this test?

(c) If you performed the pooled-variance $t$ test on this data set to solve Problem 12.13 on page 487, square the value of $t$ you computed in part (a) of Problem 12.13 and notice that it is the same (except for rounding error) as the $F$-test statistic. Express in your own words the relationship between $t$ and $F$.

## 13.2 THE RANDOMIZED BLOCK MODEL

In section 13.1, we developed the one-way ANOVA $F$ test to evaluate differences in the means of $c$ groups. The one-way ANOVA $F$ test is employed in experimental situations in which $n$ homogeneous items or individuals (i.e., *experimental units*) are randomly assigned to the $c$ levels of a factor of interest (i.e., the *treatment groups*). Such designed one-factor experiments are referred to as *one-way* or *completely randomized design models*.

Alternatively, in sections 12.3 and 12.5 we used the $t$ test for the mean difference or the Wilcoxon signed-ranks test for the median difference in situations involving repeated measurements or matched samples in order to evaluate differences between two treatment conditions. Suppose, now, we wish to extend this to situations in which there are more than two treatment groups or levels of a factor of interest. In such cases, the heterogeneous sets of items or individuals that have been matched (or on whom repeated measurements have been taken) are called **blocks**. Numerical data are then obtained as the response or outcome of each treatment group and block combination. Thus, in designing experiments of this type, there are two things to consider: treatments and blocks. However, with respect to our tests of hypotheses, we focus on the differences among the $c$ levels of the factor of interest (i.e., the treatment groups).

Experimental situations such as this are referred to as **randomized block design models**. The purpose of blocking is to remove as much variability as possible so that the focus is on differences among the $c$ treatment conditions. Thus, when appropriate, the reason for selecting a randomized block design model instead of a completely randomized design model is to provide a more efficient analysis by reducing the experimental error and thereby obtaining more precise results (see references 1, 5, 6, and 11).

## Tests for the Treatment and Block Effects

Recall from Figure 13.1 on page 541 that in the completely randomized model, the total variation in the outcome measurements (*SST*) is subdivided into that which is attributable to differences *among* the *c* groups (*SSA*) and that which is due to chance or attributable to inherent variation *within* the *c* groups (*SSW*). Among-group variation is attributable to treatment effects and within-group variation is considered experimental error.

To filter out the effects of the blocking for the randomized block design model, we need to further subdivide the within-group variation (*SSW*) into that which is attributable to differences among the blocks (*SSBL*) and that which is attributable to inherent random error (*SSE*). Therefore, as presented in Figure 13.7, in a randomized block design model the total variation in the outcome measurements is the summation of three components—among-group variation (*SSA*), among-block variation (*SSBL*), and inherent random error (*SSE*).

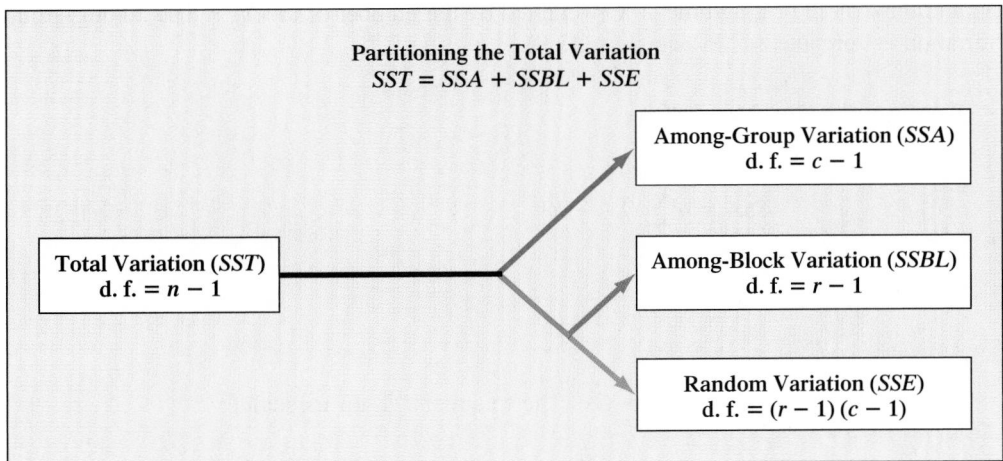

**FIGURE 13.7**  Partitioning the total variation in a randomized block design model

To develop the ANOVA procedure for the randomized block design model we need to define the following terms:

$r$ = the number of blocks

$c$ = the number of groups or levels

$n$ = the total number of observations (where $n = rc$)

$X_{ij}$ = the value in the $i$th block for the $j$th treatment level

$\overline{X}_{i.}$ = the mean of all the values in block $i$

$\overline{X}_{.j}$ = the mean of all the values for treatment level $j$

$$\sum_{j=1}^{c}\sum_{i=1}^{r} X_{ij} = \text{the grand total—i.e., the summation of the values over all blocks and all groups}$$

The total variation, also called **sum of squares total (SST)**, is a measure of the variation among all the observations. It can be obtained by summing the squared differences between each individual observation and the overall or grand mean $\overline{\overline{X}}$ that is based on all $n$ observations. SST is computed as in equation (13.8).

**Total Variation**

$$SST = \sum_{j=1}^{c} \sum_{i=1}^{r} (X_{ij} - \overline{\overline{X}})^2 \tag{13.8}$$

where

$$\overline{\overline{X}} = \frac{\sum_{j=1}^{c} \sum_{i=1}^{r} X_{ij}}{rc} \text{ (i.e., the overall or grand mean)}$$

The among-group variation, also called the **sum of squares among groups (SSA)**, is measured by the sum of the squared differences between the sample mean of each group $\overline{X}_j$ and the overall or grand mean $\overline{\overline{X}}$, weighted by the number of blocks $r$. The among-group variation is computed as in equation (13.9).

**Among-Group Variation**

$$SSA = r\sum_{j=1}^{c} (\overline{X}_j - \overline{\overline{X}})^2 \tag{13.9}$$

where

$$\overline{X}_{\cdot j} = \frac{\sum_{i=1}^{r} X_{ij}}{r} \text{ (i.e., the treatment group means)}$$

The among-block variation, also called the **sum of squares among blocks (SSBL)**, is measured by the sum of the squared differences between the mean of each block $\overline{X}_{i\cdot}$ and the overall or grand mean $\overline{\overline{X}}$, weighted by the number of groups $c$. The among-block variation is computed from equation (13.10).

**Among-Block Variation**

$$SSBL = c\sum_{i=1}^{r} (\overline{X}_{i\cdot} - \overline{\overline{X}})^2 \tag{13.10}$$

where

$$\overline{X}_{i\cdot} = \frac{\sum_{j=1}^{c} X_{ij}}{c} \text{ (i.e., the block means)}$$

The inherent random variation or error, also called the **sum of squares error (SSE)**, is measured by the sum of the squared differences among all the observations after the effect of the particular treatments and blocks has been accounted for. SSE is computed from equation (13.11).

**Random Error**

$$SSE = \sum_{j=1}^{c}\sum_{i=1}^{r}(X_{ij} - \overline{X}_{.j} - \overline{X}_{i.} + \overline{\overline{X}})^2 \qquad (13.11)$$

Because there are $c$ treatment levels of the factor being compared, there are $c - 1$ degrees of freedom associated with the sum of squares among groups (SSA). Similarly, because there are $r$ blocks, there are $r - 1$ degrees of freedom associated with the sum of squares among blocks (SSBL). Moreover, there are $n - 1$ degrees of freedom associated with the sum of squares total (SST) because each observation $X_{ij}$ is being compared with the overall or grand mean $\overline{\overline{X}}$ based on all $n$ observations. Therefore, because the degrees of freedom for each of the sources of variation must add to the degrees of freedom for the total variation, we obtain the degrees of freedom for the sum of squares error (SSE) component by subtraction and algebraic manipulation. The degrees of freedom are given by $(r - 1)(c - 1)$.

If each of the component sums of squares is divided by its associated degrees of freedom, we obtain the three *variances* or **mean square** terms (MSA, MSBL, and MSE) needed for ANOVA depicted in equation (13.12a–c).

**Obtaining the Mean Squares**

$$MSA = \frac{SSA}{c - 1} \qquad (13.12a)$$

$$MSBL = \frac{SSBL}{r - 1} \qquad (13.12b)$$

$$MSE = \frac{SSE}{(r - 1)(c - 1)} \qquad (13.12c)$$

If the assumptions pertaining to the analysis of variance are met, the null hypothesis of no differences in the $c$ population means (i.e., no treatment effects)

$$H_0: \mu_{.1} = \mu_{.2} = \cdots = \mu_{.c}$$

may be tested against the alternative that not all the $c$ population means are equal

$$H_1: \text{Not all } \mu_{.j} \text{ are equal (where } j = 1, 2, \ldots, c)$$

by computing the test statistic $F$ as in equation (13.13).

**The Randomized Block $F$-Test Statistic for Differences in $c$ Means**

$$F = \frac{MSA}{MSE} \qquad (13.13)$$

The $F$-test statistic follows an $F$ distribution with $c - 1$ degrees of freedom for the $MSA$ term and $(r - 1)(c - 1)$ degrees of freedom for the $MSE$ term. For a given level of significance $\alpha$, we may reject the null hypothesis if the computed $F$-test statistic exceeds the upper-tailed critical value $F_U$ from the $F$ distribution with $c - 1$ and $(r - 1)(c - 1)$ degrees of freedom, respectively, in the numerator and denominator (see Table E.5). That is, we have the following decision rule:

$$\text{Reject } H_0 \text{ if } F > F_U;$$

$$\text{otherwise don't reject } H_0.$$

To examine whether it is advantageous to block, some researchers suggest that the test of the null hypothesis of no block effects be performed. Thus, we test

$$H_0: \mu_{1.} = \mu_{2.} = \cdots = \mu_{r.}$$

against the alternative

$$H_1: \text{Not all } \mu_{i.} \text{ are equal (where } i = 1, 2, \ldots, r)$$

We form the $F$ statistic depicted in equation (13.14).

## The $F$-Test Statistic for Block Effects

$$F = \frac{MSBL}{MSE} \tag{13.14}$$

The null hypothesis is therefore rejected at the $\alpha$ level of significance if the $F$-test statistic exceeds the upper-tailed critical value $F_U$ from the $F$ distribution with $r - 1$ and $(r - 1)(c - 1)$ degrees of freedom, respectively, in the numerator and denominator (see Table E.5). That is, we have the following decision rule:

$$\text{Reject } H_0 \text{ if } F > F_U;$$

$$\text{otherwise don't reject } H_0.$$

However, it may be argued that this is unnecessary, that the sole purpose of establishing the blocks was to provide a more efficient means of testing for treatment effects by reducing the experimental error.

As in section 13.1, the results of an analysis-of-variance procedure are usually displayed in an ANOVA summary table, the format for which is presented in Table 13.7.

**Table 13.7**  *Analysis-of-variance table for randomized block design*

| SOURCE | DEGREES OF FREEDOM | SUM OF SQUARES | MEAN SQUARE (VARIANCE) | $F$ |
|---|---|---|---|---|
| Among treatments | $c - 1$ | $SSA$ | $MSA = \dfrac{SSA}{c - 1}$ | $F = \dfrac{MSA}{MSE}$ |
| Among blocks | $r - 1$ | $SSBL$ | $MSBL = \dfrac{SSBL}{r - 1}$ | $F = \dfrac{MSBL}{MSE}$ |
| Error | $(r - 1)(c - 1)$ | $SSE$ | $MSE = \dfrac{SSE}{(r - 1)(c - 1)}$ | |
| Total | $rc - 1$ | $SST$ | | |

To illustrate the randomized block $F$ test, suppose that a fast-food chain having four branches in a particular geographical area wants to evaluate the service at these restaurants. The research director for the chain hires 24 investigators with varied experiences in food-service evaluations to act as raters. After preliminary consultations, the 24 investigators are stratified into six blocks of four—based on food-service evaluation experience—so that the four most experienced investigators are placed in block 1, the next four most experienced investigators are placed in block 2, and so on.

Within each of the six homogeneous blocks, the four raters are then randomly assigned to evaluate the service at a particular restaurant using a rating scale from 0 (low) to 100 (high). The results are summarized in Table 13.8. The group totals, group means, block totals, block means, grand total, and grand mean are also presented in Table 13.8. Some of these statistics are highlighted along with the original data ratings in the scatter plot of Figure 13.8 to provide a visual impression of the results of the experiment.

**Table 13.8**   *Restaurant ratings for four branches of fast-food chain*

| BLOCKS OF RATERS | RESTAURANTS A | B | C | D | TOTALS | MEANS |
|---|---|---|---|---|---|---|
| 1 | 70 | 61 | 82 | 74 | 287 | 71.75 |
| 2 | 77 | 75 | 88 | 76 | 316 | 79.00 |
| 3 | 76 | 67 | 90 | 80 | 313 | 78.25 |
| 4 | 80 | 63 | 96 | 76 | 315 | 78.75 |
| 5 | 84 | 66 | 92 | 84 | 326 | 81.50 |
| 6 | 78 | 68 | 98 | 86 | 330 | 82.50 |
| Total | 465 | 400 | 546 | 476 | 1,887 | |
| Means | 77.50 | 66.67 | 91.00 | 79.33 | 78.625 | |

DATA FILE
FFCHAIN

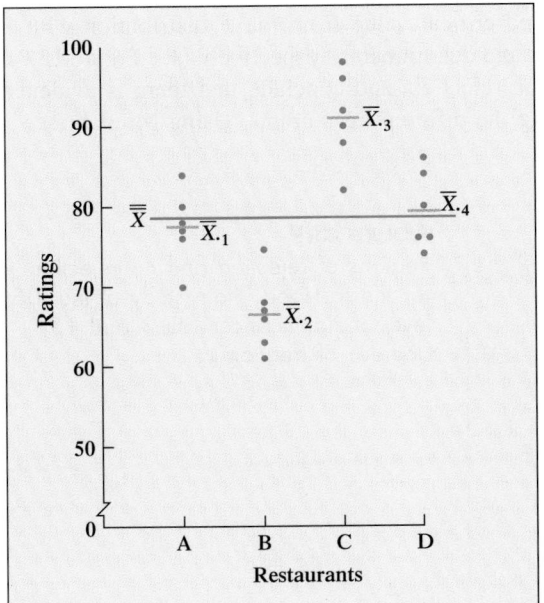

**FIGURE 13.8**
Scatter plot of ratings of services rendered at four restaurants
*Source: Table 13.8*

In addition, from Table 13.8 we have

$$r = 6 \qquad c = 4 \qquad n = rc = 24$$

and, as stated

$$\overline{\overline{X}} = \frac{\displaystyle\sum_{j=1}^{c}\sum_{i=1}^{r} X_{ij}}{rc} = \frac{1{,}887}{24} = 78.625$$

To determine the results of a randomized block design experiment, we access Microsoft Excel or Minitab on our restaurant rating data and obtain the following results:

$SSA = 1{,}787.46$; $SSBL = 283.38$; $SSE = 224.79$; $SST = 2{,}295.63$; $MSA = 595.820$; $MSBL = 56.676$; and $MSE = 14.986$

In the fast-food chain study, these computations can be summarized in the analysis-of-variance table shown in Table 13.9.

**Table 13.9** *Analysis-of-variance summary table for fast-food chain study*

| SOURCE | DEGREES OF FREEDOM | SUM OF SQUARES | MEAN SQUARE (VARIANCE) | F |
|---|---|---|---|---|
| Among groups (branches) | 3 | 1,787.46 | 595.820 | 39.758 |
| Among blocks (raters) | 5 | 283.38 | 56.676 | 3.782 |
| Error | 15 | 224.79 | 14.986 | |
| Total | 23 | 2,295.63 | | |

In using the .05 level of significance to test for differences among the restaurant branches, the decision rule is to reject the null hypothesis ($H_0$: $\mu_{.1} = \mu_{.2} = \mu_{.3} = \mu_{.4}$) if the calculated $F$ value exceeds 3.29, the upper-tailed critical value from the $F$ distribution with 3 and 15 degrees of freedom in the numerator and denominator, respectively (see Figure 13.9). Because $F = 39.758 > F_U = 3.29$, we can reject $H_0$ and conclude that there is evidence of a difference in the average rating among the different restaurants. Using Minitab (see

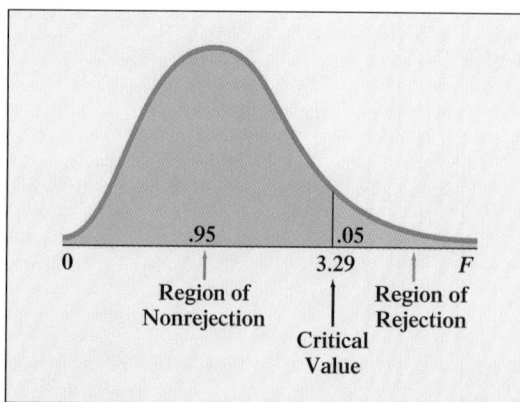

**FIGURE 13.9**

Regions of rejection and nonrejection for the fast-food chain study at the .05 level of significance with 3 and 15 degrees of freedom

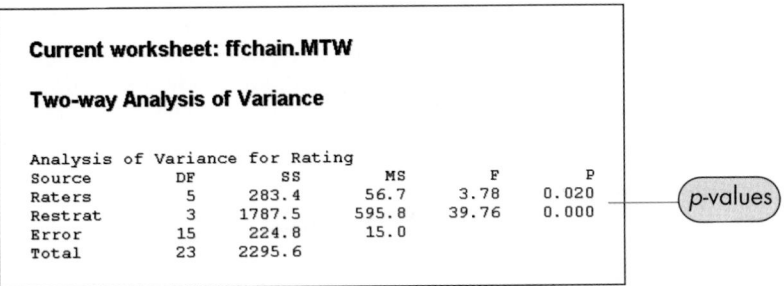

**Current worksheet: ffchain.MTW**

**Two-way Analysis of Variance**

```
Analysis of Variance for Rating
Source     DF      SS      MS      F       P
Raters      5    283.4    56.7    3.78    0.020
Restrat     3   1787.5   595.8   39.76   0.000
Error      15    224.8    15.0
Total      23   2295.6
```

p-values

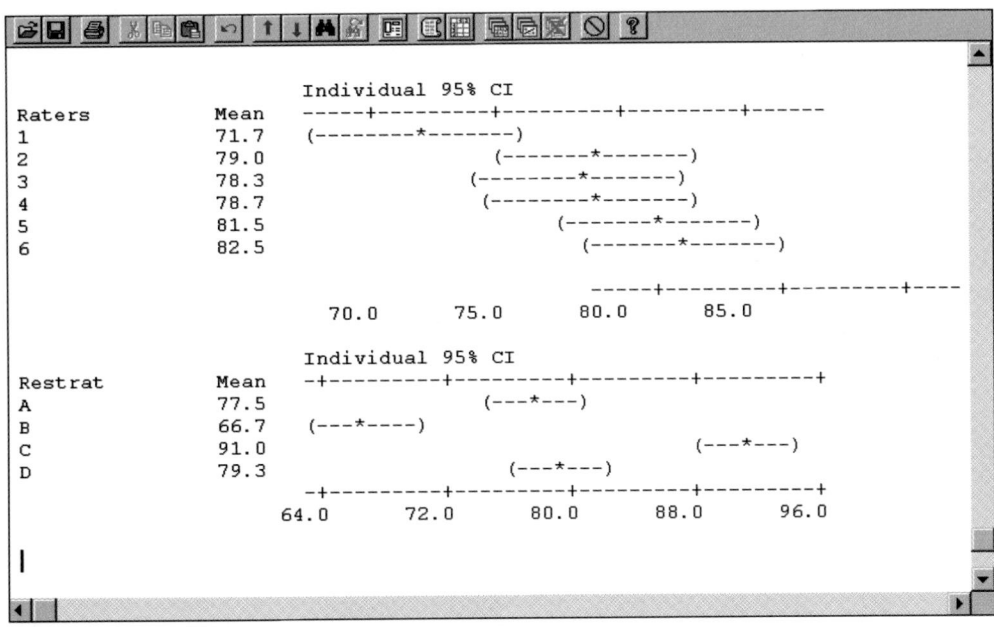

**FIGURE 13.10** Minitab output of randomized block *F* test for differences in *c* means in fast-food chain study

Figure 13.10), we obtain a *p*-value of .000 for the restaurant branches. Because .000 < .05, we reject $H_0$.

As a check on the effectiveness of blocking, we can test for a difference among the groups of raters. The decision rule, using the .05 level of significance, is to reject the null hypothesis ($H_0$: $\mu_{1.} = \mu_{2.} = \cdots = \mu_{6.}$) if the calculated *F* value exceeds 2.90, the upper-tailed critical value from the *F* distribution with 5 and 15 degrees of freedom in the numerator and denominator, respectively (see Figure 13.11 on page 570). Because $F = 3.782 > F_U = 2.90$ or the *p*-value $= .02 < .05$, we can reject $H_0$ and conclude that there is evidence of a difference among the groups of raters. Thus, we may conclude that the blocking has been advantageous in reducing the experimental error.

In addition to the assumptions of the one-way analysis of variance previously mentioned in section 13.1, we need to assume that there is no *interacting effect* between the treatments and the blocks. That is, we need to assume that any differences between the treatments (the restaurants) are consistent across the entire set of blocks (the groups of raters). The concept of *interaction* will be discussed in section 13.3.

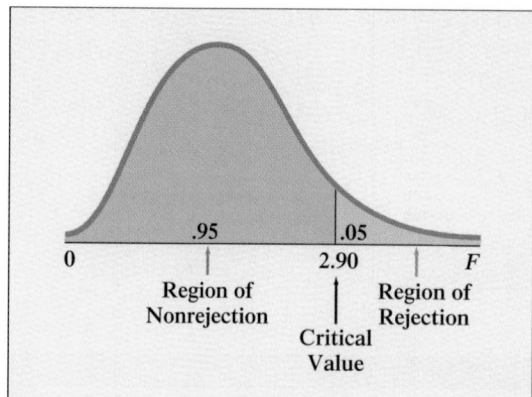

**FIGURE 13.11**
Regions of rejection and nonrejection for fast-food-chain study at the .05 level of significance with 5 and 15 degrees of freedom

Now that we have developed the randomized block model and have used it in the fast-food-chain study, the question arises as to what effect the blocking had on the analysis. That is, did the blocking result in an increase in precision in comparing the different treatment groups? To answer this, in equation (13.15) we compute the **estimated relative efficiency (RE)** of the randomized block design as compared with the completely randomized design.

**Estimated Relative Efficiency**

$$RE = \frac{(r - 1)MSBL + r(c - 1)MSE}{(rc - 1)MSE}$$

(13.15)

Thus, from Table 13.9 on page 568 we have

$$RE = \frac{(5)(56.676) + (6)(3)(14.986)}{(23)(14.986)} = 1.60$$

This means that 1.6 times as many observations in each treatment group would be needed in a one-way ANOVA design to obtain the same precision for comparison of treatment group means as would be needed for our randomized block design.

## Multiple Comparisons: The Tukey Procedure

As in the case of the completely randomized design model, once the null hypothesis of no differences between the treatment groups has been rejected, we need to determine which of these treatment groups are significantly different from the others. For the randomized block design model, because the sample sizes for each treatment group are equal, we use a procedure developed by John Tukey (see references 6 and 12). The critical range for the Tukey procedure is given in equation (13.16).

**Obtaining the Critical Range**

$$\text{Critical range} = Q_U \sqrt{\frac{MSE}{r}}$$

(13.16)

The statistic $Q_U$ is the upper-tailed critical value from a *Studentized range* distribution having $c$ degrees of freedom in the numerator and $(r - 1)(c - 1)$ degrees of freedom in the denominator.

Each of the $c(c - 1)/2$ pairs of means is compared against the one critical range. A specific pair, say group $j$ versus group $j'$, is declared significantly different if the absolute difference in the sample means $|\overline{X}_{.j} - \overline{X}_{.j'}|$ exceeds this critical range.

To apply the Tukey procedure, we return to our fast-food-chain study. Because there are four restaurants, there are $4(4 - 1)/2 = 6$ possible pairwise comparisons to be made. From Table 13.8 on page 567, the absolute mean differences are

$$1. \ |\overline{X}_{.1} - \overline{X}_{.2}| = |77.50 - 66.67| = 10.83$$
$$2. \ |\overline{X}_{.1} - \overline{X}_{.3}| = |77.50 - 91.00| = 13.50$$
$$3. \ |\overline{X}_{.1} - \overline{X}_{.4}| = |77.50 - 79.33| = 1.83$$
$$4. \ |\overline{X}_{.2} - \overline{X}_{.3}| = |66.67 - 91.00| = 24.33$$
$$5. \ |\overline{X}_{.2} - \overline{X}_{.4}| = |66.67 - 79.33| = 12.66$$
$$6. \ |\overline{X}_{.3} - \overline{X}_{.4}| = |91.00 - 79.33| = 11.67$$

To determine the critical range, use Table 13.9 on page 568 to obtain $MSE = 14.986$ and $r = 6$. From Table E.10 [for $\alpha = .05$, $c = 4$, and $(r - 1)(c - 1) = 15$], $Q_U$, the upper-tailed critical value of the test statistic with 4 degrees of freedom in the numerator and 15 degrees of freedom in the denominator, is 4.08. Using equation (13.16),

$$\text{Critical range} = 4.08\sqrt{\frac{14.986}{6}} = 6.448$$

Note that all pairwise comparisons except $|\overline{X}_{.1} - \overline{X}_{.4}|$ are greater than the critical range. Therefore, we conclude that there is evidence of a significant difference in the average rating between all pairs of restaurant branches except for branches A and D. In addition, branch C has the highest ratings (i.e., is most preferred) and branch B has the lowest (i.e., is least preferred).

---

## Problems for Section 13.2

### Learning the Basics

• **13.17** Given a randomized block experiment having a single factor of interest with five treatment levels and seven blocks, answer the following.
    (a) How many degrees of freedom are there in determining the among-group variation?
    (b) How many degrees of freedom are there in determining the among-block variation?
    (c) How many degrees of freedom are there in determining the inherent random variation or error?
    (d) How many degrees of freedom are there in determining the total variation?

• **13.18** From Problem 13.17:
    (a) If $SSA = 60$, $SSBL = 75$, and $SST = 210$, what is $SSE$?
    (b) What is $MSA$?
    (c) What is $MSBL$?
    (d) What is $MSE$?
    (e) What is the value of the test statistic $F$ for the differences in the five means?
    (f) What is the value of the test statistic $F$ for the block effects?

• **13.19** From Problems 13.17 and 13.18:
    (a) Form the ANOVA summary table and fill in all values in the body of the table.

(b) At the .05 level of significance, in testing for differences in the five means, what is the upper-tailed critical value from the $F$ distribution?

(c) State the decision rule for testing the null hypothesis that all five groups have equal population means.

(d) What is your statistical decision?

(e) At the .05 level of significance, in testing for block effects, what is the upper-tailed critical value from the $F$ distribution?

(f) State the decision rule for testing the null hypothesis that there are no block effects.

(g) What would be your statistical decision?

• **13.20** From Problems 13.17, 13.18, and 13.19:

(a) To perform the Tukey procedure, how many degrees of freedom are there in the numerator and how many degrees of freedom are there in the denominator of the Studentized range distribution?

(b) At the .05 level of significance, what is the upper-tailed critical value from the Studentized range distribution?

(c) To perform the Tukey procedure, what is the critical range?

**13.21** Given a randomized block experiment having one factor containing three treatment levels and seven blocks:

(a) How many degrees of freedom are there in determining the among-group variation?

(b) How many degrees of freedom are there in determining the among-block variation?

(c) How many degrees of freedom are there in determining the inherent random variation or error?

(d) How many degrees of freedom are there in determining the total variation?

**13.22** From Problem 13.21, if $SSA = 36$ and the randomized block $F$-test statistic is 6.0:

(a) What is $MSE$?

(b) What is $SSE$?

(c) What is $SSBL$ if the $F$-test statistic for block effects is 4.0?

(d) What is $SST$?

(e) At the .01 level of significance, is there evidence of a treatment effect?

(f) At the .01 level of significance, is there evidence of a block effect?

**13.23** Given a randomized block experiment having one factor containing four treatment levels and eight blocks, from the following ANOVA summary table fill in all the missing results.

| SOURCE | DEGREES OF FREEDOM | SUM OF SQUARES | MEAN SQUARE (VARIANCE) | F |
|---|---|---|---|---|
| Among treatments | $c - 1 = ?$ | $SSA = ?$ | $MSA = 80$ | $F = ?$ |
| Among blocks | $r - 1 = ?$ | $SSBL = 540$ | $MSBL = ?$ | $F = 5.0$ |
| Error | $(r - 1)(c - 1) = ?$ | $SSE = ?$ | $MSE = ?$ | |
| Total | $rc - 1 = ?$ | $SST = ?$ | | |

**13.24** From Problem 13.23:

(a) At the .05 level of significance, what is the upper-tailed critical value from the $F$ distribution in testing for differences among the four treatment level means?

(b) State the decision rule for testing the null hypothesis that all four groups have equal population means.

(c) What is your statistical decision?

(d) At the .05 level of significance, what is the upper-tailed critical value from the $F$ distribution in testing for block effects?

(e) State the decision rule for testing the null hypothesis of no block effects.

(f) What is your statistical decision?

## Applying the Concepts

**13.25** A taste-testing experiment has been designed so that four brands of Colombian coffee are to be rated by nine experts. To avoid any carryover effects, the tasting sequence for the four brews is randomly determined for each of the nine expert tasters until a rating on a 7-point scale (1 = extremely unpleasing, 7 = extremely pleasing) is given for each of four characteristics: taste, aroma, richness, and acidity. The following table displays the ratings accumulated over all four characteristics.

|  | BRAND | | | |
| --- | --- | --- | --- | --- |
| EXPERT | A | B | C | D |
| C.C. | 24 | 26 | 25 | 22 |
| S.E. | 27 | 27 | 26 | 24 |
| E.G. | 19 | 22 | 20 | 16 |
| B.L. | 24 | 27 | 25 | 23 |
| C.M. | 22 | 25 | 22 | 21 |
| C.N. | 26 | 27 | 24 | 24 |
| G.N. | 27 | 26 | 22 | 23 |
| R.M. | 25 | 27 | 24 | 21 |
| P.V. | 22 | 23 | 20 | 19 |

DATA FILE
COFFEE

Use either computer software or the following summary information:

| Sums of squares: | $SSA = 79.64$ | | $SSBL = 153.22$ | | $SST = 256.97$ | | | | |
| --- | --- | --- | --- | --- | --- | --- | --- | --- | --- |
| Brand: | A | B | C | D | | | | | |
| Sample means: | 24.00 | 25.56 | 23.11 | 21.44 | | | | | |
| Expert: | 1 | 2 | 3 | 4 | 5 | 6 | 7 | 8 | 9 |
| Sample means: | 24.25 | 26.00 | 19.25 | 24.75 | 22.50 | 25.25 | 24.50 | 24.25 | 21.00 |

(a) Construct an appropriate graph, plot, or chart of the data and describe any differences that might be apparent among the treatment groups and among the blocks.

(b) At the .01 level of significance, completely analyze the data to determine whether there is evidence of a difference in the summated ratings of the four brands of Colombian coffee and, if so, which of the brands are rated highest (i.e., best). What can you conclude?

• **13.26** A researcher in a pharmaceutical company wishes to perform an experiment to determine if the choice of treatment substance affects the clotting time of plasma (in minutes). Five different clotting enhancement substances (i.e., treatments) are to be compared and seven female patients, all of whom are in their first term of pregnancy, are to be studied. For each patient, five vials of blood are drawn and one vial each is randomly assigned to one of the five treatments. The clotting time data are shown at the top of page 574.

| | TREATMENT SUBSTANCE | | | | |
|---|---|---|---|---|---|
| PATIENT | 1 | 2 | 3 | 4 | 5 |
| 1 | 8.4 | 8.1 | 8.5 | 8.6 | 8.5 |
| 2 | 10.3 | 10.0 | 9.9 | 10.6 | 10.2 |
| 3 | 12.4 | 11.8 | 12.3 | 12.5 | 12.2 |
| 4 | 9.7 | 9.8 | 9.9 | 10.4 | 10.4 |
| 5 | 8.6 | 8.4 | 9.7 | 9.9 | 9.5 |
| 6 | 9.3 | 9.6 | 10.3 | 10.5 | 10.2 |
| 7 | 11.1 | 10.6 | 11.6 | 10.9 | 11.4 |

Use either computer software or the following summary information:

| Sums of squares: | $SSA = 2.5211$ | | $SSBL = 46.0309$ | | $SST = 50.7069$ | | |
|---|---|---|---|---|---|---|---|
| Substance: | 1 | 2 | 3 | 4 | 5 | | |
| Sample means: | 9.97 | 9.76 | 10.31 | 10.49 | 10.34 | | |
| Patient: | 1 | 2 | 3 | 4 | 5 | 6 | 7 |
| Sample means: | 8.42 | 10.20 | 12.24 | 10.04 | 9.22 | 9.98 | 11.12 |

(a) Construct an appropriate graph, plot, or chart of the data and describe relationships that might be apparent among the treatment groups and among the blocks.

(b) At the .05 level of significance, is there evidence of a difference in the average plasma clotting time among the five treatment substances?

(c) If appropriate, use the Tukey procedure to determine the treatment substances that differ in average clotting time. (Use $\alpha = .05$.)

(d) Determine the relative efficiency of the randomized block design as compared with the completely randomized design.

(e) What should the researcher conclude about the treatment substances?

(f) On the basis of the results of (d), why do you think that a randomized block design is preferable to a completely randomized design for these data?

**13.27** A nutritionist working for a company that manufactures weight control products wishes to compare three well-known weight loss products. Using data on girth (i.e., a function of height and weight), age, and metabolism, he matches 18 of his male clients into six groups of three each and randomly assigns one member of each group to one of the three dietary treatments. The following data represent the amount of weight (in pounds) lost by the 18 clients after 6 weeks of treatment:

| | DIETARY TREATMENT | | |
|---|---|---|---|
| CLIENT GROUPS | 1 | 2 | 3 |
| 1 | 10.4 | 12.1 | 9.0 |
| 2 | 9.8 | 14.5 | 9.6 |
| 3 | 7.3 | 10.0 | 9.8 |
| 4 | 7.5 | 9.9 | 10.7 |
| 5 | 8.6 | 14.2 | 11.1 |
| 6 | 10.7 | 10.5 | 10.5 |

Use either computer software or the following summary information:

| Sums of squares: | $SSA = 24.27$ | $SSBL = 13.72$ | $SST = 59.76$ | | | |
|---|---|---|---|---|---|
| Dietary treatment: | **1** | **2** | **3** | | |
| Sample means: | 9.05 | 11.87 | 10.12 | | |
| Client group: | **1** | **2** | **3** | **4** | **5** | **6** |
| Sample means: | 10.50 | 11.30 | 9.03 | 9.37 | 11.30 | 10.57 |

(a) Construct an appropriate graph, plot, or chart of the data and describe any differences that might be apparent among the treatment groups and among the blocks.

(b) At the .05 level of significance, is there evidence of a difference in the average amount of weight (in pounds) lost among the three dietary treatments?

(c) If appropriate, use the Tukey procedure to determine the dietary treatments that differ in average weight lost. (Use $\alpha = .05$.)

(d) Determine the relative efficiency of the randomized block design as compared with the completely randomized design.

(e) On the basis of (a)–(c), which weight loss products are best? Explain your findings.

• **13.28** The dean of a well-known business school wants to study the student-faculty evaluation process at his campus because it is used in reappointment, promotion, and tenure decisions. In particular, he is interested in determining the type of educational setting most conducive to higher faculty evaluations from students—MBA courses, advanced undergraduate courses, or required undergraduate courses. Because the faculty's semester workload at this institution is three courses, the dean randomly samples 10 faculty from his school who had been assigned one course in each of the three aforementioned types of educational settings and retrieves their end-of-semester evaluation forms. The following results are mean ratings on a 5-point scale (1 = very poor, 5 = outstanding) in response to the question "In comparison with other teachers you have had, how would you rate this individual's teaching ability?" Each of the ratings is from classes containing 25–30 students.

| FACULTY MEMBER | MBA COURSE | TYPE OF CLASS ADVANCED UNDERGRAD | REQUIRED UNDERGRAD |
|---|---|---|---|
| L.M. | 4.12 | 4.06 | 3.38 |
| N.R. | 4.87 | 4.72 | 4.60 |
| A.C. | 3.46 | 3.49 | 2.39 |
| J.K. | 3.87 | 3.61 | 3.23 |
| J.B. | 4.04 | 3.83 | 3.55 |
| D.B. | 2.90 | 3.23 | 3.52 |
| W.F. | 4.16 | 4.07 | 3.68 |
| R.S. | 4.19 | 3.76 | 3.83 |
| M.L. | 4.75 | 4.39 | 4.22 |
| V.P. | 4.29 | 4.34 | 3.67 |

DATA FILE
RATING

Use either computer software or the following summary information:

| Sums of squares: | $SSA = 1.1355$ | | $SSBL = 6.7185$ | | | $SST = 9.0605$ | | | |
|---|---|---|---|---|---|---|---|---|---|

| Course: | 1 | 2 | 3 |
|---|---|---|---|
| Sample means: | 4.065 | 3.950 | 3.607 |

| Faculty: | 1 | 2 | 3 | 4 | 5 | 6 | 7 | 8 | 9 | 10 |
|---|---|---|---|---|---|---|---|---|---|---|
| Sample means: | 3.853 | 4.730 | 3.113 | 3.570 | 3.807 | 3.217 | 3.970 | 3.927 | 4.453 | 4.100 |

(a) Construct an appropriate graph, plot, or chart of the data and describe any differences that might be apparent among the treatment groups and among the blocks.
(b) Using a level of significance of $\alpha = .05$, is there evidence of a difference in the ratings based on type of class?
(c) If appropriate, use the Tukey procedure to determine which types of classes differ in the ratings. (Use $\alpha = .05$.)
(d) Determine the relative efficiency of the randomized block design as compared with the completely randomized design.
(e) What should the dean conclude about the ratings in the different types of courses? Explain.

**13.29** The manager of a nationally known real estate agency has just completed a training session on appraisals for three newly hired agents. To evaluate the effectiveness of her training, the manager wishes to determine whether there is any difference in the appraised values placed on houses by these three different individuals. A sample of 12 houses is selected by the manager, and each agent is assigned the task of placing an appraised value (in thousands of dollars) on the 12 houses. The results are summarized below.

| HOUSE | AGENT 1 | AGENT 2 | AGENT 3 |
|---|---|---|---|
| 1 | 181.0 | 182.0 | 183.5 |
| 2 | 179.9 | 180.0 | 182.4 |
| 3 | 163.0 | 161.5 | 164.1 |
| 4 | 218.0 | 215.0 | 217.3 |
| 5 | 213.0 | 216.5 | 218.4 |
| 6 | 175.0 | 175.0 | 216.1 |
| 7 | 217.9 | 219.5 | 220.1 |
| 8 | 151.0 | 150.0 | 152.4 |
| 9 | 164.9 | 165.5 | 166.1 |
| 10 | 192.5 | 195.0 | 197.0 |
| 11 | 225.0 | 222.7 | 226.4 |
| 12 | 177.5 | 178.0 | 179.7 |

**DATA FILE**
**REAPPR3**

Use either computer software or the following summary information:

| Sums of squares: | SSA = 226.3 | | SSBL = 19,796.2 | | SST = 20,978.9 | |
|---|---|---|---|---|---|---|
| Agent: | **1** | **2** | **3** | | | |
| Sample means: | 188.2 | 188.4 | 193.6 | | | |
| House: | **1** | **2** | **3** | **4** | **5** | **6** |
| Sample means: | 182.2 | 180.8 | 162.9 | 216.8 | 216.0 | 188.7 |
| House: | **7** | **8** | **9** | **10** | **11** | **12** |
| Sample means: | 219.2 | 151.1 | 165.5 | 194.8 | 224.7 | 178.4 |

(a) At the .05 level of significance, use the randomized block $F$ test to determine if there is evidence of a difference in the average appraised values given by the three agents.

(b) If appropriate, use the Tukey procedure to determine which agents are appraising houses different from the others.

(c) What assumptions are necessary to perform this test?

(d) What conclusions about the effectiveness of the training in terms of the ability of different agents to rate the properties in a similar way can the manager reach? Explain.

**13.30** Suppose that a shoe company wants to test material for the soles of shoes. For each pair of shoes the new material is placed on one shoe and the old material is placed on the other shoe. After a given period of time a random sample of 10 pairs of shoes is selected and the wear is measured on a 10-point scale (higher is better) with the following results.

| | | | | | **PAIR NUMBER** | | | | | |
|---|---|---|---|---|---|---|---|---|---|---|
| **MATERIAL** | **I** | **II** | **III** | **IV** | **V** | **VI** | **VII** | **VIII** | **IX** | **X** |
| New | 2 | 4 | 5 | 7 | 7 | 5 | 9 | 8 | 8 | 7 |
| Old | 4 | 5 | 3 | 8 | 9 | 4 | 7 | 8 | 5 | 6 |
| Differences | −2 | −1 | +2 | −1 | −2 | +1 | +2 | 0 | +3 | +1 |

**DATA FILE**
**SHOESOLE**

Use either computer software or the following summary information:

| Sums of squares: | SSA = 0.45 | | SSBL = 64.45 | | SST = 78.95 | |
|---|---|---|---|---|---|---|
| Material: | **1** | **2** | | | | |
| Sample means: | 6.2 | 5.9 | | | | |
| Shoe pair: | **1** | **2** | **3** | **4** | **5** | |
| Sample means: | 3.0 | 4.5 | 4.0 | 7.5 | 8.0 | |
| Shoe pair: | **6** | **7** | **8** | **9** | **10** | |
| Sample means: | 4.5 | 8.0 | 8.0 | 6.5 | 6.5 | |

(a) At the .05 level of significance, use the randomized block $F$ test to determine if there is a difference in the average wear for the new material and the old material.

(b) What assumptions are necessary to perform this test?

(c) If you performed the $t$ test for the mean difference on this data set to solve Problem 12.36 on page 506, square the value of $t$ you computed in part (a) of Problem 12.36 and notice that it is the same (except for rounding error) as the $F$-test statistic. Express in your own words the relationship between $t$ and $F$.

## 13.3  THE FACTORIAL DESIGN MODEL: TWO-WAY ANALYSIS OF VARIANCE

In section 13.1 we introduced the one-way analysis-of-variance or completely randomized design model, and in section 13.2 we described the randomized block design model. In this section we shall extend our discussion to consider an experimental design model in which two factors are of interest. The two factors may differ with respect to the number of **levels** (or groups) they contain. However, we shall be concerned only with situations in which there are equal numbers of **replicates** (that is, sample sizes $n'$) for each combination of the levels of factor A with those of factor B. (See reference 1 for a discussion of two-factor ANOVA models with unequal sample sizes.)

Owing to the complexity of the calculations involved, particularly because the number of levels of each factor increases and the number of *replications* in each cell increases, we assume that in practice, a statistical software or spreadsheet package will be used when analyzing data obtained from factorial design models. Nevertheless, for purposes of illustration, we present the conceptual approach for the decomposition of the total variation for the two-factor factorial design model with equal replication. To do so, we need to define the following terms:

$r$ = the number of levels of factor A

$c$ = the number of levels of factor B

$n'$ = the number of values (replications) for each cell

$n$ = the total number of observations in the experiment (where $n = rcn'$)

$X_{ijk}$ = the value of the $k$th observation for level $i$ of factor A and level $j$ of factor B

$$\overline{\overline{X}} = \frac{\displaystyle\sum_{i=1}^{r}\sum_{j=1}^{c}\sum_{k=1}^{n'}X_{ijk}}{rcn'}$$ is the overall or grand mean

$$\overline{X}_{i..} = \frac{\displaystyle\sum_{j=1}^{c}\sum_{k=1}^{n'}X_{ijk}}{cn'}$$ is the mean of the $i$th level of factor A (where $i = 1, 2, \ldots, r$)

$$\overline{X}_{.j.} = \frac{\displaystyle\sum_{i=1}^{r}\sum_{k=1}^{n'}X_{ijk}}{rn'}$$ is the mean of the $j$th level of factor B (where $j = 1, 2, \ldots, c$)

$$\overline{X}_{ij.} = \frac{\displaystyle\sum_{k=1}^{n'}X_{ijk}}{n'}$$ is the mean of the cell $ij$, the combination of the $i$th level of factor A and the $j$th level of factor B

Recall from Figure 13.1 (page 541) that in the completely randomized design model the sum of squares total (or *SST*) is subdivided into sum of squares among groups (or *SSA*) and sum of squares within groups (or *SSW*). Also, from Figure 13.7 (page 563), in the randomized block design model, the total variation (*SST*) is subdivided into sum of squares among treatment groups (*SSA*), sum of squares among blocks (*SSBL*), and sum of squares error (*SSE*). For the two-factor factorial design model with equal replication in each cell, we subdivide the total variation (*SST*) into sum of squares due to factor A (or *SSFA*), sum of squares due to factor B (or *SSFB*), sum of squares due to the interacting effect of A and B (or *SSAB*), and sum of squares due to **inherent random error** (or *SSE*). This decomposition of the total variation (*SST*) is displayed in Figure 13.12.

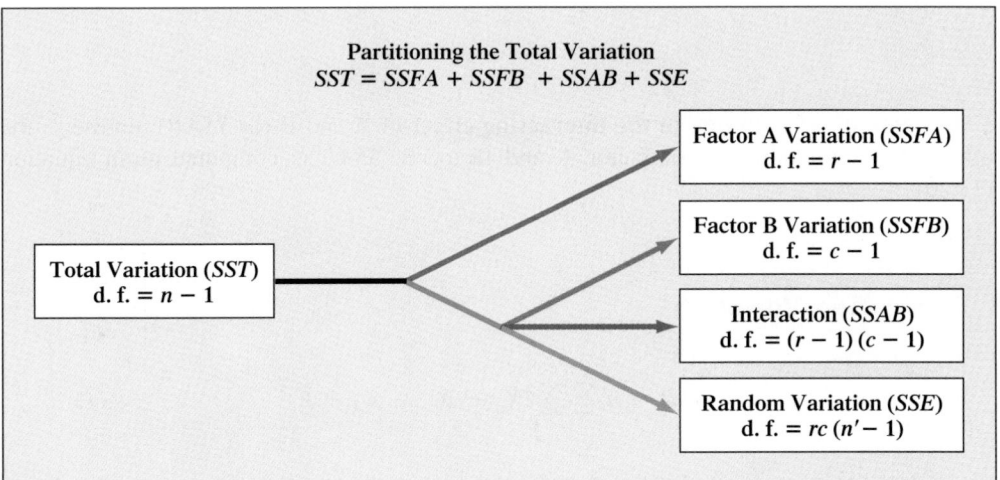

**FIGURE 13.12** Partitioning the total variation in a two-factor factorial design model

The **sum of squares total** (or ***SST***) represents the total variation among all the observations around the grand mean. *SST* is computed as presented in equation (13.17).

## Total Variation

$$SST = \sum_{i=1}^{r} \sum_{j=1}^{c} \sum_{k=1}^{n'} (X_{ijk} - \overline{\overline{X}})^2 \qquad (13.17)$$

The **sum of squares due to factor A** (or ***SSFA***) represents the differences among the various levels of factor A and the grand mean. *SSFA* is computed as in equation (13.18).

## Factor A Variation

$$SSFA = cn' \sum_{i=1}^{r} (\overline{X}_{i..} - \overline{\overline{X}})^2 \qquad (13.18)$$

The **sum of squares due to factor B** (or **SSFB**) represents the differences among the various levels of factor B and the grand mean. *SSFB* is computed as in equation (13.19).

> ### Factor B Variation
>
> $$SSFB = rn' \sum_{j=1}^{c} (\overline{X}_{.j.} - \overline{\overline{X}})^2 \qquad (13.19)$$

The **sum of squares due to the interacting effect of A** and **B** (or **SSAB**) represents the effect of the combinations of factor A and factor B. *SSAB* is computed as in equation (13.20).

> ### Interaction Variation
>
> $$SSAB = n' \sum_{i=1}^{r} \sum_{j=1}^{c} (\overline{X}_{ij.} - \overline{X}_{i..} - \overline{X}_{.j.} + \overline{\overline{X}})^2 \qquad (13.20)$$

The **sum of squares error** (or **SSE**) represents the differences among the observations within each cell and the corresponding cell mean. *SSE* is computed as in equation (13.21).

> ### Random Error
>
> $$SSE = \sum_{i=1}^{r} \sum_{j=1}^{c} \sum_{k=1}^{n'} (X_{ijk} - \overline{X}_{ij.})^2 \qquad (13.21)$$

Because there are $r$ treatment levels of factor A, there are $r - 1$ degrees of freedom associated with *SSFA*. Similarly, because there are $c$ treatment levels of factor B, there are $c - 1$ degrees of freedom associated with *SSFB*. Moreover, because there are $n'$ replications in each of the $rc$ cells, there are $rc(n' - 1)$ degrees of freedom associated with the inherent random error term. Carrying this further, there are $n - 1$ degrees of freedom associated with the sum of squares total (*SST*) because each observation $X_{ijk}$ is being compared with the overall or grand mean $\overline{\overline{X}}$ based on all $n$ observations. Therefore, because the degrees of freedom for each of the sources of variation must add to the degrees of freedom for the total variation (*SST*), we may obtain the degrees of freedom for the interaction component (*SSAB*) by subtraction. The degrees of freedom are given by $(r - 1)(c - 1)$.

If each of the sums of squares is divided by its associated degrees of freedom, we obtain the four variances or mean square terms (*MSFA*, *MSFB*, *MSAB*, and *MSE*) in equation (13.22a–d) needed for ANOVA:

## Obtaining the Mean Squares

$$MSFA = \frac{SSFA}{r-1} \tag{13.22a}$$

$$MSFB = \frac{SSFB}{c-1} \tag{13.22b}$$

$$MSAB = \frac{SSAB}{(r-1)(c-1)} \tag{13.22c}$$

$$MSE = \frac{SSE}{rc(n'-1)} \tag{13.22d}$$

In the two-factor ANOVA model there are three distinct tests that may be performed. If we assume that the levels of factor A and factor B have been *specifically selected* for analysis (rather than being *randomly selected* from a population of possible levels), we have the following three tests of hypotheses.

**1.** To test the hypothesis of no difference due to factor A

$$H_0: \mu_{1..} = \mu_{2..} = \cdots = \mu_{r..}$$

against the alternative

$$H_1: \text{Not all } \mu_{i..} \text{ are equal}$$

we form the $F$ statistic in equation (13.23).

## F Test for Factor A Effect

$$F = \frac{MSFA}{MSE} \tag{13.23}$$

The null hypothesis is rejected at the $\alpha$ level of significance if

$$F = \frac{MSFA}{MSE} > F_U$$

the upper-tailed critical value from an $F$ distribution with $r-1$ degrees of freedom in the numerator and $rc(n'-1)$ degrees of freedom in the denominator.

**2.** To test the hypothesis of no difference due to factor B

$$H_0: \mu_{.1.} = \mu_{.2.} = \cdots = \mu_{.c.}$$

against the alternative

$$H_1: \text{Not all } \mu_{.j.} \text{ are equal}$$

we form the $F$ statistic in equation (13.24).

### F Test for Factor B Effect

$$F = \frac{MSFB}{MSE} \qquad (13.24)$$

The null hypothesis is rejected at the $\alpha$ level of significance if

$$F = \frac{MSFB}{MSE} > F_U$$

the upper-tailed critical value from an $F$ distribution with $c - 1$ degrees of freedom in the numerator and $rc(n' - 1)$ degrees of freedom in the denominator.

3. To test the hypothesis of no interaction of factors A and B

$$H_0: AB_{ij} = 0 \text{ (for all } i \text{ and } j)$$

against the alternative

$$H_1: AB_{ij} \neq 0$$

we form the $F$ statistic in equation (13.25).

### F Test for Interaction Effect

$$F = \frac{MSAB}{MSE} \qquad (13.25)$$

The null hypothesis is rejected at the $\alpha$ level of significance if

$$F = \frac{MSAB}{MSE} > F_U$$

the upper-tailed critical value from an $F$ distribution with $(r - 1)(c - 1)$ degrees of freedom in the numerator and $rc(n' - 1)$ degrees of freedom in the denominator.

The entire set of steps may be summarized in an analysis-of-variance (ANOVA) table such as Table 13.10.

To motivate our discussion, let us return to the Using Statistics application at the beginning of this chapter. The operations manager for a soft-drink distributor was interested in obtaining more uniform fill heights in the bottles filled during the bottling process at the distribution center. Supposedly, available machinery fills each bottle to the correct level, but, in practice, there is variation around the specified target. In the preceding chapter we determined that an operating pressure of 25 psi is desirable for the equipment on hand. Two additional variables may still affect the filling process: percent carbonation (10% or 12%) and/or line speed (either 210, 240, 270, or 300 bottles per minute). In section 13.1 we examined the effect of line speed (in filled bottles per minute) on average deviation from the specified target fill for a given dial setting of 12% carbonation. Now we will examine the effect of varying both percent carbonation and line speed.

To determine the appropriate equipment dial settings, the operations manager decides to

## Table 13.10 Analysis-of-variance table for the two-factor model with replication

| SOURCE | DEGREES OF FREEDOM | SUM OF SQUARES | MEAN SQUARE (VARIANCE) | F |
|--------|--------------------|----------------|------------------------|---|
| A | $r - 1$ | SSFA | $MSFA = \dfrac{SSFA}{r - 1}$ | $F = \dfrac{MSFA}{MSE}$ |
| B | $c - 1$ | SSFB | $MSFB = \dfrac{SSFB}{c - 1}$ | $F = \dfrac{MSFB}{MSE}$ |
| AB | $(r - 1)(c - 1)$ | SSAB | $MSAB = \dfrac{SSAB}{(r - 1)(c - 1)}$ | $F = \dfrac{MSAB}{MSE}$ |
| Error | $rc\,(n' - 1)$ | SSE | $MSE = \dfrac{SSE}{rc(n' - 1)}$ | |
| Total | $n - 1$ | SST | | |

perform an experiment with five bottles filled at each of the eight combinations of levels of these two factors. The results of this experiment (in terms of deviation from specified target in millimeters) are displayed in Table 13.11.

## Table 13.11 Deviations from specified target fill (in mm) under two percent carbonation levels and four line speeds

| CARBONATION | LINE SPEED (IN BPM) | | | |
|-------------|:----:|:----:|:----:|:----:|
| | 210 | 240 | 270 | 300 |
| 10% | −1.4 | −0.5 | 5.7 | 0.6 |
| | −4.0 | −2.0 | −3.4 | 2.6 |
| | −3.0 | −0.9 | −1.2 | −2.4 |
| | −0.7 | 1.9 | 3.1 | 1.8 |
| | −8.8 | −6.0 | −4.3 | 5.1 |
| 12% | −3.5 | 3.4 | −1.4 | 4.3 |
| | 2.0 | −2.1 | 3.2 | 3.3 |
| | −4.8 | 0.6 | −1.2 | 2.0 |
| | −2.1 | −4.5 | 2.7 | −0.8 |
| | −4.0 | −1.6 | 0.9 | 2.5 |

Note: A "negative deviation" from target indicates the amount in millimeters a bottle is underfilled, and a "positive deviation" shows the amount in millimeters a bottle is overfilled.

**DATA FILE
LINESPD2**

From this table we have the following results:

$$r = 2, \qquad c = 4, \qquad n' = 5, \qquad n = 40$$

The overall or grand mean is $\overline{\overline{X}} = -0.4725$.

The means for the levels of factor A (percent carbonation) are as follows:

$$10\%: \overline{X}_{1..} = -0.890 \qquad 12\%: \overline{X}_{2..} = -0.055$$

The means for the levels of factor B (line speed) are as follows:

$$210 \text{ bpm}: \overline{X}_{.1.} = -3.030 \qquad 240 \text{ bpm}: \overline{X}_{.2.} = -1.170$$
$$270 \text{ bpm}: \overline{X}_{.3.} = 0.410 \qquad 300 \text{ bpm}: \overline{X}_{.4.} = 1.900$$

The treatment level cell means for the percent carbonation–line speed dial setting combinations are as follows:

$$10\% \text{ and } 210 \text{ bpm}: \overline{X}_{11.} = -3.580 \qquad 10\% \text{ and } 240 \text{ bpm}: \overline{X}_{12.} = -1.500$$
$$10\% \text{ and } 270 \text{ bpm}: \overline{X}_{13.} = -0.020 \qquad 10\% \text{ and } 300 \text{ bpm}: \overline{X}_{14.} = 1.540$$
$$12\% \text{ and } 210 \text{ bpm}: \overline{X}_{21.} = -2.480 \qquad 12\% \text{ and } 240 \text{ bpm}: \overline{X}_{22.} = -0.840$$
$$12\% \text{ and } 270 \text{ bpm}: \overline{X}_{23.} = 0.840 \qquad 12\% \text{ and } 300 \text{ bpm}: \overline{X}_{24.} = 2.260$$

Figure 13.13 on page 585 depicts the Microsoft Excel output of the ANOVA summary table for the soda fill study.

From Figure 13.13 we note that summary tables provide the sample size, sum, arithmetic mean, and variance for each percent carbonation level and line speed. The total column of the first two tables provides these statistics for each percent carbonation level, while the third table provides them for each line speed. In addition, in the ANOVA table we see that *SS* is sum of squares, *df* is degrees of freedom, *MS* is mean squares, *F* is the computed *F*-test statistic, and $F_{crit}$ is the upper-tailed critical value.

To interpret the results we start by testing whether there is an interacting effect between factor A (percent carbonation) and factor B (line speed). If the interaction effects are significant and the interaction is considered to be *interfering*, our further analysis will pertain only to this aspect. On the other hand, if the interaction effects are not significant, we focus on the main effects—potential differences in percent carbonation (factor A) and potential differences in line speed (factor B).

Using the .05 level of significance, to determine whether there is evidence of an interacting effect, the decision rule is to reject the null hypothesis $H_0$: $AB_{ij} = 0$ (for all *i* and *j*) if the calculated *F* value exceeds 2.92, the approximate upper-tailed critical value from the *F* distribution with 3 degrees of freedom in the numerator and 32 degrees of freedom in the denominator (see Figure 13.14 on page 585).[2] Because $F = 0.01 < F_U = 2.92$ or from Figure 13.13, the *p*-value = .998 > .05, we do not reject $H_0$ and we conclude that there is no evidence of an interacting effect between percent carbonation and line speed. Our focus is now on the main effects.

Using the .05 level of significance and testing for a difference between the two percent carbonation levels (factor A), the decision rule is to reject the null hypothesis $(H_0$: $\mu_{1..} = \mu_{2..})$ if the calculated *F* value exceeds 4.17, the (approximate) upper-tail critical value from the *F* distribution with 1 degree of freedom in the numerator and 32 degrees of freedom in the denominator (see Figure 13.15 on page 586). Because $F = 0.81 < F_U = 4.17$, or from Figure 13.13, the *p*-value = .375 > .05, we do not reject $H_0$ and conclude that there is no evidence of a difference between the two levels of percent carbonation in terms of the average deviation from specified target fill.

Using the .05 level of significance and testing for a difference among the four line speeds

[2]*Table E.5 does not provide the upper-tailed critical values from the F distribution with 32 degrees of freedom in the denominator. Critical values are given either for F distributions with 30 degrees of freedom in the denominator or for F distributions with 40 degrees of freedom in the denominator. When the desired degrees of freedom are not provided in the table, we suggest rounding to the closest value that is given or using the p-value approach.*

| | A | B | C | D | E | F | G | H |
|---|---|---|---|---|---|---|---|---|
| 1 | Anova: Two-Factor With Replication | | | | | | | |
| 2 | | | | | | | | |
| 3 | SUMMARY | 210BPM | 240BPM | 270BPM | 300BPM | Total | | |
| 4 | 10%Carbonation | | | | | | | |
| 5 | Count | 5 | 5 | 5 | 5 | 20 | | |
| 6 | Sum | -17.9 | -7.5 | -0.1 | 7.7 | -17.8 | | |
| 7 | Average | -3.58 | -1.5 | -0.02 | 1.54 | -0.89 | | |
| 8 | Variance | 10.202 | 8.355 | 18.397 | 7.568 | 13.12832 | | |
| 9 | | | | | | | | |
| 10 | 12%Carbonation | | | | | | | |
| 11 | Count | 5 | 5 | 5 | 5 | 20 | | |
| 12 | Sum | -12.4 | -4.2 | 4.2 | 11.3 | -1.1 | | |
| 13 | Average | -2.48 | -0.84 | 0.84 | 2.26 | -0.055 | | |
| 14 | Variance | 7.237 | 8.903 | 4.553 | 3.683 | 8.462605 | | |
| 15 | | | | | | | | |
| 16 | Total | | | | | | | |
| 17 | Count | 10 | 10 | 10 | 10 | | | |
| 18 | Sum | -30.3 | -11.7 | 4.1 | 19 | | | |
| 19 | Average | -3.03 | -1.17 | 0.41 | 1.9 | | | |
| 20 | Variance | 8.086778 | 7.791222 | 10.40544 | 5.144444 | | | |

TwoWayANOVA / Sheet1 / Sheet2 / Sheet3 / Sheet4 / S

| | A | B | C | D | E | F | G |
|---|---|---|---|---|---|---|---|
| 21 | | | | | | | |
| 22 | | | | | | | |
| 23 | ANOVA | | | | | | |
| 24 | Source of Variation | SS | df | MS | F | P-value | F crit |
| 25 | Sample | 6.97225 | 1 | 6.97225 | 0.809574 | 0.374968 | 4.149086 |
| 26 | Columns | 134.3488 | 3 | 44.78292 | 5.199909 | 0.004866 | 2.901118 |
| 27 | Interaction | 0.28675 | 3 | 0.095583 | 0.011099 | 0.998365 | 2.901118 |
| 28 | Within | 275.592 | 32 | 8.61225 | | | |
| 29 | | | | | | | |
| 30 | Total | 417.1998 | 39 | | | | |

**FIGURE 13.13**   Microsoft Excel output of ANOVA summary table for the soda fill study

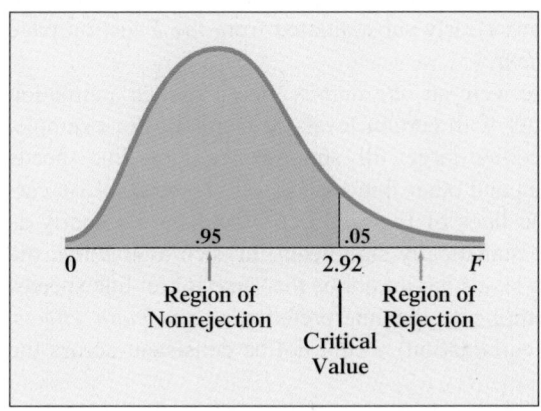

**FIGURE 13.14**
Regions of rejection and nonrejection at the .05 level of significance with 3 and 32 degrees of freedom

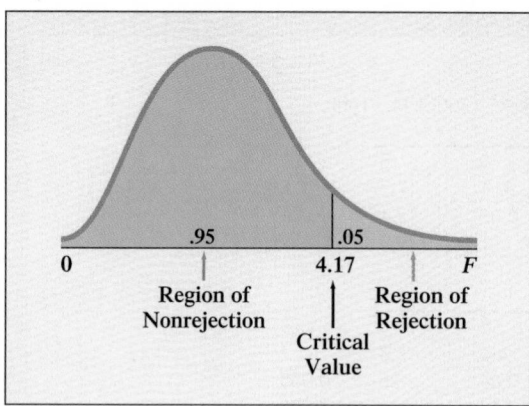

**FIGURE 13.15**
Regions of rejection and nonrejection at the .05 level of significance with 1 and 32 degrees of freedom

(factor B), the decision rule is to reject the null hypothesis ($H_0$: $\mu_{.1.} = \mu_{.2.} = \mu_{.3.} = \mu_{.4.}$) if the calculated $F$ value exceeds 2.92, the (approximate) upper-tailed critical value from the $F$ distribution with 3 degrees of freedom in the numerator and 32 degrees of freedom in the denominator (see again Figure 13.14). Because $F = 5.20 > F_U = 2.92$ or because the $p$-value from Figure 13.13 is .005 < .05, we reject $H_0$ and conclude that there is evidence of a difference among the line speeds (in bottles per minute) in terms of the average deviation from specified target fill.

## Interpreting Interaction Effects

Once the tests for the significance of factor A, factor B, and their interaction have been performed, we can get a better understanding of the interpretation of the concept of interaction by plotting the cell means as shown in Figure 13.16 on page 587. The treatment level cell means for the percent carbonation–line speed dial setting combinations are listed on page 584. By plotting the average deviation from specified target fill for each combination of percent carbonation and line speed we note that the two lines (representing the two percent carbonation levels) appear roughly parallel. We can interpret this phenomenon to mean that the *difference* in average deviation from specified target fill between the two percent carbonation levels is virtually the same for the four line speeds. In other words, there is no *interaction* between these two factors, as was clearly substantiated from the $F$ test on page 584; the two factors appear to be *independent*.

What would be the interpretation if there were an *interacting effect*? In such a situation some levels of factor A would respond better with certain levels of factor B. For example, with respect to average deviation from specified target fill, suppose that some line speeds were better for 10% carbonation dial settings and other line speeds were better for 12% carbonation dial settings. If this were true, the lines of Figure 13.16 would not be nearly as parallel and the interaction effect might be statistically significant. In such a situation, the differences between the percent carbonation levels would not be the same for all line speeds. Such an outcome would also serve to complicate the interpretation of the *main effects*, because differences in one factor (percent carbonation) would not be consistent across the other factor (line speed).

To better understand the meaning behind significant interaction effects let us look at Example 13.1.

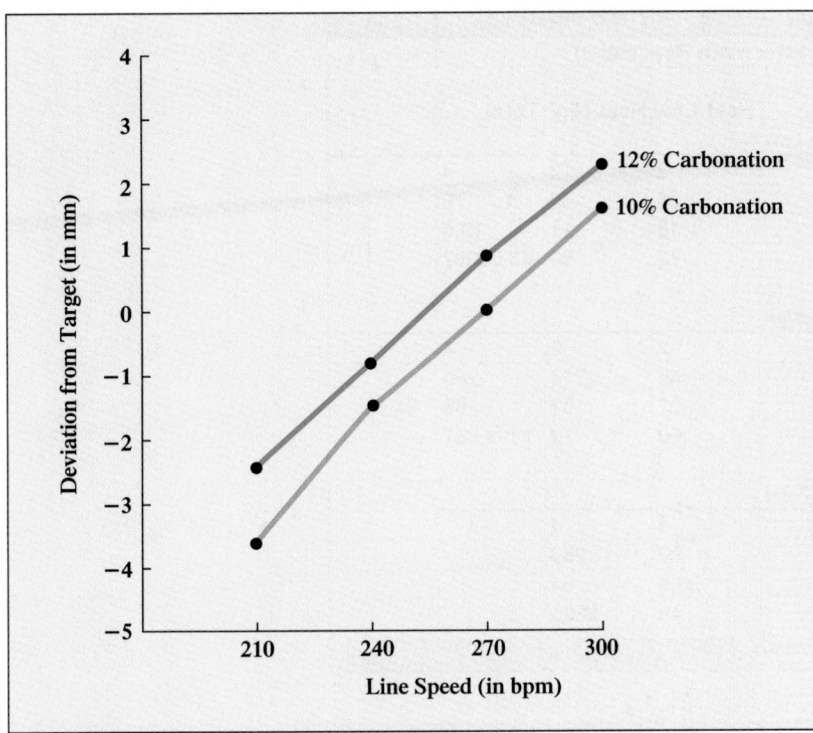

**FIGURE 13.16** Average deviation from specified target fill (in mm) based on percent carbonation levels for different line speed levels (in bpm)

## Example 13.1 *Interpreting Significant Interaction Effects*

The following data are based on an experiment concerning the manufacture of roller bearings. The two factors we examine here are the outer ring osculation and the heat treatment, each examined at a high and low setting. The results, in terms of the length of lives of the bearings, are as follows

| | **HEAT TREATMENT** | |
| **RING OSCULATION** | **LOW** | **HIGH** |
| Low | 12 | 26 |
| | 24 | 16 |
| High | 18 | 101 |
| | 28 | 113 |

**DATA FILE**
**BEARING**

What are the effects of ring osculation and heat treatment on the life of the roller bearings?

### SOLUTION

Using Microsoft Excel, the following output is produced for a two-factor factorial design with two replications per treatment level combination.

|   | A | B | C | D | E |
|---|---|---|---|---|---|
| 1 | Anova: Two-Factor With Replication | | | | |
| 2 | | | | | |
| 3 | SUMMARY | Heat-Low | Heat-High | Total | |
| 4 | *Ring-Low* | | | | |
| 5 | Count | 2 | 2 | 4 | |
| 6 | Sum | 36 | 42 | 78 | |
| 7 | Average | 18 | 21 | 19.5 | |
| 8 | Variance | 72 | 50 | 43.66667 | |
| 9 | | | | | |
| 10 | *Ring-High* | | | | |
| 11 | Count | 2 | 2 | 4 | |
| 12 | Sum | 46 | 214 | 260 | |
| 13 | Average | 23 | 107 | 65 | |
| 14 | Variance | 50 | 72 | 2392.667 | |
| 15 | | | | | |
| 16 | *Total* | | | | |
| 17 | Count | 4 | 4 | | |
| 18 | Sum | 82 | 256 | | |
| 19 | Average | 20.5 | 64 | | |
| 20 | Variance | 49 | 2506 | | |

TwoWayAnova / Data /

|   | A | B | C | D | E | F | G |
|---|---|---|---|---|---|---|---|
| 21 | | | | | | | |
| 22 | | | | | | | |
| 23 | ANOVA | | | | | | |
| 24 | *Source of Variation* | *SS* | *df* | *MS* | *F* | *P-value* | *F crit* |
| 25 | Sample | 4140.5 | 1 | 4140.5 | 67.87705 | 0.001184 | 7.70865 |
| 26 | Columns | 3784.5 | 1 | 3784.5 | 62.04098 | 0.001404 | 7.70865 |
| 27 | Interaction | 3280.5 | 1 | 3280.5 | 53.77869 | 0.00184 | 7.70865 |
| 28 | Within | 244 | 4 | 61 | | | |
| 29 | | | | | | | |
| 30 | Total | 11449.5 | 7 | | | | |

Note that in addition to the analysis-of-variance table, Excel has computed the average value for each combination of ring osculation and heat treatment, as well as the average for each level of the ring osculation and heat treatment factors. To interpret the results, we test whether there is evidence of an interacting effect between factor A (ring osculation) and factor B (heat treatment). Using a level of significance $\alpha$ of .05, we reject the null hypothesis of no interacting effect (that is, $H_0$: $AB_{ij} = 0$ for all $i$ and $j$) because the $p$-value (0.00184) is less than our selected level of significance. We also note that our calculated $F$-test statistic 53.779 exceeds 7.709, the upper-tailed critical value from the $F$ distribution with 1 degree of freedom in the numerator and 4 degrees of freedom in the denominator.

This significant interaction effect between ring osculation and heat treatment can be observed in the accompanying chart in which average life is plotted for each type of ring osculation according to type of heat treatment (low versus high). Because the lines that represent average life for the different heat treatments are not parallel for the two ring osculations, the differences in average life between low and high ring osculation are not constant for the two types of heat treatments. There is a large difference in average life between low and high heat treatments for high ring osculation but very little difference when there is low ring osculation.

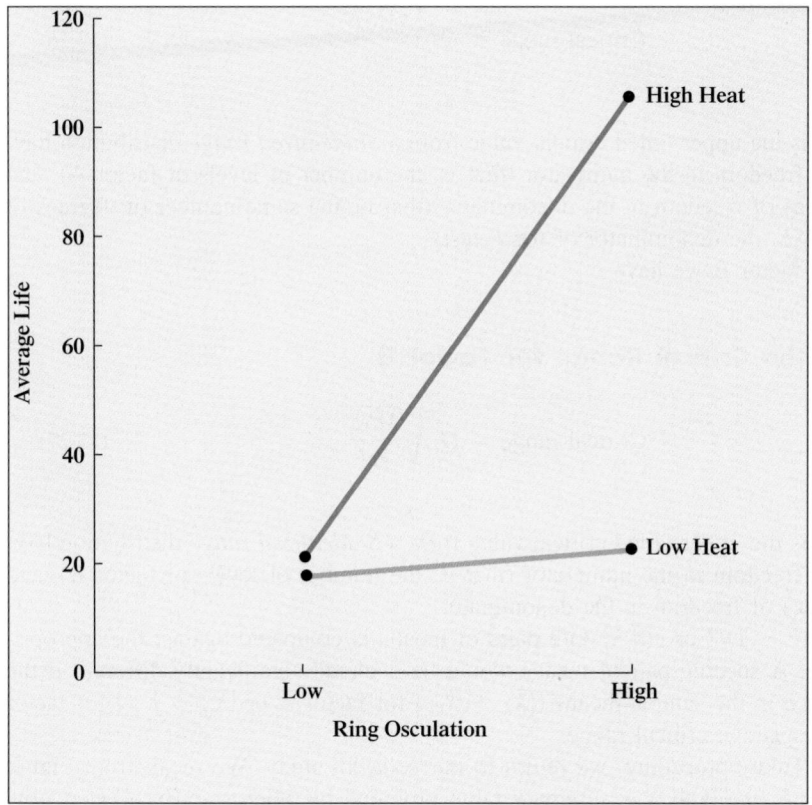

Average life of low and high ring osculation based on heat treatments

The existence of this significant interaction effect complicates the interpretation of the *main effects*. We cannot directly conclude that there is a significant difference in average life between low and high ring osculation because the difference *is not the same* over all heat treatments. Likewise, we cannot directly conclude that there is a significant difference in average life among the heat treatments because this difference *is not the same* for both types of ring osculations.

## Multiple Comparisons: The Tukey Procedure

As in the case of the one-way and randomized block models, once the null hypothesis of no differences in the levels of a factor has been rejected, we need to determine the particular groups or levels that are significantly different from each other. A procedure developed by John Tukey (references 6 and 12) may be used for factor A as well as for factor B.

For factor A we have

$$\text{Critical range} = Q_U \sqrt{\frac{MSE}{cn'}} \qquad (13.26)$$

The statistic $Q_U$ is the upper-tailed critical value from a *Studentized range* distribution having $r$ degrees of freedom in the numerator (that is, the number of levels of factor A), and $rc(n' - 1)$ degrees of freedom in the denominator (that is, the same number of degrees of freedom as in *MSE*, the denominator of the *F* test).

Similarly, for factor B we have

$$\text{Critical range} = Q_U \sqrt{\frac{MSE}{rn'}} \qquad (13.27)$$

The statistic $Q_U$ is the upper-tailed critical value from a *Studentized range* distribution having $c$ degrees of freedom in the numerator (that is, the number of levels of factor B), and $rc(n' - 1)$ degrees of freedom in the denominator.

Each of the $r(r - 1)/2$ or $c(c - 1)/2$ pairs of means is compared against the appropriate critical range. A specific pair of means would be declared significantly different if the absolute difference in the sample means ($|\overline{X}_{i..} - \overline{X}_{i'..}|$ for factor A or $|\overline{X}_{.j.} - \overline{X}_{.j'.}|$ for factor B) exceeds its respective critical range.

To apply the Tukey procedure, we return to our soda fill study. We recall from Figure 13.13 on page 585 (the ANOVA summary table provided by Microsoft Excel) that only one of our main effects was deemed significant. That is, using an $\alpha$ level of .05, there was no evidence of a significant difference between the two percent carbonation levels (10% versus 12%) that comprise factor A but there was evidence of a significant difference among the four line speed levels (210 bpm, 240 bpm, 270 bpm, and 300 bpm) that comprise factor B. Thus our multiple comparison procedure will be used to further analyze differences in the line speed levels of factor B.

With respect to factor B, because there are four levels, there are $4(4 - 1)/2 = 6$ possible pairwise comparisons to be made. The means for the levels of factor B (line speed) are:

$$210 \text{ bpm: } \overline{X}_{.1.} = -3.030 \qquad 240 \text{ bpm: } \overline{X}_{.2.} = -1.170$$
$$270 \text{ bpm: } \overline{X}_{.3.} = 0.410 \qquad 300 \text{ bpm: } \overline{X}_{.4.} = 1.900$$

The absolute mean differences for the six pairwise comparisons are:

1. $|\overline{X}_{.1.} - \overline{X}_{.2.}| = |-3.030 - (-1.170)| = 1.860$

2. $|\overline{X}_{.1.} - \overline{X}_{.3.}| = |-3.030 - 0.410| = 3.440$

3. $|\overline{X}_{.1.} - \overline{X}_{.4.}| = |-3.030 - 1.900| = 4.930$

4. $|\overline{X}_{.2.} - \overline{X}_{.3.}| = |-1.170 - 0.410| = 1.580$

5. $|\bar{X}_{.2.} - \bar{X}_{.4.}| = |-1.170 - 1.900| = 3.070$

6. $|\bar{X}_{.3.} - \bar{X}_{.4.}| = |0.410 - 1.900| = 1.490$

To determine the critical range, we use Figure 13.13 on page 585 to obtain $MSE = 8.612$, $r = 2$, $c = 4$, and $n' = 5$. From Table E.10 [for $\alpha = .05$, $c = 4$, and $rc(n' - 1) = 32$], $Q_U$, the upper-tailed critical value of the test statistic with 4 degrees of freedom in the numerator and 32 degrees of freedom in the denominator is approximated[3] as 3.84. Using equation (13.27):

$$\text{Critical range} = 3.84\sqrt{\frac{8.612}{10}} = 3.56$$

Because $4.93 > 3.56$, we note that $\bar{X}_{.1.}$ is different from $\bar{X}_{.4.}$ (that is, an average deviation of $-3.030$ mm from the specified target fill is significantly less than an average deviation of $1.900$ mm) and we may conclude that a line speed dial setting of 210 bpm results in significantly less soda bottle fill than does a dial setting of 300 bpm.

[3]*Table E.10 does not provide the upper-tailed critical values from the Studentized range distribution with 4 degrees of freedom in the numerator and 32 degrees of freedom in the denominator. When the desired degrees of freedom are not provided in the table, we suggest rounding to the closest value that is given. In our case, for a level of significance of .05, we chose the upper-tailed critical value 3.84 which corresponds to a Studentized range distribution with 4 and 30 degrees of freedom in the numerator and denominator.*

## Problems for Section 13.3

### Learning the Basics

• **13.31** Given a two-factor factorial design having three levels in factor A, three levels in factor B, and four replicates in each of the nine treatment cell combinations of factors A and B, answer the following questions.
   (a) How many degrees of freedom are there in determining the factor A variation?
   (b) How many degrees of freedom are there in determining the factor B variation?
   (c) How many degrees of freedom are there in determining the interaction variation?
   (d) How many degrees of freedom are there in determining the inherent random error variation?
   (e) How many degrees of freedom are there in determining the total variation?

• **13.32** From Problem 13.31:
   (a) If $SSFA = 120$, $SSFB = 110$, $SSE = 270$, and $SST = 540$, what is $SSAB$?
   (b) What is $MSFA$?
   (c) What is $MSFB$?
   (d) What is $MSAB$?
   (e) What is $MSE$?
   (f) What is the value of the test statistic $F$ for the interaction effect?
   (g) What is the value of the test statistic $F$ for the factor A effect?
   (h) What is the value of the test statistic $F$ for the factor B effect?
   (i) Form the ANOVA summary table and fill in all values in the body of the table.

• **13.33** Given Problems 13.31 and 13.32, answer the following.
   (a) At the .05 level of significance, what is the upper-tailed critical value from the $F$ distribution for the factor A effect?
   (b) At the .05 level of significance, what is the upper-tailed critical value from the $F$ distribution for the factor B effect?
   (c) At the .05 level of significance, what is the upper-tailed critical value from the $F$ distribution for the interaction effect?
   (d) What is your statistical decision with respect to the interaction effect?
   (e) What is your statistical decision with respect to the factor A effect?
   (f) What is your statistical decision with respect to the factor B effect?

**13.34** Given a two-way analysis of variance with two treatment levels for factor A and five treatment levels for factor B and four replicates in each of the 10 treatment cell combinations of factors A and B, and supposing that $SSFA = 18$, $SSFB = 64$, $SSE = 60$, and $SST = 150$, answer the following.

(a) What is $SSAB$?

(b) Form the ANOVA summary table and fill in all values in the body of the table.

(c) At the .01 level of significance, what is the upper-tailed critical value from the $F$ distribution for the factor A effect?

(d) At the .01 level of significance, what is the upper-tailed critical value from the $F$ distribution for the factor B effect?

(e) At the .01 level of significance, what is the upper-tailed critical value from the $F$ distribution for the interaction effect?

(f) What is your statistical decision with respect to the interaction effect?

(g) What is your statistical decision with respect to the factor A effect?

(h) What is your statistical decision with respect to the factor B effect?

**13.35** Given a two-factor experiment and the ANOVA summary table that follows, fill in all of the missing results.

| SOURCE | DEGREES OF FREEDOM | SUM OF SQUARES | MEAN SQUARE (VARIANCE) | F |
|---|---|---|---|---|
| Factor A | $r - 1 = 2$ | $SSFA = ?$ | $MSFA = 80$ | $F = ?$ |
| Factor B | $c - 1 = ?$ | $SSFB = 220$ | $MSFB = ?$ | $F = 11.0$ |
| AB interaction | $(r - 1)(c - 1) = 8$ | $SSAB = ?$ | $MSAB = 10$ | $F = ?$ |
| Error | $rc(n' - 1) = 30$ | $SSE = ?$ | $MSE = ?$ | |
| Total | $n - 1 = ?$ | $SST = ?$ | | |

**13.36** From Problem 13.35:

(a) At the .05 level of significance, what is the upper-tailed critical value from the $F$ distribution for the factor A effect?

(b) At the .05 level of significance, what is the upper-tailed critical value from the $F$ distribution for the factor B effect?

(c) At the .05 level of significance, what is the upper-tailed critical value from the $F$ distribution for the interaction effect?

(d) What is your statistical decision with respect to the interaction effect?

(e) What is your statistical decision with respect to the factor A effect?

(f) What is your statistical decision with respect to the factor B effect?

(g) To perform the Tukey procedure on factor B, how many degrees of freedom are there in the numerator and how many degrees of freedom are there in the denominator of the Studentized range distribution?

(h) At the .05 level of significance, what is the upper-tailed critical value from the Studentized range distribution?

(i) To perform the Tukey procedure, what is the critical range?

## Applying the Concepts

• **13.37** A videocassette recorder (VCR) repair service wished to study the effect of VCR brand and service center on the repair time measured in minutes. Three VCR brands (A, B, C) were specifically selected for analysis. Three service centers were also specifically selected. Each service center was assigned to perform a particular repair on two VCRs of each brand. The results are presented in the following table:

| SERVICE CENTERS | VCR BRANDS | | |
|---|---|---|---|
| | A | B | C |
| 1 | 52 | 48 | 59 |
| | 57 | 39 | 67 |
| 2 | 51 | 61 | 58 |
| | 43 | 52 | 64 |
| 3 | 37 | 44 | 65 |
| | 46 | 50 | 69 |

DATA FILE
REPAIR

Use either computer software or the following summary information:

| Sums of squares: | $SSFA = 27.44$ | $SSFB = 945.78$ | $SSAB = 361.22$ | $SST = 1,576.44$ |
|---|---|---|---|---|

| Center: | 1 | 2 | 3 |
|---|---|---|---|
| Sample means: | 53.7 | 54.8 | 51.8 |

| Brand: | A | B | C |
|---|---|---|---|
| Sample means: | 47.7 | 49.0 | 63.7 |

| Cell: | 1,A | 1,B | 1,C | 2,A | 2,B | 2,C | 3,A | 3,B | 3,C |
|---|---|---|---|---|---|---|---|---|---|
| Sample means: | 54.5 | 43.5 | 63.0 | 47.0 | 56.5 | 61.0 | 41.5 | 47.0 | 67.0 |

(a) At the .05 level of significance:
    (1) Is there an interaction due to service center and VCR brand?
    (2) Is there an effect due to service centers?
    (3) Is there an effect due to VCR brand?

(b) Plot a graph of average service time for each service center for each VCR brand.

(c) If appropriate, use the Tukey procedure to determine which service centers and which VCR brands differ in average service time. (Use $\alpha = .05$.)

(d) On the basis of the results, what conclusions can you reach concerning average service time?

**13.38** An experiment is designed to study the effect of two factors on the amplification of a stereo recording. The factors are type of receiver (two brands) and type of amplifier (four brands). For each combination of factor levels, three tests are performed in which decibel output is measured. A higher decibel output means a better result. The coded results are as follows:

| RECEIVER | AMPLIFIERS | | | |
|---|---|---|---|---|
| | A | B | C | D |
| $R_1$ | 9 | 8 | 8 | 10 |
| | 4 | 11 | 7 | 15 |
| | 12 | 16 | 1 | 9 |
| $R_2$ | 7 | 5 | 0 | 6 |
| | 1 | 9 | 1 | 7 |
| | 4 | 6 | 7 | 5 |

DATA FILE
AMPLIFY

To solve, use either computer software or the following summary information:

| Sums of squares: | $SSFA = 112.67$ | | $SSFB = 103.00$ | | $SSAB = 6.33$ | | $SST = 394.00$ | |
| --- | --- | --- | --- | --- | --- | --- | --- | --- |
| Receiver: | **1** | **2** | | | | | | |
| Sample means: | 9.17 | 4.83 | | | | | | |
| Amplifier: | **A** | **B** | **C** | **D** | | | | |
| Sample means: | 6.17 | 9.17 | 4.00 | 8.67 | | | | |
| Cell: | **1,A** | **1,B** | **1,C** | **1,D** | **2,A** | **2,B** | **2,C** | **2,D** |
| Sample means: | 8.33 | 11.67 | 5.33 | 11.33 | 4.00 | 6.67 | 2.67 | 6.00 |

(a) At the .01 level of significance:
   (1) Is there an interaction between receivers and amplifiers?
   (2) Is there an effect due to receivers?
   (3) Is there an effect due to amplifiers?
(b) Plot a graph of average decibel output for each receiver for each amplifier.
(c) If appropriate, use the Tukey procedure to determine which amplifiers differ in average decibel output. (Use $\alpha = .01$.)
(d) On the basis of the results, what conclusions can you reach concerning average decibel output?

**13.39** The manager of a supermarket chain wanted to study the effect of product location on the sales of packages of candy bars. Two factors were to be studied: location in aisle (either front or rear) and shelf location (either top or bottom). A random sample of eight equal-sized stores was selected and two stores were randomly assigned to each combination of aisle location and shelf location. The size of the display area was the same in all stores. At the end of a 1-week trial period, the sales of packages of candy bars in each store are as follows.

| | SHELF LOCATION | |
| --- | --- | --- |
| **AISLE LOCATION** | **TOP** | **BOTTOM** |
| Front | 86 | 70 |
| | 72 | 60 |
| Rear | 60 | 28 |
| | 46 | 22 |

**DATA FILE**
**CANDY**

To solve, use either computer software or the following summary information:

| Sums of squares: | $SSFA = 2,178$ | | $SSFB = 882$ | | $SSAB = 98$ | | $SST = 3,422$ |
| --- | --- | --- | --- | --- | --- | --- | --- |
| Aisle location: | **FRONT** | **REAR** | | | | | |
| Sample means: | 72 | 39 | | | | | |
| Shelf location: | **TOP** | **BOTTOM** | | | | | |
| Sample means: | 66 | 45 | | | | | |
| Cell: | **FRONT, TOP** | | **FRONT, BOTTOM** | | **REAR, TOP** | | **REAR, BOTTOM** |
| Sample means: | 79 | | 65 | | 53 | | 25 |

(a) At the .05 level of significance:
  (1) Is there an interaction between aisle location and shelf location?
  (2) Is there a difference between the aisle locations?
  (3) Is there a difference between the shelf locations?
(b) Plot a graph of the average sales for each aisle location for each shelf location.
(c) If appropriate, use the Tukey procedure to determine the aisle locations and shelf locations that differ in average sales. (Use $\alpha = .05$.)
(d) On the basis of the results, what conclusions can the manager draw?

● **13.40** The quality control director for a clothing manufacturer wants to study the effect of operators and machines on the breaking strength (in pounds) of wool serge material. A batch of the material is cut into square-yard pieces and these are randomly assigned, 3 each, to all 12 combinations of 4 operators and 3 machines chosen specifically for the experiment. The results are as follows:

| | **MACHINE** | | |
|---|---|---|---|
| **OPERATOR** | **I** | **II** | **III** |
| A | 115 | 111 | 109 |
| | 115 | 108 | 110 |
| | 119 | 114 | 107 |
| B | 117 | 105 | 110 |
| | 114 | 102 | 113 |
| | 114 | 106 | 114 |
| C | 109 | 100 | 103 |
| | 110 | 103 | 102 |
| | 106 | 101 | 105 |
| D | 112 | 105 | 108 |
| | 115 | 107 | 111 |
| | 111 | 107 | 110 |

**DATA FILE**
**BREAKSTW**

To solve, use either computer software or the following summary information:

| Sums of squares: | $SSFA = 301.111$ | $SSFB = 329.389$ | $SSAB = 86.389$ | $SST = 807.556$ | | |
|---|---|---|---|---|---|---|
| Operator: | **A** | **B** | **C** | **D** | | |
| Sample means: | 112.00 | 110.56 | 104.33 | 109.56 | | |
| Machine: | **1** | **2** | **3** | | | |
| Sample means: | 113.08 | 105.75 | 108.50 | | | |
| Cell: | **A,1** | **A,2** | **A,3** | **B,1** | **B,2** | **B,3** |
| Sample means: | 116.33 | 111.00 | 108.67 | 115.00 | 104.33 | 112.33 |
| Cell: | **C,1** | **C,2** | **C,3** | **D,1** | **D,2** | **D,3** |
| Sample means: | 108.33 | 101.33 | 103.33 | 112.67 | 106.33 | 109.67 |

(a) At the .05 level of significance:
  (1) Is there an interaction due to operator and machine?
  (2) Is there an effect due to operator?
  (3) Is there an effect due to machine?

(b) Plot a graph of average breaking strength for each operator for each machine.
(c) If appropriate, use the Tukey procedure to determine which operators and which machines differ in average breaking strength. (Use $\alpha = .05$.)
(d) What can you conclude about the effect of operators and machines on breaking strength? Explain.

**13.41** The operations manager for an appliance manufacturer wishes to determine the optimal length of time for the washing cycle of a household clothes washer. An experiment is designed to measure the effect of detergent used and washing cycle time on the amount of dirt removed from standard household laundry loads. Four brands of detergent (A, B, C, D) and four levels of washing cycle (18, 20, 22, 24 minutes) are specifically selected for analysis. In order to run the experiment, 32 standard household laundry loads (having equal weight and dirt) are randomly assigned, two each, to the 16 detergent–washing cycle time combinations. The results (in pounds of dirt removed) are as follows.

| DETERGENT BRAND | WASHING CYCLE TIME (IN MINUTES) | | | |
|---|---|---|---|---|
| | 18 | 20 | 22 | 24 |
| A | .11 | .13 | .17 | .17 |
| | .09 | .13 | .19 | .18 |
| B | .12 | .14 | .17 | .19 |
| | .10 | .15 | .18 | .17 |
| C | .08 | .16 | .18 | .20 |
| | .09 | .13 | .17 | .16 |
| D | .11 | .12 | .16 | .15 |
| | .13 | .13 | .17 | .17 |

**DATA FILE
LAUNDRY**

Use either computer software or the following summary information:

| Sums of squares: $SSFA = .0004125$; $SSFB = .0273375$; $SSAB = .0023375$; $SST = .0328875$ | | | | |
|---|---|---|---|---|
| Brand: | **A** | **B** | **C** | **D** |
| Sample means: | 0.146 | 0.153 | 0.146 | 0.143 |
| Cycle time: | **18** | **20** | **22** | **24** |
| Sample means: | 0.104 | 0.136 | 0.174 | 0.174 |

| Cell: | **A,1** | **A,2** | **A,3** | **A,4** | **B,1** | **B,2** | **B,3** | **B,4** |
|---|---|---|---|---|---|---|---|---|
| Sample means: | 0.100 | 0.130 | 0.180 | 0.175 | 0.110 | 0.145 | 0.175 | 0.180 |
| Cell: | **C,1** | **C,2** | **C,3** | **C,4** | **D,1** | **D,2** | **D,3** | **D,4** |
| Sample means: | 0.085 | 0.145 | 0.175 | 0.180 | 0.120 | 0.125 | 0.165 | 0.160 |

(a) At the .05 level of significance:
 (1) Is there an interaction due to detergent and washing cycle time?
 (2) Is there an effect due to detergent?
 (3) Is there an effect due to washing cycle time?

(b) Plot a graph of average amount of dirt removed (in pounds) for each detergent for each washing cycle time.

(c) If appropriate, use the Tukey procedure to determine which detergents and which washing cycle times differ with respect to average amount of dirt removed. (Use $\alpha = .05$.)

(d) Prepare a report for the operations manager regarding your findings on average amount of dirt removed. Be sure to offer a recommendation as to what the optimal washing cycle should be for this type of household clothes washer.

##  13.4 KRUSKAL-WALLIS RANK TEST FOR DIFFERENCES IN $c$ MEDIANS (OPTIONAL TOPIC)

The Kruskal-Wallis rank test for differences in $c$ medians (where $c > 2$) is an extension of the Wilcoxon rank-sum test for two independent samples discussed in section 12.4. Thus, the Kruskal-Wallis test enjoys the same power properties relative to the one-way ANOVA $F$ test as does the Wilcoxon rank-sum test relative to the pooled-variance $t$ test for two independent samples (section 12.1). That is, the Kruskal-Wallis procedure has proved to be almost as powerful as the $F$ test under conditions appropriate to the latter and even more powerful than the $F$ test when its assumptions (see section 13.1) are violated.

The **Kruskal-Wallis rank test** is most often used to test whether $c$ independent sample groups have been drawn from populations possessing equal medians. That is, we may test

$$H_0: M_1 = M_2 = \cdots = M_c$$

against the alternative

$$H_1: \text{Not all } M_j \text{ are equal (where } j = 1, 2, \ldots, c)$$

For such situations, it is necessary to assume that the measurements need only be ordinal over all sample groups and the $c$ populations from which the samples are drawn have the same *variability* and *shape*.

To perform the Kruskal-Wallis rank test, we first (if necessary) replace the observations in the $c$ samples with their combined ranks such that rank 1 is given to the smallest of the combined observations and rank $n$ to the largest of the combined observations (where $n = n_1 + n_2 + \cdots + n_c$). If any values are tied, they are assigned the average of the ranks they would otherwise have been assigned if ties had not been present in the data.

The Kruskal-Wallis test was developed as an alternative to the one-way ANOVA $F$ test. As such, the Kruskal-Wallis test statistic $H$ is similar conceptually to $SSA$, the *among-group variation* term [see equation (13.2) on page 543], which is part of the test statistic $F$ [see equation (13.5) on page 544]. Instead of comparing each of the $c$ group means $\overline{X}_j$ against the overall or grand mean $\overline{\overline{X}}$, we now compare the average of the ranks in each of the $c$ groups against the overall average rank based on all $n$ combined observations. If there exists a significant treatment effect among the $c$ groups, the average of the ranks assigned in each group will differ considerably from each other and from the overall average rank. In the process of squaring these differences, as we did when developing $SSA$, the test statistic $H$ becomes large. On the other hand, if there is no treatment effect present, the test statistic $H$ theoretically will have a value of 0. In practice, however, owing to random variation, if there is no treatment effect present, the $H$-test statistic will be small because the average of the ranks assigned in each group should be very similar to each other and to the overall average rank.

The Kruskal-Wallis test statistic $H$ is obtained as in equation (13.28).

## Kruskal-Wallis Rank Test for Differences in $c$ Medians

$$H = \left[ \frac{12}{n(n+1)} \sum_{j=1}^{c} \frac{T_j^2}{n_j} \right] - 3(n+1) \qquad (13.28)$$

where

$n$ = the total number of observations over the combined samples

$n_j$ = the number of observations in the $j$th sample; $j = 1, 2, \ldots, c$

$T_j$ = the sum of the ranks assigned to the $j$th sample

$T_j^2$ = the square of the sum of the ranks assigned to the $j$th sample

As the sample sizes in each group get large (greater than 5), the test statistic $H$ may be approximated by the chi-square distribution with $c - 1$ degrees of freedom. Thus, for any selected level of significance $\alpha$, the decision rule is to reject the null hypothesis if the computed value of $H$ exceeds $\chi_U^2$, the upper-tailed critical value, and not to reject the null hypothesis if $H$ is less than or equal to $\chi_U^2$ (see Figure 13.17). That is,

$$\text{Reject } H_0 \text{ if } H > \chi_U^2;$$

$$\text{otherwise don't reject } H_0.$$

The critical values from the chi-square distribution are given in Table E.4.

To illustrate the Kruskal-Wallis rank test for differences in $c$ medians, we return to our Using Statistics application. In the preceding chapter we determined that an operating pressure of 25 psi is appropriate for the machinery and equipment on hand. If, in addition, a dial setting for 12% carbonation is also used, the operations manager would still want to determine the effect of different line speeds (in filled bottles per minute) on the average deviation from the specified target fill.

Recall from section 13.1 that the operations manager performed an experiment with five bottles filled at each of the four levels of the line speed factor—210, 240, 270, and 300 bottles per minute. The results of the experiment are displayed in Table 13.2 on page 547 along with some summary computations, and a scatter plot was presented in Figure 13.5 on page 548 so that a visual, exploratory evaluation of potential trends, relationships, and

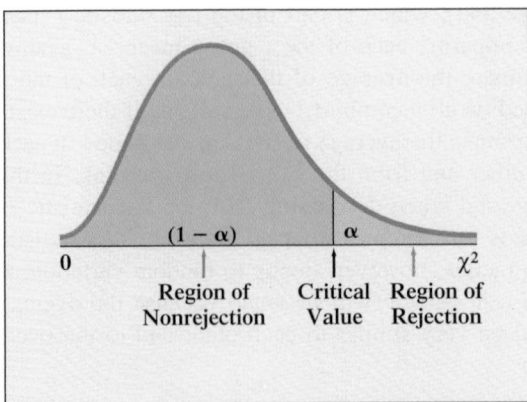

**FIGURE 13.17**
Determining the rejection region

violations in assumptions of particular testing procedures can be made. If the operations manager does not wish to make the assumption that the soda fill measurements (in mm) are normally distributed across the underlying populations, the nonparametric Kruskal-Wallis rank test for differences in the four population medians can be used.

The null hypothesis to be tested is that the median deviations from the specified target fill under the four line speed dial settings are equal; the alternative is that the median deviation for at least one of the line speeds differs from the others.

$$H_0: M_1 = M_2 = M_3 = M_4$$

$$H_1: \text{Not all the medians are equal}$$

The results of this experiment (in terms of deviation from target in millimeters) are again displayed in Table 13.12, along with the corresponding ranks.

In converting the 20 fill measurements to ranks, as in Table 13.12, we note that in the combined ranking, the third bottle filled under a 210-bpm line speed dial setting attained the lowest fill level. This underfilled bottle deviated from the specified target by 4.8 mm and received a rank of 1. The fourth bottle filled under a 240-bpm line speed dial setting attained the second lowest fill level and received a rank of 2. In addition, we note that two bottles were each underfilled by 2.1 mm—the fourth bottle filled under a 210-bpm line speed dial setting and the second bottle filled under a 240-bpm line speed dial setting. These two bottles tied for the fifth and sixth lowest fills and are each given the average rank of 5.5. Finally, we note that a rank of 20 is assigned to the first bottle filled under a 300-bpm line speed dial setting because this overfilled bottle deviated from the specified target by 4.3 mm.

After all the ranks are assigned, we obtain the following sum of the ranks for each group:

Rank sums: $T_1 = 27$   $T_2 = 44.5$   $T_3 = 62$   $T_4 = 76.5$

As a check on the rankings we have

$$T_1 + T_2 + T_3 + T_4 = \frac{n(n+1)}{2}$$

$$27 + 44.5 + 62 + 76.5 = \frac{(20)(21)}{2}$$

$$210 = 210$$

**Table 13.12** *Data on deviations from specified target fill (in mm) and converted ranks under four line speeds*

| | | | LINE SPEED (IN BPM) | | | | |
|---|---|---|---|---|---|---|---|
| **210** | | **240** | | **270** | | **300** | |
| MM | RANK | MM | RANK | MM | RANK | MM | RANK |
| −3.5 | **4** | 3.4 | **19** | −1.4 | **8** | 4.3 | **20** |
| 2.0 | **13.5** | −2.1 | **5.5** | 3.2 | **17** | 3.3 | **18** |
| −4.8 | **1** | 0.6 | **11** | −1.2 | **9** | 2.0 | **13.5** |
| −2.1 | **5.5** | −4.5 | **2** | 2.7 | **16** | −0.8 | **10** |
| −4.0 | **3** | −1.6 | **7** | 0.9 | **12** | 2.5 | **15** |

DATA FILE
LINESPD

We choose a .05 level of significance and use equation (13.28) to test the null hypothesis of equal population medians.

$$H = \left[ \frac{12}{n(n+1)} \sum_{j=1}^{c} \frac{T_j^2}{n_j} \right] - 3(n+1)$$

$$= \left\{ \frac{12}{(20)(21)} \left[ \frac{(27)^2}{5} + \frac{(44.5)^2}{5} + \frac{(62)^2}{5} + \frac{(76.5)^2}{5} \right] \right\} - 3(21)$$

$$= \left( \frac{12}{420} \right) [2{,}481.1] - 63 = 7.889$$

This statistic $H$ has a chi-square distribution with $c - 1$ degrees of freedom. Using a .05 level of significance, from Table E.4 we see that $\chi_U^2$, the upper-tailed critical value of the chi-square distribution with $c - 1 = 3$ degrees of freedom, is 7.815 (see Table 13.13). Because the computed value of the test statistic $H = 7.889$ exceeds the critical value, we can reject the null hypothesis and conclude that not all the line speed dial settings are the same with respect to median deviation from specified target fill. Using the $p$-value approach, from Figure 13.18 the $p$-value obtained from Minitab $= .048 < .05$. In addition to the $p$-value, Minitab provides the sample size, the sample median deviation from specified target fill (in mm), the average assigned rank (AVE. RANK), and the Z-value at each dial setting level. The average assigned ranks are obtained by dividing the rank sums by the respective

**Table 13.13** *Obtaining $\chi_U^2$, the approximate upper-tailed critical value for the Kruskal-Wallis test at the .05 level of significance with 3 degrees of freedom*

| DEGREES OF FREEDOM | UPPER-TAILED AREA | | | | | | | | | |
|---|---|---|---|---|---|---|---|---|---|---|
| | .995 | .99 | .975 | .95 | .90 | .75 | .25 | .10 | .05 | .025 |
| 1 | — | — | 0.001 | 0.004 | 0.016 | 0.102 | 1.323 | 2.706 | 3.841 | 5.024 |
| 2 | 0.010 | 0.020 | 0.051 | 0.103 | 0.211 | 0.575 | 2.773 | 4.605 | 5.991 | 7.378 |
| 3 | 0.072 | 0.115 | 0.216 | 0.352 | 0.584 | 1.213 | 4.108 | 6.251 → | 7.815 | 9.348 |
| 4 | 0.207 | 0.297 | 0.484 | 0.711 | 1.064 | 1.923 | 5.385 | 7.779 | 9.488 | 11.143 |
| 5 | 0.412 | 0.554 | 0.831 | 1.145 | 1.610 | 2.675 | 6.626 | 9.236 | 11.071 | 12.833 |

*Source: Extracted from Table E.4.*

```
Kruskal-Wallis Test

Kruskal-Wallis Test on Deviatio

LineSpd    N    Median    Ave Rank         Z
1          5    -3.5000        5.4     -2.23
2          5    -1.6000        8.9     -0.70
3          5     0.9000       12.4      0.83
4          5     2.5000       15.3      2.09
Overall   20                 10.5

H = 7.89   DF = 3   P = 0.048
H = 7.90   DF = 3   P = 0.048  (adjusted for ties)
```

**FIGURE 13.18**
Minitab output of Kruskal-Wallis rank test for differences in $c = 4$ medians in soda fill study

sample sizes. The overall average rank for all 20 observations is also shown. The Z-values indicate how different, in standardized units, each average rank is from the overall average rank.

At the bottom of the Minitab printout appears the test statistic $H$, the degrees of freedom (DF), and the $p$-value. If there are ties in the rankings, as is the case in our soft-drink example, Minitab provides an adjustment to the test statistic $H$ along with an adjusted $p$-value. We suggest the adjusted $H$ statistic be used for interpreting results. In our study we note that this adjustment has a minimal impact on our results. Note that these are the same conclusions we reached using the one-way ANOVA $F$ test in section 13.1.

Because we have rejected the null hypothesis and concluded that there was evidence of a significant difference among the line speed dial settings with respect to the median deviation from specified target fill, the next step is a simultaneous comparison of all possible pairs of line speed dial settings to determine which one or ones differ from the others. As a follow-up to the Kruskal-Wallis rank test, a *post hoc* or *a posteriori* multiple comparison procedure proposed by O. J. Dunn (see references 3 and 4) can be used.

To use the Kruskal-Wallis rank test for differences in $c$ medians, we make the following assumptions presented in Exhibit 13.1.

## Exhibit 13.1   Assumptions of the Kruskal-Wallis Test

✓ **1.** The $c$ samples are randomly and independently drawn from their respective populations.

✓ **2.** The underlying random phenomenon of interest is *continuous* (to avoid ties).

✓ **3.** The observed data constitute at least an ordinal scale of measurement, both within and among the $c$ samples.

✓ **4.** The $c$ populations have the same variability.

✓ **5.** The $c$ populations have the same shape.

Interestingly, the Kruskal-Wallis procedure still makes less stringent assumptions than does the $F$ test. To employ the Kruskal-Wallis procedure, the measurements need only be ordinal over all sample groups and the common population distributions need only be continuous—their common shapes are irrelevant. In fact, if we ignore the last two assumptions, the Kruskal-Wallis rank test still can be used to test the null hypothesis of no differences in the $c$ populations against the general alternative that at least one of the populations differs from at least one of the other populations in some characteristic—be it central tendency, variation, or shape. On the other hand, to use the $F$ test, the level of measurement must be more sophisticated and we must assume that the $c$ samples are coming from underlying normal populations having equal variances.

For situations involving completely randomized designs, when the more stringent assumptions of the $F$ test hold, we should select it over the Kruskal-Wallis test because it is slightly more powerful in its ability to detect significant treatment effects. On the other hand, if the more stringent assumptions cannot be met, the Kruskal-Wallis test likely is more powerful than the $F$ test and we should choose this procedure.

# Problems for Section 13.4

## Learning the Basics

- **13.42** If the Kruskal-Wallis rank test is used at the .01 level of significance when testing for the equality of the medians in six populations, what would be the upper-tailed critical value $\chi_U^2$ from the chi-square distribution?

- **13.43** From Problem 13.42:
  - (a) State the decision rule for testing the null hypothesis that all six groups have equal population medians.
  - (b) What would be your statistical decision if the computed value of the test statistic $H$ were 13.77?

## Applying the Concepts

- **13.44** An industrial psychologist desires to test whether the reaction times of assembly line workers are equivalent under three different learning methods. From a group of 25 new employees, 9 are randomly assigned to method A, 8 to method B, and 8 to method C. After the learning period, the workers are given a task to complete, and their reaction times are measured. The following data present the rankings of the reaction times from 1 (fastest) to 25 (slowest):

| METHOD | | |
|---|---|---|
| **A** | **B** | **C** |
| 2 | 1 | 5 |
| 3 | 6 | 7 |
| 4 | 8 | 11 |
| 9 | 15 | 12 |
| 10 | 16 | 13 |
| 14 | 17 | 18 |
| 19 | 21 | 24 |
| 20 | 22 | 25 |
| 23 | | |

Use either a software package or the following summary information:

| Methods: | **A** | **B** | **C** |
|---|---|---|---|
| Sample sizes: | 9 | 8 | 8 |
| Rank sums: | 104 | 106 | 115 |

Is there evidence of a significant difference in the median reaction times for these learning methods? (Use $\alpha = .01$.)

**13.45** A quality engineer in a company manufacturing electronic audio equipment is inspecting a new type of battery. A batch of 20 batteries are randomly assigned to four groups (so that there are 5 batteries per group). Each group of batteries is then subjected to a particular pressure level—low, normal, high, very high. The batteries are simultaneously tested under these pressure levels and the following times to failure (in hours) are recorded:

| PRESSURE | | | |
|---|---|---|---|
| LOW | NORMAL | HIGH | VERY HIGH |
| 8.0 | 7.6 | 6.0 | 5.1 |
| 8.1 | 8.2 | 6.3 | 5.6 |
| 9.2 | 9.8 | 7.1 | 5.9 |
| 9.4 | 10.9 | 7.7 | 6.7 |
| 11.7 | 12.3 | 8.9 | 7.8 |

DATA FILE
BATFAIL

The engineer, by experience, knows such data are coming from populations that are not normally distributed, and he wants to use a nonparametric procedure for purposes of data analysis. To solve use either computer software or the following summary information:

| Pressure levels: | **1** | **2** | **3** | **4** |
|---|---|---|---|---|
| Rank sums: | 73 | 76 | 39 | 22 |

(a) At the .05 level of significance, analyze the data to determine whether there is evidence of a significant difference in the four pressure levels with respect to median battery life.
(b) Recommend a warranty policy with respect to battery life.

**13.46** The quality engineer in a plant manufacturing stereo equipment wants to study the effect of temperature on the failure time of a particular electronic component. She designs an experiment wherein 24 of these components, all from the same batch, are randomly assigned to one of three levels of temperature and then simultaneously activated. The rank order of their times to failure (i.e., a rank of 1 is given to the first component to burn out) is as follows:

| TEMPERATURE | | |
|---|---|---|
| 150°F | 200°F | 250°F |
| 4 | 2 | 1 |
| 7 | 8 | 3 |
| 10 | 11 | 5 |
| 13 | 12 | 6 |
| 18 | 17 | 9 |
| 21 | 19 | 14 |
| 22 | 20 | 15 |
| 24 | 23 | 16 |

DATA FILE
COMPFAIL

To solve use either computer software or the following summary information:

| Temperature levels: | **1** | **2** | **3** |
|---|---|---|---|
| Rank sums: | 119 | 112 | 69 |

(a) At the .05 level of significance, is there evidence of a significant temperature effect on the median life of this type of electronic component?
(b) Do you think that temperature has an effect on failure time? Explain.

**13.47** A medical researcher decides to compare several over-the-counter sleep medications. People who have trouble sleeping come to the researcher's sleep laboratory and are randomly assigned either a placebo (a pill with no active ingredients) or one of the following products: Nighty-night, Snooze-Away, or Mr. Sandman. Their sleeping hours are given as follows:

| PILL | SLEEPING HOURS |
|------|----------------|
| Placebo | 2.5, 4.7, 3.3, 5.6, 2.2, 4.9, 3.8 |
| Nighty-Night | 3.0, 4.0, 5.4, 5.9, 3.6, 5.0, 4.8, 6.4, 5.1 |
| Snooze-Away | 6.6, 5.8, 7.3, 4.4, 8.2, 6.5 |
| Mr. Sandman | 5.2, 4.2, 7.7, 5.2, 8.3, 6.1, 7.6 |

DATA FILE
SLEEPHRS

To solve part (a) use either a software package or the following summary information:

| Medication: | 1 | 2 | 3 | 4 |
|-------------|---|---|---|---|
| Sample sizes: | 7 | 9 | 6 | 7 |
| Rank sums: | 53 | 112 | 128 | 142 |

(a) At the .05 level of significance, is there evidence of a significant difference in median hours of sleep based on sleep medication prescribed?
(b) Which sleep medications can you recommend to the medical researcher?

**● 13.48** The personnel manager of a large insurance company wishes to evaluate the effectiveness of four different sales-training programs designed for new employees. A group of 32 recently hired college graduates are randomly assigned to the four programs so that there are 8 subjects in each program. At the end of the monthlong training period, a standard exam is administered to the 32 subjects; the scores are as follows:

| PROGRAMS | | | |
|---|---|---|---|
| A | B | C | D |
| 66 | 72 | 61 | 63 |
| 74 | 51 | 60 | 61 |
| 82 | 59 | 57 | 76 |
| 75 | 62 | 60 | 84 |
| 73 | 74 | 81 | 58 |
| 97 | 64 | 55 | 65 |
| 87 | 78 | 70 | 69 |
| 78 | 63 | 71 | 80 |

DATA FILE
INSPGM

To solve, use either computer software or the following summary information:

| Programs: | A | B | C | D |
|-----------|---|---|---|---|
| Rank sums: | 197 | 106.5 | 89.5 | 135 |

(a) At an $\alpha = .05$ level of significance, is there evidence of a significant difference in the median scores among the four sales-training programs?

(b) If conditions are appropriate, which group or groups might you suspect to be significantly different from which other groups? Discuss.

(c) If you answered Problem 13.9 on page 557, are there any differences in your present results from those previously obtained? Discuss.

**13.49** The retailing manager of a food chain wishes to determine whether product location has any effect on the sale of pet toys. Three different aisle locations are to be considered: front, middle, and rear. A random sample of 18 stores is selected with 6 stores randomly assigned to each aisle location. The size of the display area and the price of the product are constant for all stores. At the end of a 1-week trial period, the sales volume (in thousands of dollars) of the product in each store is as follows:

| AISLE LOCATION | | |
|---|---|---|
| FRONT | MIDDLE | REAR |
| 8.6 | 3.2 | 4.6 |
| 7.2 | 2.4 | 6.0 |
| 5.4 | 2.0 | 4.0 |
| 6.2 | 1.4 | 2.8 |
| 4.0 | 1.6 | 2.8 |
| 5.0 | 1.8 | 2.2 |

DATA FILE
LOCATE

To solve, use either computer software or the following summary information:

| Aisle location: | FRONT | MIDDLE | REAR |
|---|---|---|---|
| Rank sums: | 88.5 | 25 | 57.5 |

(a) At an $\alpha = .05$ level of significance, is there evidence of a significant difference in median sales among the various aisle locations?

(b) If you answered Problem 13.12 on page 559, are there any differences in your present results from those previously obtained? Discuss.

**13.50** To examine effects of the work environment on attitude toward work, an industrial psychologist randomly assigns a group of 18 recently hired sales trainees to three "home rooms"—6 trainees per room. Each room is identical except for wall color. One is light green, another is light blue, and the third is deep red.

During the weeklong training program, the trainees stay mainly in their respective home rooms. At the end of the program, an attitude scale is used to measure each trainee's attitude toward work (a low score indicates a poor attitude, a high score a good attitude). The following data are obtained.

| ROOM COLOR | | |
|---|---|---|
| LIGHT GREEN | LIGHT BLUE | DEEP RED |
| 46 | 59 | 34 |
| 51 | 54 | 29 |
| 48 | 47 | 43 |
| 42 | 55 | 40 |
| 58 | 49 | 45 |
| 50 | 44 | 34 |

DATA FILE
WORKATT

Suppose that the industrial psychologist is unwilling to make the assumption that the attitude scores are normally distributed but is willing to assume that the populations have the same variability. To solve, use either computer software or the following summary information:

| Color: | GREEN | BLUE | RED |
|---|---|---|---|
| Rank sums: | 69 | 78 | 24 |

(a) Using a level of significance of $\alpha = .05$, is there evidence that work environment (i.e., color of room) has an effect on attitude toward work and, if so, which room color(s) appear(s) to significantly enhance attitude?

(b) If you answered Problem 13.13 on page 559, are there any differences in your present results from those previously obtained? Discuss.

**13.51** A senior partner in a brokerage firm wishes to determine whether there is really any difference between long-run performance of different categories of people hired as customers' representatives. The junior members of the firm are classified into four groups: professionals who have changed careers, recent business school graduates, former salespeople, and brokers hired from competing firms. A random sample of six individuals in each of these categories is selected, and a detailed performance score (a higher number indicates better performance) is obtained.

| CUSTOMER REPRESENTATIVE BACKGROUNDS | | | |
|---|---|---|---|
| **PROFESSIONALS** | **BUSINESS SCHOOL GRADS** | **SALESPEOPLE** | **BROKERS** |
| 88 | 65 | 61 | 83 |
| 85 | 73 | 67 | 87 |
| 95 | 54 | 74 | 90 |
| 96 | 72 | 65 | 84 |
| 91 | 81 | 68 | 92 |
| 88 | 69 | 77 | 94 |

**DATA FILE**
**BROKER**

To solve, use either computer software or the following summary information:

| Background: | 1 | 2 | 3 | 4 |
|---|---|---|---|---|
| Rank sums: | 117 | 40.5 | 37.5 | 105 |

(a) Is there evidence of a significant difference in the median performance score for the various categories? (Use $\alpha = .05$.)

(b) If appropriate, which customer representative backgrounds seem to result in a significantly higher performance?

(c) If you answered Problem 13.14 on page 560, are there any differences in your present results from those previously obtained? Discuss.

## 13.5 FRIEDMAN RANK TEST FOR DIFFERENCES IN $c$ MEDIANS (*OPTIONAL TOPIC*)

It often happens that although the randomized block model is deemed appropriate for a particular experiment, we prefer some nonparametric alternative to the randomized block $F$ test for analyzing the data. If the data collected are only in rank form within each block or if normality cannot be assumed, a simple but fairly powerful nonparametric approach called the **Friedman rank test** can be utilized.

The Friedman rank test is primarily used to test whether $c$-sample groups (i.e., our treatment levels) have been drawn from populations having equal medians. That is, we may test

$$H_0\colon M_{.1} = M_{.2} = \cdots = M_{.c}$$

against the alternative

$$H_1\colon \text{Not all } M_{.j} \text{ are equal (where } j = 1, 2, \ldots, c)$$

To develop the test we first replace the data by their ranks on a block-to-block basis. That is, in each of the $r$ independent blocks, we replace the $c$ observations by their corresponding ranks such that the rank 1 is given to the smallest observation in the block and the rank $c$ to the largest. If any values in a block are tied, they are assigned the average of the ranks that they would otherwise have been given. Thus $R_{ij}$ is the rank (from 1 to $c$) associated with the $j$th group (where $j = 1, 2, \ldots, c$) in the $i$th block (where $i = 1, 2, \ldots, r$).

Under the null hypothesis of no differences in the $c$ groups, each ranking within a block is equally likely. There are $c!$ possible ways of ranking within a particular block and $(c!)^r$ possible arrangements of ranks over all $r$ independent blocks. If the null hypothesis is true, there will be no real differences among the average ranks for each group (taken over all $r$ blocks).

From this discussion the following test statistic $F_R$ may be derived:

### Friedman Rank Test for Differences in $c$ Medians

$$F_R = \frac{12}{rc(c + 1)}\sum_{j=1}^{c} R_{.j}^2 - 3r(c + 1) \qquad (13.29)$$

where

$R_{.j}^2$ = the square of the rank total for group $j$ ($j = 1, 2, \ldots, c$)

$r$ = the number of independent blocks

$c$ = the number of groups or treatment levels

As the number of blocks in the experiment gets large (greater than 5), the test statistic $F_R$ may be approximated by the chi-square distribution with $c - 1$ degrees of freedom. Thus, for any selected level of significance $\alpha$, the decision rule is to reject the null hypothesis if the computed value of $F_R$ exceeds $\chi_U^2$, the upper-tailed critical value for the chi-square distribution having $c - 1$ degrees of freedom as shown in Figure 13.19. That is,

Reject $H_0$ if $F_R > \chi_U^2$;

otherwise don't reject $H_0$.

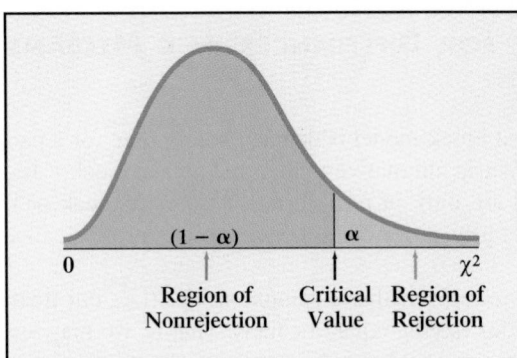

**FIGURE 13.19** Determining the rejection region

The critical values from the chi-square distribution are given in Table E.4.

To illustrate the Friedman rank test for differences in $c$ medians, we return to our fast-food-chain study from section 13.2. Recall that the research director for the chain designed a randomized block experiment in which 24 investigators were stratified into 6 blocks of 4—based on food-service evaluation experience—and the 4 members of each block were randomly assigned to evaluate the service at one of the four restaurants owned by the chain.

The results of the experiment are displayed in Table 13.8 on page 567 along with some summary computations. A scatter plot is presented in Figure 13.8 on page 567 so that a visual, exploratory evaluation of potential differences between groups and violations in assumptions of particular testing procedures can be made. If the research director does not want to make the assumption that the service ratings were normally distributed for each restaurant, the nonparametric Friedman rank test for differences in the four population medians can be used.

The null hypothesis to be tested is that the median service ratings for the four restaurants are equal; the alternative is that at least one of the restaurants differs from the others.

$$H_0: M_{.1} = M_{.2} = M_{.3} = M_{.4}$$

$$H_1: \text{Not all the medians are equal}$$

Table 13.14 provides the 24 service ratings from Table 13.8 (page 567) along with the ranks assigned within each block.

**Table 13.14** *Converting data to ranks within blocks*

| BLOCKS OF RATERS | RESTAURANTS | | | | | | | |
|---|---|---|---|---|---|---|---|---|
| | A | | B | | C | | D | |
| | RATING | RANK | RATING | RANK | RATING | RANK | RATING | RANK |
| 1 | 70 | **2.0** | 61 | **1.0** | 82 | **4.0** | 74 | **3.0** |
| 2 | 77 | **3.0** | 75 | **1.0** | 88 | **4.0** | 76 | **2.0** |
| 3 | 76 | **2.0** | 67 | **1.0** | 90 | **4.0** | 80 | **3.0** |
| 4 | 80 | **3.0** | 63 | **1.0** | 96 | **4.0** | 76 | **2.0** |
| 5 | 84 | **2.5** | 66 | **1.0** | 92 | **4.0** | 84 | **2.5** |
| 6 | 78 | **2.0** | 68 | **1.0** | 98 | **4.0** | 86 | **3.0** |
| Rank total | | **14.5** | | **6.0** | | **24.0** | | **15.5** |

**DATA FILE FFCHAIN**

From Table 13.14 we note the following rank totals for each group:

Rank totals: $R_{.1} = 14.5$    $R_{.2} = 6.0$    $R_{.3} = 24.0$    $R_{.4} = 15.5$

Equation (13.30) provides a check on the rankings.

## Checking the Rankings

$$R_{.1} + R_{.2} + R_{.3} + R_{.4} = \frac{rc(c + 1)}{2}$$   (13.30)

For our data, we have

$$14.5 + 6 + 24 + 15.5 = \frac{(6)(4)(5)}{2}$$

$$60 = 60$$

Using equation (13.29), we obtain

$$F_R = \frac{12}{rc(c + 1)} \sum_{j=1}^{c} R_{.j}^2 - 3r(c + 1)$$

$$= \left\{ \frac{12}{(6)(4)(5)} [14.5^2 + 6.0^2 + 24.0^2 + 15.5^2] \right\} - (3)(6)(5)$$

$$= \left( \frac{12}{120} \right) [1,062.5] - 90 = 16.25$$

Because the computed $F_R$ statistic exceeds 7.815, the upper-tailed critical value $\chi_U^2$ under the chi-square distribution having $c - 1 = 3$ degrees of freedom (see Table E.4), the null hypothesis is rejected at the $\alpha = .05$ level. We conclude that there are significant differences (as perceived by the raters) with respect to the service rendered at the four restaurants. Using the Minitab output that is presented in Figure 13.20, we observe that because the $p$-value $= .001 < .05$, the null hypothesis is rejected.

```
Friedman test for Rating by Restrat blocked by Raters

S = 16.25   DF = 3   P = 0.001
S = 16.53   DF = 3   P = 0.001 (adjusted for ties)

                    Est      Sum of
Restrat       N    Median    Ranks
A             6    76.87     14.5
B             6    66.50      6.0
C             6    90.38     24.0
D             6    79.25     15.5

Grand median  =    78.25
```

**FIGURE 13.20** Minitab output of Friedman rank test for differences in c medians in fast-food-chain study

Note that these are the same conclusions that were made for these data using the randomized block $F$ test in section 13.2. We observe that for each restaurant branch, the sample size, the estimated median rating, and the rank total (Sum of Ranks) are displayed. An estimate of the overall (Grand) median based on all ratings is also shown. At the top of the Minitab printout appears the Friedman test statistic $S$ (which is equivalent to our statistic $F_R$), the degrees of freedom (DF), and the $p$-value. If there are ties in the rankings, as is the case in our fast-food-chain study, Minitab provides an adjustment to the test statistic $S$ along with an adjusted $p$-value. We suggest the adjusted test statistic be used for interpreting results. Note that this adjustment has a minimal impact on our results.

Because we have rejected the null hypothesis and concluded that there is evidence of a significant difference among the restaurant branches with respect to the median ratings, the next step is a simultaneous comparison of all possible pairs of restaurant branches to determine which one or ones differ from the others. As a follow-up to the Friedman rank test, a *post hoc* multiple comparison procedure proposed by Nemenyi (see references 3 and 9) can be used.

To use the Friedman rank test for differences in $c$ medians, we make the assumptions as listed in Exhibit 13.2:

---

**Exhibit 13.2  Assumptions of the Friedman Rank Test for Differences in c Medians**

✓ **1.** The $r$ blocks are independent so that the measurements in one block have no influence on the measurements in any other block.

✓ **2.** The underlying random variable of interest is *continuous* (to avoid ties).

✓ **3.** The observed data constitute at least an ordinal scale of measurement within each of the $r$ blocks.

✓ **4.** There is no interaction between the $r$ blocks and the $c$ treatment levels.

✓ **5.** The $c$ populations have the same variability.

✓ **6.** The $c$ populations have the same shape.

---

Interestingly, the Friedman procedure still makes less stringent assumptions than does the randomized block $F$ test. To employ the Friedman procedure to test for differences in $c$ medians, the measurements need only be ordinal within each of the blocks and the common population distributions need only be continuous—their common shapes are irrelevant. In fact, if we ignore the last two assumptions, the Friedman rank test still could be used to test the null hypothesis of no differences in the $c$ populations against the general alternative that at least one of the populations differs from at least one of the other populations in some characteristic—be it central tendency, variation, or shape.

On the other hand, to use the $F$ test, the level of measurement must be more sophisticated and we must assume that the $c$ samples are coming from underlying normal populations having equal variances. Both the $F$ test and the Friedman test assume that there is no *interacting effect* between the treatments and the blocks. That is, in our fast-food-chain study we need to assume that any differences between the treatments (the restaurants) are consistent across the entire set of blocks of raters.

For situations involving randomized block designs, when the more stringent assumptions of the $F$ test hold, we should select it over the Friedman test because it will be slightly more powerful in its ability to detect significant treatment effects. However, if the more stringent assumptions cannot be met, the Friedman rank test likely will be more powerful than the $F$ test and we should choose this procedure.

## Problems for Section 13.5

### Learning the Basics

• **13.52** If the Friedman rank test is used at the .10 level of significance when testing for the equality of the medians in six populations, what would be the upper-tailed critical value $\chi_U^2$ from the chi-square distribution?

**13.53** From Problem 13.52:
(a) State the decision rule for testing the null hypothesis that all six groups have equal population medians.
(b) What is your statistical decision if the computed value of the test statistic $F_R$ is 11.56?

### Applying the Concepts

• **13.54** The President's Council on Physical Fitness and Sports asked a panel of medical experts to rank five diverse forms of exercise with respect to their special contributions to physical fitness and overall well-being. The rankings (1 = least beneficial, 5 = most beneficial) are displayed below for each of nine equally important characteristics of fitness and well-being.

| | EXERCISE | | | | |
|---|---|---|---|---|---|
| CHARACTERISTIC | BICYCLING | CALISTHENICS | JOGGING | SWIMMING | TENNIS |
| Balance | 5.0 | 2.0 | 4.0 | 1.0 | 3.0 |
| Digestion | 2.5 | 1.0 | 4.5 | 4.5 | 2.5 |
| Flexibility | 1.5 | 5.0 | 1.5 | 4.0 | 3.0 |
| Muscular definition | 4.0 | 5.0 | 2.5 | 2.5 | 1.0 |
| Muscular endurance | 3.0 | 1.0 | 4.5 | 4.5 | 2.0 |
| Muscular strength | 3.5 | 3.5 | 5.0 | 1.5 | 1.5 |
| Sleep | 3.0 | 2.0 | 4.5 | 4.5 | 1.0 |
| Stamina | 3.0 | 1.0 | 4.5 | 4.5 | 2.0 |
| Weight control | 4.0 | 1.0 | 5.0 | 2.0 | 3.0 |

DATA FILE
EXERCISE

To solve, use either computer software or the following summary information:

| Exercise: | 1 | 2 | 3 | 4 | 5 |
|---|---|---|---|---|---|
| Rank sums: | 29.5 | 21.5 | 36.0 | 29.0 | 19.0 |

(a) Is there evidence of a difference in the "perceived benefit" ratings of the five forms of exercise? (Use $\alpha = .05$.) (*Hint*: Treat the nine characteristics as blocks.)

(b) On the basis of your results in (a), comment on any exercises you think may be very beneficial.

**13.55** Billboard advertising is frequently found along highways. Because drivers must concentrate on their driving, exposure to such advertisements is very brief. To evaluate the effectiveness of such promotional materials, an advertising agency decided to conduct an experiment to determine if there are any differences in recall ability due to different levels of exposure to an object. Three levels of exposure (in msec) are considered. Eight sets of triplets are chosen as subjects. In each of the eight sets of triplets, the members are randomly assigned to be examined under an exposure level. Recall ability scores are presented below:

| SET OF TRIPLETS (SUBJECTS) | EXPOSURE LEVEL | | |
|---|---|---|---|
| | MINIMUM | MODERATE | HIGH |
| I | 55 | 68 | 67 |
| II | 78 | 83 | 84 |
| III | 34 | 53 | 54 |
| IV | 56 | 67 | 65 |
| V | 79 | 78 | 85 |
| VI | 20 | 29 | 30 |
| VII | 68 | 88 | 92 |
| VIII | 59 | 58 | 72 |

**DATA FILE RECALL**

To solve, use either computer software or the following summary information:

| Exposure level: | 1 | 2 | 3 |
|---|---|---|---|
| Rank sums: | 10 | 16 | 22 |

At the .01 level of significance, is there evidence of a difference in the median recall ability between the exposure levels? If so, what might you conclude?

**13.56** A taste-testing experiment has been designed so that four brands of Colombian coffee are to be rated by nine experts. To avoid any carryover effects, the tasting sequence for the four brews is randomly determined for each of the nine expert tasters until a rating on a 7-point scale (1 = extremely unpleasing, 7 = extremely pleasing) is given for each of the following four characteristics: taste, aroma, richness, and acidity. The following table displays the ratings accumulated over all four characteristics.

| EXPERT | BRAND A | B | C | D |
|--------|----|----|----|----|
| C.C. | 24 | 26 | 25 | 22 |
| S.E. | 27 | 27 | 26 | 24 |
| E.G. | 19 | 22 | 20 | 16 |
| B.L. | 24 | 27 | 25 | 23 |
| C.M. | 22 | 25 | 22 | 21 |
| C.N. | 26 | 27 | 24 | 24 |
| G.N. | 27 | 26 | 22 | 23 |
| R.M. | 25 | 27 | 24 | 21 |
| P.V. | 22 | 23 | 20 | 19 |

**DATA FILE
COFFEE**

To solve use either computer software or the following summary information:

| Brand: | A | B | C | D |
|--------|----|----|----|----|
| Rank sums: | 25.0 | 34.5 | 20.0 | 10.5 |

(a) At the .01 level of significance, use the Friedman rank test to determine whether there is evidence of a difference in the summated ratings of the four brands of Colombian coffee. What do you conclude?

(b) If you answered part (b) of Problem 13.25 on page 573 and performed a randomized block $F$ test, are there any differences in your present results from those previously obtained? Discuss.

• **13.57** A researcher in a pharmaceutical company wishes to perform an experiment to determine if the choice of treatment substance affects the clotting time of plasma (in minutes). Five different clotting enhancement substances (i.e., treatments) are to be compared and seven female patients, all of whom are in their first term of pregnancy, are to be studied. For each patient, five vials of blood are drawn and one vial each is randomly assigned to one of the five treatments. The clotting time data are shown below:

| PATIENT | TREATMENT SUBSTANCE 1 | 2 | 3 | 4 | 5 |
|---------|------|------|------|------|------|
| 1 | 8.4 | 8.1 | 8.5 | 8.6 | 8.5 |
| 2 | 10.3 | 10.0 | 9.9 | 10.6 | 10.2 |
| 3 | 12.4 | 11.8 | 12.3 | 12.5 | 12.2 |
| 4 | 9.7 | 9.8 | 9.9 | 10.4 | 10.4 |
| 5 | 8.6 | 8.4 | 9.7 | 9.9 | 9.5 |
| 6 | 9.3 | 9.6 | 10.3 | 10.5 | 10.2 |
| 7 | 11.1 | 10.6 | 11.6 | 10.9 | 11.4 |

**DATA FILE
CLOTTING**

To solve use either computer software or the following summary information:

| Substance: | 1 | 2 | 3 | 4 | 5 |
|------------|------|------|------|------|------|
| Rank sums: | 17.0 | 10.0 | 23.5 | 31.5 | 23.0 |

(a) At the .05 level of significance, use the Friedman rank test to determine whether there is evidence of a difference in the median plasma clotting time among the five treatment substances. What can you conclude?

(b) If you answered part (b) of Problem 13.26 on page 574 and performed a randomized block $F$ test, are there any differences in your present results from those previously obtained? Discuss.

**13.58** A nutritionist wishes to compare three well-known dietary products. Using data on girth (i.e., a function of height and weight), age, and metabolism, he matches 18 of his male clients into 6 groups of 3 each and randomly assigns 1 member of each group to 1 of the three dietary treatments. The following data represent the amount of weight (in pounds) lost by the 18 clients after 6 weeks of treatment:

| | DIETARY TREATMENT | | |
|---|---|---|---|
| **CLIENT GROUPS** | **1** | **2** | **3** |
| 1 | 10.4 | 12.1 | 9.0 |
| 2 | 9.8 | 14.5 | 9.6 |
| 3 | 7.3 | 10.0 | 9.8 |
| 4 | 7.5 | 9.9 | 10.7 |
| 5 | 8.6 | 14.2 | 11.1 |
| 6 | 10.7 | 10.5 | 10.5 |

To solve part (a) of this problem, use either a software package or the following summary information:

| Dietary treatment: | **1** | **2** | **3** |
|---|---|---|---|
| Rank sums: | 10.0 | 15.5 | 10.5 |

(a) At the .05 level of significance, use the Friedman rank test to determine whether there is evidence of a difference in the median amount of weight (in pounds) lost among the three dietary treatments. What can you conclude?

(b) If you answered part (b) of Problem 13.27 on page 574 and performed a randomized block $F$ test, are there any differences in your present results from those previously obtained? Discuss.

**13.59** The dean of a well-known business school wants to study the student-faculty evaluation process at his campus because it is used in reappointment, promotion, and tenure decisions. In particular, he is interested in determining the type of educational setting most conducive to higher faculty evaluations from students—MBA courses, advanced undergraduate courses, or required undergraduate courses. Because the faculty's semester workload at this institution is three courses, the dean takes a random sample of 10 faculty from his school who have been assigned one course in each of the three aforementioned types of educational settings and retrieves their end-of-semester evaluation forms. The following results are mean ratings on a 5-point scale (1 = very poor, 5 = outstanding) in response to the question: "In comparison with other teachers you have had, how would you rate this individual's teaching ability?" Each of the ratings is from classes containing 25–30 students.

| FACULTY MEMBER | TYPE OF CLASS | | |
| --- | --- | --- | --- |
| | MBA COURSE | ADVANCED UNDERGRAD | REQUIRED UNDERGRAD |
| L.M. | 4.12 | 4.06 | 3.38 |
| N.R. | 4.87 | 4.72 | 4.60 |
| A.C. | 3.46 | 3.49 | 2.39 |
| J.K. | 3.87 | 3.61 | 3.23 |
| J.B. | 4.04 | 3.83 | 3.55 |
| D.B. | 2.90 | 3.23 | 3.52 |
| W.F. | 4.16 | 4.07 | 3.68 |
| R.S. | 4.19 | 3.76 | 3.83 |
| M.L. | 4.75 | 4.39 | 4.22 |
| V.P. | 4.29 | 4.34 | 3.67 |

DATA FILE
RATING

To solve, use either computer software or the following summary information:

| Course: | 1 | 2 | 3 |
| --- | --- | --- | --- |
| Rank sums: | 26 | 21 | 13 |

(a) At the .05 level of significance, use the Friedman rank test to determine whether there is evidence of a difference in the median ratings based on type of class. What can you conclude?
(b) If you answered part (b) of Problem 13.28 on page 575 and performed a randomized block $F$ test, are there any differences in your present results from those previously obtained? Discuss.

# SUMMARY

In this chapter we developed the concepts of experimental design and introduced various statistical test procedures that are commonly employed in analyzing possible differences in the numerical outcomes or response measurements among the (treatment) levels of some factor of interest. Again, part of a good data analysis is to understand the assumptions underlying each of the test procedures and, using this as well as other criteria, select the one most appropriate for a given set of conditions. Thus, even when our primary purpose is a confirmatory analysis of a particular experiment or set of data, we must always perform an exploratory, descriptive analysis first so that through observation we may better understand what the data are conveying and what potential trends, relations, and effects are being indicated. Failure to take this careful look at the data is not itself unethical. It usually results, however, in a less than optimal analysis.

As observed in the accompanying summary chart for this chapter, we may distinguish among approaches for comparing $c$ groups containing numerical data based on the experimental design model used for obtaining the measured responses or outcomes. Hypothesis-testing methodology was developed separately for analyzing data obtained from one-way or completely randomized design models, randomized block design models, and two-factor factorial design models.

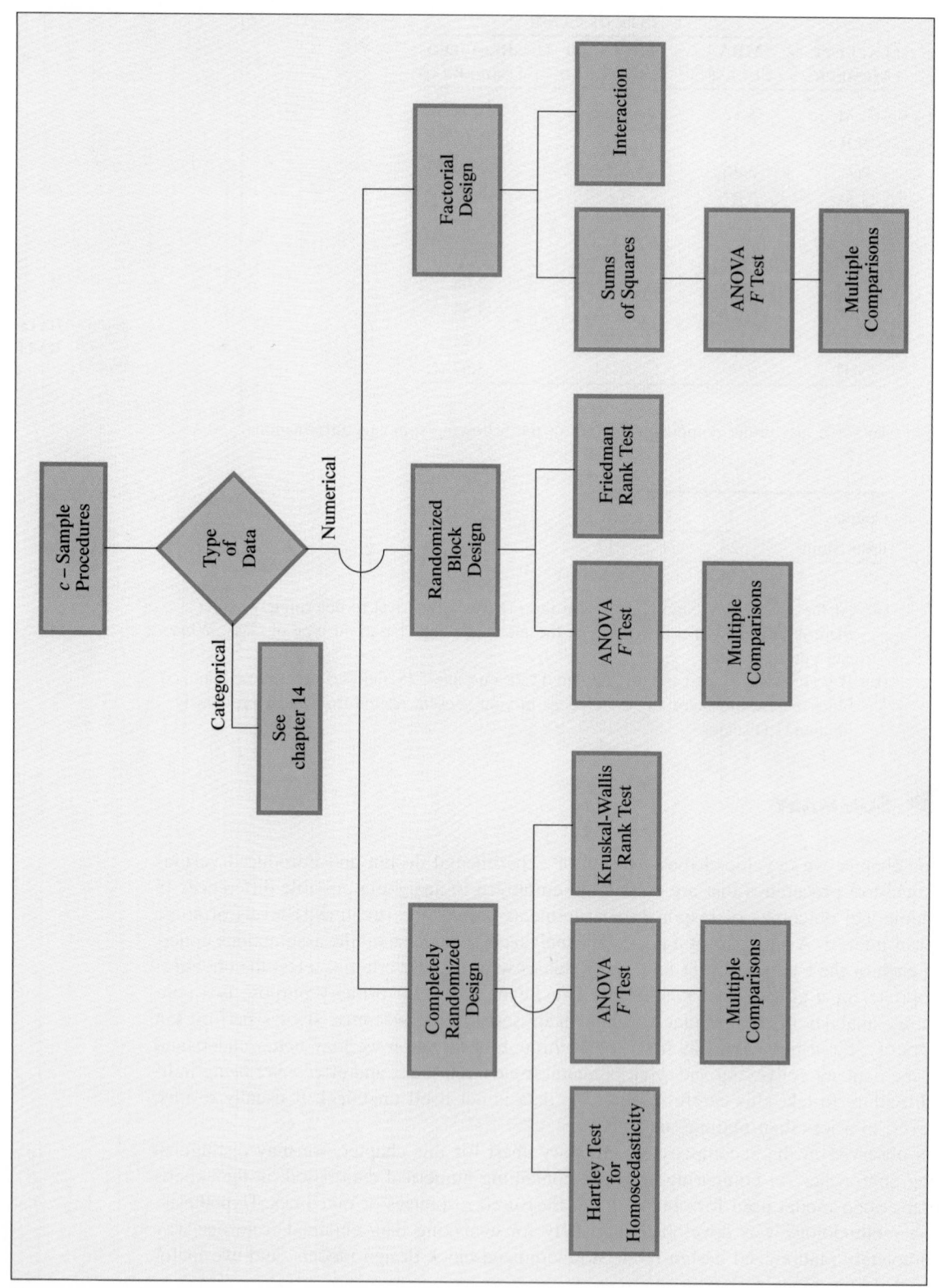

Chapter 13 summary chart

♦ *Choosing the Appropriate Test Procedure*   After focusing on an appropriate grouping of similar test procedures, we need to look carefully at the assumptions as well as at other criteria prior to selecting a particular procedure. We summarize these criteria in Exhibit 13.3.

### Exhibit 13.3   *Criteria for Test Selection*

When preparing to evaluate differences among $c$ groups containing numerical data, we must select an appropriate testing procedure. This choice is dependent on several criteria:

✓ **1.** The type of experimental design model developed (e.g., completely randomized, randomized block, or factorial).

✓ **2.** The level of measurement attained on the data (e.g., ordinal- versus interval- or ratio-scaled).

✓ **3.** The viability of the assumptions underlying alternative test procedures.

✓ **4.** The generalizability of the conclusions to be drawn.

✓ **5.** The statistical power of the test procedure.

## Key Terms

*a posteriori* analysis   551

among-block variation (*SSBL*)   564

among-group variation (*SSA*)   543

analysis of variance (ANOVA)   541

ANOVA summary table   546

blocks   562

completely randomized design model   541

critical range   551

estimated relative efficiency (*RE*)   570

experimental error   541

*F* distribution   545

*F* test for blocking effect   569

*F* test for factor A effect   580

*F* test for factor B effect   582

*F* test for interaction effect   582

factor   541

factorial design model   578

$F_{max}$ distribution   554

Friedman rank test   607

Hartley's $F_{max}$ test   553

homogeneity of variance   553

inherent random variation or error (*SSE*)   579

interacting effect   580

interaction   580

Kruskal-Wallis rank test   597

levels   578

mean squares   544, 565

multiple comparisons   570, 589

normality   553

one-factor ANOVA *F* test   544

one-way ANOVA   541

one-way ANOVA *F* test   544

overall or grand mean   542

randomized block design model   562

randomness and independence   553

replicates   578

Studentized range (*Q*) distribution   551

sum of squares among blocks (*SSBL*)   564

sum of squares among groups (*SSA*)   543, 564

sum of squares due to factor A (*SSFA*)   579

sum of squares due to factor B (*SSFB*)   580

sum of squares due to interaction (*SSAB*)   580

sum of squares error (*SSE*)   565, 580

sum of squares total (*SST*)   542, 564, 579

sum of squares within groups (*SSW*)   543

total variation (*SST*)   542, 563

treatment effect   541, 547

treatment groups (or levels)   553

Tukey procedure   570

Tukey-Kramer procedure   551

two-factor factorial design model   577

two-way ANOVA   578

within-group variation (*SSW*)   543

## Checking Your Understanding

**13.60** What is the difference between the among-groups variance *MSA* and the within-groups variance *MSW*?

**13.61** How can graphical methods be used to evaluate the validity of the assumptions of the analysis of variance?

**13.62** What is the difference between the randomized block design model and the completely randomized design model?

**13.63** What are the distinguishing features of the completely randomized design, randomized block design, and two-factor factorial design models?

**13.64** What are the major assumptions of ANOVA?

**13.65** Under what conditions should Hartley's $F_{max}$ test be used?

**13.66** Under what conditions should the one-way ANOVA *F* test to examine possible differences in the means of *c* independent populations be selected?

**13.67** What is the difference between the one-factor and two-factor ANOVA models?

**13.68** What is the difference between the randomized block design model and the two-factor factorial design model?

**13.69** Under what conditions should the Kruskal-Wallis rank test to examine possible differences in the medians of *c* independent populations be selected?

**13.70** When and how should multiple comparison procedures for evaluating pairwise combinations of the group means be used?

**13.71** Under what conditions should the randomized block *F* test to examine possible differences in the means of *c* related populations be selected?

**13.72** Under what conditions should the Friedman rank test to examine possible differences in the medians of *c* related populations be selected?

**13.73** Under what conditions should the two-way ANOVA *F* test to examine possible differences in the means of each factor in a factorial design be selected?

**13.74** What do we mean by the concept of interaction in a factorial design?

**13.75** How can we use the two-way ANOVA *F* test to examine possible interaction in the levels of the factors in a factorial design?

## Chapter Review Problems

**13.76** In a special report, *Newsweek* (June 24, 1996) rated 43 HMOs on the basis of a survey of quality characteristics. The data below present partial output from the file HMORATE in which each of the 43 companies is listed in a separate row. The data stored in column 2 are the summated ratings. In column 3 is the membership size grouping (large = 1, medium = 2, small = 3). In columns 4 and 5 are the quality monitoring ratings and quality results ratings. Column 6 displays the overall quality score.

| NAME OF HMO | SUMMATED RATING | HMO SIZE | QUAL MON | QUAL RES | Q SCORE |
|---|---|---|---|---|---|
| Fallon Community Health Plan | 21 | 3 | 3 | 4 | 28 |
| Harvard Community Health Plan | 21 | 2 | 4 | 4 | 29 |
| ⋮ | ⋮ | ⋮ | ⋮ | ⋮ | ⋮ |
| NYLCare Health Plan | 10 | 2 | 2 | 1 | 13 |

**DATA FILE
HMORATE**

Using a .05 level of significance, completely analyze these data to determine if membership size grouping has a significant effect on overall quality score. Write a report on your findings. Be sure to include information regarding the assumptions of the test procedures you selected.

**13.77** A broker at a financial investment service wishes to compare the 6-month certificates of deposit (CD) rates offered by commercial banks in the New York metropolitan area, by savings banks in the New York metropolitan area, and by other major banks outside the New York metropolitan area. The data in the accompanying table present the 6-month CD rates from samples taken at 15 New York metropolitan area commercial banks (c), 15 New York Metropolitan area savings banks (s), and 20 banks outside the New York Metropolitan area (o) in February 1997.

| COMMERCIAL | | SAVINGS | | OUTSIDE N. Y. | |
|---|---|---|---|---|---|
| 4.81 | 4.20 | 3.90 | 4.00 | 4.70 | 5.40 |
| 4.55 | 4.25 | 3.75 | 5.80 | 4.80 | 4.50 |
| 4.35 | 4.71 | 5.00 | 5.15 | 4.84 | 4.65 |
| 4.65 | 4.19 | 3.50 | 5.25 | 4.60 | 3.85 |
| 4.65 | 4.26 | 5.50 | 4.25 | 3.00 | 4.30 |
| 3.00 | 4.76 | 5.34 | 5.45 | 5.20 | 5.00 |
| 4.81 | 2.52 | 4.55 | 4.50 | 5.00 | 4.28 |
| 4.20 | | 3.75 | | 4.60 | 5.02 |
| | | | | 4.65 | 4.70 |
| | | | | 4.25 | 4.87 |

DATA FILE
BANKCD

*Reprinted from pp. 60–61 in* Newsweek, *June 24, 1996. Copyright 1996 by Newsweek, Inc. All rights reserved. Reprinted by permission of* Newsweek.

To solve use either computer software or the following summary information:

| Banks: | C | S | O | |
|---|---|---|---|---|
| Sample sizes: | 15 | 15 | 20 | |
| Sample means: | 4.261 | 4.646 | 4.611 | $\bar{\bar{X}} = 4.516$ |
| Sample standard deviations: | 0.659 | 0.757 | 0.520 | |

(a) Perform an exploratory analysis of the data in each group to evaluate the appropriateness of employing the one-way ANOVA $F$ test to compare the three group means. Discuss whether the assumptions of this test seem to be met.

(b) Using a .05 level of significance, perform a complete confirmatory analysis to determine if there is evidence of a significant difference in the average 6-month CD rates among the three groups of banks and, if so, which type of bank has the highest rate.

(c) What type of bank would you recommend? Explain.

● **13.78** Suppose an experiment was conducted that was concerned with the tensile strength of yarn spun for textile usage.

***Part I*** Suppose that a researcher wishes to examine the effect of air-jet pressure (in psi) on breaking strength. Three different levels of air-jet pressure are to be considered: 30 psi, 40 psi, and 50 psi. A random sample of 18 homogeneous/similar filling yarns were selected from the same batch and the yarns were randomly assigned, 6 each, to the three levels of air-jet pressure. The breaking strength scores are as follows:

AIR-JET PRESSURE

| 30 PSI | 40 PSI | 50 PSI |
|--------|--------|--------|
| 25.5 | 24.8 | 23.2 |
| 24.9 | 23.7 | 23.7 |
| 26.1 | 24.4 | 22.7 |
| 24.7 | 23.6 | 22.6 |
| 24.2 | 23.3 | 22.8 |
| 23.6 | 21.4 | 24.9 |

DATA FILE
YARN

To solve, use either computer software or the following summary information:

| Air-jet pressure: | 30 PSI | 40 PSI | 50 PSI | |
|-------------------|--------|--------|--------|---|
| Sample means: | 24.83 | 23.53 | 23.32 | $\bar{\bar{X}} = 23.89$ |
| Sample standard deviations: | 0.89 | 1.18 | 0.88 | |

(a) At the .05 level of significance, is there evidence of a difference in the variances of the breaking strengths for the three air-jet pressures?
(b) At the .05 level of significance, is there evidence of a difference in mean breaking strengths for the three air-jet pressures?
(c) If appropriate, use the Tukey-Kramer procedure to determine which air-jet pressures significantly differ with respect to mean breaking strength. (Use $\alpha = .05$.)
(d) What should the researcher conclude?

*Part II*   Suppose that when setting up his experiment, the researcher had access to only six samples of yarn from the batch, but was able to divide each yarn sample into three parts and randomly assign them, one each, to the three air-jet pressure levels. Thus, instead of the one-factor completely randomized design model cited, he can set up a randomized block design model, the six yarn samples being the blocks and one yarn part each assigned to the three pressure treatments. The breaking strength scores are as follows:

| | AIR-JET PRESSURE | | |
|------|--------|--------|--------|
| YARN | 30 PSI | 40 PSI | 50 PSI |
| 1 | 25.5 | 24.8 | 23.2 |
| 2 | 24.9 | 23.7 | 23.7 |
| 3 | 26.1 | 24.4 | 22.7 |
| 4 | 24.7 | 23.6 | 22.6 |
| 5 | 24.2 | 23.3 | 22.8 |
| 6 | 23.6 | 21.4 | 24.9 |

DATA FILE
YARN

To solve, use computer software or the following summary information:

| Sums of squares: | $SSA = 8.07$ | | $SSBL = 3.90$ | | $SST = 22.89$ | |
|---|---|---|---|---|---|---|
| Air-jet pressure: | **30 PSI** | **40 PSI** | **50 PSI** | | | |
| Sample means: | 24.83 | 23.53 | 23.32 | | | |
| Yarn number: | **1** | **2** | **3** | **4** | **5** | **6** |
| Sample means: | 24.50 | 24.10 | 24.40 | 23.63 | 23.43 | 23.30 |

(e) At the .05 level of significance, is there evidence of a difference in the mean break-ing strengths for the three air-jet pressures?

(f) If appropriate, use the Tukey procedure to determine the air-jet pressures that differ in mean breaking strength. (Use $\alpha = .05$.)

(g) At the .05 level of significance, is there evidence of a blocking effect?

(h) Determine the relative efficiency of the randomized block design as compared with the completely randomized design.

(i) Compare your results in parts (b) and (e). Given your results in parts (g) and (h), what do you think happened here? What can you conclude about the "impact of blocking" when the blocks themselves are not really different from each other?

*Part III* Suppose that when setting up his experiment, the researcher is able to study the effects of yarn type in addition to pressure. Thus, instead of the one-factor completely randomized design model given in Part I, he can set up a two-factor factorial design model, the first factor, side-to-side aspects, having two levels (nozzle and oppo-site) and the second factor, air-jet pressure, having three levels (30 psi, 40 psi, and 50 psi) with three replications for each side-to-side aspect and pressure combination. That is, there are two factors to be studied: (A) side-to-side aspect and (B) air-jet pressure. A sample of 18 yarns is randomly assigned, three to each of the six side-to-side aspect and pressure level combinations. The breaking strength scores are as follows:

| SIDE-TO-SIDE ASPECT | AIR-JET PRESSURE | | |
|---|---|---|---|
| | **30 PSI** | **40 PSI** | **50 PSI** |
| Nozzle | 25.5 | 24.8 | 23.2 |
| | 24.9 | 23.7 | 23.7 |
| | 26.1 | 24.4 | 22.7 |
| Opposite | 24.7 | 23.6 | 22.6 |
| | 24.2 | 23.3 | 22.8 |
| | 23.6 | 21.4 | 24.9 |

**DATA FILE YARN**

To solve use either computer software or the following summary information:

| Sums of squares: | $SSFA = 3.4672$ | $SSFB = 8.0744$ | $SSAB = 2.8078$ | $SST = 22.8894$ | | |
|---|---|---|---|---|---|---|
| Side-to-side aspect: | **1** | **2** | | | | |
| Sample means: | 24.33 | 23.46 | | | | |
| Air-jet pressure: | **30 PSI** | **40 PSI** | **50 PSI** | | | |
| Sample means: | 24.83 | 23.53 | 23.32 | | | |
| Cell: | **1,30** | **1,40** | **1,50** | **2,30** | **2,40** | **2,50** |
| Sample means: | 25.50 | 24.30 | 23.20 | 24.17 | 22.77 | 23.43 |

(j) At the .05 level of significance, answer the following.
   (1) Is there an interaction between side-to-side aspect and air-jet pressure?
   (2) Is there an effect due to side-to-side aspect?
   (3) Is there an effect due to air-jet pressure?
(k) Plot a graph of mean yarn breaking strength for the two levels of side-to-side aspect for each level of air-jet pressure.
(l) If appropriate, use the Tukey procedure to determine which air-jet pressures significantly differ with respect to mean breaking strength. (Use $\alpha = .05$.)
(m) Based on the results, what conclusions can you reach concerning yarn breaking strength? Discuss.
(n) Compare and contrast your results here with those from the one-way experiment in parts (a)–(c). Discuss fully.

**13.79** Modern software applications require rapid data access capabilities. An experiment was conducted to test the effect of data file size on the ability to access the files (as measured by read time in msec coded in terms of difference from a specified value).

***Part I*** Suppose that three different levels of data file size are to be considered: small—50,000 characters, medium—75,000 characters, or large—100,000 characters. A sample of eight files of each size were to be evaluated. The (coded) access read times in msec are as follows:

**DATA FILE ACCESS**

| DATA FILE SIZE | | |
|---|---|---|
| SMALL | MED. | LARGE |
| 2.05 | 2.24 | 2.08 |
| 2.04 | 2.21 | 2.34 |
| 2.21 | 2.23 | 2.33 |
| 2.12 | 2.09 | 2.24 |
| 2.32 | 2.52 | 2.71 |
| 2.31 | 2.62 | 2.73 |
| 2.48 | 2.57 | 2.90 |
| 2.42 | 2.61 | 2.72 |

To solve use either computer software or the following summary information:

| Data file size: | SMALL | MED. | LARGE | |
|---|---|---|---|---|
| Sample means: | 2.244 | 2.386 | 2.506 | $\overline{\overline{X}} = 2.379$ |
| Sample standard deviations: | 0.166 | 0.214 | 0.294 | |

(a) At the .05 level of significance, is there evidence of a difference in the variances of the access read times for the three file sizes?
(b) At the .05 level of significance, is there evidence of a difference in mean access read times for the three file sizes?
(c) If appropriate, use the Tukey-Kramer procedure to determine which file sizes significantly differ with respect to mean access read time. (Use $\alpha = .05$.)
(d) What should the researcher conclude?

***Part II*** Suppose that when setting up her experiment, the researcher had access to 24 programmers with different levels of training and experience. She was able to match them into eight blocks of three programmers each and randomly assign them, one each, to work on one of the three data file size levels. Thus, instead of the one-factor completely randomized design model cited, she can set up a randomized block design model, the eight groups of programmers being the blocks and one programmer in each assigned to the three data file size treatments. The (coded) access read times in msec are as follows:

| | DATA FILE SIZE | | |
| PROGRAMMER GROUP | SMALL | MED. | LARGE |
| --- | --- | --- | --- |
| 1 | 2.05 | 2.24 | 2.08 |
| 2 | 2.04 | 2.21 | 2.34 |
| 3 | 2.21 | 2.23 | 2.33 |
| 4 | 2.12 | 2.09 | 2.24 |
| 5 | 2.32 | 2.52 | 2.71 |
| 6 | 2.31 | 2.62 | 2.73 |
| 7 | 2.48 | 2.57 | 2.90 |
| 8 | 2.42 | 2.61 | 2.72 |

DATA FILE
ACCESS

To solve, use computer software or the following summary information:

| Sums of squares: | $SSA = 0.2763$ | | $SSBL = 0.9917$ | | $SST = 1.3935$ | | | |
| --- | --- | --- | --- | --- | --- | --- | --- | --- |
| Data file size: | SMALL | MED. | LARGE | | | | | |
| Sample means: | 2.244 | 2.386 | 2.506 | | | | | |
| Programmer group: | 1 | 2 | 3 | 4 | 5 | 6 | 7 | 8 |
| Sample means: | 2.123 | 2.197 | 2.257 | 2.150 | 2.517 | 2.553 | 2.650 | 2.583 |

(e) At the .05 level of significance, is there evidence of a difference in mean access read times for the three file sizes?

(f) If appropriate, use the Tukey procedure to determine the file sizes that differ in mean access read times. (Use $\alpha = .05$.)

(g) At the .05 level of significance, is there evidence of a blocking effect?

(h) Determine the relative efficiency of the randomized block design as compared with the completely randomized design.

(i) Compare your results in parts (b) and (e). Given your results in parts (g) and (h), what do you think happened here? What can you conclude about the "impact of blocking" when the blocks themselves are really different from each other?

***Part III*** Suppose that when setting up her experiment, the researcher is able to study the effects of the size of the input/output buffer in addition to the effects of data file size. Thus, instead of the one-factor completely randomized design model given in Part I, she can set up a two-factor factorial design model, the first factor, buffer size, having two levels (20 kilobytes and 40 kilobytes) and the second factor, data file size, having three levels (small, medium, and large) with four replications for each buffer size and data file size combination. That is, there are two factors to be studied: (A) buffer size and (B) data file size. A sample of four programs (replications) are to be evaluated at every buffer size–data file size combination. The (coded) access read times in msec are as follows.

| BUFFER SIZE | DATA FILE SIZE | | |
| :---: | :---: | :---: | :---: |
| (KBYTES) | SMALL | MED. | LARGE |
| 20 | 2.05 | 2.24 | 2.08 |
| | 2.04 | 2.21 | 2.34 |
| | 2.21 | 2.23 | 2.33 |
| | 2.12 | 2.09 | 2.24 |
| 40 | 2.32 | 2.52 | 2.71 |
| | 2.31 | 2.62 | 2.73 |
| | 2.48 | 2.57 | 2.90 |
| | 2.42 | 2.61 | 2.72 |

**DATA FILE ACCESS**

To solve, use computer software or the following summary information:

| | | | | | | |
| :--- | :---: | :---: | :---: | :---: | :---: | :---: |
| Sums of squares: | $SSFA = 0.9322$ | | $SSFB = 0.2763$ | $SSAB = 0.0577$ | $SST = 1.3935$ | |
| Buffer size: | 20 | 40 | | | | |
| Sample means: | 2.182 | 2.576 | | | | |
| Data file size: | SMALL | MED. | LARGE | | | |
| Sample means: | 2.244 | 2.386 | 2.506 | | | |
| Cell: | 20,S | 20,M | 20,L | 40,S | 40,M | 40,L |
| Sample means: | 2.105 | 2.193 | 2.248 | 2.383 | 2.580 | 2.765 |

(j)  At the .05 level of significance, answer the following.
  (1)  Is there an interaction between buffer size and data file size?
  (2)  Is there an effect due to buffer size?
  (3)  Is there an effect due to data file size?
(k)  Plot a graph of mean access read times (in msec) for the two buffer size levels for each of the three data file size levels. Describe the interaction and discuss why you can or cannot interpret the main effects in parts (j)(2) and (j)(3).
(l)  If appropriate, use the Tukey procedure to determine which data file sizes significantly differ with respect to mean access read times. (Use $\alpha = .05$.)
(m)  Based on the results, what conclusions can you reach concerning access read time? Discuss.
(n)  Compare and contrast your results here with those from the one-way experiment in parts (a)–(c) and the randomized block design model in parts (e)–(i). Discuss fully.

**13.80** The dean of a large and well-respected school of business was interested in evaluating the starting salaries being offered to its current MBA graduating class.

*Part I*  Suppose that the dean wishes to examine the effect of major concentration on starting salary. Four different major concentrations are to be considered: accountancy, finance, management, and marketing. Using cumulative GPAs, the dean decided to include in his study the top six academically ranked students in each major concentration. Following the job interview period, he contacted these 24 students and asked them to indicate their best annual salary package offerings (adjusted for benefits). The salary packages, in thousands of dollars, are as follows:

| SALARY PACKAGE | | | |
|------|---------|------|------|
| ACCT | FINANCE | MGT | MRKG |
| 89.3 | 81.6 | 67.8 | 85.2 |
| 98.9 | 91.7 | 72.2 | 68.3 |
| 100.4 | 75.4 | 64.7 | 69.2 |
| 87.8 | 100.2 | 82.1 | 81.9 |
| 81.7 | 93.0 | 74.4 | 77.1 |
| 83.1 | 106.5 | 84.3 | 75.3 |

DATA FILE
MBASAL

To solve, use computer software or the following summary information:

| Major: | ACCT | FINANCE | MGT | MKTG | |
|--------|------|---------|------|------|------|
| Sample means: | 90.20 | 91.40 | 74.25 | 76.17 | $\overline{\overline{X}} = 83.00$ |
| Sample standard deviations: | 7.86 | 11.49 | 7.74 | 6.73 | |

(a) At the .05 level of significance, is there evidence of a difference in the variances of the salary packages for the four major concentrations?

(b) At the .05 level of significance, is there evidence of a difference in mean salary package for the four major concentrations?

(c) If appropriate, use the Tukey-Kramer procedure to determine which major concentrations significantly differ with respect to mean salary package. (Use $\alpha = .05$.)

(d) What should the dean conclude?

***Part II*** The dean consulted Professor Berlev of the Statistics Department and wondered if the completely randomized model described previously is appropriate because the dean has the class rankings based on cumulative GPA by major area of concentration. You may recall that the dean had selected the top six academically ranked students in each major to participate in this study. This was done to create a more homogeneous study group and reduce variability based on performance when comparing the salary packages across the various major concentrations.

Professor Berlev said that the GPA rankings could be used for purposes of matching and forming blocks. He explained to the dean that variation in performance among graduating students could be reduced by forming blocks consisting of the highest-ranking student in each major, the second-highest in each major, and so on. This would also allow for a more focused analysis comparing the salary packages across the four major areas of concentration. However, if the student performances as measured by their cumulative GPAs were very close, there would likely be very little differences among the blocks. In such situations, the blocking effect would not be significant and in fact could be harmful to the analysis. He offered the dean the following advice: Use blocking only when it is appropriate to do so. Random blocking is worse than no blocking because it reduces the power of a test's ability to detect significant treatment effects. He told the dean that blocking would likely not be effective here, but had he selected students over a wide range of class rankings such as the top in each major, the first quartile in each major, the median in each major, the third quartile in each major, and the bottom rank in each major, blocking could have been very effective.

Aware of its limitations here, the dean nevertheless wanted to observe what would happen if he set up his study as a randomized block design model instead of the one-factor completely randomized design model above. Thus, using the GPA rankings within each major, the dean formed six blocks of four students each—one in each major concentration. The salary packages offered are as follows on page 626:

| GPA | SALARY PACKAGE | | | |
|---|---|---|---|---|
| RANKING | ACCT | FINANCE | MGT | MKTG |
| 1 | 89.3 | 81.6 | 67.8 | 85.2 |
| 2 | 98.9 | 91.7 | 72.2 | 68.3 |
| 3 | 100.4 | 75.4 | 64.7 | 69.2 |
| 4 | 87.8 | 100.2 | 82.1 | 81.9 |
| 5 | 81.7 | 93.0 | 74.4 | 77.1 |
| 6 | 83.1 | 106.5 | 84.3 | 75.3 |

**DATA FILE
MBASAL**

To solve, use computer software or the following summary information:

| Sums of squares: | $SSA = 1{,}473.94$ | | $SSBL = 323.30$ | | $SST = 2{,}969.21$ | |
|---|---|---|---|---|---|---|
| Major: | ACCT | FINANCE | MGT | MKTG | | |
| Sample means: | 90.2 | 91.4 | 74.3 | 76.2 | | |
| Block number: | **1** | **2** | **3** | **4** | **5** | **6** |
| Sample means: | 81.0 | 82.8 | 77.4 | 88.0 | 81.6 | 87.3 |

(e) At the .05 level of significance, is there evidence of a difference in the average salary package over the four major concentrations?

(f) If appropriate, use the Tukey procedure to determine the major concentrations that differ in average salary package. (Use $\alpha = .05$.)

(g) At the .05 level of significance, is there evidence of a blocking effect?

(h) Determine the relative efficiency of the randomized block design as compared with the completely randomized design.

(i) Compare your results in parts (b) and (e). Given your results in parts (g) and (h), what do you think happened here? What can you conclude about the "impact of blocking" when the blocks themselves are not really different from each other?

***Part III*** Suppose that when setting up his experiment, the dean is able to study the effects of gender in addition to major concentration. Thus, instead of the one-factor completely randomized design model given in Part I, he can set up a two-factor factorial design model, the first factor, gender, having two levels (male and female) and the second factor, major concentration, having four levels (accountancy, finance, management, and marketing) with three replications for each gender-major combination. That is, there are two factors to be studied: (A) gender and (B) major. Of the 24 graduating students in the study, there are three within each gender and major combination. The salary packages offered are as follows:

| | SALARY PACKAGE | | | |
|---|---|---|---|---|
| GENDER | ACCT | FINANCE | MGT | MKTG |
| M | 89.3 | 100.2 | 82.1 | 85.2 |
| | 98.9 | 93.0 | 74.4 | 68.3 |
| | 100.4 | 106.5 | 84.3 | 69.2 |
| F | 87.8 | 81.6 | 67.8 | 81.9 |
| | 81.7 | 91.7 | 72.2 | 77.1 |
| | 83.1 | 75.4 | 64.7 | 75.3 |

**DATA FILE
MBASAL**

To solve, use computer software or the following summary information:

| | | | | | |
|---|---|---|---|---|---|
| Sums of squares: | $SSFA = 518.01$ | $SSFB = 1{,}473.94$ | $SSAB = 371.12$ | $SST = 2{,}969.21$ | |
| Gender: | **MALE** | **FEMALE** | | | |
| Sample means: | 87.650 | 78.358 | | | |
| Major: | **ACCT** | **FINANCE** | **MGT** | **MKTG** | |
| Sample means: | 90.2 | 91.4 | 74.3 | 76.2 | |

| Cell: | **M,ACCT** | **M,FIN** | **M,MGT** | **M,MKTG** | **F,ACCT** | **F,FIN** | **F,MGT** | **F,MKTG** |
|---|---|---|---|---|---|---|---|---|
| Sample means: | 96.200 | 99.900 | 80.267 | 74.233 | 84.200 | 82.900 | 68.233 | 78.100 |

(j) At the .05 level of significance, answer the following:
   (1) Is there an interaction between gender and major?
   (2) Is there an effect due to gender?
   (3) Is there an effect due to major?
(k) Plot a graph of mean salary package offered for males and for females based on each major concentration. Describe the interaction and discuss why you can or cannot interpret the main effects in parts (j)(2) and (j)(3).
(l) Based on the results, what conclusions can you reach concerning the salary packages offered? Discuss.
(m) Compare and contrast your results here with those from the one-way experiment in parts (a)–(c). Discuss fully.

**13.81** On January 1, 1998, *The New York Times* (p. D3) reported that the Associated Press had compiled a list of the 10 companies on the various stock exchanges that displayed the largest percentage gains and declines in selling price over the fourth quarter of 1997. (Stocks that began the quarter with a selling price under $5 a share were excluded from the list along with stocks of closed-end investment funds and real estate investment trusts.)

The following data present partial output from the file SL&L in which each of the 60 companies is listed on a separate row. The data stored in column 1 reflect the stock exchange (NYSE = 1, ASE = 2, NASDAQ = 3). In column 2 are the companies' 4th-quarter market direction (lag = 1, lead = 2). In columns 3 through 6, respectively, are the 4th-quarter percentage changes, revised percentage changes, absolute percentage changes, and absolute revised percentage changes. In columns 7 and 8 are companies' stock prices (in dollars) on September 30 and December 31. Column 9 displays the price changes (in dollars), column 10 provides the absolute price changes, and column 11 presents the log of the absolute price changes. Column 12 shows the log of the absolute revised percentage changes.

| | | **COLUMN** | | | | | | |
|---|---|---|---|---|---|---|---|---|
| | **1** | **2** | **...** | **7** | **8** | **...** | **11** | **12** |
| **COMPANY** | **EXCH.** | **DIR.** | **...** | **SEPT. 30** | **DEC. 31** | **...** | **LACH$D-S** | **LAREV%CH** |
| Applied Magnetics | 1 | 1 | ... | $31.63 | $11.00 | ... | 3.03 | 4.57 |
| Amax Gold | 1 | 1 | ... | 6.63 | 2.31 | ... | 1.46 | 4.57 |
| ⋮ | ⋮ | ⋮ | ⋮ | ⋮ | ⋮ | ⋮ | ⋮ | ⋮ |
| THQ | 3 | 2 | ... | 11.94 | 23.00 | ... | 2.40 | 4.15 |
| Esprit Telecom | 3 | 2 | ... | 5.88 | 11.25 | ... | 1.68 | 4.14 |

The following data are presented in a two-way layout in which the log of the absolute change in the stock prices over the 4th quarter of 1997 is displayed for each of the 10 companies classified by market direction and stock exchange listing.

| | STOCK EXCHANGE | | |
|---|---|---|---|
| **MARKET DIRECTION** | **NYSE** | **ASE** | **NASDAQ** |
| Lag | 3.03 | 1.61 | 1.69 |
| | 1.46 | 2.36 | 2.23 |
| | 1.82 | 1.24 | 1.70 |
| | 1.94 | 1.16 | 2.07 |
| | 3.18 | 1.22 | 2.04 |
| | 1.10 | 1.68 | 1.63 |
| | 2.81 | 1.45 | 1.56 |
| | 2.46 | 0.92 | 1.61 |
| | 2.83 | 1.65 | 2.01 |
| | 2.63 | 1.06 | 1.96 |
| Lead | 3.16 | 1.63 | 2.40 |
| | 3.26 | 1.42 | 2.63 |
| | 2.58 | 1.63 | 2.14 |
| | 3.06 | 1.95 | 1.45 |
| | 1.63 | 2.21 | 2.00 |
| | 2.45 | 3.50 | 2.47 |
| | 2.50 | 1.29 | 1.61 |
| | 2.59 | 2.20 | 2.68 |
| | 1.64 | 1.85 | 2.40 |
| | 2.24 | 2.48 | 1.68 |

**DATA FILE SL&L**

(a) Using a .05 level of significance completely analyze these data. Write a report on your findings.
(b) Use Minitab or Excel for the SL&L file and examine some of the other variables provided. Describe the results of your analysis for a particular variable.

**13.82** According to Lisa Sedelnik (1997), "When a Latin American company lists its shares on the New York Stock Exchange through American depository receipts, it makes a firm commitment to increase the flow of information about its company to U.S. investors. The most obvious sign of that commitment is the quality of the annual report, a document which should effectively communicate the company's vision, operations and financial strength to current and prospective shareholders."

The July/August 1997 issue of *Latin Finance* described a study it conducted on the annual reports ("Review of ADR Annual Reports") of 12 Latin American companies trading as ADRs and graded them on the effectiveness of corporation communication, level of detail of the financial statements, and graphical presentation. Several judges rated these categories of information on 5-point scales (1 = lowest, 5 = highest). The data below indicate the average ratings given to each company on each of the three information categories.

| COMPANY | INFORMATION | | |
|---|---|---|---|
| | CORP. REV. | FIN. | GRAPH PRES. |
| 1. Telefonica de Argentina | 4.08 | 4.60 | 4.25 |
| 2. CTC | 3.95 | 3.77 | 4.33 |
| 3. Aracruz Celulose | 3.68 | 3.90 | 4.38 |
| 4. Telecom Argentina | 3.81 | 3.80 | 3.94 |
| 5. Telefonica del Peru | 3.90 | 3.55 | 4.00 |
| 6. Enersis | 4.16 | 4.00 | 3.25 |
| 7. Televisa | 3.08 | 4.00 | 3.25 |
| 8. Banco de Colombia | 3.37 | 3.88 | 2.83 |
| 9. Empresas Ica | 3.03 | 3.73 | 3.12 |
| 10. CanTV | 3.53 | 3.26 | 2.87 |
| 11. Telmex | 3.19 | 3.50 | 2.75 |
| 12. Tribasa | 3.50 | 3.63 | 2.00 |

*Source: L. Sedelnik, "Depository Receipts," Latin Finance 88 (July/August 1997): 41–47.*

**DATA FILE
ADR**

To solve, use either computer software or the following summary information:

| Sums of squares: | $SSA = 0.9010$ | | $SSBL = 5.4399$ | | $SST = 10.0625$ | |
|---|---|---|---|---|---|---|
| Information: | CORP. | FIN. | GRAPH | | | |
| Sample means: | 3.607 | 3.802 | 3.414 | | | |
| Rank sums: | 22 | 27 | 23 | | | |
| Company: | 1 | 2 | 3 | 4 | 5 | 6 |
| Sample means: | 4.31 | 4.02 | 3.99 | 3.85 | 3.82 | 3.80 |
| Rank sums: | 33 | 27 | 28 | 23 | 21 | 29 |
| Company: | 7 | 8 | 9 | 10 | 11 | 12 |
| Sample means: | 3.44 | 3.36 | 3.29 | 3.22 | 3.15 | 3.04 |
| Rank sums: | 19 | 15 | 11 | 11 | 7 | 10 |

(a) At the .05 level of significance, is there evidence of a difference in the average rating scores between the information categories?
(b) What assumptions are necessary in order to do (a) of this problem? Comment on the validity of these assumptions.
(c) If appropriate, use the Tukey procedure to determine the information categories that differ in average rating. (Use $\alpha = .05$.)
(d) Determine the relative efficiency of the randomized block design as compared with the completely randomized design.

(e) Ignore the blocking variable and "erroneously" reanalyze the data as a one-factor completely randomized design model where the one factor (categories of information) has three levels and each level contains a sample of 12 "independent" observations.

(f) Compare the *SSBL* and *SSE* terms in part (a) to the *SSW* term in part (e). Discuss.

(g) Using the results in parts (a), (d), (e), and (f) as a basis, describe the problems that can arise when analyzing data if the wrong procedures are applied.

(h) At the .05 level of significance, use the Friedman rank test to determine if there is evidence of a difference in the median rating scores among the information categories. Compare your results with those from part (a). Discuss.

(i) Formulate the problem from the reverse perspective, that is, compare the ratings given to the 12 companies on three "blocks" of information—communication of corporation activities, financial statement detail, and graphical presentation. At the .05 level of significance, use the Friedman rank test to determine if there is evidence of a difference in the median rating scores among the 12 companies. Compare your results to those of part (d) dealing with the effectiveness of blocking. Discuss.

**13.83** A recent wine tasting was held by the J. S. Wine Club in which eight wines were rated by club members. Information concerning the country of origin and the price was not known to the club members until after the tasting took place. The wines rated (and the prices paid for them) were

1. French white $8.59

2. Italian white $6.50

3. Italian red $6.50

4. French burgundy (red) $8.69

5. French burgundy (red) $9.75

6. California Beaujolais (red) $8.50

7. French white $7.75

8. California white $11.59

The summated ratings over several characteristics for the 12 club members were as follows:

|  | WINE | | | | | | | |
|---|---|---|---|---|---|---|---|---|
| RESPONDENT | 1 | 2 | 3 | 4 | 5 | 6 | 7 | 8 |
| A | 10 | 17 | 15 | 9 | 12 | 6 | 15 | 9 |
| B | 9 | 14 | 11 | 5 | 16 | 2 | 15 | 7 |
| C | 10 | 18 | 10 | 5 | 18 | 5 | 10 | 10 |
| D | 9 | 11 | 13 | 10 | 17 | 11 | 14 | 9 |
| E | 10 | 16 | 12 | 8 | 18 | 8 | 10 | 10 |
| F | 6 | 16 | 3 | 8 | 4 | 2 | 2 | 5 |
| G | 9 | 12 | 14 | 9 | 9 | 6 | 6 | 5 |
| H | 7 | 12 | 11 | 8 | 15 | 9 | 12 | 8 |
| I | 10 | 18 | 12 | 12 | 16 | 10 | 10 | 16 |
| J | 16 | 9 | 10 | 13 | 18 | 11 | 15 | 14 |
| K | 14 | 16 | 13 | 12 | 15 | 15 | 17 | 11 |
| L | 15 | 17 | 10 | 13 | 15 | 16 | 16 | 13 |

**DATA FILE**
**WINE**

To solve, use either computer software or the following summary information:

| Sums of squares: | $SSA = 440.33$ | | $SSBL = 521.50$ | | $SST = 1{,}592.00$ | | | |
|---|---|---|---|---|---|---|---|---|
| Wine: | **1** | **2** | **3** | **4** | **5** | **6** | **7** | **8** |
| Sample means: | 10.4 | 14.7 | 11.2 | 9.3 | 14.4 | 8.4 | 11.8 | 9.8 |
| Expert: | **1** | **2** | **3** | **4** | **5** | **6** | | |
| Sample means: | 11.6 | 9.9 | 10.8 | 11.8 | 11.5 | 5.7 | | |
| Expert: | **7** | **8** | **9** | **10** | **11** | **12** | | |
| Sample means: | 8.7 | 10.3 | 13.0 | 13.3 | 14.1 | 14.4 | | |

(a) At the .01 level of significance, is there evidence of a difference in the average rating scores between the wines?

(b) What assumptions are necessary in order to do (a) of this problem? Comment on the validity of these assumptions.

(c) If appropriate, use the Tukey procedure to determine the wines that differ in average rating. (Use $\alpha = .01$.)

(d) Answer the following based upon your results in (c):
   (1) Do you think that country of origin has had an effect on the ratings?
   (2) Do you think that the type of wine (red versus white) has had an effect on the ratings?
   (3) Do you think that price has had an effect on the ratings? Discuss fully.

(e) Determine the relative efficiency of the randomized block design as compared with the completely randomized design.

(f) Ignore the blocking variable and "erroneously" reanalyze the data as a one-factor completely randomized design model where the one factor (brands of wines) has eight levels and each level contains a sample of 12 independent observations.

(g) Compare the *SSBL* and *SSE* terms in part (a) to the *SSW* term in part (f). Discuss.

(h) Using the results in parts (a), (e), (f), and (g) as a basis, describe the problems that can arise in analyzing data if the wrong procedures are applied.

# TEAM PROJECT

**TP13.1** Refer to TP3.1 on page 115. Your group, the _____ Corporation, has been hired by the vice president for research at a financial investment service to study the financial characteristics of currently traded domestic general stock funds. The investment service is interested in evaluating the list of domestic general stock funds so that it can make purchase recommendations to potential investors. Armed with Special Data Set 1 of appendix D, the _____ Corporation is ready to:

**DATA FILE**
**MUTUAL**

(a) Determine if there is evidence of a significant difference in average net asset value (in dollars) based on the capitalization size of companies making up a fund's portfolio (large, mid, or small).

(b) Determine if there is evidence of a significant difference in average total year-to-date return based on the capitalization size of companies making up a fund's portfolio (large, mid, or small).

(c) Write and submit an executive summary describing the results in parts (a) and (b), clearly specifying all hypotheses, selected levels of significance, and the assumptions of the chosen test procedures.

(d) Prepare and deliver a 5-minute oral presentation to the vice president for research at this financial investment service.

*Note*: Additional Team Projects can be found at the following World Wide Web address:

**http://www.prenhall.com/berenson**

These Team Projects deal with the characteristics of 80 universities and colleges (see the UNIV&COL file) and the features in 89 automobile models (see the AUTO96 file).

## Case Study — TEST-MARKETING AND PROMOTING A BALL-POINT PEN

EPC Advertising has been hired by a well-established manufacturer of pens to develop a series of advertisements and national promotions for the upcoming holiday season. To prepare for this project, Nat Berry, research director at EPC Advertising, decides to initiate a study of the effect of advertising on product perception. After conferring with Milt Herfield, the chief of the statistics group, an experiment is designed in which five different advertisements are to be compared in the marketing of a ball-point pen. Advertisement A tends to greatly undersell the pen's characteristics. Advertisement B tends to slightly undersell the pen's characteristics. Advertisement C tends to slightly oversell the pen's characteristics. Advertisement D tends to greatly oversell the pen's characteristics. Advertisement E attempts to correctly state the pen's characteristics. A sample of 30 adult respondents, taken from a larger focus group, is randomly assigned to the five advertisements (so that there are six respondents to each). After reading the advertisement and developing a sense of "product expectation," all respondents unknowingly receive the same pens to evaluate. The respondents are permitted to test their pens and the plausibility of the advertising copy. The respondents are then asked to rate the pen from 1 to 7 on the following three product characteristic scales:

| | **PRODUCT RATINGS** | | | | | | |
|---|---|---|---|---|---|---|---|
| **PRODUCT CHARACTERISTICS** | **EXTREMELY POOR** | | | **NEUTRAL** | | | **EXTREMELY GOOD** |
| Appearance | 1 | 2 | 3 | 4 | 5 | 6 | 7 |
| Durability | 1 | 2 | 3 | 4 | 5 | 6 | 7 |
| Writing performance | 1 | 2 | 3 | 4 | 5 | 6 | 7 |

The *combined* scores of three ratings (appearance, durability, and writing performance) for the 30 respondents are as follows:

**PRODUCT RATINGS FOR FIVE ADVERTISEMENTS**

| A | B | C | D | E |
|---|---|---|---|---|
| 15 | 16 | 8 | 5 | 12 |
| 18 | 17 | 7 | 6 | 19 |
| 17 | 21 | 10 | 13 | 18 |
| 19 | 16 | 15 | 11 | 12 |
| 19 | 19 | 14 | 9 | 17 |
| 20 | 17 | 14 | 10 | 14 |

As a research assistant to Milt Herfield, you have been assigned to work on this project. You have an appointment to discuss this project with him at his office and when you arrive he states: "Hi, come on in and sit down. I'd offer you some coffee but I've just been called to a meeting so we'll have to make this brief. You know, Nat Berry feels he is really on to something here—test-marketing the advertising copy—and I hope he's right. I had suggested that we set up a two-factor factorial design model with gender as one factor and with advertising copy as the second factor, but Nat said he would have trouble selling a sophisticated plan to our CEO. He reminded me about the KISS principle—Keep It Sound and Simple—and said that anything more than a one-way completely randomized design model just wouldn't fly with top management. Anyway, Nat claimed he was primarily concerned with the content of the five possible ad copies, so the one-way model was what he got for this experiment. It's unfortunate, however, that we can't judge the gender factor in these potential holiday ads."

Milt continues: "I want to be prepared for next week's meeting with the research team from our public relations group, so we don't take any heat for the design model that we've used. Please prepare an executive summary showing the advantages and disadvantages of the completely randomized design model and the two-factor factorial design model. That will allow us to discuss these alternatives and move forward with the client's project in a positive manner. Also, I'd like you to thoroughly analyze the data that were obtained from the completely randomized experiment. I'd like to have a detailed report on my desk in 4 days that summarizes your findings and includes, as an appendix, a discussion of the statistical analysis utilized. Then let's get together for lunch, go over the details, and prepare for the presentations to Nat and the CEO. Do you have any questions before you get started? No? Well, good luck—and don't hesitate to give me a call if something comes up."

## One Week Later

Following your presentation at the meeting with the research team from the agency's public relations group, their chief statistician, John Mack, suggests that an appropriate nonparametric method be considered for analyzing the data.

 **DATA FILE PEN**

"Many researchers would argue," Mack observes, "that the 'product characteristic scales' used do not truly satisfy the criteria of interval or ratio scaling and, therefore, that nonparametric methods are more appropriate."

"John, that might make for an interesting statistics argument," Nat Berry exclaims. "We just have to be as sure as possible that we're practicing good data analysis."

"Well Nat," Milt Herfield intervenes, "that's just the point. I was, and still am, concerned about a potential gender effect that should be known if we really want to use effective advertising copy for our campaign. Fortunately, I'll have you know that my research assistant uncovered the fact that the first three ratings recorded in our table were provided by men and the last three by women in each of the five advertising copy samples. Now we can look at the experiment as a two-factor factorial design model and determine if there is a significant gender effect and study possible interaction as well. We'd like to meet again next week and go over these findings. It'll give us all a chance to reflect on the advantages and disadvantages of the two-factor model versus the one-factor model that my assistant discussed 20 minutes ago."

"Well, let's do it again next week, same time and place," Nat Berry remarks.

John Mack follows, "Fine, but while you are preparing for next week's meeting, would you also take a look at the following data that I've collected in a similar manner to your experiment? In this new data set the sampled audience was composed only of high school students who are part of a focus group, not adults. And the data are the ratings or responses only for students who were exposed to advertising copy E, which, as you may recall, attempted to correctly state the pen's characteristics. Please take a look at the corresponding group of adults in your study and analyze the differences in their responses."

The aforementioned combined ratings data for a sample of eight high school student respondents are as follows:

**DATA FILE**
**PENEAD**

14, 13, 15, 9, 11, 13, 12, 16

You leave the room thinking about John Mack's last remarks and you realize you've got plenty to do! In addition to analyzing the original data as a two-factor factorial design model and preparing a discussion of the differences in the results obtained using that model and those obtained using the completely randomized design model that you just reported, you also decide to answer

John's requests. First, using Milt Herfield's data, you plan to evaluate the five advertisements by using a nonparametric test and comparing the results with those you have just reported based on the one-factor model. Then, you plan to examine John's data and determine whether there is evidence of a significant difference in the combined ratings of adult versus high school student respondents subjected to advertisement E (which attempts to correctly state the pen's characteristics). Your answer to this question will identify possible differences in perceptions of adults and those of students with respect to the product.

You will be preparing a detailed report on these matters for Milt Herfield.

To solve, use either computer software or the following summary information:

## Information for Milt Herfield

Sums of squares:  $SSFA = 19.20$  $SSFB = 377.867$  $SSAB = 58.133$  $SST = 565.867$

| Gender: | **MALE** | **FEMALE** | | | |
|---|---|---|---|---|---|
| Sample sizes: | 15 | 15 | | | |
| Sample means: | 13.5 | 15.1 | | | |
| Sample standard deviations: | 5.2 | 3.5 | | | |
| Rank sums: | 214.5 | 250.5 | | | |
| Advertisement: | **A** | **B** | **C** | **D** | **E** |
| Sample sizes: | 6 | 6 | 6 | 6 | 6 |
| Sample means: | 18.0 | 17.7 | 11.3 | 9.0 | 15.3 |
| Sample standard deviations: | 1.8 | 2.0 | 3.4 | 3.0 | 3.1 |
| Rank sums: | 141.5 | 132.5 | 55.0 | 33.5 | 102.5 |
| Cell: | **M,A** | **M,B** | **M,C** | **M,D** | **M,E** |
| Sample sizes: | 3 | 3 | 3 | 3 | 3 |
| Sample means: | 16.7 | 18.0 | 8.3 | 8.0 | 16.3 |
| Sample standard deviations: | 1.5 | 2.6 | 1.5 | 4.4 | 3.8 |
| Cell: | **F,A** | **F,B** | **F,C** | **F,D** | **F,E** |
| Sample sizes: | 3 | 3 | 3 | 3 | 3 |
| Sample means: | 19.3 | 17.3 | 14.3 | 10.0 | 14.3 |
| Sample standard deviations: | 0.6 | 1.5 | 0.6 | 1.0 | 2.5 |

## Information for John Mack

| Rater: | **ADULT** | **STUDENT** |
|---|---|---|
| Sample sizes: | 6 | 8 |
| Sample means: | 15.3 | 12.9 |
| Sample standard deviations: | 3.1 | 2.2 |
| Rank sums: | 55.5 | 49.5 |

# THE SPRINGVILLE HERALD CASE

## Phase 1

The marketing department team studying new home-delivery subscriptions wanted to study the telemarketing process to increase the number of home-delivery subscriptions sold. After several brainstorming sessions involving many individuals who are familiar with all aspects of the telemarketing process, including individuals who provide training for the callers and several of the callers themselves, it was decided that it was necessary to find ways to increase the length of the phone calls because it was clear that the longer a caller can speak to a respondent, the higher is the chance that a newspaper subscription will be sold.

Initially, the team investigated the impact that time of call had on length of call and determined that calls made later in the evening (i.e., 7 to 9 P.M.) were, on average, significantly more conducive to lengthier calls than those made earlier in the evening (i.e., 5 to 7 P.M.).

Knowing that the 7 to 9 P.M. time period is superior, the team now wanted to investigate the impact of the type of presentation on the length of the call. A group of 24 female callers were randomly assigned, 8 each, to one of three presentation plans—totally scripted, semistructured, and unstructured—and were then trained how to make the telephone presentation. All calls were made between 7 and 9 P.M., the desired time period, and,

further, the callers were to provide an introductory greeting that was personal but informal ("Hi, this is Mary Jones from the *Springville Herald*—may I speak to Bill Richards?"). The callers knew that the team was observing their efforts that evening but didn't know which particular call was going to be monitored. Measurements were taken on the length of call (operationally defined as the difference, in seconds, between the time the person answers the phone and the time he or she hangs up). The results are presented in Table SH13.1.

**Table SH13.1** *Length of calls in seconds based on presentation plan*

| PRESENTATION PLAN | | |
|---|---|---|
| STRUCTURED | SEMI-STRUCTURED | UNSTRUCTURED |
| 38.8 | 41.8 | 32.9 |
| 42.1 | 36.4 | 36.1 |
| 45.2 | 39.1 | 39.2 |
| 34.8 | 28.7 | 29.3 |
| 48.3 | 36.4 | 41.9 |
| 37.8 | 36.1 | 31.7 |
| 41.1 | 35.8 | 35.2 |
| 43.6 | 33.7 | 38.1 |

 **DATA FILE SH13-1**

## Exercises

**13.1** Analyze these data and write a report for presentation to the team that indicates your findings. Be sure to include your recommendations based on your findings. Also, be sure to include an attached appendix in which you discuss the reason you selected a particular statistical test to compare the three independent groups of callers.

To solve, use either computer software or the following summary information:

| Presentation plan: | STRUCTURED | SEMISTRUCTURED | UNSTRUCTURED | |
|---|---|---|---|---|
| Sample means: | 41.46 | 36.00 | 35.55 | $\overline{\overline{X}} = 37.67$ |
| Sample standard deviations: | 4.32 | 3.82 | 4.17 | |
| Rank sums: | 142 | 81.5 | 76.50 | |

**13.2** Suppose that, instead of the completely randomized design model previously described, there were only eight callers sampled and each caller was to be trained to use all three presentation plans—totally scripted, semistructured, and unstructured—and then each caller was to be given a schedule in which the three types of presentations would be made in a particular sequence of calls (randomly determined). Calls were to be monitored three times in the evening, once under each type of presentation. Suppose that in Table SH13.1 each row represents a particular caller's three measurements. Reanalyze these data for this randomized block design and write a report for presentation to the team that indicates your findings. Be sure to include your recommendations based on your findings. Also, be sure to include an attached appendix in which you discuss the reason you selected a particular statistical test.

To solve, use either computer software or the following summary information:

| Sums of squares: | $SSA = 173.33$ | $SSBL = 255.80$ | $SST = 527.73$ | |
|---|---|---|---|---|
| Presentation plan: | **STRUCTURED** | **SEMISTRUCTURED** | **UNSTRUCTURED** | |
| Sample means: | 41.46 | 36.00 | 35.55 | $\bar{\bar{X}} = 37.67$ |
| Rank sums: | 23 | 13 | 12 | |

| Caller: | 1 | 2 | 3 | 4 | 5 | 6 | 7 | 8 |
|---|---|---|---|---|---|---|---|---|
| Sample means: | 37.8 | 38.2 | 41.2 | 30.9 | 42.2 | 35.2 | 37.4 | 38.5 |

 **Do not continue until the Phase 1 exercises have been completed.**

# Phase 2

Once the data of Table SH13.1 had been analyzed, it became evident that the totally structured/completely scripted presentation plan resulted in a significantly longer call than either the semistructured or unstructured plans. The team met and reviewed the findings in its efforts to improve the telemarketing process and, consequently, increase home-delivery newspaper subscription sales. They concluded that completely structured calls made later in the evening, from 7 to 9 P.M., afforded the best opportunity to accomplish this. The team then held another brainstorming session and determined that two additional factors need to be studied in an effort to increase the length of the phone call. These two factors are:

- Gender of the caller: male versus female.
- Type of greeting: personal but formal (i.e., "Hello, my name is Mary Jones from the *Springville Herald*—may I speak to Mr. Richards?"), personal but informal (i.e., "Hi, this is Mary Jones from the *Springville Herald*—may I speak to Bill Richards?"),

or impersonal (i.e., "I represent the *Springville Herald.* . .").

The team acknowledged that in its previous studies it had controlled for these variables. Only female callers were selected to participate in the studies, and they were trained to use a personal but informal greeting style. Now, however, it becomes necessary to determine whether these groupings of the gender and greeting variables are in fact best.

A study was designed in which a total of 30 callers were chosen to participate, 15 males and 15 females. The callers were randomly assigned to one of the three greeting style training groups so that there were five callers in each of the six combinations of the two factors, gender and greeting style. The callers knew that the team was observing their efforts that evening but didn't know which particular call was going to be monitored.

Measurements were taken on the length of call (operationally defined as the difference, in seconds, between the time the person answers and the time he or she hangs up the phone). The results are summarized in Table SH13.2.

## Table SH13.2  Length of calls in seconds based on gender and type of greeting

| | GREETING | | |
|---|---|---|---|
| GENDER | PF | PI | IM |
| M | 45.6 | 41.7 | 35.3 |
| | 49.0 | 42.8 | 37.7 |
| | 41.8 | 40.0 | 41.0 |
| | 35.6 | 39.6 | 28.7 |
| | 43.4 | 36.0 | 31.8 |
| F | 44.1 | 37.9 | 43.3 |
| | 40.8 | 41.1 | 40.0 |
| | 46.9 | 35.8 | 43.1 |
| | 51.8 | 45.3 | 39.6 |
| | 48.5 | 40.2 | 33.2 |

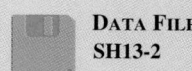

DATA FILE
SH13-2

To solve use either computer software or the following summary information:

Sums of squares: $SSFA = 57.69$   $SSFB = 279.26$   $SSAB = 31.22$   $SST = 776.01$

| Gender: | MALE | FEMALE | | | | |
|---|---|---|---|---|---|---|
| Sample sizes: | 15 | 15 | | | | |
| Sample means: | 39.33 | 42.11 | | | | |
| Sample standard deviations: | 5.28 | 4.84 | | | | |

| Greeting: | PF | PI | IM | | | |
|---|---|---|---|---|---|---|
| Sample sizes: | 10 | 10 | 10 | | | |
| Sample means: | 44.75 | 40.04 | 37.37 | | | |
| Sample standard deviations: | 4.68 | 2.95 | 4.96 | | | |

| Cell: | M,PF | M,PI | M,IM | F,PF | F,PI | F,IM |
|---|---|---|---|---|---|---|
| Sample sizes: | 5 | 5 | 5 | 5 | 5 | 5 |
| Sample means: | 43.08 | 40.02 | 34.90 | 46.42 | 40.06 | 39.84 |
| Sample standard deviations: | 4.98 | 2.59 | 4.83 | 4.20 | 3.58 | 4.09 |

## Exercises

**13.3** Completely analyze these data and write a report for presentation to the team that indicates the importance of each of the two factors and/or the interaction between them on the length of the call. Be sure to include in the report a recommendation for future experiments that might be undertaken.

**13.4** Do you believe that the length of the telephone call was the most appropriate outcome to study? What other variables should be investigated next? Discuss.

# References

1. Berenson, M. L., D. M. Levine, and M. Goldstein, *Intermediate Statistical Methods and Applications: A Computer Package Approach* (Englewood Cliffs, NJ: Prentice Hall, 1983).

2. Conover, W. J., *Practical Nonparametric Statistics*, 2d ed. (New York: Wiley, 1980).

3. Daniel, W. W., *Applied Nonparametric Statistics*, 2d ed. (Boston: PWS Kent, 1990).

4. Dunn, O. J., "Multiple Comparisons Using Rank Sums," *Technometrics* 6 (1964): 241–252.

5. Hicks, C. R., *Fundamental Concepts in the Design of Experiments*, 3d ed. (New York: Holt, Rinehart and Winston, 1982).

6. Kirk, R. E., *Experimental Design*, 2d ed. (Belmont, CA: Brooks-Cole, 1982).

7. Kramer, C. Y., "Extension of Multiple Range Tests to Group Means with Unequal Numbers of Replications," *Biometrics* 12 (1956): 307–310.

8. *Microsoft Excel 97* (Redmond, WA: Microsoft Corporation, 1997).

9. Miller, R. G., *Simultaneous Statistical Inference*, 2d ed. (New York: Springer-Verlag, 1980).

10. *Minitab for Windows Version 12* (State College, PA: Minitab, Inc., 1998).

11. Neter, J., M. H. Kutner, C. Nachtsheim, and W. Wasserman, *Applied Linear Statistical Models*, 4th ed. (Homewood, IL: Richard D. Irwin, 1996).

12. Tukey, J. W., "Comparing Individual Means in the Analysis of Variance," *Biometrics* 5 (1949): 99–114.

---

## ❖ APPENDIX 13.1  USING MICROSOFT EXCEL FOR ANOVA AND OTHER $c$-Sample Tests with Numerical Data

The Data Analysis tool of Microsoft Excel can be used for the one-way ANOVA, randomized block design, and the two-way ANOVA.

### Using Microsoft Excel for the One-Way ANOVA

To illustrate the use of Microsoft Excel for the one-way ANOVA, **open** the **LINESPD.XLS** workbook which contains the data for the soft drink example of Table 13.2 on page 547. On the Data sheet, note that the data have been set up in an unstacked format with column headings in row 1. (If the data were provided in a stacked format, it would first have to be unstacked so that each group is located in a separate column.)

To obtain the one-way ANOVA results similar to those of Table 13.4 on page 550, select **Tools | Data Analysis**. Select **Anova: Single Factor** from the Analysis tools list box. Click the **OK** button. In the Anova: Single Factor dialog box which appears, enter **A1:D6** in the **Input Range** edit box, select the **Grouped by Columns** option button, select the **Labels in First Row** check box, and enter the level of significance in the **Alpha** edit box (.05 is the default value). Select the **New Worksheet Ply** option button and enter a name such as **OneWayANOVA**. Click the **OK** button.

### Using Microsoft Excel for the Randomized Block Design

To illustrate the use of Microsoft Excel for the randomized block design, **open** the **FFCHAIN.XLS** workbook which contains the data for the restaurant ratings example of Table 13.8 on page 567. On the Data sheet, note that the data have been set up in a format that is similar to Table 13.8, except that column A provides a label for each block, and cell A1 is blank.

To obtain the results similar to those of Table 13.9 on page 568, select **Tools | Data Analysis**. Select **Anova: Two Factors without Replication** from the Analysis tools list box. Click the **OK** button. In the Anova: Two Factors without Replication dialog box which appears, enter **A1:E7** in the **Input Range** edit box, select the **Labels** check box, and enter the level of significance in the **Alpha** edit box (.05 is the default value). Select the **New Worksheet Ply** option button and enter a name such as **ANOVA**. Click the **OK** button. In addition to the ANOVA table, Excel provides the sample size, sum, arithmetic mean, and variance for each row and column in the randomized block design.

## Using Microsoft Excel for the Two-Factor ANOVA

To illustrate the use of Microsoft Excel for the two-factor ANOVA, **open** the **LINESPD2.XLS** workbook which contains the data for the soft drink example of Table 13.11 on page 583. On the Data sheet, note that the data have been set up in a format that is similar to Table 13.11, except that column A provides a label corresponding to each level of factor A, and cell A1 is blank.

To obtain the results of Figure 13.13 on page 585, select **Tools | Data Analysis**. Select **Anova: Two Factors with Replication** from the Analysis tools list box. Click the **OK** button. In the Anova: Two Factors with Replication dialog box which appears, enter **A1:E11** in the **Input Range** edit box, **5** in the **Rows per Sample** edit box, and enter the level of significance in the **Alpha** edit box (.05 is the default value). Select the **New Worksheet Ply** option button and enter a name such as **TwoWayANOVA**. Click the **OK** button. In addition to the ANOVA table, Excel provides the sample size, sum, arithmetic mean, and variance for each row, each column, and each cell in the two-factor design.

---

## ❖ APPENDIX 13.2 USING MINITAB FOR ANOVA AND OTHER c-Sample Tests with Numerical Data

### Using Minitab for the One-Way ANOVA

To illustrate the use of Minitab for the one-factor ANOVA, **open** the **LINESPD.MTP** worksheet. Note that the data have been stored in an unstacked format with each level in a separate column. Select **Stat | ANOVA | OneWay(Unstacked)**. In the **Responses (in separate columns):** edit box enter **C1 C2 C3 C4**. Click the **OK** button.

If the data are stored in a stacked format, select **Stat | ANOVA | OneWay**. Enter the column in which the response variable is stored in the Response edit box, and the column in which the factor is stored in the Factor edit box.

### Using Minitab for the Randomized Block and Two-Factor Designs

The procedure for using Minitab is similar for the randomized block design and the two-factor design. To illustrate the use of Minitab for the two-factor design, **open** the **LINESPD2.MTP** worksheet. Note that % Carbonation is stored in C1, line speed in C2, and the deviation in C3. Select **Stat | ANOVA | Two-Way**. In the Two-Way dialog box, enter **C3** or **Deviation** in the **Response** edit box, **C1** or **%Carb** in the **Row factor** edit box, and **C2** or **LineSpd** in the **Column factor** edit box. Select the **Display Means** edit box for the row and column factors. Click the **OK** button.

### Using Minitab for the Kruskal-Wallis Test

To illustrate the use of Minitab for the Kruskal-Wallis test, **open** the **LINESPD.MTP** worksheet. Note that the data have been stored in an unstacked format with each level in a separate column. In order to perform the Kruskal-Wallis test, we need to stack the data. Select **Manip | Stack/Unstack | Stack Columns**. Enter **C1–C4** in the **Stack the following Columns** edit box, **C5** in the **Store the Stacked data in:** edit box, and **C6** in the **Subscripts in:** edit box. Click the **OK** button. Enter labels for Deviation in column 5 and bottles per minute (bpm) in column 6.

Select **Stat | Nonparametrics | Kruskal-Wallis**. Enter **C5** in the **Response** edit box, and **C6** in the **Factor** edit box. Click the **OK** button. You will obtain the output displayed in Figure 13.18 on page 600.

## Using Minitab for the Friedman test

To illustrate the use of Minitab for the Friedman test, **open** the **FFCHAIN.MTW** worksheet. Select **Stat | Nonparametrics | Friedman**. Enter **C3** or **Rating** in the **Response edit box**, **C2** or **Restrat** in the **Treatment** edit box, and **C1** or **Raters** in the **Block** edit box. Click the **OK** button. You will obtain the output displayed in Figure 13.20 on page 609.

# 14

# Two-Sample and *c*-Sample Tests with Categorical Data

## CHAPTER OBJECTIVES

✓ *To test for differences in the proportions in two independent sample groups*
✓ *To test for differences in the proportions in more than two independent sample groups*
✓ *To test for the independence of two categorical variables*

## Introduction

In the preceding three chapters we were concerned with hypothesis-testing procedures that are used to analyze numerical data as well as to test for a proportion in a single population. In chapter 11 a variety of one-sample tests were presented; in chapter 12 several two-sample tests were developed for numerical data; and in chapter 13 the analysis of variance and other procedures were used to study one or more factors of interest. In this chapter we will extend our discussion of hypothesis-testing methodology to consider procedures that are used to analyze differences in population proportions based on two independent samples and $c$ independent samples. In addition, our discussions in section 5.2 on the theory of probability will be extended by presenting a more *confirmatory* analysis of the hypothesis of *independence* in the joint responses to two categorical variables. In order to do so, we consider the satisfaction of guests at a hotel chain. Once again, in this chapter, emphasis will be given to the assumptions behind the use of the various tests.

---

## ◆ USING STATISTICS: *Guest Satisfaction at a Hotel Chain*

The management of a hotel chain has to be very sensitive to the needs of its guests, particularly for its upscale branches that are located on resort islands. The perception of whether the guest is satisfied is critically important to whether or not he or she is willing to return in the future and also to recommend the location to friends and relatives. Thus, as a matter of course, hotel chains monitor the service levels at each location and analyze the results of satisfaction surveys that guests are encouraged to complete when they check out of the hotel. Among the questions to be answered is one that asks whether the guest would be likely to choose the hotel again and, if not, what the primary reason is for that response. Such a survey was taken on two resort islands. On one of the islands, the hotel chain has two locations; on the second island, the hotel chain has three locations.

##  14.1 Z TEST FOR DIFFERENCES IN TWO PROPORTIONS (INDEPENDENT SAMPLES)

Often we are concerned with making comparisons and analyzing differences between two populations in terms of some categorical characteristic. A test for the difference between two proportions based on independent samples can be performed using two different methods. In this section we present a procedure whose test statistic Z is approximated by a standard normal distribution. In section 14.2 we will develop a procedure whose test statistic $\chi^2$ is approximated by a chi-square distribution with 1 degree of freedom. We will find that the results from these two tests will be equivalent.

In evaluating differences between two proportions based on independent samples, we begin with a $Z$ test. The test statistic $Z$ used to determine the difference between the two population proportions is based on the difference between the two sample proportions $(p_{s_1} - p_{s_2})$. This test statistic is approximated by a standard normal distribution for large enough sample sizes. As shown in equation (14.1), the $Z$-test statistic is

## Z Test for the Difference between Two Proportions

$$Z \cong \frac{(p_{s_1} - p_{s_2}) - (p_1 - p_2)}{\sqrt{\bar{p}(1 - \bar{p})\left(\dfrac{1}{n_1} + \dfrac{1}{n_2}\right)}} \qquad (14.1)$$

with

$$\bar{p} = \frac{X_1 + X_2}{n_1 + n_2} \qquad p_{s_1} = \frac{X_1}{n_1} \qquad p_{s_2} = \frac{X_2}{n_2}$$

where

$p_{s_1}$ = proportion of successes in sample 1

$X_1$ = number of successes in sample 1

$n_1$ = size of the sample taken from population 1

$p_1$ = proportion of successes in population 1

$p_{s_2}$ = proportion of successes in sample 2

$X_2$ = number of successes in sample 2

$n_2$ = size of the sample taken from population 2

$p_2$ = proportion of successes in population 2

$\bar{p}$ = pooled estimate of the population proportion of successes

Under the null hypothesis it is assumed that the two population proportions are equal. We should note that $\bar{p}$, the pooled estimate for the population proportion, is based on the null hypothesis. Therefore, when testing for equality in the two population proportions, we combine or pool the two sample proportions to obtain an overall estimate of the common population proportion. This estimate $\bar{p}$ is the number of successes in the two samples combined $(X_1 + X_2)$ divided by the total sample size from the two sample groups $(n_1 + n_2)$.

A distinguishing feature of this $Z$ test for the difference in population proportions is that it can be used to determine either whether there is any difference in the proportion of successes in the two groups (two-tailed test) or whether one group has a higher proportion of successes than the other group (one-tailed test).[1]

| TWO-TAILED TEST | ONE-TAILED TEST | ONE-TAILED TEST |
|---|---|---|
| $H_0$: $p_1 = p_2$ | $H_0$: $p_1 \geq p_2$ | $H_0$: $p_1 \leq p_2$ |
| $H_1$: $p_1 \neq p_2$ | $H_1$: $p_1 < p_2$ | $H_1$: $p_1 > p_2$ |

*where*   *$p_1$ = proportion of successes in population 1*
*$p_2$ = proportion of successes in population 2*

To test the null hypothesis of no difference in the proportions of two independent populations

[1] *If the hypothesized difference is 0 (that is, $p_1 - p_2 = 0$ or $p_1 = p_2$), the numerator in equation (14.1) becomes $p_{s_1} - p_{s_2}$.*

$$H_0: p_1 = p_2$$

against the alternative that the two population proportions are not the same

$$H_1: p_1 \neq p_2$$

we may use the test statistic $Z$, given by equation (14.1), and, for a given level of significance $\alpha$, we will reject the null hypothesis if the computed $Z$-test statistic exceeds the upper-tailed critical value from the standard normal distribution or if the computed test statistic falls below the lower-tailed critical value from the standard normal distribution.

To illustrate the use of the $Z$ test for the homogeneity of two proportions, we return to our study of satisfaction at a hotel chain.

## Example 14.1 *Z Test of Equality of Two Proportions*

On one of the islands the hotel chain had facilities at two different locations. In tabulating the responses to the single question "Are you likely to choose this hotel again?" 163 of 227 guests at the Beachcomber responded yes, whereas at the Windsurfer 154 of 262 guests responded yes. At the .05 level of significance, is there evidence of a significant difference in guest satisfaction (as measured by likelihood to return to the hotel) between the two hotels?

### SOLUTION

The null and alternative hypotheses are

$$H_0: p_1 = p_2 \quad \text{or} \quad p_1 - p_2 = 0$$
$$H_1: p_1 \neq p_2 \quad \text{or} \quad p_1 - p_2 \neq 0$$

The test is to be carried out at the .05 level of significance, so the critical values are $-1.96$ and $+1.96$ (see the accompanying figure) and our decision rule is

Reject $H_0$ if $Z > +1.96$

or if $Z < -1.96$;

otherwise do not reject $H_0$.

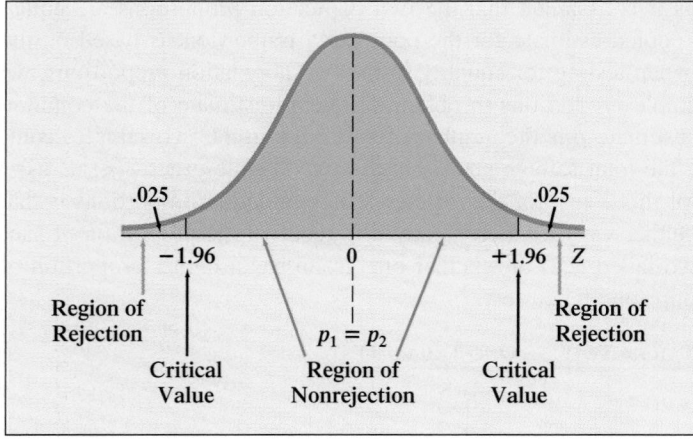

Testing hypothesis for difference between two proportions at .05 level of significance

For our data, we have

$$Z \cong \frac{(p_{s_1} - p_{s_2}) - (p_1 - p_2)}{\sqrt{\bar{p}(1 - \bar{p})\left(\dfrac{1}{n_1} + \dfrac{1}{n_2}\right)}}$$

where

$$p_{s_1} = \frac{X_1}{n_1} = \frac{163}{227} = .718 \qquad p_{s_2} = \frac{X_2}{n_2} = \frac{154}{262} = .588$$

and

$$\bar{p} = \frac{X_1 + X_2}{n_1 + n_2} = \frac{163 + 154}{227 + 262} = \frac{317}{489} = .648$$

so that

$$Z = \frac{.718 - .588}{\sqrt{(.648)(.352)\left(\frac{1}{227} + \frac{1}{262}\right)}}$$

$$= \frac{.13}{\sqrt{(.228)(.0082)}}$$

$$= \frac{.13}{\sqrt{.00187}}$$

$$= \frac{.13}{.0432} = +3.01$$

and using a .05 level of significance, the null hypothesis ($H_0$) is rejected because $Z = +3.01 > +1.96$. If the null hypothesis were true, there would be an $\alpha = .05$ probability of obtaining a $Z$-test statistic either larger than $+1.96$ standard deviations or smaller than $-1.96$ standard deviations from the center of the $Z$ distribution. The $p$-value, or probability of obtaining a difference in the two sample proportions as large as or even larger than the one observed here (which translates into a test statistic $Z$ equal to or even farther from the center than $\pm 3.01$ standard deviations) is .00262 (obtained from Table E.2). This means that if the null hypothesis were true, the probability of obtaining a $Z$-test statistic below $-3.01$ would be $.5000 - .49869 = .00131$ and, similarly, the probability of obtaining a $Z$-test statistic above $+3.01$ would be $.5000 - .49869 = .00131$. Thus, for this two-tailed test, the $p$-value is $.00131 + .00131 = .00262$. Because $.00262 < \alpha = .05$, the null hypothesis is rejected. There is evidence to conclude that the two hotels are significantly different with respect to guest satisfaction as measured by the likelihood of choosing the hotel again; that is, a greater proportion of guests were willing to return to the Beachcomber than to the Windsurfer.

## Problems for Section 14.1

### Learning the Basics

- **14.1** If $n_1 = 100$, $X_1 = 50$, $n_2 = 100$, and $X_2 = 30$, at the .05 level of significance, is there evidence of a significant difference in the proportion of successes in group 1 and group 2?

- **14.2** If $n_1 = 100$, $X_1 = 45$, $n_2 = 50$, and $X_2 = 25$, at the .01 level of significance, is there evidence of a significant difference in the proportion of successes in group 1 and group 2?

### Applying the Concepts

- **14.3** A sample of 500 respondents was selected in a large metropolitan area to determine various information concerning consumer behavior. Among the questions asked was "Do you enjoy shopping for clothing?" Of 240 males, 136 answered yes. Of 260 females, 224 answered yes.

(a) Is there evidence of a significant difference between males and females in the proportion who enjoy shopping for clothing at the .01 level of significance?

(b) Compute the $p$-value in (a) and interpret its meaning.

(c) What would be your answer to (a) and (b) if 206 males enjoyed shopping for clothing?

● **14.4** A human resources director decided to investigate employee perception of the fairness of two performance evaluation methods. To test for the differences between the two methods, 160 employees were randomly assigned to be evaluated by one of the methods: 78 were assigned to method 1, where individuals provide feedback to supervisory queries as part of the evaluation process; 82 were assigned to method 2, where individuals provide self-assessments of their work performance. Following the evaluations, employees were asked whether they considered the performance evaluation fair or unfair. Of the 78 employees in method 1, there were 63 fair ratings. Of the 82 employees in method 2, there were 49 fair ratings.

(a) Using a .05 level of significance, is there evidence of a significant difference between the two methods in the proportion of fair ratings?

(b) Compute the $p$-value in (a) and interpret its meaning.

● **14.5** A professor of accountancy was studying the readability of the annual reports of two major companies. A random sample of 100 certified public accountants was selected. Fifty were randomly assigned to read the annual report of company A, and the other fifty were to read the annual report of company B. On the basis of a standard measure of readability, 17 found company A's annual report "understandable" and 23 found company B's annual report "understandable."

(a) At the .10 level of significance, is there evidence of a significant difference between the two companies in the proportion of CPAs who find the annual reports understandable?

(b) Compute the $p$-value in (a) and interpret its meaning.

(c) What would be your answers to (a) and (b), if 33 found company B's annual report "understandable"?

● **14.6** The director of marketing for a company manufacturing laundry detergent conducts an experiment to compare satisfaction with the laundry detergent product based on level of temperature used for the wash. A random sample of 500 individuals who agree to participate in the experiment is asked to use the product on a standard-sized load under a low-temperature setting. A second random sample of 500 participants is asked to use the same product on a standard-sized load under a high-temperature setting. Of the 500 participants who use the low-temperature setting, 280 are happy with the cleansing outcome. Of the 500 participants who use the high-temperature setting, 320 are happy with the results.

(a) At the .05 level of significance, is there evidence that the detergent is significantly more preferred when used with the high-temperature setting than with the low-temperature setting?

(b) Compute the $p$-value in (a) and interpret its meaning.

**14.7** The manager of a campus bookstore conducts a survey to investigate whether there are any differences between males and females with respect to the consideration of the purchase of educational videotapes. Depending on the answer, her goal is to develop pertinent promotional material that will lead to increased sales in educational videotapes over the coming semester. Of the 40 males in the survey, 13 state they would consider purchasing educational videotapes. Of the 30 females in the survey, 15 said they would consider purchasing educational videotapes.

(a) At the .01 level of significance, is there evidence of a significant difference in the proportion of males and females who would consider purchasing educational videotapes?

(b) Compute the *p*-value in (a) and interpret its meaning.

(c) Given the results in (a) and (b), what should the bookstore manager do with respect to a future promotional campaign? Discuss your recommendations.

(d) What would be your answers to (a)–(c) if 25 females said they would consider purchasing educational videotapes?

## 14.2 $\chi^2$ TEST FOR DIFFERENCES IN TWO PROPORTIONS (INDEPENDENT SAMPLES)

In the previous section we described the *Z* test for the difference between two proportions based on independent samples. In this section, rather than directly comparing proportions of success, we view the data in terms of the frequency of success in two groups. We will develop a procedure whose test statistic $\chi^2$ is approximated by a chi-square distribution with 1 degree of freedom. The results obtained with the $\chi^2$ test are equivalent to those obtained by using the *Z* test of section 14.1.

If we are interested in comparing the tallies or counts of categorical responses between two independent groups, a two-way table of cross-classifications can be developed (see section 3.5) to display the frequency of occurrence of successes and failures for each group. Such a table is also called a **contingency table**, which was used in chapter 5 to define and study probability from an objective empirical approach. In this section, however, we develop methodology for a more confirmatory analysis of data presented in such contingency tables.

To illustrate the use of this technique, let us return to the guest satisfaction survey presented in Example 14.1 on page 644. Table 14.1 is a schematic layout of a **cross-classification** table resulting from the survey, and Table 14.2 is the contingency table displaying the actual data from the study.

### Table 14.1 *Layout of a 2 × 2 contingency table for the guest satisfaction survey*

| ARE YOU LIKELY TO CHOOSE THIS HOTEL AGAIN? | HOTEL | | TOTAL |
|---|---|---|---|
| | BEACHCOMBER | WINDSURFER | |
| Yes | $X_1$ | $X_2$ | $X$ |
| No | $n_1 - X_1$ | $n_2 - X_2$ | $n - X$ |
| Total | $n_1$ | $n_2$ | $n$ |

where
$X_1$ = *number of guests at the Beachcomber who are likely to choose the hotel again*

$X_2$ = *number of guests at the Windsurfer who are likely to choose the hotel again*

$n_1 - X_1$ = *number of guests at the Beachcomber who are not likely to choose the hotel again*

$n_2 - X_2$ = *number of guests at the Windsurfer who are not likely to choose the hotel again*

$X = X_1 + X_2$ = *total number of guests who are likely to choose the hotel again*

$n - X = (n_1 - X_1) + (n_2 - X_2)$ = *total number of guests who are not likely to choose the hotel again*

$n_1$ = *number of guests at the Beachcomber who answered the satisfaction survey*

$n_2$ = *number of guests at the Windsurfer who answered the satisfaction survey*

$n = n_1 + n_2$ = *total number of guests who answered the satisfaction survey*

**Table 14.2**   *2 × 2 contingency table for the guest satisfaction survey*

| | HOTEL | | |
|---|---|---|---|
| **CHOOSE HOTEL AGAIN?** | **BEACHCOMBER** | **WINDSURFER** | **TOTAL** |
| Yes | 163 | 154 | 317 |
| No | 64 | 108 | 172 |
| Total | 227 | 262 | 489 |

The contingency table displayed in Table 14.2 has two rows, indicating whether the guests would return to the hotel (i.e., success) or would not return to the hotel (i.e., failure), and two columns, one for each hotel. Such a table is called a **2 × 2 table**. The cells in the table indicate the frequency of successes and failures for each row and column combination. The row totals indicate the number of guests who would return to the hotel and those who would not return to the hotel; the column totals are the sample sizes for each hotel location. The proportion of guests who would return to the hotel is obtained by dividing the number of guests who say they would return to a particular hotel by the sample size for that hotel. A methodology known as the $\chi^2$ **test for homogeneity of proportions** is then used to compare the proportions for the two hotels.

To test the null hypothesis of no differences in the two population proportions

$$H_0: p_1 = p_2$$

against the alternative that the two population proportions are different

$$H_1: p_1 \neq p_2$$

we obtain the $\chi^2$-test statistic, which is given by the following:

## $\chi^2$ Test for the Difference between Two Proportions

The $\chi^2$-test statistic is equal to the squared difference between the observed and expected frequencies, divided by the expected frequency in each cell of the table, summed over all cells of the table.

$$\chi^2 = \sum_{\text{all cells}} \frac{(f_0 - f_e)^2}{f_e} \qquad (14.2)$$

where

$f_0 = $ **observed frequency** or actual tally in a particular cell of a 2 × 2 contingency table

$f_e = $ **theoretical or expected frequency** in a particular cell if the null hypothesis is true

To compute the expected frequency ($f_e$) in any cell requires an understanding of its conceptual foundation. If the null hypothesis is true and the proportion of yes responses is equal for each population, then the sample proportions computed from the two groups should differ from each other only by chance because they would each be providing an estimate of the common population proportion $p$. In such a situation, a statistic that pools or combines these two separate estimates into one overall or average estimate of the population proportion $p$ provides more information than either one of the two separate estimates. This statistic, given by the symbol $\bar{p}$, represents the overall or average proportion of yes responses for the two groups combined (i.e., the total number of yes responses divided by the total number of guests who responded). Using the notation for proportions given in section 14.1, this is stated as follows:

## Computing the Average Proportion

The average proportion $\bar{p}$ is equal to the sum of the "successes" in the two groups, divided by the sum of the sample sizes of the two groups.

$$\bar{p} = \frac{X_1 + X_2}{n_1 + n_2} = \frac{X}{n} \tag{14.3}$$

Its complement $1 - \bar{p}$ represents the overall or average proportion of "failures" over the two groups.

To obtain the expected frequency $f_e$ for each cell of yes responses (the first row in the contingency table), we multiply the sample size (or column total) for a hotel by $\bar{p}$. To obtain the expected frequency $f_e$ for each cell of no responses (the second row in the contingency table), we multiply the sample size (or column total) by $(1 - \bar{p})$.

The test statistic shown in equation (14.2) approximately follows a chi-square distribution with **degrees of freedom** equal to the number of rows in the contingency table minus 1 times the number of columns in the table minus 1:

$$\text{Degrees of freedom} = (r - 1)(c - 1)$$

where

$$r = \text{number of rows in the table}$$
$$c = \text{number of columns in the table}$$

For our $2 \times 2$ contingency table, there is 1 degree of freedom; that is,

$$\text{Degrees of freedom} = (2 - 1)(2 - 1) = 1$$

Using a level of significance $\alpha$, the null hypothesis is rejected in favor of the alternative if the computed $\chi^2$-test statistic exceeds $\chi_1^2$, the upper-tailed critical value from the **chi-square distribution** with 1 degree of freedom. The decision rule is to reject $H_0$ if

$$\chi^2 > \chi_1^2;$$

otherwise do not reject $H_0$.

This is illustrated in Figure 14.1 on page 650.

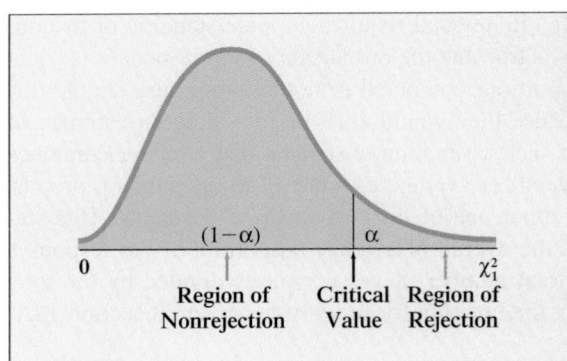

Referring to equation (14.2), if the null hypothesis is true, the computed $\chi^2$-test statistic will be close to 0 because the squared difference between what we actually observe in each cell $f_0$ and what we theoretically expect $f_e$ would be very small. If $H_0$ is false and there are significant differences in the population proportions, we should expect the computed $\chi^2$-test statistic to be large because the discrepancy between what we actually observe in each cell and what we theoretically expect will be magnified when we square the differences. However, what constitutes a large difference in a cell is relative. The same actual difference between $f_0$ and $f_e$ would contribute more to the $\chi^2$-test statistic from a cell in which only a few observations are expected ($f_e$) than from a cell where many observations are expected. This is why a standardizing adjustment is made for the size of the cell—the squared difference between $f_0$ and $f_e$ is divided by the expected frequency $f_e$ in the cell. The $\chi^2$-test statistic given in equation (14.2) is then obtained by summing each standardized value $(f_0 - f_e)^2/f_e$ over all the cells of the contingency table.

To illustrate the use of the $\chi^2$ test for the equality of two proportions, we again turn our attention to the guest satisfaction survey discussed in Example 14.1 on page 644, the results of which are displayed in Table 14.2 on page 648.

The null hypothesis ($H_0$: $p_1 = p_2$) states that when comparing the two hotels, there is no difference in the proportion of guests who are likely to choose the hotel again. From equation (14.3) on page 649, we use $\bar{p}$ to estimate the common parameter $p$, the true proportion of guests who are likely to choose either of these hotels again if the null hypothesis is true. The overall or average proportion is computed as

$$\bar{p} = \frac{X_1 + X_2}{n_1 + n_2} = \frac{X}{n}$$

$$= \frac{(163 + 154)}{(227 + 262)} = \frac{317}{489}$$

$$= .6483$$

The estimated proportion who are not likely to choose these hotels again is the complement $(1 - \bar{p})$, or .3517. Multiplying these two proportions by the sample size for the Beachcomber gives the number of guests expected to say they are likely to choose the Beachcomber again and the number not expected to choose this hotel again. In a similar manner, multiplying the two respective proportions by the Windsurfer's sample size yields the corresponding expected frequencies for that group.

## Example 14.2 *Computing the Expected Frequencies*

Compute the expected frequencies for each of the four cells of this contingency table.

### SOLUTION

Yes — Beachcomber: $\bar{p} = .6483$ and $n_1 = 227$, so $f_e = 147.16$

Yes — Windsurfer: $\bar{p} = .6483$ and $n_2 = 262$, so $f_e = 169.84$

No — Beachcomber: $1 - \bar{p} = .3517$ and $n_1 = 227$, so $f_e = 79.84$

No — Windsurfer: $1 - \bar{p} = .3517$ and $n_2 = 262$, so $f_e = 92.16$

All these expected frequencies are presented in Table 14.3, next to the corresponding observed frequencies taken from Table 14.2.

**Table 14.3** *2 × 2 contingency table for comparing observed ($f_0$) and expected ($f_e$) guest satisfaction data*

| | HOTEL | | | | |
| | BEACHCOMBER | | WINDSURFER | | |
| CHOOSE HOTEL AGAIN | OBSERVED | EXPECTED | OBSERVED | EXPECTED | TOTAL |
|---|---|---|---|---|---|
| Yes | 163 | 147.16 | 154 | 169.84 | 317 |
| No | 64 | 79.84 | 108 | 92.16 | 172 |
| Total | 227 | 227.00 | 262 | 262.00 | 489 |

To test the null hypothesis of homogeneity of proportions

$$H_0: p_1 = p_2$$

against the alternative that the true population proportions are not equal

$$H_1: p_1 \neq p_2$$

we use the actual and expected data from Table 14.3 to compute the $\chi^2$-test statistic given by equation (14.2). The calculations are presented in Table 14.4.

**Table 14.4** *Computation of $\chi^2$-test statistic for satisfaction survey*

| $f_0$ | $f_e$ | $(f_0 - f_e)$ | $(f_0 - f_e)^2$ | $(f_0 - f_e)^2/f_e$ |
|---|---|---|---|---|
| 163 | 147.16 | 15.84 | 250.9056 | 1.705 |
| 154 | 169.84 | −15.84 | 250.9056 | 1.477 |
| 64 | 79.84 | −15.84 | 250.9056 | 3.143 |
| 108 | 92.16 | 15.84 | 250.9056 | 2.723 |
| | | | | 9.048 |

**Table 14.5** *Obtaining the $\chi^2$ critical value from the chi-square distribution with 1 degree of freedom using a .05 level of significance*

| DEGREES OF FREEDOM | UPPER-TAIL AREA | | | | | | |
|---|---|---|---|---|---|---|---|
| | .995 | .99 | ... | .05 | .025 | .01 | .005 |
| 1 | — | — | ... → | 3.841 | 5.024 | 6.635 | 7.879 |
| 2 | 0.010 | 0.020 | ... | 5.991 | 7.378 | 9.210 | 10.597 |
| 3 | 0.072 | 0.115 | ... | 7.815 | 9.348 | 11.345 | 12.838 |
| 4 | 0.207 | 0.297 | ... | 9.488 | 11.143 | 13.277 | 14.860 |
| 5 | 0.412 | 0.554 | ... | 11.071 | 12.833 | 15.086 | 16.750 |

*Source: Extracted from Table E.4.*

If a .05 level of significance is chosen, the critical value of the $\chi^2$-test statistic could be obtained from Table E.4, a replica of which is presented as Table 14.5. The chi-square distribution is a skewed distribution whose shape depends solely on the number of degrees of freedom. As the number of degrees of freedom increases, the chi-square distribution becomes more symmetrical.

The values in the body of Table 14.5 refer to selected upper-tailed areas of the chi-square distribution. Because a $\chi^2$-test statistic for a 2 × 2 table has 1 degree of freedom and we are testing at the $\alpha = .05$ level of significance, the critical value of the $\chi^2$-test statistic is 3.841 (see Figure 14.2). Because our computed $\chi^2$-test statistic of 9.048 exceeds this critical value, the null hypothesis is rejected.

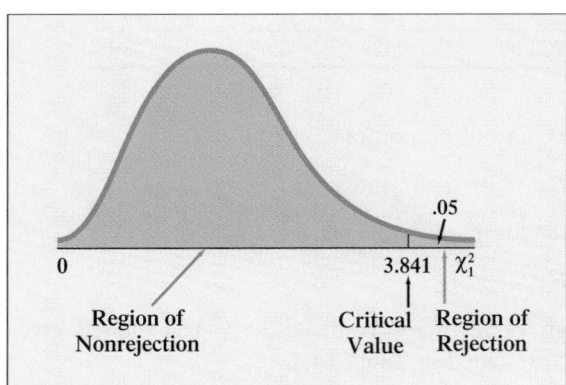

**FIGURE 14.2**
Finding $\chi^2$ critical value with 1 degree of freedom at .05 level of significance

Figure 14.3 represents output obtained using Prentice Hall's Stat Add-In for Microsoft Excel for the data of the 2 × 2 contingency table describing guest satisfaction (see Table 14.2 on page 648). From Figure 14.3 we observe that the expected frequencies, $\chi^2$-test statistic, degrees of freedom, and *p*-value have been calculated. For these data the $\chi^2$-test statistic is 9.052, which is greater than the critical value of 3.841 (or the *p*-value = .0026 < .05), so that the null hypothesis of no difference in guest satisfaction between the two hotels is rejected. There is evidence to conclude that the two hotels are significantly different with respect to guest satisfaction as measured by whether the guest is likely to return to the hotel again. An examination of Table 14.2 on page 648 indicates that a greater proportion of guests at the Beachcomber were likely to return than at the Windsurfer.

| | A | B | C | D |
|---|---|---|---|---|
| 1 | Chi-Square Test | | | |
| 2 | | | | |
| 3 | Observed | | | |
| 4 | | Hotel | | |
| 5 | Likely to Return | Beachcomber | Windsurfer | Total |
| 6 | Yes | 163 | 154 | 317 |
| 7 | No | 64 | 108 | 172 |
| 8 | Total | 227 | 262 | 489 |
| 9 | | | | |
| 10 | Expected | | | |
| 11 | | Hotel | | |
| 12 | Likely to Return | Beachcomber | Windsurfer | Total |
| 13 | Yes | 147.1554192 | 169.8445808 | 317 |
| 14 | No | 79.84458078 | 92.15541922 | 172 |
| 15 | Total | 227 | 262 | 489 |
| 16 | | | | |
| 17 | p-value | 0.002623218 | | |
| 18 | Number of Rows (R) | 2 | | |
| 19 | Number of Columns (C) | 2 | | |
| 20 | Degrees of Freedom | 1 | | |
| 21 | $\alpha$ | 0.05 | | |
| 22 | Critical Value | 3.841455338 | | |
| 23 | Chi-Square Statistic | 9.052406759 | | |
| 24 | Decision | Reject | | |

**FIGURE 14.3** Output from Prentice Hall's PHStat Add-In for Microsoft Excel for hotel guest satisfaction survey data of Table 14.2

## COMMENT: *Checking the Assumptions*

For the $\chi^2$ test to give accurate results for a 2 × 2 table, it is assumed that each expected frequency is at least 5. If this assumption is not satisfied, other procedures, such as *Fisher's exact test* (see reference 1, 2, and 5), can be used.

## Testing for the Equality of Two Proportions by $Z$ and by $\chi^2$: A Comparison of Results

We have seen in our satisfaction survey that both the $Z$ test based on the standard normal distribution and the $\chi^2$ test based on the chi-square distribution with 1 degree of freedom have led to the same conclusion. This can be explained by the interrelationship between the standard normal distribution and a chi-square distribution with 1 degree of freedom. For such situations, the $\chi^2$-test statistic will always be the square of the $Z$-test statistic. For instance, in our study the computed $Z$-test statistic is $+3.01$ and the computed $\chi^2$-test statistic is 9.05. Except for rounding error, we note that this latter value is the square of $+3.01$ [that is, $(+3.01)^2 = 9.05$]. Also, if we compare the critical values of the test statistics from the two distributions, we note that, at the .05 level of significance, the $\chi^2$ value of 3.841 is the square of the $Z$ values of $\pm 1.96$ (that is, $\chi^2 = Z^2$).

From this discussion we conclude that when testing the null hypothesis of homogeneity of proportions

$$H_0: p_1 = p_2$$

against the alternative that the true population proportions are not equal

$$H_1: p_1 \neq p_2$$

the $Z$ test and the $\chi^2$ test are equivalent methods. However, if we are specifically interested in determining whether there is evidence of a directional difference, such as $p_1 > p_2$, then the $Z$ test *must* be used with the entire rejection region located in one tail of the standard normal distribution. However, as we shall see in the next section, if we wish to make comparisons and evaluate differences in the proportions among $c$ groups or levels of some factor, we will be able to extend the $\chi^2$ test for such purposes. The $Z$ test, however, cannot be used if there are more than two groups.

## Problems for Section 14.2

### Learning the Basics

• **14.8** Given the following contingency table

|       | A  | B  | TOTAL |
|-------|----|----|-------|
| 1     | 20 | 30 | 50    |
| 2     | 30 | 45 | 75    |
| Total | 50 | 75 | 125   |

(a) Compute the expected frequencies for each cell.
(b) Compare the observed and expected frequencies for each cell.
(c) What will be the value for the $\chi^2$ statistic?

**14.9** Given the following contingency table

|       | A  | B  | TOTAL |
|-------|----|----|-------|
| 1     | 20 | 30 | 50    |
| 2     | 30 | 20 | 50    |
| Total | 50 | 50 | 100   |

(a) Compute the expected frequencies for each cell.
(b) Compute the $\chi^2$ statistic for this contingency table. Is it significant at $\alpha = .05$?

### Applying the Concepts

• **14.10** A sample of 500 respondents was selected in a large metropolitan area to determine various information concerning consumer behavior. Among the questions asked was "Do you enjoy shopping for clothing?" The results are summarized in the following contingency table.

| ENJOY SHOPPING FOR CLOTHING | GENDER | | |
| --- | --- | --- | --- |
| | MALE | FEMALE | TOTAL |
| Yes | 136 | 224 | 360 |
| No | 104 | 36 | 140 |
| Total | 240 | 260 | 500 |

(a) Is there evidence of a significant difference between males and females in the proportion who enjoy shopping for clothing at the .01 level of significance?

(b) Find the *p*-value in (a) and interpret its meaning.

(c) What would be your answer to (a) and (b) if 206 males enjoyed shopping for clothing?

• **14.11** A human resources director decided to investigate employee perception of the fairness of two performance evaluation methods. To test for the differences between the two methods, 160 employees were randomly assigned to be evaluated by one of the methods: 78 were assigned to method 1, where individuals provide feedback to supervisory queries as part of the evaluation process; 82 were assigned to method 2, where individuals provide self-assessments of their work performance. Following the evaluations, employees were asked whether they considered the performance evaluation fair or unfair. The results are summarized in the following contingency table.

| EMPLOYEE PERCEPTION | EVALUATION METHOD | | |
| --- | --- | --- | --- |
| | 1 | 2 | TOTAL |
| Fair | 63 | 49 | 112 |
| Unfair | 15 | 33 | 48 |
| Total | 78 | 82 | 160 |

(a) Using a .05 level of significance, is there evidence of a significant difference between the two methods in the proportion of fair ratings?

(b) Find the *p*-value in (a) and interpret its meaning.

• **14.12** A professor of accountancy was studying the readability of the annual reports of two major companies. A random sample of 100 certified public accountants was selected. Fifty were randomly assigned to read the annual report of company A, and the other fifty were to read the annual report of company B. The results are summarized in the following contingency table.

| UNDERSTANDABLE | COMPANY | | |
| --- | --- | --- | --- |
| | A | B | TOTAL |
| Yes | 17 | 23 | 40 |
| No | 33 | 27 | 60 |
| Total | 50 | 50 | 100 |

(a) At the .10 level of significance, is there evidence of a significant difference between the two companies in the proportion of CPAs who find the annual reports understandable?

(b) Find the *p*-value in (a) and interpret its meaning.

(c) What would be your answers to (a) and (b) if 33 found company B's annual report "understandable"?

**14.13** The manager of a campus bookstore conducts a survey to investigate whether there are any differences between males and females with respect to the consideration of the purchase of educational videotapes. Depending on the answer, her goal is to develop pertinent promotional material that will lead to increased sales in educational videotapes over the coming semester. The results are summarized in the following contingency table.

|  | GENDER | | |
| CONSIDER PURCHASING EDUCATIONAL VIDEOTAPES | MALE | FEMALE | TOTAL |
| --- | --- | --- | --- |
| Yes | 13 | 15 | 28 |
| No | 27 | 15 | 42 |
| Total | 40 | 30 | 70 |

(a) At the .01 level of significance, is there evidence of a significant difference in the proportion of males and females who would consider purchasing educational videotapes?
(b) Find the *p*-value in (a) and interpret its meaning.
(c) Given the results in (a) and (b), what should the bookstore manager do with respect to a future promotional campaign? Discuss your recommendations.
(d) What would be your answers to (a)–(c) if 25 females said they would consider purchasing educational videotapes?

**14.14** In an effort to compare the efficacy of two medical approaches to removing plaque that clogs arteries, Dr. Eric J. Topol and colleagues conducted a study in which they randomly assigned 1,012 heart patients to have either directional coronary atherectomy or balloon angioplasty. [See E. Topol et al., "A Comparison of Directional Atherectomy with Coronary Angioplasty in Patients with Coronary Artery Disease," *The New England Journal of Medicine* 329 (July 22, 1993): 221–227.] Of the 512 patients given the atherectomy, 44 died or suffered heart attacks within 6 months of treatment. Of the 500 patients given angioplasty, 23 died or suffered heart attacks within 6 months of treatment.
(a) At the .01 level of significance, is there evidence of a significant difference in the two medical approaches with respect to the proportion of deaths or heart attacks within 6 months of treatment?
(b) Find the *p*-value in (a) and interpret its meaning.
(c) Given the results in (a) and (b), what should the physicians conclude with respect to the two approaches?
(d) How should a congressional policymaker react to the results in (a) and (b)?
(e) How should a hospital CEO react to the results in (a) and (b) if the medical facility is given a fixed sum of money per treatment?
(f) How should an insurance company CEO react to the results in (a) and (b) if the company has to pay for each treatment?
(g) What would be your answers in (a) and (b) if 34 of the 512 patients given the atherectomy died or suffered heart attacks?

# 14.3 $\chi^2$ TEST FOR DIFFERENCES IN *c* PROPORTIONS (INDEPENDENT SAMPLES)

The $\chi^2$ test can be extended to the general case in which there are *c* independent populations to be compared. Thus, if there is interest in evaluating differences in the proportions among *c* groups or levels of some factor, the $\chi^2$ test can be used for such purposes. The contingency table would have two rows and $c$ columns. To test the null hypothesis of no differences in the proportions among the $c$ populations

$$H_0: p_1 = p_2 = \cdots = p_c$$

against the alternative that not all the $c$ population proportions are equal

$$H_1: \text{Not all } p_j \text{ are equal (where } j = 1, 2, \ldots, c).$$

we use equation (14.2) and compute the test statistic

$$\chi^2 = \sum_{\text{all cells}} \frac{(f_0 - f_e)^2}{f_e}$$

where

$f_0$ = observed frequency in a particular cell of a $2 \times c$ contingency table

$f_e$ = theoretical or expected frequency in a particular cell if the null hypothesis is true

To compute the expected frequency $f_e$ in any cell, we must realize that if the null hypothesis were true and the proportions were equal across all $c$ populations, then the $c$ sample proportions should differ only by chance. This is because each proportion would be providing an estimate of the common population proportion $p$. In such a situation, a statistic that would pool or combine these $c$ separate estimates into one overall or average estimate of the population proportion $p$ would provide more information than any one of the $c$ separate estimates alone. To expand on equation (14.3) on page 649, the statistic $\bar{p}$ represents the overall or average proportion over all $c$ groups combined:

$$\bar{p} = \frac{X_1 + X_2 + \cdots + X_c}{n_1 + n_2 + \cdots + n_c} = \frac{X}{n} \qquad (14.4)$$

To obtain the expected frequency $f_e$ for each cell in the first row in the contingency table, we multiply each sample size (or column total) by $\bar{p}$. To obtain the expected frequency $f_e$ for each cell in the second row in the contingency table, we multiply each sample size (or column total) by $(1 - \bar{p})$. The test statistic shown in equation (14.2) approximately follows a chi-square distribution with degrees of freedom equal to the number of rows in the contingency table minus 1 times the number of columns in the table minus 1. For a **2 $\times$ c contingency table**, there are $c - 1$ degrees of freedom:

$$\text{Degrees of freedom} = (2 - 1)(c - 1) = c - 1$$

Using a level of significance $\alpha$, the null hypothesis is rejected in favor of the alternative if the computed $\chi^2$-test statistic exceeds $\chi_U^2$, the upper-tailed critical value from a chi-square distribution having $c - 1$ degrees of freedom. That is, the decision rule is

Reject $H_0$ if $\chi^2 > \chi_U^2$;

otherwise do not reject $H_0$.

This is depicted in Figure 14.4 on page 658.

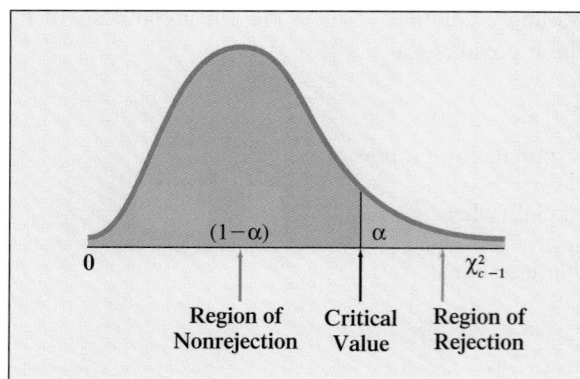

FIGURE 14.4
Testing for differences among $c$ proportions using $\chi^2$ test

---

## COMMENT: *Checking the Assumptions*

For the $\chi^2$ test to give accurate results when dealing with $2 \times c$ contingency tables, all expected frequencies must be large. For such situations there has been much debate among statisticians as to the definition of "large." Some statistical researchers (see reference 3) have found that the test gives accurate results as long as all expected frequencies equal or exceed 0.5. Other statisticians, more conservative in their approach, require that no more than 20% of the cells contain expected frequencies less than 5 and no cells have expected frequencies less than 1 (see reference 2). We suggest that a reasonable compromise between these points of view is to make sure that all expected frequencies are at least 1. To accomplish this, it may be necessary to collapse two or more low-expected frequency categories into one category in the contingency table prior to performing the test. Such merging of categories usually results in expected frequencies sufficiently large to conduct the $\chi^2$ test accurately. If the combining or pooling of categories is undesirable, alternative procedures are available (see references 1 and 5).

---

To illustrate the $\chi^2$ test for equality or homogeneity of proportions when there are more than two groups, we shall return to the guest satisfaction survey example discussed in sections 14.1 and 14.2 and consider a similar survey that was recently conducted in a different resort island area in which the hotel chain has three different properties. Table 14.6 presents the responses to the question of whether the guest would be likely to choose the hotel again for each of these three properties.

Under the null hypothesis of no differences among the three hotels with respect to the proportion of guests who would be willing to return again, we use equation (14.4) to cal-

---

**Table 14.6** *2 × 3 contingency table for the guest satisfaction survey*

| CHOOSE THIS HOTEL AGAIN? | HOTEL | | | TOTAL |
| --- | --- | --- | --- | --- |
| | GOLDEN PALM | PALM ROYALE | PALM PRINCESS | |
| Yes | 128 | 199 | 186 | 513 |
| No | 88 | 33 | 66 | 187 |
| Total | 216 | 232 | 252 | 700 |

culate an estimate of $p$, the population proportion of guests who would be willing to return again. The overall or average proportion $(\bar{p})$ of satisfied guests is computed as

$$\bar{p} = \frac{X_1 + X_2 + \cdots + X_c}{n_1 + n_2 + \cdots + n_c} = \frac{X}{n}$$

$$= \frac{(128 + 199 + 186)}{(216 + 232 + 252)} = \frac{513}{700}$$

$$= .733$$

The estimated proportion of guests who would not be likely to return again in the population is the complement $(1 - \bar{p})$, or .267. Multiplying these two proportions by the sample size taken at each hotel results in the expected numbers of guests who would and would not be likely to return again.

## Example 14.3  *Computing the Expected Frequencies*

Compute the expected frequencies for each of the six cells of this contingency table.

### SOLUTION

Yes—Golden Palm: $\bar{p} = .733$ and $n_1 = 216$, so $f_e = 158.33$

Yes—Palm Royale: $\bar{p} = .733$ and $n_2 = 232$, so $f_e = 170.06$

Yes—Palm Princess: $\bar{p} = .733$ and $n_3 = 252$, so $f_e = 184.72$

No—Golden Palm: $1 - \bar{p} = .267$ and $n_1 = 216$, so $f_e = 57.67$

No—Palm Royale: $1 - \bar{p} = .267$ and $n_2 = 232$, so $f_e = 61.94$

No—Palm Princess: $1 - \bar{p} = .267$ and $n_3 = 252$, so $f_e = 67.28$

These expected frequencies are presented in Table 14.7.

## Table 14.7  *Cross-classification of expected frequencies from the guest satisfaction survey of three hotels*

| CHOOSE THIS HOTEL AGAIN? | HOTEL GOLDEN PALM | HOTEL PALM ROYALE | HOTEL PALM PRINCESS | TOTAL |
|---|---|---|---|---|
| Yes | 158.33 | 170.06 | 184.72 | 513 |
| No | 57.67 | 61.94 | 67.28 | 187 |
| Total | 216.00 | 232.00 | 252.00 | 700 |

To test the null hypothesis of homogeneity or equality of proportions

$$H_0: p_1 = p_2 = p_3$$

against the alternative that not all the three proportions are equal

$$H_1: \text{Not all } p_j \text{ are equal (where } j = 1, 2, 3)$$

we use the observed and expected data from Tables 14.6 and 14.7 to compute the $\chi^2$-test statistic given by equation (14.2). The calculations are presented in Table 14.8 on page 660.

**Table 14.8**  *Computation of the $\chi^2$-test statistic for the three hotel properties*

| $f_0$ | $f_e$ | $(f_0 - f_e)$ | $(f_0 - f_e)^2$ | $(f_0 - f_e)^2/f_e$ |
|-------|-------|---------------|-----------------|---------------------|
| 128 | 158.33 | $-30.33$ | 919.9089 | 5.810 |
| 199 | 170.06 | 28.94 | 837.5236 | 4.925 |
| 186 | 184.72 | 1.28 | 1.6384 | 0.009 |
| 88 | 57.67 | 30.33 | 919.9089 | 15.951 |
| 33 | 61.94 | $-28.94$ | 837.5236 | 13.522 |
| 66 | 67.28 | $-1.28$ | 1.6384 | 0.024 |
| | | | | 40.241 |

If a .05 level of significance is chosen, the critical value of the $\chi^2$-test statistic could be obtained from Table E.4. In our guest satisfaction survey, because three hotel properties are being evaluated, there are $(2 - 1)(3 - 1) = 2$ degrees of freedom. The $\chi^2$ critical value with 2 degrees of freedom at the $\alpha = .05$ level of significance is 5.991. Because our computed test statistic $\chi^2 = 40.241$ exceeds this critical value, the null hypothesis is rejected (see Figure 14.5). Using Minitab (see Figure 14.6), we obtain a $p$-value of .000, which is less than $\alpha = .05$, so the null hypothesis is rejected. There is sufficient evidence to conclude that the hotel properties are different with respect to the proportion of guests who are likely to return again.

Rejecting the null hypothesis in a $\chi^2$ test of equality of proportions in a $2 \times c$ table only allows us to conclude that not all the hotel properties are equal with respect to the proportion of satisfied guests. Interest would then focus on which hotels are different from the others with respect to guest satisfaction. Because the result of the $\chi^2$ test for homogeneity of proportions does not specifically answer these questions, other approaches are needed. One such confirmatory approach that may be used following rejection of the null hypothesis of equal proportions is the **Marascuilo procedure** (see references 1, 4, and 5).

The Marascuilo procedure enables us to make comparisons between all pairs of groups. The first step involved is to compute the differences $p_{s_j} - p_{s_{j'}}$ (where $j \neq j'$) among all $c(c - 1)/2$ pairs of proportions. The corresponding critical ranges for the Marascuilo procedure are then obtained in equation (14.5):

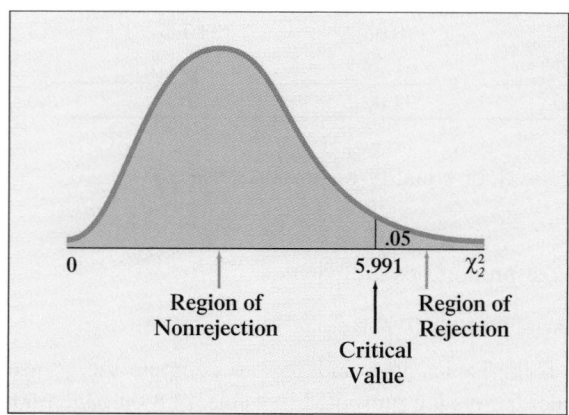

**FIGURE 14.5**
Testing for equality of three proportions at .05 level of significance with 2 degrees of freedom

## Chi-Square Test

```
Expected counts are printed below observed counts

         Golden  Royale Princess    Total
     1      128     199     186       513
          158.30  170.02  184.68

     2       88      33      66       187
           57.70   61.98   67.32

Total       216     232     252       700

Chi-Sq =   5.799 +   4.939 +   0.009 +
          15.908 +  13.548 +   0.026 = 40.228
DF = 2,  P-Value = 0.000
```

## Critical Range for the Marascuilo Procedure

$$\text{Critical range} = \sqrt{\chi_U^2}\sqrt{\frac{p_{s_j}(1 - p_{s_j})}{n_j} + \frac{p_{s_{j'}}(1 - p_{s_{j'}})}{n_{j'}}} \qquad (14.5)$$

where, for an overall level of significance, $\sqrt{\chi_U^2}$ is the square root of the upper-tailed critical value from a chi-square distribution having $c - 1$ degrees of freedom. A distinct critical range must be obtained for each pairwise comparison of sample proportions. The final step is to compare each of the $c(c - 1)/2$ pairs of proportions against its corresponding critical range. A specific pair would be declared significantly different if the absolute difference in the sample proportions $|p_{s_j} - p_{s_{j'}}|$ exceeds its critical range.

To apply the Marascuilo procedure, we return to the guest satisfaction survey. Using the $\chi^2$ test, we concluded that there was evidence of a significant difference among the population proportions. Because there are three hotels, there are $(3)(3 - 1)/2 = 3$ possible pairwise comparisons to be made and three critical ranges to compute. From Table 14.6 on page 658 the three sample proportions are:

$$p_{s_1} = \frac{X_1}{n_1} = \frac{128}{216} = .593$$

$$p_{s_2} = \frac{X_2}{n_2} = \frac{199}{232} = .858$$

$$p_{s_3} = \frac{X_3}{n_3} = \frac{186}{252} = .738$$

For an overall level of significance of .05, the upper-tailed critical value of the $\chi^2$-test statistic for a chi-square distribution having $(c - 1)$ or 2 degrees of freedom is obtained from Table E.4 as 5.991. Thus,

$$\sqrt{\chi_U^2} = \sqrt{5.991} = 2.448$$

From this we obtain the three pairs of absolute differences in proportions and their corresponding critical ranges:

| Absolute Difference in Proportions | Critical Range |
|---|---|

$$|p_{s_j} - p_{s_{j'}}|$$

$$2.448\sqrt{\frac{p_{s_j}(1-p_{s_j})}{n_j} + \frac{p_{s_{j'}}(1-p_{s_{j'}})}{n_{j'}}}$$

$$|p_{s_1} - p_{s_2}| = |.593 - .858| = .265$$

$$2.448\sqrt{\frac{(.593)(.407)}{216} + \frac{(.858)(.142)}{232}} = .099$$

$$|p_{s_1} - p_{s_3}| = |.593 - .738| = .145$$

$$2.448\sqrt{\frac{(.593)(.407)}{216} + \frac{(.738)(.262)}{252}} = .106$$

$$|p_{s_2} - p_{s_3}| = |.858 - .738| = .120$$

$$2.448\sqrt{\frac{(.858)(.142)}{232} + \frac{(.738)(.262)}{252}} = .088$$

From this we may conclude, using a .05 overall level of significance, that guest satisfaction is higher at the Palm Royale than at either the Golden Palm or the Palm Princess. Guest satisfaction is also higher at the Palm Princess than at the Golden Palm. These would clearly suggest that management should study the reasons for these differences and, in particular, should try to determine why satisfaction was significantly lower at the Golden Palm than at the other two hotels.

## Problems for Section 14.3

### Learning the Basics

**14.15** If there are two rows and five columns in a contingency table, find each of the following:
(a) The degrees of freedom
(b) The critical value for $\alpha = .05$
(c) The critical value for $\alpha = .01$

● **14.16** Given the following contingency table

|       | A  | B  | C   | TOTAL |
|-------|----|----|-----|-------|
| 1     | 10 | 30 | 50  | 90    |
| 2     | 40 | 45 | 50  | 135   |
| Total | 50 | 75 | 100 | 225   |

(a) Compute the expected frequencies for each cell.
(b) Compute the $\chi^2$ statistic for this contingency table. Is it significant at $\alpha = .05$?
(c) If appropriate, use $\alpha = .05$ and determine which groups (A, B, C) are different.

**14.17** Given the following contingency table

|       | A  | B  | C  | TOTAL |
|-------|----|----|----|-------|
| 1     | 20 | 30 | 25 | 75    |
| 2     | 30 | 20 | 25 | 75    |
| Total | 50 | 50 | 50 | 150   |

(a) Compute the expected frequencies for each cell.
(b) Compute the $\chi^2$ statistic for this contingency table. Is it significant at $\alpha = .05$?
(c) If appropriate, use $\alpha = .05$ and determine which groups (A, B, C) are different.

## Applying the Concepts

● **14.18** An employee survey was conducted by the human resources department at Leonel Industries. Responses to a questionnaire from 400 full-time employees yielded the following breakdown with respect to gender and occupational title:

| | | | | | OCCUPATIONAL TITLE | | | |
|---|---|---|---|---|---|---|---|---|
| GENDER | MGT. | PROF. | SALES | ADM. | SUPPORT SERVICE | PRODUCTION | LABORER | TOTAL |
| Male | 36 | 33 | 34 | 14 | 18 | 51 | 47 | 233 |
| Female | 29 | 33 | 23 | 51 | 11 | 3 | 17 | 167 |
| Total | 65 | 66 | 57 | 65 | 29 | 54 | 64 | 400 |

(a) At the .05 level of significance, is there evidence of a significant difference in occupational title between males and females?

(b) If appropriate, use the .05 level of significance and determine which titles have a significantly different proportion of males.

**14.19** Dr. Lawrence K. Altman reported the results of a clinical trial (*The New York Times*, May 1, 1993, 7) comparing the effectiveness of four drug regimens randomly assigned for treatment of patients following the onset of a heart attack. A total of 40,845 patients were studied. Each was given one of the four drug regimens. The outcome measure compared was the proportion of severe adverse events (i.e., death or disabling stroke) reported within 30 days of treatment. The data are presented here:

| | DRUG REGIMEN | | | | |
|---|---|---|---|---|---|
| RESULT | A | B | C | D | TOTAL |
| Severe | 714 | 785 | 754 | 820 | 3,073 |
| Not severe | 9,630 | 9,543 | 9,042 | 9,557 | 37,772 |
| Total | 10,344 | 10,328 | 9,796 | 10,377 | 40,845 |

*where*  A = *accelerated TPA with intravenous heparin*
B = *combined TPA and streptokinase, with intravenous heparin*
C = *streptokinase with subcutaneous heparin*
D = *streptokinase with intravenous heparin*

(a) At the $\alpha = .05$ level of significance, determine whether there is evidence of a significant difference among the four drug regimens with respect to the proportion of patients suffering severe adverse events (i.e., death or disabling stroke) within 30 days following treatment for heart attack.

(b) If appropriate, use the $\alpha = .05$ level of significance and determine which drug regimens are different.

(c) Discuss the impact that your findings may have on the community of health care administrators and policymakers if a dose of TPA costs $2,400 per patient and a dose of streptokinase costs $240 per patient.

**14.20** The quality control manager of an automobile parts factory would like to know whether there is a difference in the proportion of defective parts produced on different days of the work week. Random samples of 100 parts produced on each day of the week were selected with the following results given at the top of page 664:

| RESULT | MON. | TUES. | WED. | THURS. | FRI. |
|---|---|---|---|---|---|
| Number of defective parts | 12 | 7 | 7 | 10 | 14 |
| Number of acceptable parts | 88 | 93 | 93 | 90 | 86 |
| Total | 100 | 100 | 100 | 100 | 100 |

(a) At the .05 level of significance, is there evidence of a significant difference in the proportion of defective parts produced on the various days of the week?

(b) If appropriate, use the .05 level of significance and determine which days of the week are different in terms of the proportion of defective parts produced.

(c) What would be your answer to (a) and (b) if 24 of the 100 parts produced on Friday were defective?

**14.21** A fast-food chain wishes to determine whether there are any differences in three media (magazine, TV, radio) in terms of consumer recall of an ad. The results of an advertising study are as follows:

| | MEDIA | | | |
|---|---|---|---|---|
| RECALL ABILITY | MAGAZINE | TV | RADIO | TOTAL |
| Number of persons remembering ad | 25 | 10 | 7 | 42 |
| Number of persons not remembering ad | 73 | 93 | 108 | 274 |
| Total | 98 | 103 | 115 | 316 |

(a) At the .05 level of significance, determine whether there is evidence of a significant media effect with respect to the proportion of individuals who can recall the ad.

(b) If appropriate, use the .05 level of significance and determine which media are different in recall ability of the ad.

(c) What would be your answer to (a) and (b) if 17 of the 115 individuals who heard the radio ad could recall it?

• **14.22** The marketing director of a cable television company is interested in determining whether there is a difference in the proportion of households that adopt a cable television service based on the type of residence (single-family dwelling, two- to four-family dwelling, and apartment house). A random sample of 400 households revealed the following:

| | TYPE OF RESIDENCE | | | |
|---|---|---|---|---|
| PURCHASE CABLE TELEVISION? | SINGLE-FAMILY | TWO- TO FOUR-FAMILY | APARTMENT HOUSE | TOTAL |
| Yes | 94 | 39 | 77 | 210 |
| No | 56 | 36 | 98 | 190 |
| Total | 150 | 75 | 175 | 400 |

(a) At the .01 level of significance, is there evidence of a significant difference among the types of residence with respect to the proportion of households that adopt the cable TV service?

(b) If appropriate, use the .01 level of significance and determine which types of residence differ in the proportion of households that purchase cable television service.

## 14.4 ◆ $\chi^2$ Test of Independence

We have just seen how the $\chi^2$ test can be used to evaluate potential differences among the proportion of successes in any number of populations. For a contingency table that has $r$ rows and $c$ columns, the $\chi^2$ test can be generalized as a *test of independence*. In these situations, we can extend our earlier discussions on the rules of probability in section 5.2 by presenting a confirmatory analysis based on a hypothesis of independence in the joint responses to two categorical variables.

As a test of independence, the null and alternative hypotheses are

$H_0$: The two categorical variables are independent (i.e., there is no relationship between them).

$H_1$: The two categorical variables are dependent (i.e., there is a relationship between them).

And we once more use equation (14.2) to compute the test statistic

$$\chi^2 = \sum_{\text{all cells}} \frac{(f_0 - f_e)^2}{f_e}$$

The decision rule is to reject the null hypothesis at an $\alpha$ level of significance if the computed value of the $\chi^2$ test statistic exceeds $\chi^2_U$ the upper-tailed critical value from a chi-square distribution with $(r - 1)(c - 1)$ degrees of freedom (see Table E.4). That is, as depicted in Figure 14.7,

$$\text{Reject } H_0 \text{ if } \chi^2 > \chi^2_U;$$

otherwise do not reject $H_0$.

Many researchers consider the **$\chi^2$ test for independence** as an alternative approach to viewing the $\chi^2$ test for equality of proportions. The test statistics are the same and the decision rules are the same, but the stated hypotheses and the conclusion to be drawn are different. Thus, in the satisfaction survey of section 14.3, we concluded that there is evidence of a significant difference in the two hotels with respect to the proportion of guests who would be likely to return. From a different viewpoint, we could conclude that there is a significant relationship between the hotels and the likelihood the guest would return. Nevertheless, there is a fundamental and conceptual distinction between the two types of tests. The major difference is in the sampling scheme used.

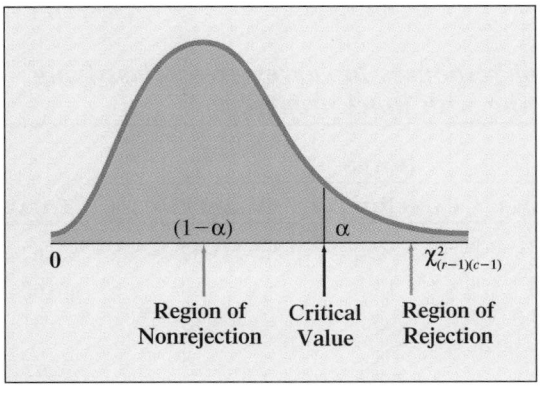

**FIGURE 14.7**

Testing for independence in $r \times c$ contingency table using the $\chi^2$ test

In a test for equality of proportions, we have one factor of interest with two or more levels. These levels represent samples drawn from independent populations. The categorical responses in each sample group or level are usually classified into two categories—*success* and *failure*. The objective is to make comparisons and evaluate differences in the proportions of success among the various levels.

However, in a test for independence, we have two factors of interest, each with two or more levels. One sample is drawn, and the joint responses to the two categorical variables are tallied into the cells of the contingency table that represent particular levels of each variable.

To illustrate the $\chi^2$ test for independence, suppose that in the survey on hotel guest satisfaction discussed in section 14.3, a second question was asked of all respondents who indicated they were not likely to return. These guests were asked to indicate the primary reason for their response. The resulting $4 \times 3$ contingency table is presented in Table 14.9.

From the totals tallied in Table 14.9, we observe that with respect to the reasons for not planning to return to the hotel, 67 were primarily due to price, 60 were primarily due to location, 31 were primarily due to room accommodation, and 29 were primarily due to other reasons. As in Table 14.6, there were 88 guests in the Golden Palm, 33 guests in the Palm Royale, and 66 guests in the Palm Princess who were not planning to return to the hotel. The observed frequencies in the cells of the $4 \times 3$ contingency table represent the joint tallies of the sampled guests with respect to primary reason for not returning and hotel property.

The null and alternative hypotheses are

$H_0$: There is no relationship between primary reason for not returning and hotel property.

$H_1$: There is a relationship between primary reason for not returning and hotel property.

To test this null hypothesis of independence against the alternative that there is a relationship between the two categorical variables, we use equation (14.2) and compute the test statistic

$$\chi^2 = \sum_{\text{all cells}} \frac{(f_0 - f_e)^2}{f_e}$$

where

$f_0$ = observed frequency or actual tally in a particular cell of the $r \times c$ contingency table

$f_e$ = theoretical frequency we would expect to find in a particular cell if the null hypothesis of independence were true

**Table 14.9** *Observed frequency of responses to survey cross-classifying reason for not returning with hotel property*

| REASON FOR NOT RETURNING | HOTEL | | | TOTAL |
|---|---|---|---|---|
| | GOLDEN PALM | PALM ROYALE | PALM PRINCESS | |
| Price | 23 | 7 | 37 | 67 |
| Location | 39 | 13 | 8 | 60 |
| Room accommodation | 13 | 5 | 13 | 31 |
| Other | 13 | 8 | 8 | 29 |
| Total | 88 | 33 | 66 | 187 |

To compute the expected frequency $f_e$ in any cell, we use the probability rules developed in chapter 5. This means that if the null hypothesis of independence is true, then we can use the multiplication rule for independent events we discussed on page 210 [see equation (5.8)] to determine the joint probability or proportion of responses expected for any cell combination. For example, under the null hypothesis of independence, the probability or proportion of responses expected in the upper-left-corner cell representing primary reason of price for the Golden Palm would be the product of the two separate probabilities

$$P(\text{price } and \text{ Golden Palm}) = P(\text{price}) \times P(\text{Golden Palm})$$

Here, the proportion of reasons due to price, $P(\text{price})$, is 67/187, or .3583, while the proportion of all responses from the Golden Palm, $P(\text{Golden Palm})$, is 88/187, or .4706. If the null hypothesis were true and the primary reason for not returning and hotel property were independent, the expected proportion or probability $P(\text{price } and \text{ Golden Palm})$ would equal the product of the separate probabilities, .3583 $\times$ .4706, or .1686. The expected frequency $f_e$ for that particular cell combination would then be the product of the overall survey sample size $n$ and this probability, 187 $\times$ .1686, or 31.53. The $f_e$ values for the remainder of the 4 $\times$ 3 contingency table would be obtained in a similar manner (see Table 14.10).

An easier way to compute **expected frequencies**, which does not require calculation of probabilities, is

## Computing the Expected Frequencies

The expected frequency in a cell is the product of its row total and column total divided by the overall sample size.

$$f_e = \frac{\text{row total} \times \text{column total}}{n} \tag{14.6}$$

where

$$\text{row total} = \text{sum of all the frequencies in the row}$$
$$\text{column total} = \text{sum of all the frequencies in the column}$$
$$n = \text{overall sample size}$$

**Table 14.10** *Expected frequency of responses to survey cross-classifying reason for not returning with hotel property*

| | HOTEL | | | |
| REASON FOR NOT RETURNING | GOLDEN PALM | PALM ROYALE | PALM PRINCESS | TOTAL |
| --- | --- | --- | --- | --- |
| Price | 31.53 | 11.82 | 23.65 | 67 |
| Location | 28.24 | 10.59 | 21.18 | 60 |
| Room accommodation | 14.59 | 5.47 | 10.94 | 31 |
| Other | 13.65 | 5.12 | 10.24 | 29 |
| Total | 88.00 | 33.00 | 66.00 | 187 |

For example, using equation (14.6) for the upper-left-corner cell (price for Golden Palm), we have

$$f_e = \frac{\text{row sum} \times \text{column sum}}{n} = \frac{(67)(88)}{187} = 31.53$$

whereas for the lower-right corner cell (other reason for the Palm Princess), we have

$$f_e = \frac{\text{row sum} \times \text{column sum}}{n} = \frac{(29)(66)}{187} = 10.24$$

All other $f_e$ values could be obtained in a similar manner as shown in Table 14.10.

The test statistic shown in equation (14.2) approximately follows a chi-square distribution with degrees of freedom equal to the number of rows in the contingency table minus 1 times the number of columns in the table minus 1. For an $r \times c$ contingency table there are $(r - 1)(c - 1)$ degrees of freedom

$$\text{Degrees of freedom} = (r - 1)(c - 1)$$

The $\chi^2$-test statistic for these data would then be computed as indicated in Table 14.11.

Using a level of significance $\alpha = .05$, our computed test statistic $\chi^2 = 27.402$ exceeds 12.592, the upper-tailed critical value from the chi-square distribution (see Table E.4) with $(4 - 1)(3 - 1) = 6$ degrees of freedom, and the null hypothesis of independence is rejected (see Figure 14.8). Using Minitab (see Figure 14.9), we observe that the $p$-value $= .000 < .05$, so that the null hypothesis of no relationship between reason for not returning and hotel property is rejected. We conclude that there is evidence of a significant relationship between reason for not returning and the specific hotel property. Examination of the observed and expected frequencies (see Table 14.11) shows that price is underrepresented as a reason for the Golden Palm but is more a reason for the Palm Princess, whereas location is overrepresented as a reason for the Golden Palm but underrepresented as a reason for the Palm Princess.

**Table 14.11** *Computation of $\chi^2$-test statistic for reason–hotel property contingency table*

| $f_0$ | $f_e$ | $(f_0 - f_e)$ | $(f_0 - f_e)^2$ | $(f_0 - f_e)^2/f_e$ |
|---|---|---|---|---|
| 23 | 31.53 | −8.53 | 72.7609 | 2.308 |
| 7 | 11.82 | −4.82 | 23.2324 | 1.966 |
| 37 | 23.65 | 13.35 | 178.2225 | 7.536 |
| 39 | 28.24 | 10.76 | 115.7776 | 4.100 |
| 13 | 10.59 | 2.41 | 5.8081 | 0.548 |
| 8 | 21.18 | −13.18 | 173.7124 | 8.202 |
| 13 | 14.59 | −1.59 | 2.5281 | 0.173 |
| 5 | 5.47 | −0.47 | 0.2209 | 0.040 |
| 13 | 10.94 | 2.06 | 4.2436 | 0.388 |
| 13 | 13.65 | −0.65 | 0.4225 | 0.031 |
| 8 | 5.12 | 2.88 | 8.2944 | 1.620 |
| 8 | 10.24 | −2.24 | 5.0176 | 0.490 |
| | | | | 27.402 |

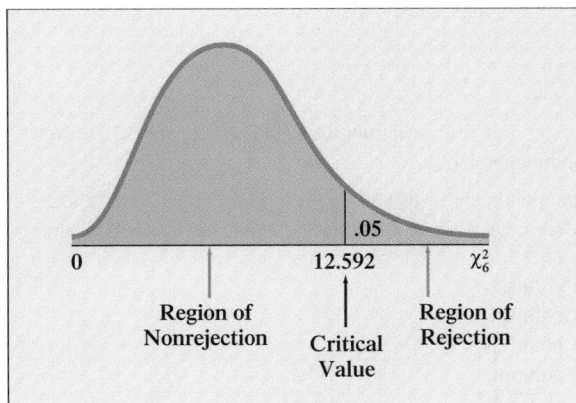

**FIGURE 14.8**
Testing for independence in hotel guest satisfaction survey example at .05 level of significance with 6 degrees of freedom

```
Expected counts are printed below observed counts

          GoldenPalm     Palm Royale  Palm Princess     Total
Price         23              7             37            67
            31.53          11.82          23.65

Location      39             13              8            60
            28.24          10.59          21.18

Room          13              5             13            31
            14.59           5.47          10.94

Other         13              8              8            29
            13.65           5.12          10.24

Total         88             33             66           187

Chi-Sq =   2.307 +   1.968 +   7.540 +
           4.104 +   0.549 +   8.199 +
           0.173 +   0.040 +   0.387 +
           0.031 +   1.623 +   0.488 = 27.410

DF = 6,  P-Value = 0.000
```

**FIGURE 14.9**  Minitab output for 4 $\times$ 3 contingency table for reason for not returning with hotel property

### COMMENT:  *Checking the Assumptions*

As in the case of the 2 $\times$ c contingency tables, to assure accurate results, use of the $\chi^2$ test when dealing with r $\times$ c contingency tables requires that all expected frequencies be "large." The same rules suggested for employing the $\chi^2$ test in the case of the 2 $\times$ c contingency tables on page 658 may be used. Again, we suggest that all expected frequencies are at least 1. For cases in which one or more expected frequencies are less than 1, the test may be performed after collapsing two or more low-frequency row categories or two or more low-frequency column categories into one category. Such merging of row or column categories will usually result in expected frequencies sufficiently large to conduct the $\chi^2$ test accurately.

# Problems for Section 14.4

## Learning the Basics

**14.23** If a contingency table has three rows and four columns, how many degrees of freedom would there be for the $\chi^2$ test for independence?

**• 14.24** When performing a $\chi^2$ test for independence in a contingency table with $r$ rows and $c$ columns, determine the upper-tailed critical value of the $\chi^2$-test statistic in each of the following circumstances:
(a) $\alpha = .05$, $r = 4$ rows, $c = 5$ columns
(b) $\alpha = .01$, $r = 4$ rows, $c = 5$ columns
(c) $\alpha = .01$, $r = 4$ rows, $c = 6$ columns
(d) $\alpha = .01$, $r = 3$ rows, $c = 6$ columns
(e) $\alpha = .01$, $r = 6$ rows, $c = 3$ columns

## Applying the Concepts

**14.25** A survey is taken in three different locations in Nassau County in New York to determine whether there is a relationship between architectural style of a house and geographic location. The results for a sample of 233 houses are as follows:

| | GEOGRAPHIC LOCATION | | | |
| STYLE | EAST MEADOW | FARMINGDALE | LEVITTOWN | TOTAL |
|---|---|---|---|---|
| Cape | 31 | 14 | 52 | 97 |
| Expanded ranch | 2 | 1 | 12 | 15 |
| Colonial | 6 | 8 | 9 | 23 |
| Ranch | 16 | 20 | 24 | 60 |
| Split-level | 19 | 17 | 2 | 38 |
| Total | 74 | 60 | 99 | 233 |

At the .05 level of significance, is there evidence of a relationship between architectural style and geographic location?

**14.26** A nationwide market research study is undertaken to determine the preferences of various age groups of males for different team sports. A random sample of 1,000 men is selected, and each individual is asked to indicate his favorite team sport. The results are as follows:

| | SPORT | | | | |
| AGE GROUP | BASEBALL | FOOTBALL | BASKETBALL | HOCKEY | TOTAL |
|---|---|---|---|---|---|
| Under 20 | 26 | 47 | 41 | 36 | 150 |
| 20–29 | 38 | 84 | 80 | 48 | 250 |
| 30–39 | 72 | 68 | 38 | 22 | 200 |
| 40–49 | 96 | 48 | 30 | 26 | 200 |
| 50 and over | 134 | 44 | 18 | 4 | 200 |
| Total | 366 | 291 | 207 | 136 | 1,000 |

(a) At the .01 level of significance, is there evidence of a significant relationship between men's ages and their preferences in sports?
(b) What would be your answer to (a) if 114 of the respondents aged 50 and over preferred baseball and 64 preferred football?

• **14.27** Suppose a survey is taken to determine whether there is a relationship between place of primary residence and automobile preference. A random sample of 500 car owners is selected with the following results:

| PRIMARY RESIDENCE | AUTOMOBILE PREFERENCE | | | | | TOTAL |
|---|---|---|---|---|---|---|
| | GM | FORD | CHRYSLER | EUROPEAN | ASIAN | |
| Large city | 64 | 40 | 26 | 8 | 62 | 200 |
| Suburb | 53 | 35 | 24 | 6 | 32 | 150 |
| Rural | 53 | 45 | 30 | 6 | 16 | 150 |
| Total | 170 | 120 | 80 | 20 | 110 | 500 |

(a) At the .05 level of significance, is there evidence of a significant relationship between place of residence and automobile preference?

(b) What would be your answer to (a) if 16 of the respondents from a large city preferred Chrysler and 18 preferred a European automobile?

**14.28** During the Vietnam War a lottery system was instituted to choose males to be drafted into the military. Numbers representing days of the year were "randomly" selected; men born on days of the year with low numbers were drafted first; those with high numbers were not drafted. The following shows how many low (1–122), medium (123–244), and high (245–366) numbers were drawn for birth dates in each quarter of the year:

| NUMBER SET | QUARTER OF YEAR | | | | TOTAL |
|---|---|---|---|---|---|
| | JAN.–MAR. | APR.–JUN. | JUL.–SEP. | OCT.–DEC. | |
| Low | 21 | 28 | 35 | 38 | 122 |
| Medium | 34 | 22 | 29 | 37 | 122 |
| High | 36 | 41 | 28 | 17 | 122 |
| Total | 91 | 91 | 92 | 92 | 366 |

(a) Is there evidence that the numbers drawn were significantly related to the time of year? (Use $\alpha = .05$.)

(b) Would you conclude that the lottery drawing appears to have been random?

(c) What would be your answers to (a) and (b) if the frequencies were

| | | | |
|---|---|---|---|
| 23 | 30 | 32 | 37 |
| 27 | 30 | 34 | 31 |
| 41 | 31 | 26 | 24 |

• **14.29** A large corporation is interested in determining whether an association exists between the commuting time of their employees and the level of stress-related problems observed on the job. A study of 116 assembly line workers reveals the following:

| | STRESS | | | |
|---|---|---|---|---|
| COMMUTING TIME | HIGH | MODERATE | LOW | TOTAL |
| Under 15 min | 9 | 5 | 18 | 32 |
| 15–45 min | 17 | 8 | 28 | 53 |
| Over 45 min | 18 | 6 | 7 | 31 |
| Total | 44 | 19 | 53 | 116 |

(a) At the .01 level of significance, is there evidence of a significant relationship between commuting time and stress?

(b) What would be your answer to (a) if the .05 level of significance were used?

## ◆ SUMMARY

As observed in the chapter summary chart, there are different approaches to categorical data analysis. We developed hypothesis-testing methodology separately for analyzing categorical response data obtained from two independent samples and $c$ independent samples. In addition, we extended our earlier discussions on the rules of probability in section 5.2 by presenting a more confirmatory analysis of the hypothesis of independence in the joint responses to two categorical variables. Once again, the assumptions and conditions behind the use of the various tests were emphasized.

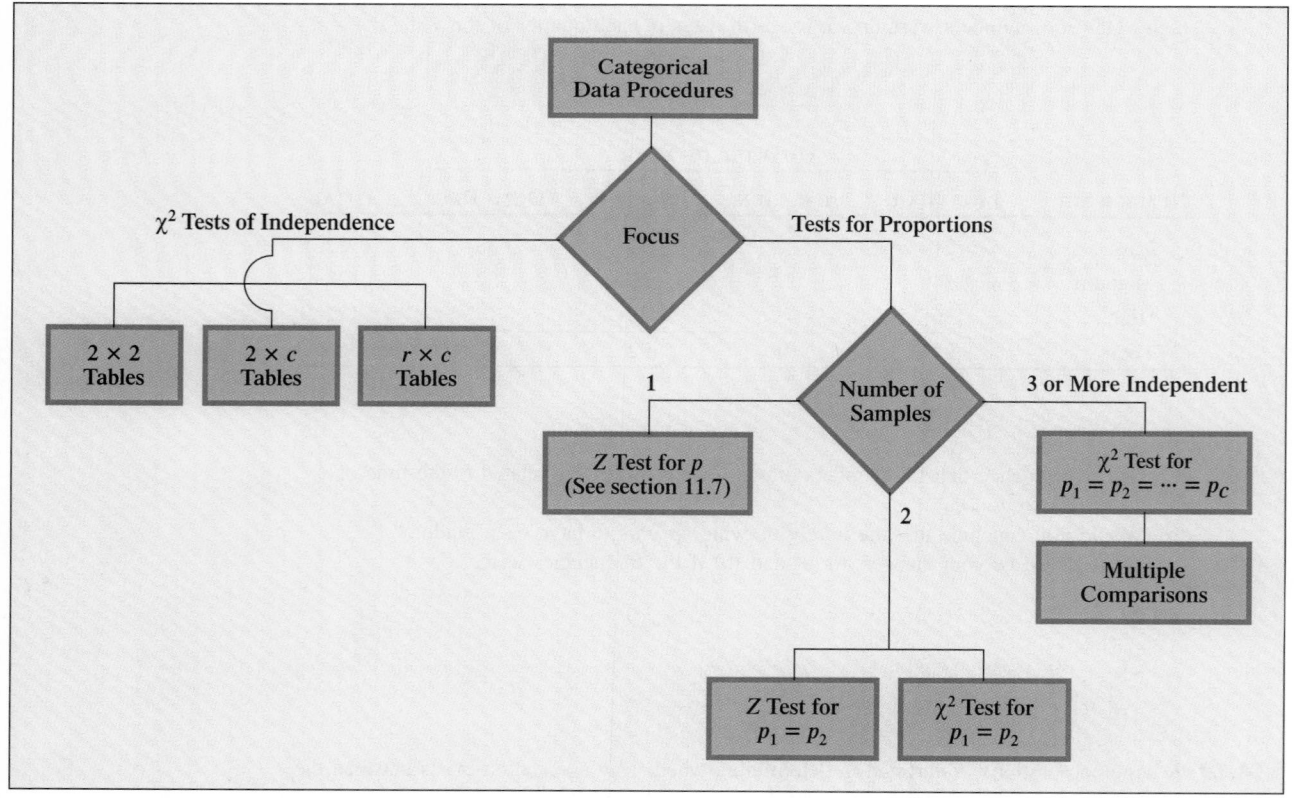

Chapter 14 summary chart

## Key Terms

chi-square distribution   649

$\chi^2$ test for differences in $c$ proportions   656

$\chi^2$ test for differences in two proportions   647

$\chi^2$ test for homogeneity of proportions   648

$\chi^2$ test for independence   665

contingency table   647

cross-classification table   647

degrees of freedom   649

expected frequencies $(f_e)$   667

Marascuilo procedure   660

observed frequencies $(f_0)$   648

pooled estimate $(\bar{p})$ of common population proportion   649

theoretical or expected frequencies   648

$2 \times c$ contingency table   657

$2 \times 2$ table   648

Z test for differences in two proportions   642

---

## Checking Your Understanding

**14.30** Under what conditions should the $Z$ test be used to examine possible differences in the proportions of two independent populations?

**14.31** Under what conditions should the $\chi^2$ test be used to examine possible differences in the proportions of two independent populations?

**14.32** What are the similarities and distinctions between the $Z$ and $\chi^2$ tests for differences in population proportions?

**14.33** Under what conditions should the $\chi^2$ test be used to examine possible differences in the proportions of $c$ independent populations?

**14.34** How can we determine which groups are different in the proportion of successes?

**14.35** Under what conditions should the $\chi^2$ test of independence be used?

---

## Chapter Review Problems

**14.36** A housing survey of single-family homes in two suburban New York state counties is conducted to determine the proportion of such homes that have gas heat. A sample of 300 single-family homes in county A indicates that 185 have gas heat, and a sample of 200 single-family homes in county B indicates that 75 have gas heat.
*Note:* Use a level of significance of .01 throughout the problem.
(a) Use two different statistical tests to determine whether there is evidence of a significant difference between the two counties in the proportion of single-family houses that have gas heat.
(b) Compute the *p*-value in (a) and interpret its meaning.
(c) Compare the results obtained by the two methods in (a). Are your conclusions the same?
(d) If you wanted to know whether there was evidence that county A had a significantly higher proportion of single-family houses with gas heat, what method would you use to perform the statistical test?
(e) What would be your answers to (a) and (b) if 95 out of the 300 sampled single-family homes in county A had gas heat?

**14.37** A "physician's health study" of the effectiveness of aspirin in the reduction of heart attacks was begun in 1982 and completed in 1987 [see C. Hennekens et al., "Findings from the Aspirin Component of the Ongoing Physician's Health Study," *The New England Journal of Medicine* 318 (January 28, 1988): 262–264]. Of 11,037 male medical doctors in the United States who took one 325-mg buffered aspirin tablet every other day, 104 suffered heart attacks during the 5-year period of the study. Of 11,034 male medical doctors in the United States who took a placebo (i.e., a pill that, unknown to the participants in the study, contained no active ingredients), 189 suffered heart attacks during the 5-year period of the study.

(a) At the .01 level of significance, is there evidence that the proportion having heart attacks is significantly lower for the male medical doctors in the United States who received the buffered aspirin every other day than for those who received the placebo?

(b) Compute the $p$-value in (a). Does this lead you to believe that taking one buffered aspirin pill every other day was effective in reducing the incidence of heart attacks? Explain.

(c) Why is it not appropriate to use the $\chi^2$ test in (a)?

(d) What would be your answers in (a) and (b) if 149 of the 11,034 male medical doctors taking the placebo suffered heart attacks?

**14.38** A statistician wishes to study the distribution of three types of cars (subcompact, compact, and full size) sold in the four geographic regions of the United States (Northeast, South, Midwest, West). A random sample of 200 cars is selected with the following results:

- Of 60 cars sold in the Northeast, 25 were subcompacts, 20 were compacts, and 15 were full size.
- Of 40 cars sold in the South, 10 were subcompacts, 10 were compacts, and 20 were full size.
- Of 50 cars sold in the Midwest, 15 were subcompacts, 15 were compacts, and 20 were full size.
- Of 50 cars sold in the West, 20 were subcompacts, 15 were compacts, and 15 were full size.

(a) At the .05 level of significance, is there evidence of a significant relationship between type of car and geographic region?

(b) Estimate with 95% confidence the true proportion of full-sized cars sold in the Northeast.

(c) From the given data can you obtain a reasonable 95% confidence interval estimate of the proportion of full-sized cars sold throughout the United States? Discuss.

(d) What would be your answer to (a) if of 40 cars sold in the South, 5 were subcompacts, 10 were compacts, and 25 were full size?

**14.39** The victory of the incumbent, Bill Clinton, in the 1996 presidential election was attributed to improved economic conditions and low unemployment. Suppose that a survey of 800 adults taken soon after the election resulted in the following cross-classification of financial condition with education level:

| | EDUCATION LEVEL | | | |
| --- | --- | --- | --- | --- |
| FINANCIAL CONDITION | H.S. DEGREE OR LOWER | SOME COLLEGE | COLLEGE DEGREE OR HIGHER | TOTAL |
| Worse off now than before | 91 | 39 | 18 | 148 |
| No difference | 104 | 73 | 31 | 208 |
| Better off now than before | 235 | 48 | 161 | 444 |
| Total | 430 | 160 | 210 | 800 |

At the .05 level of significance, is there evidence of a relationship between financial condition and education level?

**14.40** A company that produces and markets videotaped continuing education programs for the financial industry has traditionally mailed sample tapes that contain previews of the programs to prospective customers. Customers then agree to purchase the program tapes or return the sample tapes to the sales representatives when they call. A group of sales representatives studied how to increase the number of customers that agree to purchase the programs and found that many prospective customers find it difficult to tell from the sample tape alone whether or not the educational programs will meet their needs. The sales representatives performed an experiment to test whether sending the complete-program tapes for review by customers will increase sales. They selected 80 customers from the mailing list and randomly assigned 40 to receive the sample tapes and 40 to receive the full-program tapes for approval. They then recorded the number of tapes that were purchased and returned in each group. The results in their study were as follows:

**TYPE OF VIDEOTAPE RECEIVED**

| ACTION | SAMPLE | FULL | TOTAL |
|---|---|---|---|
| Purchased | 6 | 14 | 20 |
| Returned | 34 | 26 | 60 |
| Total | 40 | 40 | 80 |

(a) At the .05 level of significance, is there evidence of a difference in the proportion of tapes purchased on the basis of the type of tape that was sent?

(b) On the basis of the results of (a), which tape do you think a representative should send in the future? Explain the rationale for your decision.

The sales representatives want to determine which initial approach might result in more sales of the full-program tapes. Three approaches were to be studied: (1) a video sales-information tape mailed to prospective customers, (2) a personal sales call, and (3) a telephone call to prospective customers. A random sample of 300 prospective customers was selected, and 100 were randomly assigned to each of the three sales approaches. The results in terms of purchases of the full-program tapes were as follows:

| ACTION | SALES APPROACH | | | TOTAL |
|---|---|---|---|---|
| | VIDEOTAPE | PERSONAL SALES CALL | TELEPHONE | |
| Purchase | 19 | 27 | 14 | 60 |
| Don't purchase | 81 | 73 | 86 | 240 |
| Total | 100 | 100 | 100 | 300 |

(c) At the .05 level of significance, is there evidence of a difference in the proportion of tapes purchased based on the sales strategy that was used?

(d) If the results you obtained in (c) indicate it is appropriate, use the Marascuilo procedure (with $\alpha = .05$) to determine which sales approaches differ in the proportion of customers who purchased the full-program tape.

(e) Based on the results of (c) and (d), which sales approach do you think a representative should use in the future? Explain the rationale for your decision.

**14.41** A company is considering an organizational change by adopting the use of self-managed work teams. In order to assess the attitudes of employees of the company toward this change, a sample of 400 employees is selected and asked whether they favor the institution of self-managed work teams in their organization. Three responses were permitted: favor, neutral, or oppose. The results of the survey, cross-classified by type of job and attitude toward self-managed work teams, are summarized as follows:

| | ATTITUDE TOWARD SELF-MANAGED WORK TEAMS | | | |
|---|---|---|---|---|
| TYPE OF JOB | FAVOR | NEUTRAL | OPPOSE | TOTAL |
| Hourly worker | 108 | 46 | 71 | 225 |
| Supervisor | 18 | 12 | 30 | 60 |
| Middle management | 35 | 14 | 26 | 75 |
| Upper management | 24 | 7 | 9 | 40 |
| Total | 185 | 79 | 136 | 400 |

(a) At the .05 level of significance, is there evidence of a relationship between attitude toward self-managed work teams and type of job?
(b) If the results obtained in (a) indicate it is appropriate, use the Marascuilo procedure (with $\alpha = .05$) to determine which types of jobs differ in the proportion who oppose self-managed work teams. (*Note*: For the purpose of the analysis, combine favor and neutral into one category.)

Suppose that the survey also asked respondents their attitude toward instituting a policy whereby an employee could take one additional vacation day a month without pay. The results cross-classified by type of job were as follows:

| | ATTITUDE TOWARD VACATION TIME WITHOUT PAY | | | |
|---|---|---|---|---|
| TYPE OF JOB | FAVOR | NEUTRAL | OPPOSE | TOTAL |
| Hourly worker | 135 | 23 | 67 | 225 |
| Supervisor | 39 | 7 | 14 | 60 |
| Middle management | 47 | 6 | 22 | 75 |
| Upper management | 26 | 6 | 8 | 40 |
| Total | 247 | 42 | 111 | 400 |

(c) At the .05 level of significance, is there evidence of a relationship between attitude toward vacation time without pay and type of job?
(d) If the results obtained in (c) indicate it is appropriate, use the Marascuilo procedure (with $\alpha = .05$) to determine which types of jobs differ in the proportion who oppose additional vacation time without pay. (*Note*: For the purpose of the analysis, combine favor and neutral into one category.)

 TEAM PROJECT

TP14.1   Refer to TP3.1(h) on page 115. At the .05 level of significance, is there evidence of a significant relationship between type of fee structure and type of fund?

As chief research associate, you are attending this week's meeting of the board of directors at the invitation of Mike Drucker, the senior vice president for marketing and promotion at Air International. Mike is at the podium.

"Ladies and gentlemen, I'd like to inform you that the data from our quarterly survey have now been edited and entered into our computer system. This data set constitutes a random sample of 1,600 adult passengers who flew with us on mainland routes over the 2-week period ending last Friday. It is imperative that we continue to monitor the airline services we provide through these quarterly surveys so that by keeping tabs on our passengers and taking the market pulse, we can continue to make those improvements that will guarantee that our passengers remain loyal to Air International and that through their satisfaction they will encourage their friends and families to fly with us."

"Thank you, Mike," interrupted Lorena Martinez who recently took over as CEO of Air International, "will you kindly remind us of the central theme in this particular quarterly survey and give us your timetable for presentation and discussion?"

"Certainly, Ms. Martinez. The theme, ma'am, for this survey deals with passenger satisfaction and its potential relationships with reasons for travel and disposition of luggage. Gender differences will also be explored. As for a timetable, Dr. Jay Williamson, the director of central processing, assures me that the initial printouts will be ready by noon today. Because it takes two working days for data cleansing and preliminary analyses, I will be ready to make our presentations at next week's board meeting. I'll need 15 minutes for the presentation and I request an additional 15 minutes for questions, answers, and board discussion."

"Very good, Mike, it sounds like your marketing and promotion department has got a handle on this one. On behalf of the board, I would like to grant your requests and state that we look forward to your presentation next week. Please keep me informed if you need anything to expedite the analysis."

"Thank you, ma'am," Mike replied, and he took his seat.

## Two Days Later in Mike Drucker's Office

You are sitting in the office of the senior vice president for marketing and promotion awaiting Mike Drucker's entrance. He is on the telephone in the vestibule discussing the computer printouts that he is holding. Suddenly, the conversation ends and Mike enters his office smiling.

"Well, here it is," Mike Drucker exclaims triumphantly as he takes his seat at his desk. "Dr. Williamson says that the data appear to be clean, all error checks worked. You did a great job!" You nod and acknowledge the praise, aware that this is just the beginning. Mike continues, "Let me turn this over to you again. Take a good look at the important theme questions, along with the responses and the cross-tabulations. I'd like some confirmatory answers to the following:

1. Our well-known jingle says 'Air International is the airline of first choice for one out of two, so if you're not the one, it's time you pick us too!' I really hate that jingle—but people like it, it's catchy. But is it accurate? Is there significant evidence that the proportion of passengers who state that Air International is the airline of choice differs from .50?

2. For advertising and promotional purposes, it is important to know if a gender effect is present with respect to passenger satisfaction. Is there significant evidence of a difference between males and females in terms of the proportion of these passengers who claim Air International is the airline of choice?

3. Many of us have argued over whether the primary reason for a trip affects passenger satisfaction. Is there evidence of a significant difference among the various primary reasons for flying with respect to the proportion of the passengers who claim Air International is the airline of choice?

4. For advertising and promotional purposes, it is important to study potential associations between such factors as primary reasons for flying and luggage disposition. If handling the luggage is perceived as an important service feature, we will have to make sure Air International provides better and quicker service for

those who check their luggage in as well as have more room on the aircraft for those who carry their luggage on board. Is there evidence of a significant relationship between primary reasons for flying and luggage disposition?

I know we're under the gun on this one, but I'd like you to have this analysis on my desk first thing Monday morning. Please prepare an executive summary and attach all tables and charts. List all hypotheses that you are testing, the levels of significance you chose for the tests, and the conclusions to be drawn. Also, please prepare to give me and my staff an informal 10-minute presentation on your findings. Do you have any questions?"

Taking a deep breath, you say, "No, not at this time. I'm ready to work."

"Thanks," Mike continues, as he ushers you out of his office. "I'll see you first thing Monday, but if any questions come up don't hesitate to call me."

**Responses to Theme Portion of Air International Quarterly Satisfaction Survey**

1. What is your gender?
   Male . . . 960     Female . . . 640
2. After this trip, do you consider Air International your airline of choice?
   Yes . . . 832     No . . . 768
3. What was the primary reason for taking this trip?
   Business . . . 880
   Emergency . . . 64
   Moving/in transit . . . 96
   Pleasure . . . 560
4. What did you do with your baggage for this trip?
   Carried it all on board . . . 768
   Checked it all in . . . 592
   Carried some and checked some . . . 192
   Had no luggage . . . 48

**Theme Questions 1 and 2**

| AIRLINE CHOICE | GENDER | | |
| --- | --- | --- | --- |
| | MALES | FEMALES | TOTAL |
| Yes | 512 | 320 | 832 |
| No | 448 | 320 | 768 |
| Total | 960 | 640 | 1,600 |

**Theme Questions 2 and 3**

| AIRLINE CHOICE | PRIMARY REASON | | | | |
| --- | --- | --- | --- | --- | --- |
| | BUSINESS | EMERGENCY | MOVING/IN TRANSIT | PLEASURE | TOTAL |
| Yes | 455 | 20 | 42 | 315 | 832 |
| No | 425 | 44 | 54 | 245 | 768 |
| Total | 880 | 64 | 96 | 560 | 1,600 |

**Theme Questions 3 and 4**

| PRIMARY REASON | BAGGAGE DISPOSITION | | | | |
| --- | --- | --- | --- | --- | --- |
| | CARRY ALL | CHECK ALL | DO BOTH | NO LUGGAGE | TOTAL |
| Business | 653 | 83 | 103 | 41 | 880 |
| Emergency | 47 | 14 | 1 | 2 | 64 |
| Moving/in transit | 6 | 78 | 9 | 3 | 96 |
| Pleasure | 62 | 417 | 79 | 2 | 560 |
| Total | 768 | 592 | 192 | 48 | 1,600 |

# THE SPRINGVILLE HERALD CASE

## Phase 1

On the basis of the results of a survey, the marketing department concluded that there was a segment of the households in Springville that might be interested in subscribing to the newspaper if a discount were offered as an incentive. The team decided that an experiment should be conducted before any final decision was made concerning the type of discount that should be offered to subscribers during the trial period. Three possible incentive plans were to be offered along with a plan that offered no discount during the trial period. These plans were:

1. No discount for the newspaper. Subscribers would pay $4.50 per week for the newspaper during the 90-day trial period.

2. Moderate discount for the newspaper. Subscribers would pay $4.00 per week for the newspaper during the 90-day trial period.
3. Substantial discount for the newspaper. Subscribers would pay $3.00 per week for the newspaper during the 90-day trial period.
4. Discounted restaurant card. Subscribers would be given a card providing a discount of 15% at selected restaurants in Springville during the trial period.

Each respondent to the survey was randomly assigned to a discount plan. A random sample of 100 subscribers to each plan during the trial period was tracked to determine how many would continue to subscribe to the *Herald* after the trial period. The results are summarized in Table SH14.1.

**Table SH14.1** *Number of subscribers who continue subscriptions for four trial discount plans*

| CONTINUE SUBSCRIPTIONS AFTER TRIAL PERIOD | PLANS | | | | |
|---|---|---|---|---|---|
| | NO DISCOUNT | MODERATE DISCOUNT | SUBSTANTIAL DISCOUNT | DISCOUNT RESTAURANT CARD | TOTAL |
| Yes | 34 | 37 | 38 | 53 | 162 |
| No | 66 | 63 | 62 | 47 | 238 |
| Total | 100 | 100 | 100 | 100 | 400 |

## Exercise

**14.1** Analyze the results of the experiment. Write a report to the team that includes a recommendation for which discount plan should be used. Be prepared to discuss the limitations and assumptions of the experiment. In addition to the written report, prepare a summary that can be presented orally in less than 10 minutes.

 **Do not continue until the Phase 1 exercises have been completed.**

## Phase 2

As the marketing department team discussed the results of the survey presented in chapter 10 on page 406, the group realized that the results of the evaluation of individual questions were providing only partial information in helping focus on the marketing implications of the survey. In order to further understand the market for home-delivery subscriptions, the following cross-classification tables were obtained:

## READ OTHER NEWSPAPER

| HOME DELIVERY | YES | NO | TOTAL |
|---|---|---|---|
| Yes | 61 | 75 | 136 |
| No | 77 | 139 | 216 |
| Total | 138 | 214 | 352 |

## RESTAURANT CARD

| HOME DELIVERY | YES | NO | TOTAL |
|---|---|---|---|
| Yes | 26 | 110 | 136 |
| No | 40 | 176 | 216 |
| Total | 66 | 286 | 352 |

| | MONDAY–SATURDAY PURCHASE BEHAVIOR | | | |
|---|---|---|---|---|
| INTEREST IN TRIAL SUBSCRIPTION | EVERY DAY | MOST DAYS | OCCASIONALLY | TOTAL |
| Yes | 29 | 14 | 3 | 46 |
| No | 49 | 81 | 40 | 170 |
| Total | 78 | 95 | 43 | 216 |

| | SUNDAY PURCHASE BEHAVIOR | | | |
|---|---|---|---|---|
| INTEREST IN TRIAL SUBSCRIPTION | EVERY SUNDAY | 2–3/MONTH | ONCE/MONTH | TOTAL |
| Yes | 35 | 10 | 1 | 46 |
| No | 103 | 44 | 23 | 170 |
| Total | 138 | 54 | 24 | 216 |

| | INTEREST IN TRIAL SUBSCRIPTION | | |
|---|---|---|---|
| WHERE PURCHASED | YES | NO | TOTAL |
| Convenience store/delicatessen | 12 | 62 | 74 |
| Stationery/candy store | 15 | 80 | 95 |
| Vending machine | 10 | 11 | 21 |
| Supermarket | 5 | 8 | 13 |
| Other | 4 | 9 | 13 |
| Total | 46 | 170 | 216 |

| | MONDAY–SATURDAY PURCHASE BEHAVIOR | | | |
|---|---|---|---|---|
| SUNDAY PURCHASE BEHAVIOR | EVERY DAY | MOST DAYS | OCCASIONALLY | TOTAL |
| Every Sunday | 55 | 65 | 18 | 138 |
| 2–3/month | 19 | 23 | 12 | 54 |
| Once/month | 4 | 7 | 13 | 24 |
| Total | 78 | 95 | 43 | 216 |

## Exercise

**14.2** Analyze the results of the cross-tabulation tables obtained from the survey of households in Springville. Write a report for the marketing department team and discuss the marketing implications of the cross-tabulation results for the *Springville Herald.*

## References

1. Daniel, W. W., *Applied Nonparametric Statistics,* 2d ed. (Boston: PWS Kent, 1990).
2. Dixon, W. J., and F. J. Massey, Jr., *Introduction to Statistical Analysis*, 4th ed. (New York: McGraw-Hill, 1983).
3. Lewontin, R. C., and J. Felsenstein, "Robustness of Homogeneity Tests in $2 \times n$ Tables," *Biometrics* 21 (March 1965): 19–33.
4. Marascuilo, L. A., "Large-Sample Multiple Comparisons," *Psychological Bulletin* 65 (1966): 280–290.
5. Marascuilo, L. A., and M. McSweeney, *Nonparametric and Distribution-Free Methods for the Social Sciences* (Monterey, CA: Brooks/Cole, 1977).
6. *Microsoft Excel 97* (Redmond, WA: Microsoft Corp., 1997).
7. *Minitab for Windows Version 12* (State College, PA: Minitab, Inc., 1998).

## ❖ APPENDIX 14.1    USING MICROSOFT EXCEL FOR $\chi^2$ CONTINGENCY TABLE TESTS

### COMMENT: *PHStat Add-In Users*

If Microsoft Excel is not running, click the **PHStat** add-in icon. If Microsoft Excel is running, select **File | Open**. Select the Stat add-in file **PHSA.XLA**. Click the **Open** button.

To obtain a *Z* test for the difference between two proportions, select **PHStat | Two-Sample Test | Z Test for Two Proportions**. Enter the sample size and number of successes for groups one and two in their respective edit boxes. Enter the hypothesized difference between the two population proportions (0.00 for no difference) in its edit box. Enter the level of significance in its edit box, if it is different from the default value of 0.05. Click the **OK** button.

To obtain a chi-square test for a two-way contingency table, select **PHStat | Two-Sample Test | Chi-Square Test**. If the data have already been tabulated into a two-way table, select the **Tabulated Data** option button, and enter the cell range for the data in the Table Cell Range edit box. Be sure that the cell range given includes the row and column totals and labels. If the data need to be tabulated and the chi-square statistic computed, select the **Untabulated Data** option, and enter the cell range for the row and column variables, making sure to include the labels for the row and column variables in the cell range. Enter the level of significance in its edit box, if it is different from the default value of 0.05. Click the **OK** button.

# ❖ APPENDIX 14.2 USING MINITAB FOR $\chi^2$ CONTINGENCY TABLE TESTS

To obtain a two-way contingency table, open the file of interest. Select **Stat | Tables | Cross Tabulation**. In the Classification Variables edit box enter the two variables to be cross-classified. In the Display check box, select **Counts, Row percents, Column percents**, and **Total percents**. Select **Chi-Square** analysis. Select the **Above and expected** count button. Click the **OK** button.

If the cell frequencies are available as in the hotel satisfaction survey, enter them in columns in a Minitab worksheet. For the hotel satisfaction $2 \times 2$ table, enter 163 and 64 in column C1 and 154 and 108 in column C2. Select **Stat | Tables | Chi-Square Test**. In the Columns containing the Table edit box, enter **C1** and **C2**. Click the **OK** button.

# 15

# Statistical Applications in Quality and Productivity Management

# CHAPTER OBJECTIVES

✓ *To provide an introduction to the history of quality*
✓ *To introduce Deming's 14 points of management*
✓ *To understand the distinction between common cause variation and special cause variation*
✓ *To discuss control charts for the proportion*
✓ *To discuss a control chart for the number of nonconformances in an area of opportunity*
✓ *To discuss control charts for the mean and range*

## Introduction

In this chapter we focus on quality and productivity management. Quality and productivity have become essential for survival in the global economy. Among the areas in which quality has an impact on our everyday work and personal lives are:

- The design, production, and subsequent reliability of our automobiles
- The ever expanding capability of communication devices such as telephone and data transmission lines, paging devices, facsimile machines, cellular telephones, and so on
- The constant improvement in computer chips that make for faster and more powerful computers
- The delivery of services such as banking, communications, package deliveries, hotels, retailing operations, and mail-order companies
- The availability of new technology and equipment that has led to the improved diagnosis of illnesses and the improved delivery of health care services

We begin our study of quality and productivity with a historical perspective and discuss the evolution of management styles. The subsequent discussion of Deming's 14 points of management sets the stage for the development of a variety of control charts used for different types of data. In addition, an intriguing experiment known as the parable of the red beads will be examined to highlight the different types of variation inherent in a set of data and to reinforce the importance of management's responsibility to improve systems.

## ◆ USING STATISTICS: *Service Quality at a Hotel*

One aspect of a guest's satisfaction with a hotel relates to the perceived quality of services that the guest receives. Of particular importance to this perception of quality is the first impression the guest has when arriving at the hotel. An important aspect of this is represented by the readiness of the assigned hotel room. From the viewpoint of initial impressions, it is particularly important that all amenities that are supposed to be available (soap, towels, complimentary guest basket, etc.) are actually available in the room and equally important that all appliances such as the radio, television, and telephone are in proper working order. A second aspect of perceived quality is represented by the time it takes for luggage to be delivered to the room after the guest has checked into the hotel.

## 15.1   QUALITY AND PRODUCTIVITY: A HISTORICAL PERSPECTIVE

By the mid-1980s, it was clear that a global economy had developed in which companies located in an individual country competed not only with local and national competitors but also with competitors from all parts of the world (see reference 6). This global economy developed because of many factors, including the rapid expansion in worldwide communications and the exponential increase in the availability and power of computer systems. In such an environment it is vitally important that business organizations be able to respond rapidly to changes in market conditions by incorporating the most effective managerial approaches available.

The development of this global economy also led to a reemergence of an interest in the area of quality improvement in the United States. Evidence of the renewed interest can be seen in the importance being placed on the competition for the Malcolm Baldrige Award (see reference 7), given annually to companies making the greatest strides in improving quality and customer satisfaction with their products and services. Among the companies that have won this award are Motorola, Xerox, Federal Express, Cadillac Motor Company, Ritz-Carlton Hotels, AT&T Universal Card Services, and Eastman Chemical Company.

This renewed interest in quality in the United States followed the redevelopment of Japanese industry that began in 1950, in which individuals such as W. Edwards Deming, Joseph Juran, and Kaoru Ishikawa developed an approach that emphasized quality and continuous improvement of products and services with increased emphasis on process improvement. This process-oriented management is often referred to as **total quality management**, or **TQM**, and is characterized by the basic themes listed in Exhibit 15.1.

---

### Exhibit 15.1   *Themes of Quality Management*

✓ **1.** The primary focus is on process improvement.

✓ **2.** Most of the variation in a process is due to the system and not the individual.

✓ **3.** Teamwork is an integral part of a quality management organization.

✓ **4.** Customer satisfaction is a primary organizational goal.

✓ **5.** Organizational transformation must occur in order to implement quality management.

✓ **6.** Fear must be removed from organizations.

✓ **7.** Higher quality costs less, not more, but requires an investment in training.

---

Process or quality management has a strong statistical foundation based on a thorough knowledge of variability, a systems perspective, and belief in continuous improvement. Such statistical tools as Pareto diagrams, histograms, and control charts are an integral part of this approach.

## 15.2 DEMING'S 14 POINTS: A THEORY OF MANAGEMENT BY PROCESS

The high quality of Japanese products and the economic miracle of Japanese development after World War II are well-known facts. What is not as readily known, particularly by young people today, is that, prior to the 1950s, Japan had acquired the unenviable reputation of producing shoddy consumer products of poor quality. Thus, the question must surely be asked, what happened to change this reputation? Part of the answer lies in the fact that, by 1950, top management of Japanese companies, in alliance with the Union of Japanese Scientists and Engineers, realized that quality was a vital factor in being able to export consumer products successfully. Some Japanese engineers had been exposed to the contribution that the Shewhart control charts made toward the American war effort during World War II (see references 7 and 20). Several American experts, including W. Edwards Deming, were invited to Japan during the early 1950s. Owing primarily to his experiences in Japan, Deming developed his approach to management based on the 14 points listed in Exhibit 15.2.

**Exhibit 15.2  Deming's 14 Points for Management**

✓ **1.** Create constancy of purpose for improvement of product and service.

✓ **2.** Adopt the new philosophy.

✓ **3.** Cease dependence on inspection to achieve quality.

✓ **4.** End the practice of awarding business on the basis of price tag alone. Instead, minimize total cost by working with a single supplier.

✓ **5.** Improve constantly and forever every process for planning, production, and service.

✓ **6.** Institute training on the job.

✓ **7.** Adopt and institute leadership.

✓ **8.** Drive out fear.

✓ **9.** Break down barriers between staff areas.

✓ **10.** Eliminate slogans, exhortations, and targets for the workforce.

✓ **11.** Eliminate numerical quotas for the workforce and numerical goals for management.

✓ **12.** Remove barriers that rob people of pride of workmanship. Eliminate the annual rating or merit system.

✓ **13.** Institute a vigorous program of education and self-improvement for everyone.

✓ **14.** Put everyone in the company to work to accomplish the transformation.

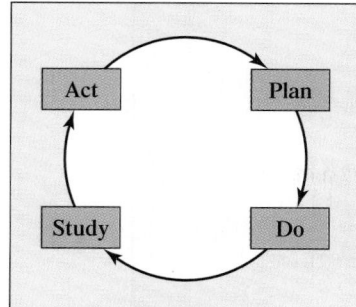

**FIGURE 15.1**

The Shewhart-Deming PDSA cycle

Point 1, create constancy of purpose, refers to how an organization deals with problems that arise both in the present and in the future. The focus is on the constant improvement of a product or service. This improvement process is illustrated by the **Shewhart-Deming cycle** of Figure 15.1. The Shewhart-Deming cycle represents a continuous cycle of "plan, do, study, and act." The first step, planning, represents the initial design phase for planning a change in a manufacturing or service process. This step involves teamwork among individuals from different areas within an organization. The second step, doing, involves implementing the change, preferably on a small scale. The third step, studying, involves an analysis of the results using statistical tools to determine what was learned. The fourth step, acting, involves the acceptance of the change, its abandonment, or further study of the change under different conditions. With this approach, the process starts with the customer as the most important element of the production or service process.

Point 2, adopt the new philosophy, refers to the urgency with which companies need to realize that we are in a new economic age of global competition. It is better to be proactive and change before a crisis occurs, rather than reacting to some negative experiences that may have occurred. Rather than taking the approach of "if it is not broke, don't fix it," it is better to continually work on improvement so that expensive fixes can be avoided.

Point 3, cease dependence on inspection to achieve quality, implies that any inspection whose purpose is to improve quality is too late because the quality is already built into the product. It is better to focus on making it right the first time. Among the difficulties involved in mass inspection (besides high costs) are the failure of inspectors to agree on nonconforming items and the problem of separating good and bad items. Such difficulties can be illustrated with an example taken from Scherkenbach (see reference 15) and depicted in Figure 15.2 on page 688.

Suppose your job involves proofreading the sentence in Figure 15.2 with the objective of counting the number of occurrences of the letter "F." Turn the page and perform this task and note the number of occurrences of the letter F that you discover.

People usually see either three F's or six F's. The correct number is six F's. The number seen is dependent on the method used in examining the sentence. One is likely to find three F's if the sentence is read phonetically and six F's if one counts the number of F's carefully. The point of the exercise is to show that if such a simple process as counting F's leads to inconsistency of "inspector's" results, what will happen when a process fails to contain a clear operational definition of nonconforming? Certainly, in such situations much more variability from inspector to inspector will occur.

Point 4, ending the practice of awarding business on the basis of price tag alone, represents the antithesis of lowest-bidder awards. It focuses on the fact that there can be no real long-term meaning to price without a knowledge of the quality of the product. A lowest-

**FINISHED FILES ARE THE RESULT OF YEARS OF SCIENTIFIC STUDY COMBINED WITH THE EXPERIENCE OF MANY YEARS**

***FIGURE 15.2*** An example of the proofreading process
*Source: W.W. Scherkenbach,* The Deming Route to Quality and Productivity: Road Maps and Roadblocks *(Washington, DC: CEEP/Press, 1987)*

bidder approach ignores the advantages in reduced variation of a single supplier and fails to consider the advantages of the development of a long-term relationship between purchaser and supplier. Such a relationship allows the supplier to be innovative and makes the supplier and purchaser partners in achieving success.

Point 5, improve constantly and forever the system of production and services, reinforces the importance of the continuous focus of the Shewhart-Deming cycle and the belief that quality needs to be built in at the design stage. Attaining quality is viewed as a never-ending process in which smaller variation translates into a reduction in the economic losses that occur in the manufacturing of a product whose characteristics are variable.

Point 6, institute training, reflects the needs of all employees including production workers, engineers, and managers. It is critically important for management to understand the differences between special causes and common causes of variation (see section 15.3) so that proper action can be taken in each circumstance.

Point 7, adopt and institute leadership, relates to the distinction between leadership and supervision. The aim of leadership should be to improve the system and achieve greater consistency of performance.

Points 8–12, drive out fear, break down barriers between staff areas, eliminate slogans, eliminate numerical quotas for the workforce and numerical goals for management, and remove barriers to pride of workmanship including the annual rating and merit system, are all related to how the performance of an employee is to be evaluated.

The quota system for the production worker is viewed as detrimental for several reasons. First, it has a negative effect on the quality of the product because supervisors are more inclined to pass inferior products through the system when they need to meet work quotas. Such flexible standards of work reduce the pride of workmanship of the individual and perpetuate a system in which peer pressure holds the upper half of the workers to no more than the quota rate. Second, the emphasis on targets and exhortations may place an improper burden on the worker because it is management's job to improve the system, not to expect workers to produce beyond the system (this will be clearly illustrated in section 15.5).

Third, the annual performance rating system can rob the manager of his or her pride of workmanship because this system of evaluation often fails to provide a meaningful measure of performance. In too many cases (see reference 19), efforts are focused on either distorting the data or distorting the system to produce the desired set of results, rather than on efforts to improve the system. Such an approach stifles teamwork because there is often a reduced tangible reward for working together across functional areas. Finally, it rewards people who work successfully within the system, rather than people who work to improve the system.

Point 13, encourage education and self-improvement for everyone, reflects the notion that the most important resource of any organization is its people. Efforts that improve the knowledge of people in the organization also serve to increase the assets of the organization.

Point 14, take action to accomplish the transformation, again reflects the approach of management as a process in which one continually strives toward improvement in a never-ending cycle.

Now that we have provided a brief introduction to the Deming philosophy, we shall introduce an important statistical tool for quality improvement, control charts. As a tool for studying the variability of a system, control charts are useful for helping managers determine how to improve a process. They will be the subject of our next section.

## 15.3 THE THEORY OF CONTROL CHARTS

If we are examining data that have been collected sequentially over a period of time, it is imperative that the variable of interest be plotted at successive time periods. One such graph, originally developed by Shewhart (see references 16, 17, and 18), is the control chart.

The **control chart** is a means of monitoring variation in the characteristic of a product or service by (1) focusing on the time dimension in which the system produces products or services and (2) studying the nature of the variability in the system. The control chart is used to study past performance and/or to evaluate present conditions. Data collected from a control chart form the basis for process improvement. Control charts are used for different types of variables—for categorical variables such as the proportion of flights of a particular airline that are more than 15 minutes late on a given day, for discrete variables such as the count of the number of paint blemishes in a panel of a car door, and for continuous variables such as the amount of apple juice contained in 1-liter bottles.

In addition to providing a visual display of data representing a process, the principal focus of the control chart is the attempt to separate special or assignable causes of variation from chance or common causes of variation.

> **Special or assignable causes of variation** represent large fluctuations or patterns in the data that are not inherent to a process. These fluctuations are often caused by changes in a system that represent either problems to be fixed or opportunities to exploit.
> **Chance or common causes of variation** represent the inherent variability that exists in a system. These consist of the numerous small causes of variability that operate randomly or by chance.

The distinction between the two causes of variation is crucial because special causes of variation are considered to be those that are not part of a process and are correctable or exploitable without changing the system, whereas common causes of variation can be reduced only by changing the system. Such systemic changes are the responsibility of management.

Control charts allow us to monitor the process and determine the presence of special causes. There are two types of errors that control charts help prevent. The first type of error involves the belief that an observed value represents special cause variation when in fact it is due to the common cause variation of the system. Treating such common cause of variation as special cause variation can result in tampering with or overadjustment of a process with an accompanying increase in variation. The second type of error involves treating special cause variation as if it is common cause variation and thus not taking immediate corrective action when it is necessary. Although these errors can still occur when a control chart is used, they are far less likely.

The most typical form of control chart will set control limits that are within $\pm 3$ standard deviations[1] of the statistical measure of interest (be it the average, the proportion, the range, etc.). In general, this may be stated as

## Obtaining Control Limits

$$\text{Process average} \pm 3 \text{ standard deviations} \qquad (15.1)$$

so that

**Upper control limit (UCL)** = process average + 3 standard deviations

**Lower control limit (LCL)** = process average − 3 standard deviations

Once these control limits are set, the control chart is evaluated from the perspective of (1) discerning any pattern that might exist in the values over time and (2) determining whether any points fall outside the control limits. Figure 15.3 illustrates three different situations.

In panel A of Figure 15.3, we observe a process that is stable and contains only common cause variation, one in which there does not appear to be any pattern in the ordering of values over time, and one in which there are no points that fall outside the 3 standard deviation control limits. Panel B, on the contrary, contains two points that fall outside the 3 standard deviation control limits. Each of these points would be investigated to determine

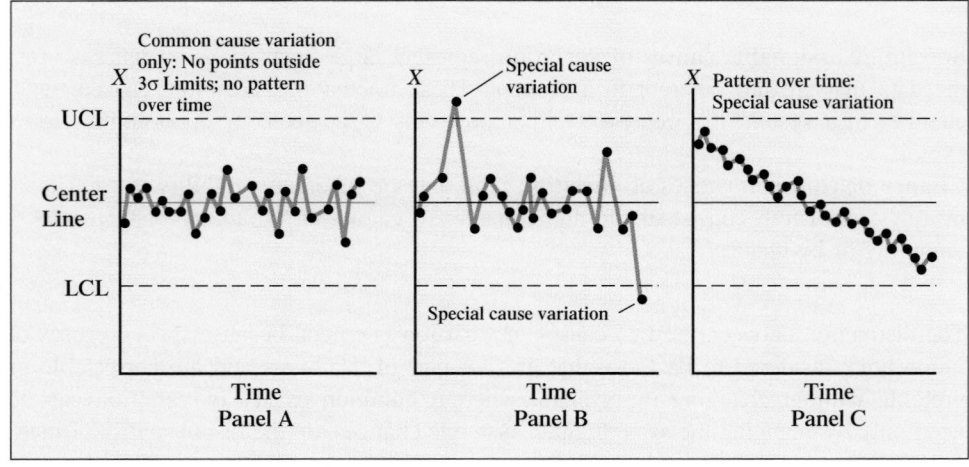

**FIGURE 15.3** Three control chart patterns

the special causes that led to their occurrence. Although panel C does not have any points outside the control limits, it has a series of consecutive points above the average value (the center line) as well as a series of consecutive points below the average value. In addition, a long-term overall downward trend in the value of the variable is clearly visible. Such a situation calls for corrective action to determine what might account for this pattern prior to initiating any changes in the system.

The detection of a trend is not always so obvious. Two simple rules (see reference 5) for indicating the presence of a trend are (1) having eight consecutive points above the center line (or eight consecutive points below the center line) or (2) having eight consecutive points that are increasing (or eight consecutive points that are decreasing).

Once all special causes of variation have been explained and eliminated, the process involved is examined on a continuing basis until there are no patterns over time or points outside the 3 standard deviation limits. When the process contains only common cause variation, its performance is predictable (at least in the near future). To reduce common cause variation, it is necessary to alter the system that is producing the product or service.

 **15.4** CONTROL CHART FOR THE PROPORTION OF NONCONFORMING ITEMS—THE *p* CHART

Let us turn our attention to various types of control charts that are used to monitor processes and determine whether special cause variation or common cause variation is present in a process. One type of commonly used control chart is the **attribute chart**, which is used when sampled items are classified according to whether they conform or do not conform to operationally defined requirements. The *p* **chart** that will be discussed in this section is based on the proportion of nonconforming items in a sample.

You may recall that we studied proportions in chapters 5 and 6 and we discussed the binomial distribution in section 6.2. In chapter 9, in equation (9.8) on page 353 we defined the proportion as $X/n$, and in equation (9.9) on page 354, we defined the standard deviation of the proportion as

$$\sigma_{p_s} = \sqrt{\frac{p(1-p)}{n}}$$

Using equation (15.1) on page 690, we establish control limits for the proportion of nonconforming[2] items from the sample or subgroup data as

[2]*In this chapter we use the term "nonconforming items," whereas in chapters 5, 6 and 9 when we discussed proportions we used the term "success."*

**Obtaining Control Limits for the Proportion**

$$\bar{p} \pm 3\sqrt{\frac{\bar{p}(1-\bar{p})}{\bar{n}}} \tag{15.2}$$

where

$X_i$ = number of nonconforming items in subgroup $i$

$n_i$ = sample or subgroup size for subgroup $i$

$p_i = X_i/n_i$

$k$ = number of subgroups taken

$\bar{n}$ = average subgroup size

$\bar{p}$ = average proportion of nonconforming items

so that

**Obtaining the Upper and Lower Control Limits for the $p$ Chart**

$$UCL = \bar{p} + 3\sqrt{\frac{\bar{p}(1 - \bar{p})}{\bar{n}}}$$ (15.3a)

$$LCL = \bar{p} - 3\sqrt{\frac{\bar{p}(1 - \bar{p})}{\bar{n}}}$$ (15.3b)

For equal $n_i$,

$$\bar{n} = n_i \quad \text{and} \quad \bar{p} = \frac{\sum_{i=1}^{k} p_i}{k}$$

or in general,

$$\bar{n} = \frac{\sum_{i=1}^{k} n_i}{k} \quad \text{and} \quad \bar{p} = \frac{\sum_{i=1}^{k} X_i}{\sum_{i=1}^{k} n_i}$$

Any negative value for the lower control limit means that the lower control limit does not exist. To show the application of the $p$ chart, we can return to the hotel services example.

Suppose that the management at one hotel has decided to study the process of room readiness for a 4-week period by taking a daily sample of 200 rooms for which guests are holding reservations. Thus, before each arrival, it determines whether the room in the sample contains any nonconformances in terms of the availability of amenities and the working order of all appliances. Table 15.1 lists the number and proportion of nonconforming rooms for each day in the 4-week period.

For these data, $k = 28$, $\sum_{i=1}^{k} p_i = 2.315$, and $n_i = \bar{n} = 200$

Thus,

$$\bar{p} = \frac{2.315}{28} = .0827$$

so that using equation (15.2) we have

$$.0827 \pm 3\sqrt{\frac{(.0827)(.9173)}{200}}$$

Thus,

$$UCL = .0827 + .0584 = .1411$$

and

$$LCL = .0827 - .0584 = .0243$$

## Table 15.1 — *Nonconforming hotel rooms at check-in over a 4-week period*

| Day | Rooms Studied | Rooms Not Ready | Proportion | Day | Rooms Studied | Rooms Not Ready | Proportion |
|-----|---------------|-----------------|------------|-----|---------------|-----------------|------------|
| 1 | 200 | 16 | .080 | 15 | 200 | 18 | .090 |
| 2 | 200 | 7 | .035 | 16 | 200 | 13 | .065 |
| 3 | 200 | 21 | .105 | 17 | 200 | 15 | .075 |
| 4 | 200 | 17 | .085 | 18 | 200 | 10 | .050 |
| 5 | 200 | 25 | .125 | 19 | 200 | 14 | .070 |
| 6 | 200 | 19 | .095 | 20 | 200 | 25 | .125 |
| 7 | 200 | 16 | .080 | 21 | 200 | 19 | .095 |
| 8 | 200 | 15 | .075 | 22 | 200 | 12 | .060 |
| 9 | 200 | 11 | .055 | 23 | 200 | 6 | .030 |
| 10 | 200 | 12 | .060 | 24 | 200 | 12 | .060 |
| 11 | 200 | 22 | .110 | 25 | 200 | 18 | .090 |
| 12 | 200 | 20 | .100 | 26 | 200 | 15 | .075 |
| 13 | 200 | 17 | .085 | 27 | 200 | 20 | .100 |
| 14 | 200 | 26 | .130 | 28 | 200 | 22 | .110 |

DATA FILE
HOTEL1

The control chart for the data of Table 15.1 obtained from Microsoft Excel is displayed in Figure 15.4. An examination of Figure 15.4 indicates a process in a state of statistical control, with the individual points distributed around $\bar{p}$ without any pattern. Thus, any improvement in this system of making rooms ready for guests must come from the reduction of common cause variation. As we have stated previously, such system alterations are the responsibility of management.

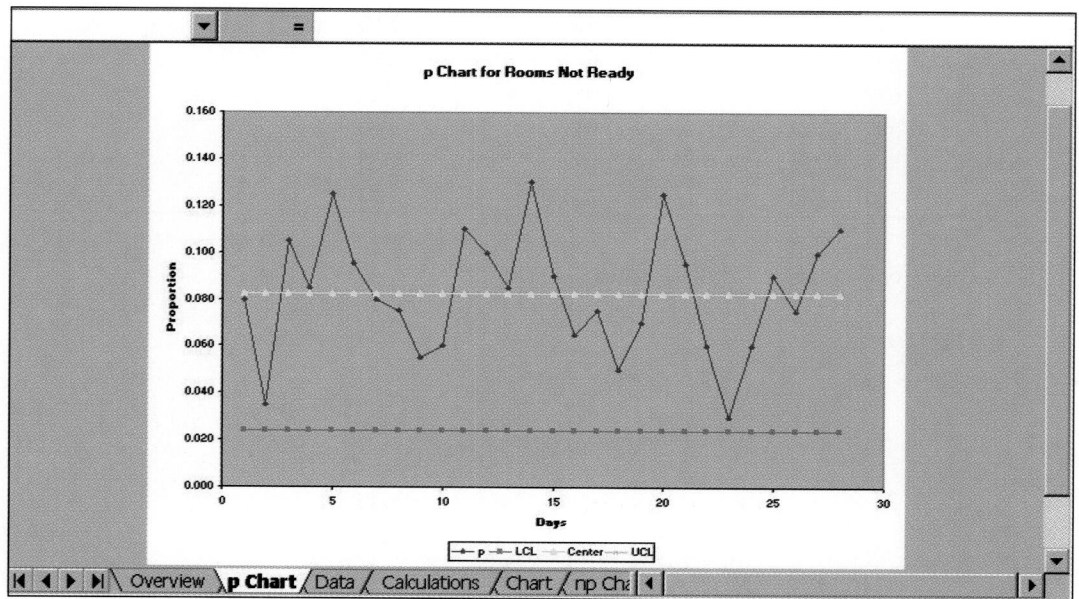

**FIGURE 15.4** The *p* chart obtained from Microsoft Excel for the nonconforming hotel room data

Now that we have examined a situation in which the sample or subgroup size does not vary, we need to turn to a more general situation in which the subgroup size varies over time. As a general rule, as long as none of the subgroup sizes $n_i$ differs from the average subgroup size $\bar{n}$ by more than $\pm 25\%$ of $n$ (see reference 5), equation (15.2) may be used to obtain the control limits for the $p$ chart.

To illustrate the use of the $p$ chart when the subgroup sizes are unequal, we will investigate the production of gauze sponges at a factory as discussed in Example 15.1.

## Example 15.1   *Using the p Chart for Unequal Subgroup Sizes*

Suppose that the number of sponges produced daily and the number of nonconforming sponges for a period of 32 days are displayed in the following table.

| Day | Sponges Produced | Non-Conforming Sponges | Proportion | Day | Sponges Produced | Non-Conforming Sponges | Proportion |
|---|---|---|---|---|---|---|---|
| 1 | 690 | 21 | .030 | 17 | 575 | 20 | .035 |
| 2 | 580 | 22 | .038 | 18 | 610 | 16 | .026 |
| 3 | 685 | 20 | .029 | 19 | 596 | 15 | .025 |
| 4 | 595 | 21 | .035 | 20 | 630 | 24 | .038 |
| 5 | 665 | 23 | .035 | 21 | 625 | 25 | .040 |
| 6 | 596 | 19 | .032 | 22 | 615 | 21 | .034 |
| 7 | 600 | 18 | .030 | 23 | 575 | 23 | .040 |
| 8 | 620 | 24 | .039 | 24 | 572 | 20 | .035 |
| 9 | 610 | 20 | .033 | 25 | 645 | 24 | .037 |
| 10 | 595 | 22 | .037 | 26 | 651 | 39 | .060 |
| 11 | 645 | 19 | .029 | 27 | 660 | 21 | .032 |
| 12 | 675 | 23 | .034 | 28 | 685 | 19 | .028 |
| 13 | 670 | 22 | .033 | 29 | 671 | 17 | .025 |
| 14 | 590 | 26 | .044 | 30 | 660 | 22 | .033 |
| 15 | 585 | 17 | .029 | 31 | 595 | 24 | .040 |
| 16 | 560 | 16 | .029 | 32 | 600 | 16 | .027 |

**DATA FILE**
SPONGE

Set up a control chart for these data.

## SOLUTION
For these data,

$$k = 32, \sum_{i=1}^{k} n_i = 19{,}926 \quad \text{and} \quad \sum_{i=1}^{k} X_i = 679$$

Thus,

$$\bar{n} = \frac{19{,}926}{32} = 622.69 \quad \text{and} \quad \bar{p} = \frac{679}{19{,}926} = .034$$

so that we have

$$.034 \pm 3\sqrt{\frac{(.034)(1 - .034)}{622.69}}$$

Thus,

$$UCL = .034 + .022 = .056$$

and

$$LCL = .034 - .022 = .012$$

The control chart for the gauze sponge data is displayed in the accompanying figure. An examination of this figure indicates that day 26 (in which there were 39 nonconforming sponges out of 651 produced) is above the upper control limit. Management needs to determine the reasons for this special cause variation and take corrective action so that if the circumstances that may have produced these results on day 26 occur again, the results will be different.

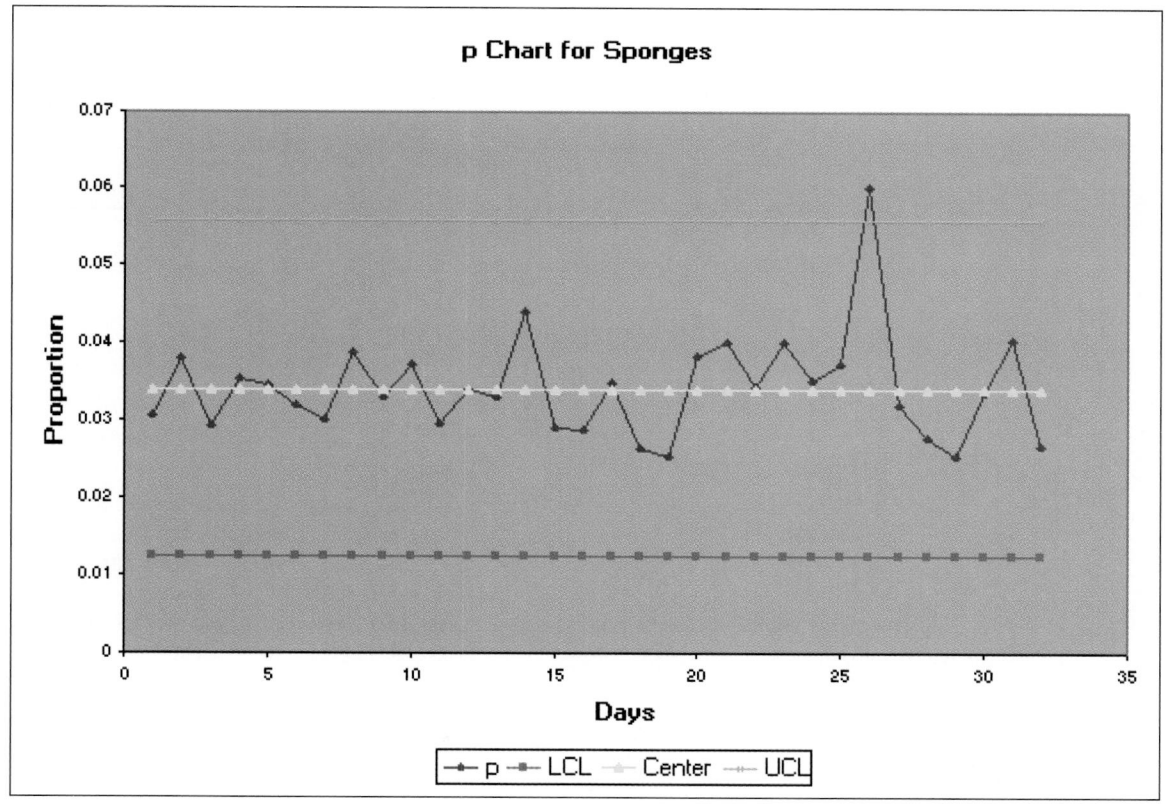

The *p* chart for the proportion of nonconforming sponges obtained from Microsoft Excel

### Learning the Basics

• **15.1** Suppose that the following data were collected on nonconformances for a period of 10 days.

| Day | Sample Size | Nonconformances | Day | Sample Size | Nonconformances |
|-----|-------------|-----------------|-----|-------------|-----------------|
| 1 | 100 | 12 | 6 | 100 | 14 |
| 2 | 100 | 14 | 7 | 100 | 15 |
| 3 | 100 | 10 | 8 | 100 | 13 |
| 4 | 100 | 18 | 9 | 100 | 14 |
| 5 | 100 | 22 | 10 | 100 | 16 |

(a) On what day is the proportion of nonconformances largest? Smallest?
(b) What are the *UCL* and *LCL*?
(c) Are there any special causes of variation?

**15.2** Suppose that the following data were collected on nonconformances for a period of 10 days.

| Day | Sample Size | Nonconformances | Day | Sample Size | Nonconformances |
|-----|-------------|-----------------|-----|-------------|-----------------|
| 1 | 111 | 12 | 6 | 88 | 14 |
| 2 | 93 | 14 | 7 | 117 | 15 |
| 3 | 105 | 10 | 8 | 87 | 13 |
| 4 | 92 | 18 | 9 | 119 | 14 |
| 5 | 117 | 22 | 10 | 107 | 16 |

(a) On what day is the proportion of nonconformances largest? Smallest?
(b) What are the *UCL* and *LCL*?
(c) Are there any special causes of variation?

### Applying the Concepts

• **15.3** The Commuters Watchdog Council of a railroad that serves a large metropolitan area wishes to monitor the on-time performance of the railroad during the morning rush hour. Suppose that a train is defined as being late if it arrives more than 5 minutes after the scheduled arrival time. A total of 235 trains are scheduled during the rush hour each morning. The results for a 4-week period (based on a 5-day work week) are as follows:

**Data File**
RRSPC

| Day | Late Arrivals | Day | Late Arrivals | Day | Late Arrivals | Day | Late Arrivals |
|-----|---------------|-----|---------------|-----|---------------|-----|---------------|
| 1 | 17 | 6 | 23 | 11 | 21 | 16 | 18 |
| 2 | 25 | 7 | 16 | 12 | 23 | 17 | 23 |
| 3 | 22 | 8 | 24 | 13 | 67 | 18 | 24 |
| 4 | 27 | 9 | 20 | 14 | 24 | 19 | 26 |
| 5 | 32 | 10 | 36 | 15 | 35 | 20 | 35 |

(a) Set up a *p* chart for the proportion of late arrivals and indicate whether the arrival process is in statistical control during this period.

(b) What effect would it have on your conclusion in (a) if you knew that there had been a 4-inch snowstorm on the morning of day 13?

(c) What effect would there be on the results obtained in (a) if the number of late arrivals on day 13 was 47?

● **15.4** A private mail delivery service has a policy of guaranteeing delivery by 10:30 A.M. of the morning after a package is picked up. Suppose that management of the service wishes to study delivery performance in a particular geographic area over a 4-week time period based on a 5-day work week. The total number of packages delivered daily and the number of packages that were not delivered by 10:30 A.M. are recorded and the results are as follows:

| DAY | PACKAGES DELIVERED | PACKAGES NOT ARRIVING BEFORE 10:30 A.M. | DAY | PACKAGES DELIVERED | PACKAGES NOT ARRIVING BEFORE 10:30 A.M. |
|-----|-----|-----|-----|-----|-----|
| 1 | 136 | 4 | 11 | 157 | 6 |
| 2 | 153 | 6 | 12 | 150 | 9 |
| 3 | 127 | 2 | 13 | 142 | 8 |
| 4 | 157 | 7 | 14 | 137 | 10 |
| 5 | 144 | 5 | 15 | 147 | 8 |
| 6 | 122 | 5 | 16 | 132 | 7 |
| 7 | 154 | 6 | 17 | 136 | 6 |
| 8 | 132 | 3 | 18 | 137 | 7 |
| 9 | 160 | 8 | 19 | 153 | 11 |
| 10 | 142 | 7 | 20 | 141 | 7 |

 **DATA FILE** MAILSPC

(a) Set up a *p* chart for the proportion of packages that are not delivered before 10:30 A.M.

(b) Does the process give an out-of-control signal?

**15.5** A hospital administrator was concerned with the time it took for patients' medical records to be processed after discharge. She determined that all records should be processed within 5 days of discharge. Any record not processed within 5 days of discharge was considered to be nonconforming. The number of patients discharged and the number of records not processed within the 5-day standard were recorded for a 30-day period as follows:

| DAY | NUMBER OF DISCHARGES | RECORDS NOT PROCESSED IN 5 DAYS | DAY | NUMBER OF DISCHARGES | RECORDS NOT PROCESSED IN 5 DAYS |
|-----|-----|-----|-----|-----|-----|
| 1 | 54 | 13 | 8 | 63 | 21 |
| 2 | 63 | 23 | 9 | 75 | 18 |
| 3 | 110 | 38 | 10 | 92 | 24 |
| 4 | 105 | 35 | 11 | 105 | 27 |
| 5 | 131 | 40 | 12 | 112 | 43 |
| 6 | 137 | 44 | 13 | 120 | 25 |
| 7 | 80 | 16 | 14 | 95 | 21 |

*continued*

| Day | Number of Discharges | Records Not Processed in 5 Days | Day | Number of Discharges | Records Not Processed in 5 Days |
|-----|-----|-----|-----|-----|-----|
| 15 | 72 | 11 | 23 | 107 | 45 |
| 16 | 128 | 24 | 24 | 135 | 53 |
| 17 | 126 | 33 | 25 | 124 | 57 |
| 18 | 106 | 38 | 26 | 113 | 28 |
| 19 | 129 | 39 | 27 | 140 | 38 |
| 20 | 136 | 74 | 28 | 83 | 21 |
| 21 | 94 | 31 | 29 | 62 | 10 |
| 22 | 74 | 15 | 30 | 106 | 45 |

**DATA FILE**
MEDREC

(a) Set up a $p$ chart for these data.
(b) Does the process give an out-of-control signal? Why?
(c) If the process is not in a state of statistical control, assume that special causes have been determined, eliminate out-of-control points, and recalculate the control limits.

**15.6** A bottling company of Sweet Suzy's Sugarless Cola maintains daily records of the occurrences of unacceptable cans flowing from the filling and sealing machine. Nonconformities such as improper filling amount, dented cans, and cans that are improperly sealed are noted. Data for 1 month's production (based on a 5-day work week) are as follows:

| Day | Cans Filled | Unacceptable Cans | Day | Cans Filled | Unacceptable Cans |
|-----|-----|-----|-----|-----|-----|
| 1 | 5,043 | 47 | 12 | 5,314 | 70 |
| 2 | 4,852 | 51 | 13 | 5,097 | 64 |
| 3 | 4,908 | 43 | 14 | 4,932 | 59 |
| 4 | 4,756 | 37 | 15 | 5,023 | 75 |
| 5 | 4,901 | 78 | 16 | 5,117 | 71 |
| 6 | 4,892 | 66 | 17 | 5,099 | 68 |
| 7 | 5,354 | 51 | 18 | 5,345 | 78 |
| 8 | 5,321 | 66 | 19 | 5,456 | 88 |
| 9 | 5,045 | 61 | 20 | 5,554 | 83 |
| 10 | 5,113 | 72 | 21 | 5,421 | 82 |
| 11 | 5,247 | 63 | 22 | 5,555 | 87 |

**DATA FILE**
COLASPC

(a) Set up a $p$ chart for the proportion of unacceptable cans for the month. Does the process give an out-of-control signal?
(b) If management wants to develop a process for reducing the proportion of unacceptable cans, how should it proceed?

**15.7** The manager of the accounting office of a large hospital is interested in studying the problem of errors in the entry of account numbers into the computer system. A group of 200 account numbers are selected from each day's output, and each is inspected to determine whether it is a nonconforming item. The results for a period of 39 days are as follows:

| Day | Nonconforming Items | Day | Nonconforming Items | Day | Nonconforming Items | Day | Nonconforming Items |
|-----|-----|-----|-----|-----|-----|-----|-----|
| 1 | 3 | 11 | 0 | 21 | 13 | 31 | 21 |
| 2 | 5 | 12 | 6 | 22 | 5 | 32 | 2 |
| 3 | 2 | 13 | 9 | 23 | 2 | 33 | 4 |
| 4 | 11 | 14 | 2 | 24 | 0 | 34 | 2 |
| 5 | 6 | 15 | 8 | 25 | 14 | 35 | 8 |
| 6 | 15 | 16 | 28 | 26 | 10 | 36 | 30 |
| 7 | 8 | 17 | 16 | 27 | 9 | 37 | 0 |
| 8 | 1 | 18 | 5 | 28 | 7 | 38 | 0 |
| 9 | 25 | 19 | 10 | 29 | 6 | 39 | 1 |
| 10 | 4 | 20 | 30 | 30 | 1 | | |

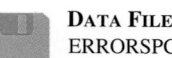

**DATA FILE
ERRORSPC**

(a) Set up a $p$ chart for the proportion of nonconforming items. Does the process give an out-of-control signal?

(b) On the basis of the results of (a), what would you now do as a manager to improve the process of account number entry?

**15.8** A manager of a regional office of a local telephone company has as one of her job responsibilities the task of processing requests for additions, changes, or deletions of telephone service. She forms a service improvement team to look at the corrections in terms of central office equipment and facilities required to process the orders issued to service requests. Data collected over a period of 30 days reveal the following:

| Day | Orders | Corrections | Day | Orders | Corrections | Day | Orders | Corrections |
|-----|--------|-------------|-----|--------|-------------|-----|--------|-------------|
| 1 | 690 | 80 | 11 | 812 | 70 | 21 | 678 | 65 |
| 2 | 676 | 88 | 12 | 759 | 83 | 22 | 915 | 74 |
| 3 | 896 | 74 | 13 | 781 | 64 | 23 | 698 | 68 |
| 4 | 707 | 94 | 14 | 682 | 64 | 24 | 821 | 72 |
| 5 | 694 | 70 | 15 | 802 | 72 | 25 | 750 | 101 |
| 6 | 765 | 95 | 16 | 831 | 91 | 26 | 600 | 91 |
| 7 | 788 | 73 | 17 | 816 | 80 | 27 | 744 | 64 |
| 8 | 794 | 103 | 18 | 701 | 96 | 28 | 698 | 67 |
| 9 | 694 | 100 | 19 | 761 | 78 | 29 | 820 | 105 |
| 10 | 784 | 103 | 20 | 851 | 85 | 30 | 732 | 112 |

**DATA FILE
TELESPC**

(a) Set up a $p$ chart for the proportion of corrections. Does the process give an out-of-control signal?

(b) What would you now do as a manager to improve the processing of requests for changes in telephone service?

## 15.5 THE RED BEAD EXPERIMENT: UNDERSTANDING PROCESS VARIABILITY

We began this chapter with a review of the history of quality and productivity that led us to a discussion of Deming's 14 points and then developed the concept of common cause variation and special cause variation. As an example of control chart procedures, we studied the *p* chart. In this section, to enhance our understanding of the two types of variation, common cause and special cause, we discuss what has become a famous parable, the **red bead experiment.**

³*Unknown to the participants in the experiment, 3,200, or 80%, of the beads are white and 800, or 20%, are red.*

The experiment involves the selection of beads from a box that typically contains 4,000 beads.[3] Several different scenarios can be used for conducting the experiment. The one that we use here begins with the following:

A facilitator (who will play the role of company foreman) asks members of the audience to volunteer for the jobs of workers (at least four are needed), inspectors (two are needed), chief inspector (one is needed), and recorder (one is needed). A worker's job consists of using a paddle that has five rows of 10 bead-size holes to select 50 beads from the box of beads.

Once the participants have been selected, the foreman explains the jobs to the particular participants. The job of the workers is to produce white beads because red beads are unacceptable to the customers. Strict procedures are to be followed. Work standards call for the production of 50 beads by each worker (a strict quota system)—no more and no less than 50. Management has established a standard that no more than 2 red beads (4%) per worker are to be produced on any given day.

The paddle is dipped into the box of beads so that when it is removed, each of the 50 holes contains a bead. Once this is done, the paddle is carried to each of the two inspectors, who independently record the count of red beads. The chief inspector compares their counts and announces the results to the audience. The recorder writes down the number and percentage of red beads next to the name of the worker.

Once all the people know their jobs, "production" can begin. Suppose that on the first "day," the number of red beads "produced" by the four workers (call them Alyson, David, Peter, and Sharyn) was 9, 12, 13, and 7, respectively. How should management react to the day's production when the standard says that no more than two red beads per worker should be produced? Should all the workers be reprimanded or should only David and Peter be given a stern warning that they will be fired if they don't improve?

Suppose that production continues for an additional 2 days: Table 15.2 summarizes the results for all 3 days.

From Table 15.2, we may observe several phenomena. On each day, some of the workers were above the average and some below the average. On day 1 Sharyn did best, but on day 2 Peter (who had the worst record on day 1) was best, and on day 3 Alyson was best.

**Table 15.2** *Red bead experiment results for four workers over 3 days*

| | DAY | | | |
| NAME | 1 | 2 | 3 | ALL 3 DAYS |
| --- | --- | --- | --- | --- |
| Alyson | 9 (18%) | 11 (22%) | 6 (12%) | 26 (17.33%) |
| David | 12 (24%) | 12 (24%) | 8 (16%) | 32 (21.33%) |
| Peter | 13 (26%) | 6 (12%) | 12 (24%) | 31 (20.67%) |
| Sharyn | 7 (14%) | 9 (18%) | 8 (16%) | 24 (16.0%) |
| All four workers | 41 | 38 | 34 | 113 |
| Average ($\overline{X}$) | 10.25 | 9.5 | 8.5 | 9.42 |
| Proportion | 20.5% | 19.0% | 17.0% | 18.83% |

How then can we explain all this variation? An answer can be provided by using equation (15.2) to develop a $p$ chart. For these data, we have

$$k = 4 \text{ workers} \times 3 \text{ days} = 12, \qquad n = 50, \qquad \text{and} \qquad \sum_{i=1}^{k} X_i = 113$$

Thus,

$$\bar{p} = \frac{113}{(50)12} = .1883$$

so that we have

$$\bar{p} \pm 3\sqrt{\frac{\bar{p}(1 - \bar{p})}{n}}$$

$$.1883 \pm 3\sqrt{\frac{.1883(1 - .1883)}{50}}$$

$$.1883 \pm .1659$$

Thus,

$$UCL = .1883 + .1659 = .3542$$

and

$$LCL = .1883 - .1659 = .0224$$

Figure 15.5 represents the $p$ chart for the data of Table 15.2. We observe from Figure 15.5 that all of the points are within the control limits and there are no patterns in the results. The differences between the workers represent common cause variation inherent in a stable system.

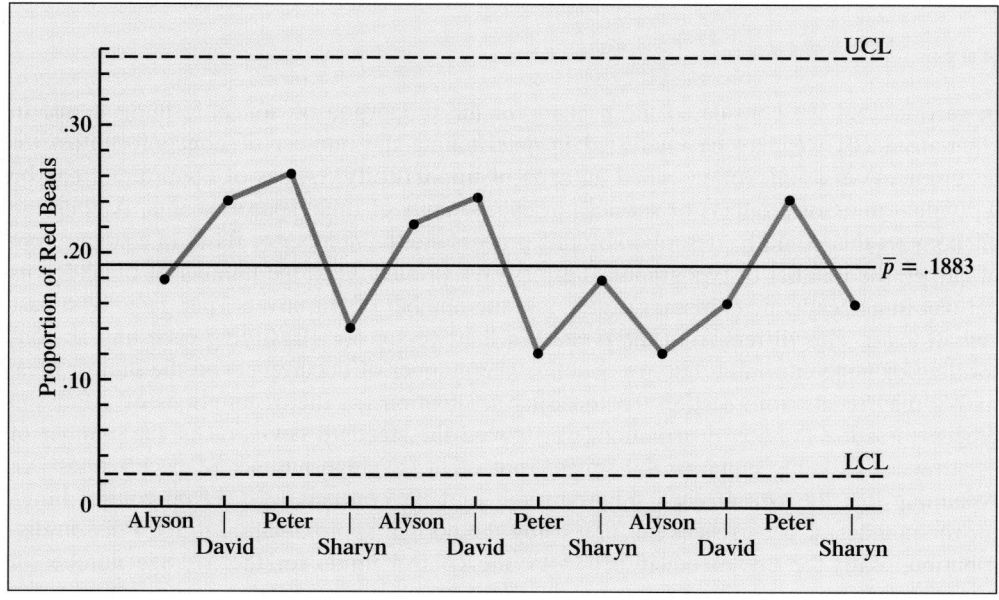

**FIGURE 15.5**   $p$ chart for red bead experiment

In conclusion, as shown in Exhibit 15.3, there are four morals to the parable of the red beads:

**Exhibit 15.3** *Morals of the Red Bead Experiment*

✓ **1.** Variation is an inherent part of any process.

✓ **2.** Workers work within a system over which they have little control. It is the system that primarily determines their performance.

✓ **3.** Only management can change the system.

✓ **4.** Some workers will always be above the average, and some workers will always be below the average.

## Problems for Section 15.5

### Applying the Concepts

**15.9** How do you think many managers would have reacted after day 1? Day 2? Day 3?

**15.10** (**Class Project**) Obtain a version of the red bead experiment for your class.
  (a) Conduct the experiment in the same way as described in this section.
  (b) Remove 400 red beads from the bead box before beginning the experiment. How do your results differ from those obtained in (a)? What does this tell you about the effect of the "system" on the workers?

 ## THE *c* CHART

In section 15.4 we considered the *p* chart for the proportion of nonconforming items. In other instances we may be interested in determining the number of nonconformities (or occurrences) in a unit (often called an **area of opportunity**). Areas of opportunity can be individual units of products or services or can be units of time, space, or area. Among the phenomena that could be described by this process are the number of flaws in a square foot of carpet, the number of typographical errors on a printed page, the number of breakdowns per day in an academic computer center, and the number of "turnovers" per game by a basketball team. This differs from the *p* chart in that we are not classifying each unit as conforming or nonconforming but are counting the number of occurrences in the unit or area.

We may recall from section 6.3 that such a situation fits the assumptions of a Poisson process. For the Poisson distribution, we defined the standard deviation of the number of occurrences as being equal to the square root of the average number of occurrences ($\lambda$). Assuming that the size of each subgroup unit remains constant,[4] we set up control limits for the number of occurrences per unit using the normal approximation to the Poisson distribution. With the use of equation (15.1), the control limits for the average number of occurrences are

[4]*If the size of the unit varies appreciably, the u chart should be used instead of the c chart (see references 5, 8, and 13).*

## Obtaining Control Limits for the c Chart

$$\bar{c} \pm 3\sqrt{\bar{c}}$$

(15.4)

where

$$\bar{c} = \frac{\sum\limits_{i=1}^{k} c_i}{k}$$

$\bar{c}$ = average number of occurrences

$k$ = number of units sampled

$c_i$ = number of occurrences in unit $i$

so that

## Obtaining Upper and Lower Control Limits for the c Chart

$$UCL = \bar{c} + 3\sqrt{\bar{c}}$$

$$LCL = \bar{c} - 3\sqrt{\bar{c}}$$

(15.5)

As an application of the $c$ chart, suppose that the operations manager of a large baking factory that makes Marilyn's pumpkin chocolate chip cupcakes for the Halloween holiday season needed to study the baking process to determine the number of chocolate chips that were present in the cupcakes being baked. A sample of 50 cupcakes was selected from the production line. The results, listed in the order of selection, are summarized in Table 15.3.

**Table 15.3** *Number of chocolate chips in a subgroup of 50 cupcakes*

| CUPCAKE | NUMBER OF CHOCOLATE CHIPS | CUPCAKE | NUMBER OF CHOCOLATE CHIPS | CUPCAKE | NUMBER OF CHOCOLATE CHIPS | CUPCAKE | NUMBER OF CHOCOLATE CHIPS |
|---------|---------------------------|---------|---------------------------|---------|---------------------------|---------|---------------------------|
| 1 | 8 | 14 | 11 | 26 | 7 | 39 | 3 |
| 2 | 10 | 15 | 10 | 27 | 5 | 40 | 3 |
| 3 | 6 | 16 | 9 | 28 | 8 | 41 | 4 |
| 4 | 7 | 17 | 8 | 29 | 6 | 42 | 2 |
| 5 | 5 | 18 | 7 | 30 | 7 | 43 | 4 |
| 6 | 7 | 19 | 10 | 31 | 5 | 44 | 5 |
| 7 | 9 | 20 | 11 | 32 | 5 | 45 | 5 |
| 8 | 8 | 21 | 8 | 33 | 4 | 46 | 3 |
| 9 | 7 | 22 | 7 | 34 | 4 | 47 | 2 |
| 10 | 9 | 23 | 8 | 35 | 3 | 48 | 5 |
| 11 | 10 | 24 | 6 | 36 | 5 | 49 | 4 |
| 12 | 7 | 25 | 7 | 37 | 2 | 50 | 4 |
| 13 | 8 | | | 38 | 4 | | |

**DATA FILE**
CHIPS

For these data

$$k = 50 \quad \text{and} \quad \sum_{i=1}^{k} c_i = 312$$

Thus,

$$\bar{c} = \frac{312}{50} = 6.24$$

so that using equations (15.4) and (15.5), we have

$$6.24 \pm 3\sqrt{6.24}$$
$$6.24 \pm 7.494$$

Thus,

$$UCL = 6.24 + 7.494 = 13.734$$

and

$LCL = 6.24 - 7.494 = -1.254$, which is less than 0, so that $LCL$ does not exist

The control chart for the data of Table 15.3 is displayed in Figure 15.6. An examination of Figure 15.6 does not indicate any points outside the control limits. However, there is a clear pattern to the number of chocolate chips per cupcake over time, with cupcakes baked in the first half of the sequence almost always having more than the average number of chocolate chips and cupcakes in the latter half of the sequence having fewer than the average number of chocolate chips. Thus, the operations manager should immediately investigate the process to determine the special causes that have produced this pattern of variation.

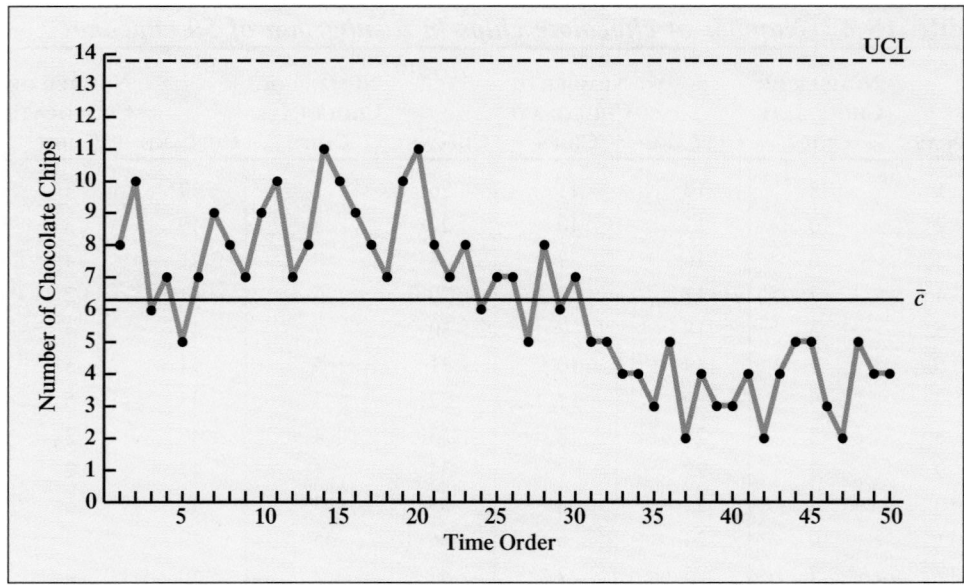

**FIGURE 15.6** *c* chart for number of chocolate chips per cupcake

## Problems for Section 15.6

### Learning the Basics

**15.11** Suppose that the following data were collected on the number of nonconformances per unit for 10 time periods:

| TIME | NONCONFORMANCES PER UNIT | TIME | NONCONFORMANCES PER UNIT |
|------|--------------------------|------|--------------------------|
| 1 | 7 | 6 | 5 |
| 2 | 3 | 7 | 3 |
| 3 | 6 | 8 | 5 |
| 4 | 3 | 9 | 2 |
| 5 | 4 | 10 | 0 |

(a) Set up the appropriate control chart and determine the *UCL* and *LCL*.
(b) Are there any special causes of variation?

**● 15.12** Suppose that the following data were collected on the number of nonconformances per unit for 10 time periods:

| TIME | NONCONFORMANCES PER UNIT | TIME | NONCONFORMANCES PER UNIT |
|------|--------------------------|------|--------------------------|
| 1 | 25 | 6 | 15 |
| 2 | 11 | 7 | 12 |
| 3 | 10 | 8 | 10 |
| 4 | 11 | 9 | 9 |
| 5 | 6 | 10 | 6 |

(a) Set up the appropriate control chart and determine the *UCL* and *LCL*.
(b) Are there any special causes of variation?

### Applying the Concepts

**● 15.13** The owner of a dry cleaning business, in an effort to measure the quality of the services provided, would like to study the number of dry-cleaned items that are returned for rework per day. Records were kept for a 4-week period (the store is open Monday–Saturday) with the results indicated as follows:

| DAY | ITEMS RETURNED FOR REWORK | DAY | ITEMS RETURNED FOR REWORK | DAY | ITEMS RETURNED FOR REWORK |
|-----|---------------------------|-----|---------------------------|-----|---------------------------|
| 1 | 4 | 9 | 8 | 17 | 10 |
| 2 | 6 | 10 | 6 | 18 | 9 |
| 3 | 3 | 11 | 5 | 19 | 6 |
| 4 | 7 | 12 | 12 | 20 | 5 |
| 5 | 6 | 13 | 5 | 21 | 8 |
| 6 | 8 | 14 | 8 | 22 | 6 |
| 7 | 6 | 15 | 3 | 23 | 7 |
| 8 | 4 | 16 | 4 | 24 | 9 |

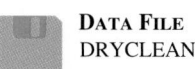

DATA FILE
DRYCLEAN

(a) Set up a $c$ chart for the number of items per day that are returned for rework. Do you think that the process is in a state of statistical control?

(b) Should the owner of the dry cleaning store take action to investigate why 12 items were returned for rework on day 12? Explain. Would your answer be the same if 20 items were returned for rework on day 12?

(c) On the basis of the results in (a), how should the owner of the dry cleaning store proceed in setting up a process to reduce the number of items per day that are returned for rework?

**15.14** The branch manager of a savings bank has recorded the number of errors of a particular type that each of 12 tellers has made during the past year. The results are as follows:

DATA FILE
TELLER

| TELLER | NUMBER OF ERRORS | TELLER | NUMBER OF ERRORS |
|--------|------------------|--------|------------------|
| Alice | 4 | Mitchell | 6 |
| Carl | 7 | Nora | 3 |
| Gina | 12 | Paul | 5 |
| Jane | 6 | Susan | 4 |
| Linda | 2 | Thomas | 7 |
| Marla | 5 | Vera | 5 |

(a) Do you think the bank manager will single out Gina for any disciplinary action regarding her performance in the last year?

(b) Set up a $c$ chart for the number of errors committed by the 12 tellers. Is the number of errors in a state of statistical control?

(c) On the basis of the $c$ chart developed in (b), do you now think that Gina should be singled out for disciplinary action regarding her performance? Does your conclusion now agree with what you expected the manager to do?

(d) On the basis of the results in (b), how should the branch manager go about setting up a program to reduce this particular type of error?

**15.15** Falls are one source of preventable hospital injury. Although most patients who fall are not hurt, a risk of serious injury is involved. The following data represent the number of patient falls per month over a 28-month period in a 19-bed AIDS unit at a major metropolitan hospital.

DATA FILE
PTFALLS

| MONTH | NUMBER OF PATIENT FALLS | MONTH | NUMBER OF PATIENT FALLS | MONTH | NUMBER OF PATIENT FALLS | MONTH | NUMBER OF PATIENT FALLS |
|-------|-------------------------|-------|-------------------------|-------|-------------------------|-------|-------------------------|
| 1 | 2 | 8 | 4 | 15 | 6 | 22 | 4 |
| 2 | 4 | 9 | 5 | 16 | 5 | 23 | 5 |
| 3 | 2 | 10 | 11 | 17 | 3 | 24 | 0 |
| 4 | 4 | 11 | 8 | 18 | 8 | 25 | 2 |
| 5 | 3 | 12 | 7 | 19 | 6 | 26 | 6 |
| 6 | 3 | 13 | 9 | 20 | 3 | 27 | 5 |
| 7 | 1 | 14 | 10 | 21 | 9 | 28 | 7 |

(a) Set up a $c$ chart for the number of patient falls per month. Is the process of patient falls per month in a state of statistical control?

(b) What effect would it have on your conclusions if you knew that the unit was started only 1 month prior to the beginning of data collection?

(c) What other factors might contribute to special cause variation in this problem?

**15.16** The director of operations for an airline was interested in studying the number of pieces of baggage that are lost (temporarily or permanently) at a large airport. Records indicating the number of lost baggage claims filed per day over a 1-month period were as follows:

| DAY | NUMBER OF CLAIMS | DAY | NUMBER OF CLAIMS | DAY | NUMBER OF CLAIMS |
|---|---|---|---|---|---|
| 1 | 14 | 11 | 15 | 21 | 38 |
| 2 | 23 | 12 | 27 | 22 | 23 |
| 3 | 17 | 13 | 41 | 23 | 28 |
| 4 | 25 | 14 | 50 | 24 | 19 |
| 5 | 27 | 15 | 23 | 25 | 26 |
| 6 | 42 | 16 | 28 | 26 | 14 |
| 7 | 35 | 17 | 20 | 27 | 30 |
| 8 | 29 | 18 | 13 | 28 | 37 |
| 9 | 30 | 19 | 26 | 29 | 17 |
| 10 | 23 | 20 | 42 | 30 | 24 |

DATA FILE
BAGGAGE

(a) Set up a control chart for the number of claims per day. Is the process in a state of statistical control? Explain.
(b) Suppose that the total number of pieces of baggage per day was available for the 30-day period. Explain how you might proceed with a different control chart than the one you used in (a). Indicate what the advantages could be of using this alternative control chart compared with the control chart that was used in (a).

**15.17** The University of Southwest North Carolina has recently completed its basketball season. Its basketball coach, the legendary Raving Rick Rawng, has maintained records of the number of turnovers (the times the ball was lost without taking a shot) per game. The results are as follows:

| GAME | NUMBER OF TURNOVERS | GAME | NUMBER OF TURNOVERS | GAME | NUMBER OF TURNOVERS |
|---|---|---|---|---|---|
| 1 | 16 | 10 | 9 | 19 | 29 |
| 2 | 12 | 11 | 13 | 20 | 11 |
| 3 | 25 | 12 | 16 | 21 | 7 |
| 4 | 17 | 13 | 21 | 22 | 15 |
| 5 | 11 | 14 | 18 | 23 | 12 |
| 6 | 19 | 15 | 26 | 24 | 17 |
| 7 | 17 | 16 | 14 | 25 | 22 |
| 8 | 23 | 17 | 12 | 26 | 14 |
| 9 | 12 | 18 | 16 | | |

DATA FILE
TURNOVER

(a) Set up a *c* chart for the number of turnovers per game. Is the process in a state of statistical control?
(b) On the basis of the results of (a), how should the coach proceed in setting up a process to reduce the number of turnovers in the future?

# CONTROL CHARTS FOR THE RANGE (R) AND THE MEAN ($\overline{X}$)

Whenever a characteristic of interest is measured on an interval or ratio scale, **variables control charts** can be used to monitor a process. Because measures from these more powerful scales provide more information than the proportion or number of nonconforming items, these charts are more sensitive in detecting special cause variation than the $p$ chart. Variables charts are typically used in pairs. One chart monitors the variation in a process; the other monitors the process average. The chart that monitors variability must be examined first because if it indicates the presence of out-of-control conditions, the interpretation of the chart for the average will be misleading. Although several alternative pairs of charts can be considered (see references 5, 8, and 13), in this text we will study the control charts for the range and average.

## The R Chart: A Control Chart for Dispersion

Before obtaining control limits for the mean, we need to develop a control chart for the range, the **R chart.** This will enable us to determine whether the variability in a process is in control or whether shifts are occurring over time. If the process range is in control, then it can be used to develop the control limits for the average.

From equation (15.1) we observe that to develop control limits for the range, we need to obtain an estimate of the average range and the standard deviation of the range. As is seen in equation (15.6), these control limits depend on two factors, $d_2$, which represents the relationship between the standard deviation and the range for varying sample sizes, and $d_3$, which represents the relationship between the standard deviation and the standard error of the range for varying sample sizes. Values for these factors are presented in Table E.11. Thus, we have the following control limits for the range over $k$ consecutive sequences or periods of time.

### Control Limits for the Range

$$\overline{R} \pm 3\overline{R}\frac{d_3}{d_2} \tag{15.6}$$

where

$$\overline{R} = \frac{\sum_{i=1}^{k} R_i}{k}$$

$R_i$ = the range of $n$ observations for subgroup $i$

$k$ = the number of subgroups or time periods, each of size $n$

so that

### Upper and Lower Control Limits for the Range

$$UCL = \bar{R} + 3\bar{R}\frac{d_3}{d_2}$$ (15.7a)

$$LCL = \bar{R} - 3\bar{R}\frac{d_3}{d_2}$$ (15.7b)

Referring to equations (15.7a) and (15.7b), we may simplify the calculations by utilizing the **$D_4$ factor**, equal to $1 + 3(d_3/d_2)$, and the **$D_3$ factor**, equal to $1 - 3(d_3/d_2)$, to obtain the control limits as shown in equations (15.8a) and (15.8b)

### Upper and Lower Control Limits for the Range

$$UCL = D_4\bar{R}$$ (15.8a)
$$LCL = D_3\bar{R}$$ (15.8b)

To illustrate the use of the $R$ chart, we return to the hotel service quality example on page 684. We mentioned that management wanted to study the aspect of service that related to the amount of time it takes to deliver luggage (as measured from the time the guest completes check-in procedures to the time the luggage arrives in the guest's room). Data are recorded over a 4-week (Sunday–Saturday) period, and subgroups of five deliveries are selected (on a certain shift) on each day for analysis. The summary results (in minutes) are recorded in Table 15.4.

---

**Table 15.4** *Subgroup average and range for luggage delivery times over 4-week period*

| DAY | SUBGROUP AVERAGE $\bar{X}_i$ (IN MINUTES) | SUBGROUP RANGE $R_i$ (IN MINUTES) | DAY | SUBGROUP AVERAGE $\bar{X}_i$ (IN MINUTES) | SUBGROUP RANGE $R_i$ (IN MINUTES) |
|---|---|---|---|---|---|
| 1 | 5.32 | 3.85 | 15 | 5.21 | 3.26 |
| 2 | 6.59 | 4.27 | 16 | 4.68 | 2.92 |
| 3 | 4.88 | 3.28 | 17 | 5.32 | 3.37 |
| 4 | 5.70 | 2.99 | 18 | 4.90 | 3.55 |
| 5 | 4.07 | 3.61 | 19 | 4.44 | 3.73 |
| 6 | 7.34 | 5.04 | 20 | 5.80 | 3.86 |
| 7 | 6.79 | 4.22 | 21 | 5.61 | 3.65 |
| 8 | 4.93 | 3.69 | 22 | 4.77 | 3.38 |
| 9 | 5.01 | 3.33 | 23 | 4.37 | 3.02 |
| 10 | 3.92 | 2.96 | 24 | 4.79 | 3.80 |
| 11 | 5.66 | 3.77 | 25 | 5.03 | 4.11 |
| 12 | 4.98 | 3.09 | 26 | 5.11 | 3.75 |
| 13 | 6.83 | 5.21 | 27 | 6.94 | 4.57 |
| 14 | 5.27 | 3.84 | 28 | 5.71 | 4.29 |

**DATA FILE**
HOTEL2

For these data,

$$k = 28 \quad \text{and} \quad \sum_{i=1}^{k} R_i = 104.41$$

Thus,

$$\overline{R} = \frac{104.41}{28} = 3.729$$

From Table E.11 for $n = 5$, we obtain $d_2 = 2.326$ and $d_3 = .864$. Using equations (15.6) and (15.7), we have

$$3.729 \pm 3 \frac{(.864)(3.729)}{2.326}$$

$$3.729 \pm 4.155$$

so that

$$UCL = 3.729 + 4.155 = 7.884$$

but

$$LCL = 3.729 - 4.155 = -0.426 \text{ so that } LCL \text{ does not exist}$$

Alternatively, using equations (15.8a) and (15.8b), from Table E.11, $D_4 = 2.114$ and $D_3 = 0$. Thus,

$$UCL = (2.114)(3.729) = 7.883$$

and

$$LCL \text{ does not exist}$$

We note that the lower control limit for $R$ does not exist because a negative range is impossible to attain. The $R$ chart is displayed in Figure 15.7. An examination of Figure 15.7 does not indicate any individual ranges outside the control limits.

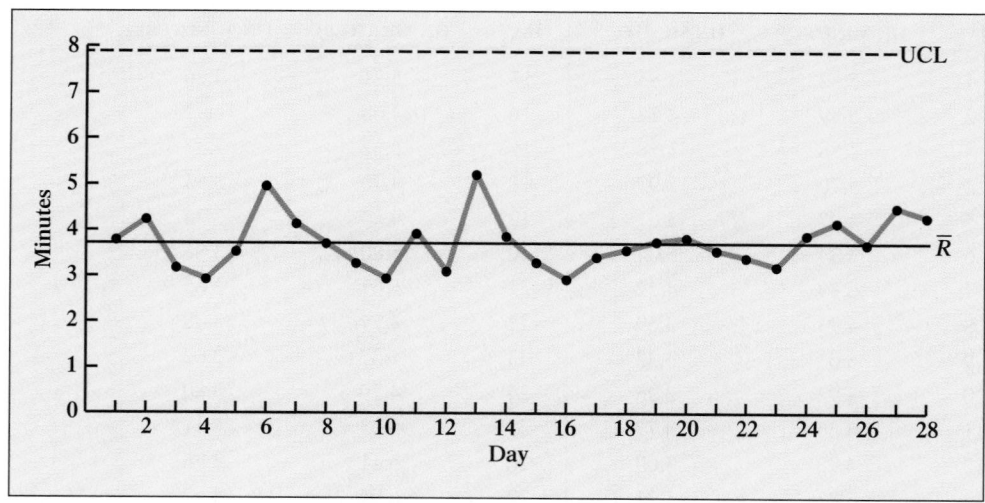

**FIGURE 15.7** R chart for luggage delivery times
*Source: Table 15.4*

## The $\overline{X}$ Chart

Now that we have determined that the control chart for the range is in control, we continue by examining the control chart for the process average, the $\overline{X}$ **chart**.

The control chart for $\overline{X}$ uses subgroups each of size $n$ that are obtained over $k$ consecutive sequences or periods of time. From equation (15.9) we observe that to compute control limits for the average, we need to obtain an estimate of the average of the subgroup averages (which we shall call $\overline{\overline{X}}$) and the standard deviation of the average (which we called the standard error of the mean $\sigma_{\overline{x}}$ in chapter 9). These control limits are a function of the $d_2$ factor, which represents the relationship between the standard deviation and the range for varying sample sizes. The range is used to estimate the standard deviation as long as the subgroup size is no more than 10 (see references 5, 8, and 13). Thus, we set up the following control limits:

---

### Obtaining Control Limits for the Mean

$$\overline{\overline{X}} \pm 3\,\frac{\overline{R}}{d_2\sqrt{n}} \tag{15.9}$$

where $\quad \overline{\overline{X}} = \dfrac{\displaystyle\sum_{i=1}^{k} \overline{X}_i}{k} \qquad \overline{R} = \dfrac{\displaystyle\sum_{i=1}^{k} R_i}{k}$

$\overline{X}_i$ = the sample mean of $n$ observations in the subgroup at time $i$

$R_i$ = the range of $n$ observations in the subgroup at time $i$

$k$ = number of subgroups

---

so that

---

### Obtaining Upper and Lower Control Limits for the Mean

$$UCL = \overline{\overline{X}} + 3\,\frac{\overline{R}}{d_2\sqrt{n}} \tag{15.10a}$$

$$LCL = \overline{\overline{X}} - 3\,\frac{\overline{R}}{d_2\sqrt{n}} \tag{15.10b}$$

---

Referring to equations (15.10a) and (15.10b), we simplify the calculations by utilizing the **$A_2$ factor**, equal to $3/(d_2\sqrt{n})$, to obtain the control limits as displayed in equations (15.11a) and (15.11b).

---

### Obtaining Upper and Lower Control Limits for the Mean

$$UCL = \overline{\overline{X}} + A_2\overline{R} \tag{15.11a}$$

$$LCL = \overline{\overline{X}} - A_2\overline{R} \tag{15.11b}$$

---

Thus, returning to our luggage delivery time example from Table 15.4, we compute

$$k = 28, \qquad \sum_{i=1}^{k} \overline{X}_i = 149.97, \qquad \text{and} \qquad \sum_{i=1}^{k} R_i = 104.41$$

so that

$$\overline{\overline{X}} = \frac{149.97}{28} = 5.356 \qquad \text{and} \qquad \overline{R} = \frac{104.41}{28} = 3.729$$

From Table E.11 for $n = 5$, we obtain $d_2 = 2.326$. Thus, using equation (15.10), we have

$$5.356 \pm 3 \frac{3.729}{(2.326)\sqrt{5}}$$

$$5.356 \pm 2.151$$

Therefore,

$$UCL = 5.356 + 2.151 = 7.507$$

and

$$LCL = 5.356 - 2.151 = 3.205$$

Alternatively, using equation (15.11), from Table E.11, we have $A_2 = .577$ and

$$UCL = 5.356 + (.577)(3.729) = 5.356 + 2.152 = 7.508$$
$$LCL = 5.356 - (.577)(3.729) = 5.356 - 2.152 = 3.204$$

These results are the same, except for rounding error.

The control chart for the luggage delivery time data of Table 15.4 is displayed in Figure 15.8. An examination of Figure 15.8 does not reveal any points outside the control limits,

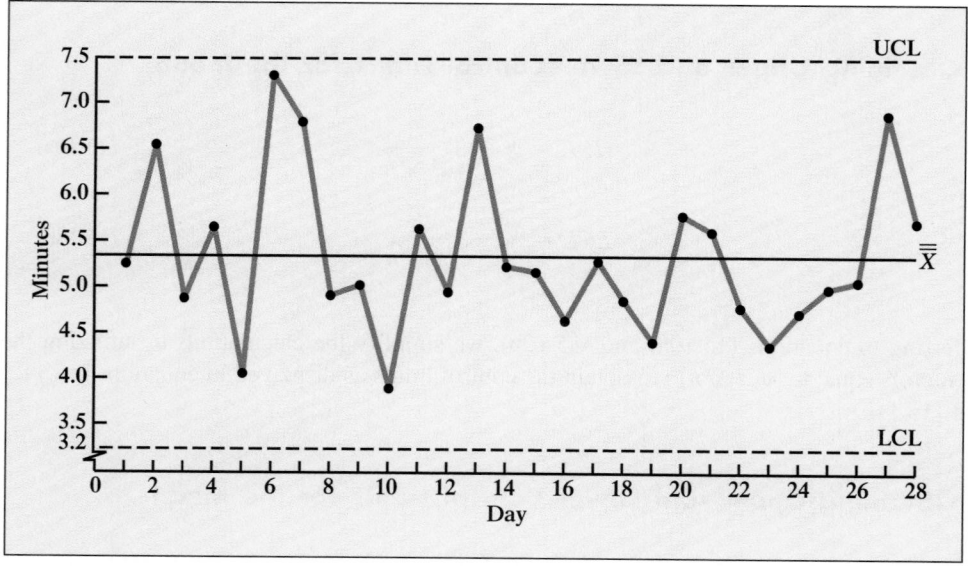

**FIGURE 15.8** $\overline{X}$ chart for average luggage delivery time
*Source: Table 15.4*

although there is a large amount of variability among the 28 subgroup means. If management wants to reduce the variation or lower the average delivery time, the process needs to be changed.

## Problems for Section 15.7

### Learning the Basics

• **15.18** For subgroups of size $n = 4$, what is the value of
   (a) the $d_2$ factor
   (b) the $d_3$ factor
   (c) the $D_3$ factor
   (d) the $D_4$ factor
   (e) the $A_2$ factor

**15.19** Given the following summary data for subgroups of $n = 4$ for a 10-day period

| DAY | AVERAGE | RANGE | DAY | AVERAGE | RANGE |
|-----|---------|-------|-----|---------|-------|
| 1 | 13.6 | 3.5 | 6 | 12.9 | 4.8 |
| 2 | 14.3 | 4.1 | 7 | 17.3 | 4.5 |
| 3 | 15.3 | 5.0 | 8 | 13.9 | 2.9 |
| 4 | 12.6 | 2.8 | 9 | 12.6 | 3.8 |
| 5 | 11.8 | 3.7 | 10 | 15.2 | 4.6 |

   (a) Set up control limits for the range.
   (b) Is there any evidence of special cause variation?
   (c) Set up control limits for the average.
   (d) Is there any evidence of special cause variation?

### Applying the Concepts

**15.20** The following data pertaining to incandescent light bulbs represent the average life and range for 30 subgroups of 5 light bulbs each.

| SUBGROUP NUMBER | SUBGROUP MEAN $\overline{X}_i$ | SUBGROUP RANGE $R_i$ | SUBGROUP NUMBER | SUBGROUP MEAN $\overline{X}_i$ | SUBGROUP RANGE $R_i$ |
|---|---|---|---|---|---|
| 1 | 790 | 52 | 16 | 845 | 42 |
| 2 | 845 | 56 | 17 | 891 | 38 |
| 3 | 857 | 116 | 18 | 859 | 65 |
| 4 | 846 | 89 | 19 | 826 | 70 |
| 5 | 843 | 65 | 20 | 828 | 37 |
| 6 | 877 | 73 | 21 | 854 | 52 |
| 7 | 861 | 38 | 22 | 847 | 49 |
| 8 | 891 | 84 | 23 | 868 | 40 |
| 9 | 866 | 76 | 24 | 851 | 43 |
| 10 | 816 | 72 | 25 | 870 | 64 |
| 11 | 806 | 61 | 26 | 857 | 53 |
| 12 | 835 | 55 | 27 | 851 | 59 |
| 13 | 797 | 59 | 28 | 834 | 68 |
| 14 | 803 | 47 | 29 | 842 | 57 |
| 15 | 818 | 69 | 30 | 825 | 74 |

**DATA FILE**
BULBLIFE

(a) Set up a control chart for the range.
(b) Set up a control chart for the average light bulb life.
(c) On the basis of the results of (a) and (b), what conclusions can you draw about the process?

**15.21** The manager of a branch of a local bank wants to study waiting times of customers for teller service during the peak 12 noon to 1 P.M. lunch hour. A subgroup of four customers is selected (one at each 15-minute interval during the hour), and the time in minutes is measured from the point each customer enters the line to when he or she begins to be served. The results over a 4-week period are as follows:

| DAY | TIME IN MINUTES | | | | DAY | TIME IN MINUTES | | | |
|-----|-----|-----|-----|-----|-----|-----|-----|-----|-----|
| 1 | 7.2 | 8.4 | 7.9 | 4.9 | 11 | 2.6 | 3.9 | 5.2 | 4.8 |
| 2 | 5.6 | 8.7 | 3.3 | 4.2 | 12 | 4.6 | 2.7 | 6.3 | 3.4 |
| 3 | 5.5 | 7.3 | 3.2 | 6.0 | 13 | 4.9 | 6.2 | 7.8 | 8.7 |
| 4 | 4.4 | 8.0 | 5.4 | 7.4 | 14 | 7.1 | 6.3 | 8.2 | 5.5 |
| 5 | 9.7 | 4.6 | 4.8 | 5.8 | 15 | 7.1 | 5.8 | 6.9 | 7.0 |
| 6 | 8.3 | 8.9 | 9.1 | 6.2 | 16 | 6.7 | 6.9 | 7.0 | 9.4 |
| 7 | 4.7 | 6.6 | 5.3 | 5.8 | 17 | 5.5 | 6.3 | 3.2 | 4.9 |
| 8 | 8.8 | 5.5 | 8.4 | 6.9 | 18 | 4.9 | 5.1 | 3.2 | 7.6 |
| 9 | 5.7 | 4.7 | 4.1 | 4.6 | 19 | 7.2 | 8.0 | 4.1 | 5.9 |
| 10 | 1.7 | 4.0 | 3.0 | 5.2 | 20 | 6.1 | 3.4 | 7.2 | 5.9 |

DATA FILE
BANKTIME

(a) Set up control charts for the range and the arithmetic mean.
(b) On the basis of the results in (a), indicate whether the process is in control in terms of these charts.

**• 15.22** The manager of a warehouse for a local telephone company is involved in a process that receives expensive circuit boards and returns them to central stock so they may be used at a later date when a circuit or new telephone service is needed. The timely return and processing of these units is critical in providing good service to field customers and reducing capital expenditures of the corporation. The following data represent the number of units handled by each of a subgroup of five employees over a 30-day period.

| DAY | EMPLOYEE | | | | |
| | 1 | 2 | 3 | 4 | 5 |
|-----|-----|-----|-----|-----|-----|
| 1 | 114 | 499 | 106 | 342 | 55 |
| 2 | 219 | 319 | 162 | 44 | 87 |
| 3 | 64 | 302 | 38 | 83 | 93 |
| 4 | 258 | 110 | 98 | 78 | 154 |
| 5 | 127 | 140 | 298 | 518 | 275 |
| 6 | 151 | 176 | 188 | 268 | 77 |
| 7 | 24 | 183 | 202 | 81 | 104 |
| 8 | 41 | 249 | 342 | 338 | 69 |
| 9 | 93 | 189 | 209 | 444 | 151 |
| 10 | 111 | 207 | 143 | 318 | 129 |
| 11 | 205 | 281 | 250 | 468 | 79 |
| 12 | 121 | 261 | 183 | 606 | 287 |

*continued*

| | EMPLOYEE | | | | |
|---|---|---|---|---|---|
| DAY | 1 | 2 | 3 | 4 | 5 |
| 13 | 225 | 83 | 198 | 223 | 180 |
| 14 | 235 | 439 | 102 | 330 | 190 |
| 15 | 91 | 32 | 190 | 70 | 150 |
| 16 | 181 | 191 | 182 | 444 | 124 |
| 17 | 52 | 190 | 310 | 245 | 156 |
| 18 | 90 | 538 | 277 | 308 | 171 |
| 19 | 78 | 587 | 147 | 172 | 299 |
| 20 | 45 | 265 | 126 | 137 | 151 |
| 21 | 410 | 227 | 179 | 298 | 342 |
| 22 | 68 | 375 | 195 | 67 | 72 |
| 23 | 140 | 266 | 157 | 92 | 140 |
| 24 | 145 | 170 | 231 | 60 | 191 |
| 25 | 129 | 74 | 148 | 119 | 139 |
| 26 | 143 | 384 | 263 | 147 | 131 |
| 27 | 86 | 229 | 474 | 181 | 40 |
| 28 | 164 | 313 | 295 | 297 | 280 |
| 29 | 257 | 310 | 217 | 152 | 351 |
| 30 | 106 | 134 | 175 | 153 | 69 |

DATA FILE
WAREHSE

(a) Set up control charts for the range and the arithmetic mean.
(b) On the basis of the results in (a), indicate whether the process is in control in terms of these charts.

● **15.23** The service manager of a large automobile dealership wants to study the length of time required for a particular type of repair in his shop. A subgroup of 10 cars needing this repair is selected on each day for a period of 4 weeks. The summary results (service time in hours) are recorded as follows:

| SUBGROUP DAY | SUBGROUP | | SUBGROUP DAY | SUBGROUP | |
|---|---|---|---|---|---|
| | AVERAGE $\bar{X}_i$ | RANGE $R_i$ | | AVERAGE $\bar{X}_i$ | RANGE $R_i$ |
| 1 | 3.73 | 5.23 | 11 | 3.64 | 5.37 |
| 2 | 3.16 | 4.82 | 12 | 3.27 | 4.42 |
| 3 | 3.56 | 4.98 | 13 | 3.16 | 4.85 |
| 4 | 3.01 | 4.28 | 14 | 3.39 | 4.44 |
| 5 | 3.87 | 5.74 | 15 | 3.85 | 5.06 |
| 6 | 3.90 | 5.42 | 16 | 3.90 | 4.99 |
| 7 | 3.54 | 4.08 | 17 | 3.72 | 4.67 |
| 8 | 3.32 | 4.55 | 18 | 3.51 | 4.37 |
| 9 | 3.29 | 4.48 | 19 | 3.34 | 4.53 |
| 10 | 3.83 | 5.09 | 20 | 3.99 | 5.28 |

DATA FILE
AUTOREP

(a) Set up all appropriate control charts and determine whether the service time process is in a state of statistical control.

(b) If the service manager wants to develop a process to reduce service time, how should he proceed?

**15.24** The director of radiology at a large metropolitan hospital is concerned about the scheduling of the radiology facilities. An average of 250 patients a day are transported each day from wards to the radiology department for treatment or diagnostic procedures. If patients do not reach the radiology unit at their scheduled times, backups will occur and other patients will experience delays. The time it takes to transport patients from wards to the radiology unit was operationally defined as the time between when the transporter was assigned to the patient and the time the patient arrived at the radiology unit. A sample of $n = 4$ patients was selected each day for 20 days, and the time to transport each patient (in minutes) was determined with the following results.

| | PATIENT | | | | | PATIENT | | | |
| DAY | 1 | 2 | 3 | 4 | DAY | 1 | 2 | 3 | 4 |
| --- | --- | --- | --- | --- | --- | --- | --- | --- | --- |
| 1 | 16.3 | 17.4 | 18.7 | 16.9 | 11 | 15.6 | 19.1 | 22.9 | 19.4 |
| 2 | 29.4 | 17.3 | 22.7 | 10.9 | 12 | 19.8 | 12.2 | 26.7 | 19.0 |
| 3 | 12.2 | 12.7 | 14.1 | 10.3 | 13 | 24.3 | 18.7 | 30.3 | 22.9 |
| 4 | 22.4 | 19.7 | 24.9 | 23.4 | 14 | 16.5 | 14.3 | 19.5 | 15.5 |
| 5 | 13.5 | 11.6 | 14.8 | 13.5 | 15 | 23.4 | 27.6 | 30.7 | 24.0 |
| 6 | 15.2 | 23.6 | 19.4 | 20.0 | 16 | 9.7 | 14.6 | 10.4 | 10.8 |
| 7 | 23.1 | 13.6 | 21.1 | 13.7 | 17 | 27.8 | 18.4 | 23.7 | 22.8 |
| 8 | 15.7 | 10.9 | 16.4 | 21.8 | 18 | 17.4 | 25.8 | 18.4 | 9.0 |
| 9 | 10.2 | 14.9 | 12.6 | 11.9 | 19 | 20.5 | 17.8 | 23.2 | 18.0 |
| 10 | 14.7 | 18.7 | 22.0 | 19.1 | 20 | 14.2 | 14.6 | 11.1 | 17.7 |

**DATA FILE**
TRANSPORT

(a) Set up control charts for the range and arithmetic mean.
(b) On the basis of the results in (a), indicate whether the process is in control in terms of these charts.

**15.25** The manager of a private swimming pool facility monitors the pH (alkalinity-acidity) level of the swimming pool by taking hourly readings from 8 A.M. to 6 P.M. daily. The results for a 3-week period summarized on a daily basis are presented as follows:

| DAY | AVERAGE $\overline{X}_i$ | RANGE $R_i$ | DAY | AVERAGE $\overline{X}_i$ | RANGE $R_i$ |
| --- | --- | --- | --- | --- | --- |
| 1 | 7.34 | 0.16 | 12 | 7.39 | 0.16 |
| 2 | 7.41 | 0.12 | 13 | 7.40 | 0.18 |
| 3 | 7.30 | 0.11 | 14 | 7.35 | 0.17 |
| 4 | 7.28 | 0.19 | 15 | 7.39 | 0.22 |
| 5 | 7.23 | 0.17 | 16 | 7.42 | 0.20 |
| 6 | 7.30 | 0.20 | 17 | 7.40 | 0.18 |
| 7 | 7.35 | 0.15 | 18 | 7.37 | 0.18 |
| 8 | 7.38 | 0.19 | 19 | 7.41 | 0.22 |
| 9 | 7.32 | 0.14 | 20 | 7.36 | 0.15 |
| 10 | 7.38 | 0.19 | 21 | 7.40 | 0.12 |
| 11 | 7.43 | 0.23 | | | |

**DATA FILE**
PHLEVEL

(a) Set up a control chart for the range.
(b) Set up a control chart for the average daily pH level.
(c) On the basis of the results of (a) and (b), what conclusions can you draw about the process?

## ◆ SUMMARY

As can be observed in the summary chart, in this chapter we have introduced the topic of quality and productivity by discussing the Deming approach to management and by developing several different types of control charts. Readers interested in the Deming approach are encouraged to examine references 1, 2, 3, 4, 8, 15, 21, and 22. Readers interested in additional control chart procedures should see references 5, 8, and 13.

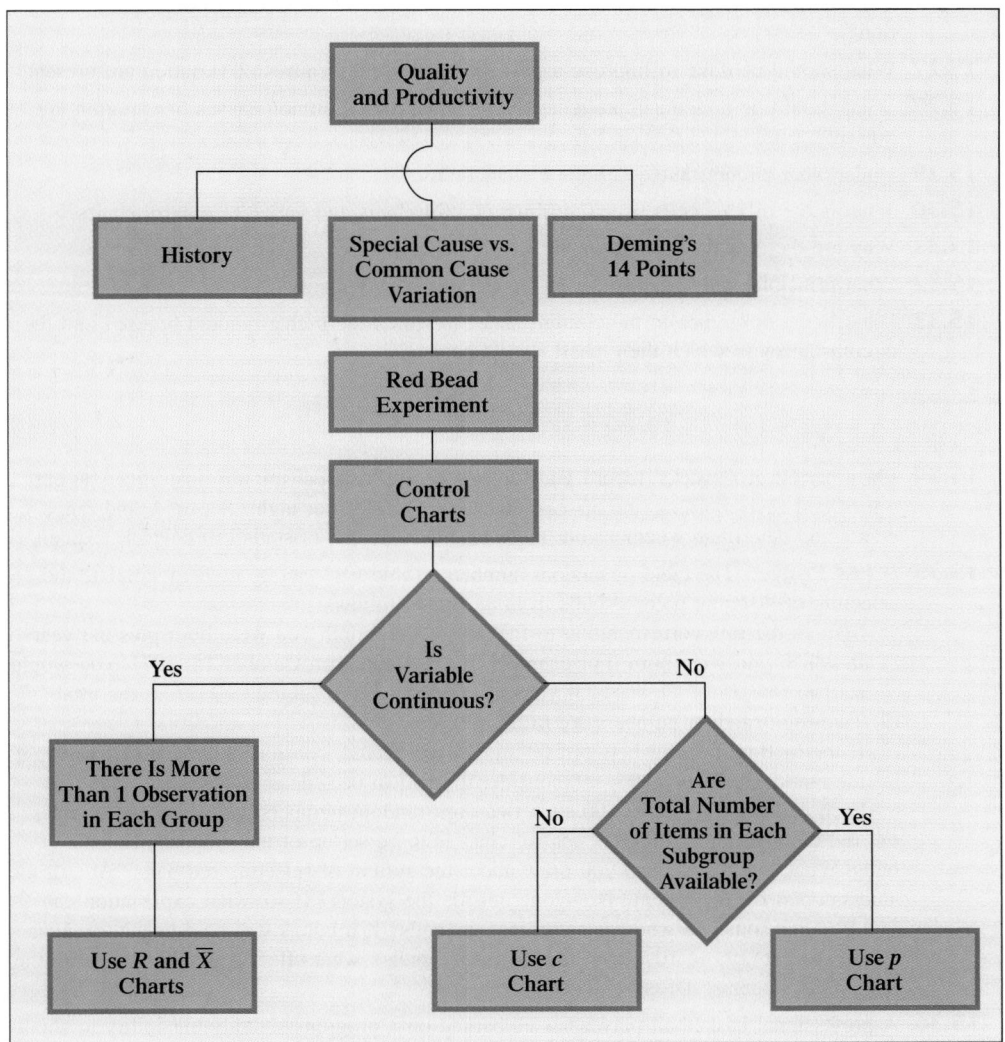

Chapter 15 summary chart

## Key Terms

$A_2$ factor  711
area of opportunity  702
attribute chart  691
$c$ chart  702
chance or common causes of variation  689
control chart  689
$d_2$ factor  708

$d_3$ factor  708
$D_3$ factor  709
$D_4$ factor  709
Deming's 14 points  686
lower control limit ($LCL$)  690
$p$ chart  691
$R$ chart  708
red bead experiment  700

Shewhart-Deming cycle  687
special or assignable causes of variation  689
total quality management (TQM)  685
upper control limit ($UCL$)  690
variables control charts  708
$\overline{X}$ chart  711

## Checking Your Understanding

**15.26** What is the difference between common causes of variation and special causes of variation?

**15.27** What should be done to improve a process when special causes of variation are present?

**15.28** What should be done to improve a process when only common causes of variation are present?

**15.29** Under what circumstances can the $c$ chart be used?

**15.30** What is the difference between attribute control charts and variables control charts?

**15.31** Why are the $\overline{X}$ and range charts used together?

**15.32** What principles did you learn from the red bead experiment?

**15.33** What is the difference in the circumstances in which the $p$ chart should be used and the circumstances in which the $c$ chart should be used?

## Chapter Review Problems

**15.34** For a period of 4 weeks, record your pulse rate (in beats per minute) just after you get out of bed each morning and also before you go to sleep at night. Set up $\overline{X}$ and range charts and determine whether your pulse rate is in a state of statistical control. Explain.

**15.35** (**Class Project**) The table of random numbers (Table E.1) can be used to simulate the selecting of different colored balls from an urn as follows:
(1) Start in the row corresponding to the day of the month you were born plus the year in which you were born. For example, if you were born October 15, 1971, you would start in row 15 + 71 = 86. If your total exceeds 100, subtract 100 from the total.
(2) Two-digit random numbers are to be selected.
(3) If the random number between 00 and 94 is selected, consider the ball to be white; if the random number is 95–99, consider the ball to be red.

   Each student is to select 100 such two-digit random numbers and report the number of "red balls" in the sample. A control chart is to be set up of the proportion of red balls. What conclusions can you draw about the system of selecting red balls? Are all the students part of the system? Is anyone outside the system? If so, what explanation can you give for someone who has too many red balls? If a bonus was paid to the top 10% of the students (those 10% with the fewest red balls), what effect would that have on the rest of the students? Discuss.

**15.36** A professional basketball player has embarked on a program to study his ability to shoot foul shots. On each day in which a game is not scheduled, he intends to shoot 100 foul shots. He maintains records over a period of 40 days of practice, with the following results:

| Day | Foul Shots Made | Day | Foul Shots Made | Day | Foul Shots Made |
|---|---|---|---|---|---|
| 1 | 73 | 15 | 73 | 29 | 76 |
| 2 | 75 | 16 | 76 | 30 | 80 |
| 3 | 69 | 17 | 69 | 31 | 78 |
| 4 | 72 | 18 | 68 | 32 | 83 |
| 5 | 77 | 19 | 72 | 33 | 84 |
| 6 | 71 | 20 | 70 | 34 | 81 |
| 7 | 68 | 21 | 64 | 35 | 86 |
| 8 | 70 | 22 | 67 | 36 | 85 |
| 9 | 67 | 23 | 72 | 37 | 86 |
| 10 | 74 | 24 | 70 | 38 | 87 |
| 11 | 75 | 25 | 74 | 39 | 85 |
| 12 | 72 | 26 | 76 | 40 | 85 |
| 13 | 70 | 27 | 75 | | |
| 14 | 74 | 28 | 78 | | |

**DATA FILE**
FOULSPC

(a) Set up a *p* chart for the proportion of successful foul shots. Do you think that the player's foul-shooting process is in statistical control? If not, why not?

(b) What if you were told that after the first 20 days, the player changed his method of shooting foul shots? How might this information change the conclusions you drew in (a)?

(c) If you knew this information prior to doing (a), how might you have done the *p* chart differently?

**15.37** The funds transfer research department of a bank is concerned with turnaround time for investigations of funds-transfer payments. A payment may involve the bank as a remitter of funds, a beneficiary of funds, or an intermediary in the payment. An investigation is initiated by a payment inquiry or query by a party involved in the payment or any department affected by the flow of funds. Once a query is received, an investigator reconstructs the transaction trail of the payment and verifies that the information is correct and the proper payment is transmitted. The investigator then reports the results of the investigation and the transaction is considered closed. It is important that investigations are closed rapidly, preferably within the same day. The number of new investigations and the number and proportion closed on the same day that the inquiry was made are as follows for a 30-day period.

| Day | New Investigations | Number Closed | Day | New Investigations | Number Closed | Day | New Investigations | Number Closed |
|---|---|---|---|---|---|---|---|---|
| 1 | 240 | 96 | 11 | 256 | 90 | 21 | 280 | 131 |
| 2 | 296 | 88 | 12 | 273 | 102 | 22 | 271 | 139 |
| 3 | 309 | 113 | 13 | 276 | 115 | 23 | 237 | 121 |
| 4 | 293 | 138 | 14 | 291 | 98 | 24 | 258 | 94 |
| 5 | 253 | 119 | 15 | 204 | 83 | 25 | 289 | 128 |
| 6 | 254 | 94 | 16 | 263 | 79 | 26 | 226 | 90 |
| 7 | 245 | 75 | 17 | 311 | 116 | 27 | 287 | 106 |
| 8 | 331 | 125 | 18 | 248 | 104 | 28 | 263 | 81 |
| 9 | 303 | 134 | 19 | 287 | 110 | 29 | 282 | 107 |
| 10 | 278 | 83 | 20 | 238 | 107 | 30 | 194 | 75 |

**DATA FILE**
FUNDTRAN

(a) Construct a control chart for these data.

(b) Is the process in a state of statistical control? Explain.

(c) On the basis of the results of (a) and (b), what should management do next to improve the process?

**15.38** The manager of a retail sales branch of a brokerage office was concerned with the number of undesirable trades made by the sales staff. A trade was considered undesirable if there was an error on the trade ticket. Trades that were in error had to be canceled and resubmitted. The cost of correcting errors was billed to the brokerage. In studying the problem, the manager wanted to know whether the proportion of undesirable trades was in a state of statistical control so she could plan the next step in a quality improvement process. Data were collected for a 30-day period with the following results:

| Day | Undesirable Trades | Total Trades | Day | Undesirable Trades | Total Trades | Day | Undesirable Trades | Total Trades |
|-----|-----|-----|-----|-----|-----|-----|-----|-----|
| 1 | 2 | 74 | 11 | 3 | 104 | 21 | 4 | 58 |
| 2 | 12 | 85 | 12 | 12 | 98 | 22 | 10 | 69 |
| 3 | 13 | 114 | 13 | 15 | 105 | 23 | 19 | 135 |
| 4 | 33 | 136 | 14 | 6 | 98 | 24 | 1 | 67 |
| 5 | 5 | 97 | 15 | 21 | 204 | 25 | 11 | 77 |
| 6 | 20 | 115 | 16 | 3 | 54 | 26 | 12 | 88 |
| 7 | 17 | 108 | 17 | 12 | 74 | 27 | 4 | 66 |
| 8 | 10 | 76 | 18 | 11 | 103 | 28 | 11 | 72 |
| 9 | 8 | 69 | 19 | 11 | 100 | 29 | 13 | 118 |
| 10 | 18 | 98 | 20 | 14 | 88 | 30 | 15 | 138 |

**DATA FILE**
**TRADE**

(a) Construct a control chart for these data.

(b) Is the process in a state of statistical control? Explain.

(c) On the basis of the results of (a) and (b), what should the manager do next to improve the process?

**15.39** As chief operating officer of a local community hospital, you have just returned from a 3-day seminar on quality and productivity. It is your intention to implement many of the ideas that you learned at the seminar. You have decided to maintain control charts for the upcoming month for the following variables: number of daily admissions, proportion of rework in the laboratory (based on 1,000 daily samples), and time (in hours) between receipt of a specimen at the laboratory and completion of the work (based on a subgroup of 10 specimens per day). The data collected are summarized as follows:

| Day | Number of Admissions | Processing Time $\overline{X}_i$ | Processing Time $R_i$ | Proportion of Rework in Laboratory |
|-----|-----|-----|-----|-----|
| 1 | 27 | 1.72 | 3.57 | 0.048 |
| 2 | 36 | 2.03 | 3.98 | 0.052 |
| 3 | 23 | 2.18 | 3.54 | 0.047 |
| 4 | 28 | 1.90 | 3.49 | 0.046 |
| 5 | 19 | 2.53 | 3.99 | 0.039 |
| 6 | 22 | 2.26 | 3.34 | 0.086 |
| 7 | 18 | 2.11 | 3.36 | 0.051 |
| 8 | 30 | 2.35 | 3.52 | 0.043 |

*continued*

| DAY | NUMBER OF ADMISSIONS | PROCESSING TIME $\overline{X}_i$ | $R_i$ | PROPORTION OF REWORK IN LABORATORY |
|---|---|---|---|---|
| 9 | 33 | 2.06 | 3.39 | 0.046 |
| 10 | 35 | 2.01 | 3.24 | 0.040 |
| 11 | 29 | 2.13 | 3.62 | 0.045 |
| 12 | 28 | 2.18 | 3.37 | 0.036 |
| 13 | 22 | 2.31 | 3.97 | 0.048 |
| 14 | 26 | 2.37 | 4.06 | 0.057 |
| 15 | 32 | 2.78 | 4.27 | 0.052 |
| 16 | 30 | 2.12 | 3.21 | 0.046 |
| 17 | 28 | 2.27 | 3.48 | 0.041 |
| 18 | 27 | 2.49 | 3.62 | 0.032 |
| 19 | 27 | 2.32 | 3.19 | 0.042 |
| 20 | 18 | 2.43 | 3.67 | 0.053 |
| 21 | 19 | 2.25 | 3.10 | 0.041 |
| 22 | 25 | 2.31 | 3.58 | 0.037 |
| 23 | 23 | 2.07 | 3.26 | 0.039 |
| 24 | 28 | 2.33 | 3.40 | 0.050 |
| 25 | 34 | 2.36 | 3.52 | 0.048 |
| 26 | 25 | 2.47 | 3.82 | 0.054 |
| 27 | 21 | 2.28 | 3.97 | 0.046 |
| 28 | 20 | 2.17 | 3.60 | 0.035 |
| 29 | 40 | 2.54 | 3.92 | 0.075 |
| 30 | 31 | 2.63 | 3.86 | 0.046 |

DATA FILE
HOSPADM

You are to make a presentation to the chief executive officer of the hospital and the board of directors. You need to prepare a report that summarizes the conclusions obtained from analyzing control charts for these variables. In addition, it is expected that you will recommend additional variables for which control charts are to be maintained. Finally, it is your intention to explain how the Deming philosophy of management by process can be implemented in the context of your hospital's environment.

## Case Study — THE HARNSWELL SEWING MACHINE COMPANY

### Phase 1

The Harnswell Sewing Machine Company is a manufacturer of industrial sewing machines that has been in business for almost 50 years. The company specializes in automated machines called pattern tackers that sew repetitive patterns on such mass production products as shoes, garments, and seat belts. Aside from the sales of machines, the company sells machine parts. The company's reputation in the industry is good, and it has been able to command a price premium because of this reputation.

Recently, Natalie York, the operations manager of the company, purchased several books relating to quality. After reading them, she began to wonder about the feasibility of beginning some type of quality program at the company. At the current time, the company has no formal quality program. Parts are 100% inspected at the time of shipping to a customer or installation in a machine, yet Natalie has always wondered why inventory of certain parts (in particular the half-inch cam roller) invariably falls short before a full year lapses, even though 7,000 pieces have been produced for a demand of 5,000 pieces per year.

After a great deal of reflection and with some apprehension, Natalie has decided that she will approach John Harnswell, the owner of the company, about the possibility of beginning a program to improve quality in the company, starting with a trial project in the machine parts area. As she is walking to Mr. Harnswell's office for the meeting, she has second thoughts about whether this is such a good idea. After all, it was just last month that Mr. Harnswell told her, "Why do you need to go to graduate school for your master's degree in business? That is a waste of your time and will not be of any value to the Harnswell Company. All those professors are just up in their ivory towers and don't know a thing about running a business like I do."

As she enters his office, Mr. Harnswell, ever courteous to her, invites Natalie to sit down across from him. "Well, what do you have on your mind this morning?" Mr. Harnswell asks her in an inquisitive tone. She begins by starting to talk about the books that she has just completed reading and about how she has some interesting ideas for making production even better than it is now and improving profits. Before she can finish, Mr. Harnswell has started to answer.

"Look, my dear young lady," he says, "everything has been fine since I started this company in 1948. I have built this company up from nothing to one that employs more than 100 people. Why do you want to make waves? Remember, if it ain't broke, don't fix it." With that he ushers her from his office with the admonishment of "What am I going to do with you if you keep coming up with these ridiculous ideas?"

## Exercises

**15.1** On the basis of what you have read, which of Deming's 14 points of management are most lacking in the Harnswell Sewing Machine Company? Explain.

**15.2** What changes, if any, do you think Natalie York might be able to institute in the company? Explain.

 **Do not continue until the Phase 1 exercises have been completed.**

## Phase 2

Natalie slowly walked down the hall after leaving Mr. Harnswell's office, feeling rather downcast. He just won't listen to anyone, she thought. As she walked, Jim Murante, the shop foreman, came up beside her. "So," he said, "did you really think that the old man would just listen to you? I've been here more than 25 years. The only way he listens is if he is shown something that worked after it has already been done. Let's see what we can plan out together."

Natalie and Jim decide to begin by investigating the production of the cam rollers, which are a precision ground part. The last part of the production process involves the grinding of the outer diameter. After grinding, the part mates with the cam groove of the particular sewing pattern. The half-inch rollers technically have an engineering specification for the outer diameter of the roller of .5075 inch (the specifications are actually metric, but in factory floor jargon they are referred to as half-inch) plus a tolerable error of .0003 inch on the lower side. Thus, the outer diameter is allowed to be between .5072 and .5075 inch. Anything larger means that the roller has to be reclassified into a different and less costly category, whereas anything smaller means that the roller cannot be used for anything other than scrap.

The grinding of the cam roller is done on a single machine with a single tool setup and no change in the grinding wheel after initial setup. The operation is done by Dave Martin, the head machinist, who has 30 years of experience in the trade and specific experience producing the cam roller part. Because production occurs in batches, Natalie and Jim sample five parts produced from each batch. Data collected over 30 batches are presented in the following table.

## Diameter of cam rollers (inch)

| BATCH | CAM ROLLER | | | | |
|---|---|---|---|---|---|
| | 1 | 2 | 3 | 4 | 5 |
| 1 | .5076 | .5076 | .5075 | .5077 | .5075 |
| 2 | .5075 | .5077 | .5076 | .5076 | .5075 |
| 3 | .5075 | .5075 | .5075 | .5075 | .5076 |
| 4 | .5075 | .5076 | .5074 | .5076 | .5073 |
| 5 | .5075 | .5074 | .5076 | .5073 | .5076 |
| 6 | .5076 | .5075 | .5076 | .5075 | .5075 |
| 7 | .5076 | .5076 | .5076 | .5075 | .5075 |
| 8 | .5075 | .5076 | .5076 | .5075 | .5074 |
| 9 | .5074 | .5076 | .5075 | .5075 | .5076 |
| 10 | .5076 | .5077 | .5075 | .5075 | .5075 |
| 11 | .5075 | .5075 | .5075 | .5076 | .5075 |
| 12 | .5075 | .5076 | .5075 | .5077 | .5075 |
| 13 | .5076 | .5076 | .5073 | .5076 | .5074 |
| 14 | .5075 | .5076 | .5074 | .5076 | .5075 |
| 15 | .5075 | .5075 | .5076 | .5074 | .5073 |
| 16 | .5075 | .5074 | .5076 | .5075 | .5075 |
| 17 | .5075 | .5074 | .5075 | .5074 | .5072 |
| 18 | .5075 | .5075 | .5076 | .5075 | .5076 |
| 19 | .5076 | .5076 | .5075 | .5075 | .5076 |
| 20 | .5075 | .5074 | .5077 | .5076 | .5074 |
| 21 | .5075 | .5074 | .5075 | .5075 | .5075 |
| 22 | .5076 | .5076 | .5075 | .5076 | .5074 |
| 23 | .5076 | .5076 | .5075 | .5075 | .5076 |
| 24 | .5075 | .5076 | .5075 | .5076 | .5075 |
| 25 | .5075 | .5075 | .5075 | .5075 | .5074 |
| 26 | .5077 | .5076 | .5076 | .5074 | .5075 |
| 27 | .5075 | .5075 | .5074 | .5076 | .5075 |
| 28 | .5077 | .5076 | .5075 | .5075 | .5076 |
| 29 | .5075 | .5075 | .5074 | .5075 | .5075 |
| 30 | .5076 | .5075 | .5075 | .5076 | .5075 |

**DATA FILE**
HARNSWELL

## Exercise

**15.3** **(a)** Is the process in a state of statistical control? Why?

**(b)** What recommendations should be made about improving the process?

**Do not continue until the Phase 2 exercise has been completed.**

## Phase 3

Natalie examined the $\overline{X}$ and $R$ charts developed from the data presented in the previous table. The $R$ chart indicated that the process was in a state of statistical control, but the $\overline{X}$ chart revealed that the average for day 17 was outside the lower control limit. This immediately gave her cause for concern because low values for the roller diameter could mean parts that had to be scrapped. Natalie went down to see Jim Murante, the shop foreman, to try to find out what had happened to batch 17. Jim looked up the production records to determine when this batch was produced. "Aha, " he exclaimed, "I think I've got the answer! This batch was produced on that really cold morning we had last month. I've been after Mr. Harnswell for a long time to let us install an automatic thermostat in the shop so that the place doesn't feel so cold when we get here in the morning. All he ever tells me is that people aren't as tough as they used to be and if I want to see real cold I should have been back in that foxhole during the winter of 1944."

Natalie stood there almost in shock. What she realized had happened is that rather than standing idle until the environment and the equipment warmed to acceptable temperatures, the machinist had opted to manufacture parts that might have to be scrapped. In fact, Natalie recalled that a major problem had occurred on that same day when several other expensive parts had to be scrapped. Natalie said to Jim, "We just have to do something. We can't let this go on now that we know what problems it is potentially causing." Natalie and Jim decided that enough money could be taken out of petty cash and other accounts to get the thermostat without having to obtain a requisition that required Mr. Harnswell's signature. They installed the thermostat and set the heating control so that the heat would turn on one-half hour before the shop opened each morning.

### *Exercises*

**15.4** What should Natalie now do concerning the cam roller data? Explain.

**15.5** Explain how the actions of Natalie and Jim to avoid this particular problem in the future have resulted in quality improvement.

 **Do not continue until the Phase 3 exercises have been completed.**

## Phase 4

Once the data for day 17 were removed from the chart because local corrective action had been taken to eliminate the special cause, the control charts for the remaining days indicated a stable system with only common causes of variation operating on the system. Thus, Natalie and Jim sat down with Dave Martin and several other machinists to try to determine all the possible causes for

the existence of oversized and scrapped rollers. Natalie was still troubled by the data that had been collected. After all, she wondered, what I really want to find out is whether or not the process is giving us oversizes (which are downgraded) and undersizes (which are scrapped). She thought about which tables and charts would really be helpful.

### *Exercise*

**15.6** **(a)** Set up a frequency distribution or a stem-and-leaf display of the cam roller diameters. Explain why you chose the tabular presentation that you used.

**(b)** On the basis of your results in (a), set up all appropriate graphs of the cam roller diameters.

**(c)** Write a report expressing your conclusions concerning the cam roller diameters. Be sure to discuss the diameters as they relate to the specifications.

 **Do not continue until the Phase 4 exercise has been completed.**

## Phase 5

Natalie noticed immediately that the overall average diameter with day 17 eliminated was .507527, which was higher than the specification value. This meant that, on average, the rollers being produced were of a diameter that was so high that they would be downgraded in value. In fact, 55 of the 150 rollers sampled (36.67 percent) were above the specification value. This meant that if this percentage was extrapolated to the full year's production, 30 percent of the 7,000 pieces manufactured, or 2,100, could not be sold as half-inch rollers, leaving only 4,900 available for sale. "No wonder we often seemed to have shortages that required costly emergency runs," she thought. She also noted that not one diameter was below the lower tolerance of .5072, so not one of the rollers had to be scrapped.

Natalie realized that there had to be a reason for all this. Along with Jim Murante, she decided to show the results to Dave Martin, the head machinist. Dave said that the results didn't surprise him that much. "You know," he said "there is only .0003 inch in diameter that I'm allowed in variation. If I aim for exactly halfway between .5072 and .5075, I'm afraid that I'll make a lot of short pieces that will have to be scrapped. I know from way back when I first started here that Mr. Harnswell and everybody else will come down on my head if they start seeing too many of those scraps. I figure that if I aim for .5075, the worst thing that will happen will be a bunch of downgrades, but I won't make any pieces that have to be scrapped."

## Exercises

**15.7** What approach do you think the machinist should take in terms of the diameter of the roller that should be aimed for? Explain.

**15.8** What do you think Natalie should do next? Explain.

# THE SPRINGVILLE HERALD CASE

## Phase 1

A team of workers in the advertising production department has been formed to begin the effort to reduce the number and dollar amount of the advertising errors, with initial focus on the ran-in-error category. While this effort is taking place, data are being routinely collected that track the number of ads with errors on a daily basis (with Sundays excluded because that is considered to involve a special type of production substantially different from the other days). Data relating to the number of ads with errors in the last month are summarized in Table SH15.1.

**Table SH15.1** *Number of ads for which customer complaints had been received and daily number of display ads*

| DAY | NUMBER OF ADS WITH ERRORS | NUMBER OF ADS | DAY | NUMBER OF ADS WITH ERRORS | NUMBER OF ADS |
|-----|-----|-----|-----|-----|-----|
| 1 | 4 | 228 | 14 | 5 | 245 |
| 2 | 6 | 273 | 15 | 7 | 266 |
| 3 | 5 | 239 | 16 | 2 | 197 |
| 4 | 3 | 197 | 17 | 4 | 228 |
| 5 | 6 | 259 | 18 | 5 | 236 |
| 6 | 7 | 203 | 19 | 4 | 208 |
| 7 | 8 | 289 | 20 | 3 | 214 |
| 8 | 14 | 241 | 21 | 8 | 258 |
| 9 | 9 | 263 | 22 | 10 | 267 |
| 10 | 5 | 199 | 23 | 4 | 217 |
| 11 | 6 | 275 | 24 | 9 | 277 |
| 12 | 4 | 212 | 25 | 7 | 258 |
| 13 | 3 | 207 | | | |

**DATA FILE**
SH15-1&2

## Exercises

**15.1** What would you suggest the team from the advertising production department should do first to reduce the errors? Explain.

**15.2** **(a)** Construct the appropriate control chart for these data.

**(b)** Is the process in a state of statistical control? Why?

**(c)** What should the team recommend as the next step to be taken to study and improve the process?

**STOP** **Do not continue until the Phase 1 exercises have been completed.**

## Phase 2

The advertising production team examined the *p* chart developed for the data of Table SH15.1. Using the rules for determining out-of-control points, they observed that point 8 is above the upper control limit. Upon investigation of the point above the upper control limit, it was determined that on that day there was an employee from another work area assigned to the processing of the ads because several employees were out ill. The group brainstormed ways of avoiding the problem in the future and recommended that a team of people from other work areas receive training on the work done by this area. Members of this team could then cover the processing of the ads by rotating in 1- or 2-hour shifts.

## Exercises

**15.3** What should the advertising production team now do concerning the data of Table SH15.1? Explain.

**15.4** Explain how the actions of the team to avoid this particular problem in the future have resulted in quality improvement.

**15.5** What other information concerning errors on a daily basis would be useful to obtain in addition to the number of ads with errors?

 **Do not continue until the Phase 2 exercises have been completed.**

## Phase 3

An important area of concern to the computer systems team related to the data management system. Each day decisions needed to be made about how information from either personnel records or the newspaper itself was to be maintained. Some information had to be maintained for 1 day, some for 7 days, some for 30 days, some for a year, and some for perpetual storage. Data that were to be maintained for more than 7 days had to be stored remotely on disk cartridges off the production site. The data cartridges used for the remote off-site storage involved both an acquisition expense and the cost of maintaining and managing the remote storage system. In an effort to study the stability of the process, weekly reports for the past 6 months were obtained. The number of data cartridges sent for remote storage each week during this period are presented in Table SH15.2.

**Table SH15.2**  *Weekly number of data cartridges sent for remote storage*

| Week | Data Cartridges Sent | Week | Data Cartridges Sent | Week | Data Cartridges Sent |
|------|----------------------|------|----------------------|------|----------------------|
| 1 | 123 | 9 | 141 | 17 | 174 |
| 2 | 116 | 10 | 142 | 18 | 176 |
| 3 | 115 | 11 | 164 | 19 | 193 |
| 4 | 116 | 12 | 148 | 20 | 173 |
| 5 | 115 | 13 | 160 | 21 | 147 |
| 6 | 120 | 14 | 134 | 22 | 159 |
| 7 | 140 | 15 | 162 | 23 | 147 |
| 8 | 137 | 16 | 174 | 24 | 147 |

 **DATA FILE**
SH15-3

### Exercise

**15.6** **(a)** Construct the appropriate control chart for these data.

**(b)** Is the process in a state of statistical control? Why?

**(c)** What should the team recommend as the next step to be taken to study and improve the process?

 **Do not continue until the Phase 3 exercise has been completed.**

## Phase 4

The production department has also embarked upon a quality improvement effort. After several brainstorming sessions, the team has chosen as its first project an issue that relates to the blackness of the print of the newspaper. Each day a determination needs to be made concerning how "black" the newspaper is printed. This is measured on a densimometer that records the results on a standard scale. Each day, five spots on the first newspaper printed are chosen and the blackness of each spot is measured. The results for 20 days are presented in Table SH15.3.

**Table SH15.3**  *Newsprint blackness for 20 consecutive weekdays*

| | SPOT | | | | | | SPOT | | | | |
|---|---|---|---|---|---|---|---|---|---|---|---|
| **DAY** | **1** | **2** | **3** | **4** | **5** | **DAY** | **1** | **2** | **3** | **4** | **5** |
| 1 | 0.96 | 1.01 | 1.12 | 1.07 | 0.97 | 11 | 0.97 | 1.13 | 0.95 | 0.86 | 1.06 |
| 2 | 1.06 | 1.00 | 1.02 | 1.16 | 0.96 | 12 | 1.00 | 0.87 | 1.02 | 0.98 | 1.13 |
| 3 | 1.00 | 0.90 | 0.98 | 1.18 | 0.96 | 13 | 0.96 | 0.79 | 1.17 | 0.97 | 0.95 |
| 4 | 0.92 | 0.89 | 1.01 | 1.16 | 0.90 | 14 | 1.03 | 0.89 | 1.03 | 1.12 | 1.03 |
| 5 | 1.02 | 1.16 | 1.03 | 0.89 | 1.00 | 15 | 0.96 | 1.12 | 0.95 | 0.88 | 0.99 |
| 6 | 0.88 | 0.92 | 1.03 | 1.16 | 0.91 | 16 | 1.01 | 0.87 | 0.99 | 1.04 | 1.16 |
| 7 | 1.05 | 1.13 | 1.01 | 0.93 | 1.03 | 17 | 0.98 | 0.85 | 0.99 | 1.04 | 1.16 |
| 8 | 0.95 | 0.86 | 1.14 | 0.90 | 0.95 | 18 | 1.03 | 0.82 | 1.21 | 0.98 | 1.08 |
| 9 | 0.99 | 0.89 | 1.00 | 1.15 | 0.92 | 19 | 1.02 | 0.84 | 1.15 | 0.94 | 1.08 |
| 10 | 0.89 | 1.18 | 1.03 | 0.96 | 1.04 | 20 | 0.90 | 1.02 | 1.10 | 1.04 | 1.08 |

**DATA FILE**
SH15-4

## Exercise

**15.7 (a)** Construct the appropriate control charts for these data.

**(b)** Is the process in a state of statistical control? Why?

**(c)** What should the team recommend as the next step to be taken to study and improve the process?

# References

1. Aguayo, R., *Dr. Deming: The American Who Taught the Japanese about Quality* (New York: Lyle Stuart, 1990).
2. Deming, W. E., *Out of the Crisis* (Cambridge, MA: MIT Center for Advanced Engineering Study, 1986).
3. Deming, W. E., *The New Economics for Business, Industry, and Government* (Cambridge, MA: MIT Center for Advanced Engineering Study, 1993).
4. Gabor, A., *The Man Who Discovered Quality* (New York: Time Books, 1990).
5. Gitlow, H., A. Oppenheim, and R. Oppenheim, *Tools and Methods for the Improvement of Quality*, 2d ed. (Homewood, IL: Irwin, 1994).
6. Halberstam, D., *The Reckoning* (New York: Morrow, 1986).
7. Holusha, J., "The Baldrige Badge of Courage—and Quality," *The New York Times*, October 21, 1990, F12.
8. Levine, D. M., P. P. Ramsey, and M. L. Berenson, *Business Statistics for Quality and Productivity* (Englewood Cliffs, NJ: Prentice Hall, 1995).
9. Main, J., "The Curmudgeon Who Talks Tough on Quality," *Fortune*, June 25, 1984, 118–122.
10. *The Memory Jogger II: A Pocket Guide of Tools for Continuous Improvement and Effective Planning* (Methuen, MA: GOAL/QPC, 1994).
11. *Microsoft Excel 97* (Redmond, WA: Microsoft Corp., 1997).
12. *Minitab for Windows Version 12* (State College, PA: Minitab, Inc., 1998)
13. Montgomery, D. C., *Introduction to Statistical Quality Control*, 3d ed. (New York: Wiley, 1996).
14. Port, O., "The Push for Quality," *Business Week*, June 8, 1987, 130–135.
15. Scherkenbach, W. W., *The Deming Route to Quality and Productivity: Road Maps and Roadblocks* (Washington, DC: CEEP Press, 1987).
16. Shewhart, W. A., "The Applications of Statistics as an Aid in Maintaining Quality of Manufactured Products,"

*Journal of the American Statistical Association* 20 (1925): 546–548.

17. Shewhart, W. A., *Economic Control of Quality of Manufactured Products* (New York: Van Nostrand and Company, 1931; reprinted by the American Society for Quality Control, Milwaukee, 1980).

18. Shewhart, W. A., and W. E. Deming, *Statistical Methods from the Viewpoint of Quality Control* (Washington, DC: Graduate School, Department of Agriculture, 1939; Dover Press, 1986).

19. Sholtes, P. R., *An Elaboration on Deming's Teaching on Performance Appraisal* (Madison, WI: Joiner Associates, 1987).

20. Wallis, W. A., "The Statistical Research Group 1942–1945," *Journal of the American Statistical Association* 75 (1980): 320–335.

21. Walton, M., *The Deming Management Method* (New York: Perigee Books, Putnam Publishing Group, 1986).

22. Walton, M., *Deming Management at Work* (New York: Putnam, 1990).

## ❖ APPENDIX 15.1   USING MICROSOFT EXCEL FOR CONTROL CHARTS

### COMMENT:  PHStat Add-In Users

If Microsoft Excel is not running, click the **PHStat** add-in icon. If Microsoft Excel is running, select **File | Open**. Select the PHStat add-in file **PHSA.XLA**. Click the **Open** button.

To obtain a *p* chart, select **PHStat | Control Charts | p Chart**. Enter the cell range for the subgroup size and the number of nonconformances in their respective edit boxes. Click the **OK** button.

To obtain $\overline{X}$ and range charts, select **PHStat | Control Charts | R & XBAR Charts**. Enter the cell range for the sample means in the Xbar cell range edit box. Enter the cell range for the sample ranges in the Subgroup range edit box. Enter the sample size for each subgroup in the Number of Observations in Sample edit box. Click the **OK** button.

Although Microsoft Excel does not have a Data Analysis tool to compute the control limits and center line of a control chart, Excel functions can be used instead. Once the control limits and center line have been computed, the Chart Wizard can be used to plot the data along with the control limits and center line.

### Using Microsoft Excel for *p* Charts

In section 15.4 we studied the *p* chart for the proportion. Referring to equation (15.2) on page 691, we see that in order to obtain the control limits for the *p* chart, we need to obtain $\overline{n}$, the average sample size and $\overline{p}$, the average proportion. For the data of Table 15.1 on page 693 concerning the nonconforming hotel rooms, the Data sheet is set up in the **HOTEL1.XLS** workbook with Days in column A, Rooms Studied in column B, Rooms Not Ready in column C. The proportion for each day is computed in column D by dividing the entry in column C by the entry in column B.

Once these four columns have been entered on the Data sheet, we can obtain the control limits and the center line on a Calculations sheet. To develop this Calculations sheet, enter appropriate labels in column A (starting in row 3) for *n*bar, *p*bar, *p* chart, *LCL*, Center Line, and *UCL*. Then compute the average sample size $\overline{n}$ in cell B3 by using the formula **=SUM(Data!B:B)/COUNT(Data!B:B)**. Note that this formula uses a special column range notation and therefore does not need the manual determination of how many rows of data there are.

The average proportion $\bar{p}$ is obtained in cell B4 using the formula **=SUM(Data!C:C)/SUM(Data!B:B)**. The lower control limit in cell B6 is obtained from the formula **=B4 − 3 * SQRT(B4 * ( 1 − B4)/B3)**, the center line in cell B7 is the contents of cell **B4**, and the upper control limit in cell B8 is obtained from the formula **=B4 + 3 * SQRT(B4 * ( 1 − B4)/B3)**.

Once the control limits and center line have been computed, we copy their values to columns E, F, and G of the Data sheet. After entering labels for *LCL*, Center, and *UCL* in E1 through G1, enter **=Calculations!731$B$6** in E2, **=Calculations!$B$7** in F2, and **=Calculations!$B$8** in G2. Then, copy the *LCL* value from E2 to E3 through E29, the center line value from F2 to F3 through F29, and the *UCL* value from G2 to G3 through G29.

We now use the Chart Wizard (see appendix 3.1) to obtain the control chart for the proportion. With the Data sheet active, select **Insert | Chart**.

In the Step 1 Dialog box, select the **Standard types** tab and then select **XY (Scatter)** from the Chart type: list box. Select the first choice of the third row of chart Sub-types, the choice designated as "Scatter with data points connected by lines." Click the **Next** button.

In the Step 2 Dialog box, select the **Data Range** tab and enter **Data!A1:A29,Data!D1:G29** in the Data range: edit box. (Be sure to include the comma as part of your entry.) Select the **Columns option** button in the Series in: group. Select the **Series** tab. Enter **=Data!A1:A29** in the Value (X) Axis edit box. Click the **Next** button.

In the Step 3 Dialog box , select the Titles tab. Enter *p* Chart for Rooms Not Ready in the Chart title edit box, enter Days in the Category (X) axis: edit box, and enter Proportion in the Value (Y) axis: edit box. Select the Gridlines tab. Deselect all check boxes. Click the **Next** button.

In the Step 4 Dialog box, select the **As new sheet: option** button and enter *p* chart in the edit box to the right of the option button. Click the **Finish** button.

## Using Microsoft Excel for *c* Charts

In section 15.6 we studied the *c* chart for the number of nonconforming items in an area of opportunity. Referring to equation (15.5) on page 703, we see that in order to obtain the control limits for the *c* chart, we need to compute $\bar{c}$, the average number of occurrences. For the data of Table 15.3 on page 703, the Data sheet is set up in the CHIPS.XLS workbook with cupcake in column A and number of chocolate chips in column B. The control limits and the center line can be computed on a Calculations sheet. To develop this Calculations sheet, enter appropriate labels in column A, starting in row 3 for *c*bar, *LCL*, Center Line, and *UCL*. Then compute the average number of nonconforming items $\bar{c}$ in cell B3 by using the formula **=SUM(Data!B:B)/COUNT(Data!B:B)**. The lower control limit is obtained in cell B4 from the formula **=B3 − 3 * SQRT(B3)**, the center line in cell B5 is the contents of cell B3, and the upper control limit in cell B6 is obtained from the formula **=B3 + 3 * SQRT(B3)**.

Now that the control limits and center line have been computed, we copy their values to columns C, D, and E of the Data sheet. After entering labels for *LCL*, Center, and *UCL* in cells C1 through E1, enter **=Calculations!$B$4** in C2, **=Calculations!$B$5** in D2, and **=Calculations!$B$6** in E2. Then, in order to plot a line for each of these variables across the days, copy the *LCL* value from C2 to C3 through C51, the center line value from D2 to D3 through D51, and the *UCL* value from E2 to E3 through E51.

We are now ready to use the Chart Wizard to obtain the control chart for the number of nonconforming items in an area of opportunity. We use the same instructions as for the *p* chart except that

1. In the Step 2 dialog box we enter **Data!A1:E51**.
2. In the Step 3 dialog box, we enter *c* Chart for Chocolate Chips in the Chart title edit box, and enter Number in the Value (Y) axis: edit box.
3. In the Step 4 dialog box, we enter *c* chart in the edit box to the right of the option button.

# Using Microsoft Excel for $R$ and $\overline{X}$ Charts

Referring to equation (15.8a) and (15.8b) on page 709 and equations (15.11a) and (15.11b) on page 711, we see that in order to obtain the control limits for the $R$ and $\overline{X}$ charts we need to obtain $R$, $\overline{X}$, and the $D_3$, $D_4$, and $A_2$ factors.

Using the data from Table 15.4 on page 709 that relate to the delivery time for a sample of five deliveries per day selected over 28 days in a hotel, the Data sheet is set up with Days in column A, $\overline{X}$ in column B, and the range in column C. If only the raw data were available, they could be stored on a separate sheet, and the range and the arithmetic mean could be computed on the Data sheet for each day by using the MAXIMUM, MINIMUM, and AVERAGE functions. Once these three columns have been entered on the Data sheet as in the HOTEL2.XLS workbook, we can develop the Calculations sheet. First enter appropriate labels in column A, starting in row 3 for $R$ chart, $R$ Bar, $D_3$ factor, $D_4$ factor, $LCL$, Center Line, and $UCL$. Then obtain the control limits and the center line for the $R$ chart on the Calculations sheet by using the formula **=AVERAGE(Data!C:C)** in B4. The values for the $D_3$ and $D_4$ factors are then entered in cells B5 and B6. The lower control limit is obtained in cell B7 from the formula **=B5 * B4**, the center line in cell B8 is the contents of cell B4, and the upper control limit in cell B9 is obtained from the formula **=B6 * B4**.

Now that the control limits and center line have been computed, we copy their values to columns D, E, and F of the Data sheet. After entering labels for $LCL$, Center, and $UCL$ in cells D1 through F1, enter **=Calculations!$B$7** in D2, **=Calculations!$B$8** in E2, and **=Calculations!$B$9** in F2. Then, in order to be able to plot a line for each of these variables across the days, copy the $LCL$ value from D2 to D3 through D29, the center line value from E2 to E3 through E29, and the $UCL$ value from F2 to F3 through F29.

We are now ready to use the Chart Wizard to obtain the control chart for the range. We use the same instructions as for the $p$ chart except that

**1.** In the Step 2 dialog box we enter **Data!A1:A29,Data!C1:F29**.
**2.** In the Step 3 dialog box, we enter $R$ Chart for Luggage Delivery in the Chart title edit box, and enter Minutes in the Value (Y) axis: edit box.
**3.** In the Step 4 dialog box, we enter $R$ chart in the edit box to the right of the option button.

Now that we have obtained the $R$ chart, we are ready to obtain the $\overline{X}$ chart. Using equation (15.11) on page 711, we need to compute $\overline{\overline{X}}$, the average of all the sample averages. With the Calculations sheet active, enter labels starting in cell A10 for XBAR chart, AVERAGE XBAR, $A_2$ Factor, $LCL$, Center Line, and $UCL$. Then compute $\overline{\overline{X}}$ in cell B11 by using the formula **=AVERAGE(Data!B:B)**. Then, enter the $A_2$ factor in cell B12. The lower control limit in cell B13 is obtained from the formula **=B11 − B12 * B4**, the center line in cell B14 is the contents of cell B11, and the upper control limit in cell B15 is obtained from the formula **=B11 + B12 * B4**.

Now that the control limits and center line for the $\overline{X}$ chart have been computed, we need to copy their values to columns G, H, and I of the Data sheet. After entering labels for $LCL$, Center, and $UCL$ in cells G1 through I1, we enter **=Calculations!$B$13** in G2, **=Calculations!$B$14** in H2, and **=Calculations!$B$15** in I2. Then in order to be able to plot a line for each of these variables across the days, copy the $LCL$ value from G2 to G3 through G29, the center line value from H2 to H3 through H29, and the $UCL$ value from I2 to I3 through I29.

We are now ready to use the Chart Wizard to obtain the control chart for the mean. We use the same instructions as for the $p$ chart except that

**1.** In the Step 2 dialog box enter **Data!A1:B29,Data!G1:I29**.
**2.** In the Step 3 dialog box, enter XBAR Chart for Luggage Delivery in the Chart title edit box, and Minutes in the Value (Y) axis: edit box.
**3.** In the Step 4 dialog box, enter XBAR chart in the edit box to the right of the option button.

## Using Minitab for the *p* Chart

We illustrate the *p* chart by referring to the sponge production data of Example 15.1 on page 694. Open the SPONGE.MTP file. Then select **Stat | Control Charts | P.** In the Variable edit box enter C3 or Nconfrm. In the subgroups edit box area there are two choices. If the subgroup sizes are equal as they were in Table 15.1 on page 693, we can select the Subgroup size option button and enter the subgroup sample size in the edit box. If, however, the subgroup sizes are different (as they were in the sponges data of Example 15.1), then select the Subgroups option button and enter **C2** or **Total** in this edit box. Then click the **OK** button.

Note that the upper control limit of .05630 is denoted by 3.0SL, the center line is labeled *p*, and the lower control limit of .01186 is called −3.0SL. Observe that the upper and lower control limit lines appear jagged. This is because Minitab is computing different control limits for each day based on the sample size on that day rather than the average sample size discussed in section 15.4.

## Using Minitab for the *c* Chart

For the data of Table 15.4 on page 709, open the CHIPS.MTP file. Select **Stat | Control Charts | C.** Enter **C2** or **Chips** in the Variable edit box. Click the **OK** button.

## Using Minitab for *R* and $\overline{X}$ Charts

*R* and $\overline{X}$ charts can be obtained from Minitab by selecting **Stat | Control Charts | Xbar-R** from the menu bar. Once data are either entered or imported into a worksheet, in the Xbar-*R* chart dialog box enter the variable name. The format for entering the name is different, depending on whether the data are stacked down a single column or unstacked across a set of columns with the data for each time period in a single row. If the data for the variable of interest are stacked down a single column, select the **Single Column** option button and enter the variable name in the Single Column edit box and the subgroup size in the Subgroup size edit box (this assumes equal sample sizes in each subgroup). If the subgroups are unstacked with each row representing the data for a single time period, the Subgroups across rows option button must be selected and the columns that contain the samples entered. Then click the **OK** button.

# 16

# Simple Linear Regression and Correlation

## CHAPTER OBJECTIVES

✓ *To develop the simple linear regression model as a means of using one variable to predict another variable*
✓ *To assess the fit of the simple linear regression model*
✓ *To study the pitfalls involved in using regression models*
✓ *To introduce correlation as a measure of the strength of the association between two variables*

## Introduction

In previous chapters we focused primarily on a single numerical response variable, such as the rate of return of mutual funds. We studied various measures of statistical description (see chapter 4) and applied different techniques of statistical inference to make estimates and draw conclusions about our numerical response variable (see chapters 10–13). In this and the following two chapters we will concern ourselves with situations involving two or more numerical variables as a means of viewing the relationships that exist between them. Two techniques will be discussed: regression and correlation.

**Regression analysis** is used primarily for the purpose of prediction. Our goal in regression analysis is the development of a statistical model that can be used to predict the values of a **dependent** or **response variable** based on the values of at least one **explanatory** or **independent variable**. In this chapter we focus on a *simple* linear regression model—one that uses a *single* numerical independent variable $X$ to predict the numerical dependent variable $Y$. In chapters 17 and 18 we develop *multiple* regression models that use *several* explanatory variables $(X_1, X_2, \ldots, X_p)$ to predict a numerical dependent variable $Y$.[1]

[1] *Regression models in which the dependent variable is categorical involve the use of logistic regression (see section 18.6).*

**Correlation analysis**, in contrast to regression, is used to measure the strength of the association between numerical variables. For example, in section 16.11 we will determine the correlation between the value of the German mark and the Japanese yen over a 10-year period. In this instance the objective is not to use one variable to predict another but rather to measure the strength of the association or covariation that exists between two numerical variables.

## ◆ USING STATISTICS: *Forecasting Sales for a Clothing Store*

Over the past 25 years a chain of discount women's clothing stores has increased market share by increasing the number of locations in the chain. A systematic approach to site selection was never used. Site selection was primarily based on what was considered to be a great location or a great lease. This year, with a strategic plan for opening several new stores, the director of special projects and planning is being asked to develop an approach to forecasting annual sales for all new stores.

## 16.1 ◆ TYPES OF REGRESSION MODELS

In section 3.3 the **scatter diagram** was used to plot the relationship between an $X$ variable on the horizontal axis and a $Y$ variable on the vertical axis. The nature of the relationship between two variables can take many forms, ranging from simple ones to extremely complicated mathematical functions. The simplest relationship consists of a straight-line or **linear relationship**. An example of this relationship is shown in Figure 16.1. The straight-line (linear) model can be represented as

### Simple Linear Regression Model

$$Y_i = \beta_0 + \beta_1 X_i + \epsilon_i \qquad (16.1)$$

where

$\beta_0 = Y$ intercept for the population

$\beta_1 =$ slope for the population

$\epsilon_i =$ random error in $Y$ for observation $i$

In this model the **slope** of the line $\beta_1$ represents the expected change in $Y$ per unit change in $X$. It represents the average amount that $Y$ changes (either positively or negatively) for a particular unit change in $X$. The **$Y$ intercept** $\beta_0$ represents the average value of $Y$ when $X$ equals 0. The last component of the model, $\epsilon_i$, represents the random error in $Y$ for each observation $i$ that occurs.

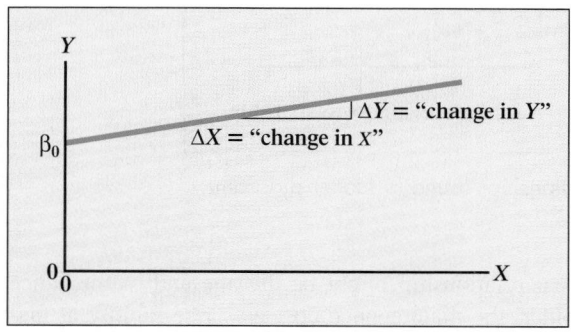

**FIGURE 16.1**

Positive straight-line relationship

The selection of the proper mathematical model is influenced by the distribution of the $X$ and $Y$ values on the scatter diagram. This can be seen readily from an examination of panels A–F in Figure 16.2 on page 736. In panel A we note that the values of $Y$ are generally increasing linearly as $X$ increases. This panel is similar to Figure 16.3 on page 738, which illustrates the positive relationship between the store size (i.e., square footage available) and the annual sales at branches of a women's clothing store.

Panel B is an example of a *negative* linear relationship. As $X$ increases, we note that the values of $Y$ are decreasing. An example of this type of relationship might be the price of a particular product and the amount of sales. Panel C shows a set of data in which there is very little or no relationship between $X$ and $Y$. High and low values of $Y$ appear at each value of $X$.

The data in panel D show a positive curvilinear relationship between $X$ and $Y$. The values of $Y$ are increasing as $X$ increases, but this increase tapers off beyond certain values of

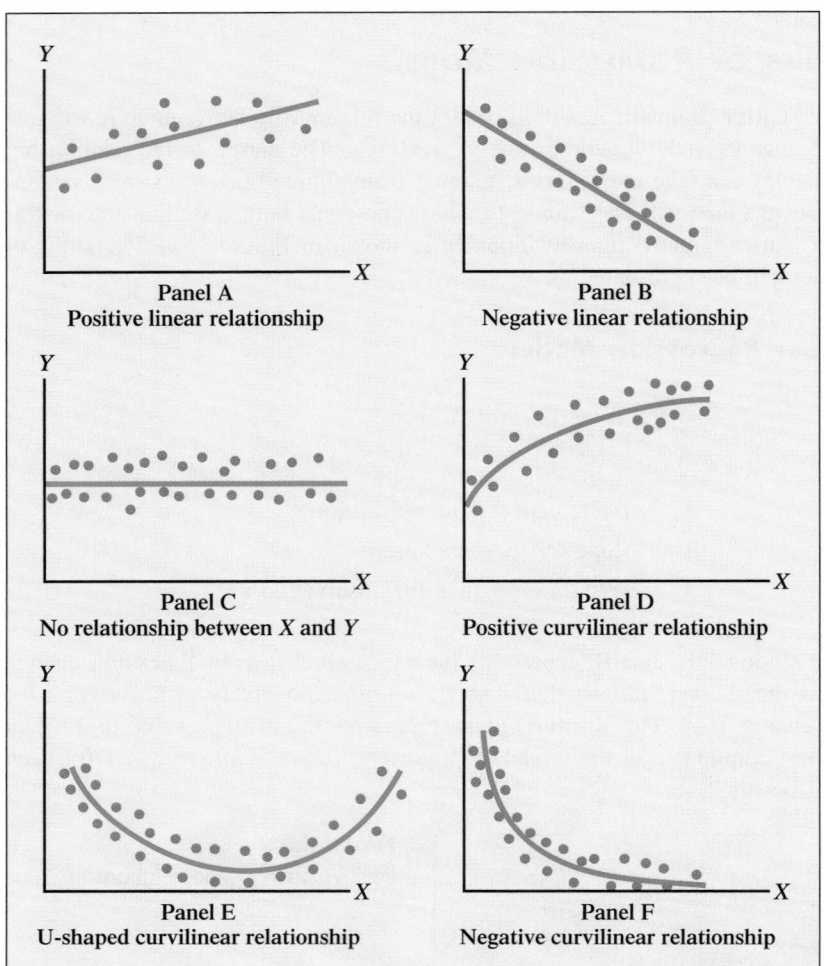

***FIGURE 16.2***   Examples of types of relationships found in scatter diagrams

*X*. An example of this positive curvilinear relationship might be the age and maintenance cost of a machine. As a machine gets older, the maintenance cost may rise rapidly at first but then level off beyond a certain number of years.

Panel E shows a parabolic or U-shaped relationship between *X* and *Y*. As *X* increases, at first *Y* decreases; but as *X* continues to increase, *Y* not only stops decreasing but actually increases above its minimum value. An example of this type of relationship could be the number of errors per hour at a task and the number of hours worked. The number of errors per hour would decrease as the individual becomes more proficient at the task but then would increase beyond a certain point because of factors such as fatigue and boredom.

Finally, panel F indicates an exponential or negative curvilinear relationship between *X* and *Y*. In this case, *Y* decreases very rapidly as *X* first increases but then decreases much less rapidly as *X* increases further. An example of this exponential relationship could be the resale value of a particular type of automobile and its age. In the first year the resale value drops drastically from its original price; however, the resale value then decreases much less rapidly in subsequent years.

In this section we have briefly examined a variety of different models that could be used to represent the relationship between two variables. Although scatter diagrams can be extremely helpful in determining the mathematical form of the relationship, more sophisticated statistical procedures are available to determine the most appropriate model for a set of variables. In subsequent sections of this chapter, we primarily focus on building statistical models for fitting linear relationships between variables.

## 16.2 DETERMINING THE SIMPLE LINEAR REGRESSION EQUATION

In the Using Statistics example introduced earlier we stated that the director of special projects wanted to develop a strategy for forecasting annual sales for all new stores. Suppose that he decided to examine the relationship between the size (i.e., square footage) of a store and its annual sales by selecting a sample of 14 stores. The results for these 14 stores are summarized in Table 16.1.

**Table 16.1** *Square footage and annual sales ($000) for sample of 14 branches of woman's clothing store chain*

| STORE | SQUARE FEET | ANNUAL SALES ($000) | STORE | SQUARE FEET | ANNUAL SALES ($000) |
|-------|-------------|---------------------|-------|-------------|---------------------|
| 1 | 1,726 | 3,681 | 8 | 1,102 | 2,694 |
| 2 | 1,642 | 3,895 | 9 | 3,151 | 5,468 |
| 3 | 2,816 | 6,653 | 10 | 1,516 | 2,898 |
| 4 | 5,555 | 9,543 | 11 | 5,161 | 10,674 |
| 5 | 1,292 | 3,418 | 12 | 4,567 | 7,585 |
| 6 | 2,208 | 5,563 | 13 | 5,841 | 11,760 |
| 7 | 1,313 | 3,660 | 14 | 3,008 | 4,085 |

DATA FILE
SITE

The scatter diagram for the data in Table 16.1 is shown in Figure 16.3 on page 738. An examination of Figure 16.3 indicates a clearly increasing relationship between square feet ($X$) and annual sales ($Y$). As the size of the store as measured by its square footage increases, annual sales increase approximately as a straight line. On this basis, if we assume that a straight line provides a useful mathematical model of this relationship, the question in regression analysis becomes the determination of the particular straight-line model that is the best fit to these data.

## The Least-Squares Method

In the preceding section we hypothesized a statistical model to represent the relationship between two variables, square footage and sales, in a chain of women's clothing stores. However, as shown in Table 16.1, we have obtained data from only a random sample of the population of stores. If certain assumptions are valid (see section 16.4), the sample $Y$ intercept $b_0$ and the sample slope $b_1$ can be used as estimates of the respective population parameters $\beta_0$ and $\beta_1$. Thus, the sample regression equation representing the straight-line regression model is

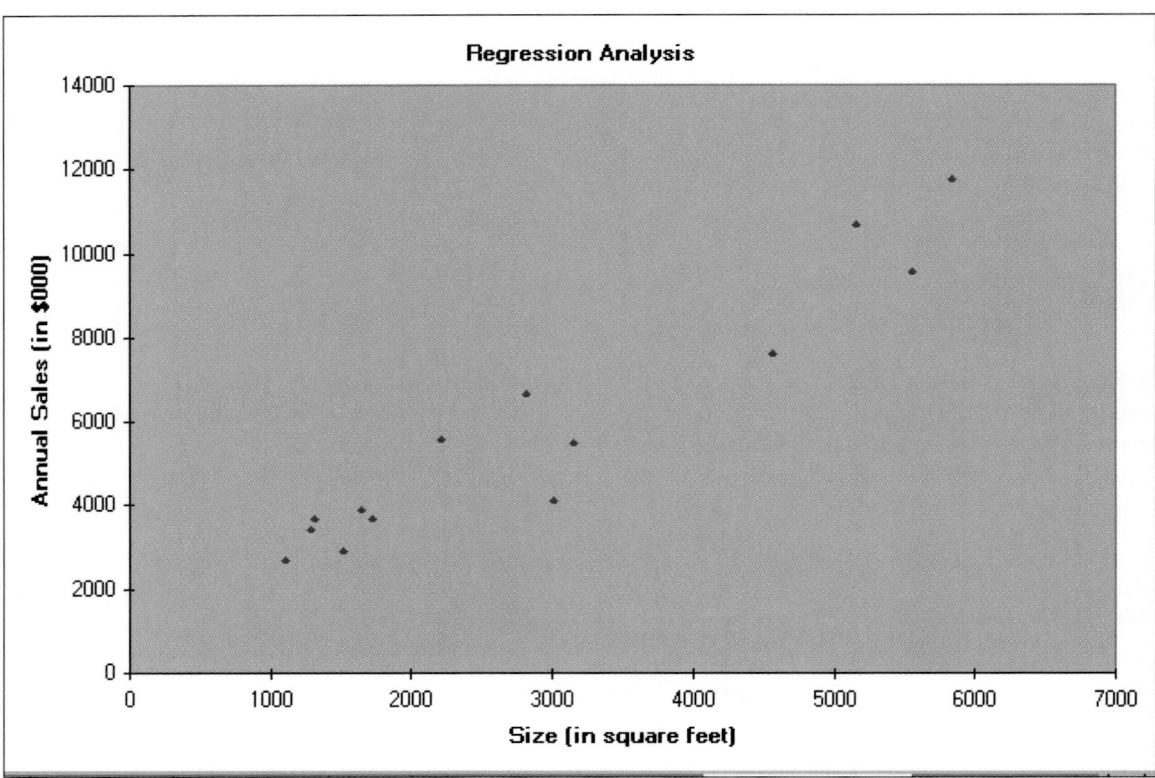

**Figure 16.3**   Scatter diagram for site selection data obtained from Microsoft Excel

## Sample Linear Regression Equation

The predicted value of $Y$ equals the $Y$ intercept plus the slope times the $X$ value.

$$\hat{Y}_i = b_0 + b_1 X_i \qquad (16.2)$$

where

$$\hat{Y}_i = \text{predicted value of } Y \text{ for observation } i$$
$$X_i = \text{value of } X \text{ for observation } i$$

This equation requires the determination of two **regression coefficients**—$b_0$ (the $Y$ intercept) and $b_1$ (the slope) in order to predict values of $Y$. Once $b_0$ and $b_1$ are obtained, the straight line is known and can be plotted on the scatter diagram. Then we can make a visual comparison of how well our particular statistical model (a straight line) fits the original data by observing whether the original data lie close to the fitted line or deviate greatly from the fitted line.

Simple linear regression analysis is concerned with finding the straight line that fits the data best. The *best* fit could be defined in a variety of ways. Perhaps the simplest way would involve finding the straight line for which the differences between the actual values ($Y_i$) and the values that would be predicted from the fitted line of regression ($\hat{Y}_i$) are as small as possible. However, because these differences will be positive for some observations and negative for other observations, mathematically we *minimize* the sum of the squared differences

$$\sum_{i=1}^{n} (Y_i - \hat{Y}_i)^2$$

where

$Y_i$ = actual value of $Y$ for observation $i$

$\hat{Y}_i$ = predicted value of $Y$ for observation $i$

Because $\hat{Y}_i = b_0 + b_1 X_i$, we are minimizing

$$\sum_{i=1}^{n} [Y_i - (b_0 + b_1 X_i)]^2$$

which has two unknowns, $b_0$ and $b_1$.

A mathematical technique that determines the values of $b_0$ and $b_1$ that minimizes this difference is known as the **least-squares method**. Any values for $b_0$ and $b_1$ other than those determined by the least-squares method result in a greater sum of squared differences between the actual value of $Y$ and the predicted value of $Y$. In using the least-squares method, we obtain the following set of equations:

## Equations from the Least-Squares Method

$$\sum_{i=1}^{n} Y_i = nb_0 + b_1 \sum_{i=1}^{n} X_i \qquad (16.3a)$$

$$\sum_{i=1}^{n} X_i Y_i = b_0 \sum_{i=1}^{n} X_i + b_1 \sum_{i=1}^{n} X_i^2 \qquad (16.3b)$$

From these two equations we must solve for $b_1$ and $b_0$. In this text we take the view that the Excel spreadsheet software or Minitab statistical software will be used to perform the calculations. However, to understand how the results displayed in the output of this software have been computed for the case of simple linear regression, in section 16.10 we illustrate many of the computations involved. Figure 16.4 on page 740 represents output from Microsoft Excel for the data of Table 16.1; Figure 16.5 on page 741 represents Minitab output.

From either Figure 16.4 or Figure 16.5 we observe that $b_1 = 1.686$ and $b_0 = 901.247$. Thus, the equation for the best straight line for these data is

$$\hat{Y}_i = 901.247 + 1.686 X_i$$

The slope $b_1$ was computed as $+1.686$. This means that for each increase of one unit in $X$, the average value of $Y$ is estimated to increase by 1.686 units. In other words, for each increase of 1 square foot in the size of the store, the fitted model predicts that the expected annual sales are estimated to increase by 1.686 thousands of dollars, or \$1,686. Thus, the slope can be viewed as representing the portion of the annual sales that are estimated to vary according to the size of the store.

The $Y$ intercept $b_0$ was computed to be $+901.247$ (thousands of dollars). The $Y$ intercept represents the average value of $Y$ when $X$ equals 0. Because the square footage size of the store cannot be 0, this $Y$ intercept can be viewed as representing the portion of the annual sales that varies with factors other than the size of the store.

To illustrate a situation where there is a direct interpretation for the $Y$ intercept $b_0$, we turn to Example 16.1.

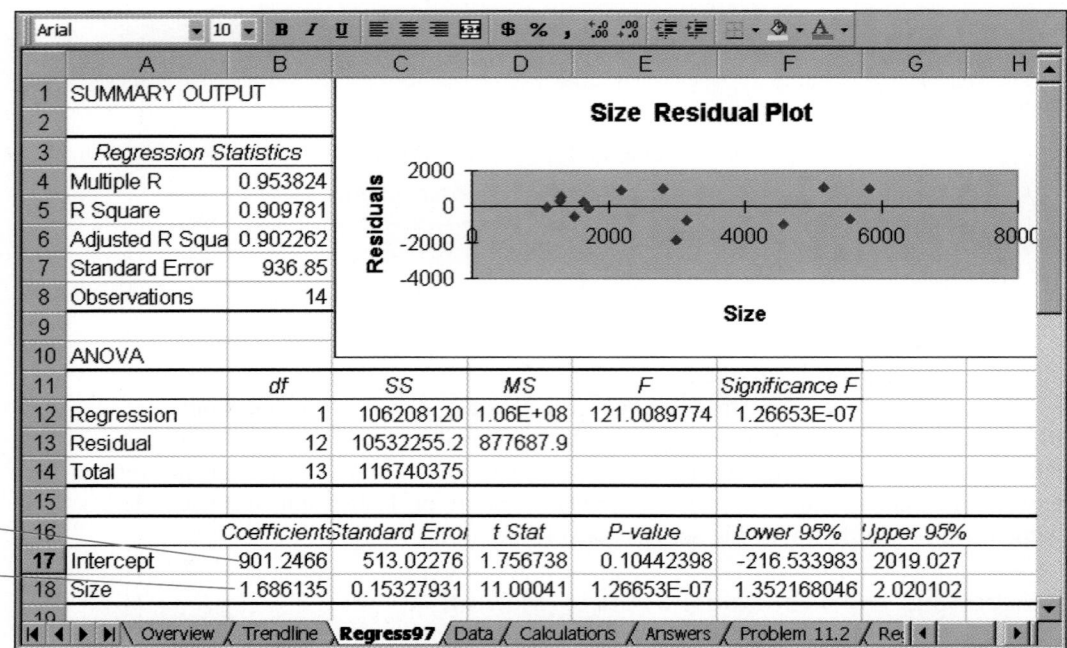

$b_0$

$b_1$

| | A | B | C |
|---|---|---|---|
| 21 | | | |
| 22 | RESIDUAL OUTPUT | | |
| 23 | | | |
| 24 | Observation | Predicted Sales | Residuals |
| 25 | 1 | 3811.515529 | -130.515529 |
| 26 | 2 | 3669.880191 | 225.119809 |
| 27 | 3 | 5649.402647 | 1003.59735 |
| 28 | 4 | 10267.72633 | -724.726331 |
| 29 | 5 | 3079.732952 | 338.267048 |
| 30 | 6 | 4624.232585 | 938.767415 |
| 31 | 7 | 3115.141786 | 544.858214 |
| 32 | 8 | 2759.367307 | -65.3673075 |
| 33 | 9 | 6214.257862 | -746.257862 |
| 34 | 10 | 3457.427185 | -559.427185 |
| 35 | 11 | 9603.389152 | 1070.61085 |
| 36 | 12 | 8601.82498 | -1016.82498 |
| 37 | 13 | 10749.96093 | 1010.03907 |
| 38 | 14 | 5973.140561 | -1888.14056 |

**FIGURE 16.4**
Microsoft Excel output for site selection problem

## Example 16.1 *Interpreting the Y Intercept $b_0$ and the Slope $b_1$*

Suppose that an economist wanted to use the yearly rate of productivity growth in the United States ($X$) to predict the percentage change in the Standard and Poor's index of 500 stocks. Suppose that a regression model was fit based upon annual data for a period of 50 years with the following results:

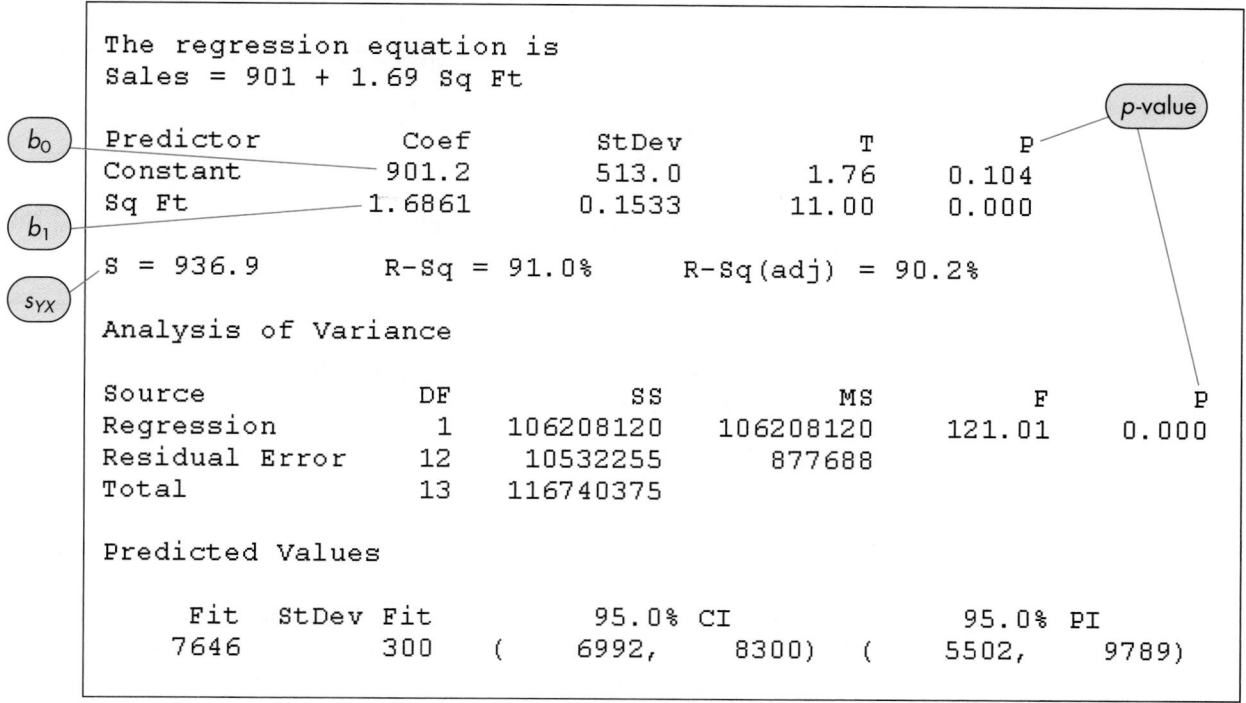

```
        The regression equation is
        Sales = 901 + 1.69 Sq Ft

                                                              ( p-value )
        Predictor           Coef         StDev           T          P
  b₀    Constant           901.2         513.0        1.76      0.104
        Sq Ft             1.6861        0.1533       11.00      0.000
  b₁

        S = 936.9       R-Sq = 91.0%      R-Sq(adj) = 90.2%
  sᵧₓ
        Analysis of Variance

        Source              DF            SS          MS          F          P
        Regression           1     106208120   106208120     121.01      0.000
        Residual Error      12      10532255      877688
        Total               13     116740375

        Predicted Values

            Fit   StDev Fit         95.0% CI            95.0% PI
           7646         300    (   6992,     8300)   (   5502,     9789)
```

**FIGURE 16.5**  Minitab output for site selection problem

$$\hat{Y}_i = -5.0 + 7X_i$$

What is the interpretation of the $Y$ intercept $b_0$ and the slope $b_1$?

### SOLUTION

The $Y$ intercept $b_0 = -5.0$ tells us that when the rate of productivity growth is zero, the expected change in the Standard and Poor's stock index is $-5.0$, meaning that the index is predicted to decrease by 5% during the year. The slope $b_1 = 7$ tells us that for each increase in productivity of 1%, we predict that the expected change in the Standard and Poor's stock index is $+7.0$, meaning that the index is predicted to increase by 7% for each 1% increase in productivity.

---

The regression model that has been fit to the site selection data can now be used to predict the average annual sales as illustrated in Example 16.2.

## Example 16.2  *Predicting Average Annual Sales Based on Square Footage*

Suppose that we would like to use the fitted model to predict the average annual sales for a store with 4,000 square feet.

## SOLUTION

We can determine the predicted value by substituting $X = 4{,}000$ into our regression equation,

$$\hat{Y}_i = 901.247 + 1.686X_i$$
$$\hat{Y}_i = 901.247 + 1.686(4{,}000) = 7{,}645.786 \text{ or } \$7{,}645{,}786$$

Thus, the predicted average annual sales for a store with 4,000 square feet is 7,645.786 thousands of dollars, or $7,645,786.

## Predictions in Regression Analysis: Interpolation versus Extrapolation

When using a regression model for prediction purposes, it is important that we consider only the **relevant range** of the independent variable in making our predictions. This relevant range encompasses all values from the smallest to the largest $X$ used in developing the regression model. Hence, when predicting $Y$ for a given value of $X$, we may *interpolate* within this relevant range of the $X$ values, but we should not *extrapolate* beyond the range of $X$ values. For example, when we use the square footage to predict annual sales, we note from Table 16.1 that the square footage varies from 1,102 to 5,841. Therefore, predictions of annual sales should be made only for stores that are between 1,102 and 5,841 square feet in size. Any prediction of annual sales for stores with size outside this range presumes that the fitted relationship holds outside the 1,102 to 5,841 range.

## Problems for Section 16.2

### Learning the Basics

• **16.1**   Fitting a straight line to a set of data yields the following regression equation

$$\hat{Y}_i = 2 + 5X_i$$

  (a) Interpret the meaning of the $Y$ intercept $b_0$.
  (b) Interpret the meaning of the slope $b_1$.
  (c) Predict the average value of $Y$ for $X = 3$.
  (d) If the values of $X$ range from 2 to 25, should you use this model to predict the average value of $Y$ when $X$ equals
   (1)  3?                    (4)  24?
   (2)  −3?                   (5)  26?
   (3)  0?

**16.2**   Fitting a straight line to a set of data yields the following regression equation

$$\hat{Y}_i = 16 - .5X_i$$

  (a) Interpret the meaning of the $Y$ intercept $b_0$.
  (b) Interpret the meaning of the slope $b_1$.
  (c) Predict the average value of $Y$ for $X = 6$.

### Applying the Concepts

*Note:* Use software such as Microsoft Excel or Minitab (or the computational formulas in section 16.10) to solve these problems.

**• 16.3** The marketing manager of a large supermarket chain would like to determine the effect of shelf space on the sales of pet food. A random sample of 12 equal-sized stores is selected with the following results:

| STORE | SHELF SPACE, X (FEET) | WEEKLY SALES, Y (HUNDREDS OF DOLLARS) | STORE | SHELF SPACE, X (FEET) | WEEKLY SALES, Y (HUNDREDS OF DOLLARS) |
|---|---|---|---|---|---|
| 1 | 5 | 1.6 | 7 | 15 | 2.3 |
| 2 | 5 | 2.2 | 8 | 15 | 2.7 |
| 3 | 5 | 1.4 | 9 | 15 | 2.8 |
| 4 | 10 | 1.9 | 10 | 20 | 2.6 |
| 5 | 10 | 2.4 | 11 | 20 | 2.9 |
| 6 | 10 | 2.6 | 12 | 20 | 3.1 |

DATA FILE
PETFOOD

Results: $b_0 = 1.45$ $b_1 = .074$

(a) Set up a scatter diagram.
(b) Assuming a linear relationship, what are the regression coefficients $b_0$ and $b_1$?
(c) Interpret the meaning of the slope $b_1$ in this problem.
(d) Predict the average weekly sales (in hundreds of dollars) of pet food for stores with 8 feet of shelf space for pet food.
(e) Suppose that sales in store 12 are 2.6. Do parts (a)–(d) with this value and compare the results.
(f) What shelf space would you recommend that the marketing manager allocate to pet food? Explain.

**16.4** Suppose that the management of a chain of package delivery stores would like to develop a model for predicting the weekly sales (in thousands of dollars) for individual stores based on the number of customers who made purchases. A random sample of 20 stores was selected from among all the stores in the chain with the following results.

| STORES | CUSTOMERS | SALES ($000) | STORES | CUSTOMERS | SALES ($000) |
|---|---|---|---|---|---|
| 1 | 907 | 11.20 | 11 | 679 | 7.63 |
| 2 | 926 | 11.05 | 12 | 872 | 9.43 |
| 3 | 506 | 6.84 | 13 | 924 | 9.46 |
| 4 | 741 | 9.21 | 14 | 607 | 7.64 |
| 5 | 789 | 9.42 | 15 | 452 | 6.92 |
| 6 | 889 | 10.08 | 16 | 729 | 8.95 |
| 7 | 874 | 9.45 | 17 | 794 | 9.33 |
| 8 | 510 | 6.73 | 18 | 844 | 10.23 |
| 9 | 529 | 7.24 | 19 | 1,010 | 11.77 |
| 10 | 420 | 6.12 | 20 | 621 | 7.41 |

DATA FILE
PACKAGE

Results: $b_0 = 2.423$ $b_1 = .00873$

(a) Set up a scatter diagram.
(b) Assuming a linear relationship, what are the regression coefficients $b_0$ and $b_1$?

(c) Interpret the meaning of the slope $b_1$ in this problem.

(d) Predict the average weekly sales (in thousands of dollars) for stores that have 600 customers.

(e) Suppose that sales in store 19 are 14.77. Do parts (a)–(d) with this value and compare the results.

(f) What other factors besides the number of customers might affect sales?

● **16.5** A company manufacturing machine parts would like to develop a model to estimate the number of worker-hours required for production runs of varying lot size. A random sample of 14 production runs (2 each for lot sizes 20, 30, 40, 50, 60, 70, and 80) is selected with the following results:

| LOT SIZE | WORKER-HOURS | LOT SIZE | WORKER-HOURS |
|---|---|---|---|
| 20 | 50 | 50 | 112 |
| 20 | 55 | 60 | 128 |
| 30 | 73 | 60 | 135 |
| 30 | 67 | 70 | 148 |
| 40 | 87 | 70 | 160 |
| 40 | 95 | 80 | 170 |
| 50 | 108 | 80 | 162 |

**DATA FILE**
**WORKHRS**

Results: $b_0 = 12.679$    $b_1 = 1.9607$

(a) Set up a scatter diagram.

(b) Assuming a linear relationship, what are the regression coefficients $b_0$ and $b_1$?

(c) Interpret the meaning of the $Y$ intercept $b_0$ and the slope $b_1$ in this problem.

(d) Predict the average number of worker-hours required for a production run with a lot size of 45.

(e) Why would it not be appropriate to predict the average number of worker-hours required for a production run with a lot size of 100? Explain.

(f) Suppose that the worker-hours for the lot size of 60 were 117 and 119. Do parts (a)–(d) with these values and compare the results.

**16.6** A company that has the distribution rights to home video sales of previously released movies would like to be able to estimate the number of units that it can be expected to sell. Data are available for 30 movies that indicate the box office gross (in millions of dollars) and the number of units sold (in thousands) of home videos. The results are as follows:

| MOVIE | BOX OFFICE GROSS ($ MILLIONS) | HOME VIDEO UNITS SOLD (000) | MOVIE | BOX OFFICE GROSS ($ MILLIONS) | HOME VIDEO UNITS SOLD (000) |
|---|---|---|---|---|---|
| 1 | 1.10 | 57.18 | 8 | 1.69 | 30.88 |
| 2 | 1.13 | 26.17 | 9 | 1.74 | 49.29 |
| 3 | 1.18 | 92.79 | 10 | 1.77 | 24.14 |
| 4 | 1.25 | 61.60 | 11 | 2.42 | 115.31 |
| 5 | 1.44 | 46.50 | 12 | 5.34 | 87.04 |
| 6 | 1.53 | 85.06 | 13 | 5.70 | 128.45 |
| 7 | 1.53 | 103.52 | 14 | 6.43 | 126.64 |

*continued*

| MOVIE | BOX OFFICE GROSS ($ MILLIONS) | HOME VIDEO UNITS SOLD (000) | MOVIE | BOX OFFICE GROSS ($ MILLIONS) | HOME VIDEO UNITS SOLD (000) |
|---|---|---|---|---|---|
| 15 | 8.59 | 107.28 | 23 | 23.13 | 280.79 |
| 16 | 9.36 | 190.80 | 24 | 27.62 | 229.51 |
| 17 | 9.89 | 121.57 | 25 | 37.09 | 277.68 |
| 18 | 12.66 | 183.30 | 26 | 40.73 | 226.73 |
| 19 | 15.35 | 204.72 | 27 | 45.55 | 365.14 |
| 20 | 17.55 | 112.47 | 28 | 46.62 | 218.64 |
| 21 | 17.91 | 162.95 | 29 | 54.70 | 286.31 |
| 22 | 18.25 | 109.20 | 30 | 58.51 | 254.58 |

DATA FILE
MOVIE

Results: $b_0 = 76.54$    $b_1 = 4.3331$

(a) Set up a scatter diagram.
(b) What are the regression coefficients $b_0$ and $b_1$?
(c) State the regression equation.
(d) Interpret the meaning of $b_0$ and $b_1$ in this problem.
(e) Predict the average video unit sales for a movie that had a box office gross of $20 million.
(f) What other factors in addition to box office gross might be useful in predicting video unit sales?

**16.7** An agent for a residential real estate company in a large city would like to be able to predict the monthly rental cost for apartments based on the size of the apartment as defined by square footage. A sample of 25 apartments in a particular residential neighborhood was selected, and the information gathered revealed the following:

| APARTMENT | MONTHLY RENT ($) | SIZE (SQUARE FEET) | APARTMENT | MONTHLY RENT ($) | SIZE (SQUARE FEET) |
|---|---|---|---|---|---|
| 1 | 950 | 850 | 14 | 1,800 | 1,369 |
| 2 | 1,600 | 1,450 | 15 | 1,400 | 1,175 |
| 3 | 1,200 | 1,085 | 16 | 1,450 | 1,225 |
| 4 | 1,500 | 1,232 | 17 | 1,100 | 1,245 |
| 5 | 950 | 718 | 18 | 1,700 | 1,259 |
| 6 | 1,700 | 1,485 | 19 | 1,200 | 1,150 |
| 7 | 1,650 | 1,136 | 20 | 1,150 | 896 |
| 8 | 935 | 726 | 21 | 1,600 | 1,361 |
| 9 | 875 | 700 | 22 | 1,650 | 1,040 |
| 10 | 1,150 | 956 | 23 | 1,200 | 755 |
| 11 | 1,400 | 1,100 | 24 | 800 | 1,000 |
| 12 | 1,650 | 1,285 | 25 | 1,750 | 1,200 |
| 13 | 2,300 | 1,985 | | | |

DATA FILE
RENT

Results: $b_0 = 177.1$    $b_1 = 1.065$

(a) Set up a scatter diagram.

(b) What are the regression coefficients $b_0$ and $b_1$?

(c) State the regression equation.

(d) Interpret the meaning of $b_0$ and $b_1$ in this problem.

(e) Predict the average monthly rental cost for an apartment that has 1,000 square feet.

(f) Why would it not be appropriate to use the model to predict the monthly rental for apartments that have 500 square feet?

(g) Your friends Jim and Jennifer are considering signing a lease for an apartment in this residential neighborhood. They are trying to decide between two apartments, one with 1,000 square feet for a monthly rent of $1,250 and the other with 1,200 square feet for a monthly rent of $1,425. What would you recommend to them? Why?

**16.8** A limousine service operating from a suburban county wants to determine the length of time it would take to transport passengers from various locations to a major metropolitan airport during nonpeak hours. A sample of 12 trips on a particular day during nonpeak hours indicates the following

| DISTANCE (MILES) | TIME (MINUTES) | DISTANCE (MILES) | TIME (MINUTES) |
|---|---|---|---|
| 10.3 | 19.71 | 18.4 | 29.38 |
| 11.6 | 18.15 | 20.2 | 37.24 |
| 12.1 | 21.88 | 21.8 | 36.84 |
| 14.3 | 24.21 | 24.3 | 40.59 |
| 15.7 | 27.08 | 25.4 | 41.21 |
| 16.1 | 22.96 | 26.7 | 38.19 |

**DATA FILE**
**LIMO**

Results: $b_0 = 3.375$    $b_1 = 1.46$

(a) Set up a scatter diagram.

(b) Assuming a linear relationship, what are the regression coefficients $b_0$ and $b_1$?

(c) Interpret the meaning of the $Y$ intercept $b_0$ and the slope $b_1$ in this problem.

(d) Use the regression model developed in (b) to predict the average number of minutes to transport someone from a location that is 21 miles from the airport.

(e) Suppose the distance for the last trip was 36.7 (instead of 26.7) miles and the time was 65 (instead of 38.19) minutes. Do parts (a)–(d) with these values and compare the results.

(f) What would the results of (e) lead you to think about the usefulness of the regression model?

## ◆16.3◆ MEASURES OF VARIATION

### Obtaining the Sum of Squares

To examine how well the independent variable predicts the dependent variable in our statistical model, we need to develop several measures of variation. The first measure, the **total sum of squares (SST)**, is a measure of variation of the $Y_i$ values around their mean $\overline{Y}$. In a regression analysis the **total variation** or sum of squares can be subdivided into **explained variation** or **regression sum of squares (SSR)**, that which is attributable to the relation-

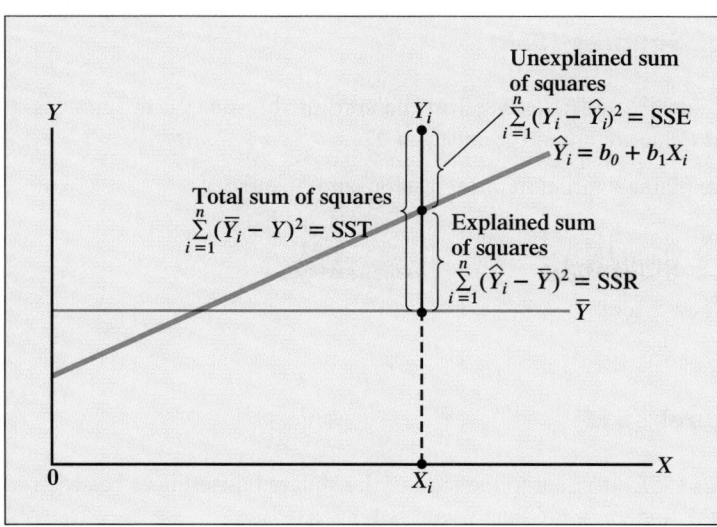

**FIGURE 16.6**    Measures of variation in regression

ship between $X$ and $Y$, and **unexplained variation** or **error sum of squares** (*SSE*), that which is attributable to factors other than the relationship between $X$ and $Y$. These different measures of variation can be seen in Figure 16.6.

The regression sum of squares (*SSR*) represents the difference between $\hat{Y}_i$ (the value of $Y$ that would be predicted from the regression relationship) and $\overline{Y}$ (the average value of $Y$). The error sum of squares (*SSE*) represents that part of the variation in $Y$ that is not explained by the regression. It is based on the difference between $Y_i$ and $\hat{Y}_i$. These measures of variation can be represented as follows:

## Measures of Variation in Regression

Total sum of squares = regression sum of squares + error sum of squares    (16.4)

$$SST = SSR + SSE$$

## Total Sum of Squares (*SST*)

The total sum of squares (*SST*) is equal to the sum of the squared differences between each observed $Y$ value and $\overline{Y}$, the average value of $Y$.

$$SST = \text{total variation or total sum of squares} = \sum_{i=1}^{n} (Y_i - \overline{Y})^2 \qquad (16.5)$$

## Regression Sum of Squares (*SSR*)

The regression sum of squares (*SSR*) is equal to the sum of the squared differences between each predicted value of *Y* and the mean of *Y*.

$$SSR = \text{explained variation or regression sum of squares} \qquad (16.6)$$

$$= \sum_{i=1}^{n} (\hat{Y}_i - \overline{Y})^2$$

$$= SST - SSE$$

## Error Sum of Squares (*SSE*)

The error sum of squares (*SSE*) is equal to the sum of the squared differences between each observed value of *Y* and each predicted value of *Y*.

$$SSE = \text{unexplained variation or error sum of squares} \qquad (16.7)$$

$$= \sum_{i=1}^{n} (Y_i - \hat{Y}_i)^2$$

Examining either Figure 16.4 or Figure 16.5 on pages 740 and 741, we observe that

$$SSR = 106,208,120, \qquad SSE = 10,532,255, \qquad \text{and} \qquad SST = 116,740,375$$

We note also, from equation (16.4), that

$$SST = SSR + SSE$$

$$116,740,375 = 106,208,120 + 10,532,255$$

The total sum of squared differences around the average value of *Y* is equal to 116,740,375. This amount is subdivided into the sum of squares that is explained by the regression (*SSR*), equal to 106,208,120, and the sum of squares that is unexplained by the regression (the error sum of squares), equal to 10,532,255.

### COMMENT: *Scientific Notation*

Note that in some versions of the Excel or Minitab software *SSR* is formatted as 1.06E+08 using a numerical format known as "scientific notation." Many software packages use this type of format to display very small or very large values. The number after the letter E represents the number of digits that the decimal point needs to be moved to the left (for a negative number) or to the right (for a positive number). For example, the number 3.7431E+02 would mean that the decimal point should be moved two places to the right, producing the number 374.31. The number 3.7431E−02 would mean that the decimal point should be moved two places to the left, producing the number .037431. Thus, a result for *SSR*, formatted as 1.06E+08, means that the decimal point should be moved eight places to the right, producing the number 106,000,000. Note that when scientific notation is used, often fewer significant digits are displayed and the numbers may appear to be rounded.

## The Coefficient of Determination

By themselves, *SSR*, *SSE*, and *SST* provide little that can be directly interpreted. However, a simple ratio of the regression sum of squares (*SSR*) to the total sum of squares (*SST*) provides a measure of the usefulness of the regression equation. This ratio is called the **coefficient of determination** $r^2$ and is defined as

### Coefficient of Determination

The coefficient of determination is equal to the regression sum of squares divided by the total sum of squares.

$$r^2 = \frac{\text{regression sum of squares}}{\text{total sum of squares}} = \frac{SSR}{SST} \qquad (16.8)$$

This coefficient of determination measures the proportion of variation in *Y* that is explained by the independent variable *X* in the regression model. For the site selection example,

with $SSR = 106{,}208{,}120$, $\qquad SSE = 10{,}532{,}255$, $\qquad$ and $\qquad SST = 116{,}740{,}375$

$$r^2 = \frac{106{,}208{,}120}{116{,}740{,}375} = .91$$

Therefore, 91% of the variation in annual sales can be explained by the variability in the size of the store as measured by the square footage. This is an example where there is a strong positive linear relationship between two variables because the use of a regression model has reduced the variability in predicting annual sales by 91%. Only 9% of the sample variability in annual sales can be explained by factors other than what is accounted for by the linear regression model that uses only square footage.

## Standard Error of the Estimate

Although the least-squares method results in the line that fits the data with the minimum amount of variation, we have seen in the computation of the error sum of squares (*SSE*) that unless all the observed data points fall on the regression line, the regression equation is not a perfect predictor. Just as we do not expect all data values to be exactly equal to their arithmetic mean, neither can we expect all data points to fall exactly on the regression line. Therefore, we need to develop a statistic that measures the variability of the actual *Y* values from the predicted *Y* values, in the same way that we developed the standard deviation in chapter 4 as a measure of the variability of each observation around its mean. This standard deviation around the line of regression is called the **standard error of the estimate**.

The variability around the line of regression is illustrated in Figure 16.7 on page 750 for the site selection data. We can see from Figure 16.7 that although many of the actual values of *Y* fall near the predicted line of regression, there are several values above the line of regression as well as below the line of regression.

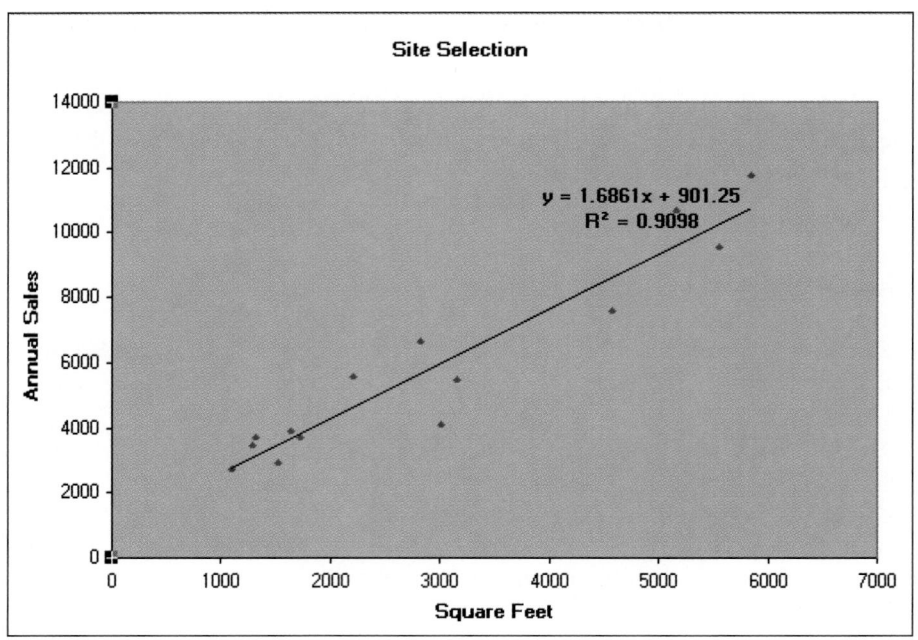

**FIGURE 16.7** Scatter diagram and line of regression for site selection data obtained from Microsoft Excel

The standard error of the estimate, given by the symbol $S_{YX}$, is defined as

**Standard Error of the Estimate**

$$S_{YX} = \sqrt{\frac{SSE}{n-2}} = \sqrt{\frac{\sum_{i=1}^{n}(Y_i - \hat{Y}_i)^2}{n-2}} \qquad (16.9)$$

where

$$Y_i = \text{actual value of } Y \text{ for a given } X_i$$
$$\hat{Y}_i = \text{predicted value of } Y \text{ for a given } X_i$$
$$SSE = \text{error sum of squares}$$

From equation (16.9), with $SSE = 10,532,255$, we have

$$S_{YX} = \sqrt{\frac{10,532,255}{14-2}}$$

$$S_{YX} = 936.85$$

This standard error of the estimate, equal to 936.85 thousands of dollars (i.e., $936,850), is labeled on the Microsoft Excel output of Figure 16.4 as Standard Error and is labeled on the Minitab output of Figure 16.5 as S. The standard error of the estimate represents a measure of the variation around the fitted line of regression. It is measured in units of the dependent variable Y. The interpretation of the standard error of the estimate is similar to that of the standard deviation. Just as the standard deviation measures variability around the arithmetic mean, the standard error of the estimate measures variability around the fitted line of regression. As we shall see in sections 16.7 and 16.8, the standard error of the estimate can be used to determine whether a statistically significant relationship exists between the two variables and to make inferences about a predicted value of $Y$.

## Problems for Section 16.3

### Learning the Basics

**16.9** If the coefficient of determination $r^2$ is equal to .80, what does this mean?

● **16.10** If $SSR = 36$ and $SSE = 4$, find $SST$, then compute the coefficient of determination $r^2$ and interpret its meaning.

**16.11** If $SSR = 66$ and $SST = 88$, compute the coefficient of determination $r^2$ and interpret its meaning.

**16.12** If $SSE = 10$ and $SST = 30$, compute the coefficient of determination $r^2$ and interpret its meaning.

**16.13** If $SSR = 120$, why is it impossible for $SST$ to equal 110?

### Applying the Concepts

● **16.14** In Problem 16.3 on page 743 the marketing manager used shelf space for pet food to predict weekly sales. Using the computer output you obtained to solve that problem or using the following summary information,

**DATA FILE**
**PETFOOD**

$$SSR = 2.0535 \quad SSE = .949 \quad SST = 3.0025$$

(a) Compute the coefficient of determination $r^2$ and interpret its meaning.
(b) Compute the standard error of the estimate.
(c) How useful do you think this regression model is for predicting sales?

**16.15** In Problem 16.4 on page 743 a manager wanted to predict weekly sales at a chain of package delivery stores based on the number of customers who made purchases. Using the computer output you obtained to solve that problem or using the following summary information,

**DATA FILE**
**PACKAGE**

$$SSR = 46.83 \quad SSE = 4.53 \quad SST = 51.36$$

(a) Compute the coefficient of determination $r^2$ and interpret its meaning.
(b) Compute the standard error of the estimate.
(c) How useful do you think this regression model is for predicting sales?

● **16.16** In Problem 16.5 on page 744 a company wanted to predict the worker-hours required for production based on the lot size. Using the computer output you obtained to solve that problem or using the following summary information,

**DATA FILE**
**WORKHRS**

$$SSR = 21{,}528.04 \quad SSE = 266.82 \quad SST = 21{,}794.86$$

(a) Compute the coefficient of determination $r^2$ and interpret its meaning.
(b) Compute the standard error of the estimate.
(c) How useful do you think this regression model is for predicting worker-hours?

**DATA FILE**
**MOVIE**

**16.17** In Problem 16.6 on page 744 a company wanted to predict home video sales based on the box office gross of movies. Using the computer output you obtained to solve that problem or using the following summary information,

$$SSR = 171,499.8 \quad SSE = 64,154.2 \quad SST = 235,654.0$$

(a) Compute the coefficient of determination $r^2$ and interpret its meaning.
(b) Compute the standard error of the estimate.
(c) How useful do you think this regression model is for predicting home video sales?

**DATA FILE**
**RENT**

**16.18** In Problem 16.7 on page 745 an agent for a real estate company wanted to predict the monthly rent for apartments based on the size of the apartment. Using the computer output you obtained to solve that problem or using the following summary information,

$$SSR = 2,268,777 \quad SSE = 870,949 \quad SST = 3,139,726$$

(a) Compute the coefficient of determination $r^2$ and interpret its meaning.
(b) Compute the standard error of the estimate.
(c) How useful do you think this regression model is for predicting monthly rent?

**DATA FILE**
**LIMO**

**16.19** In Problem 16.8 on page 746, a limousine service wants to predict travel time to an airport based on the distance from the pickup location to the airport. Using the computer output you obtained to solve that problem or using the following summary information,

$$SSR = 741.2582 \quad SSE = 66.5247 \quad SST = 807.7829$$

(a) Compute the coefficient of determination $r^2$ and interpret its meaning.
(b) Compute the standard error of the estimate.
(c) How useful do you think this regression model is for predicting travel time?

## 16.4 ASSUMPTIONS

In our study of hypothesis testing and the analysis of variance, we have stated that the appropriate application of a particular statistical procedure is dependent on how well a set of assumptions for that procedure are met. The assumptions necessary for regression and correlation analysis are analogous to those of the analysis of variance because they fall under the general heading of *linear models* (reference 7). Although there are some differences in the assumptions made by the regression model and by correlation (see reference 7), this topic is beyond the scope of this text and we will consider only the former.

The three major **assumptions of regression** are listed in Exhibit 16.1.

*Exhibit 16.1* **Assumptions of Regression**

✓ **1.** Normality of error
✓ **2.** Homoscedasticity
✓ **3.** Independence of errors

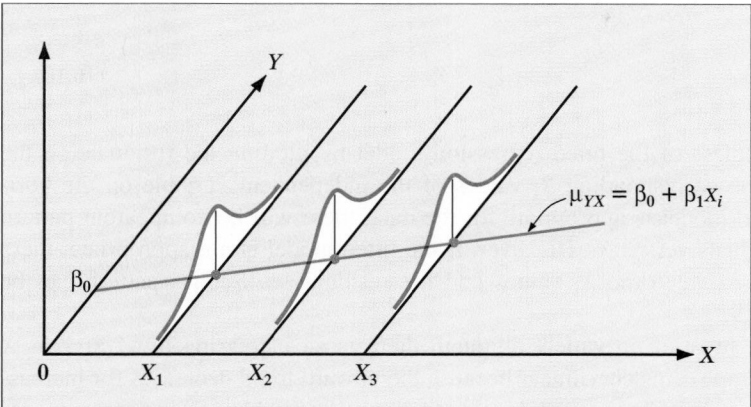

**FIGURE 16.8** Assumptions of regression

The first assumption, **normality**, requires that errors around the line of regression be normally distributed at each value of $X$ (see Figure 16.8). Like the $t$ test and the ANOVA $F$ test, regression analysis is fairly robust against departures from the normality assumption. As long as the distribution of the errors around the line of regression at each level of $X$ is not extremely different from a normal distribution, inferences about the line of regression and the regression coefficients will not be seriously affected.

The second assumption, **homoscedasticity**, requires that the variation around the line of regression be constant for all values of $X$. This means that the errors vary the same amount when $X$ is a low value as when $X$ is a high value (see Figure 16.8). The homoscedasticity assumption is important for using the least-squares method of determining the regression coefficients. If there are serious departures from this assumption, either data transformations (see section 18.3) or weighted least-squares methods (reference 7) can be applied.

The third assumption, **independence of errors**, requires that the errors be independent for each value of $X$. This assumption is particularly important when data are collected over a period of time. In such situations, the errors for a particular time period are often correlated with those of the previous time period.

## 16.5 RESIDUAL ANALYSIS

In the preceding discussion of the site selection data we have relied on a simple linear regression model in which the dependent variable is predicted based on a straight-line relationship with a single independent variable. In this section we use a graphical approach called **residual analysis** to evaluate the appropriateness of the regression model that has been fitted to the data. In addition, this approach also allows us to study potential violations of the assumptions of our regression model.

## Evaluating the Aptness of the Fitted Model

The **residual** or estimated error value ($e_i$) is defined as the difference between the observed ($Y_i$) and predicted ($\hat{Y}_i$) values of the dependent variable for a given value of $X_i$. Thus, the following definition applies:

### The Residual

The residual equals the difference between the observed value of $Y$ and the predicted value of $Y$.

$$e_i = Y_i - \hat{Y}_i \qquad (16.10)$$

We evaluate the aptness of the fitted regression model by plotting the residuals on the vertical axis against the corresponding $X_i$ values of the independent variable on the horizontal axis. If the fitted model is appropriate for the data, there will be no apparent pattern in this plot of the residuals versus $X_i$. However, if the fitted model is not appropriate, there will be a relationship between the $X_i$ values and the residuals $e_i$. Such a pattern can be observed in Figure 16.9.

Panel (a) depicts a situation in which, although there is an increasing trend in $Y$ as $X$ increases, the relationship seems curvilinear because the upward trend decreases for increasing values of $X$. Thus, a curvilinear model between the two variables seems more appropriate than a simple linear regression model. This curvilinear effect is highlighted in panel (b). Here there is a clear curvilinear effect between $X_i$ and $e_i$. By plotting the residuals, we have filtered out or removed the linear trend of $X$ with $Y$, thereby exposing the lack of fit in the simple linear model. Thus, we conclude that the curvilinear model is a better fit and should be evaluated in place of the simple linear model (see section 18.1 for further discussion of fitting curvilinear models).

Having considered Figure 16.9, let us return to the evaluation of the site selection data. Figure 16.10 provides the output that includes the values of the independent variable (square feet) along with the observed, predicted, residual, and the Studentized residual values of the response variable (annual sales) in the simple linear model we have fitted.

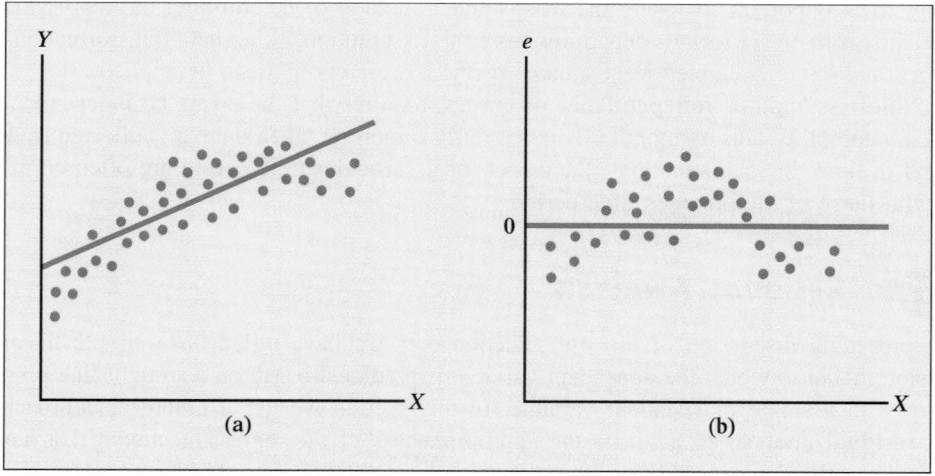

**FIGURE 16.9** Studying appropriateness of simple linear regression model

```
Obs      Sq Ft      Sales       Fit   StDev Fit    Residual   St Resid
  1       1726       3681       3812         310        -131      -0.15
  2       1642       3895       3670         318         225       0.26
  3       2816       6653       5649         251        1004       1.11
  4       5555       9543      10268         475        -725      -0.90
  5       1292       3418       3080         354         338       0.39
  6       2208       5563       4624         273         939       1.05
  7       1313       3660       3115         351         545       0.63
  8       1102       2694       2759         375         -65      -0.08
  9       3151       5468       6214         253        -746      -0.83
 10       1516       2898       3457         330        -559      -0.64
 11       5161      10674       9603         425        1071       1.28
 12       4567       7585       8602         355       -1017      -1.17
 13       5841      11760      10750         513        1010       1.29
 14       3008       4085       5973         251       -1888      -2.09R

R denotes an observation with a large standardized residual
```

**FIGURE 16.10**   Residual statistics for site selection problem obtained from Minitab

**Studentized residuals**, expressed as equation (16.11), are the **standardized residuals** (the residual divided by its standard error) adjusted for the distance from the average $X$ value. These Studentized residuals allow us to consider the magnitude of the residuals in units that reflect the standardized variation around the line of regression.

### The Studentized Residual

$$\text{Studentized residual} = SR_i = \frac{e_i}{S_{YX}\sqrt{1 - h_i}} \qquad (16.11)$$

where, for observation $i$

$$h_i = \frac{1}{n} + \frac{(X_i - \overline{X})^2}{\sum_{i=1}^{n}(X_i - \overline{X})^2}$$

To determine whether the linear model is appropriate for these data, the Studentized residuals have been plotted against the independent variable (store size in square feet) in Figure 16.11 on page 756. We observe that although there is widespread scatter in the residual plot, there is no apparent pattern or relationship between the Studentized residuals and $X_i$. The residuals appear to be evenly spread above and below 0 for the differing values of $X$. This result leads us to conclude that the fitted straight-line model is appropriate for the site selection sales data.

## Evaluating the Assumptions

◆ *Homoscedasticity*   The assumption of homoscedasticity can also be evaluated from a plot of $SR_i$ with $X_i$. For the site selection data of Figure 16.11 there do not appear to be major differences in the variability of $SR_i$ for different $X_i$ values as is the case in Figure

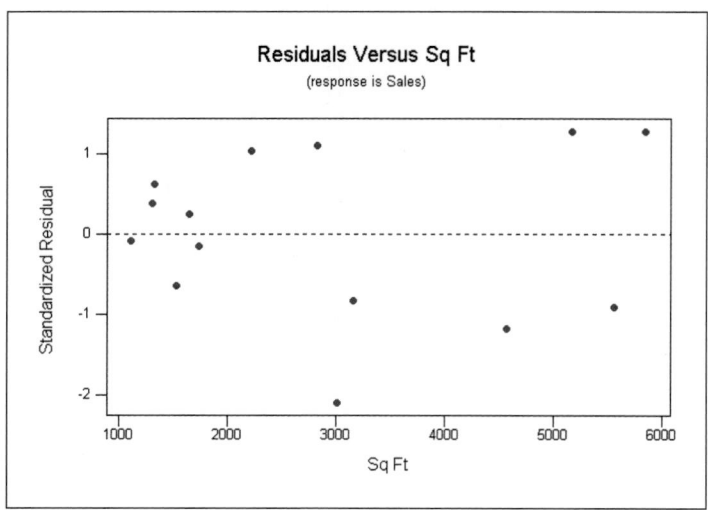

**FIGURE 16.11** Residual plot of Studentized residuals against square footage of the store for site selection problem obtained from Minitab

16.12. Thus we may conclude that, for our fitted model, there is no apparent violation in the assumption of equal variance at each level of $X$.

If we wish to observe a case in which the homoscedasticity assumption is violated, we should examine the hypothetical plot of $SR_i$ with $X_i$ in Figure 16.12. In this hypothetical plot there appears to be a *fanning* effect in which the variability of the residuals increases as $X$ increases, demonstrating the lack of homogeneity in the variances of $Y_i$ at each level of $X$.

◆ *Normality*    The assumption of normality in the errors around the line of regression can be evaluated from a residual analysis by tallying the Studentized residuals into a frequency distribution and displaying the results in a histogram (see chapter 3).

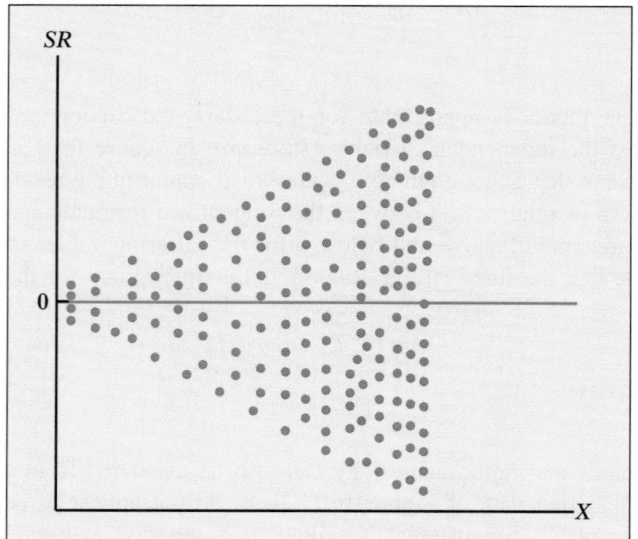

**FIGURE 16.12**
Violations of homoscedasticity

**Table 16.2** *Frequency distribution of 14 Studentized residual values for the site selection data*

| STUDENTIZED RESIDUALS | FREQUENCY |
|---|---|
| −2.25 but less than −1.75 | 1 |
| −1.75 but less than −1.25 | 0 |
| −1.25 but less than −0.75 | 3 |
| −0.75 but less than −0.25 | 1 |
| −0.25 but less than +0.25 | 2 |
| +0.25 but less than +0.75 | 3 |
| +0.75 but less than +1.25 | 2 |
| +1.25 but less than +1.75 | 2 |
| Total | 14 |

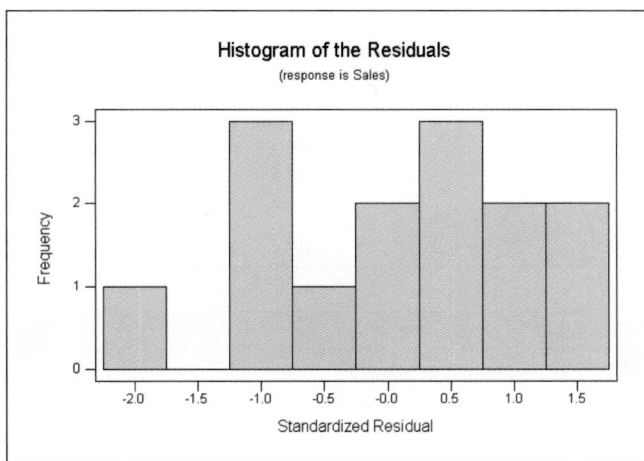

**FIGURE 16.13**  Histogram of Studentized residuals for site selection data obtained from Minitab

For the site selection data, the Studentized residuals have been tallied into a frequency distribution as indicated in Table 16.2 with the results displayed in the histogram of Figure 16.13.

It is difficult to evaluate the normality assumption for a sample of only 14 observations regardless of whether a histogram, stem-and-leaf display, box-and-whisker plot, or normal probability plot is obtained [formal test procedures are beyond the scope of this text (see reference 8)]. We can see from Figure 16.13 that although the data do not appear to be normally distributed, they also are not extremely skewed. The robustness of regression analysis to modest departures from normality, along with the small sample size, leads us to conclude that we should not be overly concerned about departures from this normality assumption in the site selection data.

◆ *Independence*   The assumption of independence of the errors can be evaluated by plotting the residuals in the order or sequence in which the observed data were obtained. Data collected over periods of time sometimes exhibit an *autocorrelation* effect among successive observations. In these instances, there exists a relationship between consecutive residuals. Such a relationship, which violates the assumption of independence, is readily apparent in the plot of the residuals versus the time in which they were collected. This effect is measured by the Durbin-Watson statistic, which will be the subject of section 16.6.

## Problems for Section 16.5

### Learning the Basics

• **16.20** The following represents the Studentized residuals and $X$ values obtained from a regression analysis along with the accompanying residual plot:

| X | STUDENTIZED RESIDUALS | X | STUDENTIZED RESIDUALS |
|---|---|---|---|
| 1 | 0.70 | 11 | 0.29 |
| 2 | −0.78 | 12 | −1.28 |
| 3 | 1.03 | 13 | 1.21 |
| 4 | 0.33 | 14 | −0.37 |
| 5 | 2.39 | 15 | 1.02 |
| 6 | −0.67 | 16 | −0.16 |
| 7 | 0.16 | 17 | 1.42 |
| 8 | 1.65 | 18 | −0.71 |
| 9 | −1.19 | 19 | −0.63 |
| 10 | 0.84 | 20 | 0.67 |

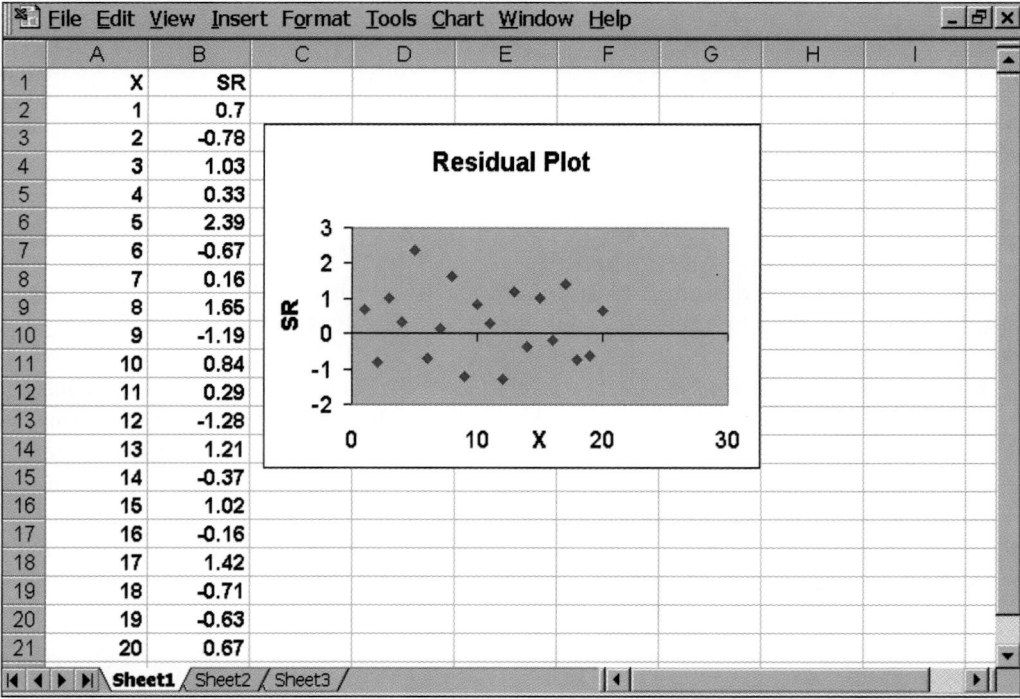

Is there any evidence of a pattern in the residuals? Explain.

**16.21** The following represents the Studentized residuals and $X$ values obtained from a regression analysis along with the accompanying residual plot:

| X | STUDENTIZED RESIDUALS | X | STUDENTIZED RESIDUALS |
|---|---|---|---|
| 1 | 0.70 | 11 | −0.29 |
| 2 | 1.58 | 12 | −1.28 |
| 3 | 1.03 | 13 | −0.21 |
| 4 | 0.33 | 14 | −0.37 |
| 5 | −0.39 | 15 | 0.22 |
| 6 | −0.67 | 16 | −0.16 |
| 7 | −0.56 | 17 | 0.82 |
| 8 | −1.65 | 18 | 0.41 |
| 9 | −1.19 | 19 | 0.63 |
| 10 | −0.84 | 20 | 0.67 |

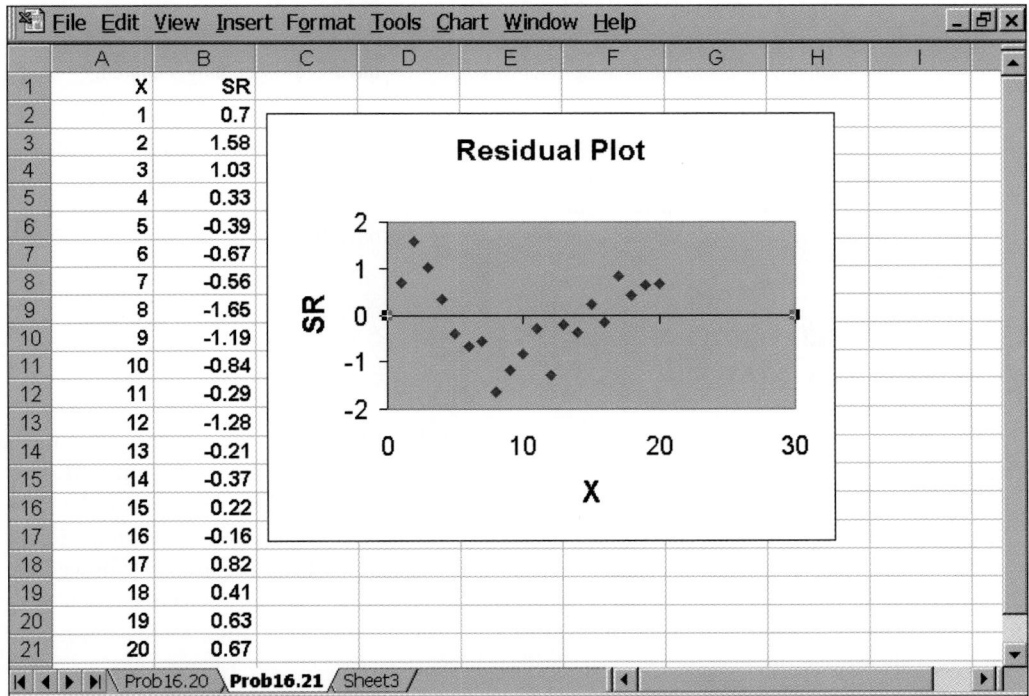

Is there any evidence of a pattern in the residuals? Explain.

## Applying the Concepts

• **16.22** In Problem 16.3 on page 743 the marketing manager used shelf space for pet food to predict weekly sales. Perform a residual analysis for these data. On the basis of the results obtained,
(a) determine the adequacy of the fit of the model.
(b) evaluate whether the assumptions of regression have been seriously violated.

DATA FILE
PETFOOD

**DATA FILE**
**PACKAGE**

**16.23** In Problem 16.4 on page 743 a manager wanted to predict weekly sales at a chain of package delivery stores based on the number of customers who made purchases. Perform a residual analysis for these data. On the basis of the results obtained,
(a) determine the adequacy of the fit of the model.
(b) evaluate whether the assumptions of regression have been seriously violated.

**DATA FILE**
**WORKHRS**

• **16.24** In Problem 16.5 on page 744 a company wanted to predict the worker-hours required for production based on the lot size. Perform a residual analysis for these data. On the basis of the results obtained,
(a) determine the adequacy of the fit of the model.
(b) evaluate whether the assumptions of regression have been seriously violated.

**DATA FILE**
**MOVIE**

**16.25** In Problem 16.6 on page 744 a company wanted to predict home video sales based on the box office gross. Perform a residual analysis for these data. On the basis of the results obtained,
(a) determine the adequacy of the fit of the model.
(b) evaluate whether the assumptions of regression have been seriously violated.

**DATA FILE**
**RENT**

**16.26** In Problem 16.7 on page 745 an agent for a real estate company wanted to predict the monthly rent for apartments based on the size of the apartment. Perform a residual analysis for these data. On the basis of the results obtained,
(a) determine the adequacy of the fit of the model.
(b) evaluate whether the assumptions of regression have been seriously violated.

**DATA FILE**
**LIMO**

**16.27** In Problem 16.8 on page 746 a limousine service wanted to predict travel time to an airport based on the distance from the pickup location to the airport. Perform a residual analysis for these data. On the basis of the results obtained,
(a) determine the adequacy of the fit of the model.
(b) evaluate whether the assumptions of regression have been seriously violated.

## 16.6   MEASURING AUTOCORRELATION: THE DURBIN-WATSON STATISTIC

One of the basic assumptions of the regression model we have been considering is the independence of the errors. This assumption is often violated when data are collected over sequential periods of time because a residual at any one point in time may tend to be similar to residuals at adjacent points in time. Thus, positive residuals would be more likely followed by positive residuals and negative residuals would be more likely followed by negative residuals. Such a pattern in the residuals is called **autocorrelation**. When substantial autocorrelation is present in a set of data, the validity of a fitted regression model may be in serious doubt.

### Residual Plots to Detect Autocorrelation

As mentioned in section 16.5, the easiest way to detect autocorrelation in a set of data is to plot the residuals or Studentized residuals in time order. If a positive autocorrelation effect is present, clusters of residuals with the same sign will be present and an apparent pattern will be readily detected. To illustrate the autocorrelation effect, we consider the following example.

Suppose that the manager of a package delivery store wants to predict weekly sales based on the number of customers making purchases for a period of 15 weeks. In this situation, because data are collected over a period of 15 consecutive weeks at the same store, we

**Table 16.3**  *Customers and sales for period of 15 consecutive weeks*

| WEEK | CUSTOMERS | SALES ($000) | WEEK | CUSTOMERS | SALES ($000) |
|------|-----------|--------------|------|-----------|--------------|
| 1 | 794 | 9.33 | 9 | 880 | 12.07 |
| 2 | 799 | 8.26 | 10 | 905 | 12.55 |
| 3 | 837 | 7.48 | 11 | 886 | 11.92 |
| 4 | 855 | 9.08 | 12 | 843 | 10.27 |
| 5 | 845 | 9.83 | 13 | 904 | 11.80 |
| 6 | 844 | 10.09 | 14 | 950 | 12.15 |
| 7 | 863 | 11.01 | 15 | 841 | 9.64 |
| 8 | 875 | 11.49 | | | |

DATA FILE
CUSTSALE

|    | A | B | C | D | E | F |
|----|---|---|---|---|---|---|
| 2 | | | | | | |
| 3 | **Regression Statistics** | | | | | |
| 4 | Multiple R | 0.810829997 | | | | |
| 5 | R Square | 0.657445284 | | | | |
| 6 | Adjusted R Square | 0.631094922 | | | | |
| 7 | Standard Error | 0.936036681 | | | | |
| 8 | Observations | 15 | | | | |
| 9 | | | | | | |
| 10 | ANOVA | | | | | |
| 11 | | *df* | *SS* | *MS* | *F* | *Significance F* |
| 12 | Regression | 1 | 21.86043264 | 21.86043264 | 24.95014 | 0.000245105 |
| 13 | Residual | 13 | 11.39014069 | 0.876164669 | | |
| 14 | Total | 14 | 33.25057333 | | | |
| 15 | | | | | | |
| 16 | | *Coefficients* | *Standard Error* | *t Stat* | *P-value* | |
| 17 | Intercept | -16.0321936 | 5.310167093 | -3.019150493 | 0.009869 | |
| 18 | Customers | 0.030760228 | 0.006158189 | 4.995011683 | 0.000245 | |
| 19 | | | | | | |

**FIGURE 16.14**  Microsoft Excel output for package delivery store data of Table 16.3

would need to be concerned with the autocorrelation effect of the residuals. The data for this store are summarized in Table 16.3. Figure 16.14 represents partial Excel output.

We note from Figure 16.14 that $r^2$ is .657, indicating that 65.7% of the variation in sales can be explained by variation in the number of customers. In addition, the $Y$ intercept $b_0$ is $-16.032$, and the slope $b_1$ is .03076. However, before we can accept the validity of this model, we must undertake proper analyses of the residuals. Because the data have been collected over a consecutive period of 15 weeks, the residuals should be plotted over time to see whether a pattern exists. Figure 16.15 represents such a plot for the 15-week sales data. From Figure 16.15, we observe that the points tend to fluctuate up and down in a cyclical pattern. This cyclical pattern would give us strong cause for concern about the autocorrelation of the residuals and, hence, a violation of the assumption of independence of the residuals.

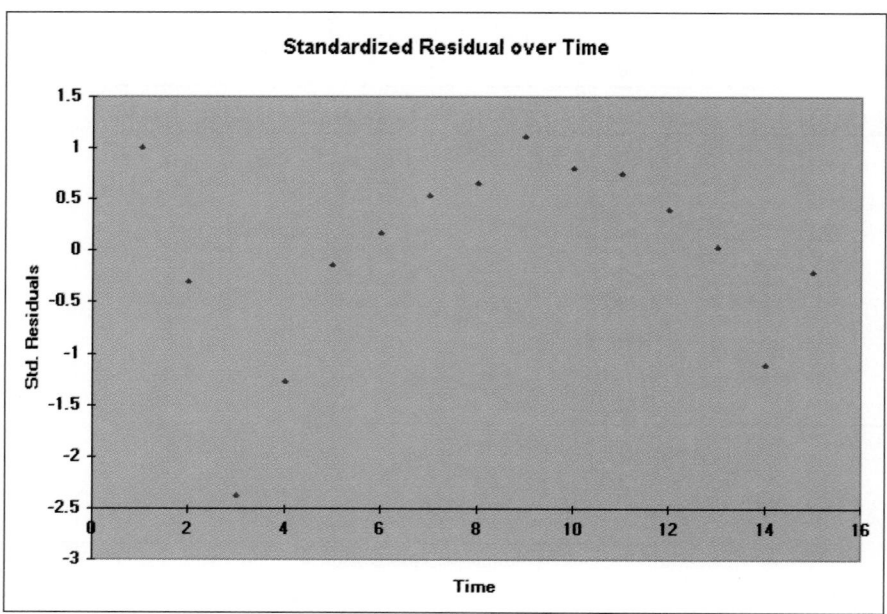

**FIGURE 16.15** Microsoft Excel residual plot for the package delivery store data of Table 16.3

## The Durbin-Watson Statistic

In addition to residual plots, autocorrelation can also be detected and measured by using the **Durbin-Watson statistic.** This statistic measures the correlation between each residual and the residual for the time period immediately preceding the one of interest. The Durbin-Watson statistic ($D$) is defined as follows:

**Durbin-Watson Statistic**

$$D = \frac{\sum_{i=2}^{n}(e_i - e_{i-1})^2}{\sum_{i=1}^{n}e_i^2} \qquad (16.12)$$

where $e_i$ = residual at the time period $i$.

To better understand what the Durbin-Watson statistic is measuring, we need to examine the composition of the $D$ statistic presented in equation (16.12). The numerator $\sum_{i=2}^{n}(e_i - e_{i-1})^2$ represents the squared difference in two successive residuals, summed from the second observation to the $n$th observation. The denominator represents the sum of the squared residuals, $\sum_{i=1}^{n}e_i^2$. When successive residuals are positively autocorrelated, the value of $D$ will approach 0. If the residuals are not correlated, the value of $D$ will be close to 2. (If there is negative autocorrelation, $D$ will be greater than 2 and could even approach its

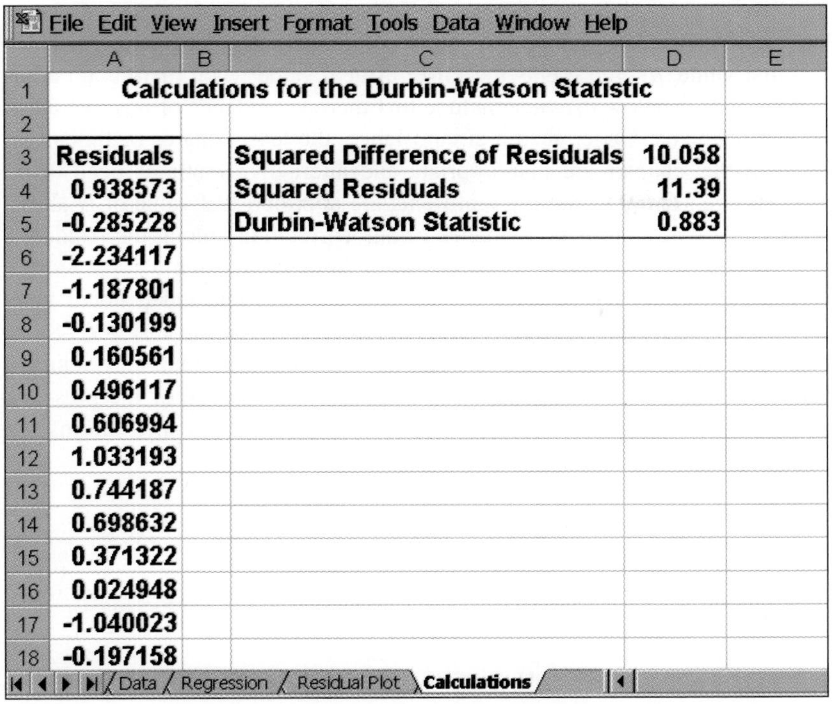

File Edit View Insert Format Tools Data Window Help

| | A | B | C | D | E |
|---|---|---|---|---|---|
| 1 | Calculations for the Durbin-Watson Statistic | | | | |
| 2 | | | | | |
| 3 | Residuals | | Squared Difference of Residuals | 10.058 | |
| 4 | 0.938573 | | Squared Residuals | 11.39 | |
| 5 | -0.285228 | | Durbin-Watson Statistic | 0.883 | |
| 6 | -2.234117 | | | | |
| 7 | -1.187801 | | | | |
| 8 | -0.130199 | | | | |
| 9 | 0.160561 | | | | |
| 10 | 0.496117 | | | | |
| 11 | 0.606994 | | | | |
| 12 | 1.033193 | | | | |
| 13 | 0.744187 | | | | |
| 14 | 0.698632 | | | | |
| 15 | 0.371322 | | | | |
| 16 | 0.024948 | | | | |
| 17 | -1.040023 | | | | |
| 18 | -0.197158 | | | | |

Data / Regression / Residual Plot / **Calculations**

***FIGURE 16.16*** Using the PHStat Add-In for Microsoft Excel to compute Durbin-Watson statistic for sales data

maximum value of 4.) The computation of the Durbin-Watson statistic obtained from Microsoft Excel (see appendix 16.1), is illustrated in Figure 16.16.

For the data in Figure 16.16, we use equation (16.12) and obtain

$$D = \frac{10.058}{11.39} = .883$$

The crux of the issue in using the Durbin-Watson statistic is the determination of when the autocorrelation is large enough to make the $D$ statistic fall sufficiently below 2 to cause concern about the validity of the model. The answer to this question is dependent on $n$, the number of observations being analyzed and $p$, the number of independent variables in the model (in simple linear regression, $p = 1$). Table 16.4 has been extracted from appendix E, Table E.12, the table of the Durbin-Watson statistic.

**Table 16.4** *Finding critical values of Durbin-Watson statistic*

$\alpha = .05$

| | $p = 1$ | | $p = 2$ | | $p = 3$ | | $p = 4$ | | $p = 5$ | |
|---|---|---|---|---|---|---|---|---|---|---|
| $n$ | $d_L$ | $d_U$ | $d_L$ | $d_U$ | $d_L$ | $d_U$ | $d_L$ | $d_U$ | $d_L$ | $d_U$ |
| 15 → | 1.08 | 1.36 | .95 | 1.54 | .82 | 1.75 | .69 | 1.97 | .56 | 2.21 |
| 16 | 1.10 | 1.37 | .98 | 1.54 | .86 | 1.73 | .74 | 1.93 | .62 | 2.15 |
| 17 | 1.13 | 1.38 | 1.02 | 1.54 | .90 | 1.71 | .78 | 1.90 | .67 | 2.10 |
| 18 | 1.16 | 1.39 | 1.05 | 1.53 | .93 | 1.69 | .82 | 1.87 | .71 | 2.06 |

*Source: Table E.12.*

From Table 16.4 we observe that two values are shown in the table for each combination of $\alpha$ (level of significance), $n$ (sample size), and $p$ (number of independent variables in the model). The first value, $d_L$, represents the lower critical value when there is no autocorrelation in the data. If $D$ is below $d_L$, we conclude that there is evidence of positive autocorrelation among the residuals. Under such a circumstance, the least-squares methods that we have considered in this chapter are inappropriate and alternative methods need to be used (see reference 7). The second value, $d_U$, represents the upper critical value of $D$ above which we would conclude that there is no evidence of autocorrelation among the residuals. If $D$ is between $d_L$ and $d_U$, we are unable to arrive at a definite conclusion.

Thus, for our data concerning the package delivery stores, with one independent variable ($p = 1$) and 15 observations ($n = 15$), $d_L = 1.08$ and $d_U = 1.36$. Because $D = 0.883 < 1.08$, we conclude that there is autocorrelation among the residuals. Our least-squares regression analysis of the data of Figure 16.14 was inappropriate because of the presence of serious autocorrelation among the residuals. We need to consider the alternative approaches discussed in reference 7.

## Problems for Section 16.6

### Learning the Basics

● **16.28** Suppose the residuals for a set of data collected over 10 consecutive time periods are as follows:

| TIME PERIOD | RESIDUAL | TIME PERIOD | RESIDUAL |
|---|---|---|---|
| 1 | $-5$ | 6 | $+1$ |
| 2 | $-4$ | 7 | $+2$ |
| 3 | $-3$ | 8 | $+3$ |
| 4 | $-2$ | 9 | $+4$ |
| 5 | $-1$ | 10 | $+5$ |

(a) Plot the residuals over time. What conclusions can you reach about the pattern of the residuals over time?
(b) Compute the Durbin-Watson statistic.
(c) Based on (a) and (b), what conclusion can you reach about the autocorrelation of the residuals?

**16.29** Suppose that the residuals for a set of data collected over 15 consecutive time periods are as follows:

| TIME PERIOD | RESIDUAL | TIME PERIOD | RESIDUAL |
|---|---|---|---|
| 1 | $+4$ | 9 | $+6$ |
| 2 | $-6$ | 10 | $-3$ |
| 3 | $-1$ | 11 | $+1$ |
| 4 | $-5$ | 12 | $+3$ |
| 5 | $+2$ | 13 | $0$ |
| 6 | $+5$ | 14 | $-4$ |
| 7 | $-2$ | 15 | $-7$ |
| 8 | $+7$ | | |

(a) Plot the residuals over time. What conclusions can you reach about the pattern of the residuals over time?

(b) Compute the Durbin-Watson statistic. At the .05 level of significance, is there evidence of positive autocorrelation among the residuals?

(c) Based on (a) and (b), what conclusion can you reach about the autocorrelation of the residuals?

## Applying the Concepts

• **16.30** In Problem 16.3 (pet food sales) on page 743 the marketing manager used shelf space for pet food to predict weekly sales.

(a) Is it necessary to compute the Durbin-Watson statistic? Explain.

(b) Under what circumstances would it be necessary to compute the Durbin-Watson statistic before proceeding with the least-squares method of regression analysis?

**16.31** The owner of a single-family home in a suburban county in the northeastern United States would like to develop a model to predict electricity consumption in his "all electric" house (lights, fans, heat, appliances, and so on) based on outdoor atmospheric temperature (in degrees Fahrenheit). Monthly billing data and temperature information were available for a period of 24 consecutive months.

| Month | Kilowatt Usage | Average Atmospheric Temperature (°F) | Month | Kilowatt Usage | Average Atmospheric Temperature (°F) |
|---|---|---|---|---|---|
| 1 | 126 | 30 | 13 | 123 | 27 |
| 2 | 132 | 25 | 14 | 121 | 33 |
| 3 | 114 | 29 | 15 | 138 | 28 |
| 4 | 87 | 42 | 16 | 99 | 39 |
| 5 | 67 | 48 | 17 | 64 | 47 |
| 6 | 50 | 61 | 18 | 52 | 63 |
| 7 | 39 | 69 | 19 | 49 | 69 |
| 8 | 45 | 78 | 20 | 41 | 73 |
| 9 | 39 | 72 | 21 | 44 | 70 |
| 10 | 43 | 62 | 22 | 53 | 64 |
| 11 | 61 | 45 | 23 | 59 | 53 |
| 12 | 92 | 36 | 24 | 118 | 27 |

**DATA FILE
ELECUSE**

(a) Set up a scatter diagram.

(b) Assuming a linear relationship, use the least-squares method to find the regression coefficients $b_0$ and $b_1$.

(c) Interpret the meaning of the slope $b_1$ in this problem.

(d) Predict the average kilowatt usage when the average atmospheric temperature is 50 degrees Fahrenheit.

(e) Compute the coefficient of determination $r^2$ and interpret its meaning.

(f) Compute the standard error of the estimate.

(g) Plot the residuals versus the average atmospheric temperature.

(h) Plot the residuals versus the time period.

(i) Compute the Durbin-Watson statistic. At the .05 level of significance, is there evidence of positive autocorrelation among the residuals?

(j) On the basis of the results of (g)–(i), is there reason to question the validity of the model?

**16.32** A mail-order catalog business selling personal computer supplies, software, and hardware maintains a centralized warehouse for the distribution of products ordered. Management is currently examining the process of distribution from the warehouse and is interested in studying the factors that affect warehouse distribution costs. Currently, a small handling fee is added to the order, regardless of the amount of the order. Data have been collected over the past 24 months indicating the warehouse distribution costs and the number of orders received. The results are as follows:

| MONTH | DISTRIBUTION COST ($000) | NUMBER OF ORDERS | MONTH | DISTRIBUTION COST ($000) | NUMBER OF ORDERS |
|---|---|---|---|---|---|
| 1 | 52.95 | 4,015 | 13 | 62.98 | 3,977 |
| 2 | 71.66 | 3,806 | 14 | 72.30 | 4,428 |
| 3 | 85.58 | 5,309 | 15 | 58.99 | 3,964 |
| 4 | 63.69 | 4,262 | 16 | 79.38 | 4,582 |
| 5 | 72.81 | 4,296 | 17 | 94.44 | 5,582 |
| 6 | 68.44 | 4,097 | 18 | 59.74 | 3,450 |
| 7 | 52.46 | 3,213 | 19 | 90.50 | 5,079 |
| 8 | 70.77 | 4,809 | 20 | 93.24 | 5,735 |
| 9 | 82.03 | 5,237 | 21 | 69.33 | 4,269 |
| 10 | 74.39 | 4,732 | 22 | 53.71 | 3,708 |
| 11 | 70.84 | 4,413 | 23 | 89.18 | 5,387 |
| 12 | 54.08 | 2,921 | 24 | 66.80 | 4,161 |

DATA FILE
WARECOST

(a) Set up a scatter diagram.
(b) Assuming a linear relationship, use the least-squares method to find the regression coefficients $b_0$ and $b_1$.
(c) Interpret the meaning of the slope $b_1$ in this problem.
(d) Predict the average monthly warehouse distribution costs when the number of orders is 4,500.
(e) Compute the coefficient of determination $r^2$ and interpret its meaning.
(f) Compute the standard error of the estimate.
(g) Plot the residuals versus the number of orders.
(h) Plot the residuals versus the time period.
(i) Compute the Durbin-Watson statistic. At the .05 level of significance, is there evidence of positive autocorrelation among the residuals?
(j) On the basis of the results of (g)–(i), is there reason to question the validity of the model?

**16.33** The owner of a large chain of ice cream stores would like to study the effect of atmospheric temperature on sales during the summer season. A random sample of 21 days is selected with the results given in the table on the next page.
*Hint:* Determine which are the independent and dependent variables.
(a) Set up a scatter diagram.
(b) Assuming a linear relationship, use the least-squares method to find the regression coefficients $b_0$ and $b_1$.
(c) Interpret the meaning of the slope $b_1$ in this problem.
(d) Predict the average sales per store for a day in which the temperature is 83°F.
(e) Compute the standard error of the estimate.
(f) Compute the coefficient of determination $r^2$ and interpret its meaning in this problem.

| DAY | DAILY HIGH TEMPERATURE (°F) | SALES PER STORE ($000) | DAY | DAILY HIGH TEMPERATURE (°F) | SALES PER STORE ($000) |
|---|---|---|---|---|---|
| 1 | 63 | 1.52 | 12 | 75 | 1.92 |
| 2 | 70 | 1.68 | 13 | 98 | 3.40 |
| 3 | 73 | 1.80 | 14 | 100 | 3.28 |
| 4 | 75 | 2.05 | 15 | 92 | 3.17 |
| 5 | 80 | 2.36 | 16 | 87 | 2.83 |
| 6 | 82 | 2.25 | 17 | 84 | 2.58 |
| 7 | 85 | 2.68 | 18 | 88 | 2.86 |
| 8 | 88 | 2.90 | 19 | 80 | 2.26 |
| 9 | 90 | 3.14 | 20 | 82 | 2.14 |
| 10 | 91 | 3.06 | 21 | 76 | 1.98 |
| 11 | 92 | 3.24 | | | |

DATA FILE
ICECREAM

(g) Plot the residuals versus the temperature.

(h) Plot the residuals versus the time period.

(i) Compute the Durbin-Watson statistic. At the .05 level of significance, is there evidence of positive autocorrelation among the residuals?

(j) On the basis of the results of (g)–(i), is there reason to question the validity of the model?

(k) Suppose that the amount of sales on day 21 was 1.75. Do (a)–(j) and compare the differences in the results.

 **16.7** **INFERENCES ABOUT THE SLOPE**

In sections 16.1–16.4, we were concerned with the use of regression solely for the purpose of description. We used the least-squares method to determine the regression coefficients and to predict the value of $Y$ from a given value of $X$. In addition, we discussed the standard error of the estimate along with the coefficient of determination.

Now that we have used residual analysis in section 16.5 to assure ourselves that the assumptions of the least-squares regression model have not been seriously violated and that the straight-line model is appropriate, we may concentrate on making inferences about the linear relationship between the variables in a population based on our sample results.

## *t* Test for the Slope

We can determine whether a significant relationship between the $X$ and $Y$ variables exists by testing whether $\beta_1$ (the true slope) is equal to 0. If this hypothesis is rejected, one would conclude that there is evidence of a linear relationship. The null and alternative hypotheses are stated as follows:

$$H_0: \beta_1 = 0 \text{ (There is no linear relationship.)}$$

$$H_1: \beta_1 \neq 0 \text{ (There is a linear relationship.)}$$

and the test statistic is given by

---

### Testing a Hypothesis for a Population Slope $\beta_1$ Using the $t$ Test

The $t$ statistic equals the difference between the sample slope and the hypothesized population slope divided by the standard error of the slope.

$$t = \frac{b_1 - \beta_1}{S_{b_1}}$$ (16.13)

where

$$S_{b_1} = \frac{S_{YX}}{\sqrt{SSX}}$$

$$SSX = \sum_{i=1}^{n}(X_i - \overline{X})^2$$

and the test statistic $t$ follows a $t$ distribution with $n - 2$ degrees of freedom.

---

Returning to our site selection example, now we will test whether there is a significant relationship between the size of the store and the annual sales at the .05 level of significance. From the Microsoft Excel output of Figure 16.4 on page 740 or the Minitab output of Figure 16.5 on page 741 we have[2]

[2]*More detailed computations of the t test statistic are contained in section 16.10.*

$$b_1 = +1.686 \qquad n = 14 \qquad S_{b_1} = .1533$$

Therefore, to test the existence of a relationship at the .05 level of significance, we have

$$t = \frac{b_1}{S_{b_1}}$$

$$= \frac{1.686}{.1533} = 11.00$$

This $t$ statistic is provided in the column titled $t$ stat by Microsoft Excel and $T$ by Minitab. Because $t = 11.00 > t_{12} = 2.1788$, we reject $H_0$. Using the $p$-value, we reject $H_0$ because the $p$-value is approximately 0 (It is labeled in scientific notation by Excel as 1.27E-07, which is equal to .000000127 and is less than $\alpha = .05$.) Hence, we can conclude that there is a significant linear relationship between average annual sales and the size of the store (see Figure 16.17).

## F Test for the Slope

An alternative approach for testing whether the slope in simple linear regression is statistically significant is to use an $F$ test, as presented in Table 16.5 on page 770. You may recall from section 12.2 that the $F$ test is used to test the ratio of two variances. In testing for the significance of the slope, the measure of random error is the error variance (the error sum of squares divided by its degrees of freedom), so the $F$ test is the ratio of the variance due to the regression (the regression sum of squares divided by the number of independent variables $p$) divided by the error variance as shown in equation (16.14).

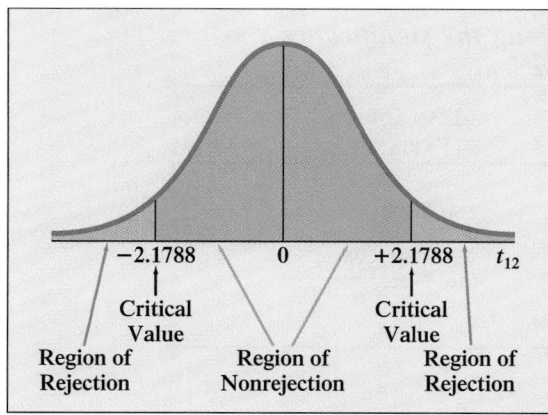

## Testing a Hypothesis for a Population Slope $\beta_1$ Using the F Test

The $F$ statistic is equal to the regression mean square (*MSR*) divided by the error mean square (*MSE*).

$$F = \frac{MSR}{MSE} \tag{16.14}$$

where

$$MSR = \frac{SSR}{p}$$

$$MSE = \frac{SSE}{n - p - 1}$$

$p$ = number of explanatory variables in the regression model

$F$ = test statistic from an $F$ distribution with $p$ and $n - p - 1$ degrees of freedom

Using a level of significance $\alpha$, the decision rule is

Reject $H_0$ if $F > F_U$, the upper-tailed critical value from the $F$ distribution with $p$ and $n - p - 1$ degrees of freedom; otherwise do not reject $H_0$.

The complete set of results is organized into an analysis of variance (ANOVA) table as illustrated in Table 16.5.

The completed ANOVA table is also available as part of the output from Excel (see Figure 16.4 on page 740) or Minitab (see Figure 16.5 on page 741). We observe from either figure that the computed $F$ statistic is 121.01 and the $p$-value is less than .001 (Excel computes the $p$-value as .000000127).

If a level of significance of .05 is chosen, we can determine from Table E.5 that the critical value on the $F$ distribution (with 1 and 12 degrees of freedom) is 4.75, as depicted in Figure 16.18 on page 770. From equation (16.14), because $F = 121.01 > 4.75$ or because the $p$-value $= .000000127 < .05$, we reject $H_0$ and conclude that the size of the store is significantly related to annual sales.

**Table 16.5** *ANOVA table for testing the significance of a regression coefficient*

| SOURCE | DF | SUMS OF SQUARES | MEAN SQUARE (VARIANCE) | F |
|---|---|---|---|---|
| Regression | $p$ | SSR | $MSR = \dfrac{SSR}{p}$ | $F = \dfrac{MSR}{MSE}$ |
| Error | $n - p - 1$ | SSE | $MSE = \dfrac{SSE}{n - p - 1}$ | |
| Total | $n - 1$ | SST | | |

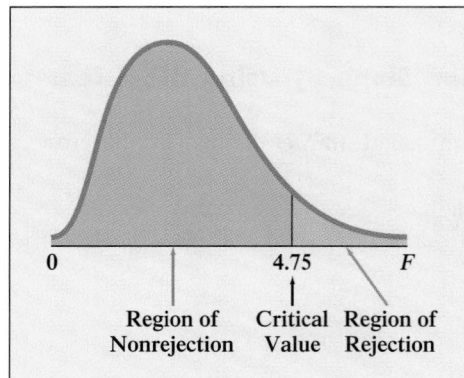

**FIGURE 16.18**
Testing for significance of slope at the .05 level of significance with 1 and 12 degrees of freedom

## Confidence Interval Estimate of the Slope ($\beta_1$)

An alternative to testing the existence of a linear relationship between the variables is to set up a confidence interval estimate of $\beta_1$ and to determine whether the hypothesized value ($\beta_1 = 0$) is included in the interval. The confidence interval estimate of $\beta_1$ would be obtained as shown in equation (16.15).

**Confidence Interval Estimate of the Slope**

The confidence interval estimate of the slope is obtained by taking the sample slope $b_1$ and adding and subtracting the critical value of the $t$ statistic multiplied by the standard error of the slope.

$$b_1 \pm t_{n-2}S_{b_1} \qquad (16.15)$$

From the Microsoft Excel output of Figure 16.4 on page 740 or the Minitab output of Figure 16.5 on page 741 we have

$$b_1 = +1.686 \quad n = 14 \quad S_{b_1} = .1533$$

Thus,

Therefore, our estimate is that the average weekly sales are between 6,992.03 and 8,299.542 (thousand dollars) for all stores with 4,000 square feet of space.

## Obtaining the Prediction Interval Estimate

In addition to obtaining a confidence interval estimate for the average value, it is often important to be able to predict the response that would be obtained for an individual value. Although the form of the prediction interval estimate is similar to the confidence interval estimate of equation (16.16), the prediction interval is estimating an individual value, not a parameter. Thus, the **prediction interval for an individual response** $Y_I$ at a particular value $X_i$ is shown in equation (16.17).

---

### Prediction Interval Estimate for an Individual Response $Y_I$

$$\hat{Y}_i \pm t_{n-2}S_{YX}\sqrt{1 + h_i} \qquad (16.17)$$

where

$h_i$, $\hat{Y}_i$, $S_{YX}$, $n$, and $X_i$ are defined as in equation (16.16) on page 773

---

Although the Prentice Hall PHStat Add-In for Microsoft Excel (see appendix 16.1) or Minitab (see appendix 16.2) can also be used to obtain a prediction interval estimate for the individual response, Example 16.4 illustrates equation (16.17) for the site selection data.

## Example 16.4 Setting Up a 95% Prediction Interval Estimate of the Individual Response $Y_I$

In the site selection example we obtained the simple linear regression model $\hat{Y}_i = 901.247 + 1.686X_i$. Set up a 95% prediction interval estimate of the annual sales for an individual store that contains 4,000 square feet.

### SOLUTION

Using our simple linear regression equation:

$$\hat{Y}_i = 901.247 + 1.686X_i$$

and for $X_i = 4,000$, we obtain

$$\hat{Y}_i = 901.247 + 1.686(4,000) = 7,645.786 \text{ (thousands of dollars)}$$

Also, given the following

$$\bar{X} = 2,921.2857; \quad S_{YX} = 936.85; \quad \sum_{i=1}^{n}(X_i - \bar{X})^2 = 37,357,090.86$$

and from Table E.3, $t_{12} = 2.1788$. Thus,

$$\hat{Y}_i \pm t_{n-2}S_{YX}\sqrt{1 + h_i}$$

where

$$h_i = \frac{1}{n} + \frac{(X_i - \overline{X})^2}{\sum_{i=1}^{n}(X_i - \overline{X})^2}$$

so that we have

$$\hat{Y}_i \pm t_{n-2}S_{YX}\sqrt{1 + \frac{1}{n} + \frac{(X_i - \overline{X})^2}{\sum_{i=1}^{n}(X_i - \overline{X})^2}}$$

and

$$7{,}645.786 \pm (2.1788)(936.85)\sqrt{1 + \frac{1}{14} + \frac{(4{,}000 - 2{,}921.2857)^2}{37{,}357{,}090.86}}$$

$$= 7{,}645.786 \pm 2{,}143.357$$

so

$$5{,}502.43 \le Y_I \le 9{,}789.143$$

Therefore, our estimate is that the annual sales for an individual store with 4,000 square feet of space is between 5,502.43 and 9,789.143 (thousand dollars).

If we compare the results of Examples 16.3 and 16.4, we observe that the width of the prediction interval for an individual store is much greater than the width of the confidence interval estimate for the average store. This is because there will be much more variation in predicting an individual value than in predicting an average value.

## Problems for Section 16.8

### Learning the Basics

**16.42** Based on a sample of 20 observations, the least-squares method was used to obtain the following linear regression equation: $\hat{Y}_i = 5 + 3X_i$. In addition, $S_{YX} = 1.0$, $\overline{X} = 2$, and

$$\sum_{i=1}^{n}(X_i - \overline{X})^2 = 20.$$

(a) Set up a 95% confidence interval estimate of the true population average response for $X = 2$.

(b) Set up a 95% prediction interval estimate of the individual response for $X = 2$.

**16.43** Based on a sample of 20 observations, the least-squares method was used to obtain the following linear regression equation: $\hat{Y}_i = 5 + 3X_i$. In addition, $S_{YX} = 1.0$, $\overline{X} = 2$, and

$$\sum_{i=1}^{n}(X_i - \overline{X})^2 = 20.$$

(a) Set up a 95% confidence interval estimate of the true population average response for $X = 4$.

(b) Set up a 95% prediction interval estimate of the individual response for $X = 4$.

(c) Compare the results of (a) and (b) with those of Problem 16.42 (a) and (b). Which interval is wider? Why?

## Applying the Concepts

• **16.44** In Problem 16.3 on page 743 the marketing manager used shelf space for pet food to predict weekly sales. Using the computer output you obtained to solve that problem or using the following summary information:

DATA FILE
PETFOOD

$$b_0 = 1.45, \ b_1 = .074, \ S_{YX} = .308, \ \overline{X} = 12.5, \ \text{and} \ \sum_{i=1}^{n} (X_i - \overline{X})^2 = 375$$

(a) Set up a 95% confidence interval estimate of the average weekly sales for all stores that have 8 feet of shelf space for pet food.
(b) Set up a 95% prediction interval of the weekly sales of an individual store that has 8 feet of shelf space for pet food.
(c) Explain the difference in the results obtained in (a) and (b).

**16.45** In Problem 16.4 on page 743 a manager wanted to predict weekly sales at a chain of package delivery stores based on the number of customers who made purchases. Using the computer output you obtained to solve that problem or using the following summary information:

DATA FILE
PACKAGE

$$b_0 = 2.423, \ b_1 = .00873, \ S_{YX} = .497, \ \overline{X} = 731.15, \ \text{and}$$
$$\sum_{i=1}^{n} (X_i - \overline{X})^2 = 614{,}603$$

(a) Set up a 95% confidence interval estimate of the average weekly sales for all stores that have 600 customers.
(b) Set up a 95% prediction interval of the weekly sales of an individual store that has 600 customers.
(c) Explain the difference in the results obtained in (a) and (b).

• **16.46** In Problem 16.5 on page 744 a company wanted to predict the worker-hours required for production based on the lot size. Using the computer output you obtained to solve that problem or using the following summary information:

DATA FILE
WORKHRS

$$b_0 = 12.679, \ b_1 = 1.9607, \ S_{YX} = 4.71, \ \overline{X} = 50, \ \text{and} \ \sum_{i=1}^{n} (X_i - \overline{X})^2 = 5{,}600$$

(a) Set up a 95% confidence interval estimate of the average worker-hours for a lot size of 45.
(b) Set up a 95% prediction interval of the worker-hours of an individual lot size of 45.
(c) Explain the difference in the results obtained in (a) and (b).

**16.47** In Problem 16.6 on page 744 a company wanted to predict home video sales based on the box office gross of movies. Using the computer output you obtained to solve that problem or using the following summary information:

DATA FILE
MOVIE

$$b_0 = 76.535, \ b_1 = 4.3331, \ S_{YX} = 47.867, \ \overline{X} = 15.925, \ \text{and}$$
$$\sum_{i=1}^{n} (X_i - \overline{X})^2 = 9{,}134.074$$

(a) Set up a 95% confidence interval estimate of the average video sales for all movies that gross 10 million dollars at the box office.

(b) Set up a 95% prediction interval of the video sales of an individual movie that grosses 10 million dollars at the box office.

(c) Explain the difference in the results obtained in (a) and (b).

**16.48** In Problem 16.7 on page 745 an agent for a real estate company wanted to predict the monthly rent for apartments based on the size of the apartment. Using the computer output you obtained to solve that problem or using the following summary information:

$$b_0 = 177.12, \ b_1 = 1.065, \ S_{YX} = 194.595, \ \overline{X} = 1{,}135.32, \ \text{and}$$

$$\sum_{i=1}^{n}(X_i - \overline{X})^2 = 1{,}999{,}747$$

(a) Set up a 95% confidence interval estimate of the average monthly rental for all apartments that are 1,000 square feet in size.

(b) Set up a 95% prediction interval of the monthly rental of an individual apartment that is 1,000 square feet in size.

(c) Explain the difference in the results obtained in (a) and (b).

**16.49** In Problem 16.8 on page 746 a limousine service wanted to predict travel time to an airport based on the distance from the pickup location to the airport. Using the computer output you obtained to solve that problem or using the following summary information:

$$b_0 = 3.375, \ b_1 = 1.461, \ S_{YX} = 2.579, \ \overline{X} = 18.075, \ \text{and}$$

$$\sum_{i=1}^{n}(X_i - \overline{X})^2 = 347.1625$$

(a) Set up a 95% confidence interval estimate of the average travel time for all trips with distances of 21 miles.

(b) Set up a 95% prediction interval of the travel time of an individual trip that has a distance of 21 miles.

(c) Explain the difference in the results obtained in (a) and (b).

## 16.9 PITFALLS IN REGRESSION AND ETHICAL ISSUES

Regression analysis is perhaps the most widely used and, unfortunately, the most widely misused statistical technique applied to business and economics. Some of the difficulties involved in using regression analysis are summarized in Exhibit 16.2.

## The Pitfalls of Regression

The widespread availability of spreadsheet and statistical software has removed the computational block that prevented many users from applying regression analysis to situations that required forecasting. With this positive development of enhanced technology comes the realization that for many users, the access to powerful techniques has not been accompanied by an understanding of how to apply regression analysis properly. How can a user be expected to know what the alternatives to least-squares regression are if a particular assumption is violated, when he or she in many instances is not even aware of the assumptions of regression, let alone how the assumptions can be evaluated?

The necessity of going beyond the basic number crunching—of computing the $Y$ intercept, the slope, and $r^2$—can be illustrated by referring to Table 16.6, a classical pedagogical piece of statistical literature that deals with the importance of observation through scatter plots and residual analysis.

**Table 16.6** *Four sets of artificial data*

| DATA SET A | | DATA SET B | | DATA SET C | | DATA SET D | |
|---|---|---|---|---|---|---|---|
| $X_i$ | $Y_i$ | $X_i$ | $Y_i$ | $X_i$ | $Y_i$ | $X_i$ | $Y_i$ |
| 10 | 8.04 | 10 | 9.14 | 10 | 7.46 | 8 | 6.58 |
| 14 | 9.96 | 14 | 8.10 | 14 | 8.84 | 8 | 5.76 |
| 5 | 5.68 | 5 | 4.74 | 5 | 5.73 | 8 | 7.71 |
| 8 | 6.95 | 8 | 8.14 | 8 | 6.77 | 8 | 8.84 |
| 9 | 8.81 | 9 | 8.77 | 9 | 7.11 | 8 | 8.47 |
| 12 | 10.84 | 12 | 9.13 | 12 | 8.15 | 8 | 7.04 |
| 4 | 4.26 | 4 | 3.10 | 4 | 5.39 | 8 | 5.25 |
| 7 | 4.82 | 7 | 7.26 | 7 | 6.42 | 19 | 12.50 |
| 11 | 8.33 | 11 | 9.26 | 11 | 7.81 | 8 | 5.56 |
| 13 | 7.58 | 13 | 8.74 | 13 | 12.74 | 8 | 7.91 |
| 6 | 7.24 | 6 | 6.13 | 6 | 6.08 | 8 | 6.89 |

*Source: F. J. Anscombe, "Graphs in Statistical Analysis,"* American Statistician *27 (1973); 17–21. Reprinted by permission of American Statistical Assn.*

**DATA FILE ANSCOMBE**

Anscombe (reference 1) showed that for the four data sets given in Table 16.6, the following results are obtained:

$$\hat{Y}_i = 3.0 + .5X_i$$

$$S_{YX} = 1.237$$

$$S_{b_1} = .118$$

$$r^2 = .667$$

$$SSR = \text{explained variation} = \sum_{i=1}^{n}(\hat{Y}_i - \overline{Y})^2 = 27.51$$

$$SSE = \text{unexplained variation} = \sum_{i=1}^{n}(Y_i - \hat{Y}_i)^2 = 13.763$$

$$SST = \text{total variation} = \sum_{i=1}^{n}(Y_i - \overline{Y})^2 = 41.273$$

Thus, with respect to these statistics associated with a simple linear regression, the four data sets are identical. Had we stopped our analysis at this point, valuable information in the data would be lost. This may be observed by examining Figure 16.20, which presents scatter diagrams for the four data sets, and Figure 16.21, which presents residual plots for the four data sets.

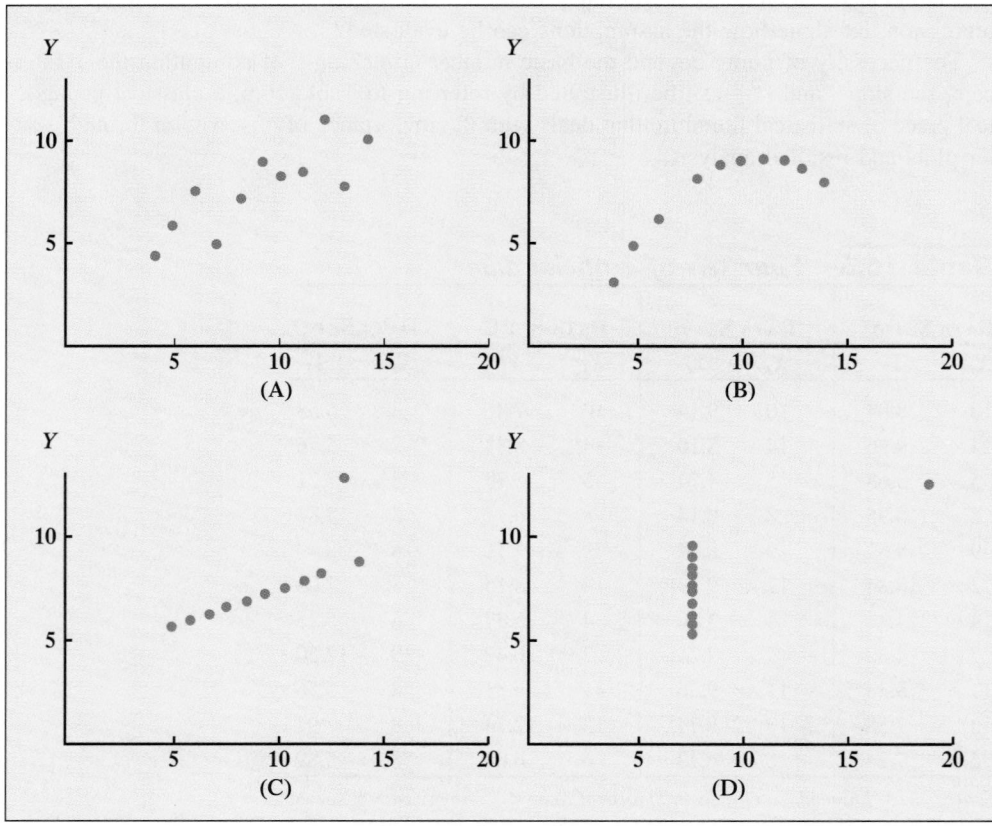

**FIGURE 16.20**    Scatter diagrams for four data sets

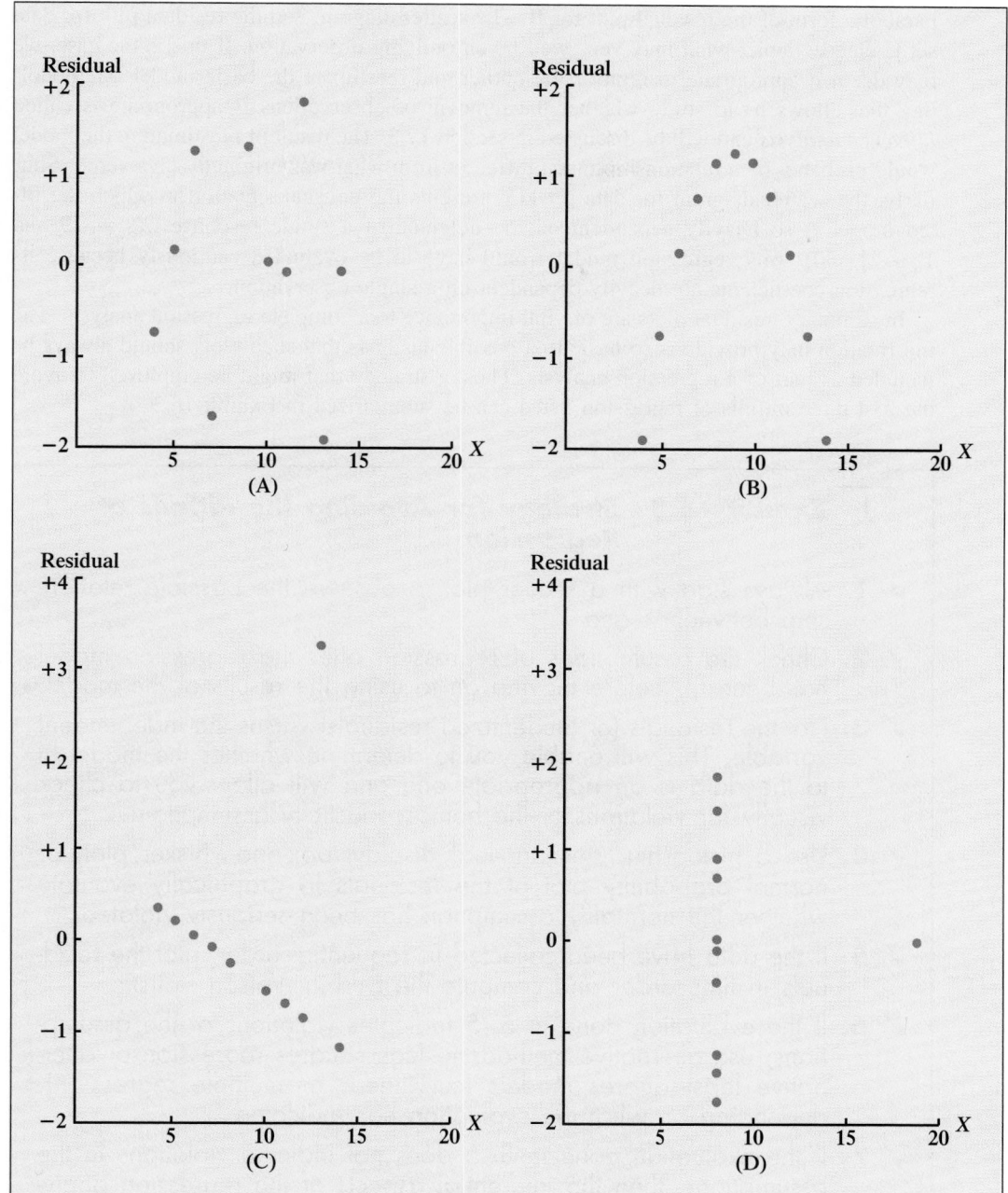

**FIGURE 16.21** Residual plots for four data sets
Reprinted by permission of American Statistical Assn.

From the scatter diagrams of Figure 16.20 and the residual plots of Figure 16.21 we see how different the data sets are. The only data set that seems to follow an approximate straight line is data set A. The residual plot for data set A does not show any obvious patterns or outlying residuals. This is certainly not the case for data sets B, C, and D. The scatter plot for data set B seems to indicate that a curvilinear regression model (to be covered in section 18.1) should be considered. This conclusion is reinforced by the clear parabolic form of the residual plot for B. The scatter diagram and the residual plot for data set C clearly depict what may very well be an outlying observation. If this is the case, we may deem it appropriate to remove the outlier and reestimate the basic model. Methodology that allows us to study whether the removal of observations is appropriate is called *influence analysis* and will be discussed in section 17.3. The result of reestimating the model would probably be a relationship much different from what was originally uncovered. Similarly, the scatter diagram for data set D represents the unusual situation in which the fitted model is so heavily dependent on the outcome of a single response ($X_8 = 19$ and $Y_8 = 12.50$). Any regression model would have to be evaluated cautiously because its regression coefficients are heavily dependent on a single observation.

In summary, residual plots are of vital importance to a complete regression analysis. The information they provide is so basic to a credible analysis that such plots should always be included as part of a regression analysis. Thus, a strategy that might be employed to avoid the first three pitfalls of regression listed can be summarized in Exhibit 16.3.

---

### Exhibit 16.3  *Strategy for Avoiding the Pitfalls of Regression*

✓ **1.** Always start with a scatter plot to observe the possible relationship between $X$ and $Y$.

✓ **2.** Check the assumptions of regression after the regression model has been fit, before moving on to using the results of the model.

✓ **3.** Plot the residuals (or Studentized residuals) versus the independent variable. This will enable you to determine whether the model fit to the data is an appropriate one and will allow you to check visually for violations of the homoscedasticity assumption.

✓ **4.** Use a histogram, stem-and-leaf display, box-and-whisker plot, or normal probability plot of the residuals to graphically evaluate whether the normality assumption has been seriously violated.

✓ **5.** If the data have been collected in sequential order, plot the residuals in time order and compute the Durbin-Watson statistic.

✓ **6.** If the evaluation done in 3–5 indicates violations of the assumptions, use alternative methods to least-squares regression or alternative least-squares models (curvilinear or multiple regression), depending on what the evaluation has indicated.

✓ **7.** If the evaluation done in 3–5 does not indicate violations in the assumptions, then the inferential aspects of the regression analysis can be undertaken. Tests for the significance of the regression coefficients can be done and confidence and prediction intervals can be developed.

---

## Ethical Considerations

Ethical considerations arise when a user wishing to develop forecasts manipulates the process of developing the regression model. The key here is intent. As listed in Exhibit 16.4, unethical behavior occurs in several ways in regression analysis.

All of these situations should make us realize even more the importance of following the steps given in Exhibit 16.3 and knowing the assumptions of regression, how to evaluate them, and what to do if any of them have been violated.

## 16.10 COMPUTATIONS IN SIMPLE LINEAR REGRESSION

In our development of the simple linear regression model we have primarily focused on using the output of software such as Microsoft Excel and Minitab. In this section we illustrate the computations that were involved in developing many of the statistics obtained for the simple linear regression model.

### Computing the Y Intercept $b_0$ and the Slope $b_1$

Using the method of least-squares, equations (16.3a) and (16.3b) on page 739 need to be solved simultaneously to obtain the regression coefficients $b_1$ and $b_0$. Because there are two equations with two unknowns, the simultaneous solution to these two equations gives the following results:

**Computational Formula for the Slope $b_1$**

$$b_1 = \frac{SSXY}{SSX} \tag{16.18}$$

where

$$SSXY = \sum_{i=1}^{n} (X_i - \overline{X})(Y_i - \overline{Y}) = \sum_{i=1}^{n} X_i Y_i - \frac{\left(\sum_{i=1}^{n} X_i\right)\left(\sum_{i=1}^{n} Y_i\right)}{n}$$

$$SSX = \sum_{i=1}^{n} (X_i - \overline{X})^2 = \sum_{i=1}^{n} X_i^2 - \frac{\left(\sum_{i=1}^{n} X_i\right)^2}{n}$$

and

## Computational Formula for the Y Intercept $b_0$

$$b_0 = \overline{Y} - b_1\overline{X} \qquad\qquad (16.19)$$

where

$$\overline{Y} = \frac{\sum\limits_{i=1}^{n} Y_i}{n} \quad \text{and} \quad \overline{X} = \frac{\sum\limits_{i=1}^{n} X_i}{n}$$

Examining equations (16.18) and (16.19), we see that there are five quantities that must be calculated to determine $b_1$ and $b_0$. These are $n$, the sample size; $\sum\limits_{i=1}^{n} X_i$, the sum of the $X$ values; $\sum\limits_{i=1}^{n} Y_i$, the sum of the $Y$ values; $\sum\limits_{i=1}^{n} X_i^2$, the sum of the squared $X$ values; and $\sum\limits_{i=1}^{n} X_iY_i$, the sum of the cross-products of $X$ and $Y$. From the data in Table 16.1 on page 737 the number of square feet is used to predict the average annual sales in a store. The computation of the various sums needed [including $\sum\limits_{i=1}^{n} Y_i^2$, the sum of the squared $Y$ values that will be used to compute the sum of squares total ($SST$)] are presented in Table 16.7.

### Table 16.7  Computations for the site selection problem

| STORE | SQUARE FEET $X$ | SALES $Y$ | $X^2$ | $Y^2$ | $XY$ |
|---|---|---|---|---|---|
| 1 | 1,726 | 3,681 | 2,979,076 | 13,549,761 | 6,353,406 |
| 2 | 1,642 | 3,895 | 2,696,164 | 15,171,025 | 6,395,590 |
| 3 | 2,816 | 6,653 | 7,929,856 | 44,262,409 | 18,734,848 |
| 4 | 5,555 | 9,543 | 30,858,025 | 91,068,849 | 53,011,365 |
| 5 | 1,292 | 3,418 | 1,669,264 | 11,682,724 | 4,416,056 |
| 6 | 2,208 | 5,563 | 4,875,264 | 30,946,969 | 12,283,104 |
| 7 | 1,313 | 3,660 | 1,723,969 | 13,395,600 | 4,805,580 |
| 8 | 1,102 | 2,694 | 1,214,404 | 7,257,636 | 2,968,788 |
| 9 | 3,151 | 5,468 | 9,928,801 | 29,899,024 | 17,229,668 |
| 10 | 1,516 | 2,898 | 2,298,256 | 8,398,404 | 4,393,368 |
| 11 | 5,161 | 10,674 | 26,635,921 | 113,934,276 | 55,088,514 |
| 12 | 4,567 | 7,585 | 20,857,489 | 57,532,225 | 34,640,695 |
| 13 | 5,841 | 11,760 | 34,117,281 | 138,297,600 | 68,690,160 |
| 14 | 3,008 | 4,085 | 9,048,064 | 16,687,225 | 12,287,680 |
| Total | 40,898 | 81,577 | 156,831,834 | 592,083,727 | 301,298,822 |

Using equations (16.18) and (16.19), we compute the values of $b_0$ and $b_1$:

$$b_1 = \frac{SSXY}{SSX}$$

$$SSXY = \sum_{i=1}^{n}(X_i - \overline{X})(Y_i - \overline{Y}) = \sum_{i=1}^{n} X_iY_i - \frac{\left(\sum\limits_{i=1}^{n} X_i\right)\left(\sum\limits_{i=1}^{n} Y_i\right)}{n}$$

$$= 301{,}298{,}822 - \frac{(40{,}898)(81{,}577)}{14}$$

$$= 301{,}298{,}822 - 238{,}309{,}724.71$$

$$= 62{,}989{,}097.29$$

$$SSX = \sum_{i=1}^{n} (X_i - \bar{X})^2 = \sum_{i=1}^{n} X_i^2 - \frac{\left(\sum_{i=1}^{n} X_i\right)^2}{n}$$

$$= 156{,}831{,}834 - \frac{(40{,}898)^2}{14}$$

$$= 156{,}831{,}834 - 119{,}474{,}743.1$$

$$= 37{,}357{,}090.86$$

so that

$$b_1 = \frac{62{,}989{,}097.29}{37{,}357{,}090.86}$$

$$= 1.68613$$

$$b_0 = \bar{Y} - b_1\bar{X}$$

and

$$\bar{Y} = \frac{\sum_{i=1}^{n} Y_i}{n} = \frac{81{,}577}{14} = 5{,}826.929$$

$$\bar{X} = \frac{\sum_{i=1}^{n} X_i}{n} = \frac{40{,}898}{14} = 2{,}921.2857$$

so that

$$b_0 = 5{,}826.929 - (1.68613)(2{,}921.2857)$$

$$= 901.2$$

## Computing the Measures of Variation

Computational formulas can be developed to compute $SST$, $SSR$, and $SSE$, which were defined in equations (16.4), (16.5), and (16.6) on pages 747 and 748.

### Computational Formula for the Total Sum of Squares (*SST*)

$$SST = \text{total variation or total sum of squares} = \sum_{i=1}^{n} (Y_i - \bar{Y})^2 \qquad (16.20)$$

$$= \sum_{i=1}^{n} Y_i^2 - \frac{\left(\sum_{i=1}^{n} Y_i\right)^2}{n}$$

## Computational Formula for the Regression Sum of Squares ($SSR$)

$SSR$ = explained variation or regression sum of squares

$$= \sum_{i=1}^{n}(\hat{Y}_i - \overline{Y})^2 = b_0\sum_{i=1}^{n}Y_i + b_1\sum_{i=1}^{n}X_iY_i - \frac{\left(\sum_{i=1}^{n}Y_i\right)^2}{n} \qquad (16.21)$$

## Computational Formula for the Error Sum of Squares ($SSE$)

$SSE$ = unexplained variation or error sum of squares

$$= \sum_{i=1}^{n}(Y_i - \hat{Y}_i)^2 = \sum_{i=1}^{n}Y_i^2 - b_0\sum_{i=1}^{n}Y_i - b_1\sum_{i=1}^{n}X_iY_i \qquad (16.22)$$

Using the summary results from Table 16.7 on page 784,

$$SST = \text{total variation or total sum of squares} = \sum_{i=1}^{n}(Y_i - \overline{Y})^2 = \sum_{i=1}^{n}Y_i^2 - \frac{\left(\sum_{i=1}^{n}Y_i\right)^2}{n}$$

$$= 592{,}083{,}727 - \frac{(81{,}577)^2}{14}$$

$$= 592{,}083{,}727 - 475{,}343{,}352.1$$

$$= 116{,}740{,}375$$

$SSR$ = explained variation or regression sum of squares

$$= \sum_{i=1}^{n}(\hat{Y}_i - \overline{Y})^2$$

$$= b_0\sum_{i=1}^{n}Y_i + b_1\sum_{i=1}^{n}X_iY_i - \frac{\left(\sum_{i=1}^{n}Y_i\right)^2}{n}$$

$$= (901.2)(81{,}577) + (1.68613)(301{,}298{,}822) - \frac{(81{,}577)^2}{14}$$

$$= 106{,}208{,}120$$

$SSE$ = unexplained variation or error sum of squares

$$= \sum_{i=1}^{n}(Y_i - \hat{Y}_i)^2$$

$$= \sum_{i=1}^{n}Y_i^2 - b_0\sum_{i=1}^{n}Y_i - b_1\sum_{i=1}^{n}X_iY_i$$

$$= 592,083,727 - (901.2)(81,577) - (1.68613)(301,298,822)$$

$$= 10,532,255.2$$

## Computing the Standard Error of the Slope

In section 16.7 the standard error of the slope was used to test the existence of a relationship between the $X$ and $Y$ variables. The computational formula can be developed as follows:

$$S_{b_1} = \frac{S_{YX}}{\sqrt{SSX}}$$

$$SSX = \sum_{i=1}^{n}(X_i - \bar{X})^2$$

$$= \sum_{i=1}^{n}X_i^2 - \frac{\left(\sum_{i=1}^{n}X_i\right)^2}{n}$$

$$= 156,831,834 - \frac{(40,898)^2}{14}$$

$$= 37,357,090.86$$

$$S_{b_1} = \frac{936.85}{\sqrt{37,357,090.86}}$$

$$= .1533$$

For a second illustration of the computations involved in regression, we turn to Example 16.5.

## Example 16.5 *Computing $b_0$, $b_1$, SST, SSR, SSE, and $r^2$*

In Table 16.6 on page 779, four data sets were considered. Data set A consisted of the following values:

| $X_i$ | $Y_i$ |
|-------|-------|
| 10 | 8.04 |
| 14 | 9.96 |
| 5 | 5.68 |
| 8 | 6.95 |
| 9 | 8.81 |
| 12 | 10.84 |
| 4 | 4.26 |
| 7 | 4.82 |
| 11 | 8.33 |
| 13 | 7.58 |
| 6 | 7.24 |

For these data, compute $b_0$, $b_1$, SST, SSR, SSE, and $r^2$.

## SOLUTION

There are five quantities that must be calculated to determine $b_1$ and $b_0$. These are $n$, the sample size; $\sum_{i=1}^{n} X_i$, the sum of the $X$ values; $\sum_{i=1}^{n} Y_i$, the sum of the $Y$ values; $\sum_{i=1}^{n} X_i^2$, the sum of the squared $X$ values, and $\sum_{i=1}^{n} X_i Y_i$, the sum of the cross-products of $X$ and $Y$. In addition, $\sum_{i=1}^{n} Y_i^2$, the sum of the squared $Y$ values is needed to compute $SST$. The computation of these sums has been obtained from Microsoft Excel as presented in the accompanying figure.

|    | A | B | C | D | E | F |
|----|-----|-------|---------|---------|--------|-----|
| 1 | X | Y | Xsquare | Ysquare | XY | |
| 2 | 10 | 8.04 | 100 | 64.6416 | 80.4 | |
| 3 | 14 | 9.96 | 196 | 99.2016 | 139.44 | |
| 4 | 5 | 5.68 | 25 | 32.2624 | 28.4 | |
| 5 | 8 | 6.95 | 64 | 48.3025 | 55.6 | |
| 6 | 9 | 8.81 | 81 | 77.6161 | 79.29 | |
| 7 | 12 | 10.84 | 144 | 117.5056 | 130.08 | |
| 8 | 4 | 4.26 | 16 | 18.1476 | 17.04 | |
| 9 | 7 | 4.82 | 49 | 23.2324 | 33.74 | |
| 10 | 11 | 8.33 | 121 | 69.3889 | 91.63 | |
| 11 | 13 | 7.58 | 169 | 57.4564 | 98.54 | |
| 12 | 6 | 7.24 | 36 | 52.4176 | 43.44 | |
| 13 | 99 | 82.51 | 1001 | 660.1727 | 797.6 | Sum |

Microsoft Excel computations for data set A

Using equations (16.18) and (16.19), we can compute the values of $b_0$ and $b_1$:

$$b_1 = \frac{SSXY}{SSX}$$

$$SSXY = \sum_{i=1}^{n} (X_i - \bar{X})(Y_i - \bar{Y}) = \sum_{i=1}^{n} X_i Y_i - \frac{\left(\sum_{i=1}^{n} X_i\right)\left(\sum_{i=1}^{n} Y_i\right)}{n}$$

$$= 797.6 - \frac{(99)(82.51)}{11}$$

$$= 797.6 - 742.59$$

$$= 55.01$$

$$SSX = \sum_{i=1}^{n} (X_i - \bar{X})^2 = \sum_{i=1}^{n} X_i^2 - \frac{\left(\sum_{i=1}^{n} X_i\right)^2}{n}$$

$$= 1{,}001 - \frac{(99)^2}{11}$$

$$= 1{,}001 - 891$$

$$= 110$$

so that

$$b_1 = \frac{55.01}{110}$$

$$= .5001$$

$$b_0 = \overline{Y} - b_1\overline{X}$$

and

$$\overline{Y} = \frac{\displaystyle\sum_{i=1}^{n} Y_i}{n} = \frac{82.51}{11} = 7.50$$

$$\overline{X} = \frac{\displaystyle\sum_{i=1}^{n} X_i}{n} = \frac{99}{11} = 9.0$$

so that

$$b_0 = 7.50 - (.50)(9.0)$$

$$= 3.0$$

Using the summary results,

$$SST = \text{total variation or total sum of squares} = \sum_{i=1}^{n} (Y_i - \overline{Y})^2 = \sum_{i=1}^{n} Y_i^2 - \frac{\left(\displaystyle\sum_{i=1}^{n} Y_i\right)^2}{n}$$

$$= 660.1727 - \frac{(82.51)^2}{11}$$

$$= 660.1727 - 618.9$$

$$= 41.2727$$

$SSR$ = explained variation or regression sum of squares

$$= \sum_{i=1}^{n} (\hat{Y}_i - \overline{Y})^2$$

$$= b_0 \sum_{i=1}^{n} Y_i + b_1 \sum_{i=1}^{n} X_i Y_i - \frac{\left(\displaystyle\sum_{i=1}^{n} Y_i\right)^2}{n}$$

$$= (3.0)(82.51) + (.5001)(797.6) - \frac{(82.51)^2}{11}$$

$$= 27.51$$

$SSE$ = unexplained variation or error sum of squares

$$= \sum_{i=1}^{n} (Y_i - \hat{Y}_i)^2$$

$$= \sum_{i=1}^{n} Y_i^2 - b_0 \sum_{i=1}^{n} Y_i - b_1 \sum_{i=1}^{n} X_i Y_i$$

$$= 660.1727 - (3.0)(82.51) - (.5001)(797.6)$$

$$= 13.763$$

### 16.11 CORRELATION—MEASURING THE STRENGTH OF THE ASSOCIATION

#### The Correlation Coefficient

In our discussion of regression analysis we have been concerned with the prediction of the dependent variable $Y$ based on the independent variable $X$. In contrast to this, in a correlation analysis our focus is on measuring the degree of association between two variables.

The strength of a relationship between two variables in a population is usually measured by the **coefficient of correlation** $\rho$, whose values range from $-1$ for perfect negative correlation up to $+1$ for perfect positive correlation. Figure 16.22 illustrates three different types of association between variables.

In panel A of Figure 16.22 there is a perfect negative linear relationship between $X$ and $Y$ so that $Y$ will decrease in a perfectly predictable manner as $X$ increases. Panel B is an example in which there is no relationship between $X$ and $Y$. As $X$ increases, there is no change in $Y$, so there is no association between the values of $X$ and the values of $Y$. Panel C depicts a perfect positive correlation between $X$ and $Y$. In this case, $Y$ increases in a perfectly predictable manner as $X$ increases.

For situations in which our primary interest is regression analysis, the sample coefficient of correlation ($r$) is obtained from the coefficient of determination $r^2$

$$r^2 = \frac{\text{regression sum of squares}}{\text{total sum of squares}} = \frac{SSR}{SST}$$

so that

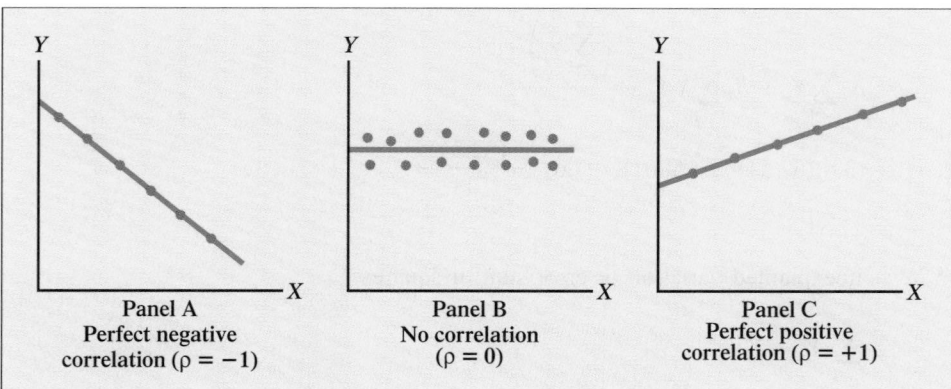

**FIGURE 16.22** Types of association between variables

## The Coefficient of Correlation

$$r = \sqrt{r^2} \qquad\qquad (16.23)$$

where $r$ takes the sign of $b_1$.

In the site selection example, because $r^2 = .91$ and the slope $b_1$ is positive, the coefficient of correlation is computed as $+.954$. The closeness of the correlation coefficient to $+1.0$ implies a strong positive association between size of the store and the annual sales.

We have now computed and interpreted the correlation coefficient from a regression perspective. As we mentioned at the beginning of this chapter, regression and correlation are two separate techniques, with regression being concerned with prediction and correlation with association. In many applications we are concerned only with measuring association between variables, not with using one variable to predict another. If we are specifically interested in measuring correlation, the sample correlation coefficient $r$ can be computed directly, using the following equation.

## The Coefficient of Correlation

$$r = \frac{SSXY}{\sqrt{SSX}\sqrt{SSY}} \qquad\qquad (16.24)$$

where

$$SSXY = \sum_{i=1}^{n} (X_i - \overline{X})(Y_i - \overline{Y})$$

$$SSX = \sum_{i=1}^{n} (X_i - \overline{X})^2$$

$$SSY = \sum_{i=1}^{n} (Y_i - \overline{Y})^2$$

One application of the correlation coefficient occurs in finance where it is important to study the association between two investments over time. In section 6.5 we introduced the *covariance* that measured the covariation between two variables. One way of viewing the correlation coefficient is from the perspective that it is the covariance in standardized form, so that its smallest possible value is $-1$ and its largest possible value is $+1$.

To illustrate an application of the correlation coefficient, suppose we want to study the association in the value of two currencies, the German mark and the Japanese yen, from 1988 to 1997. The results are summarized in Table 16.8.

For the data of Table 16.8 we use Microsoft Excel to compute $SSX$, $SSY$, $SSXY$, and $r$ as displayed in Figure 16.23.

**Table 16.8** *Exchange rate of the German mark and the Japanese yen in U.S. dollars*

| YEAR | GERMAN MARK | JAPANESE YEN |
|------|-------------|--------------|
| 1988 | 1.76 | 128.17 |
| 1989 | 1.88 | 138.07 |
| 1990 | 1.62 | 145.00 |
| 1991 | 1.66 | 134.59 |
| 1992 | 1.56 | 126.78 |
| 1993 | 1.65 | 111.20 |
| 1994 | 1.62 | 102.21 |
| 1995 | 1.50 | 103.35 |
| 1996 | 1.54 | 115.87 |
| 1997 | 1.80 | 130.38 |

DATA FILE
MARKYEN

*Source: Board of Governors of the Federal Reserve System, Table B-107.*

| | A | B | C | D | E | F |
|---|---|---|---|---|---|---|
| 1 | Year | Mark(X) | Yen(Y) | (X-XBAR)^2 | (Y-YBAR)^2 | (X-XBAR)(Y-YBAR) |
| 2 | 1988 | 1.76 | 128.17 | 0.010201 | 21.233664 | 0.465408 |
| 3 | 1989 | 1.88 | 138.07 | 0.048841 | 210.482064 | 3.206268 |
| 4 | 1990 | 1.62 | 145 | 0.001521 | 459.587844 | -0.836082 |
| 5 | 1991 | 1.66 | 134.59 | 1E-06 | 121.616784 | 0.011028 |
| 6 | 1992 | 1.56 | 126.78 | 0.009801 | 10.355524 | -0.318582 |
| 7 | 1993 | 1.65 | 111.2 | 8.1E-05 | 152.819044 | 0.111258 |
| 8 | 1994 | 1.62 | 102.21 | 0.001521 | 455.907904 | 0.832728 |
| 9 | 1995 | 1.5 | 103.35 | 0.025281 | 408.524944 | 3.213708 |
| 10 | 1996 | 1.54 | 115.87 | 0.014161 | 59.166864 | 0.915348 |
| 11 | 1997 | 1.8 | 130.38 | 0.019881 | 46.485124 | 0.961338 |
| 12 | Correlation | XBAR | YBAR | SSX | SSY | SSXY |
| 13 | 0.53566 | 1.659 | 123.562 | 0.13129 | 1946.17976 | 8.56242 |

**FIGURE 16.23** Summary computations for the correlation of the German mark and the Japanese yen obtained from Microsoft Excel

To obtain the correlation coefficient $r$, we have

$$SSXY = \sum_{i=1}^{n}(X_i - \overline{X})(Y_i - \overline{Y}) = 8.56242$$

$$SSX = \sum_{i=1}^{n}(X_i - \overline{X})^2 = .13129$$

$$SSY = \sum_{i=1}^{n}(Y_i - \overline{Y})^2 = 1,946.17976$$

so that

$$r = \frac{SSXY}{\sqrt{SSX}\sqrt{SSY}} = \frac{8.56242}{\sqrt{.13129}\sqrt{1,946.17976}}$$

$$= .53566$$

The coefficient of correlation $r = +.536$ between the German mark and the Japanese yen indicates a moderate association. A higher price of the German mark is moderately associated with a higher price of the Japanese yen.

Now that we have computed the correlation coefficient $r$, we can use these sample results to determine whether there is any evidence of a statistically significant association between these variables. The population correlation coefficient $\rho$ is hypothesized as equal to 0. Thus, the null and alternative hypotheses are

$$H_0: \rho = 0 \text{ (There is no correlation.)}$$

$$H_1: \rho \neq 0 \text{ (There is correlation.)}$$

The test statistic for determining the existence of a significant correlation is given by

## Testing for the Existence of Correlation

$$t = \frac{r - \rho}{\sqrt{\dfrac{1 - r^2}{n - 2}}} \tag{16.25}$$

where the test statistic $t$ follows a $t$ distribution with $n - 2$ degrees of freedom.

For the currency data summarized in Figure 16.23, $r = +.53566$ and $n = 10$, so testing the null hypothesis we have

$$t = \frac{r}{\sqrt{\dfrac{1 - r^2}{n - 2}}}$$

$$= \frac{.53566}{\sqrt{\dfrac{1 - (.53566)^2}{10 - 2}}} = 1.794$$

Using the .05 level of significance, because $t = 1.794 < t_8 = 2.306$, we do not reject $H_0$. We conclude that there is no evidence of an association between the value of the German mark and the Japanese yen.

When we discussed inferences concerning the population slope, we used confidence intervals and tests of hypothesis interchangeably. However, the development of a confidence interval for the correlation coefficient is more complicated because the shape of the sampling distribution of the statistic $r$ varies for different values of the true correlation coefficient. Methods for developing a confidence interval estimate for the correlation coefficient are presented in reference 7.

## Problems for Section 16.11

### Learning the Basics

- **16.50** If $r^2 = .81$ and the slope of the fitted regression line is positive, find $r$.

  **16.51** If the coefficient of determination is .49 and the slope of the fitted regression line is $-3$, find the coefficient of correlation.

  **16.52** If $SSR = SST$ and the slope is a negative value, find $r$.

  **16.53** If $SSE = 0$, and the slope is a positive value, find $r$.

  **16.54** Given the following set of data from a sample of $n = 11$ items,

  | X | 7 | 5 | 8 | 3 | 6 | 10 | 12 | 4 | 9 | 15 | 18 |
  |---|---|---|---|---|---|----|----|---|---|----|----|
  | Y | 21 | 15 | 24 | 9 | 18 | 30 | 36 | 12 | 27 | 45 | 54 |

(a) Compute the correlation coefficient $r$.

(b) At the .05 level of significance, is there evidence of a relationship between $X$ and $Y$? Explain.

## Applying the Concepts

**16.55** The following data represent the approximate retail price (in $) and the energy cost per year (in $) of nine large side-by-side refrigerators.

| BRAND | PRICE ($) | ENERGY COST PER YEAR ($) |
|---|---|---|
| KitchenAidSuperbaKSRS25QF | 1,600 | 73 |
| Kenmore(Sears)5757 | 1,200 | 73 |
| WhirlpoolED25DQXD | 1,550 | 78 |
| AmanaSRD25S3 | 1,350 | 85 |
| Kenmore(Sears)5647 | 1,700 | 93 |
| GEProfileTPX24PRY | 1,700 | 93 |
| FrigidaireGalleryFRS26ZGE | 1,500 | 95 |
| MaytagRSW2400EA | 1,400 | 96 |
| GETFX25ZRY | 1,200 | 94 |

DATA FILE
REFRIG

*Source: "The Kings of Cool," Copyright 1997 by Consumers Union of U.S., Inc. Adapted from* CONSUMER REPORTS *(January 1998): 52, by permission of Consumers Union of U.S., Inc., Yonkers, NY 10703-1057. Although these data sets originally appeared in* CONSUMER REPORTS, *the selective adaptation and resulting conclusions presented are those of the authors and are not sanctioned or endorsed in any way by Consumers Union, the publisher of* CONSUMER REPORTS.

(a) Compute the correlation coefficient $r$.

(b) At the .05 level of significance, is there a relationship between $X$ and $Y$? Explain.

(c) Would you expect the higher-priced refrigerators to have greater energy efficiency? Is this borne out by the data?

• **16.56** The following data represent the average charge (in dollars per minute) and the amount of minutes expended (in billions) for all telephone calls placed from the United States to 20 different countries during 1996.

| COUNTRY | CHARGE PER MINUTE (IN DOLLARS) | MINUTES (IN BILLIONS) | COUNTRY | CHARGE PER MINUTE (IN DOLLARS) | MINUTES (IN BILLIONS) |
|---|---|---|---|---|---|
| Canada | 0.34 | 3.049 | India | 1.38 | 0.287 |
| Mexico | 0.85 | 2.012 | Brazil | 0.96 | 0.284 |
| Britain | 0.73 | 1.025 | Italy | 1.00 | 0.279 |
| Germany | 0.88 | 0.662 | Taiwan | 0.97 | 0.273 |
| Japan | 1.00 | 0.576 | Colombia | 1.00 | 0.257 |
| Dominican Republic | 0.84 | 0.410 | China | 1.47 | 0.232 |
| France | 0.81 | 0.364 | Israel | 1.16 | 0.214 |
| South Korea | 1.09 | 0.319 | Australia | 1.01 | 0.201 |
| Hong Kong | 0.90 | 0.317 | Jamaica | 1.03 | 0.188 |
| Philippines | 1.29 | 0.297 | Netherlands | 0.78 | 0.167 |

DATA FILE
INTPHONE

*Source: The New York Times, February 17, 1997, 46. Copyright by The New York Times Company. Reprinted by permission of The New York Times.*

(a) Compute the correlation coefficient $r$.

(b) At the .05 level of significance, is there a relationship between $X$ and $Y$? Explain.

(c) One might expect that the higher the charge per minute, the lower the number of minutes that would be used. Does the correlation coefficient reflect this expected relationship? Explain.

**16.57** The following data represent the retail price (in dollars) and the printing speed (in number of pages per minute of double-spaced black text with standard margins) for a sample of 19 computer printers:

| BRAND | PRICE (IN DOLLARS) | TEXT SPEED (PAGES PER MINUTE) |
|---|---|---|
| Hewlett-PackardDeskJet855Cse | 500 | 3.0 |
| Hewlett-PackardDeskJet682C | 300 | 2.5 |
| Hewlett-PackardDeskJet600C | 250 | 2.6 |
| EpsonStylusColorII | 230 | 2.5 |
| Hewlett-PackardDeskWriter600 | 250 | 3.0 |
| CanonBJC-610 | 430 | 1.3 |
| CanonBJC-210 | 150 | 2.9 |
| AppleColorStyleWriter1500 | 280 | 3.1 |
| CanonBJC-4100 | 230 | 1.7 |
| AppleColorStyleWriter2500 | 380 | 3.4 |
| EpsonStylusColorIIs | 190 | 0.7 |
| Lexmark2070Jetprinter | 350 | 2.1 |
| Lexmark1020Jetprinter | 150 | 1.3 |
| NECSuperScript860 | 500 | 7.9 |
| PanasonicKX-P6500 | 450 | 5.5 |
| Hewlett-PackardLaserJet5L | 480 | 4.2 |
| TexasInstrumentsMicroLaserWin/4 | 380 | 4.2 |
| CanonLBP-460 | 350 | 4.1 |
| OkidataOL600e | 400 | 3.9 |

DATA FILE
PRINTER

*Source: "Computer Printers," Copyright 1996 by Consumers Union of U.S., Inc. Adapted from* CONSUMER REPORTS *(October 1996): 60–61, by permission of Consumers Union of U.S., Inc., Yonkers, NY 10703-1057. Although these data sets originally appeared in* CONSUMER REPORTS, *the selective adaptation and resulting conclusions presented are those of the authors and are not sanctioned or endorsed in any way by Consumers Union, the publisher of* CONSUMER REPORTS.

(a) Compute the correlation coefficient $r$.

(b) At the .05 level of significance, is there a relationship between $X$ and $Y$? Explain.

(c) One might expect that the higher the price, the higher the text speed. Does the correlation coefficient reflect this expected relationship? Explain.

**• 16.58** In Problem 16.3 on page 743 the marketing manager used shelf space for pet food to predict weekly sales. The coefficient of determination $r^2 = .684$.

DATA FILE
PETFOOD

(a) Compute the coefficient of correlation.

(b) Is there evidence of a significant correlation at the .05 level of significance?

(c) Compare the results of (b) to Problem 16.36(a) on page 771. What conclusion do you reach about the two tests?

**16.59** In Problem 16.4 on page 743 a manager wanted to predict weekly sales at a chain of package delivery stores based on the number of customers who made purchases. The coefficient of determination $r^2 = .913$. Compute the coefficient of correlation.

DATA FILE
PACKAGE

**DATA FILE**
**WORKHRS**

**DATA FILE**
**MOVIE**

**DATA FILE**
**RENT**

**DATA FILE**
**LIMO**

• **16.60** In Problem 16.5 on page 744 a company wanted to predict the worker-hours required for production based on the lot size. The coefficient of determination $r^2 = .9878$.
   (a) Compute the coefficient of correlation.
   (b) Is there evidence of a significant correlation at the .05 level of significance?
   (c) Compare the results of (b) to Problem 16.38(a) on page 772. What conclusion do you reach about the two tests?

**16.61** In Problem 16.6 on page 744 a company wanted to predict home video sales based on the box office gross of movies. The coefficient of determination $r^2 = .728$.
   (a) Compute the coefficient of correlation.
   (b) Is there evidence of a significant correlation at the .05 level of significance?
   (c) Compare the results of (b) to Problem 16.39(a) on page 772. What conclusion do you reach about the two tests?

**16.62** In Problem 16.7 on page 745 an agent for a real estate company wanted to predict the monthly rent for apartments based on the size of the apartment. The coefficient of determination $r^2 = .723$.
   (a) Compute the coefficient of correlation.
   (b) Is there evidence of a significant correlation at the .05 level of significance?
   (c) Compare the results of (b) to Problem 16.40(a) on page 772. What conclusion do you reach about the two tests?

**16.63** In Problem 16.8 on page 746 a limousine service wanted to predict travel time to an airport based on the distance from the pickup location to the airport. The coefficient of determination $r^2 = .918$.
   (a) Compute the coefficient of correlation.
   (b) Is there evidence of a significant correlation at the .05 level of significance?
   (c) Compare the results of (b) to Problem 16.41(a) on page 772. What conclusion do you reach about the two tests?

## SUMMARY

As seen in the chapter summary chart, we developed the simple linear regression model, discussed the assumptions of the model, and showed how these assumptions could be evaluated. We then developed the $t$ test for the significance of the slope and used the regression model for prediction. In addition, we studied the correlation coefficient and tested for its significance. In chapter 17 we will continue our discussion of regression analysis by considering a variety of multiple regression models.

## *Key Terms*

assumptions of regression   752
autocorrelation   760
coefficient of correlation   790
coefficient of determination   749
confidence interval estimate for the mean
   response   773
correlation analysis   734
dependent variable   734
Durbin-Watson statistic   762
error sum of squares (*SSE*)   747
explained variation   746
explanatory variable   734
homoscedasticity   753

independence of error   753
independent variable   734
least-squares method   737, 739
linear relationship   735
normality   753
prediction interval for an individual
   response   775
regression analysis   734
regression coefficient   738
regression sum of squares (*SSR*)   746
relevant range   742
residual analysis   753

residuals   754
response variable   734
scatter diagram   735
simple linear regression   734
slope   735
standard error of the estimate   749
standardized residuals   755
Studentized residuals   755
total sum of squares (*SST*)   746
total variation   746
unexplained variation   747
*Y* intercept   735

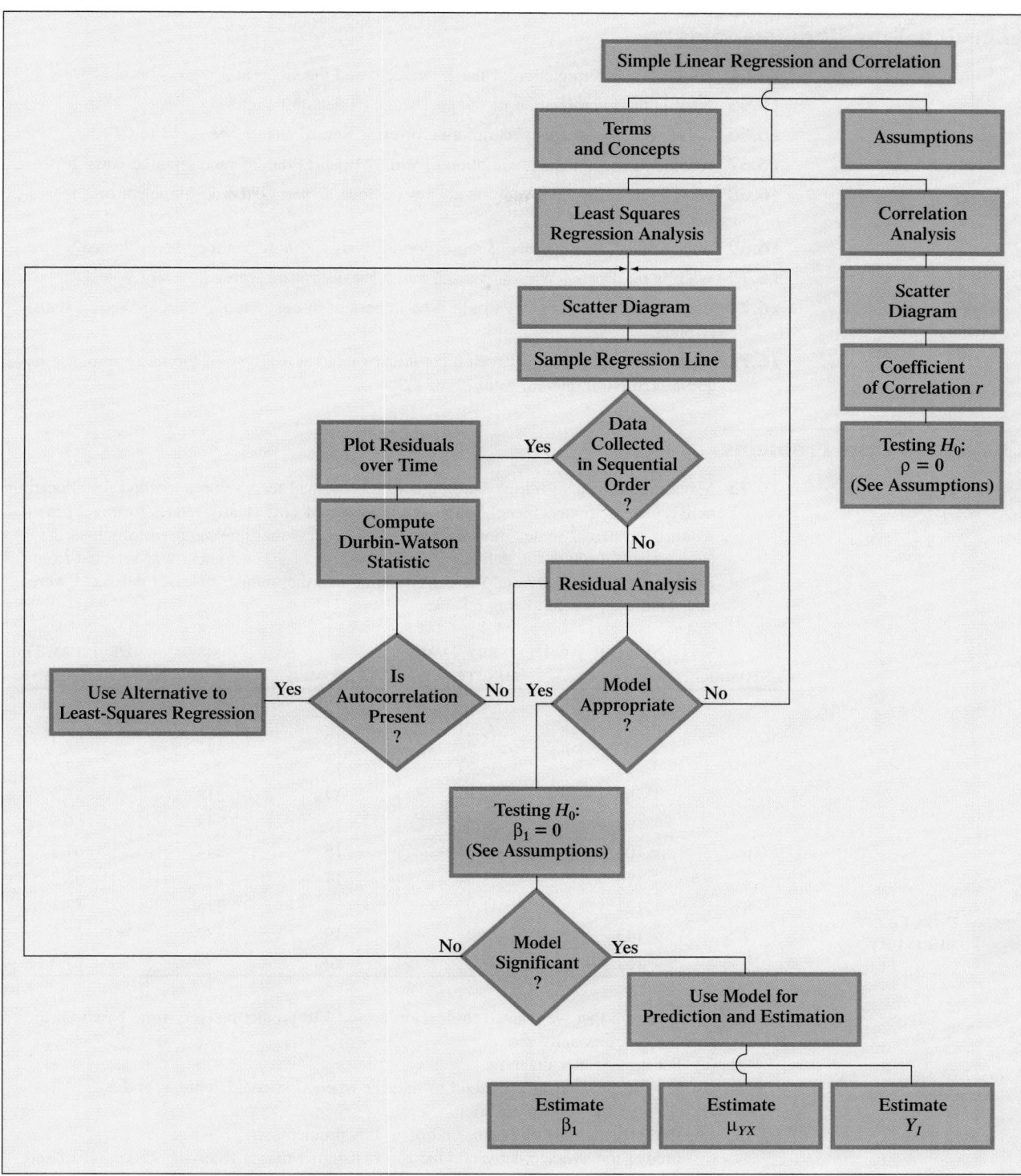

Chapter 16 summary chart

## Checking Your Understanding

**16.64** What is the interpretation of the $Y$ intercept and the slope in a regression model?

**16.65** What is the interpretation of the coefficient of determination?

**16.66** When will the unexplained variation or error sum of squares be equal to 0?

**16.67** When will the explained variation or sum of squares due to regression be equal to 0?

**16.68** Why should a residual analysis always be done as part of the development of a regression model?

**16.69** What are the assumptions of regression analysis and how can they be evaluated?

**16.70** What is the Durbin-Watson statistic and what does it measure?

**16.71** Under what circumstances would it be important to compute the Durbin-Watson statistic? Explain.

**16.72** What is the difference between a confidence interval estimate of the mean response $\mu_{YX}$ and a prediction interval estimate of $Y_I$?

## Chapter Review Problems

**16.73** Management of a soft-drink bottling company wished to develop a method for allocating delivery costs to customers. Although one aspect of cost clearly relates to travel time within a particular route, another type of cost reflects the time required to unload the cases of soft drink at the delivery point. A sample of 20 customers was selected from routes within a territory and the delivery time and the number of cases delivered were measured with the following results:

| CUSTOMER | NUMBER OF CASES | DELIVERY TIME (MINUTES) | CUSTOMER | NUMBER OF CASES | DELIVERY TIME (MINUTES) |
|---|---|---|---|---|---|
| 1 | 52 | 32.1 | 11 | 161 | 43.0 |
| 2 | 64 | 34.8 | 12 | 184 | 49.4 |
| 3 | 73 | 36.2 | 13 | 202 | 57.2 |
| 4 | 85 | 37.8 | 14 | 218 | 56.8 |
| 5 | 95 | 37.8 | 15 | 243 | 60.6 |
| 6 | 103 | 39.7 | 16 | 254 | 61.2 |
| 7 | 116 | 38.5 | 17 | 267 | 58.2 |
| 8 | 121 | 41.9 | 18 | 275 | 63.1 |
| 9 | 143 | 44.2 | 19 | 287 | 65.6 |
| 10 | 157 | 47.1 | 20 | 298 | 67.3 |

**DATA FILE**
**DELIVERY**

Assuming that we wanted to develop a model to predict delivery time based on the number of cases delivered:

(a) Set up a scatter diagram.

(b) Use the least-squares method to find the regression coefficients $b_0$ and $b_1$.

(c) State the regression equation.

(d) Interpret the meaning of $b_0$ and $b_1$ in this problem.

(e) Predict the average delivery time for a customer that is receiving 150 cases of soft drink.

(f) Would it be appropriate to use the model to predict the average delivery time for a customer who is receiving 500 cases of soft drink? Why?

(g) Compute the coefficient of determination $r^2$ and explain its meaning in this problem.

(h) Compute the coefficient of correlation.

(i) Compute the standard error of the estimate.
(j) Perform a residual analysis using either the residuals or the Studentized residuals. Is there any evidence of a pattern in the residuals? Explain.
(k) At the .05 level of significance, is there evidence of a linear relationship between delivery time and the number of cases delivered?
(l) Set up a 95% confidence interval estimate of the average delivery time for customers that receive 150 cases of soft drink.
(m) Set up a 95% prediction interval estimate of the delivery time for an individual customer that is receiving 150 cases of soft drink.
(n) Set up a 95% confidence interval estimate of the population slope.
(o) Explain how the results obtained in (a)–(n) can help allocate delivery costs to customers.

**16.74** A brokerage house would like to be able to predict the number of trade executions per day and has decided to use the number of incoming phone calls as a predictor variable. Data were collected over a period of 35 days with the following results:

| DAY | NUMBER OF INCOMING CALLS | TRADE EXECUTIONS | DAY | NUMBER OF INCOMING CALLS | TRADE EXECUTIONS |
|-----|--------------------------|------------------|-----|--------------------------|------------------|
| 1 | 2,591 | 417 | 19 | 2,328 | 365 |
| 2 | 2,146 | 321 | 20 | 2,078 | 330 |
| 3 | 2,185 | 362 | 21 | 2,134 | 312 |
| 4 | 2,245 | 364 | 22 | 2,192 | 340 |
| 5 | 2,600 | 442 | 23 | 1,965 | 339 |
| 6 | 2,510 | 386 | 24 | 2,147 | 364 |
| 7 | 2,394 | 370 | 25 | 2,015 | 295 |
| 8 | 2,486 | 376 | 26 | 2,046 | 292 |
| 9 | 2,483 | 463 | 27 | 2,073 | 379 |
| 10 | 2,297 | 389 | 28 | 2,032 | 294 |
| 11 | 2,106 | 302 | 29 | 2,108 | 329 |
| 12 | 2,035 | 266 | 30 | 1,923 | 274 |
| 13 | 1,936 | 339 | 31 | 2,069 | 326 |
| 14 | 1,951 | 369 | 32 | 2,061 | 306 |
| 15 | 2,292 | 403 | 33 | 2,010 | 352 |
| 16 | 2,094 | 319 | 34 | 1,913 | 290 |
| 17 | 1,897 | 306 | 35 | 1,904 | 283 |
| 18 | 2,237 | 397 | | | |

DATA FILE
TRADES

(a) Set up a scatter diagram.
(b) Use the least-squares method to find the regression coefficients $b_0$ and $b_1$.
(c) State the regression equation.
(d) Interpret the meaning of $b_0$ and $b_1$ in this problem.
(e) Predict the average number of trades executed for a day in which the number of incoming calls is 2,000.
(f) Would it be appropriate to use the model to predict the average number of trades executed for a day in which the number of incoming calls is 5,000? Why?
(g) Compute the coefficient of determination $r^2$ and explain its meaning in this problem.
(h) Compute the coefficient of correlation.
(i) Compute the standard error of the estimate.
(j) Plot the residuals against the number of incoming calls and also against the days. Is there any evidence of a pattern in the residuals with either of these variables? Explain.

(k) Compute the Durbin-Watson statistic for these data.

(l) On the basis of the results of (j) and (k), is there reason to question the validity of the fitted model? Explain.

(m) At the .05 level of significance, is there evidence of a linear relationship between the volume of trade executions and the number of incoming calls?

(n) Set up a 95% confidence interval estimate of the average number of trades executed for days in which the number of incoming calls is 2,000.

(o) Set up a 95% prediction interval estimate of the number of trades executed for a particular day in which the number of incoming calls is 2,000.

(p) Set up a 95% confidence interval estimate of the population slope.

(q) On the basis of the results of (a)–(p), do you think the brokerage house should focus on a strategy of increasing the total number of incoming calls or on a strategy that relies on trading by a small number of heavy traders? Explain.

**16.75** Suppose we want to develop a model to predict selling price of homes based on assessed value. A sample of 30 recently sold single-family houses in a small western city is selected to study the relationship between selling price and assessed value (the houses in the city had been reassessed at full value 1 year prior to the study). The results are as follows:

| OBSERVATION | ASSESSED VALUE ($000) | SELLING PRICE ($000) | OBSERVATION | ASSESSED VALUE ($000) | SELLING PRICE ($000) |
|---|---|---|---|---|---|
| 1 | 78.17 | 94.10 | 16 | 84.36 | 106.70 |
| 2 | 80.24 | 101.90 | 17 | 72.94 | 81.50 |
| 3 | 74.03 | 88.65 | 18 | 76.50 | 94.50 |
| 4 | 86.31 | 115.50 | 19 | 66.28 | 69.00 |
| 5 | 75.22 | 87.50 | 20 | 79.74 | 96.90 |
| 6 | 65.54 | 72.00 | 21 | 72.78 | 86.50 |
| 7 | 72.43 | 91.50 | 22 | 77.90 | 97.90 |
| 8 | 85.61 | 113.90 | 23 | 74.31 | 83.00 |
| 9 | 60.80 | 69.34 | 24 | 79.85 | 97.30 |
| 10 | 81.88 | 96.90 | 25 | 84.78 | 100.80 |
| 11 | 79.11 | 96.00 | 26 | 81.61 | 97.90 |
| 12 | 59.93 | 61.90 | 27 | 74.92 | 90.50 |
| 13 | 75.27 | 93.00 | 28 | 79.98 | 97.00 |
| 14 | 85.88 | 109.50 | 29 | 77.96 | 92.00 |
| 15 | 76.64 | 93.75 | 30 | 79.07 | 95.90 |

DATA FILE
HOUSE1

*Hint*: First determine which are the independent and dependent variables.

(a) Plot a scatter diagram and, assuming a linear relationship, use the least-squares method to find the regression coefficients $b_0$ and $b_1$.

(b) Interpret the meaning of the $Y$ intercept $b_0$ and the slope $b_1$ in this problem.

(c) Use the regression model developed in (a) to predict the average selling price for a house whose assessed value is $70,000.

(d) Compute the standard error of the estimate.

(e) Compute the coefficient of determination $r^2$ and interpret its meaning in this problem.

(f) Compute the coefficient of correlation $r$.

(g) Perform a residual analysis on your results and determine the adequacy of the fit of the model.

(h) At the .05 level of significance, is there evidence of a linear relationship between selling price and assessed value?

(i) Set up a 95% confidence interval estimate of the average selling price for houses with an assessed value of $70,000.

(j) Set up a 95% prediction interval estimate of the selling price of an individual house with an assessed value of $70,000.

(k) Set up a 95% confidence interval estimate of the population slope.

• **16.76** Suppose we want to develop a model to predict assessed value based on heating area. A sample of 15 single-family houses is selected in a particular community. The assessed value (in thousands of dollars) and the heating area of the houses (in thousands of square feet) are recorded with the following results:

| HOUSE | ASSESSED VALUE ($000) | HEATING AREA OF DWELLING (THOUSANDS OF SQUARE FEET) | HOUSE | ASSESSED VALUE ($000) | HEATING AREA OF DWELLING (THOUSANDS OF SQUARE FEET) |
|---|---|---|---|---|---|
| 1 | 84.4 | 2.00 | 9 | 78.5 | 1.59 |
| 2 | 77.4 | 1.71 | 10 | 79.2 | 1.50 |
| 3 | 75.7 | 1.45 | 11 | 86.7 | 1.90 |
| 4 | 85.9 | 1.76 | 12 | 79.3 | 1.39 |
| 5 | 79.1 | 1.93 | 13 | 74.5 | 1.54 |
| 6 | 70.4 | 1.20 | 14 | 83.8 | 1.89 |
| 7 | 75.8 | 1.55 | 15 | 76.8 | 1.59 |
| 8 | 85.9 | 1.93 | | | |

DATA FILE
HOUSE2

*Hint*: First determine which are the independent and dependent variables.

(a) Plot a scatter diagram and, assuming a linear relationship, use the least-squares method to find the regression coefficients $b_0$ and $b_1$.

(b) Interpret the meaning of the Y intercept $b_0$ and the slope $b_1$ in this problem.

(c) Use the regression model developed in (a) to predict the average assessed value for a house whose heating area is 1,750 square feet.

(d) Compute the standard error of the estimate.

(e) Compute the coefficient of determination $r^2$ and interpret its meaning in this problem.

(f) Compute the coefficient of correlation $r$.

(g) Perform a residual analysis on your results and determine the adequacy of the fit of the model.

(h) At the .05 level of significance, is there evidence of a linear relationship between assessed value and heating area?

(i) Set up a 95% confidence interval estimate of the average assessed value for houses with a heating area of 1,750 square feet.

(j) Set up a 95% prediction interval estimate of the assessed value of an individual house with a heating area of 1,750 square feet.

(k) Set up a 95% confidence interval estimate of the population slope.

(l) Suppose that the assessed value for the fourth house was 79.7. Do (a)–(k) and compare the results.

• **16.77** The director of graduate studies at a large college of business would like to be able to predict the grade point index (GPI) of students in an MBA program based on the Graduate Management Aptitude Test (GMAT) score. A sample of 20 students who have completed 2 years in the program is selected; the results are as follows on page 802.

| OBSERVATION | GMAT SCORE | GPI | OBSERVATION | GMAT SCORE | GPI |
|---|---|---|---|---|---|
| 1 | 688 | 3.72 | 11 | 567 | 3.07 |
| 2 | 647 | 3.44 | 12 | 542 | 2.86 |
| 3 | 652 | 3.21 | 13 | 551 | 2.91 |
| 4 | 608 | 3.29 | 14 | 573 | 2.79 |
| 5 | 680 | 3.91 | 15 | 536 | 3.00 |
| 6 | 617 | 3.28 | 16 | 639 | 3.55 |
| 7 | 557 | 3.02 | 17 | 619 | 3.47 |
| 8 | 599 | 3.13 | 18 | 694 | 3.60 |
| 9 | 616 | 3.45 | 19 | 718 | 3.88 |
| 10 | 594 | 3.33 | 20 | 759 | 3.76 |

DATA FILE
GPIGMAT

*Hint:* First determine which are the independent and dependent variables.

(a) Plot a scatter diagram and, assuming a linear relationship, use the least-squares method to find the regression coefficients $b_0$ and $b_1$.

(b) Interpret the meaning of the $Y$ intercept $b_0$ and the slope $b_1$ in this problem.

(c) Use the regression model developed in (a) to predict the average GPI for a student with a GMAT score of 600.

(d) Compute the standard error of the estimate.

(e) Compute the coefficient of determination $r^2$ and interpret its meaning in this problem.

(f) Compute the coefficient of correlation $r$.

(g) Perform a residual analysis on your results and determine the adequacy of the fit of the model.

(h) At the .05 level of significance, is there evidence of a linear relationship between GMAT score and GPI?

(i) Set up a 95% confidence interval estimate for the average GPI of students with a GMAT score of 600.

(j) Set up a 95% prediction interval estimate of the GPI for a particular student with a GMAT score of 600.

(k) Set up a 95% confidence interval estimate of the population slope.

(l) Suppose the GPIs of the 19th and 20th students were incorrectly entered. The GPI for student 19 should be 3.76, and the GPI for student 20 should be 3.88. Do (a)–(k) and compare the results.

**16.78** The manager of the purchasing department of a large banking organization would like to develop a model to predict the amount of time it takes to process invoices. Data are collected from a sample of 30 days with the results shown in the table on the next page. *Hint*: Determine which are the independent and dependent variables.

(a) Set up a scatter diagram.

(b) Assuming a linear relationship, use the least-squares method to find the regression coefficients $b_0$ and $b_1$.

(c) Interpret the meaning of the $Y$ intercept $b_0$ and the slope $b_1$ in this problem.

(d) Use the regression model developed in (b) to predict the average amount of time it would take to process 150 invoices.

(e) Compute the standard error of the estimate.

(f) Compute the coefficient of determination $r^2$ and interpret its meaning.

(g) Compute the coefficient of correlation $r$.

(h) Plot the residuals against the number of invoices processed and also against time.

(i) Based on the plots in (h), does the model seem appropriate?

(j) Compute the Durbin-Watson statistic and at the .05 level of significance, determine whether there is any autocorrelation in the residuals.

(k) On the basis of the results of (h)–(j), what conclusions can you reach concerning the validity of the model fit in (b)?

(l) At the .05 level of significance, is there evidence of a linear relationship between the amount of time and the number of invoices processed?

(m) Set up a 95% confidence interval estimate of the average amount of time taken to process 150 invoices.

(n) Set up a 95% prediction interval estimate of the amount of time it takes to process 150 invoices on a particular day.

| DAY | INVOICES PROCESSED | COMPLETION TIME (HOURS) | DAY | INVOICES PROCESSED | COMPLETION TIME (HOURS) |
|---|---|---|---|---|---|
| 1 | 149 | 2.1 | 16 | 169 | 2.5 |
| 2 | 60 | 1.8 | 17 | 190 | 2.9 |
| 3 | 188 | 2.3 | 18 | 233 | 3.4 |
| 4 | 19 | 0.3 | 19 | 289 | 4.1 |
| 5 | 201 | 2.7 | 20 | 45 | 1.2 |
| 6 | 58 | 1.0 | 21 | 193 | 2.5 |
| 7 | 77 | 1.7 | 22 | 70 | 1.8 |
| 8 | 222 | 3.1 | 23 | 241 | 3.8 |
| 9 | 181 | 2.8 | 24 | 103 | 1.5 |
| 10 | 30 | 1.0 | 25 | 163 | 2.8 |
| 11 | 110 | 1.5 | 26 | 120 | 2.5 |
| 12 | 83 | 1.2 | 27 | 201 | 3.3 |
| 13 | 60 | 0.8 | 28 | 135 | 2.0 |
| 14 | 25 | 0.4 | 29 | 80 | 1.7 |
| 15 | 173 | 2.0 | 30 | 29 | 0.5 |

DATA FILE
INVOICE

**16.79** Crazy Dave, a well-known baseball analyst, would like to study various team statistics for the 1997 baseball season to determine which variables might be useful in predicting the number of wins achieved by teams during the season. He has decided to begin by using the team earned run average (ERA) to predict the number of wins. The data for the 28 major league teams are as shown in the table at the top of page 804.
*Hint:* Determine which are the independent and dependent variables.

(a) Set up a scatter diagram.

(b) Assuming a linear relationship, use the least-squares method to find the regression coefficients $b_0$ and $b_1$.

(c) Interpret the meaning of the $Y$ intercept $b_0$ and the slope $b_1$ in this problem.

(d) Use the regression model developed in (b) to predict the expected number of wins for a team with an ERA of 4.00.

(e) Compute the standard error of the estimate.

(f) Compute the coefficient of determination $r^2$ and interpret its meaning.

(g) Compute the coefficient of correlation.

(h) Perform a residual analysis on your results and determine the adequacy of the fit of the model.

(i) At the .05 level of significance, is there evidence of a linear relationship between the number of wins and the ERA?

(j) Set up a 95% confidence interval estimate of the average number of wins expected for teams with an ERA of 4.00.

(k) Set up a 95% prediction interval estimate of the number of wins for an individual team that has an ERA of 4.00.

(l) Set up a 95% confidence interval estimate of the slope.

(m) The 28 teams constitute a population. In order to use statistical inference [as in (i)–(l)], the data must be assumed to represent a random sample. What "population" would this sample be drawing conclusions about?

(n) What other independent variables might be considered for inclusion in the model?

| AMERICAN LEAGUE | | | NATIONAL LEAGUE | | |
| --- | --- | --- | --- | --- | --- |
| TEAM | WINS | ERA | TEAM | WINS | ERA |
| Boston | 78 | 4.85 | Florida | 92 | 3.83 |
| Cleveland | 86 | 4.73 | Cincinnati | 76 | 4.41 |
| Kansas City | 67 | 4.70 | Chicago Cubs | 68 | 4.44 |
| Minnesota | 68 | 5.01 | San Francisco | 90 | 4.39 |
| Toronto | 76 | 3.93 | Los Angeles | 88 | 3.62 |
| Anaheim | 84 | 4.52 | Pittsburgh | 79 | 4.28 |
| Seattle | 90 | 4.78 | San Diego | 76 | 4.98 |
| Texas | 77 | 4.69 | New York Mets | 88 | 3.95 |
| Detroit | 79 | 4.56 | St. Louis | 73 | 3.88 |
| Chicago White Sox | 80 | 4.73 | Philadelphia | 68 | 4.85 |
| Milwaukee | 78 | 4.22 | Atlanta | 101 | 3.18 |
| Oakland | 65 | 5.48 | Montreal | 78 | 4.14 |
| Baltimore | 98 | 3.91 | Houston | 84 | 3.66 |
| New York Yankees | 96 | 3.84 | Colorado | 83 | 5.29 |

 **DATA FILE BB97**

---

◆ *Case Study — Predicting Sunday Newspaper Circulation*

You are employed in the marketing department of a large nationwide newspaper chain. The parent company is interested in investigating the feasibility of beginning a Sunday edition for some of its newspapers. However, before proceeding with a final decision, it needs to estimate the amount of Sunday circulation that would be expected. In particular, it wishes to predict the Sunday circulation that would be obtained by newspapers (in three different cities) that have daily circulations of 200,000, 400,000, and 600,000, respectively.

You have been asked to develop a model that would enable you to make a prediction of the expected Sunday circulation and to write a report that presents your results and summarizes your findings. Toward this end, data collected from a sample of 32 newspapers are as follows:

| | CIRCULATION (IN 000) | | | CIRCULATION (IN 000) | |
| PAPER | SUNDAY | DAILY | PAPER | SUNDAY | DAILY |
| --- | --- | --- | --- | --- | --- |
| Des Moines Register | 278,803 | 164,659 | Long Island Newsday | 646,446 | 559,233 |
| Philadelphia Inquirer | 865,989 | 422,829 | San Diego Union | | |
| New York Times | 1,644,128 | 1,107,168 | Tribune | 456,494 | 383,263 |
| New York News | 974,034 | 619,032 | Chicago Sun Times | 438,337 | 491,143 |
| Sacramento Bee | 353,366 | 285,762 | Minneapolis Star | | |
| Los Angeles Times | 1,361,988 | 1,068,812 | Tribune | 673,264 | 355,743 |
| Boston Globe | 751,377 | 466,317 | Baltimore Sun | 471,637 | 326,636 |
| Cincinnati Enquirer | 322,238 | 202,973 | Pittsburgh Post Gazette | 437,864 | 241,798 |
| Miami Herald | 492,235 | 362,184 | Rocky Mountain News | 415,962 | 326,189 |
| Chicago Tribune | 1,045,756 | 664,586 | Boston Herald | 193,462 | 285,930 |
| Detroit News | 789,666 | 236,246 | New Orleans | | |
| Houston Chronicle | 740,952 | 549,856 | Times-Picayune | 304,991 | 265,820 |
| Kansas City Star | 415,918 | 278,394 | Charlotte Observer | 301,026 | 238,216 |
| Omaha World | | | Hartford Courant | 303,191 | 217,759 |
| Herald | 291,764 | 234,106 | Rochester Democrat | | |
| Denver Post | 474,668 | 353,786 | and Chronicle | 246,520 | 147,331 |
| St. Louis | | | St. Paul Pioneer Press | 264,732 | 202,922 |
| Post-Dispatch | 539,421 | 318,994 | Providence | | |
| Portland Oregonian | 440,096 | 353,745 | Journal-Bulletin | 243,643 | 168,368 |
| Washington Post | 1,123,305 | 818,231 | | | |

DATA FILE
NEWSCIRC

*Source: From* Gale Directory of Publications, *1998, 131th edition. Edited by Carolyn Fischer. Gale Research,
1998. Copyright © 1998 by Gale Research, Inc. Reprinted by permission of Gale Research, Inc.*

# THE SPRINGVILLE HERALD CASE

In the implementation of the corporate strategic initiative of increasing home-delivery sales, the marketing department needs to work closely with the distribution department to accomplish a smooth initial delivery process for trial customers. This is of great importance in the effort to ensure that as many trial customers as possible are converted to long-term customers, because a strong negative impression will be created by any problems that occur during the first week of newspaper delivery.

As part of its role in this process, it is important for the marketing department to be able to forecast the number of new subscribers in future months. A team consisting of managers from the marketing and distribution departments was convened to de-velop a better method of forecasting new subscriptions. Melissa Hogue, the marketing department head, asked Lauren Hall, who specializes in market forecasting, to provide some ideas about how the forecasting methods used could be improved. Lauren, who was recently hired by the company to provide special skills in quantitative forecasting methods, asked the team how the forecasting of new subscriptions had been done in the past. Al Baum, a member of the team, answered that usually after examining new subscriptions in the previous 2 or 3 months, a group of three managers developed a consensus on what the final forecast should be. Lauren asked whether anyone had tried to determine what factors might be useful in helping to predict monthly new subscriptions. Al replied that the forecasts in the last year had been particularly inaccurate due to the fact that in some months a great deal of time had been spent on telemarketing, whereas in other months less effort was made. Lauren suggested that data for the past 2 years be obtained from company records. She was particularly interested in obtaining data for the number of new subscriptions and the number of hours spent on telemarketing for new subscriptions for each month. The following table indicates the number of new subscriptions for the month and the number of hours spent on telemarketing for new subscriptions.

## Number of new subscriptions and number of hours spent on telemarketing per month for 2-year time period

| TIME PERIOD | TELEMARKETING HOURS | NEW SUBSCRIPTIONS |
|---|---|---|
| 1 | 1,224 | 5,357 |
| 2 | 1,458 | 6,177 |
| 3 | 1,006 | 4,795 |
| 4 | 1,395 | 5,692 |
| 5 | 1,131 | 4,312 |
| 6 | 921 | 3,421 |
| 7 | 704 | 2,624 |
| 8 | 1,154 | 4,087 |
| 9 | 1,168 | 4,934 |
| 10 | 803 | 2,546 |
| 11 | 830 | 3,591 |
| 12 | 981 | 4,271 |
| 13 | 1,435 | 5,836 |
| 14 | 1,349 | 5,201 |
| 15 | 965 | 3,775 |
| 16 | 985 | 3,592 |
| 17 | 1,117 | 4,566 |
| 18 | 840 | 2,974 |
| 19 | 1,412 | 5,673 |
| 20 | 940 | 3,554 |
| 21 | 1,090 | 4,399 |
| 22 | 1498 | 6,143 |
| 23 | 1,240 | 4,827 |
| 24 | 1,055 | 5,418 |

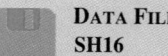

**DATA FILE
SH16**

## Exercises

**16.1** What criticism can you make concerning the previous method of forecasting that involved taking the new subscriptions for the last 3 months as the basis for future projections?

**16.2** What factors other than number of telemarketing hours spent might be useful in predicting the number of new subscriptions? Explain.

**16.3** (a) Analyze the data and develop a statistical model to predict the number of new subscriptions for a month based upon the number of hours spent on telemarketing for new subscriptions. Write a report giving detailed findings concerning the model that has been fit to the data.

**(b)** If there are expected to be 1,000 hours spent on telemarketing in the coming month, predict the number of new subscriptions expected for the month. Indicate the assumptions upon which this prediction is based. Do you think these assumptions are valid? Explain.

**(c)** What would be the danger of predicting the number of new subscriptions for a month in which 2,000 hours are spent on telemarketing? Explain.

## References

1. Anscombe, F. J., "Graphs in Statistical Analysis," *American Statistician* 27 (1973): 17–21.
2. Hoaglin, D. C., and R. Welsch, "The Hat Matrix in Regression and ANOVA," *The American Statistician* 32 (1978): 17–22.
3. Hocking, R. R., "Developments in Linear Regression Methodology: 1959–1982," *Technometrics* 25 (1983): 219–250.
4. Hosmer, D., and S. Lemeshow, *Applied Logistic Regression* (New York: Wiley, 1989).
5. *Microsoft Excel 97* (Redmond, WA: Microsoft Corp., 1997).
6. *Minitab for Windows Version 12* (State College, PA: Minitab, Inc., 1998).
7. Neter, J., M. H. Kutner, C. J. Nachtsheim, and W. Wasserman, *Applied Linear Statistical Models*, 4th ed. (Homewood, IL: Irwin, 1996).
8. Ramsey, P. P., and P. H. Ramsey, "Simple Tests of Normality in Small Samples," *Journal of Quality Technology* 22 (1990): 299–309.

## ❖ APPENDIX 16.1 USING MICROSOFT EXCEL FOR SIMPLE LINEAR REGRESSION

### COMMENT: PHStat Add-In Users

If Microsoft Excel is not running, click the **PHStat** add-in icon. If Microsoft Excel is running, select **File | Open**. Select the PHStat add-in file **PHSA.XLA**. Click the **Open** button.

To perform a regression analysis, select **PHStat | Regression | Simple Linear Regression**. Enter the cell range for the *Y* and *X* variables in their respective edit boxes. Select the Scatter Diagram check box. Select the Regression statistics, ANOVA, Coefficients, and, Residuals Table and Residual Plot check boxes if desired. If the Durbin-Watson statistic needs to be calculated, select the Durbin-Watson edit box. If confidence and prediction intervals are to be computed, select the Confidence and Prediction Interval check box, and enter a specified value in the *X* value edit box. Click the **OK** button.

### Using the Microsoft Excel Chart Wizard and TREND Function for Regression Analysis

In this chapter we have developed the least-squares method to compute the regression coefficients and used the regression model obtained to predict the average annual sales for a store with a given number of square feet. We can use the Chart Wizard that was previously discussed in chapter 3 to obtain a scatter diagram and the line of regression for these data. With the SITE.XLS workbook open, click on the Data sheet tab. Select **Insert | Chart**.

In the Step 1 Dialog box, select the **Standard types** tab and then select **XY (Scatter)** from the Chart type: list box. Select the first choice of the first row of chart Subtypes, the choice designated as "Scatter, compares pairs of values." Click the **Next** button.

In the Step 2 Dialog box, select the Data Range tab and enter **Data!B1:C15** in the Data range: edit box. Note that the first variable is the $X$ variable and the second variable is the $Y$ variable. Select the **Columns** option button in the Series in: group. Select the **Series** tab. Enter **=Data!B1:B15** in the Value(X) Axis edit box. Click the **Next** button.

In the Step 3 Dialog box, select the Titles tab. Enter Regression Analysis in the Chart title edit box, enter **Square Feet** in the Category (X) axis: edit box, and enter **Sales** in the Value (Y) axis: edit box. Select the **Gridlines** tab. Deselect all check boxes. Select the **Legend** tab. Deselect all check boxes. Click the **Next** button.

In the Step 4 Dialog box, select the **As new sheet:** option button and enter **Trend** in the edit box to the right of the option button. Click the **Finish** button. To superimpose a line of regression on this scatter diagram, right click any of the plotted points and select **Add Trendline**. In the Add Trendline dialog box that appears, select the **Type** tab. Select the **Linear** choice in the Trend/Regression type group. Select the **Options** tab of this dialog box. Select the **Display Equation on Chart** and **Display R-Squared Value on Chart** check boxes. Click the **OK** button.

Now that we have fit the regression model to a set of data, we need to be able to predict the average value of $Y$ for a given value of $X$ as was explained in section 16.2 on page 737. This may be accomplished through the use of the Excel TREND function. The general format of the TREND function is

$$=\text{TREND}(\text{range of } Y \text{ variable, range of } X \text{ variable, value of } X)$$

Suppose we want to use Excel to obtain a prediction of the average sales when there are 4,000 square feet, as we did in section 16.2. With the SITE.XLS workbook open, we can obtain the prediction by entering the formula **=TREND(Data!C2:C15,Data!B2:B15,4000)** in a cell.

## Using the Data Analysis Tool for Regression

The Data Analysis Tool of Microsoft Excel can be used instead of the TREND function to obtain a more complete regression analysis. To access the Regression option of Data Analysis, open the SITE.XLS workbook, and click the **Data** sheet tab. Select **Tools | Data Analysis**, select **Regression** in the Analysis Tools list box, and click the **OK** button. In the Regression dialog box that appears, enter **C1:C15** in the Input $Y$ Range edit box and **B1:B15** in the Input $X$ Range edit box. Select the **Labels** check box. Select the **Confidence Level** check box and set the level to 95%. Select the **New Worksheet Ply** option button and enter Regression as the name. Select the **Residuals, Standardized Residuals**, and **Residual Plots** check boxes. Click the **OK** button.

## Using the Microsoft Excel CORREL Function for Correlation Analysis

The most direct way to obtain the correlation coefficient between two variables with Excel is to use the CORREL function. The general format of the CORREL function is

$$=\text{CORREL}(\text{range of } Y \text{ variable, range of } X \text{ variable})$$

To illustrate this for the currency data of Table 16.8 on page 792, open the MARKYEN.XLS workbook and click the Data sheet tab. In cell B12, compute the correlation coefficient using the formula

$$=\textbf{CORREL(B2:B11,C2:C11)}$$

## ❖ APPENDIX 16.2 USING MINITAB FOR SIMPLE LINEAR REGRESSION

Minitab can be used for simple linear regression by selecting **Stat | Regression | Regression**. To illustrate the use of Minitab for simple linear regression with the site selection example of this chapter, open the SITE.MTP file. Select **Stat | Regression | Regression**. Enter **C3** or **Sales** in the Response edit box and **C2** or **Square Feet** in the Predictors edit box. Click the **Graphs** button. In the Graphs dialog box, for Residuals for Plots, select the **Standardized** option button. For Residual Plots, select the **Histogram of Residuals** check box. In the Residuals vs. the Variables edit box, enter **C2** or **Square Feet**. Click the **OK** button to return to the Regression dialog box. Click the **Results** button. In the Regression Results dialog box, click the **In addition, the full table of fits and residuals** button. Click the **OK** button to return to the Regression dialog box. Click the **Options** button. If the data have been collected over time, under Display, select the Durbin-Watson statistic check box. In the Prediction Interval for new Observations edit box, enter **4000**. Click the **OK** button to return to the Regression dialog box. Click the **OK** button.

This multiple linear regression model can be compared with the simple linear regression model [equation (16.1)] expressed as

$$Y_i = \beta_0 + \beta_1 X_i + \epsilon_i$$

In the case of the simple linear regression model we note that the slope $\beta_1$ represents the change in the mean of $Y$ per unit change in $X$ and does not take into account any other variables besides the single independent variable included in the model. In the multiple linear regression model [equation (17.2)], the slope $\beta_1$ represents the change in the mean of $Y$ per unit change in $X_1$, taking into account the effect of $X_2$. It is referred to as a **net regression coefficient**.

As in the case of simple linear regression, the sample regression coefficients ($b_0$, $b_1$, and $b_2$) are used as estimates of the true parameters ($\beta_0$, $\beta_1$, and $\beta_2$). Thus, the sample regression equation for a multiple linear regression model with two explanatory variables is

**Multiple Linear Regression Equation with Two Independent Variables**

$$\hat{Y}_i = b_0 + b_1 X_{1i} + b_2 X_{2i} \tag{17.3}$$

Using the least-squares method, we obtain the values of the three sample regression coefficients from Microsoft Excel (see appendix 17.1) or Minitab (see appendix 17.2). Figure 17.2 presents partial output for the monthly heating oil consumption data from Microsoft Excel, and Figure 17.3 presents partial output from Minitab.

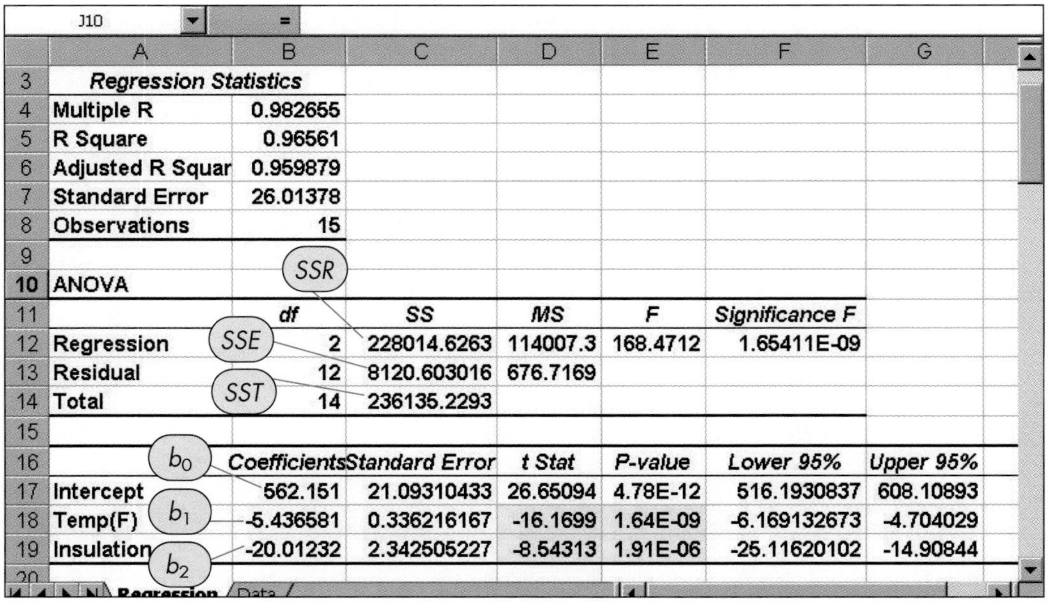

| | A | B | C | D | E | F | G |
|---|---|---|---|---|---|---|---|
| 3 | *Regression Statistics* | | | | | | |
| 4 | Multiple R | 0.982655 | | | | | |
| 5 | R Square | 0.96561 | | | | | |
| 6 | Adjusted R Squar | 0.959879 | | | | | |
| 7 | Standard Error | 26.01378 | | | | | |
| 8 | Observations | 15 | | | | | |
| 9 | | | | | | | |
| 10 | ANOVA | | | | | | |
| 11 | | *df* | *SS* | *MS* | *F* | *Significance F* | |
| 12 | Regression | 2 | 228014.6263 | 114007.3 | 168.4712 | 1.65411E-09 | |
| 13 | Residual | 12 | 8120.603016 | 676.7169 | | | |
| 14 | Total | 14 | 236135.2293 | | | | |
| 15 | | | | | | | |
| 16 | | *Coefficients* | *Standard Error* | *t Stat* | *P-value* | *Lower 95%* | *Upper 95%* |
| 17 | Intercept | 562.151 | 21.09310433 | 26.65094 | 4.78E-12 | 516.1930837 | 608.10893 |
| 18 | Temp(F) | -5.436581 | 0.336216167 | -16.1699 | 1.64E-09 | -6.169132673 | -4.704029 |
| 19 | Insulation | -20.01232 | 2.342505227 | -8.54313 | 1.91E-06 | -25.11620102 | -14.90844 |



**PANEL A**

**FIGURE 17.2** Partial output obtained from Microsoft Excel for the monthly heating oil consumption data

Continued

| | A | B | C | D |
|---|---|---|---|---|
| 23 | RESIDUAL OUTPUT | | | |
| 24 | | | | |
| 25 | Observation | Predicted Gallons | Residuals | |
| 26 | 1 | 284.6508237 | -9.350823711 | |
| 27 | 2 | 355.3263714 | 8.473628646 | |
| 28 | 3 | 144.564579 | 19.73542095 | |
| 29 | 4 | 45.20670231 | -4.406702309 | |
| 30 | 5 | 94.1359276 | 0.164072399 | |
| 31 | 6 | 257.2333452 | -26.33334524 | |
| 32 | 7 | 393.1478599 | -26.44785994 | |
| 33 | 8 | 318.5351579 | -17.93515786 | |
| 34 | 9 | 236.986449 | 0.813550957 | |
| 35 | 10 | 159.6094702 | -38.20947019 | |
| 36 | 11 | 8.650064348 | 22.74993565 | |
| 37 | 12 | 219.1772811 | -15.67728112 | |
| 38 | 13 | 387.9458549 | 53.15414512 | |
| 39 | 14 | 295.5239849 | 27.47601511 | |
| 40 | 15 | 46.70612846 | 5.793871536 | |

**PANEL B**

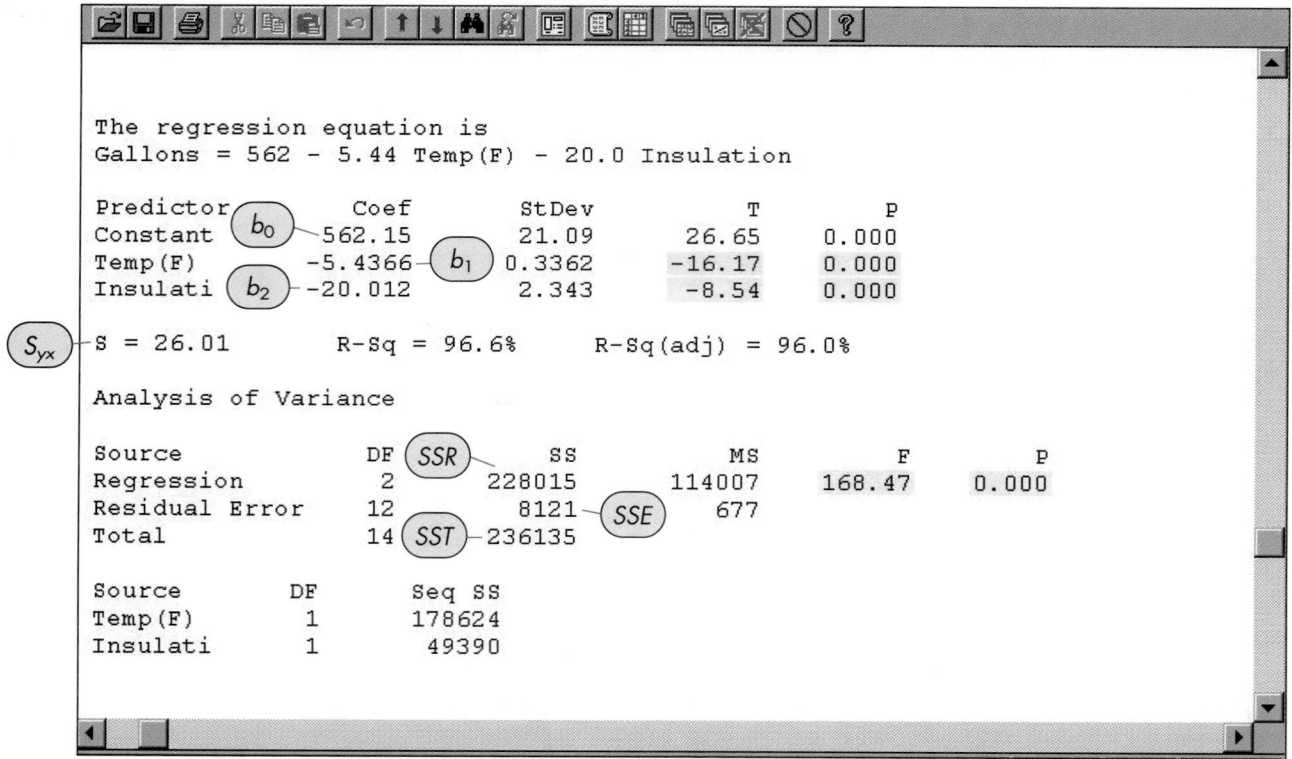

**PANEL A**

**FIGURE 17.3** Partial output obtained from Minitab for the monthly heating oil consumption data

*Continued*

| Obs | Temp(F) | Gallons | Fit | StDev Fit | Residual | St Resid |
|---|---|---|---|---|---|---|
| 1 | 40.0 | 275.30 | 284.65 | 10.30 | -9.35 | -0.39 |
| 2 | 27.0 | 363.80 | 355.33 | 11.20 | 8.47 | 0.36 |
| 3 | 40.0 | 164.30 | 144.56 | 10.90 | 19.74 | 0.84 |
| 4 | 73.0 | 40.80 | 45.21 | 12.92 | -4.41 | -0.20 |
| 5 | 64.0 | 94.30 | 94.14 | 10.46 | 0.16 | 0.01 |
| 6 | 34.0 | 230.90 | 257.23 | 7.08 | -26.33 | -1.05 |
| 7 | 9.0 | 366.70 | 393.15 | 12.49 | -26.45 | -1.16 |
| 8 | 8.0 | 300.60 | 318.54 | 15.44 | -17.94 | -0.86 |
| 9 | 23.0 | 237.80 | 236.99 | 12.39 | 0.81 | 0.04 |
| 10 | 63.0 | 121.40 | 159.61 | 12.87 | -38.21 | -1.69 |
| 11 | 65.0 | 31.40 | 8.65 | 13.67 | 22.75 | 1.03 |
| 12 | 41.0 | 203.50 | 219.18 | 6.77 | -15.68 | -0.62 |
| 13 | 21.0 | 441.10 | 387.95 | 12.13 | 53.15 | 2.31R |
| 14 | 38.0 | 323.00 | 295.52 | 10.32 | 27.48 | 1.15 |
| 15 | 58.0 | 52.50 | 46.71 | 12.39 | 5.79 | 0.25 |

**PANEL B**

From Figure 17.2 or 17.3 we observe that the computed values of the regression coefficients are

$$b_0 = 562.151 \quad b_1 = -5.43658 \quad b_2 = -20.0123$$

Therefore, the multiple regression equation can be expressed as

$$\hat{Y}_i = 562.151 - 5.43658X_{1i} - 20.0123X_{2i}$$

where

$\hat{Y}_i$ = predicted average amount of heating oil consumed (gallons) during January for house $i$

$X_{1i}$ = average daily atmospheric temperature (°F) during January for house $i$

$X_{2i}$ = amount of attic insulation (inches) for house $i$

The $Y$ intercept $b_0$, computed as 562.151, estimates the expected number of gallons of heating oil that would be consumed in January when the average daily atmospheric temperature is 0°F for a home that is not insulated (a house with 0 inches of attic insulation).

The slope of average daily atmospheric temperature with heating oil consumption ($b_1$, computed as -5.43658) means that for a home with a given number of inches of attic insulation, the expected heating oil consumption is estimated to decrease by 5.43658 gallons per month for each 1°F increase in average daily atmospheric temperature. The slope of amount of attic insulation with heating oil consumption ($b_2$, computed as -20.0123) means that for a month with a given average daily atmospheric temperature, the expected heating oil consumption is estimated to decrease by 20.0123 gallons for each additional inch of attic insulation.

We have stated that the regression coefficients in multiple regression are net regression coefficients that measure the average change in $Y$ per unit change in a particular $X$ holding constant the effect of the other $X$ variables. For example, in our study of heating oil consumption we have stated that for a home with a given number of inches of attic insulation, the expected heating oil consumption is estimated to decrease by 5.43658 gallons per month for each 1°F increase in average daily atmospheric temperature. Another way of interpreting this is to think of similar homes with an equal amount of attic insulation that are located in different geographic areas. For such homes (with attic insulation the same), expected heating oil consumption is predicted to decrease by 5.43658 gallons per month for each 1°F increase in average daily atmospheric temperature.

In a similar manner, the slope of heating oil consumption with attic insulation can be viewed from the perspective of two similar houses (except for the amount of attic insulation) that are located right next to each other. For these houses, the expected heating oil consumption is estimated to decrease by 20.0123 gallons for each additional inch of attic insulation. It is this conditional nature of the interpretation that is critical to understanding the magnitude of each slope. Otherwise, we could just compare the slopes.

## Predicting the Dependent Variable Y

Now that the multiple regression model has been fitted to these data, we can predict the monthly consumption of home heating oil and develop confidence and prediction interval estimates assuming that the regression model fitted is an appropriate one.

Suppose we want to predict the number of gallons of heating oil consumed in a house that has 6 inches of attic insulation during a month in which the average daily atmospheric temperature is 30°F. Using our multiple regression equation

$$\hat{Y}_i = 562.151 - 5.43658X_{1i} - 20.0123X_{2i}$$

with $X_{1i} = 30$ and $X_{2i} = 6$, we have

$$\hat{Y}_i = 562.151 - (5.43658)(30) - (20.0123)(6)$$

and thus

$$\hat{Y}_i = 278.9798$$

Therefore, we estimate that an average of 278.98 gallons of heating oil would be used in houses with 6 inches of insulation when the average temperature is 30°F.

Once the prediction of $\hat{Y}_i$ has been obtained after conducting a residual analysis and an influence analysis (see sections 17.2 and 17.3), the next step involves the development of a desired confidence interval estimate of the mean response and a prediction interval of the individual response. In section 16.8, methods for obtaining these estimates were examined for the simple linear regression model. However, the development of similar estimates for the multiple regression model is more computationally complex. Confidence and prediction interval estimates obtained from Minitab for the case of predicting the heating oil usage for houses with 6 inches of insulation when the average temperature is 30°F are presented in Figure 17.4.

The 95% confidence interval estimate of the average heating oil use under these circumstances is between 262.44 and 295.51 gallons; the prediction interval estimate for an

```
Predicted Values

   Fit  StDev Fit        95.0% CI              95.0% PI
 278.98        7.59   ( 262.44,  295.51)   ( 219.94,  338.02)
```

**FIGURE 17.4** Confidence and prediction interval estimates for heating oil usage example obtained from Minitab

individual house is between 219.94 and 338.02 gallons. Once again we note that because the prediction interval is for a single house, its interval is much wider than the estimate for the average house.

## Coefficients of Multiple Determination

You may recall from section 16.3 that once a regression model has been developed, we can compute the coefficient of determination $r^2$. In multiple regression, because there are at least two explanatory variables, the **coefficient of multiple determination** represents the proportion of the variation in $Y$ that is explained by the set of explanatory variables selected. For data with two explanatory variables, the coefficient of multiple determination ($r^2_{Y.12}$) is given by

### The Coefficient of Multiple Determination

The coefficient of multiple determination is equal to the regression sum of squares divided by the total sum of squares.

$$r^2_{Y.12} = \frac{SSR}{SST} \qquad (17.4)$$

where

$$SSR = \text{regression sum of squares}$$
$$SST = \text{total sum of squares}$$

In the heating oil consumption example, from Figure 17.2 or 17.3, $SSR = 228,015$ and $SST = 236,135$ (rounded). Thus,

$$r^2_{Y.12} = \frac{SSR}{SST} = \frac{228,015}{236,135} = .9656$$

This coefficient of multiple determination, computed as .9656, means that 96.56% of the variation in home heating oil consumption can be explained by the variation in the average daily atmospheric temperature and the variation in the amount of attic insulation.

However, when dealing with multiple regression models, some researchers suggest that an **adjusted** $r^2$ be computed to reflect both the number of explanatory variables in the model and the sample size. This is especially necessary when we are comparing two or more regression models that predict the same dependent variable but have different numbers of explanatory or predictor variables. Thus, the adjusted $r^2$ is

## Adjusted $r^2$

$$r^2_{adj} = 1 - \left[ (1 - r^2_{Y.12\ldots p}) \frac{n-1}{n-p-1} \right] \tag{17.5}$$

where

$$p = \text{number of explanatory variables in the regression equation}$$

Thus, for our monthly heating oil consumption data, because $r^2_{Y.12} = .9656$, $n = 15$, and $p = 2$,

$$r^2_{adj} = 1 - \left[ (1 - r^2_{Y.12}) \frac{(15-1)}{(15-2-1)} \right]$$

$$= 1 - \left[ (1 - .9656) \frac{14}{12} \right]$$

$$= 1 - .04$$

$$= .96$$

Hence, 96% of the variation in monthly heating oil consumption can be explained by our multiple regression model—adjusted for number of predictors and sample size.

## Problems for Section 17.1

### Learning the Basics

- **17.1** Suppose that you have obtained the following multiple regression model:

    $$\hat{Y}_i = 10 + 5X_{1i} + 3X_{2i} \quad \text{and} \quad r^2_{Y.12} = .60$$

    (a) Interpret the meaning of the slopes.
    (b) Interpret the meaning of the $Y$ intercept.
    (c) Interpret the meaning of the coefficient of multiple determination $r^2_{Y.12}$.

    **17.2** Suppose that you have obtained the following multiple regression model:

    $$\hat{Y}_i = 50 - 2X_{1i} + 7X_{2i} \quad \text{and} \quad r^2_{Y.12} = .40$$

    (a) Interpret the meaning of the slopes.
    (b) Interpret the meaning of the $Y$ intercept.
    (c) Interpret the meaning of the coefficient of multiple determination $r^2_{Y.12}$.

### Applying the Concepts

- **17.3** A marketing analyst for a major shoe manufacturer is considering the development of a new brand of running shoes. The marketing analyst wishes to determine which variables can be used in predicting durability (or the effect of long-term impact). Two independent variables are to be considered, $X_1$ (FOREIMP), a measurement of the forefoot shock-absorbing capability, and $X_2$ (MIDSOLE), a measurement of the change in impact properties over time, along with the dependent variable $Y$ (LTIMP), which is a measure of the long-term ability to absorb shock after a repeated impact test. A random sample of 15 types of currently manufactured running shoes was selected for testing. Using Excel, we provide the following (partial) output:

| ANOVA | df | SS | MS | F | SIGNIFICANCE F |
|---|---|---|---|---|---|
| Regression | 2 | 12.61020 | 6.30510 | 97.69 | 0.0001 |
| Residual | 12 | 0.77453 | 0.06454 | | |
| Total | 14 | 13.38473 | | | |

| VARIABLE | COEFFICIENTS | STANDARD ERROR | t STAT | p-VALUE |
|---|---|---|---|---|
| Intercept | −0.02686 | .06905 | −0.39 | |
| Foreimp | 0.79116 | .06295 | 12.57 | .0000 |
| Midsole | 0.60484 | .07174 | 8.43 | .0000 |

(a) Assuming that each independent variable is linearly related to long-term impact, state the multiple regression equation.
(b) Interpret the meaning of the slopes in this problem.
(c) Compute the coefficient of multiple determination $r_{Y.12}^2$ and interpret its meaning.
(d) Compute the adjusted $r^2$.

**17.4** A mail-order catalog business selling personal computer supplies, software, and hardware maintains a centralized warehouse for the distribution of products ordered. Management is currently examining the process of distribution from the warehouse and is interested in studying the factors that affect warehouse distribution costs. Currently, a small handling fee is added to the order, regardless of the amount of the order. Data have been collected over the past 24 months indicating the warehouse distribution costs, the sales, and the number of orders received. The results are as follows:

### Distribution cost data

| MONTH | DISTRIBUTION COST ($000) | SALES ($000) | ORDERS | MONTH | DISTRIBUTION COST ($000) | SALES ($000) | ORDERS |
|---|---|---|---|---|---|---|---|
| 1 | 52.95 | 386 | 4,015 | 13 | 62.98 | 372 | 3,977 |
| 2 | 71.66 | 446 | 3,806 | 14 | 72.30 | 328 | 4,428 |
| 3 | 85.58 | 512 | 5,309 | 15 | 58.99 | 408 | 3,964 |
| 4 | 63.69 | 401 | 4,262 | 16 | 79.38 | 491 | 4,582 |
| 5 | 72.81 | 457 | 4,296 | 17 | 94.44 | 527 | 5,582 |
| 6 | 68.44 | 458 | 4,097 | 18 | 59.74 | 444 | 3,450 |
| 7 | 52.46 | 301 | 3,213 | 19 | 90.50 | 623 | 5,079 |
| 8 | 70.77 | 484 | 4,809 | 20 | 93.24 | 596 | 5,735 |
| 9 | 82.03 | 517 | 5,237 | 21 | 69.33 | 463 | 4,269 |
| 10 | 74.39 | 503 | 4,732 | 22 | 53.71 | 389 | 3,708 |
| 11 | 70.84 | 535 | 4,413 | 23 | 89.18 | 547 | 5,387 |
| 12 | 54.08 | 353 | 2,921 | 24 | 66.80 | 415 | 4,161 |

DATA FILE
WARECOST

On the basis of the results obtained:
(a) State the multiple regression equation.
(b) Interpret the meaning of the slopes in this problem.
(c) Predict the average monthly warehouse distribution costs when sales are $400,000 and the number of orders is 4,500.
(d) Compute the coefficient of multiple determination $r_{Y.12}^2$ and interpret its meaning.
(e) Compute the adjusted $r^2$.

**17.5** Suppose that a consumer organization wanted to develop a model to predict gasoline mileage as measured by miles per gallon (MPG) based on the horsepower of the car's engine and the weight of the car. A sample of 50 recent car models was selected with the following results:

| MPG | HORSEPOWER | WEIGHT | MPG | HORSEPOWER | WEIGHT |
|---|---|---|---|---|---|
| 43.1 | 48 | 1,985 | 23.9 | 90 | 3,420 |
| 19.9 | 110 | 3,365 | 29.9 | 65 | 2,380 |
| 19.2 | 105 | 3,535 | 30.4 | 67 | 3,250 |
| 17.7 | 165 | 3,445 | 36.0 | 74 | 1,980 |
| 18.1 | 139 | 3,205 | 22.6 | 110 | 2,800 |
| 20.3 | 103 | 2,830 | 36.4 | 67 | 2,950 |
| 21.5 | 115 | 3,245 | 27.5 | 95 | 2,560 |
| 16.9 | 155 | 4,360 | 33.7 | 75 | 2,210 |
| 15.5 | 142 | 4,054 | 44.6 | 67 | 1,850 |
| 18.5 | 150 | 3,940 | 32.9 | 100 | 2,615 |
| 27.2 | 71 | 3,190 | 38.0 | 67 | 1,965 |
| 41.5 | 76 | 2,144 | 24.2 | 120 | 2,930 |
| 46.6 | 65 | 2,110 | 38.1 | 60 | 1,968 |
| 23.7 | 100 | 2,420 | 39.4 | 70 | 2,070 |
| 27.2 | 84 | 2,490 | 25.4 | 116 | 2,900 |
| 39.1 | 58 | 1,755 | 31.3 | 75 | 2,542 |
| 28.0 | 88 | 2,605 | 34.1 | 68 | 1,985 |
| 24.0 | 92 | 2,865 | 34.0 | 88 | 2,395 |
| 20.2 | 139 | 3,570 | 31.0 | 82 | 2,720 |
| 20.5 | 95 | 3,155 | 27.4 | 80 | 2,670 |
| 28.0 | 90 | 2,678 | 22.3 | 88 | 2,890 |
| 34.7 | 63 | 2,215 | 28.0 | 79 | 2,625 |
| 36.1 | 66 | 1,800 | 17.6 | 85 | 3,465 |
| 35.7 | 80 | 1,915 | 34.4 | 65 | 3,465 |
| 20.2 | 85 | 2,965 | 20.6 | 105 | 3,380 |

**DATA FILE
AUTO**

On the basis of the results obtained:
(a) State the multiple regression equation.
(b) Interpret the meaning of the slopes in this problem.
(c) Predict the average miles per gallon for a car that has 60 horsepower and weighs 2,000 pounds.
(d) Compute the coefficient of multiple determination $r_{Y.12}^2$ and interpret its meaning.
(e) Compute the adjusted $r^2$.

• **17.6** Suppose a large consumer products company wants to measure the effectiveness of different types of advertising media in the promotion of its products. Specifically, two types of advertising media are to be considered: radio and television advertising and newspaper advertising (including the cost of discount coupons). A sample of 22 cities with approximately equal populations is selected for study during a test period of 1 month. Each city is allocated a specific expenditure level for both radio and television advertising and also newspaper advertising. The sales of the product (in thousands of dollars) and the levels of media expenditure during the test month are recorded with the following results:

| City | Sales ($000) | Radio and Television Advertising ($000) | Newspaper Advertising ($000) | City | Sales ($000) | Radio and Television Advertising ($000) | Newspaper Advertising ($000) |
|---|---|---|---|---|---|---|---|
| 1 | 973 | 0 | 40 | 12 | 1,577 | 45 | 45 |
| 2 | 1,119 | 0 | 40 | 13 | 1,044 | 50 | 0 |
| 3 | 875 | 25 | 25 | 14 | 914 | 50 | 0 |
| 4 | 625 | 25 | 25 | 15 | 1,329 | 55 | 25 |
| 5 | 910 | 30 | 30 | 16 | 1,330 | 55 | 25 |
| 6 | 971 | 30 | 30 | 17 | 1,405 | 60 | 30 |
| 7 | 931 | 35 | 35 | 18 | 1,436 | 60 | 30 |
| 8 | 1,177 | 35 | 35 | 19 | 1,521 | 65 | 35 |
| 9 | 882 | 40 | 25 | 20 | 1,741 | 65 | 35 |
| 10 | 982 | 40 | 25 | 21 | 1,866 | 70 | 40 |
| 11 | 1,628 | 45 | 45 | 22 | 1,717 | 70 | 40 |

**DATA FILE ADRADTV**

On the basis of the results obtained:
(a) State the multiple regression equation.
(b) Interpret the meaning of the slopes in this problem.
(c) Predict the average sales for a city in which radio and television advertising is $20,000 and newspaper advertising is $20,000.
(d) Compute the coefficient of multiple determination $r^2_{Y.12}$ and interpret its meaning.
(e) Compute the adjusted $r^2$.

**17.7** The director of broadcasting operations for a television station wants to study the issue of "standby hours," hours in which unionized graphic artists at the station are paid but are not actually involved in any activity. The variables to be considered are:

Standby hours ($Y$)—the total number of standby hours per week
Total staff present ($X_1$)—the weekly total of people-days over a 7-day week
Remote hours ($X_2$)—the total number of hours worked by employees at locations away from the central plant

The results for a period of 26 weeks are shown as follows.

| Week | Standby Hours | Total Staff Present | Remote Hours | Week | Standby Hours | Total Staff Present | Remote Hours |
|---|---|---|---|---|---|---|---|
| 1 | 245 | 338 | 414 | 14 | 161 | 307 | 402 |
| 2 | 177 | 333 | 598 | 15 | 274 | 322 | 151 |
| 3 | 271 | 358 | 656 | 16 | 245 | 335 | 228 |
| 4 | 211 | 372 | 631 | 17 | 201 | 350 | 271 |
| 5 | 196 | 339 | 528 | 18 | 183 | 339 | 440 |
| 6 | 135 | 289 | 409 | 19 | 237 | 327 | 475 |
| 7 | 195 | 334 | 382 | 20 | 175 | 328 | 347 |
| 8 | 118 | 293 | 399 | 21 | 152 | 319 | 449 |
| 9 | 116 | 325 | 343 | 22 | 188 | 325 | 336 |
| 10 | 147 | 311 | 338 | 23 | 188 | 322 | 267 |
| 11 | 154 | 304 | 353 | 24 | 197 | 317 | 235 |
| 12 | 146 | 312 | 289 | 25 | 261 | 315 | 164 |
| 13 | 115 | 283 | 388 | 26 | 232 | 331 | 270 |

**DATA FILE STANDBY**

On the basis of the results obtained:

(a) State the multiple regression model.

(b) Interpret the meaning of the slopes in this problem.

(c) Predict the average standby hours for a week in which the total staff present is 310 people-days and the remote hours are 400.

(d) Compute the coefficient of multiple determination $r^2_{Y.12}$ and interpret its meaning.

(e) Compute the adjusted $r^2$.

## 17.2 RESIDUAL ANALYSIS FOR THE MULTIPLE REGRESSION MODEL

In section 16.5 we used residual analysis to evaluate whether the simple linear regression model is appropriate for the set of data being studied. In examining a multiple linear regression model with two explanatory variables, the residual plots listed in Exhibit 17.1 are of particular interest:

### Exhibit 17.1 Residual Plots Used in Multiple Regression

✓ **1.** Residuals versus $\hat{Y}_i$

✓ **2.** Residuals versus $X_{1i}$

✓ **3.** Residuals versus $X_{2i}$

✓ **4.** Residuals versus time

The first residual plot examines the pattern of residuals for the predicted values of $Y$. If the residuals show a pattern for different values of the predicted value of $Y$, it provides evidence of a possible curvilinear effect in at least one explanatory variable and/or the need to transform the $Y$ variable. The second and third residual plots involve the explanatory variables. Patterns in the plot of the residuals versus an explanatory variable may indicate the existence of a curvilinear effect and, therefore, lead to the possible transformation of that explanatory variable. The fourth type of plot is used to investigate patterns in the residuals when the data have been collected in time order. Associated with the residual plot versus time, as in section 16.6, the Durbin-Watson statistic can be computed and the existence of positive autocorrelation among the residuals can be determined.

The residual plots are available as part of the output of virtually all statistical and spreadsheet software. Figure 17.5 consists of the residual plots obtained from Minitab for the monthly heating oil consumption example. We can observe from Figure 17.5 that there appears to be very little or no pattern in the relationship between the residuals and either the value of $X_1$ (temperature), the value of $X_2$ (attic insulation), or the predicted value of $Y$. Thus, we may conclude that the multiple linear regression model is appropriate for predicting heating oil usage.

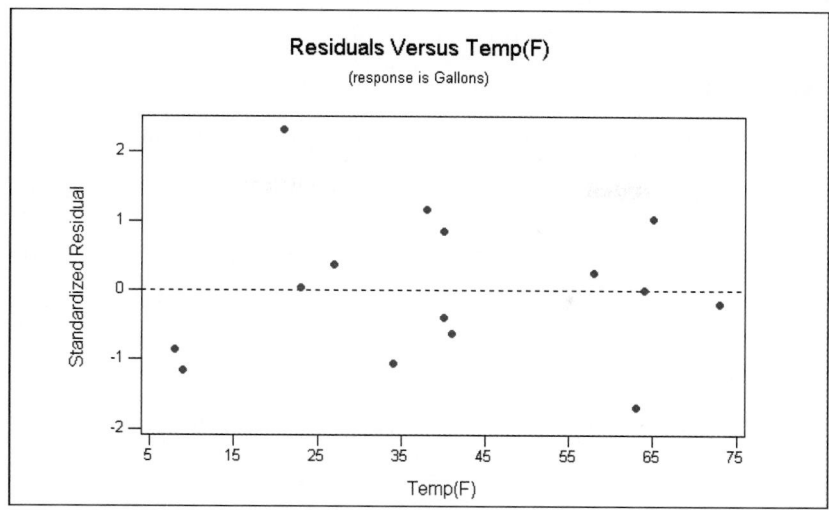

**PANEL A**

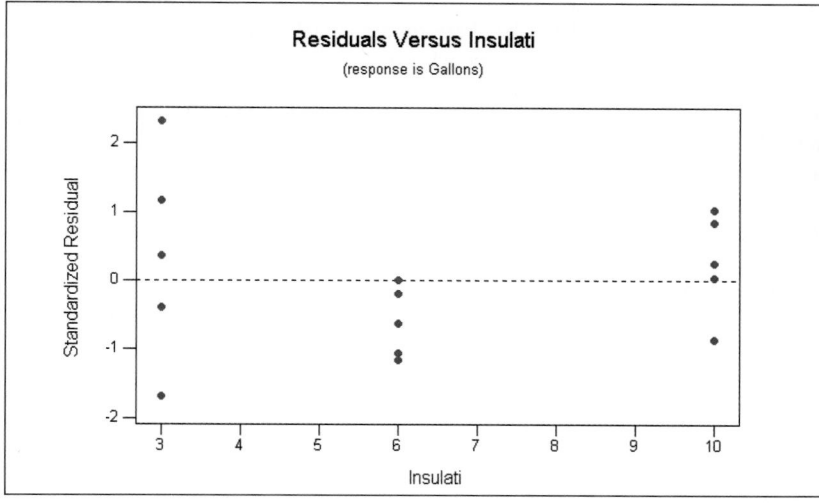

**PANEL B**

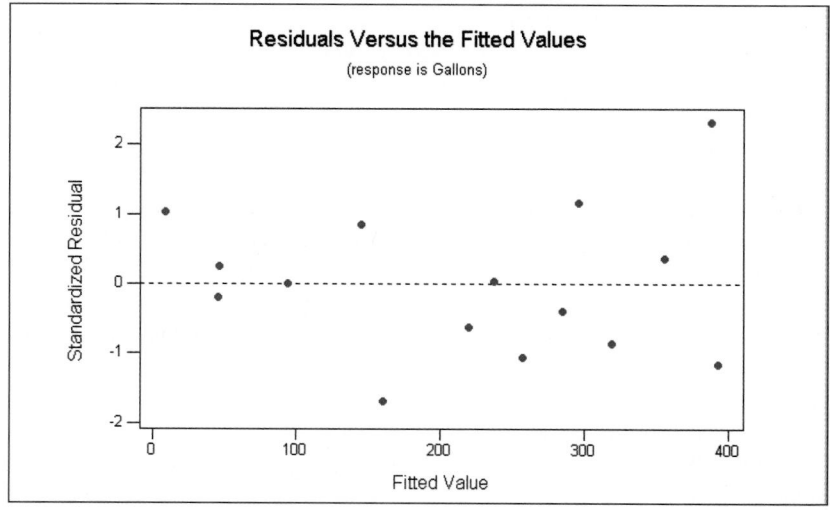

**PANEL C**

**FIGURE 17.5** Residual plots for monthly heating oil consumption model obtained from Minitab, panels A, B, and C

## Problems for Section 17.2

### Applying the Concepts

**17.8**  In Problem 17.4 on page 821 sales and number of orders were used to predict distribution cost at a mail-order catalog business.
(a)  Perform a residual analysis on your results and determine the adequacy of the fit of the model.
(b)  Plot the residuals against the months. Is there any evidence of a pattern in the residuals? Explain.
(c)  Compute the Durbin-Watson statistic.
(d)  At the .05 level of significance, is there evidence of positive autocorrelation in the residuals?

**17.9**  In Problem 17.5 on page 822 horsepower and weight were used to predict gasoline mileage. Perform a residual analysis on your results and determine the adequacy of the fit of the model.

● **17.10**  In Problem 17.6 on page 822 the amount of radio and television advertising and newspaper advertising was used to predict sales. Perform a residual analysis on your results and determine the adequacy of the fit of the model.

**17.11**  In Problem 17.7 on page 823 the total staff present and remote hours were used to predict standby hours.
(a)  Perform a residual analysis on your results and determine the adequacy of the fit of the model.
(b)  Plot the residuals against the weeks. Is there evidence of a pattern in the residuals? Explain.
(c)  Compute the Durbin-Watson statistic.
(d)  At the .05 level of significance, is there evidence of positive autocorrelation in the residuals?

## 17.3  INFLUENCE ANALYSIS

**Regression diagnostics** deals with both the evaluation of the aptness of a particular model and the potential effect or influence of each particular point on that fitted model. In sections 16.5 and 17.2 we used methods of residual analysis to study the aptness of our fitted model. In this section we consider several methods that measure the influence of particular data points. Among a variety of criteria (see references 1, 3, and 6) we consider the following:

**1.** The hat matrix elements $h_i$

**2.** The Studentized deleted residuals $t_i^*$

**3.** Cook's distance statistic $D_i$

Figure 17.6 presents the values of these statistics for the heating oil data of Table 17.1, which have been obtained from the Minitab computer package. We note from Figure 17.6 that certain data points have been highlighted for further analysis.

## The Hat Matrix Elements $h_i$

In section 16.8, when we developed a confidence-interval estimate $\mu_{YX}$ and the prediction interval estimate $Y_I$, we defined the **hat matrix diagonal elements** $h_i$ as

### Hat Matrix Diagonal Elements $h_i$

$$h_i = \frac{1}{n} + \frac{(X_i - \bar{X})^2}{\sum\limits_{i=1}^{n}(X_i - \bar{X})^2}$$

(17.6)

Each $h_i$ reflects the possible influence of each $X_i$ on the fitted regression model. If potentially influential points are present, we may need to reevaluate the necessity for keeping them in the model. In a regression model containing $p$ explanatory variables, Hoaglin and Welsch (see reference 5) suggest the following decision rule:

$$\text{If } h_i > 2(p + 1)/n$$

then $X_i$ is an influential point and may be considered a candidate for removal from the model.

| | C1 | C2 | C3 | C4 | C5 | C6 | C7 |
|---|---|---|---|---|---|---|---|
| ↓ | Gallons | Temp(F) | Insulation | t*DelRes | Hi | CookD | |
| 1 | 275.3 | 40 | 3 | -0.37720 | 0.156757 | 0.009495 | |
| 2 | 363.8 | 27 | 3 | 0.34740 | 0.185246 | 0.009870 | |
| 3 | 164.3 | 40 | 10 | 0.82438 | 0.175717 | 0.049616 | |
| 4 | 40.8 | 73 | 6 | -0.18717 | 0.246777 | 0.004161 | |
| 5 | 94.3 | 64 | 6 | 0.00660 | 0.161823 | 0.000003 | |
| 6 | 230.9 | 34 | 6 | -1.05714 | 0.074084 | 0.029517 | |
| 7 | 366.7 | 9 | 6 | -1.17765 | 0.230654 | 0.134267 | |
| 8 | 300.6 | 8 | 10 | -0.84633 | 0.352057 | 0.132868 | |
| 9 | 237.8 | 23 | 10 | 0.03405 | 0.226801 | 0.000124 | |
| 10 | 121.4 | 63 | 3 | -1.85367 | 0.244667 | 0.308398 | |
| 11 | 31.4 | 65 | 10 | 1.03043 | 0.275988 | 0.134224 | |
| 12 | 203.5 | 41 | 6 | -0.60751 | 0.067663 | 0.009424 | |
| 13 | 441.1 | 21 | 3 | 2.96740 | 0.217438 | 0.494132 | |
| 14 | 323.0 | 38 | 3 | 1.16802 | 0.157465 | 0.082488 | |
| 15 | 52.5 | 58 | 10 | 0.24317 | 0.226864 | 0.006276 | |
| 16 | | | | | | | |

**FIGURE 17.6**   Influence statistics obtained from Minitab for heating oil data

For our heating oil data, because $n = 15$ and $p = 2$, our criterion would be to flag any $h_i$ value greater than .40. Referring to Figure 17.6, we observe that none of the $h_i$ values exceed .36; therefore, on the basis of this criterion, there do not appear to be any observations that can be considered for removal from the model.

## The Studentized Deleted Residuals $t_i^*$

In section 16.5 we defined the Studentized residuals in equation (16.11) on page 755 as

$$SR_i = \frac{e_i}{S_{YX}\sqrt{1 - h_i}}$$

In an effort to better measure the adverse impact of each individual case on the model, Hoaglin and Welsch (see reference 5) also developed the **Studentized deleted residual $t_i^*$** given in equation (17.7):

### Studentized Deleted Residual

$$t_i^* = \frac{e_{(i)}}{S_{(i)}\sqrt{1 - h_i}} \qquad (17.7)$$

where

$e_{(i)}$ = the difference between the observed $Y_i$ and predicted $\hat{Y}_i$ based on a model that includes all observations except observation $i$

$S_{(i)}$ = the standard error of the estimate for a model that includes all observations except observation $i$

This Studentized deleted residual measures the difference of each observation $Y_i$ from the value predicted by a model that includes *all other observations*. For example, $t_1^*$ represents a measure of the difference between the actual monthly heating oil usage for the first house ($Y_1 = 275.3$) and the monthly heating oil usage that would be predicted for this house based on a model that included only the 2d through the 15th houses. Hoaglin and Welsch suggest that if $t_i^* > t_{n-p-2}$ or $t_i^* < -t_{n-p-2}$ using a two-tailed test with a level of significance of .10, then the observed and predicted values are so different that observation $i$ is an influential point that adversely affects the model and may be considered a candidate for removal.

For our heating oil data, because $n = 15$ and $p = 2$, our criterion would be to flag any $t_i^*$ whose absolute value is greater than 1.7959 (see Table E.3). Referring to Figure 17.6, we note that $t_{10}^* = -1.854$ and $t_{13}^* = 2.967$. Thus, the 10th and 13th observations may each have an adverse effect on the model. We note that these points were not previously flagged according to the $h_i$ criterion. Because $h_i$ and $t_i^*$ measure different aspects of influence, we consider a third influence statistic, **Cook's $D_i$ statistic**, that is based on both $h_i$ and the Studentized residual.

## Cook's Distance Statistic $D_i$

The use of $h_i$ and $t_i^*$ in the search for potential troublesome data points is complementary. Neither criterion is sufficient by itself. When $h_i$ is small, $t_i^*$ may be large. On the other hand, when $h_i$ is large, $t_i^*$ may be moderate or small because the observed $Y_i$ is consistent with the model and the rest of the data. To decide whether a point that has been flagged by either the $h_i$ or $t_i^*$ criterion is unduly affecting the model, Cook and Weisberg (see reference 4) suggest the use of the $D_i$ statistic. In the simple linear regression model, $D_i$ is shown in equation (17.8):

## Cook's $D_i$ Statistic

$$D_i = \frac{SR_i^2 h_i}{2(1 - h_i)} \qquad (17.8)$$

where $SR_i$ is the Studentized residual of equation (16.11) on page 755.

Cook and Weisberg (see reference 4) suggest that if $D_i > F_{p+1,\, n-p-1}$, the critical value of the $F$ distribution having $p + 1$ degrees of freedom in the numerator and $n - p - 1$ degrees of freedom in the denominator at a .50 level of significance, then the observation may have an impact on the results of fitting a multiple regression model and could be a candidate for removal.

For our heating oil data, from Table E.6, because $n = 15$ and $p = 2$, we flag any $D_i > F_{3,12} = .835$. Referring to Figure 17.6, we note that none of the $D_i$ values exceed .495, so that according to this criterion there are no values that may be deleted. Hence, we have no clear basis for removing any of the observations from the multiple regression model.

## Overview

In this section we have discussed several criteria for evaluating the influence of each observation on the multiple regression model. The various statistics did not lead to a consistent set of conclusions. According to both the $h_i$ and the $D_i$ criteria, none of the observations is a candidate for removal from the model. Under such circumstances, most statisticians would conclude that there is insufficient evidence for the removal of any observation from the model.

In addition to the three criteria presented here, other measures of influence have been developed (see references 1 and 6). Although different researchers seem to prefer particular measures, currently there is no consensus as to the "best" measures. Hence, only when there is consistency in a selected set of measures is it appropriate to consider the removal of particular observations.

## Problems for Section 17.3

### Applying the Concepts

**17.12** In Problem 17.4 on page 821 sales and number of orders were used to predict distribution cost at a mail-order catalog business. Perform an influence analysis on your results and determine whether any observations should be deleted from the model. If necessary, reanalyze the regression model after deleting these observations and compare your results with those of the original model.

DATA FILE
WARECOST

**17.13** In Problem 17.5 on page 822 horsepower and weight were used to predict gasoline mileage. Perform an influence analysis on your results and determine whether any observations should be deleted from the model. If necessary, reanalyze the regression model after deleting these observations and compare your results with those of the original model.

DATA FILE
AUTO

**DATA FILE**
**ADRADTV**

● **17.14** In Problem 17.6 on page 822 the amount of radio and television advertising and newspaper advertising was used to predict sales. Perform an influence analysis on your results and determine whether any observations should be deleted from the model. If necessary, reanalyze the regression model after deleting these observations and compare your results with those of the original model.

**DATA FILE**
**STANDBY**

**17.15** In Problem 17.7 on page 823 the total staff present and remote hours were used to predict standby hours. Perform an influence analysis on your results and determine whether any observations should be deleted from the model. If necessary, reanalyze the regression model after deleting these observations and compare your results with those of the original model.

## 17.4 TESTING FOR THE SIGNIFICANCE OF THE MULTIPLE REGRESSION MODEL

Now that we have used the regression diagnostic procedures of residual analysis and influence analysis to assure ourselves that the multiple linear regression model is appropriate, we can determine whether there is a significant relationship between the dependent variable and the set of explanatory variables. Because there is more than one explanatory variable, the null and alternative hypotheses can be set up as follows:

$H_0$: $\beta_1 = \beta_2 = 0$ (There is no linear relationship between the dependent variable and the explanatory variables.)

$H_1$: At least one $\beta_j \neq 0$ (There is a linear relationship between the dependent variable and at least one of the explanatory variables.)

As was done in section 16.7 for simple linear regression, this null hypothesis is tested with an $F$ test as summarized in Table 17.2.

---

### F Test for the Entire Regression Model in Multiple Regression

The $F$ statistic is equal to the regression mean square ($MSR$) divided by the error mean square ($MSE$).

$$F = \frac{MSR}{MSE} \qquad (17.9)$$

where

$p$ = number of explanatory variables in the regression model

$F$ = test statistic from an $F$ distribution with $p$ and $n - p - 1$ degrees of freedom

---

The decision rule is:

Using an $\alpha$ level of significance, reject $H_0$ if $F > F_U$, the upper-tailed critical value of an $F$ distribution with $p$ and $n - p - 1$ degrees of freedom; otherwise do not reject $H_0$.

The complete set of computations for our heating oil consumption example is shown in Figure 17.2 or Figure 17.3 on pages 815–817.

## Table 17.2 ANOVA table for testing the significance of a set of regression coefficients in a multiple regression model with p = 2 explanatory variables

| SOURCE | DF | SUM OF SQUARES | MEAN SQUARE (VARIANCE) | F |
|--------|----|----|----|---|
| Regression | $p$ | SSR | $MSR = \dfrac{SSR}{p}$ | $F = \dfrac{MSR}{MSE}$ |
| Error | $n - p - 1$ | SSE | $MSE = \dfrac{SSE}{n - p - 1}$ | |
| Total | $n - 1$ | SST | | |

If a level of significance of .05 is chosen, we can determine from Table E.5 that the critical value on the $F$ distribution (with 2 and 12 degrees of freedom) is 3.89, as depicted in Figure 17.7. Using equation (17.9), we can obtain the $F$ statistic from Figure 17.2 or Figure 17.3. Because $F = 168.47 > F_U = 3.89$ or because the $p$-value $= .000 < .05$, we can reject $H_0$ and conclude that at least one of the explanatory variables (temperature and/or insulation) is related to monthly heating oil consumption.

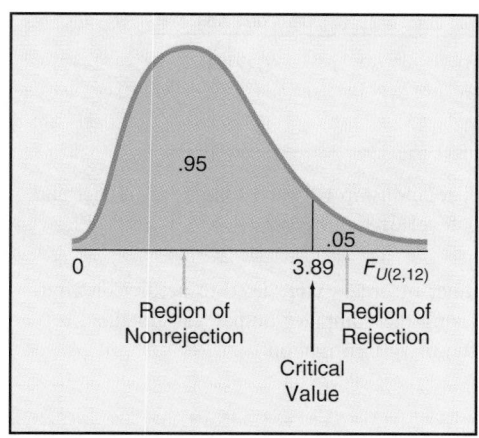

**FIGURE 17.7**

Testing for significance of set of regression coefficients at .05 level of significance with 2 and 12 degrees of freedom

## Problems for Section 17.4

### Learning the Basics

• **17.16** The following analysis of variance table was obtained from a multiple regression model with two independent variables.

| SOURCE | DEGREES OF FREEDOM | SUM OF SQUARES | MEAN SQUARE | F |
|--------|----|----|----|---|
| Regression | 2 | 60 | | |
| Error | 18 | 120 | | |
| Total | 20 | 180 | | |

(a) Determine the mean square due to regression and the mean square due to error.

(b) Determine the computed $F$ statistic.

(c) Determine whether there is a significant relationship between *Y* and the two explanatory variables at the .05 level of significance.

**17.17** The following analysis of variance table was obtained from a multiple regression model with two independent variables.

| SOURCE | DEGREES OF FREEDOM | SUM OF SQUARES | MEAN SQUARE | *F* |
|---|---|---|---|---|
| Regression | 2 | 30 | | |
| Error | 10 | 120 | | |
| Total | 12 | 150 | | |

(a) Determine the mean square due to regression and the mean square due to error.
(b) Determine the computed *F* statistic.
(c) Determine whether there is a significant relationship between *Y* and the two explanatory variables at the .05 level of significance.

## Applying the Concepts

• **17.18** In Problem 17.3 on page 820 the durability of a running shoe was predicted based on a measurement of the forefoot shock-absorbing capability and a measurement of the change in impact properties over time. The following analysis of variance table was obtained.

| ANOVA | df | SS | MS | *F* | SIGNIFICANCE *F* |
|---|---|---|---|---|---|
| Regression | 2 | 12.61020 | 6.30510 | 97.69 | 0.0001 |
| Residual | 12 | 0.77453 | 0.06454 | | |
| Total | 14 | 13.38473 | | | |

(a) Determine whether there is a significant relationship between long-term impact and the two explanatory variables at the .05 level of significance.
(b) Interpret the meaning of the *p*-value.

**DATA FILE**
**WARECOST**

**17.19** In Problem 17.4 on page 821 sales and number of orders were used to predict distribution cost at a mail-order catalog business. Using the computer output you obtained to solve that problem or using the following summary information:

$$SSR = 3,368.087 \quad SSE = 477.043 \quad SST = 3,845.13$$

(a) Determine whether there is a significant relationship between distribution cost and the two explanatory variables (sales and number of orders) at the .05 level of significance.
(b) Interpret the meaning of the *p*-value.

**DATA FILE**
**AUTO**

**17.20** In Problem 17.5 on page 822 horsepower and weight were used to predict gasoline mileage. Using the computer output you obtained to solve that problem or using the following summary information:

$$SSR = 2,451.974 \quad SSE = 819.8681 \quad SST = 3,271.842$$

(a) Determine whether there is a significant relationship between gasoline mileage and the two explanatory variables (horsepower and weight) at the .05 level of significance.
(b) Interpret the meaning of the *p*-value.

**DATA FILE**
**ADRADTV**

• **17.21** In Problem 17.6 on page 822 the amount of radio and television advertising and newspaper advertising was used to predict sales. Using the computer output you obtained to solve that problem or using the following summary information:

$$SSR = 2,028,033 \quad SSE = 479,759.9 \quad SST = 2,507,793$$

(a) Determine whether there is a significant relationship between sales and the two explanatory variables (radio and television advertising and newspaper advertising) at the .05 level of significance.

(b) Interpret the meaning of the *p*-value.

**17.22** In Problem 17.7 on page 823 the total staff present and remote hours were used to predict standby hours. Using the computer output you obtained to solve that problem or using the following summary information:

**DATA FILE
STANDBY**

$$SSR = 27,662.54 \quad SSE = 28,802.07 \quad SST = 56,464.62$$

(a) Determine whether there is a significant relationship between standby hours and the two explanatory variables (total staff present and remote hours) at the .05 level of significance.

(b) Interpret the meaning of the *p*-value.

 ## 17.5 INFERENCES CONCERNING THE POPULATION REGRESSION COEFFICIENTS

In section 16.7 a test of hypothesis was performed on the slope in a simple linear regression model to determine the significance of the relationship between $X$ and $Y$. In addition, a confidence interval was used to estimate the population slope. In this section these procedures will be extended to situations involving multiple regression.

### Tests of Hypothesis

To test the hypothesis that the population slope $\beta_1$ was 0, we used equation (16.13):

$$t = \frac{b_1}{S_{b_1}}$$

However, this equation can be generalized for multiple regression as follows:

**Testing for the Slope in Multiple Regression**

$$t = \frac{b_k}{S_{b_k}} \qquad (17.10)$$

where

$p$ = number of explanatory variables in the regression equation

$b_k$ = slope of variable $k$ with $Y$ holding constant the effects of all other independent variables

$S_{b_k}$ = standard error of the regression coefficient $b_k$

$t$ = test statistic for a $t$ distribution with $n - p - 1$ degrees of freedom

The results of this $t$ test for each of the independent variables included in the regression model are provided as part of the output obtained in Figure 17.2 for Microsoft Excel and Figure 17.3 for Minitab.

Thus, if we wish to determine whether variable $X_2$ (amount of attic insulation) has a significant effect on the monthly consumption of home heating oil, taking into account the average daily atmospheric temperature, the null and alternative hypotheses would be

$$H_0: \beta_2 = 0$$
$$H_1: \beta_2 \neq 0$$

From equation (17.10), we have

$$t = \frac{b_2}{S_{b_2}}$$

and from the data of this example,

$$b_2 = -20.0123 \qquad \text{and} \qquad S_{b_2} = 2.3425$$

so that

$$t = \frac{-20.0123}{2.3425} = -8.5431$$

If a level of significance of .05 is selected, from Table E.3 we find that for 12 degrees of freedom, the critical values of $t$ are $-2.1788$ and $+2.1788$ (see Figure 17.8). From Figure 17.2 or 17.3 on pages 815–817 we observe that the $p$-value is .00000191 or (1.91E-06 in scientific notation). Because $t = -8.5431 < -t_{12} = -2.1788$ or the $p$-value of .00000191 $< .05$, we reject $H_0$ and conclude that there is a significant relationship between variable $X_2$ (amount of attic insulation) and heating oil consumption, taking into account the average daily atmospheric temperature $X_1$.

In a similar manner, in Example 17.1 we test for the significance of $\beta_1$, the slope of monthly consumption of heating oil with the atmospheric temperature.

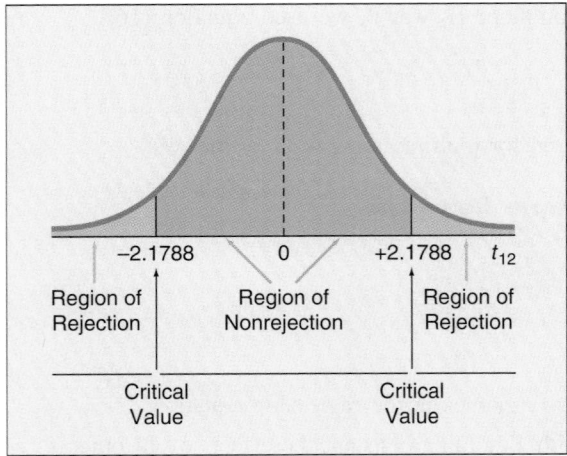

**FIGURE 17.8**

Testing for significance of regression coefficient at .05 level of significance with 12 degrees of freedom

## Example 17.1 *Testing for the Significance of the Slope of Heating Oil Consumption and Atmospheric Temperature*

At the .05 level of significance, is there evidence that the slope of heating oil consumption with atmospheric temperature is different from zero?

## SOLUTION

From Figure 17.2 or 17.3 on pages 815–817, $t = -16.17 < -2.1788$ (the critical value for $\alpha = .05$) or the $p$-value $= .00000000164 < .05$. Therefore, there is a significant relationship between atmospheric temperature ($X_1$) and heating oil consumption, taking into account the attic insulation $X_2$.

As observed with each of these two $X$ variables, the test of significance for a particular regression coefficient is actually a test for the significance of adding a particular variable into a regression model given that the other variable has been included. Therefore, the $t$ test for the regression coefficient is equivalent to testing for the contribution of each explanatory variable.

## Confidence Interval Estimation

Instead of testing the significance of a regression coefficient, we may be more concerned with estimating the population value of a regression coefficient. In multiple regression analysis, a confidence interval estimate for the population slope can be obtained from

### Confidence Interval Estimate for the Slope

$$b_k \pm t_{n-p-1} S_{b_k} \tag{17.11}$$

For example, if we wish to obtain a 95% confidence interval estimate of the population slope $\beta_1$ (the effect of average daily temperature $X_1$ on monthly heating oil consumption $Y$, holding constant the effect of attic insulation $X_2$), from equation (17.11) and Figure 17.2 or Figure 17.3 we have

$$b_1 \pm t_{12} S_{b_1}$$

Because the critical value of $t$ at the 95% confidence level with 12 degrees of freedom is 2.1788 (see Table E.3), we have

$$-5.43658 \pm (2.1788)(.33622)$$
$$-5.43658 \pm .732556$$
$$-6.169136 \le \beta_1 \le -4.704024$$

Thus, taking into account the effect of attic insulation, we estimate that the effect of average daily atmospheric temperature is to reduce the average consumption of heating oil by between approximately 4.7 and 6.17 gallons for each 1°F increase in temperature. We have 95% confidence that this interval correctly estimates the true relationship between these variables.

From a hypothesis-testing viewpoint, because this confidence interval does not include 0, we conclude that the regression coefficient $\beta_1$ has a significant effect. A confidence interval estimate for the slope of heating oil consumption with attic insulation is developed in Example 17.2.

Set up a 95% confidence interval estimate of the population slope of heating oil consumption with attic insulation.

## SOLUTION

Because the critical value of $t$ at the 95% confidence level with 12 degrees of freedom is 2.1788 (see Table E.3), we have

$$-20.0123 \pm (2.1788)(2.3425)$$
$$-20.0123 \pm 5.1039$$
$$-25.1162 \leq \beta_2 \leq -14.9084$$

Thus, taking into account the effect of average daily atmospheric temperature, we estimate that the effect of attic insulation is to reduce the average consumption of heating oil by between approximately 14.9084 and 25.1162 gallons for each inch of attic insulation. We have 95% confidence that this interval correctly estimates the true relationship between these variables. From a hypothesis-testing viewpoint, because this confidence interval does not include 0, we conclude that the regression coefficient $\beta_2$ has a significant effect.

# Problems for Section 17.5

## Learning the Basics

**17.23** Suppose that you were given the following information from a multiple regression model

$$n = 25, b_1 = 5, b_2 = 10, S_{b_1} = 2, S_{b_2} = 8$$

(a) Which variable has a larger slope?
(b) Set up a 95% confidence interval estimate of the population slope for $X_1$.
(c) At the .05 level of significance, determine whether each explanatory variable makes a significant contribution to the regression model. On the basis of these results, indicate the independent variables that should be included in this model.

**17.24** Suppose that you were given the following information from a multiple regression model

$$n = 20, b_1 = 4, b_2 = 3, S_{b_1} = 1.2, S_{b_2} = 0.8$$

(a) Which variable has a larger slope?
(b) Set up a 95% confidence interval estimate of the population slope for $X_1$.
(c) At the .05 level of significance, determine whether each explanatory variable makes a significant contribution to the regression model. On the basis of these results, indicate the independent variables that should be included in this model.

## Applying the Concepts

**17.25** In Problem 17.3 on page 820 the durability of a running shoe was predicted based on a measurement of the forefoot shock-absorbing capability and a measurement of the change in impact properties over time for a sample of 15 pairs of shoes. Using the following computer output:

| VARIABLE | COEFFICIENTS | STANDARD ERROR | t STAT | p-VALUE |
|---|---|---|---|---|
| Intercept | −0.02686 | .06905 | −0.39 | |
| Foreimp | 0.79116 | .06295 | 12.57 | .0000 |
| Midsole | 0.60484 | .07174 | 8.43 | .0000 |

(a) Set up a 95% confidence interval estimate of the population slope between long-term impact and forefoot impact.

(b) At the .05 level of significance, determine whether each explanatory variable makes a significant contribution to the regression model. On the basis of these results, indicate the independent variables that should be included in this model.

**17.26** In Problem 17.4 on page 821 sales and number of orders were used to predict distribution cost at a mail-order catalog business. Using the computer output you obtained to solve that problem or using the following summary information:

DATA FILE
WARECOST

$$b_1 = .0471 \quad b_2 = .01195 \quad S_{b_1} = .0203 \quad S_{b_2} = .00225$$

(a) Set up a 95% confidence interval estimate of the population slope between distribution cost and sales.

(b) At the .05 level of significance, determine whether each explanatory variable makes a significant contribution to the regression model. On the basis of these results, indicate the independent variables that should be included in this model.

**17.27** In Problem 17.5 on page 822 horsepower and weight were used to predict gasoline mileage. Using the computer output you obtained to solve that problem or using the following summary information:

DATA FILE
AUTO

$$b_1 = -0.11753 \quad b_2 = -0.00687 \quad S_{b_1} = .0326 \quad S_{b_2} = .0014$$

(a) Set up a 95% confidence interval estimate of the population slope between gasoline mileage and horsepower.

(b) At the .05 level of significance, determine whether each explanatory variable makes a significant contribution to the regression model. On the basis of these results, indicate the independent variables that should be included in this model.

• **17.28** In Problem 17.6 on page 822 the amount of radio and television advertising and newspaper advertising was used to predict sales. Using the computer output you obtained to solve that problem or using the following summary information:

DATA FILE
ADRADTV

$$b_1 = 13.0807 \quad b_2 = 16.7953 \quad S_{b_1} = 1.7594 \quad S_{b_2} = 2.9634$$

(a) Set up a 95% confidence interval estimate of the population slope between sales and radio and television advertising.

(b) At the .05 level of significance, determine whether each explanatory variable makes a significant contribution to the regression model. On the basis of these results, indicate the independent variables that should be included in this model.

**17.29** In Problem 17.7 on page 823 the total staff present and remote hours were used to predict standby hours. Using the computer output you obtained to solve that problem or using the following summary information:

DATA FILE
STANDBY

$$b_1 = 1.7649 \quad b_2 = -.1390 \quad S_{b_1} = .379 \quad S_{b_2} = .0588$$

(a) Set up a 95% confidence interval estimate of the population slope between standby hours and total staff present.

(b) At the .05 level of significance, determine whether each explanatory variable makes a significant contribution to the regression model. On the basis of these results, indicate the independent variables that should be included in this model.

##  17.6 TESTING PORTIONS OF THE MULTIPLE REGRESSION MODEL

In developing a multiple regression model, the objective is to use only those explanatory variables that are useful in predicting the value of a dependent variable. If an explanatory variable is not helpful in making this prediction, it could be deleted from the multiple regression model and a model with fewer explanatory variables could be used in its place.

An alternative method for determining the contribution of an explanatory variable is called the **partial $F$-test criterion**. It involves determining the contribution to the regression sum of squares made by each explanatory variable after all the other explanatory variables have been included in the model. The new explanatory variable is included only if it significantly improves the model.

To apply the partial $F$-test criterion in the home heating oil consumption example, we need to evaluate the contribution of the variable attic insulation ($X_2$) after average daily atmospheric temperature ($X_1$) has been included in the model and, conversely, we must also evaluate the contribution of the variable average daily atmospheric temperature ($X_1$) after attic insulation ($X_2$) has been included in the model.

In general, if there were several explanatory variables, the contribution of each explanatory variable to be included in the model can be determined by taking into account the regression sum of squares of a model that includes all explanatory variables except the one of interest, $SSR$ (all variables except $k$). Thus, in general, to determine the contribution of variable $k$, given that all other variables are already included, we would have

### Determining the Contribution of an Independent Variable to the Regression Model

$$SSR(X_k \mid \text{all variables } except \; k)$$
$$= SSR(\text{all variables } including \; k) - SSR(\text{all variables } except \; k) \qquad (17.12)$$

If as in the monthly heating oil consumption example, there are two explanatory variables, the contribution of each can be determined from equations (17.13a) and (17.13b).

### Determining the Contribution of $X_1$ and $X_2$ to a Regression Model

Contribution of variable $X_1$ given $X_2$ has been included:

$$SSR(X_1 \mid X_2) = SSR(X_1 \text{ and } X_2) - SSR(X_2) \qquad (17.13a)$$

Contribution of variable $X_2$ given $X_1$ has been included:

$$SSR(X_2 \mid X_1) = SSR(X_1 \text{ and } X_2) - SSR(X_1) \qquad (17.13b)$$

The terms $SSR(X_2)$ and $SSR(X_1)$, respectively, represent the sum of squares due to regression for a model that includes only the explanatory variable $X_2$ (amount of attic insulation) and only the explanatory variable $X_1$ (average daily atmospheric temperature). Output obtained from Microsoft Excel for these two models is presented in Figures 17.9 and 17.10.

| | A | B | C | D | E | F |
|---|---|---|---|---|---|---|
| 1 | SUMMARY OUTPUT | | | | | |
| 2 | | | | | | |
| 3 | *Regression Statistics* | | | | | |
| 4 | Multiple R | 0.465082527 | | | | |
| 5 | R Square | 0.216301757 | | | | |
| 6 | Adjusted R Square | 0.156017277 | | | | |
| 7 | Standard Error | 119.3117327 | | | | |
| 8 | Observations | 15 | | | | |
| 9 | | | $SSR(X_2)$ | | | |
| 10 | ANOVA | | | | | |
| 11 | | *df* | *SS* | *MS* | *F* | *Significance F* |
| 12 | Regression | 1 | 51076.46501 | 51076.46501 | 3.588017285 | 0.080660953 |
| 13 | Residual | 13 | 185058.7643 | 14235.28956 | | |
| 14 | Total | 14 | 236135.2293 | | | |
| 15 | | | | | | |
| 16 | | *Coefficients* | *Standard Error* | *t Stat* | *P-value* | |
| 17 | Intercept | 345.3783784 | 74.69065911 | 4.624117426 | 0.000476363 | |
| 18 | Insulation | -20.35027027 | 10.743429 | -1.894206241 | 0.080660953 | |
| 19 | | | | | | |

**FIGURE 17.9** Partial output obtained from Microsoft Excel of simple linear regression model for amount of heating oil consumed and amount of attic insulation

| | A | B | C | D | E | F |
|---|---|---|---|---|---|---|
| 1 | SUMMARY OUTPUT | | | | | |
| 2 | | | | | | |
| 3 | *Regression Statistics* | | | | | |
| 4 | Multiple R | 0.86974117 | | | | |
| 5 | R Square | 0.756449704 | | | | |
| 6 | Adjusted R Square | 0.737715065 | | | | |
| 7 | Standard Error | 66.51246564 | | | | |
| 8 | Observations | 15 | | | | |
| 9 | | | | | | |
| 10 | ANOVA | | | | | |
| 11 | | *df* | *SS* | *MS* | *F* | *Significance F* |
| 12 | Regression | 1 | 178624.4242 | 178624.4242 | 40.37706498 | 2.51847E-05 |
| 13 | Residual $SSR(X_1)$ | 13 | 57510.80511 | 4423.908086 | | |
| 14 | Total | 14 | 236135.2293 | | | |
| 15 | | | | | | |
| 16 | | *Coefficients* | *Standard Error* | *t Stat* | *P-value* | |
| 17 | Intercept | 436.4382299 | 38.63970893 | 11.29507033 | 4.30471E-08 | |
| 18 | Temperature | -5.462207697 | 0.859608768 | -6.354295002 | 2.51847E-05 | |
| 19 | | | | | | |

**FIGURE 17.10** Partial output obtained from Microsoft Excel of simple linear regression model for amount of heating oil consumed and average daily atmospheric temperature

We can observe from Figure 17.9 that

$$SSR(X_2) = 51,076 \text{ (rounded)}$$

and, therefore, from equation (17.13a),

$$SSR(X_1 \mid X_2) = SSR(X_1 \text{ and } X_2) - SSR(X_2)$$

we have

$$SSR(X_1 \mid X_2) = 228,015 - 51,076 = 176,939$$

To determine whether $X_1$ significantly improves the model after $X_2$ has been included, we can now subdivide the regression sum of squares into two component parts as shown in Table 17.3.

**Table 17.3** *ANOVA table dividing the regression sum of squares into components to determine the contribution of variable $X_1$*

| Source | df | Sum of Squares | Mean Square (Variance) | F |
|---|---|---|---|---|
| Regression | 2 | 228,015 | 114,007.5 | |
| $\begin{Bmatrix} X_2 \\ X_1 \mid X_2 \end{Bmatrix}$ | $\begin{Bmatrix} 1 \\ 1 \end{Bmatrix}$ | $\begin{Bmatrix} 51,076 \\ 176,939 \end{Bmatrix}$ | 176,939 | 261.47 |
| Error | 12 | 8,120 | 676.717 | |
| Total | 14 | 236,135 | | |

The null and alternative hypotheses to test for the contribution of $X_1$ to the model are

$H_0$: Variable $X_1$ does not significantly improve the model once variable $X_2$ has been included.

$H_1$: Variable $X_1$ significantly improves the model once variable $X_2$ has been included.

The partial F-test criterion is expressed by

**The Partial *F*-Test Criterion for Determining the Contribution of an Independent Variable**

$$F = \frac{SSR(X_k \mid \text{all variables } except\ k)}{MSE} \tag{17.14}$$

In equation (17.14) $F$ represents the $F$-test statistic that follows an $F$ distribution with 1 and $n - p - 1$ degrees of freedom.

Thus, from Table 17.3 we have

$$F = \frac{176,939}{676.717} = 261.47$$

Because there are 1 and 12 degrees of freedom, respectively, if a level of significance of .05 is selected, we observe from Table E.5 that the critical value is 4.75 (see Figure 17.11).

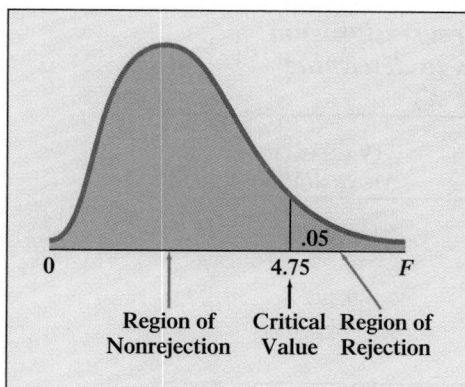

**FIGURE 17.11**

Testing for contribution of regression coefficient to multiple regression model at .05 level of significance with 1 and 12 degrees of freedom

Because the computed $F$-value exceeds this critical $F$-value $(261.47 > 4.75)$, our decision is to reject $H_0$ and conclude that the addition of variable $X_1$ (average daily atmospheric temperature) significantly improves a regression model that already contains variable $X_2$ (attic insulation).

To evaluate the contribution of variable $X_2$ (attic insulation) to a model in which variable $X_1$ has been included, we need to use equation (17.13b):

$$SSR(X_2 \mid X_1) = SSR(X_1 \text{ and } X_2) - SSR(X_1)$$

From Figures 17.2 and 17.10, we determine that

$$SSR(X_1) = 178{,}624$$

Therefore,

$$SSR(X_2 \mid X_1) = 228{,}015 - 178{,}624 = 49{,}391$$

Thus, to determine whether $X_2$ significantly improves a model after $X_1$ has been included, the regression sum of squares can be subdivided into two component parts as shown in Table 17.4 on page 842. The null and alternative hypotheses to test for the contribution of $X_2$ to the model are

$H_0$: Variable $X_2$ does not significantly improve the model once variable $X_1$ has been included.

$H_1$: Variable $X_2$ significantly improves the model once variable $X_1$ has been included.

Using equation (17.14), we obtain

$$F = \frac{49{,}391}{676.717} = 72.99$$

as indicated in Table 17.4 on page 842.

Because there are 1 and 12 degrees of freedom, respectively, if a .05 level of significance is selected, we again observe from Figure 17.11 that the critical value of $F$ is 4.75. Because the computed $F$ value exceeds this critical value $(72.99 > 4.75)$, our decision is

**Table 17.4** *ANOVA table dividing the regression sum of squares into components to determine the contribution of variable $X_2$*

| SOURCE | df | SUM OF SQUARES | (VARIANCE) MEAN SQUARE | F |
|---|---|---|---|---|
| Regression | 2 | 228,015 | 114,007.5 | |
| $\left\{\begin{array}{l} X_1 \\ X_2 \mid X_1 \end{array}\right.$ | $\left\{\begin{array}{l} 1 \\ 1 \end{array}\right.$ | $\left\{\begin{array}{l} 178,624 \\ 49,391 \end{array}\right.$ | 49,391 | 72.99 |
| Error | 12 | 8,120 | 676.717 | |
| Total | 14 | 236,135 | | |

to reject $H_0$ and conclude that the addition of variable $X_2$ (attic insulation) significantly improves the multiple regression model already containing $X_1$ (average daily atmospheric temperature).

Thus, by testing for the contribution of each explanatory variable after the other has been included in the model, we determine that each of the two explanatory variables significantly improves the model. Therefore, our multiple regression model should include both average daily atmospheric temperature $X_1$ and the amount of attic insulation $X_2$ in predicting the monthly consumption of home heating oil.

Focusing on the interpretation of these conclusions, we note that there is a relationship between the value of the *t*-test statistic obtained from equation (17.10) and the partial *F*-test statistic [equation (17.14)] used to determine the contributions of $X_1$ and $X_2$ to the multiple regression model. The *t* values were computed to be $-16.17$ and $-8.5431$, and the corresponding values of *F* were 261.47 and 72.99. This points up the following relationship[1] between *t* and *F*.

[1] *The relationship between t and F indicated in equation (17.15) holds when t is a two-tailed test.*

### The Relationship between a *t* Statistic and an *F* Statistic

$$t_v^2 = F_{1,v} \tag{17.15}$$

where $v$ = number of degrees of freedom.

### Coefficient of Partial Determination

In section 17.1 we discussed the coefficient of multiple determination ($r_{Y.12}^2$), which measured the proportion of the variation in $Y$ that was explained by variation in the two explanatory variables. Now that we have examined ways in which the contribution of each explanatory variable to the multiple regression model can be evaluated, we can also compute the **coefficients of partial determination** ($r_{Y1.2}^2$ and $r_{Y2.1}^2$). The coefficients measure the proportion of the variation in the dependent variable that is explained by each explanatory variable while controlling for, or holding constant, the other explanatory variable(s). Thus, in a multiple regression model with two explanatory variables, we have

## Coefficients of Partial Determination for a Two-Independent-Variable Model

$$r_{Y1.2}^2 = \frac{SSR(X_1|X_2)}{SST - SSR(X_1 \text{ and } X_2) + SSR(X_1|X_2)} \tag{17.16a}$$

and also

$$r_{Y2.1}^2 = \frac{SSR(X_2|X_1)}{SST - SSR(X_1 \text{ and } X_2) + SSR(X_2|X_1)} \tag{17.16b}$$

where

$SSR(X_1 \mid X_2) = $ sum of squares of the contribution of variable $X_1$ to the regression model given that variable $X_2$ has been included in the model

$SST = $ total sum of squares for $Y$

$SSR(X_1 \text{ and } X_2) = $ regression sum of squares when both variables $X_1$ and $X_2$ are included in the multiple regression model

$SSR(X_2 \mid X_1) = $ sum of squares of the contribution of variable $X_2$ to the regression model given that variable $X_1$ has been included in the model

whereas in a multiple regression model containing several ($p$) explanatory variables, for the $k$th variable we have

## Coefficients of Partial Determination for a Multiple Regression Model Containing $p$ Independent Variables

$$r_{Yk.(all\ variables\ except\ k)}^2 \tag{17.17}$$

$$= \frac{SSR(X_k \mid \text{all variables } except\ k)}{SST - SSR(\text{all variables } including\ k) + SSR(X_k \mid \text{all variables } except\ k)}$$

For the monthly heating oil consumption example, we can compute

$$r_{Y1.2}^2 = \frac{176{,}939}{236{,}135 - 228{,}015 + 176{,}939}$$

$$= 0.9561$$

and

$$r_{Y2.1}^2 = \frac{49{,}391}{236{,}135 - 228{,}015 + 49{,}391}$$

$$= 0.8588$$

The coefficient of partial determination of variable $Y$ with $X_1$ while holding $X_2$ constant ($r_{Y1.2}^2$) means that for a fixed (constant) amount of attic insulation, 95.61% of the variation in heating oil consumption in January can be explained by the variation in the average daily atmospheric temperature in that month. The coefficient of partial determination of variable $Y$ with $X_2$ while holding $X_1$ constant ($r_{Y2.1}^2$) means that for a given (constant) average daily atmospheric temperature, 85.88% of the variation in heating oil consumption in January can be explained by variation in the amount of attic insulation.

# Problems for Section 17.6

### Learning the Basics

• **17.30** The following analysis of variance table was obtained from a multiple regression model with two independent variables.

| SOURCE | DEGREES OF FREEDOM | SUM OF SQUARES | MEAN SQUARE | F |
|---|---|---|---|---|
| Regression | 2 | 60 | | |
| Error | 18 | 120 | | |
| Total | 20 | 180 | | |

$SSR(X_1) = 45$  $SSR(X_2) = 25$

(a) Determine whether there is a significant relationship between $Y$ and each of the explanatory variables at the .05 level of significance.
(b) Compute the coefficients of partial determination $r^2_{Y1.2}$ and $r^2_{Y2.1}$ and interpret their meaning.

**17.31** The following analysis of variance table was obtained from a multiple regression model with two independent variables.

| SOURCE | DEGREES OF FREEDOM | SUM OF SQUARES | MEAN SQUARE | F |
|---|---|---|---|---|
| Regression | 2 | 30 | | |
| Error | 10 | 120 | | |
| Total | 12 | 150 | | |

$SSR(X_1) = 20$  $SSR(X_2) = 15$

(a) Determine whether there is a significant relationship between $Y$ and each of the explanatory variables at the .05 level of significance.
(b) Compute the coefficients of partial determination $r^2_{Y1.2}$ and $r^2_{Y2.1}$ and interpret their meaning.

### Applying the Concepts

**DATA FILE**
**WARECOST**

**17.32** In Problem 17.4 on page 821 sales and number of orders were used to predict distribution cost at a mail-order catalog business. Using the computer output you obtained to solve that problem or using the following summary information:

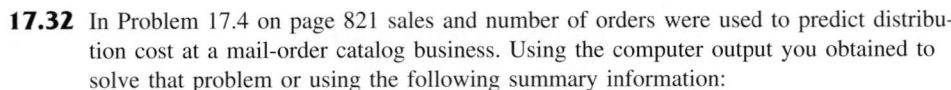

$$SSR = 3,368.087 \quad SSE = 477.043 \quad SST = 3,845.13 \quad SSR(X_1) = 2,726.822$$
$$SSR(X_2) = 3,246.062$$

(a) At the .05 level of significance, determine whether each explanatory variable makes a significant contribution to the regression model. On the basis of these results, indicate the regression model that should be used in the problem.
(b) Compute the coefficients of partial determination $r^2_{Y1.2}$ and $r^2_{Y2.1}$ and interpret their meaning.

**17.33** In Problem 17.5 on page 822 horsepower and weight were used to predict gasoline mileage. Using the computer output you obtained to solve that problem or using the following summary information:

$$SSR = 2{,}451.974 \quad SSE = 819.8681 \quad SST = 3{,}271.842 \quad SSR(X_1) = 2{,}032.546$$
$$SSR(X_2) = 2{,}225.864$$

(a) At the .05 level of significance, determine whether each explanatory variable makes a significant contribution to the regression model. On the basis of these results, indicate the regression model that should be used in the problem.

(b) Compute the coefficients of partial determination $r^2_{Y1.2}$ and $r^2_{Y2.1}$ and interpret their meaning.

**● 17.34** In Problem 17.6 on page 822 the amount of radio and television advertising and newspaper advertising was used to predict sales. Using the computer output you obtained to solve that problem or using the following summary information:

$$SSR = 2{,}028{,}033 \quad SSE = 479{,}759.9 \quad SST = 2{,}507{,}793 \quad SSR(X_1) = 1{,}216{,}940$$
$$SSR(X_2) = 632{,}259.4$$

(a) At the .05 level of significance, determine whether each explanatory variable makes a significant contribution to the regression model. On the basis of these results, indicate the regression model that should be used in the problem.

(b) Compute the coefficients of partial determination $r^2_{Y1.2}$ and $r^2_{Y2.1}$ and interpret their meaning.

**17.35** In Problem 17.7 on page 823 the total staff present and remote hours were used to predict standby hours. Using the computer output you obtained to solve that problem or using the following summary information:

$$SSR = 27{,}662.54 \quad SSE = 28{,}802.07 \quad SST = 56{,}464.62 \quad SSR(X_1) = 20{,}667.4$$
$$SSR(X_2) = 513.2846$$

(a) At the .05 level of significance, determine whether each explanatory variable makes a significant contribution to the regression model. On the basis of these results, indicate the regression model that should be utilized in the problem.

(b) Compute the coefficients of partial determination $r^2_{Y1.2}$ and $r^2_{Y2.1}$ and interpret their meaning.

# SUMMARY

In this chapter, as illustrated in the summary chart on page 846, we developed the multiple regression model with two independent variables and determined the significance of the full model and tested whether each independent variable made a significant contribution to the model. In addition, the coefficients of partial determination were studied and influence analysis was introduced. In chapter 18, we expand on our coverage of multiple regression by considering different types of models that are useful in regression model building.

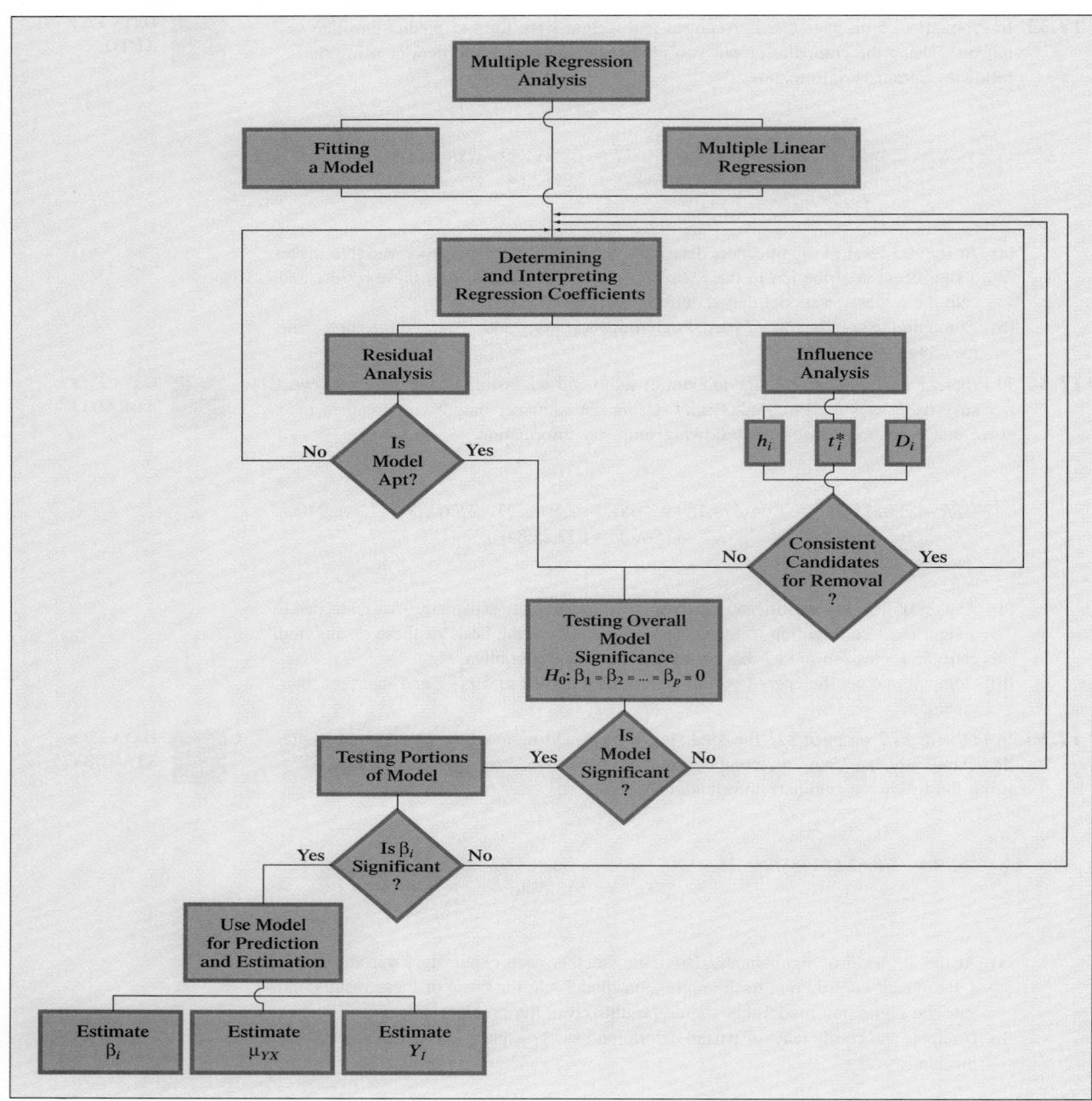

Chapter 17 summary chart

## Key Terms

## Checking Your Understanding

**17.36** How does the interpretation of the regression coefficients differ in multiple regression as compared with simple regression?

**17.37** How does testing the significance of the entire regression model differ from testing the contribution of each independent variable in the multiple regression model?

**17.38** How do the coefficients of partial determination differ from the coefficient of multiple determination?

**17.39** What is the difference between residual analysis and influence analysis?

**17.40** Under what circumstances can observations be considered for removal from the regression model?

**17.41** What is the difference between the $h_i$ statistic and the Studentized deleted residual?

## Chapter Review Problems

**17.42** Suppose we want to develop a model to predict the selling price of homes based on assessed value and the time period in which the house was sold. A sample of 30 recently sold single-family houses in a small western city is selected to study the relationship between selling price and assessed value (the houses in the city had been reassessed at full value 1 year prior to the study) as well as time period (in months since reassessment). The results are as follows:

| OBSERVATION | ASSESSED VALUE ($000) | SELLING PRICE ($000) | TIME PERIOD | OBSERVATION | ASSESSED VALUE ($000) | SELLING PRICE ($000) | TIME PERIOD |
|---|---|---|---|---|---|---|---|
| 1 | 78.17 | 94.10 | 10 | 16 | 84.36 | 106.70 | 12 |
| 2 | 80.24 | 101.90 | 10 | 17 | 72.94 | 81.50 | 5 |
| 3 | 74.03 | 88.65 | 11 | 18 | 76.50 | 94.50 | 14 |
| 4 | 86.31 | 115.50 | 2 | 19 | 66.28 | 69.00 | 1 |
| 5 | 75.22 | 87.50 | 5 | 20 | 79.74 | 96.90 | 3 |
| 6 | 65.54 | 72.00 | 4 | 21 | 72.78 | 86.50 | 14 |
| 7 | 72.43 | 91.50 | 17 | 22 | 77.90 | 97.90 | 12 |
| 8 | 85.61 | 113.90 | 13 | 23 | 74.31 | 83.00 | 11 |
| 9 | 60.80 | 69.34 | 6 | 24 | 79.85 | 97.30 | 12 |
| 10 | 81.88 | 96.90 | 5 | 25 | 84.78 | 100.80 | 2 |
| 11 | 79.11 | 96.00 | 7 | 26 | 81.61 | 97.90 | 6 |
| 12 | 59.93 | 61.90 | 4 | 27 | 74.92 | 90.50 | 12 |
| 13 | 75.27 | 93.00 | 11 | 28 | 79.98 | 97.00 | 4 |
| 14 | 85.88 | 109.50 | 10 | 29 | 77.96 | 92.00 | 9 |
| 15 | 76.64 | 93.75 | 17 | 30 | 79.07 | 95.90 | 12 |

DATA FILE
HOUSE1

(a) State the multiple regression equation.
(b) Interpret the meaning of the slopes in this equation.
(c) Predict the average selling price for a house that has an assessed value of $70,000 and was sold in time period 12.
(d) Perform a residual analysis on your results and determine the adequacy of the fit of the model.
(e) Perform an influence analysis on your results and determine whether any observations should be deleted from the model. If necessary, reanalyze the regression model

after deleting these observations and compare your results with those of the original model.

(f) Determine whether there is a significant relationship between selling price and the two explanatory variables (assessed value and time period) at the .05 level of significance.

(g) Compute the $p$-value in (f) and interpret its meaning.

(h) Interpret the meaning of the coefficient of multiple determination $r_{Y.12}^2$ in this problem.

(i) Compute the adjusted $r^2$.

(j) At the .05 level of significance, determine whether each explanatory variable makes a significant contribution to the regression model. On the basis of these results, indicate the regression model that should be used in this problem.

(k) Compute the $p$-values in (j) and interpret their meaning.

(l) Set up a 95% confidence interval estimate of the true population slope between selling price and assessed value. How does the interpretation of the slope here differ from Problem 16.75(k) on page 801?

(m) Compute the coefficients of partial determination ($r_{Y1.2}^2$ and $r_{Y2.1}^2$) and interpret their meaning.

● **17.43** Suppose we want to develop a model to predict assessed value of single-family houses based on heating area and age. A sample of 15 single-family houses is selected. The assessed value (in thousands of dollars), the heating area of the house (in thousands of square feet), and the age of the house (in years) are recorded with the following results:

| HOUSE | ASSESSED VALUE ($000) | HEATING AREA OF DWELLING (THOUSANDS OF SQUARE FEET) | AGE (YEARS) | HOUSE | ASSESSED VALUE ($000) | HEATING AREA OF DWELLING (THOUSANDS OF SQUARE FEET) | AGE (YEARS) |
|---|---|---|---|---|---|---|---|
| 1 | 84.4 | 2.00 | 3.42 | 9 | 78.5 | 1.59 | 1.75 |
| 2 | 77.4 | 1.71 | 11.50 | 10 | 79.2 | 1.50 | 2.75 |
| 3 | 75.7 | 1.45 | 8.33 | 11 | 86.7 | 1.90 | 0.00 |
| 4 | 85.9 | 1.76 | 0.00 | 12 | 79.3 | 1.39 | 0.00 |
| 5 | 79.1 | 1.93 | 7.42 | 13 | 74.5 | 1.54 | 12.58 |
| 6 | 70.4 | 1.20 | 32.00 | 14 | 83.8 | 1.89 | 2.75 |
| 7 | 75.8 | 1.55 | 16.00 | 15 | 76.8 | 1.59 | 7.17 |
| 8 | 85.9 | 1.93 | 2.00 | | | | |

DATA FILE
HOUSE2

(a) State the multiple regression equation.

(b) Interpret the meaning of the slopes in this equation.

(c) Predict the average assessed value for a house that has a heating area of 1,750 square feet and is 10 years old.

(d) Perform a residual analysis on your results and determine the adequacy of the fit of the model.

(e) Perform an influence analysis on your results and determine whether any observations should be deleted from the model. If necessary, reanalyze the regression model after deleting these observations and compare your results to the original model.

(f) Determine whether there is a significant relationship between assessed value and the two explanatory variables (heating area and age) at the .05 level of significance.

(g) Compute the $p$-value in (f) and interpret its meaning.

(h) Interpret the meaning of the coefficient of multiple determination $r_{Y.12}^2$ in this problem.

(i) Compute the adjusted $r^2$.

(j) At the .05 level of significance, determine whether each explanatory variable makes a significant contribution to the regression model. On the basis of these results, indicate the regression model that should be used in this problem.

(k) Compute the $p$-values in (j) and interpret their meaning.

(l) Set up a 95% confidence interval estimate of the true population slope between assessed value and heating area. How does the interpretation of the slope here differ from Problem 16.76(k) on page 801?

(m) Compute the coefficients of partial determination ($r_{Y1.2}^2$ and $r_{Y2.1}^2$) and interpret their meaning.

(n) The real estate assessor's office has been publicly quoted as saying that the age of the house has no bearing on its assessed value. On the basis of the results of (a)–(m), do you agree with this statement? Explain.

**17.44** The file UNIV&COL contains data on 80 colleges and universities. Among the variables included are the annual total cost (in thousands of dollars), the average total score on the Scholastic Aptitude Test (SAT), and the room and board expenses (in thousands of dollars). Suppose we wanted to develop a model to predict the annual total cost based on SAT score and room and board expenses.

DATA FILE
UNIV&COL

(a) State the multiple regression equation.

(b) Interpret the meaning of the slopes in this equation.

(c) Predict the average annual total cost for a school that has an average SAT score of 1,100 and a room and board expense of $5,000.

(d) Perform a residual analysis on your results and determine the adequacy of the fit of the model.

(e) Perform an influence analysis on your results and determine whether any observations should be deleted from the model. If necessary, reanalyze the regression model after deleting these observations and compare your results with those of the original model.

(f) Determine whether there is a significant relationship between annual total cost and the two explanatory variables (SAT score and room and board expenses) at the .05 level of significance.

(g) Compute the $p$-value in (f) and interpret its meaning.

(h) Interpret the meaning of the coefficient of multiple determination $r_{Y.12}^2$ in this problem.

(i) Compute the adjusted $r^2$.

(j) At the .05 level of significance, determine whether each explanatory variable makes a significant contribution to the regression model. On the basis of these results, indicate the regression model that should be used in this problem.

(k) Compute the $p$-values in (j) and interpret their meaning.

(l) Set up a 95% confidence interval estimate of the true population slope between annual total cost and SAT score.

(m) Compute the coefficients of partial determination ($r_{Y1.2}^2$ and $r_{Y2.1}^2$) and interpret their meaning.

(n) Explain why the slope for total annual cost with room and board expenses seems substantially different from 1.0.

(o) What other factors that are not included in the model might account for the strong positive relationship between annual total cost and SAT score?

• **17.45** The file AUTO96 contains data on 89 automobile models from the year 1996. Among the variables included are the gasoline mileage, the length (in inches), and the weight (in pounds) of each automobile. Suppose we wanted to develop a model to predict the gasoline mileage based on the length and the weight of each automobile.

DATA FILE
AUTO96

(a) State the multiple regression equation.

(b) Interpret the meaning of the slopes in this equation.

(c) Predict the average gasoline mileage for an automobile that has a length of 195 inches and a weight of 3,000 pounds.

(d) Perform a residual analysis on your results and determine the adequacy of the fit of the model.

(e) Perform an influence analysis on your results and determine whether any observations should be deleted from the model. If necessary, reanalyze the regression model after deleting these observations and compare your results with those of the original model.

(f) Determine whether there is a significant relationship between gasoline mileage and the two explanatory variables (length and weight) at the .05 level of significance.

(g) Compute the $p$-value in (f) and interpret its meaning.

(h) Interpret the meaning of the coefficient of multiple determination $r^2_{Y.12}$ in this problem.

(i) Compute the adjusted $r^2$.

(j) At the .05 level of significance, determine whether each explanatory variable makes a significant contribution to the regression model. On the basis of these results, indicate the regression model that should be used in this problem.

(k) Compute the $p$-values in (j) and interpret their meaning.

(l) Set up a 95% confidence interval estimate of the true population slope between gasoline mileage and weight.

(m) Compute the coefficients of partial determination ($r^2_{Y1.2}$ and $r^2_{Y2.1}$) and interpret their meaning.

**17.46** Crazy Dave, the well-known baseball analyst, has expanded his analysis of which variables are important in predicting a team's wins in a given season. He has collected the following data related to wins, ERA, and runs scored for a recent season (1997):

| AMERICAN LEAGUE | | | | NATIONAL LEAGUE | | | |
|---|---|---|---|---|---|---|---|
| TEAM | WINS | ERA | RUNS | TEAM | WINS | ERA | RUNS |
| Boston | 78 | 4.85 | 851 | Florida | 92 | 3.83 | 740 |
| Cleveland | 86 | 4.73 | 868 | Cincinnati | 76 | 4.41 | 651 |
| Kansas City | 67 | 4.70 | 747 | Chicago Cubs | 68 | 4.44 | 687 |
| Minnesota | 68 | 5.01 | 772 | San Francisco | 90 | 4.39 | 784 |
| Toronto | 76 | 3.93 | 654 | Los Angeles | 88 | 3.62 | 742 |
| Anaheim | 84 | 4.52 | 829 | Pittsburgh | 79 | 4.28 | 725 |
| Seattle | 90 | 4.78 | 925 | San Diego | 76 | 4.98 | 795 |
| Texas | 77 | 4.69 | 807 | New York Mets | 88 | 3.95 | 777 |
| Detroit | 79 | 4.56 | 784 | St. Louis | 73 | 3.88 | 689 |
| Chicago White Sox | 80 | 4.73 | 779 | Philadelphia | 68 | 4.85 | 668 |
| Milwaukee | 78 | 4.22 | 681 | Atlanta | 101 | 3.18 | 791 |
| Oakland | 65 | 5.48 | 764 | Montreal | 78 | 4.14 | 691 |
| Baltimore | 98 | 3.91 | 812 | Houston | 84 | 3.66 | 777 |
| New York Yankees | 96 | 3.84 | 891 | Colorado | 83 | 5.29 | 923 |

DATA FILE
BB97

(a) State the multiple regression equation.

(b) Interpret the meaning of the slopes in this equation.

(c) Predict the average number of wins for a team that has an ERA of 4.00 and scored 750 runs.

(d) Perform a residual analysis on your results and determine the adequacy of the fit of the model.

(e) Perform an influence analysis on your results and determine whether any observations should be deleted from the model. If necessary, reanalyze the regression model after deleting these observations and compare your results with those of the original model.

(f) Determine whether there is a significant relationship between number of wins and the two explanatory variables (ERA and runs) at the .05 level of significance.

(g) Compute the $p$-value in (f) and interpret its meaning.

(h) Interpret the meaning of the coefficient of multiple determination $r^2_{Y.12}$ in this problem.

(i) Compute the adjusted $r^2$.

(j) At the .05 level of significance, determine whether each explanatory variable makes a significant contribution to the regression model. On the basis of these results, indicate the regression model that should be used in this problem.

(k) Compute the $p$-values in (j) and interpret their meaning.

(l) Set up a 95% confidence interval estimate of the true population slope between wins and ERA. Compare the results with those obtained in (l) of Problem 16.79 on page 804.

(m) Compute the coefficients of partial determination ($r^2_{Y1.2}$ and $r^2_{Y2.1}$) and interpret their meaning.

(n) Which seems to be more important in predicting wins, pitching as measured by ERA or offense as measured by runs scored? Explain.

**17.47** Backpacks are commonly seen in many places, especially college campuses, shopping malls, airplanes, and hiking trails. In the August 1997 issue of *Consumer Reports* information was provided concerning different features of backpacks, including their prices ($), volume (cubic inches), and number of $5 \times 7\frac{3}{4}$-inch books that the backpacks can hold. The results are summarized below:

| PRICE | VOLUME | BOOKS | PRICE | VOLUME | BOOKS |
|-------|--------|-------|-------|--------|-------|
| 48 | 2,200 | 59 | 40 | 1,950 | 46 |
| 45 | 1,670 | 49 | 40 | 1,810 | 44 |
| 50 | 2,200 | 48 | 45 | 1,910 | 48 |
| 42 | 1,700 | 52 | 27 | 1,875 | 42 |
| 29 | 1,875 | 52 | 25 | 1,450 | 42 |
| 50 | 1,500 | 49 | 35 | 1,102 | 73 |
| 38 | 1,586 | 47 | 40 | 1,316 | 55 |
| 33 | 1,910 | 53 | 40 | 1,760 | 43 |
| 40 | 1,500 | 49 | 25 | 1,844 | 42 |
| 35 | 1,950 | 49 | 50 | 2,150 | 52 |
| 32 | 1,385 | 45 | 35 | 1,810 | 50 |
| 40 | 1,700 | 38 | 50 | 2,180 | 46 |
| 35 | 2,000 | 51 | 35 | 1,635 | 40 |
| 28 | 1,500 | 46 | 15 | 1,245 | 47 |

DATA FILE
BACKPACK

*Source: "Packs for Town and Country," Copyright 1997 by Consumers Union of U.S., Inc. Adapted from* CONSUMER REPORTS *(August 1997): 20–21, by permission of Consumers Union of U.S., Inc., Yonkers, NY 10703-1057. Although these data sets originally appeared in* CONSUMER REPORTS, *the selective adaptation and resulting conclusions presented are those of the authors and are not sanctioned or endorsed in any way by Consumers Union, the publisher of* CONSUMER REPORTS.

Suppose that we want to develop a multiple regression model to predict the price of a backpack based on the volume and the number of books it can hold.

(a) State the multiple regression equation.

(b) Interpret the meaning of the slopes in this equation.

(c) Predict the average price for a backpack that has a volume of 2,000 cubic inches and can hold 50 books.

(d) Perform a residual analysis on your results and determine the adequacy of the fit of the model.

(e) Perform an influence analysis on your results and determine whether any observations should be deleted from the model. If necessary, reanalyze the regression model after deleting these observations and compare your results with those of the original model.

(f) Determine whether there is a significant relationship between price and the two explanatory variables (volume and number of books) at the .05 level of significance.

(g) Compute the $p$-value in (f) and interpret its meaning.

(h) Interpret the meaning of the coefficient of multiple determination $r^2_{Y.12}$ in this problem.

(i) Compute the adjusted $r^2$.

(j) At the .05 level of significance, determine whether each explanatory variable makes a significant contribution to the regression model. On the basis of these results, indicate the regression model that should be used in this problem.

(k) Compute the $p$-values in (j) and interpret their meaning.

(l) Set up a 95% confidence interval estimate of the true population slope between price and number of books.

(m) Compute the coefficients of partial determination ($r^2_{Y1.2}$ and $r^2_{Y2.1}$) and interpret their meaning.

(n) Do the results of (a)–(m) surprise you? Explain.

**17.48** A headline on page 1 of *The New York Times* of March 4, 1990, read "Wine Equation Puts Some Noses Out of Joint." The article proceeded to explain that Professor Orley Ashenfelter, a Princeton University economist, had developed a multiple regression model to predict the quality of French Bordeaux based on the amount of winter rain, the average temperature during the growing season, and the harvest rain. The equation developed was

$$Q = -12.145 + .00117WR + .6164TMP - .00386HR$$

where $Q$ = logarithmic index of quality where 1961 equals 100

$WR$ = winter rain (October through March) in millimeters

$TMP$ = average temperature during the growing season (April through September) in degrees Celsius

$HR$ = harvest rain (August to September) in millimeters

You are at a cocktail party, sipping a glass of wine, when one of your friends mentions to you that she has read the article. She asks you to explain the meaning of the coefficients in the equation and also asks you what analyses that might have been done have not been included in the article. You respond . . .

## *Case Study* — EASTWESTSIDE MOVERS

The owner of an intracity moving company has typically used an estimator to determine the number of labor hours needed for the move. This has proved to be useful in the past, but he would like to be able to develop a more reliable estimate that would be more accurate in predicting the labor hours. In a preliminary effort to provide a more accurate means of estimation, he has collected data for 36 moves in which the origin and destination were within the borough of Manhattan in New York City and the travel time was an insignificant portion of the hours worked. The results were as follows:

| OBSERVATION | LABOR HOURS | ROOMS | CUBIC FEET MOVED | OBSERVATION | LABOR HOURS | ROOMS | CUBIC FEET MOVED |
|---|---|---|---|---|---|---|---|
| 1 | 24.00 | 3.5 | 545 | 19 | 25.00 | 3.0 | 557 |
| 2 | 13.50 | 2.0 | 400 | 20 | 45.00 | 5.5 | 1,028 |
| 3 | 26.25 | 2.5 | 562 | 21 | 29.00 | 4.5 | 793 |
| 4 | 25.00 | 3.0 | 540 | 22 | 21.00 | 3.0 | 523 |
| 5 | 9.00 | 1.0 | 220 | 23 | 22.00 | 3.5 | 564 |
| 6 | 20.00 | 3.0 | 344 | 24 | 16.50 | 2.5 | 312 |
| 7 | 22.00 | 3.5 | 569 | 25 | 37.00 | 4.0 | 757 |
| 8 | 11.25 | 2.0 | 340 | 26 | 32.00 | 3.5 | 600 |
| 9 | 50.00 | 5.0 | 900 | 27 | 34.00 | 4.0 | 796 |
| 10 | 12.00 | 1.5 | 285 | 28 | 25.00 | 3.5 | 577 |
| 11 | 38.75 | 5.0 | 865 | 29 | 31.00 | 3.0 | 500 |
| 12 | 40.00 | 4.5 | 831 | 30 | 24.00 | 4.0 | 695 |
| 13 | 19.50 | 3.0 | 344 | 31 | 40.00 | 5.5 | 1,054 |
| 14 | 18.00 | 2.5 | 360 | 32 | 27.00 | 3.0 | 486 |
| 15 | 28.00 | 4.0 | 750 | 33 | 18.00 | 3.0 | 442 |
| 16 | 27.00 | 3.5 | 650 | 34 | 62.50 | 5.5 | 1,249 |
| 17 | 21.00 | 3.0 | 415 | 35 | 53.75 | 5.0 | 995 |
| 18 | 15.00 | 2.5 | 275 | 36 | 79.50 | 5.5 | 1,397 |

 DATA FILE MOVING

Develop a model to predict the labor hours based on the number of rooms and the number of cubic feet to be moved from the origin apartment. Write an executive summary of no more than one page stating your conclusions. In addition, attach a technical appendix that provides and explains the statistical results.

# References

1. Andrews, D. F., and D. Pregibon, "Finding the Outliers That Matter," *Journal of the Royal Statistical Society* 40 (Ser. B., 1978): 85–93.
2. Atkinson, A. C., "Robust and Diagnostic Regression Analysis," *Communications in Statistics* 11 (1982): 2559–2572.
3. Belsley, D. A., E. Kuh, and R. Welsch, *Regression Diagnostics: Identifying Influential Data and Sources of Collinearity* (New York: Wiley, 1980).
4. Cook, R. D., and S. Weisberg, *Residuals and Influence in Regression* (New York: Chapman and Hall, 1982).
5. Hoaglin, D. C., and R. Welsch, "The Hat Matrix in Regression and ANOVA," *The American Statistician* 32 (1978): 17–22.
6. Hocking, R. R., "Developments in Linear Regression Methodology: 1959–1982," *Technometrics* 25 (1983): 219–250.
7. Marquardt, D. W., "You Should Standardize the Predictor Variables in Your Regression Models," discussion of "A Critique of Some Ridge Regression Methods," by G. Smith and F. Campbell, *Journal of the American Statistical Association* 75 (1980): 87–91.
8. *Microsoft Excel 97* (Redmond, WA: Microsoft Corp., 1997).
9. *Minitab for Windows Version 12* (State College, PA: Minitab, Inc., 1998).
10. Snee, R. D., "Some Aspects of Nonorthogonal Data Analysis, Part I. Developing Prediction Equations," *Journal of Quality Technology* 5 (1973): 67–79.
11. Tukey, J. W., "Data Analysis, Computation and Mathematics," *Quarterly Journal of Applied Mathematics* 30 (1972): 51–65.
12. Velleman, P. F., and R. Welsch, "Efficient Computing of Regression Diagnostics," *The American Statistician* 35 (1981): 234–242.

## APPENDIX 17.1   USING MICROSOFT EXCEL FOR MULTIPLE REGRESSION

### COMMENT:  PHStat Add-In Users

If Microsoft Excel is not running, click the **PHStat** add-in icon. If Microsoft Excel is running, select **File | Open**. Select the PHStat add-in file **PHSA.XLA**. Click the **Open** button.

To perform a multiple regression analysis, select **PHStat | Regression | Multiple Regression**. Enter the cell range for the $Y$ and $X$ variables in their respective edit boxes. Select the Regression statistics, ANOVA and Coefficients table, Residuals and Residual Plot check boxes if desired. Select the Durbin-Watson check box to obtain this statistic. Select the coefficients of partial determination check box to compute this statistic. Click the **OK** button.

In chapter 16 we used the Data Analysis tool and its Regression option for the simple linear regression model. In this chapter we developed a variety of multiple regression models whose computations can also be done with the Regression option of the Data Analysis tool. In using the Regression option for multiple regression models, it is important to remember that the entire set of $X$ variables must be placed in consecutive columns because the Regression tool will allow us to specify only a single contiguous range for the $X$ variable.

To illustrate the use of Microsoft Excel in multiple regression, let us return to the monthly heating oil consumption example. Open the **HTNGOIL.XLS** workbook and click the Data sheet tab to make that sheet active. Select **Tools | Data Analysis** and select **Regression** from the Analysis Tools list box and click the **OK** button.

In the Regression dialog box, enter **A1:A16** in the Input $Y$ Range edit box. Enter **B1:C16** in the Input $X$ Range edit box. Note that only a single, contiguous range is allowed in this edit box. Select the **Labels** check box. Select the **New Worksheet Ply** option button and enter Figure 17.2 as the sheet name. Select the **Residuals, Standardized Residuals**, and **Residual Plots** check boxes. Click the **OK** button to obtain the output similar to that displayed in Figure 17.2 on pages 815–816.

### Using Microsoft Excel to Obtain the Coefficients of Partial Determination

The coefficients of partial determination may be obtained using equations (17.16a) and (17.16b) on page 843 along with the output of the multiple regression model produced in Figure 17.2, the output of a regression model of insulation ($X_2$) with monthly heating oil consumption (see Figure 17.9), and the output of a regression model of temperature ($X_1$) with heating oil consumption (see Figure 17.10).

After producing the regression model outputs (on sheets named Figure 17.2, Figure 17.9, and Figure 17.10), insert a new worksheet and rename it Calculations. Then, copy the regression sum of squares for the model that includes $X_1$ and $X_2$ from cell C12 of the Figure 17.2 sheet to cell B3. Copy the regression sum of squares for the model that includes $X_2$ from cell C12 of the Figure 17.9 sheet to cell B4. Copy the regression sum of squares for the model that includes $X_1$ from cell C12 of the Figure 17.10 sheet to cell B5. Copy the total sum of squares from cell C14 of the Figure 17.2 sheet to cell B6.

Next, enter the formula **=B3−B5** in cell B7 to compute the regression sum of squares for $X_2$ given $X_1$. Enter the formula **=B3−B4** in cell B8 to compute the regression sum of squares of $X_1$ given $X_2$. Finally, compute the coefficients of partial determination by entering the formulas **=B7/(B6−B3+B7)** and **=B8/(B6−B3+B8)** in cells B9 and B10, respectively.

# ❖ APPENDIX 17.2    USING MINITAB FOR MULTIPLE REGRESSION

In appendix 16.2 instructions were provided for using Minitab for simple linear regression. The same set of instructions are valid in using Minitab for multiple regression. To obtain a regression analysis for the heating oil data, open the **HTNGOIL.MTP** worksheet and select **Stat | Regression | Regression**. Enter **C1** or **Gallons** in the Response edit box and **C2** or **Temp (F)** and **C3** or **Insulation** in the Predictors edit box. Click the **Graphs** button. In the Residuals for Plots edit box, select the **Standardized** option button. For Residual Plots, select the **Histogram of Residuals** check box. In the Residuals vs. the Variables edit box, select **C2** or **Temp (F)** and **C3** or **Insulation**. Click the **OK** button to return to the Regression dialog box. Click the **Results** button. In the Regression Results dialog box, click the **In addition, the full table of fits and residuals** option button. Click the **OK** button to return to the Regression dialog box. Click the **Options** button. If the data have been collected over time, under Display, select the **Durbin-Watson Statistic** check box. In the Prediction interval for new observations edit box, enter **30 6**. Click the **OK** button to return to the Regression dialog box. To obtain influence statistics using Minitab, click the **Storage** button. Select the **Deleted t residual, Hi, and Cook's distance** check boxes. Click the **OK** button to return to the Regression dialog box. Click the **OK** button.

# 18

# Multiple Regression Model Building

## CHAPTER OBJECTIVES

✓ *To develop the curvilinear regression model*
✓ *To introduce categorical explanatory (dummy) variables into the regression models*
✓ *To examine regression models that involve transformations of a variable*
✓ *To show how stepwise regression or best-subsets regression can be used to build and select a regression model*
✓ *To introduce the logistic regression model for predicting a categorical response variable*

## Introduction

In chapter 16 the simple linear regression model was used to predict the outcome of a response variable based on a single explanatory variable, assuming a straight-line relationship between the variables. In chapter 17 we extended the concepts of simple linear regression and developed a multiple regression model with two independent variables. In this chapter we further extend the multiple regression model to deal with a variety of situations involving curvilinear regression, categorical independent variables, and transformations of variables. We then develop strategies for selecting a single regression model from a set of alternative models. Finally, we introduce the logistic regression model for predicting a categorical response variable.

---

◆ **USING STATISTICS:** *Predicting Standby Hours for Unionized Graphic Artists*

The director of broadcasting operations for a television station wanted to study the issue of standby hours, hours in which the unionized graphic artists at the station are paid but are not actually involved in any activity. The director wanted to determine what factors most affected standby hours, so that these hours could be predicted on a weekly basis. Through study of a regression model, the process that led to standby hours could be understood, enabling the director to take actions to reduce this expensive inactivity.

### 18.1 THE CURVILINEAR REGRESSION MODEL

In our discussion of simple regression in chapter 16 and multiple regression in chapter 17 we assumed that the relationship between $Y$ and each explanatory variable is linear. However, in section 16.1 several different types of relationships between variables were introduced. One of the more common nonlinear relationships illustrated was a curvilinear relationship between two variables (see Figure 16.2, panels D–F, on page 736) in which $Y$ increases (or decreases) at a changing rate for various values of $X$. This model of a curvilinear relationship between $X$ and $Y$ can be expressed as

## Curvilinear Regression Model

$$Y_i = \beta_0 + \beta_1 X_{1i} + \beta_2 X_{1i}^2 + \epsilon_i \qquad (18.1)$$

where

$\beta_0 = Y$ intercept

$\beta_1 =$ coefficient of the linear effect on $Y$

$\beta_2 =$ coefficient of the curvilinear effect on $Y$

$\epsilon_i =$ random error in $Y$ for observation $i$

This **curvilinear regression model** is similar to the multiple regression model with two explanatory variables [see equation (17.2) on page 814] except that the second explanatory variable in this instance is the square of the first explanatory variable.

As in the case of multiple linear regression, the sample regression coefficients ($b_0$, $b_1$, and $b_2$) are used as estimates of the population parameters ($\beta_0$, $\beta_1$, and $\beta_2$). Thus, the sample regression equation for the curvilinear model with one explanatory variable ($X_1$) and a dependent variable ($Y$) is

## Sample Curvilinear Regression Equation

$$\hat{Y}_i = b_0 + b_1 X_{1i} + b_2 X_{1i}^2 \qquad (18.2)$$

In this equation, the first regression coefficient $b_0$ represents the $Y$ intercept, the second regression coefficient $b_1$ represents the linear coefficient, and the third regression coefficient $b_2$ represents the quadratic or curvilinear effect.

## Finding the Regression Coefficients and Predicting Y

To illustrate the curvilinear regression model, suppose the marketing department of a large supermarket chain wants to study the price elasticity for packages of disposable razors. A sample of 15 stores with equivalent store traffic and product placement (i.e., at the checkout counter) is selected. Five stores are randomly assigned to each of three price levels (79, 99, and 119 cents) for the package of razors. The number of packages sold over a full week and the price at each store are presented in Table 18.1 on page 860.

To help select the proper model for expressing the relationship between price and sales, a scatter diagram is plotted in Figure 18.1 on page 860. An examination of Figure 18.1 indicates that as price increases there is a decrease in sales which levels off with further increases in price. Sales for a price of 99 cents are substantially below sales at the 79 cent price, but sales for the $1.19 price are only slightly below sales at 99 cents. Therefore, it appears that a curvilinear model rather than a linear model may be the more appropriate choice to estimate sales based on price.

As in the case of multiple regression, the values of the three sample regression coefficients $b_0$, $b_1$, and $b_2$ are obtained from Microsoft Excel as illustrated in Figure 18.2 on page 861. From Figure 18.2, we observe that

$$b_0 = 729.8665 \quad b_1 = -10.887 \quad b_2 = .0465$$

**Table 18.1** *Sales and price of packages of disposable razors for sample of 15 stores*

| SALES | PRICE (CENTS) | SALES | PRICE (CENTS) |
|-------|---------------|-------|---------------|
| 142 | 79 | 115 | 99 |
| 151 | 79 | 126 | 99 |
| 163 | 79 | 77 | 119 |
| 168 | 79 | 86 | 119 |
| 176 | 79 | 95 | 119 |
| 91 | 99 | 100 | 119 |
| 100 | 99 | 106 | 119 |
| 107 | 99 | | |

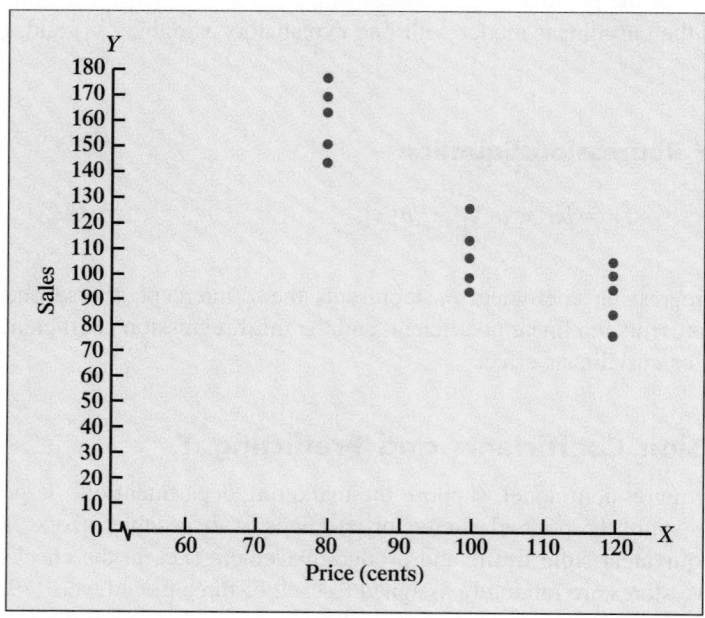

**FIGURE 18.1** Scatter diagram of price (X) and sales (Y)

Therefore, the sample curvilinear regression equation can be expressed as

$$\hat{Y}_i = 729.8665 - 10.887X_{1i} + .0465X_{1i}^2$$

where  $\hat{Y}_i$ = predicted average sales for store $i$

$X_{1i}$ = price of disposable razors in store $i$

As depicted in Figure 18.3, this curvilinear regression equation is plotted on the scatter diagram to see how well the selected regression model fits the original data.

From our curvilinear regression equation and Figure 18.3, the Y intercept ($b_0$, computed as 729.8665) has no direct interpretation for these data. It is simply a base or starting point.

| | A | B | C | D | E | F |
|---|---|---|---|---|---|---|
| 3 | *Regression Statistics* | | | | | |
| 4 | Multiple R | 0.928581176 | | | | |
| 5 | R Square | 0.862263 | | | | |
| 6 | Adjusted R Square | 0.839306834 | | | | |
| 7 | Standard Error | 12.86986143 | | | | |
| 8 | Observations | 15 | | | | |
| 9 | | | | | | |
| 10 | ANOVA | | | | | |
| 11 | | *df* | *SS* | *MS* | *F* | *Significance F* |
| 12 | Regression | 2 | 12442.8 | 6221.4 | 37.56128 | 6.82816E-06 |
| 13 | Residual | 12 | 1987.6 | 165.633333 | | |
| 14 | Total | 14 | 14430.4 | | | |
| 15 | | | | | | |
| 16 | | *Coefficients* | *Standard Error* | *t Stat* | *P-value* | |
| 17 | Intercept | 729.8665 | 169.2575176 | 4.31216592 | 0.00101 | |
| 18 | Price | -10.887 | 3.495239703 | -3.1148078 | 0.0089406 | |
| 19 | Price Squared | 0.0465 | 0.017622784 | 2.6386297 | 0.0216284 | |

$b_0$  $b_1$  $b_2$

**FIGURE 18.2**  Partial output from Microsoft Excel for razor sales data

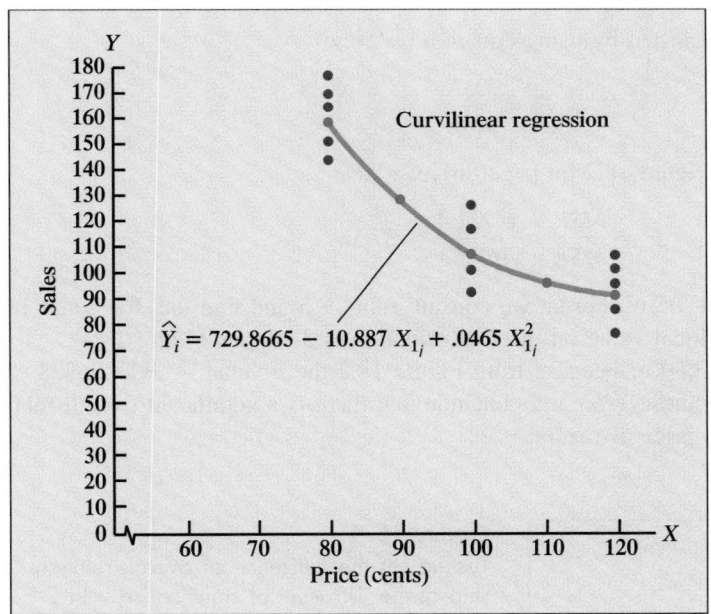

**FIGURE 18.3**  Scatter diagram expressing curvilinear relationship between price and sales for disposable razor data

Similarly, the linear term $b_1$ also has no direct interpretation in our curvilinear regression equation. To interpret the coefficient $b_2$, we see from Figure 18.3 that sales decrease with increasing price. However, we can also observe that these decreases in sales level off or become reduced with increasing price. This can be demonstrated by predicting average sales for packages priced at 79, 99, and 119 cents. Using our curvilinear regression equation,

$$\hat{Y}_i = 729.8665 - 10.887X_{1i} + .0465X_{1i}^2$$

for $X_{1i} = 79$, we have

$$\hat{Y}_i = 729.8665 - 10.887(79) + .0465(79)^2 = 160$$

For $X_{1i} = 99$, we have

$$\hat{Y}_i = 729.8665 - 10.887(99) + .0465(99)^2 = 107.8$$

For $X_{1i} = 119$, we have

$$\hat{Y}_i = 729.8665 - 10.887(119) + .0465(119)^2 = 92.8$$

Thus, a store selling the razors for 79 cents is expected to sell 52.2 more packages than a store selling them for 99 cents, but a store selling them for 99 cents is expected to sell only 15 more packages than a store selling them for $1.19 (119 cents).

## Testing for the Significance of the Curvilinear Model

Now that the curvilinear model has been fitted to the data, we can determine whether there is a significant overall relationship between sales $Y$ and price $X$. In a manner similar to multiple regression (see section 17.4), the null and alternative hypotheses can be set up as follows:

$H_0$: $\beta_1 = \beta_2 = 0$ (There is no overall relationship between $X_1$ and $Y$.)

$H_1$: $\beta_2$ and/or $\beta_1 \neq 0$ (There is an overall relationship between $X_1$ and $Y$.)

The null hypothesis can be tested by using equation (17.9):

$$F = \frac{MSR}{MSE}$$

From the Excel output in Figure 18.2 on page 861, we have

$$F = \frac{MSR}{MSE} = \frac{6{,}221.4}{165.63} = 37.56$$

If a level of significance of .05 is chosen, we consult Table E.5 and find that for 2 and 12 degrees of freedom, the critical value on the $F$ distribution is 3.89 (see Figure 18.4).

Because $F = 37.56 > 3.89$ or because from Figure 18.2 the $p$-value $= .000006828 <$ .05, we reject the null hypothesis ($H_0$) and conclude that there is a significant overall relationship between sales and price of razors.

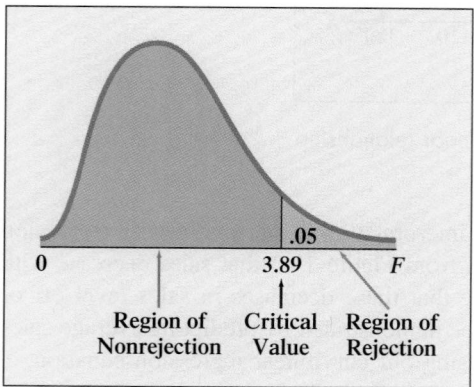

**FIGURE 18.4**
Testing for the existence of overall relationship at the .05 level of significance with 2 and 12 degrees of freedom

## Testing the Curvilinear Effect

In using a regression model to examine a relationship between two variables, we would like to fit not only the most accurate model but also the simplest model expressing that relationship. Therefore, it becomes important to examine whether there is a significant difference between the curvilinear model

$$Y_i = \beta_0 + \beta_1 X_{1i} + \beta_2 X_{1i}^2 + \epsilon_i$$

and the linear model

$$Y_i = \beta_0 + \beta_1 X_{1i} + \epsilon_i$$

We can compare these two models by determining the regression effect of adding the curvilinear term, given that the linear term has already been included $[SSR(X_1^2|X_1)]$.

You may recall that in section 17.5 we used the $t$ test for the regression coefficient to determine whether each particular variable made a significant contribution to the regression model. Because the standard error of each regression coefficient and its corresponding $t$ statistic are available as part of the Excel output (see Figure 18.2 on page 861), we test the significance of the contribution of the curvilinear effect with the following null and alternative hypotheses:

$H_0$: Including the curvilinear effect does not significantly improve the model ($\beta_2 = 0$)

$H_1$: Including the curvilinear effect significantly improves the model ($\beta_2 \neq 0$)

For our data

$$t = \frac{b_2}{S_{b_2}}$$

so that

$$t = \frac{.0465}{.01762} = 2.64$$

If a level of significance of .05 is selected, we use Table E.3 and find that with 12 degrees of freedom the critical values are $-2.1788$ and $+2.1788$ (see Figure 18.5).

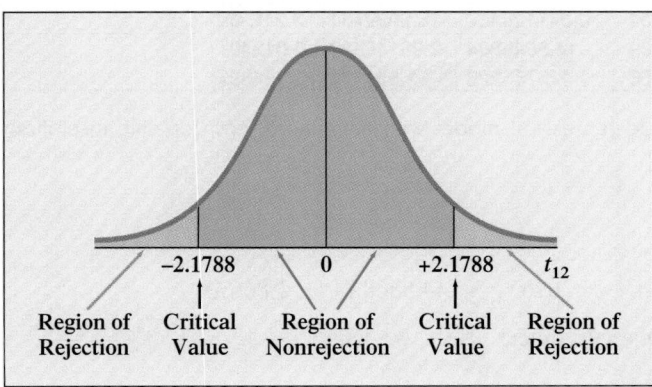

**FIGURE 18.5** Testing for contribution of the curvilinear effect to a regression model at the .05 level of significance with 12 degrees of freedom

Because $t = 2.64 > t_{12} = 2.1788$ or because the $p$-value $= .0216 < .05$, we reject $H_0$ and conclude that the curvilinear model is significantly better than the linear model in representing the relationship between sales and price.

As an additional illustration of a possible curvilinear effect, we turn to Example 18.1.

## Example 18.1 *Studying the Curvilinear Effect in a Multiple Regression Model*

In section 17.1 a multiple regression model was fit to predict monthly heating oil consumption based upon atmospheric temperature and the amount of attic insulation. Examination of the residual plot for attic insulation showed some evidence of a curvilinear effect. Fit a multiple regression model that includes a curvilinear term for attic insulation. At the .05 level of significance, is there evidence of a curvilinear effect for attic insulation?

### SOLUTION

Using Microsoft Excel, we obtain the following output:

| | A | B | C | D | E | F |
|---|---|---|---|---|---|---|
| 3 | *Regression Statistics* | | | | | |
| 4 | Multiple R | 0.9861577 | | | | |
| 5 | R Square | 0.972507 | | | | |
| 6 | Adjusted R Square | 0.96500891 | | | | |
| 7 | Standard Error | 24.2937794 | | | | |
| 8 | Observations | 15 | | | | |
| 9 | | | | | | |
| 10 | ANOVA | | | | | |
| 11 | | *df* | *SS* | *MS* | *F* | *Significance F* |
| 12 | Regression | 3 | 229643.1645 | 76547.7215 | 129.7006 | 7.26403E-09 |
| 13 | Residual | 11 | 6492.064875 | 590.187716 | | |
| 14 | Total | 14 | 236135.2293 | | | |
| 15 | | | | | | |
| 16 | | *Coefficients* | *Standard Error* | *t Stat* | *P-value* | |
| 17 | Intercept | 624.586421 | 42.43515952 | 14.7186066 | 1.39E-08 | |
| 18 | Temp(F) | -5.3626031 | 0.317128467 | -16.9098761 | 3.21E-09 | |
| 19 | Insulation | -44.586789 | 14.9546884 | -2.98145888 | 0.012487 | |
| 20 | Insu Squared | 1.86670465 | 1.123755228 | 1.661131 | 0.124892 | |

Microsoft Excel output for multiple regression model with curvilinear term for attic insulation

The regression model is

$$\hat{Y}_i = 624.5864 - 5.3626X_{1i} - 44.5868X_{2i} + 1.8667X_{2i}^2$$

To test for the significance of the curvilinear effect, we have

$H_0$: Including the curvilinear effect does not significantly improve the model ($\beta_3 = 0$)

$H_1$: Including the curvilinear effect significantly improves the model ($\beta_3 \neq 0$)

From the output, $t = 1.661 < 2.201$ or the $p$-value $= .1249 > .05$. The decision is not to reject the null hypothesis. We conclude that there is no evidence that the curvilinear effect for attic insulation is different from zero, so in the interest of keeping the model as simple as possible, the multiple linear regression model of section 17.1, $\hat{Y}_i = 562.151 - 5.43658X_{1i} - 20.0123X_{2i}$, should be used.

## Obtaining the Coefficient of Multiple Determination

In the multiple regression model, we computed the coefficient of multiple determination $r^2_{Y.12}$ (see section 17.1) to represent the proportion of variation in $Y$ that is explained by variation in the explanatory variables. In curvilinear regression analysis, this coefficient can be computed from equation (17.4):

$$r^2_{Y.12} = \frac{SSR}{SST}$$

From Figure 18.2,

$$SSR = 12,442.8 \quad SST = 14,430.4$$

Thus,

$$r^2_{Y.12} = \frac{SSR}{SST} = \frac{12,442.8}{14,430.4} = .862$$

This coefficient of multiple determination, computed as .862, means that 86.2% of the variation in sales can be explained by the curvilinear relationship between sales and price. An adjusted $r^2_{Y.12}$ can also be obtained that takes into account the number of explanatory variables and the degrees of freedom. In our curvilinear regression model, $p = 2$ because we have two explanatory variables, $X_1$, and its square, $X_1^2$. Thus, using equation (17.5) for the razor sales data, we have

$$r^2_{adj} = 1 - \left[ (1 - r^2_{Y.12}) \frac{(15 - 1)}{(15 - 2 - 1)} \right]$$

$$= 1 - \left[ (1 - .862) \frac{14}{12} \right]$$

$$= 1 - .161$$

$$= .839$$

## Problems for Section 18.1

### Learning the Basics

• **18.1** Suppose that the following curvilinear regression model has been fit for a sample of $n = 25$:

$$\hat{Y}_i = 5 + 3X_{1i} + 1.5X_{1i}^2$$

(a) Predict the average $Y$ for $X = 2$.

(b) Suppose that the $t$ statistic for the curvilinear term is 2.35. At the .05 level of significance, is there evidence that the curvilinear model is better than the linear model?

(c) Suppose that the $t$ statistic for the curvilinear term is 1.17. At the .05 level of significance, is there evidence that the curvilinear model is better than the linear model?

(d) Suppose that the regression coefficient for the linear effect was $-3.0$. Predict the average $Y$ for $X = 2$.

## Applying the Concepts

**• 18.2** A researcher for a major oil company wishes to develop a model to predict miles per gallon based on highway speed. An experiment is designed in which a test car is/ driven at speeds ranging from 10 miles per hour to 75 miles per hour in 5-mile increments over two trial periods. The results are as follows:

| OBSERVATION | MILES PER GALLON | SPEED (MILES PER HOUR) | OBSERVATION | MILES PER GALLON | SPEED (MILES PER HOUR) |
|---|---|---|---|---|---|
| 1 | 4.8 | 10 | 15 | 21.3 | 45 |
| 2 | 5.7 | 10 | 16 | 22.0 | 45 |
| 3 | 8.6 | 15 | 17 | 20.5 | 50 |
| 4 | 7.3 | 15 | 18 | 19.7 | 50 |
| 5 | 9.8 | 20 | 19 | 18.6 | 55 |
| 6 | 11.2 | 20 | 20 | 19.3 | 55 |
| 7 | 13.7 | 25 | 21 | 14.4 | 60 |
| 8 | 12.4 | 25 | 22 | 13.7 | 60 |
| 9 | 18.2 | 30 | 23 | 12.1 | 65 |
| 10 | 16.8 | 30 | 24 | 13.0 | 65 |
| 11 | 19.9 | 35 | 25 | 10.1 | 70 |
| 12 | 19.0 | 35 | 26 | 9.4 | 70 |
| 13 | 22.4 | 40 | 27 | 8.4 | 75 |
| 14 | 23.5 | 40 | 28 | 7.6 | 75 |

DATA FILE
SPEED

Assuming a curvilinear relationship between speed and mileage, based on the results obtained from Excel or Minitab:

(a) Set up a scatter diagram between speed and miles per gallon.

(b) State the equation for the curvilinear model.

(c) Predict the average mileage obtained when the car is driven at 55 miles per hour.

(d) Perform a residual analysis on your results and determine the adequacy of the fit of the model.

(e) Determine whether there is a significant curvilinear relationship between mileage and speed at the .05 level of significance.

(f) At the .05 level of significance, determine whether the curvilinear model is a better fit than the linear regression model.

(g) Interpret the meaning of the coefficient of multiple determination $r^2_{Y.12}$.

(h) Compute the adjusted $r^2$.

**18.3** An industrial psychologist would like to develop a model to predict the number of typing errors based on the amount of alcoholic consumption (in ounces). A random sample of 15 typists is selected with the following results:

| TYPIST | ALCOHOLIC CONSUMPTION | NUMBER OF ERRORS | TYPIST | ALCOHOLIC CONSUMPTION | NUMBER OF ERRORS |
|---|---|---|---|---|---|
| 1 | 0 | 2 | 9 | 2 | 9 |
| 2 | 0 | 6 | 10 | 3 | 13 |
| 3 | 0 | 3 | 11 | 3 | 18 |
| 4 | 1 | 7 | 12 | 3 | 16 |
| 5 | 1 | 5 | 13 | 4 | 24 |
| 6 | 1 | 9 | 14 | 4 | 30 |
| 7 | 2 | 12 | 15 | 4 | 22 |
| 8 | 2 | 7 | | | |

**DATA FILE ALCOHOL**

Assuming a curvilinear relationship between alcoholic consumption and the number of errors, and using Microsoft Excel or Minitab:

(a) Set up a scatter diagram between alcoholic consumption $X$ and number of errors $Y$.

(b) State the equation for the curvilinear model.

(c) Predict the average number of errors made by a typist who has consumed 2.5 ounces of alcohol.

(d) Perform a residual analysis on your results and determine the adequacy of the fit of the model.

(e) Determine whether there is a significant curvilinear relationship between alcoholic consumption and the number of errors made at the .05 level of significance.

(f) At the .05 level of significance, determine whether the curvilinear model is a better fit than the linear regression model.

(g) Interpret the meaning of the coefficient of multiple determination $r^2_{Y.12}$.

(h) Compute the adjusted $r^2$.

**18.4** Suppose an agronomist wants to design a study in which a wide range of fertilizer levels (pounds per thousand square feet) is to be used to determine whether the relationship between the yield of tomatoes and amount of fertilizer can be fit by a curvilinear model. Six rates of application are to be used: 0, 20, 40, 60, 80, and 100 pounds per 1,000 square feet. These rates are then randomly assigned to plots of land with the following results:

| PLOT | FERTILIZER APPLICATION RATE | YIELD (POUNDS) | PLOT | FERTILIZER APPLICATION RATE | YIELD (POUNDS) |
|---|---|---|---|---|---|
| 1 | 0 | 6 | 7 | 60 | 46 |
| 2 | 0 | 9 | 8 | 60 | 50 |
| 3 | 20 | 19 | 9 | 80 | 48 |
| 4 | 20 | 24 | 10 | 80 | 54 |
| 5 | 40 | 32 | 11 | 100 | 52 |
| 6 | 40 | 38 | 12 | 100 | 58 |

**DATA FILE TOMYLD2**

Assuming a curvilinear relationship between the application rate and tomato yield, and using Microsoft Excel or Minitab:

(a) Set up a scatter diagram between application rate and yield.

(b) State the regression equation for the curvilinear model.

(c) Predict the average yield of tomatoes (in pounds) for a plot that has been fertilized with 70 pounds per 1,000 square feet.

(d) Perform a residual analysis on your results and determine the adequacy of the fit of the model.

(e) Determine whether the curvilinear model indicates a significant overall relationship between the application rate and tomato yield at the .05 level of significance.

(f) What is the *p*-value in (e)? Interpret its meaning.

(g) At the .05 level of significance, determine whether there is a significant curvilinear effect.

(h) What is the *p*-value in (g)? Interpret its meaning.

(i) Interpret the meaning of the coefficient of multiple determination $r^2_{Y.12}$.

(j) Compute the adjusted $r^2$.

**18.5** An auditor for a county government would like to develop a model to predict the county taxes based on the age of single-family houses. A random sample of 19 single-family houses has been selected with the following results.

| COUNTY TAXES ($) | AGE (YEARS) | COUNTY TAXES ($) | AGE (YEARS) |
|---|---|---|---|
| 925 | 1 | 480 | 20 |
| 870 | 2 | 486 | 22 |
| 809 | 4 | 462 | 25 |
| 720 | 4 | 441 | 25 |
| 694 | 5 | 426 | 30 |
| 630 | 8 | 368 | 35 |
| 626 | 10 | 350 | 40 |
| 562 | 10 | 348 | 50 |
| 546 | 12 | 322 | 50 |
| 523 | 15 | | |

**DATA FILE**
**TAXES**

Assuming a curvilinear relationship between the age and county taxes, and using Microsoft Excel or Minitab:

(a) Set up a scatter diagram between age and county taxes.

(b) State the regression equation for the curvilinear model.

(c) Predict the average county taxes for a house that is 20 years old.

(d) Perform a residual analysis on your results and determine the adequacy of the fit of the model.

(e) Determine whether there is a significant overall relationship between age and county taxes at the .05 level of significance.

(f) What is the *p*-value in (e)? Interpret its meaning.

(g) At the .05 level of significance, determine whether the curvilinear model is superior to the linear regression model.

(h) What is the *p*-value in (g)? Interpret its meaning.

(i) Interpret the meaning of the coefficient of multiple determination $r^2_{Y.12}$.

(j) Compute the adjusted $r^2$.

## 18.2 DUMMY-VARIABLE MODELS

In our discussion of multiple regression models we have assumed that each explanatory (or independent) variable is numerical. However, there are many occasions in which categorical variables need to be included in the model development process. For example, in section 17.1 we used the atmospheric temperature and the amount of attic insulation to predict the average monthly consumption of home heating oil. In addition to these numerical independent variables, we may want to include the effect of the style of the house (for example, ranch- or non-ranch-style houses) when developing a model to predict heating oil consumption.

The use of **dummy variables** is the vehicle that permits us to consider categorical explanatory variables as part of the regression model. If a given categorical explanatory variable has two categories, then only one dummy variable will be needed to represent the two categories. A particular dummy variable $X_d$ is defined as

$$X_d = 0 \text{ if the observation is in category 1}$$
$$X_d = 1 \text{ if the observation is in category 2}$$

To illustrate the application of dummy variables in regression, we will examine a model for predicting the average assessed value from a sample of 15 houses based on the heating area (in thousands of square feet) and whether or not the house has a fireplace. The data are presented in Table 18.2. A dummy variable for fireplace ($X_2$) can be defined as

$$X_2 = 0 \text{ if the house does not have a fireplace}$$
$$X_2 = 1 \text{ if the house has a fireplace}$$

Assuming that the slope of assessed value with heating area is the same for houses that have and do not have a fireplace, the regression model to be fitted is

$$Y_i = \beta_0 + \beta_1 X_{1i} + \beta_2 X_{2i} + \epsilon_i$$

where

$Y_i$ = assessed value in thousands of dollars

$\beta_0$ = $Y$ intercept

$\beta_1$ = slope of assessed value with heating area holding constant the effect of the presence of a fireplace

$\beta_2$ = incremental effect of the presence of a fireplace holding constant the effect of heating area

$\epsilon_i$ = random error in $Y$ for house $i$

Figure 18.6 on page 870 illustrates the output for this model obtained from Minitab. From this output, the sample regression equation may be stated as

$$\hat{Y}_i = 50.09 + 16.186X_{1i} + 3.853X_{2i}$$

**Table 18.2** *Predicting assessed value based on heating area and presence of a fireplace*

| HOUSE | ASSESSED VALUE ($000) | HEATING AREA OF DWELLING (THOUSANDS OF SQUARE FEET) | FIREPLACE | HOUSE | ASSESSED VALUE ($000) | HEATING AREA OF DWELLING (THOUSANDS OF SQUARE FEET) | FIREPLACE |
|---|---|---|---|---|---|---|---|
| 1 | 84.4 | 2.00 | Yes | 9 | 78.5 | 1.59 | Yes |
| 2 | 77.4 | 1.71 | No | 10 | 79.2 | 1.50 | Yes |
| 3 | 75.7 | 1.45 | No | 11 | 86.7 | 1.90 | Yes |
| 4 | 85.9 | 1.76 | Yes | 12 | 79.3 | 1.39 | Yes |
| 5 | 79.1 | 1.93 | No | 13 | 74.5 | 1.54 | No |
| 6 | 70.4 | 1.20 | Yes | 14 | 83.8 | 1.89 | Yes |
| 7 | 75.8 | 1.55 | Yes | 15 | 76.8 | 1.59 | No |
| 8 | 85.9 | 1.93 | Yes | | | | |

DATA FILE
HOUSE3

```
The regression equation is
Value = 50.1 + 16.2 Heating + 3.85 Firepl

Predictor          Coef        StDev           T          P
Constant         50.090        4.352       11.51      0.000
Heating          16.186        2.574        6.29      0.000
Firepl            3.853        1.241        3.10      0.009

S = 2.263      R-Sq = 81.1%      R-Sq(adj) = 78.0%

Analysis of Variance

Source             DF          SS           MS          F          P
Regression          2      263.70       131.85      25.76      0.000
Residual Error     12       61.43         5.12
Total              14      325.14

Source         DF      Seq SS
Heating         1      214.37
Firepl          1       49.33
```

$b_1$

$b_2$

**FIGURE 18.6**  Minitab output for regression model that includes heating area and presence of a fireplace

For houses without a fireplace, this reduces to

$$\hat{Y}_i = 50.09 + 16.186X_{1i}$$

because $X_2 = 0$; whereas for houses with a fireplace, the regression equation is

$$\hat{Y}_i = 53.943 + 16.186X_{1i}$$

because $X_2 = 1$, so that 3.853 is added on to 50.09. In this model, we can interpret the slopes as follows:

**1.** Holding constant whether or not a house has a fireplace, for each increase of 1,000 square feet in heating area, the average assessed value is predicted to increase by 16.186 thousands of dollars (or $16,186).

**2.** Holding constant the heating area of the house, the presence of a fireplace is predicted to increase the assessed value of the house by an average of 3.853 thousand dollars (or $3,853).

We note from Figure 18.6 that the $t$ statistic for the slope of heating area with assessed value is 6.29 and the $p$-value is .000, whereas the $t$ statistic for presence of a fireplace is 3.10 and the $p$-value is .009. Thus, each of the two variables is making a significant contribution to the model at a level of significance of .01. In addition, 81.1% of the variation in assessed value is explained by variation in the heating area of the house and whether or not the house has a fireplace.

However, before we can use this model, we need to assure ourselves that the slope of assessed value with heating area is the same for houses with a fireplace as it is for houses without a fireplace. A hypothesis of equal slopes of a $Y$ variable with $X$ can be evaluated by defining an interaction term that consists of the product of the explanatory variable $X_1$

```
The regression equation is
Value = 63.0 + 8.36 Heating - 11.8 Firepl + 9.52 Ht*Fire

Predictor          Coef         StDev             T          P
Constant         62.952         9.612          6.55      0.000
Heating           8.362         5.817          1.44      0.178
Firepl          -11.84         10.65          -1.11      0.290
Ht*Fire           9.518         6.416          1.48      0.166

S = 2.157       R-Sq = 84.3%      R-Sq(adj) = 80.0%

Analysis of Variance

Source              DF             SS            MS          F          P
Regression           3        273.944        91.315      19.62      0.000
Residual Error      11         51.192         4.654
Total               14        325.136

Source          DF       Seq SS
Heating          1      214.374
Firepl           1       49.330
Ht*Fire          1       10.240
```

FIGURE 18.7    Minitab output for regression model that includes heating area, presence of fireplace, and interaction of heating area and presence of fireplace

and the dummy variable $X_2$ and then testing whether this interaction variable makes a significant contribution to a regression model that contains the other $X$ variables. If the interaction is significant, we cannot use our model for prediction. For the data of Table 18.2,

$$X_3 = X_1 \times X_2$$

The Minitab output for this regression model, which includes the heating area of the house ($X_1$), the presence of a fireplace ($X_2$), and the interaction of $X_1$ and $X_2$ (which we have defined as $X_3$), is provided in Figure 18.7.

To test the null hypothesis $H_0:\beta_3 = 0$ versus the alternative hypothesis $H_1:\beta_3 \neq 0$, from Figure 18.7 we observe that the $t$ statistic for the interaction of heating area and presence of a fireplace is 1.48. Because the $p$-value = .166 > .05, the null hypothesis is not rejected. We conclude that the interaction term does not make a significant contribution to the model given that heating area and presence of a fireplace are already included.

Now that we have examined a regression model that includes a categorical explanatory variable, we turn to Example 18.2 to study a regression model in which there is more than one numerical explanatory variable along with a categorical variable.

## Example 18.2    *Studying a Regression Model that Contains a Dummy Variable*

In the Using Statistics example in chapter 17 (see page 812) heating oil consumption was predicted based on atmospheric temperature $X_1$ and amount of attic insulation $X_2$. Suppose that, of the 15 houses in that sample, houses 1, 4, 6, 7, 8, 10, and 12 are ranch-style houses ($X_3$). Fit the appropriate regression model based on these three independent variables.

## SOLUTION

A dummy variable for ranch-style house ($X_3$) is defined as

$$X_3 = 0 \text{ if the style is not ranch}$$
$$X_3 = 1 \text{ if the style is ranch}$$

Assuming that the slope between home heating oil consumption and atmospheric temperature $X_1$ and the amount of attic insulation $X_2$ is the same for both groups, the regression model is

$$Y_i = \beta_0 + \beta_1 X_{1i} + \beta_2 X_{2i} + \beta_3 X_{3i} + \epsilon_i$$

where

$Y_i$ = monthly heating oil consumption in gallons

$\beta_0$ = $Y$ intercept

$\beta_1$ = slope of heating oil consumption with atmospheric temperature holding constant the effect of attic insulation and the house style

$\beta_2$ = slope of heating oil consumption with attic insulation holding constant the effect of atmospheric temperature and the house style

$\beta_3$ = incremental effect of the presence of a ranch-style house holding constant the effect of atmospheric temperature and attic insulation

$\epsilon_i$ = random error in $Y$ for house $i$

The figure below displays partial output obtained from Microsoft Excel.

| | A | B | C | D | E | F | G |
|---|---|---|---|---|---|---|---|
| 1 | SUMMARY OUTPUT | | | | | | |
| 2 | | | | | | | |
| 3 | Regression Statistics | | | | | | |
| 4 | Multiple R | 0.9942062 | | | | | |
| 5 | R Square | 0.9884459 | | | | | |
| 6 | Adjusted R Square | 0.9852948 | | | | | |
| 7 | Standard Error | 15.748939 | | | | | |
| 8 | Observations | 15 | | | | | |
| 9 | | | | | | | |
| 10 | ANOVA | | | | | | |
| 11 | | df | SS | MS | F | Significance F | |
| 12 | Regression | 3 | 233406.9094 | 77802.3 | 313.6822 | 6.21548E-11 | |
| 13 | Residual | 11 | 2728.319981 | 248.0291 | | | |
| 14 | Total | 14 | 236135.2293 | | | | |
| 15 | | | | | | | |
| 16 | | Coefficients | Standard Error | t Stat | P-value | Lower 95% | Upper 95% |
| 17 | Intercept | 592.54012 | 14.33698425 | 41.32948 | 2.02E-13 | 560.9846112 | 624.0956223 |
| 18 | Temp(F) | -5.5251009 | 0.204431228 | -27.0267 | 2.07E-11 | -5.97505121 | -5.075150557 |
| 19 | Insulation | -21.376128 | 1.448019304 | -14.7623 | 1.35E-08 | -24.5631986 | -18.18905733 |
| 20 | Style | -38.972666 | 8.358437237 | -4.66267 | 0.000691 | -57.3694717 | -20.57586045 |

Excel output for regression model including dummy variable (style) for home heating oil data

From this output, the sample regression equation may be stated as

$$\hat{Y}_i = 592.5401 - 5.5251 X_{1i} - 21.3761 X_{2i} - 38.9726 X_{3i}$$

| ATM Number | Withdrawal Amount ($000) | Median Assessed Value of Homes ($000) | Location of ATM |
|---|---|---|---|
| 1 | 12.0 | 225 | 1 |
| 2 | 9.9 | 170 | 0 |
| 3 | 9.1 | 153 | 1 |
| 4 | 8.2 | 132 | 0 |
| 5 | 12.4 | 237 | 1 |
| 6 | 10.4 | 187 | 1 |
| 7 | 12.7 | 245 | 1 |
| 8 | 8.0 | 125 | 1 |
| 9 | 11.5 | 215 | 1 |
| 10 | 9.7 | 170 | 0 |
| 11 | 11.7 | 223 | 0 |
| 12 | 8.6 | 147 | 0 |
| 13 | 10.9 | 197 | 1 |
| 14 | 9.4 | 167 | 0 |
| 15 | 11.2 | 210 | 0 |

**DATA FILE ATM2**

(f) At the .05 level of significance, determine whether each explanatory variable makes a contribution to the regression model. On the basis of these results, indicate the regression model that should be used in this problem.

(g) Set up 95% confidence interval estimates of the population slope for the relationship between the withdrawal amount and median assessed value of homes, and for the withdrawal amount and ATM location.

(h) Interpret the meaning of the coefficient of multiple determination $r^2_{Y.12}$.

(i) Compute the adjusted $r^2$.

(j) Compute and interpret the coefficients of partial determination.

(k) What assumption about the slope of withdrawal amount with median assessed value of homes must be made in this problem?

(l) Include an interaction term in the model and, at the .05 level of significance, determine whether it makes a significant contribution to the model.

(m) On the basis of the results of (f) and (l), which model is more appropriate? Explain.

**18.10** Referring to Problem 16.79 (relating wins to ERA) on page 803, suppose that in addition to using earned run average to predict the number of wins, Crazy Dave wants to include the league (American versus National) as an explanatory variable. On the basis of the results obtained using Microsoft Excel or Minitab:

**DATA FILE BB97**

(a) State the multiple regression equation.

(b) Interpret the meaning of the slopes in this problem.

(c) Predict the average number of wins for a team with an ERA of 4.00 in the American League.

(d) Perform a residual analysis on your results and determine the adequacy of the fit of the model.

(e) Determine whether there is a significant relationship between wins and the two explanatory variables (ERA and league) at the .05 level of significance.

(f) At the .05 level of significance, determine whether each explanatory variable makes a contribution to the regression model. On the basis of these results, indicate the regression model that should be used in this problem.

(g) Set up 95% confidence interval estimates of the population slope for the relationship between wins and ERA and between wins and league.

(h) Compare the slope obtained in (b) with the slope for the simple linear regression model of Problem 16.79 on page 803. Explain the difference in the results.

(i) Interpret the meaning of the coefficient of multiple determination $r^2_{Y.12}$.

(j) Compute the adjusted $r^2$.

(k) Compare $r^2_{Y.12}$ with the value computed in Problem 16.79(f). Explain the results.

(l) Compute the coefficients of partial determination and interpret their meaning.

(m) What assumption about the slope of wins with ERA must be made in this problem?

(n) Include an interaction term in the model and, at the .05 level of significance, determine whether it makes a significant contribution to the model.

(o) On the basis of the results of (f) and (n), which model is more appropriate? Explain.

● **18.11** A real estate association in a suburban community would like to study the relationship between the size of a single-family house (as measured by the number of rooms) and the selling price of the house. The study is to be carried out in two different neighborhoods, one on the east side of the community and the other on the west side. A random sample of 20 houses was selected with the following results:

| SELLING PRICE | NUMBER OF ROOMS | NEIGHBORHOOD | SELLING PRICE | NUMBER OF ROOMS | NEIGHBORHOOD |
|---|---|---|---|---|---|
| 109.6 | 7 | East | 108.5 | 6 | West |
| 107.4 | 8 | East | 181.3 | 13 | West |
| 140.3 | 9 | East | 137.4 | 10 | West |
| 146.5 | 12 | East | 146.2 | 10 | West |
| 98.2 | 6 | East | 142.4 | 9 | West |
| 137.8 | 9 | East | 123.7 | 8 | West |
| 124.1 | 10 | East | 129.6 | 8 | West |
| 113.2 | 8 | East | 143.6 | 9 | West |
| 127.8 | 9 | East | 160.7 | 11 | West |
| 125.3 | 8 | East | 148.3 | 9 | West |

**DATA FILE
NEIGHBOR**

Using Microsoft Excel or Minitab:
(a) State the multiple regression equation.
(b) Interpret the meaning of the slopes in this problem.
(c) Predict the average selling price for a house with nine rooms that is located on the east side of the community.
(d) Perform a residual analysis on your results and determine the adequacy of the fit of the model.
(e) Determine whether there is a significant relationship between selling price and the two explanatory variables (rooms and neighborhood) at the .05 level of significance.
(f) At the .05 level of significance, determine whether each explanatory variable makes a contribution to the regression model. On the basis of these results, indicate the regression model that should be used in this problem.
(g) Set up 95% confidence interval estimates of the population slope for the relationship

between selling price and number of rooms and between selling price and neighborhood.

(h) Interpret the meaning of the coefficient of multiple determination $r^2_{Y.12}$.

(i) Compute the adjusted $r^2$.

(j) Compute the coefficients of partial determination and interpret their meaning.

(k) What assumption about the slope of selling price with number of rooms must be made in this problem?

(l) Include an interaction term in the model and, at the .05 level of significance, determine whether it makes a significant contribution to the model.

(m) On the basis of the results of (f) and (l), which model is more appropriate? Explain.

**18.12** The file UNIV&COL contains data on 80 colleges and universities. Among the variables included are the annual total cost (in thousands of dollars), the average total score on the Scholastic Aptitude Test (SAT), and whether the school is public or private (0 = public, 1 = private). Suppose we want to develop a model to predict the annual total cost based on SAT score and whether the school is public or private:

DATA FILE
UNIV&COL

(a) State the multiple regression equation.

(b) Interpret the meaning of the slopes in this problem.

(c) Predict the average total cost for a school with an average total SAT score of 1,000 that is a public institution.

(d) Perform a residual analysis on your results and determine the adequacy of the fit of the model.

(e) Determine whether there is a significant relationship between annual total cost and the two explanatory variables (total SAT score and whether the school is public or private) at the .05 level of significance.

(f) At the .05 level of significance, determine whether each explanatory variable makes a contribution to the regression model. On the basis of these results, indicate the regression model that should be used in this problem.

(g) Set up 95% confidence interval estimates of the population slope for the relationship between annual total cost and total SAT score and between annual total cost and whether the school is public or private.

(h) Interpret the meaning of the coefficient of multiple determination $r^2_{Y.12}$.

(i) Compute the adjusted $r^2$.

(j) Compute the coefficients of partial determination and interpret their meaning.

(k) What assumption about the slope of annual total cost with total SAT score must be made in this problem?

(l) Include an interaction term in the model and, at the .05 level of significance, determine whether it makes a significant contribution to the model.

(m) On the basis of the results of (f) and (l), which model is more appropriate? Explain.

 **18.3**  USING TRANSFORMATIONS IN REGRESSION MODELS

In our discussion of multiple regression models we have thus far examined the multiple linear regression model [equation (17.1)], the curvilinear model [equation (18.1)], and a model containing a categorical explanatory (i.e., dummy) variable. In this section we discuss regression models in which the independent $X$ variable, the dependent $Y$ variable, or both are transformed in order to either overcome violations of the assumptions of regression or make a model linear in its form. Among the many transformations available (see reference 11) are the square-root transformation and transformations involving the natural logarithm.[1]

[1]*The natural logarithm, usually abbreviated ln, is the logarithm to the base e, the mathematical constant approximately equal to 2.71828.*

## The Square-Root Transformation

The **square-root transformation** is often used to overcome violations of the *homoscedasticity* assumption, as well as to transform a model that is not linear into one that is linear in form. If a square-root transformation were applied to the values of each of two explanatory variables, the multiple regression model would be

### Multiple Regression Model with a Square-Root Transformation

$$Y_i = \beta_0 + \beta_1\sqrt{X_{1i}} + \beta_2\sqrt{X_{2i}} + \epsilon_i \qquad (18.3)$$

The use of a square-root transformation is illustrated in Example 18.4.

## Example 18.4 *Using the Square-Root Transformation*

Given the following values for $Y$ and $X$,

| Y | X | Y | X |
|---|---|---|---|
| 42.7 | 1 | 100.4 | 3 |
| 50 4 | 1 | 104.7 | 4 |
| 69.1 | 2 | 112.3 | 4 |
| 79.8 | 2 | 113.6 | 5 |
| 90.0 | 3 | 123.9 | 5 |

use a square-root transformation for the $X$ variable and develop a scatter diagram.

### SOLUTION

The first figure below displays the scatter diagram of $X$ and $Y$, and the second figure plots the square root of $X$ versus $Y$. These figures are obtained from Microsoft Excel.

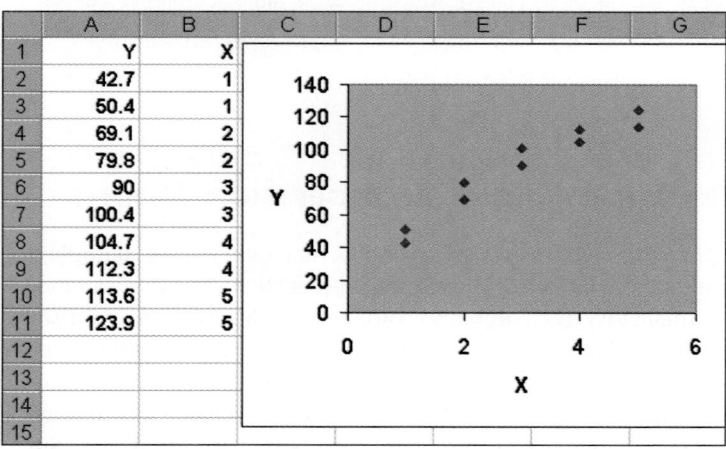

Scatter diagram of $X$ and $Y$

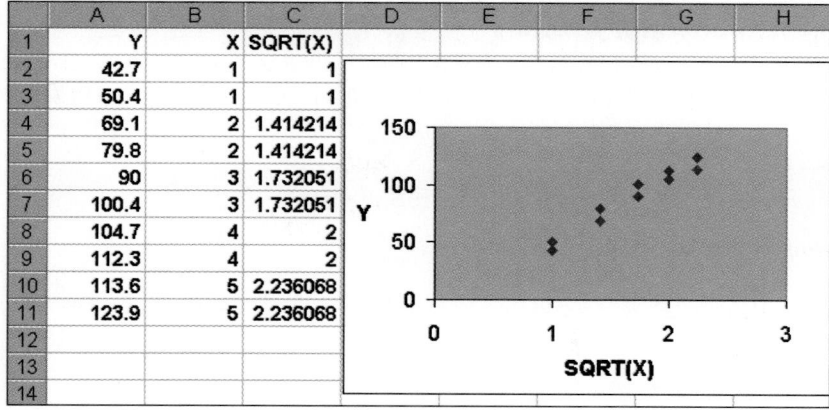

| | A | B | C | D | E | F | G | H |
|---|---|---|---|---|---|---|---|---|
| 1 | Y | X | SQRT(X) | | | | | |
| 2 | 42.7 | 1 | 1 | | | | | |
| 3 | 50.4 | 1 | 1 | | | | | |
| 4 | 69.1 | 2 | 1.414214 | | | | | |
| 5 | 79.8 | 2 | 1.414214 | | | | | |
| 6 | 90 | 3 | 1.732051 | | | | | |
| 7 | 100.4 | 3 | 1.732051 | | | | | |
| 8 | 104.7 | 4 | 2 | | | | | |
| 9 | 112.3 | 4 | 2 | | | | | |
| 10 | 113.6 | 5 | 2.236068 | | | | | |
| 11 | 123.9 | 5 | 2.236068 | | | | | |
| 12 | | | | | | | | |
| 13 | | | | | | | | |
| 14 | | | | | | | | |

Scatter diagram of square root of $X$ and $Y$

Note that the square-root transformation has taken a relationship that appears to be nonlinear and created a relationship that appears linear.

In some situations, the use of a logarithmic transformation can change a model whose form is nonlinear into a linear model. For example, the multiplicative model

### Original Multiplicative Model

$$Y_i = \beta_0 X_{1i}^{\beta_1} X_{2i}^{\beta_2} \epsilon_i \tag{18.4}$$

can be transformed (by taking natural logarithms of both the dependent and explanatory variables) to the model

### Transformed Multiplicative Model

$$\ln Y_i = \ln \beta_0 + \beta_1 \ln X_{1i} + \beta_2 \ln X_{2i} + \ln \epsilon_i \tag{18.5}$$

Hence, equation (18.5) is linear in the natural logarithms. In a similar fashion, the exponential model

### Original Exponential Model

$$Y_i = e^{\beta_0 + \beta_1 X_{1i} + \beta_2 X_{2i}} \epsilon_i \tag{18.6}$$

can also be transformed to linear form (by taking natural logarithms of both the dependent and explanatory variables). The resulting model is

## Transformed Exponential Model

$$\ln Y_i = \beta_0 + \beta_1 X_{1i} + \beta_2 X_{2i} + \ln \epsilon_i \qquad (18.7)$$

### Example 18.5 *Using the Natural Log Transformation*

Given the following values for $Y$ and $X$,

| Y | X | Y | X |
|------|---|------|---|
| 19.5 | 1 | 11.8 | 3 |
| 18.8 | 1 | 9.7 | 4 |
| 15.3 | 2 | 9.6 | 4 |
| 14.9 | 2 | 7.6 | 5 |
| 12.2 | 3 | 7.4 | 5 |

use a natural log transformation for the $Y$ variable and develop a scatter diagram.

### SOLUTION

The first figure below displays the scatter diagram of $X$ and $Y$, and the second figure plots $X$ versus the natural logarithm of $Y$. Note that the natural log transformation has taken a relationship that appears to be nonlinear and created a relationship that appears linear.

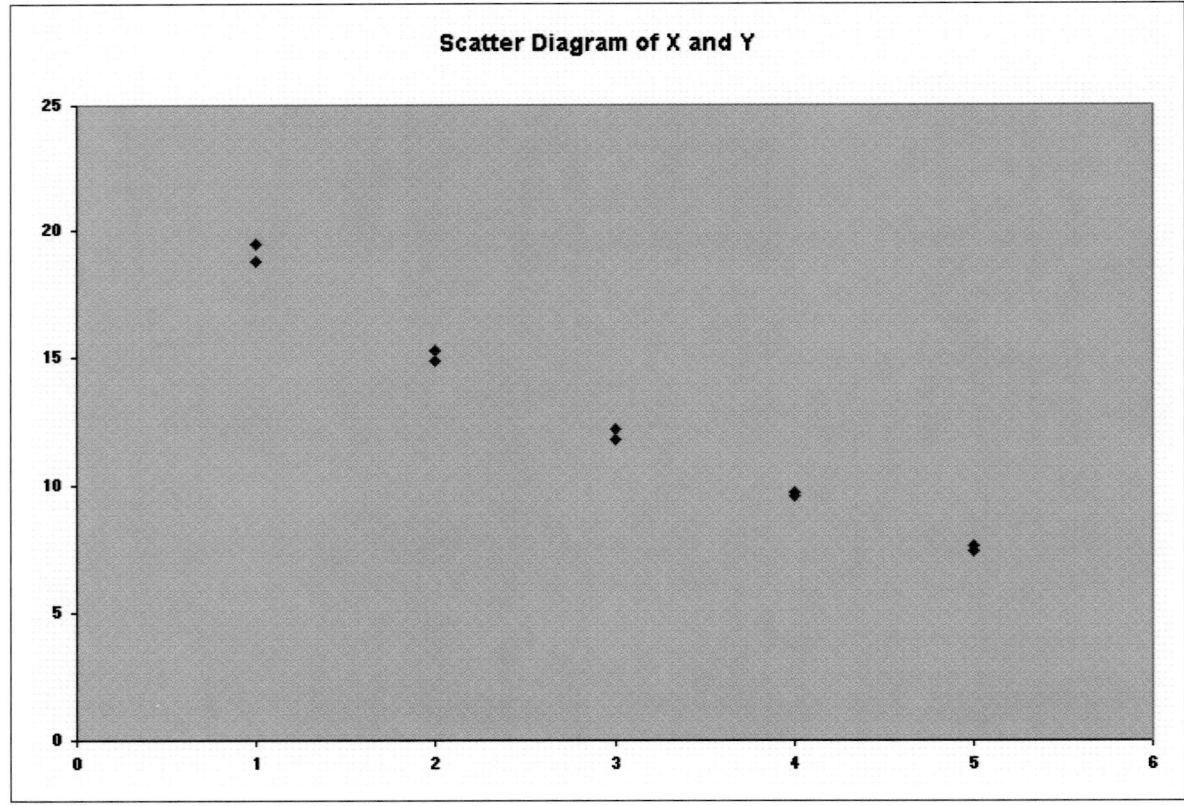

Scatter diagram of *X* and *Y* obtained from Microsoft Excel

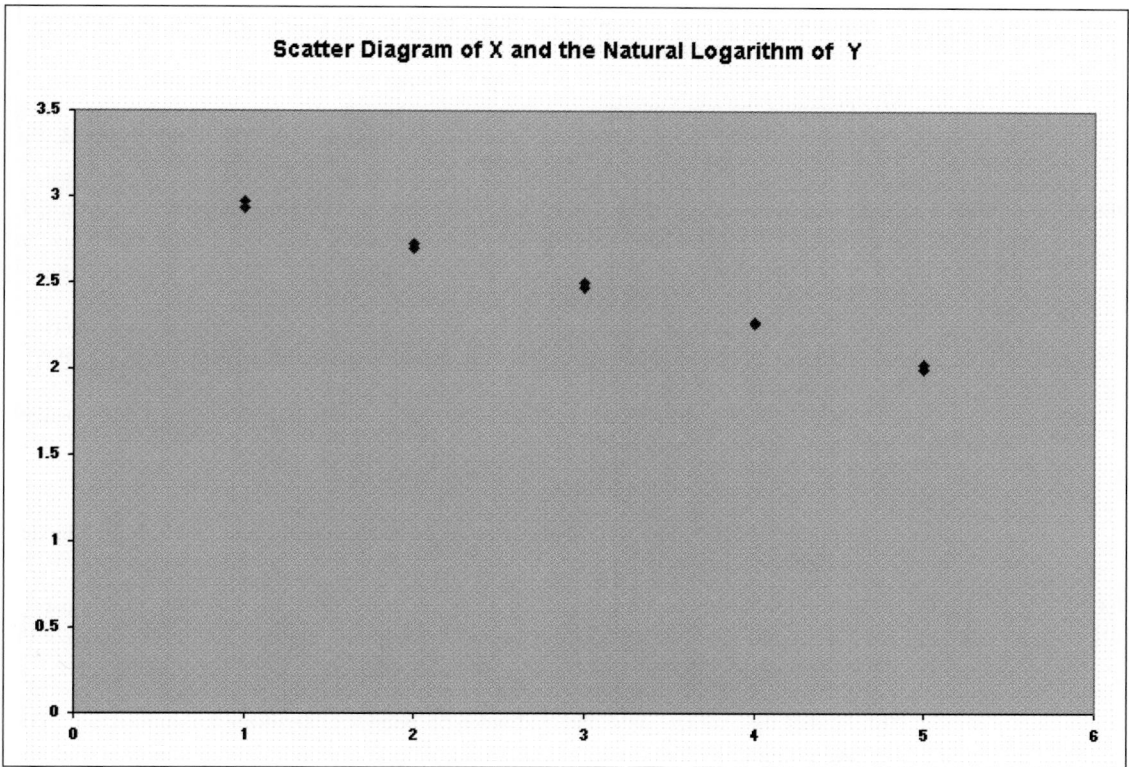

Scatter diagram of X and the natural logarithm of Y obtained from Microsoft Excel

## Problems for Section 18.3

### Learning the Basics

**18.13** Suppose that the following model has been fit to a set of data

$$\ln \hat{Y}_i = 3.07 + .9 \ln X_{1i} + 1.41 \ln X_{2i}$$

(a) Predict the value of Y for $X_1 = 8.5$ and $X_2 = 5.2$.
(b) Interpret the meaning of the slopes.

● **18.14** Suppose that the following model has been fit to a set of data

$$\ln \hat{Y}_i = 4.62 + .5 X_{1i} + .7 X_2$$

(a) Predict the value of Y for $X_1 = 8.5$ and $X_2 = 5.2$.
(b) Interpret the meaning of the slopes.

### Applying the Concepts

● **18.15** Referring to the data of Problem 18.2 on page 866 and using the file SPEED, perform a square-root transformation of the explanatory variable (speed).
(a) State the regression equation.
(b) Predict the average mileage obtained when the car is driven at 55 miles per hour.
(c) Perform a residual analysis of your results and determine the adequacy of the fit of the model.

DATA FILE
SPEED

(d) At the .05 level of significance, is there a significant relationship between mileage and the square root of speed?

(e) Interpret the meaning of the coefficient of determination $r^2$ in this problem.

(f) Compute the adjusted $r^2$.

(g) Compare your results with those obtained in Problem 18.2. Which model would you choose? Why?

**DATA FILE
SPEED**

• **18.16** Referring to the data of Problem 18.2 on page 866 and using the file SPEED, perform a natural logarithmic transformation of the response variable miles per gallon and reanalyze the data using this model. On the basis of your results:

(a) State the regression equation.

(b) Predict the average mileage obtained when the car is driven at 55 miles per hour.

(c) Perform a residual analysis of your results and determine the adequacy of the fit of the model.

(d) At the .05 level of significance, is there a significant relationship between the natural logarithm of miles per hour and speed?

(e) Interpret the meaning of the coefficient of determination $r^2$ in this problem.

(f) Compute the adjusted $r^2$.

(g) Compare your results with those obtained in Problems 18.2 and 18.15. Which model would you choose? Why?

**DATA FILE
TOMYLD2**

**18.17** Referring to the data of Problem 18.4 on page 867 and using the file TOMYLD2, perform a natural logarithmic transformation of the response variable yield and reanalyze the data. On the basis of your results:

(a) State the regression equation.

(b) Predict the average yield obtained when 55 pounds of fertilizer are applied per 1,000 square feet.

(c) Perform a residual analysis of your results and determine the adequacy of the fit of the model.

(d) At the .05 level of significance, is there a significant relationship between the natural logarithm of yield and the amount of fertilizer?

(e) Interpret the meaning of the coefficient of determination $r^2$ in this problem.

(f) Compute the adjusted $r^2$.

(g) Compare your results with those obtained in Problem 18.4. Which model would you choose? Why?

**DATA FILE
TOMYLD2**

**18.18** Referring to the data of Problem 18.4 on page 867 and using the file TOMYLD2, perform a square-root transformation of the explanatory variable amount of fertilizer and reanalyze the data. On the basis of your results:

(a) State the regression equation.

(b) Predict the average yield obtained when 55 pounds of fertilizer are applied per 1,000 square feet.

(c) Perform a residual analysis of your results and determine the adequacy of the fit of the model.

(d) At the .05 level of significance, is there a significant relationship between yield and the square root of the amount of fertilizer?

(e) Interpret the meaning of the coefficient of determination $r^2$ in this problem.

(f) Compute the adjusted $r^2$.

(g) Compare your results with those obtained in Problems 18.4 and 18.17. Which model would you choose? Why?

## 18.4 COLLINEARITY

One important problem in the application of multiple regression analysis involves the possible **collinearity** of the explanatory variables. This condition refers to situations in which some of the explanatory variables are highly correlated with each other. In such situations, collinear variables do not provide new information, and it becomes difficult to separate the effect of such variables on the dependent or response variable. In such cases, the values of the regression coefficients for the correlated variables may fluctuate drastically, depending on which independent variables are included in the model.

One method of measuring collinearity uses the **variance inflationary factor (VIF)** for each explanatory variable. $VIF_j$, the variance inflationary factor for variable $j$ is defined as in equation (18.8):

**Variance Inflationary Factor**

$$VIF_j = \frac{1}{1 - R_j^2} \qquad (18.8)$$

where $R_j^2$ is the coefficient of multiple determination of explanatory variable $X_j$ with all other explanatory variables.

If there are only two explanatory variables, $R_1^2$ is just the coefficient of determination between $X_1$ and $X_2$. It would be identical to $R_2^2$, which is the coefficient of determination between $X_2$ and $X_1$. If, for example, there were three explanatory variables, then $R_1^2$ would be the coefficient of multiple determination of $X_1$ with $X_2$ and $X_3$, $R_2^2$ would be the coefficient of multiple determination of $X_2$ with $X_1$ and $X_3$, and $R_3^2$ would be the coefficient of multiple determination of $X_3$ with $X_1$ and $X_2$.

If a set of explanatory variables is uncorrelated, then $VIF_j$ will be equal to 1. If the set is highly intercorrelated, then $VIF_j$ might even exceed 10. Marquardt (see reference 8) suggests that if $VIF_j$ is greater than 10, there is too much correlation between variable $X_j$ and the other explanatory variables. However, other researchers (see reference 12) suggest a more conservative criterion that would employ alternatives to least-squares regression if the maximum $VIF_j$ exceeds 5.

If we reexamine the monthly heating oil consumption data of section 17.1, the correlation between the two explanatory variables, temperature and attic insulation, is computed as .00892. Therefore, because there are only two explanatory variables in the model, from equation (18.8):

$$VIF_1 = VIF_2 = \frac{1}{1 - (.00892)^2}$$
$$\cong 1.00$$

Thus, we may conclude that there is no reason to suspect any collinearity for the heating oil consumption data.

## Problems for Section 18.4

### Learning the Basics

• **18.19** If the coefficient of determination between two independent variables is .20, what is the *VIF*?

**18.20** If the coefficient of determination between two independent variables is .50, what is the *VIF*?

## Applying the Concepts

- **18.21** Referring to Problem 17.4 on page 821 and doing multiple regression using the file WARECOST, determine the *VIF* for each explanatory variable in the model. Is there reason to suspect the existence of collinearity?

- **18.22** Referring to Problem 17.6 on page 822 and doing multiple regression using the file ADRADTV, determine the *VIF* for each explanatory variable in the model. Is there reason to suspect the existence of collinearity?

- **18.23** Referring to Problem 17.7 on page 823 and doing multiple regression using the file STANDBY, determine the *VIF* for each explanatory variable in the model. Is there reason to suspect the existence of collinearity?

## MODEL BUILDING

In this chapter and in chapter 17, we have developed the multiple linear regression model and subsequently discussed the curvilinear model, models involving dummy variables, and models involving transformations of variables. In this section we continue our discussion of regression by developing a model building process that considers a set of several explanatory variables.

We start by referring to the Using Statistics example at the beginning of this chapter in which four explanatory variables are to be considered in developing a regression model to predict standby hours of unionized graphic artists. The data are presented in Table 18.3.

Before we begin to develop a model to predict standby hours, we should keep in mind that a widely used criterion of model building is *parsimony*. This means that we wish to develop a regression model that includes the fewest number of explanatory variables that permit an adequate interpretation of the dependent variable of interest. Regression models with fewer explanatory variables are inherently easier to interpret, particularly because they are less likely to be affected by the problem of collinearity (described in section 18.4).

In addition, we should realize that the selection of an appropriate model when many explanatory variables are to be considered involves complexities that are not present for a model that contains only two explanatory variables. First, the evaluation of all possible regression models becomes more computationally complex. Second, although competing models can be quantitatively evaluated, there may not exist a *uniquely* best model but rather several *equally appropriate* models.

We begin our analysis of the standby hours data by first measuring the amount of collinearity that exists among the explanatory variables through the use of the variance inflationary factor [see equation (18.8)]. Figure 18.8 on page 888 represents partial Minitab output for a multiple linear regression model in which standby hours are predicted from the four explanatory variables.

We observe that all the *VIF* values are relatively small, ranging from a high of 2.0 for the total labor hours to a low of 1.2 for remote hours. Thus, on the basis of the criteria developed by Snee (see reference 12), there is little evidence of collinearity among the set of explanatory variables. We also note that the coefficient of multiple determination is .623 and the adjusted $r^2$ is .551.

## Table 18.3  Predicting standby hours based on total staff present, remote hours, Dubner hours, and total labor hours

| WEEK | STANDBY HOURS | TOTAL STAFF PRESENT | REMOTE HOURS | DUBNER HOURS | TOTAL LABOR HOURS |
|------|---------------|---------------------|--------------|--------------|-------------------|
| 1 | 245 | 338 | 414 | 323 | 2,001 |
| 2 | 177 | 333 | 598 | 340 | 2,030 |
| 3 | 271 | 358 | 656 | 340 | 2,226 |
| 4 | 211 | 372 | 631 | 352 | 2,154 |
| 5 | 196 | 339 | 528 | 380 | 2,078 |
| 6 | 135 | 289 | 409 | 339 | 2,080 |
| 7 | 195 | 334 | 382 | 331 | 2,073 |
| 8 | 118 | 293 | 399 | 311 | 1,758 |
| 9 | 116 | 325 | 343 | 328 | 1,624 |
| 10 | 147 | 311 | 338 | 353 | 1,889 |
| 11 | 154 | 304 | 353 | 518 | 1,988 |
| 12 | 146 | 312 | 289 | 440 | 2,049 |
| 13 | 115 | 283 | 388 | 276 | 1,796 |
| 14 | 161 | 307 | 402 | 207 | 1,720 |
| 15 | 274 | 322 | 151 | 287 | 2,056 |
| 16 | 245 | 335 | 228 | 290 | 1,890 |
| 17 | 201 | 350 | 271 | 355 | 2,187 |
| 18 | 183 | 339 | 440 | 300 | 2,032 |
| 19 | 237 | 327 | 475 | 284 | 1,856 |
| 20 | 175 | 328 | 347 | 337 | 2,068 |
| 21 | 152 | 319 | 449 | 279 | 1,813 |
| 22 | 188 | 325 | 336 | 244 | 1,808 |
| 23 | 188 | 322 | 267 | 253 | 1,834 |
| 24 | 197 | 317 | 235 | 272 | 1,973 |
| 25 | 261 | 315 | 164 | 223 | 1,839 |
| 26 | 232 | 331 | 270 | 272 | 1,935 |

DATA FILE
STANDBY

## The Stepwise Regression Approach to Model Building

We now continue our analysis of these data by attempting to determine the subset of all explanatory variables that yield an adequate and appropriate model without having to use the complete model. We begin with a widely used search procedure called **stepwise regression**, which attempts to find the "best" regression model without examining all possible regressions. Once a best model has been found, residual analysis is used to evaluate the aptness of the model and influence measures are computed to determine whether any observations may be deleted.

Recall that in section 17.6 the partial $F$-test criterion was used to evaluate portions of a multiple regression model. Stepwise regression extends this partial $F$-test criterion to a model with any number of explanatory variables. An important feature of this stepwise

```
The regression equation is
Standby = - 331 + 1.25 Staff - 0.118 Remote - 0.297 Dubner + 0.131 Labor

Predictor        Coef        StDev           T          P        VIF
Constant        -330.8        110.9       -2.98      0.007
Staff            1.2456      0.4121        3.02      0.006        1.7
Remote          -0.11842     0.05432      -2.18      0.041        1.2
Dubner          -0.2971      0.1179       -2.52      0.020        1.5
Labor            0.13053     0.05932       2.20      0.039        2.0

S = 31.84        R-Sq = 62.3%       R-Sq(adj) = 55.1%
Analysis of Variance

Source           DF           SS          MS          F          P
Regression        4         35182        8795       8.68      0.000
Residual Error   21         21283        1013
Total            25         56465

Source     DF    Seq SS
Staff       1     20667
Remote      1      6995
Dubner      1      2612
Labor       1      4907
```

**FIGURE 18.8** Regression model obtained from Minitab to predict standby hours based on four explanatory variables

process is that an explanatory variable that has entered into the model at an early stage may subsequently be removed once other explanatory variables are considered. That is, in stepwise regression, variables are either added to or deleted from the regression model at each step of the model-building process. The stepwise procedure terminates with the selection of a best-fitting model when no additional variables can be added to or deleted from the last model fitted.

Figure 18.9 represents partial stepwise regression output obtained from Minitab for the standby hours data. For this example, a significance level of .05 was used [as expressed by a cutoff $F$-value of 4.0 (equivalent to a $t$-value of $\pm 2.0$)] by Minitab to enter a variable into the model or to delete a variable from the model. The first variable entered into the model is total staff, the variable that correlates most highly with the dependent variable standby hours. Because the $t$-value of 3.72 is greater than 2.0, total staff is included in the regression model.

The next step involves the evaluation of the second variable to be included in this model. The variable to be chosen is the one that will make the largest contribution to the model, given that the first explanatory variable has already been selected. For this model, the second variable is remote hours. Because the $t$-value of $-2.36$ for remote hours is less than $-2.0$, remote hours is included in the regression model.

Now that remote hours has been entered into the model, we determine whether total staff is still an important contributing variable or whether it may be eliminated from the model. Because the $t$-value of 4.66 for total staff is also greater than 2.0, total staff should remain in the regression model.

The next step involves the determination of whether any of the remaining variables should be added to the model. Because none of the other variables meets the .05 criterion ($F > +4.0$ or $t > +2.0$ or $t < -2.0$) for entry into the model, the stepwise procedure terminates with a model that includes total staff present and the number of remote hours.

```
Stepwise Regression

 F-to-Enter:        4.00     F-to-Remove:        4.00

 Response is Standby  on  4 predictors, with N =    26

    Step          1        2
Constant     -272.4   -330.7

Staff          1.42     1.76
T-Value        3.72     4.66

Remote               -0.139
T-Value               -2.36

S              38.6     35.4
R-Sq          36.60    48.99
```

***FIGURE 18.9***
Stepwise regression results obtained from Minitab for predicting standby hours

This stepwise regression approach to model building was originally developed more than 30 years ago in an era in which regression analysis on mainframe computers involved the costly use of large amounts of processing time. Under such conditions, a search procedure such as stepwise regression, although providing a limited evaluation of alternative models, became widely used. In this current era of personal computers with extremely fast hardware, the evaluation of many different regression models can be done in very little time, at a very small cost. Thus, we turn to a more general way of evaluating alternative regression models, the best-subsets approach.

## The Best-Subsets Approach to Model Building

This approach evaluates either all possible regression models for a given set of independent variables or at least the best subsets of models for a given number of independent variables. Figure 18.10 represents partial output obtained from Minitab in which the best three

```
Best Subsets Regression

Response is Standby

                                                R D
                                              S e u L
                                              t m b a
                                              a o n b
                     Adj.                     f t e o
Vars     R-Sq     R-Sq      C-p          S    f e r r

   1     36.6     34.0     13.3     38.621    X
   1     17.1     13.7     24.2     44.162          X
   1      6.0      2.1     30.4     47.035        X
   2     49.0     44.6      8.4     35.387    X X
   2     45.0     40.2     10.6     36.749    X   X
   2     42.9     37.9     11.8     37.447        X X
   3     53.8     47.5      7.8     34.443    X   X X
   3     53.6     47.3      7.8     34.503    X X X
   3     50.9     44.2      9.3     35.492    X X   X
   4     62.3     55.1      5.0     31.835    X X X X
```

***FIGURE 18.10***
Best-subsets regression output obtained from Minitab for standby hours data

regression models for a given number of independent variables were provided according to two widely used criteria, the adjusted $r^2$ and the $C_p$ statistic.

The first criterion that is often used is the adjusted $r^2$, which adjusts the $r^2$ of each model to account for the number of variables in the model as well as the sample size (see section 17.1). Because models with different numbers of independent variables are to be compared, the adjusted $r^2$ is more appropriate than $r^2$.

Referring to Figure 18.10, we observe that the adjusted $r^2$ reaches a maximum value of .551 when all four independent variables plus the intercept term (for a total of five estimated parameters) are included in the model. We note that the model selected by using stepwise regression, which includes total staff present and remote hours, has an adjusted $r^2$ of .446.

A second criterion often used in the evaluation of competing models is based on the statistic developed by Mallows (see reference 11). This statistic, called $C_p$, measures the differences of a fitted regression model from a *true* model, along with random error. The **$C_p$ statistic** is defined as

**The $C_p$ statistic**

$$C_p = \frac{(1 - R_p^2)(n - T)}{1 - R_T^2} - [n - 2(p + 1)] \tag{18.9}$$

where

- $p$ = number of independent variables included in a regression model
- $T$ = total number of parameters (including the intercept) to be estimated in the full regression model
- $R_p^2$ = coefficient of multiple determination for a regression model that has $p$ independent variables
- $R_T^2$ = coefficient of multiple determination for a full regression model that contains all $T$ estimated parameters

Using equation (18.9) to compute $C_p$ for the model containing total staff present and remote hours, we have

$$n = 26 \quad p = 2 \quad T = 4 + 1 = 5 \quad R_p^2 = .490 \quad R_T^2 = .623$$

so that

$$C_p = \frac{(1 - .49)(26 - 5)}{1 - .623} - [26 - 2(2 + 1)]$$

$$C_p = 8.4$$

When a regression model with $p$ independent variables contains only random differences from a *true* model, the average value of $C_p$ is $(p + 1)$, the number of parameters. Thus, in evaluating many alternative regression models, our goal is to find models whose $C_p$ is close to or below $(p + 1)$.

From Figure 18.10 we observe that only the model with all four independent variables considered contains a $C_p$ value equal to or below $p + 1$. Therefore this model should be chosen. Although it was not the case here, the $C_p$ statistic often provides several alternative models for us to evaluate in greater depth using other criteria such as parsimony, interpretability, departure from model assumptions (as evaluated by residual analysis), and the influence of individual observations. We also note the model selected using stepwise regression has a $C_p$ value of 8.4, which is substantially above the suggested criterion of $p + 1 = 3$ for that model.

Now that the explanatory variables to be included in the model have been selected, a residual analysis should be undertaken to evaluate the aptness of the fitted model. Figure 18.11 presents partial output obtained from Minitab for these purposes. We observe from Figure 18.11 that the plots of the standardized residuals versus the total staff, the remote hours, the Dubner hours, and the total labor hours all reveal no apparent pattern. In addition, a histogram of the standardized residuals (not shown here) indicates only moderate departure from normality. Because the residual analysis appeared to confirm the aptness of

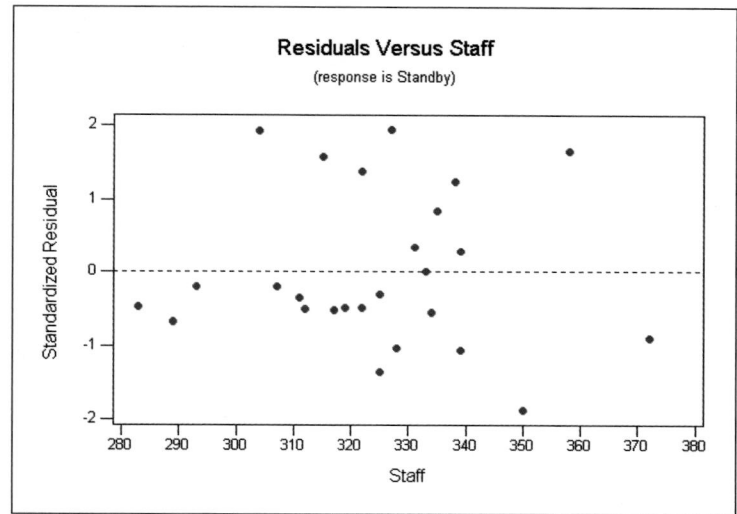

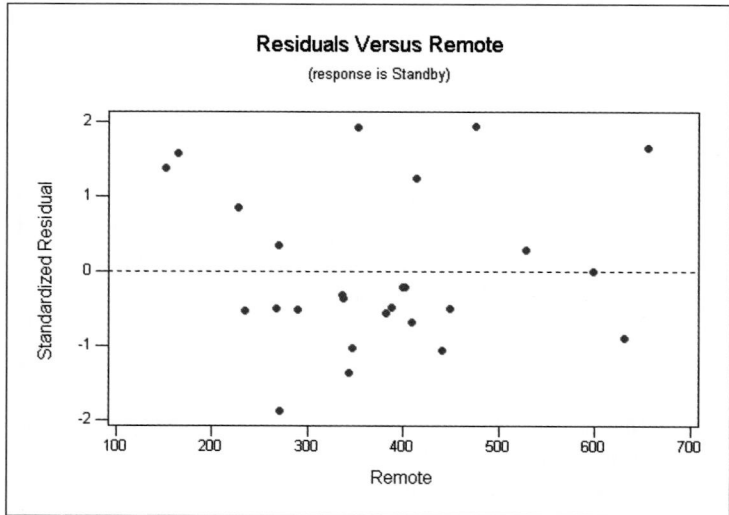

**FIGURE 18.11** Residual plots for standby hours data obtained from Minitab

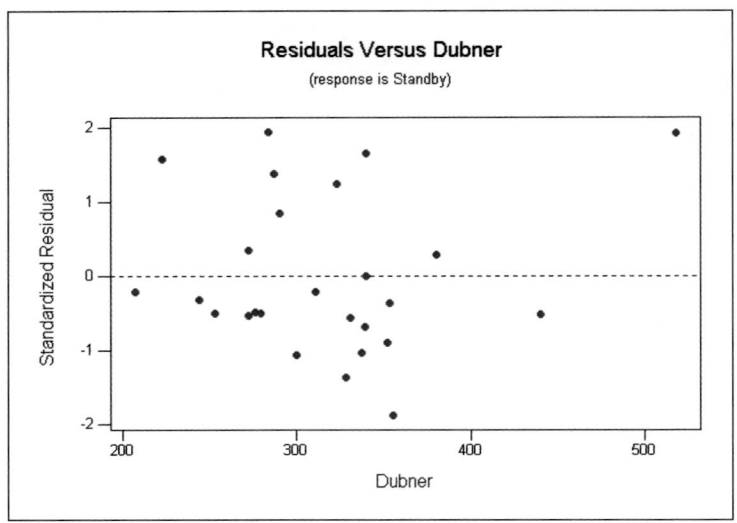

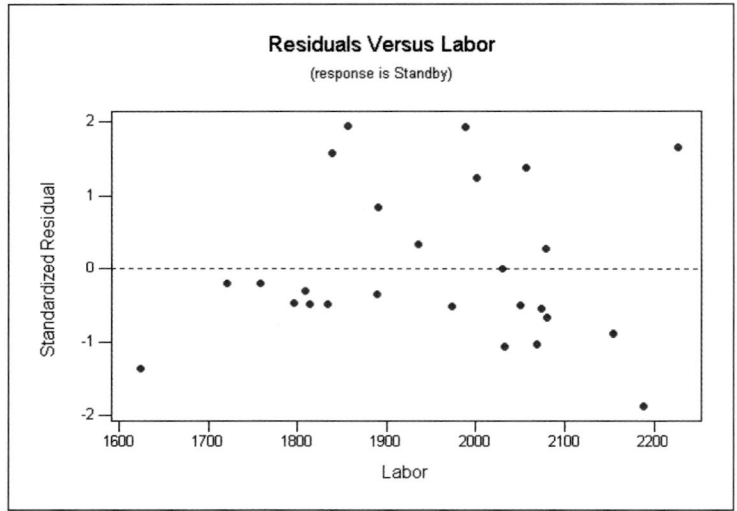

**FIGURE 18.11** *(Continued)*

the fitted model, we may now use various influence measures to determine whether any of the observations have unduly influenced the fitted model. Figure 18.12 represents the values of the $h_i$, $t_i^*$, and Cook's $D_i$ statistics for our fitted model. We note from Figure 18.12 that certain data points have been highlighted for further analysis.

For our fitted model, because $n = 26$ and $p = 4$, using the decision rule suggested by Hoaglin and Welsch (see section 17.3), our criterion would be to flag any $h_i$ value greater than $2(p + 1)/26 = .3846$. Referring to Figure 18.12, we note that observations 6 ($h_6 = .4049$), 9 ($h_9 = .4537$), and 11 ($h_{11} = .5217$) have $h_i$ values that exceed .3846 and therefore are considered to be possible candidates for deletion from the model.

Turning to the Studentized deleted residual measure $t_i^*$ for our model, because $p = 4$ and $n = 26$ and using the decision rule suggested by Hoaglin and Welsch (see section 17.3), our criterion would be to flag any $t_i^*$ value greater than 1.7247 or less than $-1.7247$ (see Table E.3). Referring to Figure 18.12, we note that $t_3^* = 1.741$, $t_{11}^* = 2.0673$,

| ↓ | C2 Staff | C3 Remote | C4 Dubner | C5 Labor | C6 DelRes | C7 Hi | C8 CookD |
|---|---------|-----------|-----------|----------|-----------|-------|----------|
| 1 | 338 | 414 | 323 | 2001 | 1.26648 | 0.057851 | 0.019147 |
| 2 | 333 | 598 | 340 | 2030 | -0.00450 | 0.159009 | 0.000001 |
| 3 | 358 | 656 | 340 | 2226 | 1.74109 | 0.308626 | 0.246769 |
| 4 | 372 | 631 | 352 | 2154 | -0.88635 | 0.317663 | 0.073903 |
| 5 | 339 | 528 | 380 | 2078 | 0.28517 | 0.117963 | 0.002275 |
| 6 | 289 | 409 | 339 | 2080 | -0.66415 | 0.404904 | 0.061665 |
| 7 | 334 | 382 | 331 | 2073 | -0.55135 | 0.066692 | 0.004493 |
| 8 | 293 | 399 | 311 | 1758 | -0.20251 | 0.177819 | 0.001859 |
| 9 | 325 | 343 | 328 | 1624 | -1.38665 | 0.453697 | 0.305928 |
| 10 | 311 | 338 | 353 | 1889 | -0.36082 | 0.080160 | 0.002367 |
| 11 | 304 | 353 | 518 | 1988 | 2.06732 | 0.521708 | 0.806606 |
| 12 | 312 | 289 | 440 | 2049 | -0.50740 | 0.239542 | 0.016814 |
| 13 | 283 | 388 | 276 | 1796 | -0.47510 | 0.267786 | 0.017142 |
| 14 | 307 | 402 | 207 | 1720 | -0.20841 | 0.219149 | 0.002554 |
| 15 | 322 | 151 | 287 | 2056 | 1.42189 | 0.241543 | 0.122799 |
| 16 | 335 | 228 | 290 | 1890 | 0.84801 | 0.155157 | 0.026771 |

| ↓ | C2 Staff | C3 Remote | C4 Dubner | C5 Labor | C6 DelRes | C7 Hi | C8 CookD |
|---|---------|-----------|-----------|----------|-----------|-------|----------|
| 17 | 350 | 271 | 355 | 2187 | -2.00716 | 0.240144 | 0.222548 |
| 18 | 339 | 440 | 300 | 2032 | -1.06250 | 0.073308 | 0.017752 |
| 19 | 327 | 475 | 284 | 1856 | 2.10290 | 0.101265 | 0.085690 |
| 20 | 328 | 347 | 337 | 2068 | -1.02770 | 0.071640 | 0.016257 |
| 21 | 319 | 449 | 279 | 1813 | -0.49356 | 0.105621 | 0.005969 |
| 22 | 325 | 336 | 244 | 1808 | -0.31659 | 0.107193 | 0.002515 |
| 23 | 322 | 267 | 253 | 1834 | -0.48404 | 0.100514 | 0.005434 |
| 24 | 317 | 235 | 272 | 1973 | -0.52597 | 0.123908 | 0.008105 |
| 25 | 315 | 164 | 223 | 1839 | 1.63790 | 0.193025 | 0.118818 |
| 26 | 331 | 270 | 272 | 1935 | 0.34618 | 0.094110 | 0.002599 |

**FIGURE 18.12** Influence statistics for standby hours data obtained from Minitab

$t^*_{17} = -2.0072$, and $t^*_{19} = 2.1029$. Thus, these observations may have an adverse effect on the model. We note that observation 11 was also flagged according to the $h_i$ criterion but observations 3, 17, and 19 were not.

Now we consider a third criterion, Cook's $D_i$ statistic, which is based on both $h_i$ and the standardized residual. For our model, in which $p = 4$ and $n = 26$, using the decision rule suggested by Cook and Weisberg (see section 17.3), our criterion is to flag any $D_i > F = .899$, the critical value for the $F$ statistic having 5 and 21 degrees of freedom at the .50 level of significance (see Table E.6). Referring to Figure 18.12, although $D_i$ for observation 11 is .807, none of the $D_i$ values exceed .899, so according to this criterion there are no values that should be deleted. Hence, we would have no clear basis for removing any observations from the multiple regression model.

Thus from Figure 18.8 on page 888 our sample regression equation can be expressed as

$$\hat{Y}_i = -330.8 + 1.2456X_{1i} - .1184X_{2i} - .2971X_{3i} + .1305X_{4i}$$

From this model we conclude that holding constant the effect of remote hours, Dubner hours, and total labor hours for each increase of one person in total staff, we predict that the average standby hours will increase by 1.2456 hours. Holding the total staff, Dubner hours, and total labor hours constant, we predict that the average standby hours will decrease by .1184 hour for each increase of 1 remote hour. Holding the total staff, remote hours, and total labor hours constant, we predict that the average standby hours will decrease by .2971 hour for each increase of 1 Dubner hour. Holding the total staff, remote hours, and Dubner hours constant, we predict that the average standby hours will increase by .1305 hour for each increase of 1 total labor hour.

To study a situation where there are several alternative models in which the $C_p$ statistic is less than or equal to $(p + 1)$, we turn to Example 18.6.

## Example 18.6 *Choosing among Alternative Regression Models*

Given the following Minitab output from a best-subsets regression analysis of a regression model with seven independent variables, determine which regression model you would choose as the *best* model.

| Vars | R-Sq | Adj. R-Sq | C-p | s | A | B | C | D | E | F | G |
|---|---|---|---|---|---|---|---|---|---|---|---|
| 1 | 12.1 | 11.9 | 113.9 | 13.240 | | | | X | | | |
| 1 | 9.3 | 9.0 | 130.4 | 13.453 | X | | | | | | |
| 1 | 8.3 | 8.0 | 136.2 | 13.526 | | | X | | | | |
| 2 | 21.4 | 21.0 | 62.1 | 12.539 | | | X | X | | | |
| 2 | 19.1 | 18.6 | 75.6 | 12.723 | X | | X | | | | |
| 2 | 18.1 | 17.7 | 81.0 | 12.796 | X | | | X | | | |
| 3 | 28.5 | 28.0 | 22.6 | 11.969 | X | | X | X | | | |
| 3 | 26.8 | 26.3 | 32.4 | 12.110 | | | X | X | X | | |
| 3 | 24.0 | 23.4 | 49.0 | 12.345 | | X | X | X | | | |
| 4 | 30.8 | 30.1 | 11.3 | 11.791 | X | X | X | X | | | |
| 4 | 30.4 | 29.7 | 14.0 | 11.831 | X | | X | X | | X | |
| 4 | 29.6 | 28.9 | 18.3 | 11.893 | X | | X | X | X | | |
| 5 | 31.7 | 30.8 | 8.2 | 11.730 | X | X | X | X | X | | |
| 5 | 31.5 | 30.6 | 9.6 | 11.751 | X | X | X | X | | | X |
| 5 | 31.3 | 30.4 | 10.7 | 11.767 | X | | X | X | X | X | |
| 6 | 32.3 | 31.3 | 6.8 | 11.695 | X | X | X | X | X | X | |
| 6 | 31.9 | 30.9 | 9.0 | 11.727 | X | X | X | X | X | | X |
| 6 | 31.7 | 30.6 | 10.4 | 11.749 | X | X | X | X | | X | X |
| 7 | 32.4 | 31.2 | 8.0 | 11.698 | X | X | X | X | X | X | X |

Minitab output from best-subsets regression

## SOLUTION

From this Minitab output, we determine which models have $C_p$ values that are less than or equal to $(p + 1)$. Two models meet this criterion. The model with six independent variables ($A$, $B$, $C$, $D$, $E$, $F$) has a $C_p$ value of 6.8, which is less than $p + 1 = 6 + 1 = 7$, and the full model with seven independent variables ($A$, $B$, $C$, $D$, $E$, $F$, $G$) has a $C_p$ value of 8.0. One way to choose among models that meet this criterion is to determine whether the models contain a subset of variables that are common and then test whether the contribution of the additional variables is significant. In this case, because the models differ only by the inclusion of variable $G$ in the full model, we test whether variable $G$ made a significant contribution to the regression model given that variables $A$, $B$, $C$, $D$, $E$, and $F$ were already included in the model. If the contribution was statistically significant, then variable $G$ would be included in the regression model. If variable $G$ did not make a statistically significant contribution, variable $G$ would not be included in the model.

Exhibit 18.1 summarizes the steps involved in model building.

---

### Exhibit 18.1  *Steps Involved in Model Building*

✓ **1.** Choose a set of independent variables to be considered for inclusion in the regression model.

✓ **2.** Fit a full regression model that includes all the independent variables to be considered so that the variance inflationary factor (*VIF*) for each independent variable can be determined.

✓ **3.** Determine whether any independent variables have a *VIF* > 5.

✓ **4.** There are three possible results that can occur.
  **(a)** None of the independent variables have a *VIF* > 5. If this is the case, proceed to step 5.
  **(b)** One of the independent variables has a *VIF* > 5. If this is the case, eliminate that independent variable and proceed to step 5.
  **(c)** More than one of the independent variables has a *VIF* > 5. If this is the case, eliminate the independent variable that has the highest *VIF* and go back to step 2.

✓ **5.** Perform a best-subsets regression with the remaining independent variables to obtain the best models (in terms of $C_p$) for a given number of independent variables.

✓ **6.** List all models that have $C_p \leq (p + 1)$.

✓ **7.** Among those models listed in step 6, choose a best model (as discussed in Example 18.6).

✓ **8.** Perform a complete analysis of the model chosen including residual analysis and influence analysis.

✓ **9.** Depending on the results of the residual analysis and influence analysis, add curvilinear terms and transform variables and/or delete individual observations as necessary, and reanalyze the data.

✓ **10.** Use the selected model for prediction and confidence interval estimation.

The following figure represents a road map for these steps in model building.

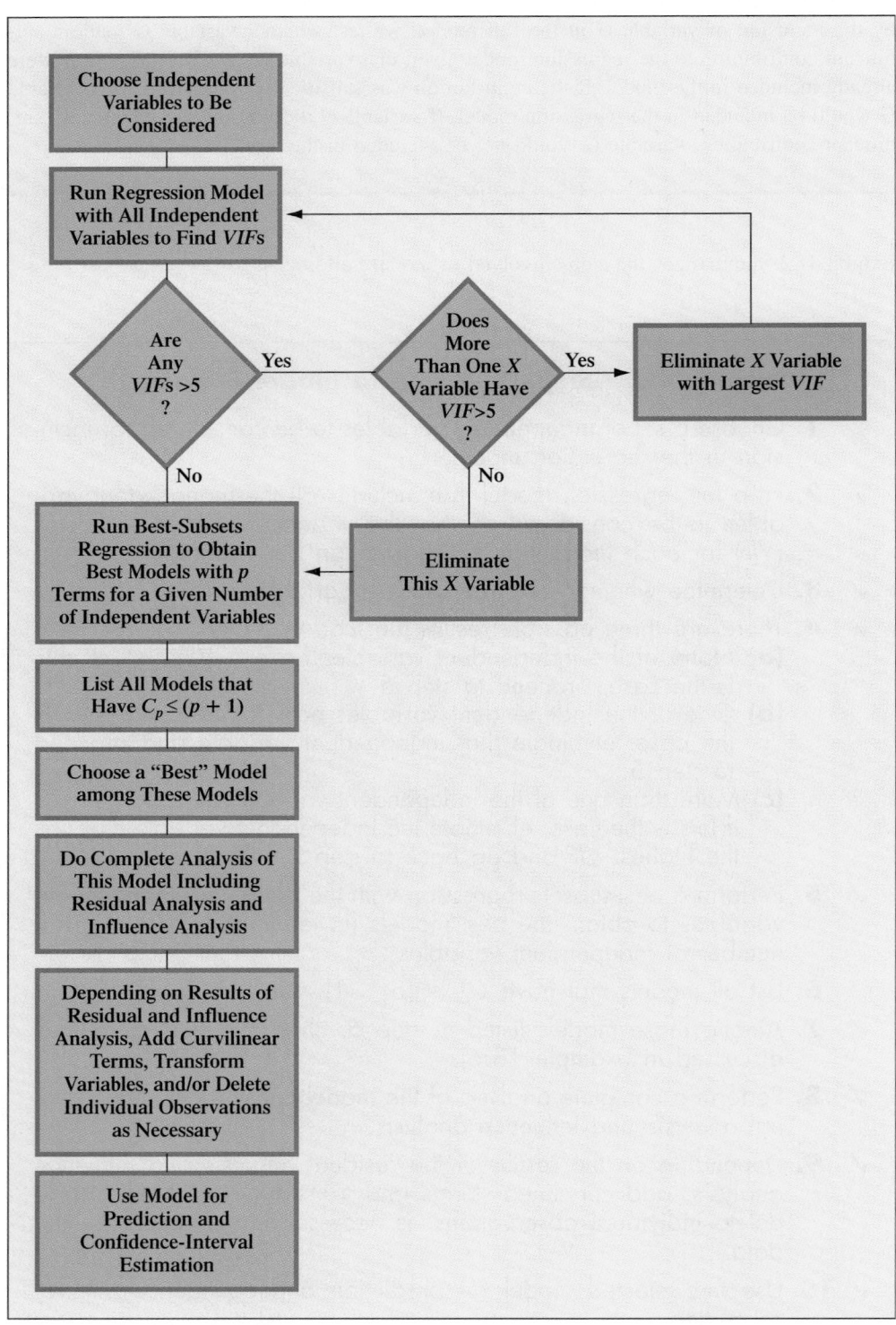

Road map for model building

## Problems for Section 18.5

### Learning the Basics

• **18.24** Suppose that six independent variables were to be considered for inclusion in a regression model. A sample of 40 observations is selected with the following results:

$$n = 40 \quad p = 2 \quad T = 6 + 1 = 7 \quad R_p^2 = .274 \quad R_T^2 = .653$$

(a) Compute the $C_p$ value for this two-independent-variable model.
(b) On the basis of the results of (a), does this model meet the criterion for further consideration as the best model to be selected? Explain.

**18.25** Suppose that four independent variables were to be considered for inclusion in a regression model. A sample of 30 observations is selected with the following results:

The model that includes independent variables $A$ and $B$ has a $C_p$ value equal to 4.6
The model that includes independent variables $A$ and $C$ has a $C_p$ value equal to 2.4
The model that includes independent variables $A$, $B$, and $C$ has a $C_p$ value equal to 2.7

(a) Based on these results, which models meet the criterion for further consideration? Explain.
(b) How would you compare the model that contains independent variables $A$, $B$, and $C$ to the model that contains independent variables $A$ and $B$? Explain.

### Applying the Concepts

• **18.26** Suppose we want to develop a model to predict the selling price of homes based on assessed value, time period in which the house was sold, and whether the house was new (0 = no, 1 = yes). A sample of 30 recently sold single-family houses in a small western city is selected to study the relationship between selling price and assessed value (the houses in the city had been reassessed at full value 1 year prior to the study). The results are as follows:

| OBSERVATION | ASSESSED VALUE ($000) | SELLING PRICE ($000) | TIME | NEW | OBSERVATION | ASSESSED VALUE ($000) | SELLING PRICE ($000) | TIME | NEW |
|---|---|---|---|---|---|---|---|---|---|
| 1 | 78.17 | 94.10 | 10 | 1 | 16 | 84.36 | 106.70 | 12 | 0 |
| 2 | 80.24 | 101.90 | 10 | 1 | 17 | 72.94 | 81.50 | 5 | 0 |
| 3 | 74.03 | 88.65 | 11 | 0 | 18 | 76.50 | 94.50 | 14 | 1 |
| 4 | 86.31 | 115.50 | 2 | 0 | 19 | 66.28 | 69.00 | 1 | 0 |
| 5 | 75.22 | 87.50 | 5 | 0 | 20 | 79.74 | 96.90 | 3 | 1 |
| 6 | 65.54 | 72.00 | 4 | 0 | 21 | 72.78 | 86.50 | 14 | 0 |
| 7 | 72.43 | 91.50 | 17 | 0 | 22 | 77.90 | 97.90 | 12 | 1 |
| 8 | 85.61 | 113.90 | 13 | 0 | 23 | 74.31 | 83.00 | 11 | 0 |
| 9 | 60.80 | 69.34 | 6 | 0 | 24 | 79.85 | 97.30 | 12 | 1 |
| 10 | 81.88 | 96.90 | 5 | 1 | 25 | 84.78 | 100.80 | 2 | 1 |
| 11 | 79.11 | 96.00 | 7 | 0 | 26 | 81.61 | 97.90 | 6 | 1 |
| 12 | 59.93 | 61.90 | 4 | 0 | 27 | 74.92 | 90.50 | 12 | 0 |
| 13 | 75.27 | 93.00 | 11 | 0 | 28 | 79.98 | 97.00 | 4 | 1 |
| 14 | 85.88 | 109.50 | 10 | 1 | 29 | 77.96 | 92.00 | 9 | 0 |
| 15 | 76.64 | 93.75 | 17 | 0 | 30 | 79.07 | 95.90 | 12 | 1 |

DATA FILE
HOUSE1

Develop the most appropriate multiple regression model to predict selling price. Be sure to perform a thorough residual analysis and evaluate the various measures of influence. In addition, provide a detailed explanation of your results.

**DATA FILE UNIV&COL**

**18.27** The file UNIV&COL contains data on 80 colleges and universities. Among the variables included are the annual total cost (in thousands of dollars), the average total score on the Scholastic Aptitude Test (SAT), the room and board expenses (in thousands of dollars), whether the institution is public or private, and whether the TOEFL criterion is at least 550.

Develop the most appropriate multiple regression model to predict annual total cost. Be sure to perform a thorough residual analysis and evaluate the various measures of influence. In addition, provide a detailed explanation of your results.

**DATA FILE AUTO96**

**18.28** The file AUTO96 contains data on 89 automobile models from the year 1996. Among the variables included are gasoline mileage, weight, width, length of each automobile, and whether the car is front wheel drive or rear wheel drive. Develop the most appropriate multiple regression model to predict gasoline mileage. Be sure to perform a thorough residual analysis and evaluate the various measures of influence. In addition, provide a detailed explanation of your results.

## 18.6 INTRODUCTION TO LOGISTIC REGRESSION (*OPTIONAL TOPIC*)

In our discussion of the simple linear regression model in chapter 16 and multiple regression models in chapter 17 and sections 18.1–18.5, we have limited ourselves to considering response variables that are numerical. However, in many instances, the response variable is categorical and takes on one of only two possible values. The use of simple or multiple least-squares regression for this type of response variable often leads to predicted values that are less than zero or greater than one, values that cannot possibly occur.

An alternative approach, **logistic regression**, originally applied to survival data in the health sciences (see reference 7), has been developed to enable us to use regression models to predict the probability of a particular categorical response for a given set of explanatory variables. This logistic regression model is based on the **odds ratio**, which represents the probability of a success compared with the probability of failure. The odds ratio may be expressed as

### Odds Ratio

$$\text{Odds ratio} = \frac{\text{probability of success}}{1 - \text{probability of success}} \tag{18.10}$$

Using equation (18.10), if the probability of success for an event was .50, the odds ratio would be

$$\text{Odds ratio} = \frac{.50}{1 - .50} = 1.0, \text{ or 1 to 1}$$

and if the probability of success for an event was .75, the odds ratio would be

$$\text{Odds ratio} = \frac{.75}{1 - .75} = 3.0, \text{ or 3 to 1}$$

The logistic regression model is based on the natural logarithm of this odds ratio. A mathematical method called *maximum likelihood estimation* is usually used to develop a regression model to predict the natural logarithm of this odds ratio. This model is expressed as

## Population Logistic Regression Model

$$\ln(\text{odds ratio}_i) = \beta_0 + \beta_1 X_{1i} + \beta_2 X_{2i} + \cdots + \beta_p X_{pi} + \epsilon_i \qquad (18.11)$$

where

$p$ = the number of independent variables in the model

$\epsilon_i$ = random error for observation $i$

For a set of data from a sample, we have

## Sample Logistic Regression Equation

$$\ln(\text{estimated odds ratio}_i) = b_0 + b_1 X_{1i} + b_2 X_{2i} + \cdots + b_p X_{pi} \qquad (18.12)$$

Once the logistic regression model has been fit to a set of data, the estimated odds ratio is obtained by raising the mathematical constant $e$ to the power equal to the natural logarithm of the estimated odds ratio. This is expressed as

## Estimated Odds Ratio

$$\text{Estimated odds ratio} = e^{\ln(\text{estimated odds ratio})} \qquad (18.13)$$

Once the estimated odds ratio has been obtained, we find the estimated probability of success from equation (18.14).

## Estimated Probability of Success

$$\text{Estimated probability of success} = \frac{\text{estimated odds ratio}}{1 + \text{estimated odds ratio}} \qquad (18.14)$$

To illustrate the logistic regression model, suppose that the marketing department for a travel and entertainment credit card company was about to embark on a periodic campaign to convince existing holders of the company's standard credit card to upgrade to one of the company's premium cards for a nominal annual fee. The major decision facing the marketing department concerns which of the existing standard credit card holders should be targeted for the campaign. Data available from a sample of 30 credit card holders who were contacted during last year's campaign indicate the following: whether the credit card holder

## Table 18.4 Purchase behavior, annual credit card spending, and possession of additional credit cards for a sample of 30 credit card holders

| Observation | Purchase Behavior | Annual Spending | Possession of Additional Credit Cards | Observation | Purchase Behavior | Annual Spending | Possession of Additional Credit Cards |
|---|---|---|---|---|---|---|---|
| 1 | 0 | 32.1007 | 0 | 16 | 0 | 23.7609 | 0 |
| 2 | 1 | 34.3706 | 1 | 17 | 0 | 35.0388 | 1 |
| 3 | 0 | 4.8749 | 0 | 18 | 1 | 49.7388 | 1 |
| 4 | 0 | 8.1263 | 0 | 19 | 0 | 24.7372 | 0 |
| 5 | 0 | 12.9783 | 0 | 20 | 1 | 26.1315 | 1 |
| 6 | 0 | 16.0471 | 0 | 21 | 0 | 31.3220 | 1 |
| 7 | 0 | 20.6648 | 0 | 22 | 1 | 40.1967 | 1 |
| 8 | 1 | 42.0483 | 1 | 23 | 0 | 35.3899 | 0 |
| 9 | 0 | 42.2264 | 1 | 24 | 0 | 30.2280 | 0 |
| 10 | 1 | 37.9900 | 1 | 25 | 1 | 50.3778 | 0 |
| 11 | 1 | 53.6063 | 1 | 26 | 0 | 52.7713 | 0 |
| 12 | 0 | 38.7936 | 0 | 27 | 0 | 27.3728 | 0 |
| 13 | 0 | 27.9999 | 0 | 28 | 1 | 59.2146 | 1 |
| 14 | 1 | 42.1694 | 0 | 29 | 1 | 50.0686 | 1 |
| 15 | 1 | 56.1997 | 1 | 30 | 1 | 35.4234 | 1 |

**DATA FILE
LOGPURCH**

upgraded from the standard to a premium card (0 = no, 1 = yes), the total amount of credit card purchases (in thousands of dollars) using the company's credit card in the 1 year prior to the campaign ($X_1$), and whether the credit card holder possessed additional credit cards (which involved an extra cost) for other members of the household ($X_2$: 0 = no, 1 = yes). The data are presented in Table 18.4.

Figure 18.13 represents partial output for the logistic regression model obtained from Minitab. We note that $X_1$ is named Spending and $X_2$ is named Extra.

The regression coefficients $b_0$, $b_1$, and $b_2$ are interpreted as follows:

**1.** The regression constant $b_0$ is equal to $-6.940$. This means that for a credit card holder who did not charge any purchases last year and who does not have additional cards, we estimate that the natural logarithm of the odds ratio of purchasing the premium card will be $-6.940$.

**2.** The regression coefficient $b_1$ is equal to 0.13947. This means that holding constant the effect of whether the credit card holder has additional cards for members of the household, for each increase of $1,000 in annual credit card spending using the company's card we estimate that the natural logarithm of the odds ratio of purchasing the premium card will increase by 0.13947.

**3.** The regression coefficient $b_2$ is equal to 2.774. This means that holding constant the annual credit card spending, we estimate that the natural logarithm of the odds ratio of purchasing the premium card will increase by 2.774 for a credit card holder who has additional cards for members of the household compared with one who does not have additional cards.

As was the case with least-squares regression models, a main purpose of undertaking

```
Factor     Levels Values
Extra         2 0 1

Logistic Regression Table
                                                   Odds        95% CI
Predictor      Coef       StDev      Z      P      Ratio    Lower    Upper
Constant (b₀) -6.940 (b₂) 2.947   -2.35 0.019
Spending       0.13947    0.06806   2.05 0.040     1.15     1.01     1.31
Extra
  1      (b₂)- 2.774       1.193     2.33 0.020    16.03     1.55   166.00

Log-Likelihood = -10.038
Test that all slopes are zero: G = 20.977, DF = 2, P-Value = 0.000

Goodness-of-Fit Tests

Method               Chi-Square    DF     P
Pearson                 18.519      27   0.887
Deviance                20.077      27   0.828
Hosmer-Lemeshow          6.517       8   0.589
Brown:
General Alternative      1.451       2   0.484
Symmetric Alternative    1.385       1   0.239
```

**FIGURE 18.13**   Partial logistic regression output for data of Table 18.4 obtained from Minitab

logistic regression analysis is to provide predictions of a response variable. Suppose we want to predict the probability that a credit card holder who used this company's card to charge $36,000 last year would purchase the premium card during the marketing campaign. If we were predicting for a credit card holder who has purchased additional cards for members of the household, we would have $X_1 = 36$ and $X_2 = 1$ and, from equation (18.12), the results for the regression model displayed in Figure 18.13 are

$$\text{ln (estimated odds of purchasing versus not purchasing)} = -6.94 + (0.13947)(36) + (2.774)(1)$$
$$= 0.85492$$

Using equation (18.13), we have

$$\text{Estimated odds ratio} = e^{.85492} = 2.3512$$

This means that the odds are 2.3512 to 1 that a credit card holder who spent $36,000 last year and has additional cards would purchase the premium card during the campaign rather than not purchase. This can be converted to a probability by using equation (18.14), so that

$$\text{Estimated probability of purchasing premium card} = \frac{2.3512}{1 + 2.3512}$$
$$= .7016$$

Thus, we would estimate that the probability is .7016 that a credit card holder who spent $36,000 last year and has additional cards would purchase the premium card during the campaign. In other words, 70.16% of such individuals could be expected to purchase the premium card.

Now that we have used the logistic regression model for prediction, we shall consider two other aspects of the model-fitting process: whether the model is a good-fitting model and whether each of the independent variables included in the model makes a significant contribution to the model. One statistic that is frequently used to evaluate the question of whether the model fit is a good-fitting one is the **deviance statistic**. This statistic measures the fit of the current model compared with a model that has as many parameters as there are data points (what is called a *saturated* model). The deviance statistic follows a chi-square distribution with $n - p - 1$ degrees of freedom. The null and alternative hypotheses for this statistic are

$$H_0\text{: The model is a good-fitting model.}$$

$$H_1\text{: The model is not a good-fitting model.}$$

Using a level of significance $\alpha$, the decision rule is:

Reject $H_0$ if deviance $> \chi^2$ with $n - p - 1$ degrees of freedom;

otherwise, don't reject $H_0$.

From Figure 18.13 on page 901 and using a .05 level of significance, we observe that deviance $= 20.08 < \chi^2 = 40.113$, or $p$-value $= .828 > .05$. Thus $H_0$ would not be rejected. Thus we conclude that the model is a good-fitting one.

Now that we have concluded that the model is a good-fitting one, we need to evaluate whether each of the independent variables makes a significant contribution to the model in the presence of the others. As was the case with linear regression in sections 16.7 and 17.5, the test statistic is based on the ratio of the regression coefficient to the standard error of the regression coefficient. In logistic regression, this ratio is called the **Wald statistic** and follows the normal distribution. From Figure 18.13 we observe that the Wald statistic is 2.05 for $X_1$ and 2.33 for $X_2$. Each of these is greater than the critical value of $+1.96$ for the normal distribution at the .05 level of significance (the $p$-values are .04 and .02). Thus, we may conclude that each of the two explanatory variables makes a contribution to the model in the presence of the other and should be included.

## Problems for Section 18.6

### Learning the Basics

**18.29** Interpret the meaning of a logistic regression coefficient equal to 2.2.

**18.30** Given an estimated odds ratio of 2.5, find the estimated probability of success.

**18.31** Given an estimated odds ratio of 0.75, find the estimated probability of success.

• **18.32** Suppose that the following logistic regression model has been fit:

$$\ln (\text{estimated odds ratio}) = 0.1 + 0.5X_{1i} + 0.2X_{2i}$$

(a) Interpret the meaning of the logistic regression coefficients.
(b) If $X_1 = 2$ and $X_2 = 1.5$, find the estimated odds ratio and interpret its meaning.
(c) On the basis of the results of (b), compute the estimated probability of success.

 **DATA FILE LOGPURCH**

### Applying the Concepts

• **18.33** Refer to the data of Figure 18.13 on page 901:

(a) Predict the probability that a credit card holder who had charged \$36,000 on the company's card last year and did not have any additional credit cards for members of the household would purchase the premium card during the marketing campaign.

(b) Compare the results obtained in (a) with those on page 901.

(c) Predict the probability that a credit card holder who had charged \$18,000 on the company's card last year and did not have any additional credit cards for members of the household would purchase the premium card during the marketing campaign.

(d) Compare the results of (a) and (c) and indicate what implications these results might have for the strategy for the marketing campaign.

**18.34** The director of graduate studies at a well-known college of business would like to predict the success of students in an MBA program. Two explanatory variables, undergraduate grade point average and GMAT score, were available for a random sample of 30 students, 20 of whom had successfully completed the program (coded as 1) and 10 of whom had not successfully completed the program in the required amount of time (coded as 0). The results are as follows:

| SUCCESS IN MBA PROGRAM | UNDERGRADUATE GRADE POINT AVERAGE | GMAT SCORE | SUCCESS IN MBA PROGRAM | UNDERGRADUATE GRADE POINT AVERAGE | GMAT SCORE |
|---|---|---|---|---|---|
| 0 | 2.93 | 617 | 1 | 3.17 | 639 |
| 0 | 3.05 | 557 | 1 | 3.24 | 632 |
| 0 | 3.11 | 599 | 1 | 3.41 | 639 |
| 0 | 3.24 | 616 | 1 | 3.37 | 619 |
| 0 | 3.36 | 594 | 1 | 3.46 | 665 |
| 0 | 3.41 | 567 | 1 | 3.57 | 694 |
| 0 | 3.45 | 542 | 1 | 3.62 | 641 |
| 0 | 3.60 | 551 | 1 | 3.66 | 594 |
| 0 | 3.64 | 573 | 1 | 3.69 | 678 |
| 0 | 3.57 | 536 | 1 | 3.70 | 624 |
| 1 | 2.75 | 688 | 1 | 3.78 | 654 |
| 1 | 2.81 | 647 | 1 | 3.84 | 718 |
| 1 | 3.03 | 652 | 1 | 3.77 | 692 |
| 1 | 3.10 | 608 | 1 | 3.79 | 632 |
| 1 | 3.06 | 680 | 1 | 3.97 | 784 |

 DATA FILE
MBA

(a) Fit a logistic regression model to predict the probability of successful completion of the MBA program based on undergraduate grade point average and GMAT score.

(b) Explain the meaning of the regression coefficients for the model fit in (a).

(c) Predict the probability of successful completion of the program for a student with an undergraduate grade point average of 3.25 and a GMAT score of 600.

(d) At the .05 level of significance, is there evidence that a logistic regression model that uses undergraduate grade point average and GMAT score to predict probability of success in the MBA program is a good-fitting model?

(e) At the .05 level of significance, is there evidence that undergraduate grade point average and GMAT score each makes a significant contribution to the logistic regression model?

(f) Fit a logistic regression model that includes only undergraduate grade point average to predict probability of success in the MBA program.

(g) Fit a logistic regression model that includes only GMAT score to predict probability of success in the MBA program.

(h) Compare the models fit in (f) and (g) to the model fit in (a). How might you evaluate whether there is a difference between the models?

**18.35** The marketing manager for a large nationally franchised lawn service company would like to study the characteristics that differentiate homeowners who do and do not have a lawn service. A random sample of 30 homeowners located in a suburban area near a large city was selected; 15 did not have a lawn service (code 0) and 15 had a lawn service (code 1). Information for these 30 homeowners was also available that indicated family income (in thousands of dollars), lawn size (in thousands of square feet), attitude toward outdoor recreational activities (0 = unfavorable, 1 = favorable), number of teenagers in the household, and age of the head of the household. The results are as follows:

| LAWN SERVICE | INCOME | LAWN SIZE | ATTITUDE | TEENAGERS | AGE |
|:---:|:---:|:---:|:---:|:---:|:---:|
| 0 | 54.3 | 3.0 | 0 | 2 | 38 |
| 0 | 65.6 | 4.3 | 1 | 1 | 45 |
| 0 | 124.7 | 1.9 | 1 | 2 | 47 |
| 0 | 71.9 | 4.5 | 1 | 0 | 37 |
| 0 | 74.2 | 1.7 | 0 | 1 | 39 |
| 0 | 54.5 | 3.2 | 0 | 2 | 37 |
| 0 | 80.0 | 4.6 | 1 | 1 | 45 |
| 0 | 66.1 | 7.9 | 1 | 1 | 46 |
| 0 | 75.3 | 5.6 | 1 | 3 | 37 |
| 0 | 84.8 | 6.0 | 1 | 2 | 39 |
| 0 | 57.9 | 4.5 | 1 | 2 | 47 |
| 0 | 104.6 | 9.1 | 1 | 3 | 36 |
| 0 | 62.3 | 4.2 | 1 | 1 | 38 |
| 0 | 80.6 | 9.4 | 1 | 2 | 44 |
| 0 | 98.9 | 2.3 | 0 | 0 | 32 |
| 1 | 107.3 | 6.9 | 1 | 1 | 43 |
| 1 | 144.1 | 8.3 | 1 | 1 | 39 |
| 1 | 94.6 | 10.8 | 0 | 2 | 40 |
| 1 | 140.1 | 10.1 | 0 | 1 | 55 |
| 1 | 141.4 | 10.3 | 1 | 1 | 49 |
| 1 | 123.1 | 6.8 | 1 | 2 | 53 |
| 1 | 164.1 | 7.2 | 0 | 0 | 51 |
| 1 | 84.7 | 3.3 | 1 | 3 | 48 |
| 1 | 66.2 | 4.7 | 0 | 2 | 41 |
| 1 | 102.9 | 5.7 | 1 | 0 | 45 |
| 1 | 79.5 | 10.9 | 0 | 2 | 43 |
| 1 | 164.6 | 8.3 | 0 | 0 | 62 |
| 1 | 137.4 | 7.8 | 0 | 3 | 52 |
| 1 | 101.6 | 6.3 | 0 | 0 | 34 |
| 1 | 106.4 | 7.2 | 1 | 1 | 45 |

**DATA FILE
LAWN**

(a) Fit a logistic regression model to predict the probability of using a lawn service based on family income (in thousands of dollars), lawn size (in thousands of square feet), attitude toward outdoor recreational activities (0 = unfavorable, 1 = favorable), number of teenagers in the household, and age of the head of the household.

(b) Explain the meaning of the regression coefficients for the model fit in (a).

(c) Predict the probability of purchasing a lawn service for a 48-year-old homeowner with a family income of $100,000, a lawn size of 5,000 square feet, a negative attitude toward outdoor recreation, and one teenager in the household.

(d) At the .05 level of significance, is there evidence that a logistic regression model that uses family income, lawn size, attitude toward outdoor recreation, number of teenagers in the household, and age of the head of the household is a good-fitting model?

(e) At the .05 level of significance, is there evidence that each of the five explanatory variables (family income, lawn size, attitude toward outdoor recreation, number of teenagers in the household, and age of the head of the household) makes a significant contribution to the logistic regression model?

##  18.7  PITFALLS IN MULTIPLE REGRESSION AND ETHICAL ISSUES

### Pitfalls in Multiple Regression

Model building is an art as well as a science. Different individuals may not always agree on the best multiple regression model. Nevertheless, we should use the process described in Exhibit 18.1 on page 895. In doing so, we must be aware of certain pitfalls that can interfere with the development of a useful model. In section 16.9 we discussed pitfalls in regression and ethical issues. Now that we have examined a variety of multiple regression models, we need to concern ourselves with some additional pitfalls related to the use of regression analysis. These are displayed in Exhibit 18.2.

> **Exhibit 18.2  Additional Pitfalls in Multiple Regression**
>
> ✓ **1.** The need to understand that the regression coefficient for a particular independent variable is interpreted from a perspective in which the values of all other independent variables are held constant.
>
> ✓ **2.** The need to evaluate residual plots for each independent variable.
>
> ✓ **3.** The need to evaluate interaction terms to determine whether the slope of other independent variables with the response variable is the same at each level of a dummy variable.
>
> ✓ **4.** The need to obtain the *VIF* for each independent variable before determining which independent variables should be included in the model.
>
> ✓ **5.** The need to use influence analysis to determine whether any observations are outliers and should be removed from the model.
>
> ✓ **6.** The need to examine several alternative models using best-subset regression in addition to or instead of stepwise regression.
>
> ✓ **7.** The need to employ logistic regression instead of least-squares regression when the response variable is categorical.

## Ethical Considerations

Ethical considerations arise when a user wishing to make predictions manipulates the development process of the multiple regression model. The key here is intent. In addition to the situations discussed in section 16.9, unethical behavior occurs when someone uses multiple regression analysis and *willfully fails* to remove variables from consideration that exhibit a high collinearity with other independent variables or *willfully fails* to use methods other than least-squares regression when the assumptions necessary for least-squares regression have been seriously violated.

## SUMMARY

In this chapter we considered curvilinear regression, dummy variables, collinearity, transformations, and model building. In addition, we developed the logistic regression model to predict a categorical variable. The summary chart on page 907 lists the topics covered.

## Key Terms

| | | |
|---|---|---|
| best-subsets approach 889 | dummy variable 869 | square-root transformation 880 |
| $C_p$ statistic 890 | exponential model 881 | stepwise regression 887 |
| collinearity 884 | logarithmic transformation 882 | variance inflationary factor (*VIF*) 885 |
| curvilinear regression model 859 | logistic regression 898 | Wald statistic 902 |
| deviance statistic 902 | odds ratio 898 | |

## Checking Your Understanding

**18.36** Why and how are dummy variables used?

**18.37** How can we evaluate whether the slope of the response variable with an independent variable is the same for each level of the dummy variable?

**18.38** What is the purpose of using transformations in multiple regression analysis?

**18.39** How do we evaluate whether independent variables are intercorrelated?

**18.40** Under what circumstances would we want to include a dummy variable in a regression model?

**18.41** What assumption concerning the slope between the response variable $Y$ and the explanatory variable $X$ must be made when a dummy variable is included in a regression model?

**18.42** What is the difference between stepwise regression and best-subsets regression?

**18.43** How do we choose among models that have been selected according to the $C_p$ statistic in best-subsets regression?

## Chapter Review Problems

**DATA FILE**
**BB97**

**18.44** Crazy Dave, the well-known baseball analyst, has expanded his analysis presented in Problem 16.79 on page 803 of which variables are important in predicting a team's wins in a given season. He has collected data related to wins, ERA, saves, runs scored, hits allowed, walks allowed, and errors for the 1997 season (see the BB97 file).

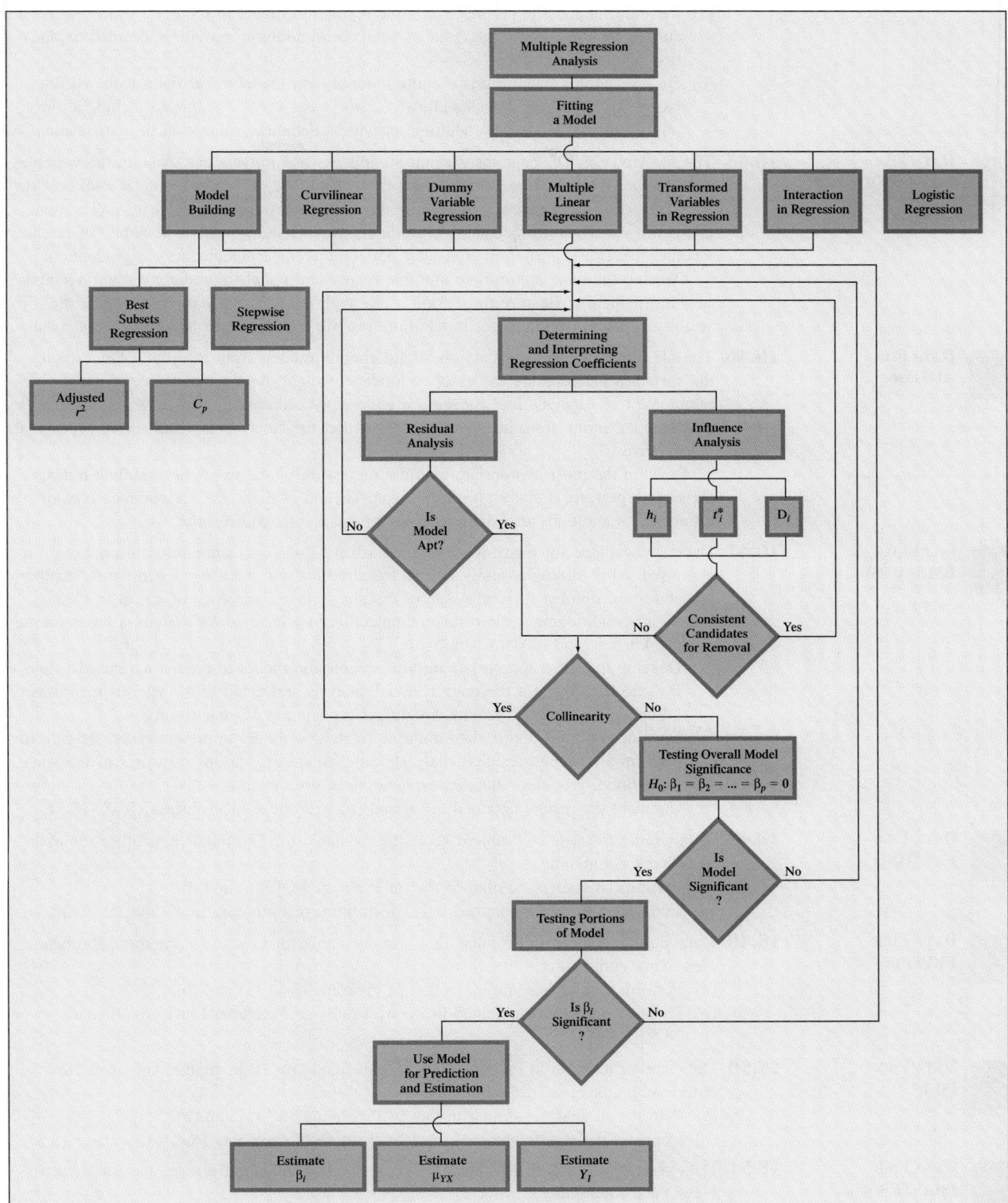

Chapter 18 summary chart

(a) Develop the most appropriate multiple regression model to predict a team's wins. Be sure to include a thorough residual analysis. In addition, provide a detailed explanation of your results.

(b) Develop the most appropriate multiple regression model to predict a team's ERA. based on hits allowed, walks allowed, errors, and saves. Be sure to include a thorough residual analysis. In addition, provide a detailed explanation of your results.

**DATA FILE**
**UNIV&COL**

**18.45** The file UNIV&COL contains data on 80 colleges and universities. Among the variables included are the academic calendar type (1 = semester, 0 = other), annual total cost (in thousands of dollars), average total score on the Scholastic Aptitude Test (SAT), room and board expenses (in thousands of dollars), whether the institution is public or private, whether the TOEFL criterion is at least 550, and average indebtedness at graduation.

Develop the most appropriate multiple regression model to predict average indebtedness at graduation. Be sure to perform a thorough residual analysis and evaluate the various measures of influence. In addition, provide a detailed explanation of your results.

**DATA FILE**
**AUTO96**

**18.46** The file AUTO96 contains data on 89 automobile models from the year 1996. Among the variables included are the gasoline mileage, weight, width, length, fuel type (0 = premium, 1 = regular), fuel capacity in gallons, wheelbase, turning circle, luggage capacity, front leg room, front head room, and whether the car is front wheel drive (1) or rear wheel drive (0).

Develop the most appropriate multiple regression model to predict gasoline mileage. Be sure to perform a thorough residual analysis and evaluate the various measures of influence. In addition, provide a detailed explanation of your results.

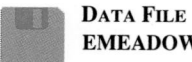

**DATA FILE**
**EMEADOW**

**18.47** Data are available for East Meadow, a suburban New York community, to predict appraised value of single-family houses based on lot size, number of bedrooms, number of bathrooms, number of rooms, age of the house, taxes, presence of an eat-in kitchen, central air-conditioning, a fireplace, a connection to a local sewer system, a basement, a modern kitchen, and modern bathrooms.

(a) Develop the most appropriate multiple regression model to predict appraised value. Be sure to perform a thorough residual analysis and evaluate the various measures of influence. In addition, provide a detailed explanation of your results.

(b) Develop the most appropriate multiple regression model to predict taxes. Be sure to perform a thorough residual analysis and evaluate the various measures of influence. In addition, provide a detailed explanation of your results.

(c) Compare the results obtained in (a) and (b) with those of Problems 18.48–18.51.

**DATA FILE**
**FARMING**

**18.48** Data similar to those in Problem 18.47 are available for Farmingdale, another suburban New York community.

(a) Perform an analysis similar to that of Problem 18.47 (a) and (b).

(b) Compare the results obtained in (a) with those of Problems 18.47 and 18.49–18.51.

**DATA FILE**
**LEVITT**

**18.49** Data similar to those in Problem 18.47 are available for Levittown, another suburban New York community.

(a) Perform an analysis similar to that of Problem 18.47 (a) and (b).

(b) Compare the results obtained in (a) with those of Problems 18.47, 18.48, and 18.50–18.51.

**DATA FILE**
**ISLIP**

**18.50** Data similar to those in Problem 18.47 are available for Islip, another suburban New York community.

(a) Perform an analysis similar to that of Problem 18.47 (a) and (b).

(b) Compare the results obtained in (a) with those of Problems 18.47–18.49 and 18.51.

**DATA FILE**
**ISLIPTER**

**18.51** Data similar to those in Problem 18.47 are available for Islip Terrace, another suburban New York community.

(a) Perform an analysis similar to that of Problem 18.47 (a) and (b).

(b) Compare the results obtained in (a) with those of Problems 18.47–18.50.

# Case Study — THE MOUNTAIN STATES POTATO COMPANY

The Mountain States Potato Company is a potato-processing firm in eastern Idaho. A by-product of the process, called a filter cake, has been sold to area feedlots as cattle feed. Recently, one of the feedlot owners complained that the cattle were not gaining weight and believed that the problem was the filter cake they purchased from the Mountain States Potato Company.

Initially, all that was known of the filter cake system was that historical records showed that the percentage of solids had been running in the neighborhood of 11.5% in years past. At present, the solids were running in the 8% to 9% range. Several additions had been made to the plant in the intervening years that had significantly increased the water and solids volume and the clarifier temperature. What was actually affecting the solids was a mystery, but because the plant needed to get rid of its solid waste if it were going to run, something had to be done quickly. The only practical solution was to determine some way to get the solids content back up to the previous levels.

Individuals involved in the process were asked to identify variables that might be manipulated that could in turn affect the percentage of solids content. This review turned up six variables that would affect the percentage of solids. The variables are:

| VARIABLE | COMMENTS |
|----------|----------|
| SOLIDS | Percent solids in filter cake. |
| PH | Acidity. This indicates bacterial action in the clarifier. As bacterial action progresses, organic acids are produced that can be measured using pH. This is controlled by the downtime of the system. |
| LOWER | Pressure of the vacuum line below the fluid line on rotating drum. |
| UPPER | Pressure of the vacuum line above the fluid line on rotating drum. |
| THICK | Cake thickness measured on the drum. |
| VARIDRIV | Setting used to control the drum speed. May differ from DRUMSPD because of mechanical inefficiencies. |
| DRUMSPD | Speed at which the drum was rotated when collecting filter cake. Measured with a stopwatch. |

Data obtained by monitoring the process several times daily for 20 days are stored in the POTATO file. The data for the first four observations are shown below.

| OBS. | SOLIDS | pH | LOWER | UPPER | THICK | VARIDRIV | DRUMSPD |
|------|--------|-----|-------|-------|-------|----------|---------|
| 1 | 9.7 | 3.7 | 13 | 14 | 0.250 | 6 | 33.00 |
| 2 | 9.4 | 3.8 | 17 | 18 | 0.875 | 6 | 30.43 |
| 3 | 10.5 | 3.8 | 14 | 15 | 0.500 | 6 | 34.00 |
| 4 | 10.9 | 3.9 | 14 | 14 | 0.500 | 6 | 34.00 |

*Source: Midwest Society for Case Research, 1994.*

**DATA FILE
POTATO**

Develop a regression model to predict the percentage of solids. Write an executive summary of your findings to the president of the Mountain States Potato Company.

# References

1. Andrews, D. F., and D. Pregibon, "Finding the Outliers That Matter," *Journal of the Royal Statistical Society* 40 (Series B, 1978): 85–93.
2. Atkinson, A. C., "Robust and Diagnostic Regression Analysis," *Communications in Statistics* 11 (1982): 2559–2572.
3. Belsley, D. A., E. Kuh, and R. Welsch, *Regression Diagnostics: Identifying Influential Data and Sources of Collinearity* (New York: Wiley, 1980).
4. Cook, R. D., and S. Weisberg, *Residuals and Influence in Regression* (New York: Chapman and Hall, 1982).
5. Hoaglin, D. C., and R. Welsch, "The Hat Matrix in Regression and ANOVA," *The American Statistician* 32 (1978): 17–22.
6. Hocking, R. R., "Developments in Linear Regression Methodology: 1959–1982," *Technometrics* 25 (1983): 219–250.
7. Hosmer, D., and S. Lemeshow, *Applied Logistic Regression* (New York: Wiley, 1989).
8. Marquardt, D. W., "You Should Standardize the Predictor Variables in Your Regression Models," discussion of "A Critique of Some Ridge Regression Methods," by G. Smith and F. Campbell, *Journal of the American Statistical Association* 75 (1980): 87–91.
9. *Microsoft Excel 97* (Redmond, WA: Microsoft Corp., 1997).
10. *Minitab for Windows Version 12* (State College, PA: Minitab, Inc., 1998).
11. Neter, J., M. Kutner, C. Nachtsheim, and W. Wasserman, *Applied Linear Statistical Models* (Homewood, IL: Irwin, 1996).
12. Snee, R. D., "Some Aspects of Nonorthogonal Data Analysis, Part I. Developing Prediction Equations," *Journal of Quality Technology* 5 (1973): 67–79.
13. Tukey, J. W., "Data Analysis, Computation and Mathematics," *Quarterly Journal of Applied Mathematics* 30 (1972): 51–65.
14. Velleman, P. F., and R. Welsch, "Efficient Computing of Regression Diagnostics," *The American Statistician* 35 (1981): 234–242.

## ❖ APPENDIX 18.1   USING MICROSOFT EXCEL FOR MODEL BUILDING

### COMMENT:  PHStat Add-In Users

If Microsoft Excel is not running, click the **PHStat** add-in icon. If Microsoft Excel is running, select **File | Open**. Select the **PHStat** add-in file **PHSA.XLA**. Click the **Open** button.

To obtain the variance inflationary factor (*VIF*) for each variable, **select PHStat | Regression | Multiple Regression**. In the multiple regression dialog box, select the **Variance Inflationary Factor** check box. To also obtain the coefficients of partial determination, check the **Coefficients of Partial Determination** check box. Click the **OK** button.

To perform a best subsets model building analysis, select **PHStat | Regression | Best Subsets**. Enter the *Y* and *X* variables in their respective Cell Range edit boxes. Select the **First cells in both ranges contain label** check box. Click the **OK** button.

### Using Microsoft Excel for Curvilinear Regression

The sample curvilinear regression model as expressed in equation (18.2) on page 859 includes both linear (*X*) and curvilinear ($X^2$) terms for each independent variable believed to have a curvilinear relationship with *Y*. To obtain a curvilinear ($X^2$) term, insert a column adjacent to the column that contains the *X* variable to hold the $X^2$ terms (by using the **Insert | Columns** command). Proceed with regression analysis using the Data Analysis tool as discussed in appendices 16.1 and 16.2.

### Using Microsoft Excel for Dummy-Variable and Other Types of Regression Models

In section 18.2 we covered the use of categorical independent variables (known as dummy variables) in regression, and in section 18.3 we introduced a variety of other regression models. Models that include dummy variables do not require any special Excel functions. Each dummy variable needs to be coded as 0 or 1 for each observation depending on whether the observation is in category 1 or category 2. If the categories are not coded into numerical values of 0 and 1, select the range of the categorical responses, and select **Edit | Replace**. Replace the category labels with values of 0 and 1 as desired. Interaction terms can be included in the model by defining a new variable as the product of two other variables.

Models involving transformations (see page 879) can also be developed using an appropriate Excel function. To apply the square-root transformation of the model shown in equation (18.3) on page 880, we can use the **SQRT** function. To apply transformations involving the natural logarithm (ln), we can use the **LN** function; we use the **LOG** function for transformations involving the common (base 10) logarithms.

## ❖ APPENDIX 18.2    USING MINITAB FOR MODEL BUILDING

In appendices 16.2 and 17.2 instructions were provided for using Minitab for simple linear regression and multiple regression. The same set of instructions can be used when there are more than two independent variables.

### Using Minitab for Curvilinear Regression

To create a new $X$ variable that is the square of another $X$ variable, select **Calc | Calculator**. In the Store result in variable edit box, enter the column number or name for the new variable. In the Expression edit box, enter {name or column number of the $X$ variable to be squared} ** 2. Click the **OK** button. A new $X$ variable that is the square of another $X$ variable has been entered in the specified column. Continue with the regression analysis as discussed previously.

### Using Minitab for Dummy Variables

In order to do regression analysis with dummy variables, the categories of the dummy variable must be coded as 0 and 1. If the dummy variable has not already been recoded as a 0–1 variable, Minitab can recode the variable. As an illustration with the data of Table 18.2 on page 869, open the HOUSE3.MTP worksheet. Note the fireplace variable in column C3 has been entered as Yes and No. To recode this variable using Minitab, select **Calc | Make Indicator Variables**. In the Indicator variables for edit box, enter **Firepl** or **C3**. In the Store results in: edit box, enter **C4 C5**, because we need to specify a column for each possible definition of the dummy variable. Click the **OK** button.

Note that no has been coded as 1 in C4 and yes has been coded as 1 in C5. To define an interaction term that is the product of heating area and the dummy variable fireplace, select **Calc | Calculator**. In the Store result in variable edit box enter **C6**. In the Expression edit box, enter the **Heating * Firepl** or **C2 * C5**. Click the **OK** button. A new $X$ variable that is the product of these two variables has been entered in column C6.

### Using Minitab for Transforming Variables

To transform a variable, select **Calc | Calculator**. In the Store result in variable edit box, enter the column number or name for the new variable. Select the function to be used for the transformation such as $\log_{10}$, natural log, or square root. In the Expression edit box, after the function has been selected, enter the name of the $X$ variable to be transformed in the parentheses of the function. Click the **OK** button. Continue with the regression analysis as discussed previously.

## Using Minitab for Stepwise Regression and Best-Subsets Regression

Minitab can be used for model building with either stepwise regression or best-subsets regression. To illustrate model building with the standby hours data, open the STANDBY.MTP worksheet. To obtain a stepwise regression select **Stat | Regression | Stepwise**. In the response edit box, enter **Standby** or **C1**. In the Predictors edit box, enter **Staff** or **C2, Remote** or **C3, Dubner** or **C4**, and **Labor** or **C5**. Click the **Options** button. The entries for $F$ to enter and $F$ to remove should be **4.0**. Click the **OK** button to return to the stepwise regression dialog box. Click the **OK** button. Output similar to that of Figure 18.9 on page 889 will be obtained.

To obtain a best-subsets regression, select **Stat | Regression | Best Subsets**. In the Response edit box, enter **Standby** or **C1**. In the Free predictors edit box, enter **Staff** or **C2, Remote** or **C3, Dubner** or **C4, and Labor** or **C5**. Click the **Options** button. Enter **3** in the Models of each size to print edit box. Click the **OK** button to return to the Best-subsets regression dialog box. Click the **OK** button. Output similar to that of Figure 18.10 on page 889 will be obtained.

## Using Minitab for Logistic Regression

To illustrate the use of Minitab for logistic regression with the credit card upgrade example, open the LOGPURCH.MTP worksheet. To obtain a logistic regression, select **Stat | Regression | Binary Logistic Regression**. In the Response edit box, enter **C2** or **Purchase**. In the Model edit box, enter **C1** or **Spending** and **C3** or **Extra**. In the Factors edit box, enter **C3** or **Extra** because it is a categorical variable. Click the **OK** button. Output similar to that of Figure 18.13 on page 901 will be obtained.

# 19

# Time-Series Analysis

# CHAPTER OBJECTIVES

✓ *To understand the components of the classical time-series model*
✓ *To introduce a variety of time-series models for forecasting purposes with annual data*
✓ *To evaluate the impact of seasonal effects when forecasting with quarterly or monthly data*

# Introduction

In the preceding three chapters we discussed the topic of regression analysis as a tool for model building and prediction. In these respects, regression analysis provides a useful guide to managerial decision making. In this chapter we develop the concept of time-series analysis and demonstrate how business forecasting methods assist in the process of managerial planning and control.

We begin with annual time-series data and illustrate two techniques for smoothing a series—moving averages and exponential smoothing (see section 19.3). We continue our analysis of annual time series by demonstrating the method of least-squares trend fitting and forecasting (see section 19.4) and other, more sophisticated forecasting methods (see sections 19.5 and 19.6). We then extend these trend fitting and forecasting models to a monthly or quarterly time series and evaluate the impact of seasonal effects (see section 19.8).

◆ **USING STATISTICS:** *Forecasting Annual Gross Revenues at Eastman Kodak Company*

Eastman Kodak, according to its 1996 annual report, has as its vision to be the world leader in imaging. Eastman Kodak's work is predicated on four business principles: mass production at low cost, international distribution, extensive advertising, and focus on the customer. To accomplish its goals, the executives at Eastman Kodak stress the fostering of growth and development through continuous research and the reinvestment of its profits to build and extend its business horizons. In sections 19.4–19.6 we assess trends in annual gross revenues from all of Eastman Kodak's products over the 22-year period 1975–1996 and make forecast extrapolations into the future. This analysis will enable company management to better understand how gross revenues have changed over time, realize where Eastman Kodak is currently positioned relative to its competitors, and permit a discussion of what gross revenues might be achieved in the future if certain strategies were implemented.

## 19.1 THE IMPORTANCE OF BUSINESS FORECASTING

Because economic and business conditions vary over time, business leaders must find ways to keep abreast of the effects that such changes will have on their operations. One technique that business leaders may use as an aid in planning for future operational needs is **forecasting**. Although numerous forecasting methods have been devised, they all have one common goal—to make predictions of future events so that these projections can then be incorporated into the decision-making process.

The need for forecasting pervades modern society. As examples, officials in government must be able to forecast such things as unemployment, inflation, industrial production, and expected revenues from personal and corporate income taxes in order to formulate policy. Marketing executives of a large retailing corporation must be able to forecast product demand, sales revenues, consumer preferences, inventory, and so on, in order to make timely decisions regarding current and future operations and to assist in strategic planning activities. To keep an inventory of expendable and replaceable parts for its fleet of planes, the directors of an airline must be able to make forecasts of usage and needs based on number of flights, number of employees, and number of passengers. The administration of your college or university must make forecasts of student enrollments based on national population projections and trends in curriculum based on technological developments in order to plan for the construction of dormitories and other academic facilities, plan for student and faculty recruitment, and make assessments of other needs.

## Types of Forecasting Methods

There are basically two approaches to forecasting: *qualitative* and *quantitative*. **Qualitative forecasting methods** are especially important when historical data are unavailable, as would be the case, for example, if the marketing department wanted to predict the sales of a new product. Qualitative forecasting methods are considered to be highly subjective and judgmental. These include the *factor listing method*, *expert opinion*, and the *Delphi technique* (see reference 4).

On the other hand, **quantitative forecasting methods** make use of historical data. The goal is to study what has happened in the past in order to better understand the underlying structure of the data and thereby provide the means necessary for predicting future occurrences.

Quantitative forecasting methods can be subdivided into two types: *time series* and *causal*. **Time-series forecasting methods** involve the projection of future values of a variable based entirely on the past and present observations of that variable.

### Time Series

A **time series** is a set of numerical data that is obtained at regular periods over time.

For example, the *daily* closing prices of a particular stock on the New York Stock Exchange constitute a time series. Other examples of economic or business time series are the *monthly* publication of the Consumer Price Index, the *quarterly* statements of gross domestic product (GDP), and the *annually* recorded total sales revenues of a particular firm.

Time series, however, are not restricted to economic or business data. For example, the dean of students at your college may wish to investigate whether there is an indication of persistent grade inflation during the past decade. To accomplish this, on an annual basis either the percentage of freshmen and sophomore students on the dean's list may be examined or the percentage of seniors graduating with honors may be studied.

**Causal forecasting methods** involve the determination of factors that relate to the variable to be predicted. These include multiple regression analysis with *lagged* variables, *econometric* modeling, *leading indicator* analysis, *diffusion* indexes, and other economic barometers that are beyond the scope of this text (see references 5 and 8). Thus, our primary emphasis here is on time-series analysis.

# COMPONENT FACTORS OF THE CLASSICAL MULTIPLICATIVE TIME-SERIES MODEL

The basic assumption underlying time-series analysis is that the factors that have influenced patterns of activity in the past and present will continue to do so in more or less the same manner in the future. Thus, the major goals of time-series analysis are to identify and isolate these influencing factors for predictive (forecasting) purposes as well as for managerial planning and control.

To achieve these goals, many mathematical models have been devised for exploring the fluctuations among the component factors of a time series. Perhaps the most fundamental is the classical multiplicative model for data recorded annually, quarterly, or monthly. It is this model that we consider in this text. We will be using the classical multiplicative model primarily for forecasting. Other applications include a detailed analysis of the particular components through *time-series decomposition*. For example, economists often study annual, quarterly, or monthly time series to filter out the cyclical component and evaluate its movement against general economic activity. Applications of time-series decomposition, however, are outside the scope of this text.

To demonstrate the classical multiplicative time-series model, we present the *actual* gross revenues for Eastman Kodak Company from 1975 to 1996 in Figure 19.1. If we may characterize these time-series data, it is clear that *actual* gross revenues have shown a tendency to increase over this 22-year period. This overall long-term tendency or impression of upward or downward movements is known as a **trend**.

However, trend is not the only component factor influencing either these particular data or other annual time series. Two other factors, the *cyclical* component and the *irregular* component, are also present in the data. The **cyclical component** depicts the up-and-down swings or movements through the series. Cyclical movements vary in length, usually lasting from 2 to 10 years; differ in intensity or amplitude; and are often correlated with a business cycle. In some years the values will be higher than what would be predicted by a simple trend line (i.e., they are at or near the *peak* of a cycle), whereas in other years the values will be lower than what would be predicted by a trend line (i.e., they are at or near the bottom or *trough* of a cycle). Any observed data that do not follow the trend curve modified by the cyclical component are indicative of the **irregular** or **random component**. When data are recorded monthly or quarterly an additional component called the *seasonal factor* is considered (see section 19.8) along with the trend, cyclical, and irregular components.

The three or four component factors that influence an economic or business time series are summarized in Table 19.1. The **classical multiplicative time-series model** states that any observed value in a time series is the product of these influencing factors; that is, when the data are obtained annually, an observation $Y_i$ recorded in the year $i$ may be expressed as in equation (19.1).

---

### Classical Multiplicative Time-Series Model for Annual Data

$$Y_i = T_i \cdot C_i \cdot I_i \tag{19.1}$$

where in the year $i$

$T_i$ = value of the trend component

$C_i$ = value of the cyclical component

$I_i$ = value of the irregular component

---

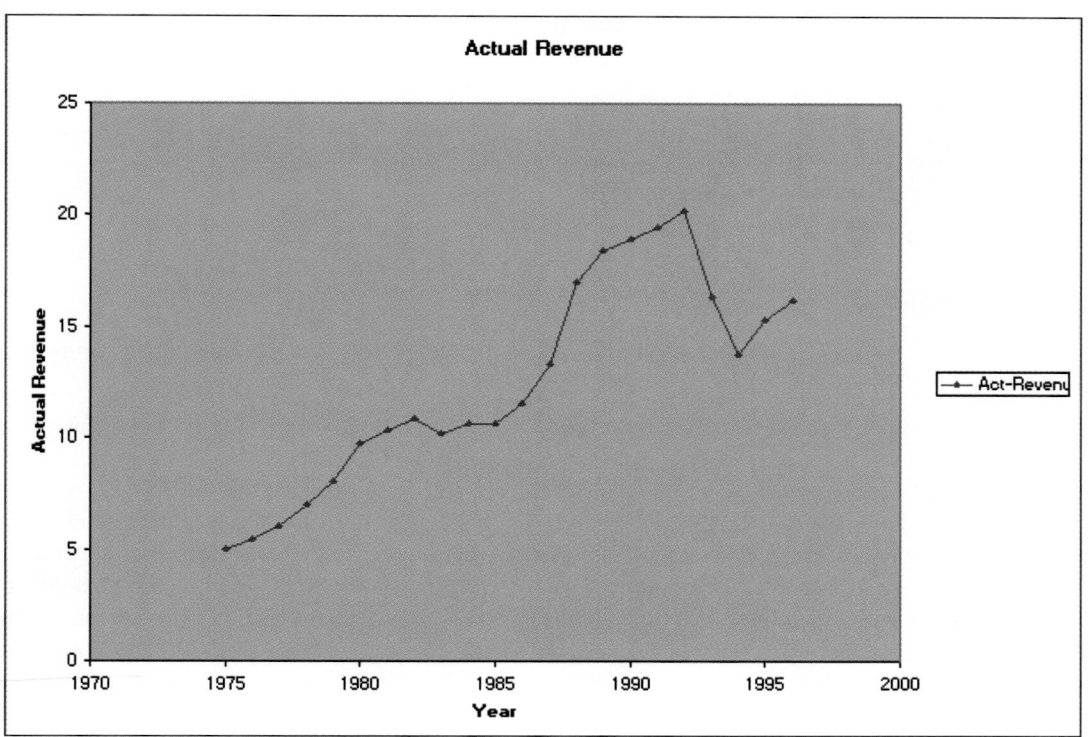

**FIGURE 19.1** Plot obtained from Microsoft Excel of *actual* gross revenues (in billions of *current* dollars) for Eastman Kodak Company (1975–1996)

*Source: Moody's Handbook of Common Stocks, 1980, 1989, 1993, 1997. Reprinted by permission of Moody's Investors Service.*

**Table 19.1**    *Factors influencing time-series data*

| COMPONENT | CLASSIFICATION OF COMPONENT | DEFINITION | REASON FOR INFLUENCE | DURATION |
|---|---|---|---|---|
| Trend | Systematic | Overall or persistent, long-term upward or downward pattern of movement | Changes in technology, population, wealth, value | Several years |
| Seasonal | Systematic | Fairly regular periodic fluctuations that occur within each 12-month period year after year | Weather conditions, social customs, religious customs | Within 12 months (or monthly or quarterly data) |
| Cyclical | Systematic | Repeating up-and-down swings or movements through four phases: from peak (prosperity) to contraction (recession) to trough (depression) to expansion (recovery or growth) | Interactions of numerous combinations of factors influencing the economy | Usually 2–10 years with differing intensity for a complete cycle |
| Irregular | Unsystematic | The erratic or "residual" fluctuations in a series that exist after taking into account the systematic effects—trend, seasonal, and cyclical | Random variations in data or due to unforeseen events such as strikes, hurricanes, floods, political assassinations, etc. | Short duration and nonrepeating |

When the data are obtained either quarterly or monthly, an observation $Y_i$ recorded in time period $i$ may be given as in equation (19.2).

The first step in a time-series analysis is to plot the data and observe their tendencies over time. We must first determine whether there appears to be a long-term upward or downward movement in the series (i.e., a trend) or whether the series seems to oscillate about a horizontal line over time. If the latter is the case (that is, there is no long-term upward or downward trend), then the method of moving averages or the method of exponential smoothing may be employed to smooth the series and provide us with an overall long-term impression (see section 19.3). On the other hand, if a trend is actually present, a variety of time-series forecasting methods can be considered (see sections 19.4–19.6) when dealing with annual data. For monthly or quarterly time-series data, forecasting will be developed in section 19.8.

## 19.3  SMOOTHING THE ANNUAL TIME SERIES

Table 19.2 presents the annual worldwide factory sales (in millions of units) of cars, trucks, and buses manufactured by General Motors Corporation (GM) over the 22-year period from 1975 to 1996, and Figure 19.2 is a time-series plot of these data. When we examine annual data such as these, our visual impression of the overall long-term tendencies or trend movements in the series is obscured by the amount of variation from year to year. It then becomes difficult to judge whether any long-term upward or downward trend effect really exists in the series.

In situations such as these, the method of *moving averages* or the method of *exponential smoothing* may be used to smooth a series and thereby provide us with an overall impression of the pattern of movement in the data over time.

### Moving Averages

The method of moving averages for smoothing a time series is highly subjective and dependent on $L$, the length of the period selected for constructing the averages. To eliminate the cyclical fluctuations, the period chosen should be an integer value that corresponds to (or is a multiple of) the estimated average length of a cycle in the series.

But what are moving averages and how are they computed?

**Table 19.2** *Factory sales (in millions of units) for General Motors*
*Corporation (1975–1996)*

| YEAR | FACTORY SALES | YEAR | FACTORY SALES | YEAR | FACTORY SALES |
|------|---------------|------|---------------|------|---------------|
| 1975 | 6.6 | 1983 | 7.8 | 1990 | 7.5 |
| 1976 | 8.6 | 1984 | 8.3 | 1991 | 7.4 |
| 1977 | 9.1 | 1985 | 9.3 | 1992 | 7.7 |
| 1978 | 9.5 | 1986 | 8.6 | 1993 | 7.8 |
| 1979 | 9.0 | 1987 | 7.8 | 1994 | 8.4 |
| 1980 | 7.1 | 1988 | 8.1 | 1995 | 8.3 |
| 1981 | 6.8 | 1989 | 7.9 | 1996 | 8.4 |
| 1982 | 6.2 | | | | |

**DATA FILE
GM**

*Note: From all sources including passenger cars, trucks and buses, and overseas plants.*
*Source:* Moody's Handbook of Common Stocks, *1980, 1989, 1993 and annual reports. Reprinted by*
*permission of Moody's Investors Service.*

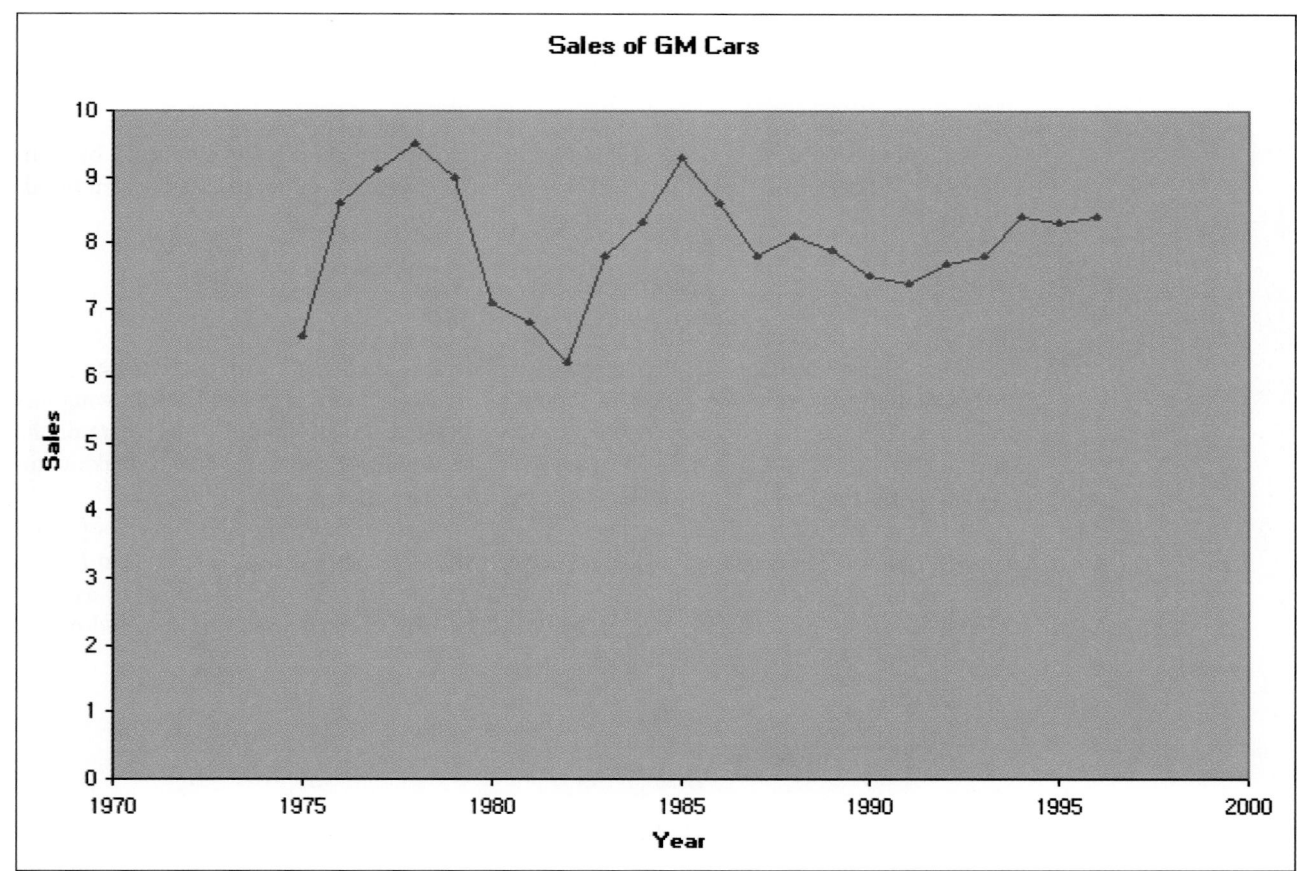

**FIGURE 19.2** Plot of factory sales (in millions of units) for General Motors Corporation
(1975–1996)
*Source: Data are taken from Table 19.2.*

## Moving Averages

**Moving averages** for a chosen period of length $L$ consist of a series of arithmetic means computed over time such that each mean is calculated for a sequence of observed values having that particular length $L$. We represent these moving averages by the symbol $MA(L)$.

To illustrate, suppose we want to compute 5-year moving averages from a series containing $n = 11$ years. Because $L = 5$, the 5-year moving averages consist of a series of means obtained over time by averaging over consecutive sequences containing five observed values. The first of these 5-year moving averages is computed by summing the values for the first 5 years in the series and dividing by 5.

$$MA(5) = \frac{Y_1 + Y_2 + Y_3 + Y_4 + Y_5}{5}$$

The second of these 5-year moving averages is computed by summing the values of years 2 through 6 in the series and then dividing by 5.

$$MA(5) = \frac{Y_2 + Y_3 + Y_4 + Y_5 + Y_6}{5}$$

This process continues until the last of these 5-year moving averages is computed by summing the values of the last 5 years in the series (i.e., years 7 through 11) and then dividing by 5.

$$MA(5) = \frac{Y_7 + Y_8 + Y_9 + Y_{10} + Y_{11}}{5}$$

When we are dealing with annual time-series data, $L$, the length of the period we choose for constructing the moving averages, should be an *odd* number of years. By following this rule, we note that no moving averages can be obtained for the first $(L-1)/2$ years or the last $(L-1)/2$ years of the series. Thus, for a 5-year moving average, we cannot make computations for the first 2 years or the last 2 years of the series.

When graphing the moving averages on a chart, each of the computed values is plotted against the middle year of the sequence of years used to compute it. If $n = 11$ and $L = 5$, our first moving average would be centered on the 3d year, our second moving average would be centered on the 4th year, and our last moving average would be centered on the 9th year. We illustrate this in Example 19.1.

## Example 19.1 *Computing a 5-Year Moving Average*

Suppose the following data represent total revenues (in millions of *constant* 1995 dollars) by a car rental agency over the 11-year period 1987–1997:

4.0   5.0   7.0   6.0   8.0   9.0   5.0   2.0   3.5   5.5   6.5

Compute the 5-year moving averages for this annual time series.

## SOLUTION

The first of the 5-year moving averages is:

$$MA(5) = \frac{Y_1 + Y_2 + Y_3 + Y_4 + Y_5}{5} = \frac{4.0 + 5.0 + 7.0 + 6.0 + 8.0}{5} = \frac{30.0}{5} = 6.0$$

That is, to compute a 5-year moving average, we first obtain the 5-year moving total and then we divide this total by 5. The moving average is then centered on the middle value—the 3d year of this time series.

To compute the second of the 5-year moving averages, we obtain the moving total of the 2d through 6th years and divide this value by 5. That is,

$$MA(5) = \frac{Y_2 + Y_3 + Y_4 + Y_5 + Y_6}{5} = \frac{5.0 + 7.0 + 6.0 + 8.0 + 9.0}{5} = \frac{35.0}{5} = 7.0$$

This moving average is centered on the new middle value—the 4th year of the time series.

The remaining moving averages are:

$$MA(5) = \frac{Y_3 + Y_4 + Y_5 + Y_6 + Y_7}{5} = \frac{7.0 + 6.0 + 8.0 + 9.0 + 5.0}{5} = \frac{35.0}{5} = 7.0$$

$$MA(5) = \frac{Y_4 + Y_5 + Y_6 + Y_7 + Y_8}{5} = \frac{6.0 + 8.0 + 9.0 + 5.0 + 2.0}{5} = \frac{30.0}{5} = 6.0$$

$$MA(5) = \frac{Y_5 + Y_6 + Y_7 + Y_8 + Y_9}{5} = \frac{8.0 + 9.0 + 5.0 + 2.0 + 3.5}{5} = \frac{27.5}{5} = 5.5$$

$$MA(5) = \frac{Y_6 + Y_7 + Y_8 + Y_9 + Y_{10}}{5} = \frac{9.0 + 5.0 + 2.0 + 3.5 + 5.5}{5} = \frac{25.0}{5} = 5.0$$

$$MA(5) = \frac{Y_7 + Y_8 + Y_9 + Y_{10} + Y_{11}}{5} = \frac{5.0 + 2.0 + 3.5 + 5.5 + 6.5}{5} = \frac{22.5}{5} = 4.5$$

These moving averages are then centered on their respective middle values, the 5th, 6th, 7th, 8th, and 9th years in the time series. We note that in obtaining the 5-year moving averages, no result can be computed for the first two or last two observed values in the time series.

---

In practice, when obtaining moving averages, we should use computer software such as Microsoft Excel or Minitab in order to avoid the tedious computations. Table 19.3 on page 922 presents the annual GM factory sales data for the 22-year period from 1975 to 1996 along with the computations for 3- and 7-year moving averages. Both of these constructed series are plotted in Figure 19.3 on page 923 with the original data.

To compute $MA(3)$, the 3-year moving averages, we first obtain a series of 3-year moving totals as indicated in column (3) of Table 19.3 and then divide each of these totals by 3. The results are given in column (4). We note that for any particular year $i$ in the series, the 3-year moving total represents the sum of the observed value for the year $i$ along with

**Table 19.3**   *3- and 7-year moving averages of GM factory sales (1975–1996)*

| (1) YEAR | (2) FACTORY SALES (IN MILLIONS OF UNITS) | (3) 3-YEAR MOVING TOTAL | (4) 3-YEAR MOVING AVERAGE | (5) 7-YEAR MOVING TOTAL | (6) 7-YEAR MOVING AVERAGE |
|---|---|---|---|---|---|
| 1975 | 6.6 | — | — | — | — |
| 1976 | 8.6 | 24.3 | 8.10 | — | — |
| 1977 | 9.1 | 27.2 | 9.07 | — | — |
| 1978 | 9.5 | 27.6 | 9.20 | 56.7 | 8.10 |
| 1979 | 9.0 | 25.6 | 8.53 | 56.3 | 8.04 |
| 1980 | 7.1 | 22.9 | 7.63 | 55.5 | 7.93 |
| 1981 | 6.8 | 20.1 | 6.70 | 54.7 | 7.81 |
| 1982 | 6.2 | 20.8 | 6.93 | 54.5 | 7.78 |
| 1983 | 7.8 | 22.3 | 7.43 | 54.1 | 7.73 |
| 1984 | 8.3 | 25.4 | 8.47 | 54.8 | 7.83 |
| 1985 | 9.3 | 26.2 | 8.73 | 56.1 | 8.01 |
| 1986 | 8.6 | 25.7 | 8.57 | 57.8 | 8.26 |
| 1987 | 7.8 | 24.5 | 8.17 | 57.5 | 8.21 |
| 1988 | 8.1 | 23.8 | 7.93 | 56.6 | 8.09 |
| 1989 | 7.9 | 23.5 | 7.83 | 55.0 | 7.86 |
| 1990 | 7.5 | 22.8 | 7.60 | 54.2 | 7.74 |
| 1991 | 7.4 | 22.6 | 7.53 | 54.8 | 7.83 |
| 1992 | 7.7 | 22.9 | 7.63 | 55.0 | 7.86 |
| 1993 | 7.8 | 23.9 | 7.97 | 55.5 | 7.93 |
| 1994 | 8.4 | 24.5 | 8.17 | — | — |
| 1995 | 8.3 | 25.1 | 8.37 | — | — |
| 1996 | 8.4 | — | — | — | — |

*Source: Data are taken from Table 19.2.*

the observed values for the year preceding it and the year following it. However, as shown in column (5), with 7-year moving totals the result computed and recorded for the year $i$ consists of the observed value in the time series for year $i$ plus the three observed values that precede it and the three observed values that follow it. The 7-year moving averages [$MA$(7)] are then obtained by dividing the series of moving totals by 7. These results are listed in column (6).

We note from columns (3) and (4) of Table 19.3 that in obtaining the 3-year moving averages, no result can be computed for the first or last observed value in the time series. We also see from columns (5) and (6) that when we compute 7-year moving averages, there are no results for the first three observed values or the last three values.

From Figure 19.3 we can see that the 7-year moving averages smooth the series a great deal more than do the 3-year moving averages because the period is of longer duration. Unfortunately, however, as we previously noted, the longer the period, the fewer the number of moving average values that can be computed and plotted. Therefore, selecting mov-

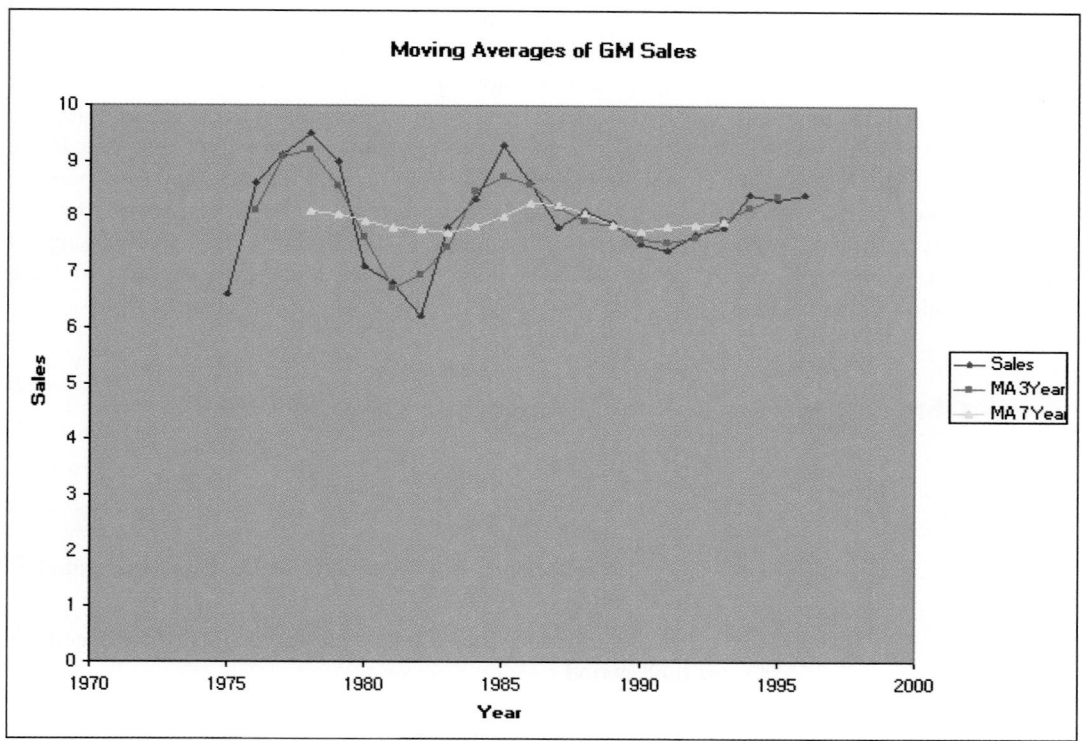

**FIGURE 19.3** Plotting 3- and 7-year moving averages for GM factory sales data using Microsoft Excel

*Source: Data are taken from Table 19.3*

ing averages with periods of length greater than 7 years is usually undesirable because too many computed data points would be missing at the beginning and end of the series, making it more difficult to obtain an overall impression of the entire series.

## Exponential Smoothing

**Exponential smoothing** is another technique that may be used to smooth a time series and thereby provide us with an impression as to the overall long-term movements in the data. In addition, we can use the method of exponential smoothing to obtain short-term (one period into the future) forecasts for such time series as the GM factory sales data depicted in Figure 19.2 (page 919) when it is questionable as to what type of long-term trend effect, if any, is present. In this respect, the technique possesses a distinct advantage over the method of moving averages.

The method of exponential smoothing derives its name from the fact that it provides us with an *exponentially weighted* moving average through the time series; that is, throughout the series each smoothing calculation or forecast is dependent on all previously observed values. This is another advantage over the method of moving averages, which does not take into account all the observed values in this manner. With exponential smoothing, the weights assigned to the observed values decrease over time so that when a calculation is made, the most recently observed value receives the highest weight, the previously observed value receives the second highest weight, and so on, with the initially observed value receiving the lowest weight. Although the magnitude of computations involved may seem formidable, exponential smoothing as well as moving average methods are available among the procedures provided in Microsoft Excel and Minitab (see appendices 19.1 and 19.2).

If we focus on the smoothing aspects of the technique (rather than the forecasting aspects), the formulas developed for exponentially smoothing a series in any time period $i$ are based on only three terms—the currently observed value in the time series $Y_i$, the previously computed exponentially smoothed value $E_{i-1}$, and some subjectively assigned weight or smoothing coefficient $W$. Thus, to smooth a series at any time period $i$, we have the following expression.

### Obtaining an Exponentially Smoothed Value in Time Period $i$

$$E_i = WY_i + (1 - W)E_{i-1} \qquad (19.3)$$

where

$E_i$ = value of the exponentially smoothed series being computed in time period $i$

$E_{i-1}$ = value of the exponentially smoothed series already computed in time period $i - 1$

$Y_i$ = observed value of the time series in period $i$

$W$ = subjectively assigned weight or smoothing coefficient (where $0 < W < 1$)

$E_1 = Y_1$

The choice of the smoothing coefficient or weight that we should assign to our time series is critical because it will directly affect our results. Unfortunately, this selection is somewhat subjective. However, in regard to smoothing ability, we observe from Figures 19.3 and 19.4 (pages 923 and 925) that a series of $L$-term moving averages is related to an exponentially smoothed series having weight $W$ as in equation (19.4)

### Relationship between $W$ and $L$

$$W = \frac{2}{L + 1} \qquad (19.4)$$

or equation (19.5)

### Relationship between $L$ and $W$

$$L = \frac{2}{W} - 1 \qquad (19.5)$$

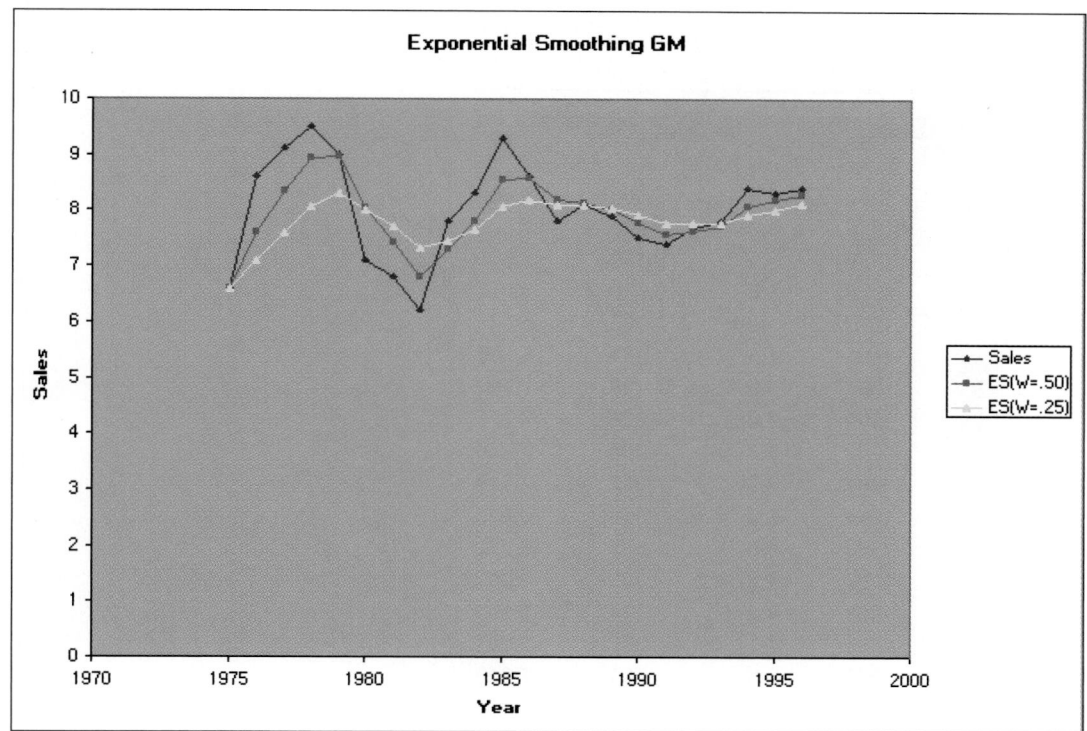

**FIGURE 19.4**  Plotting exponentially smoothed series (*W* = .50 and *W* = .25) for GM factory sales data using Microsoft Excel

*Source: Data are taken from Table 19.4 on page 926.*

From equations (19.4) and (19.5) we note that with respect to smoothing ability, similarities are found between the 3-year series of moving averages (Figure 19.3) and the exponentially smoothed series with weight *W* = .50 (see Figure 19.4). In addition, we see that the series of 7-year moving averages (Figure 19.3) corresponds to the exponentially smoothed series with weight *W* = .25 (see Figure 19.4).[1] By examining how our two smoothed series (one with *W* = .25 and the other with *W* = .50) fit the observed data in Figure 19.4, we can see that the choice of a particular smoothing coefficient *W* is dependent on the purpose of the user. If we desire only to smooth a series by eliminating unwanted cyclical and irregular variations, we should select a small value for *W* (closer to 0). On the other hand, if our goal is forecasting, we should choose a large value for *W* (closer to 1). In the former case, the overall long-term tendencies of the series will be apparent; in the latter case, future short-term directions may be more adequately predicted.

[1] *Differences in results occur because the moving averages consider only sequences of L-consecutive values in the series, whereas the exponentially smoothed averages include all the values in the series.*

◆ *Smoothing*  Table 19.4 presents the exponentially smoothed values (with smoothing coefficients of *W* = .50 and *W* = .25) for annual factory sales at GM over the 22-year period 1975–1996 obtained using Microsoft Excel. As previously indicated, the two smoothed series are plotted in Figure 19.4 along with the original time-series data.

**Table 19.4** *Exponentially smoothed series of GM factory sales (1975–1996)*

| | A | B | C | D |
|---|---|---|---|---|
| 1 | Year | Sales | ES(W=.50) | ES(W=.25) |
| 2 | 1975 | 6.6 | 6.600 | 6.600 |
| 3 | 1976 | 8.6 | 7.600 | 7.100 |
| 4 | 1977 | 9.1 | 8.350 | 7.600 |
| 5 | 1978 | 9.5 | 8.925 | 8.075 |
| 6 | 1979 | 9 | 8.963 | 8.306 |
| 7 | 1980 | 7.1 | 8.031 | 8.005 |
| 8 | 1981 | 6.8 | 7.416 | 7.704 |
| 9 | 1982 | 6.2 | 6.808 | 7.328 |
| 10 | 1983 | 7.8 | 7.304 | 7.446 |
| 11 | 1984 | 8.3 | 7.802 | 7.659 |
| 12 | 1985 | 9.3 | 8.551 | 8.069 |
| 13 | 1986 | 8.6 | 8.575 | 8.202 |
| 14 | 1987 | 7.8 | 8.188 | 8.102 |
| 15 | 1988 | 8.1 | 8.144 | 8.101 |
| 16 | 1989 | 7.9 | 8.022 | 8.051 |
| 17 | 1990 | 7.5 | 7.761 | 7.913 |
| 18 | 1991 | 7.4 | 7.580 | 7.785 |
| 19 | 1992 | 7.7 | 7.640 | 7.764 |
| 20 | 1993 | 7.8 | 7.720 | 7.773 |
| 21 | 1994 | 8.4 | 8.060 | 7.930 |
| 22 | 1995 | 8.3 | 8.180 | 8.022 |
| 23 | 1996 | 8.4 | 8.290 | 8.117 |

*Source: Data are taken from Table 19.3.*

We illustrate the exponential smoothing computations in Example 19.2.

## Example 19.2  *Computing Exponentially Smoothed Values*

Demonstrate how you would compute the exponentially smoothed values shown in Table 19.4 for the GM factory sales data using a smoothing coefficient of $W = .25$.

### SOLUTION

As a starting point, we use the initial observed value $Y_{1975} = 6.6$ as our first smoothed value ($E_{1975} = 6.6$). Then, using the observed value of the time series for the year 1976 ($Y_{1976} = 8.6$), we smooth the series for the year 1976 by computing

$$E_{1976} = WY_{1976} + (1 - W)E_{1975}$$
$$= (.25)(8.6) + (.75)(6.6) = 7.1 \text{ million}$$

To smooth the series for the year 1977, we have

$$E_{1977} = WY_{1977} + (1 - W)E_{1976}$$
$$= (.25)(9.1) + (.75)(7.1) = 7.6 \text{ million}$$

To smooth the series for the year 1978, we have

$$E_{1978} = WY_{1978} + (1 - W)E_{1977}$$
$$= (.25)(9.5) + (.75)(7.6) = 8.075 \text{ million}$$

This process continues until exponentially smoothed values have been obtained for all 22 years in the series as shown in Table 19.4 and Figure 19.4.

◆ *Forecasting*   To use the exponentially weighted moving average for purposes of forecasting rather than for smoothing, we take the smoothed value in our current period of time (say, time period $i$) as our projected estimate of the observed value of the time series in the following time period, $i + 1$, as in equation (19.6).

## Forecasting in Time Period $i + 1$

$$\hat{Y}_{i+1} = E_i \qquad (19.6)$$

We illustrate the process of forecasting in Example 19.3.

## Example 19.3   *Forecasting from Exponentially Weighted Moving Averages*

Forecast the number of units sold from all General Motors Corporation plants (see Table 19.4) during the year 1997 using a smoothing coefficient of $W = .50$.

### SOLUTION

We use the smoothed value for the year 1996 as its estimate. From Table 19.4 that projection is 8.29 million units. (How close were we with this forecast? This chapter was written in 1997. Now that time has elapsed, why don't you look up GM's performance data in a recent company annual report and find out?)

Once the observed data for the year 1997 become available, we can use equation (19.3) to make a forecast for the year 1998 by obtaining the smoothed value for 1997 as follows.

$$E_{1997} = WY_{1997} + (1 - W)E_{1996}$$

$$\text{Current smoothed value} = (W)(\text{current observed value})$$
$$+ (1 - W)(\text{previous smoothed value})$$

Or in terms of forecasting, we obtain the following.

$$\hat{Y}_{1998} = WY_{1997} + (1 - W)\hat{Y}_{1997}$$

New forecast $= (W)$(current observed value) $+ (1 - W)$(current forecast)

## Problems for Section 19.3

### Learning the Basics

- **19.1** If an exponentially smoothed series has a weight of $W = .20$, what is the length $L$ of the related $L$-term moving average?

- **19.2** If a 5-year moving average is being used to smooth a time series, what smoothing coefficient or weight $W$ should be assigned in order to obtain a related exponentially smoothed series?

  **19.3** If you are using the exponentially weighted moving average for purposes of forecasting rather than smoothing an annual time series concerning revenues (in millions of *constant* 1995 dollars), what is your forecast for next year if the smoothed value for this year is 32.4 millions of *constant* 1995 dollars?

- **19.4** Answer the following if a 9-year moving average is being used to smooth a time series that was first recorded in the year 1955.
  - (a) Which year serves as the first centered value in the smoothed series?
  - (b) How many years of observed values in the series are lost when computing all the 9-year moving averages?

  **19.5** Exponential smoothing is being used on an annual time series concerning total revenues (in millions of *constant* 1995 dollars). Answer the following if a smoothing coefficient of $W = .20$ is employed and the exponentially smoothed series for the year 1996 is expressed as $E_{1996} = (.20)(12.1) + (.80)(9.4)$.
  - (a) What is the smoothed value of this series in the year 1996?
  - (b) What is the smoothed value of this series in the year 1997 if the observed value of the series in that year were 11.5 millions of *constant* 1995 dollars?

### Applying the Concepts

- **19.6** The following data represent the annual number of employees (in thousands) in an oil supply company for the years 1978–1997.

*Number of employees (in thousands)*

| YEAR | NUMBER | YEAR | NUMBER | YEAR | NUMBER |
|------|--------|------|--------|------|--------|
| 1978 | 1.45 | 1985 | 2.04 | 1992 | 1.65 |
| 1979 | 1.55 | 1986 | 2.06 | 1993 | 1.73 |
| 1980 | 1.61 | 1987 | 1.80 | 1994 | 1.88 |
| 1981 | 1.60 | 1988 | 1.73 | 1995 | 2.00 |
| 1982 | 1.74 | 1989 | 1.77 | 1996 | 2.08 |
| 1983 | 1.92 | 1990 | 1.90 | 1997 | 1.88 |
| 1984 | 1.95 | 1991 | 1.82 | | |

**DATA FILE**
OILSUPP

- (a) Plot the data on a chart.
- (b) Fit a 3-year moving average to the data and plot the results on your chart.
- (c) Using a smoothing coefficient of $W = .50$, exponentially smooth the series and plot the results on your chart.
- (d) What is your exponentially smoothed forecast for the trend in 1998?

(e) Using a smoothing coefficient of $W = .25$, exponentially smooth the series and plot the results on your chart.

(f) Using the results of (e), what is your exponentially smoothed forecast for the trend in 1998?

(g) Compare the results of (d) and (f).

**19.7** The following data represent the annual sales (in millions of *constant* 1995 dollars) for a food-processing company for the years 1972–1997.

### Annual sales (millions of constant 1995 dollars)

| YEAR | SALES | YEAR | SALES | YEAR | SALES |
|------|-------|------|-------|------|-------|
| 1972 | 41.6 | 1981 | 53.2 | 1990 | 36.4 |
| 1973 | 48.0 | 1982 | 53.3 | 1991 | 38.4 |
| 1974 | 51.7 | 1983 | 51.6 | 1992 | 42.6 |
| 1975 | 55.9 | 1984 | 49.0 | 1993 | 34.8 |
| 1976 | 51.8 | 1985 | 38.6 | 1994 | 28.4 |
| 1977 | 57.0 | 1986 | 37.3 | 1995 | 23.9 |
| 1978 | 64.4 | 1987 | 43.8 | 1996 | 27.8 |
| 1979 | 60.8 | 1988 | 41.7 | 1997 | 42.1 |
| 1980 | 56.3 | 1989 | 38.3 | | |

DATA FILE
FOODTIME

(a) Plot the data on a chart.

(b) Fit a 7-year moving average to the data and plot the results on your chart.

(c) Using a smoothing coefficient of $W = .25$, exponentially smooth the series and plot the results on your chart.

(d) What is your exponentially smoothed forecast for the trend in 1998?

(e) Using a smoothing coefficient of $W = .50$, exponentially smooth the series and plot the results on your chart.

(f) Using the results of (e), what is your exponentially smoothed forecast for the trend in 1998?

(g) Compare the results of (d) and (f).

**19.8** The data at the top of page 930 represent the median income of families in the United States (in thousands of *constant* 1995 dollars) for all races, for whites, and for blacks, for the 16-year period from 1980 to 1995.
Answer the following for each of the three sets of data (all races, whites, and blacks).

(a) Plot the data on a chart.

(b) Fit a 3-year moving average to your data and plot the results on your chart.

(c) Using a smoothing coefficient of .50, exponentially smooth the series and plot your results on your chart.

(d) What is your exponentially smoothed forecast for the trend in 1996?

(e) Do (c), using a smoothing constant of .25.

(f) Using the results of (e), what is your exponentially smoothed forecast for the trend in 1996?

(g) Compare the results of (d) and (f).

(h) Go to your library and record the actual 1996 value from the table available from the U.S. Department of Commerce. Compare your results with the forecast you made in (d) and (f). Discuss.

(i) What conclusions can you reach concerning the trend in median family income for each of the two groups and all races combined for the period from 1980 to 1995?

### Median family income (in thousands of constant 1995 dollars) in United States (1980–1995)

| YEAR | ALL RACES | WHITES | BLACKS |
|------|-----------|--------|--------|
| 1980 | 38.9 | 40.6 | 23.5 |
| 1981 | 37.9 | 39.8 | 22.4 |
| 1982 | 37.4 | 39.2 | 21.7 |
| 1983 | 37.6 | 39.4 | 22.2 |
| 1984 | 38.8 | 40.6 | 22.6 |
| 1985 | 39.3 | 41.3 | 23.8 |
| 1986 | 41.0 | 42.8 | 24.5 |
| 1987 | 41.5 | 43.4 | 24.7 |
| 1988 | 41.5 | 43.7 | 24.9 |
| 1989 | 42.0 | 44.2 | 24.8 |
| 1990 | 41.2 | 43.0 | 25.0 |
| 1991 | 40.2 | 42.3 | 24.1 |
| 1992 | 39.7 | 42.0 | 22.9 |
| 1993 | 39.0 | 41.4 | 22.7 |
| 1994 | 39.9 | 42.0 | 25.4 |
| 1995 | 40.6 | 42.6 | 26.0 |

**DATA FILE**
MEDFAMIN

*Source:* Statistical Abstract of the United States, *116th ed., 1996, U.S. Department of Commerce, Bureau of the Census, 469.*

**19.9** The following data represent unemployment as a percentage of the civilian working population in seven European countries from 1985 to 1997.

### Percentage unemployment (1985–1997)

| YEAR | BELGIUM | DENMARK | FRANCE | ITALY | NETHERLANDS | PORTUGAL | U.K. |
|------|---------|---------|--------|-------|-------------|----------|------|
| 1985 | 10.3 | 7.1 | 10.2 | 8.5 | 8.3 | 8.7 | 11.5 |
| 1986 | 10.3 | 5.4 | 10.3 | 9.2 | 8.3 | 8.4 | 11.5 |
| 1987 | 10.0 | 5.4 | 10.4 | 9.9 | 8.0 | 6.9 | 10.6 |
| 1988 | 8.9 | 6.1 | 9.9 | 10.0 | 7.5 | 5.5 | 8.7 |
| 1989 | 7.5 | 7.4 | 9.4 | 10.0 | 6.9 | 4.9 | 7.3 |
| 1990 | 6.7 | 7.7 | 9.0 | 9.1 | 6.2 | 4.6 | 7.0 |
| 1991 | 6.6 | 8.4 | 9.5 | 8.8 | 5.8 | 4.0 | 8.8 |
| 1992 | 7.3 | 9.2 | 10.4 | 9.0 | 5.6 | 4.2 | 10.1 |
| 1993 | 8.9 | 10.1 | 11.7 | 10.3 | 6.6 | 5.7 | 10.4 |
| 1994 | 10.0 | 8.2 | 12.3 | 11.4 | 7.2 | 7.0 | 9.6 |
| 1995[a] | 9.9 | 6.8 | 11.5 | 11.8 | 7.3 | 7.2 | 8.8 |
| 1996[a] | 10.1 | 6.1 | 11.7 | 11.8 | 7.2 | 7.4 | 8.4 |
| 1997[a] | 9.8 | 5.8 | 11.7 | 11.7 | 7.0 | 7.2 | 8.0 |

**DATA FILE**
UNEMPLOY

[a] *Initial, unrevised estimates.*
*Source: Extracted from Table 3 of European Commission's* Panorama of EU Industry 97 *(1997): 22.*

For each of the seven sets of data, answer the following.

(a) Plot the data on a chart.

(b) Fit a 3-year moving average to the data and plot the results on your chart.

(c) Using a smoothing coefficient of $W = .50$, exponentially smooth the series and plot the results on your chart.

(d) What is your exponentially smoothed forecast for the trend in 1998?

(e) Do (c), using a smoothing coefficient of $W = .25$.

(f) Using the results of (e), what is your exponentially smoothed forecast for 1998?

(g) Compare the results of (d) and (f).

(h) Compare and contrast the patterns of unemployment in these seven European countries.

**19.10** For more than a decade, New Mexico has had the highest surplus in balance of payments per capita of any state in the United States. This has been achieved because that state receives a high level of government funding through programs sponsored primarily by the Department of Defense, the Department of the Interior, and the Department of Transportation. In addition, federal tax payments per capita by residents of New Mexico are substantially below average. The data below present the balance of payments per capita (in 1995 *constant* dollars), that is, the difference between federal spending per capita in New Mexico and the federal tax payments per capita from New Mexico over the 15-year period 1981–1995.

*Balance of payments per capita in New Mexico (in **constant** 1995 dollars) from 1981 to 1995*

| FISCAL YEAR | BALANCE OF PAYMENTS PER CAPITA (IN DOLLARS) | FEDERAL SPENDING PER CAPITA (IN DOLLARS) | FEDERAL TAXES PER CAPITA (IN DOLLARS) |
|---|---|---|---|
| 1981 | 2,961 | 6,212 | 3,251 |
| 1982 | 2,913 | 5,983 | 3,069 |
| 1983 | 2,426 | 5,853 | 3,427 |
| 1984 | 2,881 | 6,309 | 3,428 |
| 1985 | 2,919 | 6,414 | 3,495 |
| 1986 | 3,218 | 6,670 | 3,452 |
| 1987 | 3,322 | 6,635 | 3,313 |
| 1988 | 4,336 | 7,461 | 3,125 |
| 1989 | 3,496 | 6,578 | 3,083 |
| 1990 | 3,545 | 6,653 | 3,108 |
| 1991 | 3,462 | 6,739 | 3,277 |
| 1992 | 3,632 | 7,079 | 3,447 |
| 1993 | 3,709 | 7,272 | 3,563 |
| 1994 | 3,343 | 6,915 | 3,572 |
| 1995 | 3,300 | 6,935 | 3,635 |

 **DATA FILE** BALPAY

*Source: D. P. Moynihan, M. E. Friar, H. B. Leonard, and J. H. Walder,* The Federal Budget and the States: Fiscal Year 1995, *jointly published by the John F. Kennedy School of Government, Harvard University, and the Office of Senator Daniel Patrick Moynihan, September 30, 1996, 73.*

Answer the following for each of these three time series.

(a) Plot the data on a chart.

(b) Fit a 3-year moving average to the data and plot the results on your chart.

(c) Using a smoothing coefficient of $W = .50$, exponentially smooth the series and plot the results on your chart.

(d) What is your exponentially smoothed forecast for the trend in 1996?

(e) Do (c), using a smoothing coefficient of $W = .25$.

(f) Using the results of (e), what is your exponentially smoothed forecast for 1996?

(g) Compare the results of (d) and (f).

(h) Go to your library and record the 1996 value from an available table. Compare your results with the forecast you made in (d) and (f). Discuss.

(i) What conclusions can you reach concerning federal spending, federal taxes, and balance of payments per capita in New Mexico between 1980 and 1995?

 ## 19.4 LEAST-SQUARES TREND FITTING AND FORECASTING

The component factor of a time series most often studied is trend. First, we study trend for predictive purposes; that is, we study trend as an aid in making intermediate and long-range forecasting projections. Second, we study trend to isolate and then eliminate its influencing effects on the time-series model as a guide to short-run (1 year or less) forecasting of general business cycle conditions.

As was depicted in Figure 19.1 on page 917, to obtain some visual impression or feeling of the overall long-term movements in a time series, we constructed a chart in which the observed data (dependent variable) were plotted on the vertical axis and the time periods (independent variable) were plotted on the horizontal axis. If it appears that a straight-line trend could be adequately fitted to the data, the two most widely used methods of trend fitting are the method of least squares (see section 16.2) and the method of *double exponential smoothing* (references 1, 2, and 4). If the time-series data indicate some long-run downward or upward curvilinear movement, the two most widely used trend-fitting methods are the method of least squares (see section 18.1) and the method of *triple exponential smoothing* (references 1, 2, and 4). In this section we focus on least-squares methods for fitting linear and curvilinear trends as guides to forecasting. In sections 19.5 and 19.6 other, more elaborate forecasting approaches will be described.

### The Linear Trend Model

You may recall from section 16.2 that the least-squares method permits us to fit a straight-line (**linear trend model**) as in equation (19.7)

### The Linear Trend Model

$$\hat{Y}_i = b_0 + b_1 X_i \qquad (19.7)$$

such that the values we calculate for the two coefficients—the $Y$ intercept $b_0$ and the slope $b_1$—result in the sum of squared differences between each observed value $Y_i$ in the data and each predicted average value $\hat{Y}_i$ along the trend line being minimized. That is, we have the following, based on the *principle of least squares.*

$$\sum_{i=1}^{n}(Y_i - \hat{Y}_i)^2 = \text{minimum}$$

To obtain such a line, recall that in linear regression analysis we compute the slope $b_1$ and the $Y$ intercept $b_0$ using equations (16.18) and (16.19) on pages 783–784. Once this is accomplished and the line $\hat{Y}_i = b_0 + b_1 X_i$ is developed, we can substitute values for $X$ into equation (19.7) to predict various values for $Y$.

When using the method of least squares for fitting trends in time series, our interpretation of the coefficients is simplified if we code the $X$ values so that the first observation in our time series is selected as the origin and assigned a code value of $X = 0$. All successive observations are then assigned consecutively increasing integer codes: 1, 2, 3, .., so that the $n$th and last observation in the series has code $n - 1$. For example, for time-series data recorded annually over 22 years, the 1st year will be assigned a coded value of 0, the 2d year will be coded as 1, the 3d year will be coded as 2, . . . , and the final (22d) year will be coded as 21.

Returning to our Using Statistics example, the annual time series presented in Table 19.5 and plotted in Figure 19.1 on page 917 represents the *actual* gross revenues (in billions of *current* dollars) for the Eastman Kodak Company over the 22-year period 1975 through 1996. We then use the Bureau of Labor Statistics Consumer Price Index (CPI) to convert (and deflate) *actual* gross revenue dollars into *real* gross revenue dollars. This is achieved by multiplying each *actual* gross revenue value by the corresponding quantity $\left(\dfrac{100.0}{\text{CPI}}\right)$. The revised (i.e., *adjusted*) *real* gross revenues data in billions of *constant* 1982–1984 dollars are shown in Table 19.6 and plotted in Figure 19.5 along with the *actual* gross revenues data in billions of *current* dollars as shown on page 934.

Coding the consecutive $X$ values 0 through 21 and then using Minitab (see reference 10) on the adjusted time series, we determine that

$$\hat{Y}_i = 10.3202 + 0.1007X_i$$

where the origin is 1975 and $X$ units $= 1$ year. Partial Minitab output is displayed in Figure 19.6 on page 935.

How do we interpret these results? How can we use the linear trend model for forecasting? To answer these questions, let us look at Examples 19.4 and 19.5 on page 935.

**Table 19.5**  Actual *gross revenues (in billions of current dollars) for Eastman Kodak Company (1975–1996)*

| YEAR | SALES | YEAR | SALES | YEAR | SALES |
|------|-------|------|-------|------|-------|
| 1975 | 5.0  | 1983 | 10.2 | 1990 | 18.9 |
| 1976 | 5.4  | 1984 | 10.6 | 1991 | 19.4 |
| 1977 | 6.0  | 1985 | 10.6 | 1992 | 20.2 |
| 1978 | 7.0  | 1986 | 11.5 | 1993 | 16.3 |
| 1979 | 8.0  | 1987 | 13.3 | 1994 | 13.7 |
| 1980 | 9.7  | 1988 | 17.0 | 1995 | 15.3 |
| 1981 | 10.3 | 1989 | 18.4 | 1996 | 16.2 |
| 1982 | 10.8 |      |      |      |      |

*Source:* Moody's Handbook of Common Stocks, *1980, 1989, 1993, 1996.*
*Reprinted by permission of Moody's Investors Service.*

DATA FILE
EASTMANK

**Table 19.6** *Converting* actual *gross revenues (in billions of* current *dollars) to real gross revenues (in billions of* constant *1982–1984 dollars) for Eastman Kodak Company (1975–1996)*

| YEAR | ACTUAL | CPI | REAL | YEAR | ACTUAL | CPI | REAL |
|------|--------|------|------|------|--------|-------|------|
| 1975 | 5.0 | 53.8 | 9.3 | 1986 | 11.5 | 109.6 | 10.5 |
| 1976 | 5.4 | 56.9 | 9.5 | 1987 | 13.3 | 113.6 | 11.7 |
| 1977 | 6.0 | 60.6 | 9.9 | 1988 | 17.0 | 118.3 | 14.4 |
| 1978 | 7.0 | 65.2 | 10.7 | 1989 | 18.4 | 124.0 | 14.8 |
| 1979 | 8.0 | 72.6 | 11.0 | 1990 | 18.9 | 130.7 | 14.5 |
| 1980 | 9.7 | 82.4 | 11.8 | 1991 | 19.4 | 136.2 | 14.2 |
| 1981 | 10.3 | 90.9 | 11.3 | 1992 | 20.2 | 140.3 | 14.4 |
| 1982 | 10.8 | 96.5 | 11.2 | 1993 | 16.3 | 144.5 | 11.3 |
| 1983 | 10.2 | 99.6 | 10.2 | 1994 | 13.7 | 148.2 | 9.2 |
| 1984 | 10.6 | 103.9 | 10.2 | 1995 | 15.3 | 152.4 | 10.0 |
| 1985 | 10.6 | 107.6 | 9.9 | 1996 | 16.2 | 156.9 | 10.3 |

*Sources: Bureau of Labor Statistics, U.S. Department of Labor and Moody's Handbook of Common Stocks, 1980, 1989, 1993, 1996. Reprinted by permission of Moody's Investors Service.*

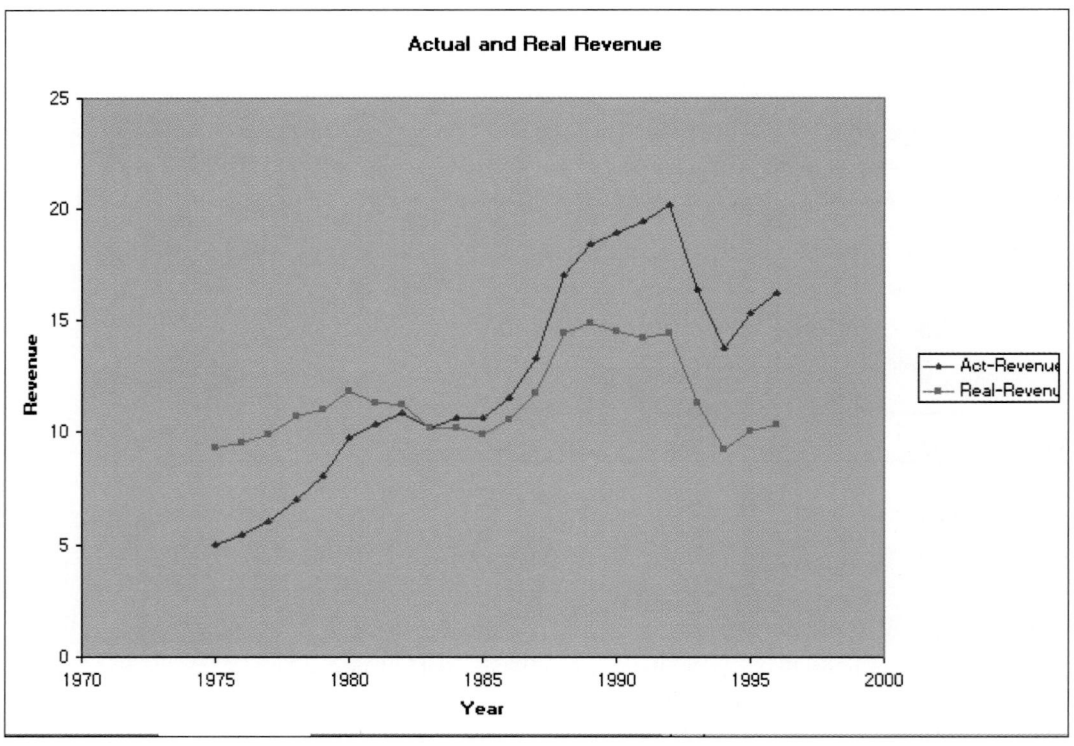

**FIGURE 19.5** Microsoft Excel time-series plots of *actual* and *real* annual gross revenues at Eastman Kodak Company (in billions of dollars): 1975–1996

```
The regression equation is
RealRev = 10.3 + 0.101 CodeYr

Predictor         Coef        StDev          T          P
Constant   (b₀)  10.3202      0.7329       14.08      0.000
CodeYr     (b₁)   0.10068     0.05974       1.69      0.107
```

**FIGURE 19.6** Minitab output for fitting linear regression model to forecast *real* annual gross revenues (in billions of *constant* 1982–1984 dollars) at Eastman Kodak Company

*Source: Data are taken from Table 19.6.*

## Example 19.4 *Interpreting the Y Intercept $b_0$ and Slope $b_1$*

How do we interpret the $Y$ intercept $b_0$ and slope $b_1$ for the least-squares linear trend model using the Eastman Kodak data?

### SOLUTION

- The $Y$ intercept $b_0 = 10.3202$ is the fitted trend value reflecting the predicted average *real* gross revenues (in billions of *constant* 1982–1984 dollars) at Eastman Kodak during the origin or base year, 1975.
- The slope $b_1 = 0.1007$ indicates that *real* gross revenues are predicted to increase by an average of 0.1007 billion dollars per year.

## Example 19.5 *Using the Linear Trend Model for Forecasting*

Project the trend in the *real* gross revenues at Eastman Kodak to the year 1997.

### SOLUTION

We substitute $X_{23} = 22$, the code for 1997, into the equation and our forecast is

1997: $\hat{Y}_{23} = 10.3202 + (0.1007)(22) = 12.536$ billions of *constant* 1982–1984 dollars

The fitted trend line projected to 1997 is plotted in Figure 19.7 along with the original time series. Although a slight upward trend is noted, a careful examination of Figure 19.7 reveals marked departures from a straight line throughout the years of the series. Perhaps, then, a curvilinear trend model would better fit the series? Two such models—a *quadratic* trend model and an *exponential* trend model—are presented next.

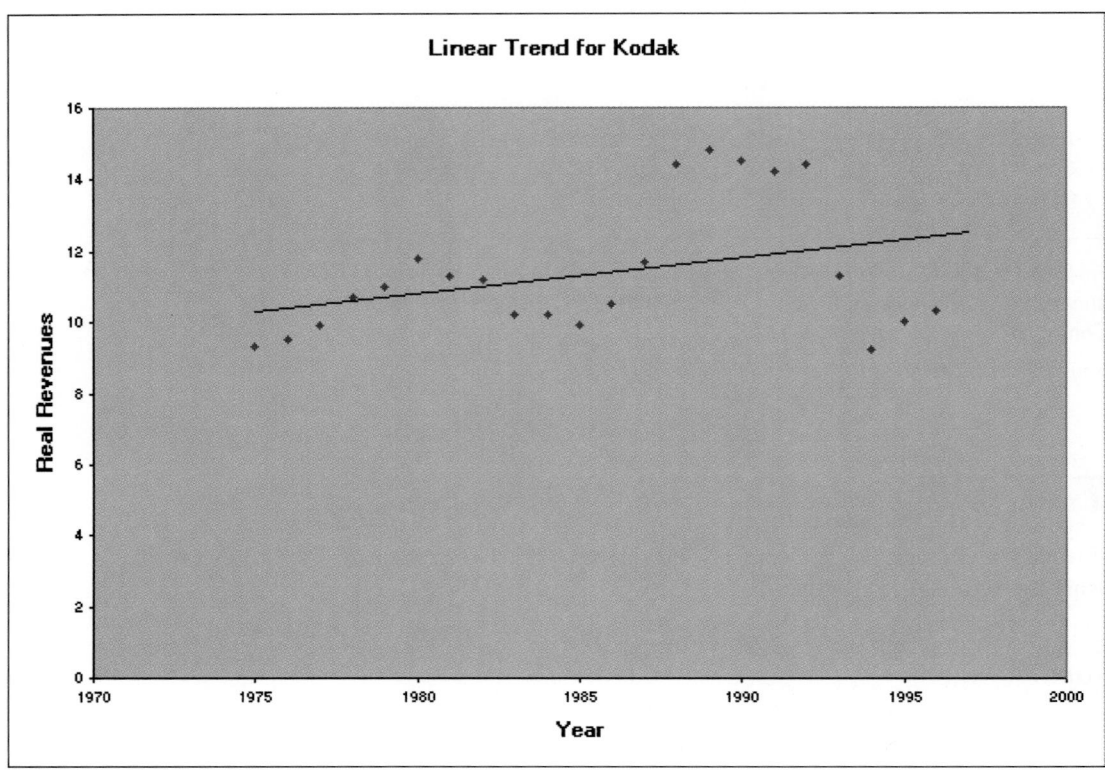

**FIGURE 19.7** Fitting least-squares trend line for Eastman Kodak Company gross revenues data using Microsoft Excel

## The Quadratic Trend Model

A **quadratic trend model** or *second-degree polynomial* is the simplest of the curvilinear models. Using the least-squares method of section 18.1, we can fit a quadratic trend equation as in equation (19.8).

### The Quadratic Trend Model

$$\hat{Y}_i = b_0 + b_1X_i + b_2X_i^2 \qquad (19.8)$$

where

$b_0$ = estimated $Y$ intercept

$b_1$ = estimated *linear* effect on $Y$

$b_2$ = estimated *curvilinear* effect on $Y$

Once again, we can access a software package such as Microsoft Excel or Minitab to perform the computations necessary to obtain the least-squares fit. Figure 19.8 provides Minitab output for the quadratic trend model representing *real* annual gross revenues at Eastman Kodak. From this we determine that

$$\hat{Y}_i = 8.7698 + 0.5658X_i - 0.0221X_i^2$$

where the origin is 1975 and $X$ units = 1 year.

```
The regression equation is
RealRev = 8.77 + 0.566 CodeYr - 0.0221 SqCodeYr

Predictor       Coef        StDev           T          P
Constant  (b₀)  8.7698  (b₁) 0.9433        9.30      0.000
CodeYr          0.5658       0.2081        2.72      0.014
SqCodeYr  (b₂) -0.022149     0.009570     -2.31      0.032
```

**FIGURE 19.8**  Minitab output for fitting a quadratic regression model to forecast *real* annual gross revenues at Eastman Kodak Company

To use the quadratic trend equation for forecasting purposes, we substitute the appropriate coded $X$ values into this equation. For example, to predict the trend in *real* gross revenues for the year 1997 (that is, $X_{23} = 22$), we have

$$1997: \hat{Y}_{23} = 8.7698 + 0.5658(22) - 0.0221(22^2)$$
$$= 10.521 \text{ billions of dollars}$$

The fitted quadratic trend equation projected to 1997 is plotted in Figure 19.9 together with the original time series. This quadratic trend model seems to provide a better fit to the time series than did the linear trend model.

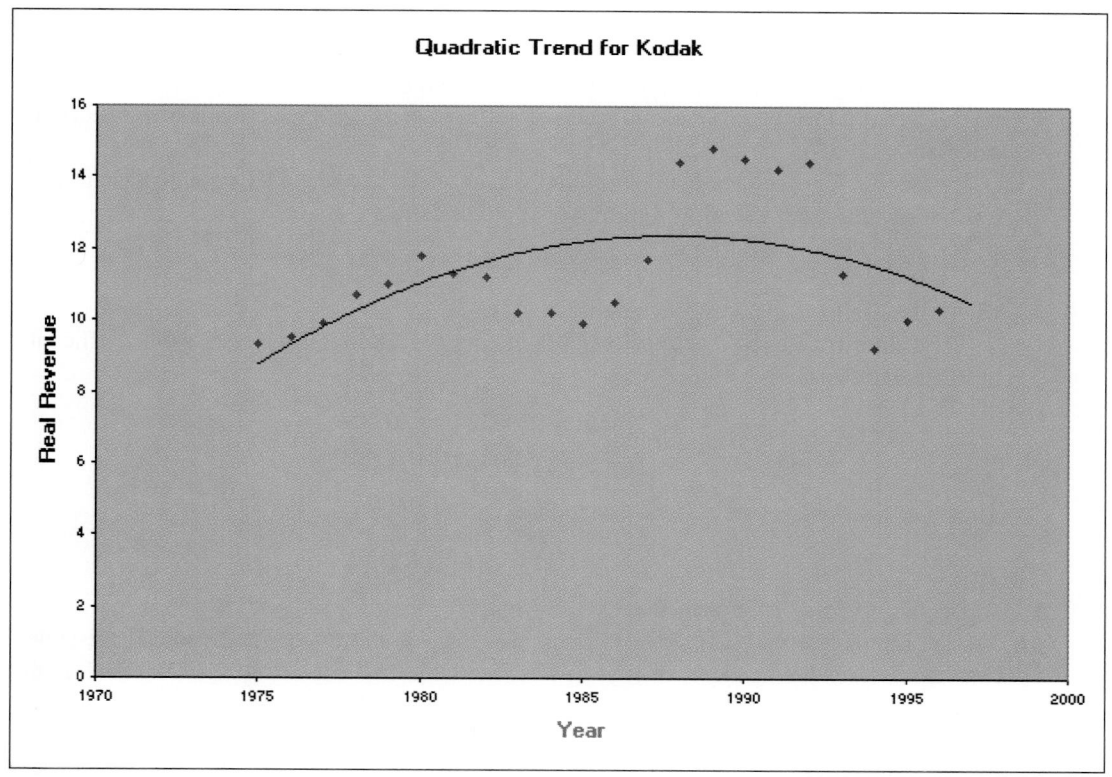

**FIGURE 19.9**  Fitting quadratic trend equation for Eastman Kodak Company *real* gross revenues data using Microsoft Excel

## The Exponential Trend Model

When a series appears to be *increasing at an increasing rate* such that the *percentage difference* from observation to observation is *constant*, we can fit an **exponential trend model**, which is presented in equation (19.9).

---

### The Exponential Trend Model

$$\hat{Y}_i = b_0 b_1^{X_i} \qquad (19.9)$$

where

$$b_0 = \text{estimated } Y \text{ intercept}$$
$$(b_1 - 1) \times 100\% = \text{estimated } \textit{annual compound growth rate } (\text{in } \%)$$

---

If we take the logarithm (base 10) of both sides of equation (19.9), we have equation (19.10).

---

### The Exponential Trend Model

$$\log \hat{Y}_i = \log b_0 + X_i \log b_1 \qquad (19.10)$$

---

Because equation (19.10) is linear in form, we can use the method of least squares by working with the $\log Y_i$ values instead of the $Y_i$ values and obtain the slope ($\log b_1$) and $Y$ intercept ($\log b_0$). Once again, we can access a software package to accomplish the necessary calculations.

Figure 19.10 represents Minitab output for an exponential model of *real* annual gross revenues at Eastman Kodak. From this we determine that

$$\log \hat{Y}_i = 1.01324 + 0.003585 X_i$$

where the origin is 1975 and $X$ units = 1 year.

The values for $b_0$ and $b_1$ are obtained by taking the antilog of the regression coefficients in this equation:

$$b_0 = \text{antilog } 1.01324 = 10.3096$$
$$b_1 = \text{antilog } 0.003585 = 1.00829$$

Thus, the fitted exponential trend equation is expressed as

$$\hat{Y}_i = (10.3096)(1.00829)^{X_i}$$

where the origin is 1975 and $X$ units = 1 year.

The $Y$ intercept $b_0 = 10.3096$ billions of dollars is the fitted trend value representing *real* gross revenues in the base year 1975. The value $(b_1 - 1) \times 100\% = 0.83\%$ is the annual compound growth rate in *real* gross revenues at Eastman Kodak.

For forecasting purposes, we can substitute the appropriate coded $X$ values into either of the two equations. For example, to predict the trend in *real* gross revenues for the year 1997 (that is, $X_{23} = 22$), we have

```
The regression equation is
LogReRev = 1.01 + 0.00358 CodeYr

Predictor        Coef        StDev         T         p
Constant      1.01324      0.02673     37.90     0.000
CodeYr       0.003585     0.002179      1.65     0.116
```

**FIGURE 19.10**   Minitab output for fitting an exponential regression model to forecast *real* annual gross revenues at Eastman Kodak Company

$$1997: \log \hat{Y}_{23} = 1.01324 + (0.003585)(22) = 1.0921$$
$$\hat{Y}_{23} = \text{antilog } (1.0921) = 12.363 \text{ billions of dollars}$$

or

$$1997: \hat{Y}_{23} = (10.3096)(1.00829)^{22} = 12.363 \text{ billions of dollars}$$

The fitted exponential trend equation projected to 1997 is plotted in Figure 19.11 together with the original time series. Among the three least-squares regression models we have just studied, the exponential trend model appears to provide the poorest fit to the time-series data.

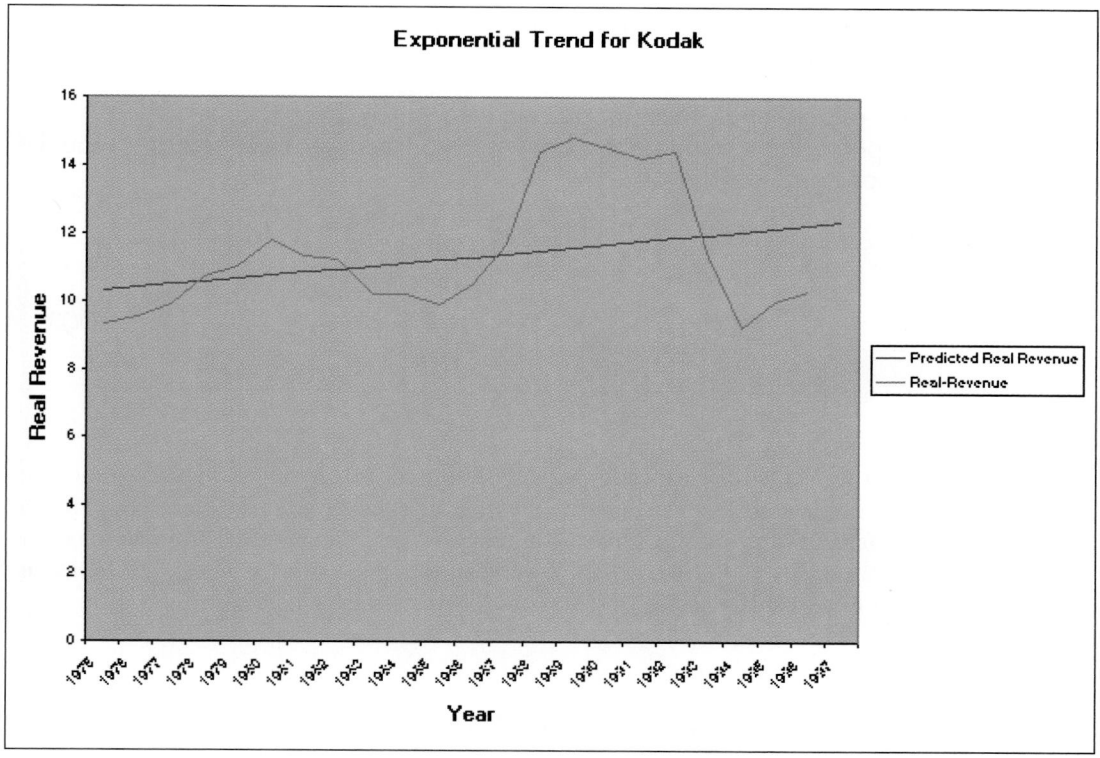

**FIGURE 19.11**   Fitting the exponential trend equation for Eastman Kodak Company *real* gross revenues data using Microsoft Excel

## Model Selection Using First, Second, and Percentage Differences

We have now seen the *real* annual gross revenues data at Eastman Kodak fitted by three different models: linear, quadratic, and exponential. How can we determine which, if any, of these models is the appropriate model to fit? Aside from visually inspecting its scatter plot, a more mathematically objective way in which we can evaluate a time series in order to determine the appropriate model to fit is to compute and examine first, second, and percentage differences. The identifying features of linear, quadratic, and exponential trend models are displayed in Exhibit 19.1.

### Exhibit 19.1  *Model Selection Using First, Second, and Percentage Differences*

- If a linear trend model were to perfectly fit a time series, then the first differences would be constant. That is, the differences between consecutive observations in the series would be the same throughout.

$$(Y_2 - Y_1) = (Y_3 - Y_2) = \cdots = (Y_n - Y_{n-1})$$

- If a quadratic trend model were to perfectly fit a time series, then the second differences would be constant. That is,

$$[(Y_3 - Y_2) - (Y_2 - Y_1)] = [(Y_4 - Y_3) - (Y_3 - Y_2)]$$
$$= \cdots = [(Y_n - Y_{n-1}) - (Y_{n-1} - Y_{n-2})]$$

- If an exponential trend model were to perfectly fit a time series, then the percentage differences between consecutive observations would be constant. That is,

$$\left(\frac{Y_2 - Y_1}{Y_1}\right) \times 100\% = \left(\frac{Y_3 - Y_2}{Y_2}\right) \times 100\%$$
$$= \cdots = \left(\frac{Y_n - Y_{n-1}}{Y_{n-1}}\right) \times 100\%$$

Although we should not expect a perfectly fitting model for any particular set of time-series data, we nevertheless can evaluate the first differences, second differences, and percentage differences for a given series as a guide for determining an appropriate model to choose. In Examples 19.6, 19.7, and 19.8 we illustrate applications of linear, quadratic, and exponential trend models having perfect fits to their respective data sets.

### Example 19.6  *A Linear Trend Model with a Perfect Fit*

You are given the following annual time series of the number of passengers (in millions) using a particular airline.

| | YEAR | | | | | | | | | |
|---|---|---|---|---|---|---|---|---|---|---|
| | **1988** | **1989** | **1990** | **1991** | **1992** | **1993** | **1994** | **1995** | **1996** | **1997** |
| Passengers | 30.0 | 33.0 | 36.0 | 39.0 | 42.0 | 45.0 | 48.0 | 51.0 | 54.0 | 57.0 |

Using first differences, show that the linear trend model provides a perfect fit to these data.

## SOLUTION

| | YEAR | | | | | | | | | |
|---|---|---|---|---|---|---|---|---|---|---|
| | **1988** | **1989** | **1990** | **1991** | **1992** | **1993** | **1994** | **1995** | **1996** | **1997** |
| Passengers | 30.0 | 33.0 | 36.0 | 39.0 | 42.0 | 45.0 | 48.0 | 51.0 | 54.0 | 57.0 |
| First differences | | 3.0 | 3.0 | 3.0 | 3.0 | 3.0 | 3.0 | 3.0 | 3.0 | 3.0 |

Note that the differences between consecutive observations in the series are the same throughout.

## Example 19.7 *A Quadratic Trend Model with a Perfect Fit*

You are given the following annual time series of the number of passengers (in millions) using a particular airline.

| | YEAR | | | | | | | | | |
|---|---|---|---|---|---|---|---|---|---|---|
| | **1988** | **1989** | **1990** | **1991** | **1992** | **1993** | **1994** | **1995** | **1996** | **1997** |
| Passengers | 30.0 | 31.0 | 33.5 | 37.5 | 43.0 | 50.0 | 58.5 | 68.5 | 80.0 | 93.0 |

Using second differences, show that the quadratic trend model provides a perfect fit to these data.

## SOLUTION

| | YEAR | | | | | | | | | |
|---|---|---|---|---|---|---|---|---|---|---|
| | **1988** | **1989** | **1990** | **1991** | **1992** | **1993** | **1994** | **1995** | **1996** | **1997** |
| Passengers | 30.0 | 31.0 | 33.5 | 37.5 | 43.0 | 50.0 | 58.5 | 68.5 | 80.0 | 93.0 |
| First differences | | 1.0 | 2.5 | 4.0 | 5.5 | 7.0 | 8.5 | 10.0 | 11.5 | 13.0 |
| Second differences | | | 1.5 | 1.5 | 1.5 | 1.5 | 1.5 | 1.5 | 1.5 | 1.5 |

Note that the second differences between consecutive pairs of observations in the series are the same throughout.

## Example 19.8 An Exponential Trend Model with a Perfect Fit

You are given the following annual time series of the number of passengers (in millions) using a particular airline.

| | YEAR | | | | | | | | | |
|---|---|---|---|---|---|---|---|---|---|---|
| | 1988 | 1989 | 1990 | 1991 | 1992 | 1993 | 1994 | 1995 | 1996 | 1997 |
| Passengers | 30.0 | 31.5 | 33.1 | 34.8 | 36.5 | 38.3 | 40.2 | 42.2 | 44.3 | 46.5 |

Using percentage differences, show that the exponential trend model provides a perfect fit to these data.

### SOLUTION

| | YEAR | | | | | | | | | |
|---|---|---|---|---|---|---|---|---|---|---|
| | 1988 | 1989 | 1990 | 1991 | 1992 | 1993 | 1994 | 1995 | 1996 | 1997 |
| Passengers | 30.0 | 31.5 | 33.1 | 34.8 | 36.5 | 38.3 | 40.2 | 42.2 | 44.3 | 46.5 |
| First differences | | 1.5 | 1.6 | 1.7 | 1.7 | 1.8 | 1.9 | 2.0 | 2.1 | 2.2 |
| Percentage differences | | 5.0 | 5.0 | 5.0 | 5.0 | 5.0 | 5.0 | 5.0 | 5.0 | 5.0 |

Note that the percentage differences between consecutive observations in the series are the same throughout.

Table 19.7 presents the first, second, and percentage differences for the annual gross revenues data at Eastman Kodak.

## Table 19.7 Comparing the first, second, and percentage differences in real annual gross revenues (in billions of constant 1982–1984 dollars) for Eastman Kodak Company (1975–1996)

| YEAR | REVENUES ($ BILLIONS) | FIRST DIFF. | SECOND DIFF. | PERCENT DIFF. | YEAR | REVENUES ($ BILLIONS) | FIRST DIFF. | SECOND DIFF. | PERCENT DIFF. |
|---|---|---|---|---|---|---|---|---|---|
| 1975 | 9.3 | — | — | — | 1986 | 10.5 | 0.6 | 0.9 | 6.1 |
| 1976 | 9.5 | 0.2 | — | 2.2 | 1987 | 11.7 | 1.2 | 0.6 | 11.4 |
| 1977 | 9.9 | 0.4 | 0.2 | 4.2 | 1988 | 14.4 | 2.7 | 1.5 | 23.1 |
| 1978 | 10.7 | 0.8 | 0.4 | 8.1 | 1989 | 14.8 | 0.4 | −2.3 | 2.8 |
| 1979 | 11.0 | 0.3 | −0.5 | 2.8 | 1990 | 14.5 | −0.3 | −0.7 | −2.0 |
| 1980 | 11.8 | 0.8 | 0.5 | 7.3 | 1991 | 14.2 | −0.3 | 0.0 | −2.1 |
| 1981 | 11.3 | −0.5 | −1.3 | −4.2 | 1992 | 14.4 | 0.2 | 0.5 | 1.4 |
| 1982 | 11.2 | −0.1 | 0.4 | −0.9 | 1993 | 11.3 | −3.1 | −3.3 | −21.5 |
| 1983 | 10.2 | −1.0 | −0.9 | −8.9 | 1994 | 9.2 | −2.1 | 1.0 | −18.6 |
| 1984 | 10.2 | 0.0 | 1.0 | 0.0 | 1995 | 10.0 | 0.8 | 2.9 | 8.7 |
| 1985 | 9.9 | −0.3 | −0.3 | −2.9 | 1996 | 10.3 | 0.3 | −0.5 | 3.0 |

*Source: Table 19.6.*

Examining Table 19.7, we conclude that none of the three models provides an excellent fit to this Eastman Kodak time series. Among the three, however, the quadratic trend model is preferable because the rule of second differences seems to be more closely observed than the others. The series of second differences appears to fluctuate more randomly above or below 0.0 than do the other two series, whose streaks above or below 0.0 seem to be more patterned.

## Problems for Section 19.4

### Learning the Basics

**19.11** Given that you are using the method of least squares for fitting trends in an annual time series containing 25 consecutive yearly observations, complete the following.
(a) What code should be given as the $X$ value for the 1st year in the series?
(b) What code should be given as the $X$ value for the 5th year in the series?
(c) What code should be given as the $X$ value for the most recent recorded year in the series?
(d) What code should be given as the $X$ value if you want to project the trend and make a forecast 5 years beyond the last observed value?

• **19.12** Suppose that the least-squares trend line to an annual time series containing 20 observations (from 1978 to 1997) on *real* total revenues (in millions of *constant* 1995 dollars) is $\hat{Y}_i = 4.0 + 1.5X_i$.
(a) Interpret the $Y$ intercept $b_0$ in this linear trend model.
(b) Interpret the slope $b_1$ in this linear trend model.
(c) What is the fitted trend value for this time series on *real* total revenues for the 5th year?
(d) What is the fitted trend value for this time series on *real* total revenues for the most recent recorded year?
(e) What is the projected trend forecast for this time series on *real* total revenues 3 years after the last recorded value on *real* total revenues?

**19.13** Suppose that the least-squares trend line to an annual time series containing 40 observations (from 1958 to 1997) on *real* net sales (in billions of *constant* 1995 dollars) is $\hat{Y}_i = 1.2 + 0.5X_i$.
(a) Interpret the $Y$ intercept $b_0$ in this linear trend model.
(b) Interpret the slope $b_1$ in this linear trend model.
(c) What is the fitted trend value for this time series on *real* net sales for the 10th year?
(d) What is the fitted trend value for this time series on *real* net sales for the most recent recorded year?
(e) What is the projected trend forecast for this time series on *real* net sales 2 years after the last recorded value on *real* net sales?

### Applying the Concepts

• **19.14** The following data reflect the annual values of the Consumer Price Index (CPI) in the United States constructed over the 33-year period 1965 through 1997 using the years 1982 through 1984 as the base period. This index measures the average change in prices over time in a fixed "market basket" of goods and services purchased by all urban consumers—urban wage earners (i.e., clerical, professional, managerial, and technical workers; self-employed individuals; and short-term workers), unemployed individuals, and retirees.

## Consumer Price Index for all urban consumers

| YEAR | CPI | YEAR | CPI | YEAR | CPI |
|------|------|------|------|------|-------|
| 1965 | 31.5 | 1976 | 56.9 | 1987 | 113.6 |
| 1966 | 32.4 | 1977 | 60.6 | 1988 | 118.3 |
| 1967 | 33.4 | 1978 | 65.2 | 1989 | 124.0 |
| 1968 | 34.8 | 1979 | 72.6 | 1990 | 130.7 |
| 1969 | 36.7 | 1980 | 82.4 | 1991 | 136.2 |
| 1970 | 38.8 | 1981 | 90.9 | 1992 | 140.3 |
| 1971 | 40.5 | 1982 | 96.5 | 1993 | 144.5 |
| 1972 | 41.8 | 1983 | 99.6 | 1994 | 148.2 |
| 1973 | 44.4 | 1984 | 103.9 | 1995 | 152.4 |
| 1974 | 49.3 | 1985 | 107.6 | 1996 | 156.9 |
| 1975 | 53.8 | 1986 | 109.6 | 1997 | 161.5 |

**DATA FILE**
CPI-U

*Source: Bureau of Labor Statistics, U.S. Department of Labor.*

(a) Plot the data on a chart.
(b) Describe the movement in this time series over the 33-year period.

● **19.15** The data given in the accompanying table represent the minimum wage rate in the United States over the 33-year period 1965 through 1997.

## Federal minimum wage rate in current dollars from 1965–1997

| YEAR | WAGE | YEAR | WAGE | YEAR | WAGE |
|------|------|------|------|------|------|
| 1965 | 1.25 | 1976 | 2.30 | 1987 | 3.35 |
| 1966 | 1.25 | 1977 | 2.30 | 1988 | 3.35 |
| 1967 | 1.40 | 1978 | 2.65 | 1989 | 3.35 |
| 1968 | 1.60 | 1979 | 2.90 | 1990 | 3.80 |
| 1969 | 1.60 | 1980 | 3.10 | 1991 | 4.25 |
| 1970 | 1.60 | 1981 | 3.35 | 1992 | 4.25 |
| 1971 | 1.60 | 1982 | 3.35 | 1993 | 4.25 |
| 1972 | 1.60 | 1983 | 3.35 | 1994 | 4.25 |
| 1973 | 1.60 | 1984 | 3.35 | 1995 | 4.25 |
| 1974 | 2.00 | 1985 | 3.35 | 1996 | 4.75 |
| 1975 | 2.10 | 1986 | 3.35 | 1997 | 5.15 |

**DATA FILE**
MINWAGE

*Source: Statistical Abstract of the United States, 117th ed., 1997, Bureau of the Census, U.S. Department of Commerce, 433.*

(a) Form a new table of "adjusted (i.e., *real*) minimum wages" by multiplying each of the *actual* minimum wages by the quantity $\left(\dfrac{100.0}{\text{CPI}}\right)$, obtained from the corresponding annual CPI values displayed in Problem 19.14.

(b) On the basis of your results, was an urban consumer earning the minimum wage "better off" in 1997, 1987, 1977, or 1967? Discuss.

(c) Fit a linear trend equation to the *real* minimum wage data and plot the line on your chart.

(d) What are your trend forecasts for the years 1998, 1999, and 2000?

(e) Suppose that legislation is proposed that would raise the minimum wage to $6.00 an hour in the year 2000. On the basis of your forecast of *real* wages for the year 2000 in part (d), what should be the *actual* minimum wage in that year to keep up with projected changes in cost of living?

**19.16** Gross domestic product (GDP) is a major indicator of the nation's overall economic activity. It consists of personal consumption expenditures, gross private domestic invest-ment, net exports of goods and services, and government consumption expenditures. The following data represent the *real* gross domestic product (in billions of *constant* 1992 dollars) for the United States over the 15-year period from 1982 to 1996.

### Real *GDP* in billions of constant 1992 *dollars, 1982–1996*

| YEAR | GDP REAL | YEAR | GDP REAL | YEAR | GDP REAL |
|------|----------|------|----------|------|----------|
| 1982 | 4,620.3 | 1987 | 5,649.5 | 1992 | 6,244.4 |
| 1983 | 4,803.7 | 1988 | 5,865.2 | 1993 | 6,386.1 |
| 1984 | 5,140.1 | 1989 | 6,062.0 | 1994 | 6,608.4 |
| 1985 | 5,323.5 | 1990 | 6,136.3 | 1995 | 6,742.2 |
| 1986 | 5,487.7 | 1991 | 6,079.4 | 1996 | 6,906.8 |

DATA FILE
GDP

*Source: U.S. Bureau of Economic Analysis—see Statistical Abstract of the United States, 117th ed., 1997, Bureau of the Census, U.S. Department of Commerce, 447.*

(a) Plot the data on a chart.

(b) Fit a linear trend equation to the data and plot the line on your chart.

(c) What are your trend forecasts for the years 1997, 1998, 1999, and 2000?

(d) What conclusions can you reach concerning the trend in *real* gross domestic product?

**• 19.17** The data given in the accompanying table represent electric power production in billions of kilowatt-hours by utility companies in the United States during the month of May over the 15-year period 1982 through 1996.

### *Electric power production in May in billions of kilowatt-hours (1982–1996)*

| YEAR | PRDCTN | YEAR | PRDCTN | YEAR | PRDCTN |
|------|--------|------|--------|------|--------|
| 1982 | 177.1 | 1987 | 206.1 | 1992 | 220.4 |
| 1983 | 174.4 | 1988 | 208.4 | 1993 | 222.4 |
| 1984 | 192.2 | 1989 | 220.1 | 1994 | 227.7 |
| 1985 | 196.8 | 1990 | 222.9 | 1995 | 236.4 |
| 1986 | 197.3 | 1991 | 234.4 | 1996 | 251.7 |

DATA FILE
EPOWERPR

*Source: Energy Information Administration, U.S. Department of Energy.*

(a) Plot the data on a chart.

(b) Fit a linear trend equation to the data and plot the line on your chart.

(c) What are your trend forecasts for the years 1997, 1998, 1999, and 2000?

(d) What conclusions can you reach concerning the trend in production?

**• 19.18** The data given in the accompanying table represent federal receipts in billions of *current* dollars over the 20-year period 1978 through 1997 obtained through individual and corporate income tax, social insurance, excise tax, estate and gift tax, customs duties, and federal reserve deposits.

### Federal receipts in billions of current dollars (1978–1997)

| YEAR | RECEIPTS | YEAR | RECEIPTS | YEAR | RECEIPTS |
|------|----------|------|----------|------|----------|
| 1978 | 399.6 | 1985 | 734.2 | 1992 | 1091.3 |
| 1979 | 463.3 | 1986 | 769.3 | 1993 | 1154.4 |
| 1980 | 517.1 | 1987 | 854.4 | 1994 | 1258.6 |
| 1981 | 599.3 | 1988 | 909.3 | 1995 | 1351.8 |
| 1982 | 617.8 | 1989 | 991.2 | 1996 | 1426.8 |
| 1983 | 600.6 | 1990 | 1032.0 | 1997a | 1505.4 |
| 1984 | 666.5 | 1991 | 1055.0 | | |

**DATA FILE**
FEDRECPT

[a] Preliminary estimate.
Source: U.S. Office of Management and Budget—see Statistical Abstract of the United States, 117th ed., 1997, Bureau of the Census, U.S. Department of Commerce, 332.

(a) Form a new table of "adjusted (i.e., *real*) federal receipts" by multiplying each of the *actual* receipts by the quantity $\left(\dfrac{100.0}{\text{CPI}}\right)$, obtained from the corresponding annual CPI values displayed in Problem 19.14 on page 944. These *real* federal receipts are in billions of *constant* 1982–1984 dollars.

(b) Plot the *revised* series of data on a chart.

(c) Fit a linear trend equation to these data and plot the line on your chart.

(d) What are your trend forecasts of *real* federal receipts for the years 1998, 1999, and 2000?

(e) Plot the *original* series of data on a chart.

(f) Fit a linear trend equation to these data and plot the line on your chart.

(g) What are your trend forecasts of the *actual* federal receipts for the years 1998, 1999, and 2000?

(h) Discuss the difference in the meaning of the forecasts in parts (d) and (g).

(i) What conclusions can you reach concerning the trends in *real* federal receipts and *actual* federal receipts between 1978 and 1997?

**19.19** The data given in the accompanying table represent the *actual* annual gross revenues (in billions of *current* dollars) at Boeing Company over the 22-year period 1975 through 1996.

### Actual gross revenues at Boeing Company (1975–1996)

| YEAR | REVENUES | YEAR | REVENUES | YEAR | REVENUES |
|------|----------|------|----------|------|----------|
| 1975 | 3.8 | 1983 | 11.3 | 1990 | 27.5 |
| 1976 | 4.0 | 1984 | 10.6 | 1991 | 29.3 |
| 1977 | 4.1 | 1985 | 14.0 | 1992 | 30.2 |
| 1978 | 5.6 | 1986 | 16.8 | 1993 | 25.4 |
| 1979 | 8.5 | 1987 | 15.8 | 1994 | 21.9 |
| 1980 | 9.8 | 1988 | 17.3 | 1995 | 19.5 |
| 1981 | 10.1 | 1989 | 20.6 | 1996 | 22.7 |
| 1982 | 9.2 | | | | |

**DATA FILE**
BOEING

Source: Moody's Handbook of Common Stocks, 1980, 1989, 1993, 1997. Reprinted by permission of Moody's Investors Service.

(a) Plot the data on a chart.

(b) Fit a linear trend equation to these data and plot the line on your chart.

(c) What are your annual trend forecasts of *actual* gross revenues for the years 1997, 1998, 1999, and 2000?

(d) Form a new table of "adjusted (i.e., *real*) gross revenues" by multiplying each of the *actual* revenues by the quantity $\left(\dfrac{100.0}{\text{CPI}}\right)$, obtained from the corresponding annual CPI values displayed in Problem 19.14 on page 944. These *real* gross revenues are in billions of *constant* 1982–1984 dollars.

(e) Plot the *revised* series of data on a chart.

(f) Fit a linear trend line to these data and plot the line on your chart.

(g) Fit a quadratic trend equation to these data and plot the results on your chart.

(h) Fit an exponential trend equation to these data and plot the results on your chart.

(i) Using the models fit in parts (f), (g), and (h), what are your annual trend forecasts of *real* gross revenues for the years 1997, 1998, 1999, and 2000?

(j) Compare the results of the forecasts in part (c) with those obtained in part (i). Discuss.

(k) What conclusions can you reach concerning the trends in *real* and *actual* gross revenues?

**19.20** The data given in the accompanying table represent the *actual* annual net operating revenues (in billions of *current* dollars) at Coca-Cola Company over the 22-year period 1975 through 1996.

## Actual *operating revenues at Coca-Cola Company (1975–1996)*

| YEAR | REVENUES | YEAR | REVENUES | YEAR | REVENUES |
|------|----------|------|----------|------|----------|
| 1975 | 2.9 | 1983 | 6.6 | 1990 | 10.2 |
| 1976 | 3.1 | 1984 | 7.2 | 1991 | 11.6 |
| 1977 | 3.6 | 1985 | 7.9 | 1992 | 13.0 |
| 1978 | 4.3 | 1986 | 7.0 | 1993 | 14.0 |
| 1979 | 4.5 | 1987 | 7.7 | 1994 | 16.2 |
| 1980 | 5.3 | 1988 | 8.3 | 1995 | 18.0 |
| 1981 | 5.5 | 1989 | 9.0 | 1996 | 18.5 |
| 1982 | 5.9 | | | | |

DATA FILE
COCACOLA

*Source:* Moody's Handbook of Common Stocks, *1980, 1989, 1993, 1997. Reprinted by permission of Moody's Investors Service.*

(a) Plot the data on a chart.

(b) Fit a quadratic trend equation to these data and plot the results on your chart.

(c) What are your trend forecasts for the years 1997, 1998, 1999, and 2000?

(d) Form a new table of "adjusted (i.e., *real*) operating revenues" by multiplying each of the *actual* revenues by the quantity $\left(\dfrac{100.0}{\text{CPI}}\right)$, obtained from the corresponding annual CPI values displayed in Problem 19.14 on page 944. These *real* operating revenues are in billions of *constant* 1982–1984 dollars.

(e) Plot the *revised* series of data on a chart.

(f) Fit a linear trend equation to these data and plot the line on your chart.

(g) Fit a quadratic trend equation to these data and plot the results on your chart.

(h) Fit an exponential trend equation to these data and plot the results on your chart.

(i) Using the models fit in parts (f), (g), and (h), what are your annual trend forecasts of *real* operating revenues for the years 1997, 1998, 1999, and 2000?

(j) Compare the results of the forecasts in part (c) with those obtained in part (i). Discuss.

(k) What conclusions can you reach concerning the trends in *real* and *actual* operating revenues?

**19.21** The data given in the accompanying table represent the *actual* annual gross revenues (in billions of *current* dollars) at Gillette Company, Inc., over the 22-year period 1975 through 1996.

### Actual *gross revenues at Gillette Company, Inc.* (1975–1996)

| YEAR | REVENUES | YEAR | REVENUES | YEAR | REVENUES |
|------|----------|------|----------|------|----------|
| 1975 | 1.4 | 1983 | 2.2 | 1990 | 4.3 |
| 1976 | 1.5 | 1984 | 2.3 | 1991 | 4.7 |
| 1977 | 1.6 | 1985 | 2.4 | 1992 | 5.2 |
| 1978 | 1.7 | 1986 | 2.8 | 1993 | 5.4 |
| 1979 | 2.0 | 1987 | 3.2 | 1994 | 6.1 |
| 1980 | 2.3 | 1988 | 3.6 | 1995 | 6.8 |
| 1981 | 2.3 | 1989 | 3.8 | 1996 | 9.7 |
| 1982 | 2.2 | | | | |

*Source:* Moody's Handbook of Common Stocks, *1980, 1989, 1993, 1997. Reprinted by permission of Moody's Investors Service.*

**DATA FILE**
GILLETTE

(a) Plot the data on a chart.

(b) Fit an exponential trend equation to these data and plot the results on your chart.

(c) What are your trend forecasts for the years 1997, 1998, 1999, and 2000?

(d) Form a new table of "adjusted (i.e., *real*) gross revenues" by multiplying each of the *actual* revenues by the quantity $\left(\dfrac{100.0}{\text{CPI}}\right)$, obtained from the corresponding annual CPI values displayed in Problem 19.14 on page 944. These *real* gross revenues are in billions of *constant* 1982–1984 dollars.

(e) Plot the *revised* series of data on a chart.

(f) Fit a linear trend equation to these data and plot the line on your chart.

(g) Fit a quadratic trend equation to these data and plot the results on your chart.

(h) Fit an exponential trend equation to these data and plot the results on your chart.

(i) Using the models fit in parts (f), (g), and (h), what are your annual trend forecasts of *real* gross revenues for the years 1997, 1998, 1999, and 2000?

(j) Compare the results of the forecasts in part (c) with those obtained in part (i). Discuss.

(k) What conclusions can you reach concerning the trends in *real* and *actual* gross revenues?

**• 19.22** The data given in the accompanying table represent the *actual* annual gross revenues (in billions of *current* dollars) at Black & Decker Corporation over the 22-year period 1975 through 1996.

## Actual *gross revenues at Black & Decker Corporation (1975–1996)*

| YEAR | REVENUES | YEAR | REVENUES | YEAR | REVENUES |
|------|----------|------|----------|------|----------|
| 1975 | 0.7 | 1983 | 1.2 | 1990 | 4.8 |
| 1976 | 0.7 | 1984 | 1.5 | 1991 | 4.7 |
| 1977 | 0.8 | 1985 | 1.7 | 1992 | 4.8 |
| 1978 | 1.0 | 1986 | 1.8 | 1993 | 4.9 |
| 1979 | 1.2 | 1987 | 1.9 | 1994 | 5.2 |
| 1980 | 1.2 | 1988 | 2.3 | 1995 | 4.8 |
| 1981 | 1.2 | 1989 | 3.2 | 1996 | 4.9 |
| 1982 | 1.2 | | | | |

*Source:* Moody's Handbook of Common Stocks, *1980, 1989, 1993, 1997. Reprinted by permission of Moody's Investors Service.*

DATA FILE
BDECKER

(a) Plot the data on a chart.
(b) Fit an exponential trend equation to these data and plot the results on your chart.
(c) What are your trend forecasts for the years 1997, 1998, 1999, and 2000?
(d) Form a new table of "adjusted (i.e., *real*) gross revenues" by multiplying each of the *actual* revenues by the quantity $\left(\dfrac{100.0}{\text{CPI}}\right)$, obtained from the corresponding annual CPI values displayed in Problem 19.14 on page 944. These *real* gross revenues are in billions of *constant* 1982–1984 dollars.
(e) Plot the *revised* series of data on a chart.
(f) Fit a linear trend equation to these data and plot the line on your chart.
(g) Fit a quadratic trend equation to these data and plot the results on your chart.
(h) Fit an exponential trend equation to these data and plot the results on your chart.
(i) Using the models fit in parts (f), (g), and (h), what are your annual trend forecasts of *real* gross revenues for the years 1997, 1998, 1999, and 2000?
(j) Compare the results of the forecasts in part (c) with those obtained in part (i). Discuss.
(k) What conclusions can you reach concerning the trends in *real* and *actual* gross revenues?

**19.23** Although we should not expect a perfectly fitting model for any particular set of time-series data, we nevertheless can evaluate the first differences, second differences, and percentage differences for a given series as a guide for determining an appropriate model to choose. Using each of the time-series data sets presented in the accompanying table:
(a) Determine the most appropriate model to fit.
(b) Develop the trend equation.
(c) Forecast the trend value for the year 2000.

| | YEAR | | | | | | | | | |
|---|------|------|------|------|------|------|------|------|------|------|
| | **1988** | **1989** | **1990** | **1991** | **1992** | **1993** | **1994** | **1995** | **1996** | **1997** |
| Time series I | 10.0 | 15.1 | 24.0 | 36.7 | 53.8 | 74.8 | 100.0 | 129.2 | 162.4 | 199.0 |
| Time series II | 30.0 | 33.1 | 36.4 | 39.9 | 43.9 | 48.2 | 53.2 | 58.2 | 64.5 | 70.7 |
| Time series III | 60.0 | 67.9 | 76.1 | 84.0 | 92.2 | 100.0 | 108.0 | 115.8 | 124.1 | 132.0 |

DATA FILE
TSMODEL1

**19.24** A time-series plot often aids the forecaster in determining an appropriate model to use. For each of the time-series data sets presented in the accompanying table, complete the following.

(a) Plot the observed data ($Y$) over time ($X$) and plot the logarithm of the observed data (log $Y$) over time ($X$) to determine whether a linear trend model or an exponential trend model is more appropriate. *Hint*: Recall that if the plot of log $Y$ versus $X$ appears to be linear, an exponential trend model provides an appropriate fit.

(b) Develop the appropriate trend equation.

(c) Forecast the trend value for the year 2000.

|  | **YEAR** | | | | | | | | | |
|---|---|---|---|---|---|---|---|---|---|---|
|  | **1988** | **1989** | **1990** | **1991** | **1992** | **1993** | **1994** | **1995** | **1996** | **1997** |
| Time series I | 100.0 | 115.2 | 130.1 | 144.9 | 160.0 | 175.0 | 189.8 | 204.9 | 219.8 | 235.0 |
| Time series II | 100.0 | 115.2 | 131.7 | 150.8 | 174.1 | 200.0 | 230.8 | 266.1 | 305.5 | 351.8 |

**DATA FILE**
TSMODEL2

**19.25** The data given in the accompanying table represent the *real* annual gross revenues (in millions of *constant* 1995 dollars) obtained by a utility company for the years 1984 through 1997.

### Real *annual gross revenues (millions of* constant *1995 dollars)*

| YEAR | REVENUES | YEAR | REVENUES |
|---|---|---|---|
| 1984 | 13.0 | 1991 | 26.2 |
| 1985 | 14.1 | 1992 | 29.0 |
| 1986 | 15.7 | 1993 | 32.8 |
| 1987 | 17.0 | 1994 | 36.5 |
| 1988 | 18.4 | 1995 | 41.0 |
| 1989 | 20.9 | 1996 | 45.4 |
| 1990 | 23.5 | 1997 | 50.8 |

**DATA FILE**
GROSSREV

(a) Compare the first differences, second differences, and percent differences to determine the most appropriate model to fit.

(b) Develop the appropriate trend equation.

(c) What has been the annual growth in *real* gross revenues over the 14 years?

(d) Forecast the trend value for the year 2000.

• **19.26** The data given in the accompanying table represent the *real* annual revenues (in millions of *constant* 1995 dollars) of an advertising agency for the years 1978 through 1997.

### Real *annual revenues (millions of* constant *1995 dollars)*

| YEAR | REVENUES | YEAR | REVENUES | YEAR | REVENUES |
|---|---|---|---|---|---|
| 1978 | 51.0 | 1985 | 93.0 | 1992 | 100.9 |
| 1979 | 54.1 | 1986 | 102.8 | 1993 | 110.9 |
| 1980 | 56.4 | 1987 | 98.0 | 1994 | 133.3 |
| 1981 | 58.1 | 1988 | 83.6 | 1995 | 192.8 |
| 1982 | 69.5 | 1989 | 81.0 | 1996 | 234.0 |
| 1983 | 79.2 | 1990 | 87.0 | 1997 | 238.9 |
| 1984 | 89.2 | 1991 | 102.9 | | |

**DATA FILE**
ADVREV

(a) Plot the data over time and plot the logarithm of the data over time to determine whether a linear trend model or an exponential trend model is more appropriate.

(b) Develop the appropriate trend equation.

(c) What has been the annual growth in *real* advertising revenues over the 20 years?

(d) Forecast the trend value for the year 2000.

 **19.5** ## THE HOLT-WINTERS METHOD FOR TREND FITTING AND FORECASTING

The **Holt-Winters method** (reference 11) is a sophisticated extension of the exponential smoothing approach described in section 19.3. Whereas the exponential smoothing procedure provides an impression of the overall, long-term movements in the data and permits short-term forecasting, the more elaborate Holt-Winters technique also allows for the study of trend through intermediate and/or long-term forecasting into the future. The differences between the two procedures are highlighted in Figure 19.12 on page 952.

From panel A we observe that exponential smoothing can be used most effectively for short-term forecasting (one period into the future). Although we can extend this forecast numerous time periods into the future, this would be meaningful only if there were no overall upward or downward trend in the series. However, if any upward or downward movement does exist, such a horizontal projection will entirely miss it. On the other hand, the Holt-Winters forecasting method of panel B is designed to detect such phenomena. The Holt-Winters technique concurrently provides for study of overall movement level and future trend in a series.

To use the Holt-Winters method at any time period $i$, we must continually estimate the level of the series ($E_i$) and the value of trend ($T_i$), as illustrated in equations (19.11a) and (19.11b).

**The Holt-Winters Method**

$$\text{Level} \quad E_i = U(E_{i-1} + T_{i-1}) + (1 - U)Y_i \qquad (19.11a)$$

$$\text{Trend} \quad T_i = VT_{i-1} + (1 - V)(E_i - E_{i-1}) \qquad (19.11b)$$

where

$E_i$ = level of the smoothed series being computed in time period $i$

$E_{i-1}$ = level of the smoothed series already computed in time period $i - 1$

$T_i$ = value of the trend component being computed in time period $i$

$T_{i-1}$ = value of the trend component already computed in time period $i - 1$

$Y_i$ = observed value of the time series in period $i$

$U$ = subjectively assigned smoothing constant (where $0 < U < 1$)

$V$ = subjectively assigned smoothing constant (where $0 < V < 1$)

To begin computations, we set $E_2 = Y_2$ and $T_2 = Y_2 - Y_1$ and choose smoothing constants for $U$ and $V$. We then compute $E_i$ and $T_i$ for all $i$ years, $i = 3, 4, \ldots, n$.

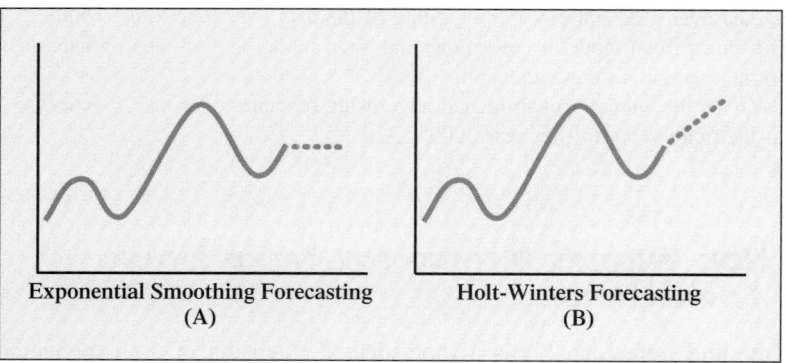

**FIGURE 19.12**   Exponential smoothing and Holt-Winters methods

**COMMENT:   *Selecting the Smoothing Constants U and V***

Our choices for the smoothing constants $U$ and $V$ affect the results. Smaller values of $U$ give less weight to the more recent levels of the time series and greater weight to earlier levels in the series. Similarly, smaller values of $V$ give less weight to the current trends in the time series and more weight to past trends in the series. Larger values of $U$ and $V$ have the opposite effect on the Holt-Winters technique.

We present Example 19.9 to illustrate the Holt-Winters method.

**Example 19.9   *Using the Holt-Winters Method to Fit a Time Series***

For the time series presented in Table 19.6 (on page 934), which represents the *real* annual gross revenues (in billions of *constant* 1982–1984 dollars) for the Eastman Kodak Company, compute the level and the trend for the 3d and 4th years (1977 and 1978) using selected smoothing constants of $U = 0.3$ and $V = 0.3$.

**SOLUTION**

To begin, we set

$$E_2 = Y_2 = 9.5$$

and

$$T_2 = Y_2 - Y_1 = 9.5 - 9.3 = 0.2$$

With the choice of smoothing constants $U = 0.3$ and $V = 0.3$, equations (19.11a) and (19.11b) become

$$E_i = (0.3)(E_{i-1} + T_{i-1}) + (0.7)(Y_i)$$

and

$$T_i = (0.3)(T_{i-1}) + (0.7)(E_i - E_{i-1})$$

For 1977, the third year, $i = 3$ and we have

$$E_3 = (0.3)(9.5 + 0.2) + (0.7)(9.9) = 9.8$$

and

$$T_3 = (0.3)(0.2) + (0.7)(9.84 - 9.5) = 0.3$$

For 1978, the fourth year, $i = 4$ and we have

$$E_4 = (0.3)(9.84 + 0.3) + (0.7)(10.7) = 10.53$$

and

$$T_4 = (0.3)(0.3) + (0.7)(10.53 - 9.84) = 0.57$$

Fortunately, we use Microsoft Excel to obtain what would otherwise be tedious computations over the remainder of the series. In Table 19.8 we display the calculated values for level and trend that we have fitted for the entire series with selected constants $U = 0.3$ and $V = 0.3$.

**Table 19.8**   *Using Microsoft Excel for the Holt-Winters method on* **real** *annual gross revenues (in billions of* **constant** *1982–1984 dollars) for Eastman Kodak Company (1975–1996)*

| | A | B | C | D | E | F |
|---|---|---|---|---|---|---|
| 1 | Year | Real-Revenue | E | T | | |
| 2 | 1975 | 9.3 | | | U | 0.3 |
| 3 | 1976 | 9.5 | 9.50 | 0.20 | V | 0.3 |
| 4 | 1977 | 9.9 | 9.84 | 0.30 | | |
| 5 | 1978 | 10.7 | 10.53 | 0.57 | | |
| 6 | 1979 | 11 | 11.03 | 0.52 | | |
| 7 | 1980 | 11.8 | 11.73 | 0.64 | | |
| 8 | 1981 | 11.3 | 11.62 | 0.12 | | |
| 9 | 1982 | 11.2 | 11.36 | -0.15 | | |
| 10 | 1983 | 10.2 | 10.50 | -0.64 | | |
| 11 | 1984 | 10.2 | 10.10 | -0.48 | | |
| 12 | 1985 | 9.9 | 9.82 | -0.34 | | |
| 13 | 1986 | 10.5 | 10.19 | 0.16 | | |
| 14 | 1987 | 11.7 | 11.30 | 0.82 | | |
| 15 | 1988 | 14.4 | 13.72 | 1.94 | | |
| 16 | 1989 | 14.8 | 15.06 | 1.52 | | |
| 17 | 1990 | 14.5 | 15.12 | 0.50 | | |
| 18 | 1991 | 14.2 | 14.63 | -0.20 | | |
| 19 | 1992 | 14.4 | 14.41 | -0.21 | | |
| 20 | 1993 | 11.3 | 12.17 | -1.63 | | |
| 21 | 1994 | 9.2 | 9.60 | -2.29 | | |
| 22 | 1995 | 10 | 9.19 | -0.97 | | |
| 23 | 1996 | 10.3 | 9.68 | 0.05 | | |

*Source: Data are taken from Table 19.6.*

To use the Holt-Winters method for forecasting, we assume that all future trend movements will continue from the most recent smoothed level $E_n$. Hence, to forecast $j$ years into the future, we have equation (19.12).

## Using the Holt-Winters Method for Forecasting

$$\hat{Y}_{n+j} = E_n + j(T_n) \qquad (19.12)$$

where

$\hat{Y}_{n+j}$ = forecasted value $j$ years into the future

$E_n$ = level of the smoothed series computed in the most recent time period $n$

$T_n$ = value of the trend component computed in the most recent time period $n$

$j$ = number of years into the future

We illustrate the process of forecasting with the Holt-Winters method in Example 19.10.

## Example 19.10  *Using the Holt-Winters Method for Forecasting*

Using the fitted values of level and trend based on smoothing constants of $U = 0.3$ and $V = 0.3$ in Table 19.8, make annual forecasts of *real* gross revenues (in billions of *constant* 1982–1984 dollars) for Eastman Kodak Company for the years 1997 through 2000.

### SOLUTION

Using $E_{22}$ and $T_{22}$, the latest estimates of current level and trend, respectively, our forecasts of *real* gross revenues for the years 1997 through 2000 are obtained from equation (19.12) as follows.

$$\hat{Y}_{n+j} = E_n + j(T_n)$$

1997: 1 year ahead $\hat{Y}_{23} = E_{22} + (1)(T_{22}) = 9.7 + (1)(.05) = 9.75$ billions of dollars

1998: 2 years ahead $\hat{Y}_{24} = E_{23} + (2)(T_{23}) = 9.7 + (2)(.05) = 9.80$ billions of dollars

1999: 3 years ahead $\hat{Y}_{25} = E_{24} + (3)(T_{24}) = 9.7 + (3)(.05) = 9.85$ billions of dollars

2000: 4 years ahead $\hat{Y}_{26} = E_{25} + (4)(T_{25}) = 9.7 + (4)(.05) = 9.90$ billions of dollars

The data, the fit, and the forecasts are plotted in Figure 19.13.

## Problems for Section 19.5

### Learning the Basics

• **19.27** Given an annual time series with 20 consecutive observations, if the smoothed level for the most recent value is 34.2 and the corresponding trend level is computed to be 5.6,

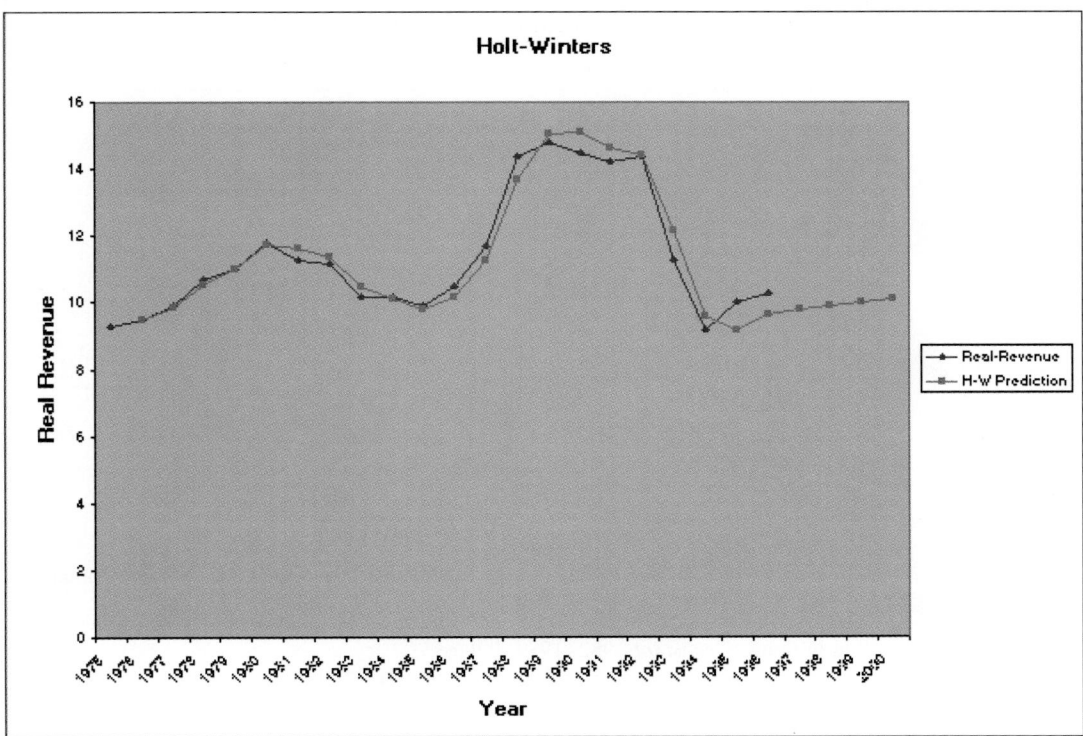

**FIGURE 19.13** Using Microsoft Excel for Holt-Winters method on Eastman Kodak Company data
*Source: Data are taken from Tables 19.6 and 19.8.*

(a) what is your forecast for the coming year?

(b) what is your forecast for 5 years from now?

**19.28** You are given the following series from $n = 15$ consecutive time periods:

3  5  6  8  10  10  12  15  16  13  16  17  22  19  24

Use the Holt-Winters method (with $U = .30$ and $V = .30$) to forecast the series for the 16th through the 20th periods.

● **19.29** You are given the following series from $n = 10$ consecutive time periods:

137  125  116  110  103  96  86  79  72  66

Use the Holt-Winters method (with $U = .20$ and $V = .20$) to forecast the series for the 11th through 14th periods.

**19.30** The Holt-Winters method was described as a sophisticated extension of the exponential smoothing approach presented in section 19.3. Under what conditions would it still be preferable to employ the exponential smoothing procedure? Discuss.

## Applying the Concepts

**19.31** The data given in the accompanying table represent the *actual* annual gross revenues (in billions of *current* dollars) at Boeing Company over the 22-year period 1975 through 1996.

### Actual *gross revenues at Boeing Company (1975–1996)*

| YEAR | REVENUES | YEAR | REVENUES | YEAR | REVENUES |
|------|----------|------|----------|------|----------|
| 1975 | 3.8  | 1983 | 11.3 | 1990 | 27.5 |
| 1976 | 4.0  | 1984 | 10.6 | 1991 | 29.3 |
| 1977 | 4.1  | 1985 | 14.0 | 1992 | 30.2 |
| 1978 | 5.6  | 1986 | 16.8 | 1993 | 25.4 |
| 1979 | 8.5  | 1987 | 15.8 | 1994 | 21.9 |
| 1980 | 9.8  | 1988 | 17.3 | 1995 | 19.5 |
| 1981 | 10.1 | 1989 | 20.6 | 1996 | 22.7 |
| 1982 | 9.2  |      |      |      |      |

DATA FILE
BOEING

*Source:* Moody's Handbook of Common Stocks, *1980, 1989, 1993, 1997. Reprinted by permission of Moody's Investors Service.*

(a) Form a new table of "adjusted (i.e., *real*) gross revenues" by multiplying each of the *actual* revenues by the quantity $\left(\dfrac{100.0}{\text{CPI}}\right)$, obtained from the corresponding annual CPI values displayed in Problem 19.14 on page 944. These *real* gross revenues are in billions of *constant* 1982–1984 dollars.

(b) Obtain annual forecasts of *real* gross revenues (in billions of *constant* 1982–1984 dollars) from 1997 through 2000 using the Holt-Winters method with the following pairs of smoothing constants:
  (1) $U = .30$ and $V = .30$
  (2) $U = .70$ and $V = .70$
  (3) $U = .30$ and $V = .70$

(c) Which of these sets of projections would you select, given the historical movement of the time series? Discuss.

**19.32** The data given in the accompanying table represent the *actual* annual net operating revenues (in billions of *current* dollars) at Coca-Cola Company over the 22-year period 1975 through 1996.

### Actual *operating revenues at Coca-Cola Company (1975–1996)*

| YEAR | REVENUES | YEAR | REVENUES | YEAR | REVENUES |
|------|----------|------|----------|------|----------|
| 1975 | 2.9 | 1983 | 6.6 | 1990 | 10.2 |
| 1976 | 3.1 | 1984 | 7.2 | 1991 | 11.6 |
| 1977 | 3.6 | 1985 | 7.9 | 1992 | 13.0 |
| 1978 | 4.3 | 1986 | 7.0 | 1993 | 14.0 |
| 1979 | 4.5 | 1987 | 7.7 | 1994 | 16.2 |
| 1980 | 5.3 | 1988 | 8.3 | 1995 | 18.0 |
| 1981 | 5.5 | 1989 | 9.0 | 1996 | 18.5 |
| 1982 | 5.9 |      |     |      |      |

DATA FILE
COCACOLA

*Source:* Moody's Handbook of Common Stocks, *1980, 1989, 1993, 1997. Reprinted by permission of Moody's Investors Service.*

(a) Form a new table of "adjusted (i.e., *real*) operating revenues" by multiplying each of the *actual* revenues by the quantity $\left(\dfrac{100.0}{\text{CPI}}\right)$, obtained from the corresponding annual CPI values displayed in Problem 19.14 on page 944. These *real* operating revenues are in billions of *constant* 1982–1984 dollars.

(b) Obtain annual forecasts for *real* operating revenues (in billions of *constant* 1982–1984 dollars) from 1997 through 2000 using the Holt-Winters method with the following pairs of smoothing constants:
   (1) $U = .30$ and $V = .30$
   (2) $U = .70$ and $V = .70$
   (3) $U = .30$ and $V = .70$

(c) Which of these sets of projections would you select, given the historical movement of the time series? Discuss.

**19.33** The data given in the accompanying table represent the *actual* annual gross revenues (in billions of *current* dollars) at Gillette Company, Inc., over the 22-year period 1975 through 1996.

## Actual *gross revenues at Gillette Company, Inc. (1975–1996)*

| YEAR | REVENUES | YEAR | REVENUES | YEAR | REVENUES |
|------|----------|------|----------|------|----------|
| 1975 | 1.4 | 1983 | 2.2 | 1990 | 4.3 |
| 1976 | 1.5 | 1984 | 2.3 | 1991 | 4.7 |
| 1977 | 1.6 | 1985 | 2.4 | 1992 | 5.2 |
| 1978 | 1.7 | 1986 | 2.8 | 1993 | 5.4 |
| 1979 | 2.0 | 1987 | 3.2 | 1994 | 6.1 |
| 1980 | 2.3 | 1988 | 3.6 | 1995 | 6.8 |
| 1981 | 2.3 | 1989 | 3.8 | 1996 | 9.7 |
| 1982 | 2.2 | | | | |

DATA FILE
GILLETTE

*Source:* Moody's Handbook of Common Stocks, *1980, 1989, 1993, 1997. Reprinted by permission of Moody's Investors Service.*

(a) Form a new table of "adjusted (i.e., *real*) gross revenues" by multiplying each of the *actual* revenues by the quantity $\left(\dfrac{100.0}{\text{CPI}}\right)$, obtained from the corresponding annual CPI values displayed in Problem 19.14 on page 944. These *real* gross revenues are in billions of *constant* 1982–1984 dollars.

(b) Obtain annual forecasts of *real* gross revenues (in billions of *constant* 1982–1984 dollars) from 1997 through 2000 using the Holt-Winters method with the following pairs of smoothing constants:
   (1) $U = .30$ and $V = .30$
   (2) $U = .70$ and $V = .70$
   (3) $U = .30$ and $V = .70$

(c) Which of these sets of projections would you select, given the historical movement of the time series? Discuss.

• **19.34** The data given in the accompanying table represent the *actual* annual gross revenues (in billions of *current* dollars) at Black & Decker Corporation over the 22-year period 1975 through 1996.

### Actual *gross revenues at Black & Decker Corporation (1975–1996)*

| Year | Revenues | Year | Revenues | Year | Revenues |
|------|----------|------|----------|------|----------|
| 1975 | 0.7 | 1983 | 1.2 | 1990 | 4.8 |
| 1976 | 0.7 | 1984 | 1.5 | 1991 | 4.7 |
| 1977 | 0.8 | 1985 | 1.7 | 1992 | 4.8 |
| 1978 | 1.0 | 1986 | 1.8 | 1993 | 4.9 |
| 1979 | 1.2 | 1987 | 1.9 | 1994 | 5.2 |
| 1980 | 1.2 | 1988 | 2.3 | 1995 | 4.8 |
| 1981 | 1.2 | 1989 | 3.2 | 1996 | 4.9 |
| 1982 | 1.2 | | | | |

**DATA FILE**
BDECKER

*Source:* Moody's Handbook of Common Stocks, *1980, 1989, 1993, 1997. Reprinted by permission of Moody's Investors Service.*

(a) Form a new table of "adjusted (i.e., *real*) gross revenues" by multiplying each of the *actual* revenues by the quantity $\left(\dfrac{100.0}{\text{CPI}}\right)$, obtained from the corresponding annual CPI values displayed in Problem 19.14 on page 944. These *real* gross revenues are in billions of *constant* 1982–1984 dollars.

(b) Obtain annual forecasts of *real* gross revenues (in billions of *constant* 1982–1984 dollars) from 1997 through 2000 using the Holt-Winters method with the following pairs of smoothing constants:
   (1) $U = .30$ and $V = .30$
   (2) $U = .70$ and $V = .70$
   (3) $U = .30$ and $V = .70$

(c) Which of these sets of projections would you select, given the historical movement of the time series? Discuss.

## ◆ 19.6 ◆ AUTOREGRESSIVE MODELING FOR TREND FITTING AND FORECASTING

[2]*It should be noted that the exponential smoothing model of section 19.3, the Holt-Winters model of section 19.5, and the autoregressive models of section 19.6 are all special cases of autoregressive integrated moving average (ARIMA) models developed by Box and Jenkins (reference 3).*

Another useful approach to forecasting with annual time-series data is based on **autoregressive modeling**.[2] Frequently, we find that the values of a series of data at particular points in time are highly correlated with the values that precede and succeed them. A **first-order autocorrelation** refers to the magnitude of the association between consecutive values in a time series. A **second-order autocorrelation** refers to the magnitude of the relationship between values 2 periods apart. A ***p*th-order autocorrelation** refers to the size of the correlation between values in a time series that are *p* periods apart. To obtain a better historical fit of our data and, at the same time, make useful forecasts of their future behavior, we can take advantage of the potential autocorrelation features inherent in such data by considering autoregressive modeling methods.

A set of autoregressive models are expressed by equations (19.13), (19.14), and (19.15).

## First-Order Autoregressive Model

$$Y_i = A_0 + A_1 Y_{i-1} + \delta_i \tag{19.13}$$

## Second-Order Autoregressive Model

$$Y_i = A_0 + A_1 Y_{i-1} + A_2 Y_{i-2} + \delta_i \tag{19.14}$$

## *p*th-Order Autoregressive Model

$$Y_i = A_0 + A_1 Y_{i-1} + A_2 Y_{i-2} + \cdots + A_p Y_{i-p} + \delta_i \tag{19.15}$$

where

$Y_i$ = the observed value of the series at time $i$

$Y_{i-1}$ = the observed value of the series at time $i-1$

$Y_{i-2}$ = the observed value of the series at time $i-2$

$Y_{i-p}$ = the observed value of the series at time $i-p$

$A_0$ = fixed parameter to be estimated from least-squares regression analysis

$A_1, A_2, \ldots, A_p$ = autoregression parameters to be estimated from least-squares regression analysis

$\delta_i$ = a nonautocorrelated random (error) component (with 0 mean and constant variance)

We note that the first-order autoregressive model [equation (19.13)] is similar in form to the simple linear regression model [equation (16.1) on page 735] and the *p*th-order autoregressive model [equation (19.15)] is similar in form to the multiple linear regression model [equation (17.1) on page 813]. In the regression models, the regression parameters were given by the symbols $\beta_0, \beta_1, \ldots, \beta_p$, with corresponding statistics denoted by $b_0, b_1, \ldots, b_p$. In the autoregressive models, the analogous parameters are given by the symbols $A_0, A_1, \ldots, A_p$, with corresponding estimates denoted by $a_0, a_1, \ldots, a_p$.

A first-order autoregressive model [equation (19.13)] is concerned only with the correlation between consecutive values in a series. A second-order autoregressive model [equation (19.14)] considers the effects of the relationship between consecutive values in a series as well as the correlation between values 2 periods apart. A *p*th-order autoregressive model [equation (19.15)] deals with the effects of relationships between consecutive values, values 2 periods apart, and so on—up to values $p$ periods apart. The selection of an appropriate autoregressive model, then, is no easy task. We must weigh the advantages due to parsimony (see section 18.5) with the concern of failing to take into account important auto-correlation behavior inherent in the data. On the other hand, we must be equally concerned with selecting a high-order model requiring the estimation of numerous, unnecessary parameters—especially if $n$, the number of observations in the series, is not too large. The reason for this is that $p$ out of $n$ data values will be lost in obtaining an estimate of $A_p$ when comparing each data value $Y_i$ with its "fairly near neighbor" $Y_{i-p}$, which is $p$ periods apart (i.e., the comparisons are $Y_{1+p}$ versus $Y_1$, then $Y_{2+p}$ versus $Y_2$, . . ., and $Y_n$ versus $Y_{n-p}$).

To illustrate this, let us look at Examples 19.11 and 19.12.

## Example 19.11 Comparison Schema for a First-Order Autoregressive Model

Suppose we have the following series of $n = 7$ consecutive annual values:

| | YEAR | | | | | | |
|---|---|---|---|---|---|---|---|
| | 1 | 2 | 3 | 4 | 5 | 6 | 7 |
| Series | 31 | 34 | 37 | 35 | 36 | 43 | 40 |

In developing a first-order autoregressive model for this series, demonstrate the comparisons that need to be made.

### SOLUTION

| YEAR $i$ | FIRST-ORDER AUTOREGRESSIVE MODEL ($Y_i$ VERSUS $Y_{i-1}$) |
|---|---|
| 1 | 31 $\leftrightarrow$ $\cdots$ |
| 2 | 34 $\leftrightarrow$ 31 |
| 3 | 37 $\leftrightarrow$ 34 |
| 4 | 35 $\leftrightarrow$ 37 |
| 5 | 36 $\leftrightarrow$ 35 |
| 6 | 43 $\leftrightarrow$ 36 |
| 7 | 40 $\leftrightarrow$ 43 |

Because there is no observation recorded prior to $Y_1$, we note that one comparison is lost for regression analysis; therefore, our first-order autoregressive model is based on six pairs of observations.

## Example 19.12  *Comparison Schema for a Second-Order Autoregressive Model*

Suppose we have the following series of $n = 7$ consecutive annual values:

| | | | YEAR | | | | |
|---|---|---|---|---|---|---|---|
| | **1** | **2** | **3** | **4** | **5** | **6** | **7** |
| Series | 31 | 34 | 37 | 35 | 36 | 43 | 40 |

In developing a second-order autoregressive model for this series, demonstrate the comparisons that would be made.

### SOLUTION

| YEAR $i$ | SECOND-ORDER AUTOREGRESSIVE MODEL ($Y_i$ VERSUS $Y_{i-1}$ AND $Y_i$ VERSUS $Y_{i-2}$) |
|---|---|
| 1 | 31 $\leftrightarrow$ $\cdots$ and 31 $\leftrightarrow$ $\cdots$ |
| 2 | 34 $\leftrightarrow$ 31 and 34 $\leftrightarrow$ $\cdots$ |
| 3 | 37 $\leftrightarrow$ 34 and 37 $\leftrightarrow$ 31 |
| 4 | 35 $\leftrightarrow$ 37 and 35 $\leftrightarrow$ 34 |
| 5 | 36 $\leftrightarrow$ 35 and 36 $\leftrightarrow$ 37 |
| 6 | 43 $\leftrightarrow$ 36 and 43 $\leftrightarrow$ 35 |
| 7 | 40 $\leftrightarrow$ 43 and 40 $\leftrightarrow$ 36 |

Because there is no observation recorded prior to $Y_1$, we note that two comparisons are lost for regression analysis; therefore, our second-order autoregressive model is based on five pairs of observations.

Once we select a model and use least-squares regression methods to obtain estimates of the parameters, our next step is to determine the appropriateness of this model. Either we can select a particular $p$th-order autoregressive model based on previous experiences with similar data or else, as a starting point, we can choose a model with several parameters and then eliminate the parameters that do not contribute significantly. In this latter approach, a $t$ test for the significance of $A_p$, the highest-order autoregressive parameter in the fitted model, may be used. The null and alternative hypotheses are:

$H_0$: $A_p = 0$ (The highest-order parameter is 0.)

$H_1$: $A_p \neq 0$ (The parameter $A_p$ is significantly meaningful.)

The test statistic is given by equation (19.16).

[3]In addition to the degrees of freedom lost for each of the p population slopes being estimated and for the Y intercept, an additional p degrees of freedom are lost because there are p fewer comparisons to be made out of the original n observations in the time series.

This t-test statistic follows a t distribution with $n - 2p - 1$ degrees of freedom.[3] For a given level of significance $\alpha$ we may reject the null hypothesis if the computed t-test statistic exceeds the upper-tailed critical value $t_{n-2p-1}$ from the t distribution or if the computed test statistic falls below the lower-tailed critical value $-t_{n-2p-1}$ from the t distribution. That is, the decision rule is

Reject $H_0$ if $t > t_{n-2p-1}$

or if $t < -t_{n-2p-1}$;

otherwise do not reject $H_0$.

The decision rule and regions of rejection and nonrejection are displayed in Figure 19.14. If the null hypothesis that $A_p = 0$ is not rejected, we conclude that the selected model contains too many estimated parameters. The highest-order term is then discarded, and an autoregressive model of order $p - 1$ is obtained through least-squares regression. A test of the hypothesis that the new highest-order term is 0 would then be repeated.

This testing and modeling procedure continues until we reject $H_0$. When this occurs, we know that our remaining highest-order parameter is significant and we are ready to use the particular model for forecasting purposes.

The fitted pth-order autoregressive model has the form expressed in equation (19.17).

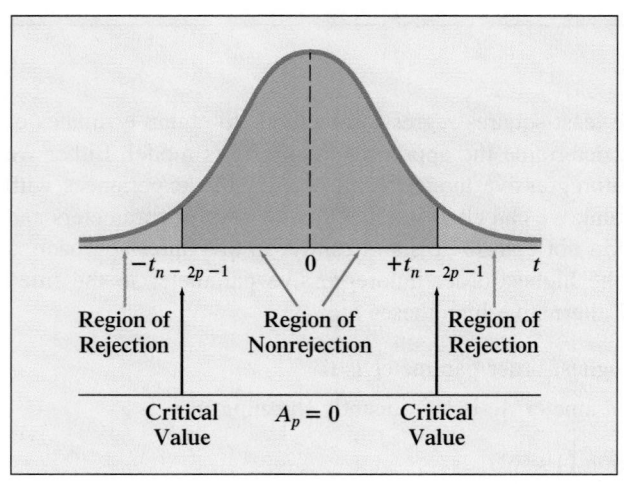

**FIGURE 19.14**

Rejection regions for two-tailed test for significance of highest-order autoregression parameter $A_p$

## The Fitted pth-Order Autoregressive Model

$$\hat{Y}_i = a_0 + a_1 Y_{i-1} + a_2 Y_{i-2} + \cdots + a_p Y_{i-p} \tag{19.17}$$

where

$$\hat{Y}_i = \text{the fitted value of the series at time } i$$
$$Y_{i-1} = \text{the observed value of the series at time } i - 1$$
$$Y_{i-2} = \text{the observed value of the series at time } i - 2$$
$$Y_{i-p} = \text{the observed value of the series at time } i - p$$
$$a_0, a_1, a_2, \ldots, a_p = \text{regression estimates of the parameters } A_0, A_1, A_2, \ldots, A_p$$

To forecast $j$ years into the future from the current $n$th time period, we have equation (19.18).

## Using the pth-Order Autoregressive Model for Forecasting

$$\hat{Y}_{n+j} = a_0 + a_1 \hat{Y}_{n+j-1} + a_2 \hat{Y}_{n+j-2} + \cdots + a_p \hat{Y}_{n+j-p} \tag{19.18}$$

where

$$a_0, a_1, a_2, \ldots, a_p = \text{regression estimates of the parameters } A_0, A_1, A_2, \ldots, A_p$$
$$j = \text{number of years into the future}$$
$$\hat{Y}_{n+j-p} = \text{forecast of } Y_{n+j-p} \text{ from the current time period for } j - p > 0$$
$$\hat{Y}_{n+j-p} = \text{the observed value for } Y_{n+j-p} \text{ for } j - p \leq 0$$

Thus, to make forecasts $j$ years into the future from a third-order autoregressive model, we need only the most recent $p = 3$ observed data values $Y_n$, $Y_{n-1}$, and $Y_{n-2}$ and the estimates of the parameters $A_0, A_1, A_2$, and $A_3$ obtained from a multiple regression analysis.

To forecast 1 year ahead, equation (19.18) becomes

$$\hat{Y}_{n+1} = a_0 + a_1 Y_n + a_2 Y_{n-1} + a_3 Y_{n-2}$$

To forecast 2 years ahead, equation (19.18) becomes

$$\hat{Y}_{n+2} = a_0 + a_1 \hat{Y}_{n+1} + a_2 Y_n + a_3 Y_{n-1}$$

To forecast 3 years ahead, equation (19.18) becomes

$$\hat{Y}_{n+3} = a_0 + a_1 \hat{Y}_{n+2} + a_2 \hat{Y}_{n+1} + a_3 Y_n$$

To forecast 4 years ahead, equation (19.18) becomes

$$\hat{Y}_{n+4} = a_0 + a_1 \hat{Y}_{n+3} + a_2 \hat{Y}_{n+2} + a_3 \hat{Y}_{n+1}$$

and so on.

Autoregressive modeling is a very useful time-series fitting and forecasting method. We summarize the steps involved in the process of autoregressive modeling in Exhibit 19.2.

**Exhibit 19.2** *Steps Involved in Autoregressive Modeling on Annual Time-Series Data*

✓ **1.** Choose a value for $p$, the highest-order parameter in the autoregressive model to be evaluated, realizing that the $t$ test for significance is based on $n - 2p - 1$ degrees of freedom.

✓ **2.** Form a series of $p$ "lagged predictor" variables such that the first variable lags by 1 year, the second variable lags by 2 years, . . . , and the last variable lags by $p$ years (see Table 19.9).

✓ **3.** Use Microsoft Excel or Minitab to run a multiple regression model containing all $p$ "lagged predictor" variables.

✓ **4.** Test for the significance of $A_p$, the highest-order autoregression parameter in the model.

  **(a)** If the null hypothesis is rejected, the autoregressive model with all $p$ predictors is selected for fitting [see equation (19.17)] and forecasting [see equation (19.18)].

  **(b)** If the null hypothesis is not rejected, the $p$th variable is discarded and steps 3 and 4 are repeated with an evaluation of the new highest-order parameter whose predictor variable lags by $p - 1$ years. The test for the significance of the new highest-order parameter is based on a $t$ distribution whose degrees of freedom are revised to correspond with the new number of predictors.

✓ **5.** Repeat steps 3 and 4 until the highest-order autoregressive parameter is statistically significant. That model is used for fitting [see equation (19.17)] and forecasting [see equation (19.18)].

To demonstrate the autoregressive modeling technique, let us return to the time series presented in Table 19.6 (on page 934) that represents the *real* annual gross revenues (in billions of *constant* 1982–1984 dollars) for Eastman Kodak Company over the 22-year period 1975 through 1996. Table 19.9 displays the setup for first-order, second-order, and third-order autoregressive models. All the columns in this table are needed for fitting third-order autoregressive models. The last column is omitted when fitting second-order autoregressive models, and the last two columns are eliminated when fitting first-order autoregressive models. Thus, we note that $p = 1$, 2, or 3 observations out of $n = 22$ are lost in the comparisons needed for developing the respective first-order, second-order, and third-order autoregressive models.

The selection of a particular autoregressive model that best fits the annual time series is demonstrated in Example 19.13. In Example 19.14 we illustrate how to use the selected autoregressive model for purposes of forecasting.

---

**Example 19.13** *Selecting an Appropriate Autoregressive Model*

Select an appropriate autoregressive model for the time series presented in Table 19.6 (on page 934), which represents the *real* annual gross revenues (in billions of *constant* 1982–1984 dollars) at Eastman Kodak Company.

**Table 19.9** *Developing first-order, second-order, and third-order autoregressive models on real annual gross revenues for Eastman Kodak Company (1975–1996)*

| YEAR | $i$ | "DEPENDENT" VARIABLE $Y_i$ | PREDICTOR VARIABLES $Y_{i-1}$ | $Y_{i-2}$ | $Y_{i-3}$ |
|------|-----|----------------------------|-------------------------------|-----------|-----------|
| 1975 | 1 | 9.3 | — | — | — |
| 1976 | 2 | 9.5 | 9.3 | — | — |
| 1977 | 3 | 9.9 | 9.5 | 9.3 | — |
| 1978 | 4 | 10.7 | 9.9 | 9.5 | 9.3 |
| 1979 | 5 | 11.0 | 10.7 | 9.9 | 9.5 |
| 1980 | 6 | 11.8 | 11.0 | 10.7 | 9.9 |
| 1981 | 7 | 11.3 | 11.8 | 11.0 | 10.7 |
| 1982 | 8 | 11.2 | 11.3 | 11.8 | 11.0 |
| 1983 | 9 | 10.2 | 11.2 | 11.3 | 11.8 |
| 1984 | 10 | 10.2 | 10.2 | 11.2 | 11.3 |
| 1985 | 11 | 9.9 | 10.2 | 10.2 | 11.2 |
| 1986 | 12 | 10.5 | 9.9 | 10.2 | 10.2 |
| 1987 | 13 | 11.7 | 10.5 | 9.9 | 10.2 |
| 1988 | 14 | 14.4 | 11.7 | 10.5 | 9.9 |
| 1989 | 15 | 14.8 | 14.4 | 11.7 | 10.5 |
| 1990 | 16 | 14.5 | 14.8 | 14.4 | 11.7 |
| 1991 | 17 | 14.2 | 14.5 | 14.8 | 14.4 |
| 1992 | 18 | 14.4 | 14.2 | 14.5 | 14.8 |
| 1993 | 19 | 11.3 | 14.4 | 14.2 | 14.5 |
| 1994 | 20 | 9.2 | 11.3 | 14.4 | 14.2 |
| 1995 | 21 | 10.0 | 9.2 | 11.3 | 14.4 |
| 1996 | 22 | 10.3 | 10.0 | 9.2 | 11.3 |

## SOLUTION

The third-order autoregressive model at the top of page 966 is fitted to the Eastman Kodak *real* annual gross revenues data using Minitab.

From this output, the third-order autoregressive model is

$$\hat{Y}_i = 4.420 + 1.109Y_{i-1} - 0.349Y_{i-2} - 0.140Y_{i-3}$$

where the origin is 1978 and $Y$ units = 1 year.

Next, we test for the significance of $A_3$, our highest-order parameter. Using our fitted model, the highest-order parameter estimate $a_3$ for the fitted third-order autoregressive model is $-0.140$ with a standard deviation $S_{a_3}$ of 0.259.

To test

$$H_0: A_3 = 0$$

```
The regression equation is
RealRev = 4.42 + 1.11 Lag1Yr - 0.349 Lag2Yr - 0.140 Lag3Yr

19 cases used 3 cases contain missing values

Predictor    (a₀)    Coef       StDev          T         P
Constant            4.420       1.944        2.27     0.038
Lag1Yr       (a₁)   1.1092      0.2578       4.30     0.001
Lag2Yr       (a₂)  -0.3485      0.3777      -0.92     0.371
Lag3Yr             -0.1396 (a₃) 0.2587      -0.54     0.597
```

Partial Minitab output for third-order autoregressive model for Eastman Kodak gross revenues data

against

$$H_1: A_3 \neq 0$$

we have, from equation (19.16) or our Minitab output,

$$t = \frac{a_3}{S_{a_3}} = \frac{-0.140}{0.259} = -0.54$$

Using a .05 level of significance, the two-tailed $t$ test with 15 degrees of freedom has critical values $t_{15}$ of $\pm 2.1315$. Because $t = -0.54 > -2.1315$, the lower-tailed critical value under the $t$ distribution (Table E.3), or because the $p$-value of .597 $> \alpha = .05$, we do not reject $H_0$. We conclude that the third-order parameter of the autoregressive model is not significant and can be deleted.

With the use of Minitab once again, a second-order autoregressive model is fitted and the following output is obtained.

```
The regression equation is
RealRev = 3.69 + 1.19 Lag1Yr - 0.507 Lag2Yr

20 cases used 2 cases contain missing values

Predictor    (a₀)    Coef       StDev          T         P
Constant            3.689       1.511        2.44     0.026
Lag1Yr       (a₁)   1.1891      0.2070       5.74     0.000
Lag2Yr       (a₂)  -0.5070      0.2030      -2.50     0.023
```

Partial Minitab output for second-order autoregressive model for Eastman Kodak gross revenues data

The second-order autoregressive model is

$$\hat{Y}_i = 3.689 + 1.189 Y_{i-1} - 0.507 Y_{i-2}$$

where the origin is 1977 and $Y$ units = 1 year.

From the Minitab output, the highest-order parameter estimate is $a_2 = -0.507$ with a standard deviation $S_{a_2} = 0.203$.

To test

$$H_0: A_2 = 0$$

against

$$H_1: A_2 \neq 0$$

we have, from equation (19.16),

$$t = \frac{a_2}{S_{a_2}} = \frac{-0.507}{0.203} = -2.50$$

To test again at the .05 level of significance, the two-tailed $t$ test with 17 degrees of freedom has critical values $t_{17}$ of $\pm 2.1098$. Because $t = -2.50 < -2.1098$, the lower-tailed critical value under the $t$ distribution (Table E.3), or because the $p$-value of .023 is less than .05, we reject $H_0$. We conclude that the second-order parameter of the autoregressive model is significantly important and cannot be deleted from the model.

Our model-building approach has led to the selection of the second-order autoregressive model as the most appropriate for the given data. In Example 19.14, we illustrate how to use this second-order autoregressive model for the purpose of forecasting.

## Example 19.14 *Using the Second-Order Autoregressive Model for Forecasting*

Use the fitted second-order autoregressive model in Example 19.13 to make annual forecasts of *real* gross revenues (in billions of *constant* 1982–1984 dollars) for Eastman Kodak Company for the years 1997 through 2000.

### SOLUTION

Using the estimates $a_0 = 3.689$, $a_1 = 1.189$, and $a_2 = -0.507$, as well as the two most recent data values $Y_{21} = 10.0$ and $Y_{22} = 10.3$, our forecasts of *real* gross revenues at Eastman Kodak for the years 1997 through 2000 are obtained from equation (19.18) as follows:

$$\hat{Y}_{n+j} = 3.689 + 1.189\hat{Y}_{n+j-1} - 0.507\hat{Y}_{n+j-2}$$

1997: 1 year ahead  $\hat{Y}_{23} = 3.689 + (1.189)(10.3) - (0.507)(10.0) = 10.9$ billions of dollars

1998: 2 years ahead  $\hat{Y}_{24} = 3.689 + (1.189)(10.9) - (0.507)(10.3) = 11.4$ billions of dollars

1999: 3 years ahead  $\hat{Y}_{25} = 3.689 + (1.189)(11.4) - (0.507)(10.9) = 11.7$ billions of dollars

2000: 4 years ahead  $\hat{Y}_{26} = 3.689 + (1.189)(11.7) - (0.507)(11.4) = 11.8$ billions of dollars

The data and the forecasts are plotted in Figure 19.15 on page 968.

On the other hand, if one's experiences with similar data permit hypothesizing that a third-order autoregressive model is appropriate for this time series, such a fitted model can be used directly for forecasting purposes without the need for testing for parameter significance. Therefore, to demonstrate the forecasting procedure for our third-order autoregressive model, we use the estimates

(a) Form a new table of "adjusted (i.e., *real*) revenues" by multiplying each of the *actual* revenues by the quantity $\left(\dfrac{100.0}{CPI}\right)$, obtained from the corresponding annual CPI values displayed in Problem 19.14 on page 944. These *real* revenues are in billions of *constant* 1982–1984 dollars.

(b) Fit a third-order autoregressive model to the *real* revenues and test for the significance of the third-order autoregressive parameter. (Use $\alpha = .05$.)

(c) If necessary, fit a second-order autoregressive model to the *real* revenues and test for the significance of the second-order autoregressive parameter. (Use $\alpha = .05$.)

(d) If necessary, fit a first-order autoregressive model to the *real* revenues and test for the significance of the first-order autoregressive parameter. (Use $\alpha = .05$.)

(e) If appropriate, provide annual forecasts of the *real* revenues from 1997 through 2000.

**19.40** The data given in the accompanying table represent the *actual* annual net operating revenues (in billions of *current* dollars) at Coca-Cola Company over the 22-year period 1975 through 1996.

### Actual *operating revenues at Coca-Cola Company (1975–1996)*

| YEAR | REVENUES | YEAR | REVENUES | YEAR | REVENUES |
|------|----------|------|----------|------|----------|
| 1975 | 2.9 | 1983 | 6.6 | 1990 | 10.2 |
| 1976 | 3.1 | 1984 | 7.2 | 1991 | 11.6 |
| 1977 | 3.6 | 1985 | 7.9 | 1992 | 13.0 |
| 1978 | 4.3 | 1986 | 7.0 | 1993 | 14.0 |
| 1979 | 4.5 | 1987 | 7.7 | 1994 | 16.2 |
| 1980 | 5.3 | 1988 | 8.3 | 1995 | 18.0 |
| 1981 | 5.5 | 1989 | 9.0 | 1996 | 18.5 |
| 1982 | 5.9 | | | | |

**DATA FILE**
**COCACOLA**

*Source:* Moody's Handbook of Common Stocks, *1980, 1989, 1993, 1997. Reprinted by permission of Moody's Investors Service.*

(a) Form a new table of "adjusted (i.e., *real*) revenues" by multiplying each of the *actual* revenues by the quantity $\left(\dfrac{100.0}{CPI}\right)$, obtained from the corresponding annual CPI values displayed in Problem 19.14 on page 944. These *real* revenues are in billions of *constant* 1982–1984 dollars.

(b) Fit a third-order autoregressive model to the *real* revenues and test for the significance of the third-order autoregressive parameter. (Use $\alpha = .05$.)

(c) If necessary, fit a second-order autoregressive model to the *real* revenues and test for the significance of the second-order autoregressive parameter. (Use $\alpha = .05$.)

(d) If necessary, fit a first-order autoregressive model to the *real* revenues and test for the significance of the first-order autoregressive parameter. (Use $\alpha = .05$.)

(e) If appropriate, provide annual forecasts of the *real* revenues from 1997 through 2000.

**19.41** The data given in the accompanying table represent the *actual* annual gross revenues (in billions of *current* dollars) at Gillette Company, Inc., over the 22-year period 1975 through 1996.

## Actual *gross revenues at Gillette Company, Inc. (1975–1996)*

| YEAR | REVENUES | YEAR | REVENUES | YEAR | REVENUES |
|------|----------|------|----------|------|----------|
| 1975 | 1.4 | 1983 | 2.2 | 1990 | 4.3 |
| 1976 | 1.5 | 1984 | 2.3 | 1991 | 4.7 |
| 1977 | 1.6 | 1985 | 2.4 | 1992 | 5.2 |
| 1978 | 1.7 | 1986 | 2.8 | 1993 | 5.4 |
| 1979 | 2.0 | 1987 | 3.2 | 1994 | 6.1 |
| 1980 | 2.3 | 1988 | 3.6 | 1995 | 6.8 |
| 1981 | 2.3 | 1989 | 3.8 | 1996 | 9.7 |
| 1982 | 2.2 | | | | |

DATA FILE
GILLETTE

*Source:* Moody's Handbook of Common Stocks, *1980, 1989, 1993, 1997. Reprinted by permission of Moody's Investors Service.*

(a) Form a new table of "adjusted (i.e., *real*) revenues" by multiplying each of the *actual* revenues by the quantity $\left(\dfrac{100.0}{\text{CPI}}\right)$, obtained from the corresponding annual CPI values displayed in Problem 19.14 on page 944. These *real* revenues are in billions of *constant* 1982–1984 dollars.

(b) Fit a third-order autoregressive model to the *real* revenues and test for the significance of the third-order autoregressive parameter. (Use $\alpha = .05$.)

(c) If necessary, fit a second-order autoregressive model to the *real* revenues and test for the significance of the second-order autoregressive parameter. (Use $\alpha = .05$.)

(d) If necessary, fit a first-order autoregressive model to the *real* revenues and test for the significance of the first-order autoregressive parameter. (Use $\alpha = .05$.)

(e) If appropriate, provide annual forecasts of the *real* revenues from 1997 through 2000.

● **19.42** The data given in the accompanying table represent the *actual* annual gross revenues (in billions of *current* dollars) at Black & Decker Corporation over the 22-year period 1975 through 1996.

## Actual *gross revenues at Black & Decker Corporation (1975–1996)*

| YEAR | REVENUES | YEAR | REVENUES | YEAR | REVENUES |
|------|----------|------|----------|------|----------|
| 1975 | 0.7 | 1983 | 1.2 | 1990 | 4.8 |
| 1976 | 0.7 | 1984 | 1.5 | 1991 | 4.7 |
| 1977 | 0.8 | 1985 | 1.7 | 1992 | 4.8 |
| 1978 | 1.0 | 1986 | 1.8 | 1993 | 4.9 |
| 1979 | 1.2 | 1987 | 1.9 | 1994 | 5.2 |
| 1980 | 1.2 | 1988 | 2.3 | 1995 | 4.8 |
| 1981 | 1.2 | 1989 | 3.2 | 1996 | 4.9 |
| 1982 | 1.2 | | | | |

DATA FILE
BDECKER

*Source:* Moody's Handbook of Common Stocks, *1980, 1989, 1993, 1997. Reprinted by permission of Moody's Investors Service.*

(a) Form a new table of "adjusted (i.e., *real*) revenues" by multiplying each of the *actual* revenues by the quantity $\left(\dfrac{100.0}{\text{CPI}}\right)$, obtained from the corresponding annual

CPI values displayed in Problem 19.14 on page 944. These *real* revenues are in billions of *constant* 1982–1984 dollars.

(b) Fit a third-order autoregressive model to the *real* revenues and test for the significance of the third-order autoregressive parameter. (Use $\alpha = .05$.)

(c) If necessary, fit a second-order autoregressive model to the *real* revenues and test for the significance of the second-order autoregressive parameter. (Use $\alpha = .05$.)

(d) If necessary, fit a first-order autoregressive model to the *real* revenues and test for the significance of the first-order autoregressive parameter. (Use $\alpha = .05$.)

(e) If appropriate, provide annual forecasts of the *real* revenues from 1997 through 2000.

 **19.7** **CHOOSING AN APPROPRIATE FORECASTING MODEL**

In sections 19.4 to 19.6 we developed seven alternative time-series forecasting methods: the linear trend model, the quadratic trend model, and the exponential trend model in section 19.4; the Holt-Winters method in section 19.5; and the first-order, second-order, and third-order autoregressive models in section 19.6.

A major question must be answered at this time: Is there a *best* model? That is, among such models as these, which *one* should we select if we are interested in time-series forecasting? In Exhibit 19.3 we offer four guidelines for determining the adequacy of a particular forecasting model. These guidelines are based on a judgment of how well the model has fit a given set of time-series data. They make the assumption that future movements in the series can be projected by a study of past behavior patterns.

---

 **Exhibit 19.3** **Guidelines for Selecting a Model for the Purpose of Forecasting**

✓ **1.** Perform a residual analysis.

✓ **2.** Measure the magnitude of the residual error through *squared* differences.

✓ **3.** Measure the magnitude of the residual error through *absolute* differences.

✓ **4.** Use the principle of parsimony.

---

A discussion of these guidelines follows.

## Residual Analysis

You may recall from our study of regression analysis in sections 16.5 and 17.2 that differences between the observed and fitted data $(Y_i - \hat{Y}_i)$ are known as *residuals* $(e_i)$. Once a particular model has been fitted to a given time series, we plot the residuals over the $n$ time periods. As depicted in panel A of Figure 19.16, if the particular model fits adequately, the residuals represent the irregular component of the time series and they should therefore be randomly distributed throughout the series. On the other hand, as illustrated in the three

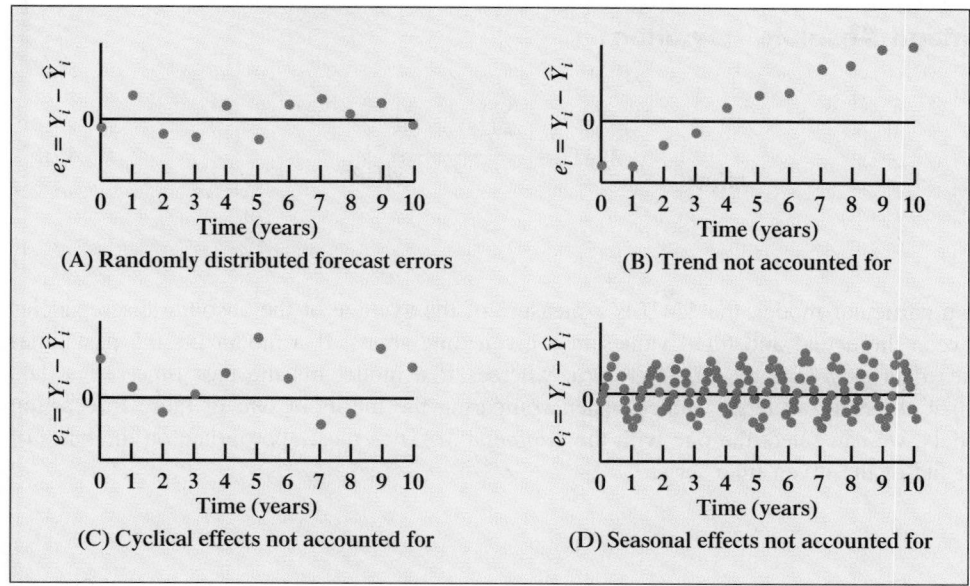

**FIGURE 19.16**   Residual analysis for studying error patterns

remaining panels of Figure 19.16, if the particular model does not fit adequately, the residuals may demonstrate some systematic pattern such as a failure to account for trend (panel B), a failure to account for cyclical variation (panel C), or, with monthly data, a failure to account for seasonal variation (panel D).

## Measuring the Magnitude of the Residual Error through Squared or Absolute Differences

If after performing a residual analysis, we still believe that two or more models appear to fit the data adequately, then a second method used for model selection is based on some measure of the magnitude of the residual error. Numerous measures have been proposed (see references 1, 2, 11, and 12). Unfortunately, there is no consensus among researchers as to which particular measure is best for determining the most appropriate forecasting model.

Based on the principle of least squares, one measure that we have already used in regression analysis (see section 16.3) is the *standard error of the estimate* ($S_{YX}$). For a particular model, this measure is based on the sum of squared differences between the actual and fitted values in a given time series. If a model fits the past time-series data *perfectly*, then the standard error of the estimate is zero. On the other hand, if a model fits the past time-series data *poorly*, the $S_{YX}$ is large. Thus, when comparing the adequacy of two or more forecasting models, we can select the one with the *minimum* $S_{YX}$ as most appropriate on the basis of the given time series.

Nevertheless, a major drawback to using $S_{YX}$ when comparing forecasting models is that it penalizes a model too much for large, individual forecasting errors. That is, whenever there is a large discrepancy between $Y_i$ and $\hat{Y}_i$, the computation for *unexplained variation* (that is, *SSE* on pages 747–748) becomes magnified through the squaring process. For this reason, a measure that many researchers seem to prefer for assessing the appropriateness of various forecasting models is the **mean absolute deviation (*MAD*)**, given in equation (19.19).

## Mean Absolute Deviation

$$MAD = \frac{\sum\limits_{i=1}^{n} |Y_i - \hat{Y}_i|}{n} \qquad (19.19)$$

For a particular model, the *MAD* is a measure of the average of the absolute discrepancies between the actual and fitted values in a given time series. If a model fits the past time-series data *perfectly*, the *MAD* is zero, whereas if a model fits the past time-series data *poorly*, the *MAD* is large. Hence, when comparing the merits of two or more forecasting models, we can select the one with the *minimum MAD* as most appropriate on the basis of past fits of the given time series.

## Principle of Parsimony

If after performing a residual analysis and comparing the obtained $S_{YX}$ and *MAD* measures, we still believe that two or more models appear to adequately fit the data, then we can use a fourth method for model selection based on the **principle of parsimony**, which is the belief that we should select the *simplest* model that gets the job done adequately.

Among the seven forecasting models studied in this chapter, the least-squares linear and quadratic models and the first-order autoregressive model are regarded by most researchers as the simplest. Their ranking likely is in the order given. The second- and third-order autoregressive models, the least-squares exponential model, and the Holt-Winters method qualify as the more complex of the techniques presented.

## A Comparison of Five Forecasting Methods

To illustrate the model selection process, we again consider the Eastman Kodak *real* annual gross revenues data. Five of the forecasting methods described in sections 19.4 to 19.6 are to be compared: the linear model, the quadratic model, the exponential model, the Holt-Winters model, and the second-order autoregressive model. (There is no need to further study the third-order autoregressive model for this time series because this model did not significantly improve the fit over the simpler second-order autoregressive model.)

Figure 19.17 on pages 975–977 displays the residual plots for the five models. In drawing conclusions from such residual plots, caution must be used because only 22 data points have been observed.

From panels A, B, and C of Figure 19.17 we note that the cyclical effects were unaccounted for in each of the least-squares models. However, the residual plot for the quadratic model seems to suggest a better fit to the series than do the linear or exponential models because the size of the residual movement above and below 0.0 in panel B is smaller and the residuals seem to display more randomness (that is, less systematic pattern) in the earlier years of the series. On the other hand, the increasing (wider) amplitude observed in the later years of all five residual plots may suggest that none of the models examined here

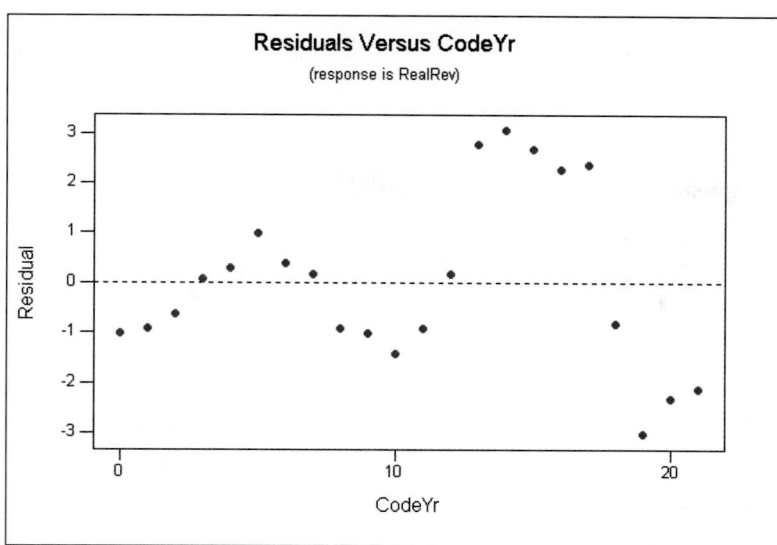

**PANEL A** Linear trend model

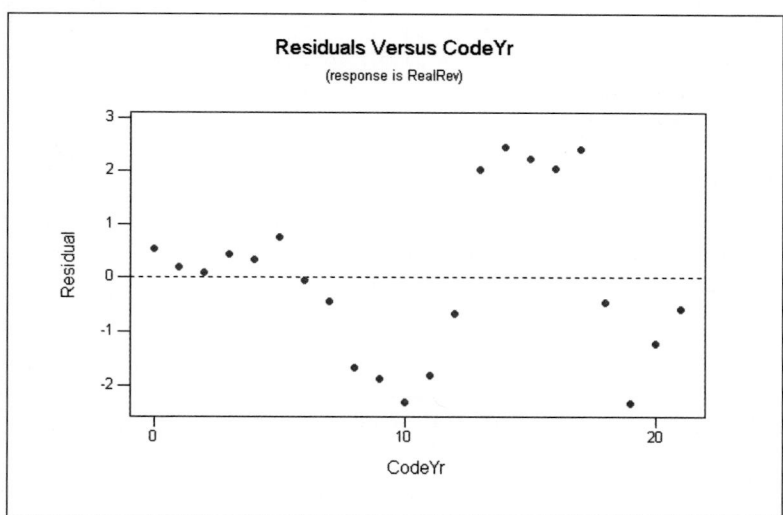

**PANEL B** Quadratic trend model

**FIGURE 19.17** Residual plots for five forecasting methods obtained from Minitab and Microsoft Excel (Continued on page 976)

*Source: Data are taken from Table 19.10 on page 977.*

performs outstandingly with respect to capturing the large *real* gross revenues movements that have occurred in these recent years. Nevertheless, from panels D and E we observe that the Holt-Winters method seems to provide the closest fit but the second-order autoregressive model exhibits the least amount of systematic structure.

To summarize, on the basis of the residual analyses of all five forecasting models, it appears that the Holt-Winters model and the second-order autoregressive model are the most

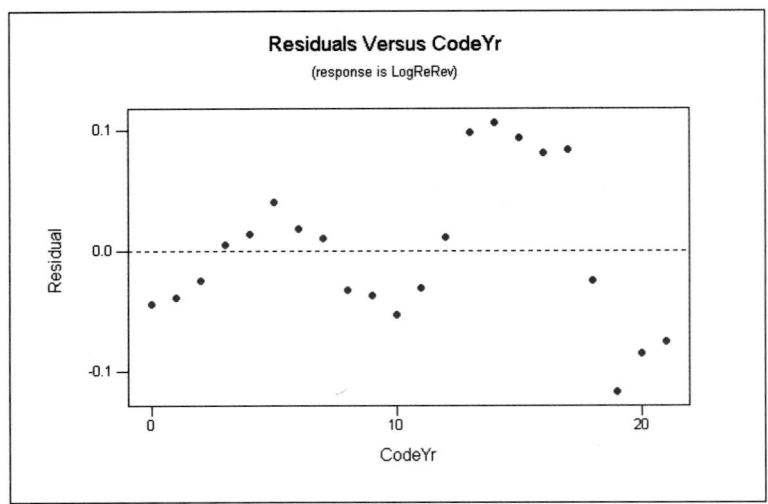

**PANEL C** Exponential trend model

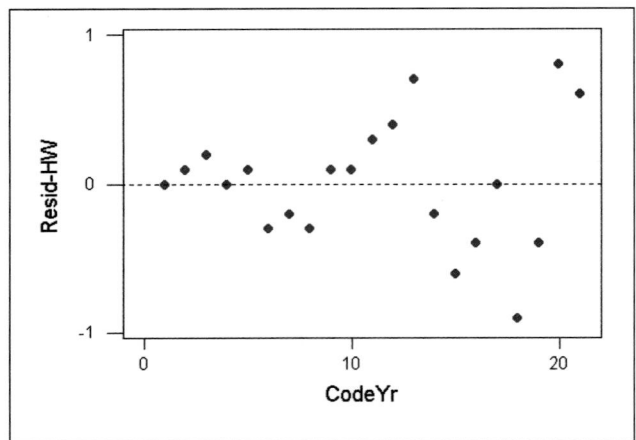

**PANEL D** Holt-Winters model with $U = .30$ and $V = .30$

**FIGURE 19.17** *(Continued)*

appropriate and the linear and exponential models are the least appropriate. To verify this, let us compare the five models with respect to the magnitude of their residual errors. Table 19.10 provides the actual values ($Y_i$) along with the fitted values ($\hat{Y}_i$) and the residuals ($e_i$) for each of the five models. In addition, the standard error of the estimate ($S_{YX}$) and the mean absolute deviation (*MAD*) for each model are displayed.

For this time series, both the $S_{YX}$ and the *MAD* measures of adequacy of fit provide us with identical results. A comparison of the $S_{YX}$ and *MAD* for each model clearly indicates that the exponential model and the linear model provide the poorest fit whereas the other least-squares model (the quadratic) shows sufficient improvement over both. As anticipated from the residual analysis (Figure 19.17), the models with the smallest $S_{YX}$ and smallest *MAD* are the Holt-Winters model and the second-order autoregressive model. Although the Holt-Winters model may be slightly superior in terms of historical fit of the data, on the

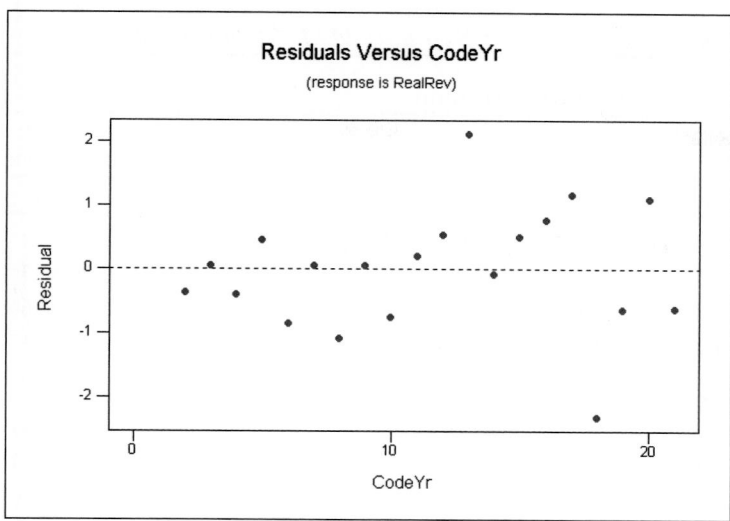

**Residuals Versus CodeYr**

(response is RealRev)

*PANEL E*  Second-order autoregressive model

*FIGURE 19.17*  (Continued)

**Table 19.10**  *Comparison of five forecasting methods using $S_{YX}$ and MAD*

| | GROSS REVENUE | LINEAR | | QUADRATIC | | EXPONENTIAL | | HOLT-WINTERS | | SECOND-ORDER AUTOREGRESSIVE | |
|---|---|---|---|---|---|---|---|---|---|---|---|
| YEAR | $Y_i$ | $\hat{Y}_i$ | $e_i$ | $\hat{Y}_i$ | $e_i$ | $\hat{Y}_i$ | $e_i$ | $\hat{Y}_i$ | $e_i$ | $\hat{Y}_i$ | $e_i$ |
| 1975 | 9.3 | 10.3 | −1.0 | 8.8 | 0.5 | 10.3 | −1.0 | — | — | — | — |
| 1976 | 9.5 | 10.4 | −0.9 | 9.3 | 0.2 | 10.4 | −0.9 | 9.5 | 0.0 | — | — |
| 1977 | 9.9 | 10.5 | −0.6 | 9.8 | 0.1 | 10.5 | −0.6 | 9.8 | 0.1 | 10.3 | −0.4 |
| 1978 | 10.7 | 10.6 | 0.1 | 10.3 | 0.4 | 10.6 | 0.1 | 10.5 | 0.2 | 10.6 | 0.1 |
| 1979 | 11.0 | 10.7 | 0.3 | 10.7 | 0.3 | 10.7 | 0.3 | 11.0 | 0.0 | 11.4 | −0.4 |
| 1980 | 11.8 | 10.8 | 1.0 | 11.0 | 0.8 | 10.7 | 1.1 | 11.7 | 0.1 | 11.3 | 0.5 |
| 1981 | 11.3 | 10.9 | 0.4 | 11.4 | −0.1 | 10.8 | 0.5 | 11.6 | −0.3 | 12.1 | −0.8 |
| 1982 | 11.2 | 11.0 | 0.2 | 11.6 | −0.4 | 10.9 | 0.3 | 11.4 | −0.2 | 11.1 | 0.1 |
| 1983 | 10.2 | 11.1 | −0.9 | 11.9 | −1.7 | 11.0 | −0.8 | 10.5 | −0.3 | 11.3 | −1.1 |
| 1984 | 10.2 | 11.2 | −1.0 | 12.1 | −1.9 | 11.1 | −0.9 | 10.1 | 0.1 | 10.1 | 0.1 |
| 1985 | 9.9 | 11.3 | −1.4 | 12.2 | −2.3 | 11.2 | −1.3 | 9.8 | 0.1 | 10.6 | −0.7 |
| 1986 | 10.5 | 11.4 | −0.9 | 12.3 | −1.8 | 11.3 | −0.8 | 10.2 | 0.3 | 10.3 | 0.2 |
| 1987 | 11.7 | 11.5 | 0.2 | 12.4 | −0.7 | 11.4 | 0.3 | 11.3 | 0.4 | 11.2 | 0.5 |
| 1988 | 14.4 | 11.6 | 2.8 | 12.4 | 2.0 | 11.5 | 2.9 | 13.7 | 0.7 | 12.3 | 2.1 |
| 1989 | 14.8 | 11.7 | 3.1 | 12.4 | 2.4 | 11.6 | 3.2 | 15.0 | −0.2 | 14.9 | −0.1 |
| 1990 | 14.5 | 11.8 | 2.7 | 12.3 | 2.2 | 11.7 | 2.8 | 15.1 | −0.6 | 14.0 | 0.5 |
| 1991 | 14.2 | 11.9 | 2.3 | 12.2 | 2.0 | 11.8 | 2.4 | 14.6 | −0.4 | 13.4 | 0.8 |

*continued*

| | GROSS REVENUE | FORECASTING METHOD | | | | | | | | |
|---|---|---|---|---|---|---|---|---|---|---|
| | | LINEAR | | QUADRATIC | | EXPONENTIAL | | HOLT-WINTERS | | SECOND-ORDER AUTOREGRESSIVE | |
| YEAR | $Y_i$ | $\hat{Y}_i$ | $e_i$ | $\hat{Y}_i$ | $e_i$ | $\hat{Y}_i$ | $e_i$ | $\hat{Y}_i$ | $e_i$ | $\hat{Y}_i$ | $e_i$ |
| 1992 | 14.4 | 12.0 | 2.4 | 12.0 | 2.4 | 11.9 | 2.5 | 14.4 | 0.0 | 13.2 | 1.2 |
| 1993 | 11.3 | 12.1 | −0.8 | 11.8 | −0.5 | 12.0 | −0.7 | 12.2 | −0.9 | 13.6 | −2.3 |
| 1994 | 9.2 | 12.2 | −3.0 | 11.5 | −2.3 | 12.1 | −2.9 | 9.6 | −0.4 | 9.8 | −0.6 |
| 1995 | 10.0 | 12.3 | −2.3 | 11.2 | −1.2 | 12.2 | −2.2 | 9.2 | 0.8 | 8.9 | 1.1 |
| 1996 | 10.3 | 12.4 | −2.1 | 10.9 | −0.6 | 12.3 | −2.0 | 9.7 | 0.6 | 10.9 | −0.6 |
| SSE | | | 63.20 | | 49.30 | | 64.06 | | 3.57 | | 17.37 |
| $S_{YX}$ | | | 1.78 | | 1.61 | | 1.79 | | 0.43 | | 1.01 |
| Absolute sum | | | 30.40 | | 26.80 | | 30.50 | | 6.70 | | 14.20 |
| MAD | | | 1.38 | | 1.22 | | 1.39 | | 0.32 | | 0.71 |

*Note: The Holt-Winters fits ($\hat{Y}_i$) are the levels of the series $e_i$.*

basis of the principle of parsimony and the fact that its residual plot seems more random, the second-order autoregressive model is the one selected for the purpose of forecasting the *real* annual gross revenues of Eastman Kodak Company.

Once a particular forecasting model is selected, it becomes imperative that we appropriately monitor the chosen model. After all, the objective in selecting the model is to project or forecast future movements in a set of time-series data. Unfortunately, such forecasting models are generally poor at detecting changes in the underlying structure of the time series. It is important then that such projections be examined together with those obtained through other types of forecasting methods (such as the use of *leading indicators*, as in reference 4). As soon as a *new* data value ($Y_t$) is observed in time period $t$, it must be compared with its projection ($\hat{Y}_t$). If the difference is too large, the forecasting model should be revised. Such *adaptive-control procedures* are described in reference 2.

## Problems for Section 19.7

### Learning the Basics

• **19.43** Suppose the following residual errors ($e_i = Y_i - \hat{Y}_i$) are obtained after fitting a least-squares trend line to an annual time series containing 12 observations on *real* total sales (in billions of *constant* 1995 dollars).

2.0, −0.5, 1.5, 1.0, 0.0, 1.0, −3.0, 1.5, −4.5, 2.0, 0.0, −1.0

(a) Compute the $S_{YX}$ and interpret your findings.
(b) Compute the MAD and interpret your findings.

• **19.44** Refer to Problem 19.43. Suppose the first residual in the time series was really 12.0 (instead of 2.0) and the last value was really −11.0 (instead of −1.0).
(a) Compute the $S_{YX}$ and interpret your findings.
(b) Compute the MAD and interpret your findings.

## Applying the Concepts

**19.45** The states of Alabama, Arizona, and Louisiana have several things in common—their populations are each roughly 4.3 million, they are each located in the southern portion of the United States, they each end in the letter "a," and depending on how residents of Louisiana pronounce their state's name, each of the states has four syllables!

The data below present *real* federal spending per capita (in *constant* 1995 dollars) in each of these states over the 15-year period 1981–1995.

### Real *federal spending per capita* (*in* constant *1995 dollars*), *1981–1995*

| FISCAL YEAR | ALABAMA | ARIZONA | LOUISIANA |
|---|---|---|---|
| 1981 | 4,091 | 3,996 | 4,142 |
| 1982 | 4,046 | 4,036 | 3,599 |
| 1983 | 4,212 | 4,084 | 3,582 |
| 1984 | 4,284 | 4,242 | 3,552 |
| 1985 | 4,497 | 4,289 | 3,864 |
| 1986 | 4,620 | 4,654 | 3,895 |
| 1987 | 4,719 | 4,784 | 3,636 |
| 1988 | 4,629 | 4,367 | 3,783 |
| 1989 | 4,664 | 4,439 | 4,136 |
| 1990 | 5,139 | 4,590 | 4,268 |
| 1991 | 5,277 | 4,526 | 4,537 |
| 1992 | 5,559 | 4,520 | 4,975 |
| 1993 | 5,599 | 4,765 | 5,261 |
| 1994 | 5,631 | 4,633 | 5,442 |
| 1995 | 5,534 | 4,686 | 5,353 |

**DATA FILE**
FEDSPEND

*Source: D. P. Moynihan, M. E. Friar, H. B. Leonard, and J. H. Walder,* The Federal Budget and the States: Fiscal Year 1995, *jointly published by the John F. Kennedy School of Government, Harvard University, and the Office of Senator Daniel Patrick Moynihan, September 30, 1996, 43, 45, 60.*

Obtain the following for each of these three time series.
(a) Plot the data on a chart.
(b) Develop the linear trend equation.
(c) Forecast the trend value for the years 1996–1999.
(d) Perform a residual analysis.
(e) Compute the standard error of the estimate ($S_{YX}$).
(f) Compute the *MAD*.
(g) On the basis of (d), (e), and (f), are you satisfied with your linear trend forecast in (c)? Discuss.

**19.46** The data given in the accompanying table represent the *actual* annual gross revenues (in billions of *current* dollars) at Boeing Company over the 22-year period 1975 through 1996.

## Actual *gross revenues at Boeing Company (1975–1996)*

| YEAR | REVENUES | YEAR | REVENUES | YEAR | REVENUES |
|------|----------|------|----------|------|----------|
| 1975 | 3.8 | 1983 | 11.3 | 1990 | 27.5 |
| 1976 | 4.0 | 1984 | 10.6 | 1991 | 29.3 |
| 1977 | 4.1 | 1985 | 14.0 | 1992 | 30.2 |
| 1978 | 5.6 | 1986 | 16.8 | 1993 | 25.4 |
| 1979 | 8.5 | 1987 | 15.8 | 1994 | 21.9 |
| 1980 | 9.8 | 1988 | 17.3 | 1995 | 19.5 |
| 1981 | 10.1 | 1989 | 20.6 | 1996 | 22.7 |
| 1982 | 9.2 | | | | |

**DATA FILE**
BOEING

*Source:* Moody's Handbook of Common Stocks, *1980, 1989, 1993, 1997. Reprinted by permission of Moody's Investors Service.*

(a) After the data are "adjusted [see Problem 19.19(d) on page 947]," the following models for predicting *real* rather than *actual* revenues for this time series should be fitted:
 (1) Linear trend model
 (2) Quadratic trend model
 (3) Exponential trend model
 (4) Holt-Winters model ($U = .3$ and $V = .3$)
 (5) Autoregressive model
(b) Perform a residual analysis for each model fitted in (a).
(c) Compute the standard error of the estimate ($S_{YX}$) for each model fitted in (a).
(d) Compute the *MAD* for each model fitted in (a).
(e) On the basis of (a), (b), (c), and parsimony, which model would you select for the purpose of forecasting? Discuss.

**19.47** The data given in the accompanying table represent the *actual* annual net operating revenues (in billions of *current* dollars) at Coca-Cola Company over the 22-year period 1975 through 1996.

## Actual *operating revenues at Coca-Cola Company (1975–1996)*

| YEAR | REVENUES | YEAR | REVENUES | YEAR | REVENUES |
|------|----------|------|----------|------|----------|
| 1975 | 2.9 | 1983 | 6.6 | 1990 | 10.2 |
| 1976 | 3.1 | 1984 | 7.2 | 1991 | 11.6 |
| 1977 | 3.6 | 1985 | 7.9 | 1992 | 13.0 |
| 1978 | 4.3 | 1986 | 7.0 | 1993 | 14.0 |
| 1979 | 4.5 | 1987 | 7.7 | 1994 | 16.2 |
| 1980 | 5.3 | 1988 | 8.3 | 1995 | 18.0 |
| 1981 | 5.5 | 1989 | 9.0 | 1996 | 18.5 |
| 1982 | 5.9 | | | | |

**DATA FILE**
COCACOLA

*Source:* Moody's Handbook of Common Stocks, *1980, 1989, 1993, 1997. Reprinted by permission of Moody's Investors Service.*

(a) After the data are "adjusted [see Problem 19.20(d) on page 947]," the following models for predicting *real* rather than *actual* revenues for this time series should be fitted:
   (1) Linear trend model
   (2) Quadratic trend model
   (3) Exponential trend model
   (4) Holt-Winters model ($U = .3$ and $V = .3$)
   (5) Autoregressive model
(b) Perform a residual analysis for each model fitted in (a).
(c) Compute the standard error of the estimate ($S_{YX}$) for each model fitted in (a).
(d) Compute the *MAD* for each model fitted in (a).
(e) On the basis of (a), (b), (c), and parsimony, which model would you select for the purpose of forecasting? Discuss.

**19.48** The data given in the accompanying table represent the *actual* annual gross revenues (in billions of *current* dollars) at Gillette Company, Inc., over the 22-year period 1975 through 1996.

## Actual *gross revenues at Gillette Company, Inc. (1975–1996)*

| YEAR | REVENUES | YEAR | REVENUES | YEAR | REVENUES |
|------|----------|------|----------|------|----------|
| 1975 | 1.4 | 1983 | 2.2 | 1990 | 4.3 |
| 1976 | 1.5 | 1984 | 2.3 | 1991 | 4.7 |
| 1977 | 1.6 | 1985 | 2.4 | 1992 | 5.2 |
| 1978 | 1.7 | 1986 | 2.8 | 1993 | 5.4 |
| 1979 | 2.0 | 1987 | 3.2 | 1994 | 6.1 |
| 1980 | 2.3 | 1988 | 3.6 | 1995 | 6.8 |
| 1981 | 2.3 | 1989 | 3.8 | 1996 | 9.7 |
| 1982 | 2.2 | | | | |

DATA FILE
GILLETTE

*Source:* Moody's Handbook of Common Stocks, *1980, 1989, 1993, 1997. Reprinted by permission of Moody's Investors Service.*

(a) After the data are "adjusted [see Problem 19.21(d) on page 948]," the following models for predicting *real* rather than *actual* revenues for this time series should be fitted:
   (1) Linear trend model
   (2) Quadratic trend model
   (3) Exponential trend model
   (4) Holt-Winters model ($U = .3$ and $V = .3$)
   (5) Autoregressive model
(b) Perform a residual analysis for each model fitted in (a).
(c) Compute the standard error of the estimate ($S_{YX}$) for each model fitted in (a).
(d) Compute the *MAD* for each model fitted in (a).
(e) On the basis of (a), (b), (c), and parsimony, which model would you select for the purpose of forecasting? Discuss.

**19.49** The data given in the accompanying table represent the *actual* annual gross revenues (in billions of *current* dollars) at Black & Decker Corporation over the 22-year period 1975 through 1996.

## Actual *gross revenues at Black & Decker Corporation (1975–1996)*

| YEAR | REVENUES | YEAR | REVENUES | YEAR | REVENUES |
|------|----------|------|----------|------|----------|
| 1975 | 0.7 | 1983 | 1.2 | 1990 | 4.8 |
| 1976 | 0.7 | 1984 | 1.5 | 1991 | 4.7 |
| 1977 | 0.8 | 1985 | 1.7 | 1992 | 4.8 |
| 1978 | 1.0 | 1986 | 1.8 | 1993 | 4.9 |
| 1979 | 1.2 | 1987 | 1.9 | 1994 | 5.2 |
| 1980 | 1.2 | 1988 | 2.3 | 1995 | 4.8 |
| 1981 | 1.2 | 1989 | 3.2 | 1996 | 4.9 |
| 1982 | 1.2 | | | | |

**DATA FILE**
BDECKER

*Source:* Moody's Handbook of Common Stocks, *1980, 1989, 1993, 1997. Reprinted by permission of Moody's Investors Service.*

(a) After the data are "adjusted [see Problem 19.22(d) on page 949]," the following models for predicting *real* rather than *actual* revenues for this time series should be fitted:
 (1) Linear trend model
 (2) Quadratic trend model
 (3) Exponential trend model
 (4) Holt-Winters model ($U = .3$ and $V = .3$)
 (5) Autoregressive model
(b) Perform a residual analysis for each fitted model.
(c) Compute the standard error of the estimate ($S_{YX}$) for each fitted model.
(d) Compute the *MAD* for each fitted model.
(e) On the basis of (a), (b), (c), and parsimony, which model would you select for the purpose of forecasting? Discuss.

## 19.8 TIME-SERIES FORECASTING OF MONTHLY OR QUARTERLY DATA

To this point in the chapter, our focus has been on time-series forecasting with annual data. However, numerous economic time series are collected quarterly or monthly; others are obtained weekly, daily, or even hourly. In particular, as displayed in Table 19.1 on page 917, when a time series is collected quarterly or monthly, the impact of seasonal effects must be considered. In this section we demonstrate a direct approach to forecasting with monthly or quarterly data through the development of regression model building described in chapter 18. To begin, let us examine a monthly time series.

Table 19.11 presents the *real* monthly private residential construction expenditures (in millions of *constant* 1995 dollars) in a small city in the United States from January 1992 through December 1997. This time series is displayed in Figure 19.18.

For such monthly time series as these the *classical multiplicative time-series model* includes the **seasonal component** in addition to the trend, cyclical, and irregular components. It is expressed by equation (19.2) on page 918 as

$$Y_i = T_i \cdot S_i \cdot C_i \cdot I_i$$

To develop a least-squares regression model that includes both the trend and seasonal components, we combine the approach to least-squares trend fitting in section 19.4 with the

**Table 19.11** Real *monthly private residential construction expenditures (in millions of* constant *1995 dollars) in small city in United States (January 1992–December 1997)*

| | YEAR | | | | | |
| MONTH | 1992 | 1993 | 1994 | 1995 | 1996 | 1997 |
|---|---|---|---|---|---|---|
| January | 10.2 | 11.2 | 12.5 | 12.6 | 13.2 | 13.0 |
| February | 9.7 | 11.0 | 12.0 | 12.0 | 12.5 | 12.7 |
| March | 11.3 | 12.7 | 13.9 | 14.2 | 14.4 | 14.8 |
| April | 12.4 | 14.3 | 15.4 | 15.6 | 15.8 | 15.9 |
| May | 13.6 | 16.2 | 17.0 | 17.1 | 17.1 | 17.1 |
| June | 14.5 | 17.7 | 18.2 | 18.3 | 18.1 | 17.7 |
| July | 14.8 | 18.4 | 18.6 | 18.9 | 18.7 | 17.9 |
| August | 15.3 | 18.6 | 18.8 | 19.3 | 18.9 | 18.0 |
| September | 15.0 | 18.1 | 18.4 | 18.7 | 18.1 | 16.8 |
| October | 15.0 | 18.0 | 18.2 | 18.7 | 17.8 | 16.3 |
| November | 14.2 | 16.7 | 17.1 | 17.7 | 16.7 | 14.7 |
| December | 12.4 | 14.2 | 14.5 | 15.0 | 14.0 | 12.2 |

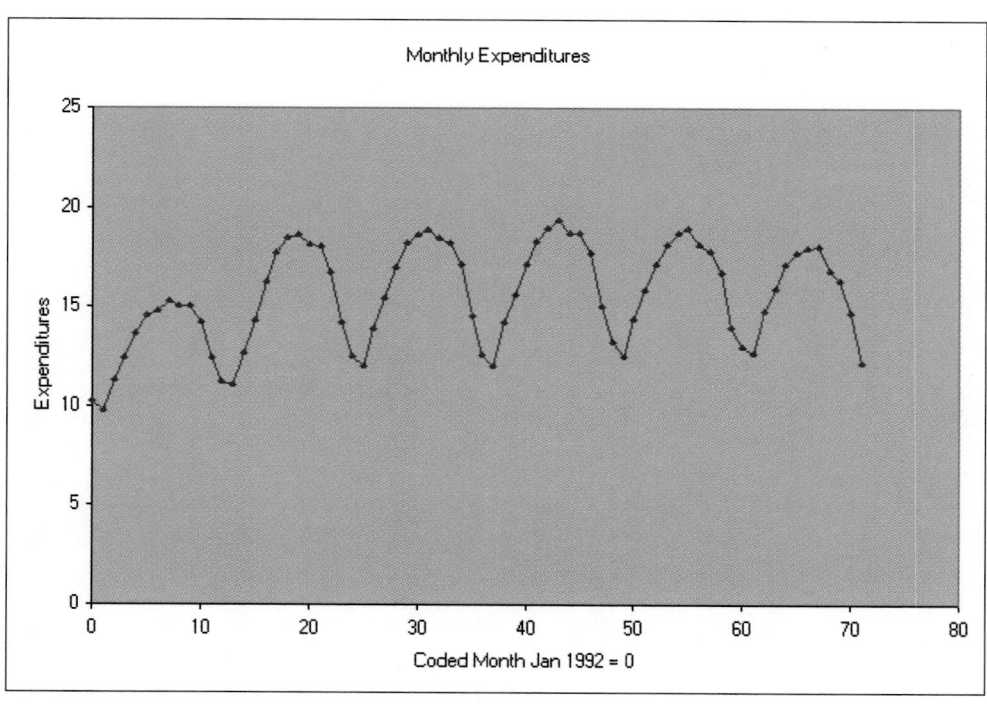

**FIGURE 19.18** *Real* private residential construction (in millions of *constant* 1995 dollars) in small city in United States from January 1992 to December 1997)
*Source: Data are taken from Table 19.11.*

approach to model building using categorical predictor variables (see section 18.2) to describe the seasonal components.

We can represent our classical multiplicative time series model [equation (19.2) on page 918] by fitting the following exponential trend equation with seasonal components denoted by equations (19.20a) and (19.20b) for monthly data or by equations (19.21a) and (19.21b) for a quarterly time series.

## Exponential Model with Monthly Data

$$\hat{Y}_i = b_0 b_1^{X_i} b_2^{M_1} b_3^{M_2} b_4^{M_3} b_5^{M_4} b_6^{M_5} b_7^{M_6} b_8^{M_7} b_9^{M_8} b_{10}^{M_9} b_{11}^{M_{10}} b_{12}^{M_{11}} \tag{19.20a}$$

where

$$b_0 = \text{estimated } Y \text{ intercept}$$
$$(b_1 - 1) \times 100\% = \text{estimated } \textit{monthly compound growth rate} \text{ (in percent)}$$
$$X_i = \text{coded } \textit{monthly} \text{ value}$$
$$b_2 = \text{"multiplier" for January relative to December}$$
$$b_3 = \text{"multiplier" for February relative to December}$$
$$b_4 = \text{"multiplier" for March relative to December}$$

$$\vdots$$

$$b_{12} = \text{"multiplier" for November relative to December}$$
$$M_1 = 1 \text{ if January, 0 if not January}$$
$$M_2 = 1 \text{ if February, 0 if not February}$$
$$M_3 = 1 \text{ if March, 0 if not March}$$

$$\vdots$$

$$M_{11} = 1 \text{ if November, 0 if not November}$$

## Exponential Model with Quarterly Data

$$\hat{Y}_i = b_0 b_1^{X_i} b_2^{Q_1} b_3^{Q_2} b_4^{Q_3} \tag{19.21a}$$

where

$$b_0 = \text{estimated } Y \text{ intercept}$$
$$(b_1 - 1) \times 100\% = \text{estimated } \textit{quarterly compound growth rate} \text{ (in percent)}$$
$$X_i = \text{coded } \textit{quarterly} \text{ value}$$
$$b_2 = \text{"multiplier" for first quarter relative to fourth quarter}$$
$$b_3 = \text{"multiplier" for second quarter relative to fourth quarter}$$
$$b_4 = \text{"multiplier" for third quarter relative to fourth quarter}$$
$$Q_1 = 1 \text{ if first quarter, 0 if not first quarter}$$
$$Q_2 = 1 \text{ if second quarter, 0 if not second quarter}$$
$$Q_3 = 1 \text{ if third quarter, 0 if not third quarter}$$

Note that $M_1$, $M_2$, $M_3$, ..., $M_{11}$ are the 11 dummy variables needed to represent the 12 months in a monthly time series, and $Q_1$, $Q_2$, $Q_3$ are the three dummy variables needed to represent the four quarter periods in a quarterly time series. If we take the natural logarithm of both sides of equations (19.20a) and (19.21a), we obtain equations (19.20b) and (19.21b), which are both in linear form.

## Exponential Model with Monthly Data

$$\ln \hat{Y}_i = \ln b_0 + X_i \ln b_1 + M_1 \ln b_2 + M_2 \ln b_3 + M_3 \ln b_4 + \cdots + M_{11} \ln b_{12} \quad (19.20b)$$

## Exponential Model with Quarterly Data

$$\ln \hat{Y}_i = \ln b_0 + X_i \ln b_1 + Q_1 \ln b_2 + Q_2 \ln b_3 + Q_3 \ln b_4 \quad (19.21b)$$

In building our model, we use the $\ln Y_i$ instead of $Y_i$ values and then obtain the actual regression coefficients by taking the antilog of the regression coefficients developed from equations (19.20b) and (19.21b).

Although at first glance these regression models look imposing, the fact is that when fitting or forecasting in any one time period, the values of all the other dummy variables in the model are set equal to 0 and the format of the equation is simplified dramatically. With a monthly time series, for example, equations (19.20b) and (19.20a), respectively, reduce as follows.

For any January:  $\ln \hat{Y}_i = \ln b_0 + X_i \ln b_1 + M_1 \ln b_2$  so that taking antilogs
$\qquad\qquad \hat{Y}_i = b_0 b_1^{X_i} b_2^{M_1}$

For any February:  $\ln \hat{Y}_i = \ln b_0 + X_i \ln b_1 + M_2 \ln b_3$  so that taking antilogs
$\qquad\qquad \hat{Y}_i = b_0 b_1^{X_i} b_3^{M_2}$

For any March:  $\ln \hat{Y}_i = \ln b_0 + X_i \ln b_1 + M_3 \ln b_4$  so that taking antilogs
$\qquad\qquad \hat{Y}_i = b_0 b_1^{X_i} b_4^{M_3}$

$$\vdots$$

For any November:  $\ln \hat{Y}_i = \ln b_0 + X_i \ln b_1 + M_{11} \ln b_{12}$  so that taking antilogs
$\qquad\qquad \hat{Y}_i = b_0 b_1^{X_i} b_{12}^{M_{11}}$

For any December:  $\ln \hat{Y}_i = \ln b_0 + X_i \ln b_1$  so that taking antilogs $\hat{Y}_i = b_0 b_1^{X_i}$

When establishing the dummy variables for each month, we note that December serves as the base period and has a coded value of zero for all the dummy variables.

With a quarterly time series, for example, equations (19.21b) and (19.21a), respectively, reduce as follows.

For any first quarter:  $\ln \hat{Y}_i = \ln b_0 + X_i \ln b_1 + Q_1 \ln b_2$  so that taking antilogs
$\qquad\qquad \hat{Y}_i = b_0 b_1^{X_i} b_2^{Q_1}$

For any second quarter:  $\ln \hat{Y}_i = \ln b_0 + X_i \ln b_1 + Q_2 \ln b_3$  so that taking antilogs
$\qquad\qquad \hat{Y}_i = b_0 b_1^{X_i} b_3^{Q_2}$

For any third quarter:  $\ln \hat{Y}_i = \ln b_0 + X_i \ln b_1 + Q_3 \ln b_4$ so that taking antilogs
$$\hat{Y}_i = b_0 b_1^{X_i} b_4^{Q_3}$$
For any fourth quarter:  $\ln \hat{Y}_i = \ln b_0 + X_i \ln b_1$ so that taking antilogs $\hat{Y}_i = b_0 b_1^{X_i}$

When establishing the dummy variables for quarterly time-series data, the fourth quarter is the base period and has a coded value of zero for each dummy variable.

To demonstrate the process of model building and least-squares forecasting with a monthly time series, we return to our *real* private residential construction expenditures data (in millions of *constant* 1995 dollars) originally displayed in Table 19.11. The data were obtained for each month from January 1992 through December 1997. Using Minitab, we provide partial output for our model in Figure 19.19.

```
The regression equation is
Lnexpen = 2.52 + 0.00241 CodeMon - 0.0986 M1 - 0.140 M2 + 0.0083 M3 + 0.101
              + 0.192 M5 + 0.253 M6 + 0.277 M7 + 0.290 M8 + 0.252 M9 + 0.239 M1
              + 0.168 M11

Predictor        Coef       StDev           T         P
Constant       2.51683     0.03525       71.39     0.000
CodeMon      0.0024091    0.0004300        5.60     0.000
M1            -0.09862     0.04343       -2.27     0.027
M2            -0.14032     0.04339       -3.23     0.002
M3             0.00831     0.04335        0.19     0.849
M4             0.10132     0.04331        2.34     0.023
M5             0.19218     0.04328        4.44     0.000
M6             0.25310     0.04325        5.85     0.000
M7             0.27688     0.04323        6.41     0.000
M8             0.28978     0.04321        6.71     0.000
M9             0.25198     0.04319        5.83     0.000
M10            0.23900     0.04318        5.53     0.000
M11            0.16756     0.04317        3.88     0.000

S = 0.07478      R-Sq = 84.4%      R-Sq(adj) = 81.3%
```

**FIGURE 19.19**  Partial Minitab output for fitting and forecasting with monthly data
*Source: Table 19.11.*

From this partial printout we note that the model seems to fit the data quite satisfactorily. The coefficient of determination $r^2$ is 84.5% unadjusted and 81.3% adjusted, and the overall test of the fit results in an $F$ statistic of 26.65 with $p$-value 0.000. Looking further, at a .05 level of significance we note that each regression coefficient is statistically significant and contributes to our classical multiplicative time-series model except for the month of March ($t$ statistic of $+0.19$ with $p$-value 0.849), which deviates only by chance from the December base period. Taking the antilogs of all the regression coefficients, we have the following table.

| REGRESSION COEFFICIENTS | $\ln b_i$ | $b_i = e^{\ln b_i}$ |
|---|---|---|
| $b_0$:$Y$ intercept | 2.51683 | 12.3893 |
| $b_1$:slope coded month | 0.00241 | 1.0024 |
| $b_2$:January | $-0.09862$ | 0.9061 |

*continued*

| REGRESSION COEFFICIENTS | $\ln b_i$ | $b_i = e^{\ln b_i}$ |
|---|---|---|
| $b_3$:February | −0.14032 | 0.8691 |
| $b_4$:March | 0.00831 | 1.0083 |
| $b_5$:April | 0.10132 | 1.1066 |
| $b_6$:May | 0.19218 | 1.2119 |
| $b_7$:June | 0.25310 | 1.2880 |
| $b_8$:July | 0.27688 | 1.3190 |
| $b_9$:August | 0.28978 | 1.3361 |
| $b_{10}$:September | 0.25198 | 1.2866 |
| $b_{11}$:October | 0.23900 | 1.2700 |
| $b_{12}$:November | 0.16756 | 1.1824 |

We present Example 19.15 to interpret these regression coefficients.

## Example 19.15  *Interpreting the Regression Coefficients*

Interpret the previous regression coefficients obtained by taking the antilogs from the regression model displayed in the partial Minitab output of Figure 19.19.

### SOLUTION

- The $Y$ intercept $b_0 = 12.3893$ (in millions of *constant* 1995 dollars) is the unadjusted trend value for private residential construction expenditures in January 1992, the initial month in our time series.
- The value $(b_1 - 1) \times 100\% = 0.24\%$ is the estimated *monthly compound growth rate* in *real* private residential construction expenditures.
- $b_2 = 0.9061$ is the seasonal "multiplier" for the month of January relative to December; it indicates that there is 9.4% less money expended on *real* private residential construction in January as compared with December.
- $b_3 = 0.8691$ is the seasonal "multiplier" for the month of February relative to December; it indicates that there is 13.1% less money expended on *real* private residential construction in February as compared with December.
- $b_4 = 1.0083$ is the seasonal "multiplier" for the month of March relative to December; it indicates that there is 0.8% more money expended on *real* private residential construction in March as compared with December.

$$\vdots$$

- $b_{12} = 1.1824$ is the seasonal "multiplier" for the month of November relative to December; it indicates that there is 18.2% more money expended on *real* private residential construction in November as compared with December.

Using the reduced format of equations (19.20b) and (19.20a), we demonstrate the process of fitting and forecasting with our classical multiplicative time-series model. As examples, to estimate what real average residential construction expenditures were expected to be in November and December 1997, we have the following.

For November 1997: $\ln \hat{Y}_{71} = 2.51683 + 70(0.00241) + 0.16756$

$$= 2.85309 \text{ so that taking antilogs}$$

$$\hat{Y}_{71} = 17.341 \text{ millions of } constant \text{ 1995 dollars}$$

For December 1997: $\ln \hat{Y}_{72} = 2.51683 + 71(0.00241)$

$$= 2.68794 \text{ so that taking antilogs}$$

$$\hat{Y}_{72} = 14.701 \text{ millions of } constant \text{ 1995 dollars}$$

To evaluate the adequacy of the fit, we would use our seasonal regression model to estimate what average residential construction expenditures were expected to be on a monthly basis over the past 6 years and then compare these results with the actual values of this monthly time series during the corresponding time period, January 1992 through December 1997. Measures such as $S_{YX}$, $MAD$, or $r^2$ enable us to evaluate the past fit to these time-series data.

To make forecasts for *real* residential construction expenditures for the months of January, February, March, November, and December during the year 2000, we have the following.

For January 2000: $\ln \hat{Y}_{97} = 2.51683 + 96(0.00241) - 0.09862$

$$= 2.64957 \text{ so that taking antilogs}$$

$$\hat{Y}_{97} = 14.148 \text{ millions of } constant \text{ 1995 dollars}$$

For February 2000: $\ln \hat{Y}_{98} = 2.51683 + 97(0.00241) - 0.14032$

$$= 2.61028 \text{ so that taking antilogs}$$

$$\hat{Y}_{98} = 13.603 \text{ millions of } constant \text{ 1995 dollars}$$

For March 2000: $\ln \hat{Y}_{99} = 2.51683 + 98(0.00241) + 0.00831$

$$= 2.76132 \text{ so that taking antilogs}$$

$$\hat{Y}_{99} = 15.821 \text{ millions of } constant \text{ 1995 dollars}$$

$$\vdots$$

For November 2000: $\ln \hat{Y}_{107} = 2.51683 + 106(0.00241) + 0.16756$

$$= 2.93985 \text{ so that taking antilogs}$$

$$\hat{Y}_{107} = 18.913 \text{ millions of } constant \text{ 1995 dollars}$$

For December 2000: $\ln \hat{Y}_{108} = 2.51683 + 107(0.00241)$

$$= 2.77470 \text{ so that taking antilogs}$$

$$\hat{Y}_{108} = 16.034 \text{ millions of } constant \text{ 1995 dollars}$$

## Problems for Section 19.8

### Learning the Basics

**19.50** In least-squares forecasting with monthly time-series data over a 5-year period from January 1993 to December 1997, the exponential model for January is

$$\ln \hat{Y}_i = 2.0 + .01 X_i + .10 \text{ January}$$

Take the antilog of the appropriate coefficient from the above equation and interpret
(a) the $Y$ intercept $b_0$.
(b) the monthly compound growth rate.
(c) the January "multiplier."

**19.51** In least-squares forecasting with *weekly* time-series data, how many dummy variables are needed to account for the seasonal categorical variable "week"?

**• 19.52** In least-squares forecasting with quarterly time series data over the 5-year period from the first quarter 1994 through the fourth quarter 1998, the exponential model is given by

$$\ln \hat{Y}_i = 3.0 + 0.10X_i - 0.25Q_1 + 0.20Q_2 + 0.15Q_3$$

where the origin is mid–first quarter 1994 and $X$ units = 1 quarter.
(a) Take the antilog of the appropriate coefficient from the above equation and interpret the $Y$ intercept $b_0$.
(b) Take the antilog of the appropriate coefficient from the above equation and interpret the quarterly compound growth rate.
(c) Take the antilog of the appropriate coefficient from the above equation and interpret the second quarter "multiplier."

**• 19.53** Refer to the exponential model given in Problem 19.52.
(a) What is the fitted value of the series in the fourth quarter of 1996?
(b) What is the fitted value of the series in the first quarter of 1997?
(c) What is the forecast in the fourth quarter of 1999?
(d) What is the forecast in the first quarter of 2000?

## Applying the Concepts

**• 19.54** The data given in the following table represent the Standard and Poor's Composite Stock Price Index recorded at the end of each quarter from 1994 through 1997.

*Quarterly Standard and Poor's Composite Stock Price Index*

| | YEAR | | | |
| --- | --- | --- | --- | --- |
| QUARTER | 1994 | 1995 | 1996 | 1997 |
| 1 | 445.77 | 500.71 | 645.50 | 757.12 |
| 2 | 444.27 | 544.75 | 670.63 | 885.14 |
| 3 | 462.69 | 584.41 | 687.31 | 947.28 |
| 4 | 459.27 | 615.93 | 740.74 | 970.43 |

DATA FILE
S&PSTKIN

*Source:* Standard and Poor's Current Statistics, *January 1998, 29.*
*Reprinted by permission of Standard & Poor's Corporation, a division of the McGraw-Hill Cos.*

(a) Plot the data on a chart.
(b) Develop an exponential trend equation with quarterly components to represent the classical multiplicative time-series model.
  (1) What is the fitted value of the series in the third quarter of 1997?
  (2) What is the fitted value of the series in the fourth quarter of 1997?
  (3) What are the forecasts for all four quarters of 1998 and 1999?
  (4) Interpret the quarterly compound growth rate.
  (5) Interpret the second quarter "multiplier."

**19.55** The data given in the accompanying table represent the quarterly gross national product (GNP), an economic indicator measured in billions of "chained 1992 (i.e., *real*) dollars," from 1990 through 1997.

### Quarterly gross national product (GNP) in billions of "chained 1992 dollars"

| QUARTER | YEAR | | | | | | | |
|---|---|---|---|---|---|---|---|---|
| | **1990** | **1991** | **1992** | **1993** | **1994** | **1995** | **1996** | **1997** |
| 1 | 6,152.6 | 6,047.5 | 6,175.7 | 6,327.9 | 6,524.5 | 6,703.7 | 6,826.4 | 7,101.6 |
| 2 | 6,171.6 | 6,074.7 | 6,214.2 | 6,359.9 | 6,600.3 | 6,708.8 | 6,926.0 | 7,159.6 |
| 3 | 6,142.1 | 6,090.1 | 6,260.7 | 6,393.5 | 6,629.5 | 6,759.2 | 6,943.8 | 7,217.6 |
| 4 | 6,079.0 | 6,105.3 | 6,327.1 | 6,436.9 | 6,688.6 | 6,796.5 | 7,017.4 | 7,250.0[a] |

**DATA FILE**
REALGNP

[a] *Initial estimate.*
*Source:* Survey of Current Business, *December 1997.*

(a) Plot the data on a chart.
(b) Develop an exponential trend equation with quarterly components to represent the classical multiplicative time-series model.
    (1) What is the fitted value of the series in the third quarter of 1997?
    (2) What is the fitted value of the series in the fourth quarter of 1997?
    (3) What are the forecasts for all four quarters of 1998 and 1999?
    (4) Interpret the quarterly compound growth rate.
    (5) Interpret the first quarter "multiplier."

● **19.56** The data given in the following table represent the *real* monthly outlays (in thousands of *constant* 1995 dollars) by a municipality to its sanitation department from January 1988 through December 1997.

### Real monthly outlays

| MONTH | YEAR | | | | | | | | | |
|---|---|---|---|---|---|---|---|---|---|---|
| | **1988** | **1989** | **1990** | **1991** | **1992** | **1993** | **1994** | **1995** | **1996** | **1997** |
| January | 262 | 259 | 271 | 251 | 298 | 260 | 275 | 315 | 354 | 417 |
| February | 295 | 276 | 241 | 231 | 283 | 291 | 321 | 342 | 365 | 408 |
| March | 333 | 310 | 301 | 252 | 315 | 307 | 352 | 370 | 389 | 416 |
| April | 252 | 238 | 265 | 293 | 287 | 293 | 322 | 316 | 198 | 398 |
| May | 274 | 270 | 255 | 278 | 301 | 279 | 309 | 361 | 366 | 397 |
| June | 245 | 292 | 301 | 447 | 185 | 287 | 314 | 320 | 389 | 452 |
| July | 377 | 289 | 278 | 216 | 368 | 344 | 299 | 324 | 341 | 423 |
| August | 291 | 289 | 262 | 247 | 310 | 359 | 355 | 320 | 413 | 456 |
| September | 273 | 273 | 246 | 267 | 313 | 250 | 324 | 344 | 387 | 356 |
| October | 266 | 271 | 249 | 281 | 312 | 368 | 310 | 300 | 384 | 479 |
| November | 286 | 272 | 246 | 297 | 325 | 359 | 339 | 350 | 415 | 425 |
| December | 285 | 284 | 221 | 288 | 326 | 345 | 320 | 333 | 328 | 499 |

**DATA FILE**
OUTLAYS

(a) Plot the data on a chart.
(b) Develop an exponential trend equation with monthly components to represent the classical multiplicative time-series model.

(1) What is the fitted value of the series in November 1997?
(2) What is the fitted value of the series in December 1997?
(3) What are the forecasts for all 12 months of 1998?
(4) Interpret the monthly compound growth rate.
(5) Interpret the June "multiplier."

**19.57** The data in the accompanying table represent the *actual* total monthly assets of commercial banks in the United States (in trillions of *current* dollars) from January 1992 to December 1997. This series excludes unearned income, reserves from losses on loans and leases, and reserves for transfer risk.

## Total monthly assets of U.S. commercial banks

| MONTH | YEAR | | | | | |
|---|---|---|---|---|---|---|
| | 1992 | 1993 | 1994 | 1995 | 1996 | 1997 |
| January | 3.41 | 3.48 | 3.67 | 3.91 | 4.24 | 4.43 |
| February | 3.41 | 3.49 | 3.69 | 3.93 | 4.23 | 4.49 |
| March | 3.42 | 3.51 | 3.71 | 3.96 | 4.25 | 4.54 |
| April | 3.43 | 3.51 | 3.73 | 4.02 | 4.28 | 4.58 |
| May | 3.42 | 3.54 | 3.74 | 4.04 | 4.27 | 4.59 |
| June | 3.43 | 3.57 | 3.75 | 4.07 | 4.28 | 4.60 |
| July | 3.42 | 3.59 | 3.79 | 4.10 | 4.29 | 4.61 |
| August | 3.44 | 3.60 | 3.80 | 4.11 | 4.30 | 4.65 |
| September | 3.46 | 3.61 | 3.81 | 4.14 | 4.33 | 4.68 |
| October | 3.46 | 3.61 | 3.83 | 4.17 | 4.35 | 4.74 |
| November | 3.48 | 3.63 | 3.85 | 4.17 | 4.39 | 4.81 |
| December | 3.49 | 3.65 | 3.88 | 4.20 | 4.42 | 4.84 |

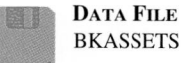

DATA FILE
BKASSETS

*Source:* Standard and Poor's Current Statistics, *January 1998, 3. Reprinted by permission of Standard & Poor's Corporation, a division of the McGraw-Hill Cos.*

(a) Form a new table of "adjusted (i.e., real) values" by multiplying each of the actual monthly values in a particular year of the time series by the quantity $\left(\dfrac{100.0}{\text{CPI}}\right)$,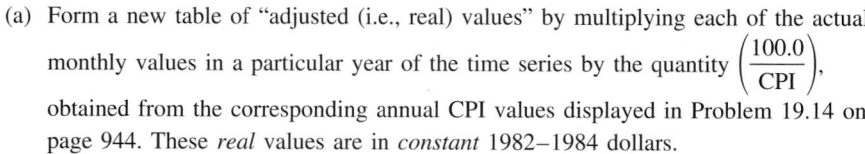
obtained from the corresponding annual CPI values displayed in Problem 19.14 on page 944. These *real* values are in *constant* 1982–1984 dollars.
(b) Plot the adjusted time-series data on a chart.
(c) Develop an exponential trend equation with monthly components to represent the classical multiplicative time-series model.
  (1) What is the fitted value of the series in November 1997?
  (2) What is the fitted value of the series in December 1997?
  (3) What are the forecasts for all 12 months of 1998?
  (4) Interpret the monthly compound growth rate.
  (5) Interpret the January "multiplier."
(d) Go to your library and, using appropriate sources, record the actual data in 1998. Use the 1998 value of the CPI to deflate the actual values. Compare the deflated values with the forecast values in part (c)(3). Discuss.

**19.58** The data in the accompanying table represent the *actual* total monthly sales of mutual funds (in billions of *current* dollars) from January 1990 through December 1997.

*Total monthly market value of mutual funds (in billions of* current *dollars)*

| MONTH | YEAR | | | | | | | |
|---|---|---|---|---|---|---|---|---|
| | 1990 | 1991 | 1992 | 1993 | 1994 | 1995 | 1996 | 1997 |
| January | 13.7 | 13.4 | 32.6 | 36.9 | 56.3 | 33.6 | 61.6 | 80.5 |
| February | 11.8 | 13.9 | 26.2 | 35.4 | 48.0 | 31.1 | 53.2 | 65.3 |
| March | 13.8 | 15.8 | 30.4 | 42.2 | 53.4 | 38.6 | 59.1 | 64.8 |
| April | 14.1 | 20.4 | 29.9 | 40.9 | 40.6 | 37.8 | 62.1 | 64.6 |
| May | 12.5 | 18.3 | 27.0 | 36.9 | 35.0 | 37.2 | 57.5 | 62.5 |
| June | 13.0 | 17.0 | 28.3 | 40.7 | 36.6 | 39.6 | 52.6 | 68.5 |
| July | 12.5 | 19.4 | 32.0 | 43.6 | 31.5 | 40.5 | 52.0 | 77.4 |
| August | 13.2 | 20.0 | 29.8 | 45.6 | 36.8 | 40.4 | 49.4 | 73.2 |
| September | 10.0 | 20.9 | 29.4 | 43.2 | 35.1 | 40.5 | 51.5 | 79.5 |
| October | 10.6 | 24.6 | 28.0 | 45.5 | 32.0 | 40.9 | 53.5 | 79.7 |
| November | 10.4 | 22.7 | 28.7 | 50.7 | 29.5 | 40.6 | 52.6 | 71.5 |
| December | 15.4 | 28.2 | 38.8 | 55.8 | 38.9 | 46.1 | 84.1 | 75.0[a] |

[a] *Initial estimate.*
*Source:* Standard and Poor's Current Statistics, *January 1998, 5. Reprinted by permission of Standard & Poor's Corporation, a division of the McGraw-Hill Cos.*

(a) Form a new table of "adjusted (i.e., real) values" by multiplying each of the actual monthly values in a particular year of the time series by the quantity $\left(\dfrac{100.0}{CPI}\right)$, obtained from the corresponding annual CPI values displayed in Problem 19.14 on page 944. These *real* values are in *constant* 1982–1984 dollars.

(b) Plot the adjusted time-series data on a chart.

(c) Develop an exponential trend equation with monthly components to represent the classical multiplicative time-series model.

   (1) What is the fitted value of the series in November 1997?
   (2) What is the fitted value of the series in December 1997?
   (3) What are the forecasts for all 12 months of 1998?
   (4) Interpret the monthly compound growth rate.
   (5) Interpret the July "multiplier."

(d) Go to your library and, using appropriate sources, record the actual data in 1998. Use the 1998 value of the CPI to deflate the actual values. Compare the deflated values with the forecast values in part (c)(3). Discuss.

**19.59** The data in the accompanying table represent average monthly retail prices (in dollars per gallon) for unleaded regular gasoline in United States cities from January 1990 through December 1997.

(a) Form a new table of "adjusted (i.e., *real*) values" by multiplying each of the *actual* monthly values in a particular year of the time series by the quantity $\left(\dfrac{100.0}{CPI}\right)$, obtained from the corresponding annual CPI values displayed in Problem 19.14 on page 944. These *real* values are in *constant* 1982–1984 dollars.

(b) Plot the adjusted time-series data on a chart.

## Average monthly retail unleaded regular gasoline prices

| | | | | YEAR | | | | |
|---|---|---|---|---|---|---|---|---|
| MONTH | 1990 | 1991 | 1992 | 1993 | 1994 | 1995 | 1996 | 1997 |
| January | 1.042 | 1.247 | 1.073 | 1.117 | 1.043 | 1.129 | 1.129 | 1.261 |
| February | 1.037 | 1.143 | 1.054 | 1.108 | 1.051 | 1.120 | 1.124 | 1.255 |
| March | 1.023 | 1.082 | 1.058 | 1.098 | 1.045 | 1.115 | 1.162 | 1.235 |
| April | 1.044 | 1.104 | 1.079 | 1.112 | 1.064 | 1.140 | 1.251 | 1.231 |
| May | 1.061 | 1.156 | 1.136 | 1.129 | 1.080 | 1.200 | 1.323 | 1.226 |
| June | 1.088 | 1.160 | 1.179 | 1.130 | 1.106 | 1.226 | 1.299 | 1.229 |
| July | 1.084 | 1.127 | 1.174 | 1.109 | 1.136 | 1.195 | 1.272 | 1.205 |
| August | 1.190 | 1.140 | 1.158 | 1.097 | 1.182 | 1.164 | 1.240 | 1.253 |
| September | 1.294 | 1.143 | 1.158 | 1.085 | 1.177 | 1.148 | 1.234 | 1.277 |
| October | 1.378 | 1.122 | 1.154 | 1.127 | 1.152 | 1.127 | 1.227 | 1.242 |
| November | 1.377 | 1.134 | 1.159 | 1.113 | 1.163 | 1.101 | 1.250 | 1.213 |
| December | 1.354 | 1.123 | 1.136 | 1.070 | 1.143 | 1.101 | 1.260 | 1.177 |

**DATA FILE**
UNLDREG

*Source: Bureau of Labor Statistics, U.S. Department of Labor, ser. ID: APU000074714, extracted February 2, 1998.*

(c) Develop an exponential trend equation with monthly components to represent the classical multiplicative time-series model.
   (1) What is the fitted value of the series in November 1997?
   (2) What is the fitted value of the series in December 1997?
   (3) What are the forecasts for all 12 months of 1998?
   (4) Interpret the monthly compound growth rate.
   (5) Interpret the July "multiplier."
(d) Go to your library and, using appropriate sources, record the actual data in 1998. Use the 1998 value of the CPI to deflate the actual values. Compare the deflated values with the forecast values in part (c)(3). Discuss.

## 19.9 PITFALLS CONCERNING TIME-SERIES ANALYSIS

The value of forecasting methodology such as time-series analysis, which uses past and present information as a guide to the future, was recognized and most eloquently expressed more than two centuries ago by the American statesman Patrick Henry, who said:

> *I have but one lamp by which my feet are guided, and that is the lamp of experience.*
> *I know no way of judging the future but by the past.* [Speech at Virginia Convention (Richmond), March 23, 1775]

If it were true (as time-series analysis assumes) that the factors that have affected particular patterns of economic activity in the past and present will continue to do so in a similar manner in the future, time-series analysis by itself would certainly be an appropriate and effective forecasting tool as well as an aid in the managerial control of present activities.

However, critics of classical time-series methods have argued that these techniques are overly naive and mechanical; that is, a mathematical model based on the past should not be used for mechanically extrapolating trends into the future without considering personal judgments, business experiences, or changing technologies, habits, and needs (see Problem 19.71 on page 996). Thus, in recent years econometricians have been concerned with including such factors in developing highly sophisticated computerized models of economic activity for forecasting purposes. Such forecasting methods, however, are beyond the scope of this text (references 2, 3, 6, and 12).

Nevertheless, as we have seen from the preceding sections of this chapter, time-series methods provide useful guides for projecting future trends (on a long- and short-term basis). If used properly, in conjunction with other forecasting methods as well as with business judgment and experience, time-series methods will continue to be an excellent managerial tool for decision making.

 **SUMMARY**

Time-series analysis is a useful tool for managerial planning and control. As we observe in the summary chart for this chapter (see page 995), we have described the components of a time series and have developed numerous approaches for time-series forecasting with annual data, including moving averages, exponential smoothing, the linear, quadratic, and exponential trend models, the Holt-Winters approach, and the autoregressive model. In addition, we have developed a least-squares regression model using dummy variables to represent the seasonal components in a direct approach to forecasting with monthly or quarterly data.

## Key Terms

autoregressive modeling   958
casual forecasting methods   915
classical multiplicative time-series model   916
cyclical component   916
exponential smoothing   923
exponential trend model   938
first-order autocorrelation   958
first-order autoregressive model   959
forecasting   914

Holt-Winters method   951
irregular component   916
linear trend model   932
mean absolute deviation (*MAD*)   973
moving averages   920
principle of parsimony   974
*p*th-order autocorrelation   958
*p*th-order autoregressive model   959
quadratic trend model   936
qualitative forecasting methods   915

quantitative forecasting methods   915
random component   916
seasonal component   982
second-order autocorrelation   958
second-order autoregressive model   959
time series   915
time-series forecasting methods   915
trend   916

## Checking Your Understanding

**19.60**  Why is forecasting methodology so important?

**19.61**  What is a time series?

**19.62**  What are the distinguishing features among the various components of the classical multiplicative time-series model?

**19.63**  What is the difference between moving averages and exponential smoothing?

**19.64**  Under what circumstances is the exponential trend model most appropriate?

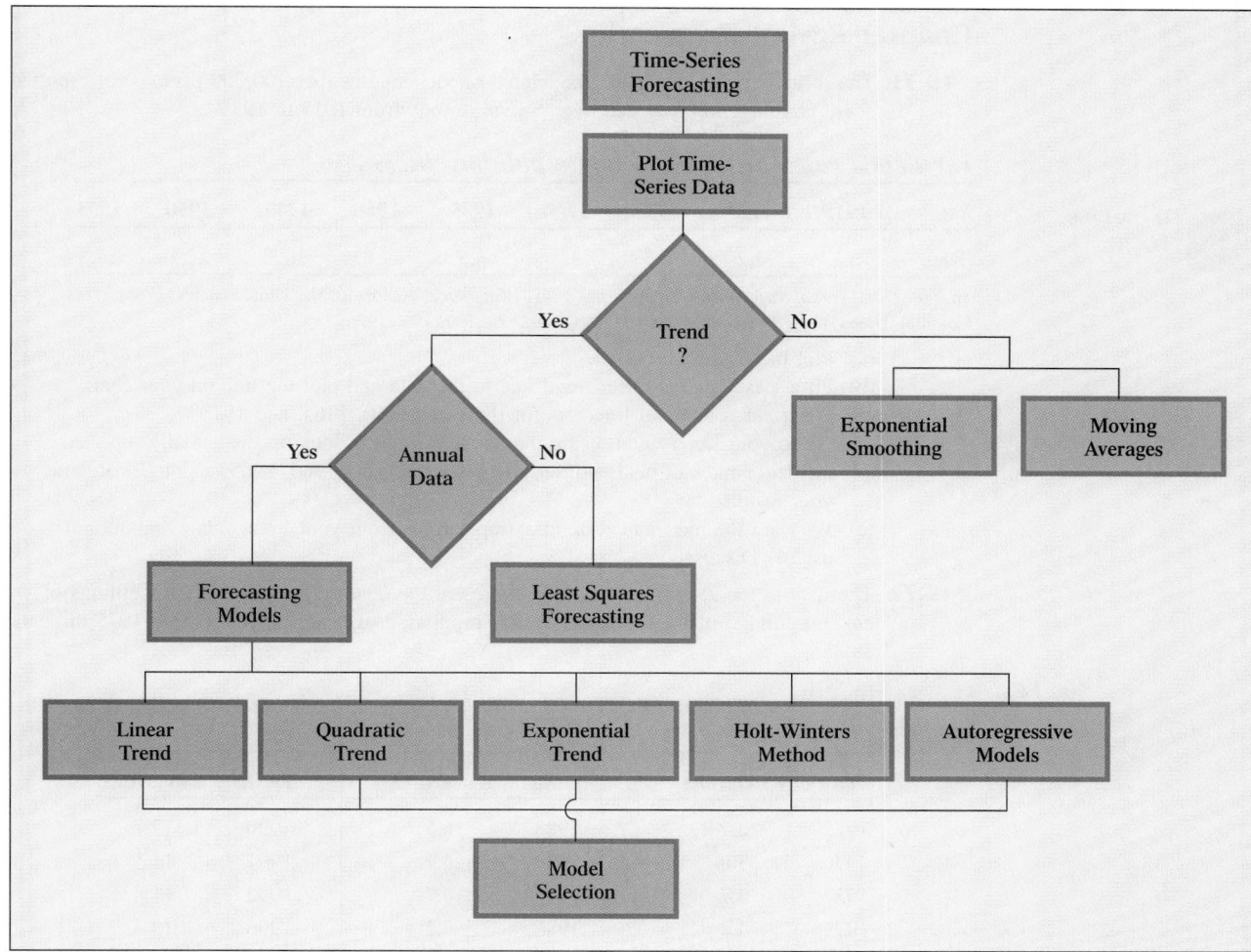

Chapter 19 summary chart

**19.65** How does the least-squares linear trend forecasting model developed in this chapter differ from the least-squares linear regression model considered in chapter 16?

**19.66** What is the difference between exponential smoothing and the Holt-Winters method?

**19.67** How do autoregressive modeling approaches differ from the other approaches to forecasting?

**19.68** What are the alternative approaches to choosing an appropriate forecasting model?

**19.69** What is the major distinction between using $S_{YX}$ and using $MAD$ for evaluating how well a particular model historically fits the data?

**19.70** How does forecasting for monthly or quarterly data differ from forecasting for annual data?

## Chapter Review Problems

**19.71** The following data represent the annual incidence rates (per 100,000 persons) of reported acute poliomyelitis recorded over 5-year periods from 1915 to 1955.

### Incidence rates of reported acute poliomyelitis

**DATA FILE**
POLIO

| YEAR | 1915 | 1920 | 1925 | 1930 | 1935 | 1940 | 1945 | 1950 | 1955 |
|------|------|------|------|------|------|------|------|------|------|
| Rate | 3.1 | 2.2 | 5.3 | 7.5 | 8.5 | 7.4 | 10.3 | 22.1 | 17.6 |

*Source: Data are taken from B. Wattenberg, ed., The Statistical History of the United States: From Colonial Times to the Present, ser. B303, (New York: Basic Books, 1976).*

(a) Plot the data on a chart.
(b) Fit a least-squares linear trend line to the data and plot the line on your chart.
(c) What are your trend forecasts for the years 1960, 1965, and 1970?
(d) Go to your library and, using the above reference, look up the actually reported incidence rates of acute poliomyelitis for the years 1960, 1965, and 1970. Record your results.
(e) Why are the mechanical trend extrapolations from your least-squares model not useful? Discuss.

• **19.72** The data in the accompanying table represent the *actual* gross revenues (in billions of *current* dollars) of the Georgia-Pacific Corporation over the 22-year period 1975 through 1996.

### Actual *gross revenues at Georgia-Pacific Corporation (1975–1996)*

| YEAR | REVENUES | YEAR | REVENUES | YEAR | REVENUES |
|------|----------|------|----------|------|----------|
| 1975 | 2.4 | 1983 | 6.5 | 1990 | 12.7 |
| 1976 | 3.0 | 1984 | 6.7 | 1991 | 11.5 |
| 1977 | 3.7 | 1985 | 6.7 | 1992 | 11.8 |
| 1978 | 4.4 | 1986 | 7.2 | 1993 | 12.3 |
| 1979 | 5.2 | 1987 | 8.6 | 1994 | 12.7 |
| 1980 | 5.0 | 1988 | 9.5 | 1995 | 14.3 |
| 1981 | 5.4 | 1989 | 10.1 | 1996 | 13.0 |
| 1982 | 5.4 |  |  |  |  |

**DATA FILE**
GAPAC

*Source: Moody's Handbook of Common Stocks, 1980, 1989, 1993, 1997. Reprinted by permission of Moody's Investors Service.*

(a) Form a new table of "adjusted (i.e., *real*) values" by multiplying each of the *actual* annual values by the quantity $\left(\dfrac{100.0}{CPI}\right)$, obtained from the corresponding annual CPI values displayed in Problem 19.14 on page 944. These *real* values are in *constant* 1982–1984 dollars.

(b) Plot the adjusted time-series data on a chart.

(c) Fit a linear trend equation to the data.

(d) Fit a quadratic trend equation to the data.

(e) Fit an exponential trend equation to the data.

(f) Use the Holt-Winters method (with $U = .30$ and $V = .30$) to fit the time series.

(g) Fit a third-order autoregressive model and test for the significance of the third-order autoregressive parameter. (Use $\alpha = .05$.)

(h) If necessary, fit a second-order autoregressive model and test for the significance of the second-order autoregressive parameter. (Use $\alpha = .05$.)

(i) If necessary, fit a first-order autoregressive model and test for the significance of the first-order autoregressive parameter. (Use $\alpha = .05$.)

(j) Perform a residual analysis for each of the fitted models in parts (c)–(f) and the most appropriate autoregressive model in parts (g)–(i).

(k) Compute the standard error of the estimate ($S_{YX}$) for each corresponding model in part (j).

(l) Compute the *MAD* for each corresponding model in part (j).

(m) On the basis of your results in parts (j), (k), and (l), along with a consideration of parsimony, which model would you select for purposes of forecasting? Discuss.

(n) Using the selected model in part (m), make an annual forecast from 1997 through 2000.

**19.73** The data in the accompanying table represent the *actual* gross revenues (in billions of *current* dollars) of Philip Morris Companies, Inc., over the 22-year period 1975 through 1996.

## Actual *gross revenues of Philip Morris Companies, Inc.* *(1975–1996)*

| YEAR | REVENUES | YEAR | REVENUES | YEAR | REVENUES |
|------|----------|------|----------|------|----------|
| 1975 | 3.6 | 1983 | 13.0 | 1990 | 51.3 |
| 1976 | 4.3 | 1984 | 13.8 | 1991 | 56.5 |
| 1977 | 5.2 | 1985 | 16.0 | 1992 | 59.1 |
| 1978 | 6.6 | 1986 | 25.9 | 1993 | 60.9 |
| 1979 | 8.1 | 1987 | 28.2 | 1994 | 65.1 |
| 1980 | 9.6 | 1988 | 31.7 | 1995 | 66.1 |
| 1981 | 10.7 | 1989 | 44.8 | 1996 | 69.2 |
| 1982 | 11.6 | | | | |

DATA FILE
PMORRIS

*Source: Moody's Handbook of Common Stocks, 1980, 1989, 1993, 1997. Reprinted by permission of Moody's Investors Service.*

(a) Form a new table of "adjusted (i.e., *real*) values" by multiplying each of the *actual* annual values by the quantity $\left(\dfrac{100.0}{\text{CPI}}\right)$, obtained from the corresponding annual CPI values displayed in Problem 19.14 on page 944. These *real* values are in *constant* 1982–1984 dollars.

(b) Plot the adjusted time-series data on a chart.

(c) Fit a linear trend equation to the data.

(d) Fit a quadratic trend equation to the data.

(e) Fit an exponential trend equation to the data.

(f) Use the Holt-Winters method (with $U = .30$ and $V = .30$) to fit the time series.

(g) Fit a third-order autoregressive model and test for the significance of the third-order autoregressive parameter. (Use $\alpha = .05$.)

(h) If necessary, fit a second-order autoregressive model and test for the significance of the second-order autoregressive parameter. (Use $\alpha = .05$.)

(i) If necessary, fit a first-order autoregressive model and test for the significance of the first-order autoregressive parameter. (Use $\alpha = .05$.)

(j) Perform a residual analysis for each of the fitted models in parts (c)–(f) and the most appropriate autoregressive model in parts (g)–(i).

(k) Compute the standard error of the estimate ($S_{YX}$) for each corresponding model in part (j).

(l) Compute the *MAD* for each corresponding model in part (j).

(m) On the basis of your results in parts (j), (k), and (l), along with a consideration of parsimony, which model would you select for purposes of forecasting? Discuss.

(n) Using the selected model in part (m), make an annual forecast from 1997 through 2000.

**19.74** The data in the accompanying table represent the *actual* gross revenues (in billions of *current* dollars) of McDonald's Corporation over the 22-year-period 1975 through 1996.

**Actual *Gross Revenues at McDonald's Corporation (1975–1996)***

| Year | Revenues | Year | Revenues | Year | Revenues |
|------|----------|------|----------|------|----------|
| 1975 | 1.0 | 1983 | 3.1 | 1990 | 6.8 |
| 1976 | 1.2 | 1984 | 3.4 | 1991 | 6.7 |
| 1977 | 1.4 | 1985 | 3.8 | 1992 | 7.1 |
| 1978 | 1.7 | 1986 | 4.2 | 1993 | 7.4 |
| 1979 | 1.9 | 1987 | 4.9 | 1994 | 8.3 |
| 1980 | 2.2 | 1988 | 5.6 | 1995 | 9.8 |
| 1981 | 2.5 | 1989 | 6.1 | 1996 | 10.7 |
| 1982 | 2.8 | | | | |

*Source:* Moody's Handbook of Common Stocks, *1980, 1989, 1993, 1997. Reprinted by permission of Moody's Investors Service.*

**DATA FILE**
MCDONALD

(a) Form a new table of "adjusted (i.e., *real*) values" by multiplying each of the *actual* annual values by the quantity $\left(\dfrac{100.0}{\text{CPI}}\right)$, obtained from the corresponding annual CPI values displayed in Problem 19.14 on page 944. These *real* values are in *constant* 1982–1984 dollars.

(b) Plot the adjusted time-series data on a chart.

(c) Fit a linear trend equation to the data.

(d) Fit a quadratic trend equation to the data.

(e) Fit an exponential trend equation to the data.

(f) Use the Holt-Winters method (with $U = .30$ and $V = .30$) to fit the time series.

(g) Fit a third-order autoregressive model and test for the significance of the third-order autoregressive parameter. (Use $\alpha = .05$.)

(h) If necessary, fit a second-order autoregressive model and test for the significance of the second-order autoregressive parameter. (Use $\alpha = .05$.)

(i) If necessary, fit a first-order autoregressive model and test for the significance of the first-order autoregressive parameter. (Use $\alpha = .05$.)

(j) Perform a residual analysis for each of the fitted models in parts (c)–(f) and the most appropriate autoregressive model in parts (g)–(i).

(k) Compute the standard error of the estimate ($S_{YX}$) for each corresponding model in part (j).

(l)  Compute the *MAD* for each corresponding model in part (j).

(m)  On the basis of your results in parts (j), (k), and (l), along with a consideration of parsimony, which model would you select for purposes of forecasting? Discuss.

(n)  Using the selected model in part (m), make an annual forecast from 1997 through 2000.

**19.75**  The data in the accompanying table represent the *actual* gross revenues (in billions of *current* dollars) of Sears, Roebuck & Company over the 22-year period 1975 through 1996.

### Actual *gross revenues at Sears, Roebuck & Company (1975–1996)*

| YEAR | REVENUES | YEAR | REVENUES | YEAR | REVENUES |
|------|----------|------|----------|------|----------|
| 1975 | 13.1 | 1983 | 35.9 | 1990 | 56.0 |
| 1976 | 17.7 | 1984 | 38.8 | 1991 | 57.2 |
| 1977 | 19.6 | 1985 | 40.7 | 1992 | 52.3 |
| 1978 | 22.9 | 1986 | 42.3 | 1993 | 50.8 |
| 1979 | 24.5 | 1987 | 48.4 | 1994 | 54.6 |
| 1980 | 25.2 | 1988 | 50.3 | 1995 | 34.9 |
| 1981 | 27.4 | 1989 | 53.8 | 1996 | 38.2 |
| 1982 | 30.0 | | | | |

**DATA FILE**
SEARS

*Source:* Moody's Handbook of Common Stocks, *1980, 1989, 1993, 1997. Reprinted by permission of Moody's Investors Service.*

(a)  Form a new table of "adjusted (i.e., *real*) values" by multiplying each of the *actual* annual values by the quantity $\left(\dfrac{100.0}{\text{CPI}}\right)$, obtained from the corresponding annual CPI values displayed in Problem 19.14 on page 944. These *real* values are in *constant* 1982–1984 dollars.

(b)  Plot the adjusted time-series data on a chart.

(c)  Fit a linear trend equation to the data.

(d)  Fit a quadratic trend equation to the data.

(e)  Fit an exponential trend equation to the data.

(f)  Use the Holt-Winters method (with $U = .30$ and $V = .30$) to fit the time series.

(g)  Fit a third-order autoregressive model and test for the significance of the third-order autoregressive parameter. (Use $\alpha = .05$.)

(h)  If necessary, fit a second-order autoregressive model and test for the significance of the second-order autoregressive parameter. (Use $\alpha = .05$.)

(i)  If necessary, fit a first-order autoregressive model and test for the significance of the first-order autoregressive parameter. (Use $\alpha = .05$.)

(j)  Perform a residual analysis for each of the fitted models in parts (c)–(f) and the most appropriate autoregressive model in parts (g)–(i).

(k)  Compute the standard error of the estimate ($S_{YX}$) for each corresponding model in part (j).

(l)  Compute the *MAD* for each corresponding model in part (j).

(m)  On the basis of your results in parts (j), (k), and (l), along with a consideration of parsimony, which model would you select for purposes of forecasting? Discuss.

(n) Using the selected model in part (m), make an annual forecast from 1997 through 2000.

**19.76** The data given in the accompanying table represent the monthly U.S. production of primary aluminum (in thousands of metric tons), both domestic and foreign ore, from January 1991 through December 1996.

### Monthly U.S. production of primary aluminum (in thousands of metric tons)

| | YEAR | | | | | |
|---|---|---|---|---|---|---|
| **MONTH** | **1991** | **1992** | **1993** | **1994** | **1995** | **1996** |
| January | 349 | 344 | 335 | 292 | 281 | 301 |
| February | 317 | 320 | 292 | 261 | 253 | 283 |
| March | 352 | 343 | 323 | 286 | 280 | 303 |
| April | 340 | 330 | 313 | 269 | 272 | 293 |
| May | 353 | 342 | 325 | 277 | 285 | 303 |
| June | 343 | 330 | 315 | 268 | 277 | 293 |
| July | 354 | 339 | 316 | 275 | 288 | 301 |
| August | 350 | 340 | 302 | 274 | 286 | 302 |
| September | 336 | 330 | 291 | 267 | 280 | 292 |
| October | 347 | 343 | 303 | 277 | 289 | 304 |
| November | 337 | 335 | 287 | 270 | 285 | 295 |
| December | 343 | 347 | 294 | 280 | 299 | 305 |

*Source: U.S. Geological Survey.*

(a) Plot the data on a chart.
(b) Develop an exponential trend equation with monthly components to represent the classical multiplicative time-series model and use this to make forecasts for all 12 months of 1998.
(c) Based on the results of (b), interpret the monthly compound growth rate and the June "multiplier."
(d) Go to your library and, using appropriate sources, record the actual data over all 12 months in 1998. Compare the data with the forecast values in (b). Discuss.
(e) Using the methods in (b), make a forecast for December 2000.

**19.77** The data given in the accompanying table represent the monthly average workweek by production workers in manufacturing from January 1992 through December 1997. This time series is considered to be a leading indicator of business and economic activity in the United States.
(a) Plot the data on a chart.
(b) Develop an exponential trend equation with monthly components to represent the classical multiplicative time-series model and use this to make forecasts for all 12 months of 1998.
(c) Based on the results of (b), interpret the monthly compound growth rate and the January "multiplier."
(d) Go to your library and, using appropriate sources, record the actual data over all 12 months in 1998. Compare the data with the forecasted values in (b). Discuss.
(e) Using the methods in (b), make a forecast for December 2000.

## Monthly average workweek of production workers in manufacturing

| | YEAR | | | | | |
| MONTH | 1992 | 1993 | 1994 | 1995 | 1996 | 1997 |
|---|---|---|---|---|---|---|
| January | 40.8 | 41.3 | 41.7 | 42.2 | 40.1 | 41.8 |
| February | 41.0 | 41.5 | 41.2 | 41.9 | 41.4 | 41.9 |
| March | 41.0 | 41.1 | 42.0 | 41.8 | 41.3 | 42.1 |
| April | 41.0 | 41.6 | 41.9 | 41.5 | 41.5 | 42.1 |
| May | 41.1 | 41.3 | 42.0 | 41.4 | 41.6 | 42.0 |
| June | 41.1 | 41.2 | 42.0 | 41.4 | 41.7 | 41.8 |
| July | 41.1 | 41.4 | 42.0 | 41.3 | 41.6 | 41.8 |
| August | 41.1 | 41.4 | 42.0 | 41.5 | 41.7 | 41.8 |
| September | 41.0 | 41.6 | 41.9 | 41.5 | 41.7 | 41.9 |
| October | 41.1 | 41.5 | 42.1 | 41.5 | 41.7 | 42.0 |
| November | 41.2 | 41.6 | 42.1 | 41.5 | 41.7 | 42.1 |
| December | 41.2 | 41.7 | 42.1 | 41.2 | 42.0 | 42.1[a] |

DATA FILE
WORKWEEK

[a] Initial estimate.

*Source: Standard and Poor's Current Statistics, January 1998, 7. Reprinted by permission of Standard & Poor's Corporation, a division of the McGraw-Hill Cos.*

## Case Study — CURRENCY TRADING

As a member of a financial firm hired by a group of investors to undertake trading in various currencies, you have been assigned the task of studying the long-term trends in the exchange rates of the Canadian dollar, the French franc, the German mark, the Japanese yen, and the English pound.

The data in the following table have been collected for the 31-year period from 1967 to 1997. All currencies are expressed in units per U.S. dollar except the English pound, which is expressed in cents per pound.

### Exchange rates of five currencies in terms of the U.S. dollar

| YEAR | CANADIAN DOLLAR | FRENCH FRANC | GERMAN MARK | JAPANESE YEN | ENGLISH POUND[a] |
|---|---|---|---|---|---|
| 1967 | 1.0789 | 4.921 | 3.9865 | 362.13 | 275.04 |
| 1968 | 1.0776 | 4.953 | 3.9920 | 360.55 | 239.35 |
| 1969 | 1.0769 | 5.200 | 3.9251 | 358.36 | 239.01 |
| 1970 | 1.0444 | 5.529 | 3.6465 | 358.16 | 239.15 |
| 1971 | 1.0099 | 5.510 | 3.4830 | 347.79 | 244.42 |
| 1972 | 0.9907 | 5.044 | 3.1886 | 303.13 | 250.34 |
| 1973 | 1.0002 | 4.454 | 2.6715 | 271.31 | 245.25 |
| 1974 | 0.9780 | 4.811 | 2.5868 | 291.84 | 234.03 |
| 1975 | 1.0175 | 4.288 | 2.4614 | 296.78 | 222.17 |

*continued*

## Exchange rates of five currencies in terms of the U.S. dollar (continued)

| YEAR | CANADIAN DOLLAR | FRENCH FRANC | GERMAN MARK | JAPANESE YEN | ENGLISH POUND[a] |
|------|-----------------|--------------|-------------|--------------|------------------|
| 1976 | 0.9863 | 4.783 | 2.5185 | 296.45 | 180.48 |
| 1977 | 1.0633 | 4.916 | 2.3236 | 268.62 | 174.49 |
| 1978 | 1.1405 | 4.509 | 2.0097 | 210.39 | 191.84 |
| 1979 | 1.1713 | 4.257 | 1.8343 | 219.02 | 212.24 |
| 1980 | 1.1693 | 4.225 | 1.8175 | 226.63 | 232.46 |
| 1981 | 1.1990 | 5.440 | 2.2632 | 220.63 | 202.43 |
| 1982 | 1.2344 | 6.579 | 2.4281 | 249.06 | 174.80 |
| 1983 | 1.2325 | 7.620 | 2.5539 | 237.55 | 151.59 |
| 1984 | 1.2952 | 8.736 | 2.8455 | 237.46 | 133.68 |
| 1985 | 1.3659 | 8.980 | 2.9420 | 238.47 | 129.74 |
| 1986 | 1.3896 | 6.926 | 2.1705 | 168.35 | 146.77 |
| 1987 | 1.3259 | 6.012 | 1.7981 | 144.60 | 163.98 |
| 1988 | 1.2306 | 5.960 | 1.7570 | 128.17 | 178.13 |
| 1989 | 1.1842 | 6.380 | 1.8808 | 138.07 | 163.82 |
| 1990 | 1.1668 | 5.447 | 1.6166 | 145.00 | 178.41 |
| 1991 | 1.1460 | 5.647 | 1.6610 | 134.59 | 176.74 |
| 1992 | 1.2085 | 5.294 | 1.5618 | 126.78 | 176.63 |
| 1993 | 1.2901 | 5.663 | 1.6533 | 111.20 | 150.20 |
| 1994 | 1.3656 | 5.552 | 1.6228 | 102.21 | 153.16 |
| 1995 | 1.3027 | 4.853 | 1.5014 | 103.35 | 152.84 |
| 1996 | 1.3704 | 5.184 | 1.5415 | 115.87 | 171.26 |
| 1997 | 1.4296 | 6.024 | 1.7986 | 130.38 | 165.18 |

[a]In cents per pound.
Source: Board of Governors of the Federal Reserve System, Table B-107.

**DATA FILE**
CURRENCY

You have decided to develop a least-squares forecasting model for the exchange rate of each of these five currencies based on these data and to provide forecasts for the years 1998, 1999, and 2000 for each currency. You are expected to write an executive summary for a presentation that is scheduled to be made to the investor's group next week. In this executive summary you plan to append a discussion regarding possible limitations that may exist in these models.

# THE SPRINGVILLE HERALD CASE

The increase of home-delivery sales has become an important part of a corporate strategic initiative for increased circulation of the newspaper. The marketing department has been assigned a leading role in monitoring this part of the newspaper's circulation, with responsibility for providing future predictions of home-delivery subscriptions and analysis of any trends that might be developing. Toward these goals, data have been collected and are presented in Table SH19.1 that indicate the number of home-delivery subscriptions for a period of the most recent 2-year (24-month) period.

**Table SH19.1**   *Home-delivery subscriptions during a 24-month period*

| MONTH | HOME-DELIVERY SUBSCRIPTIONS | MONTH | HOME-DELIVERY SUBSCRIPTIONS |
|-------|------------------------------|-------|------------------------------|
| 1 | 75,327 | 13 | 90,507 |
| 2 | 77,116 | 14 | 91,927 |
| 3 | 79,341 | 15 | 93,878 |
| 4 | 80,983 | 16 | 94,784 |
| 5 | 82,326 | 17 | 96,109 |
| 6 | 82,879 | 18 | 97,189 |
| 7 | 84,006 | 19 | 97,899 |
| 8 | 85,119 | 20 | 99,208 |
| 9 | 86,182 | 21 | 100,537 |
| 10 | 87,418 | 22 | 102,028 |
| 11 | 88,063 | 23 | 103,977 |
| 12 | 89,444 | 24 | 106,375 |

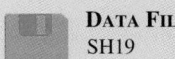

DATA FILE
SH19

## Exercise

**19.1 (a)** Analyze these data and develop a statistical model to forecast home-delivery subscriptions in the future. Be sure to indicate the assumptions of the model and its limitations.

**(b)** Forecast home-delivery subscriptions for the next 4 months.

**(c)** Would you be willing to use the model developed to forecast home-delivery subscriptions 1 year into the future? Explain.

**(d)** Compare the trend in home-delivery subscriptions to the number of new subscriptions per month provided in the table on page 806. What explanation can you provide for any differences?

## References

1. Bails, D. G., and L. C. Peppers, *Business Fluctuations: Forecasting Techniques and Applications* (Englewood Cliffs, NJ: Prentice Hall, 1982).
2. Bowerman, B. L., and R. T. O'Connell, *Forecasting and Time Series*, 3d ed. (North Scituate, MA: Duxbury Press, 1993).
3. Box, G. E. P., and G. M. Jenkins, *Time Series Analysis: Forecasting and Control*, 2d ed. (San Francisco: Holden-Day, 1977).
4. Brown, R. G., S*moothing, Forecasting, and Prediction* (Englewood Cliffs, NJ: Prentice Hall, 1963).
5. Chambers, J. C., S. K. Mullick, and D. D. Smith, "How to Choose the Right Forecasting Technique," *Harvard Business Review* 49, no. 4 (July–August 1971): 45-74.
6. Frees, E. W., *Data Analysis Using Regression Models: The Business Perspective* (Upper Saddle River, NJ: Prentice Hall, 1996).
7. Hanke, J. E., and A. G. Reitsch, *Business Forecasting*, 6th ed. (Upper Saddle River, NJ: Prentice Hall, 1998).
8. Mahmoud, E., "Accuracy in Forecasting: A Survey," *Journal of Forecasting* 3 (1984): 139–159.
9. *Microsoft Excel 97* (Redmond, WA: Microsoft Corp., 1997).
10. *Minitab for Windows Version 12* (State College, PA: Minitab, Inc., 1998).
11. Newbold, P., *Statistics for Business and Economics*, 4th ed. (Englewood Cliffs, NJ: Prentice Hall, 1994).
12. Wilson, J. H., and B. Keating, *Business Forecasting* (Homewood, IL: Irwin, 1990).

## APPENDIX 19.1 — USING MICROSOFT EXCEL FOR TIME-SERIES ANALYSIS

### Using Microsoft Excel for Moving Averages

To illustrate the computation of moving averages, open the **GM.XLS** workbook and click on the **Data** sheet tab. Select **Tools | Data Analysis**. Select **Moving Average** from the Analysis Tools list box. Click the **OK** button. In the Moving Average dialog box, enter **C1:C23** in the Input Range edit box. Select the **Labels in First Row** check box. Enter **3** in the Interval edit box to specify a 3-year moving average. Enter **D2:D23** in the Output Range edit box. Do not check the Chart Output box because the Chart Wizard can be used to plot the output from the moving averages and exponential smoothing procedures. Click the **OK** button. Microsoft Excel generates 3-year moving averages and places them in column C.

Repeat the same procedure for 7-year moving averages, changing the Interval value to **7** and the output range to **E2:E23**. Note that in both cases, Microsoft Excel has improperly placed the moving averages at the end of the series of years and not in the center of the series. (The 3-year averages were placed in the row of the third year—and not in the second—and the 7-year averages were placed in the row of the seventh year—and not in the fourth.) To correct the 3-year moving averages, select cell **D2** (the first cell of the output range). Then select **Edit | Delete** and in the Delete dialog box, select the **Shift Cells Up** option button. Click the **OK** button. Go to cell **D23** (the last cell of the output range) and enter **#N/A**. For the 7-year moving averages, select the cell range **E2:E4** (the first three cells of the output range) and use the same Edit | Delete and Shift Cells Up command. Then enter **#N/A** in the range **E21:E23** (the last three cells of the output range).

### Using Microsoft Excel for Exponential Smoothing

To illustrate the computation of exponentially smoothed values, with the Data sheet still active, select **Tools | Data Analysis** and then select **Exponential Smoothing** from the Analysis Tools list box. Click the **OK** button. In the Exponential Smoothing dialog box, enter **C1:C23** in the Input Range edit box. Select the **Labels** check box. To obtain exponentially smoothed values for $W = .25$, enter **.75** in the Damping factor edit box because the Damping factor is defined as the complement of the smoothing coefficient $(1 - W)$. Enter **F2:F23** in the Output Range edit box. Click the **OK** button.

Repeat the same procedure for $W = .50$, changing the Damping factor to **.50** (i.e., $1 - .50$) and the output range to **G2:G23**. Note that in both cases Microsoft Excel has provided exponentially smoothed forecasts 1 period into the future. To adjust these columns, shift the cells up one row for both columns (as was done for the 3-year moving averages) and then copy the formulas in cells F22 and G22 to cells F23 and G23, respectively.

Now that we have obtained the moving averages and exponentially smoothed values, the Chart Wizard (see appendix 3.1) can be used to obtain the time-series plot similar to the ones shown in Figures 19.3 and 19.4 (pages 923 and 925).

### Using Microsoft Excel for Least-Squares Trend Fitting

In chapters 16–18 we used the Data Analysis tool and its Regression option for the simple linear regression model and for a variety of multiple regression models. In this chapter we developed time-series models assuming a linear, quadratic, or exponential trend. The computations for these models can also be done with the Regression option of the Data Analysis tool. For the linear trend model, see appendix 16.1. For the curvilinear model and the exponential model, see appendix 18.1.

### Using Microsoft Excel for the Holt-Winters Model

Although procedures relating to the Holt-Winters model are not currently included in the Data Analysis tool, Excel formulas and functions can be used. Open the EASTMANK.XLS workbook and with the data sheet active, copy the year and real revenue to columns A and B of a worksheet named

**DataH-W**. Enter the labels **E** in cell C1, **T** in cell D1, **U** in cell E2, and **V** in cell E3. Enter **=B3** in cell C3 to obtain the initial $E$ value. Enter **.3**, the value for $U$, in cell F2. Enter **.3**, the value for $V$, in cell F3. Enter **=B3−B2** in cell D3 to obtain the initial T value. Enter the formula for equation (19.11a), **=$F$2*(C3+D3)+(1−$F$2)*B4** in cell C4. Enter the formula for equation (19.11b), **=$F$3*D3+(1−$F$3)*(C4−C3)** in cell D4. Copy columns C and D down to row 23 *one row at a time*. First copy from C4 to C5, then D4 to D5, C5 to C6, D5 to D6, and so on, through row 23.

## Using Microsoft Excel for Autogressive Modeling

In order to use the Data Analysis Regression option for autoregressive models, we need to create lagged variables. To accomplish this, open the EASTMANK.XLS workbook, and with the Data sheet tab active, copy the coded year and real revenue to columns A and B of a worksheet named DataAR. To create an $X$ variable that is lagged from the real revenue ($Y$) variable by 1 time period, enter the formula **=B2** in cell C3 and copy this formula down the column through row 23. To create an $X$ variable that is lagged from the real revenue ($Y$) variable by 2 time periods, enter the formula **=B2** in cell D4 and copy this formula down the column through row 23. To create an $X$ variable that is lagged from the real revenue ($Y$) variable by 3 time periods, enter the formula **=B2** in cell E5 and copy this formula down the column through row 23. Entering #N/A in cells C2, D2, D3, E2, E3, and E4 that were left empty in the above procedure, although not necessary, will prevent their use in the regression procedures should an incorrect range that included any of these cells be inadvertently entered in the Regression dialog box when using the Regression option of the Data Analysis tool (see appendix 16.1).

## Using Microsoft Excel to Obtain the Mean Absolute Deviation

Equation (19.19) on page 974 was used to compute the mean absolute deviation (*MAD*) for each of the forecasting models we studied. Although the Data Analysis Regression option does not compute the *MAD*, as long as the residuals have been computed, we can use an Excel formula instead. The Excel formula =ABS(residual) can be used for all the models in this chapter except for the exponential trend model. Enter this formula in column D of the sheet that contains the regression output, in the row corresponding to the first observation, and then copy it through the last row of data. Once this has been done, the *MAD* can be computed by entering the formula =AVERAGE(range of absolute residuals) in a row following the last row of the range containing the absolute value of the residuals.

The computation of the *MAD* for the exponential trend model is more complicated because both the predicted real revenue and the residuals are expressed not in real revenue but as the logarithm (to the base 10) of the real revenue. Thus, we first need to compute the predicted real revenue, equal to antilogarithm of the log of predicted real revenue, and subtract this value from the real revenue to obtain the residual.

To obtain the antilog of the log of the predicted value, we can use the Excel POWER function whose format is

```
POWER(number, power)
```

where

$$number = \text{the number you want to raise to a specified power}$$
$$power = \text{the power to which the number is to be raised}$$

For example, =POWER(10,2) equals 100 because the antilog of 2 base 10 is $10^2$, which is 100.

## Using Minitab for Moving Averages

To illustrate the computation of moving averages, open the **GM.MTP** worksheet. Select **Stat | Time Series | Moving Average**. In the Moving Average dialog box, enter **Sales** or **C3** in the Variable edit box. Enter **3** in the *MA* length edit box for a 3-year moving average. Select the **Center the Moving Average** check box. Click the **Results** button. Select the Output, **Summary table and results table** option button. Click the **OK** button. Click the **OK** button again.

## Using Minitab for Exponential Smoothing

To illustrate the computation of exponentially smoothed values, open the GM.MTP worksheet. Select **Stat | Time Series | Single Exp Smoothing**. In the Single Exponential Smoothing dialog box, enter **Sales** or **C3** in the Variable edit box. In the Weight to Use in Smoothing check box, select the **Use:** option button. Enter **.25** for a *W* value of .25. Click the **Options** button. In the Options dialog box, in the Output box, select the **Summary table and results table** option button. In the Set Initial Smoothed Value edit box, enter **1** in the Use Average of first value edit box. Click the **OK** button. Click the **OK** button again.

## Using Minitab for Least-Squares Trend Fitting

In chapters 16–18 we used Minitab for the simple linear regression model and for a variety of multiple regression models. In this chapter we developed time-series models assuming either a linear, quadratic, or exponential trend. The computations for these models can also be done with **Stat | Regression**. For the linear trend model, see appendix 16.2. For the curvilinear model and the exponential model, see appendix 18.2.

## Using Minitab for Autoregressive Modeling

In order to use Minitab for autoregressive models, we need to create lagged variables. To accomplish this, open the **EASTMANK.MTP** worksheet. Select **Stat | Time Series | Lag**. In the Lag dialog box, enter **C5** or **Real Rev** in the Series edit box. For a one-period lag, enter **1** in the Lag edit box. Enter **C6** in the Store Lags in edit box. Click the **OK** button. Repeat this procedure for 2- and 3-period lags by changing the lags to 2 and then 3, respectively, and the Store lags in to C7 and C8, respectively. Once the lagged variables have been stored, use Stat | Regression as in appendix 16.2.

# Answers to Selected Problems (•)

**Chapter 2**

**2.1**    (a)    The types of beverages sold yield categorical or "qualitative" responses.

         (b)    Since no order is implied among the types of beverages, the variable is a nominal level of measurement.

**2.4**    (a)    discrete numerical, ratio          (g)    categorical, nominal

         (b)    categorical, nominal               (h)    discrete numerical, ratio

         (c)    discrete numerical, ratio          (i)    continuous numerical, ratio

         (d)    continuous numerical, ratio       (j)    categorical, nominal

         (e)    categorical, nominal               (k)    categorical, nominal

         (f)    continuous numerical, ratio

**2.12**    Operational definitions of fast service in a fast-food restaurant will differ. Fast service could be defined in terms of a customer's satisfaction level with service time, the number of minutes elapsed between entering the restaurant and receiving the completed order as measured by the customer, or the number of minutes elapsed between placing and filling the order as measured by the counter clerk.

**2.19**    (a)    Row 29: 12 47 83 76 22 ~~99~~ 65 93 10 ~~65~~ ~~83~~ 61 36 ~~98~~ 89 58 86 92 71

            *Note:* All sequences above 93 and all repeating sequences are discarded.

         (b)    Row 29: 12 47 83 76 22 ~~99~~ 65 93 10 65 83 61 36 ~~98~~ 89 58 86

            *Note:* All sequences above 93 are discarded. Elements 65 and 83 are repeated.

**2.23**    (a)    Since a complete roster of full-time students exists, a simple random sample of 200 students could be taken. If student satisfaction with the quality of campus life randomly fluctuates across the student body, a systematic 1-in-20 sample could also be taken from the population frame. If student satisfaction with the quality of life may differ by gender and by experience/class level, a stratified sample using eight strata, female freshmen through female seniors and male freshmen through male seniors, could be selected. If student satisfaction with the quality of life is thought to fluctuate as much within clusters as between them, a cluster sample could be taken.

         (b)    A simple random sample is one of the simplest to select. The population frame is the registrar's file of 4,000 student names.

         (c)    A systematic sample is easier to select by hand from the registrar's records than a simple random sample, since an initial person at random is selected and then every 20th person thereafter would be sampled. The systematic sample would have the additional benefit that the alphabetic distribution of sampled students' names would be more comparable to the alphabetic distribution of student names in the campus population.

         (d)    If rosters by gender and class designations are readily available, a stratified sample should be taken. Since student satisfaction with the quality of life may indeed differ by gender and class level, the use of a stratified sampling design will not only ensure all strata are represented in the sample, it will generate a more representative sample and produce estimates of the population parameter that have greater precision.

         (e)    If all 4,000 full-time students reside in one of 20 on-campus residence halls, which fully integrate students by gender and by class, a cluster sample should be taken. A cluster could be defined as an entire residence hall, and the students of a single randomly selected residence hall could be sampled. Since the dormitories are fully integrated by floor, a cluster could alternatively be defined as one floor of one of the 20 dormitories. Four floors could be randomly sampled to produce the required 200 student sample. Selection of an entire dormitory may make distribution and collection of the survey easier to accomplish. In contrast, if there is some variable other than gender or class that differs across dormitories, sampling by floor may produce a more representative sample.

**2.46**    (a)    The target population is all customers who, over the past 12 months, purchased a videocassette recorder manufactured by the consumer electronics company.

         (b)    The sample frame is all customers who, over the past 12 months, returned a warranty card from the purchase of a videocassette recorder manufactured by the consumer electronics company.

         (c)    Not all customers routinely return warranty cards. Nonrespondents introduce bias in the results of the survey.

**Chapter 3**

**3.1**    Ordered array: 63 64 68 71 75 88 94

**3.2**    Stem-and-leaf of Finance Scores

| | |
|---|---|
| 5 | 34 |
| 6 | 9 |
| 7 | 4 |
| 8 | 0 |
| 9 | 38 |

$n = 7$

**3.10**    (a)    Ordered array:    4 5 5 6 6 6 6 7 7 7 7 7 7 8 8
    8 8 8 8 8 8 8 9 9 9 9 9 9 10 10
    10 10 10 10 10 10 11 11 12 12 13 13 14 15 15
    15 16 16 18 23

    (b)    Stem-and-leaf of Book Values

| | |
|---|---|
| 0 | 45566667777778888888888999999 |
| 1 | 000000001122334555668 |
| 2 | 3 |

$n = 50$

    (c)    Book values on the New York Stock Exchange are more likely to be low, since they are concentrated below $10. Better than half of the stocks sampled had book values below $10.

    (d)    You are much more likely to find a stock with a book value below $10 than above $20. In fact, 28 of the 50 stocks sampled had book values below $10, compared to one stock with a book value above $20.

**3.15**    (a)–(c)    Width of interval $\cong \dfrac{295{,}000 - 103{,}000}{10} = 19{,}200 \cong 20{,}000$

| Asking Price | Midpoint |
|---|---|
| $100,000 up to $120,000 | $110,000 |
| $120,000 up to $140,000 | $130,000 |
| $140,000 up to $160,000 | $150,000 |
| $160,000 up to $180,000 | $170,000 |
| $180,000 up to $200,000 | $190,000 |
| $200,000 up to $220,000 | $210,000 |
| $220,000 up to $240,000 | $230,000 |
| $240,000 up to $260,000 | $250,000 |
| $260,000 up to $280,000 | $270,000 |
| $280,000 up to $300,000 | $290,000 |

**3.19**    In constructing either a histogram or a polygon, the vertical axis must show the true zero or "origin" so as not to distort or otherwise misrepresent the character of the data.

**3.20**    In constructing an ogive, the vertical axis must show the true zero or "origin" so as not to distort or otherwise misrepresent the character of the data.

**3.23**    (a)    (1)    Width of interval $\cong \dfrac{213 - 82}{5} = 26.2 \cong 30$

| Electricity Costs | Midpoint |
|---|---|
| $80 up to $110 | $ 95 |
| $110 up to $140 | $125 |
| $140 up to $170 | $155 |
| $170 up to $200 | $185 |
| $200 up to $230 | $215 |

(2)    Width of interval $\cong \dfrac{213 - 82}{6} = 21.83 \cong 25$

| Electricity Costs | Midpoint |
|---|---|
| $75 up to $100 | $ 87.50 |
| $100 up to $125 | $112.50 |
| $125 up to $150 | $137.50 |
| $150 up to $175 | $162.50 |
| $175 up to $200 | $187.50 |
| $200 up to $225 | $212.50 |

(3)    Width of interval $\cong \dfrac{213 - 82}{7} = 18.71 \cong 20$

| Electricity Costs | Midpoint |
|---|---|
| $80 up to $100 | $ 90 |
| $100 up to $120 | $110 |
| $120 up to $140 | $130 |
| $140 up to $160 | $150 |
| $160 up to $180 | $170 |
| $180 up to $200 | $190 |
| $200 up to $220 | $210 |

(b)

| Electricity Costs | Frequency |
|---|---|
| $80 up to $100 | 4 |
| $100 up to $120 | 7 |
| $120 up to $140 | 9 |
| $140 up to $160 | 13 |
| $160 up to $180 | 9 |
| $180 up to $200 | 5 |
| $200 up to $220 | 3 |

(c)

| Electricity Costs | Frequency | Percentage |
|---|---|---|
| $80 up to $100 | 4 | 8 |
| $100 up to $120 | 7 | 14 |
| $120 up to $140 | 9 | 18 |
| $140 up to $160 | 13 | 26 |
| $160 up to $180 | 9 | 18 |
| $180 up to $200 | 5 | 10 |
| $200 up to $220 | 3 | 6 |

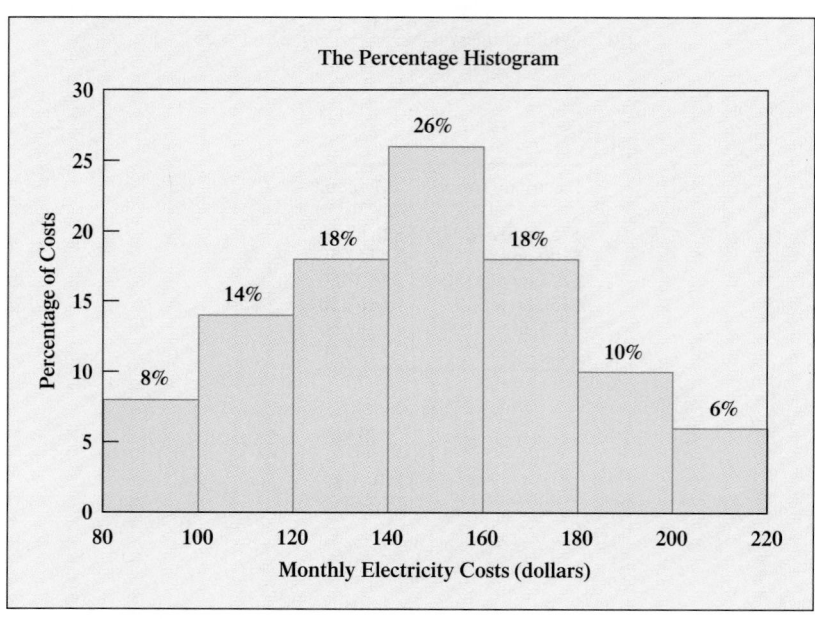

The Percentage Histogram

(f)–(g)

| Electricity Costs | (f) Frequency Less Than | (g) Percentage Less Than |
|---|---|---|
| $100 | 4 | 8 |
| $120 | 11 | 22 |
| $140 | 20 | 40 |
| $160 | 33 | 66 |
| $180 | 42 | 84 |
| $200 | 47 | 94 |
| $220 | 50 | 100 |

(i) Monthly electricity costs are most concentrated between $140 and $160 a month, with better than one-fourth of the costs falling in that interval.

(j) The percentage histogram displayed in part (d) above clearly shows the upper and lower bounds of the seven intervals as well as the percentage of the 50 electricity bills sampled that fall in each interval. In comparison, the percentage polygon [part (e) not displayed] more clearly shows the typical value for each interval (the midpoint), but, because the individual points are not labeled on this graph, only approximates the percentage of the 50 electricity bills sampled that fall in each interval. Both graphs visually depict the distribution of monthly electricity bills clearly. The ogive [part (h) not displayed] enables us to focus on the cumulative distribution, but, because it accrues the numbers of bills over each interval, is not as clear in depicting the distribution of individual monthly electricity bills.

3.25 (a)

| Gasoline Purchases (gals) | Frequency | Percentage |
|---|---|---|
| 9.0– 9.9 | 3 | 12 |
| 10.0–10.9 | 5 | 20 |
| 11.0–11.9 | 9 | 36 |
| 12.0–12.9 | 6 | 24 |
| 13.0–13.9 | 2 | 8 |

(b)

| Gasoline Purchases (gals) | Frequency Less Than | Percentage Less Than |
|---|---|---|
| 9.0– 9.9 | 3 | 12 |
| 10.0–10.9 | 8 | 32 |
| 11.0–11.9 | 17 | 68 |
| 12.0–12.9 | 23 | 92 |
| 13.0–13.9 | 25 | 100 |

(f)    Most gasoline purchases seem to be concentrated between 11 and 11.9 gallons.

**3.29**   (b)   There is strong evidence of a positive linear relationship between $X$ and $Y$—that is, as $X$ increases, $Y$ appears to increase proportionally. The data points are tightly distributed around a straight line with a positive slope.

**3.32**   (b)   Two data values appear to be atypical (Canada and Mexico). There seems to be a slight negative relationship between charges per minute ($X$) and the number of minutes consumers spent on international telephone calls ($Y$).

     (c)   One might expect the higher the charges per minute, the fewer minutes consumers are willing to buy. The scatter diagram does give some indication, but not strong evidence, of this behavior. Telephone rates alone do not provide much incentive to control and thus predict consumer telephone behavior.

**3.35**   (b)   The time-series plot presents strong evidence of a decline in the amount of soft drink filled over time. The individual data points are tightly distributed around a line with a negative slope.

     (c)   In predicting the amount of soft drink filled in the next (51st) bottle, you would predict approximately 1.87 liters because there is a decline in the amount of soft drink filled over time.

     (d)   In 3.28 (h), you predicted 2.00 liters would be filled because it was the center of the most frequently occurring interval. By taking into account the decline in the amount of drink filled over time, your prediction in 3.35 (c) is lower.

**3.38**   (a)

| Category | Frequency | Percentage |
|---|---|---|
| A | 13 | 26 |
| B | 28 | 56 |
| C | 9 | 18 |

**3.43**   (e)   Highway transportation accounted for better than half of the oil consumption in the United States in 1995.

**3.46**   (b)   To reduce the overall number of complaints, the hospital management should focus on improving food service, which accounted for 30.5% of all complaints, followed by timely response to patient buzzers and rudeness of staff, each of which accounted for 18.5% and 16.1% of complaints respectively. Together, the three areas accounted for more than 65% of all complaints registered on the patient-satisfaction survey.

**3.48**   (a)   Table frequencies for all student responses

| Gender | Student Major Categories | | | |
| | A | C | R | Total |
|---|---|---|---|---|
| Male | 14 | 9 | 2 | 25 |
| Female | 6 | 6 | 3 | 15 |
| Total | 20 | 15 | 5 | 40 |

     (b)   Table percentages based on overall student responses

| Gender | Student Major Categories | | | |
| | A | C | R | Total |
|---|---|---|---|---|
| Male | 35.0% | 22.5% | 5.0% | 62.5% |
| Female | 15.0% | 15.0% | 7.5% | 37.5% |
| Total | 50.0% | 37.5% | 12.5% | 100.0% |

(c) Table based on row percentages

| Gender | Student Major Categories | | | |
| | A | C | R | Total |
| --- | --- | --- | --- | --- |
| Male | 56.0% | 36.0% | 8.0% | 100.0% |
| Female | 40.0% | 40.0% | 20.0% | 100.0% |
| Total | 50.0% | 37.5% | 12.5% | 100.0% |

(d) Table based on column percentages

| Gender | Student Major Categories | | | |
| | A | C | R | Total |
| --- | --- | --- | --- | --- |
| Male | 70.0% | 60.0% | 40.0% | 62.5% |
| Female | 30.0% | 40.0% | 60.0% | 37.5% |
| Total | 100.0% | 100.0% | 100.0% | 100.0% |

**3.50** (a) Table based on row percentages

| Gender | Mgt | Prof | Sales | Adm | Srv | Prod | Labr | Total |
| --- | --- | --- | --- | --- | --- | --- | --- | --- |
| Male | 15.5% | 14.2% | 14.6% | 6.0% | 7.7% | 21.9% | 20.2% | 100% |
| Female | 17.4% | 19.8% | 13.8% | 30.5% | 6.6% | 1.8% | 10.2% | 100% |
| Total | 16.3% | 16.5% | 14.3% | 16.3% | 7.3% | 13.5% | 16.0% | 100% |

(c) Males are overrepresented in production, with 21.9% of all full-time male employees contrasted to 1.8% of all full-time female employees. Males are underrepresented in the area of administrative support, where only 6.0% of all full-time male employees work contrasted to 30.5% of all full-time female employees.

**3.51** (a) Table based on column percentages

| Financial Conditions | Education Level | | | |
| | H.S. Degree or Lower | Some College | College Degree or Higher | Total |
| --- | --- | --- | --- | --- |
| Worse off now | 21.2% | 24.4% | 8.6% | 18.5% |
| No difference | 24.2% | 45.6% | 14.8% | 26.0% |
| Better off now | 54.7% | 30.0% | 76.7% | 55.5% |
| Total | 100.0% | 100.0% | 100.0% | 100.0% |

(c) Financial conditions were rated as better now than before by a clear majority of the groups with the lowest and highest education levels. But the largest segment of the group with some college rated their financial conditions as no different now than before.

**3.54** (d) The row percentages are useful in showing different satisfaction rates across various banking services.

(f) Customers are not equally satisfied with all banking functions. Better than 91% were satisfied with the automatic teller machine, but only 65.4% were satisfied with waiting time for bank tellers. The bank could significantly improve overall customer satisfaction by improving wait time for tellers.

**3.75** (f) There is a great deal of variation in the number of days it took to resolve customer complaints. Better than one-quarter of all complaints were resolved in less than 20 days, over half within 30 days. But the amount of time to resolution ranged from one day to 165 days, with over 40% of the complaints requiring more than 30 days to settle and 20% requiring more than 60 days to settle.

(g) You should tell the president of the company that over half of the complaints are resolved within a month, but point out that some complaints take as long as three or four months to settle.

**3.76** (f)  Yes, there is a difference in the closing prices of stocks traded on the two exchanges. Better than 60% of the stocks traded on the American Exchange had closing prices that clustered below $10, while only 26% of the stocks traded on the New York Exchange fell in that category. Further, only 12% of the stocks on the American Exchange closed with prices at or above $20 contrasted to 58% of the stocks on the New York Exchange in the same range.

**3.85** (d)  Electrical equipment and parts, toys/games/sporting goods, and apparel/fabrics/fibers were the top three Chinese exports to the United States in 1996, totaling $24.59 billion. In contrast, machinery, mineral/chemical/plastic/rubber goods, and aircraft/spacecraft/parts were the top three U.S. exports to China in 1996, totaling $5.98 billion. Chinese exports to the United States ran more than four times the dollar value of U.S. exports to China.

---

## Chapter 4

**4.2** (a)  Mean = 7          Midrange = (3 + 12)/2 = 7.5
  Median = 7        Midhinge = (4 + 9)/2 = 6.5
  Mode = 7

(b)  Range = 9          Variance = 10.8
  Interquartile range = 5    Standard deviation = 3.286
  Coefficient of variation = (3.286/7) × 100% = 46.94%

(c)  Since the mean equals the median, the distribution is symmetrical.

**4.3** (a)  Mean = 6          Midrange = (0 + 12)/2 = 6
  Median = 7        Midhinge = (3 + 9)/2 = 6
  Mode = 7

(b)  Range = 12          Variance = 16
  Interquartile range = 6    Standard deviation = 4
  Coefficient of variation = (4/6) × 100% = 66.67%

(c)  Since the mean is less than the median, the distribution is left-skewed.

**4.6** (a)

|           | Set 1 | Set 2 |
|-----------|-------|-------|
| Mean      | 4     | 14    |
| Median    | 3     | 13    |
| Mode      | 2     | 12    |
| Midrange  | 6     | 16    |
| Midhinge  | 3.5   | 13.5  |

(b)–(c)  The data values in Set 2 are each 10 more than the corresponding values in Set 1. The measures of central tendency for Set 2 are all 10 more than the comparable statistics for Set 1.

(d)

|                          | Set 1   | Set 2   |
|--------------------------|---------|---------|
| Range                    | 8       | 8       |
| Interquartile range      | 3       | 3       |
| Variance                 | 8.33*   | 8.33*   |
| Standard deviation       | 2.89*   | 2.89*   |
| Coefficient of variation | 72.17%  | 20.62%  |

*Note: Slight differences are due to rounding.*

(e)  Since the mean is greater than the median for each data set, the distributions are both right-skewed.

(f)  Because the data values in Set 2 are each 10 more than the corresponding values in Set 1, the measures of spread among the data values remain the same across the two sets, with the exception of the coefficient of variation. The coefficients of variation are different because the sample standard deviation is divided by the set's mean; in the case of Set 2, the mean is 10 more than the mean for Set 1, resulting in a larger denominator and a smaller coefficient. Set 2 is a reflection of Set 1 simply shifted up the scale 10 units, so the distributions are also reflections of each other.

(g)  Generally stated, when a second data set is an additive shift from an original set:

- the measures of central tendency for the second set are equal to the comparable measures for the original set plus the value, or distance, of the shift;

- the measures of spread for the second set are equal to the corresponding measures for the original set, with the exception of the coefficient of variation;

- the shape of the second distribution will be a reflection of the shape of the original distribution.

**4.9**   (a)    Mean = 473.46        Midrange = (264 + 1,049)/2 = 656.5
                Median = 451             Midhinge = (307.5 + 553.5)/2 = 430.5
                There is no mode.
                The midhinge and the median seem to be better descriptive measures of the data, because they are closer to the observed values than is the midrange.

      (b)    The manufacturer should be interested in characterizing the average number of hours its batteries power a flashlight both for purposes of quality control as well as competitive market value.

      (c)    Range = 785       Variance = 44,422.44       Standard deviation = 210.77

      (d)    Six times the standard deviation is approximately 1,265, which is not equal to the range for this data set (785). The range is 785/210.77 = 3.7 times the standard deviation. The one very large observation (1,049) makes both measures large.

      (e)    From the manufacturer's viewpoint, the worst measure would be to compute the percentage of batteries that last over 400 hours (8/13 = .61). The median (451) and the mean (473.5) are both over 400, and would be better measures for the manufacturer to use in advertisements.

      (f)–(g)

| | Original Data | Altered Data |
|---|---|---|
| Mean | 473.46 | 550.38 |
| Median | 451 | 492 |
| Mode | none | none |
| Midrange | 656.5 | 803.0 |
| Midhinge | 430.5 | 452.0 |
| Range | 785 | 1,078 |
| Variance | 44,422.44 | 99,435.26 |
| Standard deviation | 210.77 | 315.33 |

                All values are significantly higher for the altered data than they are for the original data. The midhinge and the median seem to be better descriptive measures of both the original data as well as the altered data, since they are closer to their respective observed values than are the midranges for the sets. Six times the standard deviation for the altered set is approximately 1,892, which is much larger than its range (1,078). The range is 1,078/315.33 = 3.4 times the standard deviation. The two very large observations in the altered data set (1,049 and 1,342) make both measures large. From the manufacturer's viewpoint, the worst measure remains the percentage of batteries that last over 400 hours (9/13 = .69). The median (492) and the mean (550.38) are both well over 400, and would be better measures for the manufacturer to use in advertisements.

      (h)    The shape of the distribution of the original data is right-skewed, because the mean is larger than the median.

      (i)    The shape of the distribution of the altered data set is right-skewed as well, because its mean is also larger than its median.

**4.11**   (a)    (1)    Mean = 4.287
                (2)    Median = 4.5
                (3)    Midrange = 3.42
                (4)    $Q_1 = 3.20$
                (5)    $Q_3 = 5.55$
                (6)    Midhinge = 4.375
                (7)    Range = 6.08
                (8)    Interquartile range = 2.35
                (9)    Variance = 2.683
                (10)   Standard deviation = 1.638
                (11)   Coefficient of variation = 38.21%

      (b)    Since the mean is less than the median, the distribution is left-skewed.

      (c)    The mean and median are both under 5 minutes and the distribution is left-skewed, meaning that there are more unusually low observations than there are high observations. But six of the 15 bank customers sampled (or 40%) had wait times in excess of 5 minutes. So, although the customer is more likely to be served in less than 5 minutes, the manager may have been overconfident in responding that the customer would "almost certainly" not wait longer than 5 minutes for service.

**4.16**   (a)    Five-number summary: 3 4 7 9 12

(b)

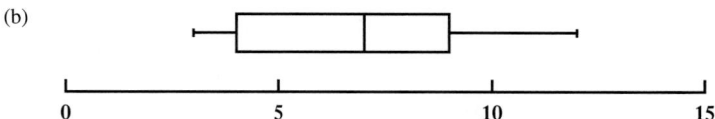

The distribution is almost symmetrical.

(c) The data set is almost symmetrical since the median line almost divides the box in half.

**4.17** (a) Five-number summary: 0 3 7 9 12

(b)

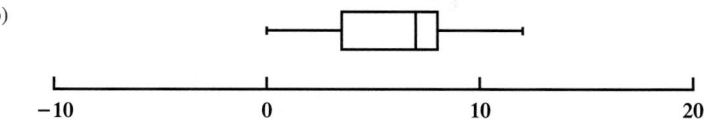

The distribution is left-skewed.

(c) The box-and-whisker plot shows a longer left box from $Q_1$ to $Q_2$ than from $Q_2$ to $Q_3$, visually confirming our conclusion that the data are left-skewed.

**4.20** (a) Five-number summary: 264 307.5 451 553.5 1,049

(b)

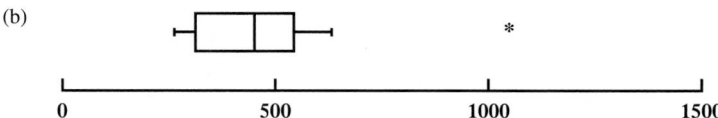

The distribution is right-skewed.

(c) Because the data set is small, one very large value (1,049) skews the distribution to the right.

**4.21** (a) Five-number summary: 1.90 2.28 2.79 3.05 3.25

(b)

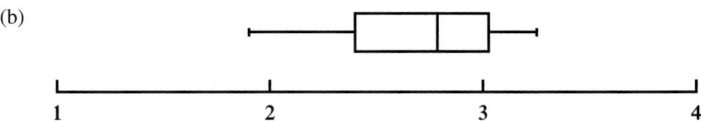

The distribution is slightly skewed to the left.

(c) The data range of 1.35 points in value is sizable given the small percentage yields over which it is calculated. Money market rates do vary among banks.

**4.27** (a) Stem-and-leaf of Quarterly Sales Tax Receipts

```
 5    3
 6    57
 7    3568
 8    04679
 9    02335689
10    00123345567
11    011125668
12    555789
13    00
14    5
15    1
```

(b) Mean = 10.28

(c) $\sigma^2 = 2.177$     $\sigma = 1.475$

(d) (1)  58%     (2)  80%     (3)  96%

(e) These percentages are lower than the empirical rule would suggest.

**4.30** Using Excel,

|   | A | B | C | D |
|---|---|---|---|---|
| 1 | $m_j$ | $f_j$ | $m_j * f_j$ | $(m_j - \overline{X})^2 * f_j$ |
| 2 | 5 | 10 | 50 | 4000 |
| 3 | 15 | 20 | 300 | 2000 |
| 4 | 25 | 40 | 1000 | 0 |
| 5 | 35 | 20 | 700 | 2000 |
| 6 | 45 | 10 | 450 | 4000 |
| 7 | Sums = | 100 | 2500 | 12000 |
| 8 |  | $\overline{X}$ = | 25 |  |
| 9 |  |  | $s^2$ = | 121.2121212 |
| 10 |  |  | $s$ = | 11.00963765 |

(a) Mean $\cong$ 25
(b) Standard deviation $\cong$ 11.01

**4.34** Using Excel,

|   | A | B | C | D | E | F | G |
|---|---|---|---|---|---|---|---|
| 1 | $m_j$ | $f_j$ A | $f_j$ B | $m_j * f_j$ A | $m_j * f_j$ B | $(m_j - \overline{X})^2 * f_j$ A | $(m_j - \overline{X})^2 * f_j$ B |
| 2 | 25 | 8 | 15 | 200 | 375 | 1905.86011 | 2099.58342 |
| 3 | 35 | 17 | 32 | 595 | 1120 | 502.126654 | 107.280302 |
| 4 | 45 | 11 | 20 | 495 | 900 | 229.253308 | 1334.65582 |
| 5 | 55 | 8 | 4 | 440 | 220 | 1697.16446 | 1320.45229 |
| 6 | 65 | 2 | 0 | 130 | 0 | 1206.89981 | 0 |
| 7 | Sums = | 46 | 71 | 1860 | 2615 |  |  |
| 8 |  |  |  | A | B |  |  |
| 9 |  |  | $\overline{X}$ = | 40.434 | 36.831 | A | B |
| 10 |  |  |  | $s^2$ = |  | 123.140097 | 69.4567404 |
| 11 |  |  |  | $s$ = |  | 11.0968508 | 8.33407106 |

|   | **Division A** | **Division B** |
|---|---|---|
| (a) | $\overline{X} \cong 40.434$ | $\overline{X} \cong 36.831$ |
| (b) | $s \cong 11.10$ | $s \cong 8.334$ |

(c) Division B employees have a lower average age than Division A employees. There are more senior employees at Division A.

**4.48** (a) Mean = 57.29     Midrange = (47.57 + 76.41)/2 = 61.99
Median = 55.355     Midhinge = (52.71 + 59.58)/2 = 56.145
Mode = 74.68
(b) Range = 28.84     Variance = 66.53
Interquartile range = 6.87     Standard deviation = 8.16
Coefficient of variation = 14.24%
(c) Five-number summary: 47.57     52.71     55.355     59.58     76.41

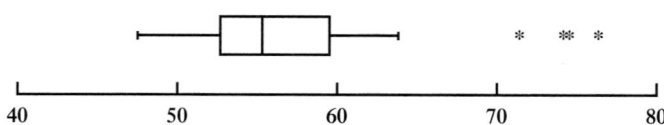

(d) The distribution is right-skewed. Evidence supporting this conclusion includes that the mean is larger than the median and that the distance between the median and $Q_3$ is larger than the distance between $Q_1$ and the median.

(e)  The mode (74.68) should not be provided since it is not truly characteristic of the data set as a whole. The mean (57.29), median (55.355), and midhinge (56.145) are good estimates of the center of the distribution, although the mean is pulled up by five very large values in the data set, as shown in the box-and-whisker plot. The midrange (61.99) is not a good estimate of location, since it is affected by the extremely large values in the set.

**4.49**  (a)

| Stem-and-leaf for Price | | Stem-and-leaf for Cups | | | Stem-and-leaf for Carafe | |
|---|---|---|---|---|---|---|
| 2 | 000025 | Ones | Tenths | | 0 | 789999 |
| 3 | 007 | 8 | 555 | | 1 | 00112244667 |
| 4 | 00 | 9 | 0000555 | | 2 | 0 |
| 5 | 002 | 10 | 555 | | 3 | |
| 6 | 05 | 11 | 000005 | | 4 | 5 |
| 7 | | | $n = 19$ | | | $n = 19$ |
| 8 | 5 | | | | | |
| 9 | 00 | | | | | |
| | $n = 19$ | | | | | |

(b)

| | Price | Cups | Carafe |
|---|---|---|---|
| Mean | 44.53 | 9.89 | 13.63 |
| Median | 40 | 9.5 | 11 |
| Mode | 20 | 11 | 9 |
| Midrange | 55 | 10 | 26 |
| Midhinge | 41 | 10 | 12.5 |

(c)

| Basic Function Stem-and-leaf for Price | | Programmable Stem-and-leaf for Price | |
|---|---|---|---|
| 2 | 000025 | 3 | 07 |
| 3 | 0 | 4 | 00 |
| 4 | | 5 | |
| 5 | 002 | 6 | 5 |
| 6 | 0 | 7 | |
| 7 | | 8 | |
| 8 | 5 | 9 | 00 |
| | $n = 12$ | | $n = 7$ |

| Basic Function Stem-and-leaf for Cups | | | Programmable Stem-and-leaf for Cups | | |
|---|---|---|---|---|---|
| Ones | Tenths | | Ones | Tenths | |
| 8 | 555 | | 8 | | |
| 9 | 0005 | | 9 | 055 | |
| 10 | 55 | | 10 | 5 | |
| 11 | 005 | | 11 | 000 | |
| | $n = 12$ | | | $n = 7$ | |

| Basic Function Stem-and-leaf for Carafe | | Programmable Stem-and-leaf for Carafe | |
|---|---|---|---|
| 0 | 78999 | 0 | 9 |
| 1 | 012467 | 1 | 01246 |
| 2 | | 2 | 0 |
| 3 | | | $n = 7$ |
| 4 | 5 | | |
| | $n = 19$ | | |

(d)

| | Basic Function | | | Programmable | | |
|---|---|---|---|---|---|---|
| | Price | Cups | Carafe | Price | Cups | Carafe |
| Mean | 37.83 | 9.71 | 13.92 | 56 | 10.21 | 13.14 |
| Median | 27.5 | 9.25 | 10.5 | 40 | 10.5 | 12 |
| Mode | 20 | 8.5, 9 | 9 | 40, 90 | 11 | none |
| Midrange | 52.5 | 10 | 26 | 60 | 10 | 14.5 |
| Midhinge | 36 | 9.75 | 12.5 | 63.5 | 10.25 | 13 |

(e)

| | Price | Cups | Carafe |
|---|---|---|---|
| Range | 70 | 3 | 38 |
| Interquartile range | 38 | 2 | 7 |
| Variance | 575.71 | 1.07 | 69.69 |
| Standard deviation | 23.99 | 1.04 | 8.35 |
| Coefficient of variation | 53.89% | 10.46% | 61.24% |

(f)

| | Basic Function | | |
|---|---|---|---|
| | Price | Cups | Carafe |
| Range | 65 | 3 | 38 |
| Interquartile range | 32 | 2.5 | 7 |
| Variance | 451.06 | 1.25 | 105.72 |
| Standard deviation | 21.24 | 1.12 | 10.28 |
| Coefficient of variation | 56.14% | 11.51% | 73.88% |

| | Programmable | | |
|---|---|---|---|
| | Price | Cups | Carafe |
| Range | 60 | 2 | 11 |
| Interquartile range | 53 | 1.5 | 6 |
| Variance | 657 | 0.74 | 14.81 |
| Standard deviation | 25.63 | 0.86 | 3.85 |
| Coefficient of variation | 45.77% | 8.41% | 29.28% |

(g) **Price:** Since the mean is greater than the median price for coffeemakers, the distribution of prices is right-skewed.
**Cup capacity:** Although the mean cup capacity (9.89) is just slightly higher than the median capacity (9.5), the distance from the first quartile to the median is one third of the distance from the median to the third quartile. The distribution is right-skewed.
**Carafe replacement cost:** The distribution of carafe replacement costs is right-skewed.

(i) Box-and-whisker plot for **Prices**

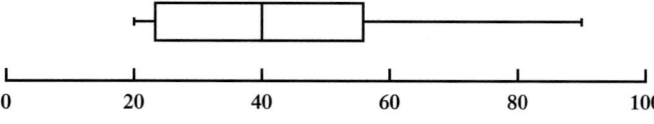

Box-and-whisker plot for **Cup Capacity**

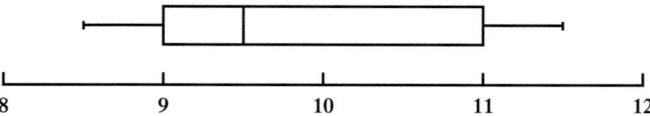

Box-and-whisker plot for **Carafe Replacement Cost**

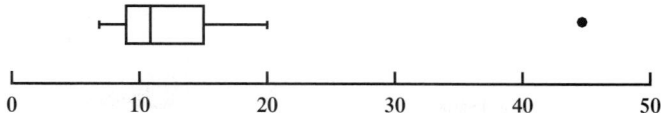

(j)  Box-and-whisker plot for **Prices, Basic Function**

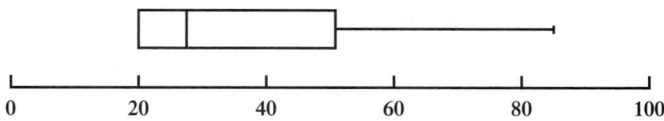

Box-and-whisker plot for **Prices, Programmable**

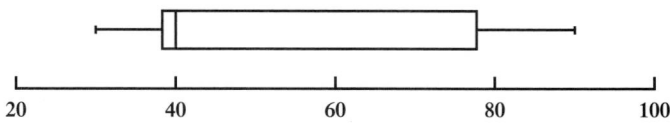

Box-and-whisker plot for **Cup Capacity, Basic Function**

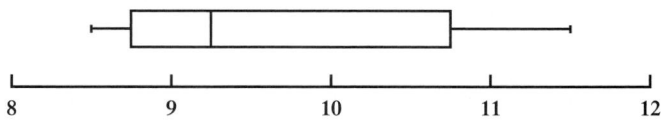

Box-and-whisker plot for **Cup Capacity, Programmable**

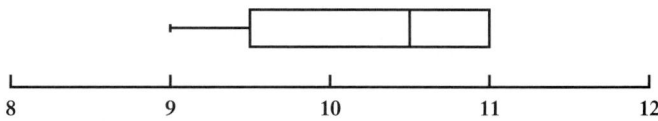

Box-and-whisker plot for **Carafe Replacement Cost, Basic Function**

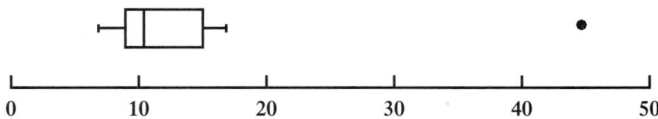

Box-and-whisker plot for **Carafe Replacement Cost, Programmable**

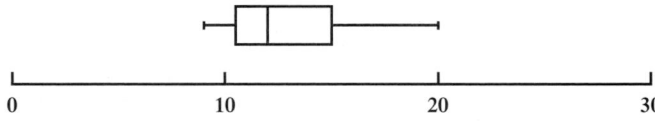

(k)  For programmable coffeemakers, the upper half of the distribution of prices is more dispersed and the cup capacity tends to be higher on average. The extreme value ($45) greatly affects the mean carafe replacement cost for basic coffeemakers.

**4.50**  (b)  Price of portable CDs is a right-skewed distribution, with a large range ($215). Price has a large standard deviation (62.3) in comparison to its mean (148.23), yielding a coefficient of variation of 42.03%. The performance scores on portable CDs is relatively symmetrical with much less dispersion among the players than price shows. Its coefficient of variation is less than 15%. Battery life is relatively symmetrical but has a higher coefficient of variation (33.6%), reflecting the small size of the mean (7.20) relative to its standard deviation (2.42). Battery cost per hour is right-skewed with moderate level of dispersion of data values around its mean.

**4.51** (a)

|       |                          | Office I | Office II |
|-------|--------------------------|----------|-----------|
| (1)   | Mean                     | 2.214    | 2.012     |
| (2)   | Median                   | 1.54     | 1.505     |
| (3)   | Midrange                 | 3.42     | 3.82      |
| (4)   | $Q_1$                    | 0.93     | 0.6       |
| (5)   | $Q_3$                    | 3.93     | 3.75      |
| (6)   | Midhinge                 | 2.43     | 2.175     |
| (7)   | Range                    | 5.8      | 7.47      |
| (8)   | Interquartile range      | 3        | 3.15      |
| (9)   | Variance                 | 2.952    | 3.579     |
| (10)  | Standard deviation       | 1.718    | 1.892     |
| (11)  | Coefficient of variation | 77.60%   | 94.04%    |

(b) Box-and-whisker plot for Office I

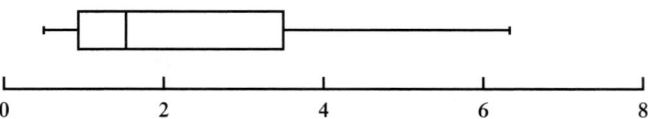

Box-and-whisker plot for Office II

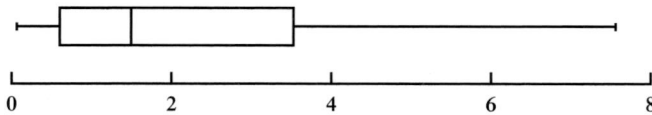

(c) Times to clear problems at both central offices are right-skewed.
(d) Times to clear problems for Office I are less dispersed about the mean than times to clear problems for Office II, even though the average for Office I times is higher (2.214) than that for Office II (2.012).
(e) If the value 7.55 were incorrectly recorded as 27.55, the mean would be one minute higher (from 2.012 to 3.012) and the standard deviation would be over three times as large (from 1.892 to 5.936).

**Chapter 5**

**5.1** (a) Simple events include tossing a head or tossing a tail.
(b) Joint events include tossing two heads (HH), a head followed by a tail (HT), a tail followed by a head (TH), and two tails (TT).
(c) Tossing a tail on the first toss

**5.4** (a) $\dfrac{40}{100} = \dfrac{2}{5} = 0.4$   (f) $\dfrac{35}{100} = \dfrac{7}{20} = 0.35$

(b) $\dfrac{35}{100} = \dfrac{7}{20} = 0.35$   (g) $\dfrac{40}{100} + \dfrac{35}{100} - \dfrac{10}{100} = \dfrac{65}{100} = \dfrac{13}{20} = 0.65$

(c) $\dfrac{60}{100} = \dfrac{3}{5} = 0.6$   (h) $\dfrac{40}{100} + \dfrac{65}{100} - \dfrac{30}{100} = \dfrac{75}{100} = \dfrac{3}{4} = 0.75$

(d) $\dfrac{10}{100} = \dfrac{1}{10} = 0.1$   (i) $\dfrac{60}{100} + \dfrac{65}{100} - \dfrac{35}{100} = \dfrac{90}{100} = \dfrac{9}{10} = 0.9$

(e) $\dfrac{30}{100} = \dfrac{3}{10} = 0.3$

**5.8** (a) Since simple events have only one criterion specified, an example could be any one of the following:
(1) Having a bank credit card,

(2) Not having a bank credit card,
(3) Having a travel/entertainment credit card,
(4) Not having a travel/entertainment credit card.

(b)  Since joint events specify two criteria simultaneously, an example could be any one of the following:
(1) Having a bank credit card and not having a travel/entertainment credit card,
(2) Not having a bank credit card and not having a travel/entertainment credit card,
(3) Having a bank credit card and having a travel/entertainment credit card,
(4) Not having a bank credit card and having a travel/entertainment credit card.

(c)  "Not having a bank credit card" is the complement of "having a bank credit card," since it involves all events other than having a bank credit card.

(d)  Having a bank credit card and having a travel/entertainment credit card is a joint event because two criteria are specified simultaneously.

(e)  $P$(has a bank credit card) $= 120/200 = 3/5 = 0.6$

(f)  $P$(has a travel/entertainment credit card) $= 75/200 = 3/8 = 0.375$

(g)  $P$(has a bank credit card *and* a travel/entertainment credit card) $= 60/200 = 3/10 = 0.3$

(h)  $P$(does not have a bank credit card *and* does not have a travel/entertainment credit card) $= 65/200 = 13/40 = 0.325$

(i)  $P$(has a bank credit card *or* has a travel/entertainment credit card) $=$
$$\frac{120}{200} + \frac{75}{200} - \frac{60}{200} = \frac{135}{200} = \frac{27}{40} = 0.675$$

(j)  $P$(does not have a bank credit card *or* has a travel/entertainment credit card) $=$
$$\frac{80}{200} + \frac{75}{200} - \frac{15}{200} = \frac{140}{200} = \frac{7}{10} = 0.7$$

**5.10**  (a)

| Enjoy Clothes Shopping | Male | Female | Total |
|---|---|---|---|
| Yes | 136 | 224 | 360 |
| No | 104 | 36 | 140 |
| Total | 240 | 260 | 500 |

(b)  Since simple events have only one criterion specified, an example could be any one of the following:
(1) Being a male,
(2) Being a female,
(3) Enjoying clothes shopping,
(4) Not enjoying clothes shopping.

(c)  Since joint events specify two criteria simultaneously, an example could be any one of the following:
(1) Being a male and enjoying clothes shopping,
(2) Being a male and not enjoying clothes shopping,
(3) Being a female and enjoying clothes shopping,
(4) Being a female and not enjoying clothes shopping.

(d)  "Not enjoying clothes shopping" is the complement of "enjoying shopping for clothes," since it involves all events other than enjoying clothes shopping.

(e)  $P$(male) $= 240/500 = 12/25 = 0.48$

(f)  $P$(enjoys clothes shopping) $= 360/500 = 18/25 = 0.72$

(g)  $P$(female *and* enjoys clothes shopping) $= 224/500 = 56/125 = 0.448$

(h)  $P$(male *and* does not enjoy clothes shopping) $= 104/500 = 26/125 = 0.208$

(i)  $P$(female *or* enjoys clothes shopping) $= 396/500 = 99/125 = 0.792$

(j)  $P$(male *or* does not enjoy clothes shopping) $= 276/500 = 69/125 = 0.552$

(k)  $P$(male *or* female) $= 500/500 = 1.00$

**5.14**  (a)  $P(A \mid B) = 10/35 = 2/7 = 0.2857$
(b)  $P(A \mid B') = 30/65 = 6/13 = 0.4615$
(c)  $P(A' \mid B') = 35/65 = 7/13 = 0.5385$
(d)  Since $P(A \mid B) = 0.2857$ and $P(A) = 0.40$, events $A$ and $B$ are not statistically independent.

**5.15**  $P(A \mid B) = \dfrac{P(A \text{ and } B)}{P(B)} = \dfrac{0.4}{0.8} = \dfrac{1}{2} - 0.5$

**5.18**  (a)  $P$(has travel/entertainment credit card | has bank credit card) $= 60/120 = 1/2 = 0.5$
(b)  $P$(has bank credit card | does not have travel/entertainment credit card) $= 60/125 = 12/25 = 0.48$
(c)  Since $P$(has travel/entertainment credit card | has bank credit card) $= 60/120$ or 0.5 and $P$(has travel/entertainment credit card) $= 75/200$ or 0.375, the two events are not statistically independent.

**5.20** (a) *P*(does not enjoy clothes shopping | female) = 36/260 = 9/65 = 0.1385

(b) *P*(male | enjoys clothes shopping) = 136/360 = 34/90 = 0.378

(c) Since *P*(male | enjoys clothes shopping) = 0.378 and *P*(male) = 240/500 or 0.48, the two events are not statistically independent.

**5.25** (a) (1) $P(2 \text{ right-handed gloves}) = \frac{7}{9} \times \frac{6}{8} = \frac{42}{72} = \frac{7}{12} = 0.5833$

(2) $P(1 \text{ right-handed and 1 left-handed glove}) = \frac{7}{9} \times \frac{2}{8} + \frac{2}{9} \times \frac{7}{8} = \frac{28}{72} = \frac{7}{8} = 0.3889$

(b) $P(3 \text{ left-handed gloves}) = 0$

(c) (a1) $P(2 \text{ right-handed gloves}) = \frac{7}{9} \times \frac{7}{9} = \frac{49}{81} = 0.6049$

(b) $P(3 \text{ left-handed gloves}) = \frac{2}{9} \times \frac{2}{9} \times \frac{2}{9} = \frac{8}{729} = 0.011$

**5.26**

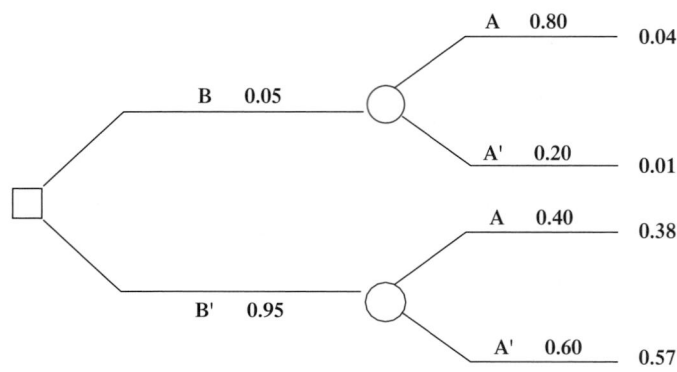

$$P(B \mid A) = \frac{P(A \mid B) \times P(B)}{P(A \mid B) \times P(B) + P(A \mid B') \times P(B')}$$

$$= \frac{0.8 \times 0.05}{0.8 \times 0.05 + 0.4 \times 0.95} = \frac{0.04}{0.42} = 0.095$$

**5.29** (a) *H* = husband watching    *W* = wife watching

$$P(H \mid W) = \frac{P(W \mid H) \times P(H)}{P(W \mid H) \times P(H) + P(W \mid H') \times P(H')}$$

$$= \frac{0.4 \times 0.6}{0.4 \times 0.6 + 0.3 \times 0.4} = \frac{0.24}{0.36} = \frac{2}{3} = 0.667$$

(b) *P*(*W*) = 0.24 + 0.12 = 0.36

**5.32** (a) *P*(A rating | issued by city) = 0.35/0.56 = 0.625

(b) *P*(issued by city) = 0.5(0.7) + 0.6(0.2) + 0.9(0.1) = 0.56

(c) *P*(issued by suburb) = 0.4(0.7) + 0.2(0.2) + 0.05(0.1) = 0.325

**5.43** (a) Since simple events have only one criterion specified, an example could be any one of the following:
(1) Being filled by machine I,
(2) Being filled by machine II,
(3) Being a conforming bottle,
(4) Being a nonconforming bottle.

(b) Since joint events specify two criteria simultaneously, an example could be
(1) Being filled by machine I and being a conforming bottle,
(2) Being filled by machine I and being a nonconforming bottle,
(3) Being filled by machine II and being a conforming bottle,
(4) Being filled by machine II and being a nonconforming bottle.

(c) (1) *P*(nonconforming bottle) = 0.01 + 0.025 = 0.035
(2) *P*(machine II) = 0.5
(3) *P*(machine I *and* conforming bottle) = 0.49
(4) *P*(machine II *and* conforming bottle) = 0.475

        (5)    $P$(machine I *or* conforming bottle) = 0.5 + 0.475 = 0.975

  (d)   $P$(nonconforming | machine II) = 0.02

  (e)   $P$(machine II | nonconforming) = 0.01/0.035 = 0.2857

  (f)   The conditions are switched. Part (d) answers $P(A \mid B)$ and part (e) answers $P(B \mid A)$.

**5.46**   (a)   (1)   $P$(dessert) = 136/600 = 17/75 = 0.227

             (2)   $P$(no beef entrée) = 413/600 = 0.688

             (3)   $P$(dessert *or* beef entrée) = 252/600 = 21/50 = 0.42

             (4)   $P$(female *and* no dessert) = 240/600 = 2/5 = 0.4

             (5)   $P$(dessert *and* beef entrée) = 71/600 = 0.118

             (6)   $P$(female *or* no dessert) = 504/600 = 21/25 = 0.84

  (b)   $P$(no dessert | female) = 240/280 = 6/7 = 0.8571

  (c)   $P$(dessert | beef entrée) = 71/187 = 0.3797

  (d)   Not statistically independent

  (e)   Not statistically independent

---

## Chapter 6

**6.1**   (a)

| Distribution A | | | Distribution B | | |
|---|---|---|---|---|---|
| X | P(X) | X*P(X) | X | P(X) | X*P(X) |
| 0 | 0.50 | 0.00 | 0 | 0.05 | 0.00 |
| 1 | 0.20 | 0.20 | 1 | 0.10 | 0.10 |
| 2 | 0.15 | 0.30 | 2 | 0.15 | 0.30 |
| 3 | 0.10 | 0.30 | 3 | 0.20 | 0.60 |
| 4 | 0.05 | 0.20 | 4 | 0.50 | 2.00 |
| | 1.00 | 1.00 | | 1.00 | 3.00 |
| | $\mu = 1.00$ | | | $\mu = 3.00$ | |

  (b)

| Distribution A | | | |
|---|---|---|---|
| X | $(X - \mu)^2$ | P(X) | $(X - \mu)^2*P(X)$ |
| 0 | $(-1)^2$ | 0.50 | 0.50 |
| 1 | $(0)^2$ | 0.20 | 0.00 |
| 2 | $(1)^2$ | 0.15 | 0.15 |
| 3 | $(2)^2$ | 0.10 | 0.40 |
| 4 | $(3)^2$ | 0.05 | 0.45 |

$$\sigma^2 = 1.50$$
$$\sigma = \sqrt{\Sigma(X - \mu)^2 \times P(X)} = 1.22$$

| Distribution B | | | |
|---|---|---|---|
| X | $(X - \mu)^2$ | P(X) | $(X - \mu)^2*P(X)$ |
| 0 | $(-3)^2$ | 0.05 | 0.45 |
| 1 | $(-2)^2$ | 0.10 | 0.40 |
| 2 | $(-1)^2$ | 0.15 | 0.15 |
| 3 | $(0)^2$ | 0.20 | 0.00 |
| 4 | $(1)^2$ | 0.50 | 0.50 |

$$\sigma^2 = 1.50$$
$$\sigma = \sqrt{\Sigma(X - \mu)^2 \times P(X)} = 1.22$$

  (c)   **Distribution A:** Because the mean of 1 is greater than the median of 0, the distribution is right-skewed.
          **Distribution B:** Because the mean of 3 is less than the median of 4, the distribution is left-skewed.

**6.4** (a)–(b)

| $X$ | $P(X)$ | $X*P(X)$ | $(X - \mu)^2$ | $(X - \mu)^2*P(X)$ |
|-----|--------|----------|---------------|---------------------|
| 0 | 0.10 | 0.00 | 4 | 0.40 |
| 1 | 0.20 | 0.20 | 1 | 0.20 |
| 2 | 0.45 | 0.90 | 0 | 0.00 |
| 3 | 0.15 | 0.45 | 1 | 0.15 |
| 4 | 0.05 | 0.20 | 4 | 0.20 |
| 5 | 0.05 | 0.25 | 9 | 0.45 |
| | **(a) Mean =** | **2.00** | variance = | 1.40 |
| | | | **(b) Stdev =** | **1.18321596** |

**6.7**  (a) 0.5997      (d) 0.4018
       (b) 0.0016      (e) 0.3874
       (c) 0.0439

**6.11**  If $p = 0.2$ and $n = 10$,
 (a)  $P(X = 0) = 0.1074$
 (b)  $P(X = 2) = 0.3020$
 (c)  $P(X \geq 2) = 1 - [P(X = 0) + P(X = 1)] = 1 - [0.1074 + 0.2684] = 0.6242$
 (d)  $P(X \leq 2) = P(X = 0) + P(X = 1) + P(X = 2)$
      $= 0.1074 + 0.2684 + 0.3020 = 0.6778$
 (e)  If $p = 0.2$ and $n = 20$,
    (a)  $P(X = 0) = 0.0115$
    (b)  $P(X = 2) = 0.1369$
    (c)  $P(X \geq 2) = 1 - [0.0115 + 0.0576] = 0.9309$
    (d)  $P(X \leq 2) = 0.0115 + 0.0576 + 0.1369 = 0.2060$
 (f)

| | If $p = 0.1$ and $n = 10$, | If $p = 0.1$ and $n = 20$ |
|---|---|---|
| (a) $P(X = 0)$ | 0.3487 | 0.1216 |
| (b) $P(X = 2)$ | 0.1937 | 0.2852 |
| (c) $P(X \geq 2)$ | 0.2639 | 0.6082 |
| (d) $P(X \leq 2)$ | 0.9298 | 0.6770 |

**6.12**  (a)  If $p = 0.7$ and $n = 5$,
      (1)  $P(X = 5) = 0.1681$
      (2)  $P(X \geq 3) = P(X = 3) + P(X = 4) + P(X = 5)$
           $= 0.3087 + 0.3601 + 0.1681 = 0.8369$
      (3)  $P(X < 2) = P(X = 0) + P(X = 1) = 0.0024 + 0.0283 = 0.0307$
 (b)  Two assumptions: (1) Independence of the repairs, (2) Only two outcomes—repair accomplished same day or repair not accomplished same day.
 (c)  Mean: $\mu = 3.5$    Standard deviation: $\sigma = 1.0247$
 (d)  If $p = 0.8$ and $n = 5$,
      (1)  $P(X = 5) = 0.3277$
      (2)  $P(X \geq 3) = P(X = 3) + P(X = 4) + P(X = 5)$
           $= 0.2048 + 0.4096 + 0.3277 = 0.9421$
      (3)  $P(X < 2) = P(X = 0) + P(X = 1) = 0.0003 + 0.0064 = 0.0067$
           Mean: $\mu = 4$    Standard deviation: $\sigma = 0.894$
 (e)  The larger $p$ is, the more likely it is that troubles reported on a given day will be repaired on the same day, and the less likely it is that troubles reported on a given day will not be repaired on the same day.

**6.14**  (a)  Using the equation, if $\lambda = 2.5$, $P(X = 2) = \dfrac{e^{-2.5} \times (2.5)^2}{2!} = 0.2565$
 (b)  If $\lambda = 8.0$, $P(X = 8) = 0.1396$
 (c)  If $\lambda = 0.5$, $P(X = 1) = 0.3033$
 (d)  If $\lambda = 3.7$, $P(X = 0) = 0.0247$
 (e)  If $\lambda = 4.4$, $P(X = 7) = 0.0778$

**6.16**  (a)  $\lambda = 3.1$, $P(X < 3) = P(X = 0) + P(X = 1) + P(X = 2)$
       $= 0.0450 + 0.1397 + 0.2165 = 0.4012$
 (b)  $P(X = 3) = 0.2237$
 (c)  $P(X \geq 3) = 1 - [P(X < 3)] = 0.5988$
 (d)  $P(X > 3) = P(X \geq 3) - P(X = 3) = 0.5988 - 0.2237 = 0.3751$

**6.18**  (a)  If $\lambda = 6.0$, $P(X < 5) = 0.0025 + 0.0149 + 0.0446 + 0.0892 + 0.1339 = 0.2851$
 (b)  $P(X = 5) = 0.1606$
 (c)  $P(X \geq 5) = 1 - P(X < 5) = 1 - 0.2851 = 0.7149$
 (d)  $P(X = 4) + P(X = 5) = 0.1339 + 0.1606 = 0.2945$
 (e)  If $\lambda = 5.0$,

(1) $P(X < 5) = 0.2650$
(2) $P(X = 5) = 0.1755$
(3) $P(X \geq 5) = 0.7350$
(4) $P(X = 4) + P(X = 5) = 0.3510$

**6.22** (a) $P(X = 3) = \dfrac{\dbinom{5}{3} \times \dbinom{10-5}{4-3}}{\dbinom{10}{4}} = \dfrac{\dfrac{5 \times 4 \times 3!}{3! \times 2 \times 1} \times \dfrac{5 \times 4!}{4! \times 1!}}{\dfrac{10 \times 9 \times 8 \times 7 \times 6!}{6! \times 4 \times 3 \times 2 \times 1}} = \dfrac{5}{3 \times 7} = 0.2381$

(b) $P(X = 1) = \dfrac{\dbinom{3}{1} \times \dbinom{6-3}{4-1}}{\dbinom{6}{4}} = \dfrac{\dfrac{3 \times 2!}{2! \times 1} \times \dfrac{3!}{3! \times 0!}}{\dfrac{6 \times 5 \times 4!}{4! \times 2 \times 1}} = \dfrac{1}{5} = 0.2$

(c) $P(X = 0) = \dfrac{\dbinom{3}{0} \times \dbinom{12-3}{5-0}}{\dbinom{12}{5}} = \dfrac{\dfrac{3!}{3! \times 0!} \times \dfrac{9 \times 8 \times 7 \times 6 \times 5!}{5! \times 4 \times 3 \times 2 \times 1}}{\dfrac{12 \times 11 \times 10 \times 9 \times 8 \times 7!}{7! \times 5 \times 4 \times 3 \times 2 \times 1}} = \dfrac{7}{44} = 0.1591$

(d) $P(X = 3) = \dfrac{\dbinom{3}{3} \times \dbinom{7-0}{3-3}}{\dbinom{10}{3}} = \dfrac{\dfrac{3!}{3! \times 0!} \times \dfrac{7!}{7! \times 0!}}{\dfrac{10 \times 9 \times 8 \times 7!}{7! \times 3 \times 2 \times 1}} = \dfrac{1}{120} = 0.0083$

**6.24** (a) (1) If $n = 6$, $A = 25$, and $N = 100$, $P(X \geq 2) = 1 - [P(X = 0) + P(X = 1)]$
$= 1 - [0.1689 + 0.3620] = 0.4691$
(2) If $n = 6$, $A = 30$, and $N = 100$, $P(X \geq 2) = 1 - [P(X = 0) + P(X = 1)]$
$= 1 - [0.1100 + 0.3046] = 0.5854$
(3) If $n = 6$, $A = 5$, and $N = 100$, $P(X \geq 2) = 1 - [P(X = 0) + P(X = 1)]$
$= 1 - [0.7291 + 0.2430] = 0.0279$
(4) If $n = 6$, $A = 10$, and $N = 100$, $P(X \geq 2) = 1 - [P(X = 0) + P(X = 1)]$
$= 1 - [0.5223 + 0.3687] = 0.1090$

(b) The probability that the entire group will be audited is very sensitive to the true number of improper returns in the population. If the true number is very low ($A = 5$), the probability is very low (0.0279). When the true number is increased by a factor of six ($A = 30$), the probability the group will be audited increases by a factor of almost 21 (0.5854).

**6.27** (a) If $n = 6$, $A = 6$, and $N = 54$, $P(X = 6) = 3.8719 \times 10^{-8} \cong 0.00000004$
(b) If $n = 6$, $A = 6$, and $N = 54$, $P(X = 5) = 1.1151 \times 10^{-5} \cong 0.00001$
(c) If $n = 6$, $A = 6$, and $N = 54$, $P(X = 4) = 0.0007$
(d) If $n = 6$, $A = 6$, and $N = 54$, $P(X = 3) = 0.0134$
(e) If $n = 6$, $A = 6$, and $N = 54$, $P(X = 0) = 0.4751$
(f) (a) If $n = 6$, $A = 6$, and $N = 40$, $P(X = 6) = 2.6053 \times 10^{-7} \cong 0.0000003$
(b) If $n = 6$, $A = 6$, and $N = 40$, $P(X = 5) = 5.3147 \times 10^{-5} \cong 0.00005$
(c) If $n = 6$, $A = 6$, and $N = 40$, $P(X = 4) = 0.0022$
(d) If $n = 6$, $A = 6$, and $N = 40$, $P(X = 3) = 0.0312$
(e) If $n = 6$, $A = 6$, and $N = 40$, $P(X = 0) = 0.3504$

**6.29** (a) $E(X) = (0.4)(\$100) + (0.6)(\$200) = \$160$
(b) $E(Y) = (0.4)(\$200) + (0.6)(\$100) = \$140$
(c) $\sigma_X = \sqrt{(0.4)(100 - 160)^2 + (0.6)(200 - 160)^2} = \sqrt{2400} = 48.99$
(d) $\sigma_Y = \sqrt{(0.4)(200 - 140)^2 + (0.6)(100 - 140)^2} = \sqrt{2400} = 48.99$
(e) $\sigma_{XY} = (0.4)(100 - 160)(200 - 140) + (0.6)(200 - 160)(100 - 140) = -2400$
(f) $E(X + Y) = E(X) + E(Y) = \$160 + \$140 = \$300$
(g) $\sigma_{X+Y} = \sqrt{2400 + 2400 + 2(-2400)} = 0$

**6.34** (a) $E(X) = \$59$     (d) $\sigma_Y = 53.75$
(b) $E(Y) = \$59$     (e) $\sigma_{XY} = 39$
(c) $\sigma_X = 78.67$
(f) Stock $Y$ gives the investor a lower standard deviation while yielding the same expected return as investing in stock $X$, so the investor should select stock $Y$.
(g) (1) $E(P) = \$59$     $\sigma_P = 49.01$
(2) $E(P) = \$59$     $\sigma_P = 44.41$
(3) $E(P) = \$59$     $\sigma_P = 47.64$
(4) $E(P) = \$59$     $\sigma_P = 57.38$
(5) $E(P) = \$59$     $\sigma_P = 71.01$
(h) Based on the results of (g), you should recommend a portfolio with 30% stock $X$ and 70% stock $Y$ because it has the same expected return as other portfolios ($59) but has the smallest portfolio risk ($44.41).

**6.36** (a) $E(X) = \$77$      (d) $\sigma_Y = 108.95$

(b) $E(Y) = \$97$      (e) $\sigma_{XY} = 4161$

(c) $\sigma_X = 39.76$

(f) Stock $Y$ gives the investor a higher expected return than stock $X$, but also has a standard deviation better than 2.5 times higher than that for stock $X$. An investor should carefully weigh the increased risk.

(g)
(1) $E(P) = \$95$      $\sigma_P = 101.88$
(2) $E(P) = \$91$      $\sigma_P = 87.79$
(3) $E(P) = \$87$      $\sigma_P = 73.78$
(4) $E(P) = \$83$      $\sigma_P = 59.92$
(5) $E(P) = \$79$      $\sigma_P = 46.35$

(h) Based on the results of (g), an investor should recognize that as the expected return increases, so does the portfolio risk.

**6.48** (a)
(1) If $p = 0.70$ and $n = 10$, $P(X \geq 7) = 0.6496$
(2) $P(X < 6) = 1 - [P(X \geq 7) + P(X = 6)] = 1 - [0.6496 + 0.2001] = 0.1503$
(3) $P(X \geq 9) = P(X = 9) + P(X = 10) = 0.1211 + 0.0282 = 0.1493$

## Chapter 7

**7.1** (a) Opportunity loss table

| Event | Optimum Action | Profit of Optimum Action | Alternative Courses of Action | |
|---|---|---|---|---|
| | | | A | B |
| 1 | B | 100 | $100 - 50 = 50$ | $100 - 100 = 0$ |
| 2 | A | 200 | $200 - 200 = 0$ | $200 - 125 = 75$ |

(b)

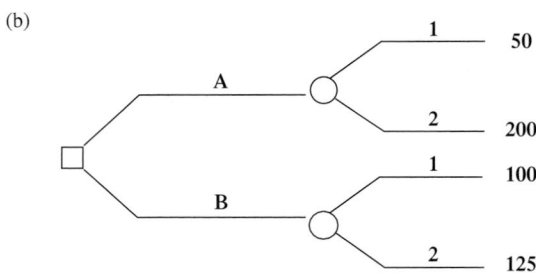

**7.4** (a)–(b) Payoff table

| Event | Action | |
|---|---|---|
| | Company A | Company B |
| 1 | $\$10,000 + \$2 \times 1,000 = \$12,000$ | $\$2,000 + \$4 \times 1,000 = \$6,000$ |
| 2 | $\$10,000 + \$2 \times 2,000 = \$14,000$ | $\$2,000 + \$4 \times 2,000 = \$10,000$ |
| 3 | $\$10,000 + \$2 \times 5,000 = \$20,000$ | $\$2,000 + \$4 \times 5,000 = \$22,000$ |
| 4 | $\$10,000 + \$2 \times 10,000 = \$30,000$ | $\$2,000 + \$4 \times 10,000 = \$42,000$ |
| 5 | $\$10,000 + \$2 \times 50,000 = \$110,000$ | $\$2,000 + \$4 \times 50,000 = \$202,000$ |

(d) Opportunity loss table

| Event | Optimum Action | Profit of Optimum Action | Alternative Courses of Action | |
|---|---|---|---|---|
| | | | A | B |
| 1 | A | 12,000 | 0 | 6,000 |
| 2 | A | 14,000 | 0 | 4,000 |
| 3 | B | 22,000 | 2,000 | 0 |
| 4 | B | 42,000 | 12,000 | 0 |
| 5 | B | 202,000 | 92,000 | 0 |

**7.6** (a) $EMV_A = 50(0.5) + 200(0.5) = 125$    $EMV_B = 100(0.5) + 125(0.5) = 112.50$

(b) $EOL_A = 50(0.5) + 0(0.5) = 25$    $EOL_B = 0(0.5) + 75(0.5) = 37.50$

(c) Perfect information would correctly forecast which event, 1 or 2, will occur. The value of perfect information is the increase in the expected value if you knew which of the events 1 or 2 would occur prior to making a decision between actions. It allows us to select the optimum action given a correct forecast.

$$EMV \text{ with perfect information} = 100\ (0.5) + 200\ (0.5) = 150$$
$$EVPI = EMV \text{ with perfect information} - EMV_A = 150 - 125 = 25$$

(d) Based on (a) and (b) above, select action $A$ because it has a higher expected monetary value (a) and a lower opportunity loss (b) than action $B$.

(e) $\sigma_A^2 = (50 - 125)^2(0.5) + (200 - 125)^2(0.5) = 5625$    $\sigma_A = 75$

$$CV_A = \frac{75}{125} \times 100\% = 60\%$$

$\sigma_B^2 = (100 - 112.5)^2(0.5) + (125 - 112.5)^2(0.5) = 156.25$    $\sigma_B = 12.5$

$$CV_B = \frac{12.5}{112.5} \times 100\% = 11.11\%$$

(f) Return to risk ratio for $A = \dfrac{125}{75} = 1.667$

Return to risk ratio for $B = \dfrac{112.5}{12.5} = 9.0$

(g) Based on (e) and (f), select action $B$ because it has a lower coefficient of variation and a higher return to risk ratio.

(h) The best decision depends on the decision criterion. In this case, expected monetary value leads to a different decision than the return to risk ratio.

**7.9** (a) $EMV = 50(0.3) + 100(0.3) + 120\ (0.3) + 200\ (0.1) = 101$

(b) $\sigma^2 = (50 - 101)^2(0.3) + (100 - 101)^2(0.3) + (120 - 101)^2(0.3)$
$\qquad + (200 - 101)^2(0.1) = 1{,}869$

$\sigma = 43.23$

(c) $CV = 42.80\%$

(d) Return to risk ratio $= 2.336$

**7.12** (a) $EMV(\text{Soft drinks}) = 50(0.4) + 60(0.6) = 56$
$EMV(\text{Ice cream}) = 30(0.4) + 90(0.6) = 66$

(b) $EOL(\text{Soft drinks}) = 18$
$EOL(\text{Ice cream}) = 8$

(d) Based on (a) and (b), choose to sell ice cream because you will earn a higher expected monetary value and incur a lower opportunity cost than choosing to sell soft drinks.

(e) $CV(\text{Soft drinks}) = \dfrac{4.899}{56} \times 100\% = 8.748\%$

$CV(\text{Ice cream}) = \dfrac{29.394}{66} \times 100\% = 44.536\%$

(f) Return to risk ratio for soft drinks $= 11.431$
Return to risk ratio for ice cream $= 2.245$

**7.13** (a) Payoff table

| | Action | | |
|---|---|---|---|
| Event | A<br>Buy 500 | B<br>Buy 1,000 | C<br>Buy 2,000 |
| 1. Sell 500 | 500 | 0 | − 1,000 |
| 2. Sell 1,000 | 500 | 1,000 | 0 |
| 3. Sell 2,000 | 500 | 1,000 | 2,000 |

(b) $EMV_A = 500(0.2) + 500(0.4) + 500(0.4) = 500$
$EMV_B = 0(0.2) + 1{,}000(0.4) + 1{,}000(0.4) = 800$
$EMV_C = -\ 1{,}000(0.2) + 0(0.4) + 2{,}000(0.4) = 600$
Based on the expected monetary value, the company should purchase 1,000 pounds of clams and will expect to net \$800 for the activity.

(c) $\sigma_A^2 = (500 - 500)^2(0.2) + (500 - 500)^2(0.4) + (500 - 500)^2(0.4) = 0$
$\sigma_A = 0$
$\sigma_B^2 = (0 - 800)^2(0.2) + (1{,}000 - 800)^2(0.4) + (1{,}000 - 800)^2(0.4) = 160{,}000$
$\sigma_B = 400$
$\sigma_C^2 = (-1{,}000 - 600)^2(0.2) + (0 - 600)^2(0.4) + (2{,}000 - 600)^2(0.4) = 1{,}440{,}000$
$\sigma_C = 1{,}200$

(d) Opportunity loss table

|  |  |  | Alternative Courses of Action | | |
| --- | --- | --- | --- | --- | --- |
| Event | Optimum Action | Profit of Optimum Action | $A$ | $B$ | $C$ |
| 1 | $A$ | 500 | 0 | 500 | 1,500 |
| 2 | $B$ | 1,000 | 500 | 0 | 1,000 |
| 3 | $C$ | 2,000 | 1,500 | 1,000 | 0 |

$EOL_A = 0(0.2) + 500(0.4) + 1,500(0.4) = 800$
$EOL_B = 500(0.2) + 0(0.4) + 1,000(0.4) = 500$
$EOL_C = 1,500(0.2) + 1,000(0.4) + 0(0.4) = 700$

(e) EMV with perfect information $= 500(0.2) + 1,000(0.4) + 2,000(0.4) = 1,300$
$EVPI = EMV$ with perfect information $- EMV_B = 1,300 - 800 = 500$
The company should not be willing to pay more than $500 for a perfect forecast.

(f) $CV_A = \dfrac{0}{500} \times 100\% = 0\%$     $CV_B = \dfrac{400}{800} \times 100\% = 50\%$

$CV_C = \dfrac{1,200}{600} \times 100\% = 200\%$

(g) Return to risk ratio for $A = \dfrac{500}{0} =$ undefined

Return to risk ratio for $B = \dfrac{800}{400} = 2.0$

Return to risk ratio for $C = \dfrac{600}{1,200} = 0.5$

(h) Choose to buy 1,000 pounds of clams. Buying 1,000 pounds has the highest expected monetary value ($800), the lowest expected opportunity loss ($500), and the larger of the two return to risk ratios with defined solutions.

(i) There is no discrepancy.

(j) (a) Payoff table

|  | Action | | |
| --- | --- | --- | --- |
|  | $A$ | $B$ | $C$ |
| Event | Buy 500 | Buy 1,000 | Buy 2,000 |
| 1. Sell 500 | 750 | 250 | $-750$ |
| 2. Sell 1,000 | 750 | 1,500 | 500 |
| 3. Sell 2,000 | 750 | 1,500 | 3,000 |

(b) $EMV_A = 750(0.2) + 750(0.4) + 750(0.4) = 750$
$EMV_B = 250(0.2) + 1,500(0.4) + 1,500(0.4) = 1,250$
$EMV_C = -750(0.2) + 500(0.4) + 3,000(0.4) = 1,250$
Based solely on the expected monetary value, the company should purchase 1,000 or 2,000 pounds of clams and will expect to net $1,250 for the activity.

(c) $\sigma_A^2 = (750 - 750)^2(0.2) + (750 - 750)^2(0.4) + (750 - 750)^2(0.4) = 0$
$\sigma_A = 0$
$\sigma_B^2 = (250 - 1,250)^2(0.2) + (1,500 - 1,250)^2(0.4)$
$\qquad + (1,500 - 1,250)^2(0.4) = 250,000$
$\sigma_B = 500$
$\sigma_C^2 = (-750 - 1,250)^2(0.2) + (500 - 1,250)^2(0.4)$
$\qquad + (3,000 - 1,250)^2(0.4) = 2,250,000$
$\sigma_C = 1,500$

(d) Opportunity loss table

|  |  |  | Alternative Courses of Action | | |
| --- | --- | --- | --- | --- | --- |
| Event | Optimum Action | Profit of Optimum Action | $A$ | $B$ | $C$ |
| 1 | $A$ | 750 | 0 | 500 | 1,500 |
| 2 | $B$ | 1,500 | 750 | 0 | 1,000 |
| 3 | $C$ | 3,000 | 2,250 | 1,500 | 0 |

$EOL_A = 0(0.2) + 750(0.4) + 2,250(0.4) = 1,200$
$EOL_B = 500(0.2) + 0(0.4) + 1,500(0.4) = 700$
$EOL_C = 1,500(0.2) + 1,000(0.4) + 0(0.4) = 700$

(j) (e) *EMV* with perfect information $= 750(0.2) + 1,500(0.4)$
$+ 3,000(0.4) = 1,950$

$EVPI = EMV$, perfect information $- EMV_{B \ or \ C} = 1,950 - 1,250 = 700$
The company should not be willing to pay more than $700 for a perfect forecast.

(f) $CV_A = \dfrac{0}{750} \times 100\% = 0\%$    $CV_B = \dfrac{500}{1,250} \times 100\% = 40\%$

$CV_C = \dfrac{1,500}{1,250} \times 100\% = 120\%$

(g) Return to risk ratio for $A = \dfrac{500}{0} =$ undefined

Return to risk ratio for $B = \dfrac{1,250}{500} = 2.5$

Return to risk ratio for $C = \dfrac{1,250}{1,500} = 0.833$

(h) Buy 1,000 or 2,000 pounds of clams, actions *B* or *C*. Buying 1,000 or 2,000 pounds has the highest expected monetary value ($1,250) and the lowest expected opportunity loss ($700). But action *B* has the higher return to risk ratio and is the best choice with respect to the return to risk.

(k) (a) Payoff table

|  | Action | | |
|---|---|---|---|
|  | *A* | *B* | *C* |
| Event | Buy 500 | Buy 1,000 | Buy 2,000 |
| 1. Sell 500 | 500 | 0 | −1,000 |
| 2. Sell 1,000 | 500 | 1,000 | 0 |
| 3. Sell 2,000 | 500 | 1,000 | 2,000 |

(b) $EMV_A = 500(0.4) + 500(0.4) + 500(0.2) = 500$
$EMV_B = 0(0.4) + 1,000(0.4) + 1,000(0.2) = 600$
$EMV_C = -1,000(0.4) + 0(0.4) + 2,000(0.2) = 0$
Based solely on the expected monetary value, the company should purchase 1,000 pounds of clams and will expect to net $600 for the activity.

(c) $\sigma_A^2 = (500 - 500)^2(0.4) + (500 - 500)^2(0.4) + (500 - 500)^2(0.2) = 0$
$\sigma_A = 0$
$\sigma_B^2 = (0 - 600)^2(0.4) + (1,000 - 600)^2(0.4)$
$+ (1,000 - 600)^2(0.2) = 240,000$
$\sigma_B = 489.90$
$\sigma_C^2 = (-1,000 - 0)^2(0.4) + (0 - 0)^2(0.4)$
$+ (2,000 - 0)^2(0.2) = 1,200,000$
$\sigma_C = 1,095.45$

(d) Opportunity loss table

|  |  |  | Alternative Courses of Action | | |
|---|---|---|---|---|---|
| Event | Optimum Action | Profit of Optimum Action | *A* | *B* | *C* |
| 1 | *A* | 500 | 0 | 500 | 1,500 |
| 2 | *B* | 1,000 | 500 | 0 | 1,000 |
| 3 | *C* | 2,000 | 1,500 | 1,000 | 0 |

$EOL_A = 0(0.4) + 500(0.4) + 1,500(0.2) = 500$
$EOL_B = 500(0.4) + 0(0.4) + 1,000(0.2) = 400$
$EOL_C = 1,500(0.4) + 1,000(0.4) + 0(0.2) = 1,000$

(k) (e) *EMV* with perfect information $= 500(0.4) + 1,000(0.4)$
$$+ 2,000(0.2) = 1,000$$
$EVPI = EMV$, perfect information $- EMV_B = 1,000 - 600 = 400$
The company should not be willing to pay more than \$400 for a perfect forecast.

(f) $CV_A = \dfrac{0}{500} \times 100\% = 0\%$  $CV_B = \dfrac{489.90}{600} \times 100\% = 81.65\%$

$CV_C = \dfrac{1,095.45}{0} \times 100\% =$ undefined

(g) Return to risk ratio for $A = \dfrac{500}{0} =$ undefined

Return to risk ratio for $B = \dfrac{600}{489.90} = 1.22$

Return to risk ratio for $C = \dfrac{0}{1,095.45} = 0$

(h) Buy 1,000 pounds of clams, action $B$. Buying 1,000 pounds has the highest expected monetary value (\$600) and the lowest expected opportunity loss (\$400). Action $B$ has the higher return to risk ratio and is the best choice with respect to the return to risk.
   Although the values of *EMV*, *EOL* and $\sigma$ are affected by \$.50/pound changes in the profit (part j above) and by shifts in the probability with which events occur (part k above), the recommendation for action $B$ remains unaffected.

**7.16** (a) $EMV_A = 12,000(0.45) + 14,000(0.2) + 20,000(0.15) + 30,000(0.1)$
$$+ 110,000(0.1) = 25,200$$
$EMV_B = 6,000(0.45) + 10,000(0.2) + 22,000(0.15) + 42,000(0.1)$
$$+ 202,000(0.1) = 32,400$$

(b) $EOL_A = 0(0.45) + 0(0.2) + 2,000(0.15) + 12,000(0.1) + 92,000(0.1)$
$$= 10,700$$
$EOL_B = 6,000(0.45) + 4,000(0.2) + 0(0.15) + 0(0.1) + 0(0.1)$
$$= 3,500$$

(c) *EMV* with perfect information $= 12,000(0.45) + 14,000(0.2) + 22,000(0.15)$
$$+ 42,000(0.1) + 202,000(0.1) = 35,900$$
$EVPI = EMV$, perfect information $- EMV_B = 35,900 - 32,400 = 3,500$
The author should not be willing to pay more than \$3,500 for a perfect forecast.

(d) Sign with company $B$ to maximize the expected monetary value (\$32,400) and minimize the expected opportunity loss (\$3,500).

(e) $CV_A = \dfrac{28,792}{25,200} \times 100\% = 114.25\%$  $CV_B = \dfrac{57,583}{32,400} \times 100\% = 177.73\%$

(f) Return to risk ratio for $A = \dfrac{25,200}{28,792} = 0.8752$

Return to risk ratio for $B = \dfrac{32,400}{57,583} = 0.5627$

(g) Signing with company $A$ will minimize the author's risk and yield the higher return to risk.

(h) Company $B$ has a higher *EMV* than $A$, but choosing company $B$ also entails more risk and has a lower return to risk ratio than $A$.

(i) Payoff table

| Event | $P$ | $A$ | $B$ |
|-------|-----|-----|-----|
| 1 | 0.3 | 12,000 | 6,000 |
| 2 | 0.2 | 14,000 | 10,000 |
| 3 | 0.2 | 20,000 | 22,000 |
| 4 | 0.1 | 30,000 | 42,000 |
| 5 | 0.2 | 110,000 | 202,000 |
| | *EMV* | 35,400 | 52,800 |
| | $\sigma$ | 37,673 | 75,346 |
| | *CV* | 106.42% | 142.70% |
| | Return to risk | 0.9397 | 0.7008 |

Opportunity loss table

| Event | P | A | B |
|---|---|---|---|
| 1 | 0.3 | 0 | 6,000 |
| 2 | 0.2 | 0 | 4,000 |
| 3 | 0.2 | 2,000 | 0 |
| 4 | 0.1 | 12,000 | 0 |
| 5 | 0.2 | 92,000 | 0 |
| | *EOL* | 20,000 | 2,600 |

The author's decision is not affected by the changed probabilities.

**7.20** (a)  $P(\text{forecast cool} \mid \text{cool weather}) = 0.80$
$P(\text{forecast warm} \mid \text{warm weather}) = 0.70$

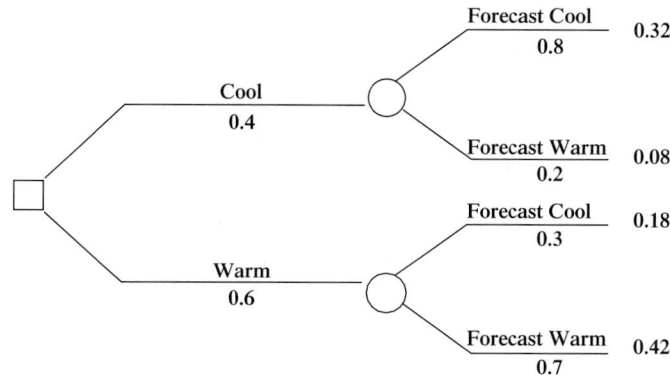

| | Forecast Cool | Forecast Warm | Total |
|---|---|---|---|
| Cool | 0.32 | 0.08 | 0.4 |
| Warm | 0.18 | 0.42 | 0.6 |
| Total | 0.5 | 0.5 | 1.0 |

Revised probabilities:   $P(\text{cool} \mid \text{forecast cool}) = \dfrac{0.32}{0.5} = 0.64$

$P(\text{warm} \mid \text{forecast cool}) = \dfrac{0.18}{0.5} = 0.36$

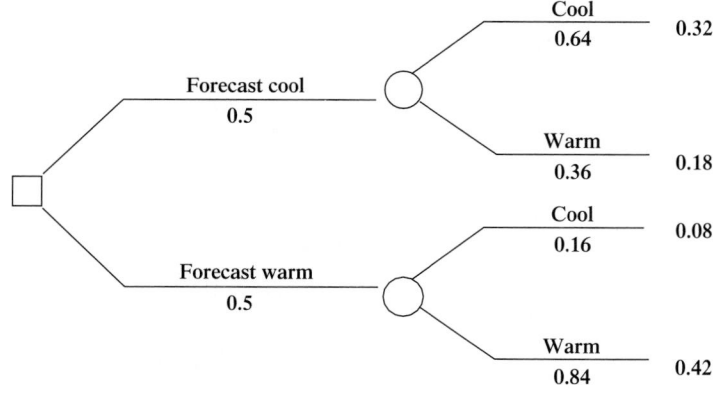

(b) $EMV$(Soft drinks) = 50(0.64) + 60(0.36) = 53.6
$EMV$(Ice cream) = 30(0.64) + 90(0.36) = 51.6

(c) $EOL$(Soft drinks) = 10.8    $EOL$(Ice cream) = 12.8

(d) $EMV$ with perfect information = 50(0.64) + 90(0.36) = 64.4
$EVPI = EMV$, perfect information $- EMV_A$ = 64.4 $-$ 53.6 = 10.8
The vendor should not be willing to pay more than $10.80 for a perfect forecast of the weather.

(e) The vendor should sell soft drinks to maximize value and minimize loss.

(f) $CV$(Soft drinks) $= \dfrac{4.8}{53.6} \times 100\% = 8.96\%$

$CV$(Ice cream) $= \dfrac{28.8}{51.6} \times 100\% = 55.81\%$

(g) Return to risk ratio for soft drinks = 11.6667
Return to risk ratio for ice cream = 1.7917

(h) Based on these revised probabilities, the vendor's decision changes because of the increased likelihood of cool weather given a forecast for cool. Under these conditions, she should sell soft drinks to maximize the expected monetary value and minimize her expected opportunity loss.

**7.38** (c), (e), (f)  Payoff table

|  | $P$ | New | Old |
|---|---|---|---|
| Weak | 0.3 | $-$ 4,000,000 | 0 |
| Moderate | 0.6 | 1,000,000 | 0 |
| Strong | 0.1 | 5,000,000 | 0 |
| $EMV$ |  | $-$ 100,000 | 0 |
| $\sigma$ |  | 2,808,914 | 0 |
| $CV$ |  | $-$2,808.94% | undefined |
| Return to risk |  | $-$ 0.0356 | undefined |

(b), (d)  Opportunity loss table

|  | $P$ | New | Old |
|---|---|---|---|
| Weak | 0.3 | 4,000,000 | 0 |
| Moderate | 0.6 | 0 | 1,000,000 |
| Strong | 0.1 | 0 | 5,000,000 |
| $EOL$ |  | 1,200,000 | 1,100,000 |

$EVPI$ = $1,100,000. The product manager should not be willing to pay more than $1,100,000 for a perfect forecast.

(g) The product manager should continue to use the old packaging to maximize expected monetary value and to minimize expected opportunity loss and risk.

(h) Payoff table

|  | $P$ | New | Old |
|---|---|---|---|
| Weak | 0.6 | $-$4,000,000 | 0 |
| Moderate | 0.3 | 1,000,000 | 0 |
| Strong | 0.1 | 5,000,000 | 0 |
| $EMV$ |  | 1,600,000 | 0 |
| $\sigma$ |  | 3,136,877 | 0 |
| $CV$ |  | $-$196.05% | undefined |
| Return to risk |  | $-$0.5101 | undefined |

Opportunity loss table

|  | P | New | Old |
|---|---|---|---|
| Weak | 0.6 | 4,000,000 | 0 |
| Moderate | 0.3 | 0 | 1,000,000 |
| Strong | 0.1 | 0 | 5,000,000 |
|  | EOL | 2,400,000 | 800,000 |

$EVPI = \$800,000$. The product manager should not be willing to pay more than $800,000 for a perfect forecast.

(i)   The product manager should use the new packaging to maximize expected monetary value and to minimize expected opportunity loss and risk.

(j)
$$P(\text{Sales decreased} \mid \text{weak response}) = 0.6$$
$$P(\text{Sales stayed same} \mid \text{weak response}) = 0.3$$
$$P(\text{Sales increased} \mid \text{weak response}) = 0.1$$
$$P(\text{Sales decreased} \mid \text{moderate response}) = 0.2$$
$$P(\text{Sales stayed same} \mid \text{moderate response}) = 0.4$$
$$P(\text{Sales increased} \mid \text{moderate response}) = 0.4$$
$$P(\text{Sales decreased} \mid \text{strong response}) = 0.05$$
$$P(\text{Sales stayed same} \mid \text{strong response}) = 0.35$$
$$P(\text{Sales increased} \mid \text{strong response}) = 0.6$$
$$P(\text{Sales decreased } and \text{ weak response}) = 0.6(0.3) = 0.18$$
$$P(\text{Sales stayed same } and \text{ weak response}) = 0.3(0.3) = 0.09$$
$$P(\text{Sales increased } and \text{ weak response}) = 0.1(0.3) = 0.03$$
$$P(\text{Sales decreased } and \text{ moderate response}) = 0.2(0.6) = 0.12$$
$$P(\text{Sales stayed same } and \text{ moderate response}) = 0.4(0.6) = 0.24$$
$$P(\text{Sales increased } and \text{ moderate response}) = 0.4(0.6) = 0.24$$
$$P(\text{Sales decreased } and \text{ strong response}) = 0.05(0.1) = 0.005$$
$$P(\text{Sales stayed same } and \text{ strong response}) = 0.35(0.1) = 0.035$$
$$P(\text{Sales increased } and \text{ strong response}) = 0.6(0.1) = 0.06$$

Joint probability table

|  | P | Sales Decrease | Sales Stay Same | Sales Increase |
|---|---|---|---|---|
| Weak | 0.3 | 0.180 | 0.090 | 0.030 |
| Moderate | 0.6 | 0.120 | 0.240 | 0.240 |
| Strong | 0.1 | 0.005 | 0.035 | 0.060 |
|  | Total | 0.305 | 0.365 | 0.330 |

(j)   Given the sales stayed the same, the revised conditional probabilities are:
$$P(\text{weak response} \mid \text{sales stayed same}) = \frac{.09}{.365} = 0.2466$$
$$P(\text{moderate response} \mid \text{sales stayed same}) = \frac{.24}{.365} = 0.6575$$
$$P(\text{strong response} \mid \text{sales stayed same}) = \frac{.035}{.365} = 0.0959$$

(k)   Payoff table

|  | P | New | Old |
|---|---|---|---|
| Weak | 0.2466 | − 4,000,000 | 0 |
| Moderate | 0.6575 | 1,000,000 | 0 |
| Strong | 0.0959 | 5,000,000 | 0 |
|  | EMV | 150,685 | 0 |
|  | σ | 2,641,457 | 0 |
|  | CV | 1752.97% | undefined |
|  | Return to risk | 0.0570 | undefined |

Opportunity loss table

|  | P | New | Old |
|---|---|---|---|
| Weak | 0.2466 | 4,000,000 | 0 |
| Moderate | 0.6575 | 0 | 1,000,000 |
| Strong | 0.0959 | 0 | 5,000,000 |
|  | EOL | 986,301 | 1,136,986 |

*EVPI* = $986,301. The product manager should not be willing to pay more than $986,301 for a perfect forecast.

The product manager should use the new packaging to maximize expected monetary value and to minimize expected opportunity loss and risk.

(l)  Given the sales decreased, the revised conditional probabilities are:

$$P(\text{weak response} \mid \text{sales decreased}) = \frac{.18}{.305} = 0.5902$$

$$P(\text{moderate response} \mid \text{sales decreased}) = \frac{.12}{.305} = 0.3934$$

$$P(\text{strong response} \mid \text{sales decreased}) = \frac{.005}{.305} = 0.0164$$

(m)  Payoff table

|  | P | New | Old |
|---|---|---|---|
| Weak | 0.5902 | −4,000,000 | 0 |
| Moderate | 0.3934 | 1,000,000 | 0 |
| Strong | 0.0164 | 5,000,000 | 0 |
|  | EMV | −1,885,246 | 0 |
|  | σ | 2,586,842 | 0 |
|  | CV | −137.22% | undefined |
|  | Return to risk | − 0.7288 | undefined |

(m)  Opportunity loss table

|  | P | New | Old |
|---|---|---|---|
| Weak | 0.5902 | 4,000,000 | 0 |
| Moderate | 0.3934 | 0 | 1,000,000 |
| Strong | 0.0164 | 0 | 5,000,000 |
|  | EOL | 2,360,656 | 475,410 |

*EVPI* = $475,410. The product manager should not be willing to pay more than $475,410 for a perfect forecast.

The product manager should continue to use the old packaging to maximize expected monetary value.

**(7.40)**  (c), (e), (f)  Payoff table*

|  | P | A: Do Not Call Mechanic | B: Call Mechanic |
|---|---|---|---|
| Very low | 0.25 | 20 | 100 |
| Low | 0.25 | 100 | 100 |
| Moderate | 0.25 | 200 | 100 |
| High | 0.25 | 400 | 100 |
|  | EMV | 180 | 100 |
|  | σ | 142 | 0 |
|  | CV | 78.96% | 0 |
|  | Return to risk | 1.2665 | undefined |

*Note:* The payoff here is cost and not profit. The opportunity cost is therefore calculated as the difference between the payoff and the minimum in the same row.

(b), (d)   Opportunity loss table

|  | P | A: Do Not Call Mechanic | B: Call Mechanic |
|---|---|---|---|
| Very low | 0.25 | 0 | 80 |
| Low | 0.25 | 0 | 0 |
| Moderate | 0.25 | 100 | 0 |
| High | 0.25 | 300 | 0 |
|  | EOL | 100 | 20 |

(g)   We want to minimize the expected monetary value because it is a cost. To minimize the expected monetary value, call the mechanic.

(h)   Given 2 successes out of 15, the binomial probabilities and their related revised conditional probabilities are:

|  | P | Binomial Probabilities | Revised Conditional Probabilities |
|---|---|---|---|
| Very low | 0.01 | 0.0092 | 0.0092/0.6418 = 0.0143 |
| Low | 0.05 | 0.1348 | 0.1348/0.6418 = 0.2100 |
| Moderate | 0.10 | 0.2669 | 0.2669/0.6418 = 0.4159 |
| High | 0.20 | 0.2309 | 0.2309/0.6418 = 0.3598 |
|  |  | 0.6418 |  |

(i)   Payoff table

|  | P | A: Do Not Call Mechanic | B: Call Mechanic |
|---|---|---|---|
| Very low | 0.0144 | 20 | 100 |
| Low | 0.2100 | 100 | 100 |
| Moderate | 0.4159 | 200 | 100 |
| High | 0.3598 | 400 | 100 |
|  | EMV | 248 | 100 |
|  | $\sigma$ | 121 | 0 |
|  | CV | 48.68% | 0 |
|  | Return to risk | 2.0544 | undefined |

Opportunity loss table

|  | P | A: Do Not Call Mechanic | B: Call Mechanic |
|---|---|---|---|
| Very low | 0.0144 | 0 | 80 |
| Low | 0.2100 | 0 | 0 |
| Moderate | 0.4159 | 100 | 0 |
| High | 0.3598 | 300 | 0 |
|  | EOL | 149.52 | 1.15 |

We want to minimize the expected monetary value because it is a cost. To minimize the expected monetary value, call the mechanic.

## Chapter 8

**8.3**  (a)  (1)  .3599  
(2)  .6401  
(3)  .0832  
(4)  .9168  
(5)  .8599  
(6)  .5832  
(7)  .4431  
(8)  .5569

| | | | | | | |
|---|---|---|---|---|---|---|
| (b) | (1) | .1401 | | (4) | .1151 | |
| | (2) | .4168 | | (5) | .1815 | |
| | (3) | .3918 | | | | |

(c)   0

(d)   $-1.00$

(e)   $+1.00$

**8.5** (a)
| | | | | |
|---|---|---|---|---|
| (1) | .9938 | | (4) | .1314 |
| (2) | .00135 | | (5) | .1515 |
| (3) | .0606 | | | |

      (b)   87.2

      (c)   87.2 and 112.8

      (d)   94.8

**8.8** (a)   .4082

      (b)   .0669

      (c)   25.08%

      (d)   749 trucks (rounded from 749.2)

      (e)   $Z = -0.84$ so that $X = 39.92$ thousand miles.

      (f)   a.   .4452

             b.   .0603

             c.   18.15%

             d.   819 trucks (rounded from 818.5)

             e.   $Z = -0.84$ so that $X = 41.6$ thousand miles.

**8.12** (a)   .1587

       (b)   .0466

       (c)   .7865

       (d)   46.4 hours

       (e)   40.0 hours

       (f)   6.7 hours

       (g)
| | | | | | |
|---|---|---|---|---|---|
| a. | .3085 | | d. | 52.8 hours | |
| b. | .0968 | | e. | 40.0 hours | |
| c. | .4796 | | f. | 13.4 hours | |

**8.16** Area under normal curve covered:   .1429, .2857, 4286, .5714, .7143, and .8571

       Standardized normal quantile value: $-1.07$, $-0.57$, $-0.18$, $+0.18$, $+0.57$, and $+1.07$

**8.17** (a)   $\overline{X} = \$106.80$

            $S = \$38.16$

            Five Number Summary: $40 $80 $100 $135 $200

**8.19** (a)   $\overline{X} = 10.07$

            $S = 2.37$

            Five Number Summary: 5.80 8.42 10.01 11.60 15.98

**8.20** Office I:

   $\overline{X} = 2.214$

   $S = 1.718$

   Five Number Summary: 0.520 0.930 1.540 3.930 6.320

   Office II:

   $\overline{X} = 2.011$

   $S = 1.892$

   Five Number Summary: 0.080 0.600 1.505 3.750 7.550

**8.22** (a)   .6321

       (b)   .3679

       (c)   .2376

       (d)   .7674

**8.26** (a)   .8647

       (b)   .99996

       (c)   a.   .6321

             b.   .9933

**8.27** (a)   .5276

       (b)   .9765

       (c)   a.   .7135

             b.   .9981

**8.40** Height: $P(X > 67) = .2119$

   Weight: $P(X > 135) = .1587$

   Weight is the slightly more unusual characteristic.

**8.44** (a)   (1)   .3413

            (2)   .3413

            (3)   .6826

        (4)   .8413
        (5)   .1587
        (6)   .1160
    (b)   10.0 million dollars
    (c)   6.8 million dollars
    (d)   3.4 million dollars

## Chapter 9

**9.1**   $\mu = 100$, $\sigma = 10$, and $n = 25$ so that $\sigma_{\bar{X}} = 2$:
    (a)   .0062
    (b)   .0994
    (c)   .1357
    (d)   .3830
    (e)   $Z = -0.39$ so $\bar{X} = 99.22$
    (f)   $\mu = 100$, $\sigma = 10$, and $n = 16$ so that $\sigma_{\bar{X}} = 2.5$:
        a.   .0228
        b.   .1359
        c.   .1894
        d.   .3108
        e.   $Z = -0.39$ so $\bar{X} = 99.025$
**9.5**   $\mu = 1.30$ and $\sigma = 0.04$:
    (a)   .1915
    (b)   .1747
    (c)   1.2664 to 1.3336
    (d)   (1)   $\mu_{\bar{X}} = 1.30$ and $\sigma_{\bar{X}} = 0.01$
        (2)   normal distribution
        (3)   .4772
        (4)   .15735
        (5)   1.2916 to 1.3084
    (e), (f)   If samples of size 16 are being taken, rather than individual values (samples of $n = 1$), then since $\sigma_{\bar{X}} = \sigma/\sqrt{n}$, more values of the sample mean will lie closer to the population mean with the increased sample size and fewer values will lie far away from the population mean.
    (g)   They are equally likely to occur (probability = .1587) since, as $n$ increases, more sample means will be closer to the population mean.
**9.8**   $\mu = 50.0$, $\sigma = 12.0$, and $n = 16$ so that $\sigma_{\bar{X}} = 3.0$:
    (a)   .0475
    (b)   .2286
    (c)   Population data are approximately normally distributed.
    (d)   If $n = 64$ then $\sigma_{\bar{X}} = 1.5$; therefore, $\bar{X} = 52.47$ thousand miles (using $Z = +1.645$).
    (e)   Central limit theorem holds if underlying population is not normally distributed.
    (f)   $\mu = 50.0$, $\sigma = 10.0$, and $n = 16$ so that $\sigma_{\bar{X}} = 2.5$:
        a.   .0228
        b.   .2037
        c.   Population data are approximately normally distributed.
        d.   If $n = 64$ then $\sigma_{\bar{X}} = 1.25$; therefore, $\bar{X} = 52.06$ thousand miles (using $Z = +1.645$).
        e.   Central limit theorem holds if underlying population is not normally distributed.
**9.10**   (a)   .75
    (b)   .0541
**9.13**   (a)   .2486
    (b)   .0918
    (c)   .1293 and .2514
    (d)   A percent defective above 10.5% is more likely to occur since it is only .33 standard deviation above the population value of 10%.
**9.16**   (a)   .4977
    (b)   44.2% to 55.8%
    (c)   .0000
    (d)   More than 60% correct in a sample of 200 is more likely since its probability is .0023.
**9.18**   .9413
**9.21**   .1483
**9.23**   (a)   .2549
    (b)   .0823

**Chapter 10**

**10.1**     $83.04 \leq \mu \leq 86.96$

**10.7**
(a)     $.9877 \leq \mu \leq 1.0023$
(b)     Since the value of 1.0 is included in the interval, there is no reason to believe that the average is below 1.0.
(c)     No, since $\sigma$ is known and $n = 50$, from the central limit theorem we may assume that $\overline{X}$ is normally distributed.
(d)     An individual value of .98 is only .75 standard deviation below the sample mean of .995 and only 1.0 standard deviation below the specified mean of 1.0. The confidence interval represents the estimate of the average of a sample of 50, not an individual value.
(e)     a.    $.9895 \leq \mu \leq 1.0005$
         b.    Since the value of 1.0 is included in the interval, there is no reason to believe that the average is below 1.0.

**10.11**     $66.88 \leq \mu \leq 83.12$.

**10.15**
(a)     $184.66 \leq \mu \leq 205.94$
(b)     Since the value of 200 is included in the interval, there is no reason to believe that the average is below 200.
(c)     An individual value of 210 is only .69 standard deviation above the sample mean of 195.3 and only .47 standard deviation above the specified mean of 200. The confidence interval represents the estimate of the average of a sample of 18, not an individual value.

**10.19**
(a)     $87.77 \leq \mu \leq 109.96$
(b)     Yes. Since the value of 90 is included in the interval, there is no reason to believe that the average is different.
(c)     Waiting time is normally distributed.
(d)     $83.42 \leq \mu \leq 140.98$. The confidence interval is much wider. In addition, the assumption of normality may not hold now and this confidence interval would no longer be appropriate. Normal probability plots and other graphic displays and descriptive summaries should be used to assess the assumption of normality and the viability of this confidence interval.

**10.21**     $.19 \leq p \leq .31$

**10.23**     (a)    $.2246 \leq p \leq .3754$

**10.25**     (a)    $.342 \leq p \leq .478$

**10.30**     $n = 35$

**10.36**     $n = 97$

**10.38**
(a)     $n = 167$
(b)     $n = 97$

**10.43**     $n = 323$

**10.44**     $n = 271$

**10.48**     $67.63 \leq \mu \leq 82.37$

**10.50**
(a)     $322.62 \leq \mu \leq 377.38$
(b)     $n = 92$
(c)     a.    $322.97 \leq \mu \leq 377.03$
         b.    $n = 88$

**10.52**
(a)     $.2284 \leq p \leq .3716$
(b)     $n = 214$
(c)     a.    $.2265 \leq p \leq .3735$
         b.    $n = 239$

**10.53**
(a)     $.344 \leq p \leq .476$
(b)     $n = 1,111$
(c)     a.    $.343 \leq p \leq .477$
         b.    $n = 1,224$

**10.56**     $721.53 \leq$ Population Total $\leq 978.47$

**10.59**     $\$457.52 \leq$ Population Total $\leq \$544.48$

**10.62**     $\$5,125.99 \leq$ Population Difference $\leq \$54,546.57$

**10.70**
(a)     $14.085 \leq \mu \leq 16.515$
(b)     $.530 \leq p \leq .820$
(c)     $n = 25$
(d)     $n = 784$
(e)     The sample size should be 784 to satisfy the requirements for both questions.

**10.74**
(a)     $\$25.80 \leq \mu \leq \$31.24$
(b)     $.304 \leq p \leq .496$
(c)     $n = 97$
(d)     $n = 423$
(e)     The sample size should be 423 to satisfy the requirements for both questions.

**Chapter 11**

**11.1** Null hypothesis

**11.2** Alternative hypothesis

**11.3** $\alpha$

**11.4** $\beta$

**11.11** It will increase.

**11.15** $H_0$: $\mu$ = $1,000,000
$H_1$: $\mu \neq$ $1,000,000

**11.16** $H_0$: $\mu$ = 20
$H_1$: $\mu \neq$ 20

**11.20** Reject $H_0$ if $Z >$ +2.58 or if $Z <$ −2.58; otherwise do not reject $H_0$.

**11.21** Reject $H_0$.

**11.23** (a) $H_0$: $\mu$ = $675
$H_1$: $\mu \neq$ $675
(b) Yes. $Z =$ −3.65 < −2.58. Reject $H_0$.
(c) Reject $H_0$. $Z =$ −2.74 < −2.58.
(d) Do not reject $H_0$. $Z =$ −1.83 > −2.58.

**11.24** (a) $H_0$: $\mu$ = 8
$H_1$: $\mu \neq$ 8
(b) No. −1.96 < $Z =$ −0.80 < +1.96. Do not reject $H_0$.
(c) Reject $H_0$. $Z =$ −2.40 < −1.96.
(d) Reject $H_0$. $Z =$ −2.26 < −1.96.

**11.25** (a) $H_0$: $\mu$ = $160
$H_1$: $\mu \neq$ $160
(b) Yes. $Z =$ +2.40 > +1.96. Reject $H_0$.
(c) Reject $H_0$. $Z =$ +3.00 > +1.96.
(d) Do not reject $H_0$. $Z =$ +2.40 < +2.58.

**11.26** .0456

**11.27** Reject $H_0$ since $p =$ .0456 < .10.

**11.31** (a) $p$ value = .00026. The probability of obtaining a sample whose mean deviates from the claim by $50 or more when the null hypothesis is true is .00026.
(b) Reject $H_0$ since $p$ value = .00026 < .01.
(c) Yes
(d) Same conclusions

**11.32** (a) $p$ value = .4238. The probability of obtaining a sample whose mean deviates from the claim by .017 ounces or more when the null hypothesis is true is .4238.
(b) Do not reject $H_0$ since $p$ value = .4238 > .05.
(c) No
(d) Same conclusions

**11.33** (a) $p$ value = .0164. The probability of obtaining a sample whose mean deviates from the claim by $12 or more when the null hypothesis is true is .0164.
(b) Reject $H_0$ since $p$ value = .0164 < .05.
(c) Yes
(d) Same conclusions

**11.34** (a) $H_0$: $\mu$ = 1
$H_1$: $\mu \neq$ 1
(b) No. −2.58 < $Z =$ −1.77 < +2.58. Do not reject $H_0$.
(c) Same conclusions. The confidence interval includes the hypothesized value of 1.

**11.39** −1.28

**11.40** Do not reject $H_0$.

**11.41** .0228

**11.42** Reject $H_0$.

**11.46** (a) $H_0$: $\mu \geq$ 2.8
$H_1$: $\mu <$ 2.8
(b) $Z =$ −1.75 < −1.645. Reject $H_0$. The average is significantly less than 2.8 feet and we can conclude that the process is not working properly.
(c) $p$ value = .0401 < .05. Reject $H_0$.
(d) The probability of obtaining a sample whose mean is 2.73 feet or less when the null hypothesis is true is .0401.
(e) Same conclusions

**11.48** (a) $H_0$: $\mu \geq$ 8
$H_1$: $\mu <$ 8
(b) $Z =$ −0.80 > −1.645. Do not reject $H_0$. There is no evidence that the average amount dispensed is less than 8 ounces.

(c)  $p$ value $= .2119 > .05$. Do not reject $H_0$.

(d)  The probability of obtaining a sample whose mean is 7.983 ounces or less when the null hypothesis is true is .2119.

(e)  Same conclusions

**11.49**  (a)  $H_0: \mu \le \$160$
$H_1: \mu > \$160$

(b)  $Z = +2.40 > +1.645$. Reject $H_0$. The average is significantly greater than \$160 and we can conclude that the bank branch is not meeting customer needs.

(c)  $p$ value $= .0082 < .05$. Reject $H_0$.

(d)  The probability of obtaining a sample whose mean is \$172 or more when the null hypothesis is true is .0082.

(e)  Same conclusions

**11.51**  $t = +2.00$

**11.52**  15

**11.55**  No. The $t$ test assumes the underlying population is normally distributed. With small sample sizes ($n < 30$) the $t$ test should not be used in situations in which the population is known to be left-skewed.

**11.57**  (a)  $t = +3.55 > t_{99} = +1.9842$. Reject $H_0$. There is evidence that the average balance is different from \$75.

(b)  $t = +2.25 > t_{99} = +1.9842$. Reject $H_0$. There is evidence that the average balance is different from \$75.

(c)  $t = +1.61 < t_{99} = +1.9842$. Do not reject $H_0$. There is no evidence that the average balance is different from \$75.

**11.60**  (a)  $t = +3.30 > t_{35} = +2.0301$. Reject $H_0$. There is evidence that the average EER is different from 9.

(b)  The data are approximately normally distributed.

(c)  $p$ value $= .0022 < .05$. Reject $H_0$. The probability of obtaining a sample whose mean deviates from the claim by 0.2111 or more when the null hypothesis is true is .0022.

(d)  $t = +2.28 > t_{35} = +2.0301$. Reject $H_0$. There is evidence that the average EER is different from 9.

**11.63**  (a)  $t = -2.57 < t_{19} = -1.7291$. Reject $H_0$. There is evidence that the manufacturer's claim is overstated.

(b)  The data are approximately normally distributed.

(c)  Using a normal probability plot, stem-and-leaf, or box-and-whisker plot, the assumption of normality appears to hold.

(d)  $t = -0.75 > t_{19} = -1.7291$. Do not reject $H_0$. There is no evidence that the manufacturer's claim is overstated.

**11.65**  $p_s = .22$

**11.66**  (a) and (b)  $Z = +1.00$

**11.71**  (a)  $Z = -1.60 > -2.33$. Do not reject $H_0$. There is no evidence that the proportion is less than .25.

(b)  $p$ value $= .0548$.

(c)  $Z = -2.92 < -2.33$. Reject $H_0$. There is evidence that the proportion is less than .25.

**11.72**  (a)  $Z = +2.93 > +1.645$. Reject $H_0$. There is evidence that the proportion is different from .30.

(b)  $p$ value $= .0034$.

(c)  $Z = +1.54 < +1.645$. Do not reject $H_0$. There is no evidence that the proportion is different from .30.

**11.78**  (a)  $\chi_L^2 = 10.520$ and $\chi_U^2 = 46.928$.

(b)  $\chi_L^2 = 6.908$ and $\chi_U^2 = 28.845$.

(c)  $\chi_L^2 = 5.892$ and $\chi_U^2 = 22.362$.

**11.79**  $\chi^2 = 10.42$

**11.80**  15

**11.81**  (a)  $\chi_L^2 = 6.262$ and $\chi_U^2 = 27.488$.

(b)  $\chi_U^2 = 24.996$

**11.82**  (a)  Do not reject $H_0$.

(b)  Do not reject $H_0$.

**11.84**  (a)  $\chi^2 = 88.81 > \chi_U^2 = 42.557$ based on 29 degrees of freedom. Reject $H_0$. There is evidence that the population standard deviation has increased above $1.2°$ F.

(b)  The data are approximately normally distributed.

(c)  $p$ value $= 12.401$ in upper tail. The probability of obtaining a sample whose standard deviation of the temperature is $2.1°F$ or more when the null hypothesis is true is approximately .0000.

**11.85** (a) $\chi_L^2 = 12.401 < \chi^2 = 33.85 < \chi_U^2 = 39.364$ based on 24 degrees of freedom. Do not reject $H_0$. There is no evidence that the population standard deviation is different from $200.

    (b) The data are approximately normally distributed.

    (c) $p$ value = .1748. The probability of obtaining a sample whose standard deviation deviates from the claim by $37.52 or more when the null hypothesis is true is .1748 from Excel.

**11.89** (a) $\chi^2 = 21.49 < \chi_U^2 = 30.144$ based on 19 degrees of freedom. Do not reject $H_0$. There is no evidence that the population standard deviation has increased above 2.5 ampere-hours.

    (b) The data are approximately normally distributed.

    (c) $p$ value = .3103 from Excel. The probability of obtaining a sample whose standard deviation of the battery capacity is 2.659 or more ampere-hours when the null hypothesis is true is .3103.

**11.90** (a) Power = .6387; $\beta$ = .3613

    (b) Power = .9908; $\beta$ = .0092

**11.91** (a) Power = .3707; $\beta$ = .6293

    (b) Power = .9525; $\beta$ = .0475

    (c) The decrease in $\alpha$ has increased $\beta$ and decreased power.

**11.92** (a) Power = .8037; $\beta$ = .1963

    (b) Power = .9996; $\beta$ = .0004

    (c) The increase in sample size has increased power.

**11.108** (a) $t = -1.58 > t_{74} = -1.6657$. Do not reject $H_0$. There is no evidence that the average reimbursement is less than $100.

    (b) $p_s = 0.16$ and $Z = +1.73 > +1.645$. Reject $H_0$. There is evidence that the proportion of incorrect reimbursements is greater than .10.

    (c) $\chi^2 = 98.15$ and, with 74 degrees of freedom, converting from $\chi^2$ to $Z$, $-1.96 < Z = +1.89 < +1.96$. Do not reject $H_0$. There is no evidence that the standard deviation amount of reimbursement differs from $30.

    (d) The data are approximately normally distributed.

    (e) $t = -2.51 < t_{74} = -1.6657$. Reject $H_0$. There is evidence that the average reimbursement is less than $100.

    (f) $p_s = 0.20$ and $Z = +2.89 > +1.645$. Reject $H_0$. There is evidence that the proportion of incorrect reimbursements is greater than .10.

**11.109** (a) $t = -1.69 > t_{14} = -1.7613$. Do not reject $H_0$. There is no evidence that the average waiting time is less than 5 minutes.

    (b) The data are approximately normally distributed.

    (c) Based on the sample of only 15 customers, the data seem to be slightly left-skewed. If approximate normality can be assumed, parts (a), (d), and (e) are appropriate.

    (d) $\chi^2 = 37.56 > \chi_U^2 = 26.119$ with 14 degrees of freedom. Reject $H_0$. There is evidence that the standard deviation of waiting time differs from 1 minute.

    (e) $p$ value = .0569 from Excel. The probability of obtaining a sample whose mean is 4.287 minutes or less when the null hypothesis is true is .0569.

**11.111** (a) (1) Power = .3707; $\beta$ = .6293

        (2) Power = .99988; $\beta$ = .00012

    (b) (1) Power = .6387; $\beta$ = .3613

        (2) Power = 1.0; $\beta$ = 0

    (c) The increase in $\alpha$ has reduced $\beta$ and increased power.

    (d) (1) Power = .6331; $\beta$ = .3669

        (2) Power = 1.0; $\beta$ = 0

    (e) The increase in sample size has increased power.

**11.112** (a) $Z = 3.32 > 2.33$. Reject $H_0$. There is evidence that the average order will exceed $14. Institute the bagel and breakfast delivery service.

    (b) $p$ value = .00045

---

**Chapter 12**

**12.1** $Z = +1.73$

**12.2** $-2.58 < Z = +1.73 < +2.58$. Do not reject $H_0$.

**12.3** $p$ value = .0836

**12.6** (a) $Z = +0.39 < +1.96$. Do not reject $H_0$. There is no evidence of a difference in the average life of bulbs produced by the two machines.

    (b) $p$ value = .6966. The probability of obtaining such samples whose means differ by 13 hours or more when the null hypothesis is true is .6966.

**12.9**   (a)   $t = +1.91 > t_{198} = +1.645$. Reject $H_0$. There is evidence of a difference in output between the day and evening shift.

    (b)   $p$ value $= .0562$ estimated from a normal distribution. The probability of obtaining such samples whose means differ by 4.6 parts per hour or more when the null hypothesis is true is .0562.

**12.13**   (a)   $t = -2.19 < t_{48} = -2.0106$. Reject $H_0$. There is evidence of a difference in the average talking time prior to recharge. The newly developed battery lasts longer.

    (b)   Approximate normality of the data in each population.

    (c)   $p$ value $= .0337$ from Excel. The probability of obtaining such a result or a more extreme result when the null hypothesis is true is .0337.

    (d)   $t = -2.19 < t_{47} = -2.0117$. Reject $H_0$. There is evidence of a difference in the average talking time prior to recharge. The newly developed battery lasts longer.

    (e)   Approximate normality of the data in each population.

    (f)   $p$ value $= .0338$. The probability of obtaining such a result or a more extreme result when the null hypothesis is true is .0338.

    (g)   The results are very similar.

**12.14**   $v = 78$ degrees of freedom. $t = +4.18 > t_{78} = +1.9908$. Reject $H_0$. There is evidence of a difference in average appraised values in the two communities.

**12.18**   (a)   $F_U = 2.20$ and $F_L = 0.429$

    (b)   $F_U = 2.57$ and $F_L = 0.362$

    (c)   $F_U = 3.09$ and $F_L = 0.297$

    (d)   $F_U = 3.50$ and $F_L = 0.258$

    (e)   As $\alpha$ gets smaller, the region of nonrejection gets wider; $F_L$ gets smaller (approaching zero) and $F_U$ gets larger.

**12.20**   (a)   $F_L = 0.429$

    (b)   $F_L = 0.362$

    (c)   $F_L = 0.297$

    (d)   $F_L = 0.258$

    (e)   As $\alpha$ gets smaller, the region of nonrejection gets wider; $F_L$ gets smaller (approaching zero).

**12.25**   The $F$ test for the equality of two population variances should not be used if the underlying populations from which the samples were drawn are very right-skewed.

**12.26**   (a)   $F_L = 0.338 < F = 1.30 < F_U = 3.18$ where the degrees of freedom are 15 and 12, respectively. Do not reject $H_0$. There is no evidence of a difference in the two population variances.

    (b)   $F_U = 2.62$. Do not reject $H_0$. There is no evidence of a difference in the two population variances.

    (c)   $F_L = 0.403$. Do not reject $H_0$. There is no evidence of a difference in the two population variances.

**12.30**   (a)   $F_L = 0.441 < F = 0.87 < F_U = 2.27$ where the degrees of freedom are 24 and 24, respectively. Do not reject $H_0$. There is no evidence of a difference in the two population variances.

    (b)   If the assumption of underlying normality in the two populations is at least approximately met, the pooled-variance $t$ test should be used.

**12.35**   (a)   Since $-2.201 < t = -0.303 < +2.201$ based on 11 degrees of freedom, do not reject $H_0$. There is no evidence of a difference in the appraised values.

    (b)   The data (i.e., differences between the two appraisals) are approximately normally distributed.

    (c)   $p$ value $= .7674$ from Excel. The probability of obtaining a $t$ statistic $> +0.303$ or $-0.303$ or more when the null hypothesis is true is .7674.

**12.37**   (a)   Since $-2.2622 < t = -0.46 < +2.2622$ based on 9 degrees of freedom, do not reject $H_0$. There is no evidence of a difference in the average gasoline mileage when using the two gasoline types.

    (b)   The data (i.e., differences between the two recorded mileage per gallon results) are approximately normally distributed.

    (c)   $p$ value $= .6567$ from Excel. The probability of obtaining a $t$ statistic $> +0.46$ or $< -0.46$ when the null hypothesis is true is greater than .6567.

**12.42**   (a)   The lower and upper critical values are 31 and 59, respectively.

    (b)   The lower and upper critical values are 29 and 61, respectively.

    (c)   The lower and upper critical values are 25 and 65, respectively.

    (d)   As the level of significance $\alpha$ gets smaller, the width of the region of nonrejection gets wider.

**12.44**   (a)   The lower critical value is 31.

    (b)   The lower critical value is 29.

    (c)   The lower critical value is 27.

    (d)   The lower critical value is 25.

(e) As the level of significance $\alpha$ gets smaller, the width of the region of nonrejection gets wider.

**12.48** (a) The ranks for Sample 1 are 1, 2, 4, 5, and 10, respectively. The ranks for Sample 2 are 3, 6.5, 6.5, 8, 9, and 11, respectively.
(b) $T_1 = 22$
(c) $T_2 = 44$
(d) $22 + 44 = 66$

**12.49** The lower-tailed critical value is 20.

**12.50** Do not reject $H_0$.

**12.51** Do not reject $H_0$. There is no evidence of a difference in performance based on the two methods.

**12.55** (a) Let the nickel-cadmium sample be group 1. Thus $T_1 = 502.5$; since $Z = -2.62 < -1.96$, reject $H_0$. There is evidence of a difference.
(b) Equal variability in the two populations.
(c) The results are all similar.

**12.58** (a) The lower and upper critical values are 13 and 53, respectively.
(b) The lower and upper critical values are 10 and 56, respectively.
(c) The lower and upper critical values are 7 and 59, respectively.
(d) The lower and upper critical values are 5 and 61, respectively.
(e) As the level of significance $\alpha$ gets smaller, the width of the region of nonrejection gets wider.

**12.60** (a) The lower critical value is 13.
(b) The lower critical value is 10.
(c) The lower critical value is 7.
(d) The lower critical value is 5.
(e) As the level of significance $\alpha$ gets smaller, the width of the region of nonrejection gets wider.

**12.64** $W = 67.5$, the sum of the "+" ranks.

**12.65** The upper tail critical value is 61.

**12.66** Reject $H_0$. There is evidence that $M_D > 0$.

**12.69** (a) Since $5 < W = 18.5 < 40$, don't reject $H_0$. There is no evidence of a difference.
(b) Distribution of difference scores is approximately symmetric.
(c) These results are the same as those obtained previously.

**12.80** (a) $\$104.64 \le \mu \le \$115.36$
(b) $t = -10.0 < t_{24} = -2.7969$. Reject $H_0$. The average monthly balance of Plan A accounts is not equal to $105.
(c) $F_L = 0.37 < F = 1.125 < F_U = 2.40$ where the degrees of freedom are 24 and 49, respectively. Do not reject $H_0$. There is no evidence of a difference in the variances between Plan A and Plan B.
(d) $t = -9.903 < t_{73} = -2.6449$. Reject $H_0$. There is evidence of a difference in the average monthly balance between Plan A and Plan B. Plan A's balance is lower.
(e) The respective $p$ values from Excel are .0000, .7080, and .0000.

**12.84** Examining stem-and-leaf displays, box-and-whisker plots, and normal probability plots, the assumption of approximate normality seems to hold for both sampled populations. A level of significance $\alpha$ is chosen as .05 throughout. Testing for equality of population variances, $F = 1.62$ with 14 and 14 degrees of freedom. Since $F_L = 0.336 < F = 1.62 < F_U = 2.979$, do not reject $H_0$. There is no evidence of a difference in the variances between the two populations. Using the pooled-variance $t$ test with 28 degrees of freedom, $t = -4.13$. Since the $p$ value = .0029 < .05, reject $H_0$. There is evidence of a difference in the mean waiting times between the two populations. The waiting times on Friday evening are significantly longer than during the lunch period.

**12.85** Examining stem-and-leaf displays, box-and-whisker plots, and normal probability plots, the assumption of approximate normality does not hold for both sampled populations. Both sampled data sets are right-skewed. However, examining the standard deviations, interquartile ranges, and ranges, the assumption of equal variability between the two sampled populations seems to hold. Using a level of significance $\alpha$ of .05, $Z$ (the large-sample approximation formula for the Wilcoxon rank sum test statistic) = +0.66. Since the $p$ value = .507 > .05, do not reject $H_0$. There is no evidence of a difference in the mean processing times between the two production plants.

## Chapter 13

**13.1** (a) 4
(b) 30
(c) 34

**13.2** (a) $SSW = 150$

(b) $MSA = 15$

(c) $MSW = 5$

(d) $F = 3.00$

**13.3** (b) $F_U = 2.69$ with 4 and 30 degrees of freedom.

(c) Reject if $H_0$ if $F > F_U = 2.69$ with 4 and 30 degrees of freedom; otherwise do not reject $H_0$.

(d) Reject $H_0$.

**13.9** (b) From (a), the exam scores from Program A stand out from the others.

(c) Yes. $F_{max} = 1.184 < F_{max_U} = 8.44$ with 4 and 7 degrees of freedom. Do not reject $H_0$.

(d) Yes, we can proceed. $F = 4.22 > F_U = 2.95$ with 3 and 28 degrees of freedom. Reject $H_0$. There is evidence of a difference in the four sales training programs.

(e) Program A is superior to B and C.

**13.12** (a) The assumption of homogeneity of variances appears to hold. $F_{max} = 6.37 < F_{max_U} = 10.8$ with 3 and 5 degrees of freedom so do not reject $H_0$. Proceeding with ANOVA, $F = 14.10 > F_U = 3.68$ with 2 and 15 degrees of freedom. Reject $H_0$. There is evidence of a difference in sales among the various aisle locations.

(b) Sales are higher in the front than in the middle or in the rear.

(c) The front aisle is best for this product. The manager would have to evaluate the trade-off in switching the location of this product and the one that is currently intended for the front location.

**13.17** (a) 4

(b) 6

(c) 24

(d) 34

**13.18** (a) $SSE = 75$     (d) $MSE = 3.125$

(b) $MSA = 15$     (e) $F = 4.80$

(c) $MSBL = 12.5$     (f) $F = 4.00$

**13.19** (b) $F_U = 2.78$ with 4 and 24 degrees of freedom.

(c) Reject $H_0$ if $F > F_U = 2.78$ with 4 and 24 degrees of freedom; otherwise do not reject $H_0$.

(d) Reject $H_0$.

(e) $F_U = 2.51$ with 6 and 24 degrees of freedom.

(f) Reject $H_0$ if $F > F_U = 2.51$ with 6 and 24 degrees of freedom; otherwise do not reject $H_0$.

(g) Reject $H_0$.

**13.20** (a) 5 and 24 degrees of freedom, respectively.

(b) $Q_U = 4.17$ with 5 and 24 degrees of freedom.

(c) Critical range = 2.79

**13.26** (b) $F = 7.02 > F_U = 2.78$ with 4 and 24 degrees of freedom. Reject $H_0$. There is evidence of a difference in average plasma clotting time among the five treatment substances.

(c) Critical range = 0.472. Treatment substance 2 results in a significantly faster clotting time than does substance 3, 4, or 5. Treatment substance 1 is also significantly faster than 4. Other pairwise differences are not significant.

(d) $RE = 15.9$

(e) If faster clotting time is desired, treatment substances 2 or 1 may be chosen, assuming costs to administer the various treatments are similar.

(f) There is a significant patient-to-patient effect.

**13.28** (b) $F = 8.47 > F_U = 3.55$ with 2 and 18 degrees of freedom. Reject $H_0$. There is evidence of a difference in average ratings based on type of class.

(c) Critical range = 0.295. Required undergraduate courses yield significantly lower ratings than do other types of courses.

(d) $RE = 4.15$

(e) Depending on priorities, if the Dean is primarily interested in stimulating undergraduate student interest in the educational experience, only top rated teachers would be assigned to the required undergraduate courses.

**13.31** (a) 2     (d) 27

(b) 2     (e) 35

(c) 4

**13.32** (a) $SSAB = 40$     (e) $MSE = 10$

(b) $MSFA = 60$     (f) $F = 1.00$

(c) $MSFB = 55$     (g) $F = 6.00$

(d) $MSAB = 10$     (h) $F = 5.50$

**13.33** (a) $F_U = 3.35$ with 2 and 27 degrees of freedom.

(b) $F_U = 3.35$ with 2 and 27 degrees of freedom.

(c) $F_U = 2.73$ with 4 and 27 degrees of freedom.

(d) Do not reject $H_0$. $F = 1.00 < F_U = 2.73$ with 4 and 27 degrees of freedom.

(e)   Reject $H_0$. $F = 6.00 > F_U = 3.35$ with 2 and 27 degrees of freedom.

(f)   Reject $H_0$. $F = 5.50 > F_U = 3.35$ with 2 and 27 degrees of freedom.

**13.37**   (a)   (1) $F = 3.36 < F_U = 3.63$ with 4 and 9 degrees of freedom. Do not reject $H_0$. Interaction is not significant.

           (2) $F = 0.51 < F_U = 4.26$ with 2 and 9 degrees of freedom. Do not reject $H_0$. There is no effect due to service center.

           (3) $F = 17.58 > F_U = 4.26$ with 2 and 9 degrees of freedom. Reject $H_0$. There is evidence of a brand effect.

    (c)   Critical range = 8.36. Brand C requires a significantly greater amount of time for repair than either of the others.

    (d)   Management of the repair service may want to take into effect the differences in repair times among brands and charge for labor by the minute rather than charging a flat rate for repair.

**13.40**   (a)   (1) $F = 3.81 > F_U = 2.51$ with 6 and 24 degrees of freedom. Reject $H_0$. There is evidence of a significant interaction between operator and machine.

           (2) $F = 26.55 > F_U = 3.01$ with 3 and 24 degrees of freedom. Reject $H_0$. There is evidence of an operator effect.

           (3) $F = 43.57 > F_U = 3.40$ with 2 and 24 degrees of freedom. Reject $H_0$. There is evidence of a machine effect.

    (c)   The Tukey procedure for pairwise comparisons is not used. The significant interaction makes the study of the main effects difficult.

    (d)   One suggestion is to use the 12 operator–machine combinations as the levels of a single factor and completely analyze the data performing a one-way ANOVA.

**13.42**   $\chi_U^2 = 15.086$ with 5 degrees of freedom.

**13.43**   (a)   Reject if $H > \chi_U^2 = 15.086$; otherwise, do not reject $H_0$.

    (b)   Do not reject $H_0$.

**13.44**   $H = 0.635 < \chi_U^2 = 9.210$ with 2 degrees of freedom. Do not reject $H_0$. There is no evidence of a difference in the reaction times for these learning methods.

**13.48**   (a)   $H = 9.51 > \chi_U^2 = 7.815$ with 3 degrees of freedom. Reject $H_0$.

    (b)   Program A appears to be superior to Programs B and C.

    (c)   The results are similar.

**13.52**   $\chi_U^2 = 9.236$ with 5 degrees of freedom.

**13.54**   (a)   $F_R = 8.244 < \chi_U^2 = 9.488$ with 4 degrees of freedom. Do not reject $H_0$.

    (b)   There is no evidence that any of the five exercises is superior or worse based on the ratings assigned for the nine characteristics.

**13.57**   (a)   $F_R = 14.71 > \chi_U^2 = 9.488$ with 4 degrees of freedom. Reject $H_0$. There is evidence of a difference in median plasma clotting time among the five treatment substances. Substance 2 appears to have a significantly faster clotting time than substance 4.

    (b)   The results are similar.

**13.78**   (a)   $F_{max} = 1.83 < 10.8$ with 3 and 5 degrees of freedom. Do not reject $H_0$. There is no evidence of a violation in the assumption of homogeneity of variances.

    (b)   $F = 4.09 > F_U = 3.68$ with 2 and 15 degrees of freedom. Reject $H_0$. The $p$ value is 0.038. There is evidence of a difference in mean breaking strengths for the three air-jet pressures.

    (c)   $Q_U = 3.67$ with 3 and 15 degrees of freedom. Breaking strength scores under 30 psi are significantly higher than under 50 psi.

    (d)   Other things being equal, use 30 psi.

    (e)   $F = 3.71 < F_U = 4.10$ with 2 and 10 degrees of freedom. Do not reject $H_0$. The $p$ value exceeds .05. There is no evidence of a difference in mean breaking strengths for the three air-jet pressures.

    (f)   The Tukey procedure should not be used since the null hypothesis in (e) was not rejected.

    (g)   $F = 0.72 < F_U = 3.33$ with 5 and 10 degrees of freedom. Do not reject $H_0$. The $p$ value exceeds .05. There is no evidence of a blocking effect.

    (h)   $RE = 0.92$.

    (i)   If blocking is not effective, it should be avoided. In this study there is no evidence of a blocking effect so the completely randomized design model is superior to the randomized complete block design model.

    (j)   (1) $F = 1.97 < F_U = 3.89$ with 2 and 12 degrees of freedom. Do not reject $H_0$. The $p$ value is 0.182. Interaction is not significant.

           (2) $F = 4.87 > F_U = 4.75$ with 1 and 12 degrees of freedom. Reject $H_0$. The $p$ value is 0.048. There is evidence of an effect due to side-to-side aspect. Breaking strength scores are higher under the nozzle side-to-side aspect than under the opposite side-to-side aspect.

           (3) $F = 5.67 > F_U = 3.89$ with 2 and 12 degrees of freedom. Reject $H_0$. The $p$ value is 0.018. There is evidence of an effect due to air-jet pressure.

(l)    $Q_U = 3.77$ with 3 and 12 degrees of freedom. Critical range $= 1.30$. Breaking strength scores under 30 psi are significantly higher than under 40 psi or 50 psi.

(m)    Yarn breaking strength is highest under 30 psi.

(n)    The two-factor experiment gave a more complete, refined set of results than the one-factor experiment. Not only was the side-to-side aspect factor significant, the application of the Tukey *a posteriori* procedure on the air-jet pressure factor determined that breaking strength scores are significantly highest under 30 psi.

## Chapter 14

**14.1**    $Z = +2.89 > +1.96$. Reject $H_0$. Yes, there is evidence of a significant difference in the two proportions.

**14.3**    (a)    $Z = -7.34 < -2.58$. Reject $H_0$. Yes, there is evidence of a difference between males and females in the proportion who enjoy shopping for clothing.

(b)    $p$ value is virtually zero. The probability of obtaining a difference in two sample proportions as large as .295 or more when the null hypothesis is true is virtually zero.

(c)    $Z = -0.13 > -2.58$. Do not reject $H_0$. No, there is no evidence of a difference between males and females in the proportion who enjoy shopping for clothing. $p$ value $= .8966$. The probability of obtaining a difference in two sample proportions as large as .004 or more when the null hypothesis is true is .8966.

**14.4**    (a)    $Z = +2.90 > +1.96$. Reject $H_0$. Yes, there is evidence of a difference between the two performance evaluation methods with respect to employee perception of fairness. A greater proportion of employees found method 1 (feedback) fairer than method 2 (self-assessment).

(b)    $p$ value $= .0038$. The probability of obtaining a difference in two sample proportions as large as .21 or more when the null hypothesis is true is .0038.

**14.5**    (a)    $Z = -1.22 > -1.645$. Do not reject $H_0$. No, there is no evidence of a difference between the two companies in the proportion of CPAs who find the annual reports understandable.

(b)    $p$ value $= .2224$. The probability of obtaining a difference in two sample proportions as large as .12 or more when the null hypothesis is true is .2224.

(c)    $Z = -3.20 < -1.645$. Reject $H_0$. Yes, there is evidence of a difference between the two companies in the proportion of CPAs who find the annual reports understandable. $p$ value $= .00138$. The probability of obtaining a difference in two sample proportions as large as .32 or more when the null hypothesis is true is .00138.

**14.6**    (a)    $Z = +2.58 > +1.645$. Reject $H_0$. Yes, there is evidence that a high temperature setting is preferred.

(b)    $p$ value $= .0049$. The probability of obtaining a difference in two sample proportions as large as .08 or more when the null hypothesis is true is .0049.

**14.8**    (b)    The expected frequencies perfectly match the observed frequencies in each cell.

(c)    Since the observed and expected frequencies in each cell are equal to each other, the test statistic $\chi^2 = 0$.

**14.10**    (a)    $\chi^2 = 53.826 > \chi_U^2 = 6.635$ with 1 degree of freedom. Reject $H_0$. Yes, there is evidence of a difference between males and females in the proportion who enjoy shopping for clothing.

(b)    $p$ value is virtually zero. The probability of obtaining a difference in two sample proportions as large as .295 or more when the null hypothesis is true is virtually zero.

(c)    $\chi^2 = 0.011 < \chi_U^2 = 6.635$ with 1 degree of freedom. Do not reject $H_0$. No, there is no evidence of a difference between males and females in the proportion who enjoy shopping for clothing. $p$ value $= .918$ from Minitab. The probability of obtaining a difference in two sample proportions as large as .004 or more when the null hypothesis is true is .918. The $p$ value differs from that in Problem 14.3(c) only because of rounding.

**14.11**    (a)    $\chi^2 = 8.405 > \chi_U^2 = 3.841$ with 1 degree of freedom. Reject $H_0$. Yes, there is evidence of a difference between the two performance evaluation methods with respect to employee perception of fairness. A greater proportion of employees found method 1 (feedback) fairer than method 2 (self-assessment).

(b)    $p$ value $= .0038$. The probability of obtaining a difference in two sample proportions as large as .21 or more when the null hypothesis is true is .0038.

**14.12**    (a)    $\chi^2 = 1.50 < \chi_U^2 = 2.706$ with 1 degree of freedom. Do not reject $H_0$. No, there is no evidence of a difference between the two companies in the proportion of CPAs who find the annual reports understandable.

(b)    $p$ value $= .2224$. The probability of obtaining a difference in two sample proportions as large as .12 or more when the null hypothesis is true is .2224.

(c)    $\chi^2 = 10.24 > \chi_U^2 = 2.706$ with 1 degree of freedom. Reject $H_0$. Yes, there is evidence of a difference between the two companies in the proportion of CPAs who find the annual reports understandable. $p$ value $= .00138$. The probability of obtaining a difference in two sample proportions as large as .32 or more when the null hypothesis is true is .00138.

**14.16** (a) In the first row the expected frequencies are 20, 30, and 40, respectively. In the second row the expected frequencies are 30, 45, and 60, respectively.

(b) $\chi^2 = 12.5 > \chi_U^2 = 5.991$ with 2 degrees of freedom. Reject $H_0$. Yes, there is evidence of a difference in the proportions among the three groups.

(c) B > A since critical range $= .196$ and C > A since critical range $= .185$. The other pairwise difference (B versus C) is due to chance.

**14.18** (a) $\chi^2 = 73.47 > \chi_U^2 = 12.592$ with 6 degrees of freedom. Reject $H_0$. Yes, there is evidence of a difference in the proportions of males among the seven occupational titles.

(b) There is a significantly lower proportion of administrative support jobs held by males than there are in all other occupational groups. Also, there is a significantly higher proportion of production jobs held by males than there are management jobs, professional jobs, and sales jobs. All other pairwise differences in the proportions of jobs held by males in the various occupational groups are due to chance.

**14.22** (a) $\chi^2 = 11.29 > \chi_U^2 = 9.210$ with 2 degrees of freedom. Reject $H_0$. Yes, there is evidence of a difference among the three types of residences in the proportion of households that adopt the cable TV service.

(b) Residents of single-family dwellings adopt a cable TV service significantly more than do residents of apartment houses. Other pairwise differences are due to chance.

**14.24** (a) $\chi_U^2 = 21.026$ with 12 degrees of freedom.

(b) $\chi_U^2 = 26.217$ with 12 degrees of freedom.

(c) $\chi_U^2 = 30.578$ with 15 degrees of freedom.

(d) $\chi_U^2 = 23.209$ with 10 degrees of freedom.

(e) $\chi_U^2 = 23.209$ with 10 degrees of freedom.

**14.27** (a) $\chi^2 = 22.78 > \chi_U^2 = 15.507$ with 8 degrees of freedom. Reject $H_0$. There is evidence of a relationship between type of area of residence and manufacturer preference in an automobile purchase.

(b) $\chi^2 = 34.58 > \chi_U^2 = 15.507$ with 8 degrees of freedom. Reject $H_0$. There is evidence of a relationship between type of area of residence and manufacturer preference in an automobile purchase.

**14.29** (a) $\chi^2 = 9.83 < \chi_U^2 = 13.277$ with 4 degrees of freedom. Do not reject $H_0$. There is no evidence of a relationship between commuting time and stress.

(b) $\chi^2 = 9.83 > \chi_U^2 = 9.488$ with 4 degrees of freedom. Reject $H_0$. There is evidence of a relationship between commuting time and stress.

**14.36** (a) $Z = +5.30 > +2.58$ and $\chi^2 = 28.078 > \chi_U^2 = 6.635$ with 1 degree of freedom. Reject $H_0$. There is evidence of a difference between the two counties in the proportion of single-family houses that have gas heat.

(b) $p$ value $\cong .0000$. The probability of obtaining a difference in two sample proportions as large as .242 or more when the null hypothesis is true is approximately .0000.

(c) Except for errors due to rounding, the two types of tests provide equivalent results.

(d) Only the $Z$ test should be used if interest is in one-tailed (i.e., directional) tests.

(e) $Z = +1.35 < +2.58$ and $\chi^2 = 1.82 < \chi_U^2 = 6.635$ with 1 degree of freedom. Do not reject $H_0$. There is no evidence of a difference between the two counties in the proportion of single-family houses that have gas heat. $p$ value $\cong .177$. The probability of obtaining a difference in two sample proportions as large as .058 or more when the null hypothesis is true is approximately .177.

**14.39** $\chi^2 = 86.02 > \chi_U^2 = 9.488$ with 4 degrees of freedom. Reject $H_0$. There is evidence of a relationship between financial condition and educational level.

## Chapter 15

**15.1** (a) The proportion of nonconformances is largest (.22) on day 5 and smallest (.10) on day 3.

(b) $\bar{p} = .148$; $LCL = .041$; $UCL = .255$.

(c) There are no special causes of variation indicated. The process is in control.

**15.3** (a) $\bar{p} = .1145$; $LCL = .0522$; $UCL = .1768$. The proportion of late arrivals on day 13 is substantially out of control. Possible special causes of this value should be investigated. In addition, the next four highest points all occur on Friday.

(b) The snowstorm would explain why the proportion of late arrivals was so high on day 13.

(c) $\bar{p} = .1102$; $LCL = .0489$; $UCL = .1715$. The proportion of late arrivals on day 13 is out of control. Possible special causes of this value (e.g., a snowstorm) should be investigated. In addition, the next four highest points all occur on Friday.

**15.4** (a) $\bar{p} = .04617$; $UCL = .09882$. $LCL$ does not exist.

(b) Although none of the points are outside the control limits, there is evidence of a pattern over time.

15.6 (a) $\bar{p} = .0129$; $LCL = .0082$; $UCL = .0175$. Although none of the points are outside the control limits, there is evidence of a pattern over time, since the last eight points are all above the mean and most of the earlier points are below the mean. Thus, the special causes that might be contributing to this pattern should be investigated before any change in the system of operation is contemplated.

(b) Once special causes have been eliminated and the process is stable, management may take steps to increase process knowledge. Then Deming's 14 points can be applied to improve the system.

15.12 (a) The $c$ chart is used. $\bar{c} = 11.5$; $LCL = 1.33$. $UCL = 21.67$.

(b) The process is not in control because the first data point exceeds the upper control limit.

15.13 (a) $\bar{c} = 6.458$; $UCL = 14.082$. $LCL$ does not exist. The process appears to be in control since there are no points outside the upper control limit and there is no pattern in the results over time.

(b) The value of 12 is within the control limits, so that it should be identified as a source of common cause variation. Thus, no action should be taken concerning this value. If the value was 20 instead of 12, $\bar{c}$ would be 6.792 and $UCL$ would be 14.61. In this situation, a value of 20 would be substantially above the $UCL$, and action should be taken to explain this special cause of variation.

(c) Since the process is in control, management may take steps to increase process knowledge. Then Deming's 14 points can be applied to improve the system.

15.18 (a) $d_2 = 2.059$        (d) $D_4 = 2.282$
(b) $d_3 = 0.880$        (e) $A_2 = 0.729$
(c) $D_3 = 0$

15.22 (a) $\bar{R} = 271.57$; $UCL = 574.20$. $LCL$ does not exist. There are no points outside the control limits and no evidence of a pattern in the $R$ chart. $\bar{\bar{X}} = 198.67$; $LCL = 41.97$; $UCL = 355.36$. There are no points outside the control limits and no evidence of a pattern in the $\bar{X}$ chart.

(b) The process seems to be in control.

15.23 (a) $\bar{R} = 4.8325$ and $\bar{\bar{X}} = 3.549$. For the $R$ chart, $LCL = 1.0776$ and $UCL = 8.5874$. For the $\bar{X}$ chart, $LCL = 2.06$ and $UCL = 5.038$. The process appears to be in control since there are no points outside the lower and upper control limits and there is no pattern in the results over time.

(b) Since the process is in control, it is up to management to reduce the common cause variation by application of the 14 points of the Deming theory of management by process after increasing the process knowledge

---

# Chapter 16

16.1 (a) $b_0 = 2$; when $X = 0$, the average value of $Y$ is 2.
(b) $b_1 = 5$; for each increase of one unit of $X$, the value of $Y$ is expected to increase on average by 5 units.
(c) $\hat{Y}_i = 17$
(d) (1) Yes
    (2) No
    (3) No
    (4) Yes
    (5) No

16.3 (b) $b_0 = 1.45$; $b_1 = .074$
(c) For each increase of 1 foot of shelf space, sales are expected to increase on average by $7.40 per week.
(d) $\hat{Y}_i = 2.042$ or $204.20
(e) $b_0 = 1.5333$; $b_1 = .064$; $\hat{Y}_i = 2.0453$ or $204.53
(f) This depends on a trade-off—what else the particular amount of shelf space can be used for.

16.5 (b) $b_0 = 12.6786$; $b_1 = 1.9607$
(c) The $Y$ intercept $b_0$ (equal to 12.6786) represents the portion of the worker hours that is not affected by variation in lot size. The slope $b_1$ (equal to 1.9607) means that for each increase in lot size of one unit, worker hours are predicted to increase on average by 1.9607.
(d) $\hat{Y}_i = 100.91$
(e) Lot size varied from 20 to 80, so that predicting for a lot size of 100 would be extrapolating beyond the range of the $X$ variable.

(f)    $b_0 = 13.1607$; $b_1 = 1.9125$; $\hat{Y}_i = 99.22$

**16.10**   $SST = 40$ and $r^2 = 0.90$. The proportion of variation in $Y$ that is explained by the model is 0.90.

**16.14**   (a)   $r^2 = .684$; 68.4% of the variation in sales can be explained by variation in shelf space.
      (b)   $S_{YX} = 0.308$
      (c)   Based on (a) and (b), the model should be useful for predicting sales.

**16.16**   (a)   $r^2 = .988$; 98.8% of the variation in worker hours can be explained by variation in lot size.
      (b)   $S_{YX} = 4.71$
      (c)   Based on (a) and (b), the model should be very useful for predicting sales.

**16.20**   A residual analysis of the data indicates no apparent pattern. The assumptions of regression appear to be met.

**16.22**   (a) and (b)   Based on a residual analysis the model appears to be adequate.

**16.24**   (a) and (b)   Based on a residual analysis the model appears to be adequate.

**16.28**   (a)   An increasing linear relationship exists.
      (b)   $D = .109$
      (c)   There is strong positive autocorrelation among the residuals.

**16.30**   The data have been collected for a single time period from a set of stores. There is no sequential nature about the set of stores. Therefore it is not necessary to compute the Durbin-Watson statistic.

**16.34**   (a)   $t = +3.00$
      (b)   With 16 degrees of freedom the critical values are $t_{16} = \pm2.1199$.
      (c)   Reject $H_0$. There is evidence that the fitted linear regression model is useful.
      (d)   $+1.32 \le \beta_1 \le +7.68$

**16.36**   (a)   $t = +4.653 > t_{10} = +2.2281$ with 10 degrees of freedom. Reject $H_0$. There is evidence that the fitted linear regression model is useful.
      (b)   $+.039 \le \beta_1 \le +.109$

**16.38**   (a)   $t = +31.15 > t_{12} = +2.1788$ with 12 degrees of freedom. Reject $H_0$. There is evidence that the fitted linear regression model is useful.
      (b)   $+1.8236 \le \beta_1 \le +2.0978$

**16.44**   (a)   $1.787 \le \mu_{YX} \le 2.296$
      (b)   $1.310 \le Y_I \le 2.774$
      (c)   (b) provides an estimate for an individual response and (a) provides an estimate for an average predicted value.

**16.46**   (a)   $98.08 \le \mu_{YX} \le 103.74$
      (b)   $90.27 \le Y_I \le 111.56$
      (c)   (b) provides an estimate for an individual response and (a) provides an estimate for an average predicted value.

**16.50**   $r = +.9$.

**16.56**   (a)   $r = -.67$.
      (b)   $t = -3.78 < t_{18} = -2.1009$ with 18 degrees of freedom. Reject $H_0$. There is evidence of a relationship between charge per minute and number of minutes used.
      (c)   Yes. As suspected, the relationship between the two variables is negative.

**16.58**   (a)   $r = +.827$
      (b)   $t = +4.652 > t_{10} = +2.2281$ with 10 degrees of freedom. Reject $H_0$. There is evidence of a linear relationship between the two variables.
      (c)   Except for rounding error, the results from the two $t$ tests are identical.

**16.60**   (a)   $r = +.994$
      (b)   $t = +31.15 > t_{12} = +2.1788$ with 12 degrees of freedom. Reject $H_0$. There is evidence of a linear relationship between the two variables.
      (c)   Except for rounding error, the results from the two $t$ tests are identical.

**16.76**   (a)   $b_0 = 51.915$; $b_1 = 16.633$
      (b)   The $Y$ intercept $b_0$ represents the portion of the assessed value ($51,915) that does not vary with heating area. The slope $b_1$ (equal to 16.633) can be interpreted to mean that for each increase in 1,000 square feet in heating area, the assessed value is expected to increase on average by $16,633.
      (c)   $\hat{Y}_i = 81.024$ (i.e., $81,024)
      (d)   $S_{YX} = 2.919$ (i.e., $2,919)
      (e)   $r^2 = .659$; 65.9% of the variation in assessed value can be explained by variation in heating area.
      (f)   $r = +.812$
      (g)   There is no pattern in the residual plot. The model appears to be adequate.
      (h)   $t = +5.02 > t_{13} = +2.1604$ with 13 degrees of freedom. Reject $H_0$. There is evidence of a linear relationship between the two variables. The regression model is useful.
      (i)   $79.279 \le \mu_{YX} \le 82.769$ (in thousands of dollars).

(j)　$74.479 \le Y_I \le 87.569$ (in thousands of dollars).

(k)　$+9.469 \le \beta_1 \le +23.797$ (in thousands of dollars).

(l)　$b_0 = 52.805$; $b_1 = 15.849$; $\hat{Y}_i = 80.541$ (in thousands of dollars); $S_{YX} = 2.598$ (in thousands of dollars); $r^2 = .689$; and $r = +.83$. There is no pattern in the residual plot. The model appears to be adequate. $t = +5.37 > t_{13} = +2.1604$ with 13 degrees of freedom. Reject $H_0$. There is evidence of a linear relationship between the two variables. The regression model is useful. The respective confidence interval estimates are:

Mean response:　　$78.987 \le \mu_{YX} \le 82.096$ (in thousands of dollars)

Individual value:　$74.716 \le Y_I \le 86.367$ (in thousands of dollars)

Slope:　　　　　　$+9.471 \le \beta_1 \le +22.227$ (in thousands of dollars)

The results are similar. The change in assessed value for the one house did not affect the model.

**16.77**　(a)　$b_0 = +0.30$; $b_1 = +.00487$

(b)　The $Y$ intercept $b_0$ represents the portion of the GPI that varies with factors other than GMAT score. The slope $b_1$ can be interpreted to mean that for each increase of one point in GMAT score, GPI is predicted to increase on average by .00487 point (or for each increase of 100 points in GMAT score, GPI is predicted to increase by 0.487 point).

(c)　$\hat{Y}_i = 3.222$

(d)　$S_{YX} = .158$

(e)　$r^2 = .793$; 79.3% of the variation in GPI can be explained by variation in GMAT score.

(f)　$r = +.891$

(g)　There is widespread scatter in the residual plot, but there is no pattern in the relationship between the residuals and $X_i$.

(h)　$t = +8.31 > t_{18} = +2.1009$ with 18 degrees of freedom. Reject $H_0$. There is evidence of a linear relationship between GMAT score and GPI. The regression model is useful.

(i)　$3.144 \le \mu_{YX} \le 3.301$

(j)　$2.886 \le Y_I \le 3.569$

(k)　$+.00366 \le \beta_1 \le +.00608$

(l)　$b_0 = +.258$; $b_1 = +.00494$; $\hat{Y}_i = 3.221$; $S_{YX} = .147$; $r^2 = .820$; and $r = +.906$. There is no pattern in the residual plot. The model appears to be adequate. $t = +9.06 > t_{13} = +2.1009$ with 18 degrees of freedom. Reject $H_0$. There is evidence of a linear relationship between the two variables. The regression model is useful. The respective confidence interval estimates are:

Mean response:　　$3.147 \le \mu_{YX} \le 3.295$

Individual value:　$2.903 \le Y_I \le 3.539$

Slope:　　　　　　$+.00380 \le \beta_1 \le +.00609$

The results are similar but the new model appears to be slightly improved.

**Chapter 17**

**17.1**　(a)　Holding constant the effect of $X_2$, for each additional unit of $X_1$ the response variable $Y$ is expected to increase on average by 5 units. Holding constant the effect of $X_1$, for each additional unit of $X_2$ the response variable $Y$ is expected to increase on average by 3 units.

(b)　The $Y$ intercept $b_0$ represents the portion of the $Y$ that varies with factors other than $X_1$ and $X_2$.

(c)　60% of the variation in $Y$ can be explained or accounted for by the variation in $X_1$ and the variation in $X_2$ in this multiple linear regression model.

**17.3**　(a)　$\hat{Y}_i = -.02686 + .79116X_{1i} + .60484X_{2i}$.

(b)　For a given midsole impact, each increase of one unit in forefoot impact absorbing capability is expected to result in an average increase in the long-term ability to absorb shock by .79116 unit. For a given forefoot impact absorbing capability, each increase in one unit in midsole impact is expected to result in an average increase in the long-term ability to absorb shock by .60484 unit.

(c)　$r^2_{Y.12} = .9421$; 94.21% of the variation in the long-term ability to absorb shock can be explained by variation in forefoot impact-absorbing capability and variation in midsole impact.

(d)　$r^2_{adj} = .9324$

**17.6**　(a)　$\hat{Y}_i = 156.4 + 13.081X_{1i} + 16.795X_{2i}$ where $X_1$ = radio and television advertising in thousands of dollars and $X_2$ = newspaper advertising in thousands of dollars.

(b)　Holding the amount of newspaper advertising constant, for each increase of $1,000 in radio and television advertising, sales are predicted to increase on average by $13,081.

(h) $r_{Y.12}^2 = .821$; 82.1% of the variation in mileage per gallon can be explained by variation in length and variation in weight.

(i) $r_{adj}^2 = .816$

(j) $t = -0.51 > t_{86} = -1.9879$ with 86 degrees of freedom. Do not reject $H_0$. There is no evidence that variable $X_1$ (length) significantly contributes to a model already containing variable $X_2$ (weight). $t = -7.90 < t_{86} = -1.9879$ with 86 degrees of freedom. Reject $H_0$. There is evidence that variable $X_2$ (weight) significantly contributes to a model already containing variable $X_1$ (length). Since variable $X_1$ does not significantly contribute in the presence of variable $X_2$, only variable $X_2$ should be included and a simple linear regression model should be developed.

(k) For variable $X_1$ the $p$-value is .613. That is, the probability of obtaining a $t$-test statistic which differs from 0 by 0.51 or more when the null hypothesis is true is .613. For variable $X_2$ the $p$-value is less than 0.001. That is, the probability of obtaining a $t$-test statistic which differs from 0 by 7.90 or more when the null hypothesis is true is less than 0.001.

(l) $-0.009289 \le \beta_2 \le -0.005553$. This is a net regression coefficient. That is, taking into account the insignificant predictor $X_1$ (length), the slope measures the expected average decrease in mileage per gallon for each additional pound of weight.

(m) $r_{Y1.2}^2 = .0030$. For a given weight, 0.30% of the variation in mileage per gallon can be explained by variation in length. $r_{Y2.1}^2 = .4192$. For a given length, 41.92% of the variation in mileage per gallon can be explained by variation in weight.

Note the following simple linear regression model using weight to predict mileage per gallon:

| | |
|---|---|
| Regression equation: | $\hat{Y}_i = 47.885 - 0.00785X_{2i}$ |
| Prediction: | $\hat{Y}_i = 24.324$ miles per gallon |
| Residual analysis: | Both residual plots indicate that the fitted model appears to be adequate. |
| Influence analysis: | All 89 observations should be retained in the model. |
| Test of significance: | For variable $X_2$ (weight), $t = -19.91 < t_{87} = -1.9876$ with 87 degrees of freedom. Reject $H_0$. There is evidence that variable $X_2$ (weight) significantly contributes to a model. |
| $p$-value: | Probability of obtaining a simple regression model whose $t$-test statistic based on 87 degrees of freedom is 19.91 or more when the null hypothesis is true is less than 0.001. |
| RSquare: | $r^2 = .820$; 82.0% of the variation in mileage per gallon can be explained by variation in weight. |
| Slope: | $-0.008638 \le \beta_2 \le -0.007070$. The slope measures the expected average decrease in mileage per gallon for each additional pound of weight. |

## Chapter 18

**18.1** (a) $\hat{Y}_i = 17$

(b) $t_{22} = \pm 2.0739$. Since $t = +2.35$, the curvilinear effect is significant.

(c) $t_{22} = \pm 2.0739$. Since $t = +1.17$, the curvilinear effect is not significant.

(d) $\hat{Y}_i = 5$

**18.2** (b) $\hat{Y}_i = -7.56 + 1.27X_{1_i} - 0.0145X_{1_i}^2$

(c) $\hat{Y}_i = 18.52$ miles per gallon.

(d) Based on a residual analysis, some pattern appears to remain. The fitted model should be used with caution.

(e) $F = 141.46 > 3.89$. Reject $H_0$. The overall model is significant. The $p$-value is less than 0.001.

(f) $t = -16.63 < -2.0595$. Reject $H_0$. The curvilinear effect is significant. The $p$-value is less than .001.

(g) $r_{Y.12}^2 = .919$; 91.9% of the variation in miles per gallon can be explained by the curvilinear relationship between miles per gallon and highway speed.

(h) $r_{adj}^2 = .912$

**18.6** (a) Taking into account variable $X_2$, for each increase of one unit of $X_1$, the dependent variable $Y$ increases on average by 4 units.

(b) Holding constant the effects of $X_1$, the presence of $X_2$ is expected to increase the dependent variable $Y$ on average by 2 units.

(c) $t = +3.27 > +2.1098$. Reject $H_0$. The curvilinear effect is significant.

**18.8** (a) $\hat{Y}_i = 1.30 + .074X_{1_i} + .45X_{2_i}$, where $X_1 =$ shelf space, $X_2 = 0$ for back of aisle and 1 for front of aisle.

(b)  Holding constant the effect of aisle location, for each additional foot of shelf space, sales are expected to increase on average by .074 hundreds of dollars ($7.40). For a given amount of shelf space, a front-of-aisle location is expected to increase sales on average by .45 hundreds of dollars ($45).

(c)  $\hat{Y}_i = 1.892$ or $189.20

(d)  Based on a residual analysis, the model appears adequate.

(e)  $F = 28.53 > 4.26$. Reject $H_0$. There is evidence of a relationship between sales and the two independent variables.

(f)  $t = +6.72 > +2.2622$ and $t = +3.45 > +2.2622$. Therefore each explanatory variable makes a significant contribution and should be included in the model.

(g)  $+.049 \le \beta_1 \le +.099$
$+.155 \le \beta_2 \le +.745$

(h)  The slope here takes into account the effects of the other predictor variable. This did not happen in Problem 16.3.

(i)  $r^2_{Y.12} = .864$; 86.4% of the variation in sales can be explained by variation in shelf space and variation in aisle location.

(j)  $r^2_{adj} = .834$

(k)  $r^2_{Y.12} = .864$ while $r^2 = .684$. The inclusion of the aisle-location variable has resulted in an increase.

(l)  $r^2_{Y1.2} = .834$. Holding constant the effect of aisle location, 83.4% of the variation in sales can be explained by variation in shelf space; $r^2_{Y2.1} = .569$; for a given amount of shelf space, 56.9% of the variation in sales can be explained by variation in aisle location.

(m)  The slope of sales with shelf space is the same regardless of whether the aisle location is front or back.

(n)  $\hat{Y}_i = 1.20 + .082X_{1_i} + .75X_{2_i} - .024X_{1_i}X_{2_i}$, where $X_1$ = shelf space, $X_2 = 0$ for back of aisle and 1 for front of aisle. $t = -1.03 > -2.306$. Do not reject $H_0$. There is no evidence that the interaction term makes a contribution to the model.

(o)  The two-variable model in (e) should be used.

**18.11**  (a)  $\hat{Y}_i = 43.737 + 9.219X_{1_i} + 12.967X_{2_i}$, where $X_1$ = number of rooms, $X_2 = 0$ for east and 1 for west.

(b)  Holding constant the effect of neighborhood, for each additional room, selling price is expected to increase on average by 9.219 thousands of dollars ($9,219). For a given number of rooms, a west side neighborhood is expected to increase the selling price on average by 12.967 thousands of dollars ($12,967).

(c)  $\hat{Y}_i = 126.710$ or $126,710.

(d)  Based on a residual analysis, the model appears adequate.

(e)  $F = 55.39 > 3.59$. Reject $H_0$. There is evidence of a relationship between selling price and the two independent variables.

(f)  $t = +8.95 > +2.1098$ and $t = +3.59 > +2.1098$. Therefore each explanatory variable makes a significant contribution and should be included in the model.

(g)  $+7.0466 \le \beta_1 \le +11.3913$
$+5.2377 \le \beta_2 \le +20.1557$

(h)  $r^2_{Y.12} = .867$; 86.7% of the variation in selling price can be explained by variation in number of rooms and variation in neighborhood.

(i)  $r^2_{adj} = .851$

(j)  $r^2_{Y1.2} = .8251$. Holding constant the effect of neighborhood, 82.51% of the variation in selling price can be explained by variation in number of rooms; $r^2_{Y2.1} = .4314$; for a given number of rooms, 43.14% of the variation in selling price can be explained by variation in neighborhood.

(k)  The slope of selling price with number of rooms is the same regardless of whether the neighborhood is on the east side or on the west side.

(l)  $\hat{Y}_i = 53.95 + 8.032X_{1_i} - 5.90X_{2_i} + 2.089X_{1_i}X_{2_i}$, where $X_1$ = number of rooms, $X_2 = 0$ for east side neighborhood and 1 for west side neighborhood. $t = 1.01 < 2.119$. Do not reject $H_0$. There is no evidence that the interaction term makes a contribution to the model. The two-variable model in (a) should be used.

**18.14**  (a)  $\hat{Y}_i = 271,034.12$

(b)  Holding constant the effects of $X_2$, for each additional unit of $X_1$ the natural logarithm of $Y$ is expected to increase on average by 0.5. Holding constant the effects of $X_1$, for each additional unit of $X_2$ the natural logarithm of $Y$ is expected to increase on average by 0.7.

**18.15**  (a)  $\hat{Y}_i = 9.04 + 0.852\sqrt{X_{1_i}}$

(b)  $\hat{Y}_i = 15.36$ miles per gallon

(c)  The residual analysis indicates a clear curvilinear pattern. This model does not adequately fit the data.

(d) $t = +1.35 < +2.0555$. Do not reject $H_0$. The model does not provide a significant relationship.

(e) $r^2_{Y.12} = .066$; only 6.6% of the variation in miles per gallon can be explained by variation in square root of highway speed.

(f) $r^2_{adj} = .030$

(g) The curvilinear model in Problem 18.2 is far superior to the inadequate model here. The square root transformation on highway speed did nothing to enhance the fit.

**18.16** (a) $\ln \hat{Y}_i = 2.3882 + 0.004557X_1,$

(b) $\ln \hat{Y}_i = 2.6388$; 14.00 miles per gallon

(c) The residual analysis indicates a clear curvilinear pattern. This model does not adequately fit the data.

(d) $t = +1.10 < +2.0555$. Do not reject $H_0$. The model does not provide a significant relationship.

(e) $r^2_{Y.12} = 0.045$; only 4.5% of the variation in the natural logarithm of miles per gallon can be explained by variation in highway speed.

(f) $r^2_{adj} = 0.008$

(g) The curvilinear model in Problem 18.2 is far superior to the inadequate models here and in Problem 18.15. Neither the natural logarithm nor square root transformation on highway speed enhanced the fit.

**18.19** $VIF = 1.25$

**18.21** $VIF_1 = 2.8$ and $VIF_2 = 2.8$. There is no reason to suspect the existence of collinearity.

**18.24** (a) $C_p = 35.04$

(b) $C_p$ overwhelmingly exceeds $p + 1 = 3$, the number of parameters, so this model does not meet the criterion for further consideration as a *best* model.

**18.26** The $VIF$ values are 1.3, 1.0, and 1.2 respectively, so there is no evidence of collinearity. Stepwise regression selects a model with assessed value and time. The $C_p$ for the model with assessed value and time period is equal to 2.8 which is less than or equal to $p + 1$. Therefore this model will be selected. The fitted model is:

Selling price = $-44.988 + 1.7506$ assessed value $+ .368$ time

There is no evidence of a pattern in any of the residual plots and there is no evidence of any serious departure in the normality of the residuals. House 4 with $h = .20007$, Studentized deleted residual $= -3.84$, and Cook's $D = 815$ need to be deleted from the model. With this observation deleted, stepwise regression selects a model with assessed value and time. Using the $C_p$ criteria the model with assessed value and time period has a value of 2.2, so this model is selected. The fitted model is:

Selling price = $-39.62 + 1.66009$ assessed value $+ .507$ time

The overall model is significant: $F = 301.27$, $p < 0.0001$. Each independent variable significantly contributes to the model at the .05 level.

There is no evidence of a pattern in any of the residual plots and there is no evidence of any serious depature in the normality of the residuals. None of the points need to be deleted from the model due to inconsistency in the influence measures. Observations 8, 11, and 24 are flagged according to the $h$ criteria, observations 7, 8, and 22 are flagged based on the Studentized deleted residual, and none of the points are flagged based on Cook's $D$ statistic.

95.9% of the variation in selling price can be explained by variation in assessed value and the time period in which the house is sold. Holding constant the time period in which the house is sold, for each increase of \$1,000 in assessed value, the average selling price is predicted to increase by \$1,660.09. Holding constant the assessed value of the house, for each additional time period, the average selling price is predicted to increase by \$507.

Holding constant the effect of time period, 95.1% of the variation in selling price can be explained by variation in assessed value. Holding constant the effect of assessed value, 78.5% of the variation in selling price can be explained by variation in time period.

**18.32** (a) Holding constant the effects of $X_2$, for each additional unit of $X_1$ the natural logarithm of the odds ratio is expected to increase on average by 0.5. Holding constant the effects of $X_1$, for each additional unit $X_2$ of the natural logarithm of the odds ratio is expected to increase on average by 0.2.

(b) Estimated odds ratio = 4.055. The odds of "success" to "failure" are 4.055 to 1.

(c) Estimated probability of "success" is .802.

**18.33** (a) $\ln$ (estimated odds ratio) = $-1.91623$ so that the estimated probability = .1283.

(b) 70.16% of individuals who charge \$36,000 per annum and possess additional cards can be expected to purchase the premium card whereas from part (a), only 12.83% of individuals who charge \$36,000 per annum but do not possess additional cards can be expected to purchase the premium card. For a given amount of money charged per annum, the likelihood of purchasing a premium card is substantially higher among individuals who already possess additional cards than for those who do not possess additional cards.

(c)   In (estimated odds ratio) = −4.42273 so that the estimated probability = .0119.

(d)   Among individuals who do not possess additional cards, the likelihood of purchasing a premium card diminishes dramatically with a corresponding decrease in the amount of money charged per annum.

**Chapter 19**

**19.1**   $L = 9$

**19.2**   $W = .33$

**19.4**   (a)   1959

(b)   8

**19.6**   (b), (c), (e)

| Pd. | Year | $Y_i$ | 3-Year Moving Total | 3-Year Moving Avg. | $W$ .50 $E_i$ | $W$ .25 $E_i$ |
|---|---|---|---|---|---|---|
| 1 | 1978 | 1.45 | — | — | 1.45 | 1.45 |
| 2 | 1979 | 1.55 | 4.61 | 1.54 | 1.50 | 1.48 |
| 3 | 1980 | 1.61 | 4.76 | 1.59 | 1.55 | 1.51 |
| 4 | 1981 | 1.60 | 4.95 | 1.65 | 1.58 | 1.53 |
| 5 | 1982 | 1.74 | 5.26 | 1.75 | 1.66 | 1.58 |
| 6 | 1983 | 1.92 | 5.61 | 1.87 | 1.79 | 1.67 |
| 7 | 1984 | 1.95 | 5.91 | 1.97 | 1.87 | 1.74 |
| 8 | 1985 | 2.04 | 6.05 | 2.02 | 1.95 | 1.81 |
| 9 | 1986 | 2.06 | 5.90 | 1.97 | 2.01 | 1.88 |
| 10 | 1987 | 1.80 | 5.59 | 1.86 | 1.90 | 1.86 |
| 11 | 1988 | 1.73 | 5.30 | 1.77 | 1.82 | 1.82 |
| 12 | 1989 | 1.77 | 5.40 | 1.80 | 1.79 | 1.81 |
| 13 | 1990 | 1.90 | 5.49 | 1.83 | 1.85 | 1.83 |
| 14 | 1991 | 1.82 | 5.37 | 1.79 | 1.83 | 1.83 |
| 15 | 1992 | 1.65 | 5.20 | 1.73 | 1.74 | 1.79 |
| 16 | 1993 | 1.73 | 5.26 | 1.75 | 1.74 | 1.77 |
| 17 | 1994 | 1.88 | 5.61 | 1.87 | 1.81 | 1.80 |
| 18 | 1995 | 2.00 | 5.96 | 1.99 | 1.90 | 1.85 |
| 19 | 1996 | 2.08 | 5.96 | 1.99 | 1.99 | 1.91 |
| 20 | 1997 | 1.88 | — | — | 1.94 | 1.90 |

(d)   $\hat{Y}_{1998} = E_{1997} = 1.94$

(f)   $\hat{Y}_{1998} = E_{1997} = 1.90$

(g)   The results are similar.

**19.12**   (a)   The $Y$ intercept $b_0 = 4.0$ is the fitted trend value reflecting the *real* total revenues (in millions of *constant* 1995 dollars) during the origin or base year 1978.

(b)   The slope $b_1 = 1.5$ indicates that the *real* total revenues are increasing at a rate of 1.5 million dollars per year.

(c)   1982: $\hat{Y}_4 = 10.0$ million dollars

(d)   1997: $\hat{Y}_{19} = 32.5$ million dollars

(e)   2000: $\hat{Y}_{22} = 37.0$ million dollars

**19.14**   (b)   The series has been increasing continuously over the years.

**19.15**   (a)

| Year | Real | Year | Real | Year | Real |
|---|---|---|---|---|---|
| 1965 | 3.97 | 1976 | 4.04 | 1987 | 2.95 |
| 1966 | 3.86 | 1977 | 3.80 | 1988 | 2.83 |
| 1967 | 4.19 | 1978 | 4.06 | 1989 | 2.70 |
| 1968 | 4.60 | 1979 | 3.99 | 1990 | 2.91 |
| 1969 | 4.36 | 1980 | 3.76 | 1991 | 3.12 |
| 1970 | 4.12 | 1981 | 3.69 | 1992 | 3.03 |
| 1971 | 3.95 | 1982 | 3.47 | 1993 | 2.94 |
| 1972 | 3.83 | 1983 | 3.36 | 1994 | 2.87 |
| 1973 | 3.60 | 1984 | 3.22 | 1995 | 2.79 |
| 1974 | 4.06 | 1985 | 3.11 | 1996 | 3.03 |
| 1975 | 3.90 | 1986 | 3.06 | 1997 | 3.19 |

(b) A consumer was "better off" in 1967 and "worse off" in 1987. In 1967 the *actual* \$1.40 minimum wage was worth \$4.19 in adjusted (*real*) dollars while in 1987 the actual \$3.35 was worth \$2.95.

(c) $\hat{Y}_i = 4.3068 - 0.0488X_i$ where the origin is 1965 and $X$ units = 1 year.

(d) 1998: \$2.70;    1999: \$2.65;    2000: \$2.60

(e) A linear trend projection for CPI-U in the year 2000 is 173.1. A quadratic trend projection for CPI-U in the year 2000 is 184.6. If the actual minimum wage is raised to \$6.00, the adjusted (*real*) minimum wage would be expected to be \$3.47 based on a linear trend projection and \$3.25 based on a quadratic trend projection. The linear trend model is more parsimonious, the quadratic trend model provides a significantly better fit. In either case your legislators should know that such action on their part will enable minimum wage consumers to enjoy the same earning power that they had in the early 1980s, but still far short of the earning power that they had in the late 1960s and the entire decade of the 1970s.

**19.17** (b) $\hat{Y}_i = 179.691 + 4.695X_i$ where the origin is 1982 and $X$ units = 1 year.

(c) 1997: 250.1;    1998: 254.8;    1999: 259.5;    2000: 264.2

**19.18** (c) $\hat{Y}_i = 584.18 + 16.642X_i$ where the origin is 1978 and $X$ units = 1 year.

(d) 1998: 917.0;    1999: 933.7;    2000: 950.3

(f) $\hat{Y}_i = 373.26 + 55.44X_i$ where the origin is 1978 and $X$ units = 1 year.

(g) 1998: 1,482.0;    1999: 1,537.4;    2000: 1,592.8

(h) The forecasts in (g) are actual (*current*) dollars while the forecasts in (d) are in adjusted real (*constant*) dollars.

**19.22** (b) $\hat{Y}_i = (0.649)(1.113)^{X_i}$ where the origin is 1975 and $X$ units = 1 year.

(c) 1997: 6.8;    1998: 7.6;    1999: 8.5;    2000: 9.4

(f) $\hat{Y}_i = 0.827 + 0.1241X_i$ where the origin is 1975 and $X$ units = 1 year.

(g) $\hat{Y}_i = 1.226 + 0.0042X_i + 0.0057X_i^2$ where the origin is 1975 and $X$ units = 1 year.

(h) $\hat{Y}_i = (1.0673)(1.0586)^{X_i}$ where the origin is 1975 and $X$ units = 1 year.

(i) Linear:       1997: 3.6;    1998: 3.7;    1999: 3.8;    2000: 3.9
Quadratic:    1997: 4.1;    1998: 4.3;    1999; 4.6;    2000: 4.9
Exponential: 1997: 3.8;    1998: 4.0;    1999; 4.2;    2000: 4.5

(j) The forecasts in (c) are actual (*current*) dollars while the forecasts in (i) are in adjusted real (*constant*) dollars.

**19.26** (b) $\hat{Y}_i = (50.049)(1.0705)^{X_i}$ where the origin is 1978 and $X$ units = 1 year.

(c) The annual compound growth rate is 7.05%.

(d) 2000: 224.0 millions of *constant* 1995 dollars.

**19.27** (a) $\hat{Y}_{21} = 39.8$

(b) $\hat{Y}_{25} = 62.2$

**19.29** $\hat{Y}_{11} = 59.43;$    $\hat{Y}_{12} = 53.16;$    $\hat{Y}_{13} = 46.89;$    $\hat{Y}_{14} = 40.62.$

**19.34** (b) (1)  1997: 2.96;    1998: 2.81;    1999: 2.66;    2000: 2.51
(2)  1997: 3.82;    1998: 3.92;    1999: 4.02;    2000: 4.12
(3)  1997: 3.16;    1998: 3.13;    1999: 3.10;    2000: 3.07

**19.35** (a) 5

(b) 6

(c) The most recent five observed values—$Y_{36}$, $Y_{37}$, $Y_{38}$, $Y_{39}$, and $Y_{40}$

(d) $\hat{Y}_i = a_0 + a_1Y_{i-1} + a_2Y_{i-2} + \cdots + a_5Y_{i-5}$

(e) $\hat{Y}_{n+j} = a_0 + a_1\hat{Y}_{n+j-1} + a_2\hat{Y}_{n+j-2} + \cdots + a_5\hat{Y}_{n+j-5}$

**19.42** (b) $\hat{Y}_i = 0.2321 + 1.2526Y_{i-1} - 0.3708Y_{i-2} + 0.0417Y_{i-3};$ $t = 0.146 < 2.1315$ so the third order term can be deleted.

(c) $\hat{Y}_i = 0.2353 + 1.2429Y_{i-1} - 0.3233Y_{i-2};$ $t = -1.397 > -2.1098$ so the second order term can be deleted.

(d) $\hat{Y}_i = 0.1840 + 0.9533Y_{i-1};$ $t = 12.49 > 2.093$. Reject $H_0$. First order model is significant.

(e) 1997: 3.16;    1998: 3.20;    1999: 3.23;    2000: 3.27.

**19.43** (a) $S_{YX} = 2.121$; the standard error of estimate or square root of the average squared differences between the observed and fitted values is 2.121 billions of *constant* dollars.

(b) MAD = 1.50; the average of the absolute differences between the actual and the fitted values in the time series is 1.50 billions of *constant* dollars.

**19.44** (a) $S_{YX} = 5.523$; the standard error of estimate or square root of the average squared differences between the observed and fitted values is 5.523 billions of *constant* dollars.

(b) MAD = 3.167; the average of the absolute differences between the actual and the fitted values in the time series is 3.167 billions of *constant* dollars.

**19.49**
(a)

| | Linear Model | Quadratic | Exponential | Holt-Winters | Autoregressive |
|---|---|---|---|---|---|
| | Model OK | Model OK | Model OK | Model OK | Model OK |
| (b) | $S_{YX} = 0.481$ | $S_{YX} = 0.441$ | $S_{YX} = 0.454$ | $S_{YX} = 0.115$ | $S_{YX} = 0.315$ |
| (c) | MAD = 0.405 | MAD = 0.327 | MAD = 0.362 | MAD = 0.081; | MAD = 0.196 |

**19.50** (a) The $Y$ intercept $b_0 = 7.389$ is the fitted trend value reflecting the series during the origin or base month January 1993, prior to adjustment by the January multiplier.

(b) The slope $b_1 = 1.01005$ indicates that the series is expected to increase on average at a rate of 1.005% per month over this five-year period. The "slope" $b_2 = 1.1052$, the monthly compound growth rate, indicates that the January "multiplier" is 10.5% more than December.

**19.52** (a) The $Y$ intercept $b_0 = 20.09$ is the fitted trend prior to adjustment by the seasonal value during the origin or first quarter, 1994.

(b) The value $(b_1 - 1) \times 100\% = 10.52\%$ is the estimated quarterly compound growth rate in the series.

(c) $b_3 = 1.2214$ is the seasonal "multiplier" for the second quarter relative to the fourth quarter and indicates that there is 22.1% higher value in the series in the second quarter as compared to the fourth quarter.

**19.53** (a) $\hat{Y}_{11} = 60.34$

(b) $\hat{Y}_{12} = 51.94$

(c) $\hat{Y}_{23} = 200.34$

(d) $\hat{Y}_{24} = 172.43$

**19.54** (b) $\ln \hat{Y}_i = 6.01119 + 0.05537X_i + 0.01042Q_1 + 0.02389Q_2 + 0.01934Q_3$

(d) (1) $\hat{Y}_{15} = 903.02$    (2) $\hat{Y}_{16} = 936.15$

(3) Forecasts: 1998: $Q_1 = 999.81$   $Q_2 = 1071.06$   $Q_3 = 1126.91$   $Q_4 = 1168.25$
               1999: $Q_1 = 1247.70$   $Q_2 = 1336.62$   $Q_3 = 1406.31$   $Q_4 = 1457.90$

(4) The estimated quarterly compound growth rate in the Standard & Poor's stock index is 5.69%.

(5) There is a 2.42% increase in the second quarter as compared with the fourth quarter.

**19.56** (b) $\ln \hat{Y}_i = 5.52 + 0.00358X_i - 0.0399\text{Jan} - 0.0146\text{Feb} + 0.0779\text{Mar} - 0.0882\text{Apr} - 0.0097\text{May} + 0.0102\text{June} + 0.0315\text{July} + 0.0392\text{Aug} - 0.0434\text{Sep} + 0.0052\text{Oct} + 0.0353\text{Nov}$

(1) $\hat{Y}_{118} = 396.44$    (2) $\hat{Y}_{119} = 384.06$

(3) Forecasts for 1998:

| | | | |
|---|---|---|---|
| Jan = 370.36 | Feb. = 381.20 | March = 419.66 | April = 356.69 |
| May = 387.22 | June = 396.43 | July = 406.39 | Aug. = 411.01 |
| Sept = 379.80 | Oct. = 400.12 | Nov = 413.84 | Dec = 400.92 |

(4) The estimated monthly compound growth rate in outlays is 0.36%.

(5) For the month of June relative to December there is a 1.03% increase in real monthly outlays.

**19.72** (c) $\hat{Y}_i = 5.221 + 0.1876X_i$ where the origin is 1975 and $X$ units = 1 year.

(d) $\hat{Y}_i = 5.190 + 0.1968X_i - 0.00044X_i^2$ where the origin is 1975 and $X$ units = 1 year.

(e) $\hat{Y}_i = (5.323)(1.0272)^{X_i}$ where the origin is 1975 and $X$ units = 1 year.

(g) $\hat{Y}_i = 1.4037X_i + 0.6754Y_{i-1} + 0.1765Y_{i-2} - 0.0228Y_{i-3}$; $t = -0.08 > 2.1315$; third order term is not significant.

(h) $\hat{Y}_i = 1.6479 + 0.6815Y_{i-1} + 0.1166Y_{i-2}$; $t = 0.479 < 2.1098$; second order term is not significant.

(i) $\hat{Y}_i = 1.7401 + 0.7818Y_{i-1}$; $t = 7.197 > 2.093$. Reject $H_0$. First order model is significant.

(j)–(l)

| | Linear Model | Quadratic | Exponential | Holt-Winters | Autoregressive |
|---|---|---|---|---|---|
| $S_{YX}$: | 0.703 | 0.721 | 0.714 | 0.259 | 0.685 |
| | Linear Model | Quadratic | Exponential | Holt-Winters | Autoregressive |
| MAD: | 0.523 | 0.521 | 0.524 | 0.180 | 0.502 |

(m) Holt-Winters model is least parsimonious but clearly the best.

(n) 1997: 8.48;    1998: 8.29;    1999: 8.11;    2000: 7.93.

# Appendix A

## Review of Arithmetic and Algebra

### A.1 RULES FOR ARITHMETIC OPERATIONS

The following is a summary of various rules for arithmetic operations with each rule illustrated by a numerical example.

| RULE | EXAMPLE |
|------|---------|
| 1. $a + b = c$ and $b + a = c$ | $2 + 1 = 3$ and $1 + 2 = 3$ |
| 2. $a + (b + c) = (a + b) + c$ | $5 + (7 + 4) = (5 + 7) + 4 = 16$ |
| 3. $a - b = c$ but $b - a \neq c$ | $9 - 7 = 2$ but $7 - 9 = -2$ |
| 4. $a \times b = b \times a$ | $7 \times 6 = 6 \times 7 = 42$ |
| 5. $a \times (b + c) = (a \times b) + (a \times c)$ | $2 \times (3 + 5) = (2 \times 3) + (2 \times 5) = 16$ |
| 6. $a \div b \neq b \div a$ | $12 \div 3 \neq 3 \div 12$ |
| 7. $\dfrac{a + b}{c} = \dfrac{a}{c} + \dfrac{b}{c}$ | $\dfrac{7 + 3}{2} = \dfrac{7}{2} + \dfrac{3}{2} = 5$ |
| 8. $\dfrac{a}{b + c} \neq \dfrac{a}{b} + \dfrac{a}{c}$ | $\dfrac{3}{4 + 5} \neq \dfrac{3}{4} + \dfrac{3}{5}$ |
| 9. $\dfrac{1}{a} + \dfrac{1}{b} = \dfrac{b + a}{ab}$ | $\dfrac{1}{3} + \dfrac{1}{5} = \dfrac{5 + 3}{(3)(5)} = \dfrac{8}{15}$ |
| 10. $\dfrac{a}{b} \times \dfrac{c}{d} = \dfrac{a \times c}{b \times d}$ | $\dfrac{2}{3} \times \dfrac{6}{7} = \dfrac{2 \times 6}{3 \times 7} = \dfrac{12}{21}$ |
| 11. $\dfrac{a}{b} \div \dfrac{c}{d} = \dfrac{a \times d}{b \times c}$ | $\dfrac{5}{8} \div \dfrac{3}{7} = \dfrac{5 \times 7}{8 \times 3} = \dfrac{35}{24}$ |

## A.2    RULES FOR ALGEBRA: EXPONENTS AND SQUARE ROOTS

The following is a summary of various rules for algebraic operations with each rule illustrated by a numerical example:

| RULE | EXAMPLE |
|------|---------|
| 1. $X^a \cdot X^b = X^{a+b}$ | $4^2 \cdot 4^3 = 4^5$ |
| 2. $(X^a)^b = X^{ab}$ | $(2^2)^3 = 2^6$ |
| 3. $(X^a/X^b) = X^{a-b}$ | $\dfrac{3^5}{3^3} = 3^2$ |
| 4. $\dfrac{X^a}{X^a} = X^0 = 1$ | $\dfrac{3^4}{3^4} = 3^0 = 1$ |
| 5. $\sqrt{XY} = \sqrt{X}\sqrt{Y}$ | $\sqrt{(25)(4)} = \sqrt{25}\sqrt{4} = 10$ |
| 6. $\sqrt{\dfrac{X}{Y}} = \dfrac{\sqrt{X}}{\sqrt{Y}}$ | $\sqrt{\dfrac{16}{100}} = \dfrac{\sqrt{16}}{\sqrt{100}} = .40$ |

# Appendix B

## Summation Notation

Because the operation of addition occurs so frequently in statistics, the special symbol $\Sigma$ (sigma) is used to denote "taking the sum of." Suppose, for example, that we have a set of $n$ values for some variable $X$. The expression $\sum_{i=1}^{n} X_i$ means that these $n$ values are to be added together. Thus

$$\sum_{i=1}^{n} X_i = X_1 + X_2 + X_3 + \cdots + X_n$$

The use of the summation notation can be illustrated in the following problem. Suppose that we have five observations of a variable $X$: $X_1 = 2$, $X_2 = 0$, $X_3 = -1$, $X_4 = 5$, and $X_5 = 7$. Thus

$$\sum_{i=1}^{5} X_i = X_1 + X_2 + X_3 + X_4 + X_5 = 2 + 0 + (-1) + 5 + 7 = 13$$

In statistics we are also frequently involved with summing the squared values of a variable. Thus

$$\sum_{i=1}^{n} X_i^2 = X_1^2 + X_2^2 + X_3^2 + \cdots + X_n^2$$

and, in our example, we have

$$\begin{aligned}
\sum_{i=1}^{5} X_i^2 &= X_1^2 + X_2^2 + X_3^2 + X_4^2 + X_5^2 \\
&= 2^2 + 0^2 + (-1)^2 + 5^2 + 7^2 \\
&= 4 + 0 + 1 + 25 + 49 \\
&= 79
\end{aligned}$$

We should realize here that $\sum_{i=1}^{n} X_i^2$, the summation of the squares, is not the same as $\left(\sum_{i=1}^{n} X_i\right)^2$, the square of the sum, that is,

$$\sum_{i=1}^{n} X_i^2 \neq \left(\sum_{i=1}^{n} X_i\right)^2$$

In our example the summation of squares is equal to 79. This is not equal to the square of the sum, which is $13^2 = 169$.

Another frequently used operation involves the summation of the product. That is, suppose that we have two variables, $X$ and $Y$, each having $n$ observations. Then,

$$\sum_{i=1}^{n} X_i Y_i = X_1 Y_1 + X_2 Y_2 + X_3 Y_3 + \cdots + X_n Y_n$$

Continuing with our previous example, suppose that there is also a second variable $Y$ whose five values are $Y_1 = 1$, $Y_2 = 3$, $Y_3 = -2$, $Y_4 = 4$, and $Y_5 = 3$. Then,

$$\sum_{i=1}^{5} X_i Y_i = X_1 Y_1 + X_2 Y_2 + X_3 Y_3 + X_4 Y_4 + X_5 Y_5$$
$$= (2)(1) + (0)(3) + (-1)(-2) + (5)(4) + (7)(3)$$
$$= 2 + 0 + 2 + 20 + 21$$
$$= 45$$

In computing $\sum_{i=1}^{n} X_i Y_i$ we must realize that the first value of $X$ is multiplied by the first value of $Y$, the second value of $X$ is multiplied by the second value of $Y$, and so on. These cross products are then summed in order to obtain the desired result. However, we should note here that the summation of cross products is not equal to the product of the individual sums, that is,

$$\sum_{i=1}^{n} X_i Y_i \neq \left( \sum_{i=1}^{n} X_i \right) \left( \sum_{i=1}^{n} Y_i \right)$$

In our example, note that $\sum_{i=1}^{5} X_i = 13$ and $\sum_{i=1}^{5} Y_i = 1 + 3 + (-2) + 4 + 3 = 9$ so that $\left( \sum_{i=1}^{5} X_i \right) \left( \sum_{i=1}^{5} Y_i \right) = (13)(9) = 117$. This is not the same as $\sum_{i=1}^{n} X_i Y_i$, which equals 45.

Before studying the four basic rules of performing operations with summation notation, it would be helpful to present the values for each of the five observations of $X$ and $Y$ in a tabular format.

| OBSERVATION | $X_i$ | $Y_i$ |
|---|---|---|
| 1 | 2 | 1 |
| 2 | 0 | 3 |
| 3 | -1 | -2 |
| 4 | 5 | 4 |
| 5 | 7 | 3 |
| | $\sum_{i=1}^{5} X_i = 13$ | $\sum_{i=1}^{5} Y_i = 9$ |

**RULE 1:** The summation of the values of two variables is equal to the sum of the values of each summed variable.

$$\sum_{i=1}^{n} (X_i + Y_i) = \sum_{i=1}^{n} X_i + \sum_{i=1}^{n} Y_i$$

Thus, in our example,

$$\sum_{i=1}^{5}(X_i + Y_i) = (2 + 1) + (0 + 3) + (-1 + (-2)) + (5 + 4) + (7 + 3)$$

$$= 3 + 3 + (-3) + 9 + 10$$

$$= 22 = \sum_{i=1}^{5}X_i + \sum_{i=1}^{5}Y_i = 13 + 9 = 22$$

**RULE 2:** The summation of a difference between the values of two variables is equal to the difference between the summed values of the variables.

$$\sum_{i=1}^{n}(X_i - Y_i) = \sum_{i=1}^{n}X_i - \sum_{i=1}^{n}Y_i$$

Thus, in our example,

$$\sum_{i=1}^{5}(X_i - Y_i) = (2 - 1) + (0 - 3) + (-1 - (-2)) + (5 - 4) + (7 - 3)$$

$$= 1 + (-3) + 1 + 1 + 4$$

$$= 4 = \sum_{i=1}^{5}X_i - \sum_{i=1}^{5}Y_i = 13 - 9 = 4$$

**RULE 3:** The summation of a constant times a variable is equal to that constant times the summation of the values of the variable.

$$\sum_{i=1}^{n}cX_i = c\sum_{i=1}^{n}X_i$$

where $c$ is a constant.

Thus, in our example, if $c = 2$,

$$\sum_{i=1}^{5}cX_i = \sum_{i=1}^{5}2X_i = (2)(2) + (2)(0) + (2)(-1) + (2)(5) + (2)(7)$$

$$= 4 + 0 + (-2) + 10 + 14$$

$$= 26 = 2\sum_{i=1}^{5}X = (2)(13) = 26$$

**RULE 4:** A constant summed $n$ times will be equal to $n$ times the value of the constant.

$$\sum_{i=1}^{n}c = nc$$

where $c$ is a constant. Thus, if the constant $c = 2$ is summed five times, we would have

$$\sum_{i=1}^{5} c = 2 + 2 + 2 + 2 + 2$$

$$= 10 = (5)(2) = 10$$

To illustrate how these summation rules are used, we may demonstrate one of the mathematical properties pertaining to the average or arithmetic mean (see section 4.2), that is,

$$\sum_{i=1}^{n} (X_i - \overline{X}) = 0$$

This property states that the summation of the differences between each observation and the arithmetic mean is zero. This can be proved mathematically in the following manner.

**1.** From equation (4.1),

$$\overline{X} = \frac{\sum_{i=1}^{n} X_i}{n}$$

Thus, using summation rule 2, we have

$$\sum_{i=1}^{n} (X_i - \overline{X}) = \sum_{i=1}^{n} X_i - \sum_{i=1}^{n} \overline{X}$$

**2.** Because, for any fixed set of data, $\overline{X}$ can be considered a constant, from summation rule 4 we have

$$\sum_{i=1}^{n} \overline{X} = n\overline{X}$$

Therefore,

$$\sum_{i=1}^{n} (X_i - \overline{X}) = \sum_{i=1}^{n} X_i - n\overline{X}$$

**3.** However, from equation (4.1), because

$$\overline{X} = \frac{\sum_{i=1}^{n} X_i}{n} \quad \text{then} \quad n\overline{X} = \sum_{i=1}^{n} X_i$$

Therefore,

$$\sum_{i=1}^{n} (X_i - \overline{X}) = \sum_{i=1}^{n} X_i - \sum_{i=1}^{n} X_i$$

Thus, we have shown that

$$\sum_{i=1}^{n} (X_i - \overline{X}) = 0$$

## Problem

Suppose that there are six observations for the variables $X$ and $Y$ such that $X_1 = 2$, $X_2 = 1$, $X_3 = 5$, $X_4 = -3$, $X_5 = 1$, $X_6 = -2$, and $Y_1 = 4$, $Y_2 = 0$, $Y_3 = -1$, $Y_4 = 2$, $Y_5 = 7$, and $Y_6 = -3$. Compute each of the following:

(a) $\displaystyle\sum_{i=1}^{6} X_i$

(b) $\displaystyle\sum_{i=1}^{6} Y_i$

(c) $\displaystyle\sum_{i=1}^{6} X_i^2$

(d) $\displaystyle\sum_{i=1}^{6} Y_i^2$

(e) $\displaystyle\sum_{i=1}^{6} X_i Y_i$

(f) $\displaystyle\sum_{i=1}^{6} (X_i + Y_i)$

(g) $\displaystyle\sum_{i=1}^{6} (X_i - Y_i)$

(h) $\displaystyle\sum_{i=1}^{6} (X_i - 3Y_i + 2X_i^2)$

(i) $\displaystyle\sum_{i=1}^{6} (cX_i)$, where $c = -1$

(j) $\displaystyle\sum_{i=1}^{6} (X_i - 3Y_i + c)$, where $c = +3$

---

## References

1. Bashaw, W. L., *Mathematics for Statistics* (New York: Wiley, 1969).
2. Lanzer, P. *Video Review of Arithmetic* (Roslyn Heights, NY: Video Aided Instruction, 1990).
3. Levine, D. *Video Review of Statistics* (Roslyn Heights, NY: Video Aided Instruction, 1989).
4. Shane, H., *Video Review of Elementary Algebra* (Roslyn Heights, NY: Video Aided Instruction, 1990).

# Appendix C

## Statistical Symbols and Greek Alphabet

 **C.1 STATISTICAL SYMBOLS**

| | | | |
|---|---|---|---|
| + | add | × | multiply |
| − | subtract | ÷ | divide |
| = | equals | ≠ | not equal |
| ≅ | approximately equal to | | |
| > | greater than | < | less than |
| ≥ or ⩾ | greater than or equal to | ≤ or ⩽ | less than or equal to |

 **C.2 GREEK ALPHABET**

| GREEK LETTER | | GREEK NAME | ENGLISH EQUIVALENT | GREEK LETTER | | GREEK NAME | ENGLISH EQUIVALENT |
|---|---|---|---|---|---|---|---|
| A | α | Alpha | a | N | ν | Nu | n |
| B | β | Beta | b | Ξ | ξ | Xi | x |
| Γ | γ | Gamma | g | O | o | Omicron | ŏ |
| Δ | δ | Delta | d | Π | π | Pi | p |
| E | ε | Epsilon | ĕ | P | ρ | Rho | r |
| Z | ζ | Zeta | z | Σ | σ | Sigma | s |
| H | η | Eta | ē | T | τ | Tau | t |
| Θ | θ | Theta | th | Υ | υ | Upsilon | u |
| I | ι | Iota | i | Φ | φ | Phi | ph |
| K | κ | Kappa | k | X | χ | Chi | ch |
| Λ | λ | Lambda | l | Ψ | ψ | Psi | ps |
| M | μ | Mu | m | Ω | ω | Omega | ō |

# Appendix D

## Special Data Set (for Team Projects)

This is a file containing data on 194 domestic general stock funds with highest Morningstar performance ratings 4 or 5.

*Notes*: To use the file MUTUAL, please note the following codes for the data:

- Fund—Name of fund.
- Type—Type of fund: 1 = LG; 2 = MG; 3 = SG; 4 = LB; 5 = MB; 6 = SB (where L, M, and S refer to Size and G and B refer to Objective).
- NAV—Net asset value (in dollars).
- 1Yr%Ret—Total year-to-date return (in percent).
- FeeSch—Fee schedule: 1 = b (From fund assets); 2 = d (Deferred fees); 3 = f (Front-load fees); 4 = m (Multiple fees); 5 = n (No-load).
- FeeGp—Fee structure group: 1 = N (No-load); 2 = F (Fee).
- Obj—Objective of fund: 1 = G (Growth fund); 2 = B (Blend fund).
- Size—Size of fund: 1 = L (Large); 2 = M (Mid-Cap); 3 = S (Small).

*Source: Data taken from* The New York Times, *section 3, Money & Business, January 19, 1997. Copyright © by the New York Times Company. Reprinted by permission.*

### Mutual

| FUND | TYPE | NAV | 1YR%RET | FEESCH | FEEGP | OBJ | SIZE |
|---|---|---|---|---|---|---|---|
| AARP Investment GrowInc | LB | 47.19 | 27.4 | n | N | B | L |
| AIM BlueCh A | LG | 25.75 | 32.3 | m | F | G | L |
| Accessor Growth | LB | 20.49 | 28.7 | n | N | B | L |
| ⋮ | ⋮ | ⋮ | ⋮ | ⋮ | ⋮ | ⋮ | ⋮ |
| Wright Yacktman | MB | 13.53 | 28.6 | b | F | B | M |

# Appendix E

## Tables

## Table E.1 *Table of Random Numbers*

| Row | 00000 12345 | 00001 67890 | 11111 12345 | 11112 67890 | 22222 12345 | 22223 67890 | 33333 12345 | 33334 67890 |
|-----|-------|-------|-------|-------|-------|-------|-------|-------|
| 01 | 49280 | 88924 | 35779 | 00283 | 81163 | 07275 | 89863 | 02348 |
| 02 | 61870 | 41657 | 07468 | 08612 | 98083 | 97349 | 20775 | 45091 |
| 03 | 43898 | 65923 | 25078 | 86129 | 78496 | 97653 | 91550 | 08078 |
| 04 | 62993 | 93912 | 30454 | 84598 | 56095 | 20664 | 12872 | 64647 |
| 05 | 33850 | 58555 | 51438 | 85507 | 71865 | 79488 | 76783 | 31708 |
| 06 | 97340 | 03364 | 88472 | 04334 | 63919 | 36394 | 11095 | 92470 |
| 07 | 70543 | 29776 | 10087 | 10072 | 55980 | 64688 | 68239 | 20461 |
| 08 | 89382 | 93809 | 00796 | 95945 | 34101 | 81277 | 66090 | 88872 |
| 09 | 37818 | 72142 | 67140 | 50785 | 22380 | 16703 | 53362 | 44940 |
| 10 | 60430 | 22834 | 14130 | 96593 | 23298 | 56203 | 92671 | ·15925 |
| 11 | 82975 | 66158 | 84731 | 19436 | 55790 | 69229 | 28661 | 13675 |
| 12 | 39087 | 71938 | 40355 | 54324 | 08401 | 26299 | 49420 | 59208 |
| 13 | 55700 | 24586 | 93247 | 32596 | 11865 | 63397 | 44251 | 43189 |
| 14 | 14756 | 23997 | 78643 | 75912 | 83832 | 32768 | 18928 | 57070 |
| 15 | 32166 | 53251 | 70654 | 92827 | 63491 | 04233 | 33825 | 69662 |
| 16 | 23236 | 73751 | 31888 | 81718 | 06546 | 83246 | 47651 | 04877 |
| 17 | 45794 | 26926 | 15130 | 82455 | 78305 | 55058 | 52551 | 47182 |
| 18 | 09893 | 20505 | 14225 | 68514 | 46427 | 56788 | 96297 | 78822 |
| 19 | 54382 | 74598 | 91499 | 14523 | 68479 | 27686 | 46162 | 83554 |
| 20 | 94750 | 89923 | 37089 | 20048 | 80336 | 94598 | 26940 | 36858 |
| 21 | 70297 | 34135 | 53140 | 33340 | 42050 | 82341 | 44104 | 82949 |
| 22 | 85157 | 47954 | 32979 | 26575 | 57600 | 40881 | 12250 | 73742 |
| 23 | 11100 | 02340 | 12860 | 74697 | 96644 | 89439 | 28707 | 25815 |
| 24 | 36871 | 50775 | 30592 | 57143 | 17381 | 68856 | 25853 | 35041 |
| 25 | 23913 | 48357 | 63308 | 16090 | 51690 | 54607 | 72407 | 55538 |
| 26 | 79348 | 36085 | 27973 | 65157 | 07456 | 22255 | 25626 | 57054 |
| 27 | 92074 | 54641 | 53673 | 54421 | 18130 | 60103 | 69593 | 49464 |
| 28 | 06873 | 21440 | 75593 | 41373 | 49502 | 17972 | 82578 | 16364 |
| 29 | 12478 | 37622 | 99659 | 31065 | 83613 | 69889 | 58869 | 29571 |
| 30 | 57175 | 55564 | 65411 | 42547 | 70457 | 03426 | 72937 | 83792 |
| 31 | 91616 | 11075 | 80103 | 07831 | 59309 | 13276 | 26710 | 73000 |
| 32 | 78025 | 73539 | 14621 | 39044 | 47450 | 03197 | 12787 | 47709 |
| 33 | 27587 | 67228 | 80145 | 10175 | 12822 | 86687 | 65530 | 49325 |
| 34 | 16690 | 20427 | 04251 | 64477 | 73709 | 73945 | 92396 | 68263 |
| 35 | 70183 | 58065 | 65489 | 31833 | 82093 | 16747 | 10386 | 59293 |
| 36 | 90730 | 35385 | 15679 | 99742 | 50866 | 78028 | 75573 | 67257 |
| 37 | 10934 | 93242 | 13431 | 24590 | 02770 | 48582 | 00906 | 58595 |
| 38 | 82462 | 30166 | 79613 | 47416 | 13389 | 80268 | 05085 | 96666 |
| 39 | 27463 | 10433 | 07606 | 16285 | 93699 | 60912 | 94532 | 95632 |
| 40 | 02979 | 52997 | 09079 | 92709 | 90110 | 47506 | 53693 | 49892 |
| 41 | 46888 | 69929 | 75233 | 52507 | 32097 | 37594 | 10067 | 67327 |
| 42 | 53638 | 83161 | 08289 | 12639 | 08141 | 12640 | 28437 | 09268 |
| 43 | 82433 | 61427 | 17239 | 89160 | 19666 | 08814 | 37841 | 12847 |
| 44 | 35766 | 31672 | 50082 | 22795 | 66948 | 65581 | 84393 | 15890 |
| 45 | 10853 | 42581 | 08792 | 13257 | 61973 | 24450 | 52351 | 16602 |
| 46 | 20341 | 27398 | 72906 | 63955 | 17276 | 10646 | 74692 | 48438 |
| 47 | 54458 | 90542 | 77563 | 51839 | 52901 | 53355 | 83281 | 19177 |
| 48 | 26337 | 66530 | 16687 | 35179 | 46560 | 00123 | 44546 | 79896 |
| 49 | 34314 | 23729 | 85264 | 05575 | 96855 | 23820 | 11091 · | 79821 |
| 50 | 28603 | 10708 | 68933 | 34189 | 92166 | 15181 | 66628 | 58599 |

| | Column | | | | | | | |
|---|---|---|---|---|---|---|---|---|
| Row | 00000<br>12345 | 00001<br>67890 | 11111<br>12345 | 11112<br>67890 | 22222<br>12345 | 22223<br>67890 | 33333<br>12345 | 33334<br>67890 |
| 51 | 66194 | 28926 | 99547 | 16625 | 45515 | 67953 | 12108 | 57846 |
| 52 | 78240 | 43195 | 24837 | 32511 | 70880 | 22070 | 52622 | 61881 |
| 53 | 00833 | 88000 | 67299 | 68215 | 11274 | 55624 | 32991 | 17436 |
| 54 | 12111 | 86683 | 61270 | 58036 | 64192 | 90611 | 15145 | 01748 |
| 55 | 47189 | 99951 | 05755 | 03834 | 43782 | 90599 | 40282 | 51417 |
| 56 | 76396 | 72486 | 62423 | 27618 | 84184 | 78922 | 73561 | 52818 |
| 57 | 46409 | 17469 | 32483 | 09083 | 76175 | 19985 | 26309 | 91536 |
| 58 | 74626 | 22111 | 87286 | 46772 | 42243 | 68046 | 44250 | 42439 |
| 59 | 34450 | 81974 | 93723 | 49023 | 58432 | 67083 | 36876 | 93391 |
| 60 | 36327 | 72135 | 33005 | 28701 | 34710 | 49359 | 50693 | 89311 |
| 61 | 74185 | 77536 | 84825 | 09934 | 99103 | 09325 | 67389 | 45869 |
| 62 | 12296 | 41623 | 62873 | 37943 | 25584 | 09609 | 63360 | 47270 |
| 63 | 90822 | 60280 | 88925 | 99610 | 42772 | 60561 | 76873 | 04117 |
| 64 | 72121 | 79152 | 96591 | 90305 | 10189 | 79778 | 68016 | 13747 |
| 65 | 95268 | 41377 | 25684 | 08151 | 61816 | 58555 | 54305 | 86189 |
| 66 | 92603 | 09091 | 75884 | 93424 | 72586 | 88903 | 30061 | 14457 |
| 67 | 18813 | 90291 | 05275 | 01223 | 79607 | 95426 | 34900 | 09778 |
| 68 | 38840 | 26903 | 28624 | 67157 | 51986 | 42865 | 14508 | 49315 |
| 69 | 05959 | 33836 | 53758 | 16562 | 41081 | 38012 | 41230 | 20528 |
| 70 | 85141 | 21155 | 99212 | 32685 | 51403 | 31926 | 69813 | 58781 |
| 71 | 75047 | 59643 | 31074 | 38172 | 03718 | 32119 | 69506 | 67143 |
| 72 | 30752 | 95260 | 68032 | 62871 | 58781 | 34143 | 68790 | 69766 |
| 73 | 22986 | 82575 | 42187 | 62295 | 84295 | 30634 | 66562 | 31442 |
| 74 | 99439 | 86692 | 90348 | 66036 | 48399 | 73451 | 26698 | 39437 |
| 75 | 20389 | 93029 | 11881 | 71685 | 65452 | 89047 | 63669 | 02656 |
| 76 | 39249 | 05173 | 68256 | 36359 | 20250 | 68686 | 05947 | 09335 |
| 77 | 96777 | 33605 | 29481 | 20063 | 09398 | 01843 | 35139 | 61344 |
| 78 | 04860 | 32918 | 10798 | 50492 | 52655 | 33359 | 94713 | 28393 |
| 79 | 41613 | 42375 | 00403 | 03656 | 77580 | 87772 | 86877 | 57085 |
| 80 | 17930 | 00794 | 53836 | 53692 | 67135 | 98102 | 61912 | 11246 |
| 81 | 24649 | 31845 | 25736 | 75231 | 83808 | 98917 | 93829 | 99430 |
| 82 | 79899 | 34061 | 54308 | 59358 | 56462 | 58166 | 97302 | 86828 |
| 83 | 76801 | 49594 | 81002 | 30397 | 52728 | 15101 | 72070 | 33706 |
| 84 | 36239 | 63636 | 38140 | 65731 | 39788 | 06872 | 38971 | 53363 |
| 85 | 07392 | 64449 | 17886 | 63632 | 53995 | 17574 | 22247 | 62607 |
| 86 | 67133 | 04181 | 33874 | 98835 | 67453 | 59734 | 76381 | 63455 |
| 87 | 77759 | 31504 | 32832 | 70861 | 15152 | 29733 | 75371 | 39174 |
| 88 | 85992 | 72268 | 42920 | 20810 | 29361 | 51423 | 90306 | 73574 |
| 89 | 79553 | 75952 | 54116 | 65553 | 47139 | 60579 | 09165 | 85490 |
| 90 | 41101 | 17336 | 48951 | 53674 | 17880 | 45260 | 08575 | 49321 |
| 91 | 36191 | 17095 | 32123 | 91576 | 84221 | 78902 | 82010 | 30847 |
| 92 | 62329 | 63898 | 23268 | 74283 | 26091 | 68409 | 69704 | 82267 |
| 93 | 14751 | 13151 | 93115 | 01437 | 56945 | 89661 | 67680 | 79790 |
| 94 | 48462 | 59278 | 44185 | 29616 | 76537 | 19589 | 83139 | 28454 |
| 95 | 29435 | 88105 | 59651 | 44391 | 74588 | 55114 | 80834 | 85686 |
| 96 | 28340 | 29285 | 12965 | 14821 | 80425 | 16602 | 44653 | 70467 |
| 97 | 02167 | 58940 | 27149 | 80242 | 10587 | 79786 | 34959 | 75339 |
| 98 | 17864 | 00991 | 39557 | 54981 | 23588 | 81914 | 37609 | 13128 |
| 99 | 79675 | 80605 | 60059 | 35862 | 00254 | 36546 | 21545 | 78179 |
| 00 | 72335 | 82037 | 92003 | 34100 | 29879 | 46613 | 89720 | 13274 |

*Source: Partially extracted from The Rand Corporation.* A Million Random Digits with 100,000 Normal Deviates *(Glencoe, IL: The Free Press, 1955).*

## Table E.2a  *The Standardized Normal Distribution*

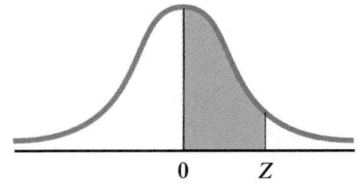

Entry represents area under the standardized normal distribution from the mean to Z

| Z | .00 | .01 | .02 | .03 | .04 | .05 | .06 | .07 | .08 | .09 |
|---|---|---|---|---|---|---|---|---|---|---|
| 0.0 | .0000 | .0040 | .0080 | .0120 | .0160 | .0199 | .0239 | .0279 | .0319 | .0359 |
| 0.1 | .0398 | .0438 | .0478 | .0517 | .0557 | .0596 | .0636 | .0675 | .0714 | .0753 |
| 0.2 | .0793 | .0832 | .0871 | .0910 | .0948 | .0987 | .1026 | .1064 | .1103 | .1141 |
| 0.3 | .1179 | .1217 | .1255 | .1293 | .1331 | .1368 | .1406 | .1443 | .1480 | .1517 |
| 0.4 | .1554 | .1591 | .1628 | .1664 | .1700 | .1736 | .1772 | .1808 | .1844 | .1879 |
| 0.5 | .1915 | .1950 | .1985 | .2019 | .2054 | .2088 | .2123 | .2157 | .2190 | .2224 |
| 0.6 | .2257 | .2291 | .2324 | .2357 | .2389 | .2422 | .2454 | .2486 | .2518 | .2549 |
| 0.7 | .2580 | .2612 | .2642 | .2673 | .2704 | .2734 | .2764 | .2794 | .2823 | .2852 |
| 0.8 | .2881 | .2910 | .2939 | .2967 | .2995 | .3023 | .3051 | .3078 | .3106 | .3133 |
| 0.9 | .3159 | .3186 | .3212 | .3238 | .3264 | .3289 | .3315 | .3340 | .3365 | .3389 |
| 1.0 | .3413 | .3438 | .3461 | .3485 | .3508 | .3531 | .3554 | .3577 | .3599 | .3621 |
| 1.1 | .3643 | .3665 | .3686 | .3708 | .3729 | .3749 | .3770 | .3790 | .3810 | .3830 |
| 1.2 | .3849 | .3869 | .3888 | .3907 | .3925 | .3944 | .3962 | .3980 | .3997 | .4015 |
| 1.3 | .4032 | .4049 | .4066 | .4082 | .4099 | .4115 | .4131 | .4147 | .4162 | .4177 |
| 1.4 | .4192 | .4207 | .4222 | .4236 | .4251 | .4265 | .4279 | .4292 | .4306 | .4319 |
| 1.5 | .4332 | .4345 | .4357 | .4370 | .4382 | .4394 | .4406 | .4418 | .4429 | .4441 |
| 1.6 | .4452 | .4463 | .4474 | .4484 | .4495 | .4505 | .4515 | .4525 | .4535 | .4545 |
| 1.7 | .4554 | .4564 | .4573 | .4582 | .4591 | .4599 | .4608 | .4616 | .4625 | .4633 |
| 1.8 | .4641 | .4649 | .4656 | .4664 | .4671 | .4678 | .4686 | .4693 | .4699 | .4706 |
| 1.9 | .4713 | .4719 | .4726 | .4732 | .4738 | .4744 | .4750 | .4756 | .4761 | .4767 |
| 2.0 | .4772 | .4778 | .4783 | .4788 | .4793 | .4798 | .4803 | .4808 | .4812 | .4817 |
| 2.1 | .4821 | .4826 | .4830 | .4834 | .4838 | .4842 | .4846 | .4850 | .4854 | .4857 |
| 2.2 | .4861 | .4864 | .4868 | .4871 | .4875 | .4878 | .4881 | .4884 | .4887 | .4890 |
| 2.3 | .4893 | .4896 | .4898 | .4901 | .4904 | .4906 | .4909 | .4911 | .4913 | .4916 |
| 2.4 | .4918 | .4920 | .4922 | .4925 | .4927 | .4929 | .4931 | .4932 | .4934 | .4936 |
| 2.5 | .4938 | .4940 | .4941 | .4943 | .4945 | .4946 | .4948 | .4949 | .4951 | .4952 |
| 2.6 | .4953 | .4955 | .4956 | .4957 | .4959 | .4960 | .4961 | .4962 | .4963 | .4964 |
| 2.7 | .4965 | .4966 | .4967 | .4968 | .4969 | .4970 | .4971 | .4972 | .4973 | .4974 |
| 2.8 | .4974 | .4975 | .4976 | .4977 | .4977 | .4978 | .4979 | .4979 | .4980 | .4981 |
| 2.9 | .4981 | .4982 | .4982 | .4983 | .4984 | .4984 | .4985 | .4985 | .4986 | .4986 |
| 3.0 | .49865 | .49869 | .49874 | .49878 | .49882 | .49886 | .49889 | .49893 | .49897 | .49900 |
| 3.1 | .49903 | .49906 | .49910 | .49913 | .49916 | .49918 | .49921 | .49924 | .49926 | .49929 |
| 3.2 | .49931 | .49934 | .49936 | .49938 | .49940 | .49942 | .49944 | .49946 | .49948 | .49950 |
| 3.3 | .49952 | .49953 | .49955 | .49957 | .49958 | .49960 | .49961 | .49962 | .49964 | .49965 |
| 3.4 | .49966 | .49968 | .49969 | .49970 | .49971 | .49972 | .49973 | .49974 | .49975 | .49976 |
| 3.5 | .49977 | .49978 | .49978 | .49979 | .49980 | .49981 | .49981 | .49982 | .49983 | .49983 |
| 3.6 | .49984 | .49985 | .49985 | .49986 | .49986 | .49987 | .49987 | .49988 | .49988 | .49989 |
| 3.7 | .49989 | .49990 | .49990 | .49990 | .49991 | .49991 | .49992 | .49992 | .49992 | .49992 |
| 3.8 | .49993 | .49993 | .49993 | .49994 | .49994 | .49994 | .49994 | .49995 | .49995 | .49995 |
| 3.9 | .49995 | .49995 | .49996 | .49996 | .49996 | .49996 | .49996 | .49996 | .49997 | .49997 |

# Table E.2b  *The Cumulative Standardized Normal Distribution*

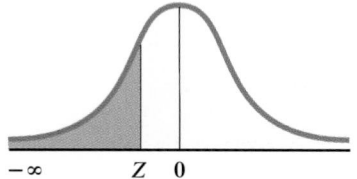

$-\infty$  $Z$  $0$

*Entry represents area under the cumulative standardized normal distribution from $-\infty$ to $Z$*

| Z | .00 | .01 | .02 | .03 | .04 | .05 | .06 | .07 | .08 | .09 |
|---|-----|-----|-----|-----|-----|-----|-----|-----|-----|-----|
| −3.9 | .00005 | .00005 | .00004 | .00004 | .00004 | .00004 | .00004 | .00004 | .00003 | .00003 |
| −3.8 | .00007 | .00007 | .00007 | .00006 | .00006 | .00006 | .00006 | .00005 | .00005 | .00005 |
| −3.7 | .00011 | .00010 | .00010 | .00010 | .00009 | .00009 | .00008 | .00008 | .00008 | .00008 |
| −3.6 | .00016 | .00015 | .00015 | .00014 | .00014 | .00013 | .00013 | .00012 | .00012 | .00011 |
| −3.5 | .00023 | .00022 | .00022 | .00021 | .00020 | .00019 | .00019 | .00018 | .00017 | .00017 |
| −3.4 | .00034 | .00032 | .00031 | .00030 | .00029 | .00028 | .00027 | .00026 | .00025 | .00024 |
| −3.3 | .00048 | .00047 | .00045 | .00043 | .00042 | .00040 | .00039 | .00038 | .00036 | .00035 |
| −3.2 | .00069 | .00066 | .00064 | .00062 | .00060 | .00058 | .00056 | .00054 | .00052 | .00050 |
| −3.1 | .00097 | .00094 | .00090 | .00087 | .00084 | .00082 | .00079 | .00076 | .00074 | .00071 |
| −3.0 | .00135 | .00131 | .00126 | .00122 | .00118 | .00114 | .00111 | .00107 | .00103 | .00100 |
| −2.9 | .0019 | .0018 | .0018 | .0017 | .0016 | .0016 | .0015 | .0015 | .0014 | .0014 |
| −2.8 | .0026 | .0025 | .0024 | .0023 | .0023 | .0022 | .0021 | .0021 | .0020 | .0019 |
| −2.7 | .0035 | .0034 | .0033 | .0032 | .0031 | .0030 | .0029 | .0028 | .0027 | .0026 |
| −2.6 | .0047 | .0045 | .0044 | .0043 | .0041 | .0040 | .0039 | .0038 | .0037 | .0036 |
| −2.5 | .0062 | .0060 | .0059 | .0057 | .0055 | .0054 | .0052 | .0051 | .0049 | .0048 |
| −2.4 | .0082 | .0080 | .0078 | .0075 | .0073 | .0071 | .0069 | .0068 | .0066 | .0064 |
| −2.3 | .0107 | .0104 | .0102 | .0099 | .0096 | .0094 | .0091 | .0089 | .0087 | .0084 |
| −2.2 | .0139 | .0136 | .0132 | .0129 | .0125 | .0122 | .0119 | .0116 | .0113 | .0110 |
| −2.1 | .0179 | .0174 | .0170 | .0166 | .0162 | .0158 | .0154 | .0150 | .0146 | .0143 |
| −2.0 | .0228 | .0222 | .0217 | .0212 | .0207 | .0202 | .0197 | .0192 | .0188 | .0183 |
| −1.9 | .0287 | .0281 | .0274 | .0268 | .0262 | .0256 | .0250 | .0244 | .0239 | .0233 |
| −1.8 | .0359 | .0351 | .0344 | .0336 | .0329 | .0322 | .0314 | .0307 | .0301 | .0294 |
| −1.7 | .0446 | .0436 | .0427 | .0418 | .0409 | .0401 | .0392 | .0384 | .0375 | .0367 |
| −1.6 | .0548 | .0537 | .0526 | .0516 | .0505 | .0495 | .0485 | .0475 | .0465 | .0455 |
| −1.5 | .0668 | .0655 | .0643 | .0630 | .0618 | .0606 | .0594 | .0582 | .0571 | .0559 |
| −1.4 | .0808 | .0793 | .0778 | .0764 | .0749 | .0735 | .0721 | .0708 | .0694 | .0681 |
| −1.3 | .0968 | .0951 | .0934 | .0918 | .0901 | .0885 | .0869 | .0853 | .0838 | .0823 |
| −1.2 | .1151 | .1131 | .1112 | .1093 | .1075 | .1056 | .1038 | .1020 | .1003 | .0985 |
| −1.1 | .1357 | .1335 | .1314 | .1292 | .1271 | .1251 | .1230 | .1210 | .1190 | .1170 |
| −1.0 | .1587 | .1562 | .1539 | .1515 | .1492 | .1469 | .1446 | .1423 | .1401 | .1379 |
| −0.9 | .1841 | .1814 | .1788 | .1762 | .1736 | .1711 | .1685 | .1660 | .1635 | .1611 |
| −0.8 | .2119 | .2090 | .2061 | .2033 | .2005 | .1977 | .1949 | .1922 | .1894 | .1867 |
| −0.7 | .2420 | .2388 | .2358 | .2327 | .2296 | .2266 | .2236 | .2006 | .2177 | .2148 |
| −0.6 | .2743 | .2709 | .2676 | .2643 | .2611 | .2578 | .2546 | .2514 | .2482 | .2451 |
| −0.5 | .3085 | .3050 | .3015 | .2981 | .2946 | .2912 | .2877 | .2843 | .2810 | .2776 |
| −0.4 | .3446 | .3409 | .3372 | .3336 | .3300 | .3264 | .3228 | .3192 | .3156 | .3121 |
| −0.3 | .3821 | .3783 | .3745 | .3707 | .3669 | .3632 | .3594 | .3557 | .3520 | .3483 |
| −0.2 | .4207 | .4168 | .4129 | .4090 | .4052 | .4013 | .3974 | .3936 | .3897 | .3859 |
| −0.1 | .4602 | .4562 | .4522 | .4483 | .4443 | .4404 | .4364 | .4325 | .4286 | .4247 |
| −0.0 | .5000 | .4960 | .4920 | .4880 | .4840 | .4801 | .4761 | .4721 | .4681 | .4641 |

*continued*

# Table E.2b  *The Cumulative Standardized Normal Distribution (Continued)*

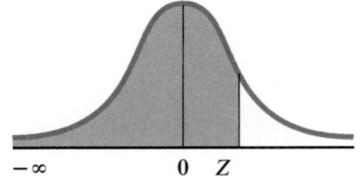

$-\infty$     0   Z

*Entry represents area under the cumulative standardized normal distribution from $-\infty$ to Z*

| Z | .00 | .01 | .02 | .03 | .04 | .05 | .06 | .07 | .08 | .09 |
|---|---|---|---|---|---|---|---|---|---|---|
| 0.0 | .5000 | .5040 | .5080 | .5120 | .5160 | .5199 | .5239 | .5279 | .5319 | .5359 |
| 0.1 | .5398 | .5438 | .5478 | .5517 | .5557 | .5596 | .5636 | .5675 | .5714 | .5753 |
| 0.2 | .5793 | .5832 | .5871 | .5910 | .5948 | .5987 | .6026 | .6064 | .6103 | .6141 |
| 0.3 | .6179 | .6217 | .6255 | .6293 | .6331 | .6368 | .6406 | .6443 | .6480 | .6517 |
| 0.4 | .6554 | .6591 | .6628 | .6664 | .6700 | .6736 | .6772 | .6808 | .6844 | .6879 |
| 0.5 | .6915 | .6950 | .6985 | .7019 | .7054 | .7088 | .7123 | .7157 | .7190 | .7224 |
| 0.6 | .7257 | .7291 | .7324 | .7357 | .7389 | .7422 | .7454 | .7486 | .7518 | .7549 |
| 0.7 | .7580 | .7612 | .7642 | .7673 | .7704 | .7734 | .7764 | .7794 | .7823 | .7852 |
| 0.8 | .7881 | .7910 | .7939 | .7967 | .7995 | .8023 | .8051 | .8078 | .8106 | .8133 |
| 0.9 | .8159 | .8186 | .8212 | .8238 | .8264 | .8289 | .8315 | .8340 | .8365 | .8389 |
| 1.0 | .8413 | .8438 | .8461 | .8485 | .8508 | .8531 | .8554 | .8577 | .8599 | .8621 |
| 1.1 | .8643 | .8665 | .8686 | .8708 | .8729 | .8749 | .8770 | .8790 | .8810 | .8830 |
| 1.2 | .8849 | .8869 | .8888 | .8907 | .8925 | .8944 | .8962 | .8980 | .8997 | .9015 |
| 1.3 | .9032 | .9089 | .9066 | .9082 | .9099 | .9115 | .9131 | .9147 | .9162 | .9177 |
| 1.4 | .9192 | .9207 | .9222 | .9236 | .9251 | .9265 | .9279 | .9292 | .9306 | .9319 |
| 1.5 | .9332 | .9345 | .9357 | .9370 | .9382 | .9394 | .9406 | .9418 | .9429 | .9441 |
| 1.6 | .9452 | .9463 | .9474 | .9484 | .9495 | .9505 | .9515 | .9525 | .9535 | .9545 |
| 1.7 | .9554 | .9564 | .9573 | .9582 | .9591 | .9599 | .9608 | .9616 | .9625 | .9633 |
| 1.8 | .9641 | .9649 | .9656 | .9664 | .9671 | .9678 | .9686 | .9693 | .9699 | .9706 |
| 1.9 | .9713 | .9719 | .9726 | .9732 | .9738 | .9744 | .9750 | .9756 | .9761 | .9767 |
| 2.0 | .9772 | .9778 | .9783 | .9788 | .9793 | .9798 | .9803 | .9808 | .9812 | .9817 |
| 2.1 | .9821 | .9826 | .9830 | .9834 | .9838 | .9842 | .9846 | .9850 | .9854 | .9857 |
| 2.2 | .9861 | .9864 | .9868 | .9871 | .9875 | .9878 | .9881 | .9884 | .9887 | .9890 |
| 2.3 | .9893 | .9896 | .9898 | .9901 | .9904 | .9906 | .9909 | .9911 | .9913 | .9916 |
| 2.4 | .9918 | .9920 | .9922 | .9925 | .9927 | .9929 | .9931 | .9932 | .9934 | .9936 |
| 2.5 | .9938 | .9940 | .9941 | .9943 | .9945 | .9946 | .9948 | .9949 | .9951 | .9952 |
| 2.6 | .9953 | .9955 | .9956 | .9957 | .9959 | .9960 | .9961 | .9962 | .9963 | .9964 |
| 2.7 | .9965 | .9966 | .9967 | .9968 | .9969 | .9970 | .9971 | .9972 | .9973 | .9974 |
| 2.8 | .9974 | .9975 | .9976 | .9977 | .9977 | .9978 | .9979 | .9979 | .9980 | .9981 |
| 2.9 | .9981 | .9982 | .9982 | .9983 | .9984 | .9984 | .9985 | .9985 | .9986 | .9986 |
| 3.0 | .99865 | .99869 | .99874 | .99878 | .99882 | .99886 | .99889 | .99893 | .99897 | .99900 |
| 3.1 | .99903 | .99906 | .99910 | .99913 | .99916 | .99918 | .99921 | .99924 | .99926 | .99929 |
| 3.2 | .99931 | .99934 | .99936 | .99938 | .99940 | .99942 | .99944 | .99946 | .99948 | .99950 |
| 3.3 | .99952 | .99953 | .99955 | .99957 | .99958 | .99960 | .99961 | .99962 | .99964 | .99965 |
| 3.4 | .99966 | .99968 | .99969 | .99970 | .99971 | .99972 | .99973 | .99974 | .99975 | .99976 |
| 3.5 | .99977 | .99978 | .99978 | .99979 | .99980 | .99981 | .99981 | .99982 | .99983 | .99983 |
| 3.6 | .99984 | .99985 | .99985 | .99986 | .99986 | .99987 | .99987 | .99988 | .99988 | .99989 |
| 3.7 | .99989 | .99990 | .99990 | .99990 | .99991 | .99991 | .99992 | .99992 | .99992 | .99992 |
| 3.8 | .99993 | .99993 | .99993 | .99994 | .99994 | .99994 | .99994 | .99995 | .99995 | .99995 |
| 3.9 | .99995 | .99995 | .99996 | .99996 | .99996 | .99996 | .99996 | .99996 | .99997 | .99997 |

# Table E.3    *Critical Values of t*

*For particular number of degrees of freedom,*
*entry represents the critical value of t*
*corresponding to a specified upper tail area (α)*

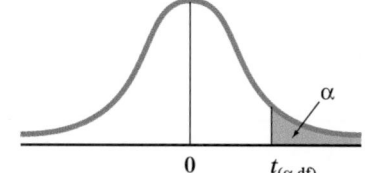

| Degrees of Freedom | Upper Tail Areas | | | | | |
|---|---|---|---|---|---|---|
| | .25 | .10 | .05 | .025 | .01 | .005 |
| 1 | 1.0000 | 3.0777 | 6.3138 | 12.7062 | 31.8207 | 63.6574 |
| 2 | 0.8165 | 1.8856 | 2.9200 | 4.3027 | 6.9646 | 9.9248 |
| 3 | 0.7649 | 1.6377 | 2.3534 | 3.1824 | 4.5407 | 5.8409 |
| 4 | 0.7407 | 1.5332 | 2.1318 | 2.7764 | 3.7469 | 4.6041 |
| 5 | 0.7267 | 1.4759 | 2.0150 | 2.5706 | 3.3649 | 4.0322 |
| 6 | 0.7176 | 1.4398 | 1.9432 | 2.4469 | 3.1427 | 3.7074 |
| 7 | 0.7111 | 1.4149 | 1.8946 | 2.3646 | 2.9980 | 3.4995 |
| 8 | 0.7064 | 1.3968 | 1.8595 | 2.3060 | 2.8965 | 3.3554 |
| 9 | 0.7027 | 1.3830 | 1.8331 | 2.2622 | 2.8214 | 3.2498 |
| 10 | 0.6998 | 1.3722 | 1.8125 | 2.2281 | 2.7638 | 3.1693 |
| 11 | 0.6974 | 1.3634 | 1.7959 | 2.2010 | 2.7181 | 3.1058 |
| 12 | 0.6955 | 1.3562 | 1.7823 | 2.1788 | 2.6810 | 3.0545 |
| 13 | 0.6938 | 1.3502 | 1.7709 | 2.1604 | 2.6503 | 3.0123 |
| 14 | 0.6924 | 1.3450 | 1.7613 | 2.1448 | 2.6245 | 2.9768 |
| 15 | 0.6912 | 1.3406 | 1.7531 | 2.1315 | 2.6025 | 2.9467 |
| 16 | 0.6901 | 1.3368 | 1.7459 | 2.1199 | 2.5835 | 2.9208 |
| 17 | 0.6892 | 1.3334 | 1.7396 | 2.1098 | 2.5669 | 2.8982 |
| 18 | 0.6884 | 1.3304 | 1.7341 | 2.1009 | 2.5524 | 2.8784 |
| 19 | 0.6876 | 1.3277 | 1.7291 | 2.0930 | 2.5395 | 2.8609 |
| 20 | 0.6870 | 1.3253 | 1.7247 | 2.0860 | 2.5280 | 2.8453 |
| 21 | 0.6864 | 1.3232 | 1.7207 | 2.0796 | 2.5177 | 2.8314 |
| 22 | 0.6858 | 1.3212 | 1.7171 | 2.0739 | 2.5083 | 2.8188 |
| 23 | 0.6853 | 1.3195 | 1.7139 | 2.0687 | 2.4999 | 2.8073 |
| 24 | 0.6848 | 1.3178 | 1.7109 | 2.0639 | 2.4922 | 2.7969 |
| 25 | 0.6844 | 1.3163 | 1.7081 | 2.0595 | 2.4851 | 2.7874 |
| 26 | 0.6840 | 1.3150 | 1.7056 | 2.0555 | 2.4786 | 2.7787 |
| 27 | 0.6837 | 1.3137 | 1.7033 | 2.0518 | 2.4727 | 2.7707 |
| 28 | 0.6834 | 1.3125 | 1.7011 | 2.0484 | 2.4671 | 2.7633 |
| 29 | 0.6830 | 1.3114 | 1.6991 | 2.0452 | 2.4620 | 2.7564 |
| 30 | 0.6828 | 1.3104 | 1.6973 | 2.0423 | 2.4573 | 2.7500 |
| 31 | 0.6825 | 1.3095 | 1.6955 | 2.0395 | 2.4528 | 2.7440 |
| 32 | 0.6822 | 1.3086 | 1.6939 | 2.0369 | 2.4487 | 2.7385 |
| 33 | 0.6820 | 1.3077 | 1.6924 | 2.0345 | 2.4448 | 2.7333 |
| 34 | 0.6818 | 1.3070 | 1.6909 | 2.0322 | 2.4411 | 2.7284 |
| 35 | 0.6816 | 1.3062 | 1.6896 | 2.0301 | 2.4377 | 2.7238 |
| 36 | 0.6814 | 1.3055 | 1.6883 | 2.0281 | 2.4345 | 2.7195 |
| 37 | 0.6812 | 1.3049 | 1.6871 | 2.0262 | 2.4314 | 2.7154 |
| 38 | 0.6810 | 1.3042 | 1.6860 | 2.0244 | 2.4286 | 2.7116 |
| 39 | 0.6808 | 1.3036 | 1.6849 | 2.0227 | 2.4258 | 2.7079 |
| 40 | 0.6807 | 1.3031 | 1.6839 | 2.0211 | 2.4233 | 2.7045 |
| 41 | 0.6805 | 1.3025 | 1.6829 | 2.0195 | 2.4208 | 2.7012 |
| 42 | 0.6804 | 1.3020 | 1.6820 | 2.0181 | 2.4185 | 2.6981 |
| 43 | 0.6802 | 1.3016 | 1.6811 | 2.0167 | 2.4163 | 2.6951 |
| 44 | 0.6801 | 1.3011 | 1.6802 | 2.0154 | 2.4141 | 2.6923 |
| 45 | 0.6800 | 1.3006 | 1.6794 | 2.0141 | 2.4121 | 2.6896 |
| 46 | 0.6799 | 1.3002 | 1.6787 | 2.0129 | 2.4102 | 2.6870 |
| 47 | 0.6797 | 1.2998 | 1.6779 | 2.0117 | 2.4083 | 2.6846 |
| 48 | 0.6796 | 1.2994 | 1.6772 | 2.0106 | 2.4066 | 2.6822 |
| 49 | 0.6795 | 1.2991 | 1.6766 | 2.0096 | 2.4049 | 2.6800 |
| 50 | 0.6794 | 1.2987 | 1.6759 | 2.0086 | 2.4033 | 2.6778 |

## Table E.3 *Critical Values of t (Continued)*

| Degrees of Freedom | Upper Tail Areas | | | | | |
|---|---|---|---|---|---|---|
| | .25 | .10 | .05 | .025 | .01 | .005 |
| 51 | 0.6793 | 1.2984 | 1.6753 | 2.0076 | 2.4017 | 2.6757 |
| 52 | 0.6792 | 1.2980 | 1.6747 | 2.0066 | 2.4002 | 2.6737 |
| 53 | 0.6791 | 1.2977 | 1.6741 | 2.0057 | 2.3988 | 2.6718 |
| 54 | 0.6791 | 1.2974 | 1.6736 | 2.0049 | 2.3974 | 2.6700 |
| 55 | 0.6790 | 1.2971 | 1.6730 | 2.0040 | 2.3961 | 2.6682 |
| 56 | 0.6789 | 1.2969 | 1.6725 | 2.0032 | 2.3948 | 2.6665 |
| 57 | 0.6788 | 1.2966 | 1.6720 | 2.0025 | 2.3936 | 2.6649 |
| 58 | 0.6787 | 1.2963 | 1.6716 | 2.0017 | 2.3924 | 2.6633 |
| 59 | 0.6787 | 1.2961 | 1.6711 | 2.0010 | 2.3912 | 2.6618 |
| 60 | 0.6786 | 1.2958 | 1.6706 | 2.0003 | 2.3901 | 2.6603 |
| 61 | 0.6785 | 1.2956 | 1.6702 | 1.9996 | 2.3890 | 2.6589 |
| 62 | 0.6785 | 1.2954 | 1.6698 | 1.9990 | 2.3880 | 2.6575 |
| 63 | 0.6784 | 1.2951 | 1.6694 | 1.9983 | 2.3870 | 2.6561 |
| 64 | 0.6783 | 1.2949 | 1.6690 | 1.9977 | 2.3860 | 2.6549 |
| 65 | 0.6783 | 1.2947 | 1.6686 | 1.9971 | 2.3851 | 2.6536 |
| 66 | 0.6782 | 1.2945 | 1.6683 | 1.9966 | 2.3842 | 2.6524 |
| 67 | 0.6782 | 1.2943 | 1.6679 | 1.9960 | 2.3833 | 2.6512 |
| 68 | 0.6781 | 1.2941 | 1.6676 | 1.9955 | 2.3824 | 2.6501 |
| 69 | 0.6781 | 1.2939 | 1.6672 | 1.9949 | 2.3816 | 2.6490 |
| 70 | 0.6780 | 1.2938 | 1.6669 | 1.9944 | 2.3808 | 2.6479 |
| 71 | 0.6780 | 1.2936 | 1.6666 | 1.9939 | 2.3800 | 2.6469 |
| 72 | 0.6779 | 1.2934 | 1.6663 | 1.9935 | 2.3793 | 2.6459 |
| 73 | 0.6779 | 1.2933 | 1.6660 | 1.9930 | 2.3785 | 2.6449 |
| 74 | 0.6778 | 1.4931 | 1.6657 | 1.9925 | 2.3778 | 2.6439 |
| 75 | 0.6778 | 1.2929 | 1.6654 | 1.9921 | 2.3771 | 2.6430 |
| 76 | 0.6777 | 1.2928 | 1.6652 | 1.9917 | 2.3764 | 2.6421 |
| 77 | 0.6777 | 1.2926 | 1.6649 | 1.9913 | 2.3758 | 2.6412 |
| 78 | 0.6776 | 1.2925 | 1.6646 | 1.9908 | 2.3751 | 2.6403 |
| 79 | 0.6776 | 1.2924 | 1.6644 | 1.9905 | 2.3745 | 2.6395 |
| 80 | 0.6776 | 1.2922 | 1.6641 | 1.9901 | 2.3739 | 2.6387 |
| 81 | 0.6775 | 1.2921 | 1.6639 | 1.9897 | 2.3733 | 2.6379 |
| 82 | 0.6775 | 1.2920 | 1.6636 | 1.9893 | 2.3727 | 2.6371 |
| 83 | 0.6775 | 1.2918 | 1.6634 | 1.9890 | 2.3721 | 2.6364 |
| 84 | 0.6774 | 1.2917 | 1.6632 | 1.9886 | 2.3716 | 2.6356 |
| 85 | 0.6774 | 1.2916 | 1.6630 | 1.9883 | 2.3710 | 2.6349 |
| 86 | 0.6774 | 1.2915 | 1.6628 | 1.9879 | 2.3705 | 2.6342 |
| 87 | 0.6773 | 1.2914 | 1.6626 | 1.9876 | 2.3700 | 2.6335 |
| 88 | 0.6773 | 1.2912 | 1.6624 | 1.9873 | 2.3695 | 2.6329 |
| 89 | 0.6773 | 1.2911 | 1.6622 | 1.9870 | 2.3690 | 2.6322 |
| 90 | 0.6772 | 1.2910 | 1.6620 | 1.9867 | 2.3685 | 2.6316 |
| 91 | 0.6772 | 1.2909 | 1.6618 | 1.9864 | 2.3680 | 2.6309 |
| 92 | 0.6772 | 1.2908 | 1.6616 | 1.9861 | 2.3676 | 2.6303 |
| 93 | 0.6771 | 1.2907 | 1.6614 | 1.9858 | 2.3671 | 2.6297 |
| 94 | 0.6771 | 1.2906 | 1.6612 | 1.9855 | 2.3667 | 2.6291 |
| 95 | 0.6771 | 1.2905 | 1.6611 | 1.9853 | 2.3662 | 2.6286 |
| 96 | 0.6771 | 1.2904 | 1.6609 | 1.9850 | 2.3658 | 2.6280 |
| 97 | 0.6770 | 1.2903 | 1.6607 | 1.9847 | 2.3654 | 2.6275 |
| 98 | 0.6770 | 1.2902 | 1.6606 | 1.9845 | 2.3650 | 2.6269 |
| 99 | 0.6770 | 1.2902 | 1.6604 | 1.9842 | 2.3646 | 2.6264 |
| 100 | 0.6770 | 1.2901 | 1.6602 | 1.9840 | 2.3642 | 2.6259 |
| 110 | 0.6767 | 1.2893 | 1.6588 | 1.9818 | 2.3607 | 2.6213 |
| 120 | 0.6765 | 1.2886 | 1.6577 | 1.9799 | 2.3578 | 2.6174 |
| ∞ | 0.6745 | 1.2816 | 1.6449 | 1.9600 | 2.3263 | 2.5758 |

## Table E.4   Critical Values of $\chi^2$

For a particular number of degrees of freedom,
entry represents the critical value of $\chi^2$
corresponding to a specified upper tail area ($\alpha$)

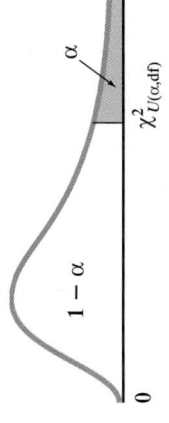

| Degrees of Freedom | Upper Tail Areas ($\alpha$) | | | | | | | | | | | | | |
|---|---|---|---|---|---|---|---|---|---|---|---|---|---|---|
| | .995 | .99 | .975 | .95 | .90 | .75 | .25 | .10 | .05 | .025 | .01 | .005 |
| 1 | 0.010 | 0.020 | 0.001 | 0.004 | 0.016 | 0.102 | 1.323 | 2.706 | 3.841 | 5.024 | 6.635 | 7.879 |
| 2 | 0.072 | 0.115 | 0.051 | 0.103 | 0.211 | 0.575 | 2.773 | 4.605 | 5.991 | 7.378 | 9.210 | 10.597 |
| 3 | 0.207 | 0.297 | 0.216 | 0.352 | 0.584 | 1.213 | 4.108 | 6.251 | 7.815 | 9.348 | 11.345 | 12.838 |
| 4 | 0.412 | 0.554 | 0.484 | 0.711 | 1.064 | 1.923 | 5.385 | 7.779 | 9.488 | 11.143 | 13.277 | 14.860 |
| 5 | | | 0.831 | 1.145 | 1.610 | 2.675 | 6.626 | 9.236 | 11.071 | 12.833 | 15.086 | 16.750 |
| 6 | 0.676 | 0.872 | 1.237 | 1.635 | 2.204 | 3.455 | 7.841 | 10.645 | 12.592 | 14.449 | 16.812 | 18.548 |
| 7 | 0.989 | 1.239 | 1.690 | 2.167 | 2.833 | 4.255 | 9.037 | 12.017 | 14.067 | 16.013 | 18.475 | 20.278 |
| 8 | 1.344 | 1.646 | 2.180 | 2.733 | 3.490 | 5.071 | 10.219 | 13.362 | 15.507 | 17.535 | 20.090 | 21.955 |
| 9 | 1.735 | 2.088 | 2.700 | 3.325 | 4.168 | 5.899 | 11.389 | 14.684 | 16.919 | 19.023 | 21.666 | 23.589 |
| 10 | 2.156 | 2.558 | 3.247 | 3.940 | 4.865 | 6.737 | 12.549 | 15.987 | 18.307 | 20.483 | 23.209 | 25.188 |
| 11 | 2.603 | 3.053 | 3.816 | 4.575 | 5.578 | 7.584 | 13.701 | 17.275 | 19.675 | 21.920 | 24.725 | 26.757 |
| 12 | 3.074 | 3.571 | 4.404 | 5.226 | 6.304 | 8.438 | 14.845 | 18.549 | 21.026 | 23.337 | 26.217 | 28.299 |
| 13 | 3.565 | 4.107 | 5.009 | 5.892 | 7.042 | 9.299 | 15.984 | 19.812 | 22.362 | 24.736 | 27.688 | 29.819 |
| 14 | 4.075 | 4.660 | 5.629 | 6.571 | 7.790 | 10.165 | 17.117 | 21.064 | 23.685 | 26.119 | 29.141 | 31.319 |
| 15 | 4.601 | 5.229 | 6.262 | 7.261 | 8.547 | 11.037 | 18.245 | 22.307 | 24.996 | 27.488 | 30.578 | 32.801 |
| 16 | 5.142 | 5.812 | 6.908 | 7.962 | 9.312 | 11.912 | 19.369 | 23.542 | 26.296 | 28.845 | 32.000 | 34.267 |
| 17 | 5.697 | 6.408 | 7.564 | 8.672 | 10.085 | 12.792 | 20.489 | 24.769 | 27.587 | 30.191 | 33.409 | 35.718 |
| 18 | 6.265 | 7.015 | 8.231 | 9.390 | 10.865 | 13.675 | 21.605 | 25.989 | 28.869 | 31.526 | 34.805 | 37.156 |
| 19 | 6.844 | 7.633 | 8.907 | 10.117 | 11.651 | 14.562 | 22.718 | 27.204 | 30.144 | 32.852 | 36.191 | 38.582 |
| 20 | 7.434 | 8.260 | 9.591 | 10.851 | 12.443 | 15.452 | 23.828 | 28.412 | 31.410 | 34.170 | 37.566 | 39.997 |
| 21 | 8.034 | 8.897 | 10.283 | 11.591 | 13.240 | 16.344 | 24.935 | 29.615 | 32.671 | 35.479 | 38.932 | 41.401 |
| 22 | 8.643 | 9.542 | 10.982 | 12.338 | 14.042 | 17.240 | 26.039 | 30.813 | 33.924 | 36.781 | 40.289 | 42.796 |
| 23 | 9.260 | 10.196 | 11.689 | 13.091 | 14.848 | 18.137 | 27.141 | 32.007 | 35.172 | 38.076 | 41.638 | 44.181 |
| 24 | 9.886 | 10.856 | 12.401 | 13.848 | 15.659 | 19.037 | 28.241 | 33.196 | 36.415 | 39.364 | 42.980 | 45.559 |
| 25 | 10.520 | 11.524 | 13.120 | 14.611 | 16.473 | 19.939 | 29.339 | 34.382 | 37.652 | 40.646 | 44.314 | 46.928 |
| 26 | 11.160 | 12.198 | 13.844 | 15.379 | 17.292 | 20.843 | 30.435 | 35.563 | 38.885 | 41.923 | 45.642 | 48.290 |
| 27 | 11.808 | 12.879 | 14.573 | 16.151 | 18.114 | 21.749 | 31.528 | 36.741 | 40.113 | 43.194 | 46.963 | 49.645 |
| 28 | 12.461 | 13.565 | 15.308 | 16.928 | 18.939 | 22.657 | 32.620 | 37.916 | 41.337 | 44.461 | 48.278 | 50.993 |
| 29 | 13.121 | 14.257 | 16.047 | 17.708 | 19.768 | 23.567 | 33.711 | 39.087 | 42.557 | 45.722 | 49.588 | 52.336 |
| 30 | 13.787 | 14.954 | 16.791 | 18.493 | 20.599 | 24.478 | 34.800 | 40.256 | 43.773 | 46.979 | 50.892 | 53.672 |

For larger values of degrees of freedom (df) the expression $Z = \sqrt{2\chi^2} - \sqrt{2(df) - 1}$ may be used and the resulting upper tail area can be obtained from the
table of the standardized normal distribution (Table E.2a).

# Table E.5  Critical Values of F

For a particular combination of numerator and denominator degrees of freedom, entry represents the critical values of F corresponding to a specified upper tail area (α)

$F_{U(\alpha, df_1, df_2)}$

$\alpha = .05$

| Denominator $df_2$ | \multicolumn{19}{c}{Numerator $df_1$} |
| | 1 | 2 | 3 | 4 | 5 | 6 | 7 | 8 | 9 | 10 | 12 | 15 | 20 | 24 | 30 | 40 | 60 | 120 | ∞ |
|---|---|---|---|---|---|---|---|---|---|---|---|---|---|---|---|---|---|---|---|---|
| 1 | 161.4 | 199.5 | 215.7 | 224.6 | 230.2 | 234.0 | 236.8 | 238.9 | 240.5 | 241.9 | 243.9 | 245.9 | 248.0 | 249.1 | 250.1 | 251.1 | 252.2 | 253.3 | 254.3 |
| 2 | 18.51 | 19.00 | 19.16 | 19.25 | 19.30 | 19.33 | 19.35 | 19.37 | 19.38 | 19.40 | 19.41 | 19.43 | 19.45 | 19.45 | 19.46 | 19.47 | 19.48 | 19.49 | 19.50 |
| 3 | 10.13 | 9.55 | 9.28 | 9.12 | 9.01 | 8.94 | 8.89 | 8.85 | 8.81 | 8.79 | 8.74 | 8.70 | 8.66 | 8.64 | 8.62 | 8.59 | 8.57 | 8.55 | 8.53 |
| 4 | 7.71 | 6.94 | 6.59 | 6.39 | 6.26 | 6.16 | 6.09 | 6.04 | 6.00 | 5.96 | 5.91 | 5.86 | 5.80 | 5.77 | 5.75 | 5.72 | 5.69 | 5.66 | 5.63 |
| 5 | 6.61 | 5.79 | 5.41 | 5.19 | 5.05 | 4.95 | 4.88 | 4.82 | 4.77 | 4.74 | 4.68 | 4.62 | 4.56 | 4.53 | 4.50 | 4.46 | 4.43 | 4.40 | 4.36 |
| 6 | 5.99 | 5.14 | 4.76 | 4.53 | 4.39 | 4.28 | 4.21 | 4.15 | 4.10 | 4.06 | 4.00 | 3.94 | 3.87 | 3.84 | 3.81 | 3.77 | 3.74 | 3.70 | 3.67 |
| 7 | 5.59 | 4.74 | 4.35 | 4.12 | 3.97 | 3.87 | 3.79 | 3.73 | 3.68 | 3.64 | 3.57 | 3.51 | 3.44 | 3.41 | 3.38 | 3.34 | 3.30 | 3.27 | 3.23 |
| 8 | 5.32 | 4.46 | 4.07 | 3.84 | 3.69 | 3.58 | 3.50 | 3.44 | 3.39 | 3.35 | 3.28 | 3.22 | 3.15 | 3.12 | 3.08 | 3.04 | 3.01 | 2.97 | 2.93 |
| 9 | 5.12 | 4.26 | 3.86 | 3.63 | 3.48 | 3.37 | 3.29 | 3.23 | 3.18 | 3.14 | 3.07 | 3.01 | 2.94 | 2.90 | 2.86 | 2.83 | 2.79 | 2.75 | 2.71 |
| 10 | 4.96 | 4.10 | 3.71 | 3.48 | 3.33 | 3.22 | 3.14 | 3.07 | 3.02 | 2.98 | 2.91 | 2.85 | 2.77 | 2.74 | 2.70 | 2.66 | 2.62 | 2.58 | 2.54 |
| 11 | 4.84 | 3.98 | 3.59 | 3.36 | 3.20 | 3.09 | 3.01 | 2.95 | 2.90 | 2.85 | 2.79 | 2.72 | 2.65 | 2.61 | 2.57 | 2.53 | 2.49 | 2.45 | 2.40 |
| 12 | 4.75 | 3.89 | 3.49 | 3.26 | 3.11 | 3.00 | 2.91 | 2.85 | 2.80 | 2.75 | 2.69 | 2.62 | 2.54 | 2.51 | 2.47 | 2.43 | 2.38 | 2.34 | 2.30 |
| 13 | 4.67 | 3.81 | 3.41 | 3.18 | 3.03 | 2.92 | 2.83 | 2.77 | 2.71 | 2.67 | 2.60 | 2.53 | 2.46 | 2.42 | 2.38 | 2.34 | 2.30 | 2.25 | 2.21 |
| 14 | 4.60 | 3.74 | 3.34 | 3.11 | 2.96 | 2.85 | 2.76 | 2.70 | 2.65 | 2.60 | 2.53 | 2.46 | 2.39 | 2.35 | 2.31 | 2.27 | 2.22 | 2.18 | 2.13 |
| 15 | 4.54 | 3.68 | 3.29 | 3.06 | 2.90 | 2.79 | 2.71 | 2.64 | 2.59 | 2.54 | 2.48 | 2.40 | 2.33 | 2.29 | 2.25 | 2.20 | 2.16 | 2.11 | 2.07 |
| 16 | 4.49 | 3.63 | 3.24 | 3.01 | 2.85 | 2.74 | 2.66 | 2.59 | 2.54 | 2.49 | 2.42 | 2.35 | 2.28 | 2.24 | 2.19 | 2.15 | 2.11 | 2.06 | 2.01 |
| 17 | 4.45 | 3.59 | 3.20 | 2.96 | 2.81 | 2.70 | 2.61 | 2.55 | 2.49 | 2.45 | 2.38 | 2.31 | 2.23 | 2.19 | 2.15 | 2.10 | 2.06 | 2.01 | 1.96 |
| 18 | 4.41 | 3.55 | 3.16 | 2.93 | 2.77 | 2.66 | 2.58 | 2.51 | 2.46 | 2.41 | 2.34 | 2.27 | 2.19 | 2.15 | 2.11 | 2.06 | 2.02 | 1.97 | 1.92 |
| 19 | 4.38 | 3.52 | 3.13 | 2.90 | 2.74 | 2.63 | 2.54 | 2.48 | 2.42 | 2.38 | 2.31 | 2.23 | 2.16 | 2.11 | 2.07 | 2.03 | 1.98 | 1.93 | 1.88 |
| 20 | 4.35 | 3.49 | 3.10 | 2.87 | 2.71 | 2.60 | 2.51 | 2.45 | 2.39 | 2.35 | 2.28 | 2.20 | 2.12 | 2.08 | 2.04 | 1.99 | 1.95 | 1.90 | 1.84 |
| 21 | 4.32 | 3.47 | 3.07 | 2.84 | 2.68 | 2.57 | 2.49 | 2.42 | 2.37 | 2.32 | 2.25 | 2.18 | 2.10 | 2.05 | 2.01 | 1.96 | 1.92 | 1.87 | 1.81 |
| 22 | 4.30 | 3.44 | 3.05 | 2.82 | 2.66 | 2.55 | 2.46 | 2.40 | 2.34 | 2.30 | 2.23 | 2.15 | 2.07 | 2.03 | 1.98 | 1.94 | 1.89 | 1.84 | 1.78 |
| 23 | 4.28 | 3.42 | 3.03 | 2.80 | 2.64 | 2.53 | 2.44 | 2.37 | 2.32 | 2.27 | 2.20 | 2.13 | 2.05 | 2.01 | 1.96 | 1.91 | 1.86 | 1.81 | 1.76 |
| 24 | 4.26 | 3.40 | 3.01 | 2.78 | 2.62 | 2.51 | 2.42 | 2.36 | 2.30 | 2.25 | 2.18 | 2.11 | 2.03 | 1.98 | 1.94 | 1.89 | 1.84 | 1.79 | 1.73 |
| 25 | 4.24 | 3.39 | 2.99 | 2.76 | 2.60 | 2.49 | 2.40 | 2.34 | 2.28 | 2.24 | 2.16 | 2.09 | 2.01 | 1.96 | 1.92 | 1.87 | 1.82 | 1.77 | 1.71 |
| 26 | 4.23 | 3.37 | 2.98 | 2.74 | 2.59 | 2.47 | 2.39 | 2.32 | 2.27 | 2.22 | 2.15 | 2.07 | 1.99 | 1.95 | 1.90 | 1.85 | 1.80 | 1.75 | 1.69 |
| 27 | 4.21 | 3.35 | 2.96 | 2.73 | 2.57 | 2.46 | 2.37 | 2.31 | 2.25 | 2.20 | 2.13 | 2.06 | 1.97 | 1.93 | 1.88 | 1.84 | 1.79 | 1.73 | 1.67 |
| 28 | 4.20 | 3.34 | 2.95 | 2.71 | 2.56 | 2.45 | 2.36 | 2.29 | 2.24 | 2.19 | 2.12 | 2.04 | 1.96 | 1.91 | 1.87 | 1.82 | 1.77 | 1.71 | 1.65 |
| 29 | 4.18 | 3.33 | 2.93 | 2.70 | 2.55 | 2.43 | 2.35 | 2.28 | 2.22 | 2.18 | 2.10 | 2.03 | 1.94 | 1.90 | 1.85 | 1.81 | 1.75 | 1.70 | 1.64 |
| 30 | 4.17 | 3.32 | 2.92 | 2.69 | 2.53 | 2.42 | 2.33 | 2.27 | 2.21 | 2.16 | 2.09 | 2.01 | 1.93 | 1.89 | 1.84 | 1.79 | 1.74 | 1.68 | 1.62 |
| 40 | 4.08 | 3.23 | 2.84 | 2.61 | 2.45 | 2.34 | 2.25 | 2.18 | 2.12 | 2.08 | 2.00 | 1.92 | 1.84 | 1.79 | 1.74 | 1.69 | 1.64 | 1.58 | 1.51 |
| 60 | 4.00 | 3.15 | 2.76 | 2.53 | 2.37 | 2.25 | 2.17 | 2.10 | 2.04 | 1.99 | 1.92 | 1.84 | 1.75 | 1.70 | 1.65 | 1.59 | 1.53 | 1.47 | 1.39 |
| 120 | 3.92 | 3.07 | 2.68 | 2.45 | 2.29 | 2.17 | 2.09 | 2.02 | 1.96 | 1.91 | 1.83 | 1.75 | 1.66 | 1.61 | 1.55 | 1.50 | 1.43 | 1.35 | 1.25 |
| ∞ | 3.84 | 3.00 | 2.60 | 2.37 | 2.21 | 2.10 | 2.01 | 1.94 | 1.88 | 1.83 | 1.75 | 1.67 | 1.57 | 1.52 | 1.46 | 1.39 | 1.32 | 1.22 | 1.00 |

## Table E.5  Critical Values of F (Continued)

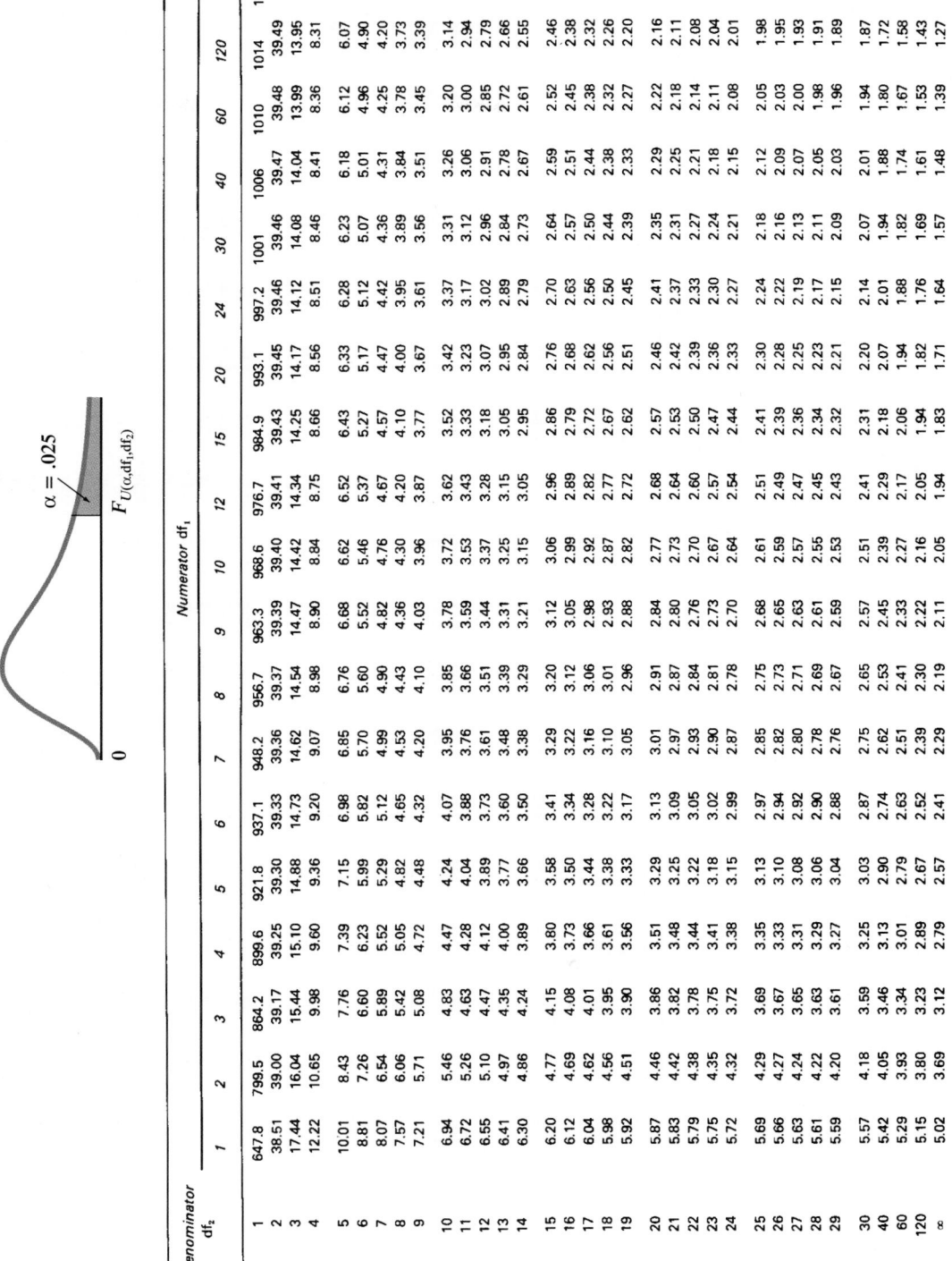

$\alpha = .025$

$F_{U(\alpha, df_1, df_2)}$

| Denominator $df_2$ | Numerator $df_1$ | | | | | | | | | | | | | | | | | | |
|---|---|---|---|---|---|---|---|---|---|---|---|---|---|---|---|---|---|---|---|
| | 1 | 2 | 3 | 4 | 5 | 6 | 7 | 8 | 9 | 10 | 12 | 15 | 20 | 24 | 30 | 40 | 60 | 120 | ∞ |
| 1 | 647.8 | 799.5 | 864.2 | 899.6 | 921.8 | 937.1 | 948.2 | 956.7 | 963.3 | 968.6 | 976.7 | 984.9 | 993.1 | 997.2 | 1001 | 1006 | 1010 | 1014 | 1018 |
| 2 | 38.51 | 39.00 | 39.17 | 39.25 | 39.30 | 39.33 | 39.36 | 39.37 | 39.39 | 39.40 | 39.41 | 39.43 | 39.45 | 39.46 | 39.46 | 39.47 | 39.48 | 39.49 | 39.50 |
| 3 | 17.44 | 16.04 | 15.44 | 15.10 | 14.88 | 14.73 | 14.62 | 14.54 | 14.47 | 14.42 | 14.34 | 14.25 | 14.17 | 14.12 | 14.08 | 14.04 | 13.99 | 13.95 | 13.90 |
| 4 | 12.22 | 10.65 | 9.98 | 9.60 | 9.36 | 9.20 | 9.07 | 8.98 | 8.90 | 8.84 | 8.75 | 8.66 | 8.56 | 8.51 | 8.46 | 8.41 | 8.36 | 8.31 | 8.26 |
| 5 | 10.01 | 8.43 | 7.76 | 7.39 | 7.15 | 6.98 | 6.85 | 6.76 | 6.68 | 6.62 | 6.52 | 6.43 | 6.33 | 6.28 | 6.23 | 6.18 | 6.12 | 6.07 | 6.02 |
| 6 | 8.81 | 7.26 | 6.60 | 6.23 | 5.99 | 5.82 | 5.70 | 5.60 | 5.52 | 5.46 | 5.37 | 5.27 | 5.17 | 5.12 | 5.07 | 5.01 | 4.96 | 4.90 | 4.85 |
| 7 | 8.07 | 6.54 | 5.89 | 5.52 | 5.29 | 5.12 | 4.99 | 4.90 | 4.82 | 4.76 | 4.67 | 4.57 | 4.47 | 4.42 | 4.36 | 4.31 | 4.25 | 4.20 | 4.14 |
| 8 | 7.57 | 6.06 | 5.42 | 5.05 | 4.82 | 4.65 | 4.53 | 4.43 | 4.36 | 4.30 | 4.20 | 4.10 | 4.00 | 3.95 | 3.89 | 3.84 | 3.78 | 3.73 | 3.67 |
| 9 | 7.21 | 5.71 | 5.08 | 4.72 | 4.48 | 4.32 | 4.20 | 4.10 | 4.03 | 3.96 | 3.87 | 3.77 | 3.67 | 3.61 | 3.56 | 3.51 | 3.45 | 3.39 | 3.33 |
| 10 | 6.94 | 5.46 | 4.83 | 4.47 | 4.24 | 4.07 | 3.95 | 3.85 | 3.78 | 3.72 | 3.62 | 3.52 | 3.42 | 3.37 | 3.31 | 3.26 | 3.20 | 3.14 | 3.08 |
| 11 | 6.72 | 5.26 | 4.63 | 4.28 | 4.04 | 3.88 | 3.76 | 3.66 | 3.59 | 3.53 | 3.43 | 3.33 | 3.23 | 3.17 | 3.12 | 3.06 | 3.00 | 2.94 | 2.88 |
| 12 | 6.55 | 5.10 | 4.47 | 4.12 | 3.89 | 3.73 | 3.61 | 3.51 | 3.44 | 3.37 | 3.28 | 3.18 | 3.07 | 3.02 | 2.96 | 2.91 | 2.85 | 2.79 | 2.72 |
| 13 | 6.41 | 4.97 | 4.35 | 4.00 | 3.77 | 3.60 | 3.48 | 3.39 | 3.31 | 3.25 | 3.15 | 3.05 | 2.95 | 2.89 | 2.84 | 2.78 | 2.72 | 2.66 | 2.60 |
| 14 | 6.30 | 4.86 | 4.24 | 3.89 | 3.66 | 3.50 | 3.38 | 3.29 | 3.21 | 3.15 | 3.05 | 2.95 | 2.84 | 2.79 | 2.73 | 2.67 | 2.61 | 2.55 | 2.49 |
| 15 | 6.20 | 4.77 | 4.15 | 3.80 | 3.58 | 3.41 | 3.29 | 3.20 | 3.12 | 3.06 | 2.96 | 2.86 | 2.76 | 2.70 | 2.64 | 2.59 | 2.52 | 2.46 | 2.40 |
| 16 | 6.12 | 4.69 | 4.08 | 3.73 | 3.50 | 3.34 | 3.22 | 3.12 | 3.05 | 2.99 | 2.89 | 2.79 | 2.68 | 2.63 | 2.57 | 2.51 | 2.45 | 2.38 | 2.32 |
| 17 | 6.04 | 4.62 | 4.01 | 3.66 | 3.44 | 3.28 | 3.16 | 3.06 | 2.98 | 2.92 | 2.82 | 2.72 | 2.62 | 2.56 | 2.50 | 2.44 | 2.38 | 2.32 | 2.25 |
| 18 | 5.98 | 4.56 | 3.95 | 3.61 | 3.38 | 3.22 | 3.10 | 3.01 | 2.93 | 2.87 | 2.77 | 2.67 | 2.56 | 2.50 | 2.44 | 2.38 | 2.32 | 2.26 | 2.19 |
| 19 | 5.92 | 4.51 | 3.90 | 3.56 | 3.33 | 3.17 | 3.05 | 2.96 | 2.88 | 2.82 | 2.72 | 2.62 | 2.51 | 2.45 | 2.39 | 2.33 | 2.27 | 2.20 | 2.13 |
| 20 | 5.87 | 4.46 | 3.86 | 3.51 | 3.29 | 3.13 | 3.01 | 2.91 | 2.84 | 2.77 | 2.68 | 2.57 | 2.46 | 2.41 | 2.35 | 2.29 | 2.22 | 2.16 | 2.09 |
| 21 | 5.83 | 4.42 | 3.82 | 3.48 | 3.25 | 3.09 | 2.97 | 2.87 | 2.80 | 2.73 | 2.64 | 2.53 | 2.42 | 2.37 | 2.31 | 2.25 | 2.18 | 2.11 | 2.04 |
| 22 | 5.79 | 4.38 | 3.78 | 3.44 | 3.22 | 3.05 | 2.93 | 2.84 | 2.76 | 2.70 | 2.60 | 2.50 | 2.39 | 2.33 | 2.27 | 2.21 | 2.14 | 2.08 | 2.00 |
| 23 | 5.75 | 4.35 | 3.75 | 3.41 | 3.18 | 3.02 | 2.90 | 2.81 | 2.73 | 2.67 | 2.57 | 2.47 | 2.36 | 2.30 | 2.24 | 2.18 | 2.11 | 2.04 | 1.97 |
| 24 | 5.72 | 4.32 | 3.72 | 3.38 | 3.15 | 2.99 | 2.87 | 2.78 | 2.70 | 2.64 | 2.54 | 2.44 | 2.33 | 2.27 | 2.21 | 2.15 | 2.08 | 2.01 | 1.94 |
| 25 | 5.69 | 4.29 | 3.69 | 3.35 | 3.13 | 2.97 | 2.85 | 2.75 | 2.68 | 2.61 | 2.51 | 2.41 | 2.30 | 2.24 | 2.18 | 2.12 | 2.05 | 1.98 | 1.91 |
| 26 | 5.66 | 4.27 | 3.67 | 3.33 | 3.10 | 2.94 | 2.82 | 2.73 | 2.65 | 2.59 | 2.49 | 2.39 | 2.28 | 2.22 | 2.16 | 2.09 | 2.03 | 1.95 | 1.88 |
| 27 | 5.63 | 4.24 | 3.65 | 3.31 | 3.08 | 2.92 | 2.80 | 2.71 | 2.63 | 2.57 | 2.47 | 2.36 | 2.25 | 2.19 | 2.13 | 2.07 | 2.00 | 1.93 | 1.85 |
| 28 | 5.61 | 4.22 | 3.63 | 3.29 | 3.06 | 2.90 | 2.78 | 2.69 | 2.61 | 2.55 | 2.45 | 2.34 | 2.23 | 2.17 | 2.11 | 2.05 | 1.98 | 1.91 | 1.83 |
| 29 | 5.59 | 4.20 | 3.61 | 3.27 | 3.04 | 2.88 | 2.76 | 2.67 | 2.59 | 2.53 | 2.43 | 2.32 | 2.21 | 2.15 | 2.09 | 2.03 | 1.96 | 1.89 | 1.81 |
| 30 | 5.57 | 4.18 | 3.59 | 3.25 | 3.03 | 2.87 | 2.75 | 2.65 | 2.57 | 2.51 | 2.41 | 2.31 | 2.20 | 2.14 | 2.07 | 2.01 | 1.94 | 1.87 | 1.79 |
| 40 | 5.42 | 4.05 | 3.46 | 3.13 | 2.90 | 2.74 | 2.62 | 2.53 | 2.45 | 2.39 | 2.29 | 2.18 | 2.07 | 2.01 | 1.94 | 1.88 | 1.80 | 1.72 | 1.64 |
| 60 | 5.29 | 3.93 | 3.34 | 3.01 | 2.79 | 2.63 | 2.51 | 2.41 | 2.33 | 2.27 | 2.17 | 2.06 | 1.94 | 1.88 | 1.82 | 1.74 | 1.67 | 1.58 | 1.48 |
| 120 | 5.15 | 3.80 | 3.23 | 2.89 | 2.67 | 2.52 | 2.39 | 2.30 | 2.22 | 2.16 | 2.05 | 1.94 | 1.82 | 1.76 | 1.69 | 1.61 | 1.53 | 1.43 | 1.31 |
| ∞ | 5.02 | 3.69 | 3.12 | 2.79 | 2.57 | 2.41 | 2.29 | 2.19 | 2.11 | 2.05 | 1.94 | 1.83 | 1.71 | 1.64 | 1.57 | 1.48 | 1.39 | 1.27 | 1.00 |

## Table E.5  Critical Values of F (Continued)

$\alpha = .01$

$F_{U(\alpha, df_1, df_2)}$

Numerator $df_1$

| Denominator $df_2$ | 1 | 2 | 3 | 4 | 5 | 6 | 7 | 8 | 9 | 10 | 12 | 15 | 20 | 24 | 30 | 40 | 60 | 120 | ∞ |
|---|---|---|---|---|---|---|---|---|---|---|---|---|---|---|---|---|---|---|---|
| 1 | 4052 | 4999.5 | 5403 | 5625 | 5764 | 5859 | 5928 | 5982 | 6022 | 6056 | 6106 | 6157 | 6209 | 6235 | 6261 | 6287 | 6313 | 6339 | 6366 |
| 2 | 98.50 | 99.00 | 99.17 | 99.25 | 99.30 | 99.33 | 99.36 | 99.37 | 99.39 | 99.40 | 99.42 | 99.43 | 99.45 | 99.46 | 99.47 | 99.47 | 99.48 | 99.49 | 99.50 |
| 3 | 34.12 | 30.82 | 29.46 | 28.71 | 28.24 | 27.91 | 27.67 | 27.49 | 27.35 | 27.23 | 27.05 | 26.87 | 26.69 | 26.60 | 26.50 | 26.41 | 26.32 | 26.22 | 26.13 |
| 4 | 21.20 | 18.00 | 16.69 | 15.98 | 15.52 | 15.21 | 14.98 | 14.80 | 14.66 | 14.55 | 14.37 | 14.20 | 14.02 | 13.93 | 13.84 | 13.75 | 13.65 | 13.56 | 13.46 |
| 5 | 16.26 | 13.27 | 12.06 | 11.39 | 10.97 | 10.67 | 10.46 | 10.29 | 10.16 | 10.05 | 9.89 | 9.72 | 9.55 | 9.47 | 9.38 | 9.29 | 9.20 | 9.11 | 9.02 |
| 6 | 13.75 | 10.92 | 9.78 | 9.15 | 8.75 | 8.47 | 8.26 | 8.10 | 7.98 | 7.87 | 7.72 | 7.56 | 7.40 | 7.31 | 7.23 | 7.14 | 7.06 | 6.97 | 6.88 |
| 7 | 12.25 | 9.55 | 8.45 | 7.85 | 7.46 | 7.19 | 6.99 | 6.84 | 6.72 | 6.62 | 6.47 | 6.31 | 6.16 | 6.07 | 5.99 | 5.91 | 5.82 | 5.74 | 5.65 |
| 8 | 11.26 | 8.65 | 7.59 | 7.01 | 6.63 | 6.37 | 6.18 | 6.03 | 5.91 | 5.81 | 5.67 | 5.52 | 5.36 | 5.28 | 5.20 | 5.12 | 5.03 | 4.95 | 4.86 |
| 9 | 10.56 | 8.02 | 6.99 | 6.42 | 6.06 | 5.80 | 5.61 | 5.47 | 5.35 | 5.26 | 5.11 | 4.96 | 4.81 | 4.73 | 4.65 | 4.57 | 4.48 | 4.40 | 4.31 |
| 10 | 10.04 | 7.56 | 6.55 | 5.99 | 5.64 | 5.39 | 5.20 | 5.06 | 4.94 | 4.85 | 4.71 | 4.56 | 4.41 | 4.33 | 4.25 | 4.17 | 4.08 | 4.00 | 3.91 |
| 11 | 9.65 | 7.21 | 6.22 | 5.67 | 5.32 | 5.07 | 4.89 | 4.74 | 4.63 | 4.54 | 4.40 | 4.25 | 4.10 | 4.02 | 3.94 | 3.86 | 3.78 | 3.69 | 3.60 |
| 12 | 9.33 | 6.93 | 5.95 | 5.41 | 5.06 | 4.82 | 4.64 | 4.50 | 4.39 | 4.30 | 4.16 | 4.01 | 3.86 | 3.78 | 3.70 | 3.62 | 3.54 | 3.45 | 3.36 |
| 13 | 9.07 | 6.70 | 5.74 | 5.21 | 4.86 | 4.62 | 4.44 | 4.30 | 4.19 | 4.10 | 3.96 | 3.82 | 3.66 | 3.59 | 3.51 | 3.43 | 3.34 | 3.25 | 3.17 |
| 14 | 8.86 | 6.51 | 5.56 | 5.04 | 4.69 | 4.46 | 4.28 | 4.14 | 4.03 | 3.94 | 3.80 | 3.66 | 3.51 | 3.43 | 3.35 | 3.27 | 3.18 | 3.09 | 3.00 |
| 15 | 8.68 | 6.36 | 5.42 | 4.89 | 4.56 | 4.32 | 4.14 | 4.00 | 3.89 | 3.80 | 3.67 | 3.52 | 3.37 | 3.29 | 3.21 | 3.13 | 3.05 | 2.96 | 2.87 |
| 16 | 8.53 | 6.23 | 5.29 | 4.77 | 4.44 | 4.20 | 4.03 | 3.89 | 3.78 | 3.69 | 3.55 | 3.41 | 3.26 | 3.18 | 3.10 | 3.02 | 2.93 | 2.84 | 2.75 |
| 17 | 8.40 | 6.11 | 5.18 | 4.67 | 4.34 | 4.10 | 3.93 | 3.79 | 3.68 | 3.59 | 3.46 | 3.31 | 3.16 | 3.08 | 3.00 | 2.92 | 2.83 | 2.75 | 2.65 |
| 18 | 8.29 | 6.01 | 5.09 | 4.58 | 4.25 | 4.01 | 3.84 | 3.71 | 3.60 | 3.51 | 3.37 | 3.23 | 3.08 | 3.00 | 2.92 | 2.84 | 2.75 | 2.66 | 2.57 |
| 19 | 8.18 | 5.93 | 5.01 | 4.50 | 4.17 | 3.94 | 3.77 | 3.63 | 3.52 | 3.43 | 3.30 | 3.15 | 3.00 | 2.92 | 2.84 | 2.76 | 2.67 | 2.58 | 2.49 |
| 20 | 8.10 | 5.85 | 4.94 | 4.43 | 4.10 | 3.87 | 3.70 | 3.56 | 3.46 | 3.37 | 3.23 | 3.09 | 2.94 | 2.86 | 2.78 | 2.69 | 2.61 | 2.52 | 2.42 |
| 21 | 8.02 | 5.78 | 4.87 | 4.37 | 4.04 | 3.81 | 3.64 | 3.51 | 3.40 | 3.31 | 3.17 | 3.03 | 2.88 | 2.80 | 2.72 | 2.64 | 2.55 | 2.46 | 2.36 |
| 22 | 7.95 | 5.72 | 4.82 | 4.31 | 3.99 | 3.76 | 3.59 | 3.45 | 3.35 | 3.26 | 3.12 | 2.98 | 2.83 | 2.75 | 2.67 | 2.58 | 2.50 | 2.40 | 2.31 |
| 23 | 7.88 | 5.66 | 4.76 | 4.26 | 3.94 | 3.71 | 3.54 | 3.41 | 3.30 | 3.21 | 3.07 | 2.93 | 2.78 | 2.70 | 2.62 | 2.54 | 2.45 | 2.35 | 2.26 |
| 24 | 7.82 | 5.61 | 4.72 | 4.22 | 3.90 | 3.67 | 3.50 | 3.36 | 3.26 | 3.17 | 3.03 | 2.89 | 2.74 | 2.66 | 2.58 | 2.49 | 2.40 | 2.31 | 2.21 |
| 25 | 7.77 | 5.57 | 4.68 | 4.18 | 3.85 | 3.63 | 3.46 | 3.32 | 3.22 | 3.13 | 2.99 | 2.85 | 2.70 | 2.62 | 2.54 | 2.45 | 2.36 | 2.27 | 2.17 |
| 26 | 7.72 | 5.53 | 4.64 | 4.14 | 3.82 | 3.59 | 3.42 | 3.29 | 3.18 | 3.09 | 2.96 | 2.81 | 2.66 | 2.58 | 2.50 | 2.42 | 2.33 | 2.23 | 2.13 |
| 27 | 7.68 | 5.49 | 4.60 | 4.11 | 3.78 | 3.56 | 3.39 | 3.26 | 3.15 | 3.06 | 2.93 | 2.78 | 2.63 | 2.55 | 2.47 | 2.38 | 2.29 | 2.20 | 2.10 |
| 28 | 7.64 | 5.45 | 4.57 | 4.07 | 3.75 | 3.53 | 3.36 | 3.23 | 3.12 | 3.03 | 2.90 | 2.75 | 2.60 | 2.52 | 2.44 | 2.35 | 2.26 | 2.17 | 2.06 |
| 29 | 7.60 | 5.42 | 4.54 | 4.04 | 3.73 | 3.50 | 3.33 | 3.20 | 3.09 | 3.00 | 2.87 | 2.73 | 2.57 | 2.49 | 2.41 | 2.33 | 2.23 | 2.14 | 2.03 |
| 30 | 7.56 | 5.39 | 4.51 | 4.02 | 3.70 | 3.47 | 3.30 | 3.17 | 3.07 | 2.98 | 2.84 | 2.70 | 2.55 | 2.47 | 2.39 | 2.30 | 2.21 | 2.11 | 2.01 |
| 40 | 7.31 | 5.18 | 4.31 | 3.83 | 3.51 | 3.29 | 3.12 | 2.99 | 2.89 | 2.80 | 2.66 | 2.52 | 2.37 | 2.29 | 2.20 | 2.11 | 2.02 | 1.92 | 1.80 |
| 60 | 7.08 | 4.98 | 4.13 | 3.65 | 3.34 | 3.12 | 2.95 | 2.82 | 2.72 | 2.63 | 2.50 | 2.35 | 2.20 | 2.12 | 2.03 | 1.94 | 1.84 | 1.73 | 1.60 |
| 120 | 6.85 | 4.79 | 3.95 | 3.48 | 3.17 | 2.96 | 2.79 | 2.66 | 2.56 | 2.47 | 2.34 | 2.19 | 2.03 | 1.95 | 1.86 | 1.76 | 1.66 | 1.53 | 1.38 |
| ∞ | 6.63 | 4.61 | 3.78 | 3.32 | 3.02 | 2.80 | 2.64 | 2.51 | 2.41 | 2.32 | 2.18 | 2.04 | 1.88 | 1.79 | 1.70 | 1.59 | 1.47 | 1.32 | 1.00 |

# Table E.5  Critical Values of F (Continued)

$\alpha = .005$

$F_{U(\alpha,df_1,df_2)}$

| Denominator $df_2$ | Numerator $df_1$ | | | | | | | | | | | | | | | | | | |
|---|---|---|---|---|---|---|---|---|---|---|---|---|---|---|---|---|---|---|---|
| | 1 | 2 | 3 | 4 | 5 | 6 | 7 | 8 | 9 | 10 | 12 | 15 | 20 | 24 | 30 | 40 | 60 | 120 | ∞ |
| 1 | 16211 | 20000 | 21615 | 22500 | 23056 | 23437 | 23715 | 23925 | 24091 | 24224 | 24426 | 24630 | 24836 | 24940 | 25044 | 25148 | 25253 | 25359 | 25465 |
| 2 | 198.5 | 199.0 | 199.2 | 199.2 | 199.3 | 199.3 | 199.4 | 199.4 | 199.4 | 199.4 | 199.4 | 199.4 | 199.4 | 199.5 | 199.5 | 199.5 | 199.5 | 199.5 | 199.5 |
| 3 | 55.55 | 49.80 | 47.47 | 46.19 | 45.39 | 44.84 | 44.43 | 44.13 | 43.88 | 43.69 | 43.39 | 43.08 | 42.78 | 42.62 | 42.47 | 42.31 | 42.15 | 41.99 | 41.83 |
| 4 | 31.33 | 26.28 | 24.26 | 23.15 | 22.46 | 21.97 | 21.62 | 21.35 | 21.14 | 20.97 | 20.70 | 20.44 | 20.17 | 20.03 | 19.89 | 19.75 | 19.61 | 19.47 | 19.32 |
| 5 | 22.78 | 18.31 | 16.53 | 15.56 | 14.94 | 14.51 | 14.20 | 13.96 | 13.77 | 13.62 | 13.38 | 13.15 | 12.90 | 12.78 | 12.66 | 12.53 | 12.40 | 12.27 | 12.14 |
| 6 | 18.63 | 14.54 | 12.92 | 12.03 | 11.46 | 11.07 | 10.79 | 10.57 | 10.39 | 10.25 | 10.03 | 9.81 | 9.59 | 9.47 | 9.36 | 9.24 | 9.12 | 9.00 | 8.88 |
| 7 | 16.24 | 12.40 | 10.88 | 10.05 | 9.52 | 9.16 | 8.89 | 8.68 | 8.51 | 8.38 | 8.18 | 7.97 | 7.75 | 7.65 | 7.53 | 7.42 | 7.31 | 7.19 | 7.08 |
| 8 | 14.69 | 11.04 | 9.60 | 8.81 | 8.30 | 7.95 | 7.69 | 7.50 | 7.34 | 7.21 | 7.01 | 6.81 | 6.61 | 6.50 | 6.40 | 6.29 | 6.18 | 6.06 | 5.95 |
| 9 | 13.61 | 10.11 | 8.72 | 7.96 | 7.47 | 7.13 | 6.88 | 6.69 | 6.54 | 6.42 | 6.23 | 6.03 | 5.83 | 5.73 | 5.62 | 5.52 | 5.41 | 5.30 | 5.19 |
| 10 | 12.83 | 9.43 | 8.08 | 7.34 | 6.87 | 6.54 | 6.30 | 6.12 | 5.97 | 5.85 | 5.66 | 5.47 | 5.27 | 5.17 | 5.07 | 4.97 | 4.86 | 4.75 | 4.64 |
| 11 | 12.23 | 8.91 | 7.60 | 6.88 | 6.42 | 6.10 | 5.86 | 5.68 | 5.54 | 5.42 | 5.24 | 5.05 | 4.86 | 4.76 | 4.65 | 4.55 | 4.44 | 4.34 | 4.23 |
| 12 | 11.75 | 8.51 | 7.23 | 6.52 | 6.07 | 5.76 | 5.52 | 5.35 | 5.20 | 5.09 | 4.91 | 4.72 | 4.53 | 4.43 | 4.33 | 4.23 | 4.12 | 4.01 | 3.90 |
| 13 | 11.37 | 8.19 | 6.93 | 6.23 | 5.79 | 5.48 | 5.25 | 5.08 | 4.94 | 4.82 | 4.64 | 4.46 | 4.27 | 4.17 | 4.07 | 3.97 | 3.87 | 3.76 | 3.65 |
| 14 | 11.06 | 7.92 | 6.68 | 6.00 | 5.56 | 5.26 | 5.03 | 4.86 | 4.72 | 4.60 | 4.43 | 4.25 | 4.06 | 3.96 | 3.86 | 3.76 | 3.66 | 3.55 | 3.44 |
| 15 | 10.80 | 7.70 | 6.48 | 5.80 | 5.37 | 5.07 | 4.85 | 4.67 | 4.54 | 4.42 | 4.25 | 4.07 | 3.88 | 3.79 | 3.69 | 3.58 | 3.48 | 3.37 | 3.26 |
| 16 | 10.58 | 7.51 | 6.30 | 5.64 | 5.21 | 4.91 | 4.69 | 4.52 | 4.38 | 4.27 | 4.10 | 3.92 | 3.73 | 3.64 | 3.54 | 3.44 | 3.33 | 3.22 | 3.11 |
| 17 | 10.38 | 7.35 | 6.16 | 5.50 | 5.07 | 4.78 | 4.56 | 4.39 | 4.25 | 4.14 | 3.97 | 3.79 | 3.61 | 3.51 | 3.41 | 3.31 | 3.21 | 3.10 | 2.98 |
| 18 | 10.22 | 7.21 | 6.03 | 5.37 | 4.96 | 4.66 | 4.44 | 4.28 | 4.14 | 4.03 | 3.86 | 3.68 | 3.50 | 3.40 | 3.30 | 3.20 | 3.10 | 2.99 | 2.87 |
| 19 | 10.07 | 7.09 | 5.92 | 5.27 | 4.85 | 4.56 | 4.34 | 4.18 | 4.04 | 3.93 | 3.76 | 3.59 | 3.40 | 3.31 | 3.21 | 3.11 | 3.00 | 2.89 | 2.78 |
| 20 | 9.94 | 6.99 | 5.82 | 5.17 | 4.76 | 4.47 | 4.26 | 4.09 | 3.96 | 3.85 | 3.68 | 3.50 | 3.32 | 3.22 | 3.12 | 3.02 | 2.92 | 2.81 | 2.69 |
| 21 | 9.83 | 6.89 | 5.73 | 5.09 | 4.68 | 4.39 | 4.18 | 4.01 | 3.88 | 3.77 | 3.60 | 3.43 | 3.24 | 3.15 | 3.05 | 2.95 | 2.84 | 2.73 | 2.61 |
| 22 | 9.73 | 6.81 | 5.65 | 5.02 | 4.61 | 4.32 | 4.11 | 3.94 | 3.81 | 3.70 | 3.54 | 3.36 | 3.18 | 3.08 | 2.98 | 2.88 | 2.77 | 2.66 | 2.55 |
| 23 | 9.63 | 6.73 | 5.58 | 4.95 | 4.54 | 4.26 | 4.05 | 3.88 | 3.75 | 3.64 | 3.47 | 3.30 | 3.12 | 3.02 | 2.92 | 2.82 | 2.71 | 2.60 | 2.48 |
| 24 | 9.55 | 6.66 | 5.52 | 4.89 | 4.49 | 4.20 | 3.99 | 3.83 | 3.69 | 3.59 | 3.42 | 3.25 | 3.06 | 2.97 | 2.87 | 2.77 | 2.66 | 2.55 | 2.43 |
| 25 | 9.48 | 6.60 | 5.46 | 4.84 | 4.43 | 4.15 | 3.94 | 3.78 | 3.64 | 3.54 | 3.37 | 3.20 | 3.01 | 2.92 | 2.82 | 2.72 | 2.61 | 2.50 | 2.38 |
| 26 | 9.41 | 6.54 | 5.41 | 4.79 | 4.38 | 4.10 | 3.89 | 3.73 | 3.60 | 3.49 | 3.33 | 3.15 | 2.97 | 2.87 | 2.77 | 2.67 | 2.56 | 2.45 | 2.33 |
| 27 | 9.34 | 6.49 | 5.36 | 4.74 | 4.34 | 4.06 | 3.85 | 3.69 | 3.56 | 3.45 | 3.28 | 3.11 | 2.93 | 2.83 | 2.73 | 2.63 | 2.52 | 2.41 | 2.29 |
| 28 | 9.28 | 6.44 | 5.32 | 4.70 | 4.30 | 4.02 | 3.81 | 3.65 | 3.52 | 3.41 | 3.25 | 3.07 | 2.89 | 2.79 | 2.69 | 2.59 | 2.48 | 2.37 | 2.25 |
| 29 | 9.23 | 6.40 | 5.28 | 4.66 | 4.26 | 3.98 | 3.77 | 3.61 | 3.48 | 3.38 | 3.21 | 3.04 | 2.86 | 2.76 | 2.66 | 2.56 | 2.45 | 2.33 | 2.21 |
| 30 | 9.18 | 6.35 | 5.24 | 4.62 | 4.23 | 3.95 | 3.74 | 3.58 | 3.45 | 3.34 | 3.18 | 3.01 | 2.82 | 2.73 | 2.63 | 2.52 | 2.42 | 2.30 | 2.18 |
| 40 | 8.83 | 6.07 | 4.98 | 4.37 | 3.99 | 3.71 | 3.51 | 3.35 | 3.22 | 3.12 | 2.95 | 2.78 | 2.60 | 2.50 | 2.40 | 2.30 | 2.18 | 2.06 | 1.93 |
| 60 | 8.49 | 5.79 | 4.73 | 4.14 | 3.76 | 3.49 | 3.29 | 3.13 | 3.01 | 2.90 | 2.74 | 2.57 | 2.39 | 2.29 | 2.19 | 2.08 | 1.96 | 1.83 | 1.69 |
| 120 | 8.18 | 5.54 | 4.50 | 3.92 | 3.55 | 3.28 | 3.09 | 2.93 | 2.81 | 2.71 | 2.54 | 2.37 | 2.19 | 2.09 | 1.98 | 1.87 | 1.75 | 1.61 | 1.43 |
| ∞ | 7.88 | 5.30 | 4.28 | 3.72 | 3.35 | 3.09 | 2.90 | 2.74 | 2.62 | 2.52 | 2.36 | 2.19 | 2.00 | 1.90 | 1.79 | 1.67 | 1.53 | 1.36 | 1.00 |

*Source: Reprinted from E. S. Pearson and H. O. Hartley, eds., Biometrika Tables for Statisticians, 3d ed., 1966, by permission of the Biometrika Trustees.*

# Table E.6    *Selected Critical Values of F for Cook's $D_i$ Statistic*

|  | $\alpha = .50$ | | | | | | | | | | | |
|---|---|---|---|---|---|---|---|---|---|---|---|---|
|  | Numerator df = P + 1 | | | | | | | | | | | |
| Denominator df = n − P − 1 | 2 | 3 | 4 | 5 | 6 | 7 | 8 | 9 | 10 | 12 | 15 | 20 |
| 10 | .743 | .845 | .899 | .932 | .954 | .971 | .983 | .992 | 1.00 | 1.01 | 1.02 | 1.03 |
| 11 | .739 | .840 | .893 | .926 | .948 | .964 | .977 | .986 | .994 | 1.01 | 1.02 | 1.03 |
| 12 | .735 | .835 | .888 | .921 | .943 | .959 | .972 | .981 | .989 | 1.00 | 1.01 | 1.02 |
| 15 | .726 | .826 | .878 | .911 | .933 | .949 | .960 | .970 | .977 | .989 | 1.00 | 1.01 |
| 20 | .718 | .816 | .868 | .900 | .922 | .938 | .950 | .959 | .966 | .977 | .989 | 1.00 |
| 24 | .714 | .812 | .863 | .895 | .917 | .932 | .944 | .953 | .961 | .972 | .983 | .994 |
| 30 | .709 | .807 | .858 | .890 | .912 | .927 | .939 | .948 | .955 | .966 | .978 | .989 |
| 40 | .705 | .802 | .854 | .885 | .907 | .922 | .934 | .943 | .950 | .961 | .972 | .983 |
| 60 | .701 | .798 | .849 | .880 | .901 | .917 | .928 | .937 | .945 | .956 | .967 | .978 |
| 120 | .697 | .793 | .844 | .875 | .896 | .912 | .923 | .932 | .939 | .950 | .961 | .972 |
| ∞ | .693 | .789 | .839 | .870 | .891 | .907 | .918 | .927 | .934 | .945 | .956 | .967 |

*Source: Extracted from E. S. Pearson and H. O. Hartley, eds.,* Biometrika Tables for Statisticians, *3d ed., 1966, by permission of the* Biometrika *Trustees.*

## Table E.7 Critical Values of Hartley's $F_{max}$ Test $\left( F_{max} = \dfrac{S^2_{largest}}{S^2_{smallest}} \sim F_{max_{1-a(c,v)}} \right)$

### Upper 5% points ($\alpha = .05$)

| $v$ \ $c$ | 2 | 3 | 4 | 5 | 6 | 7 | 8 | 9 | 10 | 11 | 12 |
|---|---|---|---|---|---|---|---|---|---|---|---|
| 2 | 39.0 | 87.5 | 142 | 202 | 266 | 333 | 403 | 475 | 550 | 626 | 704 |
| 3 | 15.4 | 27.8 | 39.2 | 50.7 | 62.0 | 72.9 | 83.5 | 93.9 | 104 | 114 | 124 |
| 4 | 9.60 | 15.5 | 20.6 | 25.2 | 29.5 | 33.6 | 37.5 | 41.1 | 44.6 | 48.0 | 51.4 |
| 5 | 7.15 | 10.8 | 13.7 | 16.3 | 18.7 | 20.8 | 22.9 | 24.7 | 26.5 | 28.2 | 29.9 |
| 6 | 5.82 | 8.38 | 10.4 | 12.1 | 13.7 | 15.0 | 16.3 | 17.5 | 18.6 | 19.7 | 20.7 |
| 7 | 4.99 | 6.94 | 8.44 | 9.70 | 10.8 | 11.8 | 12.7 | 13.5 | 14.3 | 15.1 | 15.8 |
| 8 | 4.43 | 6.00 | 7.18 | 8.12 | 9.03 | 9.78 | 10.5 | 11.1 | 11.7 | 12.2 | 12.7 |
| 9 | 4.03 | 5.34 | 6.31 | 7.11 | 7.80 | 8.41 | 8.95 | 9.45 | 9.91 | 10.3 | 10.7 |
| 10 | 3.72 | 4.85 | 5.67 | 6.34 | 6.92 | 7.42 | 7.87 | 8.28 | 8.66 | 9.01 | 9.34 |
| 12 | 3.28 | 4.16 | 4.79 | 5.30 | 5.72 | 6.09 | 6.42 | 6.72 | 7.00 | 7.25 | 7.48 |
| 15 | 2.86 | 3.54 | 4.01 | 4.37 | 4.68 | 4.95 | 5.19 | 5.40 | 5.59 | 5.77 | 5.93 |
| 20 | 2.46 | 2.95 | 3.29 | 3.54 | 3.76 | 3.94 | 4.10 | 4.24 | 4.37 | 4.49 | 4.59 |
| 30 | 2.07 | 2.40 | 2.61 | 2.78 | 2.91 | 3.02 | 3.12 | 3.21 | 3.29 | 3.36 | 3.39 |
| 60 | 1.67 | 1.85 | 1.96 | 2.04 | 2.11 | 2.17 | 2.22 | 2.26 | 2.30 | 2.33 | 2.36 |
| $\infty$ | 1.00 | 1.00 | 1.00 | 1.00 | 1.00 | 1.00 | 1.00 | 1.00 | 1.00 | 1.00 | 1.00 |

### Upper 1% points ($\alpha = .01$)

| $v$ \ $c$ | 2 | 3 | 4 | 5 | 6 | 7 | 8 | 9 | 10 | 11 | 12 |
|---|---|---|---|---|---|---|---|---|---|---|---|
| 2 | 199 | 448 | 729 | 1036 | 1362 | 1705 | 2063 | 2432 | 2813 | 3204 | 3605 |
| 3 | 47.5 | 85 | 120 | 151 | 184 | 21(6) | 24(9) | 28(1) | 31(0) | 33(7) | 36(1) |
| 4 | 23.2 | 37 | 49 | 59 | 69 | 79 | 89 | 97 | 106 | 113 | 120 |
| 5 | 14.9 | 22 | 28 | 33 | 38 | 42 | 46 | 50 | 54 | 57 | 60 |
| 6 | 11.1 | 15.5 | 19.1 | 22 | 25 | 27 | 30 | 32 | 34 | 36 | 37 |
| 7 | 8.89 | 12.1 | 14.5 | 16.5 | 18.4 | 20 | 22 | 23 | 24 | 26 | 27 |
| 8 | 7.50 | 9.9 | 11.7 | 13.2 | 14.5 | 15.8 | 16.9 | 17.9 | 18.9 | 19.8 | 21 |
| 9 | 6.54 | 8.5 | 9.9 | 11.1 | 12.1 | 13.1 | 13.9 | 14.7 | 15.3 | 16.0 | 16.6 |
| 10 | 5.85 | 7.4 | 8.6 | 9.6 | 10.4 | 11.1 | 11.8 | 12.4 | 12.9 | 13.4 | 13.9 |
| 12 | 4.91 | 6.1 | 6.9 | 7.6 | 8.2 | 8.7 | 9.1 | 9.5 | 9.9 | 10.2 | 10.6 |
| 15 | 4.07 | 4.9 | 5.5 | 6.0 | 6.4 | 6.7 | 7.1 | 7.3 | 7.5 | 7.8 | 8.0 |
| 20 | 3.32 | 3.8 | 4.3 | 4.6 | 4.9 | 5.1 | 5.3 | 5.5 | 5.6 | 5.8 | 5.9 |
| 30 | 2.63 | 3.0 | 3.3 | 3.4 | 3.6 | 3.7 | 3.8 | 3.9 | 4.0 | 4.1 | 4.2 |
| 60 | 1.96 | 2.2 | 2.3 | 2.4 | 2.4 | 2.5 | 2.5 | 2.6 | 2.6 | 2.7 | 2.7 |
| $\infty$ | 1.00 | 1.0 | 1.0 | 1.0 | 1.0 | 1.0 | 1.0 | 1.0 | 1.0 | 1.0 | 1.0 |

$s^2_{largest}$ is the largest and $s^2_{smallest}$ the smallest in a set of c independent mean squares, each based on v degrees of freedom.

*Source: Reprinted from E. S. Pearson and H. O. Hartley, eds.,* Biometrika Tables for Statisticians, *3d ed., 1966, by permission of the* Biometrika *Trustees.*

## Table E.8 *Lower and Upper Critical Values W of Wilcoxon Signed-Ranks Test*

| n | One-Tailed: $\alpha = .05$ Two-Tailed: $\alpha = .10$ | $\alpha = .025$ $\alpha = .05$ | $\alpha = .01$ $\alpha = .02$ | $\alpha = .005$ $\alpha = .01$ |
|---|---|---|---|---|
| | | (Lower, Upper) | | |
| 5 | 0,15 | —,— | —,— | —,— |
| 6 | 2,19 | 0,21 | —,— | —,— |
| 7 | 3,25 | 2,26 | 0,28 | —,— |
| 8 | 5,31 | 3,33 | 1,35 | 0,36 |
| 9 | 8,37 | 5,40 | 3,42 | 1,44 |
| 10 | 10,45 | 8,47 | 5,50 | 3,52 |
| 11 | 13,53 | 10,56 | 7,59 | 5,61 |
| 12 | 17,61 | 13,65 | 10,68 | 7,71 |
| 13 | 21,70 | 17,74 | 12,79 | 10,81 |
| 14 | 25,80 | 21,84 | 16,89 | 13,92 |
| 15 | 30,90 | 25,95 | 19,101 | 16,104 |
| 16 | 35,101 | 29,107 | 23,113 | 19,117 |
| 17 | 41,112 | 34,119 | 27,126 | 23,130 |
| 18 | 47,124 | 40,131 | 32,139 | 27,144 |
| 19 | 53,137 | 46,144 | 37,153 | 32,158 |
| 20 | 60,150 | 52,158 | 43,167 | 37,173 |

*Source: Adapted from Table 2 of F. Wilcoxon and R. A. Wilcox,* Some Rapid Approximate Statistical Procedures *(Pearl River, NY: Lederle Laboratories, 1964), with permission of the American Cyanamid Company.*

## Table E.9 Lower and Upper Critical Values $T_1$ of Wilcoxon Rank Sum Test

| $n_2$ | α One-Tailed | α Two-Tailed | $n_1$ 4 | 5 | 6 | 7 | 8 | 9 | 10 |
|---|---|---|---|---|---|---|---|---|---|
| 4 | .05 | .10 | 11,25 | | | | | | |
| | .025 | .05 | 10,26 | | | | | | |
| | .01 | .02 | —,— | | | | | | |
| | .005 | .01 | —,— | | | | | | |
| 5 | .05 | .10 | 12,28 | 19,36 | | | | | |
| | .025 | .05 | 11,29 | 17,38 | | | | | |
| | .01 | .02 | 10,30 | 16,39 | | | | | |
| | .005 | .01 | —,— | 15,40 | | | | | |
| 6 | .05 | .10 | 13,31 | 20,40 | 28,50 | | | | |
| | .025 | .05 | 12,32 | 18,42 | 26,52 | | | | |
| | .01 | .02 | 11,33 | 17,43 | 24,54 | | | | |
| | .005 | .01 | 10,34 | 16,44 | 23,55 | | | | |
| 7 | .05 | .10 | 14,34 | 21,44 | 29,55 | 39,66 | | | |
| | .025 | .05 | 13,35 | 20,45 | 27,57 | 36,69 | | | |
| | .01 | .02 | 11,37 | 18,47 | 25,59 | 34,71 | | | |
| | .005 | .01 | 10,38 | 16,49 | 24,60 | 32,73 | | | |
| 8 | .05 | .10 | 15,37 | 23,47 | 31,59 | 41,71 | 51,85 | | |
| | .025 | .05 | 14,38 | 21,49 | 29,61 | 38,74 | 49,87 | | |
| | .01 | .02 | 12,40 | 19,51 | 27,63 | 35,77 | 45,91 | | |
| | .005 | .01 | 11,41 | 17,53 | 25,65 | 34,78 | 43,93 | | |
| 9 | .05 | .10 | 16,40 | 24,51 | 33,63 | 43,76 | 54,90 | 66,105 | |
| | .025 | .05 | 14,42 | 22,53 | 31,65 | 40,79 | 51,93 | 62,109 | |
| | .01 | .02 | 13,43 | 20,55 | 28,68 | 37,82 | 47,97 | 59,112 | |
| | .005 | .01 | 11,45 | 18,57 | 26,70 | 35,84 | 45,99 | 56,115 | |
| 10 | .05 | .10 | 17,43 | 26,54 | 35,67 | 45,81 | 56,96 | 69,111 | 82,128 |
| | .025 | .05 | 15,45 | 23,57 | 32,70 | 42,84 | 53,99 | 65,115 | 78,132 |
| | .01 | .02 | 13,47 | 21,59 | 29,73 | 39,87 | 49,103 | 61,119 | 74,136 |
| | .005 | .01 | 12,48 | 19,61 | 27,75 | 37,89 | 47,105 | 58,122 | 71,139 |

*Source: Adapted from Table 1 of F. Wilcoxon and R. A. Wilcox,* Some Rapid Approximate Statistical Procedures *(Pearl River, NY: Lederle Laboratories, 1964), with permission of the American Cyanamid Company.*

# Table E.10   Critical Values[a] of the Studentized Range Q

*Upper 5% points ($\alpha = .05$)*

| $v$ \\ $r$ | 2 | 3 | 4 | 5 | 6 | 7 | 8 | 9 | 10 | 11 | 12 | 13 | 14 | 15 | 16 | 17 | 18 | 19 | 20 |
|---|---|---|---|---|---|---|---|---|---|---|---|---|---|---|---|---|---|---|---|
| 1 | 18.0 | 27.0 | 32.8 | 37.1 | 40.4 | 43.1 | 45.4 | 47.4 | 49.1 | 50.6 | 52.0 | 53.2 | 54.3 | 55.4 | 56.3 | 57.2 | 58.0 | 58.8 | 59.6 |
| 2 | 6.09 | 8.3 | 9.8 | 10.9 | 11.7 | 12.4 | 13.0 | 13.5 | 14.0 | 14.4 | 14.7 | 15.1 | 15.4 | 15.7 | 15.9 | 16.1 | 16.4 | 16.6 | 16.8 |
| 3 | 4.50 | 5.91 | 6.82 | 7.50 | 8.04 | 8.48 | 8.85 | 9.18 | 9.46 | 9.72 | 9.95 | 10.15 | 10.35 | 10.52 | 10.69 | 10.84 | 10.98 | 11.11 | 11.24 |
| 4 | 3.93 | 5.04 | 5.76 | 6.29 | 6.71 | 7.05 | 7.35 | 7.60 | 7.83 | 8.03 | 8.21 | 8.37 | 8.52 | 8.66 | 8.79 | 8.91 | 9.03 | 9.13 | 9.23 |
| 5 | 3.64 | 4.60 | 5.22 | 5.67 | 6.03 | 6.33 | 6.58 | 6.80 | 6.99 | 7.17 | 7.32 | 7.47 | 7.60 | 7.72 | 7.83 | 7.93 | 8.03 | 8.12 | 8.21 |
| 6 | 3.46 | 4.34 | 4.90 | 5.31 | 5.63 | 5.89 | 6.12 | 6.32 | 6.49 | 6.65 | 6.79 | 6.92 | 7.03 | 7.14 | 7.24 | 7.34 | 7.43 | 7.51 | 7.59 |
| 7 | 3.34 | 4.16 | 4.68 | 5.06 | 5.36 | 5.61 | 5.82 | 6.00 | 6.16 | 6.30 | 6.43 | 6.55 | 6.66 | 6.76 | 6.85 | 6.94 | 7.02 | 7.09 | 7.17 |
| 8 | 3.26 | 4.04 | 4.53 | 4.89 | 5.17 | 5.40 | 5.60 | 5.77 | 5.92 | 6.05 | 6.18 | 6.29 | 6.39 | 6.48 | 6.57 | 6.65 | 6.73 | 6.80 | 6.87 |
| 9 | 3.20 | 3.95 | 4.42 | 4.76 | 5.02 | 5.24 | 5.43 | 5.60 | 5.74 | 5.87 | 5.98 | 6.09 | 6.19 | 6.28 | 6.36 | 6.44 | 6.51 | 6.58 | 6.64 |
| 10 | 3.15 | 3.88 | 4.33 | 4.65 | 4.91 | 5.12 | 5.30 | 5.46 | 5.60 | 5.72 | 5.83 | 5.93 | 6.03 | 6.11 | 6.20 | 6.27 | 6.34 | 6.40 | 6.47 |
| 11 | 3.11 | 3.82 | 4.26 | 4.57 | 4.82 | 5.03 | 5.20 | 5.35 | 5.49 | 5.61 | 5.71 | 5.81 | 5.90 | 5.99 | 6.06 | 6.14 | 6.20 | 6.26 | 6.33 |
| 12 | 3.08 | 3.77 | 4.20 | 4.51 | 4.75 | 4.95 | 5.12 | 5.27 | 5.40 | 5.51 | 5.62 | 5.71 | 5.80 | 5.88 | 5.95 | 6.03 | 6.09 | 6.15 | 6.21 |
| 13 | 3.06 | 3.73 | 4.15 | 4.45 | 4.69 | 4.88 | 5.05 | 5.19 | 5.32 | 5.43 | 5.53 | 5.63 | 5.71 | 5.79 | 5.86 | 5.93 | 6.00 | 6.05 | 6.11 |
| 14 | 3.03 | 3.70 | 4.11 | 4.41 | 4.64 | 4.83 | 4.99 | 5.13 | 5.25 | 5.36 | 5.46 | 5.55 | 5.64 | 5.72 | 5.79 | 5.85 | 5.92 | 5.97 | 6.03 |
| 15 | 3.01 | 3.67 | 4.08 | 4.37 | 4.60 | 4.78 | 4.94 | 5.08 | 5.20 | 5.31 | 5.40 | 5.49 | 5.58 | 5.65 | 5.72 | 5.79 | 5.85 | 5.90 | 5.96 |
| 16 | 3.00 | 3.65 | 4.05 | 4.33 | 4.56 | 4.74 | 4.90 | 5.03 | 5.15 | 5.26 | 5.35 | 5.44 | 5.52 | 5.59 | 5.66 | 5.72 | 5.79 | 5.84 | 5.90 |
| 17 | 2.98 | 3.63 | 4.02 | 4.30 | 4.52 | 4.71 | 4.86 | 4.99 | 5.11 | 5.21 | 5.31 | 5.39 | 5.47 | 5.55 | 5.61 | 5.68 | 5.74 | 5.79 | 5.84 |
| 18 | 2.97 | 3.61 | 4.00 | 4.28 | 4.49 | 4.67 | 4.82 | 4.96 | 5.07 | 5.17 | 5.27 | 5.35 | 5.43 | 5.50 | 5.57 | 5.63 | 5.69 | 5.74 | 5.79 |
| 19 | 2.96 | 3.59 | 3.98 | 4.25 | 4.47 | 4.65 | 4.79 | 4.92 | 5.04 | 5.14 | 5.23 | 5.32 | 5.39 | 5.46 | 5.53 | 5.59 | 5.65 | 5.70 | 5.75 |
| 20 | 2.95 | 3.58 | 3.96 | 4.23 | 4.45 | 4.62 | 4.77 | 4.90 | 5.01 | 5.11 | 5.20 | 5.28 | 5.36 | 5.43 | 5.49 | 5.55 | 5.61 | 5.66 | 5.71 |
| 24 | 2.92 | 3.53 | 3.90 | 4.17 | 4.37 | 4.54 | 4.68 | 4.81 | 4.92 | 5.01 | 5.10 | 5.18 | 5.25 | 5.32 | 5.38 | 5.44 | 5.50 | 5.54 | 5.59 |
| 30 | 2.89 | 3.49 | 3.84 | 4.10 | 4.30 | 4.46 | 4.60 | 4.72 | 4.83 | 4.92 | 5.00 | 5.08 | 5.15 | 5.21 | 5.27 | 5.33 | 5.38 | 5.43 | 5.48 |
| 40 | 2.86 | 3.44 | 3.79 | 4.04 | 4.23 | 4.39 | 4.52 | 4.63 | 4.74 | 4.82 | 4.91 | 4.98 | 5.05 | 5.11 | 5.16 | 5.22 | 5.27 | 5.31 | 5.36 |
| 60 | 2.83 | 3.40 | 3.74 | 3.98 | 4.16 | 4.31 | 4.44 | 4.55 | 4.65 | 4.73 | 4.81 | 4.88 | 4.94 | 5.00 | 5.06 | 5.11 | 5.16 | 5.20 | 5.24 |
| 120 | 2.80 | 3.36 | 3.69 | 3.92 | 4.10 | 4.24 | 4.36 | 4.48 | 4.56 | 4.64 | 4.72 | 4.78 | 4.84 | 4.90 | 4.95 | 5.00 | 5.05 | 5.09 | 5.13 |
| $\infty$ | 2.77 | 3.31 | 3.63 | 3.86 | 4.03 | 4.17 | 4.29 | 4.39 | 4.47 | 4.55 | 4.62 | 4.68 | 4.74 | 4.80 | 4.85 | 4.89 | 4.93 | 4.97 | 5.01 |

# Table E.10  Critical Values^a of the Studentized Range Q (Continued)

Upper 1% points ($\alpha = .01$)

| $\nu$ \ $\eta$ | 2 | 3 | 4 | 5 | 6 | 7 | 8 | 9 | 10 | 11 | 12 | 13 | 14 | 15 | 16 | 17 | 18 | 19 | 20 |
|---|---|---|---|---|---|---|---|---|---|---|---|---|---|---|---|---|---|---|---|
| 1 | 90.0 | 135 | 164 | 186 | 202 | 216 | 227 | 237 | 246 | 253 | 260 | 266 | 272 | 277 | 282 | 286 | 290 | 294 | 298 |
| 2 | 14.0 | 19.0 | 22.3 | 24.7 | 26.6 | 28.2 | 29.5 | 30.7 | 31.7 | 32.6 | 33.4 | 34.1 | 34.8 | 35.4 | 36.0 | 36.5 | 37.0 | 37.5 | 37.9 |
| 3 | 8.26 | 10.6 | 12.2 | 13.3 | 14.2 | 15.0 | 15.6 | 16.2 | 16.7 | 17.1 | 17.5 | 17.9 | 18.2 | 18.5 | 18.8 | 19.1 | 19.3 | 19.5 | 19.8 |
| 4 | 6.51 | 8.12 | 9.17 | 9.96 | 10.6 | 11.1 | 11.5 | 11.9 | 12.3 | 12.6 | 12.8 | 13.1 | 13.3 | 13.5 | 13.7 | 13.9 | 14.1 | 14.2 | 14.4 |
| 5 | 5.70 | 6.97 | 7.80 | 8.42 | 8.91 | 9.32 | 9.67 | 9.97 | 10.24 | 10.48 | 10.70 | 10.89 | 11.08 | 11.24 | 11.40 | 11.55 | 11.68 | 11.81 | 11.93 |
| 6 | 5.24 | 6.33 | 7.03 | 7.56 | 7.97 | 8.32 | 8.61 | 8.87 | 9.10 | 9.30 | 9.49 | 9.65 | 9.81 | 9.95 | 10.08 | 10.21 | 10.32 | 10.43 | 10.54 |
| 7 | 4.95 | 5.92 | 6.54 | 7.01 | 7.37 | 7.68 | 7.94 | 8.17 | 8.37 | 8.55 | 8.71 | 8.86 | 9.00 | 9.12 | 9.24 | 9.35 | 9.46 | 9.55 | 9.65 |
| 8 | 4.74 | 5.63 | 6.20 | 6.63 | 6.96 | 7.24 | 7.47 | 7.68 | 7.87 | 8.03 | 8.18 | 8.31 | 8.44 | 8.55 | 8.66 | 8.76 | 8.85 | 8.94 | 9.03 |
| 9 | 4.60 | 5.43 | 5.96 | 6.35 | 6.66 | 6.91 | 7.13 | 7.32 | 7.49 | 7.65 | 7.78 | 7.91 | 8.03 | 8.13 | 8.23 | 8.32 | 8.41 | 8.49 | 8.57 |
| 10 | 4.48 | 5.27 | 5.77 | 6.14 | 6.43 | 6.67 | 6.87 | 7.05 | 7.21 | 7.36 | 7.48 | 7.60 | 7.71 | 7.81 | 7.91 | 7.99 | 8.07 | 8.15 | 8.22 |
| 11 | 4.39 | 5.14 | 5.62 | 5.97 | 6.25 | 6.48 | 6.67 | 6.84 | 6.99 | 7.13 | 7.25 | 7.36 | 7.46 | 7.56 | 7.65 | 7.73 | 7.81 | 7.88 | 7.95 |
| 12 | 4.32 | 5.04 | 5.50 | 5.84 | 6.10 | 6.32 | 6.51 | 6.67 | 6.81 | 6.94 | 7.06 | 7.17 | 7.26 | 7.36 | 7.44 | 7.52 | 7.59 | 7.66 | 7.73 |
| 13 | 4.26 | 4.96 | 5.40 | 5.73 | 5.98 | 6.19 | 6.37 | 6.53 | 6.67 | 6.79 | 6.90 | 7.01 | 7.10 | 7.19 | 7.27 | 7.34 | 7.42 | 7.48 | 7.55 |
| 14 | 4.21 | 4.89 | 5.32 | 5.63 | 5.88 | 6.08 | 6.26 | 6.41 | 6.54 | 6.66 | 6.77 | 6.87 | 6.96 | 7.05 | 7.12 | 7.20 | 7.27 | 7.33 | 7.39 |
| 15 | 4.17 | 4.83 | 5.25 | 5.56 | 5.80 | 5.99 | 6.16 | 6.31 | 6.44 | 6.55 | 6.66 | 6.76 | 6.84 | 6.93 | 7.00 | 7.07 | 7.14 | 7.20 | 7.26 |
| 16 | 4.13 | 4.78 | 5.19 | 5.49 | 5.72 | 5.92 | 6.08 | 6.22 | 6.35 | 6.46 | 6.56 | 6.66 | 6.74 | 6.82 | 6.90 | 6.97 | 7.03 | 7.09 | 7.15 |
| 17 | 4.10 | 4.74 | 5.14 | 5.43 | 5.66 | 5.85 | 6.01 | 6.15 | 6.27 | 6.38 | 6.48 | 6.57 | 6.66 | 6.73 | 6.80 | 6.87 | 6.94 | 7.00 | 7.05 |
| 18 | 4.07 | 4.70 | 5.09 | 5.38 | 5.60 | 5.79 | 5.94 | 6.08 | 6.20 | 6.31 | 6.41 | 6.50 | 6.58 | 6.65 | 6.72 | 6.79 | 6.85 | 6.91 | 6.96 |
| 19 | 4.05 | 4.67 | 5.05 | 5.33 | 5.55 | 5.73 | 5.89 | 6.02 | 6.14 | 6.25 | 6.34 | 6.43 | 6.51 | 6.58 | 6.65 | 6.72 | 6.78 | 6.84 | 6.89 |
| 20 | 4.02 | 4.64 | 5.02 | 5.29 | 5.51 | 5.69 | 5.84 | 5.97 | 6.09 | 6.19 | 6.29 | 6.37 | 6.45 | 6.52 | 6.59 | 6.65 | 6.71 | 6.76 | 6.82 |
| 24 | 3.96 | 4.54 | 4.91 | 5.17 | 5.37 | 5.54 | 5.69 | 5.81 | 5.92 | 6.02 | 6.11 | 6.19 | 6.26 | 6.33 | 6.39 | 6.45 | 6.51 | 6.56 | 6.61 |
| 30 | 3.89 | 4.45 | 4.80 | 5.05 | 5.24 | 5.40 | 5.54 | 5.65 | 5.76 | 5.85 | 5.93 | 6.01 | 6.08 | 6.14 | 6.20 | 6.26 | 6.31 | 6.36 | 6.41 |
| 40 | 3.82 | 4.37 | 4.70 | 4.93 | 5.11 | 5.27 | 5.39 | 5.50 | 5.60 | 5.69 | 5.77 | 5.84 | 5.90 | 5.96 | 6.02 | 6.07 | 6.12 | 6.17 | 6.21 |
| 60 | 3.76 | 4.28 | 4.60 | 4.82 | 4.99 | 5.13 | 5.25 | 5.36 | 5.45 | 5.53 | 5.60 | 5.67 | 5.73 | 5.79 | 5.84 | 5.89 | 5.93 | 5.98 | 6.02 |
| 120 | 3.70 | 4.20 | 4.50 | 4.71 | 4.87 | 5.01 | 5.12 | 5.21 | 5.30 | 5.38 | 5.44 | 5.51 | 5.56 | 5.61 | 5.66 | 5.71 | 5.75 | 5.79 | 5.83 |
| ∞ | 3.64 | 4.12 | 4.40 | 4.60 | 4.76 | 4.88 | 4.99 | 5.08 | 5.16 | 5.23 | 5.29 | 5.35 | 5.40 | 5.45 | 5.49 | 5.54 | 5.57 | 5.61 | 5.65 |

^aRange/S ~ $Q_{1-\alpha;\eta,\nu}$. $\eta$ is the size of the sample from which the range is obtained, and $\nu$ is the number of degrees of freedom of S.

Source: Reprinted from E. S. Pearson and H. O. Hartley, eds., Table 29 of Biometrika Tables for Statisticians, Vol. 1, 3d ed., 1966, by permission of the Biometrika Trustees, London.

## Table E.11  *Control Chart Factors*

Source: Reprinted from ASTM-STP 15D by kind permission of the American Society for Testing and Materials.

| NUMBER OF OBSERVATIONS IN SAMPLE | $d_2$ | $d_3$ | $D_3$ | $D_4$ | $A_2$ |
|---|---|---|---|---|---|
| 2 | 1.128 | 0.853 | 0 | 3.267 | 1.880 |
| 3 | 1.693 | 0.888 | 0 | 2.575 | 1.023 |
| 4 | 2.059 | 0.880 | 0 | 2.282 | 0.729 |
| 5 | 2.326 | 0.864 | 0 | 2.114 | 0.577 |
| 6 | 2.534 | 0.848 | 0 | 2.004 | 0.483 |
| 7 | 2.704 | 0.833 | 0.076 | 1.924 | 0.419 |
| 8 | 2.847 | 0.820 | 0.136 | 1.864 | 0.373 |
| 9 | 2.970 | 0.808 | 0.184 | 1.816 | 0.337 |
| 10 | 3.078 | 0.797 | 0.223 | 1.777 | 0.308 |
| 11 | 3.173 | 0.787 | 0.256 | 1.744 | 0.285 |
| 12 | 3.258 | 0.778 | 0.283 | 1.717 | 0.266 |
| 13 | 3.336 | 0.770 | 0.307 | 1.693 | 0.249 |
| 14 | 3.407 | 0.763 | 0.328 | 1.672 | 0.235 |
| 15 | 3.472 | 0.756 | 0.347 | 1.653 | 0.223 |
| 16 | 3.532 | 0.750 | 0.363 | 1.637 | 0.212 |
| 17 | 3.588 | 0.744 | 0.378 | 1.622 | 0.203 |
| 18 | 3.640 | 0.739 | 0.391 | 1.609 | 0.194 |
| 19 | 3.689 | 0.733 | 0.404 | 1.596 | 0.187 |
| 20 | 3.735 | 0.729 | 0.415 | 1.585 | 0.180 |
| 21 | 3.778 | 0.724 | 0.425 | 1.575 | 0.173 |
| 22 | 3.819 | 0.720 | 0.435 | 1.565 | 0.167 |
| 23 | 3.858 | 0.716 | 0.443 | 1.557 | 0.162 |
| 24 | 3.895 | 0.712 | 0.452 | 1.548 | 0.157 |
| 25 | 3.931 | 0.708 | 0.459 | 1.541 | 0.153 |

# Appendix F

## Documentation for CD-ROM Files

 **F.1** ◆ **CD-ROM OVERVIEW**

The CD-ROM that accompanies this text contains all of the data files (.TXT), Excel workbook files (.XLS), and Minitab worksheet files (.MTW or .MTP) used in the text. The data file icon (■) in the margin of the text names the appropriate file for a particular topic or end-of-section problem. In addition, the CD-ROM contains the *PHStat Add-In* for Excel.

 **F.2** ◆ **FILE CONTENTS**

The CD-ROM that accompanies this text contains three types of files. Files with the extension .TXT are text files (sometimes known as ASCII files) that contain raw data sets. Files with the extension .XLS are Microsoft Excel workbook files. Files with the extension .MTW or .MTP are Minitab worksheet files. Text files, Microsoft Excel workbook files, and Minitab worksheet files exist for every selected end-of-section text problem or particular topic for which a data file icon (■) is displayed.

Presented below is an alphabetical listing and description of the 232 raw data text files.

### Raw Data Text Files

| *Name* | *Description* |
| --- | --- |
| ACCESS | Coded access read times (in msec), file size (small = 1, medium = 2, large = 3), programmer group, and buffer size (20 kbytes = 1, 40 kbytes = 2). See Problem 13.79 on pages 622–624. |
| ACCRES | Processing time in seconds and type (Research = 0, Accounting = 1) of computer jobs. See Problem 12.82 on page 531. |
| ADR | Company, type of information (corporate review = 1, financial data = 2, graphical presentation = 3), and average ratings. See Problem 13.82 on page 629. |
| ADRADTV | Sales (in thousands of dollars), radio/TV ads (in thousands of dollars), and newspaper ads (in thousands of dollars) for 22 cities. See Problems 17.6 on page 823, 17.14 on page 830, 17.21 on page 832, 17.28 on page 837, 17.34 on page 845, and 18.22 on page 886. |
| ADVREV | Data showing year, coded year (1978 = 0), and annual revenues (in millions of dollars) over the 20-year period 1978–1997. See Problem 19.26 on page 950. |
| ALCOHOL | Alcohol consumption (in ounces), and number of errors from 15 typists. See Problem 18.3 on page 867. |

| | |
|---|---|
| ALUMINUM | Data showing coded month (January 1991 = 0), production amount (in thousands of metric tons), and 11 monthly dummy variables over the six-year period January 1991–December 1996. See Problem 19.76 on page 1000. |
| AMPHRS | Capacity (in ampere-hours) for 20 batteries. See Problems 11.63 on page 441 and 11.89 on page 454. |
| AMPLIFY | Coded db ratings for three recordings based on two receivers ($R_1 = 1$, $R_2 = 2$) and four amplifiers (A = 1, B = 2, C = 3, D = 4). The respective variables are receiver, amplifier, and coded decibel output. See Problem 13.38 on page 593. |
| ANSCOMBE | Data sets A, B, C, and D—each with 11 pairs of $X$ and $Y$ values. See Table 16.6 on page 779. |
| ATM1 | Cash withdrawals by 25 customers at a local bank. See Problem 8.17 on page 323. |
| ATM2 | Amount withdrawn, median assessed value of home, and location (not a shopping center = 0, shopping center = 1). See Problem 18.9 on page 877. |
| ATTACHE | Price of 29 business brief cases. See Problem 3.9 on page 58. |
| AUTO | Miles per gallon, horsepower, and weight for a sample of 50 car models. See Problems 17.5 on page 822, 17.13 on page 829, 17.20 on page 832, 17.27 on page 837, and 17.33 on page 845. |
| AUTO96 | Model, type of drive (rear = 0, front = 1), mileage per gallon, fuel type (premium = 0, regular = 1), fuel capacity in gallons, length in inches, wheelbase in inches, width in inches, turning circle in feet, weight in pounds, luggage capacity in cubic feet, front leg room in inches, and front head room in inches. See Problems 17.45 on page 849, 18.28 on page 898, and 18.46 on page 908. |
| AUTOBAT | Lengths of life (in months) for 28 automobile batteries. See Problem 11.106 on page 466. |
| AUTOREP | Day, average service time, and range in service time (over a 20-day period). See Problem 15.23 on page 715. |
| BACKPACK | Price of backpacks (in dollars), volume (in cubic inches), and number of 5 × 7¾-inch books that each of 30 backpack models can hold. See Problem 17.47 on page 851. |
| BAGGAGE | 30 days of baggage claims. See Problem 15.16 on page 707. |
| BALPAY | Year, coded year (1981 = 0), balance of payments, federal spending, and federal taxes per capita over the 15-year period 1981–1995. See Problem 19.10 on page 931. |
| BANK1 | Waiting time (in minutes) spent by a sample of 15 "lunch time" bank customers. See Problems 4.11 on page 156, 11.109 on page 467, and 12.84 on page 532. |
| BANK2 | Waiting time (in minutes) spent by a sample of 15 "evening" bank customers. See Problems 4.12 on page 157 and 12.84 on page 532. |
| BANKCD | Type (NY commercial = 1, NY savings = 2, outside NY = 3), and six-month CD rates. See Problem 13.77 on page 619. |

| | |
|---|---|
| BANKTIME | Waiting times of four bank customers per day for 20 days. See Problems 4.53 on page 183 and 15.21 on page 714. |
| BATFAIL | Times to failure (in hours) for groups of five batteries exposed to four pressure levels (low = 1, normal = 2, high = 3, very high = 4). See Problem 13.45 on page 603. |
| BB97 | League (American = 0, National = 1) wins, E.R.A., runs scored, hits allowed, walks allowed, saves, and errors for 28 teams. See Problems 16.79 on page 804, 17.46 on page 850, 18.10 on page 877, and 18.44 on page 906. |
| BBSALARY | Team, league (American = 0, National = 1), salary of pitcher (in millions of dollars), and salary of outfielder (in millions of dollars) for 28 teams. See Problem 12.87 on page 534. |
| BDECKER | Data showing year, coded year (1975 = 0), and revenues (in billions of dollars) at Black & Decker Corp. over the 22-year period 1975–1996. See Problems 19.22 on page 949, 19.34 on page 958, 19.42 on page 971, and 19.49 on page 981. |
| BEARING | Outer ring osculation (low = 0, high = 1), heat treatment (low = 0, high = 1), life of roller bearings. See Example 13.1 on page 587. |
| BEER | Brand, price in dollars, calories, percentage of alcoholic content, type (craft lager = 1, craft ale = 2, imported lager = 3, regular and ice beer = 4, light and no alcohol beer = 5) and country of origin (USA = 1, Imported = 0). See Case Study on page 186. |
| BKASSETS | Data showing coded month (January 1992 = 0), actual total monthly assets (in trillions of current dollars), and 11 monthly dummy variables over the six-year period January 1992–December 1997. See Problem 19.57 on page 991. |
| BKPRICE | Prices of 12 books, sold on campus and sold off campus. See Problem 12.39 on page 507. |
| BLACKJ | Profits (in dollars) from five sessions in each of four strategies (dealer's = 1, five count = 2, basic ten count = 3, advanced ten count = 4). See Problem 13.10 on page 558. |
| BOEING | Data showing year, coded year (1975 = 0), and total revenues (in billions of dollars) at Boeing Co. over the 22-year period 1975–1996. See Problems 19.19 on page 946, 19.31 on page 956, 19.39 on page 969, and 19.46 on page 979. |
| BREAKSTW | Data showing operators (A = 1, B = 2, C = 3, D = 4), three machines (I = 1, II = 2, III = 3) and breaking strength (in pounds). The respective variables are operator, machine, and breaking strength. See Problem 13.40 on page 595. |
| BROKER | Performance scores of three customer representatives based on gender (males = 1, females = 2) and four background (professionals = 1, business school graduates = 2, salesmen = 3, brokers = 4) combinations. The respective variables are gender, background, and performance score. See Problems 13.14 on page 560 and 13.51 on page 606. |

| | |
|---|---|
| BULBLIFE | Thirty days of data on the mean life, range, and subgroup number for subgroups of five bulbs. See Problem 15.20 on page 713. |
| BULBS | Length of life of 40 lightbulbs from Manufacturer A (= 1) and 40 lightbulbs from Manufacturer B (= 2). See Problem 3.24 on page 71. |
| CALLSDLY | Day and number of calls received over 30 consecutive workweek days. See Problem 3.79 on page 108. |
| CANDY | Aisle (front, rear), shelf location (top, bottom), and sales of candy bars. See Problem 13.39 on page 594. |
| CHIPS | Number of chocolate chips in 50 consecutive baked cupcakes. See Table 15.3 on page 703. |
| CLOTTING | Plasma clotting times (in minutes) for seven patients whose blood is studied under each of five different treatment substances. The respective variables are patient, treatment substance, and clotting time. See Problems 13.26 on page 574 and 13.57 on page 613. |
| COCACOLA | Data showing year, coded year (1975 = 0), and operating revenues (in billions of dollars) at Coca-Cola Co. over the 22-year period 1975–1996. See Problems 19.20 on page 947, 19.32 on page 956, 19.40 on page 970, and 19.47 on page 980. |
| COFFEE | Ratings by nine experts on each of four brands of coffee (A = 1, B = 2, C = 3, D = 4). The respective variables are expert, brand, and rating. See Problems 13.25 on page 573 and 13.56 on page 613. |
| COFMKR | Brand, price in dollars, actual number of cup fills attained, price to replace a carafe in dollars, and type (basic = 0, programmable = 1) for 19 coffeemakers. See Problem 4.49 on page 181. |
| COLASPC | Day, total number of cans filled, and number of unacceptable cans (over a 22-day period). See Problem 15.6 on page 698. |
| COMPFAIL | Failure time ranks for samples of eight stereo components under three different temperature levels (150 = 1, 200 = 2, 250 = 3). See Problem 13.46 on page 603. |
| COMPTIME | Completion times (in seconds) by 10 applications project users employing the current market leading product and a new software package. The respective variables are user, completion time with current market leader, and completion time with new software package. See Tables 12.5 on page 502 and 12.8 on page 523. |
| CPI-U | Data showing year, coded year (1965 = 0), and value of CPI-U, the Consumer Price Index, over the 33-year period 1965–1997 with 1982–1984 as the base. See Problem 19.14 on page 944. |
| CURRENCY | Data showing year, coded year (1967 = 0), and average annual exchange rates (against the U.S. dollar) for the Canadian dollar, French franc, German mark, Japanese yen, and English pound over the 31-year period 1967–1997. See Case Study on page 1001. |
| CUSTSALE | Week number, number of customers, and sales (in thousands of dollars) over a period of 15 consecutive weeks. See Table 16.3 on page 761. |

| DELIVERY | Delivery time (in days), number of options ordered, and shipping mileage (in hundreds of miles) for 16 cars. See Problem 16.73 on page 798. |
|---|---|
| DENTAL | Annual family dental expenses for 10 employees. See Problems 10.18 on page 379 and 10.60 on page 399. |
| DIET | Weight losses (in pounds) for six client groups under three dietary treatments. The respective variables are client group, dietary treatment, and amount of weight lost. See Problems 13.27 on page 574 and 13.58 on page 614. |
| DIFFTEST | Differences in the sales invoices and actual amounts from a sample of 50 vouchers. See Example 10.9 on page 397. |
| DISCOUNT | The amount of discount taken from 150 invoices. See Problem 10.62 on page 399. |
| DISPRAZ | Price and sales of disposable razors in 15 stores. See Table 18.1 on page 860. |
| DRINK | Amount of soft drink filled in a subgroup of 50 consecutive two-liter bottles. See Problems 3.28 on page 72 and 3.35 on page 78. |
| DRYCLEAN | Twenty-four days of items returned for rework. See Problem 15.13 on page 705. |
| EASTMANK | Year, coded year (1975 = 0), actual revenues (in billions of dollars), the CPI-U, and real revenues (in billions of constant 1982–1984 dollars) for Eastman Kodak Company. See Table 19.5 on page 933. |
| EER | Average energy efficiency ratings (EER) for 36 air-conditioning units. See Problem 11.60 on page 440. |
| ELECUSE | Electricity consumption (in kilowatts) and average temperature (in degrees Fahrenheit) over a consecutive 24-month period. See Problem 16.31 on page 765. |
| EMEADOW | Appraised value, lot size, number of bedrooms, number of bathrooms, number of rooms, age, taxes, location = 1, eat-in kitchen, central air-conditioning, fireplace, connection to local sewer system, basement, modern kitchen, and modern bathrooms for 74 homes in East Meadow. See Problem 18.47 on page 908. |
| EPOWERPR | Data showing year, coded year (1982 = 0), and electric power production (in billions of kilowatt hours) over the 15-year period 1982–1996. See Problem 19.17 on page 945. |
| ERRORSPC | Number of nonconforming items and number of accounts processed over 39 days. See Problem 15.7 on page 699. |
| EXERCISE | Ratings of nine medical experts on five diverse forms of exercise (1 = bicycling, 2 = calisthenics, 3 = jogging, 4 = swimming, 5 = tennis). The respective variables are characteristic, exercise, and rating. See Problem 13.54 on page 611. |
| FARMING | Appraised value, lot size, number of bedrooms, number of bathrooms, number of rooms, age, taxes, location = 2, eat-in kitchen, central air-conditioning, fireplace, connection to local sewer system, basement, modern kitchen, and modern bathrooms for 60 homes in Farmingdale. See Problem 18.48 on page 908. |

| | |
|---|---|
| FEDRECPT | Data showing year, coded year (1978 = 0), and federal receipts (in billions of current dollars) over the 20-year period 1978–1997. See Problem 19.18 on page 946. |
| FEDSPEND | Year, coded year (1981 = 0), and federal spending per capita for Alabama, Arizona, and Louisiana over the 15-year period 1981–1995. See Problem 19.45 on page 979. |
| FFCHAIN | Six raters of four restaurant branches (A = 1, B = 2, C = 3, D = 4) and ratings for a fast-food chain. See Tables 13.8 on page 567 and 13.14 on page 608. |
| FIFO | Historical cost (in dollars), and audited value (in dollars) for a sample of 120 inventory items. See Problem 10.63 on page 399. |
| FINTEST | Midterm and final exam test scores in Finance for 11 students. See Problem 12.68 on page 527. |
| FLASHBAT | Time to failure (in hours) for 13 flashlight batteries. See Problems 4.9 on page 155 and 4.20 on page 163. |
| FOODTIME | Data showing year, coded year (1972 = 0), and annual sales (in millions of dollars) over the 26-year period 1972–1997. See Problem 19.7 on page 929. |
| FOULSPC | Number of foul shots made and number taken over 40 days. See Problem 15.36 on page 719. |
| FUNDTRAN | Number of new investigations and number closed over a 30-day period. See Problem 15.37 on page 719. |
| FUNRAISE | Amounts pledged (in thousands of dollars) in a fund-raising campaign by nine alumni. See Problem 4.47 on page 179. |
| FURNCOMP | Days between receipt and resolution of a sample of 50 complaints regarding purchased furniture. See Problems 3.75 on page 104, 4.54 on page 184, and 11.110 on page 468. |
| GAPAC | Data showing year, coded year (1975 = 0), and revenues (in billions of dollars) at Georgia-Pacific Corp. over the 22-year period 1975–1996. See Problem 19.72 on page 996. |
| GAS1 | Amount of gasoline filled (in gallons) in 24 automobiles. See Problem 8.19 on page 324. |
| GASERVE | Length of time (in days) to establish gasoline heating service in 15 houses. See Problem 10.19 on page 379. |
| GASMILE | Miles per gallon on 10 cars, each obtained with regular gas and with high octane gas. See Problems 12.37 on page 506 and 12.69 on page 527. |
| GDP | Data showing year, coded year (1982 = 0), and real gross domestic product (in billions of constant 1992 dollars) over the 15-year period 1982–1996. See Problem 19.16 on page 945. |
| GILLETTE | Data showing year, coded year (1975 = 0), and revenues (in billions of dollars) at Gillette Company, Inc. over the 22-year period 1975–1996. See Problems 19.21 on page 948, 19.33 on page 957, 19.41 on page 971, and 19.48 on page 981. |

| GM | Data showing year, coded year (1975 = 0), and factory sales (in millions of vehicles sold) at General Motors Inc. over the 22-year period 1975–1996. See Table 19.2 on page 919. |
| --- | --- |
| GPIGMAT | GMAT scores and GPI for 20 students. See Problem 16.77 on page 802. |
| GROCERY | Grocery bills for 28 customers in a supermarket. See Problem 8.18 on page 323. |
| GROSSREV | Data showing year, coded year (1984 = 0), and real annual gross revenues (in millions of constant 1992 dollars) over the 14-year period 1984–1997. See Problem 19.25 on page 950. |
| HARNSWELL | Diameters of cam rollers (in inches) for samples of five parts produced in each of 30 batches. See Case Study on page 723. |
| HMO | Waiting times (in minutes) for 25 patients in an HMO. See Problem 10.20 on page 379. |
| HMOFRATE | Annual family premium rates for 36 HMOs. See Problem 3.11 on page 59. |
| HMORATE | Name, summated rating, HMO size (large = 1, medium = 2, small = 3), quality monitor rating, quality results rating, and quality score for a sample of 43 HMOs. See Problem 13.76 on page 618. |
| HOSPADM | Day, number of admissions, average processing time (in hours), range of processing times, and proportion of laboratory rework (over a 30-day period). See Problem 15.39 on page 721. |
| HOSPITAL | Occupancy rates (in percentages) at 16 urban hospitals (= 0) and 16 suburban hospitals (= 1). See Problems 12.16 on page 488, 12.31 on page 497, and 12.56 on page 519. |
| HOTEL1 | Day, number of rooms, and number of nonconforming rooms per day over a 28-day period. See Table 15.1 on page 693. |
| HOTEL2 | Day, average delivery time and range based on subgroups of five luggage deliveries per day over a 28-day period. See Table 15.4 on page 709. |
| HOUSE1 | Selling price (in thousands of dollars), assessed value (in thousands of dollars), type (new = 0, old = 1), and time period of sale for 30 houses. See Problems 16.75 on page 800, 17.42 on page 847, and 18.26 on page 897. |
| HOUSE2 | Assessed value (in thousands of dollars), heating area (in thousands of square feet), and age (in years) for 15 houses. See Problems 16.76 on page 801 and 17.43 on page 848. |
| HOUSE3 | Asssessed value (in thousands of dollars), heating area (in thousands of square feet), and presence of a fireplace (no = 0, yes = 1) for 15 homes. See Table 18.2 on page 869. |
| HTNGOIL | Monthly consumption of heating oil (in gallons), temperature (in degrees Fahrenheit), and attic insulation (in inches) from Table 17.1 on page 813. |

| | |
|---|---|
| ICECREAM | Daily temperature (in degrees Fahrenheit) and sales (in thousands of dollars) for 21 days. See Problem 16.33 on page 767. |
| INDPSYCH | Reaction time rankings of assembly-line workers for three groups of 9, 8, and 8 using different assembly methods. See Problem 13.44 on page 602. |
| INSPGM | Test scores of eight employees in each of four groups (A = 1, B = 2, C = 3, D = 4). See Problems 13.9 on page 557 and 13.48 on page 604. |
| INTPHONE | Country, average charge per minute (in dollars), and number of minutes used (in billions) in calls placed from the United States to 20 countries. See Problems 3.32 on page 76 and 16.56 on page 794. |
| INTRANK | Preference ranks for 10 MBA students (= 0) and 12 MPH students (= 1). See Problem 12.52 on page 517. |
| INVOICE | Number of invoices processed and amount of time (in hours) for 30 days. See Problem 16.78 on page 803. |
| INVOICES | Amount recorded (in dollars) from a sample of 12 sales invoices. See page 434. |
| ISLIP | Appraised value, lot size, number of bedrooms, number of bathrooms, number of rooms, age, taxes, location = 4, eat-in kitchen, central air-conditioning, fireplace, connection to local sewer system, basement, modern kitchen, and modern bathrooms for 84 homes in Islip. See Problem 18.50 on page 908. |
| ISLIPTER | Appraised value, lot size, number of bedrooms, number of bathrooms, number of rooms, age, taxes, location = 5, eat-in kitchen, central air-conditioning, fireplace, connection to local sewer system, basement, modern kitchen, and modern bathrooms for 45 homes in Islip Terrace. See Problem 18.51 on page 908. |
| ITEMERR | Amount of error (in dollars) from a sample of 200 items. See Problem 10.57 on page 398. |
| LAUNDRY | Dirt (in pounds) removed from two laundry loads based on four detergent brands (A = 1, B = 2, C = 3, D = 4) and four cycle times (18 minutes, 20 minutes, 22 minutes, 24 minutes). The respective variables are brand, cycle time, and pounds of dirt removed. See Problem 13.41 on page 596. |
| LAWN | Lawn service (no = 0, yes = 1), family income (in thousands of dollars), lawn size (in thousands of square feet), attitude toward activities (unfavorable = 0, favorable = 1), number of teenagers, and age of household head at 30 houses from Problem 18.35 on page 904. |
| LEVITT | Appraised value, lot size, number of bedrooms, number of bathrooms, number of rooms, age, taxes, location = 3, eat-in kitchen, central air-conditioning, fireplace, connection to local sewer system, basement, modern kitchen, and modern bathrooms for 99 homes in Levittown. See Problem 18.49 on page 908. |
| LIMO | Distance (in miles) and time (in minutes) for 12 trips. See Problems 16.8 on page 746, 16.19 on page 752, 16.27 on page 760, 16.41 on page 772, 16.49 on page 778, and 16.63 on page 796. |

| LINESPD | Bottle, fill deviation from specified target (in mm), and line speed in bottles per minute (210, 240, 270, 300). See Tables 13.2 on page 547 and 13.12 on page 599. |
|---|---|
| LINESPP2 | Bottle, percent carbonation (10 or 12), line speed (210, 240, 270, or 300 bpm) and deviation from specified target fill (in mm) for 40 bottles. See Table 13.11 on page 583. |
| LOCATE | Sales volume (in thousands of dollars) at two stores based on three aisle locations (front = 1, middle = 2, rear = 3) and three shelf heights (top = 1, middle = 2, bottom = 3). The respective variables are aisle location, height of shelf, and sales volume. See Problems 13.12 on page 559 and 13.49 on page 605. |
| LOGPURCH | Annual spending (in thousands of dollars), purchasing behavior (no = 0, yes = 1), and possession of additional credit cards (no = 0, yes = 1) for 30 people from Table 18.4 on page 900 and Problem 18.33 on page 902. |
| MAILORD | Monthly billing records of 20 unpaid accounts. See Problem 3.8 on page 58. |
| MAILSPC | Day, total number of packages, and late packages (over a 20-day period). See Problem 15.4 on page 697. |
| MARKYEN | Exchange rate of the German mark and the Japanese yen (in U.S. dollars) over the 10-year period 1988–1997. See Table 16.8 on page 792. |
| MBA | Success in program (no = 0, yes = 1), GPA, and GMAT score for 30 students from Problem 18.34 on page 903. |
| MBASAL | Student, salary package offer (in thousands of dollars), major (accountancy = 1, finance = 2, management = 3, marketing = 4), GPA ranking, and gender (male = 1, female = 2) for 24 graduating MBA candidates. See Problem 13.80 on pages 625 and 626. |
| MCDONALD | Data showing year, coded year (1975 = 0), and annual total revenues (in billions of dollars) at McDonald's Corp. over the 22-year period 1975–1996. See Problem 19.74 on page 998. |
| MEDFAMIN | Data showing year, coded year (1980 = 0), median family income for all races, median family income for Whites, and median family income for Blacks over the 16-year period 1980–1995. See Problem 19.8 on page 930. |
| MEDICARE | Difference in amount reimbursed and amount that should have been reimbursed for office visits. See Problem 10.80 on page 405. |
| MEDREC | Number of discharged patients and number of records not processed for a 30-day period. See Problem 15.5 on page 698. |
| MINWAGE | Data showing year, coded year (1965 = 0), and the minimum wage rate (in current dollars) over the 33-year period 1965–1997. See Problem 19.15 on page 944. |
| MONEYMKT | Annual yields on money market funds from 15 commercial banks. See Problem 4.21 on page 164. |
| MOVIE | Box office gross (in millions of dollars) and number of home video units sold (in thousands) for a sample of 30 movies. See Problems |

16.6 on page 745, 16.17 on page 752, 16.25 on page 760, 16.39 on page 772, 16.47 on page 777, and 16.61 on page 796.

| | |
|---|---|
| MOVING | Labor hours, number of rooms, and cubic feet of packaged items transported in a sample of 36 clients moved by a particular company. See Case Study on East-West Side Movers on page 853. |
| MUTFUNDS | Data showing coded month (January 1990 = 0), actual total monthly sales (in billions of current dollars), and 11 monthly dummy variables over the eight-year period January 1990–December 1997. See Problem 19.58 on page 992. |
| MUTUAL | Name of fund, type of fund (large growth = 1, medium growth = 2, small growth = 3, large blend = 4, medium blend = 5, small blend = 6), net asset value (in dollars), total year-to-date return (in percent), fee schedule (b—from fund assets = 1, d—deferred fees = 2, f—front-load fees = 3, m—multiple fees = 4, n—no load = 5), fee structure group (no load = 1, fee = 2), fund objective (growth = 1, blend = 2), and size (large = 1, midcap = 2, small = 3) for 194 highly rated domestic general stock funds. See TP3.1 on page 116, TP4.1 on page 185, TP8.1 on page 330, TP10.1 on page 406, TP12.1 on page 534, TP13.1 on page 631, and TP14.1 on page 676. |
| NAR | Median prices (in thousands of dollars) in the third quarter of 1997 and the third quarter of 1996 of previously owned single-family homes from a sample of 15 metropolitan areas. See Problem 12.40 on page 508. |
| NEIGHBOR | Selling price (in thousands of dollars), number of rooms, and neighborhood location (East = 0, West = 1) for 20 houses. See Problem 18.11 on page 878. |
| NEWSCIRC | Sunday and Daily circulation (in thousands) for 32 newspapers. See Case Study on page 805. |
| NICKBAT | Talking times (in minutes) prior to recharging for 25 cadmium batteries (= 0) and 25 metal hydride batteries (= 1). See Problems 12.13 on page 487, 12.30 on page 497, 12.55 on page 518, and 13.16 on page 562. |
| NYSEAX | Stock prices and exchange for 25 AMEX (= 1) and 50 NYSE (= 2) companies. See Problem 3.76 on page 105. |
| OILSUPP | Data showing year, coded year (1978 = 0), and number of employees (in thousands) over the 20-year period 1978–1997. See Problem 19.6 on page 928. |
| OILUSE | Data on annual amount of heating oil consumed (in gallons) in a sample of 35 single-family houses. See Example 10.3 on page 376. |
| OUTLAYS | Data on coded months (January 1988 = 0) and real monthly outlays (in thousands of constant 1995 dollars) over the 120-month period January 1988–December 1997. See Problem 19.56 on page 990. |
| PACKAGE | Number of customers and weekly sales (in thousands of dollars) at 20 stores. See Problems 16.4 on page 743, 16.15 on page 751, 16.23 on page 760, 16.37 on page 771, 16.45 on page 777, and 16.59 on page 795. |

| PEN | Product ratings of three ballpoint pens under gender (males = 1, females = 2) and five advertisement (A = 1, B = 2, C = 3, D = 4, E = 5) combinations. The respective variables are gender, ad, and product rating. See Case Study on page 633. |
|---|---|
| PENEAD | Product ratings of ballpoint pens by six adults (= 0) and eight high school students (= 1). See Case Study on page 634. |
| PERFORM | ID number, performance ratings before and after motivational training, and difference scores for a sample of 35 employees. See Problem 12.41 on page 508. |
| PETFOOD | Data on shelf space (in feet), weekly sales (in hundreds of dollars), and aisle location (back = 0, front = 1). See Problems 16.3 on page 743, 16.14 on page 751, 16.22 on page 759, 16.30 on page 765, 16.36 on page 771, 16.44 on page 777, 16.58 on page 795, and 18.8 on page 876. |
| PHLEVEL | Day, average pH level, and range in pH level (over 21 days). See Problem 15.25 on page 716. |
| PHONE | Time (in minutes) to clear telephone line problems and location (I and II) for samples of 20 customer problems reported to the two office locations. See Problems 4.51 on page 182, 8.20 on page 324, and 12.85 on page 532. |
| PHONRATE | Monthly long-distance phone rate for a sample of 34 plans. See Problem 4.48 on page 180. |
| PIZZA | Product, pie weight, cost per slice, amount of calories per slice, amount of fat (in grams) per slice, and type of product (pizza-chain cheese = 1, supermarket cheese = 2, supermarket pepperoni = 3) for 40 pizza products. See Problem 3.77 on page 106. |
| PLASTIC | Hardness measurements (in Brinell units) for 50 plastic blocks. See Problem 11.61 on page 440. |
| PLUMBINV | Differences (in dollars) between actual amounts recorded on sales invoices and the amounts entered into the accounting system for a sample of 100 invoices. See page 397. |
| PMORRIS | Data showing year, coded year (1975 = 0), and operating revenues (in billions of dollars) at Philip Morris Companies, Inc. over the 22-year period 1975–1996. See Problem 19.73 on page 997. |
| POLIO | Year and annual incidence rates per 100,000 persons of reported poliomyelitis. See Problem 19.71 on page 996. |
| PORTCD | Brand, price in dollars, overall performance score, battery life, and cost per hour of usage for a sample of 22 portable CDs. See Problem 4.50 on page 182. |
| POTATO | Percent solids content in filter cake, acidity (in pH), lower pressure, upper pressure, cake thickness, varidrive speed, and drum speed setting for 54 measurement from Case Study on page 909. |
| POTCHIP | Formulation method (A = 1, B = 2, C = 3, D = 4) and shelf life (in days) for six batches of tortilla chip product. See Problem 13.11 on page 558. |

| | |
|---|---|
| PRESSURE | Bottle, pressure setting (in psi), and deviation from specified target (in mm) for a sample of 20 bottles. See Using Statistics on page 472 and Table 12.1 on page 475. |
| PRINTER | Brand, price in dollars, and text speed in pages per minute of 19 computer printers. See Problems 3.33 on page 77 and 16.57 on page 795. |
| PRIRECON | Data on coded months (January 1992 = 0), real monthly private residential construction expenditures (in millions of constant 1995 dollars), and 11 monthly dummy variables over the 72-month period January 1992–December 1997. See Table 19.11 on page 983. |
| PROTEIN | Calories (in grams), protein, percent calories from fat, percent calories from saturated fat, and cholesterol (in mgs) for 25 popular protein foods. See Problem 3.80 on page 109. |
| PTFALLS | Month and number of patient falls. See Problem 15.15 on page 706. |
| RAISINS | Weights (in ounces) of 30 consecutively filled packages of raisins. See Problems 11.62 on page 441 and 11.88 on page 454. |
| RATING | Student ratings of ten faculty based on three classes they taught (MBA course = 1, advanced undergraduate course = 2, required undergraduate course = 3). The respective variables are faculty member, course, and rating. See Problems 13.28 on page 575 and 13.59 on page 615. |
| REALGNP | Data on coded quarters (first quarter 1990 = 0), quarterly gross national product (in billions of "chained 1992 dollars"), and three quarterly dummy variables over the 32-quarter period 1990–1997. See Problem 19.55 on page 990. |
| REAPPR | Appraised values (in thousands of dollars) on 12 houses, each appraised by two real estate agents. The respective variables are house and appraised value by each of the two agents. See Problem 12.35 on page 505. |
| REAPPR3 | Appraised values (in thousands of dollars) on 12 houses, each appraised by three real estate agents. The respective variables are house and appraised value by each of three agents. See Problem 13.29 on page 576. |
| RECALL | Recall ability scores for eight sets of triplets examined under three stimuli (minimum = 1, moderate = 2, high = 3). The respective variables are set of triplets, exposure level, and recall ability score. See Problem 13.55 on page 612. |
| REFRIG | Brand, price (in dollars), and energy cost per year (in dollars) for nine large side-by-side refrigerators. See Problems 3.31 on page 75 and 16.55 on page 794. |
| RENT | Monthly rental cost (in dollars) and apartment size (in square footage) for a sample of 25 apartments. See Problems 16.7 on page 745, 16.18 on page 752, 16.26 on page 760, 16.40 on page 772, 16.48 on page 778, and 16.62 on page 796. |
| REPAIR | Repair times (in minutes) of two VCRs based on three service centers (1, 2, 3) and three VCR brands (A = 1, B = 2, C = 3). The |

|  | respective variables are center, brand, and repair time. See Problem 13.37 on page 593. |
| RRSPC | Number of late arrivals and total arrivals over 20 days. See Problem 15.3 on page 696. |
| S&PSTKIN | Data on coded quarters (first quarter 1994 = 0), end-of-quarter values of the Quarterly Standard & Poors Composite Stock Price Index, and three quarterly dummy variables over the 16-quarter period 1994–1997. See Problem 19.54 on page 989. |
| SALAD | Week and number of cases of salad dressing purchased by a supermarket chain over a 30-week period. See Problems 3.27 on page 72 and 3.34 on page 77. |
| SALESCMP | Store sales (in thousands of dollars) at 13 matched pairs of stores, one with a sales campaign and one without a sales campaign. See Problems 12.38 on page 507 and 12.70 on page 528. |
| SALESVOL | Sales volume (in thousands of dollars) for 12 salespersons paid on an hourly rate (= 0) and 12 paid on a commission basis (= 1). See Problems 12.12 on page 486, 12.29 on page 497, and 12.54 on page 518. |
| SEARS | Data showing year, coded year (1975 = 0), and annual total revenues (in billions of dollars) at Sears, Roebuck & Co. over the 22-year period 1975–1996. See Problem 19.75 on page 999. |
| SH3&4 | Number of data cartridges accessed per job in a sample of 111 jobs. See Table SH3.4 on page 119 and see *Springfield Herald* Case on page 187. |
| SH10 | Amount (in dollars) customers would be willing to pay for home delivery from a sample of 46 potential customers. See *Springfield Herald* Case on page 408. |
| SH12 | Length of early calls (in seconds), length of late calls (in seconds), and difference (in seconds). See Table SH12.1 on page 536. |
| SH13–1 | Call, presentation plan (structured = 1, semistructured = 2, unstructured = 3), and length of call (in seconds). See Table SH13.1 on page 635. |
| SH13–2 | Gender of caller (male = 1, female = 2), type of greeting (personal but formal = 1, personal but informal = 2, impersonal = 3), and length of call (in seconds). See Table SH13.2 on page 637. |
| SH15–1&2 | Day, number of ads with errors, number of ads, and number of errors over a 25-day period. See Table SH15.1 on page 726. |
| SH15–3 | Week and number of data cartridges sent for remote storage over 24 consecutive weeks. See Table SH15.2 on page 727. |
| SH15–4 | Pay and newsprint blackness measure for each of five spots made over 25 consecutive weekdays. See Table SH15.3 on page 728. |
| SH16 | Hours per month spent telemarketing and number of new subscriptions per month over a 24-month period. See table on page 806. |
| SH19 | Month and number of home-delivery subscriptions over the most recent 24-month period. See Table SH19.1 on page 1003. |

| SHOESOLE | Sole wear "scores" for 10 pairs of shoes, one using new material and one using old material. The variables are pair number, material (new = 1, old = 2), and score in columns 4, 5, and 6, respectively. See Problems 12.36 on page 506 and 13.30 on page 577. |
|---|---|
| SITE | Store number, square footage, and sales (in thousands of dollars) in 14 stores. See Table 16.1 on page 737. |
| SL&L | Exchange (NYSE = 1, ASE = 2, NASDAQ = 3), direction (lag = 1, lead = 2), percent change, revised percent change, absolute percent change, absolute revised percent change, stock prices (in dollars) for the third and fourth quarters, price change (in dollars), absolute price change, log of the absolute price change, and the log of the absolute revised percent change for a sample of 60 companies. See Problem 13.81 on pages 627 and 628. |
| SLEEPHRS | Sleep medication amount of sleep (in hours) for four groups of 7, 8, 6, and 7 subjects taking different sleep medications. See Problem 13.47 on page 604. |
| SPEED | Miles per gallon and speed (in miles per hour) on 28 automobile test trials. See Problems 18.2 on page 866, 18.15 on page 883, and 18.16 on page 884. |
| SPONGE | Day, number of sponges produced, and number of sponges nonconforming over a 32-day period. See Example 15.1 on page 694. |
| STANDBY | Standby hours, staff, remote hours, Dubner hours, and labor hours for 26 weeks. See Problems 17.7 on page 823, 17.15 on page 830, 17.22 on page 833, 17.29 on page 837, 17.35 on page 845, 18.23 on page 886, and Table 18.3 on page 887. |
| STATEINC | State, bottom fifth income (in thousands of dollars), and top fifth income (in thousands of dollars) for all 50 states and the District of Columbia. See Problems 3.78 on page 107 and 4.29 on page 171. |
| STOCK | Book values of 50 stocks. See Problems 3.10 on page 59 and 3.26 on page 72. |
| STOREDOL | Date and amount of "store dollars" distributed during April. See Problem 3.36 on page 78. |
| STUDIO | Monthly rents based on location—10 studio apartments in inner city (= 0) and 10 studio apartments in outer city (= 1). See Problems 4.10 on page 156 and 4.22 on page 164. |
| TAX | Quarterly sales tax receipts (in thousands of dollars) for all 50 business establishments. See Problem 4.27 on page 169. |
| TAXES | County taxes (in dollars) and age of house (in years) for 19 single-family homes. See Problem 18.5 on page 868. |
| TAXI | Daily mileage recorded from a sample of 16 taxis. See Problem 11.64 on page 441. |
| TAXRET | Taxpayer and amount of money owed by 11 taxpayers, as computed by a tax preparation company and by the individual. See Problem 12.67 on page 527. |
| TELESPC | Number of orders and number of corrections over 30 days. See Problem 15.8 on page 699. |

| TELLER | Errors by 12 bank tellers. See Problem 15.14 on page 706. |
|---|---|
| TESTRANK | Rank scores for 10 students taught by a "traditional" method (T = 0) and 10 students taught by an "experimental" method (E = 1). See Problem 12.51 on page 517. |
| TOMYLD2 | Amount of fertilizer (in pounds per 100 square feet) and yield (in pounds) for 12 plots of land. See Problems 18.4 on page 867, 18.17 on page 884, and 18.18 on page 884. |
| TRADE | Day, number of undesirable trades, and number of total trades made over a 30-day period. See Problem 15.38 on page 720. |
| TRADES | Number of incoming calls and number of trade executions per day over a 35-day period. See Problem 16.74 on page 799. |
| TRAINING | Assembly time and training program (team-based = 0, individual-based = 1). See Problems 12.17 on page 488, 12.32 on page 498, and 12.57 on page 519. |
| TRAIN1 | Time (in minutes) early or late with respect to scheduled arrival for 10 trains. See Problems 4.13 on page 157 and 4.23 on page 164. |
| TRAIN2 | Time (in minutes) early or late with respect to scheduled arrival for 10 LIRR trains (= 0) and 12 NJT trains (= 1). See Problem 12.53 on page 517. |
| TRAIN3G | Methods (A = 1, B = 2, C = 3) and assembly time (in minutes) for three groups of workers. The group sizes were 9, 9, and 8, respectively. See Problem 13.15 on page 561. |
| TRANSPORT | Days and patient transport times (in minutes) for samples of four patients per day over a 30-day period. See Problem 15.24 on page 716. |
| TSMODEL1 | Data on years, coded years (1988 = 0), and three time-series (I, II, III) over the 10-year period 1988–1997. See Problem 19.23 on page 949. |
| TSMODEL2 | Data on years, coded years (1988 = 0), and two time-series (I, II) over the 10-year period 1988–1997. See Problem 19.24 on page 950. |
| TURNOVER | Day and number of turnovers. See Problem 15.17 on page 707. |
| UNEMPLOY | Data on years, coded years (1985 = 0), and annual unemployment as a percentage of the civilian working population in seven European countries (Belgium, Denmark, France, Italy, Netherlands, Portugal, and United Kingdom) from 1985–1997. See Problem 19.9 on page 930. |
| UNIV&COL | School, type of term (semester = 1, other = 0), location (urban = 1, suburban = 2, rural = 3), type of school (public = 0, private = 1), average total SAT score, TOEFL score (less than 550 = 0, at least 550 = 1), room and board expenses (in thousands of dollars), annual total cost (in thousands of dollars), average indebtedness at graduation (in thousands of dollars), and indebtedness to annual total cost ratio (in percent). See Problems 17.44 on page 849, 18.12 on page 879, 18.27 on page 898, and 18.45 on page 908. |
| UNLDREG | Data on coded months (January 1990 = 0), average monthly retail prices (in dollars per gallon), and 11 monthly dummy variables over |

| | the 96-month period January 1990–December 1997. See Problem 19.59 on page 992. |
|---|---|
| UTILITY | Utility charges for 50 three-bedroom apartments. See Problem 3.23 on page 70. |
| VB | Time (in minutes) for nine students to write and run a visual basic program. See Problem 12.83 on page 531. |
| VCR | Retail price (in dollars) for 22 VCR models. See Problem 3.12 on page 59. |
| VOUCHER | Population of 50 sales voucher amounts (in dollars). See Table 4.2 on page 165. |
| WARECOST | Distribution cost (in thousands of dollars), sales (in thousands of dollars), and number of orders for 24 months. See Problems 16.32 on page 766, 17.4 on page 821, 17.12 on page 829, 17.19 on page 832, 17.26 on page 837, 17.32 on page 844, and 18.21 on page 886. |
| WAREHSE | Number of units handled per day, day, and employee number. See Problem 15.22 on page 715. |
| WATER | Annual water consumption (in thousands of gallons) for 15 families. See Problems 4.14 on page 158 and 4.24 on page 164. |
| WINE | Summated ratings by 12 experts of eight wines. The respective variables are expert, wine, and rating. See Problem 13.83 on page 630. |
| WIP | Processing times for samples of 20 books at each of two plants (A = 1, B = 2). See Problems 4.52 on page 183, 8.21 on page 324, and 12.86 on page 533. |
| WORKATT | Attitude scale scores for three trainees based on gender (males = 1, females = 2) and three room color (green = 1, blue = 2, red = 3) combinations. The variables are gender, room color, and attitude scale score. See Problems 13.13 on page 559 and 13.50 on page 605. |
| WORKHRS | Lot sizes and worker hours for 14 production runs. See Problems 16.5 on page 744, 16.16 on page 751, 16.24 on page 760, 16.38 on page 772, 16.46 on page 777, and 16.60 on page 796. |
| WORKWEEK | Data on coded months (January 1992 = 0), monthly average workweek (in hours), and 11 monthly dummy variables over the 72-month period January 1992–December 1997. See Problem 19.77 on page 1000. |
| YARN | Breaking strength score, pressure (30, 40, or 50 psi), yarn sample, and side-to-side aspect (nozzle = 1, opposite = 2). See Problem 13.78 on pages 620–621. |

 **F.3** INSTALLATION INSTRUCTIONS FOR THE PHStat ADD-IN FOR MICROSOFT EXCEL AND THE DATA FILES ON THE CD-ROM

To make full use of Microsoft Excel with this text, you need to install the Analysis Tool-Pak and Analysis ToolPak–VBA add-ins that are supplied with Microsoft Excel and use the Prentice Hall PHStat add-in supplied on this CD-ROM. You must install the two Analysis

ToolPak add-ins first in order to use PHStat, as PHStat will refuse to run if it detects that the ToolPak add-ins are not installed.

## Installing the Analysis ToolPak Add-Ins

To install the two Microsoft Excel Analysis add-ins, do the following:

1. Run Microsoft Excel.
2. Select Tools | Add-Ins.
3. In the Add-Ins dialog box:
    a. Select the Analysis ToolPak *and* Analysis ToolPak–VBA check boxes in the Add-Ins available: list box.
    b. Select any other checkboxes in the Add-Ins available: list box as desired.
    c. Click the OK Button.

If Analysis ToolPak and Analysis ToolPak–VBA do not appear as choices in the Add-Ins available: list box, they were not selected when Microsoft Excel was originally setup. (If you selected the "Typical" choice during the Microsoft Excel or Microsoft Office setup program, these add-ins were **not** selected.) Rerun the Microsoft Excel (or Office) setup program to reinstall Microsoft Excel, choose the Custom choice, and select the add-ins. Then follow the instructions above to install the Analysis ToolPak add-ins.

## The Prentice Hall PHStat Add-In

The Prentice Hall PHStat Microsoft Excel add-in enhances Microsoft Excel to better support the statistical analyses taught in an introductory statistics course. Using PHStat lessens the technical training needed to use Microsoft Excel to perform analysis and allows you to generate results that would otherwise be very tedious or impossible to produce from worksheets built from scratch. PHStat requires the following:

- Any Windows 95 (or later) system.
- Microsoft Excel 95 (also known as version 7) or Microsoft Excel 97 (also known as version 8) with all service packs updates applied. (See the Microsoft web site to download service packs.)
- 32 MB of main memory; 64 MB required when running sampling distribution simulations and data-intensive regression analyses (see Notes for PHStat Version 1.0 below).
- Approximately 5 MB free hard disk space during setup process and 3 MB hard disk space after installation.

PHStat will run with any display settings, but for best results set the Desktop area to 800 by 600 pixels with Small Fonts. (Use the Settings tab of the Display applet of the Control Panel to change settings.)

PHStat should be installed to individual computer systems. It is not designed to run as a shared copy in a network setting. Microsoft Excel with PHStat is best used as a tool for learning statistics and not as an all-purpose substitute for using a standard statistical package in all situations. Very large data sets or data sets with unusual statistical properties can cause Excel with PHStat to produce invalid results.

◆ *Installing the Prentice Hall PHStat Add-In*   To use the Prentice Hall PHStat Microsoft Excel add-in, you first need to run the setup program (Setup.exe) located in the PHStat directory on this CD-ROM. The setup program will install the PHStat program files to your system and add icons on your Desktop and Start Menu for PHStat. Depending on the age of your Windows 95 system files, some Windows system files may be updated during the setup process as well. During the Setup program you will have the opportunity to specify:

   **a.** The directory into which to copy the PHStat files (default is \Program Files\Prentice Hall\PHStat).

   **b.** The name of the Start Programs folder to contain the PHStat icon.

Setup also adds an entry to the Install/Uninstall list of the Control Panel Add/Remove Programs applet. You should use this entry to uninstall PHStat if later you decide to remove the PHStat files.

◆ ***Using the Prentice Hall PHStat Add-In***   To begin using the Prentice Hall PHStat Microsoft Excel add-in, click the appropriate Start Menu or Desktop icon for PHStat that was added to your system during the setup process. Select the PHStat for Excel 95 if your system has Excel 95 installed or select PHStat for Excel 97 if your system has Excel 97 installed. In either case, Microsoft Excel—if it is available on your system—automatically loads.

Once PHStat is installed, you can set up Microsoft Excel to automatically load PHStat as an alternative to the previous. To have Microsoft Excel automatically load PHStat, do the following:

   **1.** Run Microsoft Excel.

   **2.** Select Tools | Add-Ins.

   **3.** In the Add-Ins dialog box:

   **a.** Verify that the Analysis ToolPak **and** Analysis ToolPak -VBA check boxes in the Add-Ins available: list box have been selected.

   **b.** Click the Browse button and locate and open the PHStat add-in file (PHStat.xla) in the directory into which the file was copied during setup.

   **c.** Click the OK Button.

Until this procedure is reversed, Microsoft Excel will automatically load PHStat every time Microsoft Excel opens.

◆ ***Macro Virus Warning Dialog Box***   Depending on your system configuration and method for using PHStat, opening the PHStat add-in may trigger the Microsoft macro virus dialog box that contains a warning about the possibility of viruses. Should this dialog box appear, click the Enable Macros button to allow this (virus-free) add-in to be loaded.

◆ ***Notes for PHStat Version 1.0***

**Tips:**

   • If you encounter problems when first attempting to use PHStat, make sure the Analysis ToolPak and Analysis ToolPak–VBA add-ins are installed and that all updates have been applied to Microsoft Excel.

- Generally, PHStat expects values for a variable to be placed in a single column, although it is capable of processing row-wise values as well. If you get unexpected results with your row-wise data, rearrange your data into columns.

Check the Prentice Hall web site **www.prenhall.com/berenson** for the latest information about and updates to the PHStat add-in.

**Known issues:**

- PHStat will not run properly on a system in which two versions of Microsoft Excel have been installed, such as Excel 95 and Excel 97. To use PHStat on such systems, first remove one of the Excel versions and then reinstall the other (very important).
- For procedures that require sorted data, such as Stem-and-Leaf Display, PHStat sorts the input data in place without regard to other data on the same worksheet. If you would like to preserve the order and arrangement of your data, copy the data to a new worksheet before selecting the PHStat procedure.
- In most implementations of Microsoft Excel, the Probability Distributions | Sampling Distributions Simulation choice of PHStat requires 64 MB of main memory. Attempting to use this function with less memory will cause Microsoft Excel to end with a fatal error (most likely to occur with Excel 95).
- Using any of the Regression choices with very large data sets is not recommended and may lead to a fatal error, especially on systems with less than 64 MB of main memory.

Depending on the configuration of your machine, you may have to restart Windows in cases of unexpected or fatal errors.

*Note: Microsoft and Windows are registered trademarks of the Microsoft Corporation.*

# Index

# LICENSE AGREEMENT AND LIMITED WARRANTY

READ THE FOLLOWING TERMS AND CONDITIONS CAREFULLY BEFORE OPENING THIS CD-ROM PACKAGE. THIS LEGAL DOCUMENT IS AN AGREEMENT BETWEEN YOU AND PRENTICE-HALL, INC. (THE COMPANY). BY OPENING THIS SEALED DISK PACKAGE, YOU ARE AGREEING TO THE TERMS AND CONDITIONS OF THIS AGREEMENT. IF YOU DO NOT AGREE WITH THESE TERMS AND CONDITIONS, DO NOT OPEN THE DISK PACKAGE. PROMPTLY RETURN THE UNOPENED DISK PACKAGE AND ALL ACCOMPANYING ITEMS TO THE PLACE YOU OBTAINED THEM. [[FOR A FULL REFUND OF ANY SUMS YOU HAVE PAID.]]

**GRANT OF LICENSE:**
In consideration of your payment of the license fee, which is part of the price you paid for this product, and your agreement to abide by the terms and conditions of this Agreement, the Company grants you to a nonexclusive right to use and display the copy of PHStat and the data files on the enclosed CD (hereinafter the SOFTWARE). The Company reserves all rights not expressly granted to you under this Agreement.

**OWNERSHIP OF SOFTWARE:**
You own only the magnetic or physical media (the enclosed disks) on which the SOFTWARE is recorded or fixed, but the Company retains all the rights, title, and ownership to the SOFTWARE recorded on the original disk copy(ies) and all subsequent copies of the SOFTWARE, regardless of the form or media on which the original or other copies may exist. This license is not a sale of the original software, or any copy to you.

**RESTRICTIONS ON USE AND TRANSFER:**
This SOFTWARE (PHStat and data files) are the subject of copyright and is licensed to you only. You may not sell or license copies of the SOFT-WARE or the documentation to others and you may not transfer or distribute it, except to instructors and students in your school who are users of the Company textbook that accompanies this SOFTWARE. You have the right to place this SOFTWARE on the university network as long as you are a user of the company textbook that accompanies this SOFTWARE. You may not reverse engineer, disassemble, decompile, modify, adapt, translate or create derivative works based on the SOFTWARE or the Documentation without the prior written consent of the Company. You may be held legally responsible for any copying or copyright infringement which is caused or encouraged by your failure to abide by the terms of these restrictions.

**TERMINATION:**
This license is effective until terminated. This license will terminate automatically without notice from the Company and become null and void if you fail to comply with any provisions or limitations of this license. Upon termination, you shall destroy the Documentation and all copies of the SOFTWARE. All provisions of this Agreement as to warranties, limitation of liability, remedies or damages, and our ownership rights shall survive termination.

**MISCELLANEOUS:**
THIS AGREEMENT SHALL BE CONSTRUED IN ACCORDANCE WITH THE LAWS OF THE UNITED STATES OF AMERICA AND THE STATE OF NEW YORK, APPLICABLE TO CONTRACTS MADE IN NEW YORK, AND SHALL BENEFIT THE COMPANY, ITS AFFILIATES AND ASSIGNEES.

**LIMITED WARRANTY AND DISCLAIMER OF WARRANTY:**
The Company warrants that the SOFTWARE, when properly used in accordance with the Documentation, will operate in substantial conformity with the description of the SOFTWARE set forth in the Documentation. The Company does not warrant that the SOFTWARE will meet your requirements or that the operation of the SOFTWARE will be uninterrupted or error-free. The Company warrants that the media on which the SOFTWARE is delivered shall be free from defects in materials and workmanship under normal use for a period of thirty (30) days from the date of your purchase. Your only remedy and the Company's only obligation under these limited warranties is, [[at the company's option,]] return of the warranted item for [[a refund of any amounts paid by you or]] replacement of the item. Any replacement of SOFTWARE or media under the warranties shall not extend the original warranty period. The limited warranty set forth above shall not apply to any SOFTWARE which the Company determines in good faith has been subject to misuse, neglect, improper installation, repair, alteration, or damage by you. EXCEPT FOR THE EXPRESSED WARRANTIES SET FORTH ABOVE, THE COMPANY DISCLAIMS ALL WARRANTIES, EXPRESS OR IMPLIED, INCLUDING WITHOUT LIMITATION, THE IMPLIED WARRANTIES OF MERCHANTABILITY AND FITNESS FOR A PARTICULAR PURPOSE. EXCEPT FOR THE EXPRESS WARRANTY SET FORTH ABOVE, THE COMPANY DOES NOT WARRANT, GUARANTEE, OR MAKE ANY REPRESENTATION REGARD-ING THE USE OR THE RESULTS OF THE USE OF THE SOFTWARE IN TERMS OF ITS CORRECTNESS, ACCURACY, RELIABILITY, CURRENTNESS, OR OTHERWISE. IN NO EVENT, SHALL THE COMPANY OR ITS EMPLOYEES, AGENTS, SUPPLIERS, OR CONTRAC-TORS BE LIABLE FOR ANY INCIDENTAL, INDIRECT, SPECIAL, OR CONSEQUENTIAL DAMAGES ARISING OUT OF OR IN CONNEC-TION WITH THE LICENSE GRANTED UNDER THIS AGREEMENT, OR FOR LOSS OF USE, LOSS OF DATA, LOSS OF INCOME OR PROFIT, OR OTHER LOSSES, SUSTAINED AS A RESULT OF INJURY TO ANY PERSON, OR LOSS OF DAMAGE TO PROPERTY, OR CLAIMS OF THIRD PARTIES, EVEN IF THE COMPANY OR AN AUTHORIZED REPRESENTATIVE OF THE COMPANY HAS BEEN ADVISED OF THE POSSIBILITY OF SUCH DAMAGES. [[IN NO EVENT SHALL LIABILITY OF THE COMPANY FOR DAMAGES WITH RESPECT TO THE SOFTWARE EXCEED THE AMOUNTS ACTUALLY PAID BY YOU, IF ANY, FOR THE SOFTWARE.]]

SOME JURISDICTIONS DO NOT ALLOW THE LIMITATION OF IMPLIED WARRANTIES OR LIABILITY FOR INCIDENTAL, INDIRECT, SPECIAL, OR CONSEQUENTIAL DAMAGES, SO THE ABOVE LIMITATIONS MAY NOT ALWAYS APPLY. THE WARRANTIES IN THIS AGREEMENT GIVE YOU SPECIFIC LEGAL RIGHTS AND YOU MAY ALSO HAVE OTHER RIGHTS WHICH VARY IN ACCORDANCE WITH LOCAL LAW.

**ACKNOWLEDGMENT:**
YOU ACKNOWLEDGE THAT YOU HAVE READ THIS AGREEMENT, UNDERSTAND IT, AND AGREE TO BE BOUND BY ITS TERMS AND CONDITIONS. YOU ALSO AGREE THAT THIS AGREEMENT IS THE COMPLETE AND EXCLUSIVE STATEMENT OF THE AGREEMENT BETWEEN YOU AND THE COMPANY AND SUPERSEDES ALL PROPOSALS OR PRIOR AGREEMENTS, ORAL, OR WRITTEN, AND ANY OTHER COMMUNICATIONS BETWEEN YOU AND THE COMPANY OR ANY OTHER REPRESENTATIVE OF THE COMPANY RELATING TO THE SUBJECT MATTER OF THIS AGREEMENT.

Should you have any questions concerning this agreement or if you wish to contact the Company for any reason, please contact Customer Service at (800) 922-0579.